MAY 22 1997

D0384822

NEBRASKA WESTERN COLLEGE
LIBRARY

Darkest Hours

Books by *Jay Robert Nash*

Fiction
ON ALL FRONTS

Nonfiction
DILLINGER: DEAD OR ALIVE?

CITIZEN HOOVER, A Critical Study of the Life and Times of J. Edgar Hoover and His FBI

BLOODLETTERS AND BADMEN, A Narrative Encyclopedia of American Criminals from the Pilgrims to the Present

HUSTLERS AND CON MEN, An Anecdotal History of the Confidence Man and His Games

Poetry
LOST NATIVES & EXPATRIATES

A narrative encyclopedia
of worldwide disasters
from ancient times to the present

Darkest Hours

Jay Robert Nash

NEBRASKA WESTERN COLLEGE
LIBRARY

NO LONGER
PROPERTY OF
WNCC Library

Nelson-Hall Chicago

Library of Congress Cataloging in Publication Data

Nash, Jay Robert.
Darkest hours.

Bibliography: p.
Includes index.
1. Disasters. I. Title.
D24.N3 904 76-7390
ISBN 0-88229-140-8

Copyright © 1976 by Jay Robert Nash

All rights reserved. No part of this book may be reproduced in any form without permission in writing from the publisher, except by a reviewer who wishes to quote brief passages in connection with a review written for broadcast or for inclusion in a magazine or newspaper.
For information address Nelson-Hall Inc.,
325 W. Jackson Blvd., Chicago, Illinois 60606.

Manufactured in the United States of America

This book is dedicated to my friend and associate researcher James Patrick Agnew, who labored alongside me through the purgatorial realms of this work, and to Robert J. Dundon, my friend and editor, whose faith and professional encouragement brought it to print.

Contents

Preface

This book grew out of the research on a series of articles that I wrote some years ago. Examining the then available records, I found that no one volume existed that provided a thorough, all-encompassing, and exact (as far as verifiable records will permit) chronology of the world's major disasters. I felt that a need existed not only for just such a reliable factual narrative of these calamities but also for insight into the human involvement and reaction to what are frequently called acts of God.

Although this is a book of momentous events, it is the people involved in the events who receive the narrative attention—and necessarily so. As I researched and wrote this volume, I became acutely aware that, in almost all instances, people become extensions of nature in any holocaust. They fuse their lives and deaths onto the calamity, becoming its voice of fear, its hands of courage or cowardice, its legs of survival; they climax catastrophe with terror.

It is almost always the unexpected and instantaneous event that produces in one generation after another a painful (and long after the event, nostalgic) sense of loss for survivors of disasters and provides a seemingly vital sense of vulnerability in those wholly untouched and distant from the scene of destruction. The inability to control one's destiny in the face of total chaos creates a phenomenon impossible to observe under any other circumstances. This sharp alienation from reality was once described by Charles Darwin, who viewed an earthquake in Concepcion, Chile, in 1835: "A bad earthquake at once destroys our oldest associations: the earth, the very emblem of solidity, has moved beneath our feet like a thin crust over a liquid; one second of time has created in the mind a strange idea of insecurity, which hours of reflection would not have produced."

Further, catastrophes produce, as these extensive accounts repeatedly show, a panoply of extraordinary emotions and actions exhibited by those who would consider themselves quite ordinary under other circumstances, thus accenting human commitment and heightening, perhaps only for a single moment in the lives of those affected, unforgettable human drama.

Faced with calamity and its invisible undermining of self, individuals have responded in the past with great courage; the indomitable fireman Van Haag during the Newhall House fire in Milwaukee, Wisconsin, in 1883; the valiant Dr. Edwards who sawed soldiers free from the burning wreck of a British troop train at Gretna Green, Scotland, in 1915; the incomparable act of heroism performed by H. S. Began at the pinnacle of the 1906 Hong Kong hurricane; Edward

Spencer's incredible swimming feats in saving seventeen passengers from the sinking *Lady Elgin* in 1860; the cool bravery of stewardess Doris Steele directing survivors off a crashed Northeast Airlines plane in 1957; the valor of sailor William Hunt who dragged several victims from the Exeter Theater fire in England in 1887; young Hugh McIlrath, son of an Ohio police chief, whose love for his classmates, caught in the blazing Lake View School fire in 1908, led him to the sacrifice of his own life while saving others; the Hungarian prima donna, Mme. Karalech, who jumped from a high perch in her hotel when Messina, Sicily, was devastated by an earthquake in 1908, but gave a performance a week later with her broken arms in casts; the British troops standing at attention, defying death, as their loved ones were rowed away from the sinking *Birkenhead,* in 1852. Hundreds more reached a spiritual zenith that, but for a particular disaster involving their fellow creatures, would perhaps have evaded them all their days.

On the darker side of human character evoked by disaster, the reader will discover cowardice, egotistical stupidity, brutal indifference, desertion, despair, and bestiality: Roman Emperor Trajan deserting his subjects in the middle of a vast earthquake in Antioch, Syria, in A.D. 115; the desertions of Captain Inglefield from the sinking *Centaur* in 1782 and Captain de Chaumareys from the foundering *Medusa* in 1816, both leaving their crews to drown; Chicago's prostitutes celebrating in the fiery midst of the great fire of 1871; the Sultan of Constantinople entertaining guests aboard his yacht as he watched his city gutted by fire in 1848; the vile and often murderous "remedies" prescribed by pocket-lining quacks during the three-century reign of the Black Death; the ghouls who stripped the frozen bodies on board the stranded liner *Deutschland* in 1875, and those who cut off the fingers of the dead in the splintered aftermath of the Galveston hurricane of 1900; the pistol-wielding officer on board the Chinese coastal steamer *Kiangya,* sinking with 2,750 on board, who killed old people out of berserk compassion in 1948; and scores more who compounded the horror and tragedy of catastrophe.

And there is grim humor to be found, such as the shop girl who jumped three stories from a blazing Binghamton, New York, factory in 1913 and somehow survived to joke with startled rescuers moments later, or the unforgettable man, who, while salvaging a piano in the blaze that engulfed Chelsea, Massachusetts, in 1908, suddenly sat down and played "There'll Be a Hot Time in the Old Town Tonight" as the flames closed around him.

Eerie superstitions permeate almost all disasters, exemplified in one way by the rich women of the *Titanic* and the *Andrea Doria* shipwrecks who ripped away their glittering jewels and threw them into the sea in the belief that it might aid in their salvations, and in another way by the tribe of headhunters in Borneo, who upon hearing the volcanic explosion of Krakatoa in 1883, took it as a sign of displeasure from their gods concerning their gruesome activities and committed suicide *en masse* by hurling themselves over a cliff. The mysterious disappearance of ships and planes through the centuries in the Bermuda Triangle has baffled the best twentieth-century scientific minds.

In all the havoc there are the miraculous survivals, which upon reflection, might cause one to turn to the Scriptures. Why, the reader might ask, did 36,000 people perish in the eruption of Pelée on Martinique in 1902, while a convicted murderer was found safe in the St. Pierre dungeon? How did Margaret Sue Martin, the wife of a United States Air Force lieutenant, manage to survive beneath tons of fallen debris that once was the magnificent Hotel Saada in the earthquake that leveled Agadir, Morocco, in 1960? The answers to these questions and hundreds more raised here are left, quite naturally, to the reader.

Perhaps these accounts come as close as is possible to describing how the average person meets an abrupt, on-rushing fate, the unknown, and death. Amassing this material has provided me with a more substantial appreciation of mortality.

For the serious student, researcher, historian and teacher seeking in-depth reference, hard data sections precede the narratives of major accounts. Complete hard data lists are given in appendices. Statistics remain problematic. In the almost endless research of this subject, the general works available were used primarily as guidelines; from there the research involved tracing literally thousands of sources through time to the local levels of parish priests, constables, clerks, on-the-spot correspondents (such as those working for the *London Times*) who sifted through the ruins and ashes, meticulously taking the count of life and death. It is worth mentioning that the types of disasters chosen for inclusion are natural disasters or accidents and not man-made, albeit the appendices do contain comprehensive lists of notable wartime marine sinkings and the world's war dead, which are intended for use by special researchers.

Twenty lives or more lost was a prerequisite for the inclusion of any catastrophe, an arbitrary number based on the journalistic notion that the loss of human life in large numbers demands and receives the biggest news story of the day.

Unfortunately there can be no conclusion to this work; widespread disasters of all types are happening now, at the moment of this writing. It is hoped, however, that this work will serve as an informational source of what has gone before, as well as provide a unique history of humanity at its very best and its very worst inside the vortex of destruction.

Jay Robert Nash

Acknowledgments

I would like to thank scores of people who over the years contributed their time and effort in the production of this work. My undying gratitude goes to James Agnew, who inched his way through dozens of archives, libraries, and museums checking and re-checking; to Carolyn Zozak, the most dedicated typist any writer ever had; to Jan, who read the seemingly endless proofs; to the host of foreign consulate offices that extended marvelous cooperation; to E. J. McAvoy, Air Safety Investigator, National Transportation Safety Board, Bureau of Aviation Safety; to William Kilbride of the American Red Cross; and the National Weather Service Forecast Office.

Special thanks for photos, data, published material, reminiscences goes to (U.S. Midwest) John Agnew, Jr.; James Elkins; Patrick Agnew; John Agnew, Sr.; Bob Connelly; Ed Crawford; Tom Buckley; Mary and Tom McComas; Marc Davis; Norbert Blei; Curt Johnson; Edgar Krebs; William and Edie Kelly at Wide World Photos, Chicago Bureau; Henry Scheafer and Louis Tempke of UPI's Compix, Chicago Bureau; Jerrie Lynne Klein; Neil H. Nash; Jack J. Klein, Jr.; Arthur Von Kluge; James Small; Ed and Barbara Kida; Hank Oettinger; Raymond Louis Peuchner; Ken Petchenik; Wendy Clare Oldham; Daniel McConnell; Chester Clayton Long; Roxanne Clark; Leonard Des Jardins; Jack Lane; P. Michael O'Sullivan; Sidney Harris; James and Edie McCormick (U.S. East); Robert Abel; Jeff Kamen; John Miller; David A. Edwards; Charles B. Victor (U.S. West); Raymond Friday Locke; William Peck; Jay Odell; Neal and Joan Amidei; Ann Bogazianos; Arnold L. Kaye; Charles Bukowski.

My grateful thanks go out to the scores of librarians and archivists who cooperated promptly and efficiently with a host of invaluable materials, chiefly Susan Bruchman, Librarian, Insurance Library of Chicago; the staff of the Chicago Public Library, especially Joseph C. Lutz and James Downes; Robert C. Miller, assistant director for general services at the Joseph Regenstein Library at the University of Chicago; to the staff of the Newberry Library of Chicago, especially Peter Weil; to the staff at the Cudahy Library at Loyola University; the staff at Northwestern University; the staff at John Crerar Library at IIT; Chicago Historical Society; the staff at the Smithsonian Institution, especially the Department of Military History; the staff at the New York Public Library; the New York Historical Society; the San Francisco Historical Society; Peter A. Evans, Librarian of the California Historical Society; James H. Davis, Picture Librarian of the Denver Public Library; William Kirby, Associate Director of the

Louisiana Division of the New Orleans Public Library; Holly B. Ulseth, Curator of Special Exhibits & Collections, Detroit Historical Museum; Kansas State Historical Society; Malcolm Freiberg, Massachusetts Historical Society; William M. Roberts, Reference Librarian, University of California, Berkeley; The Mariners Museum at Newport News, Va.; U.S. Department of Commerce; U.S. Signal Corps.

My sincere appreciation goes to the many newspaper and magazine reporters, editors and columnists who provided me with staggering background material from clips to personal memories. These include: Jerry Goldberg of the Capitol News Service in California; Mike Royko, Barry Felcher, Donald W. Gormley, Henry Kisor, and Thomas S. Maley of the *Chicago Daily News*; Tom Fitzpatrick, Roger Ebert, Herman Kogan, William Granger, Paul McGrath, Paul Galloway of the *Chicago Sun-Times*; Mike Lavelle of the *Chicago Tribune*; Joseph Longmeyer of the *Chicago Defender*.

A

ABERFAN, WALES

LANDSLIDE
October 21, 1966

background: One of the many giant slag heaps surrounding the giant colliery in Aberfan, Wales, was weakened by the natural spring beneath it. The 800-foot-high mound gave way on the morning of October 21, 1966, releasing a two-million-ton torrent of rock, coal and mud, which cascaded onto the Pantglas Junior and Infants School and seventeen other buildings in the town. Crushed to death and buried alive were 145 persons, of whom 116 were children. Hundreds more escaped. The landslide was the worst in Welsh history. Stricken families were awarded 200 pounds each by the government, and additional relief and compensation funds sent from the world over amounted to more than 300,000 pounds.

Some call them "mountains of doom." Dotting the landscape of once-green Wales to this day are the stygian slag heaps resulting from centuries-old collieries, mammoth piles of debris that tower above the mining towns. They are cheerless sights, which one writer likened to "spiritless cathedrals of the industrial age." As was proven in horror at Aberfan on October 21, 1966, these looming giants are killers.

For days residents of Aberfan thought they saw the slag heap move slightly. They reported this to the authorities. Little was done. Two years earlier, Gwyneth Williams of the Marthyr Tydfil Council had warned at a meeting: "We have a lot of trouble from slurry causing flooding. If the tip moves, it could threaten the whole school."

A sea of mud flows into one of the damaged schoolrooms at Aberfan, where 116 children were crushed to death in the worst landslide in Welsh history. *(UPI)*

She was referring to the Pantglas Junior and Infants School, which housed an average of 250 students each day and was situated almost at the base of the monstrous slag heap. Another Aberfan citizen later recalled how the school's headmaster, W. J. Williams, "always claimed that the tip would collapse on the school one day." Another man was to recall grimly how he watched the mountain of mine refuse growing "higher and higher, and, with a stream filtering through beneath it, it was always liable to shift."

Not far from the minds of the Aberfan citizens was the horror of the slag-heap disaster in Belgium in 1961 when a landslide of mine debris buried a village in seconds, killing twenty and injuring another thirty persons.

To allay the mounting fears of complaining residents, the mine sent a maintenance man, David John Evans, to investigate. Just after dawn on October 21, he climbed laboriously to the top of the slag heap and looked about. Nothing seemed wrong, until, in shock, he suddenly "saw the heap shifting. We could see the tip moving 300 yards away from us. Down it went, but we could not see the result because of the thick fog.

"It was like a summer's day on top, and down below visibility was poor. The movement was like thunder. We could hear the trees on the side of the tip being crushed. It was frightening. I ran for nearly a quarter of a mile, but by the time I reached the colliery, the alarm had been given. They could hear the crash a mile away."

At the sound of the two million tons of rock, coal and mud crashing downward on Aberfan, hundreds of miners, their faces still grimy from work, poured from the mines and ran pell-mell to the Pantglas school, which was directly in the path of the landslide. As the landslide crashed forward, Thomas Davies and two friends, all late for school, looked up in wonder. The debris roared toward Davies on a quarter-of-a-mile-wide path, crushing everything in its way, including seventeen houses. Ten-year-old Thomas blinked as his two friends disappeared, engulfed by the debris. "I could not see at first, because it was very foggy," the boy later told newsmen. "When I could, it looked like water pouring down the hillside. It uprooted a great tree on its way. The other two boys ran the other way. It just sucked them away and they ran right into it. It hit the school like a big wave, spattering all over the place and crushing the building. It was like a dream, and I was very scared."

Pearl Crowe, whose home was near the school, heard the great rumble and looked out her window. "I saw a black mass of moving waste pouring steadily into the school, and part of the school collapsed. I was paralyzed."

Black slime was everywhere, rushing down the streets of Aberfan. On the run women arrived at the school, frantically calling for their children. Evylen Jones found "the school buried. It was little more than a mass of tangled wreckage. Sludge started to pour down the high ground into the streets."

S. O. Davies ran through the town toward the school. "I and others have been concerned about this tip. We had a dread that sooner or later it would give way. I saw scores of houses, some with a slime-like river running through them. Running down the mountainside was a cataract, working itself through the tip, which had collapsed." This great amount of water had accumulated from what chief geologist Robert Price would later term a "geological freak," an underground spring that came into being after the tip was created.

Petite Pauline Evans ran to the school, where other housewives helped her through a window. "When I got inside," she weepingly told reporters later, "there were about a dozen children screaming in one classroom, which had only half collapsed. With the help of a nurse, I handed them through a window to safety. We found some more children in another classroom and we helped them out, too. . . . Then we went to another classroom which was terribly damaged, and we could hear the voice of a girl but we could not get to her because there were other children trapped nearby, and if we moved anything, it would have collapsed on them. We could not rescue that little girl who said her name was Katherine."

Ten-year-old Dilys Pope was one of the few lucky ones in his class to survive the disaster. His classmates had just finished their morning prayers and were laughing and joking as they waited for their teacher to begin the roll-call. Suddenly he "heard a noise and saw stuff flying about. The room seemed to be flying around. The desks were falling over and the children were falling and screaming. We could not see anything but then the dust began to go away. My leg was caught in the desk, and I could not move, and my arm was hurting. The children were lying all over the place. The teacher was also on the floor. His leg was caught."

The teacher somehow freed his leg and hobbled to the door, which was wedged shut by four-foot-high debris. He used a large stone to smash the glass in the door. By that time Dilys Pope had gotten loose. His teacher lifted him through the opening in the door. The boy made his way down the shattered hallway and outside. He then came around to one of the outside windows and managed to get it open. His teacher handed one child after another out to him. Before collapsing on the window sill, he told them quietly, "Go home, children, go home."

By then hundreds of miners and housewives were

Desperate diggers attempt to reach children trapped beneath the slag heap on October 21, 1966. *(UPI)*

outside the school clawing wildly at the huge mounds of debris from the landslide that surrounded the school. Everywhere pitiable, painful sights greeted rescuers. One man found a small boy so tightly wedged under debris that to free him he was compelled, while sobbing great tears, to break the youngster's leg.

When a group of miners did manage to force their way into the crushed school, they found teacher David Beynon, surrounded by students, beneath the rubble. "David was clutching the five little children in his arms," a rescuer stated, "as if to protect them." All were dead.

There was seemingly no end to the heart-wrenching sights that day in Aberfan. One mining boss who had led a large party in breaking into one of the collapsed rooms stumbled from the ruined building and sputtered, "We found four children underneath a lot of brickwork which had slipped down on top of them. One small boy was still alive. He was standing against the heater in the schoolroom and was crying because his leg had been caught in something. By his seat were three other children. They were dead."

Another man from the same party carried out some dead children, one of them his own child. He suddenly slumped to the ground. "Their work was on the wall," he said dazedly. "One paper in colored letters said, 'I went, I saw, I am going.' Another tot had drawn the picture of a zebra going across a road. 'Safe crossing,' it said, 'safe crossing.'" He began to rock crazily, holding his dead child in his arms.

Bulldozers and battalions of miners, some 2,000 persons in all, including hundreds of miners from other valleys, appeared. They relentlessly dug away at the oozing muck that engulfed the building. Few were left to save. The groaning, shouting work force would not give up. One man, near exhaustion, was told to rest. He turned his tear-streaked face upward and cried out: "God, man! My two sons are in there! I can't stop digging, I'll never stop digging!"

The digging went on into the next day, broken off every few minutes when a supervisor yelled through a bullhorn, "Silence! Silence!" The diggers would then listen, thousands of heads pressed hard against the

Prince Philip inspects the ruins of the Pantglas Junior and Infants School in Aberfan, Wales, October 1966. *(UPI)*

heavy slag, listening for any muffled sound that would pinpoint a trapped child. A faint voice would be heard, and one of the rescuers would desperately cry out, "Here! Here!" The digging recommenced.

Of the 250 children trapped in the pulverized school, 134 were saved. The remaining 116 students and several teachers were placed in long rows for burial. The catastrophe caused George Thomas, Minister for Wales, to lament, "A whole generation has been wiped out."

At an official inquest investigating the tragedy, angry Aberfan citizens shouted, "Mark the death certificate, 'Buried alive by the National Coal Board!'" and "Our children have been murdered!"

John Collins, whose wife and two small sons were buried in the slag heap that cascaded down on his house, which was located next to the school, was adamant with the coroner Benjamin Hamilton. "Buried alive by the National Coal Board," he insisted. "I want that recorded." Collins and dozens of others felt that the board could have prevented the disaster had they properly dealt with the dangerous slag heap, a hill that was known to shift periodically. "He's right, he's right," dozens chorused. "Our children have been murdered!"

"I know that your grief is such that you do not know what you are saying," Hamilton soothed.

Collins was on his feet with others. The miner again shouted, "I want that recorded." It was written down in the book.

Queen Elizabeth sent the town a message that read: "I am shocked and distressed to learn of the terrible disaster which has taken place in Aberfan. Please convey a message of heart-felt sympathy from my husband and myself to the children's parents and to the families of those who have lost their lives." The Queen also went to Aberfan, where she stood at the mass grave containing many of the bodies of the dead children, a grave marked by a one hundred-foot cross upon which hung countless garlands sent by miners from all over the world. She was spared the sight of the burial when women threw teddy bears into the open grave, and hardened police sergeants covered their faces and burst into uncontrollable sobbing. Yet the pain of the great Aberfan disaster worked across her face, and she was reported by dozens to have been "near tears, but she kept fighting them back."

Originally 200 pounds was given to each family involved in the tragedy, but donations of more than 300,000 pounds poured into Aberfan from sympathizers all over the world.

To many the money meant nothing. Their sons were dead; their daughters were dead, and the slag heaps still poked their ugly, menacing peaks into the skies of Wales. John Collins, his young wife and small sons in fresh graves, buried his face in his hands and told reporters: "I'm forty-one years old. The law of averages says I have thirty-one years left. What can I do with that? I can't *live.* I can only exist."

AFFRAY

MARINE DISASTER
April 16, 1951

The British submarine *Affray* was a thoroughly modern vessel and one of the largest, best equipped in the navy. Her disappearance beneath the waters of the English Channel on April 16, 1951, while on a training cruise between Portsmouth and Falmouth, is to this day shrouded in mystery.

The *Affray,* running on the surface, sailed from Portsmouth at about 4:00 P.M. That night, at about 9:00 P.M., the submarine, with seventy-five officers, sailors and marines (twenty-four of whom were not regular members of the crew but on a training cruise), radioed that she was about to submerge. It was the last message the outside world received from the submarine.

Unlike the long delays that had taken place when the British submarines *Truculent* and *Thetis* vanished, the British Admiralty immediately put into effect "Operation Subsmash," and within a few hours more than forty surface vessels, including those of Belgium, France and the United States, were searching for the ship. Minesweepers, destroyers, and frigates plumbed the depths of the Channel with asdic and sonar equipment. Spotters in fighters, bombers and helicopters scanned the choppy waters from above, but they found nothing. The *Affray,* under the command of Lieutenant J.

Blackburn, was nowhere to be found. A grim irony in this disaster is that Lieutenant A. A. Frew was on board the missing ship—he had been one of the lucky survivors to escape the stricken submarine *Truculent*.

For sixty-nine hours, the churlish, unpredictable waters of the Channel were scoured, and then the search was called off. The Admiralty tersely stated: "The Board of Admiralty announces with the deepest regret that there is now no reasonable hope of the rescue of any survivors from H.M.S. Submarine *Affray*. . . ."

The matter would probably have been dropped except for technicians at the Teddington Research Laboratory who developed an underwater television apparatus that could be lowered into great depths of water and connected to a viewing screen on board a deep-diving vessel, the *Reclaim*. This ship, which had participated in the initial search for the *Affray*, began a careful scan of the Channel with her television equipment; on June 14, 1951, she spotted what looked like a fairly new wreck on the lip of Hurd Deep.

After the camera had taken shots from many angles, the viewing screen finally revealed the name on the sunken submarine: *Affray*. Her shortmast was dismantled and appeared to have been blown away. Her tubular mast was also broken off (this was the only portion of the *Affray* that could be recovered; inspection proved that the welding on the mast had been faulty).

Despite the ship's huge supply of oxygen candles and available escape hatches, it was assumed at this late date that all on board were dead. Though the cause of the *Affray*'s sinking was never fully learned, authorities suspected a powerful explosion had crippled the sub and taken her down with all hands on board.

(ALSO SEE: Thetis, Truculent)

A lonely marker buoy bobbing in the choppy waters of the English Channel indicates where the British submarine *Affray* went to her doom on April 16, 1951. *(UPI)*

AGADIR, MOROCCO

EARTHQUAKE
February 29, 1960

background: The Moroccan seaport of Agadir at the base of the Atlas Mountains with a population of 48,000 was hit by a twelve-second earthquake at 11:45 P.M., on February 29, 1960, snapping the earth four feet to one side and then returning it; a *tsunami* swept three hundred feet inland almost at the same instant. More than 70 percent of the city was destroyed and 12,000 persons killed. The quake measured 6.25 on the Richter Scale.

"We were a peaceful union of Moslem and Christian, Arab and European. This was a prosperous city, and we had a future. We worked and behaved ourselves. We were growing. What in God's name do you suppose we did wrong?" These were the anguished words of a French cafe proprietor only hours after his city, Agadir, Morocco, had been destroyed by one of the most devastating earthquakes of modern times.

There was only a brief tremor on February 28, 1960, not felt by all in Agadir, to suggest the mass destruction that followed the next day. The resort town's hotels were packed with European and American tourists, hundreds of whom relaxed on its milk-white beaches. A British tourist, Mrs. Philip Mole, noticed the first tremor when she saw the pictures in her Marhaba Hotel room tilt, but she dismissed the event. The first earthen tug woke Mrs. Andre Alabert from her afternoon nap in a five-story apartment building. "Some one is knocking on the door," she called drowsily to her husband. "I didn't hear anything," he replied. "Go back to sleep."

On the following night, Agadir was again stirred, this time by a larger shock that alarmed the entire city. This jolt came at 10:50 P.M. About seventy-five Moslems hurried to their mosque in the Talborjt quarter to pray; it was the third day of the fast-by-day, feast-by-night religious Moslem observance, Ramadan.

At 11:45 P.M., never dreaming that "Allah would strike us while we are paying homage to his strength," the praying Moslems looked up in terror to see the dome of their mosque descend upon them.

The earthquake struck with such force that it wrenched the earth under the entire city four feet apart in six seconds and then returned the earth to its original place. Inside of that time, Agadir fell to ruins. Houses, hotels, office buildings, apartment houses, even the ancient dwellings perched high on the heights known as the Casbah, collapsed upon their inhabitants; 70 percent of all standing structures were crushed to their foundations.

Mains burst, lights went out, and sewers exploded, releasing tens of thousands of rats onto the streets. Fires erupted, but there was no one to fight them. Equipment

French soldiers dig into the ruins of the Saada Hotel in an attempt to rescue Mrs. Margaret Sue Martin, one of the thousands trapped in the quake that struck Agadir, Morocco, on February 29, 1960. Twelve thousand died. *(UPI)*

and men had been all wiped out in their fire houses.

The death toll shot skyward, most of the lives lost during the few seconds of the quake. Of the 2,200 Jews living in the city, 1,500 were instantly crushed to death. A tidal wave then raced from the sea, sweeping everything before it inland for 300 yards.

Ship captains at sea ordered their vessels outward bound as they were heaved back and forth by boiling, churning waters. Many noted the great gushes of steam coming from the ocean floor and immediately concluded that a volcanic eruption was imminent.

A lone plane circled Agadir, its pilot later gasping, "It looked like a giant foot had stepped on the city and squashed it flat."

In hours the town was cacophonous with the wails of the thousands trapped by the debris of their own homes. By dawn, an army of French soldiers from nearby military bases and sailors from the U.S. Sixth Fleet spread themselves throughout the city, digging out survivors, shooting plague-carrying rats and, in one instance, fighting off a pack of jackals attempting to ferret out a trapped child.

Spraying DDT everywhere, rescuers masked their faces to fight off the intense stench of dead bodies and open sewers. One survivor, a long-time resident, only thought to escape the carnage: "The only thing I'm thinking of is getting away, really away. The quicker they destroy this place, the better. I doubt if they can ever get rid of the odor."

King Mohammed V of Morocco guaranteed his personal fortune of $100 million to rebuild Agadir to its original splendor. It was of little comfort to the dead, the dying and the homeless.

One of the most dramatic rescues of the quake involved Margaret Sue Martin, the wife of U.S. Air Force Lieutenant Jerald Martin. Margaret Sue Martin was in the bathroom of their third-floor suite in the luxurious Hotel Saada when the quake hit. Suddenly she was hurled downward in a hailstorm of falling debris: ". . . everything dropped. It was like going down in a fast elevator." Seconds later she found herself trapped, her legs and right arm solidly pinned by wreckage. Her husband and one-year-old baby, Diane, had fallen at the same moment, and she soon heard Diane crying. Lieutenant Martin called to her, telling her that he thought he could reach the baby.

Martin smashed his way through the wreckage like a madman, burrowing toward the direction of the child's screams. He found her, as Mrs. Martin later described, answering his own shouts by "pushing with her baby hands in his direction." Both Martin and his child escaped the wreckage after struggling for several hours. Mrs. Martin was left behind. She had been in voice contact with her husband for several hours and then heard nothing.

"I didn't really think I would die," she later remembered. About fourteen hours later, French soldiers heard Mrs. Martin calling from the rubble. They rushed to the spot above her and began to dig.

One Frenchman, Lieutenant Hubert Monteus, began to talk to Sue Martin in a soft, encouraging voice. "He called me *petit poulet*—little chicken." As his soldiers burrowed downward through the debris toward Mrs. Martin, they encountered several other bodies—fifty-two of the seventy-four hotel guests had been crushed to death. They continued working.

At one point, to keep up Mrs. Martin's spirits, Lieutenant Monteus said, "Sue, you are very beautiful."

By that time, workers had cleared a patch of debris that exposed Mrs. Martin's legs. "How do you know that when all you can see is my feet?" Sue Martin asked.

"To have your courage, you *must* be beautiful," Monteus responded with typical French gallantry.

Soon a doctor was summoned to crawl down through the hollowed-out area of debris and examine the still-trapped woman. Noting that her legs were stiffening, he quietly told Monteus she would be dead in an hour. The officer refused to give up and ordered his men to renew their frantic labors. Hours later, the last bit of wreckage was cleared away, and Mrs. Martin was removed alive. She was reunited with her husband and child within minutes.

"At the top of the hole," Mrs. Martin recalled as she was being lifted out, "I felt the sunlight on my face.

People were crowding around. They were all cheering. They seemed to be crying. I think I was crying, too, with sheer happiness, as they put me on a stretcher and into an ambulance and rushed me to the French aid station. . . ." She had been trapped for almost forty hours.

Burying the dead of Agadir became a problem. Thousands of decaying corpses littered the streets. A bulldozer dug out a trench two feet deep and a hundred feet long; soldiers wearing gauze masks rolled bodies by the hundreds into it while relatives wailed.

The polyglot population of Agadir also made for burial problems. Moslems, according to religious tradition, insisted that their dead be buried close to the surface. Jews begged that their dead be buried separately from Christian and Moslem victims.

Most of the more than 12,000 dead wound up in universal graves, sprinkled with lime, and forgotten.

AGNES

HURRICANE
June 21-26, 1972

Hurricane Agnes struck full force against seven Atlantic Coast states on June 21, 1972; she pounded 116,000 homes to shreds and killed 118 persons over a five-day period. Agnes cascaded 28.1 trillion gallons of water across a five-thousand-square-mile area, leaving more than 200,000 homeless.

Federal aid was slow in coming, particularly in Pennsylvania. The Secretary of Housing and Urban Development, George Romney, flew to hard-hit Wilkes-Barre to see the thousands of frustrated victims who demanded immediate relief.

Romney met publicly with hundreds of angry, shrieking residents, led by Pennsylvania Governor Milton Shapp. The finger-wagging Shapp unloosed a torrent of his own, stating that America had sent relief to "Germany and all those other countries after World

A helicopter hovers over the stricken city of Wilkes-Barre, Pennsylvania, chief victim of hurricane Agnes. *(Red Cross)*

War II," plucked Penn Central Railroad and Lockheed Aircraft from financial ruin and should do the same for Pennsylvania, chiefly by offering full compensation for victims, even to the extent of paying off every mortgage on every home destroyed by the hurricane.

In response, Romney angrily called Shapp "unrealistic and demagogic" and accused him of playing politics with a national tragedy.

When a vituperative woman shouted, "You don't care whether we live or die!" Romney walked away red-faced and sputtering. Federal relief did arrive, but nowhere near the $3 billion demanded by residents.

One Wilkes-Barre citizen was beyond caring. "When I first looked at my house [demolished by the storm]," he said, "I wanted to change my name, leave my job, and move to California.

AGUNG — VOLCANIC ERUPTION
March 20, 1963

For 485 years the natives of Bali have considered their 10,308-foot-high mountain Agung (or Gunung Agung) "the navel of the world." According to Balinese religious thought, this volcano was chosen as a sacred throne by Hindu gods who were disgusted with losing Java to Mohammedanism. Halfway up the eastern slope of the sacred volcano, the Balinese constructed an elaborate mother temple called Besakih and have worshipped there every hundred years to rid their island of evil spirits.

During the centennial celebration of 1963, Agung was apparently disturbed, for the volcano interrupted the natives' sacred rites with loud rumbles. A month before, the god-mountain had spewed forth a cloud of brimstone that had killed seventeen villagers. Even though high priests had attemped to appease Agung, the volcano erupted on a titanic scale on March 20, 1963, as thousands prayed around the temple. Clouds of black poisonous gas rolled down the mountain, killing hundreds as they knelt in prayer.

Then came the gray-black lava that poured over the helpless villages of Sebudi, Sebih and Sorgah. Rains formed by the heat of the volcano (hot ash was measured at 230 degrees) mixed with sulfurous ash and created poisonous gases that eradicated all living things within an area of ten miles.

The volcanic torrent went uninterrupted for five days until 1,200 Balinese were dead and 200,000 more were homeless.

Agung volcano in northeast Bali brought death to 1,200 worshippers on March 20, 1963. *(Wide World)*

These giant boulders, which smashed the village of Subagan on Bali, March 20, 1963, were part of the death torrent spewed forth by the volcano Agung. *(Wide World)*

The remains of the Air Canada DC-8 that crashed near Toronto International Airport on July 5, 1970. *(UPI)*

AIR CANADA DC-8 — **AIR CRASH July 5, 1970**

On July 5, 1970, an Air Canada DC-8, piloted by forty-nine-year-old Captain Peter Hamilton, crashed outside of Toronto International Airport. The reason for the crash, which killed all 108 passengers on board, remains controversial to this day. Hamilton had disagreed with Air Canada's procedures for deploying the spoilers of his plane. Spoilers are the slats on the wings of the DC-8's that brake the jets while they taxi after landing. Hamilton especially disagreed with using them while still 2,000 feet in the air.

Captain Hamilton strongly believed that this practice led to dangerous "inadvertent" deployment in the air and he made it his private practice not to deploy the spoilers until touchdown. Hamilton's regular copilot and first officer, Donald Rowland, was, according to later testimony, "surprised and annoyed" at the captain's delayed deployment of the spoilers. In a stopover in Vienna in early 1970, Hamilton and Rowland had argued about the use of the spoilers, but according to one report they had "worked out a compromise."

That compromise was in effect on July 5, when Hamilton was bringing his stretched DC-8 into Toronto International Airport at 8:13 A.M. Rowland deployed the spoilers at a height of sixty feet. Just as the plane touched down, the outboard engine on the right side inexplicably fell off, suddenly making the plane 4,000 pounds lighter and bouncing it back into the air.

Captain Hamilton, without giving any reason, stated to the control tower that he would again circle and attempt another landing on the runway. He powered the DC-8 upward and began the circle. At this point, a second engine, the inboard engine on the right side, fell off and landed in a clump of trees. With part of the right wing gone, the DC-8 began to break up.

The tension in the cockpit that existed between Hamilton and Rowland was later affirmed by an air controller who heard Rowland apologize several times for activating a braking device prematurely. The plane suddenly dived earthward and crashed, splattering seats, baggage and bodies for hundreds of yards.

Mary Day was about to prepare breakfast for her family of ten when she "heard a very loud roaring and windows cracking and rattling." Looking out a window, she could see huge fragments of the plane hurling over her house and skidding toward her on the ground. The scene was "all flames and smoke." She grabbed her five-month-old daughter, ran outside, and hid behind a barn until the screaming, hissing mass of debris came to a halt.

AIR FRANCE BOEING 707 — **AIR CRASH June 3, 1962**

When Air France's 707 jetliner crashed in a small cherry orchard near Orly Airport in Paris during takeoff on June 3, 1962, almost the complete membership of the Atlanta, Georgia, Art Association perished. Of the 132 passengers and crew on board, only 2 stewardesses who were seated near the tail were found alive, both of them having been thrown clear.

It was a staggering loss for Atlanta; the lives of their most active and influential cultural leaders had been snuffed out in an instant, ironically, after the association had just completed a tour of the great art centers of Europe.

The mayor of Atlanta, Ivan Allen, Jr., surveying the wrecked jet only hours after the crash, wept as he pointed out clothes and jewelry that had belonged to his friends. "I recognize that tie," he said, "and that dress . . . I went to school with some of them. I was in business with others . . . I was in love with some of the ladies when they were girls . . . This was my generation . . . my friends."

Thousands of miles away in Los Angeles, Malcolm X, leader of the Black Muslims, heard of the crash and addressed followers with these words: "I would like to announce a very beautiful thing that has happened. . . . I got a wire from God today . . . well, all right, somebody came and told me that he really had answered our prayers over in France. He dropped an airplane out of the sky with over 120 white people on it because the Muslims believe in an eye for an eye and a tooth for a tooth. But thanks to God, or Jehovah, or Allah, we will continue to pray, and we hope that every day another plane falls out of the sky."

Among those who fell were Robert and Nancy Pegram, Sidney Wein and his wife and daughter, Tom-Chris Allen, Mrs. David Black, and the art association's president, Del Paige, art patrons and sponsors all, people who had brought great collections to Atlanta and had inspired the entire community to an intense appreciation of art. It was "the greatest tragedy to strike Atlanta since the Civil War," remarked Milton Bevington, who saw his wife off at the airport and watched, in horror, as the plane crashed before his eyes. (He had made a pact with his wife that they would always take different planes. If one of them crashed, the other would be alive to take care of their children.)

Bevington watched the huge Boeing 707 taxi to the runway. He noticed that the plane's movements seemed sluggish, lacking the power of a usual jet takeoff. Reaching the 8,000-foot mark, the plane, which should have been traveling at 190 m.p.h., hopped briefly into the air—Bevington said about eight feet— and then thumped down again on the runway, heading off the strip.

The pilot realized that by not lifting off, the plane faced disaster. Desperately he applied the full brakes and threw all jet engines into reverse, an act which probably knocked all the passengers unconscious. Continuing on its fatal path, the 707 went off the runway and into a small cherry orchard where it exploded. Before it exploded, the tail section broke free and two stewardesses, Francoise Authie and Jacqueline Gillet, were thrown clear. They were the only survivors.

When Bevington saw the plane explode, he ran toward a gate. A man held him back, saying, "You can't go out there. . . . There's nothing you can do."

"My wife is on that plane!" Bevington shouted.

The man continued to hold him back, staring grimly at the plane. "I'm sorry. My brother is, too."

Three hours later, Bevington learned that his wife and 129 others were dead.

The tragedy was highlighted a week later when cards that had been mailed by the victims from Paris to friends in Atlanta began to arrive. The messages were full of praise and delight over the art treasures the members had seen in the Louvre, the Doge's Palace, St. Mark's, St. Peter's, the Tate and Uffizi galleries.

Mrs. Ezekiel Chandler sent a card to her daughter that read: "If I don't come back, don't worry. Don't cry. I will have died happy in Europe."

All 117 passengers and crew members of an Air India flight died when their 707 jet crashed into Mont Blanc, Europe's highest peak, on January 24, 1966. The black specks on the slope are fragments of the plane. *(UPI)*

Only the tail of an Air France 707 remains after the plane, failing to take off at Orly Airport, exploded at the end of the runway, killing 130 people, June 3, 1962. *(UPI)*

AIR FRANCE BOEING 707

AIR CRASH
June 22, 1962

Attempting to land on the steamy French Caribbean island of Guadaloupe, an Air France 707 smashed into the jagged slopes of the island's major air hazard, Dos d'Ane—the Donkey's Back—and all 113 people aboard were instantly killed. This was the fifth crash of a 707 within the space of five months for a combined death toll of 456 persons.

Investigations into the reliability of the 707's by the Federal Aviation Agency yielded nothing.

AIR INDIA BOEING 707

AIR CRASH
January 24, 1966

The serenity of snow-blanketed 15,771-foot Mont Blanc was disturbed at 8:25 A.M. on January 24, 1966, when an intercontinental Air India flight en route from Bombay to New York with a stop in Geneva crashed into its side. All 117 occupants were killed—the worst disaster to befall Air India to that date.

Captain J. T. D'Souza was just preparing to land at Geneva when a violent snow storm at the top of Mont Blanc began sucking the plane, believed to be traveling 600 m.p.h., into its side. D'Souza had been the pilot who had flown Pope Paul VI to India, a historic flight in December, 1964.

The plane was crammed with dignitaries and the famous, including India's greatest atomic research scientist, Dr. Homi Jehangir Bhabha and Belgium's Baroness Degley. Among the twisted human remains and scattered debris of the plane, searchers later found the bodies of fifteen monkeys that were being transported to a zoo. They apparently had survived the crash but had frozen to death.

Ironically this crash had happened in almost the same spot where an Air India transport in which forty-eight were killed smashed to bits on November 3, 1950. In the earlier crash were the bodies of forty Indian seamen en route to pick up a ship. On the 1966 flight forty-six Indian seamen were on board, also en route to pick up a ship.

AKRON

AIR CRASH
April 14, 1933

background: The U.S. Navy dirigible *Akron* was built by the Goodyear Zeppelin Corporation at a cost of $5 million. Helium-filled, the airship contained 7.4 million cubic feet, was 785 feet in length and 132 feet in diameter. She was propelled by eight 12-cylinder Maybach engines totalling 4,480 horsepower and was christened on August 8, 1931, by Mrs. Herbert Hoover. The largest airship in the world to date, the *Akron,* after twenty months of service, broke up in a vicious storm off the New Jersey coast and washed into the Atlantic on April 14, 1933; seventy-three of her seventy-six-man crew died. The following day the Navy's J-3, a nonrigid blimp, also crashed in a rescue attempt with two of her seven-man crew killed. An inquiry showed that the dirigible was improperly constructed.

The death of the giant dirigible *Akron,* the Navy's proud queen of the air, which had all compartments contained in the hull, the control car to the fore and special enclosures that permitted five airplanes to take off and land while the ship was in flight, was terrifyingly abrupt. The disaster later proved that the airship, despite her majestic appearance, was miserably constructed, ill-equipped and, most probably, mismanaged by her officers.

Before the end came, the *Akron* had been plagued by mishaps. The dirigible was damaged considerably on February 22, 1932, when she was torn by a violent wind from her mooring mast at Lakehurst, N.J. Her first transcontinental flight on May 8, 1932, ended with the deaths of two ground crewmen who were attempting to moor the ship at San Diego's Camp Kearney. A sudden gust of wind took the ship upward with several sailors clinging to her mooring ropes. They dangled horribly in space while those on board attempted to pull them up into the ship. Two men whose strength gave out fell, struggling in vain, to their deaths.

On the trip to California, two longitudinal girders collapsed near the bay section of the ship. During the 2,300-mile return flight, the girders were shored up with timber backing. The *Akron* was simply unsafe—wires, frames, and girders were constantly buckling; she was jerrybuilt and most of her anxious crewmen knew she was doomed.

The ill-fated dirigible *Akron* on her accident-prone trip to California in 1932. *(UPI)*

On April 14, 1933, the *Akron,* with a full crew of seventy-six bluejackets, was suddenly swept out to sea and sucked into the center of a ripping storm that lashed at the Atlantic Coast. As the leviathan plunged from an altitude of 1,600 to 700 feet, Lieutenant Commander Herbert V. Wiley frantically ordered the ship's water ballast dumped into the sea. With a rush the water was jettisoned, and the dirigible shot upward.

The rudder cables gave way under the strain. The upper controls cracked, and the steering wheels became useless, crazily spinning ornaments. In the words of one observer, the *Akron* "was as helpless as a goose feather in a tornado."

The sailors on board grimaced as they were ordered to take landing positions, a stark directive that meant only one thing: prepare to die. The descent was swift. The altimeter man had time to call out only two signals, "Eight hundred feet—three hundred feet."

Only the storm-stripped remains of the once mighty dirigible *Akron* are left to be salvaged after her destruction over the New Jersey coast on April 14, 1933. *(UPI)*

Wiley pressed his face against the window of the control cabin and watched in horror as the ship smashed downward into a blue-black fog hovering over a raging ocean. The pit of his stomach felt hollow. He was sick with the sensation of falling, as if he were in a plunging, cableless elevator. "Stand by for a crash!" Wiley yelled over the intercom.

In a moment the *Akron* smacked nose first into the churning sea. The dirigible's steel girders snapped like toothpicks, its wires and cables sprang pinging into the air, and seventy-three men were doomed to instant death in the freezing water. Wiley and two others somehow swam clear of the *Akron*'s giant silver skin as it flattened over the towering waves and drifted off.

Hours later, Navy officials notified of the disaster by coastal viewers sent out the little J-3, a nonrigid blimp, to rescue survivors. The commander of the J-3's seven-man crew grunted the words "suicidal attempt" on liftoff and was proved correct when the blimp, bucking forty-five-mile-an-hour winds, also crashed into the ocean and lost two of its crew to the sea.

News of the tragedy went out through official channels, and all ranking Naval officers were notified, one of whom was Rear Admiral Moffett, leading exponent and mentor of the Navy's lighter-than-air craft. It was a grim phone call.

The phone rang at 2:30 A.M. in the admiral's quiet home on Massachusetts Avenue in Washington, D.C. With a dressing gown thrown hastily around her body, Mrs. Moffett answered the call.

"This is the Navy Department," a voice blurted. "Will you please inform the admiral that the *Akron* has just crashed."

For a moment there was silence, and then, in painfully spoken words, Mrs. Moffett replied, "The . . . Admiral . . . is . . . on . . . board."

While planes and boats were still circling the crash area and plucking wreckage and bodies from the water, a hastily assembled Naval Board of Inquiry, headed by Rear Admiral Henry V. Butler, met at Lakehurst, New Jersey (which would be the scene of another dirigible disaster four years later) to determine the cause of the crash. Lieutenant Commander Wiley was on hand to tell his story.

Dr. Hugo Eckener, the genius behind the construction of the dirigible *Graf Zeppelin,* which had toured 300,000 accident-free miles, criticized the dumping of the water ballast, saying, "It is very well possible . . . the airship was no longer properly trimmed."

Fog and wind had grounded all scheduled passenger planes in the area on the day of the takeoff, Wiley explained, and even though weather conditions "probably would be unfavorable for attaining the object of the flight," which was to take radio compass dimensions along the New England coastline, the ship was ordered airborne. Regardless of the dirigible's history of mishaps and her acknowledged faulty construction, authorities incongruously felt "it was quite sturdy enough to withstand any condition."

Wiley then shocked the board by stating that the ship's commander, Captain McCord, after seeing a wall of lightning ahead, ordered the course shifted to fifteen degrees. The order was misunderstood as fifty degrees. The difference of thirty-five degrees, Wiley reasoned, drove the ship into the eye of the storm and made her a deathtrap.

The final official statement concerning the disaster was emphatically uttered by Chairman Vinson of the Naval Affairs Committee: "You can take it from me, there won't be any more big airships built. We have built three and lost two."

(ALSO SEE: Hindenburg *and* Shenandoah*)*

ALABAMA

TORNADO
March 21-22, 1932

On March 21, 1932, Marion, Alabama, was the first town struck in one of the most destructive series of tornadoes to wreak havoc across seven states. From this point at least a dozen vicious twisters ravaged the tornado belt, as they moved northeast toward Georgia and then splayed out into Tennessee, South Carolina, Kentucky and Virgina.

In Chilton County, Alabama, Sheriff Gore was eating supper with his family. When the tornado struck, he was knocked unconscious. Coming to, he found himself in the yard wedged under a tree truck. He wriggled out. "The wind was howling like mad," he told a correspondent later. "It was flashing brilliant, blinding lightning, and I heard my son call to me from across the yard. He was lying against the stump of a tree. We almost feared to rise against that wind, but both of us thought of his wife and four children, and immediately went to find them."

Gore and his son found the family in a corn patch where they had been blown; all were unhurt. Then the Gores raced to the neighboring farm of Battle Hamilton.

"His house was nowhere to be seen," Gore said in semishock. "Down the road a piece we found him cut to pieces by barbed wire, hanging on a fence. . . . Battle's wife had been blown into their corn field and was badly injured. They don't expect her to pull through [she didn't]. Then there was Battle's six-month-old son, Jack. We found his body in a creek. . . . He had been drowned, if he hadn't been killed before reaching the creek."

The tornadoes raged on, killing twenty-nine at Demopolis, five in Pulaski, Tennessee, and thirty-four in the vicinity of Rome, Dalton, Athens and Cartersville in northeastern Georgia. In Cleveland, Tennessee, the wind from a tornado snatched an infant from its mother's arms and dropped it to its death down a well.

Two national guardsmen stand in the ruins of a Northport, Alabama, home, one of hundreds destroyed by a series of vicious tornadoes that struck on March 21 and 22, 1932, killing 268 people in four states. *(UPI)*

Several freakish events were caused by the erratic fury of the twisters. In Dalton a man was blown to the top of a tree and a piece of wood impaled him there in a crucifixion of nature. He hung there until the next day when he was taken down and moved to a hospital, where he died.

Hundreds of rural dwellings were demolished by this army of tornadoes, and 268 persons were killed.

ALASKA

EARTHQUAKE
March 27, 1964

background: The worst earthquake in United States history occurred on March 27, 1964, one hundred miles southeast of Anchorage, Alaska, along the shores of Prince William Sound. It was estimated to be thirty to sixty miles beneath the earth's surface. The jolt registered a staggering 8.6 on the Richter Scale (as compared to the 1906 San Francisco Quake which registered 8.25). The quake began somewhere in the Fairweather Fault, and tremors struck as far south as Seattle, Washington, and Crescent City, California, where a twelve-foot *tsunami* roared ashore, destroying four square blocks and killing six persons. The hardest hit areas were the towns of Anchorage, Seward, Kodiak and Valdez in Alaska where 118 were killed and damage ran to $500 million. The seismic force unleashed by the Alaskan earthquake was estimated to be ten million times stronger than the atomic bomb dropped on Hiroshima.

For five bewildering minutes, starting at 5:36 P.M. on March 27, 1964, the worst quake ever experienced in the United States ravaged Anchorage and other towns in Alaska and spread as far south as Oregon and California to shred property and slash away life.

As Anchorage's fifty thousand residents scurried home to their evening meals, none had any warning of what was to come.

Sam Krogstad had just parked his car in the family garage when the earth suddenly erupted. His car, a Volkswagen, and the garage were hurled, with him still at the wheel, to a neighbor's yard. He was uninjured: "It was the fastest parking I ever did."

The downtown area began to break apart. Pavement and buildings undulated, signs fell into the streets, large chasms of earth gaped open and people slipped inside.

Celebrating his sixty-second birthday, ex-pilot and onetime barnstormer Bob Reeve was sitting in the posh confines of the Petroleum Club, fifteen floors atop the Anchorage Westward Hotel. Just as he lifted his drink to his lips, he was hurled backward and sent flying twenty-five feet, the room's tables, chairs, glasses, whiskey bottles and silverware rushing crazily at him. Reeve, no doubt, wondered "what was in that highball?"

Everything in Anchorage was swaying—no place was safe. Watching in amazement as his home was split in half and then disappeared into a crevice, Robert B. Atwood, editor of the *Anchorage Daily Times,* described the abrupt, devastating motion as "a giant taffy pull." Atwoood was alone at home and about to begin his trumpet lessons. On the first note, the world seemed to come to an end. He ran outside just in time to turn and see his house shattered to pieces by the quake. Great fissures opened, and he toppled into one of these, his arm and legs caught by the soft, warm earth below. He realized that the chasm could close any minute and crush him to death, but his right arm seemed permanently pinned until he realized that it was his trumpet that was wedged in the earth and that he was still holding on to it; he let go, worked his arm free, and climbed out of the crevice just in time.

The new J. C. Penney store started to come apart. Two

Anchorage streets looked like this after one of the greatest earthquakes in U.S. history struck on March 27, 1964. *(Wide World)*

teen-age girls were trapped in the swaying elevator. They thought they had pushed the wrong button (they were stuck in the elevator shaft for several hours, finally extricated by workers with acetylene torches). It took Carol Tucker, who was inside the Penney store, several moments to realize that a quake was in progress. China crashed noisily to the floor, glassware shattered, the walls swayed, light fixtures danced, then broke loose and exploded loudly. She ran through the darkened store, fell down the inanimate escalator and made it to a doorway where she watched in horror as the facade of the building gave way in great sheets of concrete, some several tons in weight. One of these smashed down upon a car outside, squashing it to a height of three feet. A woman was trapped inside, screaming as she threw herself to the floor.

Clarence Myers, an Army private from Fort Richardson, seeing the car flattened, ran through the street and gathered men to help remove the slab of concrete. They couldn't budge it. Someone brought a wrecker and in an hour, by using a blowtorch, the badly injured woman was taken out, only to die the next day.

During the five-minute upheaval, Anchorage's citizens fought for their lives; people ran madly into the streets, away from the crashing buildings and held on to anything to prevent them from slipping into the dozens of huge fissures that opened up, buckling back highway and sidewalks. A human chain was formed by at least one hundred persons. One of these was a man who had dashed from a sauna. He was completely naked, but no one noticed.

Anchorage's exclusive suburb, Turnagain-by-the-sea, was demolished. "My God, what's happening," a ham operator talking to a friend in Seattle suddenly exclaimed on his specially built car radio.

"The land has become the ocean, the streets are rippling like waves." Mrs. Jean Chance watched, horrified, as cars slammed into each other. "The earth started to roll," she later recalled. "It rolled for five minutes. . . . People were clinging to each other, to lampposts, to buildings." The two deepest fissures measured twelve feet deep and fifty feet wide.

Death was everywhere. Dr. Perry Mead, Anchorage's only neurosurgeon, was operating on victims when he was told that his twelve-year-old son had attempted to rescue his baby brother and had been killed along with the baby. The valiant doctor, tears streaming down his face, continued his operation.

The sixty-foot control tower at Anchorage International Airport began to sway and then snapped off, killing air controller Bill Taylor.

Phones went dead, power ceased and with it all electricity. Mains burst and there was no water. There was no heat. Fortunately no children were inside the two wrecked grade schools and the shattered high school. The Denali Theatre, which was complete flattened, was also empty. The quake struck only minutes before it was due to open its doors.

The great Alaskan earthquake produced a *tsunami* (seismic sea wave) that destroyed the port of Kodiak and drove fishing vessels far inland. *(Wide World)*

The shock wave stretched out its quaking arms on this Good Friday to other parts of Alaska. The peaceful port of Valdez was struck. Around the dock area a gigantic hole yawned open and a father picnicking with his two small children disappeared into it. The town's long dock had collapsed in a shudder of flying splinters, and thirty people were tossed into the water.

The island city of Kodiak was hit by a seventeen-foot *tsunami* (seismic sea wave) that destroyed most of the downtown section and sent fishing boats far inland. The radio on board William Cuthbert's eighty-six-foot crab boat, *Selief,* crackled: "*Selief, Selief,* where are you?"

Cuthbert dazedly looked about and reported, "It looks as though I'm in the back of the Kodiak schoolhouse five blocks from the shoreline." Nearby Kaguyak, a fishing village, simply vanished.

The town of Seward was on fire. Oil storage tanks had been ruptured, and flames were everywhere.

The quake spread to Oregon. At Depoe Bay in Beverly Beach State Park, a *tsunami* roared in and swept away four children who had been camping on the sand in bedrolls. Next came Crescent City, California, where a twelve-foot *tsunami* rushed ashore and smashed four square blocks, destroying 150 stores of the downtown section, drowning ten, injuring seventy and sending three thousand more in a desperate scramble to safety.

When the earth was again in repose, 125 persons had

Seward, Alaska, was ripped apart and trains were overturned by sea waves, which also ruptured and exploded oil storage tanks, setting the entire town on fire. *(UPI)*

been killed, 118 in Alaska. The new state was bankrupted by the quake, an estimated $500 million in damage having been done. It would take, according to Edward McDermott, federal director of the Office of Emergency Planning, $33 million to repair vital public services in Anchorage alone, not to mention the ruined cities of Valdez, Kodiak and Seward.

An official from Washington's Bureau of Public Roads called Alaska's state highway commissioner, D. A. McKinnon, as soon as telephone lines were restored.

"How much in matching funds can your state provide for the repair of roads?"

The weary McKinnon grimly illustrated the financial ruin of Alaska when he replied, "Not a damned cent."

In admirable response to Governor William A. Egan's plea for help, the 40,000 United States servicepeople stationed in Alaska began to supply vital necessities, along with medical teams and armies of workers to clear away the wreckage. President Johnson declared Alaska a national disaster area, and millions of dollars of aid began to flow northward to the stricken state.

Egan stated publicly: "Along with so many thousands of others, I shed tears unashamed at what my eyes saw in a land of love." Surprisingly, the governor was right. In the pioneer land of Alaska where people were held together in a tight-knit community, selfless and humane efforts on the part of more fortunate residents to aid the homeless and bankrupt abounded. There was hardly any looting in the snowbound state and no outbreak of disorder.

A stubborn people, most Alaskans refused to be driven out by the quake. On Government Hill, a housing area near Elmendorf Air Force Base, destruction was rampant. One man, however, let the world know how he felt by pinning a sign to his half-destroyed home: "My neighbors have left . . . I'M STAYING!"

Down in a large hole in Anchorage were the ruins of an office building. Its owner had nailed a droll sign to what had once been the front door: "I knew it would be tough to make a living in Alaska, but I never thought I'd go this far in the hole."

When the first batch of newsmen arrived from the "Lower 48," they stumbled along the main streets of Anchorage, aghast at the destruction. They saw a haggard-looking policeman, his uniform torn, his eyes bloodshot, his face black with beard stubble (he had been awake for forty hours, digging out trapped people from the rubble). As he passed the clot of newsmen, the officer gave a weak salute. "Good morning, gentlemen," he said. "Welcome to hell."

ALASKA AIRLINES BOEING 727 — AIR CRASH, September 4, 1971

Flight 1866 of Alaska Airlines with 109 persons on board became a mangled funeral pyre when it slammed into 15,300-foot Mount Fairweather at midnight on September 4, 1971. The plane, piloted by Captain Richard Adams, was flying from Anchorage to Seattle and making stops at Cordova, Yakutat, Sitka and Juneau.

While attempting an instrument landing at Juneau, Adams got lost in his approach. At that time the Juneau Municipal Airport lacked two important elements of an instrument-landing system: a glide slope device, which could tell a pilot if his craft was veering away from the proper approach, and a localizer, which would line up an in-coming plane with the center of the landing strip.

All on board died.

AL BASRAH, IRAQ — MASS POISONING, September, 1971

One of the best-kept secrets of a national catastrophe was the mass poisoning that occurred in Iraq, chiefly in its main port of Al Basrah, in September, 1971. Early that month huge cargoes of American barley and Mexican wheat that had been treated with a mercury solution arrived. The grain, intended as seed only, had been chemically treated to prevent rot. It had been sprayed with a bright pink dye to indicate the presence of the lethal substance. In addition the shipments had been clearly marked in Spanish and English, but no such warnings in Iraqi were printed on the grain sacks.

The grain was stolen from the docks of Al Basrah on a wholesale basis and then sold to starving residents. A monstrous epidemic of mercury poisoning ensued, but the Iraqi government hushed up the story.

American newsman Ed Hughes ferreted out the story two years later in September, 1973, and pressured authorities to admit that 6,530 hospital cases of mercury poisoning had occurred. Of these, officials stated that 459 had died. Hughes began an exhaustive investigation into the secret disaster and discovered that "as many as 6,000 may have died and perhaps 100,000 were injured."

The injured were physically crippled, blinded, made deaf and brain damaged.

ALEXANDRIA, EGYPT — EARTHQUAKE, July 21, A.D. 365

A catastrophe of worldwide measure occurred on July 21, A.D. 365, during the second year of the reigns of both Valentinian and Valens when, according to the historian Gibbon, "The greater part of the Roman world was shaken by a violent and destructive earthquake." The waters surrounding Sicily, Dalmatia, Greece and Egypt drew back several hundred feet from the shore and then dashed forward again in giant *tsunamis* that created widespread destruction.

Alexandria, Egypt, was hardest hit. The quake and subsequent waves destroyed some of the world's finest architecture, including the fourth wonder of the world, the incredible 600-foot-high lighthouse whose beacon could be seen thirty miles out to sea. Its stump remained for another 500 years.

More than 50,000 people in Alexandria perished with the magnificent lighthouse.

The lighthouse at Alexandria, Egypt, towering 600 feet, was destroyed by an earthquake on July 21, A.D. 365.

ALITALIA AIRLINES — AIR CRASH, May 5, 1972

The worst air crash in Alitalia Airlines history occurred when a DC-8 jetliner crashed into 12,250-foot-high Montagna Lunga (Long Mountain) while attempting to land at Palermo, Sicily's Punta Raisi Airport, on May 5, 1972.

All 115 passengers and crew members were killed on impact. The plane, on a routine flight from Rome, was attempting to avoid the ring of mountains surrounding the Palermo airport, one of the most dangerous landing fields in Europe, especially at night. Authorities concluded that the pilot was flying too low. The crash created fires in the woods on the mountain that raged for several days.

National police inspect the ruins of an Alitalia DC-8 jetliner, which crashed near Palermo, Sicily, on May 5, 1972, killing all 115 on board. *(UPI)*

ALLEGHENY AIRLINES DC-9

AIR CRASH
August 9, 1969

All eighty-three persons on board an Allegheny Airlines DC-9 flight attempting to land at Weir Cook Airport in Indianapolis, Indiana, were killed on August 9, 1969, after being hit by a small plane. The student pilot of the single-engine Piper Cherokee, a plumber flying a solo training flight, sheared away the DC-9's tail. The Allegheny flight spiraled to earth out of control and crashed outside of Shelbyville, Indiana.

Radar control did not detect the small plane in the vicinity of the DC-9 since it was not equipped with a transponder (standard equipment on all commercial airlines), which would have bounced back a radar signal to airport controllers and would have probably averted the accident.

State police and officials search a debris-strewn field near Indianapolis, Indiana, the site of an Allegheny Airlines crash which took the lives of eighty-three persons. *(Wide World)*

ALL-NIPPON AIRWAY BOEING 727

AIR CRASH
February 4, 1966

There was never a complete explanation for the destruction of All-Nippon's 727 flight arriving in Tokyo from Sapporo. Masaki Takahashi, an experienced pilot, had made the trip dozens of times. The only divergence in procedures on this February 4, 1966, trip was that Takahashi told ground control that he was making a visual landing. Controllers thought there might have been some slight malfunctioning of equipment.

The weather over Tokyo at 6:59 P.M. was clear, and 133 passengers and crew members strapped themselves in for the landing. As the 727 was making its airport approach, it suddenly vanished from the radar screen. The minutes silently dragged by while controllers scanned the Tokyo Bay area in search of the plane. More than one hundred persons waiting for their relatives at the airport became nervous when the plane failed to appear.

The smashed tail section of an All-Nippon Airway 727 jet is lifted from the bottom of Tokyo Bay; 133 people were killed when the jet crashed on February 4, 1966. *(UPI)*

A report came in stating that fishermen had seen "a pillar of fire" plummet into Tokyo Bay and then disappear. When this information was released to the waiting crowd, people began to shout.

"Were there enough preservers?" asked one.

"Did the plane carry rescue crafts?" another anxiously quizzed.

Many of the answers came at dawn when 25 bodies were recovered from Tokyo Bay after the corpse-clogged fuselage was brought up by grappling hooks. The bodies were brought ashore and placed in plain wooden coffins waiting on the dock. All 133 persons on board the 727 were killed.

ALL-NIPPON BOEING FLIGHT 58 and JAPANESE AF F-86

AIR CRASH
July 30, 1971

background: A midair collision between passenger airliner Flight 58 of the All-Nippon Airways and a Japanese military F-86 Sabre jet over Morioka, Japan, on July 30, 1971, caused the deaths of all 162 on board the passenger plane. This was the largest recorded number of people to die in a single air crash to date. The pilot of the military craft was arrested and tried for negligence.

Almost all of the 155 passengers on All-Nippon's Flight 58, which had just taken off at Chitose Airport, were members of a society dedicated to the memory of the war dead. The group had finished touring shrines on the island of Hokkaido before boarding their homeward-bound plane. Takeoff was accomplished without incident, and soon the jam-packed Boeing 727 was comfortably cruising at 28,000 feet.

The 1971 skies over Japan were crowded with heavy air traffic. The 727's pilot was well aware that 200 near-collisions each year was normal (there were an estimated 600 in the United States that year), and yet he was relatively unconcerned. It was merely another fact of life—and death—in his profession. A half hour after takeoff, the pilot spotted an F-86 Sabre jet. His craft was almost on top of it, and the 727 pilot barely managed to get off a distress signal before impact. The passenger plane burst apart immediately, the fragments of debris and 162 bodies—all 155 passengers and a crew of seven—scattering for miles.

Sergeant Yoshimi Ichikawa, pilot of the Sabre jet, and the lone survivor of the collision, managed to parachute to safety. A trainee who had only logged twenty-one hours in the air, Ichikawa had been performing formation turns under the guidance of Captain Tamotsu Kuma, who was in another jet. Both Sabre jets were without radar, and Kuma saw the fast-approaching 727 only at the last second when he called out to his student to climb and turn immediately. It was too late.

Student pilot Yoshimi Ichikawa was arrested after crashing into the All-Nippon Airways jetliner with his F-86 jet. *(UPI)*

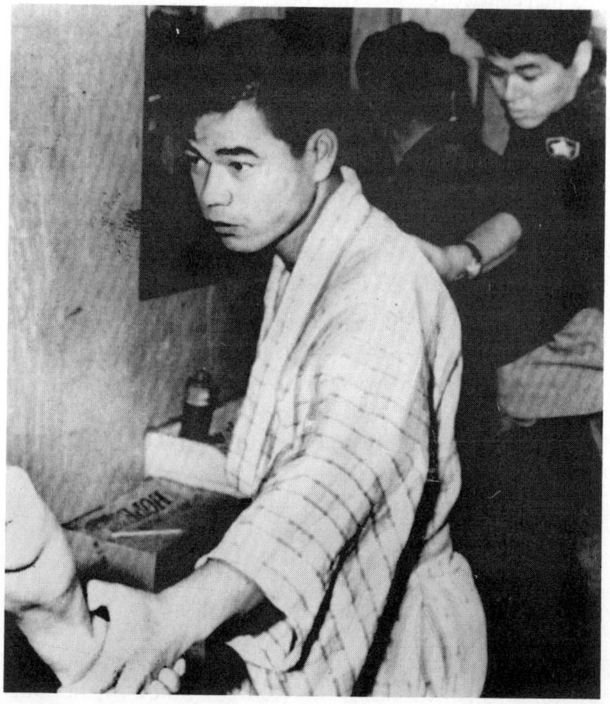

"I saw a civilian plane approach from the rear," the apprentice airman later stated, "and felt a jolt in my tail."

Upon parachuting to earth, Ichikawa was arrested for involuntary homicide. He was later tried, but acquitted.

The crash was the worst ever involving aircraft, with the possible exception of a Russian Aeroflot airliner that crashed on October 10, 1972, near Moscow's International Airport, killing 176 persons, including more than 50 foreigners. The Soviet government refused to release details concerning the disaster.

ALPENA

MARINE DISASTER
October 15, 1880

background: The 653-ton interlake passenger steamer *Alpena,* first launched in 1865 with an overall length of 175 feet and a width of 35 feet, foundered in a Lake Michigan storm on the evening of October 15, 1880. All 101 passengers and crew on board were lost.

After picking up passengers and freight at Grand Haven and Muskegon, Michigan, Captain Nelson W. Napier headed his steamship, *Alpena,* toward Chicago, 108 miles to the west. October 15, 1880, changed rapidly from a warm fall day to a stormy afternoon, purple black clouds hustling monstrous waves across Lake Michigan in a matter of minutes. It was one of the worst natural disasters in Great Lakes history. The storm destroyed groves of trees and fishing shacks along the shore and trapped and severely damaged ninety ships, many of which were in the harbor. By the time the storm struck, the *Alpena* was far from shore. She began to break up rapidly. None of the 101 persons on board survived.

For four days, flotsam from the steamer washed ashore, first thousands of apples that had escaped from the hold. Next came small pieces of debris, then buckets and flags marked "Alpena" (this storm was known by mariners afterward as the "Alpena Storm"). Then human bodies and whole wooden slabs from the shredded cabins of the doomed ship drifted ashore.

From behind one of these dismembered walls, a college professor, searching the wreckage, plucked a note that read: "This is terrible. The steamer is breaking up fast. I am aboard from Grand Haven to Chicago." It was signed George Connor.

ALPS

AVALANCHES
218 B.C.

In October of 218 B.C. the struggling army of Hannibal reached the heights of the still-unknown pass the Carthaginians took through the Alps en route from Spain to Italy to conquer the Romans. According to the writings of Polybius and Livy, the African general led an army of 38,000 soldiers, 8,000 horsemen and 37 elephants.

Their descent proved disastrous, mainly because the soldiers were inexperienced climbers. As the Italian plains spread before them, the descent became a race among the legions to get into the warm Italian lowlands. The rush of troops created a series of avalanches that engulfed and killed 18,000 men, 2,000 horses and several elephants in a single day. Many contemporary historians believe the pass was the Col de la Traversette.

The poet Silius Italicus (A.D. 25-101) refers to the catastrophe in his epic poem, *Punici:* "There where the path is intercepted by the glistening slope, he [Hannibal] pierces the resistant ice with his lance. Detached snow drags the men into the abyss and snow falling rapidly from the high summits engulfs the living squadrons."

AMAZON — MARINE DISASTER — January 4, 1852

background: The 3,000-ton British passenger liner, *Amazon,* of the Royal Mail Steam Packet Company, launched at Blackwell, England, June 28, 1851, sank on her maiden voyage, January 4, 1852, 110 miles off the Scillies at the northern end of the Bay of Biscay, due to fire; 140 of the 161 passengers and crew members on board were killed.

By the time the British Admiralty ordered the construction of the then immense passenger ship, *Amazon,* she was already obsolete, being a paddle steamer with a wooden hull. Eight years prior to this, the trend had already been set for iron hulls and screw propellers exemplified by the P&O Company, owners of such modern steamers as the *Pacha* and *Shanghai.* Still, the Admiralty mistakenly placed its confidence in wooden-hulled ships and insisted that the ship, described in one source as "the largest timber-built steamship ever constructed in England," be completed by mid-1851.

On fire and sinking fast with 140 still aboard, the *Amazon* succumbs to wild seas in the Bay of Biscay, January 4, 1852.

There was trouble with the *Amazon* right from the beginning, when she sailed on January 2, 1852, on her maiden voyage to the West Indies with Captain William Symons commanding. The passenger list was low at fifty wealthy travelers with 111 crew members to service them. All became apprehensive when the *Amazon* smacked into a terrific gale off Portland Bill. Alarm spread when the ship was stopped because of hot bearings.

Two days later the *Amazon* burst into flames amidships while 110 miles off the Scillies. Huge amounts of water were pumped into the fire, but to no avail. Captain Symons kept the engines churning either to keep the ship heading into the wind (which only succeeded in fanning the flames) or, as later reported, because the fire prevented crewmen from turning them off. When all lifeboats were ordered lowered, calamity ensued. Most of the lifeboats were released prematurely by their aft-end falls, which gave way and caused them to hang vertically from the fore-end falls, thus spilling passengers and crew into the boiling ocean waters surrounding the ship.

Those who managed to cling to the lifeboats in this precarious position soon lost strength and slipped into the heavy waves. Only one boat was safely lowered, and it contained twenty-one persons—only three passengers—who eventually reached safety.

The debacle that was the *Amazon* soon caused the wholesale conversion to iron-hulled ships and screw propellers as standard construction in ocean-going vessels.

AMERICA and UNITED STATES — MARINE DISASTERS — December 4, 1868

A bone-chilling wind blowing down the Ohio River on the night of December 4, 1868, embraced two large steamboats, the *America* and the *United States.* Both were United States mail boats and regularly passed each other, tooting friendly greetings. On this night, however, they were to meet in disaster.

The *America* traveled upbound, doing about 10 m.p.h. Most of her passengers had retired to their cabins for the night. An elderly pilot, Napoleon B. Jenkins, had replaced the regular pilot on board the *America,* and for some inexplicable reason Jenkins ordered the boat to proceed along the Indiana shore instead of following the customary route along the Kentucky side of the Ohio

River. This put the *America* directly in the path of the *United States,* which routinely hugged the Indiana shore in order to avoid the passage of her sister ship.

The *America* was dark, except for her signal lanterns, and the *United States,* driving downstream at 20 m.p.h., was aglow with dozens of lights as a double wedding party celebrated loudly by singing in the saloon. They became so boisterous, in fact, that Captain Wade of the *United States* left the wheelhouse to quiet them down lest they disturb those already asleep in their cabins.

Near Warsaw, Kentucky, Jenkins blew the whistle on the *America.* A faint reply could be heard, but Jenkins did not alter his course. Moments later, at approximately 11:15 P.M., the *America* rammed into the *United States,* bow to bow. Barrels of petroleum had been lashed to the bow of the *United States,* and these crashed open into the river, on board the *America* and onto its own furnaces. In seconds the entire stretch of river was a mass of flames. Cotton piled high on the bow of the *America* caught fire at once. Flames shot up on the *United States* and reached as high as her hurricane roof. Captain Wade ordered the *United States* to back off, which she did sluggishly. For two hundred yards between and around the two burning ships, the water was a solid sheet of fire from the oil slick.

The *America,* under Captain Whitten (who was in his cabin when Jenkins chose his fatal course), lost all power and, sinking slowly, drifted toward shore. Her half-dressed passengers gathered on the upper deck. As the ship came close to shore, a woman clad in a thin negligee jumped from the upper deck and caught hold of a tree branch overhanging the river. She shouted wildly and another figure in a negligee, her daughter, also sprang from the deck and clutched the tree branch. Both women dangled there for a moment, the flames from the river casting weird shadows upon their squirming forms until their combined weight caused the branch to break off. They fell into the river and disappeared.

Another passenger, a young husband, on the *America* fastened a lifebelt around his wife and with a rope dragged her through the flaming water to shore. When the ship grounded, a Norwegian violinist, Ole Bull, and three of his troupe, waded ashore, their hair and clothes singed but the violin cases they held over their heads intact and dry.

Those on board the *United States* were in worse condition. Upon impact, the entire forward part of the ship burst into flames. Captain Wade stood on the roof bellowing orders to his scurrying crew, but few of his commands could be carried out. The vessel was dying. The flames ran up the boat's stairways and were soon as high as the chimneys. Women, mostly from the wedding parties, their hair and clothes on fire, raced along the sides of the ship and screamed horribly as they fell into the river. About two dozen persons climbed into a yawl suspended by a derrick at the stern of the ship and desperately attempted to lower the boat into the water. The derrick broke under the strain of the weight, and the yawl was thrown down into the river where it capsized. All were drowned.

In five minutes both great steamboats were smoldering wrecks. An estimated seventy-two persons had either drowned or burned to death. About 10:00 A.M. the following day the small packet steamer *C. T. Dumont* puffed up the channel and rescued survivors.

The burned-out hull of the *United States* was eventually towed to Cincinnati where a new *United States* was erected on her. The *America* was wrecked beyond repair, and her sunken remains rested near Bryant's Creek, Indiana, for thirty years. When the waters were low, small boys, mindless of the great tragedy she represented, played upon her bones.

(ALSO SEE: Sultana)

AMERICAN AIRLINES CONVAIR 6780

AIR CRASH
January 22, 1952

Captain John J. Reid, pilot of American Airlines Flight 6780, was making an approach to Newark, New Jersey's airport. The Convair aircraft had only twenty-three passengers and crew aboard, and though rain and fog limited Reid's visibility to three-quarters of a mile, it was still a routine landing on the afternoon of January 22, 1952.

Firemen of Elizabeth, New Jersey, water down the smoldering wreckage of a Convair that crashed on January 22, 1952, killing all twenty-three on board and six on the ground. *(UPI)*

The landing was made through instruments, which meant that Reid would be "talked" down by ground controllers at Newark. The pilot also could rely on several instruments. First, a low-frequency radio beam signaled through Morse Code—A, dot-dash to the left, and N, dash-dot to the right—until a steady whine of both signals indicated that the plane was approaching the runway on course. An automatic direction finder and an instrument landing system television beam in the cockpit also pinpointed the landing strip. In addition ground controllers tracked the ship accurately and could warn Reid if he veered off course.

Just as Reid swung his ship to the right of the Union County Courthouse, towering 320 feet above Elizabeth, New Jersey, which was usual flying practice for all pilots in foul weather, his plane's "blip" vanished from the radar scope at ground control.

The controller, puzzled, was on the air, calling, "American 6780. American 6780. This is Newark radar. We've lost your target, sir, after you drifted well to the right there. I don't have you in radar contact at present. We'll try to pick you up . . . American 6780. This is Newark radar. Still unable to pick up a target on you .,. . could you advise us your position . . . American 6780. This is Newark radar. Do you hear? Over . . . American 6780 . . . American 6780 . . . This is Newark radar .,. . One, two, three, four, five, five, four, three, two, one . . . Do you hear Newark radar? Over . . ."

No one on Flight 6780 could hear. Reid, his crew, and all passengers, including a former Secretary of War, Robert P. Patterson, were dead, along with six others on the ground, twenty-nine all told. The American Convair had suddenly plunged straight down while on its approach, smashed into several houses and burned to cinders.

It was one of the strangest air mishaps in history and was not solved until another pilot flew Reid's exact course several days later, and it was determined that, at an altitude of eight hundred feet, Reid, who had not misread his instruments, was suddenly dealing with a runaway plane. Apparently, one of the four propellers had reversed its pitch and freakishly began spinning backward, which would cause the plane to plummet instantly to earth. Similar accidents had occurred previously.

But no one ever knew for sure.

Bundled against the cold is eight-year-old Robert Sullivan, one of the few survivors of an American Airlines Electra that crashed into New York's East River, February 3, 1959. *(UPI)*

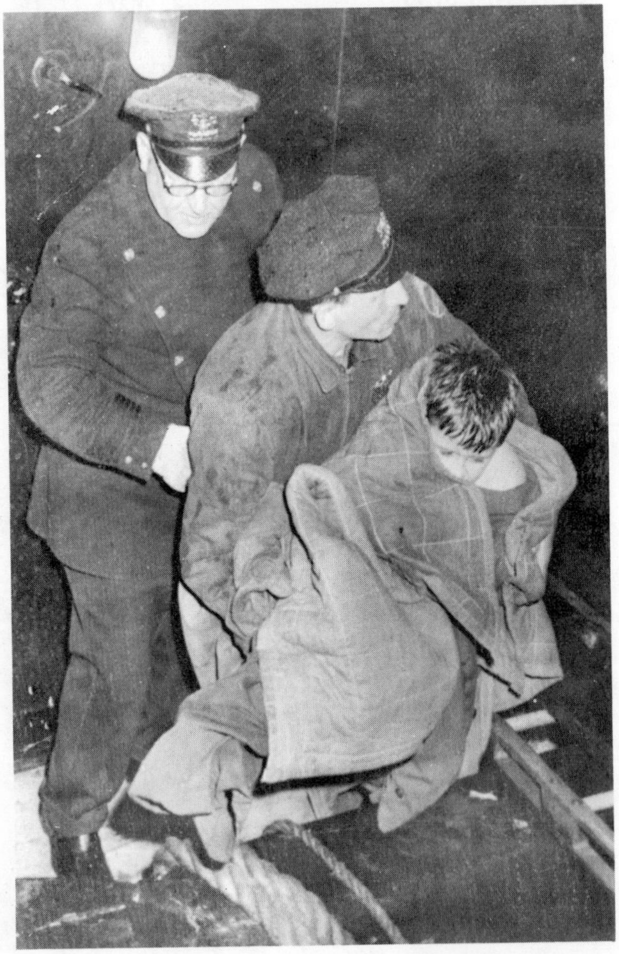

AMERICAN AIRLINES LOCKHEED ELECTRA — AIR CRASH, February 3, 1959

Heading from Chicago to New York, fifty-nine-year-old Captain Albert DeWitt had just announced to his seventy-two passengers and crew that they would be landing at La Guardia Airport in five minutes. The new Lockheed Electra prop-jet DeWitt was flying had been in service just twelve days; he had asked to be named its pilot and was full of praise for the luxury airliner.

There was fog and rain over the city on the night of February 3, 1959, and just after DeWitt switched off the intercom and began an instrument landing, the plane plunged downward at terrific speeds. One passenger, Herbert Forman, later stated, "There was a sudden jolt and a shudder. There was a terrific bang, and the plane went in splinters and bits." Suddenly Forman was in the East River, swimming for his life. Thrashing about next to him was Edward Gottlieb, a Manhattan advertising executive famous for dreaming up the slogan: "Which twin has the Toni?"

When the plane hit the water at 135 m.p.h., part of the fuselage and tail stayed intact and remained afloat. Seymour Kemach, a salesman from Brooklyn, had been sitting in the lounge at the rear of the plane talking to two stewardesses. After the crash he found himself still in the plane with water rising to his knees. The overhead lights were out, but a blue emergency light was still on, and in this dim glare he could see a young boy's head protruding from the wreckage and water. There was an emergency exit next to him; he kicked it open and helped the stewardesses onto the tail of the plane, which rose up out of the East River.

Kemach then went back for the boy, Bobby Sullivan, who was still alive, and pulled him from the rising water. By the time he and the youngster got out onto the tail, Kemach was surprised to see that the boy's mother, Lorraine Sullivan, who was pregnant, was also there, having worked her way through a window. Holding on to the tail, the five called for help and tried to see through the inky darkness surrounding them.

Tugboat Captain Samuel Nickerson was dragging several valuable barges with his tug, *H. Thomas Teti, Jr.*, when he spotted the survivors 800 feet away through the mist. He cut loose the barges (a risky act in itself; he would have to face the owner later) and made straight for the people.

Gottlieb, who had sunk several times before resurfacing and swimming on with a seat cushion for support, heard cries all about him, "My God! I'm drowning. Save me!" "Help me! This way, this way!" Then he heard another voice ask, "Can you swim over here?" It was Kemach, who was on the Electra's wing.

Forman reached the wing, too. He and Gottlieb climbed onto it, encouraged by a man swimming next to them whose face was coated with blood. He was the badly injured flight engineer Warren Cook, thirty-six. "Go on, go on, you can make it," he shouted. Cook had repeatedly saved Forman's life in the water.

Kemach and one of the stewardesses, Joan Zeller, had already left the tail section and were swimming toward the tugboat to direct Nickerson to the other survivors. They were pulled aboard with boat hooks. The *Teti* raced up to the fast-sinking Electra.

As it took off the remaining survivors (the other stewardess had slipped off the wingtip and disappeared into the dark waters), a piece of the plane's fuselage bumped into the tug. It contained a door partly opened; a human arm waved frantically from it. Everett Phelps, the *Teti*'s mate, vainly tried to pry the door open and save the unknown person behind it, but the current swept the wreckage under.

"I'll never forget that feeling," Phelps said later as he recalled helplessly watching the debris sink with its human cargo.

Out of the seventy-three on board the Electra, seven were saved. It was a miracle. Why the prop-jet crashed in the first place remains a mystery. Some have speculated

Seven persons clung to the tail of an Electra turboprop that dived into New York's East River on February 3, 1959. Sixty-five persons were killed. *(UPI)*

that Captain DeWitt had not read his altimeter, a new type, properly and that this caused him to come in too low. Another theory was that La Guardia's runway 22 lacked a radio beam that would have told DeWitt his exact altitude.

AMUDE, SYRIA — **FIRE** — **November 13, 1960**

About 175 children were gathered for a special children's film program on the night of November 13, 1960, in the small town of Amude, Syria, near the Turkish border. Shortly after the film began, a violent explosion ripped open the projection booth. Strands of burning film flew into the audience, and within minutes the entire theater was ablaze, trapping and killing 152 children. Twenty-three badly injured youngsters managed to escape.

The dead children were buried in a mass funeral the next day.

ANATOLIA, ASIA MINOR (TURKEY) — **EARTHQUAKE** — **October 16, 1883**

The earth shook once in the province of Anatolia, Asia Minor, now part of Turkey, on October 16, 1883. The tremor lasted only a few seconds. But in those moments the homes of 20,000 persons were completely destroyed, and more than 1,000 others were killed as the walls of their houses collapsed upon them or they fell into huge crevices that snapped open and shut in seconds.

Homeless thousands took to the open fields, and several hundred of these later died of cold and starvation before relief arrived from Constantinople.

The elegant luxury liner *Andrea Doria,* empty of life, rolls over in placid Atlantic waters leaving splintered lifeboats in her wake. *(Wide World)*

ANDREA DORIA and STOCKHOLM **MARINE DISASTER July 25-26, 1956**

background: The elegant Italian passenger liner, *Andrea Doria,* built at the Ansaldo Shipyards at Sestri (Genoa) from 1949 to 1951, was 697 feet long, 11 decks high, had a 90-foot beam, and displaced 29,083 tons. This ship, powered by twin turbine engines of 35,000 horsepower, made her maiden voyage from Genoa to New York in January, 1953. On her fifty-first voyage, with 1,134 passengers and a crew of 572 on board, the ship was struck by the 12,644-ton Swedish-American liner *Stockholm* on July 25, 1956, off Nantucket Island, Massachusetts, sinking the next day; 52 persons were killed, 1,654 were saved by rescue ships *Cape Ann, Private William H. Thomas* and the *Ile de France* in one of the most dramatic rescue operations ever witnessed at sea.

The *Andrea Doria* was one of the most elegant, luxurious passenger liners in the world, the pride of Italian Lines, which had lavished three years of design and decoration on her during construction and provided the ship with three outdoor pools (the only ship in the world to offer so many), hand-painted murals throughout the lounges, three movie theaters, air conditioning, deluxe private accommodations and cuisine that was unmatched by any other ocean liner.

She was a product of grace and art, an attempt by the Italian Lines to offer in the immediate postwar years, not the largest, fastest ship afloat—although the *Andrea Doria* had a twenty-six-knot capacity and cruised at twenty-three—but one of total convenience and utter relaxation. She was named after a sixteenth-century admiral, a military savior of Italy.

On July 7, 1956, the *Andrea Doria* embarked from Genoa on her fifty-first voyage to New York, with leisurely stops along the Riviera before heading past the Azores and into the open sea. For years the Nantucket Lightship had functioned as a navigational guidepoint for all ships entering the dangerous Nantucket shoals, one of the most hazardous seafaring lanes in the world. (The liners *Republic* and *Florida* had collided twenty-five miles from the lightship on January 23, 1909. On May 16, 1934, the giant liner *Olympic* smashed into the Nantucket Lightship in dense fog and seven of the lightship's crew were killed.)

The same kind of fog enveloped the *Andrea Doria* as she approached the lightship on the night of July 25, 1956. In the spacious wheelhouse with its two helms and two radar sets to detect nearby ships, Captain Piero Calamai, fifty-eight, a veteran of thirty-nine years at sea, maintained a cruising speed of twenty-two knots. Calamai was confident that his radar would pick up any ship hazarding his path.

The small 12,644-ton Swedish-American liner, *Stockholm,* which had departed New York that

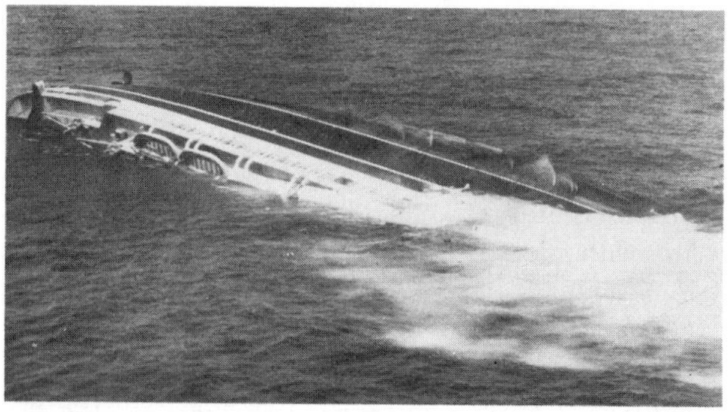

morning at 11:30 A.M., was outward bound, also enveloped in the thick, soupy fog. She was cruising at eighteen knots. At 11:45 P.M. as Third Officer Ernst Johannsen-Carstens stood a solitary watch in the *Stockholm*'s wheelhouse, the ships collided.

"It's a ship!" yelled the *Doria*'s Second Officer Curzio Franchini to Captain Calamai, as they watched the all white *Stockholm* emerge from the fog. "I can see a ship coming against us." The *Doria* was presenting her starboard side to the onrushing bow of the *Stockholm.*

Third Officer Eugenio Giannini spotted the lights of the *Stockholm* and screamed: "She is turning, she is turning! She is showing the red light! She is coming toward us!"

Captain Calamai ordered "All left," and the helmsman spun the wheel desperately. The *Doria*'s whistles screeched and Calamai gripped the rails, waiting for the impact. The *Stockholm*'s bow sliced the *Doria*'s hull like a butter knife. The Italian liner, using all her power to escape the collision, dragged the smaller Swedish ship until the *Stockholm,* her bow sheered away, disengaged and slipped back into the fog.

Captain H. Gunnar Nordenson raced to the wheelhouse of the *Stockholm* to hear a sputtering explanation from Third Officer Carstens, who had prudently ordered all of the watertight doors of the Swedish ship closed.

Nordenson peered at the fast disappearing *Doria* as she churned away into the nightfog. "Who is she?" he asked.

"I don't know," Carstens replied.

Thousands of tons of water roared into the *Andrea Doria,* already a doomed ship. The gash in her side was thirty feet deep. She immediately listed to her right, making her lifeboats on that side useless—it was impossible to lower them from that angle. To avoid panic, Calamai refused to sound an alarm and intended to save his vessel by beaching her. He ordered an SOS alert.

The reaction of the *Doria*'s passengers was mixed but far from chaotic. The then mayor of Philadelphia, Richardson Dilworth, and his wife were knocked from their beds to the floor of their cabin. "I think we hit an iceberg, like the *Titanic,*" Mrs. Dilworth said as they dressed to leave their cabin.

Several people, like ship's surgeon Dr. Bruno Donati, thought the boiler had exploded. Morris Novik, head of New York radio station WOV, minimized the rumble. "It's really nothing," he told others. "Let's sit tight until we find out what's wrong."

Ruth Roman, Hollywood actress, was more apprehensive. She stopped dancing in the first-class lounge, slipped off her high heels and raced to her double cabin where she awakened her three-year-old son, Dickie, quickly dressed him and said, "We're going on a picnic."

Throughout the night the *Doria* listed closer and closer to the water. The SOS brought two ships, a Navy transport, *Pvt. William H. Thomas,* and the *Cape Ann,* to the vicinity. These ships, coupled to the few boats Captain Calamai could get away, however, were incapable of handling the 1,600 persons attempting to escape the sinking *Doria.*

At the last minute, a ship altered her Europe-bound

The Swedish liner *Stockholm* en route to New York, minus her bow, after a collision with the *Andrea Doria* on July 25, 1956. *(Wide World)*

course and raced through the night heroically to answer the SOS. Hundreds of the *Doria*'s passengers, beginning to feel themselves lost, saw the huge white letters of the liner, *Ile de France*.

They applauded, sang, wept and prayed their thankfulness.

Captain de Baudean ordered every light on board his great ship set ablaze. "Turn on the lights, all the lights, and let them know we are here." The glow from the *Ile de France,* lowering her huge lifeboats as she came alongside the sinking *Doria,* was one of the most inspiring sights ever witnessed at sea. In what has been heralded as the most dramatic ocean rescue operation ever conducted, the *Ile de France* and the other ships saved all but fifty-two lives.

As if to propitiate the gods, wealthy women in the lifeboats threw their costly jewelry into the water.

The luxurious rooms and spacious decks empty of human life, the *Andrea Doria* sank to a depth of 225 feet at 10:09 A.M. Her resting place has been permanently marked by a yellow buoy. Her passing brought improvements in radar devices that could detect the true course of ships, rather than their relative positions, and made double watches in wheelhouses mandatory.

Months later, Captain Calamai sorrowfully remarked, "When I was a boy, and all my life, I loved the sea; now I hate it."

ANGOLA, NEW YORK

RAILWAY WRECK
December 18, 1867

The general nonconformity in track sizes of early American railroads was the cause of what was later called the "Angola Horror." From the beginning of the nineteenth century through the late 1860's, track widths varied with the scores of independent railroad lines crisscrossing the land. The variance was from four feet, eight and one-half inches to seven feet, and several lines used "compromise" cars, interchangeable vehicles equipped with extra wide flanges to compensate for the different track widths.

A compromise car was the last coach on the Lake Shore Railroad's New York Express as it made its way past Angola, New York, on December 18, 1867, at a speed of 30 m.p.h. As engineer Charles Carscadin pulled away from Angola, John Martin, a resident standing on the platform, noticed the last car joggle unsteadily.

Martin ran after the train and waved his hat in warning as the train picked up steam. The train moved toward a trestle bridge that loomed fifty feet above Big Sisters Creek. When on the bridge, engineer Carscadin heard the alarm bell in his cabin and yanked his whistle cord to alert brakemen to stop their individual cars. Only two brakemen were on board, and they simply did not have enough time to stop the seven cars.

By the time one of them began working his way

The railway tragedy at Angola on December 18, 1867, was caused by oversized wheels on narrow-gauge rails. *(Harper's Weekly)*

Rescuers attempt to free those trapped in the burning coach, Angola, New York, December 18, 1867. *(Harper's Weekly)*

toward the end of the train, the last car was already derailed and being dragged sideways across the bridge. Its coupling snapped, and the car dived into the ravine onto an ice-covered slope. The second-to-the-last car, according to Martin, who was still running after the train and bringing other Angola residents, "scooted the other way . . . it rolled off sideways like a saw log."

Only two persons were able to escape from the first car before it crashed, and only by sheer clawing on ice did they manage to scramble up the frozen slope where the wooden car burned, its stoves coating its splintered walls with flames. Forty-one people were trapped in the burning wreckage. Rescuers from Angola failed to reach the car; they either slid uncontrollably down the ice-packed slopes or could not make their ways up the slippery incline. From inside the car, several shots were heard. A reporter later speculated that someone had been carrying a pistol, and the intense heat from the flaming car had ignited the bullets. Another person insisted that some merciful soul had dispatched those helplessly pinned in the wreckage rather than see them roast alive. From the top of the trestle, a human chain was made and extended down to the top of the smashed car. One-by-one survivors were hauled out this way, passed over linked bodies until they reached the trestle. Flames drove the rescuers back, and there was little they could do but listen in anguish as the remaining trapped passengers died.

On the other side of the bridge, the second-to-the-last car had flopped onto a more secure bank, striking a tree and killing a man. Passengers easily escaped or were helped from this car.

The "Angola Horror" became a *cause cèlébre.* It prompted authorities to develop better safety devices. Had engineer Carscadin been able to operate the brakes of his train from the cab, in all probability there would have been no accident. As a direct result of this accident, George Westinghouse invented and refined the air brake eighteen months later; this was the single most important safety device in railroad history. As a result of this disaster, the use of "compromise" cars ceased and track gauges were standardized.

ANNAPOLIS, MISSOURI — TORNADO

March 18, 1925

The most violent tornado recorded in American history occurred on March 18, 1925. It began in Annapolis, Missouri, and moved in a straight line 219 miles to Petersburg, Indiana. The main funnel was of giant proportions and estimated to be almost a mile in width.

Thousands were victimized by this twister. Several witnesses described it as "a hundred Niagaras," "a hundred fast freight trains sweeping by," "a horrific whistling roar."

As this monster tornado swept across Missouri, Illinois and Indiana, it destroyed property valued at $16.5 million and killed 689 persons.

More than three years later a similar high-velocity tornado swept through Kansas. Striking mostly rural areas, it caused considerably less damage and loss of life. No accurate description remains of the terrible 1925 tornado, but one of the best illustrations of any twister resulted from the 1928 Kansas funnel, given by a farmer named Will Keller.

Keller reported, "On the afternoon of June 22, 1928, the air had that peculiar oppressiveness that nearly always precedes a tornado. Between three and four my family and I were out in a field when I saw in the west an umbrella-shaped cloud. Dangling from its greenish-black base like great ropes were three tornadoes, the central and largest one perilously near and apparently headed for our place.

"We hurried to the cyclone celler, and as I was about to close the door I turned for a last look. While I watched the lower end of the funnel-shaped cloud, which had been sweeping the ground, began to rise, and I knew we were comparatively safe until it dipped again. In a few seconds the great shaggy end of the funnel was directly overhead. There was a strong gassy odor and I could scarcely breathe.

"Looking up, I saw right into the heart of the tornado. The circular opening in the center of the funnel, entirely hollow except for what looked like a detached cloud moving up and down, was fifty to one hundred feet in diameter and extended upward for at least half a mile; its walls were of rotating clouds. The whole was made brilliantly visible by constant flashes of lightning which zigzagged from side to side. Around the lower rim of the great vortex small tornadoes were constantly forming and breaking away. They looked like tails as they writhed about and made hissing and screaming sounds.

"I had plenty of time for a good view, as the tornado cloud was not traveling at great speed. It dipped again after it passed my place and demolished the neighboring house and barn, whirling the wreckage round and round in the air. Then it zigzagged away across the country."

ANNIE JANE — MARINE DISASTER

September 29, 1853

An immigrant ship, the *Annie Jane,* was caught in a wild gale on September 29, 1853, and driven onto the rocks of Bara Island, one of the Hebrides. All 348 steerage passengers taken on at Liverpool were drowned within minutes. Most of the crew escaped.

ANTIOCH, SYRIA — EARTHQUAKES 115 A.D., 526 A.D.

Great crowds streamed into the ancient capital of Syria in the early part of A.D. 115. Antioch was the gathering place of hundreds of tribes in the East that had converged to pay homage to the Roman Emperor Trajan. Early scribes tell of the violent earthquake that took place at the height of the ceremonies, killing thousands. Emperor Trajan, as one account recorded the event, "escaped by creeping through a window, for the shaken earth is no respecter of persons, and as readily engulfs the master of the world of men as it does the meanest slave."

In the reign of Justinian, Antioch was again struck by a thundrous earthquake on May 20, A.D. 526. Ironically, great throngs again had assembled, this time to celebrate the Festival of the Ascension. This was the most violent of quakes ever endured by Antioch and, destroying all but a few buildings, it toppled many magnificent temples and tombs. The shrines, some as high as ten stories, collapsed on the gathered crowds and more than 250,000 persons were either crushed outright or buried alive.

ARCTIC — MARINE DISASTER September 27, 1854

The loss of the *Arctic,* an ocean-going wooden paddlewheeler of the United States Mail Steamship Company, occurred when Captain Luce misjudged the damage done to her after she collided with the small French steamer, *Vesta,* on September 27, 1854, about fifty miles off Cape Race in Newfoundland. The collision was assured by dense, rolling fog, and Luce, believing that the smaller *Vesta* was sinking, humanely sent one of his lifeboats to pick up survivors.

His second mistake that day was thinking his ship was slightly damaged, when the *Vesta,* in fact, had actually ripped open a good chunk of the *Arctic's* bow. Told that his ship was taking on heavy water, Luce ordered full speed toward land. Giant swells flooded the boiler rooms by the time the *Arctic's* lookout spotted land twenty miles distant. But it was too late; the ship was sinking rapidly.

Luce ordered his 367 passengers and crew members on deck, began to organize the lowering of boats, and instructed everyone that women and children would go first. The "black gang"—stokers—rebelled *en masse;* with shouts and curses they made for the lifeboats, knocking passengers to the deck. One ship's officer drew his gun, but before he could fire, a stoker killed him with a vicious smash on his head with a shovel. As a result of the panic, only one boat and a raft hastily constructed of spars and wooden rails took off forty-five passengers. Among the 322 people lost were Mary Collins and her two children, Henry and Mary; the family of a shipping line owner, Edward Knight Collins, who hounded Captain Luce, a survivor, from the seas. Collins screamed that he "had practically murdered" his family.

ARMAGH, IRELAND — RAILWAY WRECK June 12, 1889

The great train wreck near Armagh in Northern Ireland on June 12, 1889, which killed 75 persons and brutally injured another 160, was the result of bad judgment.

Teachers of a Methodist Church Sunday School in Armagh had arranged a holiday excursion for over 1,200 members of the congregation, mostly young persons ranging from seven to sixteen years old. The plan was to take two special trains of the Great Northern Railway line to the resort town of Warrenpoint on Carlingford Bay. The first train carried 940 persons in thirteen carriages and two vans. The second train with the remaining students and teachers followed a mile behind.

Joseph Elliott, conductor of the first train, was a punctilious and authoritarian employee of the railway, a stickler for regulations, a martinet of terse orders and timetables. His taciturn nature and performance made his subsequently illogical orders all the more curious.

Both trains left the Armagh station at 10:20 A.M. Two miles away, the first train labored up a steep incline called Kilooney Ridge. Seeing that he was gaining on the first train, the engineer of the second halted at Annaclare Bridge.

Halfway up Kilooney Ridge, the first train, pulling its excessive burden, ground to a halt. Conductor Elliott jumped from a car and surveyed the scene. Engineer Thomas Magrath came on the run and told Elliott that he could not make it up the grade with so many carriages in tow; his engine lacked the power.

Without hesitation Elliott ordered the last seven carriages of the train uncoupled. Assistant guard William Moorhead shook his head as he looked down the hill, where he could see the second train waiting on Annaclare Bridge.

"I wouldn't do that, Mr. Elliott," Moorhead said.

"Do as you're told, Mr. Moorhead," Elliott responded. "It's the only way to gain the ridge."

Two passengers overhearing this conversation jumped from a car and shouted at Elliott that the action was lunacy.

"I am in charge here," Elliott imperiously stated. "Uncouple those cars, Moorhead."

Moorhead, still shaking his head, walked off to perform this duty, muttering, "You're wrong, Mr. Elliott."

The excursion train telescoped into another train at Armagh. *(Illustrated London News)*

It was only after the last seven wooden carriages were uncoupled and had begun to gently roll backward that Elliott ordered the brakes applied on the cars. Several men ran alongside the carriages and attempted to jam large rocks behind the wheels as they gained momentum in their downward roll; these merely popped outward like the pulp of grapes squeezed from their skins.

Faster, ever faster, the carriages plunged downward until they were almost lifted from their tracks by speeds undreamed of at that time. Panic gripped passengers in the carriages.

Open-mouthed, the engineer of the second train froze at his station as he watched the carriages rumble toward him. He jumped at the last moment, the roaring carriages smashing into his train, telescoping several carriages and splintering others to bits. The second train was stopped on a seventy-foot-high embankment and at collision, debris and bodies soared into space and then tumbled to earth, broken, dead cargo.

Hundreds of dead, dying and injured littered the embankment. What few teachers were still alive (most, oddly, were aboard the seven uncoupled carriages) lifted their long skirts and ran after bloody children stumbling wildly along the tracks and down the embankment.

All of those in the last two carriages were killed outright, except two men and two young girls who had somehow gotten pinned beneath the engine of the second train, which, according to the *London News,* "was twisted and battered in an extraordinary manner."

An army of rescuers streamed from Armagh, but it took hours to extricate the bodies of the dead and those pinned beneath the wreckage.

Board of Trade Inspector Major-General Hutchinson convened an inquiry later, and conductor Joseph Elliott was given a reprimand.

ASAMAYAMA — VOLCANIC ERUPTION 1783

Of Japan's many volcanoes, the most active and feared is the deadly Asamayama, standing 8,131 feet high. The most violent eruption of this volatile monster recorded in historic times came in the year 1783. Asamayama spewed forth tons of giant sizzling rocks. These landed like meteors on forty-eight villages, crushing them to pulp and killing an estimated 5,000 inhabitants. One rock, reported to be 264 by 120 feet, smashed down into a river and created a permanent island.

ASANSOL, INDIA — MINE DISASTER February 19, 1958

Three interlocking coal mines near Asansol exploded when gases inside were somehow ignited on February 19, 1958. The explosion led to the flooding of several shafts, which trapped more than 200 miners. For six hours rescuers attempted to reach the trapped men, but were driven back by intense smoke after saving only seventeen men. Authorities stated 181 men perished in the disaster.

A bridge collapsed at Ashtabula, Ohio, on December 29, 1876, and took in its fall the lives of ninety-two railway passengers. *(Frank Leslie's Illustrated Newspaper)*

ASHTABULA, OHIO

RAILWAY WRECK
December 29, 1876

background: On its regular run from New York to Chicago on December 29, 1876, the Pacific Express of the Lake Shore & Michigan Southern Railway, eleven cars pulled by two engines, was destroyed when the double-tracked iron bridge over Ashtabula Creek collapsed, killing ninety-two persons. Though officials of the rail line faced a board of inquiry and were acquitted of constructing a faulty iron truss bridge, this accident led to the first federal legislation requiring an investigation of rail disasters in which lives were lost.

Engineer Daniel McGuire, a seventeen-year railroad veteran, could barely see twenty feet beyond the head lamp of his locomotive, "Socrates," as the Pacific Express chugged along at a conservative 10 m.p.h. A snowstorm of violent proportions tore across Lake Erie on the night of December 29, 1876, and blew wild, blinding gusts of snow along the train's path as it groped its way, almost four hours late, toward Chicago.

Behind McGuire's lead engine was another locomotive, the "Columbia," driven by an old engineer called "Dad" Folsom. Eleven cars—three sleepers, a smoker, a parlor car, two coaches and four baggage cars—made up the train's complement. At about 7:30 P.M. McGuire nosed his engine across the iron truss bridge spanning the Ashtabula Creek 75 feet below. The dense blizzard prevented any true vision of the bridge's condition.

Just as "Socrates" reached the opposite end of the 152-foot span, engineer McGuire felt the bridge start to sink beneath his locomotive. Then followed a muffled explosion, which McGuire later described as a "fog torpedo."

Looking back in horror through the intermittent blasts of snow, McGuire could see the bridge disintegrating rapidly as tierods and braces began to snap and disappear. Opening the throttle all the way, McGuire attempted to "shoot" the train forward but only succeeded in breaking "Socrates" away from the second engine, which pitched upward on the tracks, and then in a sickening grind of splintering metal, fell with the rest of the train down into the ravine.

McGuire's engine scooted forward and stopped. The engineer sent out long warning blasts from his whistle and then jumped from the cabin and ran back to the gap where the bridge had stood. He could see the cars telescoping into each other as they fell. The entire wreck piled in the creek and caught fire. McGuire slid down the snow-covered embankment and found Folsom, the Columbia's engineer, who had been thrown clear into a snowbank. Before collapsing from severe injuries, Folsom gasped, "It's another Angola Horror, Dan," referring to an earlier, nearby train wreck.

In the cars all was carnage and chaos. One survivor, Charles Tyler, who had been playing cards with three others in the first sleeping car, remembered yelling, "My God, we're going down!" He and his companions held on to guard rails "in breathless suspense for what seemed to me to be ten minutes, it was so agonizing before we struck the bottom of the ravine." Though jolted by the impact and squashed by the weight of his friends hurtling against his body, Tyler managed to work his way up the vertical position of the car, where he could see that several cars were mashed on top of each other and that the wood- and coal-burning stoves and the sperm-oil candle lamps had burst and spread their flames everywhere.

Tyler found a woman named Shepherd, one of the few persons not killed outright by the crash, attempting to get out a window high above the ravine. He broke the glass, climbed out and hung from the sill by his hands as she slid down the length of his body to safety. At first he thought she had slipped into the creek and drowned, but it was only a snowbank, and he soon heard her shout, "All right." He bathed his singed hands in the soothing snow.

Most of the other passengers found no such salvation. Those not instantly crushed by the fall were burned in their seats and berths. Only fifty-two persons managed to escape; ninety-two were killed. The townsfolk of Ashtabula, Ohio, having heard McGuire's plaintive train whistles, rushed to the scene and dragged away the injured.

A subsequent inquiry into the causes of the accident, chiefly the failure of the iron-constructed truss bridge, resulted in no criminal charges, but because of this train horror, federal legislation was introduced the following year by a future president, James A. Garfield, that established a permanent committee to investigate train wrecks involving loss of human life, to determine causes and to suggest preventatives. Ironically, the bill incorporated into the Interstate Commerce Act of 1887 was largely written by Charles F. Adams, Jr., grandson of President John Quincy Adams, who had been in the first train wreck in America in which lives had been lost.

A curious aftermath to this accident involved two executives of the Lake Shore & Michigan Southern Railway line, Amasa Stone, its director, and Charles Collins, chief engineer. Both were questioned about the unsafe trestle bridge built under their guidance at Ashtabula, but were found innocent of any criminal negligence.

Two days later Collins sat down on his bed with two pistols and a razor. He chose one revolver, lifted it to his head and pulled the trigger. Stone, five years later, also committed suicide.

(ALSO SEE: Angola, N.Y., Camden, N.J.)

ASIA — MARINE DISASTER
September 14, 1882

The Great Lakes steamer *Asia* was a resurrected ghost ship. Owned by the Northwestern Transportation Company, the steamer sank in 1881. The 350-ton passenger-freighter was raised, refitted and sent out again on routine voyages.

On September 13 the ship sailed from Collingwood with 125 passengers and crew members, headed for the French River and Sault Ste. Marie. Even with her repairs, the nine-year-old ship proved cumbersome under the wheel and used up a great deal of wood. Captain John Savage fought her through rising waters the first night out while most of the passengers became seasick and stayed in their bunks. At dawn Savage put in at a small landing and sent some sailors ashore to chop down trees for fuel.

When the steamer was again under way, the lake became increasingly choppy, and finally a full-fledged gale was upon the ship. Cargo stacked on the open deck broke loose from its moorings and skidded back and forth. Keeping the *Asia* on an even keel became impossible. Captain Savage spotted Lonely Island and headed straight for land. About a half mile away, the steamer suddenly foundered and passengers dived madly into the water.

Eighteen persons managed to climb into a small metal lifeboat and leave the sinking *Asia*. Savage, his first mate and others soon found themselves once again in trouble. The boat pitched wildly about, turning over several times. Each time the boat capsized, more lives were lost, until only Christena Ann Morrison and seventeen-year-old Duncan A. Tinkiss were left alive; they were at opposite ends of the boat and each time it overturned, they managed to hold on to the ends and then climb back inside. They were the only survivors, 123 persons having drowned. The small lifeboat bobbed into a wilderness cove.

An Indian found Miss Morrison and Tinkiss hours later and said he would guide them to the nearby village at Parry Sound. It was a three-day trip, he warned, and for such a trek he must be rewarded. Tinkiss wordlessly handed over his gold watch, which no longer worked, and the trio started back to civilization.

ASSAM, INDIA — EARTHQUAKE
August 15, 1950

Eternal watchers of the Richter Scale, seismologists across the world, were flabbergasted on August 15, 1950, to see their delicate machines record the most violent earthquake known to people, one so traumatic, in fact, that their recording indicators raced off the paper. At first seismologists could not pinpoint the disaster area. In America scientists thought the quake was in Japan. Japanese technicians thought it to be in America.

Instead it was the agrarian province of Assam, India, which had already experienced the second most violent quake ever recorded in 1897 (death toll: 1,542 persons), that bore the brunt of this catastrophe.

Village after village disappeared; thousands wildly raced into open fields, shouting "Hari bol! Hari bol!"

More than 1,000 were killed by the earthquake that devastated Assam, India, on August 15, 1950. Shown here is a fissure in the Sukerting Road. *(UPI)*

(God speaks!) A British tea planter stated that the quake "sounded like an express train rushing through a tunnel." Natives likened it to the crunch of stampeding elephants.

Landslides from the mountains were created by the great quake, and the fall of rock blocked tributaries flowing into the Brahmaputra River. These muddy rock-and-earth dams then gave way, flooding and destroying everything in their path. Villagers raced to the jungle and climbed trees (one woman gave birth to a child in a tree). For five days the earth of Assam trembled, great fissures opened, geysers of hot water and steam shot upward. At the end more than 1,000 persons had been killed and 2,000 homes demolished; damage totaled more than $25 million.

ATLANTA — MARINE DISASTER
January 31, 1880

Originally christened the *Juno,* a British frigate built in 1844, the renamed *Atlanta* served as a training ship for English seamen. On her third instruction cruise, the ship sailed from Portsmouth, England, to the West Indies. The discovery of two cases of yellow fever on board compelled the redoubtable Captain Francis Stirling to put in at Bermuda on January 29, 1880. For two days, each member of the crew was checked and found free of the illness. Two days later, the *Atlanta* again set sail.

It was the last anyone ever saw of the ship or the 290 men who sailed in her. Though the British Admiralty ordered a squadron of ships to search from Bermuda to Bantry Bay, it was thought that the ship had been wrecked in a storm during her return voyage to England. The gunboat *Avon,* returning from the China station, reported immense wreckage floating about the Azores, particularly in Fayal Harbor. Upon close inspection, however, it was determined that none of the debris could have come from the vanished *Atlanta.*

The disappearance, it was noted in some quarters, seemed to be part of the historical fate that had befallen many another vessel in what was then ominously called "the sea of lost ships"—now known as the Bermuda Triangle.

(ALSO SEE: Bermuda Triangle)

ATLANTA, GEORGIA — MASS POISONING
October 22, 1951

In many areas of the Deep South it is a practice on the part of poor people to buy moonshine or bootleg liquor to avoid paying the expensive price and tax on legitimate whiskey. On October 22, 1951, this practice caused pain, blindness and death. To save on the cost of distilling whiskey, bootlegger Jack Howell spiked 300 gallons of whiskey with close to a barrel of methyl alcohol. This poisonous fluid was then dispersed by his ten salesmen throughout a black neighborhood.

The following day, Atlanta's Grady Hospital was swamped with hundreds of Howell's victims, who were complaining of stomach cramps and loss of breath and vision. The onrush of the sick was so overwhelming that medical students and apprentice nurses were pressed into service. Then the dying began. No one was available to attend to the removal of the dead. The poisoned numbered 433, and of these, inside of a week, 39 died. Seven people were blinded.

Howell was tracked down, arrested, convicted and sentenced to life imprisonment.

One black hospital attendant at Grady Hospital, an elderly, superstitious man, told a resident doctor that the mass poisoning was God's way of purging his people of their sins. "He used a hurricane in Florida. Here, He uses poison liquor to get rid of bad niggers."

ATLANTIC — MARINE DISASTER
August 20, 1852

background: The 1,155-ton Great Lakes sidewheeler *Atlantic,* built at Newport, Michigan, and launched in 1848 was 267 feet in length and had a 33-foot beam. In 1849 this ship made the trip between Buffalo and Detroit at the then unheard of time of 16½ hours. The *Atlantic* collided with the steamer *Ogdensburg* on August 20, 1852. Of the 500 to 600 passengers and crew aboard, 250 to 350 drowned.

The night of August 20, 1852, was hazy, but the stars could be seen by the hundreds of passengers on the decks of the sidewheeler *Atlantic* as she passed about six miles above Long Point on Lake Erie. Suddenly the steamer *Ogdensburg* appeared as if from nowhere and rammed into the *Atlantic,* striking the ship just forward of the

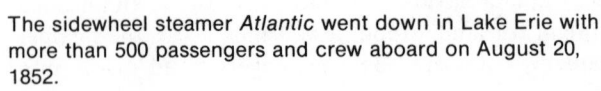

The sidewheel steamer *Atlantic* went down in Lake Erie with more than 500 passengers and crew aboard on August 20, 1852.

wheelhouse. The *Ogdensburg* crunched into the sidewheeler's baggage room, then broke free and continued on her way.

Atlantic passengers, 426 of whom were immigrants who spoke little English, panicked. Captain Pettys was unconscious, having been knocked into a yawl at the moment of collision. The officers and crews failed to maintain order and wildly shouting passengers flung themselves into the lake and thrashed away from the sinking ship without any thought of direction. One of the small boats was half lowered before it broke from its mooring and dumped its human cargo into the water.

The ship continued to sink slowly; her stern floated for some time and the returning *Ogdensburg* found 250 persons clinging to her. These were saved. From 250 to 350 persons drowned—the clerk failed to save his trip sheet—in a major disaster on the Great Lakes.

ATLANTIC

MARINE DISASTER
April 1, 1873

background: The *Atlantic* was built in 1871 and was owned by the British White Star Line. The ship was 435 feet long, displaced 3,607 tons, and had a 41-foot beam. She was powered by four 150 horsepower engines. Constructed of angle iron the *Atlantic* had three 8-foot iron decks supported by wooden bulkheads and seven watertight compartments. An expensively appointed luxury liner for her day, the ship was considered one of the finest afloat before her foundering near Halifax, Nova Scotia, on April 1, 1873, a tragedy that resulted in 560 dead, mostly women and children.

Despite vast experience at sea, Captain John A. Williams, skipper of the relatively new ocean liner, *Atlantic,* was hopelessly incompetent at sailing his ship responsibly to safe harbor. Perhaps it was Williams's misfortune to be professionally active in the time when ships were in transition from sail to steam. He relied upon his sails—the *Atlantic* had four 150-foot ship-rigged masts—to do a job the engines might fail at. And in that dependency upon the mariner's old ways, Captain Williams was palpably wrongheaded. Coupled to this archaic attitude was his indifference toward charts illustrating dangerous landfalls. Although he proved himself courageous in saving hundreds from his sinking ship, it was Williams alone who had to bear the responsibility for the deaths of close to 600 persons on the ill-fated *Atlantic.*

Departing from Queenstown, England, in late March, 1873, the *Atlantic* sailed for New York on tranquil seas for four days. Then winds whipped the waters until they were choppy, and the ship had rough going, using up great quantities of fuel. The storm increased, and Williams ordered passengers to stay in their cabins; it was extremely hazardous to move between decks since the *Atlantic* was lurching terribly, pitching and rolling as she struggled to maintain even a slow pace of three knots. When the ship was about 1100 miles out of New York, the captain was informed that only 419 tons of coal remained to power the engines. Williams thought it sufficient fuel to complete the voyage, and added that if the supply ran out, the vessel could always rely on her sails to get her into the closest harbor. By March 31 the *Atlantic* was about 460 miles out to sea and down to her last 100 tons of coal. It was clear to Williams that he could not make port without resupplying his fuel. He ordered the ship to make for Halifax, Nova Scotia, one of the most dangerous harbors for any ship to enter, due to numerous reefs and rocky landfalls that jutted from the sea. Williams himself had never sailed into this harbor and turned the entire job over to his third officer named Cornelius Brady.

The captain, failing to consult maps and charts, concluded that the red light he spotted in the distance at 11:50 P.M. was that of Sambro Light, which was near the entrance to Halifax harbor. It was, in fact, Peggy's Point Light. (Sambro Light was white, while Peggy's Point Light, which warned of dangerous reefs, was red, a fact that most sailing masters of the day knew.)

"Keep the same course until six bells [three o'clock] and then call me," Williams told Brady before he retired to his cabin. It is inconceivable to this day that any ship's captain would take to his berth at a time when his ship was about to enter one of the most dangerous harbors in the world, but Captain Williams did, falling asleep immediately.

At 3:00 A.M., a lookout on the bow shouted back to

The sail-and-steam ship *Atlantic* foundered off Halifax, April 1, 1873.

the bridge, "Breakers ahead! Breakers ahead!" By the time Captain Williams scrambled from his bunk and made his way to the bridge, it was all over. The *Atlantic,* foundering upon huge rocks, shuddered as the wild tide drove her upward and backward, ripping open her hull and drowning close to 300 passengers. Those in upper deck cabins ran half-naked to the decks, and many men, leaving their wives and children to cling to the slippery, listing decks and wash overboard into the sea, began climbing into the ship's rigging. All the fine manners usually flaunted by these elegant first-class dandies, products of the genteel Victorian era, were forgotten.

To his credit, Captain Williams acted quickly and had a line from the ship taken ashore. Williams and his crew passed survivors along this rope for several hours, while the storm raged and the winds picked off scores of wailing persons from the decks and masts of the stricken ship.

Bathed in an icy spray, the few women who had managed to climb to the rigging froze in their places, their hair matted with ice, their faces contorted in ghastly, open-mouthed expressions. Exhorting those still alive to rub their limbs and take heart was First Officer John W. Firth. He died later from the frost, although he was saved temporarily by jumping into a small boat brought alongside the sinking *Atlantic* at the insistence of a local pastor.

Williams and 414 others, including 60 crewmen, survived. Not one woman was brought alive to shore, and only one child, twelve-year-old John Henly, pulled from a porthole by his hair by crew member Richard Reynolds, was saved.

Captain Williams stood before a Canadian board of inquiry four days later and was stripped of his sailing certificate for two years. He broke down, "I was too confident. I thought I knew where the vessel was. I thought that I was a long way eastward of Sambro Light. To think that while hundreds of men were saved, every woman should have perished. It's horrible. If I'd been able to save just one I could bear the disaster, but to lose every woman on board, it's too terrible, it's too terrible."

A passenger coach of the West Jersey Railroad is hauled out of the bay near Atlantic City, New Jersey, following the head-on collision which took sixty lives on July 30, 1896.

ATLANTIC CITY, NEW JERSEY — RAILWAY WRECK, July 30, 1896

background: Two trains, one a seven-car special excursion train of the West Jersey Railroad leaving Atlantic City, the other an express of the Reading line from Philadelphia, collided at an overworked Atlantic City crossing at approximately 7:00 P.M. on July 30, 1896. Hundreds were injured, many crippled for life; sixty persons were killed. Engineer Edward Farr of the Reading train, who was killed, was found responsible.

It was only minutes after the crash when policemen rushed up the wooden stairs of the block tower overlooking "Death Trap" crossing and arrested signal operator William Thurlow for gross negligence. From the tower Thurlow and the officers saw two trains, wrecked and on fire, and heard the wails and screeches of those staggering from the ruins.

"You better come with us," one policeman said.

"Why?" Thurlow said.

The officer pointed to the flaming carnage below. "For that."

"It was that damned Farr. Not me."

"Who's Farr?"

"The engineer of the Philadelphia Express. He had the red light. The Atlantic train had the white. Farr was supposed to stop, damn him."

"That train's engineer is dead."

"Then he's double-damned," Thurlow said as he was led stonily down the stairs.

The crossing in Atlantic City where many tracks intersected had been dubbed the "Death Trap" by engineers of both the Pensylvania and West Jersey railroads because of the "heavily loaded trains dodging each other at that point for years."

It was never fully determined who was entirely to blame for the horrible wreck that occurred on the evening of July 30, 1896, but Edward Farr, engineer of the Philadelphia Express, was held officially responsible.

As Farr approached the crossing at about 7:00 P.M., his throttle wide open, he apparently ignored the red signal shining from the control tower where Thurlow stood. Engineer John Greiner, running the West Jersey excursion train out of Atlantic City, saw the Reading train but proceeded, since Thurlow had given him the white or go-ahead light. His engine had barely rolled across the crossing when his train was struck by Farr's locomotive.

"My train left Atlantic City at 6:46," he later told officials. "My fireman was Morris Newell. We were about two minutes in reaching the drawbridge. Just as my engine left the bridge, I looked out of one of the cab windows and saw the Reading Express. She was flying shoreward. I should judge that she was about two miles away when I first saw her, and she was traveling in a cloud of dust. There was a Camden and Atlantic train . . . moving toward me also, and in the same direction as the Express, and from what I saw, I think they were racing [upon investigation this claim was later discovered to be unfounded].

"I had whistled for signals on leaving the drawbridge, and as I approached the crossing I looked up and saw that I had a clear track. I knew that the white [light] being set against me, the red must be showing against the Reading train. It could not be otherwise. I started off, believing that the Reading train would stop. When I was on the crossing, I saw the train coming with unslackened speed, and I shouted to Newell, 'My God, Morris, he's not going to stop!' Then I followed the first impulse, and leaped from my seat to the floor, and then to the step. I hesitated about jumping after I was on the step, and then, through some unaccountable impulse, I sprang back into the cab. Had I leaped I would have been buried beneath the wreck. My fireman also stayed on the engine and was uninjured. When the crash came, my engine broke loose and ran down the track. When I ran back, the sights and sounds I witnessed unnerved me, and I have been in a tremble ever since. I shall never forget the sight of that Reading engine as she rushed toward us. . . . "

The side of the West Jersey train was the last sight the eyes of engineer Farr would ever behold. His engine ploughed into the side of the first car behind the West Jersey engine at 50 m.p.h., smashing it off the tracks with such force that it crashed down an embankment and sank into a marsh. The second car on this train was also torn from the tracks and collapsed down the embankment. The third and fourth cars telescoped into each other, devastating the occupants.

Farr's engine was tossed to the opposite side of the track, and the first car behind it was carried with it into a ditch. Many people clambering from the wreck of this car momentarily escaped death only to be overtaken by the scalding steam of the exploding boiler of Farr's engine.

Most of the wooden cars, both on and off the tracks, were burning. Inside the cars of both trains gruesome death scenes scarred the minds of survivors for life.

Charles Blue, a passenger on the excursion train, recalled, "After the crash there was an indescribable scene. . . . I do not know how I escaped being killed. Two children sat in front of me. They were crushed into a shapeless mass, while I was merely turned around in my seat. I noticed one family in particular who were sitting in the center of the car. The family consisted of father, mother and two children. The father evidently saw that there was going to be a collision, and just before the shock came he seized the youngest child and threw it out of an open window. Then followed the collision and the rest of the family was killed. The child was found apparently uninjured. . . . A number of people escaped by jumping from windows before the cars came together."

The residents of Atlantic City were drawn to the burning trains by the hundreds, immediately attempting to yank the living and dead from the flames. The owner of the Union Market, John Meyer, recoiled in horror when he looked down to see a small child sobbing, "I won't leave you, Mama." The bloodstained girl held a headless corpse in her tiny arms.

Rescuers found a mother and father who had formed a tent with their bodies over their child who survived (she, too, had to be torn away from her dead parents). Huge bonfires were built from the train wreckage to enable rescuers to find those still pinned under the debris. The shooting flames made the grisly scene all the more macabre.

One party of searchers, stumbling through the Pennsylvania Line's destroyed car, saw a human heart impaled upon a splintered portion of wall. They also found a man's severed leg, later identified as belonging to engineer Farr. The impact had occurred with such force that his leg, blown off by the exploding boiler, was hurtled the entire length of the car behind the engine.

Fires raged through the fourth car of the excursion train as Charles W. Seeds smashed his way through a closed window. He humped out and then pulled his wife after him. "The others, Charlie," Mrs. Seeds mumbled, "the others." With blood dripping from his cut legs, Seeds worked his way back into the car. He found a small girl pinioned by two seats and pulled her out. Seeds made several trips through the car. Other than the little girl, no one was alive. He thought it indecent to leave the dead to the flames and he pulled eleven bodies from the car before it was consumed by the blaze.

Julius B. Price, on his way to relax in Atlantic City, was in the smoker of the Reading train's second car. Moments after the crash, Price, uninjured, made his way forward. Other men on the same train joined him. Entering the next car, Price saw "half a dozen people lying about amid the wreckage of seats. It was here that we fully realized the horror of the accident. The first woman that we took out had her leg cut off between the knee and the ankle. A man we took out afterward had evidently had his back broken. . . . We got out as many as we could, but the cars were so smashed that it was impossible to remove all by the doors."

Price and others climbed the roof of the second car and broke through, taking out many through this opening. Price then stumbled along the embankment. Dozens of bodies were being laid out by the tracks. He heard the screams of those still trapped beneath the wreckage, tried to help them and then realized that only heavy equipment (which arrived later) could aid them. "I helped carry a man who had been internally injured," Price remembered, "to a spot where a number of others lay who had been hurt. On the way he told us in broken words that he feared that his entire family was destroyed—his wife, his child, and his wife's mother and father. As we lowered him to the ground, a woman all bandaged came up panting and sank beside the sufferer, crying: 'Harry, Harry! Oh, my God! He's dying!' "

That night hundreds of injured and groggy passengers, propped up by torch-carrying residents of Atlantic City, searched the debris for their families and were then escorted to the city, many taken to the Excursion House, which had been converted into a temporary morgue.

The Atlantic City hospital filled up quickly. One man, delirious, babbled how he had been in the thoroughly wrecked second car of the express from Philadelphia and how, upon impact, bodies had been hurtled the complete distance of the car. A reporter leaned forward and asked who he was. "When he was asked his name," the writer stated, "he stared in a silly manner as if his tongue had suddenly forgotten to speak. On this point, his memory faded entirely."

In the morning, the famous Atlantic City boardwalk was cluttered with bandaged survivors, many of them still searching for missing relatives and friends. Henry Muta of Bridgeton had searched all night for his sister and father. He finally went to the Excursion House where the dead were kept, all of whom had been placed in crudely built wooden caskets.

The first box opened to his gaze contained his father, the next his sister. Muta fainted.

At dawn the rescuers were still at work, and the last corpse to be removed from the wreckage was the one-legged body of engineer Edward Farr. It required two men to release Farr's deathgrips on the throttle and air brake.

The last fatality of the Atlantic City crash was recorded miles from the scene of the disaster. Authorities stood on the porch of Mrs. Edward Farr and told the woman her husband had just been killed. Her eyes grew large, her face went white, and she fell toward them in shock, quite dead.

Though Dr. Cecil Clark of Cameron, Louisiana, lost three children to hurricane Audrey's winds and floods, he heroically stayed with his trapped patients. *(Wide World)*

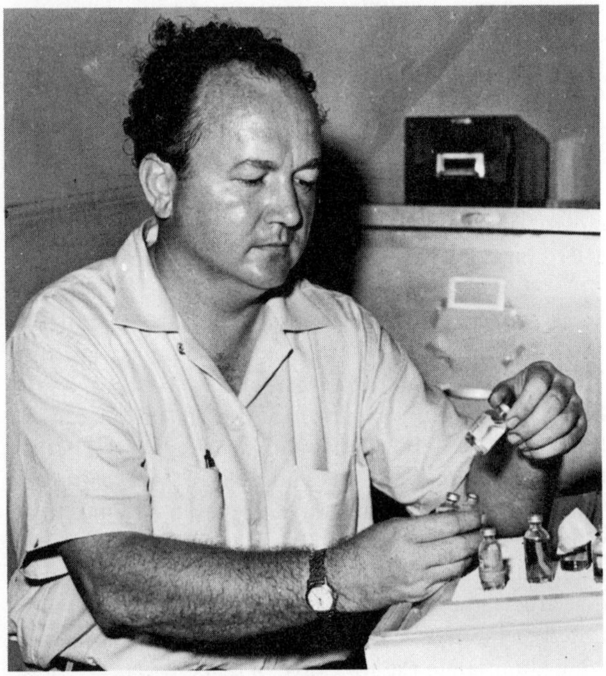

AUDREY **HURRICANE**
June 27-30, 1957

It was two months ahead of time, though residents along the Gulf states had been warned by the United States Weather Bureau to expect tropical storms as early as June. The hurricane season, however, traditionally begins in August, which may account for the staggering loss of life brought by unexpected Audrey, a hurricane born as an atmospheric depression in the Gulf of Mexico about 350 miles southeast of Brownsville, Texas. Audrey hurled herself at 105 m.p.h. into the bayou lowlands of Texas and Louisiana on June 27, 1957.

A Navy pilot in a P2V flew over the eye of the storm only hours before it hit land. He reported that the disturbance had developed into a full-fledged hurricane. Audrey was christened, and her first victim was a seventy-eight-ton fishing smack that she hurled into an oil rig, killing nine men.

Warnings went out to the residents of Galveston, which had been devastated by a hurricane and tidal wave in 1900, to Port Arthur and to the low-lying swamp towns in Louisiana to evacuate. The Texans, for the most part, pulled out. They knew by their grim history what they might expect, but the inhabitants of

Cameron, Louisiana, was one of the delta towns that were reduced to rubble by hurricane Audrey, which killed 534 persons in June 1957. *(Wide World)*

the bayou villages stayed where they were, not believing for an instant that Audrey could reach them.

One fundamentalist, an elderly woman, stated later, "I wasn't much afraid because the Lord told us he would never destroy this earth with water again."

After bruising Galveston and Port Arthur, Texas, Audrey drove lustily inward toward the Louisiana coastal towns of Cameron, Creole and Grand Chenier with a rage never seen before by the living of the bayou country.

Grand Chenier had been destroyed by a tidal wave decades previously, when it was the posh vacationing spot for the landed gentry. Yet its inhabitants, whose forefathers had cleared away a blanket of human bones to reestablish the community, refused to flee.

This attitude was reflected by eighty-year-old Jethro Broussard, a resident of Pecon Island. "Never in my memory," said the isle's oldest resident, "has a tidal wave crossed over the island." He stared vacantly ahead, and then added: "We didn't leave here because we didn't think it would turn out this bad." His son, Stephen, lost three children to Audrey and a fourth died of snakebite when the hurricane blew thousands of poisonous reptiles, alligators and toads into village streets.

Cameron, Louisiana, the worst-hit town, was obliterated. An hour before Audrey struck, the sky was filled with purple, swirling clouds, and dozens of Cameron citizens listened impatiently to Robert Jeffers, a young mechanic, as he yelled at them to flee. "Get your cars and get out!" he shouted. "And if there's no room, lie on top of them. But get going!" Only a few took his advice and left.

The storm struck Cameron at 97 m.p.h., uplifting trees, smashing houses, throwing cars for blocks as if they were toy models. And killing.

Norman Wood, twenty-seven, gathered his family about him, embracing them in his arms; he saved his wife and two older boys, but his seven-year-old son and nine-month-old twins disappeared into the crushing tidal wave accompanying Audrey. "I held my babies close," he said later, choking on sorrow. "I held tight to a tree because the water was forcing me under. And I held tight to them. But sometimes the body doesn't do what the brain tells it to. I wanted to hold onto my babies, but. . . . "

Similar stories were told by others. Albert January,

thirty-eight, managed to get his wife and three children onto the roof of a house. It was wrenched away by the storm and floated about crazily. "There were thirty-two of us on this roof, riding it like a raft. Then a big wave hit us and a lot fell off. My wife and kids slid off. I jumped in and pulled them back on. They slid off four times. I got to them three times. The fourth time I didn't even see them in the dark. By the time daylight came and they found us, another fellow and me was all there was on the raft."

A lull in Audrey's torrent caused the crippled and the lost to stumble through high water, searching for relatives and friends amidst the floating bodies. A fisherman sobbed loudly, telling everyone who would listen that his father, pregnant wife and two children had drowned. A small boy sat high on the courthouse steps dwarfed by a pair of man's overalls that someone had given him after his clothes had been ripped away. "My brothers are all dead," he wept, "and I don't know where my daddy's gone."

The horror was everywhere, even high in a whirring helicopter. It was the first skyride for Mrs. Elcide Miller, ninety-one. The chopper had picked her up, along with a man and his son. "In the helicopter," she later remembered, shaking her head in disbelief, "was a man and a little boy. The little boy was dead, but the man didn't realize it. He kissed the boy's body and talked to it. He kept saying they would be safe soon. . . . It was the saddest thing I've ever seen."

The most heroic man in Cameron that day was mild-mannered Dr. Cecil Clark, who had left his wife and two children to see to patients at his medical center. He stayed with his patients and the hundreds more who streamed in for aid throughout the storm and then went out to treat others who could not be removed, even though he knew his own house had been ripped apart and his family swept away. His wife was later found alive clinging to driftwood after having been washed twenty miles away; he never saw his children again.

Audrey roared on with winds of 80 m.p.h. into Ohio and Pennsylvania, spending herself there after destroying 40,000 homes and killing 534 persons, most of whom were caught in little Cameron.

After the storm had passed, residents found a shrimp boat squatting in the middle of the main street. It had been tossed several hundred yards onto land from its moorings. They stared at its name, boldly imprinted on the stern: *Audrey*.

(ALSO SEE: Galveston, Texas, 1900)

AVRO TUDOR V

AIR CRASH
March 12, 1950

background: A four-engine Avro Tudor V was chartered by a group of seventy-eight rugby enthusiasts returning from Belfast matches via Dublin to Cardiff, Wales, on March 12, 1950. Coming in too low for a landing at Llandow Airport, the Avro jackknifed and crashed, killing eighty and leaving three survivors.

The group of seventy-eight happy Welshmen who had witnessed the championship rugby matches in Belfast had loaded up with souvenirs—nylons, canned fruit, toys, even a string of pearls—before the return flight to Cardiff from Dublin. Jubilantly, the seventy-two men and six women sang out chorus after chorus of "Land of My Father" while going through Irish customs.

An hour later, the Avro prop-engine plane swooped in toward Llandow Airport at Cardiff. Tom Newman, standing in a field nearby where he had been playing football with his father and five others, looked up, spotted the plane, and gasped: "He's coming in too low . . . something is going to happen."

At that moment, the Avro inexplicably flopped, coming to a halt on its back with an ear-deafening thud. But no flames emitted from the craft. "The smoke from the engines was curling from the wreckage," Evan Thomas, a farmer on the run to the scene, later reported. "Through it walked two men. They were the only things that moved."

An eerie silence inside the plane after impact caused passenger Handel Rogers, hanging almost upside down in his seat, to call through the cabin of crushed and lifeless humans. His cry for help was heard by his brother-in-law, Gwyn Anthony: "The nose seemed suddenly to go up and then there was a crash. I heard a cry. It was Handel. We called to each other and found we were both alive."

One other survivor, Melville Thomas, later stumbled from the smashed plane. All the rest on board, seventy-five passengers and five crew members, were dead.

B

BABB SWITCH SCHOOL — FIRE

December 24, 1924

A Christmas celebration ended in tragedy on the night of December 24, 1924, in the small Babb Switch School in Hobart, Oklahoma. Grade-school children were in the middle of their annual Christmas songfest when a candle on a Christmas tree fell among the branches and set the tree afire. As the crisp, dry branches crackled into flames, parents watching the show jumped up wildly and raced toward the stage to save their children. This panicked the children and caused someone to knock over the burning tree, setting the wooden stage on fire.

The children were performing at the rear of the one-room school, far from the exit so that, as the enveloping blaze forced them backward on the stage, they had no avenue of escape. Clutching their offspring, parents dashed *en masse* through the flames toward the only door. Men on the outside yanked as many through the clogged doorway as possible before the entire building was swept by a severe winter wind to become totally engulfed by flames.

"It was a madhouse," one man said. "Listening to those children cry for their folks and the elders shouting for them kids . . . nearly drove me crazy." Dozens escaped with their clothes on fire, raced to snowbanks and dived desperately into the drifts to put out the flames.

In minutes the building was gone, and thirty-six persons, mostly small children, were dead. It was the kind of panic that would occur in other schoolhouse fires through the years, most horribly in Chicago at Our Lady of the Angels School.

(ALSO SEE: Our Lady of the Angels School)

Stunned parents and relatives mill about the charred ruins of Babb Switch School near Hobart, Oklahoma, where thirty-six died in a fire, on December 24, 1924. *(UPI)*

Collapse of the Mönchenstein Bridge near Bale, Switzerland, on June 14, 1891, caused a train wreck and the deaths of 120. *(Illustrated London News)*

BACKERGUNGE, INDIA CYCLONE
October 31, 1876

Straight up the Bay of Bengal, on October 31, 1876, came one of the most savage cyclones ever to strike the mainland of India. Hardest hit was the city of Backergunge, which sat at the mouth of the Megna River. An above-average high tide had already flooded the shores and river, and an enormous storm wave added to this inundated all the islands in the area and most of the towns, some submerged by forty feet of water.

On the day the cyclone struck, 100,000 immediately drowned. Another 100,000 died later from disease spread as a result of the storm.

(ALSO SEE: Bay of Bengal)

BALDWYN, MISSISSIPPI TORNADO
March 16, 1942

The tornado is probably the most freakish of natural phenomena. Its path is erratic and impossible to chart. Its force is immeasurable, and no one can predict its conclusion. One thing is known: tornadoes often strike several times in the same place, which happened on March 16, 1942, in Baldwyn, Mississippi. Two monstrous tornadoes, only twenty-five minutes apart, hit the town, killed sixty-five people and caused $1 million in damages. Most of those killed had made the mistake of emerging from shelter after the first tornado passed, only to be struck down by the second.

BALE, SWITZERLAND RAILWAY WRECK
June 14, 1891

En route to Delsberg, Switzerland, on June 14, 1891, a Swiss train, consisting of two engines and twelve carriages, passed over the newly built Mönchenstein Bridge skirting the Birs River.

Just after departing from Bale, the train edged across the bridge, which gave way almost at once, taking three passenger carriages with it. The engines made it to the other side, but the violent uncoupling of the cars behind them flipped them over on their sides and killed two stokers and two engineers. Everyone in the first two carriages that crashed into the swollen river—120 men, women and children—were killed instantly. Scores more in the third car, which telescoped into the other two, were crippled for life.

It took hours to retrieve only a dozen of the bodies. These were left lying by the riverbank until relatives from Bale arrived to cart them off. The bloated bodies of other victims floated down the Birs River for days and drifted in at small hamlets, where they were plucked from the water by horrified peasants. It was one of the worst railway catastrophes in Swiss history.

BALLANTYNE'S DEPARTMENT STORE FIRE
November 18, 1947

One of the worst fires in a crowded department store was the one that inched through Ballantyne's in Christchurch, New Zealand, on the afternoon of November 18, 1947. Of the forty-one persons who lost their lives, few succumbed to the blaze itself; smoke was the slayer.

Starting in the basement of the three-story building, the fire began as a small blaze that crept through packed displays of carpeting, linoleum and clothing. The sprinkler system was not activated, since it did not detect the smoke and the fire was of low intensity.

Great walls of smoke coming up the stairways from the basement finally trapped dozens on the upper floors, and by the time the store erupted in a blaze, most were dead from smoke inhalation.

(ALSO SEE: Bogotá, Colombia)

BALTIMORE, MARYLAND

FIRE
February 7-8, 1904

background: The second greatest fire in U.S. history in terms of damage—$85 million—occurred in Baltimore, Maryland, on February 7-8, 1904, when combustible materials broke into flames in a dry-goods warehouse, and spread through 140 acres of the business district, destroying 2,500 buildings. Surprisingly, only one person, a fireman, was killed.

One of the most startling great conflagrations in United States history was one that consumed Baltimore on February 7-8, 1904. It was startling in that though the blaze destroyed all of the business district, only one person, a fireman killed by a falling wall, lost his life. The fire that obliterated Baltimore made it the second worst in property damages at $85 million (Chicago's fire of 1871 was first, the Boston fire of 1872, third), began on a Sunday morning at 11:00 A.M. in the sprawling wholesale dry-goods warehouse owned by John E. Hurst & Co.

At first everything was in favor of the fire department. The streets were clear of traffic, all hydrants were in working order, and there was no snow to impede the rush of engines to the scene. Then the wind came up. By the time firemen began to fight the blaze in the Hurst warehouse, a full gale was in progress, and the wind quickly drove the flames to other buildings across Baltimore's narrow, winding streets. Most of the buildings in the business district were ancient wooden structures—out of the 2,500 that were gutted by the fire, less than 100 could be considered modern—and these crackled into flames like tinderboxes.

A critic writing in the *Review of Reviews* chastised the fire department: "The fire should not have got away from a competent chief of a well-equipped fire department, but it did, and in short order, too."

The fire chief on the spot, however competent, was not able to direct his men after a few minutes at the scene. An electric line snapped and fell upon the chief, rendering him unconscious. The leaderless firemen then acted independently and, for the most part, ineffectively, as they formed separate clots of firefighters attempting to water down different burning buildings instead of establishing a fireline or solid wall of water. Seeing that their efforts were useless, some men gave up in disgust.

The militia was called in to ring the 140-acre area with ropes and wires. Most of Baltimore, which then numbered 538,957, gathered to watch the blaze consume the Merchants Club, the Stock Exchange Building, the First National Bank. (When the bank burst into flames, dozens of impoverished citizens let out a rousing cheer.) Then the first iron building to be constructed in America, which housed the influential *Baltimore Sun,* went up in flames. Within two hours only four pillars of the *Sun* building were left standing.

Though ruined, the *Sun* had managed to get out an extra before its building collapsed. To compensate for the loss of its building, the paper was sold by hawking newsboys for ten cents per copy instead of the usual one cent. The two other newspapers in town, not to be outdone or outscooped with news of the fire, put out extras that also sold for ten cents each. The situation became bizarre with thousands of persons avidly reading about the fire while they stood at firelines nervously looking up from the banner headlines to see it in action, destroying the city's mercantile area.

The fire was everywhere. Firemen began to drop after twenty hours of continuous firefighting in the streets. A fire captain awakened one fireman who was sleeping dangerously close to a burning building.

"How long have you been asleep?" the captain asked.

"I don't know," the fireman said drowsily. "I really don't remember . . . a long time . . . three days."

Firemen staggered back to their houses to be treated

Firefighters battle the fire that consumed the once stylish Ballantyne's Department Store in Christchurch, New Zealand, on November 18, 1947. *(Wide World)*

for burns and cuts, and then returned to the fight.

Fire Captain Jordan, who had been knocked unconscious by the electric wire, was revived in a firehouse, bolted upright, and instantly gave an interview to reporters gathered about him (the *Sun*'s reporters were there on the job even though they knew their paper had gone up in flames): "My first effort in order to get a line of hose into the burning building [the Hurst warehouse] was to break open the door. I had hardly put my shoulder against it when I was warned by a cry from the men to run for my life, and at that instant there was a tremendous explosion, and flames burst through the roof of the building and were carried immediately to the buildings adjoining."

The fire reached epic proportions, huge cinders and flying debris the size of a man's fist showering down on the thousands watching the inferno. Obviously prepared for such an event, hundreds of men and women produced umbrellas and held them against the strange firefall.

Lexington, Calvert and St. Paul streets were soon charred caverns of gutted buildings—all the great business buildings had disappeared. The blaze raced on toward the docks. Though two dozen pieces of fire equipment and extra men had come from Philadelphia and another dozen men from New York, 200 miles away, nothing seemed to be able to stop it.

At the docks the blaze wiped out the oyster industry's packing plants and warehouses and destroyed hundreds of thousands of tobacco bales (the shortage was felt throughout the nation for months). The lumber companies were also obliterated.

At the end of thirty-eight hours, the wind suddenly died, and the fire went out. Neither fire hoses nor dynamite, nor the combined energy of a thousand firemen had stopped the blaze.

The mood of the crowd changed as it religiously watched the fire from Sunday to Monday. According to one reporter, "The expression on the faces of the crowd in the afternoon was chiefly that of intense interest, sometimes jovial; late at night the prevailing expression was that of awe, and on Monday, there were looks of agony, added to the haggardness from loss of sleep."

There was also drunkenness. In their sorrow thousands of men, bankrupted and ruined by the fire, men of position dressed in expensive clothes, guzzled liquor from solid silver flasks as they lurched and lumbered through the crowds. One account stated that the flashes of flasks in the night sent up glitters of bright light. Even the militiamen drank heavily but mostly to keep warm against the biting-cold February night.

"I saw one of the soldier boys," stated eyewitness Samuel H. Ranck, curator of the Enoch Pratt Free Library, "—a mere boy he was—drink the greater part of a pint bottle of whiskey without once stopping to take a breath."

Told of such libertine reactions by some of Baltimore's more prominent businessmen, President Ira

Baltimore, Maryland, February 8, 1904: Gutted skeletons of buildings are all that remain of the city's business district at Fayette and Guilford avenues. City Hall, at right, was spared. *(Wide World)*

Remsen of Johns Hopkins University became incensed and angrily told newsmen, "This is not the hour for anybody to whine. Every citizen who is worthy of the name must set his shoulder to the wheel and lend his aid to make our city better and bigger and handsomer than ever before."
(ALSO SEE: Boston, Mass., Chicago, Ill., 1871)

BANDAISAN — **VOLCANIC ERUPTION**
July 15, 1888

The ancient volcano of Bandaisan in northern Honshu, Japan, about 190 miles from Tokyo, erupted with extreme ferocity on July 15, 1888, hurling four- to five-ton boulders from its top and killing 461 persons.

Bandaisan, which exploded from the top of its crater, had been dormant for centuries until the 1888 outbreak. When it did erupt, its force was mighty. Luckily, the agrarian population surrounding the volcano was sparse, so loss of life in the ten-square-mile area was small. The eruption, according to vulcanologist John Milne, sent sixteen hundred-million cubic yards of rock and earth into the valley beneath. Milne hypothesized that if the amount of lava from this explosion—it raced down the mountain at 48 m.p.h. to form a depth of one hundred feet over dozens of miles—had been cut into chunks each the size of a streetcar, the train could have encircled the earth five times. Milne estimated that were the lava to be cut into chunks the size of large ships, equaling 15,000 tons displacement for each ship, the string of ships would "bridge the Pacific from San Francisco to Yokohama."

Bandaisan's most recent eruption was in 1972, but it did relatively little damage.

BAQUET THEATER — **FIRE**
March 21, 1888

In Portugal's second largest city, Oporto, on the evening of March 21, 1888, there occurred one of the country's most devastating theater fires, one so savage and quick that more than 200 lives were lost within minutes. During the last act of a performance, a gaslight used to illuminate the stage somehow exploded and set the stage on fire. The flaming gas shot in jets onto those seated closest to the stage, and in moments dozens of first-nighters were immolated.

Seeing this, those in the gallery and in the third tier of box seats panicked and made a screaming dash *en masse* for the exits and stairs. Like the rush to escape the fire in Chicago's Iroquois Theater fifteen years later, many people were crushed, and many more trapped in their seats. According to the *London Illustrated News,* many of the theater patrons, their elegant evening dress in tatters and still smoking, "who succeeded in reaching

The resplendent Baquet Theater in Oporto, Portugal, burned on March 21, 1888. *(Illustrated London News)*

Due to panic in the gallery, 120 theater-goers died in the Baquet Theater fire. *(Illustrated London News)*

the street were severely injured and vomited blood."

Within an hour, the theater had been totally gutted by the sweeping fire. It took two days for firemen to remove all the bodies. All were taken to a cemetery, where only 63 persons of the 200 dead were identified.
(ALSO SEE: Iroquois Theater)

BAR, NORTH CAROLINA **HURRICANE**
September 2, 1775

As American Minutemen and British Redcoats began to jockey for military position, a violent storm that had been born in the tropics roared ashore at South and North Carolina coastal towns on September 2, 1775, and devastated the little hamlet of Bar, North Carolina, where 150 persons lost their lives. Thirteen more were killed by the hurricane at neighboring Matamisket before the storm moved through Virginia and evaporated in Pennsylvania, a storm path now only too familiar to residents in the area, particularly those ravaged by Hazel in 1954.

The 1775 hurricane utterly wiped out the corn crop in North Carolina's Pasquotank County, and the state legislature voted extra pay to feed the county's fighting men.

BARBADOS, WEST INDIES **HURRICANE**
October 10, 1780

What has come to be known as the "Great Hurricane of 1780" began on October 10 around Barbados and raged for eight days through the islands, then heavily populated with new colonists. Almost 20,000 persons died in the wake of this killer storm. The island of Barbados itself was completely flattened. Not a tree or building was left standing as the storm, passing directly over the island, killed 6,000 inhabitants and then demolished a British fleet anchored off nearby St. Lucia.

The hurricane then raced on to Martinique, where it destroyed a French fleet of more than forty ships and drowned 4,000 soldiers. Martinique, like Barbados and St. Lucia, was also leveled; twenty towns were wiped out and 9,000 persons killed. The storm dissipated after sweeping through the islands of St. Vincent, St. Eustatius and Puerto Rico, where several dozen more ships foundered.

The historian Elisée Reclus stated: "At Barbados, where the cyclone had commenced its terrible spiral, the wind was unchained with such fury, that the inhabitants hiding in their cellars did not hear their houses falling above their heads; they did not feel the shocks of earthquake, which, according to Rodney [British Admiral George Rodney], accompanied the storm." It was popularly and mistakenly believed in that era that earthquakes acted in unison with violent hurricanes.

Major General Vaughan, commander in chief of British forces in the area, wrote to England on October 30, 1780: ". . . Whole families were buried in the ruins of their inhabitations; and many, in attempting to escape, were maimed and disabled: a general convulsion of nature seemed to take place, and a universal destruction ensued. The strongest colours could not paint to your Lordship the miseries of the inhabitants: on the one hand, the ground covered with the mangled bodies of their friends and relations and on the other, reputable families, wandering through the ruins, seeking for food and shelter: in short, imagination can form but a faint idea of the horrors of this dreadful scene."

The only eyewitness account to survive, a letter written by Major General Cunningham, who was then governor of Barbados, was published in the *London Gazette* in December, 1780. Cunningham described the sky on the evening before the storm struck as "surprisingly red and fiery." Then the torrential downpour followed. On the morning the hurricane struck, there "was much rain and wind from the N.W. . . . Soon after, by six o'clock, the wind had torn up and blown down many trees, and foreboded a most violent tempest."

Cunningham and his family took refuge in the Government House, the strongest building on the island, with walls three feet thick. " . . . [T]he doors and windows were barricaded up, but it availed little." The wind ripped open parts of the walls of the circular building—its design was thought to be protective against the straight blast of the hurricane—and Cunningham's family retreated "to the cellar, the wind having forced its way into every part, and [having] torn off most of the roof."

When he emerged, Cunningham viewed the devastation with poetic reaction: " . . . the most luxuriant spring changed in this one night to the dreariest winter." He added imperiously, "It is as yet impossible to make any accurate calculation of the number of souls that have perished in this dreadful calamity; whites and blacks together, it is imagined to exceed some thousands, *but fortunately few people of consequence are among the number* [Italics added]. Many were buried in the ruins of the houses and buildings. Many fell victims to the violence of the storm and the inclemency of the weather, and great numbers were driven into the sea, and there perished. . . ."

The British warship *Albermarle* left Barbados harbor on the morning of October 10 and set sail, running before the hurricane. She was one of the few ships to survive the storm but not before, as her log later showed, her captain ordered every mast cut off. The frigate endured the full blast of the hurricane for an amazing twenty-four hours.

BARBADOS, WEST INDIES

HURRICANE
August 10-11, 1831

One of the great hurricanes of the nineteenth century began near Barbados on August 10, 1831, and swept through the West Indies, into the Gulf of Mexico and onto the mainland of Louisiana. Though the death toll reached 1,500 in this hurricane, compared to the 19,000 slain by the killer storm that hit Barbados and neighboring islands in 1780, the storm proved to be one of the most destructive on record.

Lieutenant Colonel William Reid of the Royal British Engineers estimated property damage caused by the hurricane at $7.5 million. Reid's investigation of the storm led to a lifelong study of hurricanes, culminating in his massive book, *An Attempt to Develop the Law of Storms* (1838).

The *Bridgetown Press* published the only description of the 1831 Barbados hurricane: "On reaching the summit of the cathedral tower, to whichever point of the compass the eye was directed, a grand but distressing ruin presented itself. The whole face of the country was laid waste; no sign of vegetation was apparent, except here and there small patches of a sickly green. The surface of the ground appeared as if fire had run through the land, scorching and burning up the production of the earth. The few remaining trees, stripped of the boughs and foliage, wore a cold and wintry aspect; and numerous seats in the environs of Bridgetown, formerly concealed amid thick groves, were now exposed and in ruins."

The renowned student of hurricanes and storms, William C. Redfield, traced this hurricane from Barbados to Haiti, where it struck a day later, to Cuba, where it hit on the fourteenth, through the Gulf of Mexico and then inland at New Orleans to strike on the sixteenth. The once-feared haven of Jean Laffitte and other pirates, the island of Barrataria, was completely submerged by tidal waves emanating from this hurricane.

BARCELONA, SPAIN

FLOODS
September 26, 1962

The worst floods to strike Barcelona, Spain, and neighboring towns in modern times occurred on September 26, 1962, where 445 were killed, their homes ripped to pieces by torrential waters. The small towns of Sabadell and Tarrasa were completely submerged, and overall damage ran to 2,386 million pesetas. To aid the 10,000 homeless, painters Salvador Dali and Pablo Picasso auctioned off some of their paintings.

BAY OF BENGAL

CYCLONE
October 7, 1737

The greatest toll of death by cyclone tidal waves occurred on October 7, 1737, when a massive cyclone, centering its fury at the mouth of the Hooghly River, struck the Bay of Bengal. The Bay of Bengal, especially when a cyclone approaches from the south, is curiously suited to tidal waves because of the great accumulation of water at the north end of the bay. When a cyclone strikes at full tide, it inflates the waters to gigantic proportions, creating huge tidal waves.

This is exactly what happened in 1737, when the cyclone caused a storm wave to rise to a height of forty feet as it drove inward toward the densely populated land. The wave destroyed more than 20,000 ships of all types and, engulfing the seaports, annihilated 300,000 persons.

A similar tidal wave, though less catastrophic, happened in 1864, when 50,000 seacoast residents were drowned along with 100,000 head of cattle within an hour.

BAYONNE, NEW JERSEY

RAILWAY WRECK
September 15, 1958

background: The New Jersey Central Railroad's commuter train Number 3314 en route to Newark from Bay Head crashed into Newark Bay at Bayonne, New Jersey, September 15, 1958, after it failed to stop for an open drawbridge. Of the fewer than one hundred passengers on board, forty-eight were killed and twenty injured. The train was made up of five coaches and two 1,500 horsepower locomotives.

Lloyd Nelson was a man blessed twice by incredible luck. An insurance claims adjuster, Nelson had survived one of the worst New York City area railway disasters in history when riding a Pennsylvania train that was derailed at Woodbridge, New Jersey, on February 6, 1951. Though eighty-four had been killed in this crash and hundreds injured, Nelson escaped without a broken button.

It was a few minutes before 10:00 A.M. on September 15, 1958, when Nelson, riding in the third car of a five-car two-engine train heading toward Newark, noticed something peculiar. As the train took a small bend, he could see that the drawbridge spanning Newark Bay just ahead was open; he instantly realized that the train, traveling at 30 m.p.h., could not stop in time to avoid hurling into the forty-foot water and that the bridge could not be closed fast enough to allow the train to cross safely. He threw open the window next to him. Seconds later, Nelson felt the sickening dive of the train going downward and water gushing past him.

Struggling out the window, Nelson swam upward to the surface and fortunately bumped into a piece of floating timber that he clung to until he was rescued by a river boat. A few other heads bobbed to the surface, including Gustav Planitz and seventy-year-old Campbell Jeffrey, both of whom, ironically, had also survived the Woodbridge catastrophe.

For dozens of others it was their first disaster—and their last. Most of the passengers on train Number 3314 were sitting in the first three cars, and all in the first two were dead.

Mystery shrouds the Bayonne crash since there was a more-than-ample warning system that should have caused the train to halt while the drawbridge was up.

Even the captain of the ship going under the bridge, Peder Pederson, could see that as the *Sand Captain* made her way past the trestle, the train was about to plunge into the bay. He sounded his boat's whistle as a warning. But train Number 3314 kept coming.

Three warning lights, two amber and one red, were placed three quarters of a mile from the trestle as a signal that the train should stop. Yet engineer Lloyd Wilburn and fireman Peter Andrew, positioned in the first cars, did nothing to prevent the train from plunging into Newark Bay.

Commuter Train No. 3314 of the Jersey Central raced through an open drawbridge at Bayonne, New Jersey, September 15, 1958, killing forty-eight passengers. *(UPI)*

Days later huge cranes had lifted the submerged cars from the muddy bay and recovered the bloated bodies—forty-eight in all lost their lives; several bodies had floated as far as Staten Island. An investigation revealed a theoretical reason for the crash.

With the help of physicians and a pathologist checking the bodies of the dead engineer and fireman, an inquiry board placed the blame on "unexplained human failure." It was thought that the engineer, Wilburn, sixty-three, and Andrew, forty-two, had *both* suffered attacks at the moment the train approached the warning lights along the track. Wilburn, it was known, had a slight heart condition, and Andrew suffered from high blood pressure.

Examining the tape that recorded the engine's speed, authorities determined it was going 58 m.p.h. when it left the trestle. This was startling in that it was also discovered that the brakes had been applied seconds before the fatal plunge. The high speed was attributed to the wheels of the engine as they spun wildly in midair after leaving the tracks. The brakes had been applied by either Andrew or Wilburn, but too late.

Since it was determined that Andrew was dead before the train crashed, it was thought that Wilburn probably had undergone a mild seizure just as the train approached the warning lights. This so undid Andrew that he, too, suffered a seizure—and it killed him. Wilburn recovered, saw what was happening and jammed on the brakes.

The Bayonne disaster brought about important safety measures, chiefly the installation in New Jersey passenger trains of "dead man's controls," a device that automatically brings a train to a halt should the engineer die at the throttle.

(ALSO SEE: Woodbridge, New Jersey)

BELIZE, HONDURAS — HURRICANE

September 10, 1931

Moving west-northwest from Barbados, a small but forceful hurricane worked its way across the Caribbean. In four days this storm built up mammoth force, and by 3:30 P.M. on September 10, 1931, it smashed into Belize, Honduras, and drove dozens of broken ships before it like a battering ram. Its winds reached 132 m.p.h.

For ten minutes the hurricane battered an unprepared Belize, flooding almost the entire city and drowning more than 1,500 people. Damages were reported as high as $7.5 million.

The 32,000-ton aircraft carrier *Bennington* returns to Quonset Naval Air Station after a disastrous fire on board, on May 26, 1954, took 103 lives. *(Wide World)*

BENGAL, INDIA

CYCLONE
October 16, 1942

Winds approaching 150 m.p.h., according to one report, swept across the coast of India, turned inland, raged through the province of Bengal on October 16, 1942, and reached the heart of densely populated Calcutta. In a single day, more than 40,000 lives were lost in one of the fiercest storms ever to hit India. Most of the dead had lived in coastal villages that were completely flattened by the cyclone.

The aftermath of the violent hurricane that struck Belize, Honduras, on September 10, 1931. *(UPI)*

BENNINGTON

MARINE DISASTER
May 26, 1954

The 32,000-ton, United States aircraft carrier *Bennington,* which boasted a 2,300-man crew, was seventy-five miles off Newport and in the process of launching planes on May 26, 1954. Captain William F. Raborn, Jr., was on the navigation bridge directing operations when, at 6:20 A.M., he noticed smoke billowing from both sides of the ship. Seconds before, he had received a report that the starboard catapult had malfunctioned. Then a huge explosion rocked the ship.

Below, the third deck was awash with fire and smoke. The blast tore through dozens of wardrooms, corridors and mess areas, where scores of sailors were eating breakfast. A gaseous mixture filtered through the ventilating system, and those in the immediate area not killed outright by the explosion dropped to the deck as the poison filled their lungs.

Before the fire was brought under control, 107 sailors and officers were dead. The cause of the explosion was left in doubt, but several officers claimed they had smelled "hydraulic oil" just after the catapult system failed, an occurrence that had spelled disaster on other United States carriers.

The loss of life on board the *Bennington* made it one of the worst noncombat disasters in United States Naval history up to that time, exceeded only by the 218 men killed on board the destroyer *Ingraham* sunk in 1942 as a result of a mid-Atlantic collision.

(ALSO SEE: Leyte)

Students hurriedly move furniture and belongings from a fraternity house before it is consumed by the wind-driven blaze that decimated Berkeley, California, on October 26, 1923. *(UPI)*

BENWOOD, WEST VIRGINIA — MINE DISASTER, April 28, 1924

The morning shift of 119 men at the Benwood Mine owned by the Wheeling Steel Corporation climbed into five train cars at 7:30 A.M. on April 28, 1924, and began a mile-long ride downward into the shaft. None would ever see the sun again.

Five minutes after the miners' train left the main entranceway of the shaft, a loud, rolling explosion that reverberated through all the auxiliary shafts was heard. As relatives of the miners rushed to the gates of the mine and waited in a drenching rain for news, hundreds of rescuers poured into the main Benwood mineshaft. Reaching the 3000-foot level, diggers found their way blocked by a solid wall of fallen rock and timber. Burrowing through this, the men were instantly driven back when poisonous gas burst upon them. They retreated, bringing 14 bodies back with them.

For three hours rescuers combed the many air shafts searching for miners who might have escaped. Two men were found in one air shaft. They were barely alive, and by the time they were carted to the surface, their lungs had given out. Two more men, their bodies burned beyond recognition, were found draped over a motor in another shaft.

A special rescue train loaded with doctors roared down another shaft, but it was derailed and several persons were injured. Red Cross nurses and doctors streaming into the area waited to administer aid to those brought out of the mine. It wasn't necessary. Inspector A. E. Lafferty, who had organized efforts to test all the air hoses leading to the main shaft, reported that it was full of poison gas.

Lafferty walked down to the hundreds of relatives standing silent at the gates of the mine area. Though it was 2:30 P.M., the overcast sky was heavy with black clouds from the mines. The lurid glow from the steel furnaces played upon the hollow-eyed faces of the women and children.

"There is no hope for any of them," Lafferty said. "Absolutely no hope at all. Go home."

Nobody moved; no one went home until all 119 bodies of the dead crew were eventually brought to the surface, the death toll making the explosion one of the worst in United States mine history.

BERKELEY, CALIFORNIA — FIRE

October 26, 1923

In 1923 a grass fire three miles from the city of Berkeley swept into the town and devastated forty square blocks, gutting 600 homes with damage running to $10 million. Oddly, the public water supply then was provided by a private concern, and no emergency fire provisions to fight such a large fire had been made.

A heavy wind fanned the flames. The blaze raced unmolested from rooftop to rooftop; the heat from the flames reached 2000 degrees F. Thousands of volunteer firemen formed a human circle around the University of California buildings in Berkeley and managed, by digging ditches and forming bucket brigades, to save them from the holocaust. At least twenty-four persons were killed, most roasted alive in their homes by the lightning-quick inferno.

BERLIN — MARINE DISASTER

February 21, 1907

background: Built in 1895, the *Berlin* was a steel steamer of 1,775 tons; she functioned as a mail packet and passenger liner plying between England and the Continent. During an exceptionally heavy gale on February 21, 1907, the ship, while attempting to navigate around the Hook of Holland, hit dangerous shoals and broke up; 127 were killed or drowned; 14 survived.

The demise of the British-owned mail ship *Berlin* could be attributed to nothing more than rough weather in the English Channel, but historians are convinced to this day that her Captain Procious might have been more attentive in navigating his ship around the always threatening but passable Hook of Holland.

En route to Rotterdam from Harwich, England, the *Berlin* was buffeted violently by high-velocity winds and mammoth swells (albeit dozens of smaller vessels were making similar voyages at the same time without mishap) on February 21, 1907. There were but forty-eight passengers on board, nineteen of whom were members of the German Opera Company, which had just triumphed in a Covent Garden performance. Palefaced, anxious people stepped from their cabins at dawn in time to see land. Moving shakily in their wrinkled finery up and down the first- and second-class decks, they congratulated each other for having weathered the stomach-turning trip.

The Hook of Holland, an ugly-looking jetty of rocks capped by a light beacon, loomed into view. Captain Procious attempted to bring the *Berlin* around this point and then sail into the entrance of the Maas River. Passengers and crew alike gripped the side rails as the *Berlin* lurched heavily in her turn around the Hook. A gale was blasting, and the waters slashed against the ship in six-foot combers. As the liner was abreast of the Hook, just yards away from sharp, jutting rocks, she suddenly swirled, "as if lifted out of the water," according to one survivor. In a moment she crunched up onto the vicious rocks and broke in two.

Captain Procious, a sailing master of fourteen years, and his pilot were knocked from the bridge into the sea, where they disappeared. Close to one hundred persons standing in shock on the foredeck were tossed like rag dolls into the water and soon drowned. A Captain Parkinson, traveling from Amsterdam to join his ship, was hurtled from the stern into the water. He was knocked out by a wooden beam but regained consciousness and began to swim against the towering waves.

Parkinson was able to grab hold of a floating board and held onto this as he made his tortuous way to shore. As he struggled, he pushed away at least twenty floating bodies bumping into him as he swam.

The stern of the *Berlin* was wedged high in the rocks, and a score of passengers and crew members hovered at the rail, wailing for help. Several hours passed before rescuers could rig a line to the light beacon and begin removing people. Only 14 of the 143 on the vessel were

The steamer *Berlin* broke in two and 127 on board met their doom off the Hook of Holland, February 21, 1907. *(Illustrated London News)*

saved in this way. The death count was fixed at 127, including all the leading members of the opera company and a king's messenger, Arthur Herbert, who was on a diplomatic mission.

There were several diamond merchants on board when the *Berlin* sank, and their gems, valued at a half million dollars, were locked in the captain's safe, and, with their owners, rest at the bottom of the North Sea.

BERMUDA TRIANGLE — MARINE and AIR DISASTERS 1554-1972

background: Within an area of a half-million square miles of ocean, encompassing a triangle from Miami to Bermuda to Puerto Rico, more than sixty ships and a dozen airplanes have mysteriously disappeared in the span of 400 years; that these ships and planes met with disaster is certain, but the specific type of disaster remains unknown.

The mystery of the Bermuda Triangle in the waters and air of the Atlantic Ocean has for years bedeviled scientists, frustrated officials, delighted occultists and struck terror in those who, for one reason or another, have ventured forth into the area by sea or air. It is a proven death trap.

As early as 1554 ships had disappeared in this area at times when there were no known weather hazards. Three large ships of General Angel de Villafane's immense armada were lost in a fog in 1554, drifted into the Triangle and were never heard from again. A huge treasure fleet, laden with gold and destined for the ports of Spain, set sail into the Triangle. Commanded by Don Antonio Manrique (one ship alone carried 400,000 gold pesos), the fleet vanished in 1577. A huge galleon disappeared here in 1618, another in 1621. In 1689 the N.S. *de Concepcion y San Josef* met the same fate. Sailing down into the Triangle from Fort Lauderdale, a frigate disappeared in 1734. In 1771 it was *El Nauva Victoriosa.*

No fewer than ten ships of considerable size, usually manned by large crews, vanished in the Triangle during the nineteenth century—all under enigmatic circumstances. Until the turn of the century and the development of sophisticated instruments and equipment to measure storms and make possible thorough searches of the area, it was felt that ships lost in this watery belt were victims of sudden, freak storms.

Others, seeking a more romantic explanation, darkly suggested that it was something more. Some said a giant creature—an octopus, a whale, or Poseidon himself—lurked in the deep and dragged the hapless ships to death and destruction. For the most part the stories of early victims of the Triangle were shrugged off with a "lost-at-sea" report and forgotten in musty archives.

Then the *Cyclops* incident happened, and the Triangle's sinister history as a cryptic graveyard became widely noted. The *Cyclops,* ominously named for the one-eyed giant of Greek mythology, was a United States Navy ship with 307 crewmen and passengers that sailed into the Triangle from Barbados in March, 1918, en route to Baltimore. She was a large steamship, close to 600 feet in length and fully equipped with the latest radio equipment. She vanished in the Triangle.

When the *Cyclops* failed to appear in Baltimore, a flotilla was sent out to scour the route of the missing ship. Not a survivor, not a trace of wreckage was located. Wild speculation as to the ship's fate was rampant in the press, and the disappearance of the *Cyclops* is still a mystery.

Next came the ill-fated *Raiuke Maru,* a Japanese freighter that reported her position a hundred miles north of Cuba in 1924. The ship did not die silently. Her panic-stricken radio operator screamed over his set: "It's like a dagger! Come quick! We cannot escape!" She, too, joined the *Cyclops.*

Two years later an American freighter, the *Sudoffco,* vanished with her twenty-six crewmen. In 1931 the *Stavenger,* a Norwegian vessel, disappeared. Then in 1945 the *Nereus* and the *Proteus,* American ships, were lost in the Triangle. In all instances the area was searched by planes and ships, and not a shred of wreckage was ever found.

Also in 1945 an event occurred that made the Triangle a match for any man-made transport, no matter how scientifically advanced. Above this clear blue patch of sea soared five Grumman TBM-3 Avenger torpedo bombers manned by fourteen men equipped with life jackets and parachutes; each plane had a life raft. This was United States Navy Flight 19 on maneuvers. After only an hour's flight from the Fort Lauderdale Naval air station, the flight commander's taut voice was heard by the control tower operator. He was signaling distress.

"Emergency, emergency," he said. "We cannot see land. Repeat, we cannot see land."

"What is your position?" the tower radioed.

The flight commander, a veteran of thousands of hours in the air, gave a tense, garbled response.

"Repeat, repeat," the tower operator shouted.

"We are not sure where we are. . . . It would appear we are lost."

"Assume bearing due west," ordered the tower.

Then despite the sophisticated instruments on board his ship, the flight commander replied, "We don't know which way is west." From the sound of his voice, the pilot appeared to be struggling to keep his senses. "Everything is . . . somehow . . . strange. . . . Direction is unclear. . . . Even the ocean looks different. . . ." The contact went dead.

Navy officials were aghast. It would have been impossible, they reasoned, for Flight 19 to have been out of sight of land since the scant hour of flying time would have put it approximately 250 miles away. Quickly a search mission was organized, and a PBM Flying Boat with thirteen Marines aboard, all experienced in the techniques of search and rescue, was sent out. For twenty minutes the rescue plane stayed in contact with the tower, and then its transmission was cut off in mid-sentence. It failed to respond to calls and a half-dozen Coast Guard vessels slashed into the area where the pilots were thought to be down. Nothing. The search lasted the night, and at dawn an armada of surface craft, including destroyers and a baby aircraft carrier, scoured the ocean. Hundreds of Army, Navy and Royal Air Force planes joined the search, flying close to 1,000 sorties. There was no trace of the twenty-seven men and six airplanes claimed by the Triangle.

This tragedy was only one more disaster in a continuing, inexplicable series. The British passenger plane *Star Tiger* evaporated in the Triangle in 1948. Another British plane, the *Star Ariel,* followed it into oblivion the next year.

On December 28, 1948, Captain R. Lindquist was flying a chartered DC-3 into Miami, Florida, carrying thirty-three passengers from San Juan, Puerto Rico. He radioed that he was about fifty miles from the city and could see the bright lights of Miami as he was preparing to drop to landing altitude. The control tower operator could hear the passengers singing Christmas carols. This plane and its jubilant passengers disappeared without a trace.

The next fatality attributed to the Triangle was the racing yacht *Renovac,* lost as she sped toward Miami on January 1, 1958.

Another ship, the *Marine Sulphur Queen,* a freighter en route to Norfolk, Virginia, in February, 1963, disappeared. A massive 1,700-hour search was conducted by the Air Force, but again there were no clues.

One of the strangest Triangle victims was the cabin cruiser *Witchcraft* (a name quite suited to the area), which was lying off Miami on December 24, 1967. Her captain radioed that he was just offshore at 9 P.M. and that his ship's propeller had been damaged—he stated that the *Witchcraft* had struck a strange, submerged object. A Coast Guard cutter raced out to the *Witchcraft*—and found nothing but open stretches of quiet ocean. The cabin cruiser and her crew had disappeared.

Four "ghost" ships were found within a two-week span in 1969, their crews vanished. The four ships were in perfect order. At this writing the last mysterious disaster to occur was in March, 1973, when an 18,000-ton freighter with a crew of thirty-two men sailed out of Newport News, Virginia, and disappeared into the Triangle. Naval officials have no explanation. Many wild theories, however, are offered by self-styled experts on the mysteries of the Triangle, which is still one of the most heavily traveled (both by ship and plane) areas in the world. Some theorists believe that there is a time warp in this area, similar to one in the Devil's Sea, south of Japan and east of the Bonin Island group in the Pacific. A time warp functions, it is claimed, like a trap door into another dimension into which its victims inadvertently slip.

Others side with flying saucer exponents, who insist that ships, planes, and, in particular, humans are grabbed from the Triangle and taken into outer space for experimental examination. (Their return might be explained, perhaps, by the report of human flesh and blood raining down upon a roadway between Rio de Janeiro and Sao Paulo on August 27, 1968: laboratory discards?)

None of these imaginative and bizarre theories have been, of course, proven. On the other hand the mystery of the Triangle remains to haunt, perplex and terrify.

BIEL, SWITZERLAND — AVALANCHE 1869

Early in 1869 the village of Biel, located in the heart of the Valais, Switzerland, was struck by an avalanche that killed twenty-seven of its residents in seconds. The avalanche created strange havoc. One family, a man and a woman and their four children, were hurled bodily into the street while still in their beds. The parents were killed outright but the children were unharmed. A three-year-old child, Peter Ruppen, who later became chief forester for the town of Saas, was sent shooting from a second-story window by the avalanche but failed to receive a scratch.

Avalanches have a long history of weird pranks. At Calancathal in the Grisons, an avalanche struck in 1806, carried a forest *en masse* to the other side of the valley and left it standing without a fallen tree, thus providing villagers with firewood for a decade. In March, 1824, an avalanche struck a wooden chalet near Aloerthal, uprooting it and rolling it for several miles with several children inside of it. When their agonized parents arrived and chopped their way into the upside-down building, they found to their relief all their offspring intact.

(ALSO SEE: Leukerbad, Switzerland)

BINGHAMTON CLOTHING COMPANY

FIRE
July 22, 1913

background: Several hundred seamstresses working for the Binghamton Clothing Company in Binghamton, N.Y., were trapped by a fire which raged through the four-story building on July 22, 1913, destroying it in approximately twenty minutes and claiming the lives of fifty and seriously injuring one hundred more. The cause of the blaze was attributed to a burning cigarette and the loss of life was due, owners later stated, to tardiness on the part of the women in responding to the alarm, though inadequate fire exits caused most of the fatalities.

The Binghamton Clothing Company was a sweatshop that typified the long, arduous hours; cramped working space; low pay and haphazard safety precautions of the robber baron era. Like the awful Triangle Shirt Factory fire in New York in 1911, this fire raged through premises strewn with fabric, thread and other highly flammable materials. Also like the Triangle fire, the Binghamton shop had narrow halls and stairways and had been built with no thought for proper fire exits, all of which spelled death for dozens of its workers.

The four-story factory building located at 7 Wall Street emitted small puffs of smoke from the top floor on the morning of July 22, 1913. A passerby, several blocks away, noticed the smoke and turned to a nearby alarm box to send out the alert. This act of Good Samaritanism proved deadly in that Binghamton's company of firemen raced to the fire alarm box instead of the factory and lost precious time.

During this time the factory became engulfed with flames, fed by the oil-soaked floors (oil had spilled from the sewing machines onto the floors for years, and the management had never cleaned it). Within five minutes all the floors were ablaze and hundreds of screaming, panicking women struggled vainly to escape.

Apparently someone in the building had set off the alarm in an attempt to warn the women. A survivor, Ruth Crotty, stated: "We girls on the top floor were not alarmed when the fire gong rang. We thought it was a false alarm. We took our time getting ready to march out, and when the signal was given, we passed slowly down the stairs. A man stood on the stairs and clapped his hands, saying, 'Hurry up, girls!' Then we saw it was a fire and the girls got frightened and refused to go further. They turned around and ran back upstairs. The flames chased us. Some of us reached the window and jumped out. There must have been scores burned to death on the floor from which I jumped."

Another survivor, Esther Rankin, nineteen, later testified that the fire alarm had been used in the past on occasion by some prankster to falsely alarm the women; and that this was the real reason why their reaction to the alarm was slow. "When the fire alarm was sent in, everybody thought they were fooling us, because they did it two weeks ago. But when I heard everybody yelling 'Fire' I got up from my chair and ran down the stairs."

When Miss Rankin reached the third floor, her path was blocked by a wall of flames, but she ran through them to the second floor. She was caught up by a dozen hysterical girls trapped there by the fire. Fighting her way to the windows, the heat searing her lungs, she jumped to an alleyway and broke a leg. A group of men rushed to her and pulled her away from the burning debris falling about her. "That was the first time in my life I had so many fellows," Miss Rankin later joked.

There was little humor for the women on the top floor, all trapped by the flames and driven to the windows, where they would either be suffocated, consumed by the fire or injured by jumping. Ida Prentice wrapped an awning about her and plummeted downward four floors; the awning acted like a parachute and saved her life. She looked up and "saw scores of girls" at the windows. "There must have been many left," she said, "to burn alive."

Passersby attempted but failed to catch the jumping women, and their crumpled bodies lay lifeless in heaps on the sidewalk. George Dearce watched helplessly as a group of women trapped on a narrow fire escape "burned to death before they could reach the ground. . . . the flames darted out all the windows and wiped the women off the fire escape."

Superintendent of service at the factory, Vernon Wilbur, dropped several women to men waiting below who used their bodies to cushion the falls. He climbed down a ladder to safety, his fingers charred by the flames. Weeping openly, Wilbur sobbed: "They were standing five or six deep in each window with the flames waving directly behind them. They were mad with pain and the sound of their cries was as if the wind were howling in our ears. . . ."

By the time the fire department companies arrived at the scene, the building had been gutted and there was little to do but cool off the smoking ashes with their hoses. Then began the gruesome chore of counting bodies; fifty in all were discovered and identified, and more then one hundred were hospitalized.

Owners Reed B. Freeman and Harry Evans, blaming the women themselves for their deaths, stated that they had responded too slowly to the factory alarm gong. They insisted that the $100,000 fire was caused by careless smoking habits on the part of a woman worker. The actual cause of the fire was a spark from one of the machines that ignited the oil-coated floors, and the staggering death toll was easily attributed to inadequate safety measures.

(ALSO SEE: Triangle Shirtwaist Factory)

BIRKENHEAD

MARINE DISASTER
February 26, 1852

background: The iron-hulled paddle frigate *Birkenhead* was built in 1846 by Laird Brothers. Operating for several years as a troopship, the vessel also assisted in salvage operations for the British Admiralty such as the raising of the *Great Britain* in Dundrum Bay. The troopship with 680 people on board, 56 of whom were women and children, sailed from Queenstown to Algoa Bay, South Africa, on January 17, 1852, and, while rounding the Cape of Good Hope on February 26, 1852, struck a giant rock and in a matter of twenty-five minutes split in two and sank while the troops she bore stood at attention and went under without a murmur; 455 died, 193 survived.

Of all the sagas of the sea, where men faced inevitable death in the deep, none was more heroic than the sinking of the British troopship *Birkenhead* on February 26, 1852.

For five years the massive *Birkenhead* had been employed by the Admiralty as a troopship, especially in transporting regiments to South Africa, where seemingly unending wars of attrition sapped the British soldiery. On one such reinforcement voyage the troopship left Queenstown with 680 troopers, sailors and passengers on board with Captain Robert Salmond in command.

The ship rocked its way through a vicious gale in the Bay of Biscay until its stop at the Simonstown naval base, where it took on provisions and disembarked several women, children and some of the soldiers too sick to travel (three women had died in childbirth—the children lived—and one more of consumption). Dozens of officers' horses were loaded onto the *Birkenhead* before it continued its voyage.

On February 25, 1852, the *Birkenhead* made for Algoa Bay, where its troops were to land. Most of these were fledgling recruits under the command of Major Alexander Seton of the 74th Highlanders (unknown to him he had been promoted to lieutenant colonel while on the voyage). Seton was one of the army's finest officers, according to his peers and superiors, an extraordinarily gifted linguist and leader. The thirty-seven-year-old major had imbued in his young replacements the rigid code of discipline and honor that so distinguished the British troops of that era. This superb military bearing showed itself to the world on the night of February 26, when the *Birkenhead* cut across a

British troopship *Birkenhead* sank on February 26, 1852, off the Cape of Good Hope. Four hundred fifty-five perished.

gigantic rock jutting from the end of the appropriately named Danger Point.

The ship, which did not have the normal number of bulkhead compartments in order to provide more space for troops—a commonly lethal practice of the Admiralty—began to fill rapidly with torrents of sea water. Dozens of soldiers in the forward area were drowned while sleeping in their hammocks.

Captain Salmond ordered his engines reversed, and the *Birkenhead* backed off the reef. The ship filled all the more quickly. Major Seton ordered his troops to the deck where, in their immaculate uniforms, they stood at attention. Seton did this to prevent panic and to allow the twenty women and several children on board to be lowered safely into lifeboats. Sixty soldiers manned the pumps, and another sixty soldiers helped lower the boats; the rest continued to stand at attention, mute and unblinking.

As the ship began to list badly, the scenes along her decks were dramatic. Wives reached out for their husbands in the ranks; children sobbed and tugged at their fathers' sleeves. Not a soldier moved from the ranks. The fifes piped and the drums rolled and the women cried out from the departing lifeboats, as Major Seton and his troops stood silently at attention and waited for the water.

Even the horses, which were whipped from the stern of the ship into the water, were given a chance to survive before the order to break ranks was barked. Five animals somehow managed to swim ashore through the shark-infested waters. A little after 2 A.M. the *Birkenhead* began to sink. Half a dozen boats were lowered for the troops when the vessel broke in half, its funnel collapsing on a group of men. At this moment Seton ordered his men to save themselves by jumping overboard and swimming to the small lifeboats. It was a useless order, for hundreds could not swim. Many men held their formations and went down with the ship. Seton drowned; Captain Salmond drowned. A Captain Wright and sixty-eight others made it to land. Fifty more soldiers climbed to the masts of the still-floating after-section of the ship and were later rescued by the schooner *Lioness.*

All of the women and children aboard were among the 193 survivors. Of the valiant troopers whose heroic deed would find its way into scores of paintings and dozens of books, 458 died at their posts.

The hoary campaigner and martial poet Rudyard Kipling wrote their unforgettable epitaph:

To take your chance in the thick of a rush,
with firing all about,
Is nothing so bad when you've cover to 'and,
an' leave an' likin' to shout;
But to stand an' be still to the Birken'ead drill
is a damn tough billet to chew.
An' they done it, the Jollies—
'Er Majesty's Jollies—soldier an' sailor too.

The bodies of thirty-seven miners killed in a coal mine explosion on February 4, 1957, were taken from a shaft. *(UPI)*

BISHOP, VIRGINIA — MINE DISASTER
February 4, 1957

At 1:55 A.M. on February 4, 1957, coal gases exploded in the giant Bishop coal mine on the Virginia-West Virginia line, trapping 180 men who were working 337 feet below the surface. As dozens of miners stumbled from the various shafts of the mines, they told of hearing a blast and then smelling acrid dust-laden fumes.

Miner Charles Vaughan heard the blast while he worked in another part of the mine and described it as "almost gentle . . . it wasn't loud at all."

Another said, after catching his breath, that it was like "a big puff of wind."

Rescuers combed the many galleries of the mine and recovered all but thirty-seven men. This group was far down in the mine, but they were reached by telephone. On the other end was Raymond Owensby.

"We'll be okay if the fumes die down," Owensby reported. Those were his last words. Hours later the thirty-seven men were found dead, many still holding their picks. They were asphyxiated.

BLACK DEATH — BUBONIC PLAGUE
1348-1666

background: The Bubonic Plague, better known as the Black Death, is believed to have originated in China and Turkistan and was carried to Genoa, Italy, in January, 1348, from the Crimean port of Kaffa (now Feodosiya) by merchant ships. The plague, which eradicated one-third of Europe's population, did not dissipate until 1666, proving to be the supreme catastrophe afflicting the human race in recorded time, killing an estimated 25 million persons.

It was everywhere, killing. And there was nothing to stop it.

The signs were unmistakable. The victims caught headaches and then developed fevers. Next came shivering and dizziness. Black hard boils appeared in the groin and armpits, and there was swelling of the lymph nodes—buboes.

Finally the victims vomited blood. Death was a certainty in three days.

That was the Black Death.

The time was January, 1348, and medieval doctors could do nothing to prevent this most massive killer, the greatest human calamity that ever struck the earth.

Germs were unknown to the medical profession. Remedies doctors recommended were useless, foolish and often fatal in themselves.

Physicians all over Europe could suggest only one thing to the terrorized people: "Flee quickly, go far, come back slowly."

But flee to where? The Black Death was in every

country; there was no escape. Inside of fifty years, this killer annihilated one-third of the population of Europe. It raged for five centuries.

It began quietly enough. The plague first crept through China and Turkistan and reached the Crimea in 1347, withering the army commanded by Kipchak Khan Janibeg who was laying siege to the Genoese port of Kaffa. His army crumbling, the desperate Janibeg ordered all of the corpses catapulted over Kaffa's walls. The Italians were the next stricken. Three Italian ships returning to Genoa from Kaffa in 1348 were loaded with two commodities—spices and disease-ridden rats.

The rats landed first, thousands of them, lean and starving, big-eared black rats that raced down the anchor lines and vanished in the city streets.

Soon the rats died. Then the people began to die. In ten years, the Bubonic Plague, spread by the infected rats, raced across Europe and, carried by ships and invaders, to England.

As the Black Death went unchecked through 200,000 towns and villages in Europe, slaying like a giant reaper, wolves and vultures became the sole surviving inhabitants, feeding savagely off the corpses.

Hundreds of ships at sea became derelicts as their crews died. In the streets of London, Paris, Rome and Berlin, "dead men," as they were called, pushed huge carts, stacked with the stricken—some still alive—upon them like cordwood.

The number of dead in Europe's major cities was astronomical. In the Russian town of Smolensk, only five persons remained alive by 1386. Half the population of Italy died. In Vienna over 700 persons died daily of the plague for many years.

Nine out of ten in London died. The populations of Iceland and Cyprus were wiped out to the last person. In what is now Germany, the least affected region of Europe lost 1,244,434 in the year 1348.

Such monstrous carnage drove even the most level-headed leaders to absurd actions. They slaughtered prize oxen to the gods; they lit big bonfires to "purify" the air; they resorted to astrology, witchcraft and alchemy to effect cures.

Doctors suggested that afflicted persons drink melted gold and ground emeralds—if their stomachs could stand it. Few doctors admitted defeat. Only one of the most eminent physicians of the day, Calin de Vinario, honestly stated: "Every pronounced case of the plague is incurable."

Yet physicians resorted to black magic and strange superstitious acts. Fresh milk was ordered placed on platters in the centers of rooms to absorb the "poisonous air." Toads and lizards—"if dried"—were applied to the boils to suck out the evil poison. Leeches, ever popular with medical men of those days, were constantly applied to the body.

German and Balkan peoples fanatically believed that "stinks" would fumigate the air and prevent the Black Death. This included leather, dead dogs thrown into the streets, and live and stinking billy goats kept in the bedroom!

A physician named Paracelsus advocated the wearing of human excrement to beat off the plague. A physician named Rommel disagreed: "Such filth-mongers may be left to enjoy their stinks and may, if they wish for nothing better, absorb them to their fill."

The "stink" theory held sway with many. One doctor suggested "bottled wind," but did not suggest how to bottle it. Goat urine was recommended by a monk.

Abraham Hossmann encouragingly stated: "A wash with urine does more than any other preventive, more particularly when in addition, the urine was drunk."

Menstrual blood was also quaffed as a suggested remedy.

Witchcraft enthusiasts urged pregnant women to drink deep red wine in which hot steel had been cooled, to wear jewelry and touch their left breasts many times

Carriers were burned alive to prevent the spreading of the Plague; one of the 80,000 fanatical flagellants who wandered through France whipping themselves in penance for the Black Death; the macabre "Dance of Death" performed by the dying chorisants afflicted by the Bubonic Plague.

with the gems, and to make fists about bloodstones, interchanging them between hands.

Potions were tried. Charms, talismans and secret amulets containing special occult messages were worn about the necks of millions of tortured, superstitious people.

One dying carpenter tore off his amulet and broke it open. Inside he found the words:

"To him who bears this note along
A joyful hour never belong.
Who in these words with trust confides
Within his skin a great fool hides."

The crackpot remedies kept coming as the Black Death continued. Lard and butter were spread into open wounds, testicles were pierced, blood from the torn chests of pigeons was pressed to feverish foreheads. "In the same manner," one doctor wrote, "a puppy dog of one month old may be used."

The plague victims in Warsaw were fed the boils of those already slain by the Black Death—after the boils had been cut out, dried and powdered. People grasped at any preventative measure. Many, one historian relates, "were so courageous that they swallowed the pus from the mature boils in spoonfuls."

Guy de Chauliac was, perhaps, the most successful doctor to treat plague victims. He cut open the boils of the afflicted and inserted red hot pokers into the open wounds, thus purifying the diseased areas. Many survived this operation—if they could stand the intense pain without going mad or dying from a heart attack.

As the plague spread and governments began to totter, authorities imposed severe, weird laws.

Dice shooting was prohibited in churchyards. Drunkards, beggars, gypsies and lepers were banished from all towns. Corpse-bearers had to wear bells. Strangers were whipped mercilessly.

One servant girl, Barbara Thutin, fatally infected herself and her master by stealing the clothes of plague victims. According to a new law, the authorities of Koenigsberg dug up her coffin, and it was hanged and then burned at the foot of the gallows as an example to others.

The royal and the wealthy fled from the cities to their country estates, some not returning for decades, some choosing to lose their thrones rather than risk the plague.

Pope Clement sat for days on end between two roaring fires to keep the Black Death from him.

But it touched his followers in the millions, also infecting their minds. They turned away from the Church and prayed to Lucifer and old pagan images. Gangs of deranged persons, like wild beasts, roamed the roads of Europe, waylaying and killing everyone in sight.

One of these was Werner of Urslingen, who had enjoyed a good reputation until the plague transformed him into a monster. He wore a medal about his neck with these words engraved upon it: "Enemy of God, all charity and mercy."

Another good-man-turned-animal was Joachim Burghard, who with his sons killed his sister and cannibalized her. She had the plague, and Burghard's barbarity killed him.

With the advent of the Black Death, erotic elements entered society. Boccaccio stated that "bishops, prelates, and temporal lords worshipped voluptuousness in the most disgraceful manner."

In Rome festivals and drunken revels burst forth as if those of wealth and royalty were resigned to burning themselves out before the plague struck them down.

Paris was the worst. Here elaborate balls, banquets, tournaments and orgies of all kinds ran round the clock.

"The French," one historian reported, "so to say, danced on the corpses of their relations. It was actually as if they wished to display their joy at the upset in their houses and at the death of their friends."

Also born in that miserable time were the most corrupt governments known to man. Public officials pillaged funds and food and medicine until nothing was left to plunder. Few were punished.

Also flagellants by the thousands traveled through Europe beating themselves in mistaken penance for the Black Death's appearance.

The most sinister of all were the chorisants who danced uncontrollably in the city streets until they dropped, others trampling on them in awkward dance steps, until they too dropped and died. This was known as the dance of death. Thousands died this way.

In Cologne, Liege and Strasbourg dancers took over the streets in wild abandon. An observer, Daniel Specklin, watched in horror as feverish and afflicted souls crazily spent their lives in 1518 in Strasbourg during another outbreak of the plague.

"Several guildhalls were allotted to them, and in the horse and corn market a platform was erected for them and people were appointed to dance with them and make music with drums and pipes, but it was all of no avail. Many of them danced themselves to death."

Suddenly, as quickly as it had begun, the Black Death disappeared. Some claimed that the London Fire of 1666 stopped it. Others said it was the change of seasons.

The best reason was the increase of sanitation and personal hygiene. The germ was being destroyed by simple soap and water!

The Black Death is a remote, historical nightmare now that modern science and medicine have the means to protect people from it, but isolated cases do occasionally appear. The latest, in California in 1963, was quickly checked.

BLACK RIVER, JAMAICA

HURRICANE
November 18, 1912

After having been battered by several tropical storms in the early part of 1912, Jamaica, particularly in the area of Black River, where 100 persons were killed instantly, was attacked by one of the most savage hurricanes on record on November 18, 1912. At 6:00 A.M. hurricane watchers at Negril Point gaped as the barometer fell to 28.48 and winds approaching 120 m.p.h. swept in from the northeast. Tidal waves of great proportion followed in the wake of the fierce storm, which dissipated in eastern Cuba.

As the hurricane passed over Black River, Rev. J.J. Williams, a missionary, observed its initial havoc, "Then succeeded a breathless calm for a few hours that seemed to indicate that the very vortex of the storm was passing over us. This lull lasted for about three hours. The unnatural stillness, marred only by an occasional drizzle, was itself portentous of approaching trouble. As there had been no change in the wind, the knowing ones prepared for the worst . . . suddenly we seemed to be standing in the midst of a blazing furnace.

"Around the entire horizon was a ring of blood-red fire, shading away to a brilliant amber at the zenith. The sky, in fact [it was near the hour of sunset], formed one great fiery dome of reddish light that shone through the descending rain. . . . Then burst forth the hurricane afresh, and for two hours or more (I have lost track of the hours that night), it raged and tore asunder what little had passed unscathed through the previous blow."

BOAC BOEING 707

AIR CRASH
March 5, 1966

Among the 124 persons on board BOAC's Flight 911 taking off from Tokyo International Airport on March 5, 1966, 75 were dealers and executives and their wives of the Minneapolis Thermo King Corporation; they were finishing a fourteen-day all-expense-paid tour, a company bonus for record sales. The weather was bright and sunny, and the contented passengers were, no doubt, taking in the majesty of Mount Fuji.

There were strong winds swirling about the mountain, however, that probably proved lethal to the climbing Boeing 707 jetliner, which reached 6,000 feet smoothly and then, as horrified spectators watched from the ground, began to emit white and then black smoke. Moments later, the airliner seemed to explode in midair, sending down a shower of wreckage and pieces of bodies.

Sections of the plane, the wings, the tail section, "fluttered to the ground like dry leaves," according to one report. There were no survivors. The cause of the crash was undetermined, but there was speculation that the BOAC flight either suffered some sort of midair explosion or was literally ripped apart by the tornado-like winds that often circle Mount Fuji.

Had they been superstitious, some of the passengers might have looked into their own doom when BOAC Flight 911 taxied down its takeoff runway past the wreckage of a Canadian Pacific DC-8 that had crashed while landing the previous night.

(ALSO SEE: Canadian Pacific DC-8)

The smoking fragments of a BOAC Boeing 707 jetliner falling onto Mount Fuji on March 5, 1966, were photographed by a Japanese school teacher; 124 passengers and crew members died. *(UPI)*

BOGOTA, COLOMBIA — FIRE

December 16, 1958

One of the worst department store fires happened in Bogota, Colombia, on December 16, 1958, when the colored lights over a manger scene short-circuited and set ablaze the straw on which a figure of Christ was lying. Soon plastic toys on a counter began to burn, and the flames quickly spread to other counters in the toy department.

Panic-stricken people raced for the front of the store, but found the entranceway blocked by shooting flames. Several men kicked out windows and dozens escaped by running over the shattered glass to the street. Eighty-four people were cut off in the rear of the store, where there were no exits. For these there was no escape, and they burned to death in shrieking agony. One was an eight-year-old boy whose face was burned off, who was found still clutching a toy.

The store's ironic name was The Almacen Vidá, which means "The Life Department Store."

Smoke gushes from the entrance of the sprawling Vida Department Store in Bogota, Colombia, where eighty-four died on December 23, 1958. *(Wide World)*

BOMBAY, INDIA — EXPLOSION

April 14, 1944

> **background:** The 7,142-ton cargo vessel, *Fort Stikine,* laden with 1,390 tons of high explosives (shells, torpedoes, mines, signal rockets, magnesium flares, incendiary bombs) anchored in Bombay Harbor on April 12, 1944. The ship caught fire at 1:30 P.M. two days later, and though a fire company fought the blaze for two hours, the ship exploded twice, wiping out the entire harbor, destroying 100,000 tons of the Allies' materiel, killing 1,376 and injuring 3,000.

It was the greatest gunpowder-dynamite explosion of World War II, and it totally wrecked the Allies' port in Bombay, India—all because of rotten fish.

The Canadian-built cargo ship, *Fort Stikine,* was part of the lend-lease package to Britain, and her twelve dismantled Spitfires were intended for the garrison at Karachi when she sailed from Birkenhead on February 24, 1944. More than 1,390 tons of explosives would then be taken on to Bombay, India.

The Captain of the *Fort Stikine,* Alexander J. Naismith, was ordered to keep his dangerous ship at the outskirts of a convoy, lest it be torpedoed and blow up her sister ships in the voyage. Naismith did not fly the usual red warning flag from his bridge when in convoy or when the ship anchored at Karachi and later Bombay on April 12, 1944. To do so would have invited possible saboteurs to single out his ship for destruction.

After unloading the Spitfires in Karachi, the *Fort Stikine* took on 8,700 bales of raw cotton, hundreds of barrels of lubricating oil, scrap metal and several tons of fish manure. The odor of the stinking fish nauseated everyone as it wafted upward from the holds and hovered throughout the ship during the entire voyage to Bombay. When the ship docked in Bombay, the odor became more intense, and there were no ocean breezes to disperse it. When an Indian foreman, Shapoojee Desai, arrived with five gangs of stevedores to unload the ship, Chief Officer William D. Henderson told him, "If you can't make a start on the explosives yet, we'd be glad if you could get rid of that stinking fish pretty soon. We've had that awful smell in the cabins for three days now."

The Indian workers began unloading the fish manure on April 13. They were still working the next day when smoke began to drift out of number two hold. The dock workers, knowing the ship was packed with explosives, scrambled out of the hold, yelling "Fire!" A squad of men from the Bombay fire brigade climbed aboard with a hose and sent a stream of water into the hold. There was a call for additional men and equipment, but it was blundered. The man sent out to make the call found a phone in a nearby shed, but it had no dial and he did not wait for the operator to come on the line. Instead he raced down the dock and broke an alarm box, which meant that only a routine fire was in progress and that a minimum crew should respond.

As the fire in the hold worked toward the stacked explosives, Captain Naismith ordered his crew to abandon ship. Indian firemen stayed on board fighting the fire with thirty-two hoses. The fire continued to burn in the cotton bales; then the small arms ammunition exploded, driving the firefighters off the ship.

Captain Naismith became befuddled. As he debated whether to scuttle his ship or take her out into the harbor, the *Fort Stikine,* at 3:30 P.M., blew up. Naismith's indecision cost him his life and the lives of 1,376 other men. At the first explosion the entire forward portion of the ship, from the bridge to the bow, blew away and scudded across the water into the bay, igniting other ships as she went.

The 400-foot vessel *Japlanda,* anchored next to the *Fort Stikine* was blown 60 feet out of the water and tossed by the blast onto the roof of a shed at dockside. All the Indian firemen on or near the doomed ship were blown onto the dock or into the water. They were dead or dying. Many who survived were horribly disfigured. An English officer who arrived at the scene after the blasts thought the Indians were Europeans at first, but then realized that the explosion had torn away the outer layer of flesh from each man, making them appear light-skinned. None of the fatally injured firemen was whole; each man was either missing arms or legs.

Several minutes later another explosion came, finishing the ship and the port of Bombay, sinking every vessel in the harbor, destroying the docks and setting part of the city afire. One million pounds in gold brick that the ship had been carrying were sent flying. One brick flew a mile into the air and landed on a man's porch, barely missing him.

Just before the second explosion, a Colonel Eric Bain sauntered up to the smoldering dock and in proper British indignation inquired: "Hello, what's this?"

After the last explosion, which produced a cloud 3,000 feet high, Bain was felled. Two officers examined him, one of whom said, "We'd better try to get him to hospital quickly. . . . Look, his brain is exposed." Bain died hours later.

Hundreds of bodies of seamen and dockworkers were floating in the bay. More were mangled on the destroyed docks. The last explosion sent a shower of scrap metal, which the *Fort Stikine* had been carrying, in every direction throughout the city. More than a mile away two officers were walking to their offices. One of them, Captain Sidney Kielly, was cut in half by flying metal. The other man was unharmed.

Roy Hayward, a sailor on the *Belray,* survived the blast and spent the next hour picking up the mangled bodies of Indian firemen and dockworkers, whose cries of "Sahib, Sahib" were everywhere, and ran with them in his arms down the battered dock to cars and trucks that raced them to the hospital.

The blast tore off the tiled rooftops of hundreds of buildings and smashed almost every window in Bombay. People on the streets fell in clumps, writhing with wounds from flying scrap metal and gold bricks. A seismograph in a meteorological station in Simla in the Himalayas, a thousand miles away, recorded the blast. At first, the shudder was thought to be an earthquake.

Residents of the city took cover everywhere as debris rained down upon them. Some dived into cars that were subsequently flattened by huge hunks of flying metal, killing those inside. A panicked soldier, whose mind had snapped, ran wildly down Frere Road screaming at the top of his lungs: "Get out of it! The whole city is going to go up!"

Victoria dock and the twenty-seven ships berthed along it were gone. All the homes, buildings and sheds around the harbor were on fire. It took several days for the hopelessly unprepared fire department, aided by thousands of Allied troops of all nations, to subdue the fires. More than 7,000 troops working day and night took six months to clear away the debris and restore the "Gateway to India."

The cause of the *Fort Stikine's* fire was never determined.

BONE, ALGERIA

EXPLOSION
July 23, 1964

The detonation of the *Star of Alexandria* in the port of Bone, Algeria, caused eighty-five deaths, including the entire ship's crew and the dockers unloading its dangerous cargo, ammunition and arms. On the day the ship docked in the eastern Algerian port, scores of workers began taking off a vast shipment of guns and explosives. Reports later varied as to the cause of the disaster. One news source stated, "Algerians are not highly skilled in handling such lethal materials" and blamed a careless

Debris littered the docks of Bone, Algeria, after the *Star of Alexandria* blew up, July 23, 1963, killing 100 workmen. *(Wide World)*

Algerian worker for being responsible for the blast.

Algeria's President Benbella called it sabotage, pointing to "a foreign hand in league with the 'counterrevolution' " (meaning Marxists such as Mohammed Khider and Mohammed Harbi, editor of *Revolution Africaine,* leaders of the opposition). Proof of Benbella's claim was never forthcoming since his detectives had nothing to study; the *Star of Alexandria* and all eighty-five men were literally blown to bits.

(ALSO SEE: Bombay, India)

BOQUERON — VOLCANIC ERUPTION
June 6, 1917

background: Rising to the west of the city of San Salvador in volcano-dotted El Salvador is the towering Boqueron whose crater is 1,300 feet in diameter and contains a rainwater lake 1,200 feet below the edge of its pit. On June 6, 1917, the volcano erupted at 6:55 P.M. destroying San Salvador, leaving 100,000 homeless and 450 people dead.

The cone of the giant volcano Boqueron on the northwestern flank of San Salvador exploded on June 6, 1917, throwing out huge showers of ash and cinders and pouring a thunderous flow of lava. The shock occurred at 6:55 P.M. and lasted fifteen seconds, but during this brief span the city of San Salvador was virtually wiped out; the thatched rooftops over 100,000 persons were burned away, and 450 people were killed, most of whom were burned to death by walls of flying cinders.

For twenty miles around the volcano, destruction was total. Several plantations were eradicated, including the expansive Las Granadillas, where dozens of houses were a mere fifty feet from the point of eruption. The rainwater lake that had nestled inside Boqueron's crater spewed forth scalding water that submerged fifteen towns. In some depressed areas of land the lava was 160 feet deep, the ash 4 feet deep.

An unusual volcanic phenomenon occurred: Boqueron's poisonous gases mixed with the acid ash shower and fell on fleeing villagers, causing their hair to fall out.

The 1917 explosion of Boqueron marked the thirteenth time the city of San Salvador had been wrecked by volcanoes, and previous devastating ones had occurred in 1575 and 1765.

BORUSSIA — MARINE DISASTER
December 2, 1879

Hit by a wild gale off the Spanish coast, the steamship *Borussia* of the Dominion and Mississippi Line was abandoned at sea on December 2, 1879. Of her 180 passengers and 54 crew men, 174 perished. The seventy survivors were mostly sailors. The high number of deaths was attributed to the hopelessly inadequate life-saving equipment.

BOSTON, MASSACHUSETTS — FIRE
November 9, 1872

background: The business district of Boston, Massachusetts, approximately sixty-five acres which incorporated 930 buildings and several historic landmarks such as Trinity Church, was devastated in a fire that began on November 9, 1872, and burned until noon of the following day. More than $75 million in damage was done and twelve persons, mostly firemen, were killed.

In 1872 the city of Boston was no more equipped to handle the inferno that gutted its sixty-five-acre business district, caused $75 million in damage and killed twelve persons than Chicago was when it was destroyed by fire the year before. Instead of eating through the clapboard homes of the poor, as it did in Chicago, the fire in Boston struck down the business buildings and mansions of the wealthy. In no other city, however, were conditions more ripe to produce a blaze such as the one in Boston.

The business section, beginning at Sumner Street, was tightly-packed with office buildings, their highly combustible mansard roofs crowding each other. The narrow streets predated the American Revolution. On the night of November 9, at 7:15 P.M., crowds at the corner of Sumner and Kingston streets stood petrified as they watched a tower of flame shoot from the basement to the fourth floor of a business building in a matter of minutes.

None of the onlookers turned in the fire alarm when the blaze was spotted, each thinking the person next to him had summoned the horse-drawn fire wagons. When the alarm was finally given, the firemen were slow in answering the call; most of the horses in their stalls were unfit for duty, as they were suffering from an epidemic.

By the time the first contingents of firemen arrived, almost all the buildings along Sumner and Kingston streets were devoured by flames that fed on the mansard roofs and easily jumped the narrow streets until the buildings on Otis Street and its neighboring streets caught fire. An 18 m.p.h. wind fanned the flames.

Trinity Church, even then an historic landmark, caught fire and burned to an ember in seconds. The offices of the *Boston Transcript* on Washington Street were gutted. The editor, his writers and printers desperately attempted to save their type and important papers by rushing armloads to the basement, which housed the presses, in the belief that the fireproof first-story would offer protection. It did, but only for a few hours. The blaze tore with such ferocity through the *Transcript* offices that all the floors in the building collapsed upon the first floor, caving it in and instantly reducing the precious galleys of type and presses to debris.

The fire licked at the granite sides of Boston's mammoth new post office building. One of the first officials to react to the blaze was Postmaster General William L. Burt. Most other officials had been dumbfounded by the disaster into ineffectual gestures, palsied indecision and panic. Burt took charge. He ordered all the mail removed from the post office and placed in the custom house and Faneuil Hall, far removed from the conflagration. Hundreds of postal employees struggled with sacks of mail, dragging them through the streets and carting them on wagons and in carriages. Not one letter was lost to the fire, and on the following Monday carriers were in the streets making deliveries, albeit the addresses to which they were brought were, for the most part, burned-out.

Racing to city hall, Burt ordered the entire building lighted and summoned the mayor. He then sent to the Navy Yard for explosives, knowing that the fire could only be stopped by dynamiting certain blocks and creating a large vacant area beyond which the fire could not move. Burt also sent for a troop of marines to halt the sure-to-come scavengers of all disasters, the looters.

Toughs came by the trainloads as soon as word of the great fire was telegraphed. An estimated 200 toughs from New York arrived in Boston late that night, while firemen were vainly attempting to contain the blaze. The hoodlums, intent on burglary, skirmished with police as they tried to enter the burning business district. The police lines held.

Sixty-five acres burned all that night. The fire drew

The newspaper offices of the *Pilot* burned during the great Boston fire of 1872.

thousands from Boston and neighboring Lowell, Worcester, Andover and Manchester. Fire departments from these towns sent every available piece of equipment and men to assist in combating the blaze.

A man wearing a sandwich board walked at the fringe of the fire advertising the relocation of the Shawmut Bank. Confusion was everywhere. A shoe manufacturer in an expensive suit, dangling gold watch chain and angled bowler hat shouted at police that Purchase Street, where he stood, was really what was left of Pearl Street. When an officer attempted to lead him away, he shouted, "I am a respectable businessman!" and then dashed into the raging fire and disappeared. A woman quaking with grief moved up and down the police lines crying out, "Clara! Clara!" Her wailing made spectators shudder, thinking she had lost a child. The woman suddenly stopped moaning and dashed to the side of a building where she reached out in great relief to a large white cat, her Clara. The cat, its tail singed, arched its back in terror, leaped forward and scratched the woman's face before running off with the woman in pursuit, her bonnet fluttering while the crowds jeered, laughed and hooted.

The reaction to the fire by the crowds was bizarre. While firemen, heroically trying to stem the blaze, were dying of smoke inhalation or were being crushed to death by falling walls, spectators enjoyed themselves. *Harper's Weekly* later stated, "Pressing against this line [of police] all the way around the sixty acres of ruin was a crowd of sight-seers peering curiously into the smoke and dust, pleading for a passage through, or begging for some relic of the great fire; and beyond, in the streets nearby, on the piers on one side and the paths of the Common on the other, strangers thronged unceasingly from morning till night, looking contented, interested and happy, watching the cavalry as they cantered by, examining the wares of itinerant peddlers on the Tremont Mall, studying the smoky sky through the big telescope, or trying the lung-testers—carrying themselves for all the world as if it was a festival they had journeyed to see, rather than the destruction of a great section of a great city by fire."

The French steamer *Bourgogne* sank off Sable Island, Nova Scotia, July 4, 1898. *(Illustrated London News)*

The next day, Sunday, while the fire still burned down Boston's great thoroughfares of trade, Franklin, Federal, Pearl, Milk, Broad, Congress and Washington streets, spectators continued to arrive, filling the hotels and buying all sorts of odd souvenirs from street urchins. Pieces of twisted iron culled from the burned-out business district brought a nickel each. Broken bits of crockery were sold, scraps of leather from the large and gutted shoe manufacturing district, even blackened hard-boiled eggs.

By noon on Sunday, the firemen, troops and sailors from the Navy Yard had blown up several blocks of buildings and managed to stop the fire. It smoldered for several days. The heat of the blaze was so intense that it had melted lampposts and curbstones. A Signal Corps officer, standing 2,000 feet from the fire and "dead to windward of it," held up a thermometer and the mercury shot up five degrees.

At the height of the inferno, the same officer reported, "a flock of ducks passed at a great height overhead and the light reflected from their plumage made them appear as fireballs passing rapidly through the air. . . . Many who saw them called them meteors. . . ."

Though the great Boston fire took only twelve lives, it destroyed the heart of the city, obliterated 930 buildings and caused $75 million in damage. Insurance covered $56 million, but only $36 million was paid; a host of small underwriters were bankrupted. As a result of this and the Chicago fire of 1871, the National Board of Fire Underwriters was established to research and investigate fires, establishing future preventatives and strong fire codes.

(ALSO SEE: Chicago, Illinois)

BOURGOGNE — MARINE DISASTER

July 4, 1898

The staggering death toll that accompanied the sinking of the *Bourgogne,* a French transatlantic liner, on July 4, 1898, can be attributed to panic, barbarity and outright murder.

Two days out of New York and bound for LeHavre, France, the *Bourgogne* ran into fog six miles south of Sable Island, near Nova Scotia. Captain Deloncle felt no need to reduce the speed of his fast ship as she dashed into the fog bank. The crew and passengers were relatively unconcerned by hidden dangers.

At 5 A.M., the *Bourgogne* and a British sailing vessel, the *Cromartyshire,* collided head-on. Immediately after the impact the French ship, its plates torn open, began to list badly. Confusion reigned on the stricken liner. Captain Deloncle bellowed orders from the bridge, but his polyglot crewmen responded by running about dazedly and shouting wildly in a dozen languages.

"Hopeless, hopeless," Deloncle was heard to mutter.

There were more than 500 passengers on board the *Bourgogne,* and many reacted like maniacs. As crew members lowered boats and attempted to place women and children in them, scores of Italian steerage passengers, mostly men, burst from the lower decks like wide-eyed savages. One report stated: "These fought desperately with knives to obtain places in the boats. . . . They forced back, trampled on, and stabbed women and children, and little could be done by the officers, who bravely stood by their ship to the end."

The end was quick in coming. The *Bourgogne* careened onto its side and sank within minutes. Only about twenty passengers and crew members managed to swim free of the suction created by the ship as it sank, pulling hundreds of frantic, thrashing victims with it to the bottom.

The *Cromartyshire* picked up the survivors, some of whom were later tried for murder but acquitted. Of the close to 600 persons on board the *Bourgogne,* 571 were lost, including Captain Deloncle.

One of the *Bourgogne* victims was Anthony Pollock, who was seen moving rapidly on an upper deck in search of a free lifeboat before he disappeared beneath the waves. Pollock was a wealthy patent attorney in Washington, and his heirs offered a prize of $20,000 for the best lifesaving device for use at sea. A hundred devices were submitted; the contest was held in Paris, and from this event evolved a number of safety measures still employed by vessels today, notably the watertight bulkhead door, which is operated electrically from the bridge of a ship.

BRANIFF INTERNATIONAL AIRLINES — AIR CRASH, May 3, 1968

The early history of the Electra, a four-engine turboprop built by Lockheed Aircraft, was marked by disaster. First introduced in 1959, one crashed that year and another in 1960. A wing of each plane was ripped off on both occasions. Lockheed recalled all Electras in 1960 at a cost of $25 million and launched intensive studies. The defect was found to be in the mounts holding the engines in place. When these became loose, a vibration known as "whirl mode" developed in flight and was transmitted to the wing. At very high speeds, the wing would fall off.

The remains of Braniff International Airlines' Flight 352 after it "exploded in a red ball of fire" over Dawson, Texas, on May 3, 1968, killing all eighty-five on board. *(Wide World)*

Though Lockheed apparently solved this problem, the firm could not explain why the Braniff Electra flight en route from Houston to Dallas, Texas, on the night of May 3, 1968, suddenly erupted in flames and crashed, killing all eighty-eight persons on board.

The Electra went down about a mile from the small town of Dawson. Postmaster Cloyce Floyd saw it go. As he drove along a back road in a rainstorm, he spotted "a red flash. I looked over to the left and I could see this red ball of fire hanging back there about the size of the sun. From the glare of the fire, I could see the fuselage sort of fishtailing down. Then it hit and exploded."

The cause of this crash was never determined. Wreckage and bodies were spread over a mile of rain-soaked earth. A Braniff spokesman later stated: "It appears that this plane exploded prior to hitting the ground inasmuch as it scattered over a large area."

BRISTOL — MARINE DISASTER, November 21, 1836

The American bark, *Bristol,* was chiefly an immigrant vessel, transporting wealthy passengers to England and Irish homesteaders to the United States. She made her maiden voyage to Liverpool in the fall of 1836 and left that port on a return trip on October 16, 1836.

Twenty-two persons survived the crash of a four-engine turboprop Britannia airliner near Ljubljana, Yugoslavia, September 1, 1966. *(Wide World)*

More than a month later, the *Bristol,* with 116 crew and passengers on board, came within sight of the Atlantic highlands off Sandy Hook, New Jersey. It was the evening of November 21, 1836, and rough seas hammered away at the small vessel. Captain McKown ordered all passengers to stay below decks and sent sailors to secure the hatches. Then he flashed signals for the pilot to come on board. After an hour McKown realized that the pilot would not appear.

At 1:00 A.M. the wind increased and for three hours the ship headed into the wind, riding at the center of a fast-developing gale. The *Bristol* was ultimately driven onto the shoals of Far Rockaway. Through swirling fog and huge waves, McKown kept his ship afloat, though he was unable to back her off the reef. He thought he could wait out the storm, but one gigantic wave hit the vessel and tore away all lifeboats. The savage waves and wind began to break up the *Bristol;* the water beat against the closed hatches. They gave way under pressure and most of the immigrants in the hold were immediately drowned except those closest to the hatches who managed to scramble out.

Rescuers sent out boats and brought back thirty-two survivors. As the *Bristol* went to pieces in the storm, Captain McKown and the others still on the ship roped themselves to the mizzenmast. That, too, snapped in the wind and most were drowned. By midnight eighty-four passengers and crew members were lost, and all that remained of the *Bristol* was an ugly hulk jutting stern first from the sea.

BRITANNIA AIRWAYS — AIR CRASH
September 1, 1966

Approaching Ljubljana Airport in northern Yugoslavia on September 1, 1966, a four-engine turboprop suddenly dipped too low, scraped a ridge lined with fir trees, rose again and then crashed in flames only two miles from its runway. Rescuers were amazed to discover 22 out of the 117 on board still alive. (Two died later, bringing the death toll to 97.)

The Britannia Airways plane had been chartered by British vacationers and, according to later investigations, was 110 yards off its course during its approach. This fact was relayed to the pilot, Captain Ronald A. Smith. Officials inferred that Smith failed to adjust both his altitude, which was six hundred feet below the prescribed altitude, and his course when the plane crashed.

People who were awakened in the vicinity (the crash occurred at 11:30 P.M.) later described it as a "sound like an earthquake in a thunderstorm."

One rescuer, Franc Korencen, raced to the scene of the crash. "I saw three women limping out of the flaming inferno. One collapsed and died. The other two we took to the hospital."

A Briton, Arthur Rowcliff, who amazingly survived with his wife and daughter, gave the only firsthand account of the disaster: "The plane slowed down. Then it started to vibrate. A few seconds later we crashed, bounced back in the air and finally fell down. We were thrown clear with our seats."

BRITISH EAGLE INTERNATIONAL AIRLINES — AIR CRASH
February 29, 1964

Landing at Innsbruck, Austria, airport has been compared to landing a plane in the middle of Times Square. The Austrian ski resort town is completely ringed by mountains averaging 8,000 feet or more and requiring a rapid descent from an altitude of 10,000 feet to get safely inside the bowl, a landing that usually frightens the wits out of any experienced traveler. For eighty-three passengers, mostly Britons on their way to a winter ski vacation, on February 29, 1964, it would be their last landing.

Captain E. Williams was at the controls of a four-engined Bristol Britannia owned by England's largest independent airline, British Eagle International. He was in contact with Innsbruck tower just before his signal went dead. A farmer in Wattenstal, twelve miles from Innsbruck, later told authorities he heard engines in the dense fog above him as he moved through his fields. "First I hear engines. Then no more. No crash, but no more engines."

It was first thought that the plane had crashed into 7,373-foot-high Mount Patscherkofel, but rescue planes soon spotted the blackened tail of the Bristol jutting from a gorge between Mount Glungezer and Mount Gamslahner, both towering more than 8,000 feet. The plane, authorities later figured, hit the former and slid down the gorge. There were no survivors.

Deputy security director of Tyrol Province, Dr. Eduard Obrist, stated Williams was flying too low. "Even one hundred feet more altitude would have been enough for the plane to clear the mountain and escape the disaster."

BRITISH EUROPEAN AIRWAYS **AIR CRASH**
October 12, 1967

A four-jet Comet belonging to British European Airways was on its way to Nicosia, Cyprus, from Athens when it crashed at 4:30 A.M. on October 12, 1967. All sixty-six persons on board perished when the plane dived into the sea near Turkey.

The pilot of the plane had been talking to Nicosia control tower only seconds before the crash. Although thunderstorms were in the area at the time, they did not cause the crash—indeed, no cause was ever given. The plane would not have been affected by the storms since it was flying at an altitude of 29,000 feet just before it crashed.

BRITISH EUROPEAN AIRWAYS **AIR CRASH**
June 18, 1972

A Brussels bound Trident-1 aircraft owned by British European Airways barely made it off the runway from Heathrow Airport (London) before it crashed into fields four miles away and killed 118 on board.

Hundreds of observers saw the plane take off, and then watched in horror as it crashed into a field and broke up. First the tail snapped off, then the fuselage

Just after takeoff from London's Heathrow Airport, this British European Airways Trident jet fell to earth, killing 118, June 18, 1972. *(Wide World)*

A British Midland Airways Argonaut crashed into Stockport, England, homes on June 4, 1967. *(Wide World)*

splintered, one piece screeching for fifty yards until it smashed into a line of trees.

"The pilot got his undercarriage up," an official later reported. "This indicates that he made a good takeoff. But he landed with no undercarriage, and it's a complete mystery what could have gone wrong."

One reason given for the unusually full plane was that many passengers were attempting to beat the intended worldwide pilots strike protesting the lax measures taken by authorities against skyjackers.

All but two persons, a young girl and an Irish businessman, died on impact. The girl was dragged to safety by a policeman, but she died before ambulances arrived; the businessman lingered for an hour in the hospital.

BRITISH MIDLAND AIRWAYS — AIR CRASH June 4, 1967

A chartered Argonaut DC-4 returning from Palma, Majorca, with eighty-four well-tanned Britons aboard suddenly fell from the sky over Stockport, England, the plane breaking into pieces and killing seventy-two of those on board. Miraculously, the plane struck the only spot in the center of the city where there were no houses. It was also a miracle that twelve persons survived the crash.

A teenager, Hayden Holden, who was watching the plane through binoculars, saw it pass low over a chain of warehouses. "It seemed to swerve, then dive, and then part of it burst into flames."

Luggage, bodies, snapshots showing smiling faces in the Spanish sun, littered the ground. One survivor, bleeding from a headwound, pounded furiously on the battered fuselage, attempting to rescue his trapped wife (she was dead). People rushed to the site and began dragging out the living. Still alive, Captain Harry Marlow, the pilot, was yanked from his crushed cockpit, just as it exploded into flames. Residents also managed to save the unconscious copilot and one of the two hostesses on board.

A Roman Catholic priest picked up a small boy bleeding from wounds as he staggered away from the wreck. After getting him off to the hospital, the priest turned and gave the last rites to the dead sprawled in the square. A little girl with a broken leg was also taken from the plane alive.

BRITISH ROYAL AIR FORCE C-130 HERCULES — AIR CRASH, November 9, 1971

The worst military air crash in Italian air history occurred on November 9, 1971, when a British Royal Air Force C-130, en route to Sardinia, dived into the Ligurian Sea near Leghorn, Italy. Of the fifty-one killed on board, forty-six were Italian paratroopers on their way to take part in a joint English-Italian paratroop exercise, ironically called Coldstream. The rest were British crew members. The huge British aircraft had taken off at San Gusto Airport in Pisa and was last heard from at 5:41 A.M. Authorities thought the crash was due to equipment malfunction. There were no survivors.

BROOKLYN, NEW YORK — RAILWAY WRECK, November 2, 1918

background: A five-car Brooklyn Rapid Transit train, just entering the Malbone Street Tunnel on the evening of November 2, 1918, derailed, obviously out of control, and the resulting crash killed ninety-seven persons, mostly women, on their way from work, and injured ninety-five more. Motorman Edward Anthony Lewis, a conductor, and a guard were arrested for negligence, but were later acquitted on the grounds of brake failure.

New York Mayor John F. Hylan was boiling mad. News had reached his office that a rush-hour Brooklyn Rapid Transit (B.R.T.) train had been derailed just before entering the Malbone Street Tunnel on the evening of November 2, 1918. There were bodies strewn all over the tracks, he was told. Hylan learned that a twenty-five-year-old motorman, Edward Anthony Lewis, had been arrested along with Samuel Russof, a guard, and a conductor, Michael Turner (Turner was hospitalized for head injuries).

Major Hylan soon appeared in a Flatbush courtroom, where he spied Borough Inspector Murphy. "What has happened here?" he demanded.

Murphy replied, "The motorman and guard were held without bail for the Grand Jury."

"No complaints against the big fellows?" quizzed Hylan.

"No, sir."

The Mayor stomped off to the hospital to interview injured survivors. In the next few days he would be involved in a controversial battle over the inadequate safety precautions of the Brighton Beach Line, accusing the line's commissioners of malfeasance. The commissioners would retort that Hylan was attempting "to make political capital out of a disaster. . . . " None of the bickering mattered to the ninety-seven persons who had been killed in the railway wreck and little of it mattered to the ninety-five who clung to life as their bodies were stitched and sewn together in the Kings County Hospital.

The Mayor personally interviewed some of the victims and later turned over important notes. One damning witness was Mrs. John Barnett of East Flatbush, the only survivor who was in the second car of the train.

"The first thing I knew," she said, "the lights went out, and the car jumped the track, and I was pitched on top of everybody. It was the motorman's fault. He was only a boy. He raced the car just like he was running an automobile. It looked so terrible. It was crowded—those lives. They were lying all over me, dead. In order to reach me, they had to lift the bodies off me. I could not move. I screamed and screamed. They finally pulled me out."

Another survivor, Mrs. Helen Hartley, who was in the third car, stated: "All the lights went out. The people were thrown back. My trouble was that I hit my back and head, and then we were all thrown forward in the car and everybody screamed. The men helped the women. I knew that some of the women in our car were killed, and there was nothing to do but wait and be taken out of the car. I screamed. There was a most frantic time, awful. We did not know at the time that there were so many dead."

Mayor Hylan leaned over this injured woman and asked, "How fast was the train going before the accident?"

"To my mind we were going about 100 miles an hour. We all knew the end was coming."

Motorman Lewis denied the speed and stated that the train was moving about 30 m.p.h. (the regulation speed was six m.p.h. before entering the tunnel) as he approached the Malbone Street Tunnel. Lewis insisted that he had applied the brakes and that they had failed to work, thus causing the train to increase its speed until

Actress Kate Claxton and others on the stage of the Brooklyn Theater, December 5, 1876, attempt to quiet the panicking audience.

Though the actors tried to avert panic, 295 persons were trampled and burned to death in the Brooklyn Theater on December 5, 1876. *(Harper's Weekly)*

it derailed at the curve and he was thrown clear.

Lewis admitted that he was a tired man. He had worked as a train dispatcher for a full day and then took over the duties of motorman during the rush hour, in order to earn extra money. He also admitted missing a switch earlier on the run. He was arrested at his home in Brooklyn hours after the wreck.

His wife pleaded with detectives: "Three weeks ago my husband had an attack of influenza. The next Friday our baby died. . . . now this terrible accident." Lewis was taken away and locked up.

Although Lewis was later acquitted, the controversy over the Malbone Tunnel accident raged for months, culminating in the charge by Public Service Commissioner Travis H. Whitney that Mayor Hylan was responsible for the use of decrepit wooden cars on the Brighton Beach Line (the wooden cars had been demolished; two steel cars and their passengers survived with little damage). Hylan, Whitney insisted, had done nothing for ten months with an agreement awaiting his signature that would compel the line to employ all-steel cars.

BROOKLYN THEATER FIRE

December 5, 1876

background: The Brooklyn Theater, built by the wealthy socialites Mr. and Mrs. F.B. Conway, was ravaged by a fire that began among fly curtains on the night of December 5, 1876, during a performance attended by more than 900 persons; the theater was gutted by the blaze, which killed 295 persons.

Miss Kate Claxton reclined on a pallet of straw as she played the part of Louise, the blind girl in the popular melodrama, *The Two Orphans.* A voice whispered through the curtains behind her: "Fire. The flies are on fire." Miss Claxton, and the rest of the actors on stage, all of whom had heard the warning, went on nervously with their performance. Backstage, men were frantically attempting to put out a fire that ate its way up the fly curtains. Since there was no hydrant or hose in the Brooklyn Theater that night of December 5, 1876, anxious stagehands were compelled to use their coats and hands to stifle the blaze. One ran to the waterbuckets, usually filled each night before performances and set along a wall for just such emergencies. They were empty. He returned with a pole and tried to beat out the flames, but this only fanned them higher.

"Fire!" yelled one of the 900 spectators in the theater, jumping from his seat.

Actor H. S. Murdoch, playing the part of a cripple named Pierre, suddenly dashed to the front of the stage. "Now, now," he soothed. "None of that."

Another actor, J. B. Studley, stepped forward and

said: "There is a small flame, but it will be put out. Please stay calm and keep your seats."

But as soon as one person was quieted, another arose shouting "Fire!"

A prop man ran on stage and grabbed the long hair of Kate Claxton. Thinking her unconcerned with the blaze, he yanked her hair downward to pull her face back so that, when staring upward, she could see the flames racing along the curtains above her. Miss Claxton knocked the man's arm away, stood up and clasped hands with her fellow performers as they stood to the footlights.

"We are between you and the fire," Kate Claxton said loudly to the audience. "Sit still, for God's sake, sit still."

The only persons who listened to her plea, at least momentarily, were those seated in the first rows of the orchestra. Everywhere else, the panic had begun. *Frank Leslie's Weekly* reported: "The dress circle and galleries seemed from the stage to be filled with raving lunatics."

As the musicians calmly placed their instruments aside and began to file out, the orchestra patrons slowly got up and walked to the side exits. At first they walked. Everyone attempted to remain calm, but some people began to push those in front until most were running. Almost all of those in the orchestra escaped.

The galleries were a different matter. A crush of people surging from the galleries down a single flight of stairs smashed headlong into the fleeing orchestra patrons. People were knocked down; children were trampled; women fainted and their husbands fought with fists to retrieve them from the floor. Dozens of unconscious women were held aloft above the crowd by their husbands until they were taken outside.

Flames shot from the stage—now empty of the actors—and black, billowing clouds poured outward and up to the gallery, further panicking the horde trying to escape. Most of the actors left the theater by the rear entrance, but actors Harry Murdoch and Claude Burroughs went to their dressing rooms to change into street clothes. Both men emerged on a stairway carrying their walking canes and wearing top hats. They stared briefly down the stairs, now a sheet of flames, and, according to witnesses, shrugged and returned to their dressing rooms.

Outside, several companies of firemen had already drawn up and were pumping water onto the theater's roof, which was sending up a huge tower of flame. Suddenly they saw a window being thrown up. It was Murdoch, attempting to escape. He managed to get his head and a portion of his body through the half-raised window opening before it fell down on him, trapping him. He was silent as he struggled to raise it again. Firemen hosed down his face and hands as he worked the window upward. He then slipped backward and disappeared. The floor under him had burned away and he dropped, as did hundreds of others caught in immovable human wedges, to the basement. Their bodies fed the flames like a human furnace and sent up great wreaths of firebrands and showers of sparks.

Several hours later, firemen managed to get into the still burning theater, which had been constructed entirely of wood, and found great heaps of ashes that, when disturbed, proved to be human remains. An order went out to "Bring coffins, hundreds of them." Police and firemen spent the next day disinterring corpses and placing them into pine coffins that were carried from the theater by a stream of workers who filled dead wagons to the roofs.

At 10:00 P.M. that night a Captain Smith was given several baskets filled with purses, shawls, wallets, books, watches and jewelry. Then the firemen ran out of coffins and began carrying out bodies wrapped in sheets. The morgue filled up, so bodies were taken to Brooklyn's Old Adam Street Market and placed along the walls with candles held by wooden blocks on the chest of each victim. More candles, to help relatives identify the remains, were impaled on meat hooks. In this dank and eerily lighted place moved solemn masses of people searching out relatives and friends; loud, echoing cries burst forth as each identification was made.

After sifting through the odorous ruins of the demolished Brooklyn Theater for several days, 295 bodies had been removed. Most of these were buried at Greenwood Cemetery in a cylindrical ditch. Lengthy services were held, at which politicians, much concerned with an upcoming election, appeared primarily to canvass the crowds for votes.

(ALSO SEE: Baquet Theater, Iroquois Theater)

BROUGHTON ISLAND, GEORGIA

HURRICANE
September 12, 1804

background: A West Indies hurricane raced up the islands in early September, 1804, and struck the American coastline near Savannah, Georgia, bringing great destruction to several islands at the entrance of the Savannah River. The greatest loss of life, seventy-five slaves, occurred on Broughton Island.

By the time the Great Gale of 1804 turned landward on September 12, its hurricane force had reached killer proportions. One of the hardest hit islands was Broughton, where William Brailsford owned a plantation. The highest piece of land had been man-made and on it perched a large barn. Instead of taking refuge here when the hurricane struck, Brailsford's slaves attempted to escape the storm by setting out for the mainland in a large boat.

No sooner had they shoved off than the boat was swamped by huge combers, and 75 slaves drowned. Their bodies were found floating about the large barn, the only thing not submerged on the entire island.

Other islands in the group also suffered severe damage during this hurricane. Fort Green on Cockspur Island was flattened, its 4,800-pound cannons sent flying hundreds of feet in the air as they were tossed about by the storm. Sunbury Island's towering bluff was ground down to a flat beach by the hurricane. St. Catherine and St. Simon islands were all but destroyed.

Aaron Burr happened to be on St. Simon Island when the hurricane passed over it, and he wrote of it to his daughter Theodosia.

"In the morning the wind was still higher. It continued to rise, and by noon blew a gale from the north, which together with the swelling of the water became alarming. From twelve to three, several of the outhouses had been destroyed; most of the trees about the house were blown down. The house in which we were shook and rocked so much that Mr. C. began to express his apprehensions for our safety. Before three, part of the piazza was carried away; two or three of the windows burst in. The house was inundated with water, and presently one of the chimneys fell. Mr. C. then commanded a retreat to a storehouse about fifty yards off, and we decamped, men, women, and children.

"You may imagine, in this scene of confusion and dismay, a good many incidents to amuse one if one had dared to be amused in a moment of such anxiety. The house, however, did not blow down. The storm continued till four, and then very suddenly abated, and in ten minutes it was almost calm. I seized the moment to return home. Before I had got quite over, the gale rose from the southeast and threatened new destruction. It lasted a great part of the night, but it did not attain the violence from that of the north; yet it contributed to raise still higher the water, which was the principal instrument of devastation. The flood was about seven feet, about the height of an ordinary high tide. This has been sufficient to inundate great parts of the coast; to destroy all the rice; to carry off most of the buildings, which were on lowlands, and to destroy the lives of many blacks. The roads are rendered impassable, and scarcely a boat has been preserved. Thus all intercourse is suspended."

Sweeping up the coastal plantation areas of Georgia and South Carolina, the hurricane hit Charleston with such fury that dozens of large ships were wrecked and five were sunk. The Charleston *City Gazette* stated that shipping goods stacked high on the docks were destroyed by the torrent: "The whole of the wharves from Gadsden's on Cooper river, to the extent of South-Bay, have received very considerable damage, the heads and sides of most of them are washed away."

The hurricane reached all the way to Cape Fear River where the *Wilmington Packet,* a large brig, was tossed about like a corkscrew and set adrift. Running up the Atlantic spine of the country to New England, the hurricane dipped inland several times, its fierce winds roaring 100 miles from the coast to snap trees and crush houses.

BUTTE, MONTANA — MINE DISASTER
June 8, 1917

There were 415 men working the night shift in the Speculator, Diamond and High Ore mines outside Butte, Montana, on June 8, 1917, when fire broke out. The blaze erupted when a power cable carrying electricity to the underground pumps broke, emitting a shower of sparks that set timbers aflame. The lower levels of all three interconnecting mines were suddenly filled with smoke and gas. The miners ran for their lives, racing blindly up various shafts leading to the surface.

The first two men taken from the shafts alive were John Coffemetten and John Boyce. Both men had been working at the 700-foot level when billows of smoke gushed in, followed by the lethal gas. An air hose lowered to the trapped miners served as their means of rescue. Boyce and Coffemetten cut the hose and sucked air from it until a rescue party found them, close to death.

Officials for the Speculator and Granite Mountain properties first felt the death toll would be low when they counted 213 men escaping from the mines and only 50 bodies were recovered. Then the dead began to appear in large numbers, dragged out by helmeted men on sledges and in small ore cars. The final number of fatalities was 163.

BYZANTINE — MARINE DISASTER
December 18, 1878

En route from Marseilles to Constantinople, the large French steamship *Byzantine* collided with the British steamer *Rinaldo* near Gallipoli in the Sea of Marmora while attempting to pass through the Dardanelles Straits. The collision occurred in a pitch black night, and 210 lives were lost. The *Byzantine* sank almost immediately, and the crippled *Rinaldo,* after picking up the few survivors, limped into port.

C

CACERES, SPAIN — TRAFFIC ACCIDENT
June 25, 1972

One of the worst traffic accidents in history occurred when a bus carrying fifty-six persons skidded off a road near Caceres on the night of June 25, 1972, and plunged down a forty-foot ravine. All aboard were football fans returning home from a game. Twenty-two people were killed by the time the bus came to rest at the bottom of the gorge.

CALABRIA, ITALY — EARTHQUAKE
February 5, 1783

Beginning on February 5, 1783, the entire western side of southern Italy was hit by a devastating series of earthquakes, five shocks in all, that were to continue for two months. The area that took most of the upheaval was around Calabria, Italy, where the first quake took an estimated 30,000 lives. More than 10,000 others later died of epidemics traceable to the quake. (There were 949 shocks recorded throughout the year; the center of the action was beneath the towns of Oppido and Monteleone.)

The first great Calabrian quake was odd in that thermal springs erupted from great fissures, some estimated by scientists on the spot to be 150 feet wide and 225 feet deep. In many instances the fissures opened so rapidly that hundreds of humans and animals were swallowed up, only to be vomited back by boiling geysers of spray. There were a few who even survived this phenomenon, but were burned so badly they were crippled for life.

The quake destroyed 181 towns, and along the seacoast, where terrified residents took to fragile rafts, landslips produced twenty-foot high waves that engulfed and drowned another 1,600 hapless people.

(ALSO SEE: Messina)

CALABRIA, ITALY — EARTHQUAKE
December 16, 1857

More than 10,000 lives were lost in Calabria, Italy, on December 16, 1857, when an earthquake rumbled from the Mediterranean to the Adriatic. Calabria, near Naples, was apparently at the center of the quake. Around the city, according to one report, "Complete villages were engulfed in the gigantic yawning fissures."

The historian, Lacaita, estimated that between 1783 and 1857, the period of the most violent earthquakes to plague the Naples-Calabria area, 111,000 inhabitants lost their lives, which meant 1,500 per year from an average population of 6 million.

CALCUTTA, INDIA — CYCLONE
October 5, 1864

The great Calcutta cyclone of October 5, 1864, struck that populous city at 10:00 A.M. after raging up the Bay of Bengal for a day and shooting through the Hooghly River. Ironically, at the nearby coastal town of Contai, where the barometer plummeted to 28.025, there was a serene calm between 9:45 and 11:00 A.M. while Calcutta was being ripped to shreds.

For those in Calcutta there was little hope. Residents helplessly watched as the cyclone furiously drove a sea wave estimated to be forty feet high toward an enormous amount of water normally accumulated at the northwest area of the bay, which was at high tide. Crashing into the harbor, the sea wave destroyed more that 200 ships and submerged most of the city in moments. More than 50,000 inhabitants were instantly drowned and another 30,000 died weeks later from

The 1783 earthquake near Calabria, Italy, killed more than 30,000 people.

disease brought on by the destruction of water systems.

Such sea waves whipped up by cyclones are normal along that coastal area of India because the Bay of Bengal, which serves as a giant reservoir at full tide, is easily upset by any substantial storm.

(ALSO SEE: Backergunge, India; Bay of Bengal)

CALI, COLOMBIA — EXPLOSION

August 7, 1956

Twenty trucks of ammunition and dynamite, after disembarking at the Pacific port of Buenaventura, Colombia, arrived at Cali, Colombia, on August 6, 1956. Thirteen trucks went on to the capital, Bogotá, that night to supply the garrisoned troops of the Colombian dictator, General Gustavo Rojas Pinilla. The remaining seven trucks were parked in front of Cali's railway terminal.

Shortly after midnight, August 7, the entire seven-truck convoy exploded with a deafening roar, instantly obliterating eight city blocks and causing extensive damage. The heart of Cali's downtown district was leveled, and more than 1,200 people were killed; several thousand more were injured.

Heavy casualties were sustained by the troops and military police stationed at the Codazzi army regiment barracks, which was close to the blast. More than 500 soldiers, asleep in their quarters at the time, were killed.

The offices of American companies with heavy interests in Colombia at the time (Ford, General Motors and Abbott Laboratories) were destroyed. A huge crater was created by the blast, which shattered windows in every building within a three-mile radius and blew the massive bronze doors off Cali's elegant St. Peter's Cathedral, thirteen blocks away.

Though President Pinilla said the explosion was

Devastation stretched for blocks in Cali, Colombia, after seven trucks loaded with dynamite exploded, killing 1,200, on August 7, 1956. *(Wide World)*

the work of "treacherous and criminal conspirators" working against the government, the cause of the blast was never fully determined.

CALIFORNIA

EARTHQUAKE
October 21, 1868

Prior to the Great Earthquake that eradicated San Francisco in 1906, one of the largest, most devastating quakes to hit north-central California occurred on October 21, 1868. Eight major cities were affected by the quake; more than forty persons were killed, mostly by falling chimneys. Damage in San Francisco alone was estimated to be $300,000.

The quake was attributed to movements of the San Andreas and Hayward faults, and one expert reported that "Mt. Tamalpais was apparently displaced 5.4 feet." Beginning at 8:00 A.M., the quake lasted forty-two seconds and was followed by seven more tremors within the next half hour.

In San Francisco in the older area along Montgomery, Sansome and Battery Streets, where flimsy wooden buildings rested on sandfill and old pilings, damage was extensive. None of the brick buildings in the city, however, were affected. Just the opposite happened across the bay in Oakland, where more than a dozen brick buildings were severely damaged and hundreds of brick chimneys were toppled. In San Jose the Presbyterian church was wrecked at a cost of $1,000. The towns of Santa Clara, Santa Rosa, Stockton, Petaluma, Healdsburg and Gilroy also suffered damage and several deaths.

The 1868 quake was the first one recorded in California history in which there were fatalities. Almost all the deaths were due to falling structures, and the *Daily Alta* thundered on October 22, 1868: "Every fatal casualty was the result of criminal carelessness in constructing brick cornices, without supports or proper attachments to the walls."

(ALSO SEE: San Francisco, California, 1906)

CALVADOS

MARINE DISASTER
March 1, 1913

The 353-ton British steamer *Calvados,* was an aging vessel—it was built in 1878—and was considered seaworthy only for short distances, such as its normal sixty-mile run between Constantinople and Panderma. On March 1, 1913, an unexpected blizzard engulfed the ship while it plodded through the Sea of Marmora. A small gale soon caused the ship to founder, and it went down in minutes, taking 200 passengers and crew members with her. Only a handful survived.

CAMP HILL, PENNSYLVANIA

RAILWAY WRECK
July 17, 1856

background: Two trains of the North Pennsylvania Railroad, one a picnic special from Philadelphia to Fort Washington, the other, a local en route to Philadelphia from Gwynedd, were traveling the same track when they met in a head-on collision on the morning of July 17, 1856. The picnic special was thoroughly demolished, and sixty-six persons on board, mostly children, were killed; sixty more were critically injured. No one on the local was killed. Conductor of the special, Alfred Hoppel, was tried for murder but was acquitted.

"Head-On Joe" Connolly was a colorful promoter of what was best described in the nineteenth century as "cornfield meets" in which two locomotives were purposely run into each other with wooden coaches coupled behind them and well soaked in kerosene to make sure they would burst into flames on impact. Connolly, who set up about 150 such monumental "shows" during his heyday, made his fortune by edifying the thrill-seeking rural crowds flocking to state fairs throughout the country. The largest crowd ever assembled to view two trains wrecked in a head-on collision gathered in 1896 at the Des Moines State Fair, where ninety thousand gapers cheered, laughed and shrieked in ecstasy at the violent destruction.

Ironically, what Connolly's spectators witnessed for a price has been repeated in reality dozens of times in the annals of railroad history. The most horrible head-on collision occurred at Camp Hill, Pennsylvania, on the morning of July 17, 1856. Punctilious men, not machines, men who feared timetables more than wholesale destruction and staggering loss of life, created this disaster.

The diminutive North Pennsylvania Railroad (later the Reading), ran its trains on a single track like most small lines of that day. Engineers, who were supposed to adhere to a strict timetable, were expected to either pull onto sidings and wait until priority trains passed them or assume the right-of-way. Such methods required absolute obedience to schedules with usually no more than a fifteen-minute leeway for running late.

In the case of the Camp Hill calamity, the conductors relied on each other to follow the rules, and both erred. William Vanstavoren, twenty-nine years old, had only recently been made a conductor after serving as a molder and brakeman. He had replaced conductor Alfred Hoppel as conductor of the line's regular morning run from Gwynedd to Philadelphia. He was a highly ambitious young man, eager to impress his superiors with his ability to direct his train, especially his scrupulous faith and loyalty to the company's strict timetables.

Ironically his predecessor, Hoppel, a man of many more years of experience, who, on July 17, 1856, was in command of a special picnic train from Philadelphia to Fort Washington, thought to stretch those very rules.

For weeks the youngsters belonging to St. Michael's Catholic Church in Philadelphia had been looking ahead to the grand picnic planned for them in the grass-laden glens of Fort Washington. More than 1,500 children, herded by several priests, lined up at the Philadelphia Master Street station in the early dawn hours. They watched sandwiches, milk cans and ice cream as it was loaded on the first of two trains to take them to their picnic. The baggage car carrying the ice cream was hooked to the end of the first ten-car train (two trains, one departing at 5:00 A.M., the other at 8:00 A.M. would carry the children, mostly of Irish immigrant stock, to the campgrounds). At the suggestion of one of the priests, the baggage car was locked in the event any snack-hungry youngster had ideas of a premature feast.

With engineer Henry Harris, twenty-one, at the throttle, conductor Hoppel boarded the first picnic special after making sure the more than 700 young, squirming riders had taken their seats. Just as Hoppel was about to give the signal to pull out, the stationmaster told him to wait and take on more passengers. The ten-minute delay worried Hoppel. He told Harris, who fidgeted at the controls of his engine, "Shackamaxon," that they might be compelled to pull over to a siding to let the local through to Philadelphia.

When the train pulled out, the deep blue summer sky was streaked with amber slices of dawn; an hour later the early dew on the rails caused the engine, laboring to pull its unusually long train, to slow down on hills. Several times Hoppel jumped from the engine to spread sawdust on the wet tracks to prevent the wheels from spinning.

Hoppel became breathless with such activity and complained to a brakeman, "If this keeps up, we'll have to take the siding at Edge Hill." Foremost in his mind was young conductor William Vanstavoren, who was bringing in the local from Gwynedd. Hoppel's train, according to the timetable, had a clear route to Fort Washington only if the train arrived there by 6:00 A.M. The conductor knew that after that time he would be allowed an additional fifteen minutes to make his destination. Beyond that he knew it was mandatory that he order his train to a siding and allow Vanstavoren's train through. "The local's got to wait for us," he murmured. "Excursion Number One has the right-of-way."

"That's right," the brakeman replied. "Better keep to the main track and let the local take the siding. There are dump cars on that siding. Not enough room for us."

Coming down the track from the other end of the line was the local, consisting of the engine, "Aramingo," driven by William Lee, a baggage car and a lone passenger car. Only twelve persons were riding the train into Philadelphia that morning, and when the local pulled onto the siding at Fort Washington, conductor William Vanstavoren nervously glanced at his watch. It was exactly 6:12 A.M.

Vanstavoren grabbed a passenger who was boarding by the arm. "Hasn't the special arrived yet?"

"No, not yet."

"It should be up by now."

Stephen Winslow, a Philadelphia newspaperman, was returning on the local from an assignment to the city. He had overheard the conductor's remarks and said to him, "You do intend to wait for the special, don't you?"

Vanstavoren barked, "I'm not waiting for anybody."

On the assumption that the special had pulled off to the siding at Edge Hill and was waiting for him, Vanstavoren told the engineer, William Lee, "It's stupid for us to be waiting for each other."

"What do your orders say?" Lee inquired.

"I have no orders."

"What are you going to do?"

Vanstavoren closed the face of his pocket watch, tucked it into his vest and said, "Go ahead."

"All right," Lee said slowly, shaking his head. "But I think you'd better not."

Vanstavoren then replied with what has become in railroad history one of the most irresponsible statements on record, "It's all right. Just sound your whistle like hell and go slow."

"I was very fearful," Lee later told investigating officials. "But he was in charge, and I did not wish to be reported for disobeying his orders." Frightened or not, engineer Lee moved out the local and was soon crawling toward Philadelphia at 10 m.p.h. He yanked the cord of his whistle constantly as he went. Reporter Winslow and others became apprehensive when they heard the shrieking warning signal and moved to the platform at the end of the last car.

The local began to work its way through the cut at Camp Hill where twenty-foot embankments on either side shot upward. Entering a long S-curve, the engineer peered forward from his perch in the cabin as he continued to blow the whistle. The special just then entered the long curve at the other end of the S, roaring down the track at 35 m.p.h., a dangerous speed considering the fact that its heavy load would be almost impossible to stop with its antiquated hand brakes.

Then engineer Lee's blood froze as he saw the joggling, racing shadow of the oncoming train. He pulled frantically at the throttle, reversing the engine. As he shut off the steam and pulled the whistle twice to signal brakemen to apply the hand brakes or "down brakes," he turned to his fireman and yelled, "My God, here they come! Oh, here they come!"

There was nothing left to do but jump, and this Lee and his fireman did, tumbling over and over down an embankment.

As soon as engineer Harris on the special saw the local charging toward him, he, too, jumped, failing in his panic, however, to either reverse the engine or call "down brakes." His fireman was cut and bruised by the fall; Harris was killed. He miscalculated the leap from the engine's cabin and fell between the engine and tender and was crushed to death.

Then came the collision. The special raced right up the snout of the almost stopped local and then careened sideways onto the embankment. Its boilers exploded and its firebox shot flames, which quickly ignited five coaches immediately behind it and reduced them to ruins. The coaches of the special crumpled into one another, crushing children and sending them flying through the glass windows onto both embankments.

A priest in the first car, Father Daniel Sheridan, was found by a parish member, Tom Harkins, crushed between the engine and the first car, his arms protectively encircling the bodies of several children. Harkins could not reach the fallen group. Flames that were quickly spreading throughout the first six cars drove him back.

Conductor Hoppel had been thrown clear upon impact and came to his senses in a field far from the burning wreck. When he staggered to his feet, he glimpsed a child's blood-soaked pink dress and grabbed it. He tore it in half and told two dazed passengers to wave the strips as danger flags, sending them both ways along the tracks to stop any approaching trains.

Minutes later, while shouting orders to rescuers pouring into the area from Camp Hill and Chestnut Hill, which had sent their entire fire department when the roaring crash was first heard, Hoppel collapsed. As he was being carried away to the hospital, he groaned, "Oh, my Lord, why didn't Bill Vanstavoren wait out his fifteen minutes?"

Vanstavoren was on the other side of the burning debris, shaken so terribly by the accident that he appeared temporarily insane. He staggered about on wobbly legs staring dazedly at the Chestnut Hill firemen working hand pumps and spraying the remaining five cars of the special that were still on the track to prevent them from catching fire. Aside from the engine, the local, incredibly, was intact, and no one other than the baggagemaster, who had his legs broken, was seriously injured.

All about the conductor were cries and moans from the wrecked five cars of the special. "The scene was the most awful I ever witnessed," said William Swain from Chestnut Hill. "Of five cars, nothing was left standing but the wheels. Every bit of woodwork was totally destroyed."

Legs and arms stuck up in grotesque positions from the burning wreck. There were hundreds of cries for help. Children called out for their parents. The flames forced back everyone trying to save the youngsters. One man could no longer bear the pathetic pleadings and shouted "Good God, help me," and with that, dashed into the towering, blazing wreck of one car, smashing away broken timbers with his huge hands, charging forward with his head as a battering ram until he disappeared into the flames and died.

Vanstavoren watched as he repeated over and over to engineer Lee, "All of it, all of it is my fault." He and Lee decided to take the news of the disaster to Philadelphia. They ran to Edge Hill where, mounting a handcar, they pushed on. Several miles away from Philadelphia, they borrowed a buggy and rode like madmen into the city. All the while Vanstavoren shouted to Lee, "If I had a dose of arsenic, I'd take it!"

One horse dropped dead in its own lather as the buggy tore through the Philadelphia streets. Vanstavoren jumped from the buggy and raced to a drugstore, where he purchased an ounce of arsenic and some morphine. He then dashed to the offices of the North Pennsylvania Railroad. Before one of his nonplussed superiors he calmly swallowed the arsenic and morphine, reported the disaster, and claimed the guilt. Within minutes he grew violently ill, vomited and was then carried to his home where he died shortly before 5:00 P.M.

At Camp Hill there was chaos. Hundreds of parents, hearing of the disaster, had fought bloody battles with their fists and clubs to take handcars and board a baggage train going in the direction of the disaster. Dozens of frenzied parents riding the cowcatcher of the baggage train came upon the scene and their shrieks of anguish "mingled with those of the dying." The five remaining cars became a somber, funereal procession hauling the dead and injured back to Philadelphia, where thousands of grief-stricken parents waiting at the station rioted, struggling with haggard policemen who had been restraining them for hours. For that era the death count was monumental. Sixty-six had been killed, mostly small children. Another sixty had been, in the words of a district attorney, "maimed and crippled, perhaps for life."

The public wrath demanded the heads of those responsible. Engineer William Lee was arrested, but was soon declared blameless by a coroner's jury. Conductor Hoppel, after recovering from his injuries, was held solely responsible for the accident. The jury's decision was that Hoppel had written orders directing him to take his train onto a siding if it were more than fifteen minutes late. It was twenty-three minutes behind time. Hoppel was imprisoned close to the scene of the wreck at Norristown, and he was later charged with murder. He stood trial in November, 1856, and was judged not guilty, mostly since local vengeance had abated; also Vanstavoren's suicide, jurors had reckoned, somehow paid for the mistake both conductors committed.

"Railroad Butchery" continued, however, to be the standing headline employed by the *New York Times* in its ongoing editorials against the railroad lines.

CANADIAN PACIFIC AIRLINES — AIR CRASH, March 3, 1953

The first fatal crash of a jet airliner occurred when a de Havilland-built Comet 1A with four turbojets failed to take off from the Karachi, Pakistan, airport on March 3, 1953, crashed through a wall and exploded, killing all eleven technicians and crew members on board.

The Comet, at this stage, was still plagued with mechanical problems. Six months before the Karachi crash, another Comet had crashed in Rome, but all on board were unharmed. At Karachi the accident was attributed to pilot error. Observers later stated that, in attempting to take off, the plane had "an excessive nose-up attitude." The plane was carrying 5,000 extra gallons of fuel; the load was apparently too much for a liftoff.

At a point halfway down the Karachi runway, the pilot made a decision to try for takeoff. He overshot the runway by 750 feet, became airborne by a few feet, missed some concrete blocks marking the end of the runway, and then his starboard suspension hit a low brick culvert. At full throttle the plane smashed through the wall and disappeared in a burst of flames.

After several other Comets crashed in the ensuing months, de Havilland experts went to work on the plane's design and solved the problem a year later. The Comet, it was discovered, developed stress concentration in the pressurized cabin of about 45,000 pounds per square inch two or three times during a routine flight. This pressure was 70 percent of the static strength of the metal and probably made the plane a deathtrap. It was also learned that the Comet's metal skin did not possess the fatigue life necessary to sustain safe flight.

In the foreground is the wreckage of a Canadian Pacific DC-8 which crashed at Tokyo Airport, March 4, 1966, killing fifty-four. The plane in background also crashed moments later (see BOAC). *(UPI)*

CANADIAN PACIFIC AIRLINES — AIR CRASH, March 4, 1966

Dense fog shrouded Tokyo International Airport on March 4, 1966, as the pilot of a Canadian Pacific DC-8 attempted to bring in his plane for a landing. He was forced to circle the airport for an hour to wait for the ceiling to lift.

The pilot then announced to his passengers that he was going to fly to Taiwan and land there. Suddenly, Tokyo tower called to tell him that the fog was thinning out and that an instrument landing was possible.

The jetliner came down much too fast and much too low, according to control tower authorities. An air controller later reported that the plane was "dangerously low." He shouted at the pilot over his microphone, "Raise your altitude! Try relanding . . . go back!"

But there was no going back, and as these commands were given, the lunging DC-8 smacked into a concrete breakwater at the lip of the airport, crumpled its nose and then cartwheeled down the runway before it burst into bright, rushing flames. Out of the splintered wreckage staggered eight survivors. Sixty-four others died inside the flaming hulk, including the fifty-three-year-old vice president of the American Broadcasting Company, Jesse Zousmer, and his wife, Ruth.

Japanese workmen still hadn't cleared away the debris by the following afternoon when a British Overseas Airways' Boeing 707 taxied past it. Passengers grimly viewed the wreckage from their windows. This plane, within minutes, shared the fate of the Canadian liner by crashing into Mount Fuji; all 124 persons on board were killed. The death toll, 188 within a twenty-four-hour period, made it the worst day in the history of commercial aviation.

(ALSO SEE: BOAC Boeing 707)

CAPE GIRARDEAU, MISSOURI — TORNADO
May 21, 1941

The tornado that touched down and ripped through Cape Girardeau, Missouri, on May 21, 1941, was a major Missouri catastrophe of the twentieth century. Touching down at 6:55 P.M., the tornado, within five minutes, cut a swath 200 yards wide through the town and pulverized 233 homes, killing 23 persons. Another 135 people were seriously injured by collapsing buildings and flying debris. Before the tornado moved off to dissipate in Illinois, ten miles distant, it had caused $4 million in damage.

CAPITANAS — MARINE DISASTER
July 31, 1715

background: The eleven-ship Spanish flota that embarked on July 24, 1715, from Havana en route to Spain was laden with one of the greatest treasures ever to be shipped from the New World (fourteen million gold and silver pesos newly minted in Veracruz, pearls, emeralds and gold bars culled from the treasure troves of Peru and Colombia). The armada sailed for six days and was struck by a massive hurricane on July 31, 1715, off the Florida coast; only one ship, the *Grifon,* stayed afloat. The two flagships, known as *Capitanas,* both 1000-ton, cannon-stacked galleons, were destroyed, along with seven other escort vessels; more than 1,000 men were drowned, an equal number surviving.

General Juan Esteban Ubilla was mindful of the hurricane season that was about to begin in the Caribbean. For two years his soldiers had been collecting a vast treasure to lay before King Philip of Spain. Resting beneath the polished decks General Ubilla and his helmeted captains trod were more than 4,000 chests of silver, gold, emeralds, pearls, silks and porcelain.

Ubilla knew, as he watched his eleven-ship armada make ready to sail in Havana harbor, that he was running the risk of encountering hurricanes, but he nervously told subordinates that once past the Florida Straits, the flota could safely reach Spain. The hurricanes were not expected until August, and he had a good chance of beating them. He was under royal orders to deliver the treasure in his ships' holds and the edicts of Philip of Spain always took precedence over the weather. The general raised his arm and give the signal to sail.

The heavy, snout-nosed galleons, groaning with the weight of their rich burdens, creaked out of Havana. More than 2,000 sailors and soldiers working the sails were unconcerned with possible disaster. The pale blue skies were clear of clouds; the breeze filling the canvases was mild. It was July 24, 1715.

By July 29 the treasure-laden fleet moved northeast into sultry weather. The air was thick and hot, the wind blew in heavy gusts and the sea rolled in wide waves that dashed forcefully against the sluggish galleons. Ubilla and his men became apprehensive when a strange mist enveloped the fleet. On the following day the wind turned to unpredictable courses, whipping the ships from several directions.

The flota was well into the Florida Straits early on the thirty-first, and General Ubilla, who had stood ramrod stiff on deck for several hours during the night, turned to an aide and said laconically, "It's coming."

"What's coming, sir?" the aide responded.

Ubilla remained silent, staring east.

The hurricane struck a little after 2:00 A.M. The sailors were already worn out, having exhausted themselves in repairing torn sails and broken halyards from the previous day's gales. They were caught in the eye of the storm—winds of 100 m.p.h. drove the ships toward the Florida reefs.

Ubilla and his officers shouted orders that could not be heard above the wind. Masts began to crash downward, killing scores of seamen. Each ship, attempting to escape the hurricane, crazily made for open seas, but the gigantic waves drove them back toward the deadly shoals. Several ships disappeared.

Only the *Grifon,* captained by Antonio Darie, escaped destruction because it was sailing far outside the hurricane's perimeter. The other ten vessels of the treasure flota met their doom in the vortex of the storm. Ubilla's *Capitana* was the first to strike the reefs and was hull-ripped, its stores and treasure chests popping into the sea, its sides stove in and its crewmen spilling overboard, plunging downward to death; 230 men, including General Ubilla, were lost in moments.

The second *Capitana* was thrown onto its side and scudded awkwardly before the wind into the shoals. General Antonio de Echeverz and 115 others drowned. Merchant and men-of-war ships followed them into oblivion, each heavy vessel shredded to pieces.

There were survivors, odd ones. An escort ship was hit broadside by a towering wave and its deck was wrenched from the hull. Clinging to the free-sailing deck, which was more like a skipping stone than a raft, 150 sailors rode safely to shore. Another ship was lifted from the water and hurled bodily onto a reef where, miraculously, all of its crew found shelter.

Within the span of five minutes the crown of Spain suffered a fleet disaster second only to the infamous Spanish Armada obliterated in the English Channel in 1588. More than a thousand men were killed, most dashed to death against the rocks. About 1,000 survived and made their way north to St. Augustine. Sailors found with looted treasure were strangled to death on orders of the provisional governor. Spanish salvagers spent three years attempting to recover the lost fourteen-million peso treasure but recouped only six million. The man in charge of the salvage operations, Juan de Hoyo Solorzano, compelled 300 Indian divers, driven by a whip and lance, to dive unceasingly for the scattered treasure. Half died groveling through the murky waters off Florida in quest of sand-covered gold and silver coins.

(ALSO SEE: Spanish Armada)

CARACAS, VENEZUELA — EARTHQUAKE
March 26, 1812

Superstition was rampant in Venezuela during the dark hours of Holy Thursday, March 26, 1812, when one of the worst earthquakes in its history destroyed nine-tenths of Caracas. The quake was most devastating near the mountain of La Silla, at the northern point of the city. Here the churches of Trinity and Alta Gracia caved onto praying multitudes. Alta Gracia Church was a 150-foot structure supported by pillars 15 feet thick. Not a person in the churches escaped.

The San Carlos barracks, which was housing a regiment of crack troops, was swallowed by giant fissures that killed every soldier. Almost every building in the city had been smashed by the one-minute quake, and throughout the night rescuers labored under a full moon to extract more than 2,000 trapped people from the ruins. Hundreds were evacuated from the hospital and taken to the banks of the bloated Guaya River.

Fearing plague, the civil authorities ordered troops to burn the thousands of bodies strewn about the streets. The entire town blazed with giant funeral pyres that night.

In addition to the estimated 10,000 killed in Caracas, another 5,000 were reported dead in the neighboring towns of La Guaya, Antimano, Baruta, Mayquetia, La Vega, Merida and San Felipe. During the weeks following the quake, famine, along with disease, soon spread, mostly from impure water (all the conduits carrying fresh water had been smashed by the quake), and another 5,000 died, bringing the death toll to 20,000 by mid-April.

The poor, led by zealous priests, considered the quake an omen from God, a sign of His displeasure with their efforts to break away from Spanish rule and join with Simón Bolívar in the establishment of the United States of Colombia.

Survivors followed the advice of their priests and betrayed their revolutionary leader, Miranda, whose troops deserted wholesale from the fortress of Puerto Cavello (commanded at the time by the great Bolívar, then a colonel), which they had won at a great cost. The Royalists regained control of the country by capitalizing on the fears of an illiterate population.

CARACAS, VENEZUELA — STAMPEDE
April 14, 1953

Moving among a great crowd assembled to pray in a Caracas church at the beginning of Holy Week, April 14, 1953, a pickpocket eagerly sought out victims. The quiet, kneeling throng, however, offered little opportunity to get close enough to anyone's wallet.

The thief resorted to an ancient criminal ploy and shouted, "Fire! Fire!" He expected that the resultant stampede to the church doors would provide him with several careless, unguarded persons from whom he could filch wallets at random.

The congregation immediately bolted in panic, and hundreds of persons charged toward the back of the church, punching, clubbing and kicking their way forward over the fallen bodies of their fellow parishioners and ignoring cries of "mercy, mercy."

By the time the church was emptied of the living, horrified priests counted the smashed corpses of fifty-three persons, twenty-two of whom were small children, some infants.

CARMICHAELS, PENNSYLVANIA — MINE DISASTER
December 6, 1962

Rescuers directed by Lewis Evans, Pennsylvania's secretary of mines, hurriedly moved to save thirty-seven men who had been trapped by a methane gas explosion in the United States Steel Corporation's Robena Number 3 mine near Carmichaels, Pennsylvania. The shaft had been shaken by two explosions, one at 1:15 P.M., the other at 2:00 P.M. on December 6, 1962.

Great clouds of black smoke were seen by Mary Ullom, who lived near the mine. "But there was no noise," she reported. The noise was certainly heard by the eighty men working throughout the mine, especially those at the 650-foot level. Forty-three men led by Alec Holowich came staggering out of the mine shortly after the explosion. Thirty-seven more were unaccounted for and Evans considered them trapped.

Publicity and attention was focused on the rescue operations for many hours. Relatives of those trapped gathered close to the mine and waited. Mrs. Eugene Zuzak held on to the quaking hand of her fourteen-year-

A miner rushes timber into the collapsed Robena No. 3 mine at Carmichaels, Pennsylvania, where thirty-seven men died, December 1962. *(UPI)*

old son Eugene, waiting to hear of her husband's fate. "I just feel empty," she mumbled to reporters. Edith Seper's brother and husband were also with the thirty-seven trapped miners. "I hate mines," she told the newsmen. "I've always hated mines."

The rescuers toiled on, making their way deeper into the shaft, pausing several times to obtain more air. At 3,900 feet, they stopped and found the first body, fifty-nine-year-old Hurley Stalnaker, a motorman. They found the rest too, a little further on, all dead.

CAROL

HURRICANE
August 26-31, 1954

background: Originating in the Cape Verde Islands, Hurricane Carol began as a small storm with 15 m.p.h. winds on August 15, 1954, and within ten days hit the Atlantic seacoast, on August 26, 1954, and struck, at 135 m.p.h. hitting areas of Virginia, Maryland, Delaware, New Jersey, New York, Connecticut, Rhode Island, Massachusetts, New Hampshire and Maine. Within six days, Carol killed 60 persons, injured 1,000 more and created $461 million in damages.

It was not the greatest hurricane ever to tear into the Atlantic seacoast, but in terms of damage, it was one of the most destructive, its rage seemingly directed at some of the oldest historical sites on the American continent. A ship named *Robin Hood* initially reported the hurricane near the Cape Verde Islands, which are often the birthplace of Western Hemisphere hurricanes. Carol was then no more than a timid squall. Its winds were a mere 15 m.p.h. gust.

Eleven days later the puny storm had swirled itself into a full-fledged hurricane. While moving through the southern Bahamas, Florida Straits and the Gulf of Mexico, the storm seemed to spend itself, with only its northern tip clustering and running as a low pressure area toward Daytona Beach, Florida. It again gathered momentous winds and seawaves. For five days Carol's powerful winds, roaring inland at 135 m.p.h., ripped out avenues of destruction through ten states.

Long Island was, as with the violent hurricane of 1938, hit first and hard by Carol's blast. Thousands were driven from the beaches, and more than 13,000 telephones were ripped out of service by her winds. More than $50,000 worth of carefully pampered elm trees snapped and died.

Rhode Island was next. The storm forced a quarter of a million men to stop work and scurry to cover. The howling winds swept through Newport, knifing into historic landmarks such as the Newport Casino, where F. Scott Fitzgerald's pleasure-lusting rich once romped. Carol tore apart the lavish structure and threw great walls of water against the coastal homes of the wealthy. The prestigious Philadelphia architect Will Van Alen and his wife caught a glimpse of an oncoming tidal wave just in time to hold on to a huge rock and save themselves, but three of the five servants with them were not as fortunate and drowned.

Two hundred homes were bashed down by the hurricane as it sliced through Misquamicutt Beach. Mrs. William J. Boudreau found herself clinging to her two children and to the roof of her beach cottage, which had been ripped away by the storm. They floated in towering seas for several hours before they were rescued.

Cars traveling along seacoast roads were clutched in the grip of Carol's winds and tossed into the sea. A car of three men returning from an outing was blown into the sea as if it had been on strings. Ensign Thomas Farrey was driving toward Jamestown when he was washed away by a giant sea wave. Providence was flooded to the first floor of almost every building.

The elegant, quiet harbors of New Bedford, Marblehead and Narragansett Bay, where once proud yachts and sailing fleets poked their gleaming masts toward the sun, were wrecked in seconds. In New Bedford, children were blown down the bay, and fishermen were sucked overboard from the rails of their fishing ships. The bodies of several babies floated in the water. Carol assailed a one hundred-year-old stone house in Wareham in which two elderly sisters, Henrietta and Lucy Berry, waited, killing them.

Half of the seventy-one boats assembled in Point Judith Bay for the annual Atlantic Tuna Tournament were wrecked by the storm. The shambles of ships piled on land or sunk deep in the harbor ran to $250,000 in damage.

Twisting up the coast, Carol vented more of her spleen on Massachusetts by attacking Martha's Vineyard and Nantucket. Here 2,500 people ran for cover following warnings of the approaching storm. Many returned home to find their houses in rubble.

Carol jabbed viciously with its solid walls of gray rain and wind at Boston, hammering at the tower of the Old North Church from which that famous lantern signal had once been flashed to Paul Revere (the spire had been rebuilt once before, after its destruction in the Great New England Hurricane of 1804). An enterprising newsman looked up in time to see the church tower swaying and clicked off a photo as it finally cracked and gave way.

In Worcester, several miles inland, businessman Harry R. Davis opened a window in his tenth story office and was sucked to his death by the howling winds.

Unwarned Maine then took the final blows Carol had to offer before she angled into Canada and died. In her six-day rampage, Carol had killed 60 people, seriously injured 1,000 more, and wreaked $461 million in damages, not the least of which was a million pounds of foodstuffs spoiled in Massachusetts for lack of electricity. This last disaster caused Governor Christian A. Herter to suspend blue laws and allow Sunday shopping. For several days, national guardsmen patrolled streets and shores to prevent looting. The Small Business Administration listed twenty-seven counties as disaster areas, and President Eisenhower ordered $1.5 million in hurricane-disaster relief funds for Massachusetts. Carol had proved to be one of the most expensive hurricanes in modern recorded history.

(ALSO SEE: Long Island, New York; New England)

CARR'S POINT, NEW YORK — RAILWAY WRECK, April 15, 1868

Harper's Weekly roared its wrath over the rail disaster at Carr's Point, New York, on April 15, 1868, by holding the Erie Railroad "guilty of the frightful massacre. We mean exactly what we say. The train was running at an extraordinary speed on what is naturally the most dangerous part of the road."

The speed of the Erie passenger train that day may or may not have caused the accident. It was determined that an unattended rail that had worked loose from its moorings caused the train to derail as it rounded a curve.

The engine and tender stayed on the track, but the four passenger cars behind these broke away and roared down a one hundred-foot gorge, each car telescoping into the one ahead as it fell. The splintered wooden cars were quickly ignited by exploding stoves and before the screaming, terrified passengers could escape the carnage, twenty-six of them were roasted to death. Sixty-three others crawled from the wreckage with serious injuries.

CARTAGO, COSTA RICA — EARTHQUAKE, August 27, 1841

Costa Rica is regularly beset with quakes, but none was more devastating than one that struck the city of Cartago, squatting in the middle of the earthquake belt, on August 27, 1841. Records of seismic upheavals were first documented only a year before. Of the 17,000 inhabitants, close to four thousand perished. Most of the deaths were caused when the city's 4,205 homes and 600 beautiful government buildings collapsed.

The homeless survivors were compelled to live in thin, cheaply constructed huts out of fear that larger, more substantial structures might collapse, while hundreds of minor quakes shook the land for the next twenty-one months.

The quake of 1841 remained the most destructive in Costa Rican history, although a smaller earthquake on May 4, 1910, did kill 242 persons, injured hundreds and caused much damage.

CASTLE GATE, UTAH

MINE DISASTER
March 8, 1924

Details are sketchy concerning the mine explosion at the Utah Fuel Company's mine outside Castle Gate on March 8, 1924. A sudden blast rocked one of the main shafts, and within hours 173 dead miners were dragged out. The cause of the blast was never fully described, but "exploding gas" was reported on several occasions.

Oddly enough, inspectors for the firm had checked the mine's ventilation and sprinkling systems only three weeks before the explosion and pronounced them safe. The Castle Gate tragedy touched off a widespread newspaper campaign lobbying for better safety measures in the mines.

"Is something seriously wrong with our Federal mine regulations?" asked the *Grand Rapids Herald*. "Is there a need for drastic revision of our coal-mine safety codes?"

There apparently was, for local authorities began to institute new codes shortly after the explosion.

CATHAY PACIFIC AIRLINES

AIR CRASH
June 15, 1972

Most of the passengers aboard the Cathay Pacific flight zooming above South Vietnam at 35,000 feet on June 15, 1972, were tourists, oblivious to the war raging beneath them in the body-littered jungles. The British-owned airline jet was Hong Kong based and was return-

A rescue team takes out a mine disaster victim at Castle Gate, Utah, March 8, 1924. *(UPI)*

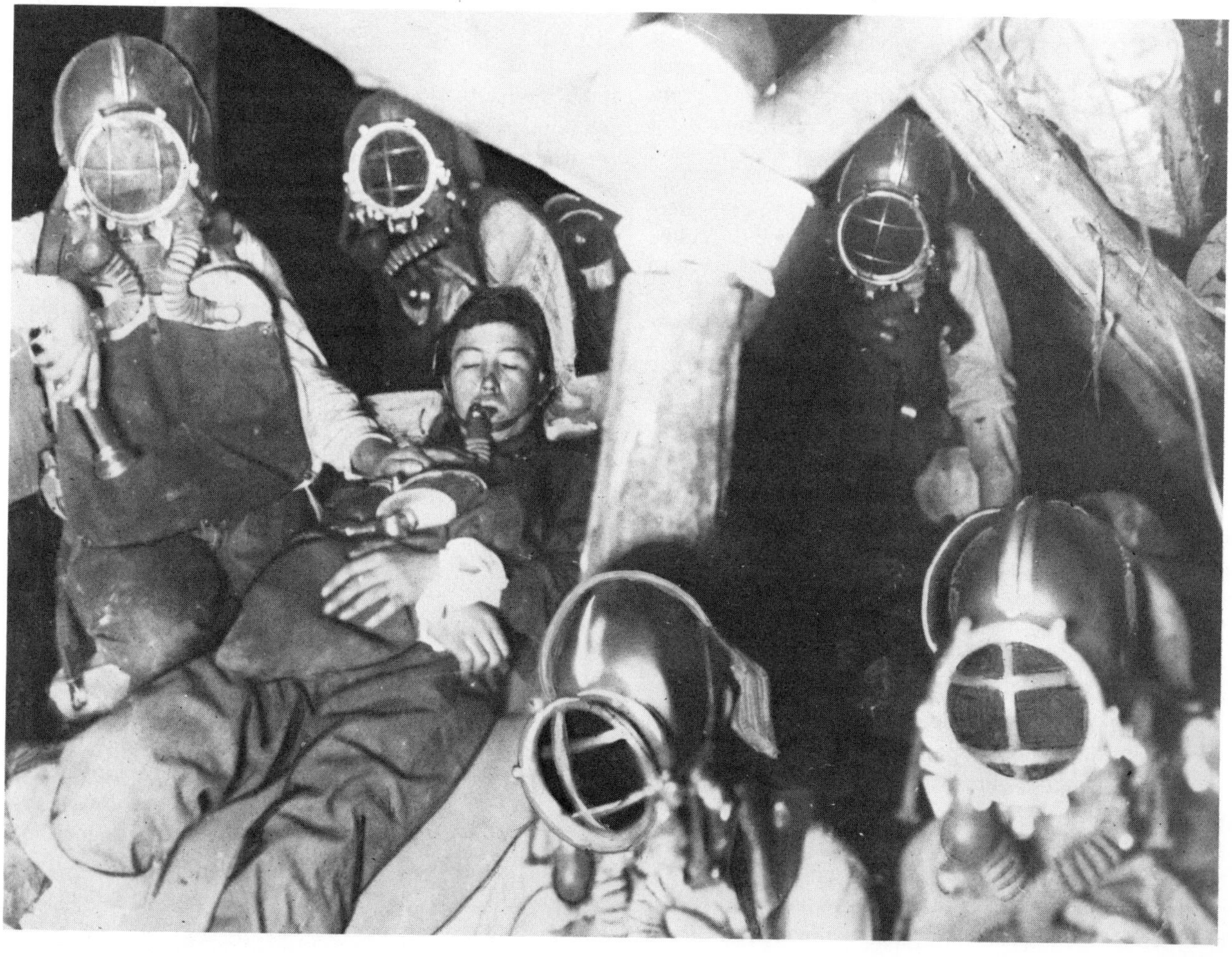

ing there after visiting Singapore and Bangkok. All but a few of the seventy-one passengers aboard carried cameras, which they had used constantly in their travels.

What brought the giant plane down from the clear skies of Vietnam to the mud flats of Cheoreo, reducing it to tiny strips of metal, was never determined. Ruled out completely was any effect from ground fire directed by Viet Cong in the area. The jetliner was simply too high to be reached.

No one on board lived to explain the plane's fate; all eighty-one (which included a crew of ten) were killed upon impact. Among the dead was Thomas J. Kenny, a fifty-year-old Wisconsin man and vice president of the B. C. Ziegler Company of West Bend, Wisconsin, along with his wife Roberta and four children, the only American fatalities.

United States troops reached the crash site via helicopters, retrieving bodies and driving off Viet Cong guerrillas who had been rummaging through the ruins of the behemoth Convair 880 jet.

CENTAUR

MARINE DISASTER
September, 1782

background: A huge West Indies convoy consisting of merchant ships, British man-of-war frigates and French warships captured by Admiral George Rodney from Admiral DeGrasse in an April, 1782, battle was caught in a violent mid-Atlantic gale in early September, 1782, as it attempted to reach England. Admiral Graves's flagship, *Ramillies*, foundered, but all of its 600-man crew were saved; other notable sinkings of this convoy included the *Ville de Paris*, which disappeared along with its 800-man crew, and the *Centaur*, which sank with more than 400 on board, its crew deserted by Captain Inglefield, who was later tried by the British Admiralty.

Dispersed and driven before hurricane winds, the huge fleet of British Admiral Graves, ninety-three vessels in all, was making for England in September of 1782. Most of the ships in the fleet had been taken as prizes from French Admiral DeGrasse in a titanic sea battle the previous April, a battle from which British Admiral George Rodney had emerged victorious. Now Admiral Graves was shepherding the 110-gun *Ville de Paris*, the *Glorieux*, the *Hector*, the *Ardent*, the *Caton* and the *Jason* across a turbulent Atlantic with other vessels.

Both the British and the French ships were barely seaworthy, only slight repairs to their battle damages having been made. One of the most severely injured ships was the British man-of-war, *Centaur*, whose crew of more than 400 under the command of Captain Inglefield battled the gale at the pumps. The storm increased with such fury that the ship was tossed on her beam ends and appeared to capsize. Inglefield ordered all masts cut away. This done, the *Centaur* abruptly righted, but then the ship's armament became lethal. The violent storm wrenched three heavy cannons free from their moorings and crushed the lockers that held the round shot.

Scores of sailors chased the rolling cannons and round shot as they crashed into railings, deck beams and bulkheads. Several men were crushed to death by the cannons, others were lanced by huge slivers splintered away from stanchions as the shot and cannons crunched into them. After battering holes in the side of the oaken ship, the cannons were finally lashed down. Captain Inglefield was warned that the ship was in a perilous condition, but he ignored the warning and pointed toward the majestic three-decker *Ville de Paris*, which heaved into view. Inglefield told his officers that the captured French prize now proudly bearing the British ensign would come to their aid.

There was a sudden lull in the storm, and those on the *Centaur* happily watched the *Ville de Paris* make for them. She was the only ship of Graves's entire command not crippled by the storm, and the sight of her defiantly crashing through huge waves, her sails billowing, cheered the despondent *Centaur* bluejackets. Inglefield fired off a distress rocket and, watching the great ship through his telescope, thought she had responded and was making directly for his stricken vessel. So confident was the captain that the *Ville de Paris* would come to his aid that he waved off several merchant vessels passing by, declining their help.

Then the inexplicable happened. The tall French ship, commanded by Captain Wilkinson, veered onto an opposite course and within an hour sailed beyond sight, never to appear again, carrying her crew, 800 men, into oblivion. Her unknown fate became one of the great mysteries of the sea.

Aboard the *Centaur* conditions worsened by the minute. The warship was taking great amounts of water, and almost all of her crewmen were manning the pumps. Inglefield wrote in his log: "The people worked without a murmur and indeed with cheerfulness."

All through the night the *Centaur* groaned with the sound of her chain pumps, and men staggered forward in wobbly-legged groups to bale and pump the rising water. She was alone, the rest of Graves's storm-battered fleet scattered over the roiling ocean. In the dark distance Captain Inglefield and his sweating men could hear the pop of cannons from other ships of the fleet. They caught glimpses of flashing gunpowder far away. They knew these were the farewell signals of sinking ships. It was almost over for the *Centaur*, too.

No matter how fast or how much the crew bailed and pumped, the ocean beat them by inches until the lower decks were awash. The exhausted bluejackets began to collapse at their posts. Captain Inglefield went to each party of men and encouraged them to continue their labors, but he, too, knew they were beaten: ". . . seeing their efforts useless, many of them burst into tears and wept like children." It was time to take their chances in the open sea. But all knew there were only a few lifeboats available.

Leaving the pumps, many sailors, resigned to death, went to their hammocks and had their friends lash them down. Others, such as the carpenter's gang, hastily attempted to construct rafts from gratings, spars and booms.

Inglefield recorded, "The most predominant idea was that of putting on their best and cleanest clothing." Such an act was not unheard of but, rather, was a strange ritual of the sea observed by sailors anticipating death.

Captain Inglefield was not prepared at all to don his finest uniform and sink with the *Centaur*. Unlike most of his peers in that stoic sailing epoch, Inglefield's love of life was more important than the ancient mariner custom of the captain going down with his ship. Spying a pinnace near his cabin, Inglefield motioned to the master, Rainey, a young midshipman, a surgeon's mate, a coxswain, a quartermaster and six burly seamen. He directed these men to lower the small boat and scooped up a blanket he intended to use for a sail.

Once in the boat, Inglefield ordered the makeshift sail rigged, and the twelve men drifted away from the sinking *Centaur*. More than 400 men, most of whom did not see the pinnace being lowered, stood at the railing and watched their captain desert them. Everyone in the boat averted his eyes from the ship, except Captain Inglefield. He continued to stare back silently at his trapped men, who cursed and damned him. It was sunset on the sea, and the small boat skipped along under a heavy wind until no one in the pinnace could sight the *Centaur*.

For thirteen days, Inglefield later related, he and his men sailed toward the Azores, "in a leaky boat, with one of the gunwhales stove . . . without compass, quadrant or sail; wanting greatcoat or cloak, all very thinly clothed, in a gale of wind and with a great sea running." Their provisions consisted of a small ham, some pork, a bag of bread, two quart bottles of water and two French cordials.

The small boat drifted into the port of Fayal thirteen days later. Only one seaman had died. The rest were taken to a hospital. After recovering, Captain Inglefield was arrested for abandoning his command and held for court-martial by the British Admiralty.

His defense was a deftly worded speech of self-exoneration: "As evening approached, the ship [*Centaur*] seemed little more than suspended in the water. There was no certainty that she would swim from one minute to another; and the love of life, now began to level all distinctions. It was impossible, indeed, for any man to deceive himself with the hopes of being saved on a raft on such a sea; besides, it was probable that the ship in sinking would carry everything down with her in a vortex.

A sailor on board the sinking *Centaur* chops away decking to use for a raft. *(From an old print)*

"It was near five o'clock, when coming from my cabin, I observed a number of people gazing very anxiously over the side; and looking myself, I saw that several men had forced the pinnace and that more were attempting to get in. I had thoughts of securing this boat before she might be sunk by numbers; there appeared not a moment for consideration; to remain and perish with the ship's company to whom I could no longer be of any use, or seize the opportunity, which seemed the only one of escaping and leave the people with whom on a variety of occasions I had been so well satisfied that I thought I could give my life to preserve them. This was, indeed, a painful conflict and of which, I believe, no man could form a just idea who had not been placed in a similar situation.

"The love of life prevailed. I called to Mr. Rainey, the master, the only officer on deck, and desired him to follow me, and we immediately descended into the boat by the after port of the chains. But it was not without great difficulty that we got her clear of the ship, twice the number that she could carry pushing in, and many leaping into the water. Mr. Baylis, a young gentleman of fifteen years of age [the midshipman], leaped from the chains after the boat had got off and was taken in. . . ."

Admiralty officers nodded their understanding. Some praised his open boat voyage and seamanship much the same way Captain William Bligh of the ill-starred *Bounty* received acclaim from his peers. The high court honorably acquitted Captain Inglefield of any blame, and his personal dossier remained unblemished for the balance of his career. No one spoke for the 400 dead.

CENTRAL AMERICA — EARTHQUAKES
August 13-15, 1868

Great earthquakes began to shake dozens of cities in Central America on the morning of August 13, 1868, continuing for two days and destroying the cities of Arica, Arequipa, Iquique, Tacna, Chencha and dozens of smaller towns and villages. More than 25,000 lost their lives, and an additional 30,000 became homeless overnight.

Along the coasts the ocean waters drew back long distances and then rushed forward with seismic waves that engulfed villages and cities. The damage was estimated at $300 million, adding up to one of the worst catastrophes along the earthquake belt. Relief funds were collected worldwide to aid the distraught survivors, the bulk of which, $55 million, was collected in London, England.

CHANDKA FOREST, INDIA — STAMPEDE
July 10, 1972

An excessive drought and burning heat wave around the Chandka Forest in India was the reason given when herds of wild elephants went berserk on July 10, 1972, and raced through five villages, killing twenty-four persons.

Many weeks before the tragedy villagers had reported to authorities that they were afraid to farm their land because the elephants in the district had become crazed from the heat and drought.

CHANG TYONG-HO — MARINE DISASTER
January 9, 1953

The decrepit 146-ton Korean passenger ship, *Chang Tyong-Ho,* was a leaky, unstable coastal steamer. It was never really built for travel on the high seas, and on January 9, 1953, it became a death trap for 249 passengers and crewmen.

On its regular run from Yosu to Pusan, the ship fumbled its way through a growing storm flecked with mounting whitecaps. By 9:00 P.M. Captain Ha Ryang Moh had taken control of the steering wheel to battle the cyclonic seas. Then he saw the wave approaching, a colossal wall of water, since described as the much-dreaded *tsunami.* The steamer took the wave broadside and instantly rolled over. Decks and compartments in which most of the passengers were attempting to sleep were completely engulfed.

Captain Ha and 6 others were blown into the water upon impact and survived. The rest drowned. Had there been time to abandon ship, it is unlikely that even a third of the 249 lost would have lived. The *Chang Tyong-Ho* had only 60 life preservers and a single lifeboat on board.

Chang Dok Yong, an official of the South Korean Ministry of Transportation, held a press conference the next day and stated that rescue vessels sent out eight hours following the disaster found no wreckage or survivors. Chang pointedly stated that the tragedy "was no fault of the captain" and went on to utter much concern over the possibility that the sunken vessel had carried any important South Korean officials on their way to Pusan and a meeting of the National Assembly.

The discovery that none of the dead possessed any political importance came as a great relief.

CHAOUIA — MARINE DISASTER
January 17, 1919

The devastation wrought by the two world wars went on long after hostilities ceased, notably on the sea in the form of unswept mine fields. The instances of peacetime vessels destroyed by these partly submerged hazards were less pronounced following World War I than World War II, but one awesome casualty was the 4,334-ton French liner, *Chaouia* (formerly the *Koningen Wilhelmina*). En route to Constantinople from Piraeus, the ship hit a mine in the Straits of Messina and went down in four minutes. The 690 passengers and crew had no time whatever to abandon ship, and 460 people drowned.

(ALSO SEE: Chimara, Kiangya)

CHARLESTON, SOUTH CAROLINA — TORNADO
September 10, 1811

One of the worst tornadoes ever recorded in American history struck Charleston, South Carolina, on September 10, 1811. According to historian Lorin Blodget, the tornado came on the heels of a strong southerly gale, punctuated by a calm in which the clouds above the city took on a reddish tint. The air became thick, and then a strange funnel-shaped cloud approached. The tornado shot to earth shortly after 12:30 P.M., destroying great sections of the city and killing uncounted numbers. One death figure given was more than 500.

(ALSO SEE: Natchez, Mississippi, 1940)

An earthquake rattled Charleston, South Carolina, on August 31, 1886, killing 100 citizens.

CHARLESTON, SOUTH CAROLINA

FIRE
April 27-28, 1838

Half of Charleston, South Carolina, was burned to the foundations of its antebellum mansions by a raging inferno that began in a paint store at King and Beresford streets on April 27, 1838. The blaze began about 8:30 A.M. and, due to the city's inadequate firefighting equipment and forces, went unchecked until noon of the following day. By then it had destroyed more than half the city. There were 1,158 buildings gutted at a cost of $3 million.

Engineers, troops and wealthy plantation owners began a backfire the following day by blowing up buildings in the fire's path. According to one account, "the worst feature of the catastrophe was the loss of life which occurred while the houses were being blown up. Through the careless manner in which the gunpowder was used four of the most prominent citizens of the city were killed. . . . " Dozens more were injured by the blast.

CHARLESTON, SOUTH CAROLINA

EARTHQUAKE
August 31, 1886

The Great Charleston Earthquake, which took the lives of one hundred persons on August 31, 1886, was one of the most widely felt quakes in America. Quakes had been known to occur in Charleston as early as 1687 (as reported by Harriott H. Ravenal in her book, *Charleston, The Place and the People.*) The killer quake of 1886 produced many fissures from which sulfuric clouds emanated, and its damage to buildings in Charleston was extensive.

Shocks were felt as far north as New York, to Mobile, Alabama in the south, and as far west as Omaha, Nebraska. For ten seconds, chandeliers shook, gas jets flickered, and a general swaying motion was felt in New York. One report said that in the Western Union office on Broadway "desks seemed to be on rockers and move like cradles." Walls cracked in Harlem. In Brooklyn a telegraph operator reported that he had been "spilled" from his chair.

A Professor Capen, whom the *New York Times* called "the weather prophet of this city," was busily penning his forecast for the next day. He had warned of the approaching quake with the ominous prediction that it would be "awful and terrible." Capen worked for the *Republican* newspaper, and when the quake was felt in its offices, all the editors, reporters and compositors ran out. Capen, the *Times* took pains to later point out, "remained at his desk in blissful ignorance of the fact that his prediction had been fulfilled."

In Richmond, Virginia, prisoners in the penitentiary rioted until wardens allowed them out into the exercise yard, and then, fearing a mass escape attempt, called up National Guard units to surround the prison walls. More than 10,000 amused spectators stood outside the prison listening to "the shrieks of the male and female prisoners which could be heard for a quarter of a mile."

The shock waves reached Vicksburg, Mississippi, and interrupted a city council meeting. For a full minute the "oscillations" gently shook the city, and many at the city council session became ill and vomited, causing a speedy adjournment.

Women boarders at the Peabody Hotel in Memphis, Tennessee, which received a violent ten-minute shock, became hysterical and threw themselves down stairways, screaming that the building was falling.

In Chicago three or four shocks, lasting several seconds each, were felt. Clerks working in the Government Building listened, frightened, as the windows of their offices began banging loudly in their frames. In another Chicago office a government employee named Harrold, writing at his desk when the quake came, reported that his head "was wobbling around without any particular reason." Citizens on the streets with no knowledge of the quake, an account states, "found themselves growing dizzy and thought they were suffering from vertigo."

The quake struck at 9:16 P.M. in Cincinnati and was particularly violent. Compositors of the *Commercial Gazette* panicked and jumped from windows to lower roofs, and it took a great deal of persuasion to get them back into the building.

Patients in the Central Asylum for the Insane in Columbus, Ohio, then the largest mental hospital in the world, ran amuck of their attendants after seeing the furniture tilt and turn with the tremor.

In Indianapolis an injury occurred when a piece of coping fell from the Denison Hotel, beaned Pool Commissioner Doherty, and knocked him senseless.

The wildest panic was, however, in Charleston itself, at the center of the quake. Dozens of buildings, many of them historic landmarks, toppled. Falling buildings

Kingston, Jamaica, was left in ruins after a visit from hurricane Charlie, August 17, 1951. *(UPI)*

killed most of the 100 people slain in the quake. Oddly, most of the dead were blacks who had panicked at the first shockwaves and run wildly through the streets proclaiming the end of the world.

CHARLESTON, SOUTH CAROLINA — TORNADO — September 29, 1938

Charleston, South Carolina, long besieged by tornadoes, experienced an epidemic of twisters, a group of five at once, on September 29, 1938, from 6:45 A.M. to 8:30 A.M. The worst of the onslaught were the second and third tornadoes, touching down a little more than two miles apart. The third tornado destroyed everything in its 1,600 foot path.

The third tornado first touched down on James Island and moved toward the city from there. Thirty-two persons were killed and 150 more were hospitalized for injuries. Property damage was estimated at $2 million.

CHARLIE — HURRICANE — August 17, 1951

Before the United States Weather Bureau decided to name hurricanes after women, it made an attempt to dub them with military call signals. The twelve 1951 hurricanes were labeled Able, Baker, Charlie and so on. Charlie was the worst of the lot.

Sweeping in from the Antilles, the hurricane struck Jamaica with intensive force at 8:30 P.M. on August 17, 1951. Before its hollow-sounding scream, Charlie drove all the cocoa palms along the elegant avenues of Morant Bay into the sea. Almost every wooden structure on the island was smashed to pieces by the fury of the storm, and at Kingston and the old pirate haven of Port Royal, 125 m.p.h. winds broke apart dozens of ships and flattened wharves and warehouses before moving on to destroy Savanna-la-Mar and Spanish Town.

An hour after Charlie roared back out to sea, more than 50,000 Jamaicans found themselves homeless. Dead were 154 victims of the storm who had been struck down by flying debris and crushed under falling walls. More than 2,000 were injured.

It would be a full five years before Jamaica recovered, close to a year before most of its citizens could move from tents provided by Great Britain (along with $2 million in relief funds) to city barracks. But, led by the Red Cross, the Central Hurricane Relief Committee, organized on the spot as soon as Charlie left, made great efforts to revive the island. Free fresh milk to babies and thousands of pounds of clothing and food were given out. Gradually, the paradise island returned to its former beauty and serenity.

CHARTRES, FRANCE — HAIL STORM — 1359

Within a few miles of Chartres in 1359, Edward III, his heavily armored army moving forward to the attack, was, according to the *Old Chronicle,* enveloped in a raging storm of rain and lightning that rapidly changed to hail. The "hailstones [were] so prodigious as to instantly kill 6,000 of his horses and 1,000 of his best troops." Edward's warriors wore heavy metal helmets, and when the hailstones, the size of "goose eggs," struck these, the death toll was increased.

CHATSWORTH, ILLINOIS — RAILWAY WRECK — August 10, 1887

background: An excursion train made up of fifteen cars pulled by two engines en route from Peoria, Illinois, to Niagara Falls with more than 600 passengers on board crashed through a fifteen-foot trestle bridge between Chatsworth and Piper City, Illinois. The bridge caught fire on the night of August 10, 1887. The second engine and the next eleven cars of the near bankrupt Toledo, Peoria & Western train were destroyed; eighty-two persons were killed and more than a hundred were horribly mangled by their injuries. The wreck was one of the worst disasters in American train history. Negligence on the part of road gangs and inadequate safety equipment were held responsible for the tragedy.

Notorious robber barons in the United States during the late nineteenth century, men like Jim Fisk and Jay Gould, were responsible for more than bilking the public and swindling the government. In the case of the monstrous railroad disaster near Chatsworth, Illinois, on August 10, 1887, which claimed eighty-two lives and crippled a hundred more, the blame could be pinned to the tails of Jay Gould's frock coat.

Gould had eliminated the Toledo, Peoria & Western line as a competitor to his Wabash Road by leasing the railroad for fifty years, draining it of all its assets and dumping it bankrupt in the laps of trustees holding the first mortgage. In a desperate attempt to bolster the financial standing of the Peoria line and to cover its 247 miles of track with trains filled with paying passengers, the railroad began to offer extensive excursions at cut-rate prices.

Though the firm realized some immediate profit, its tracks and trestles were allowed to fall into disrepair; its trains were in shoddy condition, and its employees, underpaid and overworked, became unconcerned and irresponsible about their duties and passenger safety.

As more than 600 passengers paid the incredibly low excursion fare of $7.50 for a round trip from Peoria to Niagara Falls, on August 10, 1887, a TP&W road

The tragic end of a holiday occurred near Chatsworth, Illinois, on August 10, 1887, when an excursion train crashed.

gang, headed by foreman Tim Coughlan, was burning away high prairie grass near the tracks running between Chatsworth and Piper City in eastern Illinois. Passing freight trains had sent sparks into the grass, now crackling dry in August, and ignited the reeds on several occasions. As a safety measure Coughlan and four others were sent to clear these dangerous patches of high grass. As it turned out, their efforts proved more dangerous than fires beginning from train wheel sparks.

The men worked until 5:00 P.M., Coughlan a half-hour longer as he made sure none of the burned-out patches of grass were still smoldering. Seventy miles to the west and three hours later, more than 600 jubilant tourists, their cheap tickets in hand, boarded one of the longest trains ever to be pulled down the TP&W's line, fifteen cars towed by two engines.

One man watching the throng board the train, engineer Edward McClintock, scowled and shook his head. He turned to the conductor, J. W. Stillwell, and said, "This train is too long and too damned heavy. It's dangerous." He looked at the two engines coupled together, Number 21 and Number 13 (the latter was his engine), which would pull the train. "This excursion should be divided into two trains, an engine for each section. If anything happens, the whole train will go."

Stillwell was a company man, adamant about instructions. "I got my orders and you got yours, Ed. Roll it out."

Swallowing his prophecy and studying the controls, McClintock climbed aboard the second engine. He peered down the track at the waiting train. Behind the two engines were a baggage car, a passenger coach brimming with TP&W officials, five more coaches, two parlor cars and six Pullman sleepers.

The passengers were a mixed lot, their ranks swollen with the poor, dragging dozens of children on board. It was the one excursion trip, a high point in their lives, they could afford. Jostling next to them, Superintendent N. E. Armstrong was told by conductors, were many thugs and sneak thieves, some even carrying pistols that were easily detected when the flaps of their coats were brushed back. An hour after the train pulled out, Armstrong became more alarmed when he began to receive reports that handbags and valises were mysteriously missing. Preoccupied by this epidemic of widespread pilferage on the speeding train, Armstrong and others took little note of either the condition of the tracks or the distant flickers of flame far ahead on the dark prairie.

At about 11:30 P.M., some evening strollers in Chatsworth looked across the prairie to the east to see specks of flame jerking skyward. They felt the strong wind that had arisen surprisingly in the arid night and then heard the excursion special approaching, its whistles piercing the thick, murky air. The train roared through the town of Chatsworth without stopping. The engineers were behind schedule and were trying to make up for lost time.

Beneath a fifteen-foot trestle bridge spanning a parched six-foot-deep gully were several bales of hay, stored by a farmer. The patches of field grass Coughlan and the others had attempted to burn away in the afternoon had somehow ignited other clumps of dry grass. The flames from these snaked to the hay bales and ignited them. The old wooden trestle was soon smoking at its low supports.

In the lead engine, Number 21, engineer Sutherland blinked as he stared ahead. There were bright red flames directly in his path. First he thought it was only a grass fire, which was quite common this time of year. Then he realized, as his engine roared forward, that the trestle was aflame. At 300 yards from the culvert, Sutherland applied the manual brakes (air brakes, although available, had not been introduced on the TP&W line because they were too expensive).

It was much too late. Sutherland's engine raced over the flaming bridge at 35 m.p.h., but McClintock's engine, Number 13 (as luck and his own premonition would have it), offered too much weight for the already weakened trestle, and it crashed downward through the flames. McClintock was killed instantly as nine cars behind his engine toppled, one onto the other, into the chasm.

Superintendent Armstrong was hurtled through a window and injured seriously. He looked up to receive a scalding blast of steam escaping from the mangled engine and then crawled away, groaning for help. Stillwell, the conductor, was thrown the length of three cars and landed in the arms of a startled passenger. He was uninjured.

But eighty-two others were either dead or dying. "From all sides," sleeping-car passenger E. A. Van Zandt recalled, "came groans and cries, so we went to work, and we had to work hard, too. If the wreck ever caught fire, three hundred people would have been burned to death, and the only thing we could do was to smother the fire with dirt."

The passengers were divided by fate into three groups: the dead and injured, the unharmed who worked feverishly to extinguish flames creeping up the walls of the wooden coaches and extract the living, and the unconscionable thieves who raced through the stricken cars looting and robbing.

Engineer Sutherland paused only a moment after clearing the bridge, then raced his engine at full throttle to Piper City, where he enlisted an army of rescuers in minutes and roared back to the scene of disaster. In Chatsworth word of the crash spread, and soon all the bells in the church towers were clanging the alarm and calling volunteers to the rescue.

The dead and injured were removed from the train wreck at Chatsworth, Illinois, and placed in rows along the track; many were never identified. *(Frank Leslie's Illustrated Newspaper)*

Theft and suicide added to the Chatsworth horror; hundreds were pinned under wreckage for hours. *(Harper's Weekly)*

When the residents of these two towns arrived, they found bodies stretched out in rows, placed along the track by other passengers. Clusters of injured wailed and begged for help. The passengers who had saved their fellows from the burning train held up bloody hands. Most had ripped away their nails by clawing in the sun-hardened earth to scoop dirt upon the flames.

Some of the plug-uglies who had taken the trip to rob their fellow passengers and were subsequently pinned beneath the wreckage now found another and unexpected use for their secreted revolvers. Pistol shots began to bark out, puncturing the steady hum of groans and moaning. Many of the burly men killed themselves when unable to remove the seats and beams that straddled and impaled their bodies.

These self-inflicted *coups-de-grace* were but added irony and bizarre pockets of violence to the flaming, bloody horror the inhabitants of Chatsworth and Piper City saw strewn along the forlorn tracks of the TP&W.

Jay Gould had his quick millions. The TP&W had, by virtue of its economic plight, precipitated the catastrophe. And the Niagara Excursion Special had eighty-two dead and more than a hundred seriously injured from its once "happy as children" passenger list.

Official inquiries into the Chatsworth disaster were held, and road-gang-boss Coughlan was censured for failing to notice the smoldering grass he left to burn on the open prairie. The authorities then quickly forgot the disaster. The townspeople in the region incorporated the tragedy into local folklore, especially when T.P. Westendorf penned his maudlin ballad, "The Bridge Was Burned at Chatsworth." One luridly melodramatic stanza is:

The mighty crash of timbers
A sound of hissing steam
The groans and cries of anguish
A woman's stifled scream.
The dead and dying mingled.
With broken beams and bars
An awful human carnage
A dreadful wreck of cars.

CHELSEA, MASSACHUSETTS — FIRE — April 12, 1908

background: The great Chelsea, Massachusetts, fire broke out in the poorer section of the town at 11:00 A.M., Sunday, April 12, 1908, raging for several hours and devastating 492 acres. More than 17,450 were left homeless with damage running to $6 million; more than a dozen were killed.

Just what caused the great Chelsea fire of 1908 was never determined. Much like the Chicago fire thirty-seven years earlier, it was reasoned that it began in one of the cardboardlike houses in the rundown East End section, where wooden houses had been built close together and served as tinder boxes to the inferno.

Though a minimum of human lives were lost, family pets, horses and livestock suffered greatly. Officials of the Animal Rescue League estimated that 2,000 cats burned to death inside houses they were reluctant to leave.

Deacons of the Universal Church, trying to save precious books and documents, piled archives on a horsedrawn wagon and covered them with church pew cushions. As they dashed away from the burning church, the cushions caught fire, gutted the wagon and destroyed its revered cargo. Flames billowing from the cushions shot upward in a wind reaching almost cyclonic proportions and touched off several houses in a two-block area.

The flames rushed through and over the residential area known as "the foreign section" and toward the business district at Broadway between Third and Fourth streets. Here the city's valiant fire department, its horse-drawn engines lined up, its smoke-stained legion of firemen in rows with hoses drawn, waited for the blaze to reach them. The wall of water thrown up at the flames was not enough to stop it. The blaze jumped the broad business streets, ignited awnings over shops and was soon eating its awful way through the heart of town. Bellingham Station was on fire. So was the new six-story YMCA structure. Firemen were powerless to stop the flames now; their hoses were burning up.

Then it became a matter of saving mementos. A hundred men suddenly decided to preserve a trolley car on Broadway and shoved the heavy vehicle for several blocks to safety. Elderly women stumbled down the sidewalks away from the row of mansions on Hawthorne Street carrying frying pans or pieces of crockery under their arms. Dozens were prostrate in the street, pounding the pavements with fists and sobbing at the loss of their prestigious homes.

A fireman spotted one of the town's leading society matrons who dazedly walked past him carrying a broken statue. "Why bother with that, Ma'am?" he said, pointing to the headless statue. The woman glanced down to the statue tucked under her arm and, as if seeing it for the first time, threw it into the gutter in disgust.

A militiaman raced into a burning house and ordered a woman from her kitchen. The housewife complied, but not before she filled her teakettle and placed it on the stove, never bothering to explain her action to the anxious, perplexed soldier.

Temporary insanity gripped many that day. In Union Park a distinguished-looking gentleman, noting the flames on all four sides closing in on those huddled about him, calmly withdrew a pistol from his long coat, murmured a soft "goodbye" and put a bullet in his head. Another man, his clothes all but burned from his body, stood in the middle of the Washington Avenue Bridge and shrieked at the poor, fleeing wretches about him to "turn back" and fight the fire. Later, addressing crowds of the homeless, he raved that he had saved the destroyed city.

Heat exhaustion took its toll. Firemen, the water in their hoses gone, phlegmatically walked into the advancing wall of fire and disappeared. One, seeing his own reflection in a smoke-filled drug store mirror and thinking it to be another fireman, walked through the glass and knocked himself unconscious. A woman carried her dog so tightly while escaping the flames that the animal could not lie down for several days.

The ludicrous happened. Two burly men attempted to salvage an upright piano when it caught fire. One man fled. The other shrugged, flipped open the keyboard lid, sat down and deliriously plunked out "There'll be a hot time in the old town tonight," as the house in which he played was destroyed by flames.

Eli C. Bliss, a rich man, walked calmly from his mansion on Chestnut Street to an embankment nearby where a freight train had come to a halt. A work gang on the train announced that two of the freight's boxcars were empty. Bliss enlisted the aid of the brawny workers, and slaving in the intense heat, the crew filled the boxcars with Bliss's treasures—expensive mahogany furniture, paintings, books—just before the mansion burst into flames. The train, its cars beginning to smoke, pulled out just in time.

A hideous scene occurred in Garden Cemetery. Fleeing the flames, hundreds of people crowded into the burial ground and hid behind marble tombstones to escape. Some broke into mausoleums but died of the intense heat inside.

The inferno reached epic force, whipped by a raging wind. Historian Walter Pratt, who was present, gave his impressions:

"We fled down the hill [away from ex-Mayor Thomas Strahan's magnificent, hill-perched estate, which was in flaming ruins] in the direction of Orient Heights. Hun-

The great fire that swept Chelsea, Massachusetts, on April 12, 1908, killed twenty persons and destroyed 17,450 homes with a loss totaling $32 million. *(Wide World)*

dreds were going the same way; poor and rich were on equal terms. The wind blew with such force that women were blown into fences and trees or lost their balance and fell. Great pieces of furniture went bounding end over end down the hill, blown by the wind. Horses were running away, and the scene was one of terrifying confusion. Escape was possible only by enduring the hostile breath of the flames, running, tripping over abandoned furniture in the blinding, sickening smoke, towards the marshes to the northeast, where, although safe from the flames, the refugees suffered untold agony from the hail storm of stones and showers of blazing embers that fell upon them, burning holes in their clothes and starting grass fires in every direction."

The bridges to east Boston began to burn, cutting off that route of escape. Yachts moored near the bridges caught fire and burned. One flaming vessel drifted across the river and ignited the Standard Oil Works on the other side; the oil tanks exploded into towers of flame. Eighty thousand volumes and priceless historical records burned to ashes in the public library.

The fire raged all day and all night, its titanic glow seen as far as Portland, Maine (ninety miles away), where residents thought it to be fireworks from York Beach.

By morning Chelsea was gone except for the shells of a few sturdy brick buildings. Even the ashes from 10,000 homes did not remain. The gale had swept all away.

CHERRY, ILLINOIS — MINE DISASTER November 13, 1909

background: The St. Paul Coal Company mine at Cherry, Illinois, caught fire and exploded on November 13, 1909, as a result of smoldering hay, which ignited timbers and thus exploded escaping gases; of the more than 400 men in the mine at the moment of explosion and fire, 259 were killed, making this the worst mine disaster in Illinois history.

At about 1:00 P.M. on November 13, 1909, a careless miner tossed a burning torch into a stack of hay near the entrance of the huge St. Paul Coal Company mine just outside Cherry, Illinois. In the three main shafts of the mine worked more than 400 miners. The hay smoked for several minutes before two workers noticed it, loaded the bales onto a car and began to wheel the burning hay from the mine. They were too late. Flames shot up and instantly inflamed dry, rotting timbers bolstering the shaft. In seconds fire coated the entrance to the shaft, and gases then exploded.

The mules used to pull the mine carts, for which the hay was intended, reared back, crazed and honking, from the fire. Men fled by the scores deeper into the mine shafts to escape the flames, fumes and smoke.

Seven men had been standing at the entrance of the mine when the explosion came. Six of them—Alexander Nerberg, John Flood, Isaac Lewis, a merchant in Cherry, Dominic Fonenti and a miner named Rubinski—led by mine superintendent John Bundy, made a dash for the elevator cage. Another man, Dr. W. Howe, ran after them. The men jumped into the cage. Bundy pushed back Dr. Howe.

"They will need you at the top," Bundy shouted to Dr. Howe, "if we get anyone out. You must not risk your life down here."

Dr. Howe stayed behind and waited. The cage descended, and within minutes the six would-be rescuers reached the bottom of the shaft and were instantly overcome by gas fumes. Nerberg, seeing the men drop, loaded them back into the elevator cage and, with a final effort, fell across the body of the last man as he yanked the signal bell to be hauled up. The cage rose slowly and at the surface Dr. Howe yanked them out. They were all dead.

By this time, flames were great yellow and orange tongues shooting from the mouth of the shaft entrance. Mine superintendent James Steele ordered the entrance sealed off, in the archaic belief that this would suffocate the fire; only the elevator cages were left as a way of escape for the miners.

At the reverberating sound of the mine explosion, more than 5,000 persons rushed to the entrance of the shaft. A great wail went up from relatives whose husbands, fathers and brothers were trapped inside. Dozens of volunteers, more than could be used, offered to go down the cages in search of the trapped miners, and six men were selected. They slung oxygen bags over their shoulders and wedged down steel and glass-faced hoods. They went down into the shaft three times, but the extreme heat from three separate veins drove them to the surface each time. They waited for the earth to cool.

Hours crawled by. Women and children waiting at the entrance became frantic with grief and worry. One account relates: "Wives and mothers grouped about the shafts of the mine, narrowly watching every movement of the rescuers . . . kept up a low moaning. Others who had kept silent fell to the ground and still others shrieked themselves into hysteria."

Mrs. John Buddon, who was unkindly told that her husband would die if fresh air was not pumped to him and the others, became mad. Wandering through the agonized crowd was Mrs. James Leandreck, with her ten-year-old daughter, Annie, clinging to her skirt. They begged for information about the fate of their husband and father, who was in the deepest part of the mine. Only shaking heads met their questions.

Clara Governor, seventeen, walked with her sister Martha, fifteen, to the entrance of the mine. An official

Canvas-wrapped bodies await identification beneath a circus tent only hours after the St. Paul Coal Company mine exploded, November 13, 1909. *(Wide World)*

asked her what she wanted. "We live over there," she said and pointed to a small soot-covered cottage down the road from the mine. "Mama is over there and our little brother Theodore. Papa didn't come up with the rest of the men. Maybe he is dead. Martha and I are trying to find out." Governor was dead, and many more were dying in the blackened bowels of the mine.

A quarter of a mile away a farmer heard soft thuds beneath his land and recognized the sounds. The mine shafts led directly under his farmland, and he thought the miners were signaling with pistol shots that they still lived.

All along the dark shafts men groped through dense black smoke, choking and falling, and then crawled toward the escape routes leading to the elevator cages. Many, like Andrew McFadden, twenty-two, were dead minutes after the fire began. A foreman ordered McFadden to stay with the mules near the main shaft entrance. "It's only a little smoke. It'll soon blow over," the foreman told him. Although dozens of escaping miners ran past McFadden shouting at him to "run for it," he obeyed the foreman's order and was burned to death.

Rescuers began to descend and enter the various mine shafts toward morning of the following day. One of these, a man named Eddy, his headlamp flickering along the chiseled walls of a shaft, stumbled over dozens of dead men in one vein as he followed the weak calls of dying men. He was responsible for dragging out at least twenty miners, placing them in the elevator cage and then returning for more. "On the last trip," he remembered, "I found two helpless men not more than eight feet from the main shaft. The air fans had been reversed and that caused a hot backfire around the foot of the main shaft. I helped these two men—they were Poles—into the cage, but that was all I could do. There were no other men near, and I no longer heard the calls for help."

At the gate of the cage, Eddy's uncle George worked to help his nephew place the last two men in the cage.

"There's nobody left alive down here," Eddy told his uncle. "Please come up now with me and save yourself."

The old miner, a veteran of the pit for more than twenty years, grinned white teeth through a soot-smeared face. "Go on, boy. I'll come up on the next trip."

"The next trip," Eddy recalled, "was the one that took twelve good men [rescuers] down to death in the cage. That was the last I heard of my uncle."

John Phillips stumbled over a fallen miner named Edward Surrock. He began to drag Surrock toward the waiting cages, but with every breath his lungs filled with unbearable smoke. He withdrew a tobacco pouch and placed it over his face, using it to filter the air. Phillips and Surrock survived.

The stricken men William Vicker saw as he crawled his way toward freedom were not as fortunate. He inched down the roadbed, grasping the rails and calling to a friend who was moving behind him, both men low and sucking for air beneath the hovering smoke wafting above them.

"At one point," Vicker later reported, "we passed about sixty-five miners sitting by the roadside, almost in a stupor. I tried to rouse them and encourage them to go on, but they seemed to have given up all hope, and did not stir. I had no time to lose and continued on, expecting to send back relief from the shaft. The sight of my doomed comrades is something that will haunt me until my dying day. . . . I escaped death by just three minutes. When I arrived at the bottom of the shaft, the last cage was about to ascend. I shouted as the signal bell was ringing. Two men broke their way to me and dragged me to the cage. I then lost consciousness. When I came to, I was safely on top. My buddy had followed closely all the way and, encouraged by the light held by the cage men, managed to reach the shaft, and he was carried with me to safety."

These two were the last men out alive. After thirty-six hours of rescue operations, 170 men had been saved; 259 were dead. The muffled shots heard by the farmer from the shafts angling beneath his land had not been signals after all. An older miner, seeing six youngsters, all about fifteen, dying of smoke inhalation, withdrew a pistol and benevolently, he no doubt thought, executed them. He then sat beside them to slowly gag to death on the killing smoke.

CHIAVENNA, ITALY — LANDSLIDE

September 4, 1618

Two towns nestling in the Italian valley of Chiavenna were destroyed by a massive landslide that caused mountains to fall away at tremendous speeds, crushing every dwelling in its path and killing 2,427 persons on the morning of September 4, 1618. Only three persons survived and by hand dug their ways to freedom over a period of several days. It was one of the worst landslide disasters in history.

CHICAGO, ILLINOIS — FIRE

October 8-9, 1871

background: The Great Chicago Fire of 1871, considered the greatest calamity of the nineteenth century, began in the barn of Mrs. Patrick O'Leary on DeKoven Street on Chicago's West Side on October 8, 1871, about 9:00 P.M. The fire quickly spread to the entire West Side, mostly tarpaper shacks of Irish and Bohemian poor. The blaze quickly spread to the South and North sides, leveling them to the ground. The fire continued until the dawn of October 10, 1871. Of the 335,000 inhabitants only 250 to 300 had been killed, but 90,000 were homeless, and three and a third square miles of buildings had been devastated with damage estimated at $200 million, making the fire the most destructive in American history.

Gaunt-eyed fanatics shuffled down the sweltering streets shouting—high-pitched voices cracked like the early October earth then laden with gnarled, dead oak leaves—"The earth is drying up, preparatory to burning up! Repent ye!" No one in Chicago seemed to repent.

Reformer Ignatius Donnelly riveted his eyes skyward and moaned loudly that a fiery comet two thousand years gone arching into space had made the very soil flammable. Zealots of God hacked their way with placards through throngs in the bordello-laced Conely's Patch on the Near South Side, evangelical tales of Sodom and Gommorah thick in their throats. The long, hot, dry summer and fall with temperatures in the 100's without the pity of rain had brought forth these angry talismans of salvation.

Doom and prophecy cluttered the minds of educated men, too. Even the indefatigable traveler and author, George Francis Train, while lecturing a large crowd in Farwell Hall on the night of October 7, 1871, became suddenly fitful with telepathy. "This is the last public address that will be delivered within these walls!" His startled audience blinked. "A terrible calamity is impending over the City of Chicago! More I cannot say; more I dare not utter."

The looming specter of catastrophe slipped its way into the editorial pages of the stoic *Chicago Tribune*: "For days past alarm has followed alarm, but the comparatively trifling losses have familiarized us to the pealing of the Courthouse bell, and we had forgotten that the absence of rain for three weeks had left everything in so dry and inflammable a condition that a spark might set a fire which could sweep from end to end of the city."

The *Tribune,* however, was not delving into the murky mists of soothsaying but was dealing, as usual, with the facts at hand. Thirty alarms had been turned in and answered during the first week of October. The worst of this series, like a vanguard to the major onslaught, had devastated four square miles on the West

Side with damages running to $750,000 on the night of October 7, 1871, only hours after Train's ominous outcry.

This fire had required a large portion of Chicago's pitifully small fire department to be called into service, and the blaze had exhausted the men. Following the fire, as was then the custom, the firefighters consumed great quantities of whiskey. The *Evening Post* later claimed that drunkenness or, at least, an *en masse* hangover, had reduced the firemen's effectiveness by the time the great inferno began. Although later branded "stupid and listless," the meager ranks of firemen, numbering no more than 200 (to serve a population of 350,000), were to prove marrow-brave in the hours to come. They were, in the end, simply outnumbered and underequipped. They would go blind, be burned and crippled; some would die miserably in a cauldron of fire never before seen on the North American continent.

The department possessed only seventeen fire engines, eighteen ladder trucks and 48,000 feet of hose with which to patrol 56 miles of wooden block pavement, 651 miles of wooden sidewalks, and 60,000 buildings, 40,000 of which were constructed of wood. (There was only one pumping station—and it had a wooden roof.) Most structures, especially office buildings, department stores and the ornate homes of the rich, were bedecked with awnings, taut-dry by the intense heat. These striped hussies would later invite the flames to ravage the heart of the city.

There were no awnings spreading shade over the windows of the ramshackle house at 137 DeKoven Street. The wooden structure on the near West Side was the home of a "big, burly" stevedore named Patrick O'Leary. The subsequent wrath of Chicago residents immediately following the fire was aimed like a javelin at O'Leary as the cause of their woes, but it was the stout Mrs. O'Leary and her infamous cow who were to become part of the folklore of Chicago.

Catherine O'Leary, later described as "an old hag and a witch" by Chicago newspapers, was about thirty-five years old at the time of the fire. She worked hard at a milk route, her product taken from five cows, one of which was kept in a shed directly behind her cottage. Of her five children, only one came to later prominence, Big Jim O'Leary who was a successful politician and gambler (actor Tyrone Power was cast in his role in the $3 million Zanuck film, *In Old Chicago,* a fanciful fabrication of the Great Fire).

Mrs. O'Leary and her family retired early on the night of October 8, 1871. They slept in the rear portion of a double-framed home, the front part occupied by Patrick McLaughlin. The McLaughlins were having a party, and Irish jigs could be heard across the street and down the block.

What happened at approximately 8:45 P.M. in the O'Leary shed that sultry night has never become fully known. The scapegoat-seeking press adamantly insisted that Mrs. O'Leary went into her barn at that time to milk an unruly cow who, though she "was a grand milker," was obstinate about coal-oil lanterns and kicked over the one Catherine O'Leary had carried into the barn, thus beginning the great conflagration.

The O'Learys remained steadfast in their denials of this occurrence. Neighbors Daniel "Pegleg" Sullivan and Dennis Rogan swore that the O'Learys were in bed by 8:30 P.M., Mrs. O'Leary complaining of a sore foot. It was a fact that she ritually milked her cows at 5:00 A.M.

Big Jim later claimed that the fire in his mother's shed was caused by tramps or boys carelessly smoking in secret.

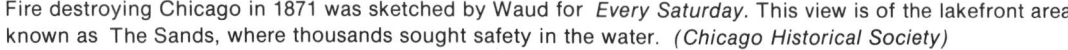

Fire destroying Chicago in 1871 was sketched by Waud for *Every Saturday.* This view is of the lakefront area known as The Sands, where thousands sought safety in the water. *(Chicago Historical Society)*

Another story was that several youngsters were not only smoking in the shed that night but were playing poker by the light of the coal-oil lamp that they accidentally knocked over.

The most believable story did not appear until October 25, 1927, when the *Chicago Tribune* ran an exclusive interview with Mrs. Nellie L. Hayes, grandmother and distinguished socialite. Recalling that long-ago evening of disaster when she was thirteen years old, Nellie Mahoney, who lived down the block from the O'Learys at 214 West Taylor Street, laughed at the cow-and-lantern story.

It was the McLaughlins who caused the whole thing, said she. Though the McLaughlins said they had gone out to supper, the christening party they held was replete with food. "In those days oyster soup was always the big dish," Mrs. Hayes told a *Tribune* reporter. "The day had been so hot that the milk spoiled." Someone, she inferred, left the party to go into the shed to obtain fresh milk and in the process dropped a burning candle or lantern, and fire erupted on the hay-strewn floor.

Several persons loitering about in the street that night later claimed to have seen the first glowing flames dancing behind the wooden slats of the O'Leary shed. Pegleg Sullivan told police that he was standing across the street staring at the O'Leary house. He not only claimed that he spotted the fire first but that he hobbled on his wooden leg to the barn, saved several animals, and then roused the O'Leary clan. (Sullivan's actions were thoroughly suspect; he had been kicked out of the O'Leary homestead. He wanted to talk; Pat O'Leary wanted to go to sleep. Sullivan, himself not the kindest man in the world, could very likely have started the fire himself in reaction to the snub, real or imaginary.)

Nellie Mahoney saw the fire first, she insisted, from the windows of her mother's bedroom, which faced down the alley toward the O'Leary barn. Nellie ran outside and down the alley. "I saw flames coming out from between the boards of the O'Leary barn. There was no one about, no one in the barn. I ran to the house and tapped on the windows.

" 'The barn's on fire!' I cried, then ran back to watch the fire. I was not interested in anything else. It had been a hot day, and the wind was blowing from the northwest. In a few minutes, the barn was in flames." Nellie never saw Pegleg Sullivan, but she did see the O'Learys and almost everyone else in the shantytown neighborhood where wooden pigsties, wooden chicken coops, wooden sheds, barns and cottages nestled tightly against each other. "The flames began to spread to the adjoining barns and the people began to save things from their houses. One woman tried to throw a feather bed tick from an upper window. A spark caught it. That was the second big blaze. There was not a fire engine in sight."

Patients, doctors and nurses fled from the Marine Hospital as flames approached the building during the Chicago fire of 1871. *(Gross cyclorama reconstruction, Library of Congress)*

The home of James Dalton, close to the O'Leary barn, soon caught fire. The O'Learys and the McLaughlins successfully kept the flames from consuming their cottages, though the walls smoldered for three days. The Daltons were less fortunate. Theirs was the first house to burn to the ground.

Another neighbor, William Lee, saw the fire and raced from his house to Canal and Twelfth Streets, where he threw open the police telegraph alarm box. Newly installed, the boxes were elaborate affairs, and Lee took several moments to study the metal arrow poised on a dial with points marked CALL WAGON—THIEVES—FORGERS—RIOT—DRUNKARD—MURDER—ACCIDENT—VIOLATION OF CITY ORDINANCE—FIGHTING—TEST OF LINE—FIRE. He spun the arrow to the last mark and prayed.

Either the alarm box malfunctioned, or as later stories

had it, Lee did not really turn in the warning but told a local druggist named Goll to do it. The alarm did not get through to the Courthouse, but firewatcher Mathias Schafer, high in the tower of that imposing edifice, scanned the tumbledown area to the southwest and saw bright flames dancing upward into the night sky. Schafer signaled to fire operator William Brown to mark the spot at Call Box 342. Another mistake. This call box was more than a mile from the blazing O'Leary shed, and fire engines in that area were sent while those in the vicinity of the blaze stayed put.

Firewatcher Schafer took a closer look at the fire through a spyglass and then called down a correction to Brown, that the fire was near alarm box 319. With an air of incredible aloofness, Brown refused to send out the second alarm because it might be confusing.

Schafer argued with him. He, not Brown in the bowels of the Courthouse, could spot the true area of the fire. He could see it now, right now.

No, the obstinate Brown said. It would lead to confusion among the fire squads. Had he merely done his job and sent out the correction, the two most powerful engines in the city, stationed only a few blocks from the fire, could have easily reached the area and put out the fire. Brown's truculent attitude and downright refusal to send out the second alarm, more than any other occurrence during the next thirty hours, contributed to the destruction of Chicago. He, not the much-maligned Mrs. O'Leary and her legendary cow, was the true culprit of the calamity. (Oddly enough, Brown was still on duty a month after the fire, defying all accusers and holding himself entirely blameless.)

The fire was on. At Dekoven Street, two fire engines did appear about 10:00 P.M. They fought the spurting blazes haphazardly. They would turn their hoses on one fire, splatter it with water and, without waiting for it to be completely extinguished, attend to another roaring blaze. Patrick O'Leary raced up to one engine and asked a fireman to save his house, which was smoking at the rear. They gave it "two or three splashes."

One of the firemen turned to O'Leary and said, "What company carries your insurance?"

"None," O'Leary had to admit. "I have no insurance, none at all."

The fireman shook his head and waved off the other firemen. They moved down the block to fight more blazes, and O'Leary rejoined his exhausted family in beating out flames on the side of his house.

Fires began to break out all over the shanty town area on the West Side (Chicago at that time was about equally separated into three divisions, north, south and west, each divided by branches of the Chicago River). It became clear in a matter of hours that the two engines battling the spreading flames were losing. Saloons, homes, sheds, barns—all were crackling into fire aided by an increasingly forceful wind.

Assistant Fire Marshal Mathias Benner told his firemen to round up the able-bodied citizens gaping at the blaze and use them to form another fire brigade. At first the rowdies, Irish workers and boys, worked at the pumps and hoses, but they soon grew tired of the chore; many became frightened when the flames shot as high as thirty and forty feet. One by one they slipped away. A final handful broke and fled when a building exploded into flames.

From the moment the fire broke out of the DeKoven block, the firefighters had lost and would continue losing building after building, block after block, section by section. Benner saw it happening and rubbed his eyes, which had already begun to swell. He had been up all night and in charge of the battle the previous evening. The fire marshal grabbed fireman John Schank. "Where has the fire gone to, John?"

Schank shot back, "She has gone to hell-and-gone!"

Furniture store proprietor Jacob Beiersdorf rushed up to Benner, his arms flailing wildly in the smoke-filled air. "My building," he gasped excitedly. "I'll give you one thousand dollars to save it."

Benner merely glanced in the direction of the store, already aflame. "You might as well offer a million," the fire marshal responded in a sigh. "I can't stop it."

As if to insure the disaster, the wind swept in behind the fire from the southwest prairie. It was estimated to be traveling at 60 m.p.h. by a Sergeant Kaufman at the United States Weather Signal Office. He had measured the force of the gale winds with an anemometer from a LaSalle Street perch near the resplendent, so-called fireproof courthouse. He wired Washington a report and then went home, never dreaming the fire would not be contained on the west side of the Chicago River.

In three hours, however, the fire had eaten its way through seven square blocks consuming at great speed huge lumberyards, mills and old St. Paul's Church. The strange thing was that spectators by the thousands, many of whom had now lost their homes to the fire, were awe-stricken by the towering inferno that now moved in twin columns.

"What's burning now?" an elderly Irish woman asked a beleaguered fireman.

"Why, it's St. Paul's. Can't you see?"

She smiled knowingly. "God will put it out."

At that moment the church roof caved in with a thunderous sound and sent a shower of firebrands hurtling skyward along with the anabatic fury of the wind. Fire Marshal Robert A. Williams arrived to survey the scene and realized at once his small fire department had no way of stopping the blaze. He thought that perhaps the burned-out area of the previous night might stop the fire, for there was little fuel in that area upon which it might feed. Looking up, he moaned. The sky for a hundred feet, perhaps two hundred feet, was crimson with burning firebrands, billions of sparks, some the size of baseballs. Carried by the high wind, the fire would jump the vacant area and leap across the river into the South District. He ordered several fire engines out of the West Division to the North, where he was stopped by Commissioner James Chadwick.

The commissioner was blood-faced. "Don't you know the fire is getting ahead of you, Williams?"

At the moment, Williams sounded the death knell for Chicago: "Yes. It is getting ahead of me in spite of all I can do. . . . It's just driving me along."

In the South and North districts of the city, life went on as usual. Rich and poor alike retired. In Conley's Patch in the South District close to the river, the saloons and bordellos were overflowing. Had Williams the foresight, he would have abandoned the Patch, an ugly, jam-packed quarter of squalid wooden buildings, and consolidated all his equipment about the mercantile district nearer the Lake and North Side. But even then, his scant firefighters might not have stopped the blaze. Even then.

As homeless residents fled west to the open prairies, and firemen, their equipment and clothes steaming and smoking from the intense heat, raced toward the South District, the fire roared upward and across the Chicago River striking at the motley stretch of buildings making up the scabrous Conley's Patch. For years the Patch had been known as a twenty-four-hour red light district where robbery, murder and white slavery were rampant. Huge firebrands, mostly from the West District's roaring lumberyards, blew into the Patch on great gusts of wind and ignited the creaking rooftops with great speed.

People raced to keep ahead of the fire at Clark and Randolph streets. *(Chicago Historical Society)*

In minutes the brothels, saloons, gambling dens and sleazy rooming houses emptied out thousands of the most notorious persons in the city. The shrill screams of prostitutes mingled with the hurrahs of drunks staggering down the narrow streets even as sheets of flame dropped down and set many of them on fire. Fights broke out as toughs attempted to loot vacated buildings. It was the beginning of widespread lawlessness, a special havoc within the larger catastrophe.

One man on the West Side, Jacob Klein, was killed by looters. Several toughs rushed him as he was carrying goods from his building. He fought for his property and was murdered when a man crushed his head with a shovel. The thieves made off with two bolts of cloth.

The scene was much worse in Conley's Patch, which even squads of well-armed police feared to enter. The firemen in this district not only battled the fire but also fought the denizens wild with fright or mad with liquor. One woman on Adams Street had to be carried from her rickety house three times. Each time she broke away and ran back into her house. Weary firemen tired of prying her loose from her possessions, and she soon perished. Saloonkeepers refused to leave their bars and were burned alive; one was seen toasting the flames all about him before the ceiling crushed him to death.

The nearby gasworks caught fire and burned quickly. Conscientious workers, thankfully, had turned off all the gas leading into the direction of the fire and thereby prevented massive explosions. Conley's Patch was no more by 1:00 A.M.

Gone was Lizzie Allen's bordello. Lizzie and her girls dressed quickly, many of them wearing several of their best robes, climbed into a buggy and made off toward the comparative safety of the North Side (where many of Lizzie's more prominent patrons resided). Gone, too, was the infamous Ramrod Hall, run by the sadistic Katie Hawkins who buggy-whipped her sixty girls into action each night. Katie, a white slaver, stood cracking her whips at her fleeing, half-naked girls, and vowed terrible beatings and even murder for those who fled. But the flames, where reformer groups, police and relatives had failed in the past, freed her fleshly menagerie from her demoniac presence. This towering woman with gaudy orange hair and scarlet-smeared face was last seen in the archway of her house of pleasure. Her throaty rage was cut short by collapsing walls. One policeman saw her head protruding from a pile of bricks, flames dancing about her. "Her mouth was open, her eyes near bursting. . . . Cut off in the middle of a bellow, she was."

The fire ran forward, great walls of flame now, toward the center of the South District, the very crux of the city, its government offices, businesses, theater section, great department stores and newspaper offices. Fire Marshal Williams ordered four of his best fire engines to halt the fire before it consumed the living heart of the city along a line at Fifth Avenue (now Wells Street). Puny streams of water vaporized in the curls and eddies of flames.

Ex-alderman James Hildreth, seeing that the situation was hopeless, first grew angry, then determined. If the firemen could not stop the wholesale leveling of the city, he, Hildreth, would. Without authority he broke into an armory magazine and had three thousand pounds of explosives removed. These were carted to the basement of the courthouse where Hildreth managed to corner a much-harassed Mayor Roswell B. Mason.

The mayor was perspiring heavily as he moved from office to office. Scooping up reports from the West and South Districts, he realized as he read the accounts that the fire had already moved on and that the reports were useless. Hildreth demanded that the mayor authorize him to blow up certain buildings on a line that would halt the fire.

Survivors stand in the rubble of the Twenty-Second Street Station a day after the great fire. *(Chicago Public Library)*

Wagons remove debris hours after the fire. This is a view of the city looking south from the courthouse. *(Chicago Historical Society)*

Mason would try anything. He drew up an order of authorization. Handing it to Hildreth, he said: "Who will carry this out?"

"I will," Hildreth vowed and ran down the corridor to the basement stairs to retrieve his precious explosives, his paper authority in his hand.

Aided by a few policemen Hildreth made his way through the smoking streets and past the fleeing crowds, forced at times to drive his wagons directly into clusters of panicking people, until he reached Fire Marshal Williams under whose orders he was to act. They surveyed the corner of LaSalle and Madison. Williams, by then, was a beaten man. "You know the engines cannot halt the fire. We may as well try to stop it by blowing up buildings on some fixed point." Williams returned to his firefight.

Hildreth's first detonation was a failure. The powder only blew out windows and one wall, making the structure more vulnerable to the fire. Doggedly Hildreth selected more buildings to be razed, but he was uncertain. The fire was not cooperating. It did not move in a straight line but darted forth in jets, in quick shooting streams, whirlpools of flame that danced madly in long, quivering fingers, erratically and indiscriminately chewing at the city in several directions. Hildreth and ten policemen did their best while the residents of Chicago dashed into full flight before the flames. In the distance the terrified mass could hear the steady gong from the huge bell in the courthouse tower, as it pealed disaster.

Like dozens of vastly expensive buildings in the business district, the courthouse was considered "fireproof," but its huge buttresses and fancily molded cornices and cupolas, its limestone facade had never felt the heat of a fire such as this. The tower caught fire. Flames invaded the basement. Smoke billowed through the marble hallways. It was lost.

For the scores of prisoners locked in cells in the building's basement, it was a nightmare. Smoke crept beneath the doors and through the narrow window slots of their cells. They screamed, wailed and begged to be released. Police Captain Hickey ordered their cells unlocked. His complement of officers certainly could not control so many men. He made a quick decision.

"Take the murderers out the other way, boys," he told his men. "We'll hold onto them. March them to the North Side . . . and keep your guns on them."

"What about the others?" a sergeant asked.

"Let 'em all go. They're free as birds . . . God help 'em."

Except for a small knot of accused and convicted murderers who were herded quickly away, the prisoners stepped from their cells and were told to run for their lives. One man, so much in terror of burning alive in his cell, fainted when his cell door was opened. There was no time to revive him. As the others scurried, hooting and hollering out of the subterranean passage, the unconscious prisoner was left to the fire.

The prisoners ran pell-mell up Clark Street. A few stopped in their tracks at the corner of Randolph and, at first, were bewildered by A. H. Miller, a prominent jeweler who stood with a sardonic grin on his face at the entrance to his store, which was already smoldering. He held out his hands, loaded with gems, necklaces and bracelets. "Help yourselves, gentlemen," he told the thieves. Miller realized he could not save his stock and so resignedly decided to give away his jewels rather than leave them to melt in the fire.

A few of the thieves raced ecstatically through his store, scooping up handfuls of diamonds, rubies and pearls, stuffing their pockets, their faces agleam with half-mad grins. Miller, taking his most precious stones, sauntered from the store and casually began to make his way to his home and family on the North Side.

Southsiders had gone to the West District at the outbreak of the fire to view it, much the same way hundreds of foolish Washington residents went to picnic before the bloody battlefields of Bull Run ten years before, only to become part of the battle. When the fire turned and jumped the river, the onlookers battled each other across the clogged bridges and poured northward. Each carried what he thought most important to him. One man, the tails of his frock coat burned away, staggered along clutching a large frying pan and a feather duster. Women dragged small, crying children. The children dragged goats, pigs, chickens, dogs and cats. As the fire soared the firebrands cascaded down. People found themselves beating furiously as their clothes and hair were quickly ignited.

Behind them trailed the groping firemen, indifferently spraying buildings. Shopkeepers, their fists clenched with money, pleaded with them to save their stores, offering hundreds, sometimes thousands, of dollars.

Mayor Mason and a horde of clerks attempted to protect the courthouse, but it was beyond saving. The tower was soon ablaze, and its giant bell, rope and planking burned away, soon crashed the length of the steeple, through floor after floor, smashing into the basement with a thunderous roar heard for miles.

Joseph and Sam Medill rounded up the printers and newsmen who had been preparing an extra edition and fought the blaze atop the *Tribune* Building, but that, too, was hopeless. They gave up the fight and went home to bed. (After the fire, which had destroyed invaluable historic documents and editions of the newspaper, searchers found only a linen duster and a box of matches in the huge *Tribune* safe.)

The great hotels—the Tremont, the Grand Pacific and the Sherman House—emptied with relative order. For several hours in the morning of October 9, the wealthy visitors at the Sherman House had their large trunks brought to the lobby only to be told that the fire would not reach the hotel. Dozens of guests, disgusted with the scare, milled about the grand foyer and then demanded breakfast. An hour later, they were running for their lives when the hotel burst into flames at the top floors.

Mothers, exhausted from running, loosened holds on their children and lost them underfoot; others were swept away from their families by the jostling, shoving crowds, brutal in their desperation. Horses drawing every type of vehicle nosed nervously through clots of pedestrians. Draymen charged exorbitant fees to those wanting to save their goods and lives. Many took on loads, snatched up fares as high as $1,000, and then, without waiting for their passengers, drove off alone.

By Monday morning all the theaters in the South District were gutted. Aiken's Opera House was destroyed; so were the Farwell and Hooley halls. The Academy of Music operated by Dr. Florenz Ziegfield was burned to cinders. It was Ziegfield's son, four decades later, who would become the king of Broadway.

The crowds, thigh to thigh, moved across the remaining bridges to the far West Side and to the North District. The great cry "To the North! To the North!" rippled loudly through the undulating masses. They streamed through the LaSalle Street tunnel, jets of churlish smoke chasing after them. In their midst were the looters. They plucked with deft hands the scant memorabilia the fleeing managed to save. They literally stole the clothes from men's backs. On Wabash Avenue at the Drake and Farwell building, scores of looters fought a head-splitting battle with police, hand to hand, club to club, over smoking merchandise.

Street urchins, raised in apprentice hoodlumism by Fagins in Conley's Patch, ran with those escaping to the North, pilfering as they went. One, a twelve-year-old called Darby the Cobbler, was seen by an out-of-town visitor, Alexander Frear. Darby's patched pockets bulged with illicit swag. But he would never enjoy the gain. Frear spotted this "ragamuffin on the Clark Street bridge who had been killed by a marble slab thrown from a window, with white kid gloves on his hands."

Frear, who had escaped the fire by seconds as it closed down upon the Sherman House, witnessed some of the most terrifying spectacles the calamity had to offer, not the least of which was the small girl "whose golden hair, worn loose on her back, caught fire. She ran screaming past me, and someone threw a glass of liquor upon her, which flared up and covered her with a blue flame."

By that time Frear was beyond shock. He had stumbled north with the rest after seeing, at Wabash and Adams Streets, a woman kneeling "with a crucifix held up before her and the skirt of her dress on fire." Drunks in rags and in finery lurched everywhere. One mounted a piano that had been abandoned in the middle of the street and lifted his arms as if to embrace the flames.

"The fire is our friend!" he screamed to his fellow sots. "We are poor men . . . the fire is the friend of the poor . . . it destroys the rich . . . and gives us things. Liquor! Liquor!" He raved on, shouting to all who would listen, encouraging them to strip the bars and liquor warehouses. A bored listener, another drunk weaving in the smoke-gusted street, threw a bottle at the orator, knocked him from his musical perch and split his skull.

Whiskey was everywhere in the business district. Frear watched as firemen bathed their heads in it to cool their blistered skin. At Fifth and Monroe herds of drunks discovered to their whooping delight dozens of whiskey kegs in the street. They were smashed open, and men slavishly lapped up the spillage from the gutter. Frear heard "explosions that followed each other in quick succession on all sides, to the accompaniment of a crackling noise as of an enormous number of dry twigs burning." The heat was a searing, killing thing. In Heath & Milligan's paint store on Randolph Street, an officious city clerk took time to discover that the temperature of the fire exceeded 3,000 degrees.

Those who stayed in the path of the fire in the South District were mad from the heat. A businessman named Garrick could save nothing from his Harrison Street building; in delirium, he snatched an American flag from the wall of his office, wrapped it about himself and paraded into the street. In the home of clothing merchant Solomon Witkowsky at Van Buren and Harrison, lunacy reigned. As majestic glass chandeliers began to crack and melt under the heat of the flames, Witkowsky came unhinged. He stared at wallpaper withering and peeling before him, glass heirlooms shattering, expensively bound books steaming. Witkowsky withdrew a revolver from his desk, loped upstairs, threw open large windows, and, cursing hoarsely, fired round after round into the fire pressing in on him.

All of the city's official records were burned when the courthouse was consumed by the fire, but John G. Shortall, whose firm kept the records of most of Chicago's businesses, managed to save the priceless documents in his charge. Hackmen still cruised about the littered, burning streets, and Shortall stopped one of these. The man demanded an outrageous fee for hauling the records. Shortall's friend, James Nye, hopped on the wagon, drew a revolver and jammed it into the driver's neck. "You'll take this load, mister." The drayman accepted with alacrity.

But where there were thieves, looters and gougers, there were also modest heroes. One such was professional gymnast, William Haskell. As James Hildreth and his ragged group of policemen attempted to turn the fire from the far South Side with their powder, he noticed the steeple of Wabash Avenue Methodist Church catch fire. This was a vital spot from which the fire could pivot and run southward, destroying everything in its path. There was no time to explode the building, and the trickling streams of water thrown up by a few engines (the waterworks was already failing) could not reach the spire. Haskell stepped forward.

"I think I can put that fire out," he told Hildreth. Then, taking off his coat and before thousands of spectators, the agile gymnast scaled the tower. Others climbed part of the way up the steeple, and they formed

Charred buildings edge the Chicago River the day after the great fire. *(Chicago Public Library)*

a human chain with buckets of water worked hand over hand to Haskell, who managed to put out the fire eating up the floorboards in the steeple. The church was saved and so was the far South Side.

Thousands cheered and applauded the young man as he made his way down the steeple. A sharper moved rapidly through the grateful crowd while Haskell made his descent. "That grand boy deserves a reward," the slippery one intoned. "I'm taking up a collection for him right now." He moved quickly through the throng, smiling, nodding appreciatively, bowing to the ladies as his large hat was filled to the sweatband with currency.

By the time Haskell reached the ground, the collector had disappeared with a young fortune. Haskell knew nothing of the con man. He spoke to no one, put on his coat and walked home.

While Hildreth was attempting to halt the fire at the Methodist Church, several policemen under the command of a Sergeant Mahoney were preparing to dynamite buildings along Michigan Avenue where the homes of the rich were aflame, the blaze fed by their own window awnings. Smoke driven by powerful winds whirled about the policemen carrying kegs of explosives. Fire towering as high as two hundred feet overhead blotted out the sun. And into this blistering nightmare, mounted on a black charger, his long Toledo blade clanking in its scabbard, his mustache flowing, rode the hero of Shenandoah, the magnificent General Philip H. Sheridan, commandant of the military district encompassing Chicago.

He drew his horse up imposingly before Sergeant Mahoney.

"What are you doing?" the general demanded.

"I'm blowing up these buildings, as you can see," came Mahoney's laconic reply.

Sheridan told him that the effort was ineffective. He, General Sheridan, knew best how to use the explosives to thwart this monster fire. Turn them over, he ordered.

Mahoney, his face streaked with sweat and soot, his uniform in tatters, was under Hildreth's orders not to release the explosives to anyone. He vowed to obey and told Sheridan to depart. He did, but he returned within minutes, bringing along a policeman. Under the glare of Sheridan's hot eyes, the policeman told Mahoney to turn over the explosives.

The intrepid police sergeant continued directing his men and then turned toward Sheridan and drew his revolver. "If you get any of this powder, it will be after my weapon has been emptied." He aimed the revolver directly at General Sheridan's heart.

The Civil War titan's wrath caused his face to go purple. He gripped the reins of his horse so tightly that his knuckles showed white. Through gritted teeth Sheridan hissed: "Do you know who I am?"

Mahoney gave him back a tired look and kept the pistol level. "I do not care a damn who you are. No powder."

Spitting disgust, the general spurred his horse and rode away in fury, determined to save the city of Chicago. If any single human, he felt, could perform such a miraculous deed, it was Philip H. Sheridan.

By noon on Monday, chaos ruled the North Side, once thought to be a bastion of safety. Everyone felt the river would stem the rush of the fire. And for a while it did. The bridges were swung away so the flames could not creep across their wooden planking. Burning ships on the South Side of the river were held at anchor or towed by tugs into the lake.

To the north were the opulent estates of the Ryersons, McCormicks, Arnolds, Greeleys, Newberrys, Armours and Fields, with their Victorian homes bedecked with curlicued balustrades, carved cupolas, pompous minarets and turrets, these many-winged mansions moated by filigreed spike fences, grotesque in any other age but this. Here, too, were the fabulous homes of world-famous artists Joseph Jefferson, Parepa Rosa, the violinist Ole Bull (who had survived the steamboat wreck between the *America* and the *United States* on the Ohio River in 1868) and the great opera singer Christine Nilsson.

The magnificent North Side was the essence of security, a monument to the success and grandeur of America's greatest inland city. Yet it would die more horribly than the seared sections of the West and South Sides. (Of the 17,500 homes and buildings destroyed by the fire, 13,300 of these were on the North Side.)

At first those who had managed to flee to the North Side and those living there felt unreachable by the fire. North Siders stepped from their homes and walked south to watch the inferno and the "poor unfortunates" ruined by its devastation. Women ordered their cooks to make sandwiches for the homeless. Wealthy dowagers fanned themselves on their broad verandas as their cooks served soup to homeless children.

Then the unthinkable happened: A huge firebrand, a flying, burning plank, was lifted by the unrelenting gale-like wind and hurled hundreds of feet skyward to the north. It smashed down with all its bad luck on the wooden roof of the waterworks, crashed through and ignited the ceiling, walls and floorboards. In minutes the waterworks was gutted, forcing the fire engines in all districts to be abandoned. There was no water to fight the fire and no time to draw more water from the lake or the river. As the flames lunged from the waterworks through the North Side, they destroyed everything before them.

As in Conley's Patch, the toughs and prostitutes inhabiting the lower portions of Wells and Clark Streets near the riverfront, went berserk with liquor. Half-dressed whores staggered in the street with obscenities and curses bubbling on their lips. One absurd ditty they chanted was: "Chickey, chickey, craney crow, I went to the well to wash my toes."

An eyewitness, Alfred Sewell, later lamented that "scores of the wretched women, some gaudily bedecked, others almost naked, and some in their nightclothes, came pouring out of the long lines of frame houses into the street to escape the swift-coming flames. . . . Some ran through the middle of the streets, frantic with terror, while others of them, wild with drink or reckless with depravity, yelled, and swore, and laughed, like the suddenly released inmates of a mad-house. . . ."

Fire Marshal Williams surveyed the North Side and gave up. Even though engines and fire crews were on their way by rail from Milwaukee and as far away as Pittsburgh, he felt the fight was lost. Williams was notified that his own house was on fire, and he raced there. He and several others threw the furniture out windows and managed to save his prized carpet.

The rich saved more, thanks to their servants. Before the fire reached their magnificent homes, they loaded their heirlooms, paintings, silverware, crockery and clothing into wagons and drove away to Fullerton Avenue, the city limits to the north, or beyond to country estates. Left behind were those who worked for them, many told to watch the mansions and try to save them while their own homes burned to the ground unattended.

Financier Mahlon Ogden's huge mansion was saved, oddly enough, through his own generosity. Ogden had donated a square block of land to the city to be used as a public park. This area was just south of his home, and when reaching the park, the fire had little upon which to feed. It died at the gates of the Ogden mansion. (Newberry Library stands where the house was, and Washington Park, also known as "Bughouse Square," is still opposite.)

Only one other home on the North Side survived the holocaust. A young policeman named Richard Bellinger, who was home on honeymoon when the fire broke out, strove to save his small cottage. As the fire ate its way toward Lincoln Place, where the cottage sat, Bellinger and his brother-in-law quickly stripped the area about the house, scattering picket fences, tearing away shutters, rooting up clumps of dry grass and spreading dirt everywhere. They soaked the small frame building with water, heavily dousing the roof. They waited, buckets ringed about the tiny house. When the fire reached them, they used all the water and even employed several kegs of apple cider to extinguish the flames. The sides of the house became smoked and charred, its slats steaming with heat, but it did not burn. (It stood until 1956, torn down to be replaced by a firemen's training school.)

Many of those who could not carry off their possessions chose to bury them. Davis Fales, a lawyer, dug a large pit behind his luxurious home and buried his piano. Only then would Fales leave with his wife, Mary, who later wrote: "Everybody was out of their houses without one exception, and the sidewalks were covered with furniture and bundles of every description. The middle of the street was a jam of carts, carriages, wheelbarrows, and every sort of vehicle, and many horses being led along, all excited and prancing, some running away. I scarcely dared look right or left as I kept my seat by holding tightly to the trunk. The horse would not be restrained, and I had to use all my powers to keep on. I was glad to go fast, for the fire behind us raged and crackled, and the whole earth, or all we saw of it, was lurid yellowish red."

Persons trapped in upper floors of buildings tossed their cherished belongings to those in the streets. One woman, a large German housewife with a thick accent, threw down a heavy bundle of linen to a man beneath her window. He ran away. Her baby was in the bundle. Screaming, the woman, followed by two of her children, chased the thief through the mass heaving over the Clark Street bridge, but he disappeared. Wailing despair, the mother leaned over the railing with thoughts of suicide heavy in her head. At that moment, she saw her infant, ten feet down, squirming on some sooty cotton bales where the thief had discarded him. She climbed down a girder and saved her child.

Others jumped from three- and four-story windows when the stairways and halls burst into flame. Some suffered only broken legs and arms; others dashed themselves to death. One businessman, remaining in his third-floor offices, tossed valuables to his clerks who stood in an alley. As smoke and flames darted through the floor above him, his clerks shouted for him to come down.

He jiggled a rope fastened to the window sill. "Don't worry, boys," he said jovially. "Here is my ladder." Abruptly, he turned to see his office engulfed in flames. The businessman climbed onto the sill and then wrapped himself about the rope and lowered himself slowly. The fire licked with heavy tongues from the window and the twisting rope soon snapped. He tumbled head-first into the alley, his head cracked wide open, his brains scattered over the shoes of his horrified clerks.

While the North Side emptied of people and animals, a great, unselfish effort was made by Samuel Stone and others to save the treasured artifacts of Chicago. Stone, assistant librarian of the Chicago Historical Society, which was then close to the river at Dearborn and Ontario Streets, spent several hours lugging the society's important documents to the basement. The building was considered "fireproof," but Stone was taking no chances. He had been in the basement for some time before he realized how close and perilous the fire was. When informed, his first thought was of Chicago's most precious document, the original copy of Abraham Lincoln's Emancipation Proclamation.

Stone ran to the reception room, where, finding the frame holding the Lincoln document too large to carry, he attempted to smash the glass covering it with his fists. The flames were all about him, shooting down the stairs, swooping up from the basement, overhead, gnawing. The librarian beat on the sturdy glass, but it would not give way. He began to choke. "At this moment again the wind and fire filled the whole heavens," he said, "dashing firebrands against the reception room windows." He heard the ceiling give way. It was too late. He threw a shawl over his head and ran through the flaming front doors and saved himself. Behind him the words that freed slaves curled and went to ashes under the closing yellow fingers of fire.

The fire gutted the *Chicago Tribune* building. *(Chicago Public Library)*

Others tried to escape the fire by seeking refuge in solidly built churches. In one, the Unity Church, hundreds huddled in deep prayer. Their pastor, the Reverend Robert Collyer, stood in the pulpit. He was a man of abrupt and final decision. A one-time abolitionist and Union zealot, Reverend Collyer, at the outbreak of the Civil War, had announced from the same pulpit, "This place is closed. I am going to war." Now he took his Bible under one arm and shouted, "The steeple is on fire. This place is closed. Run for your lives."

They ran, along with everyone else. They ran until they fell from exhaustion and either stayed unconscious and were roasted in the fire or picked themselves up and ran again.

There is no truth to the story that Reverend Moody of the Moody Bible Institute escaped naked on horseback carrying a portrait of himself in one hand and his favorite sermon in the other. His wife, at the time of their flight, merely asked him to take along her favorite portrait of him, and he refused, saying, "How would it appear if I met a friend and he asked what I had saved, and all I could display was my own portrait?"

For many the only escape route left on the North Side was toward the lake. Hundreds, then thousands, streamed onto a small peninsula called The Sands. They waded into the neck-high water to escape the intense heat, which had already been fatal to some.

One man brought his family there. He dug quickly in the sand and then buried his wife, two daughters and young son, leaving air holes for them that faced the lake and away from the fire. He watered down the sand and then waded into the lake, while for seven hours all about him towering granaries, mills and lumberyards along the lakefront blazed.

He later described his ordeal: "Those seven hours seemed like a whole year. Often, while the flames were raging in the adjacent street, I thought I must drop down in despair, so intense was the heat, and so thick the volumes of smoke that drove out upon me. Had I been alone—had it not been for my family, the thought of their safety, and the necessity of my preserving my life for their sake, I surely would have sunk down in the water and ended my agony. While my head and face were burning, the rest of my body, being in the icy-cold lake, was chilled and numbed so that I lost all sensation, except the boiling hot blood in my head."

All through the night, he and others fought death, and waited. Toward morning, small tugs that had performed valiant service in the Chicago River by removing burning hulks into Lake Michigan, appeared at the end of a nearby pier and began to take people off the scalding beach. The man who had buried his family scooped away the earth from their bodies, and they stumbled to the pier and were saved. The tug took them to Hyde Park where the father described his family as being "black as Negroes and covered with sand from head to foot—about as woe-begone and hard-looking a set as would be a crew of escaped imps from Tophet."

Among the people who escaped with this group was a black man who had been hired by banker Edward Ilsley Tinkham to save a trunk. He was given a modest sum and ordered to race his horses to safety. The driver drove them furiously toward the lake and onto The Sands, urging his horses far into the water, where one immediately collapsed from the strain. The drayman sat on the trunk for hours until he dragged it to a pier and was taken away by tug. He delivered the trunk the following day and was tipped a dollar. He then stood bug-eyed as Tinkham opened the trunk and began to count more than $1 million in currency he had saved for his bank.

At approximately 3:00 A.M. on October 10, 1871, the wind slackened and died. Rain came in quiet drops, splattering onto the charred wreck that was Chicago. Slowly the residents gathered their slim belongings and moved from the prairies and lake into their desolate city.

High atop a far South Side mansion, his shirtsleeves rolled up, stood General Philip H. Sheridan, whacking away at the cornices of a house he felt had to be destroyed before the fire could be checked.

James Hildreth found him there with the owner of the house, who was also chopping away under Sheridan's orders. "That's no longer necessary, General," Hildreth said. "The fire's out." Sheridan rested his axe against a chimney. He clucked his tongue and then gave orders for martial law to descend upon Chicago. Now he would save the city from looters.

Within two days Chicago's feisty newspapers were reborn and blathering the story of Mrs. O'Leary's cow. The cry rang out from a thousand throats. "Where's O'Leary! Lynch him!" Patrick O'Leary became a hunted man, marked by people's misery for the rope. For a week, the hapless O'Leary family hid in the attic of a home owned by Kevin McCarthy.

One bright, moonlit night, Patrick O'Leary was led, dressed as a woman, by little Nellie Mahoney to a distant place through the cinders of what had once been his neighborhood.

(ALSO SEE: Baltimore, Boston, Peshtigo)

CHICAGO, ILLINOIS — TORNADO

March 28, 1920

background: Of the six great tornadoes ever to strike metropolitan Chicago (these include the twisters of May 25, 1896, April 6, 1912, March 28, 1920, May 18, 1926, April 1, 1929, and May 1, 1933), the one touching down on March 28, 1920, was the most destructive, killing 28 persons—10 in Melrose Park alone—injuring 325 and destroying 113 buildings at a property loss of $3 million. This was the worst of a series of tornadoes that drove through southern and midwestern states, chiefly Illinois, Mississippi, Alabama, Tennessee, Georgia, North Dakota and Nebraska. Throughout this area, where dozens of tornadoes struck on a single day, a total of 220 deaths was recorded with over $3.5 million in damages.

"First we were pelted with hailstones as big as pigeons' eggs. Then we were soaked in a deluge of rain. We saw a funnel-shaped cloud coming toward us and stopped the machine." These were the words of a seventeen-year-old boy who, while driving a car down Milwaukee Avenue, was one of thousands to witness the wildest tornado ever to strike Chicago.

Beginning eight miles south of Joliet, Illinois, at 12:15

P.M. on March 28, 1920, the tornado took an hour to work its way through northwestern Chicago, especially devastating Melrose Park before it careened into Lake Michigan.

The seventeen-year-old on Milwaukee Avenue saw "shingles flying off roofs. Chickens carried high up in the air. Telephone poles snapped off and went swirling off in a cloud of dust. Houses shook and collapsed. One of them seemed to fold right up. Another jumped up in the air and fell down all in pieces. Birds were flung down in the road, their lives crushed out.

"All this happened quicker than I can tell it. We [he and a friend] were about to crawl out of the car when it began to rise. We jumped and the car turned over. We were both blown into a ditch and were soaking wet when we picked ourselves up. A repair car came along towing another light machine. The repair car didn't upset, but the other did. We helped those fellows right their machine and they helped us with ours. While we were working, a house a short distance away burst into flames and was destroyed before firemen came."

The tornado caused freakish things to happen. When its large funnel passed over homes, the vacuum at its center caused the natural pressure inside a house to increase and thereby blow the walls outward. One house was completely turned over and was standing on its chimney. One man was hauled out of a gigantic pile of debris and told his rescuers, when he regained consciousness, that he thought he had "awakened some place way below." Looking deep into the hole from which he had just been extracted, rescuers discovered two stoves still burning briskly. The man had been wedged tightly between them.

Women's lingerie was scooped up from the store window of one town and blown to the trees facing the courthouse of another, later drooping there in pinkish splendor. Eight persons were crushed to death in hard-hit Elgin, Illinois. An enterprising photographer scrambled through the ruins and then spotted another body. He threw down his camera and began to dig crazily, shouting over his shoulder to a reporter, "Call my paper and tell them there are *nine* dead in Elgin!" The reporter

A jumble of debris was left by the tornado that struck Chicago on March 28, 1920, and took the lives of twenty-eight residents. *(UPI)*

raced off and word was flashed to Chicago. The ninth body proved to be a wax clothing model.

One of the few buildings in Melrose Park to survive the twister, even though it was in the tornado's direct path, was a two-story brick structure loaded from cellar to roof with $500,000 worth of manure. Its weight was simply too much to budge. The tornado, however, had enough strength to lift a freight car laden with 1,500 pounds of goods and send it forty feet in the air before depositing it on the roof of a train station.

Just after the tornado passed, Chicago's newspapermen scampered through the ruins, photographing the rubble and interviewing survivors. Photographers grouped around one old woman sitting forlornly in the debris that had once been her home. About her head was wrapped a bloody towel. She said nothing, only moaned and rocked and wept. Her picture was run on the front page of one afternoon paper with the caption: "The whole story of the tornado."

CHICAGO, ILLINOIS — STREETCAR WRECK
May 25, 1950

background: A CTA streetcar, operated by Paul Manning, forty-two, was inadvertently rerouted from its regular tracks and smashed into a gasoline truck carrying 8,000 gallons of gas, which was ignited and engulfed the streetcar, burning thirty-three persons to death on May 25, 1950. The ensuing fire burned eight buildings and dozens of automobiles with damage estimated by Fire Marshal Anthony J. Mullaney to be in excess of $150,000. It was the worst streetcar accident on record.

It had rained heavily only hours before streetcar operator Paul Manning began his run down State Street through Chicago's South Side during the rush hour of May 25, 1950. A block south of 63rd Street an underpass was flooded, and a flagman had been sent out to stop all southbound cars and reroute them. The flagman waved repeatedly at Manning's oncoming streetcar. Its seats and aisles were full to capacity.

Manning either ignored his signal or did not see it. He was unaware that his car was being rerouted and expected to travel straight through to the underpass. He approached the intersection with great speed, and then his car unexpectedly lurched onto the open switch, turning it violently at the corner.

Just at that moment, Mel Wilson was turning his oversized gasoline truck to the north, and the lunging streetcar hit its side. The crash was thunderous and was immediately followed by a huge spray of sparks and metal gnashing into metal. Moments later a yellow-red gas explosion tore down the street, blistering concrete and cracking cobblestones. The entire front of the streetcar was enveloped in rushing, shooting flames. Manning was roasted to death at his post. The intense gasoline-fed flames burst through windows and inflamed all the passengers who were seated. Those standing, led by conductor William Lidell, twenty-nine, stampeded toward the rear of the car where for an instant they were trapped.

Edward W. White, Jr., was sitting at the rear of the car when the collision took place. "The whole car was in flames within a second," he stated later. "I kicked the glass out of the back door and jumped out. The flames were right behind me. It was so hot I just rolled over to the curb. A woman put her coat around me."

In kicking out the glass White had saved several lives, those who followed him out, but he had gashed his leg so severely that he almost lost his own life. A pedestrian used his tie to apply a tourniquet that stopped the blood flow. White was taken to Provident Hospital and eventually recovered from his injury.

Mrs. Ora Mae Bryant was one of those who jumped out after White had smashed his way to freedom. "Everyone was screaming and yelling. We couldn't get the door open. . . . Finally someone broke a window, and we crawled out."

Mary Poornay, who was later treated for injuries at Englewood Hospital, was standing in the aisle, close to the front of the car, when the vehicles collided. "I heard someone shout 'Look out!' and then there was a crash. The car tilted a little and then righted itself. People were thrown to the floor. Suddenly there were black smoke and flames all around. People tried to get off, but the doors were locked. Someone finally forced the back door. I followed others and leaped off the car and ran as fast as I could . . . "

She was running through the flames, for half the block was literally a wall of flames on one side of the street where the fire zoomed up the walls of eight buildings, breaking windows and burning rooftops; it danced and slid in lightning flashes under and over dozens of parked cars.

When the crash was first heard, the Reverend Robert J. Sidney looked up the street. At first he was puzzled. "Something like air blew over the streetcar." Then he saw that it was "enveloped in flames. In a second the entire car was hidden by fire. The flames went in all the open windows. One woman thrust her head out, but couldn't get her body through the opening. She raised her clenched fists over her head and just shuddered and then slumped to the floor. I saw people with their hair on fire. It was miserable."

Sitting in the front window of his house, Walter Skonicki gaped at the disaster before him. He watched helplessly as "a number of persons jumped off the back

Thirty-three bodies were removed from a gutted Chicago streetcar, May 25, 1950. The trolley crashed into a gas truck which exploded. A priest, center, is administering last rites. *(UPI)*

end of the streetcar, some of them with their clothing afire, some of them with their legs and arms cut by glass." Skonicki raced outside to save his daughter's car, parked in front of the house, but the spreading inferno caused him to retreat into his house. The house itself caught fire, and Skonicki gathered his family, led them out the back door and turned back to view the sickening sight of his front windows melting from the blazing heat.

Another witness, seventy-six-year-old Ella Flowers, had seen the crash from her second-story apartment window. She had little time to view the carnage as the flames shot up the walls to her window. She and others ran down the backstairs of the building to save themselves.

The first person to think of calling the fire department was tavern owner Peter Simadis. He was strolling down the street and turned around upon hearing the crash. A wall of colorful flame rolled toward him. "The fire was traveling like a series of explosions," he later recalled, "spreading so fast that no one could have escaped its path. . . . I ran to the telephone, but before I could complete a call to the fire department the front window of the tavern cracked under the intense heat and then fell inside the tavern."

Six men sat at the bar, all turned bug-eyed at the sight of the raging inferno bursting on their peaceful hour of libation. They rose as one man, and, following Simadis, "ran like hell" out of the back of the burning tavern.

When the fire department finally did appear, its firefighters worked for several hours to extinguish the flames on the street. Several walls of buildings collapsed, and half of the block was in ruins by 9:00 P.M. The dead, most charred beyond recognition, numbered thirty-three, and these were placed in a row along the sidewalk for removal to the morgue.

Then began, as epilogue to the most disastrous streetcar accident in history, the tedious, grim task of contacting relatives: the phone calls, the letters.

CHICAGO, ILLINOIS

RAILWAY WRECK
October 30, 1972

An Illinois Central commuter train, a modern double-decker, overshot one of its stops four miles from the IC's main terminal south of the Loop on October 30, 1972. It backed up to pick up passengers. Moments later another train proceeding north, its engineer, Robert Cavanaugh, apparently unwarned of the unusual action on the part of the train in front, slammed into the train. The almost new cars crumpled as they telescoped into one another. (This fact later caused Governor Richard Ogilvie to withhold funds for the purchase of modern train cars until their safety was determined.)

One passenger, Cliff Retis, who was riding in the modern train, later stated, "I was thrown into the seat in front of me. Then the windows started crashing down on top of me. The floor was gone, and people were screaming for help."

"I don't know what caused it," engineer Robert Cavanaugh later told *Chicago Daily News* reporter Barry Felcher. "When I knew it [the crash] was imminent, I set the brakes and tried to warn the passengers." Cavanaugh ran back to the passenger cars and shouted, "Quick! Quick! Get to the rear of the car! Get away from the front! We are going to crash!"

Cavanaugh's much older, heavier train, it was later estimated, was traveling at about 30 m.p.h. Officials also stated that a yellow warning light that was a signal to Cavanaugh to reduce speed was in working order.

After warning passengers Cavanaugh closed the double steel door leading to the passenger compartment, ". . . and that's all I can remember. The roof caved in, and the doors fell on me, pinning me in the wreckage where I was trapped for more than four hours before the firemen got me out."

Forty-five persons were killed in the wreck, and more than 350 were injured. "I'm sorry for those who didn't make it," Cavanaugh later said from his hospital bed.

Forty-four died when one Illinois Central commuter train slammed into the rear of another train on October 30, 1972. *(American Red Cross)*

CHILE — EARTHQUAKE
November 19, 1822

The quake that destroyed a great number of villages and towns along the western coast of Chile on November 19, 1822, struck Valparaiso hardest, killing close to 10,000 persons. The coastal area was permanently raised by the upheaval.

Maria Graham, the president of Quintero, a town close to Valparaiso, traveled along the coast following the quake. Her discoveries appeared later in her *Journal of a Residence in Chile.* Mrs. Graham related that "part of the bed of the sea remained bare and dry at high water, with beds of oysters and mussels and other shells adhering to the rocks on which they grew, the fish being all dead and exhaling [a] most offensive effluvia. An old wreck of a ship, the *Aquila,* which could not normally be approached became accessible from the land although its distance from the original sea-shore had not altered."

Mrs. Graham noted that the land itself had risen four feet.

CHILE — EARTHQUAKE
January 24, 1939

background: More than 450 miles of Chile was caught in a three-minute earthquake beginning at 11:35 P.M. on January 24, 1939. Most affected were the towns of Concepcion, Chillan, Coihueco, Coronel and Angol. More than 50,000 were killed (with half of the dead in Chillan alone), 60,000 injured and 700,000 left homeless with damage in the millions of dollars. The 1939 Chilean quake had the highest casualty list of any South American disaster in modern times.

Though Chile is rich in minerals, grains and timber, the long, angular country (if stretched across Europe, Chile would reach from Moscow to Madrid) is the most earthquake-vexed on the planet, receiving 21 percent of the average 9,000 quakes recorded worldwide every year. For centuries its people have accustomed themselves to the steady tremors that move menacingly beneath them each month, but none was prepared for the monster earthquake that struck Chile on the night of January 24, 1939.

In the ancient cities of Concepcion, Coihueco and Chillan, where dwellings butted up against each other down narrow, twisting streets, the quake did its worst damage. On Chillan's 144 city blocks, only three buildings remained standing. The historic town, some 250 miles south of the capital, Santiago, lost all of its landmarks including the revered birth site of the Chilean man known as the "father of his country," Bernardo O'Higgins. (Born of a Chilean mother and Irish father, Ambrosio O'Higgins, Bernardo was educated in Europe and returned to Chile where he fought alongside liberator José de San Martin against the Spanish, whose rule had lasted since the conquistadors. O'Higgins became a benevolent dictator over Chile's first independent government in 1817.)

More than 300 persons were watching a motion picture in Chillan's National Theater when the quake hit. The audience had only a few seconds to look up before walls and ceiling collapsed on them, killing all. The United States Ambassador to Chile, Norman Armour, flew from Santiago to Chillan after hearing of the disaster. One of the first places he visited was the theater.

"I walked over the ruins of this theater," he later reported. "The walls had collapsed and the roof fallen almost at once so that the majority of the people were killed outright. But for several hours, even days, cries and groans came from below, and only the day before I was there, . . . a man was dug out alive but delirious from his terrible experience. . . . "

Blinking in disbelief at the total devastation, Armour moved through the city. Half of its 50,000 population had been wiped out. Survivors shuffled dazedly through the ruins, feebly looking for relatives. One man came up to Armour and said, "And where is one to go, Señor, when the earth beneath your feet gives way? I staggered on. All the world seemed to crash about me. Finally, somehow, I reached my house, or the place where my house had once been, but there was nothing there, only brick and plaster and my wife and three little ones beneath. We have found only two of them [they were dead]." He pointed solemnly to the rubble. "The others are still there."

The shocks that hit Concepcion and several other cities were equally devastating, and Armour noted that about 70 percent of the staggering 50,000 dead were children, most of whom were sleeping when the quake folded the walls of their homes over their beds.

Out of the Chillan horror emerged the story of a young hero, a night watchman barely out of his teens who worked at the main power plant. Moments after the quake struck, the young man saw dozens of live wires fall, splattering sparks to earth. He realized that these wires, jumping with current in the main streets, would electrocute scores of unwary people. He ran into the power plant and, as the building began to topple in on him, turned off the main switch. A second later he was crushed to death by the collapsing building.

Concepcion lost 70 percent of its buildings. Hundreds of coal mine shafts caved in, burying miners in them. Fifteen majestic cathedrals were utterly wrecked. Six provinces in Chile's industrial and agricultural southern region had been razed.

Communication with the stricken areas was cut off

for several days, but when the news of the mammoth disaster reached the outside world, aid began to flow toward Chile. Supplies from Brazil and Peru were sent. Two trainloads of food and ambulances were sent by Argentina's President Roberto Ortiz. Chilean President Pedro Aguirre Cerda was on hand to see two British cruisers arrive with medical and food supplies from their berths in Valparaiso. United States Army bombers flew in from the Panama Canal under orders from President Roosevelt. They carried serums to check the spread of typhoid, tetanus and gangrene.

It was several years before Chile recovered from this quake, which had literally destroyed a generation of its young.

CHILE — EARTHQUAKES May 21-30, 1960

background: Beginning on May 21, 1960, central Chile was struck by a series of quakes, five occurring in the first two days, and several more throughout the following three days. In addition six dormant volcanoes sprang to life; three more volcanoes were born, and a great *tsunami* struck the coast, killing more than 5,700 people. (The initial quake registered 8.9 on the Strasbourg scale.) More than 100,000 homes were destroyed, along with 20 percent of the country's industrial complex, at a cost of $400 million. Through the Red Cross, thirty-five nations sent relief supplies and funds. The twenty-four foot *tsunami* that struck Chile later rolled back to strike Japan, where it killed 150 people.

The dodging boy, all of six years, had no idea why he had been chosen to be killed. Wide-eyed and screaming, he attempted to flee from his murderers, but crowds of male adults surrounded him and struck him with clubs until he dropped into a pathetic little heap at their feet, dead. His assailants then ceremoniously ripped out his young heart, and with loud chants and drums beating the men marched down to the pulsating sea and offered the bloody heart to placate their angry gods.

Two of the culprits, superstitious Mapuche Indians, were arrested by the police and questioned about their ghastly deed. One said, "We were asking for calm in the sea and on the earth."

Their act of horror was but one of many that occurred when titanic earthquakes in a seven-day ordeal all but obliterated Chile. The attack began on May 21, 1960, at a little past 6:00 A.M. Warning shocks, slight murmurs and tremblings of the earth had gone on for days previous. The apprehensive Chileans in Concepcion were as prepared as they could be, and when the first shock came, most of the citizens poured into streets that had been widened following the devastating quakes of 1939. One *National Observer* reporter, Patrick O'Donovan, rushed outside with the rest and watched ancient buildings "dissolve with a weary slowness like lumps of sugar in hot tea. And then came the long-drawn-out appalling noise of wrecking, of tearing and falling, and a continuous silly tinkle of breaking glass. Sometimes fissures opened in the ground, wavering for a hundred yards in parallel ripples imitating the waves of the sea shore. And when it was all over, the birds began to sing very loudly and discordantly together . . . "

As the walls of the city of Puerto Montt began to crumble, a newsman saw a six-year-old boy snatch up two of his infant brothers and seek a place of safety, dancing madly about the inside of his teetering home, a brother under each arm. But the walls closed on him. burying him to his neck. He survived, but his brothers were crushed to death.

Like a giant hammer blow, the quakes continued, ripping and shredding more than 90,000 square miles of Andean countryside, reshaping the contour of the earth in many places; in one spot, a twenty-five-mile area sank one thousand feet. Ravaged and flattened were the exquisite white cities of Concepcion, Valdivia, Osorno and Puerto Montt. Lakes disappeared; new ones formed. Two small mountains vanished.

Six ancient volcanoes violently sprang to life, and in their wake three more were born. Crusted lava beds split open and boiling lava streamed into steaming Lake Ranco, which broke its banks and hurled downward gushing water, creating landslides, killing everything in its way. The sky upwards of 23,000 feet was filled with volcanic ash.

Following the first upheaval, the waters along the Chilean coast retreated a great distance. One account described the movement "as though the water was being drained away through a large straw." It returned to the fishing villages of Lebu, Quelin and Anoud traveling at 520 m.p.h., according to one estimate, one of the greatest *tsunamis* ever to strike Chile. The seismic seawave drove inland for 500 yards, wiping out every building and drowning every soul in its path.

Between the ongoing quakes Chileans everywhere began to sort through the rubble and rebuild their lives. Most of the buildings in the major cities were gone, and the population was forced to camp in the streets and parks with nothing to protect them from the sleetlike rains that followed the quakes.

Within hours a massive airlift from the United States was under way. Through the ash-filled skies of Chile flew seventy-four Globemaster transports carrying 1,000 tons of emergency equipment, two 400-bed army field hospitals, 800 doctors, nurses, technicians ("You sent people, not just supplies," one long-time anti-American newspaper gratefully stated.), portable radio stations, water purification systems and $4,500,000 in nongovernment aid. The crews of the Globemasters flew several flights along the 5,000-mile journey. Many worked nonstop for 50 hours.

It was weeks before the United States and Red Cross supplies (thirty-three other nations contributed hundreds of tons of supplies to the stricken country through the Red Cross) could be distributed.

In remote Valdivia the Chilean government decided to evacuate as many people as possible by trains. When one train moved out, those left behind wailed, "We are starving . . . please send us bread and milk."

Over 5,700 were dead, and it seemed the living were not much better off. Homeless, foodless, more than 100,000 persons throughout the country were reduced to rioting over crusts of bread, and men fought death duels with knives for cans of beans. For weeks army troops were compelled to disperse mobs berserk with hunger by firing over their heads and sometimes into the crowds themselves. Some instances of murder and cannibalism were reported.

Fortunately the destruction of Agadir, Morocco, on February 29, 1960, three months before the Chilean tragedy, had caused worldwide earthquake relief organizations to be more prepared, and Chile, within a month of its tragedy, was already rebuilding.

(ALSO SEE: Agadir, Morocco)

CHILE

EARTHQUAKES
March 28, 1965

Central Chile was hit by several earthquake tremors at noon on March 28, 1965, with most of the damage confined to a dozen villages. Dead were 470 people, most of them wives and children of farmers and workers.

The quake itself did little direct damage, but it caused several dams, especially the one high above the village of El Cobre, to burst. Here the waters quickly broke through the earthen dam, cascaded onto the small hamlet, and buried its sixty houses in mud seven feet deep.

One man, Sergio Villagran, hurrying to the village in a truck, witnessed the catastrophe and was almost killed when the truck was hurled to the edge of a mountain road. When he reached his home, he began to dig wildly down into the mud. His twelve-year-old son helped him. The boy had explained that his mother, sister and three brothers had escaped with him, but had raced back to their house to turn off the electricity. Several hours later Villagran reached the bodies of his family. In one of the dead hands was a transistor radio, turned on and still blaring music.

CHILIE-LINCA AERA NACIONALE

AIR CRASH
February 6, 1965

The lure of the sharp, cloud-dusted peaks of the Andes was, perhaps more than any other factor, the cause of the worst air crash in Chilean history. Plane passengers as late as 1965 insisted upon traveling in propeller-driven craft in order to view the magnificent mountains better, particularly the Christ of the Andes monument soaring high above the Chilean-Argentine border. Jet planes simply flew at altitudes too great to afford the view.

Tourists, sightseers and a soccer team boarded a Chilean DC-6B airliner at Santiago on February 6, 1965. Twenty minutes later, as the pilot was making his way through heavy clouds hovering about the 11,700-foot El Volcan Pass (an ancient gorge slashed into the San Jose Mountain, an extinct volcano), contact with the plane was lost.

At that moment a waterworks engineer high in the mountains saw the plane plunge behind the volcano and then heard a crash. His report was immediately followed up by search planes. The old DC-6B was spotted hours later, its debris and bodies strewn for 1,000 feet over the mountain slopes. All of the eighty-seven persons on board perished.

CHIMARA

MARINE DISASTER
January 19, 1947

More than a year and a half after World War II, the seas of the world were still afloat with hundreds of thousands of mines. By the beginning of 1947, 6,300 lives had been lost on board peacetime ships due to the explosions of these deadly mines that menaced shipping in the North Sea, the English Channel and almost the whole of the Mediterranean (only the American coasts had been swept free of these bobbing perils).

The 1,800-ton Greek passenger liner *Chimara,* like the Chinese steamer *Kiangya* a year later, was one of the most notable ships to befoul itself on a mine. Sailing from Salonika to the Athenian port of Piraeus off the tip of the Attica peninsula on January 19, 1947, the *Chimara*'s port bow was torn away by an unseen mine at 3:50 A.M. This one-time German hospital ship had no chance to survive, for her engine room was immediately enveloped in flames and her lower compartments quickly flooded.

The 548 passengers and 87 crew members stumbled down the vessel's blackened passageways and, amid screams and many-tongued curses, attempted to make their way to the upper decks. Those who did fought wildly for places in the few lifeboats that managed to get away. For most, however, it was a quick death. Chained in a hold were forty Greek leftist guerrillas who were left to drown.

Women and children suffered most as they were knocked down and trampled by crazed male passengers and crewmen who knuckled their way into the eight lifeboats. Some 200 survived; 393 died.
(ALSO SEE: Kiangya)

CHINA — EARTHQUAKE
February 2, 1556

The most destructive earthquake in recorded history occurred in three provinces of China—Honan, Shansi and Shensi—with an estimated death toll of 830,000 persons. The facts surrounding this colossal disaster, however, are skimpy, and many historians and scientists disagree over the magnitude of the Great China Quake.

In his *Theoretical and Applied Seismology* the prominent seismologist Akitune Imamura states, "However, by tracing on a map the recorded area of fallen dwellings, it will be found that it [the quake] follows the valley of the river Wei-ho, a tributary of the Hoang-ho, and involves an immense territory." He concludes that "the figure may not be exaggerated."

CHINA — FAMINE
1877-78

Lack of communication coupled with the xenophobic reclusiveness practiced by the Ch'ing (Manchu) dynasty prevented the outside world from obtaining early knowledge of China's worst famine. Details of this mammoth disaster are sketchy to this day, yet it has been reliably determined that between 9.5 and 13 million people perished in northern and central China during the years 1877-78.

Drought began the catastrophe in 1876; almost no rain fell for a period of three years, and inside of these years China, for all its centuries of high culture and gentility, was reduced to a giant horror pit where human slavery, cannibalism, murder, disease and death went unchecked in all strata of society.

Much of this was due to the Manchus, who sought to conceal China's internal ills (which, no doubt, encouraged the collapse of the Ch'ing dynasty in 1911). The rare and fragmentary accounts of the famine dribbled out of the country in the form of letters and statements of Western missionaries and travelers.

Frederick H. Balfour, a European resident of Shanghai at the height of the famine, chronicled what he saw. "The people's faces are black with hunger; they are dying by thousands upon thousands. Women and girls and boys are openly offered for sale to any chance wayfarer. When I left the country, a respectable married woman could be easily bought for six dollars and a little girl for two. In cases, however, where it was found impossible to dispose of their children, parents have been known to kill them sooner than witness their prolonged sufferings, in many instances throwing themselves afterwards down wells, or committing suicide by arsenic."

In one province stricken by the famine, the only method by which the countless dead bodies littering the roadways and fields could be buried was by placing them in huge pits which later became known as "ten thousand men holes." In desperation the populace slaughtered the oxen, mules, camels and donkeys that were the primary transportation across the vast stretches of China. Every traveler was on guard to protect his beasts. One account verifies that "so many [animals] were killed by the desperate people in the hills, for the sake of their flesh, that the transit could only be carried on by banded vigilance. . . . Night traveling was out of the question." The account also confirms the existence of widespread cannibalism. "The way was marked by the carcasses or skeletons of men and beasts, and the wolves, dogs and foxes soon put an end to the sufferings of any wretch who lay down to recover from or die of his sickness in those terrible defiles."

More than 70 million Chinese were affected by the famine. The first official word of its existence reached British officials through a telegram sent by an investigating envoy on January 28, 1878. It read: "Appalling famine raging throughout four provinces North China. Nine million people reported destitute. Children daily sold in markets for food. Foreign Relief Committee appeal to England and America for assistance."

Secretary Mayers at the British Legation at Peking reported more fully on the millions dying of the famine in China's interior, including areas about Chefoo and Tientsin, where foreign settlements came in contact with those afflicted. For the most part Manchu officials prohibited travel by foreigners into the area bordered by the Yangtze to Peking and eastward to the Korean border. The failure of the monsoons to appear since 1876 in this vast tract of land caused the drought that led to the famine. In ironic contrast the neighboring provinces of Kwangtung and Fuhkien were inundated by crop-killing floods.

A commissioner of Emperor Yen King-Ming traveling through hard-hit Shansi Province noted from his elaborate man-carried cab that "the roads are lined with corpses in such numbers as to distance all efforts for their interment, while women and children, starving and in rags, know not where to look for the means of

keeping body and soul together." The commissioner had to turn back after his entourage was repeatedly attacked by ravenous crowds. For the most part the authorities turned their backs on their dehydrated millions and left them to die in guarded obscurity.
(ALSO SEE: India)

CHINA **FLOODS**
Spring, 1887

The northwest provinces of China have experienced perennial deluges since the beginning of recorded time, the first great flood in the area being recorded in 2297 B.C., at which time the Yellow River overflowed and drowned tens of thousands of villagers living along the water's edge.

Often called "China's Sorrow," the Yellow River has acted more like a rampaging dragon than a benevolent, life-giving waterway. Through the centuries, the Chinese have attempted to dam the Yellow at the most vulnerable breaking points to protect the residents [1,000-3,000 per square mile] living in its vast province.

In the thirteenth century, Marco Polo visited the Chinese city of Hangchow and observed, "Beyond the city and enclosing it on that side, there is a ditch about forty miles in length, very wide, and full of water that comes from the river. . . . This was excavated by the ancient kings of the province, in order that when the river should overflow its banks, the superfluous water might be diverted into this channel."

These methods, and most since, have proved futile in holding back the Yellow River. In the spring of 1887, following heavy rains in Honan Province, the river rushed over its banks at a sharp bend where the town of Cheng Chou was located. The entire population raced for the protective walls and attempted to shore them up, but a gap widened to 1,200 yards in width. The workers could not hold back the river and soon fled for their lives, the river in demonic pursuit. It engulfed the city in twenty feet of water within seconds and then turned to inflate the small stream known as the Luchia. These waters combined to rush eastward for twenty miles until they roared up against the walled city of Chungmow. In minutes the walls were washed away, and the city ceased to exist. The torrent continued day after day, swallowing villages and towns—600 in number—and, broadening to a width of thirty miles. At Kaifeng the waters rose even higher, forty, perhaps fifty feet, pouring down into a low-lying plain where 1,500 more villages were quickly inundated.

The result was unbelievable destruction and an astronomical death toll. One authority did attempt an estimate. A.H. Godbey stated, "Not far beyond this locality (the plain below Kaifeng) the flood passed into the province of Anhwei, where it spread very widely. The actual loss of life could not be computed accurately, but the lowest intelligent estimate placed it at 1.5 million, and one authority placed it at 7 million." These claims would make the Great China Flood of 1887 the worst such calamity in world history.

CHINA **FLOODS**
September, 1911

The snaking Yangtze River burst over its earthen embankments in early September, 1911, making an inland sea of the Chinese provinces of Nganhwei, Ichang, Hupei, Hunan and the city of Shanghai, an area of about 700 square miles. Living inside this water basin, the most fertile country of the nation, were 2 million persons, and of these 100,000 were immediately drowned in the floods.

For several weeks starvation took another 100,000 lives, and the area was subject to pillage and murder by roving bands of starving men. The most notable of these attacks was the sacking of the American Baptist Chapel near Quisan by marauders from Suchow, a town that had been completely submerged within an hour of the first flood.

Missionaries traveling by steamboat to Hangkow on September 6 observed thousands of wooden coffins floating down the bloated Yangtze. The swelling waters of the river had swept away one of the largest cemeteries in the district.

More than half a million refugees fled to Manchuria and Mongolia as a result of the immense floods.

CHINA **FLOODS-FAMINE**
September-November, 1939

The great floods that inundated the northern provinces of China from September to November in 1939 obliterated all grain and rice crops, destroyed most housing and made close to 25 million persons destitute. Hopei and Shantung provinces suffered the greatest damage, and famine spread rapidly throughout the Yellow River basin.

Though the Red Cross attempted to send food and supplies into the area, most of these relief efforts were cut off by Japanese troops that controlled a large part of the afflicted area. About 90 of Hopei's 130 districts were in ten feet of water for several months, making 10 million homeless. The death toll from the flooding was moderate, but over 500,000 bushels of grain were de-

Tientsin, China, was under water during the floods of 1939 which claimed 200,000 lives. *(UPI)*

stroyed, and famine soon spread. Within three months more than 200,000 perished.

As always in this land of practical ironies, other provinces such as Hunan, Kiangsi and Anhwei produced so much rice that autumn (25 million bushels) that the overproduction caused widespread depression in its going rate, and hundreds of tons of rice were destroyed.

CHINA — FLOOD
August, 1950

The Chinese provinces of Anhwei, Kiangow, and to a lesser degree Honan, Hopei, Hupei, Hunan, Kiangsi and Kwangtung were devastated by flooding from the Hwai and Yangtze rivers in early August, 1950. Hardest hit was Anhwei, where Communist officials reported 489 persons killed (although this figure was probably a low estimate) and 10 million persons homeless.

Authorities were reluctant to admit that more than 890,000 houses had been "ruined," and 5 million acres of cultivated land (3.5 million of which were unsalvageable as grain producers that year) had been inundated.

From the ancient battlements of the walled city of Hwaiyuan in north Kiangow, an observer in that Grand Canal city described the scene as a "vast ocean of water stretching beyond the horizon."

CHINA — FLOODS
August, 1954

background: One of China's worst and best recorded floods was that which turned the country's "rice bowl," the 3,400-mile Yangtze River basin, into an inland sea in August, 1954. More than 40,000 drowned within several days of the flooding in the Tungting Lake region. More than 600,000 persons were employed on a slave labor basis to combat the floods.

China's greatest flood, abetted by the "heaviest rainfall in a hundred years," according to Radio Peking, swamped the country's rice bowl when the Yangtze and Hwai Rivers broke through their embankments in August, 1954. The rising waters caused this vast area, about twice the size of Texas, to turn into an inland sea. The rivers rose to a record-breaking 96.06-foot level, and their torrents inundated hundreds of villages and towns and drowned more than 40,000 persons.

The previous high-water mark had been set in 1931 when these killer rivers burst their dams, killed 140,000 and made 10 million homeless. John E. Baker directed relief supplies from the United States at that time, and Charles A. Lindbergh flew medicine and food to hard-hit areas.

The sunken Peking-Shanghai-Hankow triangle has been a deathtrap for the more than 160 million persons who have dwelled there for centuries. Between the years 1851 and 1866 it has been estimated that 40 to 50 million persons perished in this area due to nightmare floods.

Prior to the deluge of 1954, and Communist control of China, the United States spent $500,000 on an American-designed plan to build massive TVA-like dams to protect this area against the fourth largest river in the world. Damming of the Yangtze and also the Hwai came to a halt when Communists took over China in 1948 and 1949. The American plan, which called for building the world's largest dam 300 miles east of Chungking, allowing a 250-mile reservoir to irrigate 10 million acres of land, was thrown out in favor of what was later termed the Bukhov Plan.

Unlike the American device of building dams that rested on subsurface piles, the Bukhov Plan (named after an engineer sent to China from Moscow), "the new Soviet method of dam construction," called for dams to rest completely on the surface soil. The leading Chinese Communist engineer in the field, a woman named Chien Chen Ying, followed this concept and ordered 3 million workers pressed into construction of this type of dam. Ying sneered at the West and was quoted as saying, "We learned from the Soviet experts that clay from the other side of the Hwai River was just as effective as pine from the other side of the Pacific."

Then the floods of 1954 came, and the dams proved useless against the mountainous waters. They crumbled quickly. The Chinese desperately pressed more then 600,000 men to work on the quaking dams, handling sandbags. At one break in a Soviet-inspired dam, 200 soldiers and 10,000 peasants with mats on their backs stood shoulder to shoulder for three hours to hold back the flood. But the river won and swept past these arm-locked men, several thousand of whom were drowned.

The fact that the Communists had lost their fight with the waters was at first covered up with propaganda by Peking's New China News Agency, which proudly proclaimed: "People are confident that everything has been foreseen. There will be no panic, no hunger, nothing like the bad old days when there was no hold from above. . . . "

When the waters topped the 96-foot embankment at Wuhan and gushed over into the city, the "bad old days" were back in full force despite the Bukhov Plan, boisterous propaganda and human walls. Mao's first Five Year Plan crumbled with the clay dams of China.

CHUNGKING, CHINA — FIRE

September 2, 1949

More than 1,700 bodies were recovered after an eighteen-hour fire slashed through central Chungking on September 2, 1949. The Nationalist Central News Agency stated that upwards of 10,000 homes had been gutted by the inferno, leaving 100,000 homeless. The fire was mysterious in origin, breaking out in Chungking's slums at 4:00 P.M. It soon spread to the residential and business districts and ate its way down to the rickety wooden piers of the waterfronts of the Chialing and Yangtze Rivers, where thousands had sought refuge and hundreds were burned to death while attempting to flee in open boats.

The Nationalists quickly rounded up suspected Communists and from their catch selected an "underground worker." A week later this man was charged with arson and was executed.

CIMBRIA — MARINE DISASTER

January 19, 1883

The elegant steamship, *Cimbria,* of the Hamburg-American Line, was reported as having been sunk by an iceberg in the North Sea on January 19, 1883, with 340 hands and passengers going to the chilly bottom of the Atlantic. The true fate of that tragic liner, however, involves the word "murder" if one ocean-going vessel can murder another through irresponsible navigation and then callously steam away, leaving the stricken ship to founder and its hapless passengers to drown. Perhaps certain historians are more willing to ascribe such dire events to God than to compassionless captains of the sea, whose universal image through the centuries is shored up in baroque prose and studded with stylish words like "heroic," "valiant," "unswerving."

But in the case of the steamship *Cimbria,* it was murder, plain and simple. And the killing "iceberg" was the steamer *Sultan.*

The *Cimbria* sailed from Hamburg on the morning of January 18, 1883. That night the North Sea was shrouded in a soupy bank of fog. Captain Hansen ordered his ship's engines brought to half speed, then slow, and the *Cimbria,* with 402 passengers (most of whom were in steerage) and 94 officers and men, groped its way forward. The whistles were sounded every few minutes. At a little after 2:00 A.M., what was first thought to be an eerie echo of a whistle was heard. The sound then became more distinct, and Captain Hansen realized another ship was bearing down upon the *Cimbria,* whose officers blinked in amazement on the bridge as they saw the green signal lights of the *Sultan,* only 150 feet away, as it dashed full speed out of the fog.

"Collision," Captain Hansen stated, and First Officer Karlowa and Second Officer Spruthzen dashed from the bridge shouting the alarm and ordering crewmen to swing out the lifeboats and prepare to lower away. The *Sultan* came on with such speed that, when it made impact, the *Cimbria*'s portside bulkheads collapsed at once, and the ship began to sink. Hundreds of women and children poured onto the upper decks shrieking. The *Cimbria* possessed only eight large lifeboats, and four of these on the port side were useless. Though filled they could not be lowered since the ship was sinking to port and the angle prevented descent. The first boat on the starboard side was lowered safely into the water, but the great number of people caused the boat to capsize. All aboard drowned. (The eight boats could hold about 250 persons, about half of those on board the sinking liner.)

Three lifeboats with 56 crew and passengers were lowered safely, and they pulled away from the dying *Cimbria.* The rescue operations were admirable. First Officer Karlowa held two blazing torches to light the way to the starboard boats and was last seen grasping the twin flames until he disappeared beneath the waves. Spruthzen, wielding an axe, chopped large sections from the wooden railings and tossed these into the sea to struggling survivors (he was eventually pulled from the ocean).

Most people who had jumped into the freezing water were German immigrants from the province of Posen. Their heavy winter garments helped to drag them under. Only three women survived. One was a Polish woman on her way to join her parents in America. She struggled with her aging aunt in the water, but the effort was too much for the elderly woman and she soon slipped beneath the waves. Another woman held on to the side of a lifeboat for an hour and a half before she was rescued.

Amid the screams and shouts for help the captain of the *Sultan,* discovering that his ship was intact, ignored the distress rockets and flares sent up by Captain Hansen from the bridge of the *Cimbria.* The *Sultan* was only two ship's lengths away from the *Cimbria* when the latter was clearly sinking, yet the *Sultan* never stopped to lower boats or give assistance of any kind. It sailed on and on into the fog bank until its green signal lights vanished.

The *Cimbria*'s water-soaked officers stood in the lifeboats cursing the *Sultan*'s captain loudly. One later testified that had he "taken the trouble to act humanely he might have saved a hundred lives." As it was, 340 died and 56 survived to see the officers of the *Sultan* arrested. But there was no trial. The disaster was recorded as a "regrettable accident," and some less-than-conscientious almanac researchers have even concluded that the *Sultan* never existed and that the *Cimbria* met its fate at the hands of a nameless, blameless "iceberg."

CINCINNATI, OHIO — FLOOD

January, 1937

Military men, for the most part, determined the sites of early American cities. A young officer of engineers, Jefferson Davis, later to become the first and only president of the Confederate States of America, selected the site of Fort Dearborn from which sprang Chicago. Cincinnati, Ohio, was first begun in 1789 as Fort Washington, established by Major John Doughty. In Davis's case he chose well. In Doughty strutted the fool.

Fort Washington was not constructed with foresight. Doughty built the fort almost on the lip of the surging Ohio River, which had been known for decades to flood its banks to great heights. A friendly Shawnee Indian made this quite clear to Doughty and suggested that the soldiers construct their fort on a nearby hill. Doughty ignored him.

As a result, the city of Cincinnati has been subject to violent, murderous floods ever since, the worst occurring in January, 1937. The flooding that month swelled the Ohio River more than 80 feet above the usual level and wiped out almost all transportation and business for 700 miles along the riverfront.

In Cincinnati the river flooded most of the business and residential districts, and more than one million persons in and about the city fled their homes. Damages of the great Ohio River flood ran upwards of $400 million and sixty-five persons lost their lives in the rising waters.

CIRCASSIAN — MARINE DISASTER

December 29, 1876

background: The British-built, two hundred eighty-foot *Circassian,* was launched before the Civil War and was the victim of several storms in which it was almost wrecked. During salvage attempts to free the vessel from a bar off Long Island on December 29, 1876, a great gale tore the ship in two, killing twenty-eight repairmen.

Sailors in all ages religiously talk of ill-fated ships that are born and die without luck. From its grim history the iron-hulled sailing ship *Circassian* appears to be one of these, perhaps the unluckiest ship to ever glide upon the waves. First seeing service for the British, the ship was then employed as a Confederate blockade-runner during the Civil War. This activity was cut short when the

Cincinnati, Ohio, was inundated by the flooding Ohio River, January 1937. Sixty-five lost their lives. *(UPI)*

Circassian was captured by a refitted ferry boat, the *Somerset,* off Cuba, an ignominious defeat in which $500,000 in goods fell into Union hands.

Following the war the *Circassian* suffered a series of dismal groundings and wrecks, each time being salvaged, refitted and pressed into passenger service between Liverpool and New York. On December 11, 1876, the ship, returning from Liverpool, was engulfed by a sea blizzard. Captain Richard Williams lost his way immediately, thanks to the ship's malfunctioning compass. The vessel drove blindly onto a reef only a few hundred yards from land. Spotters at the Shinnocock Life Saving Post on Long Island sighted the ship and, when the storm abated, took off the passengers and crew in longboats.

A salvaging firm, the New York Coast Wrecking Company, put thirty-two repairmen to work on the vessel. While on board and attempting to free the ship from the reef (it was lodged amidships) on December 26, a gale blew in from the northeast and trapped the men.

The storm increased and prevented land rescuers from reaching the ship. By December 29, the "buster" had reached hurricane proportions, and great clouds of sand kicked up by the storm all but obscured the *Circassian.* The raging sea made it impossible to send out lifeboats to rescue the thirty-two workmen aboard. Several attempts were made to shoot a line to the wind-tossed ship, but none reached that far. It was a futile gesture anyway. No man could hoist himself hand over hand from ship to shore in such a gale.

Presently people watching in horror from shore saw most of the men on board climb the iron mizzenmast and cling there while the enormous waves pounded the ship and caused the mast to sway back and forth like a colossal, sinister-looking metronome until the vessel, creaking amidships on the reef, literally snapped in two. As it did so, the iron spar, clustered with desperate men whose howls merged with those of the wind, began to whip faster back and forth from port to starboard until it settled into the sea. Still the men hung on. A cross sea with waves coming from different directions soon pried the men loose and swept them away.

Four men somehow managed to stay afloat on a five-foot piece of cork. They rode this as it spun frantically in the teeming surf, submerging several times and finally being tossed onto shore. Twenty-eight others were lost. The *Circassian* was finished, her bad luck having played itself out.

Divers look for bodies in the half-submerged *City of Columbus* which foundered off Martha's Vineyard, Massachusetts, January 18, 1884. *(Harper's Weekly)*

An hysterical mother identifies the body of her child on the tug *Storm King* following the sinking of the *City of Columbus*. *(Frank Leslie's Illustrated Newspaper)*

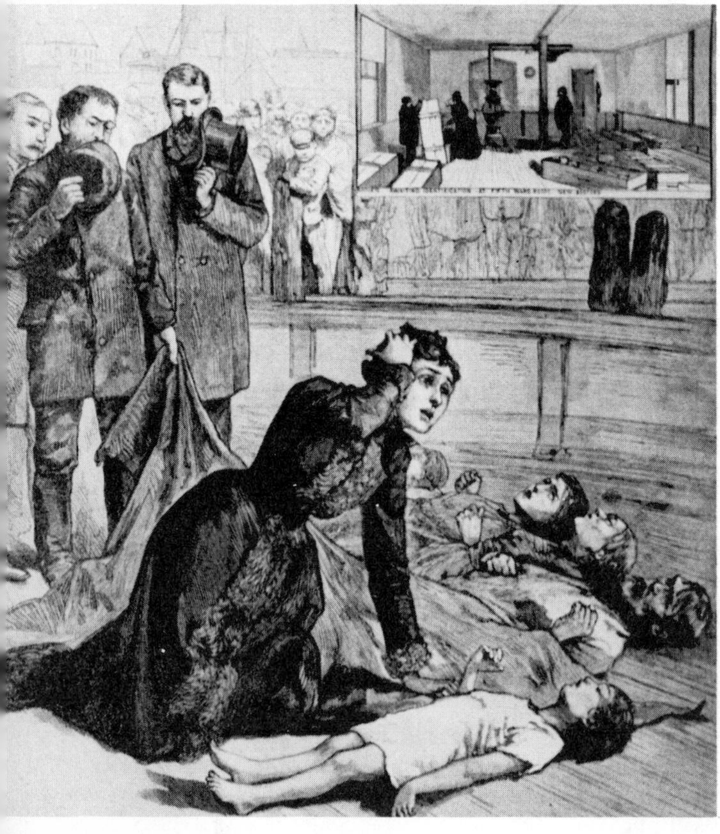

CITY OF BOSTON — MARINE DISASTER

January 31, 1870

After leaving New York on January 25, 1870, with 191 crew and passengers, the American steamer, *City of Boston,* was sighted off Halifax three days later, but nothing of the ship or her crew was ever heard again. A steam and sailing vessel, the *City of Boston,* early on January 31, 1870, was thought to have been the victim of a hurricane that swept the seas about Sable Island, long a disastrous stretch of water, the depths of which are laced with hundreds of sunken ships.

Though sailing in heavily trafficked sea lanes, the *City of Boston* was extremely well built and more than adequately endowed with lifesaving equipment. The ship was seen only once on that last day of January. The schooner *Charles Tupper* was fighting to stay afloat in the hurricane when her master, Captain Hackett, spotted to the southward of Sable Island, "a steamer, which threw up rockets three times and shifted her position round all points of the compass, so that I could not make out her position."

This eerie storm sighting is reminiscent of the controversial story of the freighter *California,* which was trapped in an Atlantic ice field near the doomed *Titanic* and watched the fiery rockets signaling her distress a few miles away.

The vanishing of the *City of Boston* remains one of the great mysteries of the sea.

(ALSO SEE: Titanic)

CITY OF COLUMBUS — MARINE DISASTER

January 18, 1884

background: The *City of Columbus,* built in 1878 by John Roach and Son, was a fixture of the Savannah line. The ship displaced 1,999 tons, was 270 feet long, had a 30-foot beam, was built at a cost of $300,000 and insured for $244,980. Sailing from Boston, the ship hit the reef of Devil's Bridge buoy in a storm near Martha's Vineyard, Massachusetts, on January 18, 1884, and foundered for many hours. Out of the 126 persons on board the passenger ship, only 29 survived.

It was one of the most terrifying stories of the sea. The proud *City of Columbus,* a luxury liner of its day in every sense, set sail from Boston on January 16, 1884, moving out into tranquil waters toward its destination, Savannah, Georgia. At 3:45 A.M. the following Friday morning, the steam-and-sail vessel, after passing the most dangerous point in a channel near Martha's Vineyard, struck the reef at the Devil's Bridge buoy off Gay Head promontory.

A gale raked the length of the ship and great waves lashed at her. Water gushed into the main hold, and on that bitterly cold and dark winter morning passengers and crew began the struggle to save their lives.

With the water rushing down the decks, passengers shaken awake by the impact partially dressed and dashed from their staterooms. Women and children, who lacked the strength to hold on to lifelines, were the first victims of the wreck. Within twenty minutes of the crash all the eighteen women and several children on board were swept away by the storm.

One wife embraced her husband in rushed goodbyes and both were torn into the raging sea. A woman carrying her infant child and running up the stairs was washed overboard; neither was seen again. The next day, the body of a woman floated to the southeastern end of Martha's Vineyard. Frozen to the front of her dress was a pair of tiny shoes, all that remained of her child who had been ripped from her fierce grasp.

The crew behaved badly from the start. It was clear to the passengers that, above all, the sailors were interested in saving their own lives. The first lifeboat lowered by frantically shouting crewmen went down bow first and was smashed to splinters against the hull of the ship. The second was freed so haphazardly that it drifted out to sea empty. A third was lowered so rapidly that crewmen jumped into it before it hit the water and capsized it.

The last boat was lowered safely, and several officers and sailors, their backs purposely turned away from the fast-disintegrating *City of Columbus,* headed for shore without a single pleading passenger. (None of these men were ever tried for desertion.)

About forty men, all that remained of the passengers on the wallowing ship, struggled up the rigging and clung to frozen ropes that were wind-whipped about the masts. One survivor stated: "To the men in the rigging it became a test of endurance against death."

When dawn broke the storm was still upon them, pounding the *City of Columbus* to slivers. The smokestack gave away, breaking in two and taking with it several men who clung with frozen hands to the stays about it. Six men jumped into the rigging and squirmed upward, when the wheelhouse they were lying on collapsed.

"They were in all sorts of positions," the survivor elaborated. "Two were supported upon a loose swinging rope between the masts. They dangled there in the wind for hours, with the rope supporting them under their armpits. The gale swung them back and forth like clothes upon a clothes line, while the spray of every wave breaking over the ship drenched them. They grew numb, and probably died as they hung, the stiffening in their muscles in the cold holding them in place. One of them was swept away about nine o'clock, and the other disappeared at about eleven."

There were only about twenty men left alive holding on, one above another, in the crosstrees of the masts. When some of them attempted to sit on the ropes and put their legs through the crosstrees, their legs froze.

Two of these men, looking down, cried out in anguish, for directly below them floated the corpses of their young wives. They watched the bodies until they drifted out to sea and disappeared. Their tears froze in rivulets of ice to their cheeks.

A band of Indians, rowing furiously against the roaring tide, bravely set out from Gay Head Point and attempted to reach the remains of the *City of Columbus.* When it became apparent to those still alive in the rigging that they would have to make a swim for it, the survivors jumped from their perches into the ocean below. Only seven heads surfaced—the strongest of the group—and these men swam leadenly to the boat and were taken aboard. They lived.

It became the grim chore of those on land to count the dead (ninety-seven men, women and children were listed as lost) and identify the bloated bodies washing up on the beach all that week. These included some noteworthy victims: the Reverend C. A. Rand, Dean of the Episcopal clergy of the Eastern Convocation; his brother, the famous lawyer Edward S. Rand; renowned manufacturer of agricultural implements Joel Nourse; and Oscar Tasigi, consul-general to Turkey.

CITY OF PORTLAND — MARINE DISASTER

November 26, 1898

background: The $250,000 sidepaddle steamer *City of Portland,* built at Bath in 1890, displaced 1,517 tons, was 230 feet long and had a 42-foot beam. Departing from Boston at 7:00 P.M. on the evening of November 26, 1898, under the command of Captain Blanchard, the ship, bound for Portland with 157 passengers and crew and carrying 100 tons of merchandise, was caught up in a gale two hours later and foundered. All on board perished.

The gale that blew against the sea walls of Massachusetts Bay on the night of November 26, 1898, was one of the worst in weather history to that date, with winds measured up to 70 m.p.h. The *City of Portland,* commanded by veteran Captain Blanchard, was a steam sidewheeler destined that night for Portland, Maine.

B. Lincoln, manager of the steamship line, had been studying weather reports all day and informed his Boston agent, a man named Williams, to tell Captain Blanchard to postpone sailing until weather permitted. The message was sent along. Yet, with the storm raging along the New England coast, Blanchard ordered the *City of Portland,* its holds crammed with 100 tons of lard and its cabins full of passengers, to sail.

For two hours the lumbering steamship, fighting near-hurricane winds, nosed its way far out into the bay.

A fisherman last saw her being buffeted wildly by towering sea walls as the steamship lurched past Thacher's Island. Then she disappeared. Her broad, almost unseaworthy hull, many experts agreed, was probably not up to battling the raging ocean, and she soon foundered, around 9:00 P.M., in what was termed "the graveyard" near Cape Cod. None of her 157 passengers and crewmen were ever seen alive again, but dozens of bodies did float to shore the following morning. The first was a black deck hand with a life preserver marked "City of Portland" encircling his waist.

Dr. Maurice Richardson stepped from his summer home at Wellfleet, walked to the storm-gouged beach and began to turn over bodies collected there like so much driftwood. "One was probably that of a deckhand . . . the other body was that of a stout woman. She, too, wore a lifebelt with the steamer's name on it. Wreckage was coming ashore for fifteen miles along the coast. I picked up three piano keys and a piano cage, but, of course, I do not know if they were from the *Portland* [they were from the ship's saloon]. Among the wreckage was a large quantity of furniture upholstered in red plush. Then there were the cases of lard directed to Portland."

At Orleans, the body of a girl about twenty washed ashore. She, too, wore a life preserver marked "City of Portland," and it appeared that before the ship went down there was an attempt to take to the lifeboats. The girl, never identified, wore a ring marked "J.G.E." and a gold watch that had stopped at 9:17 P.M.

The body of Captain Blanchard was never recovered. His disobedience to orders was curtly reported by Williams to Manager Lincoln.

"Did you give him my order not to sail?" Lincoln asked Williams at a hearing.

"Yes, to his face."

"What did the captain say?"

"He said: 'I think not. I am sailing at 7 o'clock.' And he did."

CLEO — HURRICANE
August 22-27, 1964

Caribbean-born hurricane Cleo rampaged through the islands for four days, beginning on August 22, 1964. Its 100 m.p.h. winds hurled storm waves hardest against the silky shores of Guadaloupe and Haiti. Hours later, 120 persons were dragged from beneath the debris that had crushed them to death. By the time Cleo roared ashore on August 27, at densely populated Miami, Florida, her winds were estimated to be in excess of 135 m.p.h.

Hurricane Cleo's 135 m.p.h. winds littered Miami's streets with debris on August 27, 1964, and killed 138. *(Wide World)*

Miami's swanky Gold Coast hotels met the face of the storm and instantly became a shambles of broken glass. This decorous debris littered the wind-slashed beaches for many days. More than 1,200 homes and offices were damaged. At the marinas boats and yachts were overturned, sunk or smashed. The damages raced up to $200 million. Worse, 13 more persons were killed, bringing Cleo's death toll to 138.

CLEVELAND NATIONAL FOREST

FIRE
November 25, 1956

"I've never seen anything like this fire. It burns without a sound. There isn't a bit of moisture in the underbrush to cause crackling." This is how firefighting specialist Ralph L. Fenner described the soaring, avaricious blaze that tore through Cleveland National Forest on November 25, 1956, destroying 40,000 acres and killing eleven men.

Fenner spoke for the more than 1,400 men who fought the fire for three days from the mountaintop hamlet of Julian, California, to the town of Lakeside, a San Diego suburb. "Until the winds die down or shift, or unless it rains, the whole United States Air Force and one hundred million dollars can't stop this fire."

At one point dozens of men were driven against a perpendicular clay cliff by the flames while they attempted to build a backfire. All but eleven men—three United States Forest Service employees, seven county prisoners and a guard—escaped. Others who successfully dashed through the flames turned to watch the trapped men, unable to scale the cliff, as they were engulfed by the fire and died shrieking. The prisoners had volunteered to fight the fire.

Two days later, after the fire had burned itself out and blackened the most verdant area of the forest, United States Forest Investigator Elwood Stone detained a sixteen-year-old Inaja Indian named Gilbert Paipa, who admitted setting the fire. "I just got a crazy idea to throw a match in the grass to see if it would burn," Paipa said.

CLEVELAND, OHIO

FIRE
May 15, 1929

At that time one of the most modern hospitals in the country, the Cleveland Clinic became a smoking deathtrap for a host of patients when a fire broke out on May 15, 1929, in the X-ray room. (X-ray film was made of nitrocellulose, which proved highly noxious when ignited.)

Seconds after the fire broke out, nurses and doctors attempted to close allegedly fireproof doors. They would not budge. The hospital's large supply of X-ray film burned instantly, sending clouds of poisonous gas into the corridors. The staff members scrambled to place patients on rolling stretchers, but only a few were available. The gases found most of the patients before the nurses did, and 121 were asphyxiated.

(ALSO SEE: Paisley, Scotland)

Fire in the X-ray room of the Cleveland Clinic in 1929 caused the deaths of 121 persons. *(UPI)*

CLEVELAND RURAL GRADE SCHOOL

FIRE
May 17, 1923

background: Fire broke out on the second story of the Cleveland Rural Grade School on May 17, 1923, while children were enacting a play. The school, about six miles from Camden, South Carolina, quickly burned to the ground. In a wild attempt to escape the burning second floor seventy-six persons, forty-one of them children, were burned or crushed to death.

"Miss Topsy-Turvy" was in progress, and to the delight of their parents, eight young school children were performing on the stage of the Cleveland Rural Grade School on the night of May 17, 1923. The school was six miles from Camden, South Carolina, and the small auditorium in which the play was being presented was on the second floor of the two-story frame building.

All the lights in the auditorium were out except a small kerosene lamp hanging behind a gauzelike curtain on stage which threw its yellow rays upon the diminutive actors. In the rush of changing scenes the lamp was knocked from its holder, and it exploded into flames when it hit the stage.

The audience, mostly parents, rose quickly, but several older boys on stage assured their fathers they could easily extinguish the flames. Dozens of parents, as

Stunned parents and bystanders walk through the gutted ruins of the Cleveland Rural Grade School outside of Camden, South Carolina, where seventy-six persons burned to death on May 17, 1923. *(UPI)*

a precaution, walked quietly down the stairs and waited in a hallway. The flames, however, were out of control.

Screams from children and women burst forth, and a general panic ensued with everyone still on the second floor racing to the narrow stairway that had two small landings. The parents already downstairs unthinkingly rushed up the stairs to retrieve their children. Both groups met at the second landing. By that time the entire building was aflame.

Dozens of struggling persons wedged themselves so tightly together on the landing that it became impossible to move. The weight was also too much for the ancient structure, and the stairway collapsed in burning splinters. Seeing this, many mothers herded their children to the second-floor windows of the school. They broke open the locked windows with their fists and with bloody hands held out their children to those waiting beneath.

Scores of men caught the children, whose clothing was already on fire. The men outside realized that the weight of the adults jumping from the windows would be too much for them to handle, so they ripped automobile seats from their parked cars and placed them beneath the windows. Most of the adults who jumped survived without injuries.

The worst calamity took place on the stairway just before it collapsed. Here mothers held on to their children and burned to death. Later one woman was found with "the stumps of her arms near the charred bodies of two children" she had been protecting. A black girl taking care of a small white child was found burned to death with her arms still locked about her charge.

Of the eight children acting in the play, four died on stage in the flames. Of the 300 persons in the building, 76 died. Fifty men, women and children were buried in a single grave the following day.

Ironically, the school, which collapsed inward within five minutes of the fire's eruption, had been condemned, and the play was to be the last held in the old building; the new one, already built, awaited pupils for the next term.

(ALSO SEE: Babb Switch School, Iroquois Theater, Our Lady of the Angels School)

COCOANUT GROVE — FIRE

November 28, 1942

background: Boston's Cocoanut Grove nightclub, jammed to twice its capacity—more than 1,000—caught fire on November 11, 1942, through accident, as a result of inadequate fire exits and a lack of fire-resistant materials, coupled with the *en masse* panic of patrons, 491 persons burned to death.

It was Saturday night and the bistros in Boston's South End were teeming with revelers, servicemen and civilians alike in this war year. The Cocoanut Grove, a sprawling cabaret which boasted three bars, a main dining room for dancing and an impressive floor show, was jammed to the hilt. More than 1,000 persons thronged inside to its bars and struggled on its postage-stamp dance floor. The Grove's legal capacity was 500 patrons, and in addition to its two-level construction, it was, thanks to its highly flammable accoutrements, a firetrap.

For all of its popularity and fame, the Grove was only an inch above the typical sleezy clubs that lined Tremont Street. Built by gangsters during Prohibition, the Cocoanut Grove's three cocktail lounges and main cabaret area were decked out in cloth ceilings, leather-faced walls and, at almost every table and chair, cheaply constructed artificial palm trees.

The Grove was unusually packed this night, its normally heavy crowd padded by hundreds of collegiate football fans celebrating the outcome of the day's game. Buck Jones, the silent screen cowboy star, and a group of people had just taken their showside seats while chorines tittered his name in the wings and prepared to swing into their dance routines.

Downstairs in the heavily decorated Melody Lounge, a basement appendix to the club, a sixteen-year-old busboy watched a patron reach up and unscrew a light fixture, obviously preferring a subtler light in which to woo his date. The busboy clucked his tongue and looked at his watch. It was a few minutes before 10:00 P.M. He was going to have a long night.

Balancing on a chair in the darkened corner, the busboy reached upward to insert a new lightbulb in the fixture. He held a lighted match. It burned his fingers and he dropped it into an artificial palm tree, which immediately burst into flames.

"Fire!" a woman's piercing voice announced. Panic followed instantly. Dozens jumped from their small tables and, in doing so, knocked more artificial palm trees into those already burning. The leather-lined walls were burning; the cloth ceiling was burning. Then people began to burn as one hundred persons, like a giant wedge of struggling flesh, attempted to get up the stairs. The fire was ahead of them, working its way up the ceiling of the stairs into the main cabaret and shooting into two more lounges—the Broadway Cocktail Lounge and the Caricature Bar.

Just before the floorshow was about to go on, a woman, her hair and dress ablaze, raced screaming into the main cabaret area, lighting up the linen cloths on tables as she passed. Poisonous smoke and gases gushed everywhere, overcoming scores of panic-stricken customers looking for exits.

Those attempting to escape the downstairs Melody Lounge packed the stairs and a long corridor on the main floor that led to a locked door. They jammed themselves too tightly against this door that there was no room to turn. More than a hundred were roasted; more were crushed to death.

Passers-by outside were alarmed to see basement windows being smashed and desperate men and women climbing out, their expensive evening gowns and tuxedoes singed and ripped. These were the lucky few, level-headed survivors from the Melody Lounge. Others on the street floor came diving through windows from the Caricature Bar and the Broadway Cocktail Lounge. The door leading from the latter opened inward, and when the crazed crowd dashed for it, they piled up against it like driftwood, blocking it. A hundred charred corpses were found there.

Ear-bursting pandemonium was rampant in the main cabaret area. Many who fell in the panic were crushed to death. Some were murdered, it was later claimed, by patrons driven insane by the heat and fire who, using chairs and bottles, tried to club their way to the outside. A stampede smashed against the Grove's revolving door, jamming it. Two hundred died in the main cabaret area.

A total of 491 humans died in this holocaust, and several hundred more were either crippled or scarred for life. The Cocoanut Grove was no more. It died of fire inside of two minutes.

Smoke billows from the Cocoanut Grove, a Boston nightclub, November 28, 1942, where 491 revelers were trapped and burned to death. *(Wide World)*

Firemen inspect the highly flammable materials in one of the Grove's bars. *(Wide World)*

A flash flood caused the railroad bridge across Cole Creek to collapse, sending several cars of the CB&Q line into the water, killing thirty-one passengers. *(UPI)*

COLE CREEK, WYOMING **RAILWAY WRECK**
September 27, 1923

At approximately 8:00 P.M., September 27, 1923, a railway inspector tramped across the trestle bridge spanning Cole Creek that skirted the small town of Lockett, Wyoming. He meticulously checked the bridge girders and supports. "It's fine," he said to an aide and moved off.

An hour and fifteen minutes later a speeding passenger train of the Chicago, Burlington & Quincy line rushed across the bridge, and, to the horror of those on board, plunged downward into the creek. The bridge collapsed under the weight of the train, and car after car squealed its way downward, slipping into the murky, roaring stream. Disappearing almost immediately were the locomotive, tender, mail car, baggage car, parlor and smoker cars, followed by the first of three Pullmans at the end of the train.

There was no time for panic or distress on the part of the passengers. They were under water too fast. It was a quick drowning for thirty-one of eighty passengers whose unlucky circumstances caused them to be riding the train that night.

The flash flood of Cole Creek apparently had occurred when a river reservoir held back by a sand bar gave way, and the resulting avalanche of waters tore loose the girders of the bridge. A half-dozen bodies were carried in the quick flood many miles south to the Platte River and were discovered floating there days later. Those corpses trapped inside the submerged cars were not recovered for close to a week, until the flood ebbed. Several cars, it was discovered, were buried to their roofs in mud. It was one of the quickest disasters on record—about twenty seconds.

(ALSO SEE: Ashtabula, Ohio)

COLOMBIA, SOUTH AMERICA **EARTHQUAKE**
May 15, 1875

An earthquake lasting forty-five seconds ripped through Colombia on May 15, 1875, and shattered Santiago, San Cayetano and several other towns. In Cucuta (in the Republic of Santander) residents reported a local volcano erupting at the same time as the earthquake, throwing out huge fireballs that smashed and burned all the churches and business buildings in the city.

The total fatalities throughout Colombia, mostly along the Venezuelan frontier, numbered more than 16,000.

COLOMBIAN MILITARY PLANE **AIR CRASH**
July 24, 1938

"I do not like the stunting of the aviators over the crowd," Dr. Eduardo Santos, president-elect of Colombia, remarked to War Minister Alberto Pumarejo. As he spoke on that hot afternoon of July 24, 1938, several Colombian military planes were performing aerial stunts to commemorate the new Campo de Marte, a military exercise field.

Looping and banking sharply, the planes whined dangerously close to the stands, which contained more than 50,000 jubilant spectators. The planes, as if dueling, came closer and closer to earth with each pass, slicing through the wild cheers of the masses.

"They are much too close," Pumarejo said to Santos, and he motioned for an aide to order the planes to break off the acrobatics. At that moment a plane flown by a Lieutenant Abadia attempted to pass between two of the reviewing stands, flying no higher than ninety feet. Abadia's plane rolled sideways, and the wingtip struck one of the stands, sheered away a set of steps and burst into flames. (Abadia was incinerated.)

The shrieks of hundreds of viewers in the plane's fiery path mingled with the sound of the crash. The plane tore through a metal roof on one stand and then burst into flaming, scythelike bits through the crowd, its propellers still spinning wildly, cutting down dozens and decapitating several.

In panic the terrorized spectators bolted onto the field, many with their clothes on fire. Santos and dozens of other dignitaries narrowly missed being struck by the flying debris, but fifty-three persons were, hours later, listed as dead on this one hundred fifty-fifth anniversary of the birth of the South American liberator, Simon Bolivar.

COLORADO — FLOODS

June 16-26, 1965

In a very bad flood the Arkansas River and several others overflowed, bringing $102 million in damages to Colorado in June, 1965. Also hard hit were the states of Montana, Kansas, Wyoming and New Mexico. Twenty-three persons were killed, fourteen of these in Colorado.

The town of Wiggins was inundated and Fort Morgan, Brush and Sterling, all in northeastern Colorado, were hard-pressed by the rising floods. In Denver the flood waters covered a mile-wide area of city streets. North of Denver, two boys on horses were swept away by the South Platte River. The horses reappeared riderless in the surging waters.

The Arkansas's raging waters rushed through Dodge City, Kansas. Claude Fare and three other employees endured a horrible experience in Dodge City when the water rushed into the Peoples Gas Company building. "In a matter of five minutes," Fare later recalled, "we were standing in water to our waists. The water soon reached the ceilings, which are nine feet. We crawled up to the building's roof from the back and stayed there until we were rescued by boat."

COLUMBIA — MARINE DISASTER

July 20, 1907

The passenger steamer *Columbia,* operated by the San Francisco and Portland Steamship Company, sailed off its course on the night of July 20, 1907, lost in a dense fog rolling along the California coast. The ship, carrying 249 persons, smashed without warning into the steamer *San Pedro* and disappeared beneath the waves in minutes. Quick action by *San Pedro*'s crew members who lowered lifeboats immediately saved 149 persons on board the *Columbia;* 100 were lost.

COLUMBIA — MARINE DISASTER

July 5, 1918

The ancient sternwheeler *Columbia,* which ran summer excursions along the Illinois River, had been condemned as unfit eight years before it sank on July 5, 1918. The vessel regularly sprang leaks, and the wooden timbers supporting its decks had been rotten for years. Crammed with close to 500 persons, the *Columbia,* making its way along a wide stretch of the Illinois waterway in dense fog, struck a submerged object (probably a small logjam) and broke it in half, drowning 87 persons. The disaster could have resulted in a greater loss of life but for the fact that the ship sank in shallow water and the banks of Pekin, Illinois, were close at hand for survivors to reach.

COLUMBIA RIVER — FLOOD

May-June, 1948

background: In May and June of 1948 the Columbia River basin inundated great portions of British Columbia, Washington and Oregon causing $100 million in damages and killing fifty-one persons.

The most disastrous flood of the Columbia River in this century occurred in May-June, 1948, when temperatures in the nearby mountain ranges remained below average, not allowing snow to melt at the usual rate. When the weather did turn warm, this snow, egged on by three days of intense rain, flooded the basin. The Clark, Oreille and Spokane rivers burst their banks and broke through decades-old dikes. Then the huge Columbia River dashed over its banks at Hanford, Washington, which was soon under water. Within a matter of hours more than 5,000 persons fled.

Station master Sidney Jacobs wades through the deserted Union Station, Portland, Oregon, during the floods of June 1948. *(UPI)*

By the time the floodwaters of the Columbia reached Vanport City, Oregon, its waters were estimated to be rushing forward at one million cubic feet per second. The city was evacuated on May 30, when a dike near a railroad embankment burst. All 19,000 residents of the town raced by car, bicycle and foot from the area with no more "than the clothing they were wearing."

Every house not immediately broken up by the towering wall of water that crashed over the city was, within minutes, floating in fourteen feet of water.

Portland, Oregon, was saved by thousands of troops from the Army Corps of Engineers and thousands of civilians who worked day and night on temporary sandbag dikes. More than $3 million in relief foodstuffs was supplied by the Red Cross in Washington and Oregon alone. When the floodwaters finally receded, fifty-one bodies, mostly in dozens of flooded Oregon towns, were counted.

COLUMBUS, NEW JERSEY — RAILWAY WRECK
August 29, 1855

Of the many causes of train derailments, none are so frightening as those involving people attempting to cross tracks in the face of on-coming locomotives. Since the birth of train travel, such accidents have strewn the tracks with the mutilated dead and the twisted remains of once-elegant passenger cars. At the beginning, railway lines made serious attempts to ward off such mishaps by directing engineers to ring their bells at all crossings, as did the Boston and Worcester line in 1835; by employing whistles—the first steam whistle was installed on the engine "Sandusky" by Thomas Rogers in 1837; and by using headlights, first kerosene lamps and, after 1900, electric beams.

Yet the accident toll mounted despite such precautions. In the early days of train travel, when speed was limited, almost all the fatalities involved in such accidents were those at crossings.

One such victim was a seventy-five-year-old Aaron Pratt, who was deaf. He was killed at the Framington, Massachusetts, station in 1839. He simply did not hear the clanging bell of the oncoming train. "I am grieved to say," the Framington stationmaster wrote to his superiors, "that our gravel train, in coming into the depot this forenoon, ran over Mr. Aaron Pratt, a worthy citizen of this village. . . . Four of the cars passed over his body, and he was instantly killed. . . ."

By the 1850's, with trains running at higher speeds, deaths in large numbers began to involve passengers. One of the first crossing disasters involved two trains crossing each other's path near Chicago at Grand Crossing on April 25, 1853. A Toledo-bound express failed to stop and yield the right-of-way to a slow-moving local carrying dozens of immigrant workers to the city. The fast-moving express smashed at top speed into the side of the local, derailing it and ripping its wooden cars to pieces. Twenty-one people, mostly immigrants who cried out their agony in foreign tongues, died.

One survivor described the carnage as "an immense heap of iron splinters, doors, and baggage with the crushed locomotive of the express train hissing steam from its ruptured boiler. . . . Time will not efface the memory of that terrible and heart-rending spectacle from the mind of the unwilling beholder. A heap of ruins, from beneath which shrieked out upon the midnight air cries for help, mingled in strong discord with the deeper groans of the dying. . . ."

A similar, more destructive crossing derailment happened at Columbus, New Jersey, on August 29, 1855. Hot, late morning sun beat down on Dr. John T. Hannigan as he steered his team of horses en route to a house call in nearby Burlington.

Mrs. Mary Cook, a crossing guard, became frantic at Dr. Hannigan's approach. From where she stood she could see a Camden & Amboy train backing at high speed toward the crossing. Mrs. Cook violently waved her guard's flag in Hannigan's direction. Not until the last moment did the doctor notice Mrs. Cook or the oncoming train.

He jerked at the reins so hard that the horses bolted forward in front of the train. One horse was struck, pulled under the train and derailed three cars which tumbled awkwardly down a steep embankment, their flimsy wooden frames breaking up almost immediately. Twenty-three persons were killed in their seats. Hannigan survived by leaping out of the way at the last minute.

"I don't understand it," the engineer said minutes later as he surveyed the incredible damage done by one dead horse. "I yanked that whistle until my hand was raw from the rope." Such warnings, however, were useless to Dr. Hannigan. He, like Aaron Pratt, was deaf.

CONCEPCION, CHILE — EARTHQUAKE
1757

The earthquake that struck Concepcion in the summer of 1757 was scantily recorded, but one report stated that half the city was "sunk beneath the waves" of a seismic sea wall. About 5,000 persons were killed, and twice as many were injured during the quake.

Reporting from the scene of the disaster a religious historian, Daniel Riquelme, wrote: ". . . the net moral result of that distressing time was that the blasphemy

Amid the ruins of Concepcion, Chile, stand the remains of its grand cathedral. The city was destroyed by an earthquake in 1835.

and immorality and drunkenness of the men and the indecency in the dress of the women was put away for a long time, and four hundred couples, who had been living in sin, went to the priests to have a true marriage rite performed."

CONCEPCION, CHILE — EARTHQUAKE — February 20, 1835

More than 5,000 people in Concepcion and Santiago, Chile, met violent, quick death when an earthquake struck on February 20, 1835.

One of the most astute firsthand reports of any early quake was provided by Charles Darwin, who at the time was traveling with Captain Fitzroy on the *Beagle.* Darwin later aptly observed that "a bad earthquake at once destroys our oldest associations: the earth, the very emblem of solidity, has moved beneath our feet like a thin crust over a fluid; one second of time has created in the mind a strange idea of insecurity, which hours of reflection would not have produced."

Going ashore at the small coastal hamlet of Talcahuano, the young Darwin proceeded to Concepcion. His findings were later related in his book, *Journal of Research.* "Both towns presented the most awful yet interesting spectacle I ever beheld." He reported: ". . .the earthquake commenced at half past eleven in the forenoon. If it had happened in the middle of the night, the greater number of the inhabitants . . . must have perished, instead of less than a hundred: as it was, the invariable practice of running out of doors at the first trembling of the ground alone saved them. In Concepcion each house, or row of houses stood by itself, a heap or a line of ruins; but in Talcahuano, owing to the great wave, little more than one layer of bricks, tiles and timber, with here and there part of a wall left standing, could be distinguished.

"From this circumstance Concepcion, although not so completely desolated, was a more terrible, and if I may so call it, picturesque sight. The first shock was very sudden. The major-domo at Quiriquina told me that the first notice he received of it was finding both the horse he rode and himself rolling together on the ground. Rising up, he was again thrown down. He also told me that some cows which were standing on the steep side of the island were rolled into the sea. The great wave caused the destruction of many cattle; on one low island near the head of the bay, seventy animals were washed off and drowned. . . .

"As shock succeeded shock at the interval of a few minutes, no one dared approach the shattered ruins; and no one knew whether his dearest friends and relations were not perishing from the want of help. Those who had saved any property were obliged to keep a constant watch, for thieves prowled about, and at each little trembling of the grounds, with one hand they beat their breasts and cried 'misericordia' and then with the other filched what they could from the ruins. The thatched roofs fell over the fires, and flames burst forth in all parts. Hundreds knew themselves ruined, and few had the means of providing food for the day."

In awe, Darwin, Fitzroy and others watched as a colossal seismic seawave neared the Chilean coastline.

Darwin wrote: "Shortly after the shock a great wave was seen from a distance of three or four miles, approaching in the middle of the bay with a smooth outline; but along the shore it tore up cottages and trees, as it swept onwards with irresistible force. At the head of the bay it broke into a fearful line of white breakers, which rushed up to a height of twenty-three vertical feet above the highest spring tides.

"Their force must have been prodigious; for at the Fort a cannon with its carriage, estimated a four tons in weight, was moved fifteen feet inwards. A schooner was left in the midst of the ruins, 200 yards from the beach. The first wave was followed by two others, which in their retreat carried away a vast wreck of floating objects. In one part of the bay, a ship was pitched high and dry on shore, was carried off, again driven on shore, and again carried off. In another part two large vessels anchored near together were whirled about, and their cables were thrice wound round each other; though anchored at a depth of thirty-six feet, they were for some minutes aground.

"The great waves must have travelled slowly, for the inhabitants of Talcahuano had time to run up the hills behind the town; and some sailors pulled out seaward, trusting successfully to their boat riding securely over the swell, if they could reach it before it broke. One old woman with a little boy, four or five years old, ran into a boat, but there was nobody to row it out; the boat was consequently dashed against an anchor and cut in twain; the old woman was drowned but the child was picked up some hours afterwards clinging to the wreck."

CONNEAUT, OHIO — RAILWAY WRECK

March 27, 1953

Speeding east on the New York Central Railroad near Conneaut, Ohio, on the night of March 27, 1953, a fast freight train suddenly began to disgorge stacks of metal pipes that broke loose from one of its gondola cars. A westbound freight passed the eastbound freight, and the flagman noticed the pipes flying onto the opposite tracks. He leaped into the caboose and returned holding a lantern with which he frantically attempted to signal the passenger train coming up the same track, the elegant *Mohawk,* speeding along at 76 m.p.h.

A three-train collision at Conneaut, Ohio, caused the deaths of twenty-one persons on March 27, 1953. *(Wide World)*

The *Mohawk* did not see the signal and smashed into a loose pipe lying at awkward angles along the tracks, causing it to derail and veer into the last cars of the eastbound freight. The eastbound freight was also derailed.

Moments after this crash, the *Southwestern Limited,* roaring eastward at 70 m.p.h. with a full load of passengers, crashed into the wreckage of the *Mohawk* and the eastbound freight. The wreckage was immense. The *Mohawk* lost its first six cars, which were totally destroyed. Completely demolished also were the first two cars of the *Southwestern Limited* and several more cars were derailed.

Frenzied rescuers dragged hundreds from the passenger cars, their steel frames twisted and shredded. Hours later, authorities counted twenty-one bodies from the wreckage of all three trains, proving it to be one of the worst train disasters in New York Central's history.

CONNIE (and DIANE) HURRICANES

August 4-18, 1955

background: Hurricane Connie, born in the Atlantic, was first spotted about seven hundred miles east of the French West Indies on August 4, 1955, with winds measured at 100 m.p.h. and struck the Atlantic wall, her fury spending itself on the Carolinas, Delaware, New York and Connecticut the hardest before dissipating in Pennsylvania. Immediately following Connie came Hurricane Diane, sweeping in from the Atlantic out of the Bermuda area on August 11, 1955, and, combined with gale winds at Connie's outer fringe, it devastated the Carolinas, Virginia, Maryland, Pennsylvania, New Jersey, New York and New England. An estimated $1.5 billion in damage and 310 deaths were attributed to the two hurricanes, the worst to visit the Atlantic seacoast in this century.

Hurricane Connie was first spotted well into the Atlantic on August 4, 1955, when a Navy Neptune plane flew into its eye and measured its winds at 125 m.p.h. The Weather Bureau and the Red Cross warned of its severity, and by the time the hurricane lashed onto the beaches of the Carolinas, thousands had already fled inland. Connie drove ten-foot swells of water into Wilmington, North Carolina, wrecked Myrtle Beach, South Carolina, and struck down everything in its path along Pamlico Sound.

At New Bern, North Carolina, forty-one deaths by drowning, auto crashes and electrocution (after the electric and power systems were smashed by the storm) were recorded on August 11-12. Terrific rains driven by gale winds blew through New York, and Connie then moved into Pennsylvania. At its tail came Hurricane Diane, even more powerful and deadly.

Diane tore along the same path taken by Connie but continued up the New England coastline and went back out to sea off Boston. Before it moved off, the hurricane flooded almost all the Connecticut rivers, particularly the Naugatuck, Still and Mad rivers. The Mad River, bloated by Diane's rains and winds, tore through Winsted, flooding the town with twelve feet of water. The coffins of Revolutionary soldiers were torn from the antique graveyards of Woonsocket, Rhode Island, and sent floating down raging rivers. The most bizarre incident occurred in Putnam, Connecticut, when the roaring waters smashed a magnesium plant and carried off hundreds of barrels of burning magnesium, which floated menacingly down the town's flooded streets, exploding unexpectedly and sending showers of white-hot metal 250 feet in the air.

Massachusetts was also devastated, and before Diane returned to the sea she splintered the historic fifty-foot bridge across the Concord River where "the shot heard round the world" was fired. President Eisenhower declared six eastern states disaster areas, and money, food and supplies, thanks to newly coordinated relief systems on the part of local, state, federal and private organizations, were made available immediately.

The damage, estimated at $1.5 billion, was never fully repaired. There were 310 dead.

CONSTANTINOPLE, TURKEY FIRE

August 16, 1848

The triple metropolises of Constantinople, Galata and Pera had suffered a long, dry summer of intense heat in 1848. On the evening of August 16, with no wind whatsoever rustling through the dark cypress coves standing like black marble, a column of smoke rose out of the dried fruit bazaar in Constantinople. At first authorities and firemen had trouble locating the fire. Alarm guns were sounded at 7:30 P.M., and this added to the general confusion as residents, particularly the poor, ran in all directions, spreading panic and fear through the city.

By 8:00 P.M. the Yagh Kapan region, where there were oil depots, lumberyards and warehouses stacked with flammable materials, was ablaze. The whole city was soon burning. The *London Morning Herald*'s correspondent wrote: "Kaiks darted in all directions over the Golden Horn, some containing a few curious and idle foreigners, rowing along the shore to view the scene, others transporting from the flames what property had been saved. The towers, the mosques, with their elegant and delicate minarets, the reflection of the roofs of houses, and minute lines of carved woodwork in the windows, were discernible from a great distance, on account of the blaze of light that filled the heavens. Among the many sights that such scenes necessarily

Constantinople's Yagh Kapan district burned on August 16, 1848. The Sultan and his friends viewed the inferno from his private steamer in the bay. *(Illustrated London News)*

The Sultan amused himself by traversing the ruins of Constantinople while wearing a disguise. *(Illustrated London News)*

furnish to the observer, none were more striking than the innumerable groups congregated in the burying grounds that line the declivities of Pera, from whence an excellent view of the fire could be obtained."

Separate fires joined together to make great pyramids of flames in the night sky. While Constantinople burned, wealthy merchants, whose homes and businesses were protected by private firemen, and English women, attired as if for a ball or play, sat together sipping aperitifs and watching the fire. The Sultan also watched. At 2:00 A.M. the fire, unaffected by the puny efforts of scampering firemen, died out when it had no more fuel on which to feed.

Officials carefully inspected the ruins and counted more than 200 bodies in the slum district of Oun Kapan. They then counted more than 2,500 ruined shops. They set the then-staggering amount of damage at $15 million, which would be fifty times that sum today.

Wearing a disguise, the Sultan, accompanied by dozens of guards, toured the devastated area, which consisted of about half of Constantinople. He then retired to his private steamer anchored nearby and had deck chairs placed on the bridge so he and his guests could observe the inhabitants seeking lost children and rummaging through the ruins.

CONSTANTINOPLE, TURKEY — FIRE

June 5, 1870

It was Sunday, June 5, 1870, and a great portion of the city of Constantinople was deserted. Most of the residents were enjoying the balmy weather in the country. The large Armenian population of the city had cleared out almost to a person to celebrate a national holiday in honor of the tenth anniversary of their civil and religious constitution.

One Armenian family, too poor for even such a simple country sojourn, stayed behind. The mother of this household told her small daughter to go upstairs and fetch a pan of burning charcoal for supper. The child spilled the burning embers on the stairs, and through the open windows of the small house a wind of near-gale proportion swept these up and blew the burning flakes onto the roof of the adjoining house. The cheaply constructed wooden houses with wooden roofs and balconies in the Valide Tchesme district were soon ablaze. The fire raced through the Armenian Quarter and the adjacent Christian Quarter in a matter of hours.

More than a square mile of Constantinople burned furiously, racing down to the ramshackle docks edging into the Bosphorus and up the grand street, Feridje, along which rested elegant shops, churches, hospitals, legations and consulates. The fire, like a sea wave, rolled up against the thick walls of the British Embassy.

The ambassador, Sir Henry Elliott, dressed in a flapping silken nightgown, personally directed the two British fire engines within the spacious grounds. Although flying firebrands ignited the embassy roof and burned it through, the only other loss was Sir Henry's robe, which was considerably singed.

The Armenian district was gutted. More than 3,000 dwellings and shops were destroyed, and 900 persons were burned to death.

CONSTELLATION

MARINE DISASTER
December 19, 1960

background: Her keel first laid in the Brooklyn Naval Yard on September 14, 1957, the *Constellation* aircraft carrier displaced 80,000 tons and was the world's largest vessel at that time, built at a cost of $275 million. The ship, 1,047 feet long, with four steam turbine engines of 300,000 horsepower, would be capable of 31 knots and could carry 100 jet aircraft. On December 19, 1960, with 85 percent of her construction completed, a fire started on board while the ship was still in the Brooklyn Naval Yard berth. It raged for four hours, injuring 154 and killing 50.

Her history was as proud as the backbone of the American Revolution. Christened on October 8, 1959, the *Constellation* was one of the largest aircraft carriers (Forrestal Class) in the United States Navy up to that time. (The other five super attack-carriers of her class were the *Saratoga,* the *Ranger,* the *Forrestal,* the *Kitty Hawk* and the *Independence.*) From keel to masthead, the *Constellation* rose twenty-five stories, and if stood on end, her 1,047-foot-long hull almost matched the height of the Empire State Building.

More than $275 million had been pumped into the vessel's construction by December, 1960, and 85 percent of the ship had been completed. When finished the 80,000-ton *Constellation* would boast four steam turbines with a total of more than 300,000 horsepower providing a 31-knot capability. She could carry one hundred missile-bearing aircraft. She was to be launched by four giant steam catapults. More than two million pounds of quarter-inch weld metal had been installed in the ship along with 185 miles of piping and 300 miles of electrical cables. Her peacetime crew would number 3,412. The *Constellation* was to be one of America's greatest warships, reflecting the history of its name, which dated back to the late eighteenth century.

The first *Constellation* was a war frigate launched in Baltimore in 1797, and it performed notable service in the undeclared war with France that year and the next. Its speed earned it the nickname "Yankee Race Horse."

Constellation number two was a sloop of war built in 1855. The third *Constellation* was a huge battle cruiser half-built before it was scrapped as a result of naval restrictions effected by the Washington Treaty of 1922.

The giant carrier *Constellation* burned in the Brooklyn Navy Yard, December 19, 1960. *(Wide World)*

The fourth and last *Constellation* almost went the way of the third, when, on December 19, 1960, a massive fire erupted in her hull while she was in the Brooklyn Naval Yards berth. In the flurry to finish the ship, the 4,000 workmen had become sloppy, and one of the vehicles racing about a hangar deck accidentally knocked a valve from a fuel tank. The highly flammable liquid seeped down to another deck where a welder was busy with an acetylene torch. Sparks jumped to the liquid, and the burning fuel poured downward from one deck to another, the flames feeding on the wooden scaffolding throughout the ship. In minutes the *Constellation* was an inferno. Workers scrambled to get off.

Hundreds of men ran for the gangplanks. About thirty men on the hangar deck, cut off from this avenue of escape, were driven back toward the stern. A crane operator on the deck saw their predicament and swung his gigantic crane, which held a narrow thirty-foot gangway in its teeth, to the stern of the ship. The workmen clambered onto the gangway and were lifted to safety. Ropes dangling from the sides of the carrier were soon knotted with hundreds of men sliding wildly down to the dock on one side and into the river on the other. Two hundred men landed on a nearby barge and almost swamped it until a tug raced over and took them off.

For many, unfortunately, there would be no miraculous escape. Scores of fear-struck men ran through the bowels of the ship seeking refuge from the dense black smoke gushing after them. Many fell choking to death on smoke and poisonous fumes. The interior of the ship was truly a deathtrap. The *Constellation* was an all-welded ship and totally compartmentalized to limit her vulnerability to sinking under attack. Consequently the workmen trapped as far below as four decks were pocketed in a lightless, smoke-filled maze with dozens of fires springing up around them.

The heroic New York Fire Department responded to the towering ten-alarm blaze almost at once and rushed to the scene with more than 350 firemen and 120 pieces of large equipment. The *Constellation* itself could offer no assistance; its fire-prevention sprinkler systems had not yet been installed.

There were more than 1,200 compartments on the carrier. Shouting, running workmen, tools still grasped in their hands, moved through the dark labyrinth without direction. As one report later stated: "This class of ship is so extensively compartmented that it is very difficult to find one's way about [it], even with full illumination. If lights were out or dimmer or visibility was obscured by clouds of billowing smoke, the task might well be impossible."

One group of thirty men, each holding on to the shirt tail of the man in front, followed a foreman holding a flashlight and were led to safety. Painter Arthur Storm escaped in a similar manner. "The lights went out," he recalled later. "I got on my hands and knees. Someone said, 'Follow me.' It was just dumb luck. I followed him up a ladder out of the compartment. Once on deck I ran off the ship before the fire itself got there."

Many raced into compartments and sealed the watertight doors to escape the smoke. Then they began banging loudly on bulkheads with their tools, hoping rescuers would hear them. Twenty-six men, clanging away with wrenches on the steel, waited patiently. One of their number peered from a porthole. Through the clouds of smoke outside he could see a ladder from a firetruck working its way toward a sponson (a type of abutment) near the porthole.

Firemen climbed the ladder and then extended a horizontal ladder from the upright on which they were perched to the porthole. One by one, the workmen slowly crawled to safety. "It was one of the most spectacular rescues the fire department ever made," said Fire Commissioner Cavanagh.

For others it was a matter of tense waiting and wondering if the flames had reached the corridors outside their closed compartment doors. Walter R. Knoll remembered: "We went into a compartment and locked the door. We were in there an hour and a half. Some of the fellows were pretty worried, but most of us just kidded and said silly things. We banged on the walls and heard banging from other walls. The fire rescue squad came along, but I refused to open the door. I was afraid that it was still too smokey. Finally I opened the door and found most of the smoke gone."

Compartment by compartment the rescue squads, oxygen tanks on their backs, cut their way to the trapped workmen and recovered those who had collapsed in the smoke-filled corridors.

Within four hours all the trapped workmen had been located, along with the dead and the dying, these carried down the gangplanks on stretchers. Behind them in a receding swirl of smoke were two-and-a-quarter-inch steel armor platings buckled by the heat, part of the more than $75 million in damage.

The stretcher bearers took away 154 badly burned men. Then came the dead, fifty in all.

An elderly foreman who had escaped from the ship and then joined the rescuers stood with half his clothes burned away. As he spied the bodies being removed from the crippled *Constellation,* he sobbed uncontrollably, "Oh, those poor boys, those poor boys."

A stern-faced sergeant of police walked over and put his arm around the grieving man. "Go away," he said. "There's nothing you can do for them now."

This had been a pleasant street in Cordele, Georgia, before a monstrous twister struck, killing twenty-three, on April 2, 1936. *(UPI)*

CORDELE, GEORGIA

TORNADO
April 2, 1936

The twister that touched down just west of Cordele, Georgia, on April 2, 1936, was one of the worst ever experienced in that part of the state. It moved with great speed through the heart of the town, mowing down everything in a 400-yard-wide path for twelve miles.

Within twenty minutes the tornado threw down 289 buildings, killed twenty-three people and injured 600 more, leaving in its wake damages estimated at $3 million.

CORINGA, INDIA

CYCLONE
December, 1789

When the Imperial East India Company sent Henry Piddington to Calcutta as an emissary to oversee British business interests, the world gained one of the first experts on storms, particularly those raging across the deadly Bay of Bengal. Piddington witnessed several storms before he wrote the first definitive analysis of such storms, *Conversations about Hurricanes: for the use of Plain Sailors*. It was Piddington who first coined the word "cyclone" (employing the Greek word for circle, *Kyklos*).

Without his investigative research nothing at all would have been made known of the great cyclone that struck Coringa, India, in the early part of December, 1789. The city, he discovered, was destroyed in a single day when "the unfortunate inhabitants of Coringa saw with terror three monstrous waves coming in from the sea, and following each other at short distances."

The first wave unraveled everything before it—ships at anchor, government buildings, dwellings—and flooded the city. The second wave broke into the low countryside and flooded that area; the third wave supplemented the first two and carried the roaring flood to nearby Yanaon.

"The sea in retiring left heaps of sand and mud," Piddington reported in 1860, "which rendered all search for the property or bodies impossible, and shut up the mouth of the river for large ships. The only trace of the ancient town which now remains is the house of the master attendant and the dockyards surrounding it."

More than 20,000 persons were drowned or killed by floating debris in this cyclone. Coringa itself was rebuilt and flourished. But another cyclone, even more devastating than that of 1789, struck the city in 1839 with a forty-foot wave that crushed 20,000 vessels of all dimensions and killed an estimated 300,000 inhabitants.

CORPUS CHRISTI, TEXAS — HURRICANE
September 14, 1919

background: A slow-moving storm appearing first on August 2, 1919, in the southwest Atlantic moved to hurricane proportions by the time it reached the Florida Straits—property damage at Key West was $2 million—and finally went ashore at Corpus Christi, Texas, on September 14, 1919, where 284 persons were killed and $20 million in damage done.

The hurricane of 1919 that raged along the southern coast of the United States is considered to be the worst in that area of the twentieth century. After running over the central Bahamas, the storm cut across the Florida Straits and demolished almost every building on Key West. Winds striking the key at the time were in excess of 100 m.p.h. Almost fourteen inches of rainfall sloshed down in its wake.

Ten ships were lost in the hurricane as it passed sixty miles west of Key West on September 9. Of these the largest was the Spanish liner *Valbanera,* which disappeared with 400 passengers and 88 crew members.

The hurricane had a huge diameter and moved at a tortuous pace for those anxiously awaiting its arrival on the Texas shore. The wall of rain, waves and wind drove ashore just south of Corpus Christi, Texas, on September 14. The hurricane's winds measured 72 m.p.h. The roaring tide engulfed the docks and lower parts of the city in sixteen-foot waves, crushing everything before it.

It took days following the hurricane to extract from the wreckage the 284 persons killed. It was years before the citizens could restore the $20 million in damages.

Corpus Christi would not experience anything like this hurricane until 1955 when Hurricane Gladys smashed ashore on September 6. With tides four and a half feet above normal, she was still a pygmy compared to the monster storm of 1919.

Debris litters the waterfront of Corpus Christi, Texas, in the wake of the hurricane of September 14, 1919. *(UPI)*

COSEGÜINA — VOLCANIC ERUPTION
January 20, 1835

For three days beginning on January 20, 1835, the ancient volcano Cosegüina in western Nicaragua exploded. On the twenty-second, the entire top of the mountain was blown away. Natives in Bogata, 1,100 miles away, and in Jamaica, 800 miles away heard the awful din. Hundreds of Nicaraguans near the base of the volcano were killed under the tumble of rocks and by searing blasts of heat.

The superintendent of Belize, about 800 miles away from the explosion, thought the noise was an invading fleet and called his army together to repel a military expedition.

So thick were the skies with ash that daylight was snuffed out, and the brightest lights could be seen only from a few feet. A twelve-mile crater at the top of the volcano was created. From it emanated great seas of lava, which flowed steaming into the Gulf of Fonseca. Two days later a captain reported sailing along the coast through fifty leagues of solid pumice without spotting an open space of water.

The natives in the immediate area were hardest hit and thought the end of the world was at hand. Many of their descendants to this day superstitiously believe that the only way to pacify the dreaded Cosegüina is to sacrifice a three-month-old infant by throwing it into the crater every twenty-five years.

COSPATRICK — MARINE DISASTER
November 17, 1874

background: The 1,200-ton *Cospatrick* was a teak-hulled sailing frigate 190 feet long with a 34-foot beam. She was built in the Moulmein shipyards of Burma and completed in 1856. The ship was first owned by the Blackwell firm as a passenger vessel, and she helped to lay the submarine cable in the Persian Gulf in 1863. Later used as an immigrant carrier for Shaw, Savill & Co., the vessel caught fire on November 17, 1874, off Auckland, New Zealand, and sank; 468 drowned or later died of thirst in lifeboats; five survived.

The British frigate *Cospatrick* enjoyed a decade-long reputation as a first-class passenger ship before it was turned into an immigrant vessel transporting steerage patrons to Australia and New Zealand. Its crew of forty-four men under the command of Captain Elmsley maintained the ship in excellent condition. She sailed for Auckland on September 11, 1874, with 429 immigrants on board.

The elegant sailing frigate *Cospatrick* caught fire off New Zealand, causing the deaths of 468 persons.

It was a smooth voyage with the vessel making close to 200 miles a day, even past the doldrum area near the equator. Off Auckland, on November 17, 1874, a small fire broke out in the boatswain's cabin, where oil and paints were stored. The crew fought the blaze effectively for a while, but Captain Elmsley unaccountably sailed the *Cospatrick* directly into the wind. One report has it that the helmsman mistook the captain's order and headed the ship into the wind, but the responsibility for the error mattered little since the wind instantly caused the fire to shoot upward, where it licked away at the halliards and consumed the head sails.

Seeing the front part of the ship aflame, the immigrants rushed to the deck in panic. Within two hours the *Cospatrick* was blazing almost from bow to stern. The first lifeboat foundered under the weight of too many immigrants jumping into it. Another boat caught fire as it was being lowered. Second Mate Henry MacDonald managed to get away two boats with eighty-one passengers and crew in them. The rest of the boats burned in their checks as hundreds of frantic passengers still trapped on board called out to those in the lifeboats to rescue them.

But no rescue attempt was made; the two lifeboats were brimming with injured survivors, many of whom were already dying. For thirty-six hours those in the lifeboats watched in agony as the *Cospatrick* was in her death throes.

MacDonald saw Captain Elmsley approach the railing and throw his small boy and wife overboard and then follow them. All drowned. The huge masts then fell, still burning, and crashed onto and through the deck of the groaning ship, killing scores of terrified passengers.

When the ship finally went down, piercing screams shot across the water. The lifeboats drifted off without provisions, and for three days, they bobbed together aimlessly. A storm came up on November 21 and the boats separated; one was never to reappear. MacDonald's boat drifted on. The lifeboats sighted several passing ships, one coming as close as one hundred yards, but after suffering days without food and water, the survivors were too weak to call out. The *British Sceptre* spotted a lifeboat on the morning of the twenty-sixth and took aboard five survivors—MacDonald, three crewmen and one passenger. MacDonald's long ordeal had made him permanently insane.

COTOPAXI — VOLCANIC ERUPTION

June 26, 1877

Cotopaxi, the highest active volcano on earth, 19,550 feet, sits in the highlands of north central Ecuador. It is the best-known volcano in the Andes Mountains and the most feared. Symmetrically shaped, a perfect 4,400 foot high cone at its upper portion, Cotopaxi resembles Mount Fujiyama. The legendary volcano has a long history of violent eruptions, dating back thousands of years, but the earliest recorded outbreaks date back to 1532-33.

In 1698 Cotopaxi erupted, killing hundreds and obliterating the city of Tacunga at its base. The worst eruption on record, however, was that of June 26, 1877. This eruption, which tore a large piece of the mountain away with it, vomited forth great rocks and spewed lava on several villages in adjoining valleys. More than 1,000 were killed instantly.

The highest volcano on earth, Cotopaxi in Ecuador, erupted on June 26, 1877, killing more than 1,000 natives. *(Humboldt engraving)*

CRESTED BUTTE, COLORADO

MINE DISASTER
February 24, 1884

The mine operated by the Colorado Coal and Iron Company at Crested Butte in 1884 was considered by most experienced miners to be one of the most dangerous in the country. One report said that "the amount of gas generated [in the mine] was usually large and very deadly."

To disperse the gas and to pump clean air into the shaft, the company installed a huge, cumbersome fan. It wasn't enough. On the morning of February 24, with fifty-nine miners working in the main tunnel, the gas exploded with a great roar, battering and breaking cars and snapping the rails beneath them as they stood at the entranceway waiting to be loaded. The fan was crumpled and twenty-five feet of tunnel collapsed from the entrance inward.

Twelve men, subsequently aided by others racing up the slopes from Crested Butte, ferreted their way into the shaft. The reassembled fan pumped air behind them. When the rubble was cleared away, all fifty-nine miners trapped inside were found dead.

CUARTLA, MEXICO

RAILWAY WRECK
June 24, 1881

background: A ten-car military train operating near Cuartla, Mexico, on the newly opened Morelos Rail Line fell through a bridge span weakened by heavy rains on June 24, 1881, and the ensuing crash killed 216 persons, mostly military personnel, making it one of the worst railway wrecks in history.

The long military train pulled by two engines slowly made its way along the San Antonio River on June 24, 1881. Next to the embankments the passengers, a full company of troops and about 60 civilians, saw the evidence of flooding from the heavy rains that had fallen throughout the week. A large wooden bridge spanning the San Antonio was barely above the flooded river swiftly moving under its weakened timbers.

As the train moved onto the trestle the bridge began to sway and then suddenly collapsed. The engines and cars struck an embankment instead of plummeting into the river. Sparks from one of the engine's boilers flew upward and ignited the flood from 100 broken barrels of brandy that had spilled downward from a freight car onto the smashed cars and trapped passengers. The burning fluid doused 197 enlisted men and 17 officers, who had been in the forward part of the train and now were thrashing about in the debris. The 60 civilians, two-thirds of whom were seriously injured, managed to scramble to safety and watched in horror as the troopers roasted to death.

The *New York Times* described the scene: "The dead and the living were wrapped in a sheet of flame, and slowly burned before the eyes of the survivors, who were unable to save them." The engineer and firemen working the two engines were scalded to death. This worst of Mexico's rail accidents ran a fatality toll of 216 persons. The *Times* was quick to capitalize on the anti-Mexican sentiment then in vogue by stating that the Mexicans, who had not properly maintained the rail line, were fully responsible.

(ALSO SEE: Angola, New York; Ashtabula, Ohio)

CUBA

HURRICANE
October 20, 1926

background: The hurricane that struck Cuba on October 20, 1926, reached wind velocities of 120 to 130 m.p.h., bringing $100 million in damages to Havana, Matanzas and Pinar del Rio provinces, wiping out towns, scores of villages, and making 10,000 homeless; 650 were killed, mostly by falling buildings. Dozens of vessels in Havana harbor were sunk or permanently damaged.

The tropical hurricane that struck Cuba at 10:30 A.M. on October 20, 1926, was the most ferocious felt by the island in eighty years. The storm's straight-line winds reached 130 m.p.h. and threw down thousands of dwellings. Havana was hardest hit. Here the winds broke every glass window in the downtown section, unroofed most of the houses and sent dozens of policemen and firemen hurling down streets with cars and trolleys tumbling after them and over them, crushing some to death.

One historic victim of the hurricane was a huge monument erected in honor of the 266 American sailors killed when the United States battleship *Maine* blew up in Havana harbor in 1898. The monument's towering twin marble columns were sliced in half by the storm, and the eagles perched on top were blown away, never to be recovered. Inside of an hour, 325 buildings, at a cost of $5 million, were toppled in Havana.

There was little shelter in or outside the buildings. A four-year-old boy, running with the wind, was slammed against the concrete wall of a hospital and killed. A policeman was sent rolling over and over the length of a block until he grabbed a tree and held on. When the tree was ripped to pieces he clung with bloody hands to the roots. Not more than five trees remained standing in the whole of Havana after the storm.

As the sky turned purple-black, the hurricane's unusual voice was a deep and steady growl that sometimes changed to a terrifying shriek. "It was a sound I never heard before," a fireman later said, "and I never want to hear it again."

Waves as high as twenty-five feet lashed at the seawall and gushed over onto the resplendent Malecon Drive,

Buildings in Havana's harbor were destroyed by a hurricane which killed 650 persons, October 20, 1926. *(UPI)*

tore up the roadway and snapped with ten-pin accuracy every tree.

Camp Columbia, the Cuban army headquarters, was destroyed; every building in the Marianao suburb leveled. An officer ran onto the parade grounds and fired a bullet into his temple. Most of the troops joined police and firemen in digging out those trapped in collapsed houses. Hundreds dug away at what had been their homes, now reduced to piles of debris along Escobar Street. Some were blown away from their digging, but they fought the wind and returned again and again until eight families were removed alive.

In Havana Harbor all was chaos. Giant steamers bobbed like new corks and careened crazily into each other. The Cuban cruiser *Patria* was severely damaged. The steamer *Maximo Gomez* was sent reeling about the harbor, ramming other ships and sinking scores before it was driven to land by the hurricane. The large steamer *Puerto Tarafa* raised itself sharply and went to the bottom bow first with all hands. A dozen schooners followed her.

The southern end of Havana Province was in ruins. In the small town of Batapano, 300 out of 2,000 residents were crushed to death when their flimsy homes caved in on them. Villages like Guanabocoa, Jaruco, Minas, Fajardo, Tapaste and Santa Maria del Rosario ceased to exist.

There was little anyone could do but either endure or die in the hurricane, which gushed over the hapless island on a gigantic front, taking six hours to pass out again to sea, veering off toward Key West at 4:30 P.M.

The reports of the dead, more than 650, dribbled into Havana all week long.

CUBA (and UNITED STATES EAST COAST) — HURRICANE, October 13-21, 1944

The hurricane which swept across Cuba on October 17, 1944, had begun in the Caribbean four days before, and its blasting winds struck four provinces of the vulnerable island, killed three hundred and tumbled hundreds of homes. Downtown Havana suffered greatly, its graceful trees uprooted and almost every store window shattered by violent winds.

W. S. Hall, writing in *Publishers Weekly,* described a visit to the island only days later: "I have seen desolation from typhoons in the Orient, but I never saw the power of pure wind so tragically demonstrated as here. Later, what struck me about the damage was the Chinese stoicism of the people as they went about repairing it."

The city was without fresh water for a week, every

main having been broken by the howling storm. According to resident Rene de Smedt: "The separate big blows came heralded by a slowly mounting wail, climaxed at the height of the wind with a sound exactly like the sound of a baby."

Cubans were extremely resourceful, for even in this wartime year when supplies were scarce, they had replaced every bit of broken glass along the tourist-glutted boulevards within twelve hours of the storm. The thousands of trees ripped from their roots, magnificent palms, pines and laurels, were another matter. It would take a generation to replace them.

CURTISS-REID AIRTOURS, LTD — AIR CRASH November 13, 1950

"Now we are going through the unknown." These were the written words of one of the fifty-eight persons aboard a chartered flight making its way back to Canada. The group had made a Holy Year pilgrimage to Rome and had, on that morning of November 13, 1950, visited with Pope Pius XII.

While attempting to avoid 8,500-foot Mont Obiou in the French Alps, the group's plane lost its way in rain and fog and hit the mountain. The plane shattered to pieces and killed all on board. Only ten days before, an Air India plane had slammed into nearby Mont Blanc, and forty-eight persons met death.

One of the pilgrims was a Canadian, Alphonse Michaud, a farmer whose wife had nineteen children. Another, Antoine Dussault, had been reluctant to make the trip because his wife was expecting their fifth child. She insisted that he go, stayed behind and was baking an apple pie in her kitchen for his return when she was informed of the crash. Arthur Pelletier, another ill-fated passenger, left a wife and seven children.

When told of the crash, the Pope broke down and wept, cancelling his mass. When they scaled the treacherous Mont Obiou Alpinists from Grenoble found dozens of the Pontiff's pictures clutched in the hands of the mangled victims.

(ALSO SEE: Air India)

The blanket-wrapped bodies of passengers who died on Mount Obiou when a chartered plane crashed on November 13, 1950, are carried from the slopes by French alpine guides. *(UPI)*

CUSTOIAS, PORTUGAL — RAILWAY WRECK July 26, 1964

The *Automara* Express, carrying people on holiday from the sunny Atlantic beaches of Povoà de Varzim back to Oporto, Portugal, suddenly met with disaster on July 26, 1964. Six miles away from Oporto, near Custoias, the last car of the tow train came uncoupled, and the car, at 50 m.p.h. jumped the track and hurtled down an embankment, breaking up as it went.

Death came instantly to sixty-nine persons. Another ninety-two, all seriously injured, were dug out from the debris after seven hours of wild all-night work by firemen. Of these, another twenty-five died hours later, bringing the total of fatalities to ninety-four and making this the worst train accident in Portugal's history.

The car in which the 161 travelers had been riding was not supposed to carry more than seventy.

CUYAHOGA FALLS, OHIO — RAILWAY WRECK July 31, 1940

background: Two trains of the Pennsylvania Railroad—a gasoline-propelled motor coach shuttling from Hudson to Akron, Ohio, and a seventy-three-car freight train enroute from Columbus to Cleveland—met in a head-on collision at Cuyahoga Falls, Ohio, on July 31, 1940, and all forty-one passengers on the coach were killed; the engineers of both trains survived.

The "doodlebug," as the one-car, gas-fed motor coach for commuters was then called, was shuttling its way toward Akron on the evening of July 31, 1940, its engineman and conductor oblivious to the onrushing death approaching them and their forty-one passengers.

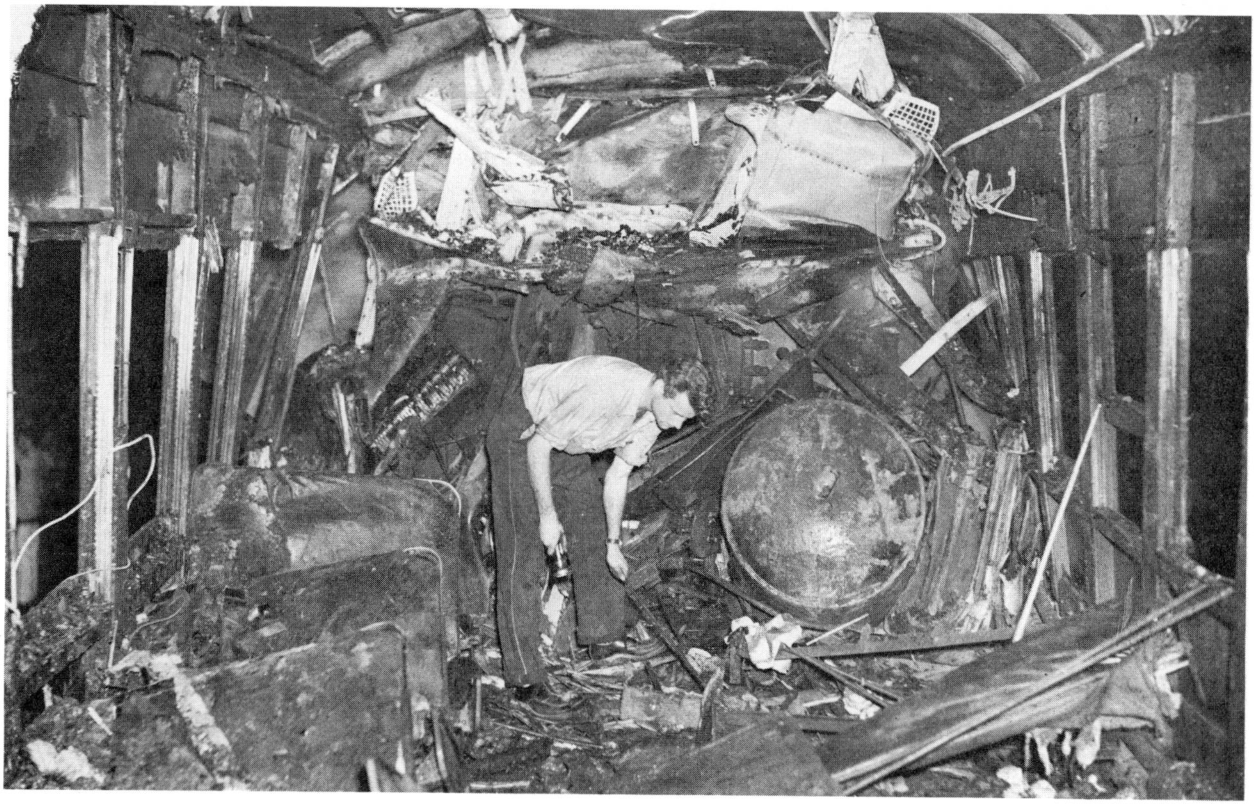

A shuttle coach and a freight train on the Pennsylvania line collided, causing the deaths of forty-one persons, July 31, 1940. *(UPI)*

Roaring toward Cleveland, in the opposite direction, was a ponderous freight train, seventy-three cars long and pulled by two locomotives. At the controls of the first engine was Engineer O.M. Lodge. He suddenly bolted upright and stared in disbelief at the single headlamp glaring down the single track at his own train. "We just came around the bend in the road when I saw the gas-electric loom up in front of us. We jammed on the brakes, and there was a terrible explosion."

The commuter coach was smashed, burning and spreading its blazing fuel under the track as the enormous freight train violently shoved it backward two hundred yards before both trains came to a stop. By that time the freight had run over the track where the fuel was burning and it, too, was set afire.

Engineer Lodge said, "B. E. Reynolds, my fireman, stayed with her through the fire and explosion until she came to a stop, then we jumped through a wall of flame that had surrounded the whole wreckage."

Others were also jumping. The engineman of the "doodlebug" left the train just before impact. Conductor H.B. Shaffer ran through the single doomed car and shouted, "We are going to crash!" He threw open a door, leaped out and sustained major injuries from his fall. Tod Wonn, a trainman, followed him out the door. Wonn later stated, "My clothing caught fire. I rolled in some bushes at the side of the track and put out the flames. . . . My pal, Bruce Kell, who lives at the same place I do, was with me in the car and I did not see any more of him."

Flames totally engulfed the commuter car and sent up a bright yellow beacon in the sultry night. Firemen from Cuyahoga Falls, Kent, Barberton, Ravenna and Akron arrived with sirens screaming and poured water on the coach. It took forty-five minutes before the fire subsided.

Charles Taylor, who lived a few blocks from the disaster scene, was on hand and looked inside the coach just after the fire was put out. "Seats and bodies were scattered around," he said. "Bodies were wedged in the windows and we could see legs and arms hanging outside. . . . It was the most terrible scene I ever witnessed."

Forty-one persons had been roasted to death. An inquiry board blamed the operator of the coach by stating that he "ran by its leaving point and so collided with the northbound freight."

(ALSO SEE: Tipton Ford, Missouri)

An Ilyushin 18 crashed at Casablanca on July 12, 1961, killing all seventy-two persons on board. *(UPI)*

CZECHOSLOVAKIAN AIRLINES **AIR CRASH July 12, 1961**

One of the strangest air crashes in history occurred on July 12, 1961, when a Czechoslovakian Soviet-built turboprop Ilyushin-18 smacked to earth while attempting a landing at Casablanca, Morocco. The crash killed all seventy-two passengers on board.

The Prague and Zurich-born flight was captained by Josef Mikus, a highly-decorated World War II hero. His actions on this flight were more than curious. Upon learning that Casablanca was closed in with weather, Mikus insisted on landing there anyway. Tower control told him that the United States air base at Nouasseur, fifteen miles away, was open for landings. Mikus refused to land there and began to nose down his four-engine plane.

In the middle of its glide path the plane struck a power line and dragged down two huge cable pylons. Two of the plane's engines tore away from the wings and flew off hundreds of yards, exploding in midair. The fuselage crashed and some bodies were catapulted away from the burning wreck.

But many were still alive inside. One, Kouli Baly, thirty-one, of the Mali Republic, was somehow thrown clear, and he staggered into the arms of emergency crewmen. (He died an hour later.) The strange thing was that for twenty-five minutes, until police arrived, there was no attempt to extract those still alive inside the plane. When policemen did arrive and "heard calls coming from the wreckage . . . an attempt was made to rescue the passengers, but a fire started, and it became impossible to continue operations." All alive in the plane burned to death.

Strange still was why Captain Mikus had stubbornly risked landing at fog-bound Casablanca instead of at the military base a few miles away. An unofficial answer came days later when a Zurich airport officer reported that the Czech plane was loaded down with communist documentary films and pamphlets for distribution to Guinea and Ghana insurrectionists. The same officer stated that on board the plane were several Soviet flying instructors who were on their way to train the African rebels.

This, then, was the reason why Captain Mikus refused to land anywhere near a United States-controlled base. He feared that the material and persons "not fully described on the manifest" might be identified.

D

DAKAR — MARINE DISASTER
January 25, 1968

It is ironic that the British government, which had long held the Israelis in check through their peace-keeping role as the Protectorate of Palestine, should have sold Israel one of its first submarines, the *Dakar,* which had seen twenty years' service in Her Majesty's fleet. The ironic became the inexplicable when this submarine, completely refitted by the British before its sale, disappeared west of Cyprus on January 25, 1968.

Sixty-nine Israeli crew members on the vessel on its maiden voyage to Haifa were running under water. Suddenly all messages from the 1,800-ton *Dakar* ceased, and the ship vanished forever.

Incredibly another submarine, the 800-ton French *Minerve,* with crew of 52, disappeared forty-eight hours later, just outside its home port of Toulon. The submarine radioed that it was running forty feet under water, and then it completely disappeared. This double disaster, which claimed the lives of 121 sailors, was never explained, but authorities advanced the theories that the submarines underwent mechanical or electrical failures. After searching for four days—the amount of time in which all oxygen would have been used up in the subs—the books were closed on the *Dakar* and the *Minerve.*

(*ALSO SEE:* Affray, Dumlupinar, L-24, K-13, Squalus, Thetis, Thresher, Truculent)

DAN-AIR AIRLINES — AIR CRASH
July 3, 1970

Vacationers and residents walking along the hot sands of the Costa Brava on the evening of July 3, 1970, watched a large plane sink perilously close to the sea. Dozens of squinting viewers saw it disappear into the water about twenty miles from Mataro. They were the last to see the chartered British-made Dan-Air Airlines plane, which had 112 persons on board.

The jet's pilot had talked to ground control in Barcelona, his destination, at 7:00 P.M. He reported that he was then twelve miles out and at an altitude of 6,000 feet. Moments later, the plane, coming from Manchester, England, and loaded down with sun-seeking tourists, disappeared from the radar screens.

All on board died, and no bodies were ever recovered. The cause of the crash was never fully determined although the Comet jet had had a long history of fatal accidents.

DANIEL STEINMANN — MARINE DISASTER
April 3, 1884

The steamer *Daniel Steinmann,* bound for Halifax and New York with ninety-four passengers and thirty-nine seamen, left Antwerp, Belgium, on March 20, 1884. Captain Van Schoonhoven had negotiated the tricky, treacherous shoals near Sambro Light several times before, but the waters on those occasions had been peaceful. On this trip, a hurricane drove the *Daniel Steinmann* through soupy banks of fog and vicious seas.

At 10:00 P.M. on the night of April 3 Van Schoonhoven was on the bridge and attempting to negotiate the ship into Halifax Harbor. He was much too far to the north, and his ship was suddenly dashed upon the rocks of Sambro Island, less than 300 yards from the lighthouse.

The steamer soon went to pieces in the storm. Its passengers attempted to claw their way over each other's backs to the water. Only Van Schoonhoven and eight

On April 3, 1884, the Sambro Light station claimed another victim, the Halifax-bound steamer *Daniel Steinmann* with 124 passengers aboard. *(Harper's Weekly)*

others managed to reach the island; 124 drowned in the attempt.

Making passage around Sambro Island had always meant possible disaster, and the area is still a graveyard for dozens of lost ships. The White Star *Atlantic,* running at a speed of twelve knots, had been wrecked in a storm near Sambro Light (546 persons were killed) eleven years before the *Steinmann*'s destruction.

Harper's Weekly, ranting at the violent passing of the *Daniel Steinmann,* blamed the captain: "If later particulars shall show him to have been guilty of neglect of the ordinary precautions which should be observed under such circumstances, he should be held to a strict accountability. . . . No punishment can be too severe for a crime that involves a disaster like this, costing untold distress and the loss of scores of human lives."

No action was taken against Van Schoonhoven.
(ALSO SEE: Atlantic, *1873)*

DAPHNE

MARINE DISASTER
July 3, 1883

The packet steamer *Daphne* was launched in Glasgow by builders Alexander Stephen & Sons on July 3, 1883, and immediately sank into the River Clyde, taking the lives of the 195 workmen on board. The 460-ton ship, it was discovered on salvage, had little stability when it was launched, rolling over forty-five degrees and taking huge amounts of water through a large deck opening.

There was little or no ballast on the ship other than the 195 startled workmen who went to their unexpected deaths in seconds. Because of the *Daphne* disaster, shipbuilders in the future took care to provide the necessary stability and ballast in all launchings. It was one of marine history's grim lessons.

DARA

MARINE DISASTER
April 8, 1961

background: The 5,030-ton passenger ship *Dara,* owned by the British India Steam Navigation Company, was, along with her sister ships *Daressa, Dwarka* and *Dumrah,* used as a weekly service shuttling between Basra and Bombay. Carrying 19 officers, 113 crew and 584 passengers (her maximum capacity was 1,158), the ship embarked for Basra on March 23, 1961, and was ripped by an explosion on April 8, 1961 (later claimed to be an act of sabotage), which caused her to burn and founder the next day with 236 on board perishing.

Tension and strain were everywhere on board the British steamer *Dara* when she left Bombay on March 23, 1961. Most of the ship's passengers were Arabs, many openly hostile to the British, whose interests stretched along the North African coast. The nineteen officers of the ship were British, but the *Dara*'s crew was a polyglot of various Arab nationals who, it was later alleged, secretly worked for insurrectionist groups. Several officers on British ships during this time had been attacked and even killed by vengeful sailors. Beneath their immaculate whites the *Dara*'s officers all wore specially made "stab-proof" vests.

Sailing up the Persian Gulf and just off Dubai at the tip of the Omani coast, the *Dara* was rocked by a deafening explosion. It was daybreak of April 8, 1961. The ship was suddenly on fire, flames shooting up from the bridge deck through a hole to the promenade deck above. Fearing that there had been a crankcase explosion, the captain ordered the engines stopped, but all crankcase doors had been sealed.

With flames shooting all along the superstructure of the ship and the fire alarms clanging loudly, Captain Charles Elson soon realized that his ship was doomed. He gave the order to abandon ship. The *Dara*'s Second Radio Officer, Francis Terrace, later stated, "The explosion seemed to have taken place in the engine room. I was told to send out an SOS. Immediately afterward the order was given to abandon ship and everyone made a frenzied scramble to get into the sea."

As hundreds of passengers and crew hurtled themselves into the warm Gulf waters, several ships in the heavily trafficked sea lane arrived. The tanker *British Energy,* the frigate *Empire Guillemot,* the *Barpeta,* the *Thorsholm,* the Japanese *Yogu Maru* and three British frigates began to pick up survivors.

Captain Elson, who remained forever puzzled about why the second and fifth engineers chose to close down their engines without orders from the bridge, was the last to leave the sinking *Dara.* A year later at a board of inquiry, Elson stated that he and a cluster of other officers were driven from the sundeck of the bridge by the fire and were momentarily trapped on the deck below. "We waited for I can't say how long and it was obvious that we would either have to stay and burn or jump over the side." Chief Officer P. E. Jordan vaulted over the rail to the accommodation ladder and suddenly yelled up to the others: "I can't stop! It's too hot!" He fell into the sea.

Cadet John Grimwood was one of the last officers to go over the rail. He had herded scores of passengers through menacing patches of soaring fire to the side of the ship and helped them over the side. "It was like a nightmare," he said. The fire eventually drove him, too, into the water. (He was later cited for bravery by the Solicitor General of England.)

Elson and the senior radio officer looked around. The deck beneath them was burning quickly. "Come on," Elson shouted. "We shall have to go!" They leaped into the sea and swam to the nearby *Barpeta.*

The *Dara* did not sink immediately; she smoldered and shuddered sluggishly through the Gulf waters. Captain Elson returned to the ship with several other officers. As this party made its way through the still burning ship they noted dozens of passengers, their bodies reduced to skeletons by the fire, stretched out on the decks. It would be days before a full check of the manifest revealed that 236 on board the burning ship, most of them overcome in their sleep by lack of oxygen, had perished.

After checking the bridge deck and salvaging a few items, Elson and his party were again driven back by the mounting fire. They heard a loud whoosh, saw oil quickly spread from the ship into the water and thought the entire vessel was about to blow up. "We jumped over the side because it was a question of getting off quickly," Elson stated.

The *Dara* did not blow up; she lingered for hours. A tow attempt was made by the *Ocean Salvor* the next day while the ship was still spewing smoke, but her list increased drastically and, three miles from shore, the *Dara* rolled over and sank in ten murky fathoms.

A year later, Solicitor General Sir John Hobson revealed at a court of inquiry that the *Dara* had been sabotaged and that the fire was not attributable to a minor collision with the Panamanian steamship *Zeus* two days previous to its foundering, as was initially thought. Hobson blamed Omani terrorists on board, stating that they had placed a twenty-pound plastic explosive charge near the bridge and it was this that caused the disaster. What they hoped to achieve by such sabotage was never made clear. Of those killed on the *Dara,* many were Arabs.

DAWSON, NEW MEXICO — MINE DISASTER, October 22, 1913

background: Mine Number 2 of the Stag Canyon Fuel Company exploded at 3:00 P.M. on October 22, 1913, as 284 men worked in various shafts. Rescue attempts were immediately made, but only 21 were saved with 263 dying. The explosion started in a dusty pillar section and was caused by coal dust ignited by dynamite blasting.

The Stag Canyon Fuel Company's coal mines in Dawson, New Mexico, were considered one of the safest until Mine Number 2 blew up on October 22, 1913. Although sprayers were placed at intervals to wet the dust in the tunnels, they reached out only to an area of six feet, so

The British liner *Dara* burned on April 8, 1961, and 236 passengers perished. *(UPI)*

the mine was generally dry. Firedamp, a poisonous gas, mostly methane, was not present, except in occasional pockets coming from the roof. Miners were usually careful when they used explosives. Charges were ignited electrically from outside, yet the blasts set off at 3:00 P.M. on October 22 ignited coal dust and trapped 284 miners when the main shaft entrance was sealed off by falling rocks.

Scores of men summoned from other mines by the general manager, T. H. O'Brien, dug away furiously at the rocks, and when they broke through they dashed inside only to be driven out by the poisonous gases accumulated in the shaft. The main air fans had been destroyed by the explosion, and it was two hours before these could be repaired. During this interval, a two-man rescue team wearing helmets and holding oxygen bottles worked its way deep into the mine. The air supply gave out, and the men were overcome by afterdamp, another poisonous gas. The team was saved by another party minutes later. Fourteen more men who had been working in an unaffected area escaped from the shaft. Eight more men were recovered from the base of the shaft; all of them were unconscious and pulmotors required to revive them. By 8:00 P.M. that evening, as the gases abated,

Grim miners remove one of the 236 employees who died in an explosion of a Dawson, New Mexico, mine on October 22, 1913. *(UPI)*

bodies by the carload were taken to the surface. One was nineteen-year-old Henry P. McShane of New York City, whose father held a heavy interest in the mine. He had just begun to work in the mine shaft to gain practical experience.

The coal company had known long before 8:00 P.M. what rescuers would bring to the surface. As the coal wagons, heavy with the weight of the dead, were rolled slowly from the shaft entrance, those working the cars were greeted with the sight of long rows of neatly stacked pine coffins, preordered and ready.

DELTA AIRLINES — AIR CRASH, July 31, 1973

background: Delta Airlines Flight 723, a DC-9 jet, flying from Manchester, New Hampshire, to Boston, Massachusetts, with eighty-nine passengers and crew members on board, crashed in a dense fog at 11:08 A.M. while attempting to land at Logan Airport, Boston; eighty-eight passengers died and one survived. There was a stiff legal contest between the airline and FAA officials over blame in the disaster.

"Help me! Help me!" Air Force Sergeant Leopold Chouinard was flat on his back in the middle of the smoking, gruesome wreckage that littered a Logan Airport runway. Chouinard kept up a steady cry for help, but he could not move; his clothes and most of his flesh had been burned away. About him were the mangled bodies of eighty-eight other passengers who had been on Delta Airlines' Flight 723, which had attempted to land in ceiling-zero fog and had crashed in a ball of fire.

Bodies all around Chouinard were motionless. Some were in bloody chunks, meshed with the charred steel remnants of the plane. Others, intact, had no shoes; they had been torn from the feet by the impact. Two dead passengers, knees bent, faces down, were still strapped to their seats. Their seats had been ripped from the fuselage.

Two airport construction workers, Harris A. Cusick and Geoffrey F. Keating, had been driving near the end of the runway and had witnessed everything. "I just happened to be looking at the horizon," Keating said, "and saw a large flame go up in the air. Then there was a big, black cloud, followed by a muffled rumble like thunder."

The two men raced to the shredded plane. Cusick spotted Chouinard among the debris. "From the neck up, it was as if he was in perfect health, . . . but, God, from the neck down, nobody would want to see what Geoffrey and I saw . . . he was fully conscious, fully awake. He was begging for help. I found a magazine in the debris and ripped a page out as he was talking. I got a pen and began writing. He said his name. He said he was in the military and was coming from his home in Vermont. . . . We kept talking to him. One of us would stay with him and the other would go around looking for other people who were alive."

Cusick and Keating were the only ones at the scene for a full six minutes. Apparently tower control had not realized the big DC-9 had crashed, and a precious six minutes were lost before emergency vehicles responded to a fire alarm. Scattered on the runway were eighty-one dead bodies and seven critically injured passengers in addition to Chouinard. The seven died a few hours later in the hospital.

An eighty-ninth fatality was avoided in Manchester, New Hampshire, two hours before when businessman Charles R. Mealy had decided to get off the star-crossed Flight 723. The plane had taxied out to the Manchester runway. Mealy suddenly grabbed the hostess's hand and told her, "I want to get off this plane." The stewardess hesitated. Mealy then got up and asked the pilot if he could get off. "He told me to go back to my seat and he would return to the terminal," Mealy remembered later.

The DC-9 taxied back to the terminal, and the pilot switched on the intercom and said, "I am letting a passenger off. Anyone else who so desires can deplane at this time." None of the other passengers moved. Mealy got off, and Flight 723 went on its way to destruction and death. Mealy later explained that he figured he would be late for a business appointment in New York City and that that was his real reason for deplaning.

A hearing the following month turned into a legal battle between Delta Airline's lawyers and FAA representatives. Delta maintained that control tower personnel were understaffed and confused at the time of the crash. The hearings officer, James W. Kuehl, commented: "Some crashes are clearcut from the beginning. We knew this one was a controversial crash and not one that could be pinned down to one cause."

The causes listed were the plane's reported history of malfunctioning instruments and those precious six minutes in which no aid was sent out by the control tower to the crash victims.

At that time the only two able-bodied men sifting through the ruins and keeping Chouinard's spirits up were Keating and Cusick. "I figured by talking to him, we could keep him conscious," Cusick stated. "You're going to be all right," Cusick chanted to Chouinard. "Hold on, kid. Help is coming, help is coming, help is coming. . . ."

In the hospital, Chouinard told his mother: "They'll never take my legs." But twenty-year-old Leopold Chouinard from Marshfield, Vermont, who was to be married to his high school sweetheart, did lose his legs.

A fireman stares in shock at the twisted, smoking remains of Delta Airlines Flight 723 at Boston's Logan Airport, July 31, 1975. *(UPI)*

DEUTSCHLAND — MARINE DISASTER

December 6, 1875

background: The *Deutschland,* an ocean-going iron passenger liner regularly running between Bremen and New York, was owned by the North German Lloyd's Company. Built in 1866 by Caird Brothers, the vessel was 328 feet long, had a 40-foot beam and possessed two 300 horsepower engines. She weighed 2,898 tons. Commanded by Captain Brickenstein, the ship, on December 6, 1875, attempting to avoid a storm, struck the Kentish Knock shoals in the height of a gale; 157 drowned, 155 were saved; 136 of these rescued by the tug *Liverpool* the following day.

Safety, often ignored in the early steamship days of the nineteenth century, was a potent feature on board the sturdy passenger liner *Deutschland.* The vessel carried eight large boats and more than 1,000 life preservers, more capacity and equipment than were really required for her average 300 passengers and crew members.

On the morning of December 6, 1875, Captain Brickenstein was alarmed by a storm blowing from the northeast, and to avoid wrecking the *Deutschland,* then en route to New York with a mere 113 passengers, mostly immigrants occupying steerage space (third class), he sailed the ship in a westerly course. As a result the *Deutschland* steamed in ignorance onto the Thames shoals, where she struck at 5:00 A.M.

To this day the fact that the liner struck at all is a bit incredible since two experienced pilots, one German and one British, were both on board the ship and were familiar with such dangerous waters.

There was no panic, at first, on the *Deutschland.*

Considered one of the safest ocean-going vessels of its era, the *Deutschland* struck a reef off Kentish Knock; 157 froze to death or drowned. *(Illustrated London News)*

Land was in sight and boats and life preservers were plentiful. In fact the middle deck, where most of the steerage passengers were still sleeping, was "roofed" with more than 800 life preservers. At the head of each bed in first and second class was a life belt. The lifeboats were extremely large and easily lowered. It was the storm, however, and the position in which the ship had been reefed that was the problem.

The storm was hard from the northeast and thick with snow and sleet when the vessel, going at slow speed, struck. Brickenstein ordered the engines reversed at high speed, and the propeller was instantly broken. The storm then drove the powerless ship further onto the shoals. The captain ordered two of his boats lowered.

Eight persons climbed into the first boat, which was commanded by the fourth officer. Great combers whipped by the wind immediately caused the boat to swamp and drowned all in the boat. A boat in the charge of Quartermaster Auguste Bock was then let down into the foamy brine. This boat, too, was filled when a three-inch lowering rope snapped under the pressure of the wind and waves, pitching Bock and three others into the water. The boat capsized, but Bock and two passengers managed to right her and climb inside, baling for life. The boat drifted away from the *Deutschland.*

For thirty-eight hours Bock and his two companions drifted and were buffeted by an unceasing wind. Twice the boat was swamped, and each time the three men managed to bale it out and reenter. One of the men had been hit in the head by a blow from the boat, and he died within six hours. His corpse froze in the gale. The other sank slowly into a death sleep. Bock shouted at him and rubbed him vigorously, attempting to keep him awake and alive but it was no good: he was soon frozen. The next day the lifeboat bumped to shore with Bock barely alive, staring as if transfixed at his two dead companions in the boat.

The quartermaster later told authorities that all was well on board the *Deutschland* until Brickenstein ordered the boats away and then the passengers, especially the women, panicked, shrieking not to be sent into the sea. This problem was solved quickly when the storm ripped all the remaining boats from their davits and made instant debris out of them.

Seeing that the situation was hopeless for the moment, Brickenstein ordered the passengers to find shelter, but most, now desperate with terror, took to the rigging and in these lofty positions, scores of men (and a few women) froze to death or fell to the sea or to the deck of the ship. By the time the powerful tug *Liverpool* managed to come alongside the stricken ship at about noon the following day, the *Deutschland* was littered with the dead, their bodies sprawled and stretched in grotesque positions. An artist from the *Illustrated London News* who sailed with the tug to sketch the disaster for his newspaper noticed that "one corpse was . . . sticking in the ventilating shaft, head downwards, the feet protruding at the top."

Ice-covered bodies of women and children were skidded back and forth on the watery decks by crashing waves. Many corpses had been washed down the hatchways and into the hold. While the *Liverpool* began its arduous task of taking off survivors, about fourteen fishing smacks, hovering like jackals, surrounded the partly submerged stern of the ship. From these leaped burly boatmen who ignored the pleas of the living to be saved and went directly to the bodies of the dead, stripping them of all valuable clothes. They were seen removing wedding rings of dead women. They took the mufflers from the frozen blue necks of dead infants. Hardy crewmen from the *Liverpool* cursed them, and the "smackers" grunted back obscenities while the storm continued in its rage.

After stripping the dead these boatmen, many of whom were later located, arrested and charged with their ghoulish thefts, lumbered into the *Deutschland*'s elegant saloon and first-class cabins and ripped away any salable accoutrements—lamps, paintings, fixtures, even expensive teakwood paneling. Hours later many of these men were apprehended while hawking their wares on the beaches of Harwich.

Since the passenger manifest sank with the *Deutschland,* the number of dead was never verified, but one reliable estimate lists the dead at 157. The valiant little tug *Liverpool* took off 21 women and children, 48 men and 86 crewmen. About 20 crew members perished, dying at their exposed stations. Bodies drifted to shore for a week. Of these, 5 were young Franciscan nuns from

Westphalia. It was ruefully noted that even their meager valuables, including their rosaries, had been taken by the scurrilous boatmen.

DHARBAD, INDIA — MINE DISASTER
May 28, 1965

One of the largest, most destructive mine explosions ever recorded occurred in Dharbad, India, on May 28, 1965. The East Indian coal mine, 225 miles northwest of Calcutta, was suddenly thick with coal dust from blasting. Either an electrical spark or a small flame ignited the dust, and a gigantic explosion rocked the mine, thundering outward, killing at least 100 miners on the surface, blowing huge timbers like straw through the air, and flattening the engine room structure, the record office, and several houses nearby. The blast rattled a four-square-mile area.

Flames tore through the whole of the main shaft; it was several hours before rescue parties dared to enter, and when they did they dragged out an appalling number of dead. The total fatalities reached 375. Prime Minister Lal Behadur Shastri donated 40,000 rupees to aid survivors and their families. This amounted to roughly $8,000.

DIERKS, ARKANSAS — TORNADO
March 21, 1952

A violent storm moved rapidly in from the Gulf of Mexico on March 21, 1952, and out of its tremulous cloud banks, a tornado first touched down at Dierks, Arkansas, and gouged out a block-wide path. The twister exploded dozens of houses, sheared pine trees, and scalped animals.

One young man, Carl Young, Jr., hurried his family into his parked car, rolled down the windows and jammed down the emergency brakes. Young's house was demolished as if detonated; only its concrete porch remained. The tires of his car burst and the auto was bounced several feet into the air, but no one inside was injured. All of his neighbors within a block, however, representing several generations of the Allen family, were killed.

After destroying Dierks, the storm moved through Arkansas like a scythe, its tornados chopping up the towns of Bald Knob, Marked Tree, Carlisle, Hazen and Cotton Plant. A flurry of tornadoes from this storm front also struck the states of Alabama, Kentucky, Missouri and Tennessee, where at Henderson twenty houses were flattened by a single twister in only a few seconds. The series of twisters killed 208 persons and injured close to 2,500. More than 2,500 homes and buildings were either totally demolished or badly damaged.

Indian women mourn their husbands who were killed when the East Indian coal mine in Dharbad blew up on May 28, 1965. *(UPI)*

DIXMUDE — AIR CRASH
December 21, 1923

background: Built by Germany during World War I, the LZ.114 or L.72 dirigible was turned over to the French on July 9, 1920, when her name was changed to the *Dixmude*. After completing several historic flights, the dirigible, on a voyage to Africa, exploded and all fifty-two crew members were killed on December 21, 1923.

The *Dixmude* was the pride of the French dirigible fleet. The one-time German military zeppelin, turned over to France with a number of other dirigibles following the war, had made an historic first flight from Maubeuge to Cuers in 24 hours and 25 minutes on August 10, 1920.

A world endurance record was shattered by the French dirigible, then used as a survey craft for the navy, on September 25, 1923, when she flew from France to Tunisia and returned in 118 hours and 41 minutes. In the golden age of the dirigibles, the French considered the *Dixmude* one of the best. Her glory vanished, however, on December 21, 1923, when she disappeared over the Mediterranean with fifty-two crew members. All on board were killed.

Commanded by Lieutenant de Vaisseau du Plessis de Grenadan, the dirigible left her mooring mast at Cuers-Pierrefeu and set a course for Algeria. Her mission was to fly over the Sahara Desert so that experts could chart maps and locate fresh water sources. While in flight over the Mediterranean, Lieutenant de Grenadan talked by radio to weather authorities along the African coast. De Grenadan informed the control points that he estimated his ship to be about fifty miles south of Biskra. He was told that the *Dixmude* was headed straight into a violent storm. He then said he was changing course to avoid the storm.

Nothing was heard from de Grenadan until early morning of December 21 when his voice, shouting above a whining gale, told of the *Dixmude*'s wild battle with a thunderclapping storm. An hour and a half later the commander was again on the radio, stating in a hoarse, quick voice that "we must make an emergency landing." The *Dixmude* was sinking fast toward the raging waters of the Mediterranean, and her captain had decided that those on board must take their chances in the sea.

Dozens of radio operators along the African coast tuned into the radio frequency, but de Grenadan did not make further contact. Planes and ships were sent out to scour the Mediterranean where the airship had most likely crashed. Planes also flew over the northern areas of the Sahara in the event that the dirigible had been blown into that desolate wasteland by the storm.

Villages along the coast reported that the sky had been lit up by a fireball at the height of the storm, and authorities figured that the light-framed *Dixmude*'s hydrogen had been ignited by lightning and the ship had detonated. Days later two Sicilian fishermen hauled in their nets and discovered in their catch the body of Lieutenant de Grenadan. His was the only corpse recovered of the fifty-two killed on board the ill-fated dirigible.

The end of the *Dixmude* spelled the end of the French adventure with lighter-than-air dirigibles.

(ALSO SEE: Akron, Hindenburg, Roma, Shenandoah)

DOMINICA, GUADELOUPE — HURRICANE
September 9, 1806

One of the most severe hurricanes ever to strike the pleasure island of Guadeloupe occurred on September 9, 1806, when the city of Dominica was flooded, particularly by the swollen waters of the Roseau River. One hundred thirty-one persons were killed in this violent storm.

The *American Journal of Science* described the storm: "The spectacle which presented itself on the return of daylight was horrid beyond every power of description. Heaps of mud and sand through all parts of the town; the form of a street hardly to be discerned; two large streams, or rather torrents, running through the midst of the town; ruins of houses blown down . . . the carcasses of several of the unfortunate victims of this event drawn out from the ruins and lying in the streets, while numbers almost distracted were searching for some near relation or friend who had perished.

Hurricane Donna killed 143 persons in 1960; here its 150 m.p.h. winds lash a Miami estate. *(UPI)*

DONNA — HURRICANE

September 4-12, 1960

Hurricane Donna, born in the mid-Atlantic, traversed more than 5,000 miles before she died in the Gulf of St. Lawrence. The sluggish storm first struck the Leeward Islands on September 4, 1960, and then moved across Puerto Rico, which bore the brunt of its fury. Here 106 lives were taken by the storm. Donna then swept over northern Cuba and shoved her 150 m.p.h. winds and rains through the Florida Keys.

At Key Largo, the hurricane's winds gusted up to a piercing 180 m.p.h. Power lines were torn away, boats smashed and sunk and homes flattened. Scores of residents scurried to the cement warehouse owned by the Florida Keys Electric Cooperative Association. Huddled behind its steel doors, they waited in terror. *Newsweek*'s James C. Jones, who had been covering an auto show in nearby Miami Beach, was in the warehouse and later wrote: "The steel doors boomed like block-busting bombs. The transformer threw whole cascades of sparks. One power line went down. Soon, as the wind roared up to 150 m.p.h., all electricity failed, including the emergency generator. Lamps were lit and the night wore on."

Before the storm pivoted and spun up the Atlantic seaboard, the United States Weather Bureau had no less than four planes flying inside the storm's eye to calculate its speed and movement. Because of such accurate surveys coastal areas were warned far enough in advance to prevent great loss of life. Twenty-two persons were killed by Donna in the United States, mostly in Florida. Still the final death toll was 143.

DONNER PARTY — FAMINE

October 28, 1846-April 21, 1847

background: The Donner Party, organized by George and Jacob Donner and James F. Reed, was a frontier expedition of more than one hundred persons who immigrated from Springfield, Illinois, to California, departing on April 14, 1846. By October 28, 1846, the party, then numbering about ninety, reached what is now known as Donner Lake near California's Truckee River, high in the Sierras. Penned in by snow, the party suffered famine throughout the winter and lost half its members; charges of cannibalism and murder were later made. Survivors finally struggled across the mountains to Fort Sutter on April 21, 1847.

The ill-starred Donner Party was far from a struggling, ragamuffin clot of immigrants when it began its trek from Springfield, Illinois, to California on April 14, 1846. The group was well outfitted, its prairie schooners were the best available, and behind the caravan were large herds of cattle and horses. For the most part those in the train were prominent businessmen whose retrench in California was motivated by advent the prospects of sunny climate and larger tracts than currently were available to them in the Mi The great god gold had yet to be discovered. In fact it was in the wind-splintered cabin of Mrs. James Frazier Reed at Donner Lake in December, 1846, that John Denton, poking aimlessly at rocks used as fire-irons, first discovered gold.

Denton leaped forward and withdrew the hot stones, saying: "Mrs. Reed, this is gold. . . . If we ever get away from here, I'm coming back for more." He was a professional gunsmith and gold-beater from Sheffield, England. The thirty-year-old Denton left Donner Lake with the first relief party, but he died trying to get over the Sierras, his stomach empty, his pockets full of gold (which no one bothered to remove). His was the first discovery of what three years later would lead to the fever panic of the great California gold strike.

A great deal of good luck enhanced the Donner Party's initial travels. Though the Snake, Sioux and Pawnee tribes were viciously warlike at this time, the party lost only one member, William Trimble, to Indian attack near Scott's Bluff, Utah. Up to that point, only one other person, Mrs. Sarah Keyes, the elderly mother-in-law of James Reed, died en route. Her coffin was fashioned out of a cottonwood tree, and her grave became the site of what is now Manhattan, Kansas.

The first evidence of disaster in a series of mishaps that plagued the Donner Party occurred on October 5, 1846, as the group's wagons struggled up high embankments overlooking the Humboldt River in Nevada. John Snyder's team of oxen failed to pull his wagon up the steep incline. Normally a calm person, Snyder suddenly began to whip his cattle wildly.

One of the leaders of the group, James Reed, rode up and tried to calm Snyder and offered the assistance of his own oxen. Snyder cursed him. Reed stated, "We'll settle this when we get up on the hill."

"We will settle it now," Snyder shouted and brought his whip down on Reed's skull several times until Reed was blinded by blood running from deep gashes in his forehead. Mrs. Reed ran forward and got between the two men. Snyder raised his whip.

"John! John!" Reed shouted, but Snyder brought the whip down on Mrs. Reed and knocked her to the ground. Reed jumped forward and buried his hunting knife in Snyder's chest. Snyder died within minutes.

At first the members of the party (George and Jacob Donner, Reed's friends, were absent at the time, scouting far ahead) argued to hang Reed. He was finally banished, forced to make his way to California alone, although his family struggled on with the main party.

The financial savior of the Donner Party was California pioneer Captain J. A. Sutter.

Virginia Reed, shown here as an adult, was one of the few children to survive the Donner Party's ordeal.

James F. Reed, banished early in the Donner Party's trek, was one of the first rescuers to reach the group at the Truckee River in 1847.

Another Reed child, Mattie, shown here as an adult, ate leather and tree bark to stay alive.

Lewis Keseberg, a member of the Donner Party, turned cannibal in order to live.

By the time the caravan reached the Sierra Nevada range, winter snows blocked all the passes. The Donner Party hastily camped on October 28, 1846, at Truckee Lake (now Donner Lake). The blustery snowfall came on so rapidly that there was no time to build cabins, although a few abandoned hunters' cabins were found nearby. Leanna Donner later wrote, "The snow came on so suddenly that we had barely time to pitch our tent, and put up a brush shed, as it were, one side of which was open. This brush shed was covered with pine boughs, and then covered with rubber coats, quilts, etc. My uncle, Jacob Donner, and family, also had a tent, and camped near us."

Food supplies soon dwindled, and game in the high mountains became almost nonexistent. Hunting parties invariably returned empty-armed and bone-weary from hunger to the threadbare campsites around the lake. By mid-December, several attempts had been made to climb the summit. Mrs. Reed and her children tried once. One of her children, Virginia Reed, remembered "men and women walking in the snow up to their waists, carrying their children in their arms and trying to drive their cattle."

As the trapped immigrants slaughtered first their cattle and then their horses and dogs to obtain food, seventeen people, later called "The Forlorn Hope," attempted to cross the summit, led by the courageous C. T. Stanton, who was a gifted poet, well-educated and an expert woodsman. Stanton could not bear the starvation of the camp any longer, and he vowed: "I will bring help to these famishing people or lay down my life."

He and sixteen others, twelve men and five women, set off on December 16, 1846, to conquer the Sierras. They took only six days' rations, a pitiful allowance which came down to about a piece of shriveled beef the size of two fingers once each day. They crossed the summit and waded through the thick mantle of loose snow atop the Sierras. For three days they trudged, seldom speaking, eyes downcast. One of them, Patrick Dolan, who had given his beef supply from his slaughtered cattle to the starving Reed family back at camp, murmured incessantly about the snow: "a beautiful, white bed of snow . . . a bed of death." On the third day, Stanton went snowblind. Two days later he built a small fire, lit his pipe, wrote a poem to his dead mother and died.

Three days later, the small party was engulfed by a tornado of snow. By December 27, 1846, several men, including Dolan, had died. Without food, starving and delirious, the survivors resorted to cannibalism. One account states: "With averted eyes and trembling hand, pieces of flesh were severed from the inanimate forms and laid upon the coals. It was the very refinement of torture to taste such food, yet those who tasted lived. . . . Each of the four bodies was divested of its flesh, and the flesh was dried. Although no person partook of kindred flesh, sights were often witnessed that were blood-curdling." Sarah Foster watched horrified as the heart of her brother, Lemuel, was cut out and "thrust through with a stick and broiled upon the coals."

Their two Indian guides, Lewis and Salvador, refused to eat the human remains. They moved off a bit, camped with watchful eyes, ate their moccasins, and fled before dawn, thinking they would be the next victims. Mrs. Jay Fosdick, a day later, held her dying husband in her arms and then, hours later, turned his body over to the survivors to "be converted into food."

The small party staggered on, coming upon the exhausted Indians who had fallen with bloody feet in the snow. Two men and five women were staring down on them. William Foster, who had eaten Jay Fosdick's flesh to keep alive, leaned over the barely breathing Indians who had gone nine days without food, and apologized. "I am compelled to take your lives," he is quoted as saying to the Indians. "Forgive me." He then shot them to death, stripped their flesh, and moved off with the party.

Thirty-two days after leaving the campsite at Donner Lake, the seven survivors walked into an Indian camp on bloody, swollen feet. The five women immediately pleaded that rescue parties be sent to Donner Lake to retrieve their starving children. One of the first to mount such an expedition was the exiled James Reed.

At the campsite the remaining Donner members were reduced to eating green rawhide which was boiled down to a gluey substance. On Prosser Creek, where the Donner families lived in their wipsy tents, Jacob Donner died. Patrick Breen recorded in his diary on December 21, 1846: "Milton got back last night from Donner's camp. Sad news; Jacob Donner, Samuel Shoemaker, Rinehart and Smith are dead; the rest of them in a low situation; snowed all night with a strong southwest wind."

Women fought over hides with which to feed their children. Then the children began dying, mostly at night. They went to sleep breathing heavily and died. Bodies were strewn throughout the camps, the living too weak to bury them. Some men strong enough stripped the bodies and consumed the flesh. Milford Elliott, who had worked for the Reed family for years before accompanying them on the trip west, staggered to the Reed cabin one day, crazed with hunger. "Mrs. Reed," he said, "I am not going to starve to death. I am going to eat the bodies of the dead."

Elliott then stripped a dead body of its flesh but could not bring himself to eat it. He fell forward in the snow.

Mrs. Reed knelt beside him and, as he died, she prayed. Days later, on February 19, 1847, the first relief column broke through the high snows of the mountain passes and reached the campsite. The men of the rescue column wept upon seeing the skeletons littering the ground about the miserable campsite and viewing the sepulchral survivors.

James Reed and another relief party arrived days later, supplied, as was the first relief party, by the early West Coast pioneer, Captain J. A. Sutter, described in the *California Star* on January 16, 1847, in an editorial telling of the Donner Party's plight, as "one of the most humane and liberal men in California."

With the arrival of the third relief party, Lewis Keseberg, who had joined the Donner campsite on Alder Creek and had attempted to cross the mountains several times, once finding his own frozen child in a snowdrift, was accused of no less than six murders, robbing George Donner's gold and cannibalizing dozens of bodies.

In a subsequent hearing Keseberg was acquitted of the murders and robbery. He admitted to being a cannibal, pointing out that many others in the party had eaten the flesh of the dead to remain alive. Keseberg's wife and children had departed with the first relief columns. He was lame from an accident and could not travel.

Staying behind in a small cabin, Keseberg had become a sort of storekeeper of the unburied dead. Five corpses were housed with him. In an 1879 interview, punctured by the babbling and shrieks of his two daughters who had been turned into idiots by the savage ordeal at Donner Lake, Keseberg stated: "Five of my companions had died in my cabin, and their stark and ghastly bodies lay there day and night, seemingly gazing at me with their glazed and staring eyes. I was too weak to move them had I tried. The relief parties had not removed them. These parties had been too hurried, too horror-stricken at the sight, too fearful lest an hour's delay might cause them to share the same fate. I endured a thousand deaths. To have one's suffering prolonged inch by inch, to be deserted, forsaken, hopeless; to see that loathsome food ever before my eyes, was almost too much for human endurance."

Before their rescue Mrs. George Donner had staggered into Keseberg's cabin one night, almost incoherent but insisting on going over the mountains to see her children. She had fallen into the creek and frozen to death before Keseberg's eyes. Before dying, Mrs. Donner gave Keseberg several bags of gold to be delivered to her children if she failed to live. He promised they would get it. "I have often been accused of taking her life," Keseberg stated. "Before my God, I swear this is untrue! Do you think a man would be such a miscreant, such a damnable fiend, such a caricature on humanity, as to kill this lone woman? There were plenty of corpses lying around. . . ."

And these corpses Keseberg did eat after stripping and boiling the flesh. "There was no other resort. It was that or death. My wife and child had gone on with the first relief party. I knew not whether they were living or dead. They were penniless and friendless in a strange land. For their sakes I must live, if not for my own. . . . The flesh of starved beings contains little nutriment. It is like feeding straw to horses.

"I cannot describe the unutterable repugnance with which I tasted the first mouthful of flesh. There is an instinct in our nature that revolts at the thought of touching, much less eating, a corpse. It makes my blood curdle to think of it. It has been told that I boasted of my shame—said that I enjoyed this horrid food, and that I remarked that human flesh was more palatable than California beef. This is a falsehood. It is a horrible, revolting falsehood. This food was never otherwise than loathsome, insipid, and disgusting."

For two months the hapless Keseberg was inside the cabin, sustaining himself by cannibalism. Wolves scratched frantically at the door at night. In his disgust Keseberg claimed he thought of ending his life several times. "Suicide would have been a relief, a happiness, a Godsend. Many a time I had the muzzle of my pistol in my mouth and my finger on the trigger, but the faces of my helpless, dependent wife and child would rise up before me, and my hand would fall powerless."

When another relief party arrived, rescuers demanded the Donner money from Keseberg; they claimed he had stolen it and threatened to lynch him. He turned over the money and was led, bound by ropes, over the mountains to his hearing. Captain W. O. Fallon testified that "in the cabin with Keseberg were found two kettles of human blood, in all supposed to be over one gallon." He was, nevertheless, exonerated of his alleged crimes. But wherever Lewis Keseberg went for the remainder of his life, small children shouted "Stone him! Stone him!" and showered him with rocks.

Of those in the original Donner Party, forty-eight survived and forty-two perished.

DORT, HOLLAND — FLOOD 1421

Always in danger of the sea the Dutch built up an immense system of dikes to protect their lowland countryside, where, even in 1421, there were an average of five hundred persons to a square mile. It was in that year that Holland suffered the second worst flood in its history. The massive dikes around the city of Dort burst open, and the gushing flood quickly took the lives of

The dikes of Dort, Holland, gave way on April 17, 1421, and 100,000 people were drowned.

more than 100,000 persons.

Seventy-two villages were swept into oblivion, twenty never to be found again. The city of Dordrecht was separated permanently from the mainland. This great deluge reduced almost all of the region's nobles to penury.

(ALSO SEE: Holland, 1530, 1570)

DUGALD, ONTARIO, CANADA

RAILWAY WRECK
September 1, 1947

The head-on collision at Dugald, Ontario, on September 1, 1947, came as a result of confused orders and/or disobedience. It was never learned which, since both the engineer and fireman of the ramming train, Number 6001, were killed, along with twenty-nine others, in the crash.

Number 6001 was first ordered to meet train Number 4 at Vivian, Ontario, along the single track of the Canadian National Railway. The train proceeded on this schedule. Company authorities, however, rescinded this instruction with a later order, telling Number 6001 to meet Number 4 at Dugald, sixteen miles closer on Number 6001's route. Either the order was not seen or was purposely disobeyed, which would have certainly meant strong streaks of insanity and suicidal desires on the part of both the fireman and engineer, which, as records later proved, were not the case.

Not expecting to meet Number 4 until sixteen miles further down the track to the east, Number 6001 roared into Dugald at 30 m.p.h. and collided on a dead-heading run with Number 4, which was standing still. The

Two Canadian National trains met head-on at Dugald, Ontario, September 1, 1947; 31 passengers died. *(UPI)*

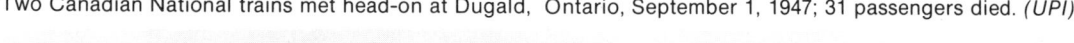

The ill-fated Turkish submarine *Dumlumpinar* sank in the Dardanelles, April 4, 1953, with eighty-one sailors aboard. *(Wide World)*

oncoming train, a vintage with nine wooden coaches lighted by gas, was wrecked completely, and the coaches were ignited and burned by gas from the ruptured gas tubes. Most of the thirty-one passengers who died burned to death in their seats.

DUMLUPINAR **MARINE DISASTER**
April 4, 1953

The Turkish submarine, the *Dumlupinar,* a 1,526-ton vessel built in the United States in 1944, saw heavy action in the Asiatic-Pacific theater during World War II (it was then known as the U.S.S. *Bumper,* and sank 2,525 tons of enemy shipping), and had been part of America's Mutual Defense Assistance program. Along with five other United States submarines, *Blower, Boarfish, Blueback, Chub,* and *Brill,* it had been turned over to the Turkish Government in 1950 after refitting in the Philadelphia Naval Yard.

Three years later while surface cruising on routine patrol with her sister submarine, *Inonu,* at 2:00 A.M. on April 4, 1953, the *Dumlupinar* was rammed by the 4,000-ton Swedish freighter *Naboland.* The night was inky black as both vessels were making their way through the perilous Dardanelles toward Istanbul. The *Naboland* backed away from the submarine and sustained only light damage, but the *Dumlupinar* was fatally struck and almost immediately sank to a depth of thirty-eight fathoms; the five men in the conning tower, including Captain Sabri Tohelebioglu, were knocked into the water and subsequently saved.

Although several vessels steamed to the rescue, including the United States destroyer *Hawkins,* the eighty-one men on board were doomed. During the hours of attempting to save the submarine, one message from the *Dumlupinar* was received: "Rescue us. We have air to last only a few hours." Although the submarine was equipped with snorkel underwater breathing devices, not one crewman apparently used them or the escape hatches. By 1:00 P.M. on the same day, the Turkish navy gave up the entire crew for dead. The submarine was never refloated.

DUNDEE, SCOTLAND — RAIL DISASTER

December 28, 1879

The loss of a seven-car train operated by the North British Railway that crashed through a wide gap of the famous Tay Bridge at Dundee, Scotland, on December 28, 1879, was a calamity of epic dimensions. The disaster was trumpeted worldwide, for the Tay was the longest bridge on earth. No survivors or even bodies were ever recovered from the swollen, gale-swept waters of the Tay River.

Up to this time train wrecks evoked much interest, particularly in the lurid tales told by survivors and reprinted with all their gory details in the otherwise dull columns of the "yellow sheets." But other train wrecks had survivors. The Dundee catastrophe offered only sullen mystery and the mute wreckage of torn clothing, traveling valises and the tops of coaches floating to shore.

The train left Edinburgh at 4:15 P.M. Two hours later, with near hurricane winds blowing along the Tay, the train rolled onto the long trestle. Whether or not the bridge was damaged before the train approached was never discovered. Most think the weight of the train was the final strain that caused already weakened spans to collapse and send the train hurtling downward 88 feet to disappear in the boiling waters of the Tay, flooded at that moment to 45 feet in depth.

Thirteen girders along the central span, each 245 feet in length, caved in, and the two-year-old bridge, considered to be an engineering marvel, was gone.

During their plunge the seventy-five passengers no doubt struggled to open their compartment doors and take their chances in the river. This was futile, as the *New York Times* pointed out, because of "the absurd rule . . . on railroads in Great Britain [that] the doors of every car were locked when the train left its last station; so that they [the passengers] were drowned without even having the chance to make a struggle for life."

DURAND, MICHIGAN — RAILWAY WRECK

August 7, 1903

The destruction of the Wallace circus train at Durand, Michigan, in the predawn hours of August 7, 1903, was attributed to brake failure. The first part of the circus train pulled into Durand yard, but its caboose jutted out dangerously onto the main tracks. A red lantern was hung at the caboose's rear platform, and those on the train went to sleep. The second train came roaring along the main track an hour later with an engineer named Probst at the controls.

Probst's line of vision was uncluttered, and the track was arrow straight. But Probst saw nothing. He was asleep. His fireman, looking down the track, turned to the engineer and was startled to see him head down and snoring. He shook Probst, who blinked at the red-lanterned caboose in his path and then lunged for the brakes. There was no response. The second circus train did not slacken its speed. Probst signaled for hand brakes. But there was no time.

The train smashed into the caboose at about 20 m.p.h., tearing it in half and instantly killing the twenty-two workmen sleeping inside. No one was injured on the second train, which consisted mostly of flatcars. In addition to the workmen, two camels and an elephant were critically injured. Animal trainers shot them quickly.

A later investigation revealed that Probst had had no sleep in thirty hours and that he had failed to recharge the train's brake line so that there would be enough pressure for the brakes to operate.

(ALSO SEE: Ivanhoe, Indiana)

E

EASTERN AIRLINES

AIR CRASH
November 1, 1949

background: While attempting to land at Washington National Airport on November 1, 1949, an Eastern Airlines' Flight 537, a DC-4, was struck by a P-38 also attempting to land on the same runway. Both planes were demolished; all fifty-four persons on the Eastern flight were killed, and the pilot of the P-38, Bolivian flying ace Eric Rios Bridoux, lingered for several hours before perishing.

Captain Eric Rios Bridoux was a Bolivian national hero and flying ace, a man who, friends stated, longed to make an epic flight similar to that of Charles A. Lindbergh and thus "make Bolivia famous." Just the opposite happened on November 1, 1949, only minutes after Bridoux took off from Washington National Airport flying a war surplus P-38. It was his job to test such planes prior to purchasing large lots for the meager Bolivian air force.

The day was brisk and bright; a panoramic view was afforded traffic controller Glen Tigner. From his perch in the tower Tigner could see for miles across the sprawling Virginia landscape. Eastern Airlines' flight 537 came on the air asking for landing instructions. Tigner gave the pilot instructions, telling him to bring his plane in on runway Number 3. The Eastern plane banked into a left-hand traffic pattern, and the pilot moved his four-engined ship in a counterclockwise direction about the field. He then descended toward the runway.

As Tigner watched the passenger plane come down, he heard Captain Bridoux call for landing instructions from his P-38. "Hold at 5,000 feet and circle," Tigner told Bridoux. There was no response. Tigner and others squinted into the bright sky and watched, horrified, as the P-38 swept over the residential section of Alexandria, Virginia, and flew over the landing Eastern DC-4, apparently oblivious to the fact that the large craft was directly beneath.

Tigner leaped for the radio mike. "Bolivia 927," he shouted, "Bolivia, Bolivia, turn left! Turn left! Traffic, Eastern DC-4 on final approach and below! Turn left!" As before there was no response from Captain Bridoux. The pilot of the Eastern plane, who was on another frequency, had no way of knowing that the fast-moving P-38 was snarling just above him and moving, landing wheels out, down on the back of his own plane.

The Eastern pilot did hear Tigner's imperative message to him, "Turn left! P-38 is traffic!" The pilot swerved his large plane to the left, but it was too late. Bridoux's hawklike fighter plane was on top of the helpless passenger craft in a matter of seconds. The P-38's still-whirling propellers slashed through the lumbering Eastern plane, broke it in two, and sent it crashing onto the runway, the men, women, and children inside spewing forth like broken dolls.

Bridoux and most of his plane caromed off the Eastern flight like a ricocheting bullet, leaped skyward for some distance, and then fell like a dead bird into the river. Before the war plane sank, Bridoux squeezed himself from the cockpit and rose to the surface, where he treaded water until United States Navy boats scooted across the placid river and hooked him into a boat just as he blacked out. But the rescue was in vain; the "pride of Bolivia" died shortly afterward, following in death all fifty-four passengers and crew of the hapless DC-4.

Though almost a hundred ambulances screamed their way from various points in Washington to the blood-soaked airfield, only one survivor, a woman, was found among the broken bodies. She died in the hospital a few hours later. Among the doomed travelers were several distinguished passengers, including Massachusetts Congressman George J. Bates and newspaper cartoonist Helen Hokinson.

It was never determined whether Bridoux misunderstood or failed to hear the desperate call of the twenty-one-year-old Tigner.

EASTERN AIRLINES

AIR CRASH
October 4, 1960

A small knot of persons gathered at Boston's Logan Airport to see off passengers on Eastern Airlines' flight 375, a four-engine prop-jet Lockheed Electra headed for Philadelphia on October 4, 1960. On board were fifteen Marine recruits headed to Parris Island, South Carolina. The parents of Frederick Abate were the only ones on hand to wave good-bye.

The Abates and others watched as the plane taxied down Runway 9 and then flew skyward, winging over Boston Harbor. It was 5:48 P.M. In seconds the port

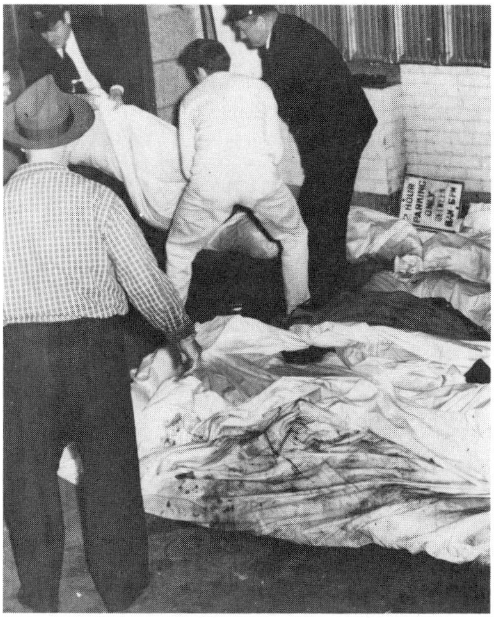

Bodies of passengers killed when an Eastern Airlines' flight crashed in Boston Harbor are stored in a police station garage. *(Wide World)*

Wreckage of Eastern Airlines' Flight 375 is hauled out of Boston Harbor, October 4, 1960. *(UPI)*

inboard engine burst into flames. With a lazy snore, the plane flopped to the left and, nose first, dove into the Pleasant Park Channel.

Skin divers from five yachts anchored nearby paddled frantically in small boats through the choppy waters, dove downward, and came up with ten survivors, many of whom were still strapped to their floating seats. Sixty-one others, including Frederick Abate, were dead.

A full-scale investigation, headed by General Elwood R. Quesada, head of the FAA, was launched, and two weeks later the Electra, a much-plagued airplane at that time, was cleared. Flight 375, it was determined, had inadvertently flown into a dense flock of starlings. The Electra's turbine engines had sucked a half-dozen of these birds into the jets, and this had caused an immediate loss of power.

EASTERN AIRLINES **AIR CRASH**
February 8, 1965

What caused the flaming crash that killed all eighty-four persons on board Eastern Airlines' Flight 663 on February 8, 1965, has never been determined. Reports from eyewitnesses on the ground first gave rise to the belief that the DC-7B might have been sabotaged. At Lido Beach, Long Island, housewife Thelma Gutman saw "a ball of fire fall into the sea" from a window of her home.

Another witness on the ground, Dale Bishop, a seaman on duty atop the seventy-five-foot watchtower at Short Beach Station, looked up to see "this red ball of fire about ten feet high above the water. . . . I heard a thud, or something that sounded like a small firecracker."

Flight 663 took off from Kennedy Airport Runway 31, the longest in the world at 14,600 feet, at 6:20 P.M. with Captain Frederick R. Carson at the controls. Carson flew the plane southward in an arching bank, apparently attempting to gain altitude. The radarman at Kennedy watched the plane's blip on the screen for about nine minutes, and just before he was to turn over ground control of the flight to New York Air Traffic Center, he lost the blip.

By that time the huge plane had plummeted into the Atlantic eight miles south of Jones Beach, crashing into seventy-five feet of water. Captain Stephen Marshall, the pilot of an incoming Pan-American flight from Puerto Rico, saw the Eastern plane "in an exceptionally deep turn" and watched it plunge into the water, where it exploded. It was hours before Coast Guard cutters searching the area discovered a large oil slick. Then bits of metal, headrests and a maroon blazer were fished from the sea. The bodies of several passengers had bobbed to the surface.

Among the dead were several executives of the Life Insurance Company of Virginia and another employee of the same firm, Marcia Childress, twenty-two, a beauty queen. Also killed were two promising young opera stars, Lillian Garabedian and Joan Gavoorian.

EASTLAND — MARINE DISASTER — July 24, 1915

background: The packet boat S.S. *Eastland* was a poorly constructed interlake steamer used for excursions on the Great Lakes. Due to gross engineering deficiencies and irresponsible passenger allotment, the ship capsized on July 24, 1915, only five years after she was built, in the Chicago River prior to her scheduled voyage to Michigan City, Indiana; 852 passengers were drowned.

Two years before the *Eastland* disaster, on August 2, 1913, a naval architect, John Devereaux York, wrote to the harbormaster of the Port of Chicago, warning that the *Eastland* tilted at precarious angles:

"You are aware of the conditions of the S.S. *Eastland,* and unless structural defects are remedied to prevent listing, there may be a serious accident," he wrote. York's warning was endorsed by naval architect W. J. Wood. After putting the *Eastland* through its "S" tests—reversing courses sharply from starboard to port to test its antilist capacity—Wood stated: "I thought the damned ship would take the turns on her side like a skipping stone."

Both of these strong and urgent warnings came to nothing; the *Eastland* went on with her excursion cruises, with as many passengers as possible packed on for each trip.

On July 24, 1915, more than 7,300 tourists had purchased tickets to attend the annual picnic sponsored by the Hawthorne Club. Most of the passengers were employed by Western Electric Company.

Five steamers led by the *Eastland* were to carry the huge crowd via Lake Michigan to Michigan City, Indiana, where they would picnic on the sand dunes.

The gala affair was heralded by a special issue of the club's paper. "Are you all set and ready for the big event? A long time ago Jonah took a trip on a whale. There is no Jonah about this, but it will be a Whale of a Success. Get your tickets early. Adults 75 cents. Children under five free! Children between five and twelve, half fare!"

The crowds were undaunted by the slight drizzle that

Moments after the excursion ship *Eastland* turned turtle in the Chicago River on July 24, 1915, hundreds of her bewildered passengers scrambled onto her hull and awaited rescue.

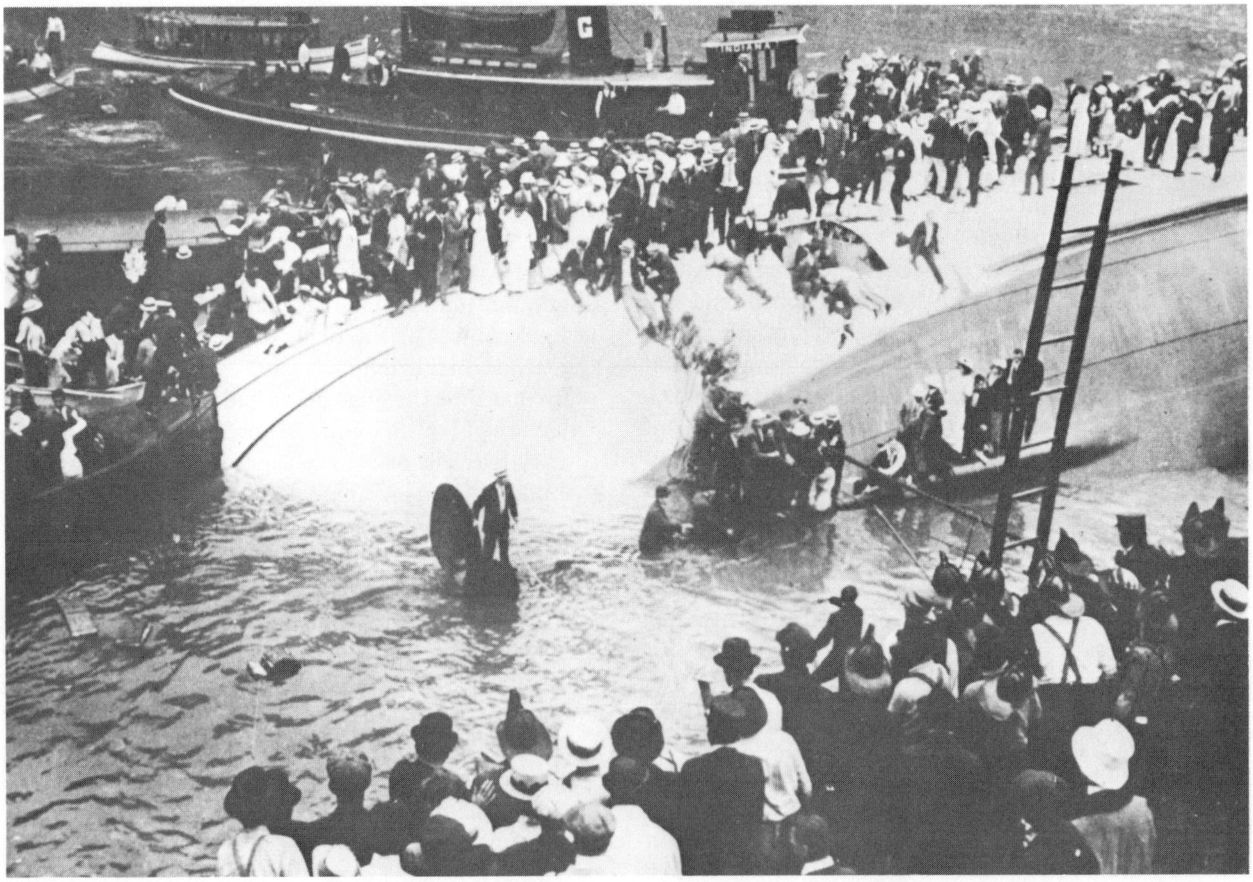

morning. They began to board the *Eastland* in droves just after 6:00 A.M. at the mouth of the Chicago River.

The *Eastland* was licensed to carry 2,500 passengers and crew members. But more than 3,500 were crammed onto her teeming decks in a half-hour.

A fiddle and mandolin band beat out a ragtime tune for the festive passengers. Thousands turned away from the *Eastland* when she was obviously full to her rails and went aboard the next ship, the *Theodore Roosevelt*.

A band on that ship was playing, "I'm on My Way to Dear Old Dublin Bay."

By 6:53 A.M. the chief engineer, Joseph M. Erickson, noticed that the ship was listing dangerously to port. The overloaded *Eastland* was tipping that way since the passengers had rushed to the port railing when someone spotted a photographer perched on a bridge taking pictures of the ship and her festive passengers.

Erickson compensated for the list by opening number two ballast tank on the starboard side. This righted the ship a little, but the listing increased, first to one side and then another, and Erickson constantly opened ballast tanks to compensate.

Exasperated the chief engineer sent several sailors topside to ask passengers to move to the right side of the *Eastland.* The request was ignored.

The harbormaster, Adam F. Wreckler, shouted from the tug *Kenosha,* waiting to help the *Eastland* from the dock, up to the *Eastland's* captain, Harry Pedersen: "Are you ready, captain?"

Passengers were alarmed to see the *Eastland* tilt even further toward the water. The sixty crew members realized what was about to happen and jumped immediately onto the dock.

Pedersen saw the terrible list the *Eastland* was making, and he shouted wildly and vainly from the bridge, "Open the inside doors and let the people off!"

But Pedersen was too late. The *Eastland* began to turn on her side, the list to port increasing from 25 to 30 to 35 degrees, going over hard in only a few seconds.

Water by the tons gushed through open ports and down three gangways. As one historian reconstructed the scene, "Passengers, furniture, picnic hampers, benches, refreshment stands, popcorn machines, barrels of lemonade and boxes of candy slid into piles on the port side amid a dreadful, overpowering volume of yelling and screaming.

"Over she went until she was flat on her port side on the river bottom. Only about eight feet of her white starboard side remained above water, giving her the appearance of a great, stranded whale."

While hundreds hung precariously to the slippery starboard sideplates, thousands of hysterical passengers fought each other for survival in the water—men, women, and children, clawing and thrashing at each other.

Another view of the capsized *Eastland;* acetylene torchmen saved forty persons trapped inside the ship's hull despite the captain's attempt to stop them.

"Above all the cataclysmic scene there was a great and dreadful wailing sound as the cries and pleas of the drowning blended in a terrible symphony with the moans and apprehensive shrieks of those who stood helplessly on the dock or watched in disbelief and torment from the other excursion vessels," wrote one reporter.

Workmen from a warehouse next to the river threw lumber, crates—anything that would float—into the river for the thrashing victims to hang onto. Tugs and other boats raced to the scene.

N. W. LeVally arrived at the scene with his workmen, who brought acetylene torches. Pounding had been heard from inside the *Eastland's* hull. One torchman, J. H. Rista, went to work cutting a hole in the hull, but, incredibly, Captain Pedersen showed up and pushed him away.

"Stop cutting a hole in my ship!" Pedersen shouted.

Rista told him there were people trapped inside, but Pedersen stood firm. Rista and his burly co-workers yelled obscenities at Pedersen and then went back to work.

"After I got rid of Pedersen," Rista testified later, "we took out forty people, all alive, out of that hole he had tried to stop me from cutting."

Pedersen and his first mate, Dell Fisher, finally had to be arrested to keep them from interfering with rescue operations.

Meanwhile the dead fished from the river were piled

up like cordwood in Chicago's Second Regiment Armory. The eventual death tally was 852.

Hundreds filed lawsuits against the St. Joseph-Chicago Steamship Company. But after twenty years of delays an Illinois court ruled that the firm was not liable for the disaster. The ruling simply said that the engineer had "neglected to fill the ballast tanks properly."

(*ALSO SEE:* General Slocum)

EAST OHIO GAS COMPANY — EXPLOSION — October 21, 1944

Constructed in 1940, the three thermos jug-shaped natural gas tanks of the East Ohio Gas Company in Cleveland exploded in a titanic blast on October 21, 1944, releasing a thick, black cloud that hung over the city to 2,800 feet. The tanks, holding 240 million cubic feet of gas that was flammable when vaporized, had leaked at times, but quick repairs had shut off the escaping gas. In the early afternoon of October 21, the yard was completely engulfed in a wall of flames. Men working around the tanks were consumed instantly, dying like moths in a flame.

The exploding tanks were similar to shooting flame throwers, their tongues of white heat darting and licking several blocks of residential dwellings in east Cleveland. The walls of houses glared red with flames and several blocks were destroyed. Manhole covers popped like tiddlywinks, shot skyward by the blue jets of flame.

Thousands of residents evacuated their homes, and thousands more, idiotically running toward the flames to get a better look, became victims. Mingled with the charred bodies of the dead were thousands of birds burned crisp by the blast.

The east Cleveland sky burned red all night, and firemen moved cautiously toward the gas works. It was not until the following dawn that the escaping gas was closed off and the fires put out. By then 112 were dead, roasted alive. Almost 1,000 were homeless, and 104 were missing.

The East Ohio Gas Company was left in a shambles after an explosion which killed 112 persons, October 21, 1944. *(UPI)*

EAST PAKISTAN — CYCLONE — October 10, 31, 1960

The lieutenant governor of East Pakistan, Mohammed Azam Khan, bumped along in a jeep as he made his way along the wide stretches of his country devastated by the monstrous cyclone of October 10, 1960. Before the Khan were thousands of huts flattened and buried by freshly turned-up mud, carts, dead animals (160,000 cattle died) and bodies scattered over the storm-ravaged earth. The Khan wept.

Following a long birth in the Bay of Bengal, the mother of so many cyclones, the 70 m.p.h. storm swept up to Chittagong and Noak, blasting East Pakistan for a full six hours and destroying more than 80 percent of every standing building. In the cyclone's wake came a huge tidal wave that capsized hundreds of fishing boats then at sea. For days afterward, dozens of fishermen were plucked from the ocean by liners and dropped off at Calcutta and other ports.

Islands in the Ganges were obliterated by the storm. A large ferry boat near Monghyr capsized when great slabs of earth from the riverbank were loosened by the storm and fell upon it. Only seven survived, and more than forty bodies were taken from the river in a three-day period. The streets of Lucknow, once the site of the bloody Sepoy Rebellion, were under twelve feet of water.

An estimated 4,000 persons lost their lives to this storm, but the catastrophe was but a forerunner to another cyclone that struck the entire country on October 31. In this storm winds of 120 m.p.h. gouged out great crevices in the country and inundated scores of islands. The islands of Kutubdia, Anwara, Bashkhali, Sandwip, Hatia and Ramgati were hardest hit by the storm. For hours Kutubdia was totally submerged under thirty-five feet of water. In Chittagong the cyclone ripped sixteen ocean-going vessels away from their moorings and sent them out to sea. Close to 10,000 were killed by this second storm, bringing the death toll to more than 14,000. More than 900,000 homes were destroyed.

EAST PAKISTAN — CYCLONE — May 28-29, 1963

On May 28, 1963, a land-ripping cyclone, estimated to be twenty times more devastating than one of 1960, struck the coastal regions of East Pakistan, where over a million people were crowded into the 179-mile stretch on the Bay of Bengal. With winds of 150 m.p.h. the storm tore through the countryside for fifteen hours, pummeling Cox's Bazaar and Chittagong; the many offshore islands were literally swept clean of people.

More than one million mud homes were squashed by the cyclone, and a tidal wave unraveled itself three miles inland at Chittagong, where 5,000 persons perished. At Cox's Bazaar another 5,000 were killed by the tidal wave. Four ocean liners were torn away from their moorings and sent by the wave almost a half mile inland. Gigantic dock cranes were snapped in two; jetties were ground to pieces.

A relief fund was established for the 300,000 left homeless, but little of this went toward the burial of the 22,000 killed by the storm.

EAST PAKISTAN — CYCLONE
June 1-2, 1965

The Pakistani authorities were meticulous in counting the dead, 12,047, after East Pakistan was struck by a cyclone on June 1, 1965. The 100 m.p.h. winds of the storm were concentrated in the Barisal region, about seventy miles south of the provincial capital, Dacca.

It was in this densely populated area that several tidal waves following the cyclone came ashore and accounted for most of the deaths. An estimated five million were made homeless, and starvation and plague took the lives of hundreds more during the subsequent summer months.

EAST PAKISTAN — CYCLONE
December 15, 1965

"The devastation wrought by the cyclone is horrible." These were the words of East Pakistan's provincial Governor Monem just after his plane set down in a foot of water covering the airfield at Cox's Bazaar. The December 15, 1965, cyclone had raced ashore from the Bay of Bengal at 12:15 A.M. with winds gauged at 100 m.p.h., striking into the heart of the Chittagong-Cox's Bazaar area and instantly flooding most of the coastal towns with tidal waves.

As usual the government was next to helpless in aiding the millions affected by the storm. (More than 60 million persons live in East Pakistan, an area roughly the size of the state of New York. The offshore islands of Kutubdia and Maiskhal bore the brunt of the savage cyclone. Thousands out of a population of 40,000 were killed and injured on the thirty-two-square-mile island of Kutubdia, which withered under the three-hour blast of the storm. At Maiskhal the destruction of life and property was almost complete. More than 80 percent of all the island's buildings were splintered, and its entire fishing fleet with 2,000 sailors was driven to the deep. The death toll topped 10,000, mostly from these two islands.

Relief supplies from the United States amounted to $25,000.

EBRO RIVER, SPAIN — MASS DROWNING
September 17, 1880

While taking part in maneuvers, a battalion of Spanish infantry, 275 officers and recruits, stationed at Logrono near the Ebro River, met death *en masse* when a pontoon raft on which they were traveling collapsed. The raft was a shaky affair and had to be towed to the other side of the river.

As the raft was being towed, the troops, all herded tightly together, kept pace with a military band playing martial music on the bank. Officers in the battalion ordered the troops to stop stomping their feet in time with the music as the raft began to roll. The young conscripts ignored the directives and marched in place, their uniform thumping striking the raft harder and harder.

Only when water sloshed over the sides of the large, unwieldy raft did the troops become alarmed. When the raft dipped first forward and then aft, the battalion panicked and rushed to the forward section; amid the confused shouting, the raft capsized.

Thrashing wildly about in the fast-moving Ebro, the young soldiers died in groups, dozens in linked arms sinking from sight. Eleven officers and ninety-seven conscripts were drowned.

The colonel emerged from the river, the medals on his chest dripping. Between gasping for air and coughing up brown water, he inquired, "Why didn't they obey?"

A battalion of young Spanish army recruits, 275 in all, drowned in the Ebro River, September 17, 1880. *(Illustrated London News)*

ECCLES, WEST VIRGINIA — MINE EXPLOSION — April 28, 1914

background: At 2:10 P.M. on April 28, 1914, Number 5 mine of the New River Collieries Company in Eccles, West Virginia, exploded, killing all 178 men inside the shaft, which was 500 feet below the earth's surface, and 8 men in Number 6 mine 250 feet above Number 5; another rescued miner died hours later, bringing the death toll to 181. Ten minutes after the first explosion another explosion occurred in Number 5 mine. Cause of the disaster was attributed to a pocket of gas that had accumulated from blasting out a coal barrier; the gas was ignited by an open light (burning fuse); coal dust carried the explosion throughout shaft Number 5.

Two shifts of workers were laboring in two mine shafts at the River Collieries Company in the small mining community of Eccles, West Virginia, on April 28, 1914, when a blasting fuse ignited huge pockets of accumulated gas and sent an enormous, flaming explosion shivering through the shaft of Number 5 mine. In that instant 172 men were killed. Eight miners laboring in Number 6, who were close to the shaft connecting both collieries, wrapped handkerchiefs over their noses and mouths and ran, but they died of asphyxiation.

Speedy rescue efforts saved sixty-six trapped in Number 6 mine, but one died later. Ironically one of those killed in the Number 5 mine had been a Charleston insurance agent, who only minutes before the fatal blast had descended to the 500-foot level to sell coverage to the men working there.

An ugly aspect of the disaster was that five of the dead miners were only fourteen years old. The mining laws of West Virginia at that time permitted child labor and no proof of age was required "except in case of doubt," at which time an affidavit from a parent was sufficient for hiring. The parents of the five youngsters had signed affidavits and filed them with the company. Following the explosion the *Survey* editorialized that "it ought to be evident by this time that it is a practice [sending youngsters to work the mines] not dissimilar from sending them to stand in the front line of battle."

Unlike previous mine disasters in the United States, the Eccles calamity followed in the wake of new workmen's compensation laws that provided some meager assistance to dependents. At that time each widow received $20 monthly until death or remarriage and $5 a month from the state for each child under fifteen. (West Virginia would not pay for more than three children in each family.)

In compliance with its new laws the state furnished two carloads of coffins and boxes and undertook burial expenses "not to exceed $75" for each of the dead miners, most of whom were so disfigured by the explosion that identification was made by the brass checks given to them before they entered the mine.

The New River Collieries Company was owned by the Guggenheims. In light of the new compensations it is interesting to note the statement that Daniel Guggenheim made a short time later to the newly established United States Industrial Relations Commission. His posture was wholly uncharacteristic of those robber barons who advocated an aristocracy of wealth and regarded humans as nameless chattel: "There is today too great a difference between the rich man and the poor man. To remedy this is too big a job for the state or the employer to tackle single-handed. There should be a combination in this work between the Federal government, the state, the employer and the employee. The men want more comforts—more of the luxuries of life. They are entitled to them. I say this because humanity owes it to them."

ECUADOR — EARTHQUAKE — August 5, 1949

background: The worst earthquake in modern Ecuadorian history occurred on August 5, 1949. The quake began at 2:10 P.M., 25 miles below the earth's surface (at 1 degree latitude 78 degrees longitude) and affected a 1,500-mile area along the eastern Andes, especially the central highland plateau of Ecuador, measuring 7.5 on the Richter scale. More than 6,000 were killed, 20,000 were injured, mostly by falling buildings, and 100,000 were left homeless; fifty-three cities and towns were devastated at a cost of $66 million. Major cities and towns shattered were Ambato, Pelileo, Latacunga, Banos and Patate.

Several tremors heralded the forceful earthquake that shivered along Ecuador's spine in the central highland plateau on the afternoon of August 5, 1949. Because of this thousands of lives were saved as people ran into the streets of fifty towns just before most of the buildings collapsed. Some people, like those in Ambato, known as the garden city of Ecuador, ran into churches where they wailed to God for protection. In the Ambato Cathedral seventy children receiving religious instruction were killed when the roof collapsed on them. The Reverend Juan Bautista Palacios was wedged under a fallen altar and was dug out alive four days later.

As the steady, sickening crash of walls deafened the ears of Ambato's frantic citizens, other priests hurried through the crowds with large, golden crucifixes in their hands, giving Extreme Unction to the dying and listening to quavering confessions in the open streets. One young priest, Aurelio de Jesus Barros, later reported: "I was strolling along slowly on the street that passes our church. Suddenly I found myself buried to my armpits. One second I was walking. The next second I stood there

Beneath the rubble of Ambato Cathedral were sixty children and a priest, buried in Ecuador's worst earthquake of modern times. *(UPI)*

looking down at my imprisoned body and legs. I was not in the least injured. It seems that I dropped into the earth. I heard the cries of the people. I saw the houses drop and collapse. . . . Those who were on the streets dropped out of sight or were covered with rubble. Nearly all of them died just as did those who were in their homes. I remained there, upright, buried up to my chest for three hours. Shortly after five o'clock an Indian got to me and dug me out. My shoes were gone, but my hat had remained upon my head."

Great sacrifices were made by the victims. One Indian woman was walking along with her child in her arms when the quake struck. She fell into a yawning fissure, and as she fell she lifted her child the full length of her arms. The gap of earth closed, crushing her to death, leaving only her dead hands protruding from the earth and in them her live child, who was saved. Days after the quake diggers found hundreds of bodies of parents and grandparents covering the bodies of their children and grandchildren in fruitless efforts to protect them.

The town of Pelileo vanished. An Ecuadorian doctor escaping from the carnage told how it "simply disappeared. Where it stood there is nothing but a waste of rubble, at some places more than twelve feet high. . . . The sides of the mountains seemed to have slid down. Landslides changed the courses of streams. Some of the country is unrecognizable."

Shock after shock hit Pelileo until its terrified people wandered without direction, stumbling over the rubble with the stark look of aphasia on their faces. Of the 3,500 people in the town, fewer than 1,000 survived. An incredulous *Newsweek* reporter at the scene a day later watched the survivors build rickety lean-tos on a hill to the west of the town. "They seem hardened to death," he later wrote, "and ignored the moans of persons buried under the rubble. They lack a sense of sorrow. Their ingrained habit of respect for the dead was overcome by relief for their own escapes, and they are anxious to repeat their stories."

Their stories were horrid and grotesque. For 117 hours, a seven-year-old boy, Enrique Mejia, lay buried beneath twelve feet of bricks. His loud cries failed to move any passing Ecuadorians to action, and it took Red Cross workers to dig him out. He died an hour after being pulled from the rubble.

In Pelileo what was left of the city was sunken twenty

feet and the beautiful river that had run through the city now spread like engulfing fingers and inundated the town. Within days its residents, shut off as they were from outside help, were reduced to eating dogs, cats and finally human flesh.

Outside the mountain town of Patate a grove of eucalyptus trees belonging to one farmer had been moved a quarter of a mile onto the property of a neighbor, which resulted in oath-shouting arguments over who now owned the grove.

Ecuador's president, Galo Plaza Lasso, flew into stricken Ambato from Quito and established his office in the middle of the park. About him gathered the crippled survivors. Lasso refused to admit either defeat or sorrow, saying, "I want dry eyes. If you wish to weep, weep silver for the destitute. . . . We have not lost our courage. Neither Ambato nor Ecuador shall cry any more, but [we shall] begin to work."

Help for Ecuador began to arrive within hours after the quake struck. South and Central American countries—Colombia, Venezuela, Peru, Cuba and Bolivia—responded with airlifts. The United States sent mercy planes, giant C-47s, loaded with supplies and Red Cross teams. A Shell Oil plane, carrying thirty-four workers who had volunteered to dig out the buried of Ambato, crashed near the city killing all on board. Relief columns to remote towns high in the Andes range were hampered by vicious attacks of the fierce and primitive Salasaca Indians, who took many lives.

Red Cross workers labored around the clock without sleep, administering in one city alone 7,200 typhoid and 2,000 whooping cough injections.

Five days later Ecuador's one hundred-fortieth birthday took place. There was no celebration.

EDDYSTONE AMMUNITION CORPORATION — EXPLOSION, April 10, 1917

background: First thought to be an act of sabotage, the explosion of the Eddystone Ammunition Corporation near Chester, Pennsylvania, on April 10, 1917, was caused by sparks from malfunctioning vibrators that caused powder being shaken into shrapnel shells to ignite. Killed were 133 workers, mostly women.

When the Eddystone Ammunition Corporation plant blew up on April 10, 1917, killing 133 workers, company owners and police officials skittishly turned in every direction to ferret out saboteurs. One official, only hours after the twenty-nine-month-old plant had been blown up, shouted, "It is the result of a diabolical plot conceived in the degenerate brain of a demon in human guise."

The only support for this claim was a note allegedly found by a Trenton, New Jersey, housewife, Anne Keating, as she was waiting for a train to Pottsville in Philadelphia's Broad Street Station. The note read: "All ready to blow up Eddystone. Send us help. N.K."

Dozens of suspects were arrested in a frenzy to trap German agents. One of the more bizarre incidents involved a Camden, New Jersey, man, Frank Miller. While finishing his dinner in a Camden restaurant, Miller engaged the cook in conversation, saying, "It's a damned lie to say the Germans blew up the Eddystone plant." Seated nearby Circuit Court Judge Lloyd overheard the remark and followed the man outside. Lloyd met two other judges about to go to dinner, and he hurriedly whispered his suspicions; the three judges then stopped a mounted policeman, and the group proceeded to follow Miller down the street.

They trailed Miller to a boarding house at 38 North Third Street. When they knocked on the door they were refused admission. "Knock that door down," ordered Judge Lloyd. The policeman, with the help of the magistrates, smashed the door down. "He's the fellow," Judge Lloyd said, and the policeman arrested Miller.

In custody Miller admitted he had been born in Germany but had lived all his life in the United States and had, in fact, served honorably as an officer in the Spanish-American War. Strange diagrams and plans were found in the forty-five-year-old man's room and authorities were sure that they represented blueprints of the Eddystone plant. They turned out to be sketches Miller had drawn of his farm in Burlington County. He was released.

Another German-born suspect was John Sickel, who had been arrested near the entrance of the plant several hours before the explosion. Sickel explained that he was seeking work, but Department of Justice officials appeared more willing to believe the fabulous tale that he was really a crew member of the German cruiser, *Prince Eitel Fredrich,* and on a nefarious assignment.

The special agent in charge of the case, Frank L. Barbarino, grilled Sickel and told reporters that "he is either insane or pretending to be. . . . I am having him removed to the hospital so as to find out what his mental condition really is." Sickel was proved sane and released.

The cause of the accident was ultimately determined when workers explained that the vibrators used to shake explosive powder down into the shrapnel shells had not been working properly for several weeks before the explosion. One employee stated: "I think the electric wires [of the vibrators] got tangled, started a short circuit and that sparks ignited the powder." Supporting this was a blinding flare seen by most of the females at work on the affected stretch of the assembly line. Dozens of them threw their hands over their eyes, and many of those killed by the resulting blast were found with their hands still covering their faces.

(ALSO SEE: Lake Denmark, New Jersey)

EDEN, COLORADO — RAILWAY WRECK
August 7, 1904

background: On the evening of August 7, 1904, Missouri Pacific Train Number 8, commonly called the Denver-St. Louis Express and also known as the World's Fair Flyer, was moving on Denver & Rio Grande tracks between Denver and Pueblo. The train crossed a ninety-six-foot bridge spanning a thirty-foot arroyo called Steele's Hollow, which was flooded to the tracks. As the train was midway across the bridge, a flash flood broke away an old wagon bridge above the trestle, and this bridge tore into the train bridge, dislodging its three spans and spilling the locomotive, baggage car, coach and chair car into the wall of water moving at a volume of 4000 cubic feet per second. There were an estimated ninety-six dead, which made this train disaster, only a mile from Eden, Colorado, the worst of its kind in railroad history.

A railway crane lifts the jumbled debris of a train washed away in a flood at Eden, Colorado, on August 7, 1904. *(Harper's Weekly)*

It had been raining for days, and the usually barren arroyos zig-zagging the route of the Denver-St. Louis Express between Denver and Pueblo were bloated with charging floodwaters. The seven-car express, also called the World's Fair Flyer, paused briefly at Eden, Colorado, on the night of August 7, 1904, before getting up steam and racing forward in the driving rain. Contrary to most reports the train had not slowed to a cautious crawl as it entered the trestle bridges yawning over heavily flooded streams. It was trying to make up for six minutes' lost time. Just as the train began to cross Steele's Hollow Bridge, an old wagon bridge upstream gave way under a torrent of water, and the debris from this bridge smashed into the train trestle and cut away its three main spans.

The Express collapsed into the racing waters. First the locomotive flopped sideways, followed by the baggage car and passenger-packed chair and smoking cars. Two partially filled sleepers and a dining car almost met the same fate, but a quick-thinking porter applied separate air brakes to the last three cars, and they stopped just short of the washed-out bridge.

In the cab of the engine, Charles Hindman applied the brakes, but it was too late. The fireman, Frank Mayfield, was thrown clear of the cab when the locomotive lumbered from the tracks and into the flood. He landed on an embankment, knocked unconscious. "Just as I was putting in the second shovelful of coal," he later recalled, "the engine gave a sudden lurch upward. I lost my balance and was thrown from the train on to the bank of the creek. . . . When I came to, I saw the Pullman cars standing near me, but could not see the engine or the rest of the train. I went up and down the stream looking for my engineer, Charles Hindman." But Hindman and ninety-five others, by most reliable counts, were dead. An hour after the crash searchers from Eden found Hindman's body washed ashore a mile from the ravine. Three men in the chair car managed to save themselves when the top of the car burst open. They swam upward through the hole and just barely reached the embankment. It was only after he climbed the embankment that Mayfield noticed that "the water was much higher than the tracks."

The flash flood carried the cars some distance, and bodies floated downstream for several miles, most of them collected by dawn of August 8. As relief trains rushed from Pueblo, more than 500 men busied themselves looking miles downstream for the dead whose arms and legs protruded from the muddy banks. The body of one elegantly dressed young woman, about twenty-five, was found twenty-three miles down the Arkansas River.

Most of the fallen cars were beyond salvaging. The large safe carried in the baggage car was one of the last items uncovered days later from the muddy riverbank. A superintendent laconically wired Denver & Rio Grande headquarters: "The express car safe was open when found, but do not think robbed."

EGYPT — FAMINE
1708 B.C.

In the course of Egypt's Middle Kingdom, when its pharaohs had been usurped by the *Hekau Khasut* ("rulers of foreign lands"), later termed by the Greek scribes as *Hyksos* from Syria and Canaan, the land was prey to large-scale killer plagues and famines. The worst of these occurred, according to historical and religious scribes, in 1708 B.C.

It was in this year that the seven years' famine, mentioned in Genesis, began: "And the famine was over all the face of the earth . . . and the famine waxed sore in Egypt." Tens of thousands were believed to have died in this famine, although few records of the day survived. Palestine was also heavily affected by the famine, where many thousands perished from starvation.

EGYPT **FAMINE 1064**

With the failure of the Nile to overflow and thus irrigate necessary food crops, in 1064 Egypt suffered a famine that depopulated two provinces and took the lives of 25,000 to 40,000 persons. Bread in Cairo sold for fourteen dirhems to the loaf at this time, and cannibalism became rampant in certain districts.

According to one source: "Organized bands kidnapped the unwary passenger in the desolate streets, principally by means of ropes furnished with hooks let down from the latticed windows." This famine extended to the year 1072 and was followed by pestilence.

EGYPT **FAMINE 1199-1202**

Probably the most severe and dehumanizing famine ever to strike that plague-ridden land of Egypt occurred early in the year 1199 and was attributed to a deficient rise in the Nile. A vivid and chilling eyewitness account of the famine was penned by Abdul Latif, a Baghdad physician and one of Saladin's intimates. He also became one of the world's first accomplished anatomists, thanks to a famine that took more than 100,000 lives.

By early 1200 Latif observed tens of thousands fleeing from Egypt to Arabia, Yemen and Syria; all were escaping the spiraling food prices which they knew would result once it was known that the Nile would not flood as usual. Cairo and neighboring cities were inundated by hordes of farmers. The bloated city populations were soon starving, and the impoverished were soon reduced to eating dogs, carrion and even the bodies of their own families.

Children, made homeless and unprotected by the deaths of their parents, were particularly prey to hunger-crazed bands of thugs. These men, who lived for months at a time, according to Latif, on the excrement of animals, began to waylay and kill the wandering orphans for food. The government retaliated by posting death notices for anyone committing cannibalism. Those caught eating the flesh of children were to be burned to death at the stake.

"I myself," Latif related, "saw a small roasted child in a basket. They carried it to the Emir and led in at the same time the mother and father of the child. The Emir sentenced both of them to be burnt alive. . . . I saw one woman wounded in the head, whom ruffians dragged across a square. They had arrested her while she was eating a roasted infant they found in her possession."

The physician recoiled in patrician shock at the indifference displayed by the general populace over such barbarism. Men became more adept at killing and cannibalizing the young than women, who were almost always caught and executed. At Misr, Latif witnessed the death of more than thirty such starved and senseless females. "I saw them lead one before the Governor, having a roasted child suspended from her neck. They gave her more than two hundred lashes to make her confess her crime, but in vain. She seemed to have lost all the faculties whi h characterize human nature."

Oddly enough, those who were burned at the stake were, when penitently dead and properly roasted themselves, turned over as legal food consumption for the insatiable masses. It therefore made sense to capture the openly practicing cannibals.

The famine even reached into remote areas of Egypt. Adults soon, too, had to fear for their lives, especially fat people. Craftsmen, who were called to homes ostensibly to perform their work, were murdered and cannibalized. Authorities discovered wholesale butchery taking place, even among the rich. One man, who bribed his way to freedom when apprehended, had invited dozens of friends, chiefly those on the portly side, to his home to partake in a dinner. They became the dinner. One of his unslaughtered guests found that her food tasted unusual.

"What kind of beef is this?" she asked a child of the house.

The daughter responded with: "Oh, a fat woman visited us and my father killed her and she's in there strung up." The small girl pointed to a pantry, and upon investigating, the visitor viewed what appeared to be a human butcher shop.

Soon relatives became victims of ravished appetites. Officials came across a woman gnawing on a human thigh. After they remonstrated with her, she looked up and blandly stated: "Why not? It's my husband." Mothers and fathers ate their children, explaining that it was better for them than for strangers to perform such grisly life-saving acts upon their own children.

Though accurate records giving exact death tolls of this most terrible of famines do not exist, it was estimated that more than 100,000 either perished by starvation or were killed to provide food; 20,000 alone died in the small city of Maks.

If nothing else, this calamity provided great study for anatomists like Abdul Latif. Up to this time Islamic laws had forbidden the dissection of bodies for medical experimentation and knowledge. Such laws were ignored, however, with such an overabundance of corpses in Egyptian streets, and the cause of medical science was advanced considerably after physicians began to perform the first crude autopsies upon the dead.

ELBE

MARINE DISASTER
January 30, 1895

The sinking of the *Elbe* with 335 persons on board (20 escaped, 5 passengers and 15 of the crew) was wholly due to the reckless navigation of the British vessel *Crathie,* which rammed the German liner and then left her to perish and her passengers to flounder in a roaring sea, much the same way the *Sultan* collided with the ill-starred *Cimbria* twelve years earlier.

Sailing from Bremen to Southampton with a destination of New York, the 4,510-ton *Elbe,* built in 1881, was capable of speeds up to sixteen knots. Captain Von Gossel was an able and conscientious seaman who was known to spend as much as thirty consecutive hours on the bridge in times of danger. He was on his bridge on the night of January 30, 1895, when he spotted the Aberdeen steamer, *Crathie,* as both vessels were forty miles off Lowestoft. The *Crathie* was sailing about a mile off the *Elbe*'s port bow and was therefore, under the rules of the sea, obligated to keep clear. Von Gossel expected the *Crathie* to alter her course to starboard, and he became increasingly alarmed when the vessel maintained what appeared to be a collision course.

On board the *Crathie* both the mate and lookout, who were supposed to be on the open bridge, had taken refuge in the galley where they sipped hot cocoa, sheltered from the bitter cold wind and roaring seas. Only the helmsman at the wheel could see the *Elbe.* He shouted repeatedly for the mate from his station in the wheelhouse, but it was several minutes before the mate responded. Captain A. Gordon was asleep in his cabin.

Dashing into the wheelhouse the mate reacted to the situation by ordering the *Crathie* to starboard, but it was too late. The ships collided with a forceful impact, made all the more destructive by the gale jamming them together. The *Elbe* had been struck behind the engine

The German steamer *Elbe* and her passengers and crew were victims of a midocean collision, January 30, 1895. *(Harper's Weekly)*

The bow of the *Crathie* was crushed when she rammed the *Elbe;* the *Crathie's* captain left survivors to drown. *(Illustrated London News)*

room, and tons of water gushed into her hull. She was a dead ship and began to fill rapidly.

With the crunch of ships Captain Gordon of the *Crathie* was awakened in his berth and jumped from his bunk into three feet of water that had rushed into his cabin. He later claimed, "I hurried on deck, and the first thing I saw was a large strange ship across the *Crathie's* bows. Immediately after the collision the *Crathie's* engines were stopped and reversed. I was not able to distinguish the name of the other ship on account of the darkness, but I was under the impression that the other steamer proceeded on her voyage."

The *Elbe* did proceed on its voyage—downward. As the *Crathie* sailed on in the dark sea, the German liner, carrying mostly immigrants journeying to America, began to list badly. Von Gossel ordered all lifeboats swung out and lowered, but the heavy seas soon swamped all but one, drowning 335 passengers and crew men. One boat with 20 persons on board watched the *Elbe* leave the surface in twenty minutes.

Only one woman, Anna Boecker, survived. After retiring for the night, fully dressed, she was shaken violently awake by the collision and then heard people running on the decks of the crippled liner. She ran on deck and two men helped her into a lifeboat. The *Elbe* was sinking so rapidly that the upper deck descended to the level of the lifeboat in minutes, swamping it. Miss Boecker then reached out and clung to the *Elbe*'s railing, pulling herself on board the liner. As the *Elbe* went under she spotted another lifeboat passing and leaped into the water, clinging to one of the boat's oars. The men inside the boat struggled for a full ten minutes to pull her from the water. The lifeboat was fast filling with water, and Anna almost drowned in the bottom of the boat as the waves washed over her and the men bailed frantically. They fought the heavy seas for five hours, and just as they were on the verge of being swamped, the fishing smack *Wildflower* came to their rescue.

Confusion reigned when the British Court of Inquiry convened to investigate the disaster. Von Gossel and most of his officers were dead. *Elbe* survivors and the crew of the *Crathie* gave vastly different versions of the collision, but the *Crathie* was eventually cited as being the culprit in the affair, although the *Elbe* was held partly to blame for not taking evasive action when it became obvious that the *Crathie* was on a collision course. It was a tragic story that would repeat itself at sea again and again.

(ALSO SEE: Cimbria, Egypt, Empress of Ireland)

ELM, SWITZERLAND — LANDSLIDE

September 11, 1881

background: Located in the Sernf valley, the Swiss village of Elm in Canton Clarus was all but destroyed when the top of the Plattenbergkopf mountain, undermined and weakened for years by slate mining, collapsed on September 11, 1881, at 5:30 P.M. and slid down the valley, demolishing thirty houses and killing 150 persons.

The mass devastation of the Swiss village of Elm on the Sunday afternoon of September 11, 1881, was caused by the greed and stupidity of its inhabitants. Beginning in 1868 villagers, under the auspices of the Swiss government, began to mine the towering mountain, Plattenbergkopf, which overlooked their peaceful hamlet of Elm. Huge amounts of profitable slate were carved from the mountain, and a deep quarry was blasted into its side, making its pinnacle, which was craggy with gigantic rocks and trees, unstable and dangerous.

Yet the haphazard mining went on without government supervision and with no concern over the increasing hazard of the weakened mountain. Cracks began to appear at the mountain's top in 1876, the largest of these widening to a gaping maw of five yards by 1881. During that year the top of the mountain creaked with rotten timber and quarry cave-ins and groaned and sent down occasional flurries of rocks to the valley beneath. The number of fatal accidents from falling rocks increased steadily.

The residents took to watching the mountain, first as an amusing pastime, then with apprehension. A schoolmaster named Wyss trained his telescope on a rumbling Plattenbergkopf about 5:30 P.M. on September 11, 1881. He was the first to see the mountain begin to disintegrate. Suddenly the trees at the top nodded and came together, and huge boulders swept them inward and downward as the roof of the quarry caved in. An immense gray-black cloud rose high above the peak. For moments it was quiet, and the residents of Elm thought that was the end of it. Then came another rumble, and those whose homes were high on the slope raced about, attempting to move the aged and sick to safety.

It was seventeen minutes between the first and second falls of the mountain. A curtain of rocks, trees and dust descended with breath-taking speed. The inn was overwhelmed, and all inside were killed. A dozen men had actually gathered in the inn to watch the daily rockfalls; Meirad Rhyner became alarmed at the first fall and left for his home deep in the valley carrying a large cheese and explaining that he did not "want to get pebbles in [his] cheese." All the houses about the inn were buried along with their occupants.

Half drunk, some of those in the inn still had the presence of mind to flee. Oswald Kubli later stated that he was one of the last to leave the inn. He and a few others were already outside when he heard a voice cry out, "My God! Here comes the whole thing down!"

"I made four or five strides," he recalled later while nursing head wounds, "and then a stone struck Geiger, and he fell without a word. Pieces from the ruined inn flew over my head. My brother Jacob was knocked down by them."

The confused villagers in the path of the rocky onslaught ran wildly about, as one observer said, "like a herd of terrified chamois." Rhyner dropped his cheese and loped down the side of the mountain. As he raced downward, his lungs and legs in pain, he saw indecision clutching most of those around him. "Of those who were before me some were for turning back to the valley to render help, but I called to them to fly. Heinrich Elmer was carrying boxes and was only twenty paces behind me when he was killed. There were also an old man and woman who were helping along their brother, eighty years old; they might have been saved if they had left him. I ran by them, and urged them to hasten."

A third fall of what was left of the mountain's top rolled everything before it. Cows, chickens, dogs, houses and humans flew into the air. More than ten million cubic yards of rock, the entire upper portion of the Plattenbergkopf, slid down the slopes and into the valley and raised immense clouds of dust. "Trees were snapped like matches," one survivor said, "and houses were lifted through the air like feathers and thrown like cards against the hillside."

Half the village of Elm had been swept away. One house had been sliced in two as if by a meat cleaver chop. The fastest runner of the village, Kasper Zentner, was just ahead of the landslide for a half mile. He saved himself by jumping over several stone walls and, with a broken leg, dropping into a deep gully while the slide passed over him.

Within an hour of the first slide, the grinding, roaring and tearing rush of rock and earth which drowned out every human shriek and cry mouthed by the 150 villagers killed and 200 more who were injured became silent. The broken mountain filled the valley 450 yards deep and a million yards in area.

The chalky clouds rolling in the wake of the slide had transformed the entire valley into a snow scene, unreal in the hot sunlight that poured down on undisturbed trees and grass coated white with dust.

Bodies stuck up awkwardly from the debris. On one mound of crushed homes, trees and rocks perched a severed head, open eyes clouded with dust and staring in the direction of the also severed mountain. Burkhard Rhyner was breathless by the time he reached his home. The slide had miraculously spared his home, but it had surrounded it with rocks, all of which had killed his fleeing family—his wife, daughter, son, son's wife and two grandchildren. Rhyner stared at his house in his grief and noted that "the doors were open, a fire burning in the kitchen, the table laid and coffee hot in the coffeepot, but no living soul was left . . . I am the sole survivor of my family."

(ALSO SEE: Aberfan, Wales; Chiavenna, Italy; Japan, 1964, 1972; Los Angeles, 1969; Rio de Janeiro, Brazil)

EL SALVADOR (and WESTERN HONDURAS) — HURRICANE, June 8, 1934

Almost all of El Salvador was overcome by a sluggish Pacific-born hurricane that crawled over the land on June 8, 1934. The excessive downpour of rain created by the storm bloated the Guija and Coatepeque lakes and swelled the Lempa River so high that most ships operating on the estuary were sunk. One reporter described a large steamboat sunk to its funnel in the middle of the Lempa and recalled seeing dozens of bodies floating around it.

Western Honduras was also heavily struck by the same hurricane, which created death-dealing floods there. The Ulua River overran its banks by forty-five feet, and the entire population of Pimienta was drowned. More than 2,000 persons in El Salvador and Honduras were killed by this hurricane.

EMPRESS OF IRELAND — MARINE DISASTER May 29, 1914

background: Built in 1906, the Canadian Pacific liner *Empress of Ireland* at 14,500 tons was an elegant ocean-going passenger ship that sailed from Quebec for Liverpool on March 28, 1914. The following day, while sailing down the St. Lawrence River in a dense fog near Rimouski, the vessel was rammed by the 3,561-ton Norwegian collier, *Storstad,* and sank to the bottom of the river in fourteen minutes, taking with her 1,024 passengers and crew members; her hull is still at the bottom.

The sinking of the great liner, *Empress of Ireland,* with the accompanying enormous loss of life was caused by pure stupidity. With 1,482 ensconced in her stately cabins and her crew manning her magnificent equipment, the *Empress* made her way down the St. Lawrence for the open sea. In the early hours of the second day of the voyage, Captain Kendall, at the bridge of his ship, noticed a collier about two miles down the St. Lawrence coming at full speed toward him.

Only a skeleton crew was about on the *Empress.* All the passengers were still asleep in their compartments. Kendall watched with apprehension as a fog bank rolled off the land and between his vessel and the approaching ship. In minutes his vision was totally obscured. "I rang for full speed astern on my engines and stopped my ship," Kendall later claimed.

He then blew three short blasts on the whistle, which was then known by mariners to mean that the *Empress* was going full speed astern.

Captain Anderson, skipper of the collier *Storstad,* who had spotted the liner coming toward him, blew three prolonged blasts on his whistle in response to the signal from the *Empress.* He slowed his ship down as fog signals were being exchanged between the two

The crumpled bow of the *Storstad* mutely testifies to the ramming of the *Empress of Ireland* on May 29, 1914. *(UPI)*

vessels, but he did not stop. Anderson watched the *Empress's* green starboard light disappear in the fog. He later insisted, "Under the circumstances the rules of navigation gave the *Storstad* the right-of-way." He continued to allow his collier to proceed at moderate speed up the St. Lawrence with no thought of stopping his engines.

On the deck of the *Empress* Captain Kendall strained his vision in search of the *Storstad* as the dense fog bank enveloped his ship. He ordered the whistle blown continually. Then out of the fog came the collier, headed straight for the liner, which was then "dead in the water." Kendall quickly grabbed his megaphone and shouted at Anderson, "Go full speed astern! Astern!" Then he spun to the helmsman and ordered the *Empress* full speed ahead, the helm hard aport. But there was nothing that could save his ship. In helpless anger Kendall watched as the *Storstad* "came right in and cut me down in a line between the funnels."

Captain Anderson blamed Kendall for "making considerable headway" and making the *Empress* an unavoidable target for the *Storstad.* Only when the collier was almost on top of the dodging liner did Anderson order his engines reversed. As the vessels collided, the *Storstad*'s ice-strengthened iron bow slashed into the *Empress* and created a gigantic hole running up half the ship. Anderson then did a peculiar thing. Instead of backing his ship off, he continued to drive her into the *Empress.* His thinking was to plug the very hole his ship had created by "holding her [the *Storstad*'s] bow against the side of the *Empress,* and thus preventing the entrance of water into the vessel."

The act did not achieve this effect as tons of water gushed into the liner. In fact driving the *Storstad*'s bow against the *Empress's* side caused her to list so badly that her more than ample lifeboats (which could hold 2,000, roughly 500 more than the number of people on board) could not be lowered safely.

There was no clamorous activity on board the *Empress* after she was hit; most of the passengers were in their beds and were drowned as the ship sank in the record time of fourteen minutes. It was miraculous that 458 passengers and crew men on the *Empress* managed to get off the liner before she went to the bottom. Captain Anderson supervised the rescue operations in the *Storstad*'s lifeboats.

Following this collision, the *Empress*'s parent firm, the Canadian Pacific Railway, lodged a claim of $2 million against the *Storstad*'s owners. Anderson was later held solely responsible for the disaster. While the claims were being settled, hundreds of bodies recovered from the *Empress* were gathered in the riverbank village of St. Luce; these were buried in a quiet ceremony near

Captain Kendall of the ill-fated *Empress of Ireland* watched helplessly as his ship was cut in two. *(UPI)*

The deck of the *Lady Grey*, en route to Montreal, is jammed with coffins holding some of the 1,024 persons who perished on the *Empress of Ireland. (UPI)*

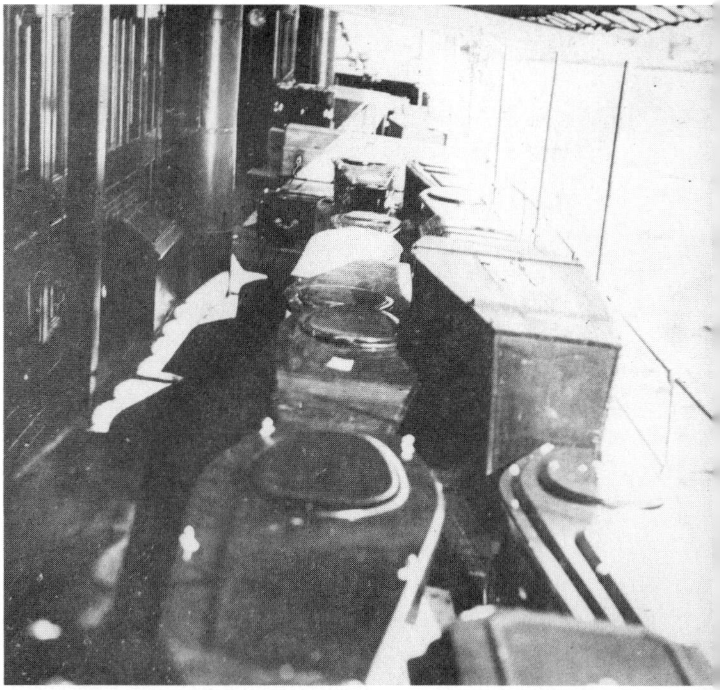

Metis Beach, where today stands a monument to their memory in a "disaster cemetery."

The *Empress* is still at the bottom of the St. Lawrence, resting in about thirty fathoms. An estimated $1 million in passengers' jewelry that had been stored in her safe has been sought by divers for more than fifty years. A year after the *Empress of Ireland* sank, a diver worked his way into the captain's room, reached the safe, and when his gear became entangled in the wreckage, suffocated and joined the grim death list on board that tragic liner.

(ALSO SEE: Andrea Doria*)*

ENGLAND — FAMINE
1069

Along with the Norman Conquest (A.D. 1066) of England, in A.D. 1069 most of the northern counties were ravaged and then stricken by famine. To stave off hunger, many, according to the *Harleian Miscellany* of the day, "ate human dog and horse flesh. . . . between Durham and Yorke lay waste, without inhabitants or people to till the ground, for the space of nine years, except only the territory of St. John of Bewlake [Beverley]. . . . other parts of his realm were so wasted with his wars that, for want both of husbandry and habitation, a great dearth did ensue, whereby many were forced to eat horses, dogs, cats, rats and other loathsome and vile vermin; yea, some abstained not from the flesh of men. . . ."

Thousands sold themselves and their families into slavery to survive. More than 50,000 died in this famine.

ENGLAND — HURRICANE
November 27, 1703

A savage Atlantic hurricane lashed the coastal cities and counties of England on November 27, 1703, devastating the southern portion of England. Little would be known of this killer storm had it not been for a then obscure pamphleteer, Daniel Defoe, who collected an amazing amount of data from victims and survivors.

Defoe reported that the hurricane mounted its fury against England for fourteen days before wreaking its greatest havoc. Rain squalls and violent gusts of wind preceded the final blast on November 27. Defoe wrote: "few people that were capable of any sense of danger, were so hardy as to lie in bed. . . . Most people expected the fall of their houses. And yet, nobody dared quit their tottering habitations: for, whatever the danger was within doors, it was worse without. The bricks, tiles and stones from the tops of the houses flew with such force and so thick in the streets. . . . The force of the wind blew the tiles point blank; where there was room for them to fly, the author of this has seen tiles blown from a house above thirty or forty yards and stuck from five to eight inches into the solid earth. Pieces of timber, iron and sheets of lead have from higher buildings been blown much farther."

Many like Defoe thought the hurricane came from the western Atlantic, from as far away as Florida. The worst damage was done to English, Russian and French fleets. All the important ports—Portsmouth, Hull, Yarmouth, Gravesend, Cowes, Plymouth, Falmouth, Bristol and Grimsby—and the river Thames were flooded by giant waves and an estimated 300 ships and 30,000 sailors were lost to the sea.

More than 5,000 houses were destroyed by the storm as it swept over Kent, Worcestershire, Warwickshire, Surrey, Sussex, Somersetshire, Northampton, Suffolk, Oxfordshire and Gloucestershire. The price of roof tiles skyrocketed from fifty shillings to six pounds per thousand.

Defoe's grim narrative continued: "Several ships that rode it out till now gave up all, for no anchor would hold. Even the ships in the river Thames were all blown away from their moorings and from Execution Dock to the Limehouse Hall there were but four ships that rid it out. . . . the rest were huddled together and drove on shore, heads and sterns, one upon another.

"There was a prodigious tide the next day but one . . . that brought up the sea raging that in some parts of England the water rising six or eight feet higher than it was ever known to do in the memory of man by which ships were fleeted up upon the firm land . . . and an incredible number of cattle and people drowned."

ENGLISH ARMADA — MARINE DISASTER
August 22, 1711

background: The sixty-one ships, transports and men-of-war making up the fleet of British Admiral Sir Hovendon Walker en route to attack Quebec were scattered in a gale and lost in fog on August 22, 1711, with eight transports, carrying 1,342 soldiers and sailors and close to 1,000 dependents, smashing to pieces on the rocky shoals of Egg Island near Labrador; all on board the transports were killed.

An ebullient expedition of English warriors sailed from the friendly waters of Great Britain on April 29, 1711, under sealed orders from Queen Anne. At sea Admiral Sir Hovendon Walker and General John Hill read with excitement their sovereign's directive. The queen had cast her lot for empire; they were to attack and capture the French fortress of Quebec, strongest bastion in the western world. They would require as allies speed and stealth, since no war then existed between England and France.

The British had mounted several offenses against

Quebec in the past, but each expedition had broken down or had suffered ignominious defeats, such as the drubbing Sir William Phips took at the hands of the French in 1690 when his proud scarlet regiments, almost 1,000 men, drowned in the perilous seas near Quebec.

Admiral Walker vowed he would be no Phips and sailed his majestic fleet under severe orders against breaking formations. The English armada, with almost 10,000 troopers and their families, numbering in the hundreds, on board, moved up the Massachusetts coastline after a stop in Boston. They encountered the French sloop, *Neptune,* under the command of Captain Paradis, on her way to Quebec with reinforcements. Taking the *Neptune* quickly in tow, Walker spoke briefly with the French captain and inexplicably became convinced that Paradis was the best man to navigate the armada through the dangerous waters of Saint Lawrence Bay. Walker's aides argued against it; the Frenchman, even though he claimed to have sailed the passage dozens of times, could not be trusted, they said. The English admiral paid Paradis 500 pistoles and felt he could rely upon such a charming, willing and helpful navigator. The armada proceeded under the direction of the Frenchman.

The sixty-one ships sped under full sail past Cape Gaspe, where Walker stopped long enough to burn some French fishing smacks. Then on toward the Gulf of Saint Lawrence the fleet moved, much too fast according to the French captain, but Walker insisted on getting to Quebec, now an easy prize in his vivid imagination.

On the night of August 22, 1711, at about 10:00 P.M., the massive fleet slipped into a dense, puffy fog and began to pitch and roll in an increasingly choppy sea. Conspiring with the fog and turbulent waves were wind gusts of gale proportions. Out of the fog, too late to be seen by the eight lumbering transports, loomed treacherous Egg Island, dreaded by all mariners for its jagged reefs and shoals. As if drawn to it by magnets, the transports—*Content, Isabella, Samuel, Merchant, Nathanial, Smyrna, Colchester,* and *Marlborough*—dashing their hulls to splinters on the island's rocks, were ground to pieces and spilled their human cargo, more than 2,000 soldiers, sailors, women and children, into a raging, black sea that shoved, tossed and eventually disgorged their lifeless bodies upon the land.

Walker's warships, faster than the transports, evaded the reefs and regrouped the following day. The British admiral, thoroughly disillusioned, made a feeble attempt to rescue possible survivors, sailing his ships far from Egg Island and staring coldly through his telescope at the skeletal remains of his transports. He gave up and sailed back to England in disgrace. (Walker was subsequently snubbed and shamed out of Great Britain and spent his last days in the colonies, dying with the works of Horace upon his chest.)

But there were survivors from the wreck of the armada, a few officers and a cluster of women and children who reached the mainland of Labrador in rags and with empty stomachs. They found no shelter or food, and when the winter of 1711 closed over them—some were later found frozen in hollow tree trunks and under wipsy shrubs where they had sought protection—the remnants of the once proud English armada ceased to exist.

Curious Frenchmen, hearing tales of the armada's destruction, visited Egg Island and Labrador and counted more than two thousand skeletons, most on the beaches, half-sunken in the sand. Edward Rowe Snow, the historian, described them: "Some of the dead bodies appeared as though they were gnashing their teeth; others seemed to be tearing out their hair; a few were joined in a final embrace. One group of seven women was discovered, their hands locked in a fatal circle."

The French benefited by much more than the staggering loss of English lives. Their Quebec-bound ships recovered more than $100,000 in armament, supplies and equipment that had washed ashore from the ill-fated British ships that ended their sailing days on that seaman's fright, Egg Island.

(ALSO SEE: Spanish Armada)

ENGLISH CHANNEL — STORM

January 16, 1974

A furious storm with fifty-foot waves beaten by 100 m.p.h. winds, the worst in twenty years, tore through the English Channel on January 16, 1974, killing thirty-five persons, most of whom were sailors.

The *Prosperity,* a 2,088-ton Cypriot freighter, was caught in the middle of the channel at the height of the storm and was soon out of control, eventually driven aground on a high reef surrounding Guernsey, one of the Channel Islands. The crew of the *Prosperity* abandoned ship, and of these, eighteen bodies later floated to shore. Eight more sailors were drowned when their ship, the *Merc Enterprises,* a 781-ton Danish freighter, sank in the storm.

Monster waves of this storm lashed the coasts of England and Europe. As a half-dozen other ships were run onto reefs, the deaths of numerous coastal residents were recorded. Two English boys walking along the sea wall at Dawlis in Devon were sucked out to sea by a giant wave. Another wave brought one back alive. A sixteen-year-old school girl was washed off a Brest ferry and disappeared. Four other Brest citizens fishing from a small boat in the harbor vanished in the storm.

Two more fishermen sailing off Brittany were lost to

the storm, which plucked what lives it could in its unpredictable course. Ten miles off Ostend, Belgium, the 2,447-ton freighter *Marta* fought the high seas. When she caught fire her captain wired that he could not launch lifeboats. One of her crew men, who had been fighting the fire, plunged into the sea, his clothes aflame. The *Marta,* badly damaged, limped into Ostend hours later.

ENTERPRISE — MARINE DISASTER

January 14, 1969

The then-largest warship afloat, the *Enterprise* (a 90,000-ton, 1,123-foot-long aircraft carrier, commissioned in 1961, the eighth American ship to bear that name) was conducting training flights off Hawaii on January 14, 1969, when she was rocked by three belching explosions. In a matter of minutes three holes were torn into the flight deck, which became a red furnace of flames.

Captain Kent Lee turned the huge ship, which could make thirty knots with her eight nuclear-powered steam turbines, into the wind in an attempt to blow out the fire from the stern of the ship where it raged. The ship's 5,400-man crew manned fire stations, but it was forty minutes before the fire was under control.

By that time twenty-seven seamen had been killed, most roasted to death by the intense flames. Another eighty-five were injured.

The cause of the explosion was attributed to a loose bomb falling onto the flight deck from a landing plane. The *Enterprise,* which had sailed nonstop around the world in sixty-five days in 1964, lost fifty yards of her flight deck following the explosion of "rockets, bombs, and twenty-millimeter ammunition," according to Captain Lee.

(*ALSO SEE:* Constellation, Forrestal, Oriskany)

ERTOGRUL — MARINE DISASTER

September 19, 1890

The wooden frigate *Ertogrul* possibly was consigned to death in the storm-tossed Sea of Japan by her own government, Turkey. Her construction and maintenance were so slovenly and slipshod that foundering on any prolonged voyage was virtually certain. The 587 crew members and passengers who drowned in her were unwitting victims, according to one claim, in the political assassination of one important passenger on the *Ertogrul's* manifest, a man whose life reads like a Kipling adventure yarn.

That man was known to the world as Osman Pasha, one of the most powerful and feared adventurers in the hierarchy of the Turkish government and one of Turkey's most renowned military heroes. For all of his fame Osman Pasha was shrouded in mystery, his origin, background and travels as nebulous as the mystical Levant itself. In one story he was supposedly a German who had appeared almost magically to aid Turkey in the Crimean War, the campaigns against Syria and the battles with Russia, much the same way that Lawrence of Arabia surfaced a century later. Another report claimed he was an American named Crawford who was wanted for murder in the United States.

Osman Pasha, also known as Osman Nurl, stated that he had been born in Tokat, Asia Minor, in 1832. On another occasion he claimed that he had been born in Amasia in 1837. Records revealed that he entered the military academy in Constantinople in 1850, joined the cavalry in 1854, and fought in that capacity six years later under the name of Omar Pasha in the Crimean War.

His career was meteoric after that, first defeating the forces of Hagia on Crete in 1867, then, as a brigadier, wiping out two Russian corps under Schackoskoy and Krudener near Plevna, earning the vaunted Turkish title of "The Ghazi," a rarely bestowed appellative meaning "The Victorious." From that point Osman Pasha returned to Constantinople and took over the army as Minister of War. His political power broadened and so did the titles strung ceremoniously after his name—commandant of the imperial guard, grand master of artillery, grand marshal of the palace. He was the closest man to the ruling sultan, and his influence in domestic and foreign affairs was as extensive as the list of enemies who plotted his demise, which points to the ill-fated *Ertogrul.*

The sultan enigmatically ordered Osman Pasha to head a political commission to the Mikado of Japan, a low-echelon errand that conveniently removed the adventurer from his seat of political influence. That he was ordered to take the ramshackle *Ertogrul* on this extended voyage when Turkey boasted of many excellent ocean-going ships attests to the claim that this was a simple way to eliminate Osman Pasha.

Half the navies of the world knew the *Ertogrul* was a jerry-built, ill-equipped, laggardly-crewed ship, hopelessly inadequate to undertake any extended ocean voyage. The trip to Japan would certainly prove fatal. Built in 1863 the unarmored, wooden-framed cruiser displaced 2,344 tons, had a 49-foot beam, was 250 feet in length and was able to move at 10 knots with her two 300 horsepower engines. She was designed, as one report stated, "on very coarse and clumsy lines."

Before Osman Pasha boarded her, the *Ertogrul* squatted in a small Mediterranean port with no money to buy fuel, her machinery broken down, her polyglot crew on the point of mutiny, and several of her officers unreliable. Once under way the ship lumbered and lurched her way into the Sea of Japan, her rotting boards giving way in the smallest swells, her engines missing and sputtering. On September 19, 1890, while attempting to return to Turkish waters, the *Ertogrul* foundered in a short-lived squall that almost any fishing skiff could have weathered. The sinking, in which 587 men drowned and 66 others survived, had been predicted by most authorities. But in Constantinople, it seems, it was a known fact.

As the ship went down one survivor related that shouts could be heard from the cabin of Osman Pasha. It appeared that someone had locked the door to his cabin, and nowhere on the ship could the key be located.

ERZINCAN, TURKEY — EARTHQUAKE

December 27, 1939

background: Seven death-dealing shocks struck Turkey, especially the provinces of Erzincan, Sivas and Samsun, on December 27, 1939, striking through the Janik mountain range throughout the upper half of Turkey, a 60,000-square-mile hinterland of the Anatolia peninsula, killing more than 50,000 persons, and leaving hundreds of thousands injured and homeless. The epicenter of the quake was estimated to be sixteen miles below the earth's surface. Damaged were eighty villages and a dozen major provincial towns of which the worst hit was Erzincan, which was totally ruined.

Erzincan, a scrubby, sprawling town of 51,000 in east-central Turkey, had known centuries of privation and disaster. Always subject to earthquakes emanating from the Janik mountain range, which is honeycombed with trembling faults, the city suffered one conqueror after another, the most devastating being the Mongol horde that defeated the Sultan of Rum in 1243 and all but reduced the city to ashes.

Not even the weather is kind to Erzincan, particularly its severe winters. Even though the town is on the same latitude as the city of New York, intense cold snaps drop the temperature to 30 degrees below zero. To insulate their homes against such piercing cold, the Turks pile mounds of dirt and rocks on their rooftops. When the worst earthquake ever to hit Turkey struck on the morning of December 27, 1939, these dirt piles became killers as rooftops and ceilings caved inward upon thousands of sleeping citizens.

Seven shocks between 2:00 and 5:00 A.M. were registered, and the buildings and homes of eighty villages and dozens of towns were wiped out. Half-dressed inhabitants dazedly moved about on quaking legs on the rolling, undulating streets to gape at swaying mosques and wiggling minarets. Rivers fanned into new streams and flooded fourteen towns in the Karacabey valley. Thousands climbed to their slippery roofs; hundreds of motorists drove off the roadways and were killed.

As the earth split, cracked and became a choppy sea, blizzards pounded the entire area, making it all the more hazardous to survive the deadly quakes. (Shocks continued the next day and were recorded on December 30, January 3, 5, and 18, 1940.) A flurry of earthquakes around the globe followed twenty-four hours later. In Los Angeles downtown buildings noticeably swayed for forty seconds. Twenty-five shocks, albeit minor ones, were recorded in South Africa's Rand. Rome's outlying districts, chiefly Bolsena, had four shocks. Those in the earthquake belt of Nicaragua, El Salvador and the Honduras felt tremors. Some argued that the Turkish quake had set off an epidemic of other trembles, but seismologist William A. Lynch of the Fordham University Observatory insisted that the minor quakes were caused locally.

It was no matter to the city of Erzincan, as one of the few survivors of that city despaired, "Erzincan is no longer a city, but a great cemetery." Every building except the barracks prison in the city was leveled by the quake. All of the town's doctors were dead. All of the nurses were dead. All of the officials, except the governor general and the chief municipal councillor, were dead. The councillor, staggering over debris, naked and babbling, was not discovered until the next day. He had become insane, and he was not alone. Hundreds of other city dwellers also lost their sanity; many committed suicide.

Ironically dozens of convicted murderers who had been saved when their prison failed to crumble, instead of fleeing, heroically dug out more than 1,000 persons trapped by debris. These same men, long hardened by prison, hurriedly built makeshift shelters for survivors, provided blankets and coats, often their own, as protection against the violent blizzard, built fires against the plunging temperatures and with sticks and fists beat off hundreds of wild dogs that scavenged the stricken city to feed on the dead and injured.

There were 50,000 dead in Turkey by dawn, and hundreds of thousands more were crippled and homeless. President Ismet Inönü arrived in Erzincan two days later, bringing with him most of his army and the Red Crescent (the Turkish Red Cross).

He was stunned at the sight of the city's vast ruins and stood stonily in the middle of what had been the town square. A grief-torn woman, her family dead, collapsed in tears on his chest. Inönü wrapped an arm around the peasant woman and consoled her.

ERZURUM, TURKEY — FIRE
December 7, 1966

On the night of December 7, 1966, a soldier attempted to light a gas stove in his barracks and succeeded in blowing up the roof of the building. The walls caught fire, and the more than 200 men sleeping inside quickly panicked and stampeded toward the door. Sixty-eight of these never got outside; they burned to death as they found their way blocked by blazing roof timbers. Another hundred men were badly injured.

The troops belonged to the Third Turkish Army stationed near Erzurum, the largest city in eastern Turkey.

ESHGHABAD — MARINE DISASTER
July 14, 1957

While transporting a cargo of fish and 270 passengers and crewmen between Salyan and Baku in the Caspian Sea, the large Russian fishing vessel *Eshghabad* struck a reef during a heavy storm on July 14, 1957, and sank. Although the Persian navy reported it had no evidence of the sinking, Soviet officials admitted the following day the loss of the vessel and all aboard.

ETNA — VOLCANIC ERUPTIONS
1226 B.C.-1928

background: Mount Etna, 10,870 feet above the Mediterranean on the eastern shore of Sicily, is the largest and highest volcano in Europe and is still active. Etna's base is eighty-seven miles in circumference, on which rest dozens of villages and towns, the chief city being Catania, which has suffered most through the volcano's historic eruptions. The worst eruption occurred in 1169, when 15,000 persons were buried in its ruins, and 1669, when 20,000 people died.

Legend has surrounded the giant volcano Etna from the time of its first recorded eruption. Early Greeks had mythological reasons for its volcanic eruptions. The eruptions of 1226 B.C., 1170 B.C. and 1149 B.C. are attributed to the expulsion of the demigod Hercules from Sicily and the wrath of the father-god Zeus. Greek writers also theorized that the volcano was the workshop of Haphaestus and the Cyclops (just as the fire-god Thor at this time was made responsible for the eruptions of the volcano Hecla in Iceland). Pythagoras pinpointed an eruption by Etna in 525 B.C. that took many lives. The Greek historian Thucydides mentioned another titanic explosion in 477 B.C.

The first full description of Etna's activity was penned by the lyric poet Pindar in the *Pythian Ode for Heiron,* written in 474 B.C. Pindar ardently believed that the giant Typhon was imprisoned in the mountain by Zeus: "He is fast bound by a pillar of the sky, even by snowy Etna, nursing the whole year through her dazzling snow. Whereat pure springs of unapproachable fire are vomited from the inmost depths; in the daytime lava streams forth a lurid rush of smoke; but in the darkness a red roiling flame sweepeth rocks with uproar to the wide, deep sea. . . . That dragon-thing [Typhon] it is that maketh issue from beneath the terrible, fiery flood."

An account by Thucydides relates, "In the first days of this spring the stream of fire issued from Etna as on former occasions, and destroyed some land of the Catanians who live upon Mount Etna, which is the largest mountain in Sicily. Fifty years, it is said, had elapsed since the last eruption, there having been three in all since the Hellenes have inhabited Sicily."

Even the poet Virgil could not ignore this ancient, belching monster:

> But Etna, with her voice of fear,
> In weltering chaos thunders near.
> Now pitchy clouds she belches forth
> Of cinders red, and vapor swarth;
> And from her caverns lifts on high
> Live balls of flame that lick the sky:
> Now with more dire convulsion flings
> Disploded rocks, her heart's rent strings.
> And lava torrents hurls today
> A burning gulf of fiery spray.

It remained for the poet Lucretius to shunt aside the mythical one-eyed Polyphamus, also said to live within Etna, and, in a burst of scientific candor astounding for its day, apply natural laws to the mountain's eruptions. "And now at last," he wrote, "I will explain in what ways yon flame, roused to fury in a moment, blazes forth from the huge furnace of Etna. First the nature of the whole mountain is hollow underneath, underpropped throughout with caverns of basalt rocks. Furthermore in all caves are wind and air, for wind is produced when the air has been stirred and put in motion. When the air has been thoroughly heated, and raging about, has imparted its heat to all the rocks around, whenever it comes in contact with them, and to the earth, and has struck out from them fire burning with swift flames, it rises up and then forces itself out on high, straight through the gorges; and so carries its heat far, and scatters far its ashes, and rolls on smoke of a thick, pitchy blackness, and flings out at the same time stones of prodigious weight—leaving no doubt that this is the stormy force of air. Again the sea to a great extent breaks its waves and sucks back its surf at the roots of the mountain. Caverns reach from this sea as far back as the deep gorges of the mountain below. Through these you must admit that air mixed up with water passes; and the nature of the case compels this air to enter in from that open sea, and pass within, and then go out in blasts and so lift up flame, and throw out stones, and raise clouds of sand; for on the summit are craters, as they name them in their own language, what we call gorges and mouths."

Roman writers like Seneca continued to build myths about Etna but constructed them around earthbound humans. Two brothers, Anapias and Amphinomus, it was related, heroically saved their elderly parents in 477 B.C. when Etna all but destroyed the city of Catania, the most volcano-plagued city in the world. They carried their parents on their shoulders to safety while dodging the snakelike rivers of lava darting about them. The apocryphal story records that the sizzling lava streams parted to allow the "pious brothers" with their parental burdens to escape. "The flames blushed to touch the filial youths, and retired before their footsteps. On their right hand fierce dangers prevailed; on their left were burning fires. Athwart the flames they passed in triumph, his brother and he, each safe beneath his filial burden. The devouring flames fled backward and checked themselves around the twin pair. At length they issued forth unharmed, and bore with them their deities in safety." This man-against-nature canard was told with such force and repetition that statues of the imaginary youths were chiseled and a temple erected in their honor.

In 396 B.C. Etna erupted with such magnitude that the Carthaginian general, Himileo, en route to Syracuse from Messino, was compelled to march his troops in the opposite direction along the west side of the mountain. This explosion devastated the town of Naxos and killed all but a few of its 500 Greek colonists. Etna was dormant until 140 B.C. when it again erupted and killed 40 persons.

Fourteen years later an Etna eruption took several hundred lives indirectly and freakishly. In 126 B.C. a huge mass of molten lava gushed into the Ionian Sea, boiling the waters about Lipari and throwing up thousands of cooked fish onto the shore. The inhabitants consumed the fish with such gusto and in such quantity that, according to one report, "a distemper appeared" in hundreds of the slothful and caused their deaths.

The much-harassed city of Catania was plagued again by an Etna eruption in 122 B.C., when the ash from its outpour was so heavy that it caved in the roofs of hundreds of dwellings. The extent of damage was so vast that Rome, then in control of Sicilian colonies, granted a stay of taxation for all inhabitants for a span of ten years, the first known relief action for disaster victims.

Shortly before the death of Julius Ceasar Etna erupted again, the tenth time in recorded history. From this time to A.D. 72 the giant volcano exploded five more times and then slept for two centuries until A.D. 252,

Etna erupted in 1852, spewing forth more than two billion cubic feet of lava. *(Illustrated London News)*

when it went on a nine-day binge that was halted, some historians allege, by the intervention of a saint. Martyred in A.D. 251 St. Agatha was revered by the townsfolk of Catania. When great rivers of lava began to flow from Etna toward the town, the terror-stricken natives rushed to St. Agatha's tomb, removed a veil that covered the saint's remains, and armed with this holy talisman, intrepidly approached the crackling lava flow. Holding the veil aloft, the story goes, the believers succeeded in halting the lava.

Mount Etna erupted again in A.D. 420 and then remained silent (with only a minor rumble in seven and a half centuries) until 1169, when "hell visited earth." The volcano erupted in a stupefying explosion, accompanied by an earthquake of great violence. Again St. Agatha's veil was employed, but it failed to turn back the flooding lava and exploding debris. From the moment of the volcano's first tremors Catania's great cathedral was jammed with frightened peasants kneeling with their bishop and forty-four Benedictine monks in fitful prayer. Near Etna's summit the side of the cone of one of its craters collapsed inward and a tremendous blast followed. More than 15,000 in Catania—everyone in the cathedral—were instantly killed as buildings collapsed into rubble. The fountains throughout Sicily, especially those at Syracuse and Ajo, celebrated for their purity, first turned blackish, and then the waters dropped and rose again, this time the color of blood. All over the island residents ran to the sea. Hundreds of Messina's natives, seeking refuge on the beaches, watched in horror as the waters of the Mediterranean drew back from the land hundreds of yards and then formed a tidal wave wall that returned in a rush, drowning scores and flooding half of the city. (Similar reactions by the sea occurred later in momentous earthquakes and volcanic eruptions.)

In almost twenty-three centuries of recorded Etna eruptions, the one in 1169 was the worst until 1669, when the volcano, after twenty-two minor outbreaks, exploded with such force that the entire island of Sicily quaked and 20,000 people met instant death. The holocaust began on March 8, 1669, when the sun was ominously obscured as a whirlwind swept across the mountain's summit. Then the land was possessed by convulsions for three days. The earthquakes destroyed several hamlets, including the town of Nicolosi, which disappeared completely. Every person on Sicily could feel the tremors of Etna growing stronger each hour; helplessly they watched, prayed and waited.

At dawn on March 11 a giant fissure twelve miles long and six feet wide opened on Etna's side, sending a blinding red-white light from the crevice. Six cavernous mouths also opened along the fissure, and great bursts of flames and towers of smoke shot from these. The volcano's roar could be heard for fifty miles. By dusk another extremely large crater gaped a mile beneath the original six, and from it shot white-hot stones. Sand and ashes blew, coating the countryside for ninety miles. This time the entire island of Sicily, it appeared, was doomed.

From Etna's seventh new crater roared a river of lava two miles wide. It encircled the town of Belpasso and killed 8,000. The new crater was enlarged further still when more mouths gaped open hideously and joined it. A seemingly endless lava flow rushed from the main crater and, by March 23, engulfed the town of Mascalucia, roasting alive hundreds of trapped inhabitants. On this day Etna's new crater gave up great quantities of ash, and a double-coned hill, now named Monti Rossi, was formed near the summit. An earthquake added to the devastation by splitting the great central crater from the mountain. This slab of mountain fell into the bowels of the volcano and caused tremendous blasts of fire and showers of rocks.

One village after another was swallowed up by the lava flow, which formed three huge rushing streams. Pietro was obliterated—then Camporotondo. Next came Mascalucia and Misterbianco. Fifty towns and villages in all were swept to destruction, and finally, the burning lava seas, almost as if aiming at an old, stubborn enemy, dashed once more toward the hapless city of Catania.

This time, however, the city had made preparations, its elders having vowed to fight the volcano after its previous carnage had wrecked their town time and again. Great walls towering to sixty feet had been erected to shield the community against the lava. Behind Catania's thick walls thousands of residents stripped the town of its religious relics, including the veil of St. Agatha, and followed their bishop, clergy and senate to Monte di Sofia, where mass was hurriedly said. According to one report the dazed parishioners moaned prayers and employed "the exorcisms accustomed upon such extraordinary occasions."

Nevertheless the lava raced toward Catania and scooped up cornfields and vineyards, which floated eerily upon the boiling surface. The burning liquid reached the city walls, welling up higher and higher until it cascaded over the top. In some instances the lava forced its way through the barrier. A third of the city was destroyed in hours.

Before the walls gave way or were surmounted, brave Catanians attempted to build new walls within the city. Baron Papalardo even tried to redirect the river of lava with dozens of determined men. Covered in skins to ward off the searing heat the Baron and fifty others,

The village of Nunziata crumbled under heavy shocks from Mt. Etna in 1928. *(UPI)*

using iron hooks and crowbars, severed a solid wall of scoriae that contained the lava and diverted the flow away from Catania. This caused the molten river to angle toward neighboring Paterno. The residents of Paterno, feeling themselves menaced, grabbed swords and lances and threatened the Baron and his followers with death if they would not desist. The Baron and his followers threw down their tools in disgust and staggered back to an already smoldering Catania.

An English ambassador, who was in Sicily to witness the devastation, reported, "I could discern the river of fire to descend the mountain, of a terrible fiery or red color, and stones of a paler red to swim thereon, and to be as big as an ordinary table. . . . of twenty thousand persons which inhabited Catania, three thousand did only remain; all their goods are carried away, the cannon of brass are removed out of the castle, some great bells taken down, the city gates walled up next the fire, and preparations made by all to abandon the city."

More than 20,000 were officially listed as dead in the 1669 outbreak, although some reports indicated that 60,000 to 100,000 had died. The loss of life to Etna's anger increased in 1693 when an eruption claimed the lives of 18,000 of Catania's residents. The wonder of Catania's determination to exist on the very slopes of volatile Etna is best explained by noting that the area offers some of the most fertile land in the world, its rich topsoil providing superb corn and vineyards sometimes yielding five crops a year. It is also home to its stoic residents.

Between 1693 and 1755 seven more eruptions were recorded, the last of which was joined by an earthquake that shuddered through a five-thousand-mile area, inflicting upon Lisbon, Portugal, one of her worst disasters. Over twenty undistinguished eruptions occurred on Etna from this time until 1843, when a crater 7,000 feet up the mountain burst apart above the village of Bronte. From this aperture shot scoriae and sand, and then a tidal wave of lava flowed downward at a speed of 180 feet per minute. Oddly the forward lip of this lava river suddenly exploded like gunpowder. The blast killed thirty-six persons instantly and injured twenty more.

Subsequent to these eruptions the mountain's other notable explosions happened in 1852 and 1928. In the first instance a small loss of life was recorded, but the eruption was distinguished by the largest overflow of lava ever witnessed. Two billion cubic feet of lava encompassed three square miles. The lava flow continued for nine months, and a central explosion emitting from the main crater on Etna produced a strange white ash, thought to be the residue of feldspathic rocks, that became clay-like when squeezed and turned to a powdery substance when heated.

The 1852 outbreak of Etna coincided with the destruction of Santiago, Cuba, by an earthquake, twin disturbances that ran hand in hand through the volcano belt.

Etna's last devastating eruption occurred in November, 1928, when the Messina-Catania rail line was overcome by rivers of lava estimated to be one hundred feet wide and moving at a speed of twenty feet per minute. When it reached the sea on November 7, the lava had already destroyed the town of Mascati and the village of Nunziata. Scores were killed.

(ALSO SEE: Krakotoa; Lisbon, Portugal; Santiago, Cuba)

EUROPE — BLIZZARD

February 1-29, 1956

For almost four weeks Europe was battered by blizzards and cold blasts in February, 1956. It was the worst record of snowstorms known to Europe in the twentieth century. Within one month the weather took the lives of 907 persons and caused more than $2 billion in damages.

The British training ship *Eurydice* sank off Bonchurch, March 24, 1878; 398 drowned. *(Frank Leslie's Illustrated Newspaper)*

EURYDICE — MARINE DISASTER

March 24, 1878

background: Built in 1843, the 921-ton twenty-six-gun British frigate, *Eurydice,* with almost 400 crew members on board, was being used as a seaman's training ship when it foundered and capsized at 3:50 P.M. on March 24, 1878, off Bonchurch on the Isle of Wight. It was making for port in Spithead after its four-month cruise in the West Indies; all but 2 on board died.

The British training ship *Eurydice,* converted from a twenty-six-gun frigate in 1877, had just completed a four-month cruise of the West Indies and was returning to England on March 24, 1878, when she met with sudden disaster. About 400 seamen, along with several army officers, soldiers in ill health and a number of military prisoners awaiting court-martial were aboard when the vessel was spotted by coastguard officials at Bonchurch at 3:30 P.M.

The seas were calm as the *Eurydice,* a wooden, full-rigged sailing ship, made her way toward Spithead, rounding the Isle of Wight and prow-dancing through usually dangerous waters. A strange, unexpected wind suddenly veered onto the ship's path, and with it came a blinding snowstorm.

Most of the crew were below assembling for prayers before the evening meal. Food was being carried into the seaman's mess. Captain Marcus Hare was on deck giving orders to weather the onrushing blast. It was 3:50 P.M. when the gale and wall of snow enveloped the *Eurydice,* and she was lost from view by those on land who were tracking her with telescopes. Within minutes the storm had ripped past the ship, but the land watchers who had been admiring "the grand, old ship" blinked in disbelief. The *Eurydice* was gone with the storm, nowhere visible on the clear sea. Not until several bodies began to float ashore and two men were rescued was the mystery explained.

When the sudden snow squall struck the ship, she was moving at eight knots and under full sail. All the main-deck ports were open to let in the air to the main-deck mess. The *Eurydice* was struck by the vicious blast of wind and snow a little before the beam and her fore and mizzen topgallant masts were snapped off and carried away. Tons of water sluiced through the open ports. As the ship began to capsize, only one man from below decks, nineteen-year-old Sydney Fletcher, first-class seaman, escaped. Hearing a loud, crunching noise, probably the masts breaking away, Fletcher raced up a hatchway and heard a voice shout, "All hands for themselves!"

Grabbing a life buoy, Fletcher jumped overboard. Seconds later the *Eurydice* capsized and sank, the suction in its wake dragging Fletcher under and downward. He held tightly to the buoy, however, and soon bobbed to the surface with it.

Before the ship went over, Captain Hare bellowed orders to Lieutenant Francis Tabor and the seaman working the sails, but the whine of the storm drowned out his words. As the ship rolled over, several men rode her like a log. Seaman Benjamin Cuddiford last "saw the Captain standing on the vessel's side near the quarter boat and the two doctors [were] struggling in the water." Cuddiford, the only other survivor, had already jumped overboard and was swimming furiously in an attempt to avoid the suction he knew the ship would cause when she sank.

Lieutenant Tabor swam past Cuddiford as he made for the shore. (Tabor reached land but fell dead on the beach.) Cuddiford held on to a life buoy and a wooden beam from one of the broken masts. He saw a group of men struggling nearby and pushed the wooden beam toward them. "I then came across the copper punt full of water, five men were in it. The sea capsized the punt, and they all got on the bottom. They asked me if there were any signs of help. I told them that the best thing they could do was to keep their spirits up." As he spoke Cuddiford saw an exhausted man let go and sink.

Swimming on, Cuddiford came across Fletcher, who was nearly dead. He helped him stay afloat until the schooner *Erma* approached and hauled them aboard.

EURYDICE — MARINE DISASTER

March 4, 1970

The disappearance of the French submarine *Minerve* in 1968 caused authorities to suspect that there might be a structural defect in France's Daphne-class submarine. In commemorating the dead—fifty-two officers and men—who vanished with the *Minerve,* and in a display of confidence, Charles De Gaulle nervelessly took a ride at a depth of 130 feet in a sister submarine, the *Eurydice.* De Gaulle's presence, however, failed to prevent the *Eurydice*'s fate two years later on March 4, 1970.

On that day the *Eurydice* left St. Tropez and made for Toulon. At a little after seven in the morning, her commander, Lieutenant Bernard de Truchis de Lays, radioed that he was diving his ship off Cape Camarat. Scientists in a geophysical lab, minutes later, were startled as their instruments recorded a massive underwater explosion. It was, as planes, helicopters, and ships verified hours later through oil slicks and marked debris, the *Eurydice* that had blown up while submerging, killing all fifty-seven men on board. The cause of the explosion was never determined.

(ALSO SEE: Dakar)

The luxury steam-and-sail vessel *Evening Star* foundered in the Atlantic, October 3, 1866; only ten survived. *(Harper's Weekly)*

EVENING STAR — MARINE DISASTER

October 3, 1866

A $500,000 steam sidewheeler and sailing vessel, *Evening Star,* was the celebrated front-running liner of the Star Line, and it was considered one of the most luxurious ships of its day, an expensive favorite of high society in the antebellum South. The *Star*'s regular run was between New York and New Orleans, and its captain, William Knapp, usually kept the ship on a course that hugged the Atlantic coastline.

On March 2, with 270 passengers and crew on board, the *Evening Star* sailed right into a full-fledged hurricane. For seventeen hours Knapp and his sailors fought the gale while their vessel slowly began to break up. To quiet the alarmed passengers fifty-nine singers of a New Orleans troupe and thirty circus performers entertained in the ship's saloon.

At 6:00 A.M., March 3, 1866, the *Star* could no longer withstand the hurricane's onslaught and began to founder about 180 miles east of Tybee Island. There was a mad scurry for the lifeboats, but most of these had been blown into the sea and wrecked. As the *Star* went down, nine persons, including two women, followed the ship's purser, E. S. Allen, as he swam to a single lifeboat that had miraculously been saved.

For two days nine people, without food or water, clung to life in the drifting lifeboat. They were finally spotted and rescued by the Southampton-bound steamer *Fleetwing.*

EXETER THEATER

FIRE
September 4, 1887

background: Built in 1886 and opened in October of that year, the Exeter Theater in Exeter, England, caught fire on the night of September 4, 1887. The cause was gaslights that set fire to the upper part of the scenery in the flies above the front of the stage. Most of the 200 spectators killed were attempting to flee the gallery down a five-foot stairway.

The newly built Exeter Theater in Exeter, England, was packed on the evening of September 4, 1887, with almost 1,400 in the audience. Just after the play began, spurting gaslights affixed to the walls set fire to the upper part of the scenery on the stage. William Keating, a spectator in the gallery, was one of the first to notice the small flame.

"I thought there was something strange in the appearance of the flies at the left-hand corner [of the stage]," he later told authorities, "and I saw a bright light behind the act-drop. Some people in the gallery called out 'Fire!' and a rush was made for the door."

As smoke gushed from the stage, the actors scurried off to easily accessible side exits, and those in the pit, dress circle, stalls and private boxes, about 900 in all, filed quietly to other exits without panic. But in the gallery, like that of the Iroquois disaster sixteen years later in Chicago, pandemonium reigned.

Keating kept his head and worked his way down the narrow steps leading from the gallery by holding on to the wall. Women and children raced forward screaming. Desperate men were at their heels, their boots snagging on the trains of women's dresses, causing them to fall forward. Their prostrate bodies were trampled. The fire had not yet reached the gallery, but the auditorium was quickly filling with smoke, and black clouds curled menacingly behind those racing down the angling stairs leading from the gallery to the street.

"It was only when we got to the last flight of stairs," Keating related, "that we came in contact with the black, suffocating smoke. I should think many persons were stifled by this smoke while on the stairs."

Though many men acted with blatant selfishness, heroism was displayed by a few conscionable persons. One of these, a soldier named Scattergood, who was stationed at Exeter, had escaped from the gallery and turned at the foot of the stairs when he heard the screams of children. He moved up the stairs again, forced the crowd to slow down and pulled youngsters around his

The elegant Exeter Theater, Exeter, England, burned down on September 4, 1887. *(Illustrated London News)*

body so they could move downstairs unhampered. Scattergood was later found burned to death.

George Cooper, another soldier in the crowd, a sailor named William Hunt, and a patron named Harry Foot ran into the theater at the first alarm and began to drag half-conscious persons to the street.

By the time Foot worked his way through the intense smoke to the gallery stairs, he was met with a grisly sight. "The staircase had been filled with a dense smoke, which had found its way there from other portions of the house, and the staircase, acting as a sort of flue, carried it up into the gallery. This smoke had suffocated those whom I saw lying dead in the second flight, because there was no sign of any crush there . . . the most fearful sight met our eyes on the third flight. . . . The bodies were lying in a heap. . . . They were all head downwards, and in nearly every instance the face was towards the floor. At the bottom of the third flight of steps were the bodies of three or four females. . . . The bodies were lying so thick that they quite occupied the entire width of the staircase; in some cases they were four and five rows deep. At the bottom of the stairs they lay thicker than at the top, almost as if shot down a shoot. In the majority of cases the arms were outstretched beyond the head, as if they had struggled to the last to drag themselves forward; but their legs were rendered immovable by the bodies of those who had followed and partly fallen on them."

Among the 200 dead on the gallery stairs a young woman was still alive, buried beneath several bodies. She was removed immediately to the London Hotel but died afterwards. Foot, Hunt, Cooper and others attempted to drag out several persons they thought were still alive, but the flames began to dart down the staircase, and the lead roof was so heated by the fire that it turned to a molten rain that seared the heads of the rescuers, who were driven back and outside. "It would have been suicidal to have continued our work," Foot concluded.

Commenting on the great Exeter fire, the *Illustrated London News* said, "The occupants of the boxes, who paid higher prices, had their safety well provided for; and so it is at most of our theaters." The paper archly added, "But shilling [gallery patrons] customers must not expect any care for their lives in these places of public entertainment."

(ALSO SEE: Brooklyn Theater, Ring Theater)

Seaman William A. Hunt, one of the heroes of the Exeter Theater fire, dragged several persons to safety. *(Illustrated London News)*

Two hundred bodies, removed from the remains of the Exeter Theater, await identification. *(Illustrated London News)*

The terror began here in the gallery of the Exeter Theater. *(Illustrated London News)*

F

FARAHZAD, IRAN — FLOOD

September 17, 1954

Several thousand Iranian pilgrims arrived in Farahzad in mid-September, 1954, to worship at Imam Zadeh David, a shrine clinging to the side of a deep gorge. Dozens of pilgrims' rest houses were also precariously built into the side of the mountain, and these, full of occupants, gave way almost at once following a thunderous rain storm on the seventeenth. Part of the shrine, which housed 3,000 worshippers wailing for "Imam to protect us" was swept away by the torrent.

Flooding the gorge, the deluge drowned more than 2,000 pilgrims and carried most of the bodies several miles downstream.

FERGUS FALLS, MINNESOTA — TORNADO

June 22, 1919

The destruction of Fergus Falls, Minnesota, on June 22, 1919, was uncanny. It was as if the twister divided the town with a bread knife, obliterating half of the community, 228 houses in all, and leaving the other half completely untouched. The death toll was fifty-nine persons.

One witness described the sound of the sudden storm as "a dozen factories filled with buzz saws."

FLINT, MICHIGAN — TORNADO

June 8, 1953

background: In a record year for tornadoes—250 from January 1, 1953, to June 1, 1953—a series of twisters spun through Michigan and Ohio; on June 8, 1953, the Ohio cities of Cygnet, Deshler, Elyria, Ceylon and Bowling Green, where 8 died, and the west side of Cleveland, where 9 were killed (the Ohio death total was 19 killed, 351 injured) were rocked. The hardest-hit area was in Michigan, where Ann Arbor, Erie, Milford, Brown City, and Tawas City were smashed; and Flint, where 116 were killed, 867 hurt and damages mounted to $19 million.

It has been estimated that an average of 150 tornadoes slice through the United States each year killing 222 people and causing about $14 million in damages. From January to June, 1953, this average figure had almost doubled in the number of twisters, and before the year was out the death toll and damages would be quadrupled. (The record of tornado-caused deaths was set in 1925 with 794.)

On June 8, 1953, Michigan was struck by the most devastating tornado in its history. The auto center of Flint was the site the twister marked for destruction.

Beginning at Flushing, Michigan, the twister rushed over a half-mile area and hit Flint at 8:45 P.M. The suburban areas along the Coldwater Road and Flint River were all but obliterated. Lifting roofs, exploding walls and flattening buildings to the foundations, the twister wiped out 386 homes, damaged another 525 and killed 116 trapped victims. The tornado that whooshed down on Flint was described by one reporter as "swirling like water draining from some giant bathtub."

Four New England states were also hit, notably Worcester, Massachusetts, where 87 were killed and 800 were injured. President Eisenhower flew to the scene, where, after personally viewing the carnage at Flint and Worcester, he declared both stricken cities disaster areas, making them eligible for federal aid.

In administering to the injured and housing the homeless, the Red Cross exhausted its disaster funds for the entire year. They reported that the tornadoes represented the worst two months of calamities in the agency's history.

FLORA — HURRICANE

September 30-October 9, 1963

Hurricane Flora was a most unpredictable, unorthodox, and vicious storm in that it did not follow the normal courses of Western Hemisphere hurricanes. The storm, emanating from Tobago on September 30, 1963, capriciously headed for the countries in the Caribbean. First Haiti, run by dictator Papa Doc Duvalier, was struck on October 3-4.

The suppressed residents suffered and died miserably as the hurricane's squall lines ripped away forests, ploughed up valleys and turned small streams into roaring rivers. Villages and towns were erased by the storm; 5,000 persons, a minimal estimate forwarded by the cagey Duvalier government, were reported dead and 100,000 were left homeless.

Next it was Cuba's turn. Tenaciously Flora hovered over the island's eastern provinces for five days, destroying 90 percent of Cuba's coffee crop and killing about

Hurricane Flora devastated Cuba in 1963. *(Wide World)*

1,000 persons. One anti-Castro leader in Florida reflected upon the hurricane, "In four days the storm did more damage to Castro's economy than we'd been able to do in more than four years." More than 175,000 Cubans were made homeless. Cuba's economic base, its sugar crop, was cut down by a fourth.

Castro accused the United States of not providing him with weather information about the approaching storm and then, paradoxically, filed for United States aid.

FLORENCE, COLORADO RAILWAY WRECK
March 16, 1906

The head-on collision of two Rio Grande trains between Florence and Adobe, Colorado, on March 16, 1906, was directly due to the exhaustion of a dispatcher who fell asleep for only one minute. In that minute's duration death came for thirty-four train travelers.

It was close to 2:00 A.M. and a blinding snowstorm raged all along the Rio Grande line. The Pueblo, Colorado, dispatcher wired twenty-five-year-old S. V. Lively in the Beaver station.

"Has train Number 3 passed your station?" Lively was asked.

"Not yet," he answered.

"Display stop signal and hold train at your station," the Pueblo operator told him. Lively said he would do that. But he was already too late. Working two shifts, Lively had been on duty nearly twenty hours. He had dozed off for a period of time later accurately estimated to be less than a minute. Within that minute train Number 3 had passed his station.

The reason for holding the train at Beaver was, hours later, regretfully obvious. The eastbound train, Number 16, had been running late, and the Pueblo dispatcher decided to send it on and allow it to pass Number 3, which was to wait on a siding at Beaver. Because of Lively's brief nap, both trains headed toward each other on a single track and met, albeit at cautious speeds, outside Florence. There were no fatalities on Number 16, but the first two day coaches of Number 3 burst into flames on impact, their stoves bursting to shower the cars and riders with flaming coals. An inferno developed. Thirty-four persons, including the two engineers, were trapped and burned to death.

Two of the dead were later found with their charred wrists encircled by handcuffs. A sheriff and his prisoner, en route to the Colorado Penitentiary, had been caught in the burning debris of the first car. The sheriff died instantly and the prisoner fought desperately to free himself from the dead man. Escaping passengers saw him fight off the flames and then suddenly fall next to his captor. The superb train historian Robert B. Shaw mused, "In fiction the prisoner should have been enabled to escape by the wreck to prove his innocence or to begin a new career under a concealed identity." In reality his corpse, burned beyond recognition, was buried in an unmarked grave.

FLORENCE, ITALY — FLOOD

November 4-6, 1966

background: Torrential rains and 90 m.p.h. winds combined to flood the Arno and Po rivers between November 4 and 6, 1966, killing 113 and injuring thousands, especially in the area of Florence. Two-thirds of Florence was inundated; 6,000 artisan shops were destroyed and countless, priceless art treasures were damaged and lost. Also hard hit by the flooding rivers were Venice, with damage to 7,000 shops; the Tuscany vineyards, where the chianti crop was obliterated, and the Trentino region, where 30,000 were made homeless. Damage, particularly to the art objects, was inestimable. The Italian parliament voted $320 million in relief aid with $2.5 million going to the restoration of damaged art works, monuments and ruined libraries.

The Florentines, sensitive to their custodianship of some of the world's greatest art treasures, as well as being perhaps the finest artisans anywhere, universally fear one shock more than war or disease or death itself—the flood. Cruel torrents had slashed through the capital of Italian art, where the Renaissance had blossomed, in 1333, 1577, 1666 and 1844. As each flood ebbed more treasures slipped down the riverbanks, sank into the mud or broke under the pressure of the water.

Dante in his beloved and imperiled Florence had seen "the green and lovely banks of the Arno" transposed into "raging froth and mud." And in the wake of its destruction he had lamented,

> So swiftly it rushed towards the royal stream,
> that naught held it back.
> My frozen body at its mouth the raging Archain found,
> and swept it into the Arno.

The Arno and its tributaries conspired again in early November, 1966, to threaten the golden city of Italy. The Arno and Po rivers were bloated by furious flood-

The once elegant Via Roso Finiguerra in Florence, Italy, is awash during the floods of 1966. *(UPI)*

waters following a cyclonic storm that rained down millions of tons of water in the mountainous region north of Florence.

From a remote vacation spa a hotel clerk shouted over a phone that he could see a nearby lake spilling wildly over its banks. He described whole forests sliding as if on skids from the slopes of mountains. By the dawn of November 4 the Arno floodwaters gushed into Florence, inundating two-thirds of the city. The exquisite jewelry shops along the Ponte Vecchio built in 1345 were gone. So, too, were the Santa Croce's artisan shops—6,000 in all—containing the works of dedicated weavers, woodworkers, leather workers and wool carders. Worse, Cimabue's magnificent thirteenth-century crucifix was submerged in brackish, oily water in the Museum of Santa Cruce for twelve hours. With 70 percent of its color gone, it could not be repaired.

Ghiberti's *Doors of Paradise,* the priceless bronze relief gates adorning the Baptistery, were at first feared ruined. Five panels had been punched out by the raging flood waters, but all were later discovered snared to an iron rail fence encircling the Baptistery.

All day the flood waters lapped at frescoes painted centuries earlier by Giotto, Ghirlandaio, Botticelli and Andrea del Sarto, and smeared oil and muck onto the sculptures by Michelangelo and Donatello. More than 600 paintings were damaged, but they, for the most part, could be restored. The priceless manuscripts and incunabula housed in the Biblioteca Nazionale, one of the first Florentine victims of the directionless Arno, could not. More than 500,000 records were lost as the flood broke through the weakened walls of the great library. It reminded many of the loss by fire of Turin's royal library in 1903 and the obliteration of Alexandria's library of classical antiquity in 500 A.D.

All was in the flood's path at the University of Florence. A million volumes inside the Library of the Faculty of Liberal Arts and Philosophy were washed away. Thousands of doctoral theses were ruined at the School of Economics and Business. One of the most cherished collections of rare documents and books on jurisprudence (covering the seventeenth to the nineteenth centuries), the only ones extant and totalling 20,000 volumes in all, were swept into oblivion from the Faculty of Law building. All scientific equipment and most of the extensive library housed in the San Salvi clinic for neurological and mental diseases were lost from the Faculty of Medicine. In a matter of hours one of the most distinguished universities in the world was robbed forever of its most precious intellectual heirlooms.

Though most of Florence's residents retreated to high rooftops to wait out the flood, the elderly Professor Umberto Baldini, director of the Uffizi Gallery, refused to leave to a watery fate the eighty-odd masterpieces stored in a subterranean vault. He and a small group of employees carried, one by one, the enormous works of Giotto (one of his polyptychs weighed several hundred pounds), Botticelli, Masaccio and Fra Filippo Lippi to the upper floors, even as the water rushed knee-high about them.

Florentines examine Ghiberti's *Doors of Paradise* after the floods of 1966. *(UPI)*

On the rooftops the Florentines called to each other, their only means of communication. Noted art historian Victor Velen and his wife Elizabeth recalled hearing residents relaying information about the flood's destruction from rooftop to rooftop. "Tell the Palazzo Vecchio that the house on the corner of the Via dei Pepi and the Via dell' Agnolo is collapsing. . . . No one is inside."

At dawn Florence was in shambles. Mud left by the receding waters was waist high. Shopkeepers drove their hands into the muck in search of their wares and tools, most of which were gone.

Designer Emilio Pucci took one look at his devastated studio and its more than a million dollars in damages, shrugged and tersely said, "I personally will begin again." For others there would be no new beginning; 113 persons were found, most in and about Florence, awkwardly dead in the upheaval of mud and smashed buildings.

While the Italian government sent a covy of helicopters (800 missions eventually were flown) over and into Florence with water and food supplies, artists, historians, professors and students immediately began to save what they could of the Italian heritage. Thousands of books, paintings and sculptures were dug up from the mud and brought to the University of Florence where restoration efforts feverishly began. Hundreds of American art students became full-time volunteers to save the treasures. Eminent experts throughout the world came to Florence to aid in the restoration. All worked until they collapsed. One mud-spattered American girl looked up briefly from her labors and told reporters, "My father should see us now. . . . He thinks our generation has no values."

FLORIDA — HURRICANE
September 15-22, 1926

background: Originating near the Cape Verde Islands, a hurricane moved north of Puerto Rico on September 15, 1926. Winds of up to 138 m.p.h. made it one of the most destructive in the twentieth century. When it moved over the Miami area, newly and lavishly built-up in the previous year's land boom, 115 were killed in Miami proper; another 300 lost their lives at Moore Haven with dozens more killed at Fort Lauderdale, Coral Gables and other towns. Damages exceeded $100 million with $76 million in the Miami area.

Jazz Age sheiks and flappers, aging red-hot mamas and their gigolos, zesty retirees joined the spritely race to Florida in 1925 in one of the greatest fevers of real-estate speculations in American history. It was called "the bubble in the sun." Penniless, brainless persons using giant advertisements blared in New York City had made fortunes overnight speculating on Florida real estate. "Why not YOU?"

From a sparsely populated area with tiny, remote villages, southern Florida was converted by the shrewdest speculators afield into an exotic Xanadu of pleasure and year-round warmth where towns mushroomed into booming cities, cities into a frenzied megalopolis. Coral Gables, started by real estate magnate George Merrick, blossomed into an American Venice replete with man-made canals. Hollywood-by-the-Sea, St. Petersburg, Orlando, Fort Lauderdale, Winter Park and, of course, Miami and Miami Beach became the fashionable places to be.

Suave realtors—brothers Addison and Wilson Mizener, whose tastes ran to Spanish stuccoes of pink, blue and cream-colored hues on their subdivision homes, ornate grillwork, authentic tile roofs imported from Spain and Mexico ("Looted," said *American Heritage*)—hawked their housing projects and profited by millions. The type of housing erected and what investors really got for their money were best reflected in Wilson Mizener's oft-quoted line: "Never give a sucker an even break." Their homes were quaint and darling and lavishly splashed with color but about as durable as cardboard (and they fell, most of them, with the 5,000 houses flattened by the hurricane the following year).

But the suckers came to Florida by the trainloads (4,000 a day) and by car (3,000 a day) and by ship (200 a day)—2.5 million people inside of six months during the 1925 boom. Mark Sullivan wrote: "All of America's gold rushes, all her oil booms, and all her free land stampedes dwindled by comparison . . . with the torrent of migration pouring into Florida." To greet them were such Jazz Age celebrities as orator, religious sachem and three-time nominee for the presidency, William Jennings Bryan, who took over the cultured Royal Palm Park on Sundays to conduct Bible classes for tourists. Other hand-clappers included boxer Gene Tunney, golfer Bobby Jones, shimmy dancer Gilda Gray, and warblers Helen Morgan and Elsie Janis.

Those who flocked to Florida were frenetic in their lust for land and buildings. Stepping into this sultry bedlam, an unemployed English journalist, T. Hamilton Weigall, who later worked as a public relations man for Florida developers, was aghast at what he saw. "Hatless, coatless men rushed about the blazing streets, their arms full of papers, perspiration pouring from their foreheads. Every shop seemed to be combined with a real estate office; at every doorway crowds of young men were shouting and speechmaking, thrusting forward papers and proclaiming to heaven the unsurpassed chances which they were offering to make a fortune. One had been prepared for real-estate madness; and here it was, *in excelsis*."

The advertising speculators plastered on billboards in northern towns gave more peaceful descriptions. One promotion read: "Florida is bathed in passionate caresses of the southern sun. It is laved by the limpid waves of the embracing seas, wooed by the glorious Gulf Stream, whose waters warmed by the tropical sun, speed northeast to temper the climate of Europe. Florida is an emerald kingdom by southern seas, fanned by zephyrs laden with ozone from stately pines, watered by Lethe's copious libation, decked with palm and pine, flower and fern, clothed in perpetual verdure and lapt in the gorgeous folds of the semitropical zone."

But the paradise had ash cans that began to overflow by the turn of the year. Swindles and frauds were rampant, and the National Better Business Bureau began to create uproars (and quick departures) with its angry investigations. Stocks in the Florida earth plunged on the New York Exchange. A mass exodus began, the roads leading north black with the disgruntled and the financially ruined. All through 1926 the promoters intensified their money-voiced pleas and there was some renewed investor interest, but the hurricane ended any immediate rejuvenation of the Florida land boom.

Born in the deep southern area of the Atlantic near the Cape Verde Islands, the hurricane stalked past Puerto Rico on September 15, and three days later came ashore at Miami. Its winds reached 138 m.p.h., and the cheap subdivision houses of "the emerald kingdom" began to fall, horribly killing the victims.

The storm at Fort Lauderdale unraveled the beach and established a new shoreline one hundred yards inland. In Coral Gables melancholy heaps of dead floated through wrecked "Venetian" canals. The intensity of the storm at this point was illustrated by a Fort Lauderdale man who lashed his wife to a tree and struggled for four hours against the roaring ten-foot waves and cyclonic wind to go a few blocks for help. The rescue party took as many hours to return to the woman (she was saved). But Miami was the real nightmare.

Here one hysterical woman ran from house to house, four in all, as each successively collapsed about her. The hurricane's first fury broke at 3:00 A.M. on September 18. Inside a lush beachfront hotel at that hour sat several hundred guests in tuxedos and evening gowns, all nervously clustered about a piano, all eyeing the windows and doors of the massive hostelry. The pianist tinkled out Broadway show tunes and one woman shouted, "Play louder, louder!" as if to drown out the sound of the shrieking hurricane.

S. K. Hicks, sitting with the tense group, heard the crashing combers slapping the shoreline, only 300 feet from the hotel. "At last came one giant wave," he remembered, "that battered down the door and rushed through the lobby, leaving it three feet deep in water." Rising as one, the large group shouted and ran.

By 8:00 A.M., there was quiet. Hicks and others thought the storm was over, so they donned bathing suits and waded happily into the troubled surf. Hundreds, even thousands, from the proud hotels changed into bathing suits and wandered into the water, splashing, playing, commenting on the storm, which upon inspection had not been so terrible; some roofs were missing from the hotels, a few houses were down; that was all.

But it wasn't all. These émigré tourists and investors had no idea of what to expect of any kind of hurricane and were ignorant of the storm's lumbering body. They were playing inside the calm eye of the hurricane and within an hour, as they paddled through the increasingly rough surf, they became puzzled at the sky, which had turned black. Now the other edge of the hurricane was upon them. Hicks motioned for his friends to swim ashore. "We tried to get back to the hotel as the wind freshened, but were unable to make it." Again the winds and waters were upon Miami, catching thousands in the water and on the streets. (Some larks had gone to work in their bathing suits, merrily wading through giant pools of water in the streets left by the first blast of the storm.) Flying timbers, glass windows, doors and roofs cut down hundreds. Hundreds more were dragged from the beaches into the sea.

Hicks and a friend, Malcolm Wisehart, made it to the nearby Beachview Apartments. The doors of the building had been torn away at either end, and the wind rushed through the hallway like a great bellows. The two men were repeatedly knocked to the floor, but they managed to crawl to the stairway. Racing into an apartment, Hicks saw "a young girl in a bathing suit seated calmly on a couch. She didn't seem to be the least bit alarmed and was watching with great interest the beat of the rain against the windows." The girl wordlessly got up and gave them blankets and cigarettes.

In the true spirit of the Lost Generation the two young men and the girl sat on the couch and watched the hurricane winds press against the buckling glass, trying to enter the room. "While we sat smoking the wind drove the glass from the window frames, showering and cutting Wisehart and the girl."

The blasting winds and pounding waves ripped through the elaborate Venetian Causeway, spilling hundreds of fleeing people into the raging water and making battered hulks of scores of cars. Elegant yachts were lifted from their berths and hurtled blocks inland onto Miami streets. The Fleetwood Hotel's manicured rooftop gardens were shredded and torn away. The dome of the Flamingo Hotel was decapitated. A dredge, *Magic City,* ironically named after Miami, split in two, one half sinking in the bay, the other dashing out to sea with six shouting men still on board who were never seen again.

Ruth Anderson from Lexington, Kentucky, and another girl raced into a house just ahead of a wall of water. Dozens of snakes and rats, also seeking shelter from the storm, crawled about, as terrified as the two women. Part of a wall collapsed and the other girl's spine was broken. Miss Anderson built a raft from flotsam inside the house and placed the girl on it, where she floated for two hours before being rescued.

Apartment buildings, flimsily built, began to collapse. One went down with more than one hundred persons inside of it. R. T. Freng, a pilot, put his weight against the storm and attempted to move down one Miami street, but the winds, estimated by him to be 140 m.p.h., blew him into a gutter, and there, hanging on to the grate of a sewer, he stayed from 9:00 A.M. to 12:30 P.M. Freng had earlier tried to save the life of a woman who had just given premature birth, and as he and two friends carried her and the child from a collapsing house, her returning husband was crushed to death by a falling telegraph pole before their eyes.

While in the gutter, Freng saw all manner of debris sail past him in the air—lumber, pipes, trees, even small autos. Children separated from their parents screamed helplessly and were blown past him down the street.

Kirby Jones was inside a large building with 150 people when the roof caved in and sent down a shower of murderous timbers. "All of us fled to a schoolhouse a block away. It was a pitiful sight to see that crowd running through the driving rain, barely able to make headway against the terrific force of the wind. . . . Women were crying hysterically, and old men whimpering that they did not want to die, their voices almost inaudible in the roar of the wind. And all the while flying timbers and glass were falling all about us."

Coral Gables with its gossamer gardens and Old World canals was a wreck. Charles G. Crosby staggered along a once-elegant street, hardly seeing a five-masted steel schooner that had been thrown by the storm onto the pavement and taking only mild notice of a naked woman breast-feeding her equally naked child on the steps in front of her home, which had been reduced to its foundation.

At the door of the Miami Morgue, George Fielding kept count until fifty-six bodies had been brought in and then could not continue his grim addition, brushing past a seemingly endless line of volunteers holding more corpses. "I wept," he said, "at the sight of children having broken limbs set and deep wounds sewed without narcotics to deaden the pain."

For the marginal speculators, it was all over. One man with a half-million in ruined houses was reported a suicide; he walked into the sea. A total of 372 persons were dead, 2,000 were injured, many crippled for life; 5,000 homes were blown down, and despite the claims of Mayor E. C. Romfh that Miami was still "the fastest growing city in America," the bubble in the sun had finally burst with one of the loudest, most lamentable bangs ever heard.

FLORIDA KEYS — HURRICANE
September 12-18, 1835

The first adequately recorded hurricane to strike the Florida Keys occurred on September 15, 1835. After brewing three days at sea, originating near Jamaica on September 12, swirling across Cuba on the fourteenth, the storm swarmed its mass of wind and rain and seawaves over the keys on the following day. Before the giant front of the storm moved off to plague Georgia and the Carolinas on the eighteenth, Key West, Key Biscayne, Fort Brooke, Cape Florida and Cape Canaveral were raked by the hurricane.

At Key Biscayne the water stood four feet deep in the small villages. Dozens of vessels were driven ashore and wrecked on Cape Florida and Cape Canaveral reefs. At least one hundred persons were killed in the storm, but accurate figures were unavailable in that then scantly populated area.

The *Key West Enquirer* glumly hinted at mysterious forces at work in bringing on the season's unexpected spate of storms: "We remember seeing, sometime since, the prognostications of an officer in the British army or navy, who judged (upon what authority we know not) that the visit of Halley's Comet, now expected, would cause the gales of wind and other atmospheric phenomena; and whether it may be considered strange coincidences or not, we cannot say, but there has certainly been an undue number of severe storms, tornadoes, gales, etc. throughout the country for the last few months."

FLORIDA KEYS — HURRICANE
October 18, 1906

The first serious hurricane to hit the Florida Keys in the twentieth century occurred on October 18, 1906, passing Havana, Cuba, the day before at 11:30 A.M. Its winds reaching 50 m.p.h., the storm was thought to be a small threat even though its diameter was intense.

At that time the Overseas Highway and the Florida East Coast Railroad to Key West were being built by Henry M. Flagler, and his workmen were strung out all along the keys industriously constructing solid rock embankments, bridges, and trestles.

The Cuban hurricane, which had whipped up its winds to 75 m.p.h., struck the keys on the early morning of the eighteenth, driving a huge wedge of rain and waves into Sand Key, where hundreds of workmen, sleeping in houseboats, were caught without a chance to flee. The wooden houseboats were easily broken up and capsized by the storm, and 124 workmen and 5 natives were drowned.

Though Flagler's much-criticized highway and railroad survived this hurricane, many, including the local *News-Record,* had warned that any substantial storm could pressure enough water to wash away the concrete embankments and destroy the railroad. It would be almost thirty years later when the critics were proved correct.

(ALSO SEE: Florida Keys, 1935)

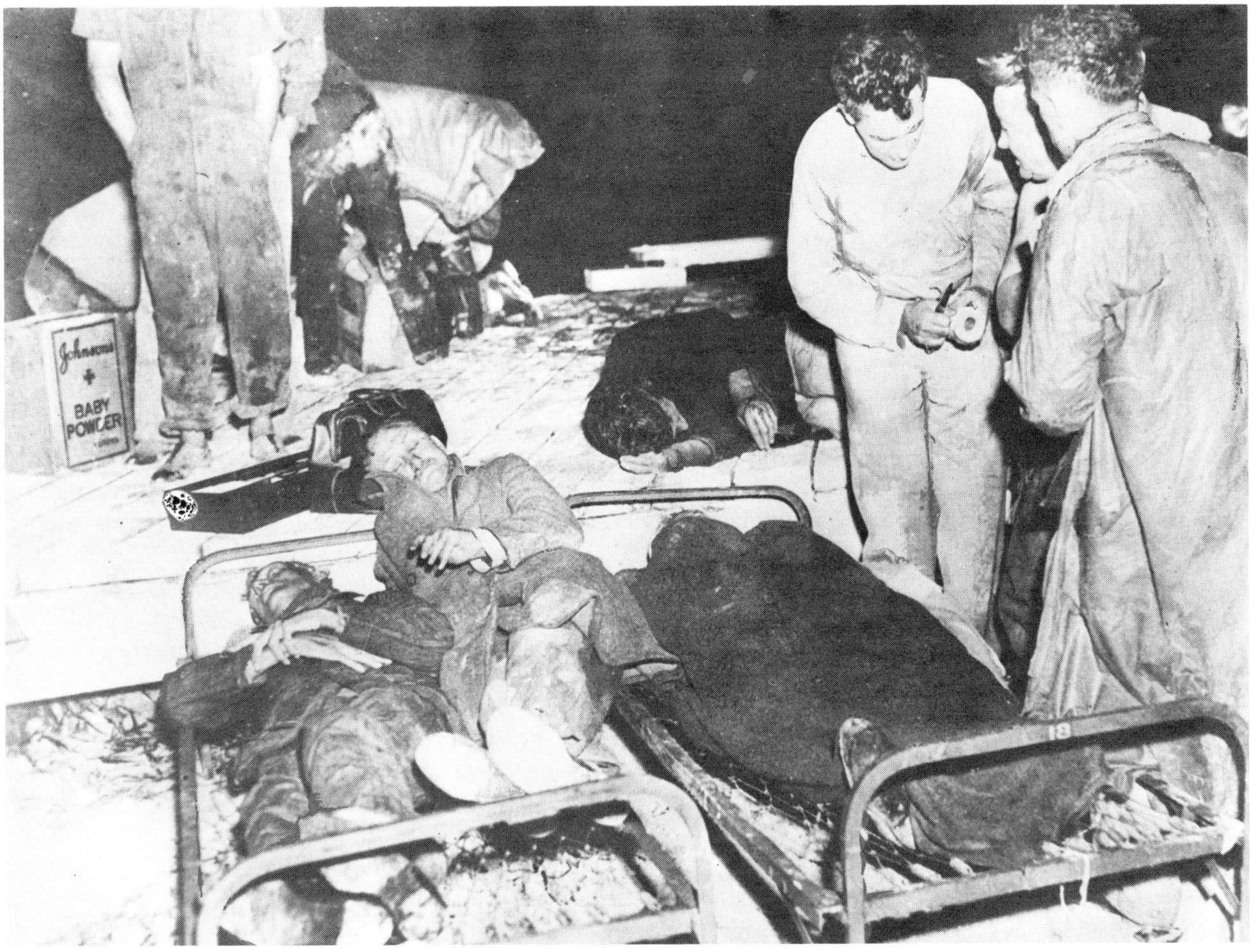

The murderous hurricane that swept through the Florida Keys in 1935 obliterated a workforce of bonus marchers, World War I Army veterans, causing Ernest Hemingway to ask who killed the vets. *(UPI)*

FLORIDA KEYS HURRICANE
September 2, 1935

background: The most furious hurricane ever to strike the Florida Keys hit on September 2, 1935, with twenty-foot waves and winds gusting to 250 m.p.h. It devastated Upper and Lower Matecumbe Keys, wiping out the villages of Rock Harbor, Islamorada, Matecumbe, Tavernier and Camp Number Five near Snake Creek on Lower Matecumbe Key, which housed 716 bonus army workers; of these 121 veterans were killed; another 279 local residents were killed. Hundreds more were injured, and the great Overseas Railroad, which ran through the keys, was destroyed.

The long, sultry summer of 1935 in the Florida Keys had already been punctured by several hurricane alerts, but the storms had veered off to die in the Atlantic. Those who lived permanently on the yawning keys were not hoodwinked by the dulcet breezes and milky clouds floating lazily overhead. Their sun-browned faces scanned those deceptive late summer skies, and day by day a certain, universal awareness crept larger into the inhabitants. The hurricane weather was upon them, they knew.

But in total ignorance were the 716 bitter men who had once been part of the 20,000-man Bonus Expeditionary Force that had marched on Washington to demand of Congress their bonus for having fought in France during World War I. These homeless, directionless men had been sent to Lower Matecumbe Key ostensibly to build a government road but in reality to be kept out of sight. Their miserable lot was that of displaced persons in their own land, jobless, futureless. Their mere presence was a gritty reminder of the bloody battle fought between the veterans and the Third U.S. Cavalry under the command of General Douglas MacArthur on July 28, 1932, a battle that left Washington's Anacostia Flats littered with bodies of ex-doughboys. It was not a pretty sight then, and the scarecrow vision of those who listlessly went to work on the government road in 1935 became a cringing national memory hidden away on Lower Matecumbe Key.

In a year the road had crept out only 200 feet from its starting point and the men mostly sat around drinking, playing cards and squandering their $30-a-month government allotment in the gin joints of Key West. They had no one to send their money to, most having no families.

Writing for the *New Masses,* Ernest Hemingway vented his spleen over the trapped situation of the broken-down bonus army marchers. "I'd known a lot of them at Josie Grunt's place and around the town when they would come in for pay day, and some of them were punch drunk and some of them were smart; some had been on the bum since the Argonne almost, and some had lost their jobs the year before last Christmas; some had wives and some couldn't remember; some were good guys and others put their pay checks in the Postal Savings and then came over to cadge in on the drinks when better men were drunk; some liked to fight and others liked to walk around the town; and they were all what you get after a war. But who sent them there to die?"

Whoever it was in the federal government that sent them also knew little about hurricanes. While the homes of long-time residents were reinforced with concrete and possessed shutters with heavy bolts, the barracks and shacks that housed the veterans were paper thin, and they were surrounded by dense, dangerous mangrove swamps. But there was a railroad nearby, the Florida East Coast Railway, which knifed through the keys over concrete embankments and spidery trestles spanning the inlets of water between the islands. If any help for the isolated veterans would come, it would arrive by this railroad.

It was the only outside link anyone on the keys had with the world, and that link was snapped on September 2, 1935. First sighted east and north of Turks Island, a hurricane swept over Andros Island hours later with winds and waves, some of the most violent and intense in recorded history. Attended by twenty-foot waves hurricane winds reached upward to 250 m.p.h. The "Labor Day Hurricane," as it is now called, crushed everything before it.

As it curved inward on the Florida Keys, aiming at Long and Matecumbe keys, the barometer plummeted to 26.35, a record in the Western Hemisphere. The hurricane traveled at about 10 m.p.h., and one authority estimated that the calm center was about nine miles in diameter. Though the storm had grown smaller by the time it struck the keys, its intensity was unbelievable.

Two ships attempting to scurry through the Florida Straits before the storm were caught up by it and scattered like twigs. One, the *Dixie,* was smashed about by twenty- and thirty-foot waves until she was tossed up on the French Reef. The other, the *Pueblo,* a tanker, was swirled about for eight hours by the storm, out of control, and she eventually ended up back at her starting place.

As authorities got sketchy reports of the approaching storm, they quickly dispatched a rescue train steaming toward Matecumbe Key to evacuate the veterans and residents there. The hurricane won the race. Fortunately 350 veterans had gone to Key West to watch a baseball game, so half the camp was empty. As the wind howled overhead and through their thin clothing, the others waited with their few belongings next to the tracks, watching through squinted eyes for the relief train that had left Miami at 4:25 P.M. Cautiously probing into the ever-increasing darkness of the southern keys, the train picked up some badly frightened residents and proceeded through screaming winds. At Islamorada, the full fist of the hurricane lashed out at the ten-car train, a wall of water estimated to be forty feet high dashing against the cars and instantly flopping them to their sides and off the cracking concrete foundation under the tracks on which they had been crawling.

William Johns, a reporter for the *New York Times,* related that he "was in the smoker when the wave hit. The car crashed over on its right side and water poured in the broken windows on the ocean side. I grabbed a seat and hung on while water poured in. Somehow I got outside the smoking compartment. . . ."

The nightmare already encompassed Long and Matecumbe keys. It was as if a giant claw had reached out to gouge out an unforgettable ten-mile scar across the land. One family named Russell, numbering seventy-five and representing several generations of residency on the lush keys, was reduced to eleven members. The rocket winds tore and burst and broke and grated houses, boats, animals and humans inside of one sustained screech of death.

The thirty-foot concrete embankments painstakingly built by the railroad across the keys burst under the pressure of the waves and wind at almost all points; the trestle bridges collapsed and sank into the mud. The air was thick with hurtling debris and dead bodies. At 8:00 P.M. inside Alligator Reef Lighthouse, attendants became frantic when they saw a gigantic wave rushing toward the ninety-foot tower. It rocked the lighthouse, and winds drove through the 3/8-inch glass surrounding the light, shattering it to grains and carrying the lenses for ten miles.

Nothing was spared from Hawk Channel to Key Vaca, especially the hapless veterans who waited for a train that would never arrive. For forty minutes the hurricane bashed its way across Matecumbe Key, pulverizing every building in Camp Five and flinging the 300-odd veterans there into the swamps. There was no escape for them. Most of them attempted to hide behind the railroad embankment, but the wind curled downward and blew them away. They fought desperately back again to reach the rails where they clung like clothesline wash flapping in the breeze. One by one the wind tore their grasps from the shuddering steel beams and rolled them into the mounting seas of water at their backs, snatched them up and hurtled them into the stumpy mangrove swamps where their bodies were cracked and broken.

For camp timekeeper Joseph Factsau it was an impossible horror. He, his wife, two daughters and two grandchildren took refuge in a quaking building, the ordeal further heightened by a score of wailing drunks huddled next to them. Between sobs he later said, "The building we were placed in lasted only an hour. I tried to make a human chain from the building to the railroad track to get all the women and children to safety, but I was washed into the Gulf by a high wave. I swam back as quickly as I could and reached shore just as the hospital collapsed. I heard my wife calling my name, but I was not able to get to her in time. They were all [his entire family] killed under the ruins."

By 10:00 P.M. when the hurricane moved off, the carnage was complete. CCC workers, National Guardsmen, even Boy Scouts scoured the area for two days, retrieving bodies. Of the local residents, 279 were dead, and many more were injured. The straggly ranks of the veterans were withered by 121 deaths; 90 more were missing, and more than 100 were seriously injured.

Coming upon the shambles of Camp Five, rescuers moaned aloud. One veteran was still alive, pinned to a tree by a 2-by-4 plank that had run through him like a Toledo blade. A doctor approached him and saw that the board had entered under the rib cage and had taken his kidneys out the back. Incredibly, he was alive and conscious.

"I'm going to give you a shot of morphine," the doctor told the ex-doughboy.

"None of that," the feisty veteran said.

"But, I've got to pull it out, and you will not stand the pain."

"When you pull it out, I'll be dead. Get me a couple of beers."

Two bottles of beer were brought, and the veteran drank them quickly. He then looked the doctor in the eye and said: "Now pull!"

The doctor pulled. Before the gory piece of timber was free, the man was dead.

Sloshing through the mangrove swamps to look for victims with veterans who had escaped the storm was Hemingway, who lived nearby. "It doesn't take a bird dog to locate them," he wrote, mingling his narrative with the comments of the searchers and addressing the reader, in such a way as to involve him in this lonely tragedy. "You can find them in the grass that's washed along the fill. Hey, there's another one. He's got low shoes, put him down, man, looks about sixty, low shoes, copper-riveted overalls, blue percale shirt without collar, storm jacket, by Jesus, that's the thing to wear, nothing in his pockets. Turn him over. Face tumefied beyond recognition. Hell he don't look like a veteran. He's too old. He's got grey hair. You'll have grey hair yourself this time next week. And across his back there was a great big blister as wide as his back and ready to burst where his storm jacket had slipped down. Turn him over again. Sure he's a veteran. I know him. What's he got low shoes on for then? Maybe he made some money shooting craps and bought them. You don't know that guy. You can't tell him now. I know him, he hasn't got any thumb. That's how I know him. The land crabs ate his thumb. You think you know everybody. Well you waited a long time to get sick, brother. Sixty-seven of them and you got sick on the sixty-eighth. . . .

"And the wind makes a noise like a locomotive passing, with a shriek on top of that, because the wind has a scream exactly as it has in books, and then the fill goes and the high wall of water rolls you over and over and then, whatever it is, you get it and we find you, now of no importance stinking in the mangroves . . . You're dead now, brother. . . ."

FLORIDA STRAITS — HURRICANE
September 2-14, 1919

Perhaps the largest hurricane ever to occur in the Western Hemisphere during the twentieth century was the one that literally crawled through the Florida Straits on September 9-10, 1919, after having inched its way from Santo Domingo, where it began as a minor disturbance on September 2. By the time the storm mass drifted past Nassau, the barometer was at 29.46 inches. Its violent, 80 m.p.h. winds, blowing away the anemometer cups off Key West, became pronounced in the Florida Straits. The barometer reading here was 28.35 inches, and Key West suffered voluminous destruction, later estimated at $2 million.

As the hurricane passed the Dry Tortugas, sixty miles west of Key West, several unfortunate ships were caught in the full fury of the storm. Ten vessels were capsized by the storm, the largest of which was the Spanish passenger steamer, *Valbanera,* which disappeared with 400 tourists and 88 crew members on board.

The angry behemoth stalked on, staggering inland at Corpus Christi, Texas, where it inflated the tide sixteen feet above normal, shredded $20 million in buildings and brought death to 284 persons. While its center pulverized Corpus Christi, its outer fingers whipped with 60 m.p.h. winds at far away Galveston, Miami and Brownsville. The death toll was 772.

FOREST HILLS, MASSACHUSETTS — RAILWAY WRECK, March 14, 1887

The crash of the Boston & Providence local train to Boston on March 14, 1887, which caused the death of 24 passengers and injured another 125, startled officials because the iron-constructed Busey Bridge, which collapsed and brought down the nine-car train, was considered prodigiously stable. Its designer, Edmund Hewins (later exposed as a fraud), was so well thought of that the line never bothered to inspect the trestle, even though dozens of loose nuts and bolts from the bridge were found by children playing nearby.

It was late morning, a Monday, when the Dedham Branch train moved across the 125-foot-long bridge. The heavier, faster express had already gone over the bridge an hour before. Yet when the local raced onto it, the bridge gave way almost immediately, and with a rushing shriek the passenger cars followed the engine and tender into the 40-foot precipice. The train's speed was so great that the roof of the fourth car was sheared off and flew to the other side of the ruptured trestle while the car itself plunged downward.

Busey Bridge collapsed near Forest Hills, dumping several railway cars into a gorge. *(Harper's Weekly)*

The Boston & Providence local crashed through Busey Bridge on March 14, 1887. *(From an old print)*

Death came horribly to the unfortunate victims. *Harper's Weekly* related one sight that sickened rescuers: "The first thing taken from the wreck was the headless body of a woman." A score of persons were pinned to the walls, ceilings and floors of the mangled cars by splinters. Two men were trapped by debris in an overturned car, and, while rescuers clawed their way to them, the pair apprehensively eyed a red-hot stove, its coals still burning, directly above their heads. They knew if it dropped, they would instantly roast to death. Unlike the bridge, the stove was sturdily bolted to the floor and did not drop. The men were saved inside of fifteen minutes.

FORRESTAL — MARINE DISASTER, July 29, 1967

background: The 75,900-ton United States carrier, *Forrestal,* while launching planes 175 miles north of Danang for a strike against North Vietnam on July 29, 1967, caught fire and eventually caused the deaths of 134 crewmen and the loss of twenty-five fighter planes. The 1,039-foot carrier, carrying 4,300 men and six squadrons of aircraft, was commissioned October 1, 1955, the first of the supercarriers built after World War II.

Just after 10:00 A.M. on July 29, 1967, the giant carrier *Forrestal* swung her bow into the wind preparatory to launching her daily fighter plane strike into North Vietnam. Hundreds of the 4,300-man crew were scurrying about the *Forrestal*'s four-acre flight deck readying planes. Without warning a 250-gallon auxiliary gas tank dropped from a Douglas A-4 Skyraider as it was warming up for takeoff.

The sloshing liquid spread quickly across the flight deck, running menacingly under the feet of scores of men. "She's gonna go," one sailor shouted just at the time the gas was ignited by steam from the carrier's four-catapult launching system. The ship was ablaze.

The crew members displayed great bravery in saving their ship. Rear Admiral Harvey P. Lanham, who was on the bridge, later commented: "I saw more heroic incidents than I could count." Crash crews calmly walked through the burning liquid. They unhooked bombs from planes and unscrewed their fuses.

"People were carrying these bombs," marveled the ship's catapult officer, Lieutenant Commander Larry Forderhase, "carrying 250-pound bombs and throwing them over the side." Some bombs ignited, and there were four large craters on the flight deck. Yet the work went on. One sailor, wearing an aluminum, fire-resistant suit, jumped on a fork-lift truck and drove the machine against a burning plane, pushing the fighter off the flight deck and into the sea. Twenty-five fighters burned, more than what North Vietnamese gunners brought down in an average month (625 planes had been lost in combat up to this time).

Sister ships of the fleet steamed to the *Forrestal*'s aid. The carriers *Oriskany* and *Bon Homme Richard* immediately dispatched helicopters with doctors to remove casualties while destroyers *Henry W. Tucker* and the *Rupertus* poured tons of water onto the carrier's flaming deck.

The *Forrestal* was brought about to starboard to cut the 40 m.p.h. winds that had been fanning the flames. She headed for the hospital ship, *Repose,* which was steaming out of Danang Harbor to aid the stricken craft.

Many would never get on board the *Repose.* Close to 80 seamen, their paths blocked by walls of flame, were driven to the edge of the flight deck and, rather than roast to death, hurtled themselves into the sea. These hapless sailors accounted for most of the 134 fatalities suffered in the worst mishap in the *Forrestal*'s history. *(ALSO SEE:* Bennington, Enterprise, Oriskany*)*

The deck of the aircraft carrier *Forrestal* smolders in Viet Nam waters in 1967; 134 sailors lost their lives. *(UPI)*

Sliced in half and seventy-four of her seamen dead, what is left of the American destroyer *Frank E. Evans* is towed to port. *(UPI)*

FRANK E. EVANS — MARINE DISASTER
June 2, 1969

background: While operating at sea on SEATO maneuvers, the Australian carrier, *Melbourne,* accidentally rammed and sliced in two the American destroyer *Frank E. Evans* on June 2, 1969, in the South China Sea, killing 74 American seamen; 199 survived from the destroyer.

The quiet May waters of Manila Bay lapped at the host of SEATO ships riding at anchor; they had gathered there to await a naval exercise called "Sea Spirit," which was to begin four days later. On board the Australian fleet's flagship, the 20,000-ton aircraft carrier, *Melbourne,* Captain John P. Stevenson sat down to dinner with his officers, impressing upon them the necessity of a smooth voyage.

The *Melbourne,* he recounted, had not been called the "Troubled Lady" for nothing. Built by the British in World War II, her history was studded with freakish accidents occurring so frequently that many of her crewmen thought her jinxed. She originally was designed for cold service in the North Atlantic, but under the Australians she was used in warm seas, and below decks she became an oven, where temperatures of 153 degrees were not unusual. Her catapult system malfunctioned shortly after the Australians took her over, and planes could not be launched from her decks for months. Her boilers were easily overstrained, frequently causing her to limp home for repairs from routine sea exercises and patrols. In 1964 the carrier had collided with an Australian destroyer, *Voyager,* which sank with eighty-two hands still on board. (It was determined later that the destroyer was at fault.) She was not even safe in port; a Japanese freighter had brushed her when she was docked and crumpled a gun turret. More than $8.2 million had been pumped into the *Melbourne* in repairs and refitting since then, and Stevenson was determined to maintain an accident-free record this trip. But for all her new hardware and paint, the *Melbourne* was still a smirking "Troubled Lady" underneath.

Four days out of Manila, June 2, 1969, the aircraft carrier was maneuvering at 3:10 A.M. in the South China Sea. Two miles ahead and about ten degrees to the port flitted the twenty-four-year-old, 2,200-ton United States destroyer, *Frank E. Evans,* positioned there so that her truck lights would serve as a beacon for the *Melbourne*'s incoming planes returning from patrol. She was ready for rescue operations should any craft have to ditch.

Most of the 273 crew members on board the *Evans*

were asleep. On the bridge the night-watch commander, Second Lieutenant Ronald Ramsey, twenty-four, could smell the fresh breakfast bread being baked in the galley below. He received an order from the *Melbourne*—"Plane Guard"—which meant move to a position astern of the carrier.

The *Evans,* instead of putting her rudder left and moving from the path of the carrier in a wide near-circle to drop astern of the *Melbourne,* violated a cardinal naval rule and ruddered right, cutting in front of the fast-moving carrier. Loud klaxons on board the *Melbourne* blared. Stevenson sent the *Evans* a radio message: "You are on a collision course. . . . Repeat, you are on a collision course."

Seeing that the *Evans* was responding improperly, Stevenson whirled swiftly on his bridge and ordered, "Reverse engines. Turn hard left." As he looked back at the destroyer and checked his action, Stevenson saw an incredible sight. The *Evans* had again turned right, placing herself directly before the bow of the on-coming carrier. In moments there was an echoing crunch of steel grinding into steel. The *Frank E. Evans,* considered a "lucky" ship in the United States fleet, was sliced in two. After surviving an epic sea battle in 1945 off Okinawa, in which she had repulsed 150 kamikaze planes, shooting down 50, the *Evans* ignobly went to her death through poor navigation. The front portion of the ship sank almost immediately in 5,500 feet of water, taking with her seventy-four crewmen.

At the point of collision several *Melbourne* sailors jumped onto the aft section of the decapitated destroyer and began to yank seamen to safety. They lashed the remaining section to the stern of the carrier. Others jumped from the sinking fore section onto the aft just in time. Dozens swam desperately to the side of the carrier and were rescued.

The last man to be plucked from the water alive was the destroyer's captain, Albert S. McLemore, who never realized what was happening until too late. "I was asleep in the sea cabin. My first recollection was a tremendous noise and fire. I thought we had been torpedoed or mined." McLemore was surrounded in his bunk by smashed bulkheads through which water poured into the cabin. "I bent back the jagged metal with my hands to force my way out. I found myself in the water with the wreckage. I don't know how I survived." Ramsey, the night-watch officer on the bridge, also survived but was injured.

Standing on the floating aft section of the destroyer was Chief Gunner's Mate Lawrence J. Reilly. As flames burst about him he wept at the spectacle of the sinking fore section of his ship. Inside the plunging hulk was his son, twenty-year-old Lawrence J. Reilly, Jr., an oil tender, who went swiftly to his death. His, perhaps, was not the greatest tragedy. Three brothers, Gary Sage, twenty-two, Gregory Sage, twenty-one, and Kelly Sage, nineteen, all from the little town of Niobrara, Nebraska, went down with the *Evans.* It was the worst family tragedy in the United States Navy since the five plucky Sullivan boys died fighting on board the cruiser *Juneau* in 1942 off Guadalcanal. (The Sage and Reilly deaths prompted Melvin R. Laird, Secretary of Defense, to order a quick investigation of Navy practices of permitting family members to serve on the same ship.)

Commander McLemore, dripping sea water, made his way to the *Melbourne*'s pilot house after being picked up. "I was still about half naked," the American skipper stated. Captain Stevenson met him there and the two embraced and simultaneously blurted, "I'm sorry!"

Days later a rear admiral in full-dress uniform stood on the stoop of the Sage home in Nebraska and broke the news. Gregory Sage's wife, Linda, said, "We don't blame anyone. We don't blame the Navy or Australia. It was the boys' wish that they serve together. That's the way they wanted it, and that's the way we accepted it. I guess it couldn't be helped."

Battered but afloat, the Australian carrier *Melbourne* arrives in Singapore after colliding with the *Evans,* June 2, 1969. *(UPI)*

FRANKFORD JUNCTION, PENNSYLVANIA — RAILWAY WRECK, September 6, 1943

background: The sixteen-car Congressional Limited, en route to New York from Philadelphia, rounded a curve at Frankford Junction in the afternoon of September 6, 1943, when the journal box—a housing for one end of an axle—caught fire and derailed the last ten cars of the train in which 541 persons were riding; 79 persons were killed and several hundred injured in one of the worst train accidents in American history.

The Pennsylvania's sleek Congressional Limited was jammed to wartime capacity on September 6, 1943, when it departed from Washington for Baltimore, Wilmington, Philadelphia and New York. Though mandatory speed laws for cars were 45 m.p.h., the trains of America, loaded down with troops under orders, were, in the words of Joseph Eastman, "under tremendous pressure and are forced to drive their equipment as it never has been driven before."

The speed scheduled for the Congressional Limited explicitly supported that statement. The top passenger train was expected to cover the distance between New York and Washington, 226 miles, in 215 minutes, quite a dash for those days. The trip was pleasant and uneventful until the train roared through Frankford Junction, Pennsylvania, after a brief stop in Philadelphia. A crew working an engine in a yard saw that the left front journal—the "hotbox"—of the forward truck of the seventh car was on fire and ran to a signal tower. The operator called the next tower about a mile down the line to halt the train, but the Limited was singing on the rails, and it passed so quickly that the second operator had no time to signal a stop.

Rounding a curve at 58 m.p.h. the train began to pass beneath a signal bridge. At this point the axle on the seventh car broke and sent the car almost straight up as it ripped away from the first six cars and engine (the forward part of the train remained coupled and proceeded down the track for 2,000 feet). In its crazy upward swing the seventh car spilled everyone inside to one end and yanked the remaining nine cars from the tracks. The eighth car, also a coach, smashed into the seventh and was bent into a U-shape. Behind these cars two diners and four parlor cars jerked and bumped wildly across the four-track yard, thumping to stops in awkward positions.

One soldier in the first dining car later stated, "People, tables and food were hurled into the aisles and a tiny child went sliding by on the floor. I tried to grab it but missed. I later learned that it was undamaged."

Death, however, came quickly to seventy-nine, most of whom were in the first two derailed coaches. There was little left of the seventh car. Its roof had been sheared off by a steel girder of the overhanging signal bridge, and, as it was hit by the coach behind, it was cut in two.

Dozens of servicemen and workers poured out of the undamaged six cars in front and ran back to the wreck, where blow torches were quickly produced. It took rescuers six hours to work their way through a mass of twisted steel surrounding one woman who, though in terrible agony, was conscious and buried to the waist (she died a few hours after being removed).

Two notables on board, newspaperman Roy Howard of the Scripps-Howard chain, and Chinese philosopher Lin Yutang, were fortunate to receive no injuries.

It was one of the most spectacular wrecks in railroad history, but it certainly was not the first time the "hotbox" had brought death to the trains. On January 23, 1881, an Erie train was derailed by a burned-out journal at Tioga Center, New York, killing five postal employees. Nineteen persons were killed on a passenger train outside of Milton, Pennsylvania, on June 15, 1945, when due to a burned out journal, it collided with a freight moving in the opposite direction.

(ALSO SEE: Ivanhoe, Indiana)

FREJUS, FRANCE — FLOOD, December 3, 1959

The Malpasset Dam, strung majestically above the town of Frejus, France, and the fertile Reyran valley, a rich peach center off the Riviera, held back a lake five miles long and two and a half miles wide. Built from 1952 to 1957 by world-famous engineer Andre Coyne, the dam provided water for Frejus and dozens of other Riviera towns, as well as irrigation for the Reyran valley.

On the night of December 3, 1959, the dam suddenly broke open and a fifteen-foot wave cascaded downward into the valley, rolling houses, autos, animals and humans, most of whom had been asleep, before it. The 14,000 inhabitants of Frejus, which is about fifteen miles from the pleasure capital of Cannes, found themselves swimming and dodging debris. The only warning they had was a "roar—like thunder" before the torrent was upon them. Everything in the town was swept away except a few buildings and an old Roman arena where gladiators had once fought to the death.

Of the displaced inhabitants 412 were killed in the flash flood, and most of these were buried the following day in three long trench-graves. As onlookers viewed the barren town with its destroyed houses, collapsed bridges, uprooted trees and the still-standing arena, one grimly remarked, "The Romans built better than we did."

FUKIEN PROVINCE, CHINA

FLOOD
August 7, 1948

The annual floods plaguing China were particularly severe in Fukien Province in early August, 1948. The swollen Min River suddenly burst its banks on the night of August 7, sending before it terrified gong beaters who shouted, "Chiu ming! Chiu ming!" ("Save life!"). The flood was the culmination of two months of steady, unmerciful cloudbursts, and it sent a million refugees crowding into the highlands and drowned 1,000 persons who were too close to the river when it rushed over its banks.

More than 80 percent of Fukien's rice harvest was destroyed, and Nationalist and Communist leaders traded propaganda over the great flood. Peking Radio blared: "It is impossible to complete dike repair work because of constant Nationalist raids. . . . We request Nationalist troops and air forces to cease their obstruction." Nanking Radio shouted back: "Since their occupation of this area, Communists have methodically destroyed dikes. With floods coming they are wildly firing accusations against the Central Government. . . . We hope they will show a sense of humanity and withdraw. . . ."

More than the immediate death toll (comparatively low for flood disasters in China), the threat of starvation and famine loomed high that year. Also hard hit was Hunan Province, where Tungting Lake overflowed and wrecked 50 percent of the rice crop. In Kiangsu Province 30 percent of the rice crop was obliterated; in Kiangsi, 60 percent. Hankow's streets were submerged, Kiukiang's teeming wharves were swept away, and the river gorges leading up to Chungking were clotted with debris and dead bodies.

FUKUOKA, JAPAN

MINE DISASTER
June 1, 1965

A total of 552 miners were laboring in the mine pits of the Yamano coal mine outside of Fukuoka, Japan, on June 1, 1965, when a tremendous blast, the result of escaping gas, shook the area. As tons of rocks crashed and reverberated through the many shafts of the mine, hundreds of miners scrambled for the elevators that would bring them to the surface and safety. Only 279 men, 37 of them injured, reached the elevators and were hauled up.

Gathered outside the pithead were more than 2,000 relatives of the 236 trapped miners. Their vigil lasted almost two days until, one by one, sealed-off chambers were entered and groups of bodies were found. All had either been crushed to death or asphyxiated.

Even before the 236 bodies were brought to the surface, Yoshio Sakurauchi, Trade and Industries Minister, had resigned his office in a statement that admitted his office had failed to introduce the proper safety measures to prevent such catastrophes. Seven men were killed and twenty-four more had been seriously injured in the same mine six years before by the same kind of explosion.

(ALSO SEE: Dharbad, India)

Half sheared away, the Malpasset Dam stands above Frejus, France, where 412 died on December 3, 1959. *(UPI)*

G

GAINESVILLE, GEORGIA — TORNADO

June 1, 1903

One of the most deadly twisters of modern times was the tornado that struck Gainesville, Georgia, on June 1, 1903. It was a freakish case of bad timing. Only a few minutes after 750 employees of a giant cotton mill reported for work, the tornado bore down on Gainesville, deliberately, it later seemed, aiming at the mill. The high-roofed, cheaply constructed building quickly caved in, and scores were instantly killed.

Total fatalities in Gainesville reached 203, and more than 900 were seriously injured.

GAINESVILLE, GEORGIA — TORNADOES

April 2-6, 1936

background: Flurries of tornadoes touched down in six southern states between April 2 and 6, 1936, the one that hit Gainesville, Georgia, being the most destructive; 630 buildings of the downtown district were demolished and 187 persons killed. Other hard-hit areas were Tupelo, Mississippi, where 195 of the 211 deaths in the state occurred, and Coffeyville, Booneville and Auburn, Mississippi; Cordelle, Acworth, Woodstock and Lavonia, Georgia; Elkwood and Red Bay, Alabama; Columbia and Fayetteville, Tennessee; and Lacrosse, Arkansas. The death toll for all states was 421 with 2,000 or more injured and $25 million in damages.

For William T. Porter, sixty-seven-year-old resident of tiny Gordo, Alabama, it was the strangest, most terrifying experience of his long life. He was in bed on the morning of April 2, 1936, his four-room house still dark even though it was 8:45 A.M. Outside loomed a turbulent purple-black storm, its high-velocity winds scudding angry clouds overhead. Porter rolled over and decided to sleep on. Then he heard a roar, like a cannon belching giant shells. A whirring gust of wind ripped away the roof of Porter's house, and as he bolted upright in bed, the storm let loose its grasp of debris and showered it down on him. Though unharmed Porter sank back to his pillow in shock as rain began to pour down on his face. It was the beginning of one of the worst tornado outbreaks in the history of the South.

Rotating at 90 m.p.h. the tornado moved on to Cordele, Georgia, pummeling and flattening a three-block area. Before the funnel spun itself into oblivion, it smacked Greensboro, North Carolina. But this was but a prelude to the funnel-shaped clouds that touched down four days later in a dozen southern towns.

On April 6, Tupelo, Mississippi, was hit by a tornado that uprooted fifteen residential blocks. It was evening when the little TVA town, the first to employ power from the Muscle Shoals Dam, was struck. A sleepy city of fewer than 10,000 persons then, the last great tragedy folks remembered was the death of a stunt flyer, Dean Swift Faulkner, brother of novelist William Faulkner, six months before. (Faulkner himself might have died that day, September 10, 1935, had he not lost the flip of the coin to determine which barnstorming brother would take up joyriding farmers in their ancient biplane.)

As the tornado swooped down on strollers and late-night drivers, it lifted up cars and tossed them a block or so. Water mains were severed, hydrants buried beneath debris, and when subsequent fires broke out there was little water with which to fight them. Hundreds of people were brought to the town's small hospital, which, like most of the town, was in darkness; the electric power had been knocked out. Doctors and nurses ordered office buildings converted into hospitals and labored over bleeding patients by using pocket flashlights.

As the tornado swirled and growled down the streets of Tupelo, hundreds raced for cover. For some there was no time. One man who realized that he was caught with his family in the middle of the street with the twister a half block distant and roaring toward them spied a manhole cover, kicked it open and thrust his wife and children inside, dropping down at the last moment before the tornado swept over him.

A woman trapped alone in her crumbling house grabbed her pet canary and jumped into a large refrigerator. (She and her bird were saved at the last moment from suffocation by rescuers.)

Tupelo was seriously threatened by fires, but rain began to fall in the tornado's wake as it rushed off to the east. This helped to extinguish the flames, but 195 Tupelo residents were already dead.

The twister's next victim felt the full weight of its havoc. Gainesville, in northeastern Georgia, fifty-five miles from Atlanta, suddenly, at 8:45 A.M., became a vast, tangled morgue of ripped up streets and crumpled

Dazed survivors make their way through tornado-smashed Gainesville, Georgia, in 1936. *(UPI)*

buildings with mangled bodies sprawling everywhere. "Bricks, wood, and tin collapsed all around us with a thunderous crash. . . . It happened with lightning swiftness," were the words one injured worker used to describe the destruction of the Cooper Pants Manufacturing Company, where there was the greatest death toll of 125. One man alone, bleeding from a head wound, dragged forty-five bodies from the smashed building.

The downtown section of this small mill town (population, 8,624) was obliterated as the twister brought down or wrecked every business structure except for the new post office and the federal courthouse dedicated a year before with much pomp by Postmaster General William Farley. The ancient, elegant Dixie Hunt Hotel was gone. The First Baptist Church was unroofed. Five persons were crushed to death as the walls of the Palmour Hardware Store collapsed. In all 630 buildings and fourteen blocks were wrecked, and 33 buildings were blown away from their foundations.

The city clerk, W. E. Dozier, was at his desk in city hall when the tornado struck. He heard one of the windows crack and got up to investigate. In a second he was blown across the room. P. O. McKinney, a storeowner, was waiting on customers. He heard a loud explosion, looked up and saw that his shop was without a roof.

Ima Pruitt was outside and saw the monster churning its way toward her. "It was a terrifying experience. I was walking down Main Street when everything suddenly got real dark and the wind began blowing. I went into a one-story drugstore building. There was a two-story structure next door. All of a sudden, the ceiling started cracking. . . ." It showered down on her: "My legs were buried beneath the debris. . . . I was suffering excruciating pain. I did not lose consciousness. One man beside me was dead and another dying. There were terrifying groans all around us. It was ten minutes after the storm passed before rescue workers reached us."

The rescuers, 2,000 in all, poured into Gainesville from Atlanta and dozens of other towns. National Guardsmen, Civilian Conservation Corps workers and chain-gang convicts labored side by side to extract the stricken and dead from tons of fallen brick and mortar. More than 2,000 were homeless even though the twister only sliced through a tip of the residential district. Soup kitchens were set up by noon, and the Red Cross mobilized 500 nurses to attend to the wounded.

Gainesville had suffered the worst storm disaster since a twister struck the city on June 1, 1903, killing 104, but in terms of damage in this brooding year of depression, the loss was staggering: $5 million alone to the business district and half as much to private homes.

Before three companies of National Guardsmen arrived to protect against looters, a squadron of young, beardless cadets from the Riverside Academy in full dress regalia smartly marched into the area shouldering empty Civil War rifles, their proud patrol preceded by a small band blaring "Dixie."

(ALSO SEE: Cordelle, Georgia)

GALLITZEN, PENNSYLVANIA — RAILWAY WRECK
February 18, 1947

The derailment of the Pennsylvania's eastbound Red Arrow (Number 68), on the morning of February 18, 1947, was caused by excessive speeds as the train rounded a curve near Gallitzen, Pennsylvania. The curve was one of the most dangerous on the line, and engineers were cautioned to take it at no more than 30 m.p.h.

The Red Arrow fairly flew around this arc of steel at more than 65 m.p.h., according to later investigators. Seven cars of the fourteen-car train were thrown off the tracks into awkward positions, but they did not crash into each other. Twenty-four persons were killed, including the crew of the second engine. The engineer had been attempting to make up for lost time.

GALUNG GUNG — VOLCANIC ERUPTIONS
October, 1822

Prior to 1822, Galung Gung, a huge but inactive volcano on Java (which possesses 125 volcanoes, 13 of which are still active), was coated with thick forests, and its slopes were dotted with numerous villages. Its cone was hollow and resembled a tranquil meadow. It was, according to missionaries, one of the most beautiful, placid sites in the world at that time.

All of this changed to horrible carnage in October, 1822, when, without any warning rumbles or tremors, Galung Gung blew its top—a gigantic waterspout mixed with steaming mud, brimstone, ashes and rocks. This debris fell to earth forty miles from the volcano's summit. The many streams flowing about and down the

Scattered like matchsticks are cars of the famed "Red Arrow" express near Gallitzen, Pennsylvania, February 18, 1947. *(Wide World)*

volcano became instantly swollen with burning mud; these floodwaters swept away one village after another, snaring in their paths the fleeing, panic-stricken villagers. Cattle and wild animals—even birds—caught in the torrent were dashed headlong toward a major river forty miles away. In other areas dozens of villages were immediately engulfed by seas of blue mud that trapped and suffocated inhabitants caught in their houses. Within five hours more than a thousand persons were dead.

Four days later the volcano erupted in a massive explosion that caused the top of the mountain to cave in and one of its sides to collapse inward. A shower of mud and slag similar to basalt beat down upon more hapless villages. There was an enormous breach in Galung Gung, and following the eruption an earthquake shook the entire area, creating new hills where once there had been level plains. Rivers altered courses and swept away 2,000 villagers whose mangled bodies were washed toward the sea over the drowned carcasses of tigers, rhinoceroses and monkeys. The destruction was total; 114 villages were obliterated and more than 4,000 were killed in the watery avalanche.

GALVESTON, TEXAS — HURRICANE
September 8, 1900

background: One of the most severe West Indian hurricanes ever to lash the United States coast struck Galveston, Texas, on September 8, 1900, with winds of 100 to 120 m.p.h. and a twenty-foot tidal wave which pushed the sea level fifteen feet above normal. More than 6,000 persons, about one-seventh of the city's total population, were killed, and an equal number were injured. The city was all but obliterated, and scores of persons were shot for looting and robbing the dead. At that time the fourth wealthiest city per capita in the United States, Galveston suffered property losses in the millions of dollars. Two thousand million tons of rain fell on Galveston during the hurricane's first twenty-four-hour period.

Parasols spun on the shoulders of women in long white dresses, and their male escorts pushed back straw boaters from sweat-streaked foreheads as they strolled the hard, white sand of Galveston's beaches on the evening of September 7, 1900. Wafting out to them was the simultaneously sad and merry music of ragtime bands. Children played in the gentle surf as the caressing Gulf breezes played across the four-mile-wide sandbar upon which stood the fourth richest city in the United States at that time (the second largest grain-shipping port in the country with a business of more than $300 million in exports and imports).

First used by the pirate Jean Lafitte as a haven, the six-mile-square Galveston Island is separated from the Texas mainland on one side by an azure bay and on the other by the Gulf of Mexico.

This sandy island rises but five feet above sea level, yet it withstood hurricane attacks in 1875 and a particularly violent storm in 1887. There were warnings, of course, from engineers and weather experts that a hurricane wall shielding the city from the gulf waters should be built, but town leaders pointed to the past performances of storms, which at the eleventh hour always veered northeast and spared the island.

Such conditions did not prevail when the slow-moving storm born 1,200 miles to the south in the West Indies moved determinedly toward Galveston. It came with squalling rains at 4:00 A.M. on September 8. Brutishly shoving the rain bursts were winds over 30 m.p.h. At 10:00 A.M., with the winds increasing rapidly, the bay area, which had been deepened at a cost of $6.2 million, began to flood. Breakers dashed up and over the wharves. Heavy ships at anchor tossed against splintered piers. The business section, which faced the bay, was soon awash, four feet of water surging along Market Street.

Alarms still did not go out. Then several buildings began to go to pieces, first copings, then sections of walls and portions of roofs blown to bits. On the gulf side of the island, where most of the residential district sprawled, all was calm. Suddenly the wind shifted from the north to the southeast. Four miles of residences along the beaches were under attack as the waters rose up and lashed into them.

The winds increased. Witless spectators stood on the beaches marveling at the gigantic storm as it advanced on a sixty-mile front. Isaac and Joseph Cline, United States Weather Bureau employees, hitched horses and rode to the beach to warn people to take cover. They were ignored. The Clines hoisted warning flags to ships in the harbor from atop the Levy Building, but these were soon torn away by winds that had increased to 84 m.p.h., at which time the anometer was blown away. (Winds intensified from 100 to 120 m.p.h., according to other reports.)

The Clines rushed home to evacuate their families. Isaac later stated, "The water rose at a steady rate from 3:00 P.M. until about 7:30 P.M., when there was a sudden rise of about four feet in as many seconds. I was standing at my front door, which was partly open, watching the water which was flowing with great rapidity from east to west. The water at this time was about eight inches deep in my residence, and the sudden rise of four feet brought it above my waist before I could change position."

Death leaped through the storm. The first to die, according to one report, were three leading citizens, toasting the storm as they sat in Rietter's Saloon on

Galveston was devastated by the killer hurricane of 1900; 6,000 died. *(UPI)*

Strand Street, Stanley G. Spencer, Charles Kellner and Richard Lord. The three were sitting at a table on the first floor scoffing at the panic screamed in the streets when the roof collapsed and crushed them to death. Dozens were saved when the roof and flooring was caught by the bar; they worked their way to freedom through this awkward lean-to. A Negro waiter was sent to find a doctor; his bloated body was found the following day washing up against buildings at Strand and Twenty-first streets.

Those along the gulf who refused to leave their patchwork cottages sealed their own doom. The hurricane clawed these flimsy buildings and soon smashed them, killing hundreds. A giant wave, estimated at twenty feet, roared ashore and bulldozed everything—people, houses, animals, trees—1200 feet back from the shoreline into a massive two-story reef of debris and dead.

Captain W. C. Rafferty, commanding Battery O, First Artillery at Fort Crockett, had watched the storm's approach perched upon the giant ten-inch gun that poked its nose solemnly into the gulf. He sent word to the barracks for the men to disperse and seek better shelter. Then he made for his home and family. Water was swirling about his waist before he reached his house. He quickly gathered up loose timbers, lashed them together to make a raft, placed his children, wife, and servant on it with their backs to the violent spray and pushed the raft back to the gun. Beneath the gun was a small steel room that offered refuge. In the dark with the steel door bolted against the storm, Rafferty and his family heard the foundation around them begin to crumble, and the gun over head creaking. The booming nightmare continued until massive waves broke through the door and plucked, as if with invisible hands, the family's servant and dragged her out to sea and death. The family survived.

Twenty-seven of Rafferty's soldiers fared less well. A sergeant named George brought the troops to attention as the barracks about them began to break up. "Boys," he told them, "it is every man for himself. This building won't stand half an hour. I am going to get out." The men followed George, attempting to gain safety in the Denver Resurvey School. Twelve remained, and these were literally blown upward and outward when the barracks building caved in. Seven were killed instantly; five others, clinging to wreckage, were furiously driven like javelins across the island and into the bay. Wading and then swimming, George and twenty-seven others reached the schoolhouse. Three nonswimmers drowned during the trek. The schoolhouse filled with water rising to five feet. A wall fell; three more men were dead beneath it. Eight men stayed with the building; sixteen others took their chances in the water, clutching debris that shot past them at millrace velocity. Fifteen were hurtled, dead, into the bay. The lone survivor jumped onto a rooftop floating by and rode it to Virginia Point, two miles inland. When the roof broke up he jumped onto a scudding telephone pole and rode it like a horse for hours before he reached land.

Telephone poles had fallen in droves. There was no electricity, and as the hurricane rose to full force during the night, all of Galveston pitched and rocked in darkness.

The two-ton bell high in the tower of St. Mary's Cathedral stopped its warning peals as the winds tore through its braces and sent it shuddering downward. On a lower floor Bishop Nicholas Gallagher and Father James Kerwin were prepared for death, but both survived. Father Kerwin later related dozens of stories of death, heroism and survival he heard from members of his parish, one of whom was a butcher named Meyer.

"He lost his wife and child and was floating along, half dazed, on a raft, when he saw two children struggling in the water. He seized them and found that their combined weight threatened to sink his raft. He jumped off, and pushed the raft against a stable which had lodged against a telegraph pole. He placed the children in the hay in the upper part of the stable, and going out on his raft, fell asleep. When he awoke, he found himself on the dry street, and, forgetting all about the children, came uptown. The next day he remembered the little ones, and returning to the stable, found them crying. They were his sister's children."

Though the winds increased at a murderous rate, the mounds of debris that had been hurled inland, some as high as fifty feet, proved to be barriers against the huge waves crashing in from the gulf. One of the buildings to survive the battering was the Ursuline Convent, five blocks from the beach. Though it was flooded to the second floor, dozens of intrepid nuns using poles and ropes drew more than 1,000 drifting, helpless persons into the substantial brick building. One of these was Mrs. William H. Heidemann, who climbed up a rope from a truck in which she had been floating. Pregnant, she gave birth to a child only a few hours afterward.

The single worst tragedy in Galveston occurred at the Catholic Orphanage Asylum, which housed one hundred children and fifteen Sisters of Charity. Located at Twenty-first Street and Avenue M the aged building soon gave way to the hurricane. At 8:00 P.M. the structure went down, killing all but two small boys, both seven years old, who clung to floating debris and were found the next day. The sisters attempted to tie the children to them before the building collapsed, but it was hopeless. They were later found in bunches of eight, strung together by the ropes that encircled the dead sisters' waists.

The rain was like a continuous volley of grapeshot, driven horizontally by the relentless winds. People were sent flying in the air along with whizzing debris and shooting timbers, which slaughtered many. One boy named Rutter jumped into a trunk after losing his father, mother, brother and sister and was carried twenty miles, landing at Hitchcock the next day. A soldier, who had been stationed at Bolivar Point, clung to debris and drifted forty miles to the mainland, staggering ashore at Cedar Bayou.

Those who stayed with their homes had less chance of surviving than those who risked the swirling, chaotic waters. Even though Richard Spillane, editor of the *Galveston Tribune,* later wrote that "to go upon the streets was to court death," most of the more than 6,000 dead were killed by their own houses, weak structures for the most part constructed of cedar posts, brick columns and brick foundations imbedded only a few feet in the sand. These quickly collapsed.

The attractive Sarah Summers, one of the most sought-after belles in Galveston, refused to leave her lavish surroundings. She was later found next to her home at Tremont Street and Avenue F, "her lips smiling but her features set in death, her hands grasping her diamonds tightly."

More than 700 persons thought the city hall would afford them protection, but 50 died inside the building and hundreds more were injured. Even the dead were not safe. The cemetery west of Thirty-fifth Street was inundated; caskets were unearthed and floated with their macabre cargoes into the bay. One metal coffin of 200 pounds floated as far as Virginia Point.

A dredge weighing several tons was sent flying in the same direction, landing two miles inland. In the harbor all was havoc; one steamer was ripped from its moorings and sent down the channel like a cannonball, ramming all three bridges—one for wagons, two for trains—that stretched to the mainland, tearing them apart and cutting off avenues of escape as well as aid.

The steamers *Alamo* and *Red Cross* were lifted bodily by the storm and dumped onto Pelican Flats. The

Kendal Castle was slammed across the turbulent waters to Texas City, four miles away, where she was buried in the mud. The *Gylla* was beached at Virginia Point.

Downtown where the storm raged less violently, the luxurious Tremont House became a source of safety. Hundreds waded and swam to the hotel, but dozens drowned on the way.

Death lurked and then pounced in other areas. Only eight persons out of one hundred survived St. Mary's Infirmary. When the Rosenberg schoolhouse fell, scores were crushed to death.

Its south wall gone and its top caved in, the old Union Depot was filled quickly by hundreds of quaking survivors seeking shelter but expecting to die at any moment. Outside the building the swelling waters reached twelve feet and bodies drifted by in dense clumps. Baggagemaster Harding plucked a dead baby girl from the waters and wept for hours as he held the lifeless child.

Galveston, the old, haughty, unprotected Galveston, was finished. In the words of one chronicler of the event: "It was nothing strange to see the dead and crippled everywhere, and the living were so fascinated by the dead they could hardly be dragged away from the spots where the corpses were piled. There were dead by the score, by the hundreds and by the thousands. It was a city of the dead; a vast battlefield, the slain being victims of flood and gale. The dead were at rest, but the living had to suffer, for no aid was at hand."

By 11:00 P.M. the storm abated somewhat and at dawn the waters began to recede. Then the miserable search for relatives living and dead commenced. Sun fell on the mud-covered face of John Bowie, propped up on a pedestal on Tremont Street; he had recently been awarded a prize as the most popular police officer in Galveston. His feet were broken, his ribs stove in, his head crusted with blood. "My house with wife and children is in the gulf," he murmured. "I have not a thing on earth for which to live."

Guns drawn, U.S. troops eye Galveston's survivors as they line up for relief packages. Dozens of persons were shot for looting. *(UPI)*

The living searched for the living and found the dead. Many went insane. Several shot themselves when discovering the crushed bodies of their loved ones. Added to the growing threat of disease arising from the masses of dead littering the shorn island was another virus, more deadly than any pestilence any corpse could give off: hundreds of looters streamed over the crumpled city, many coming by boat from the mainland cities of Texas City and Houston.

Hurling themselves with savage glee into stores, they stuffed their pockets with anything available from canned goods to feather dusters. They stripped the dead of jewelry, clothes and even gold teeth. To combat the ghouls Captain Rafferty rounded up seventy waterlogged troopers, most of them unarmed, and told them to stop the wholesale robbery. Two regiments of regular infantry moved in from Houston. Incensed at the tales of looting by thugs, a Major Faylings told his troopers, "Shoot them in their tracks, boys! We want no prisoners." By Tuesday, scores of looters had been shot. Ninety Negroes had been shot to death by citizen guards. "One of them was searched and $700 found, together with four diamond rings and two water-soaked gold watches. The finger of a white woman with a gold band around it was clutched in his hands," one report stated. Another had it that "one Negro had twenty-three human fingers with rings on them in his pocket."

Major Faylings received word that twenty Negroes were looting a house at Nineteenth and Beach streets. "Plant them!" he screamed to his men, who rushed to the area and shot all twenty to death. On Wednesday evening regular troops captured fifty ghouls rummaging through mounds of dead in a huge apartment building. All fifty, including some white women, harlots from New Orleans it was later claimed, were lined against one of the few remaining brick walls and shot to death. Ninety more Negroes were executed for looting the following day.

Mayor Walter C. Jones declared martial law on Tuesday morning, commanding "all good citizens . . . to deliver all arms and ammunition to the city and take Major Faylings' receipt."

The problem of the dead increased. Corpses floated like cordwood in the bay, in the gulf and down the streets, mixing with putrid carcasses of animals; they were jammed into pathetic, confused heaps, eddying in the water about broken buildings. The supply of lime, carbolic acid and camphor was used quickly as the living attempted to purify the city. More than 2,000 men began the task of gathering up bodies and burying them; hundreds of Negroes refused to do this work and were pressed into the labor at gunpoint.

But it seemed hopeless. There were too many bodies to bury beneath the sand of Galveston. A passenger on the Houston-bound steamer *Allen Charlotte* stated, "I saw fully fifty dead bodies floating in the water. I saw one dray with sixty-four dead bodies being drawn by four horses to the wharves, where the bodies were unloaded on a tug and taken out in the gulf for burial."

But the bodies buried at sea only washed ashore again. Then the burning began. On Tuesday, block-long trenches were dug and lined with wood. The dead were placed in these, and wood was thrown on top of them. Oil was sloshed down and the trenches set on fire. Men dug these death trenches for two days, some breaking down when they discovered a relative being tossed into the ditch. One man examined the teeth of hundreds of dead women as he sought out his wife. They wore camphor bags under their noses, but many still became so nauseated by the smell of death that they either fainted or had to quit the digging.

The huge funeral pyres burned all week, black clouds from the incinerations drifting upward and hanging like a sinister signal above the ruined city of Galveston, a smoky, gruesome reminder that it was time to build a seawall.

GALVESTON, TEXAS — HURRICANE — August 16, 1915

background: Beginning in the Cape Verde area, a tremendous hurricane with winds up to 120 m.p.h. hit Galveston, Texas, on August 16, 1915, its waves cresting at twenty-one feet and breaching the seawall. The island's business district was under six feet of water. Fifty million dollars in damage resulted, and 275 persons were killed.

Following the killer storm that battered Galveston in 1900, the city built one of the great almost hurricane-proof seawalls in the world. Stretching eleven miles is a riprap wall of granite, its timbers and concrete sixteen feet wide at the base and rising to a height of seventeen to nineteen feet. Sloping backward in a concave curve, it was thought, until 1915, that the wall could hold back any storm.

But the hurricane that roared out of the Cape Verde region past Guadaloupe and Dominica on August 10, 1915, gathered itself to gale force with 60 m.p.h. winds. When it reached the Texas coast, blasting directly at Galveston, its winds had accelerated to 120 m.p.h. The weather bureau broadcast warnings of the storm, but the residents felt secure behind their magnificent wall.

When the tide raced forward with the hurricane, it was twelve feet above normal, and waves crested at 21 feet, pouring over and in some places through the wall. The downtown district was soon awash to the second stories of most buildings. There were $50 million in damages. More appalling were the 275 deaths created by the storm.

In the wake of this hurricane Galveston elevated its seawall to 19.2 feet, a height that proved necessary when hurricane Carla, with winds of 175 m.p.h., raced toward the city on September 11, 1961. This time the wall fully resisted the storm, though water crept around the barrier and killed two persons.

GANGES DELTA, EAST PAKISTAN — CYCLONE — May 11-12, 1965

A furious cyclone, whipped on by 100 m.p.h. winds and driving thirteen-foot waves over the narrow channels of the Ganges Delta in East Pakistan on May 11-12, 1965, took more than 12,000 lives, mostly from drowning. Even the capital, Dacca, 125 miles from the menacing sea, was wrecked, its streets shredded, homes pounded to bits, its spreading mango orchards and jute crops destroyed.

Damage ran between $300 and $600 million; five million homes were wiped out. It was the worst storm to hit the area since 1960, but it would be dwarfed by the murderous torrent that inundated the Ganges district five years later.

(ALSO SEE: East Pakistan, October 10, 1960; Ganges Delta, November 12, 1970)

GANGES DELTA, EAST PAKISTAN — CYCLONE — November 12, 1970

background: On the night of November 12, 1970, an immense cyclone struck the Ganges Delta, centering on the East Pakistan coast and offshore islands with winds up to 150 m.p.h. and a seawave estimated to be fifty feet high. The death toll ranged between 300,000 and 500,000 persons, most either struck down by the wave or carried out to sea when it retreated; hardest hit were Manpura, Bhola, Hatia, Rangabali and Kukri Mukri islands. Worldwide relief efforts were put into action. Thousands more died weeks later from typhoid and cholera.

Everyone thought it was a false alarm. The Ganges Delta had previously been alerted and its myriad inhabitants badly frightened when a small but clamorous cyclone struck on October 23, 1970. Damage had been slight, injuries minimal. Then the next alarm, a report sent to the coastal areas of East Pakistan from Cox's Bazaar, warned of a gigantic cyclone lumbering across the sea near the Adaman Islands.

On November 9 an American weather satellite

pinpointed the massive storm and rough estimates had it moving at 10 m.p.h., doggedly stalking the Ganges Delta 800 miles south. Radio Pakistan, however, failed to describe the obdurate storm and its full dangers. Millions of coastal dwellers did not budge, either refusing to flee or feeling that evacuation up the Ganges and its tributaries would be hopeless.

The cyclone struck on the night of November 12, pushing before it a twenty to fifty-foot wave that raced over the puny offshore islands, most of which sat no more than twenty feet above the sea. (Most of them were made of silt deposited from the waterways of the mainland.) The residents here were simply torn from their thatched homes, hurtled out to sea to disappear, and then floated to the surface, dead, hours after the cyclone had driven inland. By the time the storm rolled over the land, its winds were estimated at 150 m.p.h. Communications were instantly broken between the stricken area and the capital, Dacca, which would remain ignorant of the disaster's magnitude for two days.

A rich farmer on the island of Manpura, Kamaluddin Chodhury, was one of the few survivors from the first-hit area. "The radio warned of a storm," he later said, "but nobody spoke of a tidal wave. At midnight we heard a great roar growing louder from the southeast. I looked out. It was pitch black, but in the distance I could see a glow. The glow got nearer and bigger, and then I realized it was the crest of a huge wave." Chodhury quickly gathered up his family and raced to the top floor of their solidly built home. The wave rushed in and flooded everything around them to the second story until the water swirled at their feet. Manpura was gone.

Bhola Island succumbed immediately when its carefully constructed eighteen-foot seawall was battered down by the wave and wind. Island after island disappeared as the cyclone moved over them and then onto the mainland, where it slew lavishly.

One coastal villager who did not take a radio warning lightly was Nomohan Das. He gathered up his large family and began to move them into a storm shelter some distance from his house. The wind began to blow them down and roll them across the land. Das, his wife and children formed a human chain by linking arms and struggled forward. They were blown down, but they began to crawl ahead. The villager realized that he and his family could not reach the shelter and crawled to his brother's house, which was nearby. They managed to climb to the roof where, for four hours, they were pelted by rain and wind. "Then we heard a roar," Das said, "like it was the end of the world and the tidal wave was on us. The roof of the house was ripped loose. I grabbed

Devastation was left in the wake of the monster cyclone that smashed the Ganges Delta in November 1970. Shown here are the shattered remains of Kachha, East Pakistan. *(UPI)*

my youngest son. The roof was floating, and I grabbed a tree and held on for hours. I was freezing from the rain. Children would be swept by, screaming for help. I tried to grab on to them and tie them to me but the current was too strong. They were swept away. I felt helpless."

At dawn the water receded and Das happily discovered all of his family alive, clinging to trees. Thousands of bodies, many of his friends, floated by. Das's son did not speak for several hours. "It was like he was dead." In the afternoon the boy suddenly sat down and began to weep.

Das's neighbor, Ginda Daz, lost two of his children. He too had retreated to a roof that was torn loose by the wave. His family slipped from the sinking roof. "My wife was tossed from tree to tree and somehow our five-year-old daughter disappeared, gone forever." When the water backed off toward the sea, Daz found his wife naked "and the front of her body was streaming with blood from clutching a thorny palm tree." Daz attempted to cross a river, but he could not move his small boat because the river was clogged with corpses. Daz noticed some movement and plucked from the stream two girls who were alive and floating on top of the dead bodies.

He staggered back to his hysterical wife. They sat and waited for nothing. Hours later his nine-year-old daughter and his sister-in-law stumbled from bushes. They explained that they had survived by hanging on to floating bamboo and had been carried several miles downstream. Their late return was due to embarrassment. They, too, were naked and hid from the sight of men as they slowly and secretly crept home through the underbrush. The partially reunited family celebrated by splitting open green cocoanuts and gulping the milk.

The number killed by the cyclone was appalling, one of the worst disasters in modern times; an estimated 300,000 to 500,000 were dead. More than 20,000 inhabitants disappeared from one island alone. On Hatia there were so many corpses that survivors took to tossing them into the sea rather than burying them. The bodies floated back to the island's serene beaches each day only to be driven out again by people using bamboo poles. Cholera spread on Rangabali. Carcasses in hideous clumps drew vultures when they gave off the sickening sweet smell of death. All along the Ganges Delta rice paddies had turned the color of blood.

When full details of the catastrophe reached Dacca, calls for sweeping relief and supplies were sent out. The world responded immediately. British and American aid proved the largest. Ten British C-130 Hercules cargo planes flew into the area with huge quantities of food and medicine. The H.M.S. *Intrepid* steamed with several other English ships into the Bay of Bengal to unload

This village in the Ganges Delta was flattened by a savage cyclone, November 12, 1970, which killed 300,000 to 500,000 people. *(Wide World)*

tons of rice, and engineers to rebuild roads and bridges. Whole fleets of American helicopters buzzed into the area with food and supplies. From one of the choppers Ambassador Joseph Farland saw thousands of starving Pakistanis close to panic as they lifted up their arms to the helicopters, shouting "*Beshi, beshi* [More, more]" to the Vietnamese-trained pilots and aides who kicked out relief bundles. They were afraid to land.

Newsweek's Maynard Parker reported: "As we hovered for a landing, the sickening smell of rotting corpses—human and cattle—came wafting up from the ground. . . . We touched down, and men, boys and girls below the age of puberty ran toward us across the ruined fields. . . . There was a mad scramble for the packages." The helicoptor was forced to take flight lest its blades kill the panicking crowds. Parker stayed on the ground and attempted to hand out the supplies with some order. The packages were soon gone, the objects of wild fights and grappling crowds. Parker recalled, "A little girl came running up to me, pointing at her swollen belly and asking for food, but I had none to give. Nearby a small boy collapsed on top of his relief bundle and broke into tears."

Water supplies were nonexistent. Most of the mains had been broken in the urban areas, and fresh water outlets had turned brackish and bloody. Typhoid and cholera spread rapidly, and Red Cross medical teams worked feverishly to check the outbreaks.

The city of Patuakhali was all but wiped out. Dead littered the streets, and over them sauntered a Pakistani minister with his valet and army aides at his side. Poet and author Dom Moraes, who had flown into the area after the cyclone had spent itself, walked up to the minister and introduced himself. The impeccably attired politician smiled broadly and said, "So you are a foreign correspondent? How fortunate for you that you have arrived at this moment. You may obtain a fine story of the details of my visit to Patuakhali. I have seen (you may quote this) the sufferings of the good people of this district, and I have shared them, both physically and mentally. Do you not have a notebook? Please take this down. It is well worth your while."

In Dacca on the afternoon following the cyclone, Moraes overheard four youths, two girls and two boys, talking.

"It would be fun to have a picnic," one of the girls suggested.

The oldest boy shrugged and said, "All the pretty places are crapped up with dead bodies and stuff like that."

"Hell, I forgot about that," the girl stated. "It's a shame, but I guess no picnic."

GASCONADE, MISSOURI — RAILWAY WRECK — November 1, 1855

The train disaster at the Gasconade bridge on November 1, 1855, which took the lives of twenty-two festive passengers and injured scores more, was attributed to excessive speed, but impatience was the primary villain. The Pacific Railroad of Missouri had almost completed the longest, largest trestle (a 750-foot, six-span iron girder bridge rising above a 35-foot gorge) on its route. Six towering concrete piers supported the span, but because of its haste to complete this section of track, the Pacific (later the Missouri Pacific) line had shored up one embankment with a makeshift wooden trestle to complete the bridge.

The structure was tested by a heavy gravel train before the VIP Special from St. Louis, its eleven cars loaded down with railroad and military dignitaries and several tooting bands, arrived with much fanfare at 6:00 P.M. Engineer William Tucker had been instructed to go over the bridge at a crawl. He later claimed his train was not exceeding 6 m.p.h., but officials who saw the Special approach the bridge estimated the speed to be more than 15 m.p.h. Just after the engine and baggage car cleared the 130-foot area between the first two piers, it broke off and took with it seven passenger cars, uncoupling and dragging with them the baggage car.

Fortunately for most of the passengers, the cars fell at different angles into the shallow Gasconade River, a tributary of the Missouri, and landed separately instead of on top of each other. This, no doubt, saved some lives, but twenty-two were killed outright and many more injured. Fires broke out in many of the cars when coal stoves burst, but rain providentially fell minutes later and squelched the flames.

Investigators later blamed Tucker for his exuberance in taking the Special across at high speed, but one engineer charged the line with "incompetency, recklessness or infatuation" in its hurried attempt to throw up "such frail structures" as the death bridge constructed over the Gasconade.

GENERAL SLOCUM — MARINE DISASTER — June 15, 1904

background: Launched in 1891, the excursion steamer, *General Slocum,* 250 feet long, had suffered a series of mishaps since her first operations out of the port of New York. The ship, commanded by William Van Schaick, departed from the Third Street pier at 9:00 A.M. on June 15, 1904. A little more than two hours later she became a burning funeral pyre, beached on North Brother Island in the East River. Of the 1,500 on board, 1,021 perished, mostly due, it was later determined, to the inadequate and faulty safety equipment on board and the gross negligence of Captain Van Schaick.

William Van Schaick was more than unlucky. His record proved him one of the most incompetent seamen in the history of New York harbor. The fact that he continued to command one of the largest excursion steamers in that port for more than ten years despite his outright recklessness is still a mystery.

Captain Van Schaick was at the helm when the *Slocum* accidentally beached herself on July 29, 1894. Once on the sand bar, neither the captain nor the crew bothered to prevent the ensuing panic in which dozens were injured. Order on board his ship apparently did not concern Van Schaick. On August 17, 1901, a panic among picnickers mounted to a riot in which, again, scores were taken to the hospital for treatment.

That husbands would leave their wives and children in care of such a notorious blunderer on the morning of June 15, 1904—of the 1,500 boarding the *Slocum* only 83 were men—attests to the naiveté of an immigrant German community and the neglect and stupidity of harbor authorities.

The brutal disaster that the *Slocum* became that day need not have happened if panic had been controlled by the crew, if the ship's firehoses and life saving equipment had been kept in repair, if her captain had been another man. Those nagging, horrifying "ifs" are, as a whole, applicable to almost every major disaster at sea, except that in the case of the *General Slocum,* they all came to bear on a single incident.

Almost all of the 1,021 souls lost on the *Slocum* on that crisp, sunny morning in 1904 were members of St. Mark's school picnic near Throg's Neck in the Bronx. The paddlewheeler's 23 crew men indifferently herded the more than 1,400 passengers onto the three decks of the ship. Many of the crew grumbled that they were "in for a long day." They would have this teeming crowd on their hands until 11:00 P.M., when the *Slocum* would return her passengers to the Third Street pier.

Captain Van Schaick ordered his steamer away from the pier a little after 9:00 A.M., while the German congregation sang the hymn "A Mighty Fortress is Our God." As the ship churned away from her berth the smell of chowder being prepared in the galley was thick in the air. Hundreds of small children raced about the decks playing. The *Slocum* was resplendent in a coat of fresh white paint and decorative banners flapping, but that is where the ship's improvements stopped. The vessel was in sloppy condition. Hatches were left open. Paint lockers were unlocked. Life preservers were largely inaccessible. So too were most of the crew members; only two reserve policemen were on board to maintain order. (One of these, Thomas Cooney, saved eleven victims that day before drowning as he swam to save a twelfth.)

For an hour the *Slocum* crawled up the East River, approaching a point known and feared as Hell's Gate, a particularly treacherous stretch of water. The *Haarlem,* a ferry, passed the ship and her crew members waved to the gay crowd.

It was 10:00 A.M. when the vessel was abeam of 130th Street. Suddenly the festive noises on the *Slocum* halted. "Fire!" a woman shouted. Indeed there was. Flames were issuing from a paint locker in the forward part of the ship. One account states that a cabin containing flammables such as gasoline, polish and oil lamps burst into flames. Another account stated that the blaze began in the galley when the cook stove exploded. It mattered little where the fire started; the *Slocum* was ripe for burning. Her rotting wooden frame was cracked and brittle; the fresh paint upon her boards was highly combustible.

Those watching through field glasses from the gas works on Long Island could see smoke billowing and flames dancing upward toward the front of the ship. They also heard the frantic crowd on board shrieking and yelling.

Mothers herded their children toward the stern of the *Slocum,* a costly mistake that lead to death for most. Captain Van Schaick, who had turned the wheel over to Pilot Edward Van Wart at 138th Street, ordered the vessel to North Brother Island, disregarding the stiff northeast wind that fanned the flames. Why Van Schaick did not turn the *Slocum* toward the Manhattan shore, only three hundred yards away, where it could have been beached in a few minutes and countless lives would have been saved, was never explained. He chose the long route to the island and thus sealed the fate of hundreds.

The excursion steamer *General Slocum* burned to the water line in New York's East River, June 15, 1904. Her captain, Van Schaick, went to prison for manslaughter. *(UPI)*

Some crew members attempted to put out the blaze, but the firehose would not work. One crew member discovered a rubber disc that had been tightly fitted over the nozzle, and it took several minutes to remove this. When the water was finally turned on, only a trickle emitted from the hose. The hose, which apparently had not been inspected, was rotten, and dozens of leaks fizzed water, leaving no pressure with which to fight the fire.

Panic was rampant at the stern of the ship where most of the excursionists had taken refuge. The flames shot backward from the bow of the vessel, lapping at the horrified women and children huddled in little clusters.

Barge and dredge captains were frantically tooting their whistles to call any nearby fireboats. One fireboat, the *Abram S. Hewitt,* responded, but she lost precious seconds by stopping at the East 67th Street pier to pick up New York City Fire Department Chief Edward F. Croker. She did not arrive upon the scene of the disaster until the *Slocum* had already crashed onto the rocky shoals of North Brother Island. Captain Van Schaick had beached the vessel in a most unreachable spot.

The hundreds of huddled, screaming people at the stern of the ship fought desperately over life preservers, almost all of which proved rotten and went to pieces in the hands of frantic mothers. (Another report stated that the manager and some employees of the Nonpareil Cork Works, manufacturer of the *Slocum's* life saving equipment, had placed iron bars inside the preservers to meet the mandatory legal weight; these men were later indicted on criminal charges by the Department of Justice.)

When the *Slocum* shuddered onto the rocks, the flames from her holds, galley and bow cabins soared upward. There was no escape for most of the passengers behind this wall of fire. Most could not swim, and they either met death in the blaze or fell or jumped from the stern of the ship, which jutted out into close to thirty feet of water. Supports for the ship's hurricane deck caught fire and snapped, causing the *Slocum's* upper decks to collapse and sending those trapped there down into the inferno now enveloping the doomed ship.

Van Schaick and his two pilots, Edward Van Wart and Edward Weaver, were on the bow of the sidewheeler when she crashed, and they jumped quickly onto the deck of the *Jack Wade,* a tugboat moored nearby. The captain, aside from minor singeing, had hardly rumpled his uniform. His actions were emulated by his untrained crew, whose members, for the most part, never bothered with attempting to save the passengers, but instead ran, jumped and dived into the swift waters to save their own lives.

Two tugs, the *Massasoit* and the *Franklin Edson,* tooting their whistles—the entire river was ablast with the high pitch of ships' whistles—drew close to the burning *Slocum* and began to rescue survivors. Albert Rappaport, a mate on the *Massasoit,* heroically leaped into the water, swam to the *Slocum,* grabbed two children from their drowning mother, and took them back to the safety of his own ship. Other tugs—*Jack Wade, Water Tracy* and *Theo*—arrived and began plucking people from the water.

Though Van Schaick and others had deserted the ship, two engineers, George Conklin and Everett Brandow, remained at their stations at the throttle. Conklin died later in the water; Brandow survived and was cited for bravery. Only one other crew man, William R. Trembly, upheld the noble traditions of the sea that day. This intrepid sailor repeatedly scooped up drowning women and children and took them to shore, then swam back to that sickening patch of water, where heads were fast disappearing, to again save more.

Two women, Mary McCann and Nellie O'Donnell, the latter having claimed that she had never swum a stroke in her life, were credited with saving thirty victims.

By the time the fireboat *Hewitt* arrived on the scene, there was little to do but gather up the jam of floating bodies. Near the bow of the ship the bodies were so thickly crowded together in the water that they formed a

Firemen and volunteers bring in the bodies of children from the East River, victims, for the most part, of the cowardice of the *Slocum's* crew. *(UPI)*

carpet upon which survivors walked to the safety of the shore.

It was noon, less than two hours after the blaze erupted on the *Slocum,* before the full impact of the disaster was felt by the living. The excursion steamer had burned to her water line, and a painfully methodical count would later reveal that 1,021 people, almost all women and children, were dead. The survivors numbered 407. The burning of the *General Slocum,* later used in the movie *Manhattan Melodrama,* was the worst harbor disaster in American history since the steamboat *Seawanhaka* sank off Ward's Island on June 28, 1880, at which time 60 passengers burned to death. Prior to that time the sinking of the *Westfield,* the Staten Island ferry, on July 20, 1871, held the record number of 50 deaths.

Following the *Slocum*'s demise, sixty-one-year-old Captain Van Schaick was arrested, charged with manslaughter and failure to train his crew members in fire prevention and life saving. (Two New York City safety inspectors were immediately dismissed from the service.) Eighteen months later Van Schaick was convicted and sentenced to ten years in Sing Sing. He was pardoned because of his advanced years by President Theodore Roosevelt in 1908.

For a month after the disaster *Slocum* survivors continued to search for and hope that their lost children might be located, perhaps living with some kindly family who had taken them in and cared for them. Newspapers printed sad appeals from mothers, running photos of children with captions that said, "Have you seen this little girl?" None were answered.

(ALSO SEE: Eastland*)*

Many of the 1,021 passengers who died on the *Slocum* could not speak English, which added to the confusion and panic. *(Wide World)*

GENERAL WARREN — MARINE DISASTER

January 28, 1852

One of the early serious marine disasters to occur in the West Coast waters was the sinking of the steamer *General Warren* on January 28, 1852. These waters were, at that time, generally uncharted, albeit the *Warren*'s pilot was aware of the danger of crossing the Columbia River bar and warned the captain, who ignored his pilot's urgings and pigheadedly crossed the bar. The *Warren* quickly foundered, and only ten persons out of the fifty-two on board managed to save themselves.

GEORGES PHILLIPAR — MARINE DISASTER

May 19, 1932

The spanking new luxury liner *Georges Phillipar,* on her maiden voyage, caught fire when only five miles off Cape Guardafui in the Gulf of Aden. The blazing 17,359-ton ship had no time to send out an SOS; her radio cabin was the first compartment to burn out. Of those on board fifty-four died in the flames and water. The French liner had cost $6 million to build and was the essence of swank and quality, but behind the expensive wall paneling in most of the staterooms, faulty wiring had been installed.

Short-circuited wires caused fires to break out all over the passenger accommodations rather than in the cargoholds as the crew first thought. As passengers ran into corridors to escape, they became lost as clouds of dense smoke met them. Doors were locked through which passengers would normally make their escape. They retreated to their cabins for the most part, threw open their portholes and squeezed out to plop into the water.

Fortunately the ship was traveling in sea lanes heavily populated by other ships and three vessels—*Mashud, Soviet-skaya Neft* and *Contractor*—soon arrived to take off 700 survivors. Valorous conduct was attributed to the crew, the sole reason why so many were rescued.

GEORGIA (and SOUTH CAROLINA) — HURRICANE

August 27, 1893

An unusual hurricane, in that it followed a northwest course rather than the usual northeast pattern, struck the coasts of Georgia and South Carolina on August 27, 1893. With it came a giant wave that submerged dozens of offshore islands. More than 1,000 persons were killed, and damages ranged upward to $10 million.

GERMANY (NORTH SEA COAST)

FLOODS
February 17, 1962

Hurricane winds drove in from the North Sea on February 17, 1962, creating one of the worst floods along Germany's coast in recent times. Hamburg suffered most as the Elbe rose to record heights (281 died here in the first few hours of flooding). The island of Krautsand, squatting in the Elbe, was cut off for days. Twenty miles of the sprawling city of Bremen were under water.

For two days the floods broke through ancient barriers, crumbled historic buildings and drowned hundreds. Lower Saxony and Schleswig-Holstein, large farming areas, lost hundreds of cattle and became marshes. At Blankenese, a rustic pleasure resort, a 1916 tablet marking the previous record flood was submerged in five feet of water.

All along Germany's North Sea coast floodwaters wrecked thousands of homes, leaving 500,000 homeless, killing 343 and causing more than $6 million in damages.

GLOUCESTER, MASSACHUSETTS

HURRICANE
February 24, 1862

Settled in 1623, Gloucester, Massachusetts, was one of the earliest fishing settlements in the United States, and a bronze statue of a fisherman stands at its harbor in memory of historical sea tragedies. The first well recorded tragedy was an awesome gale that swept across the sea beyond Gloucester on February 24, 1862, while most of the fishing fleet was out.

The unexpected hurricane caught seventy schooners along the Georges Bank, their crews busy fishing. The northwest storm came upon the fleet so quickly that most captains had no time to order anchors up, so their moorings caused the ships to remain rigid under the giant swells, and the schooners soon capsized one by one, dumping their crews into an impossible sea..

Thirteen ships went to the bottom, and two more were later abandoned. The "February blow of '62" claimed the lives of 122 fishermen, and several captains.

Iron beds from the Golden Age Nursing Home, near Fitchville, Ohio, are all that remain after a blazing fire that killed sixty-three residents. *(Wide World)*

GLOUCESTER MASSACHUSETTS — **GALE** — **February 21-22, 1879**

The hurricane that struck the coastal area near Gloucester, Massachusetts, on the night of February 21, 1879, was the fiercest ever experienced by the storm-plagued fishing fleet. Coming from the east the wind and snow thrust up gigantic combers that broke over the entire fleet nestled at anchor in shoal water. The winds quickly turned fifteen vessels over, and 157 men drowned, making it the worst disaster in Gloucester history.

GOLDAU VALLEY, SWITZERLAND — **LANDSLIDE** — **September 2, 1806**

The sight was incredible. Witnesses peering at towering Rossberg Peak on September 2, 1806, blinked in amazement as they saw the top of the mountain tremble, its dense forests swaying and then cracking. The landslide was one of the most devastating on record, and as the forest, still in place, rushed downward into the Goldau valley, the friction was so intense that vapors of steam and then flames shot upward as stone ground on stone.

In a matter of minutes the avalanche filled the entire valley and wiped out four villages, killing an estimated 800 persons.

GOLDEN AGE NURSING HOME — **FIRE** — **November 23, 1963**

"This is the most devastating thing I have ever seen," said Ohio Governor James A. Rhodes, as he inspected the still-smoldering ruins of the sixty-year-old Golden Age Nursing Home just outside Fitchville, Ohio, on November 23, 1963. Inside were sixty-three people, many of them invalids ranging in age from seventy-five to ninety, burned beyond recognition for the most part.

What caused the fire was never determined, although the one-story frame building had been certified safe eight months earlier, according to Assistant State Fire Marshal Clarence Hall. "It went up like a tinderbox," said Clifford French, a student at Midwestern Baptist Seminary, who was passing at the moment the building broke into fire.

French saw only a "trickle of flame" as he passed the home and then watched, horrified, as it burst into flames as if soaked through with gasoline. The allegedly "safe" building was engulfed in flames in seconds. French, aided by two truck drivers also driving by on U.S. Route 250 (one was a man named Henry Dahman; the other was never identified) raced toward the home and attempted to save the helpless victims. "I crawled on my hands and knees to stay below the smoke in pulling some of the people out," French said.

But by that time there were very few people left alive to save. Only twenty-one patients managed to escape the inferno. The three attendants on duty also survived. One, a kitchen employee, had attempted to phone the fire department, but the telephone wires were burned away before she could put through a call. The president of the Cleveland firm that owned and operated the nursing home, Robert Pollack, later reported that health officials had cited the establishment as "efficient, clean," and "safe."

GOLDEN GATE — **MARINE DISASTER** — **July 27, 1862**

Carrying cargo valued at more than $1.5 million, the steamer *Golden Gate* caught fire three miles off the Mexican coast in Pacific waters on July 27, 1862. Captain W. H. Hudson ordered his ship to head for land, and his 338 passengers quickly slipped on life preservers. Moments after the ship was beached, the crew and passengers panicked. With the flames all about them, they dropped into the heavy seas. Fierce breakers drowned many people who had not properly fastened their life preservers, and dozens more were crushed to death by monstrous waves that dashed them against jagged reefs.

A large group, including captains Hudson and Pearson, took their chances with the ship, expecting that it would be driven closer to shore before being demolished by the spreading fire. Their gamble paid off when the *Golden Gate* was suddenly lifted from a reef by large combers and sent wheeling toward land. The remaining passengers and crew members swam for shore.

Pearson later related how he "was overtaken by a quick succession of immense breakers, beaten and bruised by them, and was finally pitched amongst the wreck of spars attached to the foremast. The danger was imminent of being crushed, but my strength was nearly gone, and I could make no effort to free myself; but the next roller threw me clear of them and onto the beach. . . ."

All that night the survivors staggered ashore and watched the ship, which burned to the waterline. The final number of dead claimed by the sea came to 198. The *Golden Gate* is still the object of much attention by treasure seekers, her location never having been pinpointed. She rests somewhere in the shallows off Manzanillo, Mexico.

GORGONE — **MARINE DISASTER** — **December 18, 1870**

Bound for Cherbourg, the French steam-corvette *Gorgone* with 122 crew men aboard was engulfed by a hurricane off the French coast on the night of December 18, 1870. Though the ship disappeared along with her entire crew, varied reports had the *Gorgone* heroically battling the storm, attempting to make port at Brest, mistaking a reef for an entrance to the harbor and smashing to pieces.

The French navy sent out two steamers to search for the ship, but after a three-day cruise, nothing had been sighted in the area. By that time dozens of tarpaulin hats worn in the French navy marked with the *Gorgone*'s name, along with planks also carrying her name, drifted to shore. About a week later, a ship's trunk was also found floating near Toulinguet. In it was the *Gorgone*'s log. The final entry, penned hurriedly by the ship's commander, Lieutenant T. Mage, read: "We have struggled on to the end. Impossible to save the ship; there is a large leak. I put my trust in God."

GRAN CIRCO NORTE-AMERICANO — FIRE — December 17, 1961

background: The Brazilian-owned Gran Circo Norte-Americano, while performing under a nylon tent outside Niteroi, across the bay from Rio de Janeiro, caught fire on December 17, 1961, resulting in a mass stampede of the 2,500 spectators. Burned or crushed to death were 323 persons, mostly children. It was the worst single calamity to befall Brazil and the largest circus disaster on record.

The cause, though thoroughly searched for, was never found. Some said sparks from a passing freight train showered onto the circus tent and ignited it. Others claimed arson—a group of young toughs denied admission had deliberately set fire to the nylon big top.

Avidly watching trapeze artist Antonietta Estavanovich perform her high daredevil act were 2,500 spectators, most of them children, on December 17, 1961. The circus was part of Brazil's festive Christmas week. The crowds were from the historic town of Niteroi, which was across the bay from Rio de Janeiro.

Estavanovich was preparing to leap into her partner's arms when she saw the first flames below her. She didn't yell because she was afraid that her partner would fall. When he completed his swings they both dropped to nets below and escaped. It took only seconds for the flames to race up the flammable tent walls, leap across the top and burn down the supporting poles. The entire tent collapsed in three minutes. Hundreds panicked, stampeding for the exits. A group of about 300 children, without direction, ran to the sawdust covered center arena. When the burning tent collapsed upon them, they suffocated.

Dozens of others were crushed to death in the push for the outside. Brave little Sergio Pfiel Manhaes, a Boy Scout, withdrew his pocket knife when he saw the jammed exits, sliced a gaping hole in the tent wall and led his little cousin and another child to safety. He went back inside, where he grabbed a woman who had been blinded by the smoke and led her and the infant she carried out.

The woman kissed Sergio and said, "God reward you." Then she fainted.

Another hero was a cow elephant called Elisa. Chained outside the tent the elephant broke loose and, blaring like a trumpet, lunged directly through the tent. Hundreds escaped death by escaping through the giant hole. Elisa died in the flames. She was found near the center arena with the children.

Hours later, Brazilian President Joao Goulart visited the children's ward at Niteroi's Antonio Pedro Hospital. In long rows of beds were 500 badly burned youngsters. Goulart broke down and was led away in tears, saying, "My God, it's not possible."

It was, with 323 dead, the worst circus fire in history, far surpassing that of the tragic Ringling Brothers and Barnum & Bailey fire that killed 168 in 1944 in Hartford, Connecticut.

(ALSO SEE: Ringling Brothers and Barnum & Bailey)

GRAND BAZAR DE CHARITÉ — FIRE — May 4, 1897

Each year the cream of Paris society gathered to hold an elaborate bazaar for the purpose of collecting funds for the city's poor. It became one of the social events of the season and attracted mainly females from the houses of wealth. The Grand Bazar de Charité held on May 4, 1897, in Paris saw more than 1,500 uppercrust participants crowd into a flimsy, makeshift building (220 feet by 300 feet long) to auction articles for the relief of the destitute.

The building was a firetrap. The aislelike interior had been made to look like a street of medieval Paris, its booths representing ancient shops and housefronts; these façades were constructed of linen coated with turpentine and filled between the surfaces with papier-mâché. The freshly painted material was a year old, having been used in an exposition at the Palace of Industry. The building housing this highly flammable display consisted of three-quarter-inch boarding and a roof of tarred felt.

Into this bazaar poured 1,500 persons. Just as the social matrons began to hawk their charitable wares, flames from an illuminating lamp of a kinematograph shot outward and quickly ignited the roof, walls and booths.

In minutes the bazaar was an inferno with screaming women, their hats, parasols, dresses and long trains on fire. They scurried toward the single exit, all fearfully watching the flaming roof overhead, which burned with speed. According to a New York Socialite who managed to survive, it was "just like that which one would see if a sheet of paper were to be saturated with petroleum and then ignited."

The ceiling dropped in flaming pieces onto the escaping women, making human torches of more than 150 of them. The maddening spectacle and desperate women were described by one reporter "like so many poor creatures in a burning cage."

The roof collapsed completely and then the walls caved inward. More than 1,300 managed to escape, several hundred badly burned. But 150 women were roasted to death, an event so shocking, particularly in that they represented the leading families of Paris, that more stringent fire precautions were immediately put into effect in public places.

GRAND FLEET — MARINE DISASTER

August 10, 1591

Four large hurricanes swept the Western Hemisphere in a month's time during 1591. On August 10 the worst storm caught the Spanish treasure fleet, loaded down with riches, that was making its annual run from Havana to Spain. The Grand Fleet, as it was called, was caught in a severe hurricane, and a dozen vessels of its entourage were sent to the bottom. With them went 500 Spanish soldiers and sailors.

It was a brutal naval setback for Spain, coming only three years after the destruction of the Spanish Armada in the English Channel.

(ALSO SEE: Spanish Armada)

GRAND PRIX — RACING ACCIDENT

June 11, 1955

background: The most catastrophic racing accident in history occurred at Le Mans, France, during the running of the Grand Prix on June 11, 1955. At speeds varying between 125 and 160 m.p.h., two cars, an Austin-Healey driven by Lance Macklin of Britain and a Mercedes Benz driven by Pierre Levegh, collided on the straightaway. The parts of both autos ripped away and tore through the massive throng; 83 spectators were killed, and 100 more injured.

The crowd of more than 250,000 lining the historic Grand Prix roadway at Le Mans, France, on June 11, 1955, stood thirty deep. Most scorned the grandstands, preferring to press inward at the most dangerous hairpin curves along the 8.38 mile circuit. At 4:00 P.M. the sports car entries raced forward in the dash to win the twenty-four-hour race.

Before the race an ominous statement had come from forty-nine-year-old driver Pierre Levegh, who had suffered a close call with a French Gordini during the trials. "We have to get some sort of signal system working," Levegh insisted. "Our cars go too fast."

Thirty-eight laps into the race, the leader, Mike Hawthorne, driving a Jaguar, got a signal for a pit stop to refuel. Either the signal was given too late, or the British driver, then in the lead, failed to see it. He jerked his wheel violently and swung his car to the right toward the pits. Right behind him was an Austin-Healey driven by Britain's Lance Macklin, who swung his car left to avoid collision with the Jaguar.

Levegh, in his powerful Mercedes, saw the move and threw up his arm as a signal for his teammate Juan Fangio, some yards behind him, to slow down. But Levegh did not slow down in time, and, traveling at about 160 m.p.h., the Mercedes dashed ahead and smacked the smaller Austin-Healey from behind on the straightaway.

The two cars screeched ahead, locked together for several moments, then separated with a steel-grinding tear. The Austin-Healey raced over several mechanics, injuring a few, and then stopped in a cloud of smoke. Macklin dove from the burning car and escaped.

But Pierre Levegh was a dead man. His car, as if blown from a cannon, roared into a six-foot dirt retaining wall and went to pieces. The hood tore loose and sailed into the crowd like a scythe, decapitating some people. The chassis flew in another direction and knifed through the crowds. Levegh himself was decapitated, and his headless corpse was burned to a cinder in the flaming car before rescuers could approach it.

For 400 square yards, spectators were slaughtered by the splintering Mercedes. Human flesh, showers of blood and auto parts hurtled through the air. One young girl screamed and fainted as a bloody foot sailed into her. The area wreaked of blood and twisted bodies. The injured attempted to crawl away as thousands of unharmed spectators ghoulishly fought to see more.

Police and doctors wandered through the area hours later, picking up the dead and injured. Private trucks and cars were used as ambulances to remove the 105 seriously maimed to hospitals. One officer said, "Many of the injured are so mutilated they cannot live. I fought through the war, and never did I see worse carnage."

A priest walked solemnly through the body-littered area praying, occasionally lifting up the newspapers that covered victims' faces to discover if they were male or female. It was the worst catastrophe ever at any auto race, claiming a total of eighty-three dead. (More than $2 million in claims were filed against the sponsor, Automobile Club de l'Ouest.)

British racing star Sterling Moss, who was part of the Mercedes team, angrily struck out at the crowd's attitude. "This accident is a nightmare," he complained, wanting the race stopped. "I can't understand how people can go on singing, drinking and having fun at the side of the track while sixty other spectators are lying in the morgue."

GREECE **EARTHQUAKE 373 B.C.**

In the year 373 B.C. the whole of Greece was shaken by a tremendous earthquake that destroyed almost every major city and proved especially devastating to Bura and Helas. The inhabitants of lofty Peloponnesus managed to survive, but were shocked at dawn to look down from their mountainous perch and see the ocean now covering the area where the two mighty cities once stood.

Long after on clear days sailors could look downward through the Corinthian Gulf waters and gape at the once inland city of Helas, still beautiful in ruins beneath the surface, "a city of the dead" as it were, with dozens of its marble homes, temples and columns intact.

No accurate report of the dead has endured, but the fact that several thousand residents perished is accepted.

GRENADA **HURRICANE September 22, 1956**

A powerful hurricane with winds whipping up to 127 m.p.h. roared over Barbados from the Atlantic on September 21, 1956, killing 30 persons and destroying the homes of another 40,000, but this killer storm took its greatest toll of lives the following day ninety-eight miles southwest at Grenada, a rocky resort of quiet coconut and nutmeg plantations.

Weather warnings to the residents went out over the radio and were carried by shouting policemen madly pedaling bicycles. The two ancient Spanish cannon in the harbor were even fired off as a signal to take cover as the skies darkened and near-tidal waves spent themselves on the high rocks of the towering island.

In five hours the onslaught of wind, rain and waves killed 200 persons and toppled almost every building on the island. Recovery was slow, taking almost a year, but with American and British aid Grenada rebuilt its homes, warehouses and piers.

GRETNA GREEN, SCOTLAND **RAILWAY WRECK May 22, 1915**

background: The worst train wreck in British history occurred at 6:00 A.M. on May 22, 1915, when four trains of the Caledonian Railway, and a troop train carrying 500 soldiers collided near Gretna Green, Scotland. The impact and resultant fires took the lives of 227, most of whom were troopers; a signalman allowing the troop train onto an already occupied track was held accountable.

In the tenth month of World War I, the British Isles suffered its worst railway disaster in history at Gretna

Gutted by fire and still smoking are cars of a troop train that collided with two other trains at Gretna Green, Scotland, May 22, 1915. *(Illustrated London News)*

Green, Scotland, on May 22, 1915. It came about through the mistake of one man. At about 6:00 A.M. at the small village on the Scottish border, a signalman unthinkingly waved a fast-moving troop train en route to London, carrying 500 men from the Seventh Battalion of the Royal Scots, onto a single track already occupied by a local. In moments the troop train crashed into the local, telescoping both its own and the local's cars.

Seconds later the London to Glasgow Express smacked into the burning debris of both stricken trains (the gas cylinders of the troop train along with ammunition it was carrying exploded). Roaring fires raced through the mangled wrecks as hundreds called out for help.

Rescuers were driven back from the cars by the intense flames and could do little else but wait for the fire brigades to arrive. When they did scores of men, mostly soldiers who had escaped from less damaged cars, raced in behind the flames to save their comrades. In battledress, those trapped or dying in the blazing debris became lethal to their saviors. Most of the Scottish soldiers were wearing cartridge belts full of live ammunition. Bullets ignited by the searing flames began to explode killing those wearing the belts and their rescuers. Heavier ammunition exploded and killed more. A doctor named Edwards arrived on the scene and worked through the flaming cars until most of his coat was burned away and his face thoroughly singed.

Two soldiers horribly trapped by the legs in the flames called out to him. Not being able to lift the fallen beams from the train's roof, Edwards saw no method by which he could save the men other than amputation. As the flames ate away at his own face, he carefully cut away both legs of one soldier and one leg of the other (one of the men died of shock).

Scores of similar horrors filled the day as firefighters, troopers, and townspeople battled the fires and removed the charred, quivering injured and the silent dead, many of whom had already stiffened with rigor mortis. The fires were not put out until 5:00 A.M. A roll call of troopers then revealed only 52 men out of 500 present—many were still crawling through the skeletal remains of the three trains in search of friends. The final death toll was fixed at 227, most of them faceless cinders who were buried with full military honors, although they did not die at their scheduled destination, the Western Front.

The lives of 227 were lost at Gretna Green in the worst railway wreck in British history. *(Illustrated London News)*

GRIFFIN — MARINE DISASTER
September 18, 1679

A 40-ton ship, the *Griffin,* built by the French explorer Robert Cavalier, Sieur de La Salle, was a supply ship navigating the Great Lakes. After an uneventful trip from Fort Niagara in western New York to Green Bay, Wisconsin, to pick up trappers' pelts, the *Griffin* set sail to return to her home port on September 18, 1679. La Salle's chief pilot, Luc Dane, and thirty others on board the ship disappeared that day.

Several claims have been made of the *Griffin*'s presence in the waters of Lake Michigan and Lake Erie, but the ship has never been found. Indian tribes along the lakes have told stories for centuries of a mysterious ship appearing at night with a figurehead on her bow in the shape of a lion with the head and wings of an eagle, an image of a Greek monster of mythological times that La Salle had specifically ordered affixed to his ill-named ship.

G. P. GRIFFITH — MARINE DISASTER
June 17, 1850

background: En route to Chicago from Buffalo, New York, the all-wooden steamer *G. P. Griffith* caught fire in the hold on June 17, 1850, a day after sailing on Lake Erie. While her captain attempted to make for shore, she burned to the waterline; 295 perished, 26 survived. The sinking of this vessel is considered to be one of the worst marine disasters ever to occur on the Great Lakes.

Under the command of C. C. Roby the steamer G. P. *Griffith,* loaded down with 321 crew and passengers, mostly English, Irish and German immigrants, left Buffalo, New York, on June 16, 1850, bound for Chicago. On the following morning, while making her way westward across placid Lake Erie, the ship began to give up thin wisps of smoke. Frantic crew members discovered a raging fire burning in the overloaded cargo hold.

Captain Roby ordered the steamer to make for the Ohio shore, then about five miles distant, figuring that he would run the *Griffith* ashore where he could disembark his polyglot passengers in an orderly manner. The crew calmly directed the immigrants to the deck areas most remote from the fire, which then was burning out of the hold. Lining up meekly and donning life preservers, the passengers waited for the ship to outrace the fire to safety. When the ship was only a half mile from land, the fire began to spread along the decks.

Crew members, thinking to add more speed to the ship, mistakenly crowded the boilers with steam, but this only provided more drafts, which fed the fire.

With flames leaping everywhere the passengers grew frightened and desperately jumped in clusters to the water. Dozens drowned in sight of those remaining with the ship. One crew member, a good swimmer, dove into the water and raced for shore. He returned in a boat and began to pick up survivors, but by that time the *Griffith* was almost burned to the waterline.

Captain Roby, who had been a half-owner of the steam line, threw his mother, wife and two children overboard, leaped after them, and attempted to tie them together and tow them landward. All of them died. None of the children and women on board the ill-fated steamer survived, except the wife of the ship's barber. Only 25 others survived.

Most of the 295 who died aboard the *Griffith* washed ashore in the next few days, many of them charred and unrecognizable. They were buried in a common grave, a long trench running close to the beach that is now beneath Lake Erie's waters.

The tragedy brought about virulent town meetings where angry citizens demanded better regulations for passenger safety and the storing of flammable cargo. The result, however belated for the *Griffith*'s victims, was the passing of federal legislation in 1859 that brought about strict inspection of ships' hulls, boilers and lifeboat accommodations.

GRINNELL, IOWA — TORNADO
June 17, 1882

Iowa's most devastating twister of the Nineteenth Century was the one that tore through Grinnell on June 17, 1882. Beginning about ninety miles to the west of the town, the storm moved at 56 m.p.h., reaching Grinnell at 8:30 P.M. Mount Pleasant, Malcolm and Brooklyn were also hit by the ravaging tornado, killing 100 more.

Grinnell, the hardest hit, was leveled. Sixty persons perished, mostly by collapsing buildings. The total loss was estimated at $600,000.

GUADALAJARA, MEXICO — RAILWAY WRECK
January 18, 1915

Facts concerning what has been alleged to be the worst train disaster in the world, the derailment of a troop train in Guadalajara after its departure from Colima on January 18, 1915, are clouded to this day. At that time, Mexico was at the height of civil turmoil, with thousands dying daily in slaughterhouse battles. Records dealing with entire troop divisions disappeared, so it is not surprising that the only acceptable report of the train disaster in which more than 600 died was a letter written on February 14, 1915, by a missionary to the American Board of Commissioners for Foreign Missions.

The missionary stated that Carranza's troops had taken the province of Guadalajara on January 18, and on that day, at the orders of the governor, families of the soldiers were sent from Colima to join them. The letter read: "There were more than twenty cars simply packed with humanity, the roofs covered with men and women and many slung under the cars in a most perilous position even for ordinary travel.

"At the top of the steepest grade, coming down, the engineer lost control, the cars rushed down the long incline, throwing off human freight on both sides and finally plunging into an abyss.

"Nine hundred people were on the train and only six were unhurt. More than six hundred were killed outright." Mrs. John Howland, the author of the letter, who was attempting to escape from the country with her husband, added a postscript containing the information that dozens of Yaqui Indians committed suicide when told of the mass deaths of their families aboard the train.

GUADELOUPE — HURRICANE
August 4, 1666

One of the most violent hurricanes recorded in the Western Hemisphere's early history was one that struck Guadeloupe, Martinique and St. Christopher on August 4, 1666. Guadeloupe was hardest hit, its six-foot-thick rock wall barriers dashed to rubble by a gigantic sea wave and its fourteen-pound defense guns ripped from their emplacements and hurled into the sea.

Every ship anchored or sailing about the island when the storm arrived was broken up. Fifteen ships in a troop fleet were caught in the hurricane's eyewall and sunk, carrying to the bottom 2,000 soldiers.

GUADELOUPE — HURRICANE
September 12, 1928

The lack of adequate weather information and a proper warning system were, no doubt, the reasons why death came to more than 600 people on the scenic island of Guadeloupe on September 12, 1928. A sluggish, mammoth hurricane drifted out of the Atlantic, tearing across the island and slaughtering unwary residents, most of whom were caught out of doors. This storm went on to ravage Puerto Rico, drowning and crushing in wind-tossed debris another 300 persons and leaving $50 million in damages.

GUATEMALA — EARTHQUAKE
April 18, 1902

background: During the night of April 18, 1902, a series of earthquakes struck Guatemala, destroying a city and eighteen towns, killing 12,200, and making another 80,000 homeless. Fires followed the quakes, and several ancient volcanoes erupted.

A fierce thunderstorm and torrential rain preceded the massive series of earthquakes that rattled Guatemala on the night of April 18, 1902. In Guatemala City, an evening meeting of the National Commission for the Louisiana Purchase Exposition was interrupted when heavy crystal chandeliers began to swing like pendulums. The terrified commissioners raced to the streets, which were already jammed with panicking citizens.

The streets were flooding; darkness was everywhere. Groups of dazed people stumbled along fervently singing "Salve Regina." Roofs collapsed; walls caved in. Hundreds of people were buried in the rubble. Others went insane; several shot themselves. More than 80,000 were made homeless within an hour.

By 10:00 P.M. startled clusters of men holding torchlights scurried to their precious religious shrines and temples, their first concern. They wept as they inspected the crevices and cracks made by the quake in the walls of the ancient cathedral, Santa Teresa.

The first shock lasted fifty seconds, according to eyewitness D. Ingle Burton. Thirty-six shocks followed and the volcano Santa Ana, thought to be extinct, broke into violent, lava-heaving eruption. Highways leading into the resort city were split, and fissures ran downward for hundreds of feet.

"It was an awful thing to see," Burton later wrote, "how the buildings tumbled to the ground like cob houses into a mass of ruins, burying their inmates beneath the debris like so many rats."

Smaller towns—San Marcus, San Pedro, San Juan Ostancalco, Tucana, Mazatenango, Cuyotenango, Champerico and Escuintla—were ravaged. Of the 10,000 inhabitants of Escuintla, 4,000 were killed outright as a two-minute shock ran through the town. At Ocos, a Pacific port city, giant waves raced inward and flooded the town. Not one house was left standing as hundreds of lava-spewing cracks in the earth opened. The quake squeezed the banks of a river together so quickly that up from the estuary's muddy bottom rose a sailing vessel, intact, which had been sunk for decades. The railroad bridge across the river was telescoped by the contraction of the banks. The grand wharf, pride of Ocos, was twisted into a misshapen jumble.

More than 1,000 buildings fell in San Jose. Such was the magnitude of the quake that the volcano Esalco in neighboring Salvador, extinct for ten months, burst into flames.

It was the worst earthquake in Guatemalan history since the old capital Antigua was destroyed by shocks two centuries before.

GUATEMALA CITY INSANE ASYLUM — FIRE
July 14, 1960

background: The decrepit insane asylum in Guatemala City, Guatemala, built in 1890, caught fire from an undetermined source on July 14, 1960, trapping 600 of 1,500 patients and killing 225, mostly women, and injuring 300 more.

The madness of the fire was coupled to the insanity of the victims when the Guatemala City Insane Asylum caught fire in the early hours of July 14, 1960. One explanation for the fire was that a candle before a religious statue fell onto combustible material in the women's sewing room. Another attributed it to a short-circuit in the electric wiring. Whatever the reason the already crumbling seventy-year-old building was a blazing inferno within minutes, despite the heroic efforts of Guatemala's fire department, led by President Miguel Ydigoras Fuentes.

President Fuentes personally led out groups of shrieking patients. Many survivors went berserk and fought bloody battles with their rescuers. Boy Scouts, firemen and policemen were beside themselves in attempting to drag the hysterical patients from the flames.

All of the children were quickly saved, but more than 200 women were burned to death; 31 of them, locked behind bars because they were considered murderous, screamed their way into death as thousands watched their misery.

Seeing all exits blocked by the fire, firemen brought up a bulldozer and drove it through a wall by which hundreds fled to safety. At 9:00 A.M. the fire was under control. The following day, the United States flew 27,000 pounds of emergency supplies into Guatemala City. By then the death toll had reached 225, and 300 more had been badly burned.

Of the fifty inmates who escaped, all considered potentially violent, only two were recaptured. The others disappeared, and various murders, arsons and other illegal acts that occurred in subsequent years in and about the city were attributed to these escapees.

A child saves her pet from the floodwaters that destroyed her home in Gujaret, India, August 1968. *(UPI)*

GUJARET, INDIA — FLOOD

August 7-14, 1968

Record floods inundated the state of Gujaret, India, between August 7-14, 1968, when the swollen Tapti River broke over its banks and drowned more than 1,000 persons. Surat, in the state of Gujaret, was submerged for seven days under ten feet of floodwaters. Throughout the state and the neighboring state of Rajasthan, a staggering total of 80,000 head of cattle drowned. The carcasses were left to rot on the streets, and this, coupled with muddy drinking water, soon caused cholera to break out, killing many more.

GULF HOTEL — FIRE

September 7, 1943

Houston's oldest building, the Gulf Hotel, was a firetrap, and almost everyone knew it. The once-proud three-story building had deteriorated over the decades into a filthy flophouse with cheap partitions separating the "rooms." Most of the 133 men registered on the night of September 7, 1943, were old, crippled, or drunk.

The building represented the end of the line for men down on their luck. Its shoddy end came when flames suddenly engulfed the wooden partitions on the second the third floors. Dozens of naked, sleepy men ran for the two fire escapes. One was blocked by fire. The other became a slaughterhouse.

In a last attempt at life naked men punched, kicked, shoved and strangled each other to make their way down the narrow iron escapeway. Others jumped, screaming, through windows. One gaping witness, Lloyd Brown, "saw men crawling down the fire escape. . . . Some of them didn't have clothes on. . . . I saw others run down the stairway and out into the street. Many of those were unclothed."

The seedy place was all but gutted before firemen arrived. A city detective, H. P. Blanchard, who had been helplessly watching the fire from across the street, saw a naked man leap from the third floor, strike an awning and pitch out onto the street. "He was burned and crushed."

In the rubble firemen found fifty-five corpses. Thirty-two others received hospital treatment, many hurt in the bloody brawls to get to the street.

Up to that time it was the worst fire in the history of Houston, Texas, seconded only by the schoolhouse explosion in New London that claimed 294 lives on March 18, 1937.

H

HABER CORPORATION — EXPLOSION

April 16, 1953

Aluminum dust, including magnesium, was set off in a violent explosion by a polishing machine, most authorities stated, when the Haber Corporation's four-story building caught fire on April 16, 1953. Thirty-five were killed, and scores more injured.

The Chicago metalwork plant caught fire on the first floor immediately after the explosion, and the flames quickly spread to the other three floors. The company president, Kelly Tanko, was startled to see four of his employees, their clothes on fire, race onto the building's loading dock. He and others quickly smothered the flames, but there was little he could do for those trapped on the upper floors.

"Glass flew all over the street," said eyewitness Ted Mechnek. "In just a second it seemed fire burst out all of the second-floor windows. In another second a woman jumped from the third-floor window to the roof of the one-and-a-half-story receiving department. Then a man jumped and turned to catch others as they jumped. Ten or fifteen must have jumped that way, but the smoke was so dense it was hard to tell the exact number."

Damage to the building was estimated at $175,000.

The Haber Corporation building in Chicago is destroyed in a wild blaze that killed thirty-five employees on April 16, 1953. *(Wide World)*

HACKETTSTOWN, NEW JERSEY — RAILWAY WRECK

June 16, 1925

background: An engine and four cars behind it were derailed when a mudslide during a violent storm covered the Delaware, Lackawanna & Western Railroad's tracks near Hackettstown, New Jersey, at 3:30 A.M. on June 16, 1925. Though three cars remained on the tracks, fifty persons were killed and another thirty-eight were injured when the engine's boiler burst.

Two coaches, four Pullman cars and a diner were decorated with colorful banners that read: "Neuman's Party, S.S. *Republic,* Bremen, Cologne, Munich, Vienna." This special excursion train, chartered by Leopold Neuman, a steamship agent, and running on the Lackawanna line, left Chicago at 6:00 P.M. on June 15, 1925, heading for Hoboken with 182 German-Americans en route to a summer vacation in their homeland. The S.S. *Republic* of the United States line would sail them across the Atlantic.

All of the passengers were asleep when the speeding train, rushing down Rockport Sag to gain momentum for the upgrade leading into Hackettstown, smacked into a mudslide caused by a torrential cloudburst only minutes before. The engine bumped along, half on and off the track for 160 feet, and then hit the frog of a crossover switch to a siding. The impact sent the engine and the first four cars diving down a 12-foot embankment. The engine and the first car toppled to their sides: the second coach lurched crosswise on the track, one end on top of the engine, the other on the track.

The third and fourth cars, both Pullmans, flipped left and right off the tracks. Killed immediately were the engineer, two firemen and the head trainman. A few passengers in the first coach were also killed instantly, one woman being decapitated. "These were the most fortunate of those who died," stated one account.

The boiler in the engine suddenly exploded and sent

scalding steam through the crippled cars. Dozens of passengers received the full blast of the steam, and their cries of agony could be heard by farmers in the vicinity.

Joseph Snyder, whose farm was only yards from the derailment, was the first to arrive on the scene. In the darkness he helped scores of staggering women and men from the wreck, while others begged him for morphine. Some asked him to kill them, such was their excruciating pain. One man, his face burned away by the steam, dug into his pockets, produced a fat roll of bills and offered the money to anyone who would be kind enough to put a bullet in his head.

Dozens of other farmers arrived and began speedy and heroic rescue work. Of those on board thirty-eight died within the first hour of the derailment, twelve more in the hospital. Thirty-eight others were treated for injuries and then joined the unharmed passengers who boarded another Lackawanna special that took the depleted group to Hoboken, where the *Republic* held off her sailing for two hours. The group then sailed to Europe, leaving its dead to be buried by strangers.

HAITI — HURRICANE
October 22, 1935

The so-called "hairpin hurricane," the fourth to devastate the West Indies in 1935, was named for its unusual path, which began in the Western Caribbean, moved eastward near Jamaica and then headed south.

Its damage in Jamaica, where whole plantations were wrecked, was estimated to be about $2 million, but in terms of lives lost, the hurricane did its worst in Haiti on October 22. More than 2,000 were killed in the extreme southwestern districts of the country. Most of the victims were farmers caught unaware while working their fields.

This storm next moved on to Cape Gracias, Honduras, where on October 25 it killed another 150 persons before dissipating inland.

HAKODATE, JAPAN — TYPHOON
September 26, 1954

The year 1954 saw fifteen powerful, deadly typhoons sweep over Japan, the worst storm being the one that struck the main islands on September 26. Caught in the eyewall of the typhoon was the 4,300-ton open-ended ferry, *Toya Maru,* making for Honshu from Hokkaido. The storm crippled the ferry's engines in the Tsugaru Straits, but her captain and crew managed to keep her afloat until she limped into Hakodate harbor, where she struck a reef.

The heavy typhoon winds did the rest and literally knocked the *Toya Maru* over, dumping more than 1,000 passengers, including 50 Americans, into the sea, all of them drowning. Hundreds more were killed by this storm, total fatalities coming to 1,600.

The capsized ferry *Toya Maru* with more than 500 bodies still trapped inside her was only one victim of the typhoon that wrecked Hakodate, Japan, on September 26, 1954. *(Wide World)*

HALIFAX, NOVA SCOTIA, CANADA — EXPLOSION-FIRE — December 6, 1917

background: A monstrous explosion, resulting from the collision of two ships, the *Mont Blanc* and the *Imo* (the former carrying 5,000 tons of high explosives), in the narrows leading from Halifax Harbor to Bedford Basin, wiped out the suburb of Richmond on December 6, 1917, killing 1,600 persons, injuring 8,000 and destroying 3,000 dwellings; 2,000 more persons were listed missing, and total damages were estimated to be more than $30 million.

Though an anormous mishap, the explosion and fire that destroyed half of Halifax, Nova Scotia, on December 6, 1917, could indirectly be attributed to World War I, then raging in Europe, for it was the tools of war that worked the horrible proportions of this disaster. The *Savannah News* even went so far as to suggest that the Allies "look for the Kaiser's hand" in fixing the blame for the calamity.

The immediate fault, however, lay with the skipper and pilot of the 5,043-ton Belgian relief ship *Imo,* a Norwegian vessel built in Belfast in 1889 for the White Star Line. After changing hands and names—*Runic, Tampican*—over the years, she became the property of Norway's South Pacific Whaling Company. Bound for Europe and proceeding at half speed through the narrows between Halifax and Bedford Basin at 8:40 A.M., the *Imo*'s captain and pilot spied an approaching ship, the 3,121-ton *Mont Blanc,* coming in from New York. The *Mont Blanc* was laden with 5,000 tons of deadly explosives allocated for war use in Europe.

Built in 1899 and owned by the French Line (Cie Generale Transatlantique), the *Mont Blanc* carried 580 tons of TNT in her two afterholds, picric acid in the forward hold and a deck jammed with tanks of benzine. The French ship was a sailing bomb.

The two ships edged toward each other in the narrows. Both vessels began to signal each other with whistles. The weather was clear and bright, although several claims that there was a light mist were later made. The pilot on the *Mont Blanc,* Frank Mackie, who watched the *Imo* veer inexplicably toward his ship on a collision course, later stated that the ramming "was due to a confusion of whistles sounded by the *Imo.*"

Confusion ran to irresponsibility, as the captain of the *Imo,* realizing a collision imminent, reversed his engines, causing his ship to heave over to port with her bow aimed at the *Mont Blanc.* Lemodec, captain of the French ship, saw that the collision was inevitable and gave orders for his ship to be maneuvered in such a way that the *Imo* would strike his vessel at a place where there would be less danger of exploding her cargo.

The *Imo* came on with a crunch, her bow slicing one-third of the way through the *Mont Blanc*'s deck. The twenty-five barrels of benzine were ripped open and spilled into the torn compartment containing the acid and dozens of bales of gun cotton. The blazing fire was instantaneous. Captain Lemodec and his crew fought the towering fire for several minutes, retreating step by step, their fruitless efforts watched intensely by hundreds who had gathered at the nearby shoreline.

Suddenly the French skipper waved his men into lifeboats, and the scrambling seamen made for shore, rowing like wild men, knowing the explosion could come at any moment. When they reached the shore the *Mont Blanc* crew jumped fitfully from their boats and ran, yelling all the way, into a nearby woods to hide.

The slightly damaged *Imo* made for the opposite Dartmouth shore. Seventeen minutes after the collision came one of the most violent explosions ever recorded. The *Mont Blanc* disappeared completely when the fire reached the TNT in her holds. The suburb of Richmond, densely populated with old wooden structures, was literally blown off the map; the explosion was heard sixty miles away at Truro. Houses, office buildings, people and animals were sent skyward at the instant of the great concussion. The *Imo* was lifted from the water and hurled bodily ashore at Dartmouth. Freight cars were blown through the air for distances of two miles. Two-thirds of every crew on every ship in the harbor were instantly killed.

More than 500 schoolchildren were in their classrooms at the time the explosion occurred, and only 10 in both Richmond and Dartmouth survived as their schools caved in on them like falling cards. In the Dartmouth School 200 youngsters perished. Every child and matron in the Protestant Orphan Home was killed.

At the edge of the Richmond district towered the old and resplendent Queen's Hotel. In its lobby sat I. M. Soy, an official of the Maple Leaf Lumber Company. He was thrown off his chair by the terrific blast and heard hysterical cries from those who had been expecting trans-Atlantic German air raids for months. "The Zeppelins! It's the Zeppelins!"

A telegrapher, four miles from the disaster, was killed at his desk by a piece of flying metal. Only one telegraph line was left standing over which Halifax could send out its pleas for help. The one remaining operator stayed at his key for only twenty minutes and then let the wire go dead when a bleeding child ran to him to tell him that his wife was dying.

More than 1,600 persons were dead under debris or blown bodily into the next district. Either bravery or shock drove Nova Scotians to uncommonly heroic acts. A railroad telegrapher burned to death in his shack rather than leave it and allow an incoming train to continue unwarned. A dockworker dragged dozens of injured men out of burning piles of debris. When told that one of his eyes was hanging on his cheek, he refused to go to the hospital and returned to save more lives. One smartly dressed chauffeur drove scores of injured to the hospital several times, refusing to take time to have his broken ribs taped.

Many Halifax buildings of historical import were obliterated. The brown freestone and granite Dominion Building with its priceless museum of Indian artifacts was gone. Other buildings destroyed included the Government House built in 1800, the Halifax Club, the Waverly and Halifax hotels, a half-dozen churches, and the Presbyterian Ladies' College.

Fires raged moments after the explosion through Dartmouth and Richmond, rising on either side of the narrows, their sharp hills serving as a trough up through which the flames leapt in perfect drafts.

There was no fire department left to combat the fires, and they simply burned themselves out after sending pillars of black smoke rising several thousand feet that could be seen from forty miles away.

As thousands of injured limped out of Richmond and Dartmouth (more than 8,000 were wounded one way or another by the blast), every restaurant in Halifax opened kitchens, giving free food to all survivors and rescuers. Druggists gave away all their medical supplies; employers told their help to quit work and aid the stricken. Overnight Halifax was known as "The City of Comrades." (Within days, however, the public empathy switched to acrimonious chiseling; truckers extorted life savings from the homeless for moving their singed, meager belongings; a grocer was stoned for charging a starving child ten times the normal amount for a loaf of bread; landlords hiked their rents to fabulous sums and forced their tenants to pay or move into the snow-swept streets.)

Aid was on its way to Halifax even before its fires were out and its appalling list of dead completed. Consigned to the Red Cross, Maine's Governor Carl E. Milliken sent the following day by rail 2,000 blankets, 1,000 cots, 400,000 square feet of beaver board (for temporary housing), 200,000 pieces of window glass, 10,000 rolls of tarred paper. A train from Massachusetts, 450 miles from wrecked Halifax, was on its way on the night of the disaster carrying 1,100 pairs of pajamas, 350 hospital shirts, and carloads of medical supplies. This was followed by a Red Cross Special containing twenty-five doctors, including two obstetricians, sixty-eight nurses and eight orderlies. On Saturday another Red Cross train left Providence, Rhode Island, with sixty-two surgeons, sixty nurses, ten orthopedic surgeons and two hospital social workers. The United States Navy offered the Red Cross 50,000 blankets. New York City sent carloads of clothing—shoes, stockings, boots and overcoats—for women and children. It was one of the greatest outpourings of human compassion ever to sweep the continent, and these enormous supplies were soon delivered as Halifax began the tedious work of rebuilding.

The ship *Imo* was rebuilt. Her name, for obvious reasons, was changed once again, to the *Guvernoren.* She was wrecked after running aground off the Falkland Islands four years later, a hulk dying in obscurity under an alias few would connect with the great Halifax explosion.

(ALSO SEE: Bombay, India; Bone, Algeria; Cali, Colombia; Texas City, Texas)

HAMBURG, GERMANY — FIRE

April 5, 1842

The city of Hamburg, Germany, caught fire in the early hours of April 5, 1842, and the inferno raged through forty acres of the old part of the city, consuming 1,992 five- and six-story wooden tenements. About one hundred persons were killed, most burned to death while the city's firemen, unable to bring water from the dried-up canals and harbor, were powerless.

As proof of the anti-Semitism flourishing even then in Germany, one newspaper account stated: "The fire was by some thought to have originated in the street known by the name of the Stein Twite, in the warehouse of a Jew named Cohen, a cigar manufacturer, and, who, upon good grounds, has been taken up on suspicion as the incendiary."

The fire quickly spread to the business and financial districts where firemen were also hindered by tens of thousands of frenzied refugees who cluttered the street with their hastily gathered belongings. Tons of furniture

Hamburg, Germany, was consumed by flames in 1852; about 100 persons died. *(Illustrated London News)*

The great Hamburg fire of 1852 caused $35 million in damages. *(Illustrated London News)*

were stored in the massive Nicolai Church only to be burned up three hours later when the church caught fire. "The streets are crowded with carts, wagons, cabs, carriages, conveying people and goods away," wrote the *London Times* correspondent who was then in Hamburg. "People seem frantic and nothing is to be seen but goods in the public streets."

Two other famous churches, St. Peter's and St. Joseph's, were reduced to ashes. The best hotels were gutted. All of the finest bookshops and art galleries were destroyed. Total damages ran upward of $35 million.

HAMILTON, ONTARIO, CANADA — RAILWAY WRECK March 17, 1857

background: An entire train—locomotive, tender, baggage car, and two coaches—of the Great Western of Canada line (Canadian National) crashed through aging timbers of the Des Jardines Canal bridge outside of Hamilton, Ontario, late on March 17, 1857, and dove down an eighteen-foot embankment to the frozen canal; sixty persons were killed, another twenty injured.

The bridge spanning the Des Jardines Canal just outside Hamilton, Ontario, was a haphazard affair from the beginning. Its wooden ties and flooring were weak, and its designers indifferently neglected to mount a guide rail that might have prevented a derailed train from plunging eighteen feet to doom if it jumped the tracks. This is exactly what occurred on the dark night of March 17, 1857, as the engineer of a four-car local cautiously nudged his train toward the bridge. The local somehow struck the abutment and was derailed onto the rotting timbers of the bridge, which gave way immediately and sent the whole train, engine, tender, baggage car and two coaches, plummeting downward.

The locomotive dove through the heavy ice followed by the tender. Snapping free, the baggage car, with three occupants, did not crash through the heavy ice but flopped onto its side and went sliding crazily down the canal; those inside miraculously had only slight injuries.

This was not the case with the occupants of the first coach, who were all killed as it jackknifed and landed roof-down on top of the hissing locomotive. The second car drove partly onto the top of the first, and almost every traveler in it received serious injuries.

From nearby Hamilton scores of rescuers, including two companies of militia, answered the cries for help. They worked by the headlights of locomotives brought up to the severed bridge and by torchlights held over the canal. Ropes were tied to the intact timbers of the bridge, and these were let down with rescuers dangling from them. Ladders were then tied to the ropes and used as stretchers to haul up the injured lashed to them.

A woman who lived near the bridge rushed down to the canal after hearing the terrible crash. Holding a torchlight she spied an eight-year-old girl floating on a slab of ice and quickly waded into the bone-chilling stream to retrieve her. The girl explained that her mother, father, and uncle were dead inside the first coach, but her small brother was trapped inside the second. The women led other rescuers to the second coach, and the boy was taken out of a window after debris had been cleared away.

Newspapers of the day ballyhooed the Hamilton train plunge into one of the major disasters of the nineteenth century, meticulously pointing out that its death toll exceeded the lives lost on the American side in the battles of Palo Alto and Resaca de la Palma in the Mexican War.

(ALSO SEE: Angola, New York; Ashtabula, Ohio)

HANNA, WYOMING — MINE DISASTER
June 30, 1903

background: Two explosions two seconds apart, the first gas ignited by blasting, the second caused by ignited dust and firedamp, ripped wide the coal mine at Hanna, Wyoming, at 10:30 A.M. on June 30, 1903, trapping 215 miners one and a half miles underground; of these, 169 were killed and 46 rescued. Though unsafe, portions of the mine were still worked to March 28, 1908, when another explosion killed 59. The mine was then closed forever.

It was a deathtrap, the miners who worked the Hanna, Wyoming, coal mine knew, but the wages were good, and most of them possessed no skills other than mining and had little opportunity to establish themselves in the New Land other than working in the inky underground. Hanna was a Union Pacific town, where the land and houses were rented, never sold, by the railroad. Paying the rent and attempting to save enough money to either return to Europe or establish themselves in other trades were Polish, Finnish, Negro and Chinese miners.

The Finns made up most of the population, the towering wooden Hall of the Finnish Temperance Society dominating Hanna's scrubby landscape. They were hard workers and made, family by family, seasonal trips to the old country every few years, but they invariably returned to Hanna. Town authorities were edified by the Finnish deportment of sobriety and thrift. Only once, when a load of mail arrived from a Finnish bordertown, was there a riot.

The mayor at first could not decipher the meaning of their madness, unable to speak the tongue. When a wildly gesturing Finnish miner kept jabbing at the stamp from his native town, the mayor finally realized the crowd's agony. It was a Russian stamp, signifying that their birthplace had been absorbed by the czar.

Most of the male population of the Finnish community was working the day shift on June 30, 1903, when at 10:30 A.M. blasting set off a tremendous explosion one and a half miles into the shaft. Another explosion followed two seconds later. The second explosion ignited gas in the recklessly checked mine, and great bursts of flame belched into all the mine levels, knocking down miners, scorching and burning to death others in its path.

At the first explosion timbers at the mouth of the mine blew outward like toothpicks. So many tongues of flame licked outward from all the entranceways that rescuers found only a single manway to descend. One Negro miner, William Christian, worked back and forth in this narrow causeway for hours, pulling out twenty men in dozens of trips, until he collapsed.

Forty-six men were ultimately rescued over a twenty-four-hour period, but 169 were killed. One body, never recovered, was sealed off with the fourteenth level. The mine was closed partially for five months. Again no safety precautions were put into practice.

The *Independent* railed in an editorial following the 1903 explosion: "We should . . . demand for these miners the same protection to life which we would ask for if we were working underground at Hanna."

On March 28, 1908, an explosion again shredded another 59 miners. By that time everyone knew the Hanna mine was lethal—incredibly half shifts continued to work the upper levels even though gas fires below them had been raging for six days before the final 1908 explosion—but company owners did nothing to prevent the second mine disaster. Thirty-two bodies were recovered after the 1908 explosion, and days later twenty-seven were left inside when the mine was closed forever.

(ALSO SEE: Cherry, Illinois; Crested Butte, Colorado)

HANS HEDTOFT — MARINE DISASTER
January 30, 1959

Forty-seven years after the sinking of the *Titanic,* the 2,800-ton passenger freighter *Hans Hedtoft* repeated her nightmare history. Like the *Titanic* the ultramodern *Hedtoft* struck an iceberg on her maiden voyage and sank. Unlike the great White Star liner of 1912, the 288-foot *Hedtoft* was equipped with the most up-to-date safety devices available including radar. Built by the Danish government to maintain a year-round passenger and cargo service to its gigantic, isolated dominion island, Greenland, the ship was 37 miles south of Cape Farewell when she rammed into an iceberg. (The *Titanic* went down about 600 miles south of this area.)

Bitterly cold winds whipped the waves, more than twenty feet high, lashing at the ship. The *Hedtoft*'s captain, fifty-eight-year-old P. E. Rasmussen, ordered an SOS sent out. The American Coast Guard cutter *Campbell* picked up the message on January 30, 1959, at 9:55 P.M. She was approximately 280 miles away but raced immediately to the rescue.

Captain Rasmussen apparently felt his ship was secure with her double steel bottom, armored bow and stern and seven watertight compartments. This may have been the same mistake made by the *Titanic*'s Captain Smith, who failed to realize until too late the fatal damage the iceberg had inflicted upon his "unsinkable" liner. Rasmussen's laconic messages reflected the same kind of overconfidence.

His first taciturn signal said: "Collision with iceberg." Then the *Hedtoft* radioed: "Filling fast." Finally, and bluntly, came the words: "Taking a lot of water in the engine room." These were the last words from the stricken vessel as she departed to the deep. With her went fifty-five passengers and a crew of forty.

The odd thing about the disaster was that, unlike the *Titanic,* which was caught unaware of the presence of an iceberg in her path, the *Hans Hedtoft*'s captain realized he was in an area "right up where the bergs are born," as one official later put it.

Though the *Campbell* and other ships and planes joined in the search for the vessel, the *Hedtoft* had completely disappeared by the time the rescuers arrived. She was gone and the ninety-five persons in her were lost, including six children and Augo Lynge, a member of the Danish parliament. The violence of that sea, awash with looming, dipping icebergs, told the searchers that further operations were useless. It was obvious to them that Rasmussen could not have lowered one boat in such chaotic waters without having it instantly swamped. If any of those on board jumped before the liner went down, there would still be no hope of finding them. The icy water would have prevented that. One official stated that any human afloat in such water could live "just over sixty seconds."

(ALSO SEE: Titanic*)*

HARRISBURG, PENNSYLVANIA — RAILWAY WRECK, May 11, 1905

Engineer H. K. Thomas was in the locomotive of the Cincinnati Express of the Pennsylvania line that was approaching Harrisburg, Pennsylvania, on May 11, 1905. It was almost 1:30 P.M. A few minutes before a sixty-eight-car westbound freight had buckled, with two cars jumping the rails at different angles.

Thomas saw the freight cars, but it was too late to stop, and he hoped his passenger train might slip by them. The engine and three cars did manage to scrape by, but the express was brushed to a stop as coal poured out of the engine's firebox. The burning embers set fire to jets of gas escaping from some of the passenger cars.

At this moment fate had it that one of the derailed freight cars was jam-packed with 50,000 pounds of dynamite. As passengers poured out of the Pullmans,

Like the *Titanic,* the Danish cargo ship *Hans Hedtoft* struck an iceberg and sank with 130 passengers aboard. *(Wide World)*

they could hear the popping explosions of a few loose sticks ignited by the burning gas. Dozens of startled people in nightgowns rubbing sleep from their eyes were on the roadbed when the entire dynamite car exploded, blowing one passenger car off the tracks and killing twenty people. Engineer Thomas was killed along with two other crew members. The fireman was sent flying for half a block, but he landed in a mound of soft sand and survived.

Though hauled out of the burning wreckage, the noted theatrical producer Samuel Shubert was so badly burned that he died a short time after.

This arial photo shows the jumbled wrecks of three trains that collided at Harrow-Wealstone, England, on October 8, 1952; 112 persons were killed. *(Wide World)*

HARROW-WEALDSTONE, ENGLAND — RAILWAY WRECK, October 8, 1952

background: Three trains of the western region of British Railways (Great Western Railway), a local and two expresses, collided at Harrow-and-Wealdstone Station, England, eleven and a half miles from London during the businessman's rush hour at 8:19 A.M. on October 8, 1952; 112 persons were killed and 165 injured in this second-worst train accident in British history; the blame was fixed by an inquiry to engineer Jones of the Perth-London night express (he was killed).

Hundreds of commuters fidgeted in the Midlands fog just beginning to lift after 8:00 A.M. on Wednesday, October 8, 1952, as they stood waiting to board the local early businessman's train, which was eight minutes late from Tring and West Hertfordshire en route to London, a little more than eleven miles distant. The packed local was just inching out of the station when, behind it and southbound on the same track, the Perth-London Express (the Night Scot), raced up, ninety-five minutes late and going full throttle.

Engineer Jones of the express either failed to see or, less possibly, ignored the frantic signs flashed by signalman A. G. Armitage at Harrow Number 1 box, warning of the local's presence in the station. (Jones was later fixed with the blame by Lieutenant Colonel G. R. S. Wilson, chief inspector of railways, who headed a board of inquiry.)

The express dove into the local, its 130-ton engine mounting the telescoped coaches, throwing two of them onto the express line and bashing a large hole in a footbridge. Through this hole dozens of commuters dropped to their deaths. Above the hissing trains severed electric lines jiggled out dangerous electricity.

Less than ten seconds later the Manchester Express, northbound and speeding into the station at 40 m.p.h. in an attempt to make up five minutes of lost time, smashed into the two local coaches lying sideways in its path. The third impact was tremendous. The two engines of the Manchester train left the tracks, rose vertically and fell upon a platform jammed with commuters and then onto another track. The debris was piled fifty feet high.

More than 1,000 persons, crowded together in a space less than 100 square yards, were enmeshed in the steam-clouded rubble of wrenched and twisted steel. A fifth of these were instantly dead or maimed. There was at first an eerie silence soon shattered by muffled calls for help from the mound of debris. Thousands of rescuers came on the double.

Doctors, firemen, police and clergymen swarmed to the wreck. From nearby United States Air Force bases came twelve doctors and fifty medics and nurses. From one smashed car emerged a businessman who dusted off his expensive suit and complained: "I've lost my briefcase." For most of the others trapped in the wreck, the losses were more acute.

A passenger who escaped and began to dig for others stated, "One man who had lost an eye said quietly, 'Give me a cigarette.' " A sixteen-year-old girl bandaging the injured was amazed at the calm exhibited by most of the victims. "I have seen people coming here for hours with broken legs and arms and with faces smashed in," she told newsmen at the scene. "I haven't heard one complaint. There was one man lying on the platform who was talking quietly with others. It was a little time before we knew he had a broken back. He said, 'Get those others out, don't worry about me.' "

Rescuers armed with acetylene torches worked their way into the death mound for two full days and nights, attempting to reach the two rear coaches of the local where most of the dead and injured were trapped. The first man spotted deep in the debris was David Dean, a railway clerk. He joked with his rescuers as they dug toward him despite the fact that he had already lost a foot and was bleeding to death.

Holding a syringe of morphine, a doctor tried to reach Dean but could not. "If he doesn't bleed to death, the pain will kill him," he said to a man nearby. This man was Sidney Blackford, who had fought with the Royal Fusiliers. He had been passing by at the time of the triple collision and had rushed to the scene and had begun to dig for survivors. He took the needle from the doctor and, inching himself downward on his stomach, reached Dean and gave him two shots of morphine. He then bandaged Dean's severed leg and stayed in the pit while diggers began to remove the twisted steel precariously hanging overhead, all of which could have collapsed at any moment on both men.

"It was like being in the trenches after a heavy bombardment," Blackford later stated. "We talked about everything under the sun, from football to everyday events. David was very cool throughout it all and tried to help by edging himself clear."

When both men were rescued Blackford ambled down the littered tracks, shrugging off compliments and looking for more injured. But there were precious few left to save. The final count of dead ran to 112, with 165 seriously injured, making this the second-worst rail disaster in British history.

Days later a newspaper man photographed a sign swinging above the Harrow-Wealdstone platform that read: "This station has been awarded fifth prize in the best kept station competition of 1952."

(ALSO SEE: Gretna Green, Scotland)

HASTINGS, COLORADO — MINE DISASTER

April 27, 1917

Known as a "gas" mine, the coal mine in Hastings, Colorado, owned and operated by the Victor-American Company, was nearly always damp and a treacherous place to work in. The firm sent down a regular shift of 100 men and extracted about 1,000 tons of coal a day in 1917. Its safety regulations and warning systems were poor. An explosion in 1913 had killed several men, yet no improvements in guarding the workers' safety had been initiated.

Fire bosses were hired to check the intensity of gaseous fumes in the mine shafts, but they were lackadaisical. Highly dangerous electric cap lamps were used by all the miners, and the hurried inspections made by the fire bosses each day were merely perfunctory. Two fire bosses checked the mine on the morning of April 27, 1917, and emerged quickly to present "written reports that the mine was clear of gas."

A train of cars carrying 121 men then descended the main shaft to work the day shift. Just as the train entered the mine, a mine inspector was suddenly standing in darkness when his key-locked safety flame lamp went out. He lit a match to relight it, and the thick gases present erupted into flames. An explosion followed. By this time the trainload of miners had reached the 1,300-foot level, and all were enveloped in flames. Those not burned to death were asphyxiated. One man, the trip rider, had gotten off the train and was only 120 feet from the mine entrance. When he saw smoke billowing up toward him, he ran to the surface and gave the alarm.

Dozens of rescue squads were formed, carrying oxygen tanks and masks. They entered to the level of the "B" seam, which had collapsed. At this point one rescuer brushed a fallen timber and lost his mask. He was overcome by fumes. Another member also collapsed. Both men, one already dead, were dragged to the surface.

Most of the Hastings mine had collapsed, crushing the corpses of the 120 dead miners. It took days to dig them out. Total fatalities: 121. Total improvements following the disaster: none.

HATTIE — HURRICANE

October 31, 1961

British Honduras was no more prepared for the violence of Hurricane Hattie on October 31, 1961, than it had been for the hurricane that devastated the capital, Belize, thirty years before, except that a more modern warning system saved countless lives. When Hattie blew into the country, its winds were gauged from 160 to 200 m.p.h.

Hurricane Hattie slashed through British Honduras on October 31, 1961, killing more than 400 residents. This photo shows what happened to Stann Creek where thirty-eight died. *(Wide World)*

Again Belize was hardest hit, its 31,000 residents fleeing in all directions before the high velocity winds and the ten-foot tidal waves lashing its waterfront and carrying mud and debris to the third floors of most buildings. Here 275 persons perished, most by drowning. Hattie raced on to Stann Creek and demolished that town until only three buildings were left standing and scores were killed. Two islands, Turneffe Cay and Caulker Cay, were inundated, and dozens were buried beneath huge waves.

For days British officials walked dazedly through Belize and nearby villages and towns, trying to estimate the loss of life, which finally came to 400. Even that number was uncertain. Gerald Griffith, director of medical services for the colony, said, "We don't know yet what's under things."

(ALSO SEE: Belize, British Honduras)

HAZEL

HURRICANE
October 12-16, 1954

Moving slowly off the South American coast near Grenada, Hurricane Hazel's pattern was erratic. With 100 m.p.h. winds the storm lashed western Haiti, killing 100 and making 100,000 homeless, uprooting Dame-Marie, Jerémié and Aux Caves. By October 15, 1954, Hazel came ashore at Myrtle Beach, South Carolina, winds in its eyewall raging at 130 m.p.h.

After devastating the Carolinas, Virginia and Washington, D.C., the hurricane moved through Maryland, Delaware and New York and then unpredictably slanted across to the Great Lakes, moving over Toronto, Canada's second largest city, where 56 were killed. Hazel proved to be one of the most durable hurricanes on record, and she took a total of 411 lives and caused damages beyond $1 billion.

HEPPNER, OREGON

FLOOD
June 14, 1903

A freakish flash flood resulting from a cloudburst between 4:00 and 5:00 P.M. on June 14, 1903, took the lives of 325 persons in Heppner, Oregon, and created $250 million in damage. It was all over quickly. Just above Heppner the rain and hail storm raged in the foothills of the Blue Mountains on Willow Creek, blanketing a twenty-square-mile area. The storm lasted half an hour and the flood an hour, but Willow Creek was swollen to a wall of rushing water twenty to twenty-five feet high. One third of the town, more than 200 buildings, was swept away.

Debris clutters Willow Creek which flooded during a storm on June 14, 1903. The flash flood destroyed Heppner, Oregon, and killed 325. *(Frank Leslie's Illustrated Newspaper)*

HERAKLION

MARINE DISASTER
December 12, 1966

"We are sinking, help us!" This terse message was sent by the Greek passenger-freight ferry *Heraklion,* caught in a raging Aegean storm at 2:00 A.M. on December 12, 1966. The ferry was making for the Athenian port of Piraeus in a night crossing from Crete. Lashed in her lower decks were dozens of cars that broke free and began smashing into the ship's sides.

Answering the *Heraklion*'s distress signals was the Finnish freighter *Nuna Lath.* By the time the freighter arrived at the scene, the ferry had disappeared. By then a sixteen-ton refrigerator trailor had broken loose from its moorings and was pitching back and forth on the storm waves, acting like a battering ram. It tore a gaping hole in the *Heraklion*'s side through which burst thousands of tons of sea water.

Hurricane Hazel smashes ashore at Morehead City, North Carolina, October 15, 1954; 411 died in this violent storm. *(Wide World)*

Of the 281 passengers and crew on board, 230 drowned as the ferry quickly sank beneath the churlish waves. One survivor, Antonios Gofas, stated: "Cars were rolling back and forth in sloshing water from the storm, and many had broken from the retainers. I ran upstairs, grabbing a lifejacket on the way, to spread the alarm."

As ship's officer Alexandros Stefadouros was pulled aboard the *Nuna Lath* coated with oil, he sputtered, "The ship began to list. The alarm was sounded everywhere. We watched her continue to list badly. When there was nothing more to be done, I jumped into the sea. . . . In fifteen minutes she went down. God knows what happened to the captain. . . ."

HIGHTSTOWN, NEW JERSEY

RAILWAY WRECK
November 8, 1833

background: The first train wreck in the world occurred on November 8, 1833, near Hightstown, New Jersey, when a broken axle of a forward car of a Camden & Amboy train traveling west between Bordentown and South Amboy caused a derailment and subsequent pileup of the following cars; two persons were killed. These were the first passenger train fatalities recorded.

Though a number of mishaps had befallen the rickety early American trains, which were built along the lines of stagecoaches, the first serious railway wreck happened on November 8, 1833, as a Camden & Amboy train, traveling at no more than 20 m.p.h., neared Hightstown, New Jersey.

Running as a second section, or what was then termed a "brigade," the train was on the same schedule as another ahead of it. When the axle broke on the forward coach, it pitched the weight of the second coach in the opposite direction, thus lifting up the first coach momentarily and dropping it back onto the tracks. Speed, most claim, did the rest. The second coach tilted over to the opposite side, and this assured derailment.

When the train flew off the tracks, the twenty-four occupants in the second coach received most of the injuries as the coaches behind it dove into it. Inside this coach rode some of America's most distinguished gentlemen, not the least of whom was the sixty-six-year-old ex-president of the United States, John Quincy Adams. He was not harmed, but the wreck moved him to write in his diary: "Blessed, ever blessed be the name of God, that I am alive and have escaped unhurt from the most dreadful catastrophe that ever my eyes beheld!"

The train must have seemed to have been flying to those pioneer rail voyagers, and its speed was fingered as the culprit for the wreck, although the C & A had established strict speed limits. In fact the line had employed stopwatchmen to clock the speed of each train, and engineers were ordered never to exceed 20 m.p.h., maintaining an average speed of 17½ m.p.h. The derailment on a slight downgrade, no doubt, accelerated the engine's flight.

The stopwatchman was absent on this trip; he was home ill. In addition two brakemen who could have easily halted the individual coaches by merely applying the hand brakes of each car were not at their posts; one was riding atop one car, "to get some fresh air," and the other was battling a small blaze in the baggage car, where a bale of cotton had caught fire.

Adams was meticulous, surrounded as he was by horror, in recording the accident. "The train was stopped I suppose within five seconds of the time when our wheel slipped off the rail, but it was then going at the rate of sixty feet in a second, and the overturned car dragged nearly two hundred feet before it would stop."

All of the twenty-four persons in the wrecked coach were injured, and James C. Stedman, a Raleigh, North Carolina, merchant, died two hours later, railroading's first fatality. A man named Rex, or Lex (the records are unclear), from Pennsylvania was the second fatality.

Adams was anguished as he wrote: "The scene of sufferance was excruciating. Men, women, and a child scattered along the road, bleeding, mangled, groaning, writhing in torture, and dying, was a trial of feeling to which I had never before been called; and when the thought came over me that a few yards more of pressure on the car in which I was would have laid me a prostrate corpse like him who was before my eyes, or a cripple for life; and more insupportable still, what if my wife and grandchild had been in the car behind me! Merciful God!"

In the same coach was Captain Cornelius Vanderbilt of the New Brunswick Steamship Line. He and a Reverend West of Washington, D.C., received identical injuries, broken legs. Reverend West made no particular historical statement on the matter, but the future "Commodore" Vanderbilt underwent such trauma as a result of this first railroad accident that he refused to ride trains for three decades. But the financial giant in him awoke to the thought, one day, of a lost empire on tracks, and he then went busily about piecing together the great New York Central Rail Line.

Downtown Tampico, Mexico, was wrecked by Hurricane Hilda, which killed 300 people. *(UPI)*

HILDA — HURRICANE

September 19, 1955

Tampico, Mexico, and its 110,000 residents were pounded senseless in 1955 by three mammoth hurricanes and relentless flooding in their wake. The first to strike the sprawling port on the Gulf of Mexico was Hurricane Gladys, which inundated a large section of the city. Next came Hurricane Hilda, the most powerful of the three, described by Mexico's President Adolfo Ruiz Cortines as "the worst disaster in the city's history."

Hilda pounced on Tampico on September 19 and flooded fully half of the city, drowning approximately 200 persons. The Panuco River rose to its highest level in thirty years, twenty or more inches a day, to wipe out all but a few of the downtown area's blocks.

At the end of the month, Hurricane Janet came ashore to complete Tampico's destruction. Another 100 persons drowned and damages totaled from the three storms leaped to $42 million.

HILO CITY, HAWAII

TSUNAMI
April 1, 1946

Originating in the Aleutian Trench off Alaska, a giant *tsunami* washed down the Pacific to Hawaii, where, on April 1, 1946, it all but destroyed Hilo City. The forty-foot wave struck at 7:00 A.M., followed by several waves fifteen to twenty feet high. A pilot who had just taken off from Honolulu looked down to describe the *tsunami* invading the shore; he said it was swallowing all the boats and waders on Waikiki Beach "like molasses."

Oceanographer Francis L. Shepard happened to be living in a beach cottage on Kawela Bay when the "April Fool's *tsunami*" struck there. He heard it rush ashore at 400 miles an hour sounding like "a dozen steam engines blowing off steam." He and his wife, who survived, counted seven *tsunamis,* all breaking over their cottage and destroying it and dozens more along the beach.

Thinking that the attack was over, Shepard returned to his cottage. Suddenly he heard that hissing sound. "I became conscious that a very powerful mass of water was bearing down on the place. This time there was simply no island in back of the house. . . . I rushed to a nearby tree and climbed it as fast as possible and then hung on for dear life as I swayed back and forth under the impact of the wave."

Hilo City was gone, 5,000 homes crushed to kindling by the *tsunamis.* Floating in the $10 million wreckage were 179 bodies. Hundreds of injured thrashed about.

The waves, traveling a distance of more than 8,000 miles, then swept in forty feet high over Robinson Crusoe's island off Valparaiso, Chile. Seismologists tracked the pattern of the *tsunami* and attributed it to an undersea earthquake off Unimak Island, Alaska. The quake occurred 10,000 feet deep; forty-one separate shocks were counted.

At Unimak the one-hundred-foot-high lighthouse was completely wrecked by the waves and the tower crew of five was killed.

Buildings for a block inland were reduced to splinters at Hilo City, Hawaii, by a forty-foot *tsunami* on April 1, 1946. *(Wide World)*

HILO CITY, HAWAII

TSUNAMI
May 23, 1960

The earthquake that ravaged Chile in May, 1960, produced a giant *tsunami* that raced north and west across the Pacific. Six hours before the wave arrived at Hawaii, urgent warnings were sent out, but few persons heeded the alert. Even when the first waves, themselves unusual in height and power, arrived, it was business as usual. When the *tsunami* did crash inland on May 23, it caught sixty-one helpless persons in Hilo City and killed them.

The wave, as high as a two-story building, took everything down before it. An eyewitness stated: "The roar of the massive wall of water blended with the

Hilo City, Hawaii, was devastated by a *tsunami* on May 23, 1960. *(Wide World)*

crashing of dozens of stores and apartments and theaters and restaurants—and with the screams of dozens of persons for whom the final noisy warning came in the same moment with death."

The height of the *tsunami* was estimated to be thirty-five feet. Other *tsunamis* emanating from the Chilean disaster raced on to Japan, 10,000 miles distant, swamping the fishing hamlet of Kiritappu and killing 180 persons. The Philippines, especially the main island of Luzon, were hit by *tsunamis* in company with tropical storm Lucille, resulting in 258 persons, mostly fishermen, drowned and missing.

(ALSO SEE: Chile, 1960)

HINCKLEY, MINNESOTA — FIRE

September 1, 1894

background: A series of forest fires, beginning in the last two weeks of August, 1894, ravaged several towns in Minnesota, Michigan and Wisconsin. Completely devastated was Hinckley, Minnesota, where, on September 1, 1894, 413 persons were burned to death with a loss of $10 million as the entire community was gutted. A total of 600 lives were lost here and in other towns. Other towns wholly or partially destroyed included Pokegame, Sandstone, Mission Creek, Rutledge, Mansfield and Mille Lacs in Minnesota; Bashaw, Baronette, Benoit, Cartwright, Fifield, Granite Lake, Grantsburg, Gidden, Marengo, Muscado, Shell Lake, South Range, Poplar, Spencer, Highbridge, Ashland Junction and Washburn in Wisconsin; and Ewen and Trout Creek in Michigan.

Forest and peat fires had been eating their way through the north woods of Minnesota, Michigan and Wisconsin for several weeks in August, 1894; the sun-scorched summer was without rainfall. Parched vegetation and brittle-dry wood leapt to blazes by the smallest spark. And what happened in Peshtigo, Wisconsin, and Chicago, Illinois (the Great Chicago Fire), in the flammable fall of 1870 reoccurred in the small town of Hinckley, Minnesota, seventy-five miles from St. Paul. Its 1,200 residents were literally engulfed by a sea of flames bursting from the woods all about them in the afternoon of September 1, 1894.

Sudden gusting winds fanned the smoldering forest fires outside of town (which the inhabitants fairly ignored as normal for that time of year), and a raging inferno was soon lapping at houses in the quiet streets. Rushing from their homes and glimpsing the red wall of flames, the people panicked and ran to nearby shallow ponds and swamps to escape shooting arms of fire that whooshed out toward them in block-long sprays.

One pond was crowded with women and children and cattle, the foot-deep water barely affording them protection. Hundreds reached the Grindstone River, but it was so shallow that the screaming persons clawing into it could not submerge themselves and the flames found them, "trapping them like rats and roasting them alive," as one account put it. Dozens were trampled to death by crazed farm animals.

At the searing height of the fire an Eastern Minnesota Line train pulled into town and 500 persons, their clothes smoking, clambered on board and were saved as the train barely made its way through the flames.

Another train, the Limited of the St. Paul and Duluth Line, waited for the remaining residents to reach it. Hundreds tried to battle their way through the flames to the depot, but most were cut off and forced to retreat to a nearby pond. Days later 105 bodies were removed from this pond.

Those who did reach the train underwent an additional terror. Surrounded on all sides by fire, its wooden coaches dancing with eddies of flame, the train at full throttle steamed through the blaze for several miles. All the coaches were on fire and the riders prostrate on the floors. The engineer, burned to death at his post, valiantly refused to stop his engine, stayed at the controls and physically restrained his firemen from leaping off.

Upon reaching a lake the engineer brought the Limited to a stop, waved his passengers toward the water, and fell dead. Sixty-two men, women, and children staggered into the lake. Women walked out into the water until it reached their waists. One report states: "With their hands they bathed their burned faces in mud and water. Many of them were seriously burned on the train. Many lay in the mud, covering themselves with it, and as often as this became baked a fresh coat had to be added. . . . Many women had their clothes partially burned and torn from their bodies."

A third of Hinckley's population, 413, perished in the forest fires, and scores more died in similar blazes on the same day in Michigan and Wisconsin.

(ALSO SEE: Peshtigo, Wisconsin)

HINDENBURG — DIRIGIBLE EXPLOSION

May 6, 1937

background: Built in 1936 the $3.75 million German dirigible, the *Hindenburg,* was the successor to the mammoth *Graf Zeppelin,* owned and operated by the Zeppelin Transport Company. The 804-foot *Hindenburg* (largest dirigible ever constructed) had a nonstop range of 8,000 miles and could carry ninety-seven passengers in addition to her sixty-one-man crew. Powered by four 1,100 horsepower, Mercedes-Benz diesel engines, the 430,850-pound Zeppelin housed seven million cubic feet of flammable hydrogen gas, rather than helium. This caused her fiery destruction while docking at Lakehurst, New Jersey, on May 6, 1937, at which time thirty-six passengers and crew men perished in the flames.

It was a warm, almost balmy spring dusk, May 6, 1937, and over Lakehurst, New Jersey, the clear sky was punctured by the outline of a giant, silvery object that seemed to blot out the moon. It was the pride of Germany and the largest dirigible ever built, the *Hindenburg.*

The *Hindenburg* had been afloat for over a year and had startled the world with her ten speedy transoceanic trips in 1936, carrying the then unheard of passenger capacity of ninety-seven people.

Adolf Hitler took as much pride in this behemoth of the air as he did in the slashing fists of prizefighter Max Schmeling. The *Hindenburg* flaunted the dreaded Nazi swastika on her fishlike tail.

The *Hindenburg* contained over seven million cubic feet of hydrogen gas and a sixty-one-man crew. As the airship headed for Lakehurst on May 6, she carried thirty-six passengers who had paid premium fares to cross from Europe to the United States on the world's greatest air luxury liner.

While the ship sailed peacefully over New York City's busy streets, Captain Max Pruss and Captain Ernst Lehmann made final arrangements for the docking in New Jersey. The guests relaxed in the wide verandalike smoking and drinking lounges while porters scurried along corridors and bustled with luggage from the twenty-five staterooms.

They were in no hurry. This was the *Hindenburg*'s first flight of the 1937 season, and she had crossed the Atlantic in a leisurely seventy-six hours.

Bad cross winds and rain squalls had hindered the flight, slowing the colossal craft. Captain Pruss had radioed the naval air station at Lakehurst that the *Hindenburg* would not dock at her scheduled 5:00 A.M. time, but would land at sunset.

The awesome zeppelin *Hindenburg* glides past the Empire State Building in 1936.

The *Hindenburg*'s captain was Ernst Lehmann, who commanded the dirigible's maiden Atlantic crossings (shown here waving from the ship's control room); he died raving the day after her destruction.

At 3:12 P.M., as the *Hindenburg* sailed into view over Lakehurst, a sudden rainstorm came up. Pruss decided to ride it out until conditions were more favorable.

Shortly before 6:00 P.M. with more than 1,000 spectators looking on and dozens of sailors and marines waiting for the ropelines to drop from the vast belly of the dirigible, the *Hindenburg* headed toward the docking tower.

The eager hands of sailors and marines grabbed the lines thrown from the ship, and crowds waiting on the sandy docking area waved back to signaling *Hindenburg* passengers who leaned, gay and smiling, from open windows. They had paid $400 each for their one-way flight. Little trapdoors in the nose of the great ship flipped open sending wormlike ropes into the hands of the sailors and marines. It was 7:23 P.M.

Chief Boatswain's Mate R. H. Ward, a member of the ground crew, looked up and curiously noted that part of the *Hindenburg's* fabric located near the tail seemed to flutter as if a small amount of gas was escaping. To compensate for her sudden irregular trim, 1,000 gallons of water ballast were released from the ship's rear. Realizing that the zeppelin was heading toward the docking tower much too fast, Pruss had the two rear diesel engines reversed, which caused flashing exhaust sparks to shoot out.

Suddenly the clear sky was cracked open with a terrific explosion as a gigantic burst of flames shot outward and upward from the tail of the *Hindenburg*. Red and white-hot flames enveloped the entire stern of the ship, instantly eating away the swastika emblem. Helmsman Helmut Lau whipped his head back to see gas cell number 4 above him vanish into flames. "It sounded like a rifle shot," crew man Richard Killman, who was standing behind Lau, later reported.

As if she were made of tinfoil, the explosion ripped the *Hindenburg* in two. As the tail dropped down, the nose bobbed briefly skyward, hanging for seconds in the sultry air. Then the nose shuddered earthward as huge licks of flame ran alongside the *Hindenburg's* belly and sides.

Radio announcer Herbert Morrison of WLS, Chicago, was on the ground recording the arrival of the sky leviathan. "Here it comes, ladies and gentlemen," he said. "And what a sight it is, a thrilling one, a marvelous sight. . . . The sun is striking the windows of the observation deck on the westward side and sparkling like glittering jewels on the background of black velvet . . . oh, oh, oh! . . . It's burst into flames . . . get out of the way, please, oh, this is terrible, oh my, get out of the way please! It is burning, bursting into flames and is falling . . . oh! . . . This is one of the worst . . . oh! It's a terrific sight . . . oh! . . . and all the humanity! . . ."

In flight passengers doze in one of *Hindenburg's* spacious lounges. None were allowed matches or cigarettes.

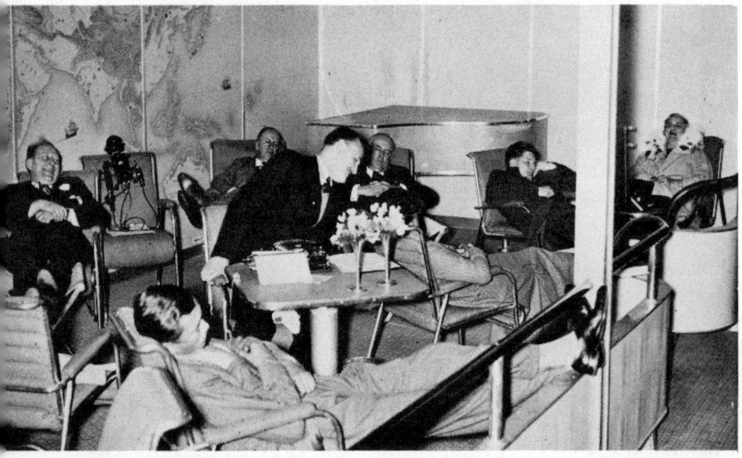

"It flew apart as if made of paper," said photographer Larry Kennedy, who was mingling with the stunned ground crew. "Pieces of flaming fabric fell around us."

Dozens of the *Hindenburg's* passengers were instantly hurtled from their perches on board into the air and fell, legs moving awkwardly in space, to the sandy earth below. Some crew members dove headlong for the guide ropes that dangled earthward and missed, plunging to their deaths.

Tailrigger Hans Freund—the only crew member to survive—had just thrown out a cable from the fin section to the ground and was suddenly engulfed by flames. The burst hurled him unconscious down the cable and freakishly saved him.

A mass shriek to "run for your lives!" came from the throats of those on the ground as the flaming *Hindenburg* began her death dive.

The intensity of the heat from the *Hindenburg's* hydrogen flames was unbearable. Another photographer on the ground, Robert Seelig, said, "There was a noise that sounded like bullets coming out of the gondolas. I saw nobody jumping. I heard everybody on the ground screaming. The heat made my face tighten up."

The explosion, never fully explained, began at number 2 gas cell at the stern of the ship. "The crew men back there never had a chance," one survivor stated.

Navy personnel rushed forward under the *Hindenburg's* burning belly, now descending in flames, and attempted to rescue those who had jumped. Additional explosions came, red and yellow walls of flame shooting across the entire ship.

As the *Hindenburg* plunged to her death, many passengers and crew members began jumping from the gondola-like compartments of the craft. Those who did not jump were catapulted out of their cabins by the massive eruptions.

One passenger, Leonard Adelt, who was on board to gather a few additional facts for a recently finished book on dirigibles, took only mild interest in the first explosion. The detonation sounded to him "no greater than a beer bottle being opened."

When the blasts increased as one gas cell after another (sixteen in all) exploded, the tail disappeared and lifted the nose of the ship; flames shot up the main body of the zeppelin, which in this position was like a chimney. Adelt immediately grasped the situation and grabbed his wife's hand. He shouted at the rest of the petrified passengers, "Through the windows, everyone!" Then Leonard and Gertrude Adelt gingerly stepped forward, mounted a window frame, and heroically plunged to earth and survival.

Not all of the passengers reacted with such

A gigantic explosion of hydrogen gas belched from *Hindenburg*'s tail section at 7:23 P.M. on May 6, 1937, at Lakehurst, New Jersey.

reasonableness. "This is the end," one resigned German businessman said, as he calmly walked into a corridor of flames to his death.

Mrs. Doehner gathered her three children, two small boys and an eleven-year-old daughter, about her. She screamed for her husband, but he was nowhere in sight. He had gone to check on the family's luggage. As flames surrounded the terrified family, she said, "Be brave, children." One by one she lifted her children to a window and threw them out, following them in a screaming dive. She and one boy were the only survivors of the family.

Others wandered through the flames hopelessly seeking loved ones. Shipping tycoon John Pannes disappeared that way looking for his wife; both burned to death. As the nose settled, the sixty-three-year-old descendant of President Ulysses S. Grant, George Grant, calmly watched the ground grow closer. When the flames tightened the flesh of his face he jumped, receiving only a sprained back and broken ankle.

Stewardess Elsa Ernst was helped onto a mooring rope by a crew man who immediately roasted to death before her eyes as she swung away from the ship. Miss Ernst slid down the rope burning her hands and legs. She noticed a crackling sound accompanying her entire slide. Her hair was on fire.

Captain Lehmann and Captain Pruss were the last to jump as the nose of the zeppelin settled fast. Both leaped, their hair and clothes sizzling with flames, from bow windows, looking like burning candles.

Some survivors were blessed by luck or cursed by false self-assurance. Margaret Mather, an American, lacked the nerve to jump and merely sat down on the floor of a forward lounge, pulling her coat over her head against the searing heat of the fire. When the *Hindenburg*'s nose touched down, valiant sailors dove through windows to drag her and several others out. Miss Mather received only minor burns. One man merely stepped from the wreckage in a nonchalant manner. Every inch of clothing had been burned from his body. When startled sailors rushed to assist him, he quizzically furrowed his brow. "What's the matter with you?" he asked them. "Can't you see I'm completely all right." The next second he dropped dead at their feet.

Firemen in wailing trucks roared toward the Lakehurst site as men scrambled away from the wreck, which now hit the ground with a resounding crash. Steel girders and thousands of web frames collapsed in a jumble of twisted wreckage. Over a ton of baggage, 340 pounds of mail and two dogs roasted in the *Hindenburg*'s baggage hold.

The 804-foot giant, which once boasted speeds of 84 m.p.h. from her four 1,100 horsepower, Mercedes-Benz diesel engines and had a nonstop range of over 8,000 miles, was crumpled, belching flames, in the dust.

Survivors crawled, ran and staggered from the wreckage in a daze, many of them naked, their clothes burned off their backs. Some were burned so badly their entire bodies were charred.

Two stewards and a little cabin boy were totally unharmed even though they had jumped from the *Hindenburg* at a height of seventy-five feet.

Others were not so lucky.

One American survivor, Herbert O'Laughlin of Chicago, waited until the ship was close to the ground and then jumped for his life.

He described the first explosion as "a blinding flash . . . the fire seemed to spread to the nose of the ship. There were two distinct explosions. She floated down gently.

"The heat was terrific. You could hear people screaming when we hit the ground. I saw bodies on the track and some of the crew walking around in a daze, nude.

"I saw the radioman, I think his name is Hartmann. There wasn't a scratch on him. He was walking in a daze. I couldn't tell how many got out alive, but I saw about six walking."

After O'Laughlin picked himself up, he saw Captain Lehmann, his clothes on fire, staggering past him. O'Laughlin put out the flames, but Lehmann was totally unaware of his presence, and continued dazedly walking and muttering, "I don't understand it, I don't understand it." Lehmann, who had won an Iron Cross for leading the World War I zeppelin raids on London, was rushed to a hospital where he deliriously shouted to doctors: "I shall live! I shall live!" Twenty hours later he was dead.

In minutes all that remained of the air giant was a flaming skeleton.

Associated Press photographer Murray Becker couldn't believe his eyes. He thought—as most people did—that the *Hindenburg* was just about the safest way there was to travel. Now she had become a deathtrap.

"The ship burst toward the tail end, toward the center," Becker later recalled. "The tail went down first and the nose seemed to hang in the air. I ran toward the ship and saw it enveloped in flames. In a fraction of a second there was nothing left but the skeleton.

"I saw a man walking toward me, assisted by two men. He had no clothes on. I saw a woman on a stretcher. There were screams from men and women on the field."

As soon as rescuers dragged survivors away from the boiling heat of the wreckage, ambulances rushed the injured to hospitals. The black smoke from the *Hindenburg* towered hundreds of feet into the air so that all neighboring communities could see it.

A member of the ground crew, Harry Wellbrook, had been holding on to one of the guidelines at the stern of the ship when the explosion took place. He dropped his line and ran for his life. After the ship crashed he was among the first to rush back to her to save injured passengers. Some were beyond saving.

"We got out three bodies from the stern of the ship," he reported, "all burned beyond recognition. One of the men was so burned that only by the fact that he was still breathing could we tell he was alive. The clothing on all of these bodies was burned to cinders."

The courage of the rescuers was amazing. Dozens of sailors and marines dove into the hull of the *Hindenburg* while the supership was still afire, searching for survivors.

Only one badly burned body was found in the sizzling control cabin.

Strangely even as the *Hindenburg* burned, passengers arrived for the return flight to Germany lugging baggage. They stood in amazement watching sailors "dive into the flames like dogs after a rabbit."

For hours hundreds of stunned spectators watched the immense dirigible burn, her rings and girders glowing white. Badly burned Captains Pruss and Stampf stumbled from the carnage.

By 10:45 P.M., with survivors and rescuers sobbing hysterically at the calamity, thirty-five persons on the *Hindenburg* were dead or dying.

Later F. W. Von Meister, an executive of the American Zeppelin Transport Company, thought that a spark from static electricity created by the rain touched off the highly flammable hydrogen gas.

State Aviation Commissioner Gill Robb Wilson hinted darkly that the explosion was unexplainable. "I repeat," he said solemnly, "there was something strange that caused this tragedy."

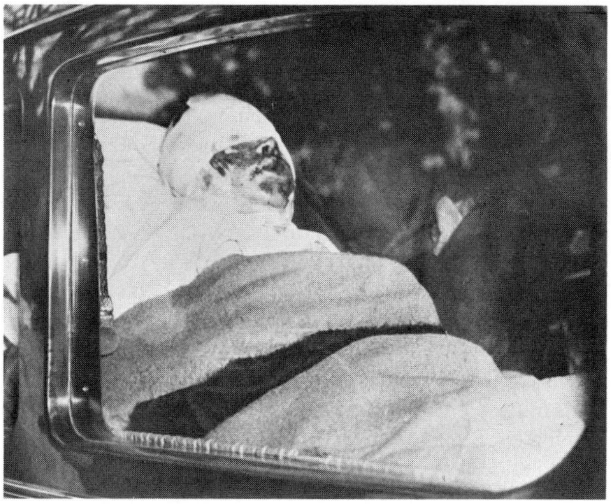

Horribly burned, Captain Max Pruss is seen through the window of an ambulance which rushed him to a hospital, where he successfully fought against death.

And though it was never proved, that "something strange" might well have been sabotage—there were many who wanted to see Hitler's pride of the sky in ruins.

No matter what the reason, the great *Hindenburg* now lay in smoldering ashes.

It was an event not easily realized, especially when one recalls an exuberant account of the *Hindenburg*'s majesty and immunity to disaster written by W. B. Courtney in a 1936 article for *Collier's,* in which he stated: "After watching their methods [the zeppelin's crew] it is the firm conviction of this reporter that only a stroke of war or an unfathomable act of God will ever mar this German dirigible's passenger safety record."

(ALSO SEE: Akron, Dixmude, R-38, Roma, Shenandoah*)*

HINDUSTAN, INDIA — FAMINE 1769-70

The first great famine in India recorded in some detail was the one that claimed the lives of an estimated three million inhabitants from 1769 to 1770 (some estimated the loss to be one-third of the province's population). Drought plagued the countryside for almost eighteen months, but ironically when new crops did manage to appear, most of their owners were dead—the crops died without harvest.

Entire villages were desolated by the famine and entire families were wiped out. One account relates: "The air was so infected by the noxious effluvia of dead bodies, that it was scarcely possible to stir abroad without perceiving it; and without hearing also the frantic cries of the victims of famine who were seen at every stage of suffering and death."

HOBOKEN, NEW JERSEY FIRE
June 30, 1900

background: At 3:55 P.M., Saturday, June 30, 1900, a smoldering fire burning in cotton bales stacked along the wooden North German Lloyd Line pier ignited one hundred barrels of whiskey nearby and set fire to four leading passenger ships of the line at the dock. The ships were the 6,398-ton *Main,* built by Blohm & Voss in 1899; the 10,000-ton *Bremen,* built in 1896 by Schichau; the 5,267-ton *Saale,* built in 1886 in Glasgow; and the elegant 20,000-ton *Kaiser Wilhelm der Grosse.* All the ships except the *Main* made for open water, and only the *Kaiser Wilhelm* survived. Also burning were eighteen lighters, canal boats and barges. Burned to death were 326 persons, mostly the line's employees and dockworkers; 250 were injured. More than $10 million in damages were done.

That Saturday, June 30, 1900, was a beautiful clear blue sun-filled day. Tourists flocked to the waters lapping gently against Manhattan and the Jersey shore. Along the imposing North German Lloyd Line pier on the New Jersey shore on the North River at Hoboken, clots of merry-making vacationers climbed aboard four large leviathans at dock. Their crews were skimpy, most of the men were ashore on leave, but hundreds of carpenters, longshoremen, stewards and stewardesses were busy preparing the vessels for departure. Mingling with these were New Yorkers who had come across the smiling rivers from Manhattan and New Jersey, families tramping the decks of the luxury liners in an afternoon "open house."

All along Pier Number 3 where the steamers *Saale* and *Bremen* were docked towered stacks of baled cotton. Next to these were one hundred barrels of whiskey ready for shipment. At Pier Number 2 stood the liner *Main,* which had completed her maiden voyage only months ago, and the pride of the German commercial fleet, the *Kaiser Wilhelm der Grosse,* 648 feet in length with a 66-foot beam, a ship that held the eastward Atlantic crossing record to Southampton to that date of five days, seventeen hours and eight minutes, her 27,000-horsepower engines capable of twenty-two and a half knots. Tending to these four proud luxury liners were eighteen canal boats, lighters and barges, all laden with oil, coal, cotton and gasoline, all floating torches.

Somewhere in the huge piles of cotton bales a fire had been smoldering for hours, the result of a careless cigarette, a spark or a match—no one ever really determined the cause. At 3:55 P.M. a huge tower of red and yellow flames shot skyward as the burning cotton set fire to the whiskey barrels piled nearby. Two hundred longshoremen froze in fear and knew what would happen next. They were standing on a wooden pier that was already crackling into flames.

Watchman William Northmaid stepped from his control box and shouted, "Alarm! Fire on the pier! Alarm!" But his shouts were drowned out by a uniform growl escaping from the longshoremen as they made a dash for the end of the pier. As they ran the flames ran with them, alongside and in front. Forty men were not fast enough, and in seconds they were enveloped by the fire.

The shooting flames and curling smoke began to rise, and more than a half million spectators normally lining the Manhattan and New Jersey shores on such days

Smoke billows from the ships and piers of the North German Lloyd line, June 30, 1900. *(Munsey's Magazine)*

turned to view the spectacle. For most it was an exciting interlude in an otherwise uneventful afternoon. One purple-prose writer, Mrs. Alexander Sullivan, sunning herself on Long Island, saw the flames and smoke shooting from the Hoboken pier and later penned, "It was as if a huge building of ebony, square and sky-reaching, had been lifted into mid-air. Its rectilinear walls appeared solid, its roof flat. Instantaneously a spiral tower of murky rose tapered from the ebony mass and quivered above its outlines. The vision changed line and hue with every glance. Wind and sun were playing upon it, the one lending the tremor of vast wings, the other imparting myriad successions of brilliant hues, an instant snow-white on the culm of the tower, an instant ruby at its base. All the time the ebony mass was firm and intact, remaining so many minutes, until a livelier gust swept a brown bar detachedly from the ebony and sent it sailing softly upward for a new base to the now vermillion tower, whose apex caught a nimbus from the declining sun. Ruskin's 'Queen of the Air' flew back from long memory. 'As upon the plumes of the bird are put the colors of the air'; on these vaporous shapes the 'gold of the cloud that cannot be gathered by covetousness'; the 'rubies of the clouds, the vermillion of the cloud bar and the flame of the cloud crest, the snow of the cloud and its shadow, and the melted blue of the deep wells of the sky.' "

Beyond and beneath Mrs. Sullivan's aesthetic gaze people were roasting to death. All of the German ships had caught fire. Flames a hundred feet high jumped from Pier Number 3 to Pier Number 2, then to Pier Number 1 and on to the piers of the Thingvalla Line. The great Campbell storehouses, built at a cost of $1.5 million, were gutted in nine minutes. Flames ran up wooden gangplanks and chewed viciously at the wooden decks of the *Saale, Bremen, Main* and *Kaiser Wilhelm.*

It was apparent from the beginning that only the *Kaiser Wilhelm,* her decks loaded with hundreds of sightseeing men, women and children, had a chance to escape. Her bow was already in flames while more than one hundred tugs from both shores scurried to the rescue. A dozen lines were tossed up to the ship's crew. A dozen tugs soon pulled the *Kaiser Wilhelm* into mid-stream. Her stern was also ablaze, and despite the shrieks and screams of terrified women and children her crew admirably stood to their posts and confidently fought the fires. Some of her officers suffocated small fires with their elegant uniforms. None of her charred crew deserted, and step by step they beat back the fires until they were out. To underscore the concept of discipline on the *Kaiser Wilhelm,* her captain stood stoically on the bridge, a pistol in either hand, uttering nothing. Not one life was lost that day on his ship.

A few survivors were rescued from the burning *Bremen.* *(Munsey's Magazine)*

It was a different and agonizing story for the other three liners. All of them were blazing from stem to stern. The stubborn, valiant little tugboats hovering about them and attempting to draw them away from the piers caught fire, too. Lighters caught fire and drifted off, one sailing to a Manhattan pier and starting a fire there, but the flames were quickly put out.

The tug *Nettie Tice* was almost swamped as it took off 104 men from the blazing *Bremen,* while it and other tugs pulled the ship into deeper waters. The tug *Westchester* took off 40 men from the hold of the *Saale* as that ship, too, was hauled away from the doomed piers. Nothing could be done for the fire-stricken *Main.* Though several tugs tried to budge her, the liner could not be freed from the dock, and the ship burned so thoroughly that her hull became cherry-red before nightfall.

Then the real horror began. Faces and arms appeared at the eleven-inch portholes of the *Saale, Bremen* and *Main,* portholes too pitiably small to permit the passage of any adult body. A woman appeared at a porthole on the *Main.* She looked down at a half-dozen tugs and one hundred men unable to help her.

The woman, a stewardess, began praying loudly. Smoke drifted past her head and flames could be seen behind her. Hoping to save her, one man grabbed a rope, clung to the red-hot side of the *Main* and with a hose climbed to an adjacent porthole, through which he sprayed water on the creeping flames. He fell.

Flames and smoke began to envelop the woman, and she called out, "Now listen! Listen! Tell my mother—she lives in Bremen—tell her my last thought was of her—tell her all my money is in the bank—tell her she can have it all—tell her. . . ." Purple fire closed over her face, and with a quick shriek she was gone.

Below decks on the *Main* dozens of stokers, engineers and stewards died miserably, waiting for death as ten feet of flames roared over their heads and ate downward to them.

It was the same on the *Saale.* Dozens of pathetic figures appeared at the portholes, unable to escape. One was a woman who waved frantically for help, her golden wedding ring gleaming in the bright sunlight. Twenty tugs fought desperately to put out the fires on this ship, more than one hundred men with axes tried to chop their way through to the woman, who kept repeating, "I know you will save me, I know you will save me." The tugboat men ripped away at rails, pulled hopelessly at those in the portholes, trying to yank them through the unyielding steel.

It took three hours for those trapped behind the portholes to die. On one of the tugs a Catholic priest, Reverend John Brosnan, lifted up his hands and face to

Trapped passengers on the doomed *Saale* could not squeeze through the eleven-inch portholes and died in the fire as rescuers watched helplessly. *(Munsey's Magazine)*

The all-wood Hoboken piers were ignited by exploding whiskey barrels. *(Munsey's Magazine)*

those begging "Wasser, wasser! Ach, Himmel, wasser!" and gave them Extreme Unction. Men in the tugboats went mad with their inability to save anyone. One tugboat captain broke down and wept, bitterly shouting as each face disappeared into flames behind the portholes: "My God, my God, will it never stop!"

By now hundreds of thousands from ferry boats and the shore were watching the death spectacle in awe and shock. Some watched in curious wonder, like the excursion ship loaded with young persons who had returned from the college races at Poughkeepsie that afternoon. They insisted that their ship's band continue to play all through the nightmare.

The fire on the *Kaiser Wilhelm* was out with $25,000 in damage done. Her captain could not bear to look at his sister ships going down in flames, so he jammed his pistols in his belt, went into his cabin and locked the door. His good friend, Captain Mirow of the *Saale,* was already dead, roasted on his bridge as he vainly tried to save his ship, now grounded in the mud and gutted off Ellis Island. The *Bremen,* on which dozens more also died burning behind the portholes, went aground on the Jersey side just below Weehawken, and she continued to burn into the night aided by the strong southwest wind which had originally fanned the flames on the piers.

It was 11:00 P.M. when a minor miracle occurred, momentarily lessening the impact of the tragedy. Though the *Main,* sunk at her dock and her plates glowing red, was given up, a tug passed her and its captain gaped to see a small oil torch signaling from the dead ship. Coming alongside, the tugboat men heard knocking on the hull and immediately began to cut into the plates. Fifteen men had survived inside the oven that was the *Main.* For eight hours they had holed up in an empty coal bunker in the very bowels of the ship. The steel plates all about them turned almost white, and to save themselves from suffocating, they stripped naked and jammed their clothing into crevices. At first they had an electric light, but the dynamo failed and they were in darkness. The air was so hot and stifling that they sank delirious to the deck, but one man managed to get his blistered arm through a porthole and signal with his little oil lamp. They were cut out of their oven an hour later; only one, an elderly seaman, was seriously injured. He had gone blind in the intense heat.

The next day bodies were collected, sixty-five from that veritable coffin, the *Saale,* dozens off the *Bremen,* scores from the *Main,* thirty-four bunched together in one eddy in the river. One account related: "There were those who had died on the decks when another step would have meant safety; there were those of whom but a bone remained. Some had been sadly charred; some were not even blemished. . . . A little heap of white ashes told the whole pitiful story better than words."

A rough and conservative count of the dead reached 326, with 250 injured, but most authorities figured there must have been more dead, many more. When these repugnant figures were turned over to the officials of the German Lloyd Line, one, in taciturn deliberation, announced: "We will rebuild our piers. This time, we use steel."

(ALSO SEE: Bombay, India; Bone, Algeria; Halifax, Nova Scotia; Texas City, Texas)

HOBSON

MARINE DISASTER
April 26, 1952

Plowing through heavy seas, three powerful ships of the United States Navy were making twenty-five knots in a black mid-Atlantic. This relief force was thrusting toward the Mediterranean. The largest was the World War II veteran aircraft carrier *Wasp,* her gigantic 27,100-tons creating great swells from her bow as she churned through a starless night. At her flanks were the destroyer-minesweepers, *Rodman* and *Hobson,* both acting as pickets should any of the flattop's routine nightflight airplanes have to ditch.

Hobson's captain, Lieutenant Commander William J. Tierney, was on the bridge and a skeleton crew manned ready stations. Most of the destroyer's 236 mates were asleep in their bunks.

Only a slight, gradually increasing wind bestirred the waters dashing against the hull of their ship. The wind, however, would bring most of them to their deaths. At a little after 10:30 P.M. on April 26, 1952, the wind shifted violently, and Captain Burnham C. McCaffree, who skippered the *Wasp,* ordered his ship turned into the wind so that his last flight of planes could land. The *Rodman* noted the turn and compensated. The *Hobson* did not. Tierney, a man who had given thousands of quick-thinking orders at sea, said, according to the official Navy report, "left rudder." (Another report had it that Tierney sailed the *Hobson* straight without altering course with the carrier.)

The bow of the U.S. aircraft carrier *Wasp* was gouged out when it collided with the destroyer *Hobson* on April 26, 1952. The *Hobson* and 175 men went to the bottom. *(Wide World)*

As the destroyer swung over, the *Wasp* ground down on her with elephantine ferocity, her great bow crunching into the smaller vessel amidships.

"All back!" shouted Captain McCaffree, and the *Wasp*'s engines went into reverse at emergency speed. It was too late. The *Hobson* was already rolling over on her port side, her death throes emphasized by the wailing clash of metal on metal as her keel knifed into the carrier's bow. In four minutes flat the *Hobson,* broken in two, slid beneath the waves as the *Wasp,* dead in the water, stood by helplessly. Then a shower of life preservers, ropes and jetsam was tossed overboard to the sailors in the sea, choking on inky black water. Clutching at these, sixty-one men were pulled to safety aboard the *Wasp.* Tierney was not among them.

"They had no time at all," lamented one officer on the *Rodman.* "For anyone who stopped to get a wallet, or watch, or rub the sleep from his eyes, it was too late."

It was not too late for a board of inquiry. High-ranking naval officers came to the quick conclusion that Tierney was entirely to blame for the loss of his ship. Tierney, they said, committed a "grave error in judgment" and was "completely confused" when he gave his disastrous order to turn left. They summed up the fatal move, saying, "As the commanding officer was not among the survivors, his reasons for turning left will never be known."

HODGES, TENNESSEE — RAILWAY WRECK

September 24, 1904

A head-on collision between two trains of the Southern Railway on September 24, 1904, near Hodges, Tennessee, resulted in the deaths of sixty-three passengers, the cause being fixed with the engineer of Number 15. Orders were sent out that day that Number 12 train en route to Bristol from Chattanooga would meet train Number 15 at New Market, one station east of Hodges. One train would take to the siding, while the other proceeded on the single track.

The crew of Number 15 either forgot their orders or ignored them as they raced through New Market, hitting Number 12 just outside of Hodges. A notable survivor was Henry Gibson, a congressman from Tennessee. Those killed were packed into flimsily constructed cars.

HOLLAND — FLOOD

November 1, 1530

Holland's dikes, which the populace at large felt would hold back the sea, gave way on November 1, 1530, and without any warning, 400,000 surprised inhabitants were drowned in floodwaters furiously driven by high winds. The loss of property would today be estimated in the billions.

HOLLAND — FLOOD

November 1, 1570

Universal ruin came to Holland on November 1, 1570, when powerful northwest winds, gusting at high tide, sent the sea ripping through the heavy dikes, wiping out dozens of villages and destroying the city of Friesland where 20,000 persons died in the violent waters. More than 50,000 lost their lives in the path of the flood.

According to one historical account: "The Spaniards [then at war with The Netherlands] imputed the flood, which occurred on All Saints' Day, to the vengeance of God upon the heresy of the land; The Netherlands looked upon it as an omen portending some violent commotions."

(ALSO SEE: Leyden, Holland)

HOLLAND — FLOODS

February 1, 1953

background: Following hurricane winds, the sea rose to the level of Holland's ten-foot primary dikes on the morning of February 1, 1953, breaking fifty dikes and flooding more than 500,000 acres. Dead were 1,835 persons, 500,000 livestock and poultry. More than 72,000 persons were evacuated, 3,000 houses were completely ruined, and another 40,000 damaged. Nine percent of the agricultural land (roughly 625 square miles) was flooded and $500 million in damages were done. England and Belgium also suffered great losses; 307 were killed in England, 32,000 evacuated, 24,000 houses wrecked, and damages totaled $120 million; Belgium lost 22 persons and suffered $60 million in damages.

Would the dikes hold? In Holland that question has always been foremost in the minds of its citizens at any given gust of wind or rise in the sea, for they live on stolen land, rich earth wrested from the ocean waters hundreds of years ago. They have constantly fought the sea to keep it. Sometimes, as in the predawn hours of February 1, 1953, the sea wins.

For days, from January 29 to 31, 1953, powerful winds drove fifteen billion cubic feet of water from the Atlantic Ocean into the North Sea, while a huge, sluggish depression moved slowly toward Holland. The Atlantic waters swelled the North Sea by two additional feet and the relentless winds, estimated at 100 m.p.h., built up the momentum and pressure of the storm until one giant dike after another began to give way. The first to go were those guarding the squatting islands in the Schlede and Maas rivers.

Thousands of tons of water began to gush into the lowlands, but strangely the ordinarily prepared Dutch were caught unaware. Some were even indifferent to the disaster. In one Dutch village a woman left a burgomaster's home, where guests toasted each other with gin, to

Submerged and all but deserted, the Dutch coastal village of Oude stands in mute testimony to the savage floods that swept over Holland on February 1, 1953, when 1,835 persons were killed. *(Wide World)*

watch the harbor swell with floodwaters. Returning she told the official, "Your new town hall may drown tonight." Above the laughter greeting this remark a man rose and toasted the water. Moments later another man entered the festivities to report that the polder was flooding.

"You're insane," the burgomaster said and waved him away.

By the next evening the top of the town hall in the hamlet was under water. As one who was at the burgomaster's gay revel later put it, "The Lord has served us with this calamity because of our godlessness."

Engineers, however, blamed the fifty dikes that broke almost simultaneously over 133 towns and villages. As the water spilled quickly into one polder after another, the residents clambered up stairs, first to the second floor, then the attic. They heard their furniture lifted noisily to the ceilings under them in swirls of water and counted the remaining stairs until they would reach their perches still above water.

One story related how the head of one household refused to save himself other than by stretching out on his dining room table. The waters poured into his home and rescuers hours later found him floating near the ceiling beams of his house.

In the town of Stavenisse a husband jumped from bed at the first sound of rushing water, running down a hall for a suitcase in which to pack a few necessities. Upon returning to the bedroom he found the door closed by the water. He pulled, his terrified wife pushed, but the water held the door fast. Her nightgown soaked, the wife barely escaped drowning by getting out a window. She climbed onto the roof and screamed for her husband. Moments later she saw the floodwaters disgorge him, dead, out the front door.

Even with the floodwaters dashing into their houses,

people refused to believe the dikes had been pierced. One woman in Kruiningen, who knew her daughter was preparing tea in the kitchen, heard the splashing, and thought "she had spilled a lot of water." Another attributed the sounds to a toilet overflowing.

In Tholen a wife and her twelve children died before her husband's eyes as he was helplessly trapped on a second story. Another husband whose wife had just given birth in a bed surrounded by floodwaters raced out for a doctor, found none and returned struggling against the whirlpools to find his wife and child swept away.

One town after another was engulfed—Burghsluis, Stellendam, Ouddorp and Kortgene. At Kortgene one hundred fishermen made a fight of it, bracing a weakening dike with their backs, straining against the immense pressure of the sea for several hours. A town constable strolled by shaking his head. The men battling to bolster the dike shouted at him to run to the alarm bell and ring it so the village would be alerted. Imperiously he continued to shake his head, coolly refusing on the grounds that the water already flooding the ground he stood upon was merely the result of a few large waves sloshing over the "impregnable" dike. In this same town the dike-keeper madly raced his small car along the top of the dike to warn farmers asleep in their beds. The dike broke in a dozen places just after his car passed.

On the day before they were to be married, a young couple held on to the embankment of a dike for thirty-six hours while the raw February gale whipped at them and the freezing water soaked them through. The woman was dead by the time a relief party came upon the two still grasping each other. The man had turned into a raving lunatic.

Everywhere thousands of persons either climbed onto their roofs or up trees and telephone poles. One person hung between telegraph wires for two days until rescued. A Spijkenisse housewife held on to her unconscious husband by the waist with one arm and grappled a chimney with the other for several hours. When they were finally hauled into a boat, she discovered that the fierce waters that had smashed her husband's leg into a metal gutter had severed his foot.

Terror was complete in every hamlet that was dashed to pieces by the crashing rapids. "The fishermen dirtied their pants with fright," one account related. Another reported: "The faces of many people were so distorted with fear that people could hardly recognize each other. There were continuous shrieks from people drowning or nearly drowning. People were seen to perish and several dead bodies were lying along the dike without any attention according to the instinct of 'first the living, then the dead.' A few children who had just come out of the water were so terror-stricken that they continued running madly although the dike was strewn with hard objects."

The dead bodies of men, women and children floated everywhere, bumping against debris and the bloated carcasses of animals. The stench of death hung thickly over a half million inundated acres. And from the 43,000 houses under water gurgled once preciously guarded heirlooms, foodstuffs—a complete untouched breakfast floated on a large platter in one instance—dolls, bedding, portraits.

A survivor with an ironic eye recalled seeing books by the hundreds floating out of one elegant house. "Most of them floated with the title page downward. The title of one of them, could be read, *Citizens in Trouble.*"

All that day, with the spring tides gushing through more and more dikes, people died in clumps and alone long before the 12,000 soldiers of the Dutch Army or the helicopters of the Royal Netherlands Air Force or the dozens of desperately weaving ships and boats of the Royal Netherlands Navy could reach them.

"It is probable," stated the austere H. A. Quarles V. Ufford of the Dutch Meteorological Institute, "that no floods of such an intensity have occurred during the past 400 or 500 years."

With 1,835 persons dead, hundreds of thousands of animals destroyed, 3,000 houses wrecked and 40,000 more in ruins, the scientist's evaluation was indeed low-key. Reminding her subjects of Zeeland's valorous motto, *Luctor et Emrgo* ("I struggle and rise again"), the queen was moved to state: "All at once, the perfect unity in which our people worked together during the war was there again. It suddenly removed all barriers and compromise in our society. We all feel the goodness of working together for one great cause, and in our enthusiasm we work on without noting that we are getting tired, and we give without realizing that we are denying ourselves."

The peoples of twenty-five other nations rushed food, medical supplies and equipment. The United States Army hurried in battalions of engineers, giant amphibious supply ships, planes and helicopters. England and Belgium, also hard hit by the North Sea storm, sent aid. Even Israel, then an infant nation, took up street collections for the Dutch and from its impoverished people sent stricken Holland more than 76,000 gilders, an act that further cemented the strong bond between the two nations, which would both suffer for that bond the financial wrath of Arab tyrants twenty years later.

It was only a matter of days before the Dutch, like the immortal boy Hans who saved the city of Haarlem, began to plug the ruptured dikes and reclaim their land from the cruel sea.

HONG KOH — MARINE DISASTER

March 18, 1921

Probably the most vicious ship sinking of modern times was that of the Chinese steamer *Hong Koh.* Her decks packed with more than 1,100 Amoy and Swatow Chinese, the steamer approached the port of Swatow drawing twenty-two feet of water on January 18, 1921. Captain Harry Holmes operated under British command, and unlike the slap-dash oriental sea captains of the day, he was quite precise in his orders and handling of the ancient ship.

Holmes picked up a pilot who warned him against entering Swatow Harbor at low tide. The captain knew the volatile nature of his passengers, who had already threatened homicide unless they reached their home ports; the Swatows insisted on going to Swatow, the Amoys demanded a landing at Amoy. Weapon wielding and shouting matches had already occurred on the voyage between the town partisans. When the pilot, stating loudly that the sand bar at its entrance would block passage, absolutely refused to guide the *Hong Koh* into the harbor, Captain Holmes announced that the Swatow Chinese would have to go on to Amoy and then return. They rioted.

Holmes ordered his crew members forward. They held guns and a hot water hose. "We will fire on the count of three!" Holmes shouted through a megaphone. Shrieks changed to grumbles as the Chinese quieted. While the arguments continued the *Hong Koh* sailed onto a rocky reef and began to list badly. Panic exploded. Then everyone rushed for the lifeboats and rafts. Knives, axes and hatchets were flourished. The fear-gripped passengers began to hack each other to death over positions in the boats. Hundreds were slain, and the decks of the steamer ran red with blood. Holmes and his crew fired several volleys into the air, but nothing could stem the stampede. Those boats that were successfully lowered were swamped almost instantly by hatchet-wielding crowds. Several boats were smashed to splinters against the side of the sinking ship.

Holmes stayed on his bridge to the end, drowning when his ship went down. His officers, all foreigners, deserted him, and the passengers escaped in the remaining lifeboat. More than 1,000 persons either drowned or were cut down by flailing knives and axes.

HONG KONG, CHINA — TYPHOON

July 21-22, 1841

A heavy typhoon wrecked Hong Kong harbor on the night and morning of July 21-22, 1841, drowning an estimated 1,000 Chinese fishermen and junk inhabitants. For several days the storm brewed about the area, dark, purple clouds sliding over the hills surrounding the harbor and incessant lightning bolting downward. The mercury in the British navy's barometers quivered downward by the hour, descending to 28.50 at 10:30 P.M. on the night of July 21. By that time the typhoon was in full force over the harbor.

Every boat in Hong Kong was either wrecked or sunk except the sturdy British frigates anchored there. Planks, spars, boats and dead bodies coated the harbor waters as howling winds swept across the bay and churned and rolled the flotsam. British naval observers on board the frigates found it barely possible to see during the typhoon's four-hour blast, so thick was the salt spray in the air.

One English officer wrote in his diary later: "The Chinese were all distracted, imploring their gods in vain for help; such an awful scene of destruction and ruin is rarely witnessed, and almost every one was so busy in thinking of his own safety as to be unable to render assistance to anyone else. Hundreds of Chinese were drowned, and occasionally a whole family, children and all, floated past the ships, clinging in apparent apathy, perhaps under the influence of opium, to the last remnants of their shattered boats, which soon tumbled to pieces and left them to their fate."

HONG KONG, CHINA — TYPHOON

September 18, 1906

background: A furious typhoon broke over Hong Kong harbor at 9:00 P.M. on September 18, 1906, sinking nine steamers, wrecking another twenty-two and capsizing thousands of sampans and junks; an estimated 10,000 persons were either drowned or killed by flying timbers and collapsing houses, particularly in the Kowloon district. Damage ran upward to $20 million.

The Reverend Doctor J. C. Hoare, bishop of Victoria, stepped aboard his pleasant houseboat, the *Pioneer,* on September 14, 1906, with four Chinese apprentice sailors who were his students. They set sail out of Hong Kong harbor under clear skies and a bright sun. Bishop Hoare was off to preach his gospel along the Chinese coast, and he joked with waving boatmen grinning from their sampans.

Four days later, still at sea, Bishop Hoare looked across the watery horizon and hurriedly crossed himself. Before him moved a massive typhoon. One of his students pointed with a trembling finger and uttered two words, "white horses." The tremendous white-capped waves galloping forward—the "white horses"—meant death for anyone and anything in their paths. The waves leaped forward and soon capsized the *Pioneer,* her cabin and hull ripping apart. Two students clung to the cabin; the bishop and four others held on to the hull of the ship as the typhoon began to swallow them.

In Hong Kong the weather observatory spotted the approaching storm and fired its typhoon gun at 8:40 P.M. Twenty minutes later the storm roared in from the west to blast the harbor. Unraveled before it were 11 heavy ships, another 22 medium-sized steamers and more than 2,000 sampans and junks, which were immediately capsized; their estimated 8,000 occupants drowned. The 1,698-ton German steamer *Petrarch* was plucked upward by the typhoon and dropped down on the hulls of the steamers *Emma Luyken* and *Monteagle* before being hurled onto a Kowloon wharf. The 2,000-ton *S. P. Hitchcock,* an American sailing vessel out of New York, was also lifted up and blown in the air across the bay and beached on shore.

Most of the French fleet then in the harbor were wrecked. The torpedo-boat destroyer *Fronde* was sent skipping over the waves to the beach where 100 m.p.h. or more winds rolled her over, killing six of her crew.

The iron cable mooring the *San Cheung,* a heavy steamer, snapped like a piece of string, and the vessel was flung about the harbor ramming dozens of ships and sinking them. Her captain, S. McGinty, stood helpless on his bridge as the ship's wheel spun dizzily back and forth. He attempted to grab it several times and got his fingers broken. "Damn you, damn you," he cursed.

Thousands of coolies rushed to the large, wooden drawbridge that spanned the waterway leading to the boat club lagoon. By hand these men, half-blinded by the storm, raised the bridge to allow surviving sampans and other small craft into the lagoon, which everyone thought would be a haven against the typhoon. Hundreds of small boats scurried into the calmer waters of the lagoon only to find themselves trapped. As the storm increased all the small ships were destroyed; so great was the wreckage that one could walk across the lagoon on it the following day.

On the 485-ton steamer *Kongnam* W. F. Donaldson and his wife and two children were also trapped. The family had lived all summer on the *Kongnam* in Yaumati Bay. A year before the Donaldsons had almost perished at sea; when they were rescued Mrs. Donaldson stated, "If we have to die someday, I want us all to go together." The typhoon granted her wish. When the storm struck the *Kongnam* giant waves washed away her deck cabins, and she began to settle. Donaldson snatched up the baby and ran for a place of shelter, but a large wave engulfed him and the child and pulled them into the sea. Mrs. Donaldson held on to her four-year-old son and together with two Chinese women huddled on the wrecked hull of the ship, which suddenly lurched sideways and pitched them all into the water. They were never found.

The district residents of Kowloon fared almost as badly as those caught in the harbor. Hundreds of houses were unroofed. Bamboo scaffolding and timbers were whisked away like shavings through the air by skin-splitting winds knifing into hundreds of persons, pinning many against buildings and trees. Telephone poles and trolley lines snapped and danced as their electricity crackled forth.

Two coolies gaped in terror as their rickshaw was torn from their shoulders and tossed in the air. Its occupant screaming, it blew away in the gale. Hundreds of Chinese employees in the Blue Building were ordered by their employer, a Mr. Rodger, to "go out there and save some of those poor devils." Many declined and ran for the safety of the shallow basement. Dozens more, however, heroically ran outside, grabbed bamboo poles and raced for the fast-splintering piers. From these shaky positions, some totally blinded by the storm, the barefoot Chinese swirled their poles downward into the water and yanked up hundreds of drowning boatmen and their families who had been spilled from their sampans.

One of the most spectacular rescues during this disaster (or inside of any disaster, for that matter) was that accomplished by H. S. Bevan, a sometime soldier of fortune down on his luck. He spotted a coolie being blown down Connaught Road by the wind. The coolie attempted to grab a lamppost at Blake Pier, but the winds rammed his head into it, and then he was blown into the water.

Bevan made a wild dash onto the pier, where an Indian constable was pointing at a swirl of water in which the coolie was drowning. The Indian, in what must be considered the rarest presence of mind, quickly unwound his turban. While he held on to one end of the long cloth, Bevan made a loop in the other end, threw his arm through the loop and swung over the pier, leaping into the water and clutching the coolie just before he went down for the last time. The intrepid Indian constable then hauled both men up to the pier. The coolie lived, coming out of a coma two days later in the hospital. After the storm H. S. Bevan disappeared.

The storm raged for almost four hours, and by the morning of September 19 Hong Kong was a wreck, with $20 million worth of damaged buildings, homes and ships littering the harbor and shoreline. Of the 10,000 persons killed in the typhoon (many bodies were jammed under piers and houses for days) only twenty were Europeans. Most of the foreigners then in Hong Kong lived in sturdy brick homes that weathered the storm and sustained little more than broken glass in damages. There was some criticism of Europeans who refused to open their doors to Chinese victims during the storm, but little of this was printed in this ebbing but still potent era of colonialism.

One European who did not escape was Bishop Hoare. After his ship was split in two by the typhoon, the bishop lashed himself to a mast on the hull. The two students who had stayed with the cabin were washed ashore, alive, two days later. The prelate was not as fortunate. A Chinese fisherman spotted the *Pioneer*'s hull floating aimlessly days later and poled his sampan toward it. Bishop Hoare was still tied to the mast, his body sagging, his face flecked with salt water and his eyes staring. Seeing that he was dead, the fisherman, a superstitious fellow, thrust out his pole and sent the *Pioneer* with her lifeless cargo out to the open sea.

HONSHU, JAPAN — TSUNAMI

December 21, 1946

Beginning forty-five miles offshore at 4:20 A.M. on December 21, 1946, an undersea earthquake estimated to be five times stronger than the one that devastated Japan in 1923, began to rattle Honshu, Shikoku and Kyushu Islands. Japanese and Allied occupation troops poured into the subfreezing streets as buildings began to topple. In bomb-devastated Hiroshima twenty-five new buildings were razed to their foundations.

Then came the *tsunamis,* seismic sea waves from seven to ten feet high, lashing the mainland every half hour, tearing through the slit or sea known as the Kii Strait and dashing across the Inland Sea. An estimated 2,000 ships were wrecked or sunk as the waves engulfed them. When the waves reached the shores, especially of Honshu, utter damage ensued with fifty cities and towns in ruins. The violent *tsunamis* crushed more than 40,000 houses, making 500,000 homeless and drowning 2,000 persons. More than 60,000 square miles of ravaged countryside were inundated.

(ALSO SEE: Japan, 1923)

HSIN-YU — MARINE DISASTER

August 29, 1916

A heavy fog bank shrouded the choppy waters off the Chusan Islands on the night of August 29, 1916, while the Chinese navy was transporting troops to Foochow. The captain of the cruiser *Hai-Yung* apparently became confused in the fog and gave contradictory orders; his ship was soon zig-zagging crazily through the sea, narrowly missing several ships.

Suddenly the steamer *Hsin-Yu* appeared in the fog, and the *Hai-Yung* rammed her broadside, cutting the transport almost in two. More than 1,000 Chinese soldiers were pitched into the water and drowned. Twenty soldiers, nine sailors and a foreign engineer were saved.

Fire sweeps through Shingu City in southern Japan following an earthquake and tidal wave that killed 2,000 persons on December 21, 1946. *(Wide World)*

HUASCARÁN — AVALANCHE

January 10, 1962

background: The fifth worst natural avalanche in terms of human life lost was the one that occurred on January 10, 1962, when the 22,205-foot extinct Peruvian volcano Huascarán shuddered down a slide of ice and rock, estimated to be 13 million cubic yards, weighing 20 million tons, falling 13,000 feet, and traveling ten miles. The avalanche destroyed six villages, ruined another three and killed 4,000 persons and 10,000 animals; $1.2 million in crop damage was done.

Towering out of the Andes range in northern Peru is the lofty peak of Huascarán, a dying, blazing white glacier at its top (its local name is Nevado Huascarán, *nevado* meaning white or snow-covered). Ice had continually fallen from this giant; in 1941 an avalanche pierced a glacial lake, and the resulting flood obliterated the town of Huaras, and killed almost 5,000 persons.

Hearing a distant popping sound a telephone operator in a small village looked out her window to see

This Peruvian Air Force photo shows the path of the avalanche that roared down Mt. Huascarán and took 4,000 lives on January 10, 1962. *(Wide World)*

a piece of the mountain's ice cap break off and fall downward to the lower glacier (the first mass was estimated to be about three million cubic yards). She looked at her watch. It was 6:13 P.M., January 10, 1962. In seven minutes, more than 4,000 persons, most of whom lived in the town of Ranrahirca at the mountain's base, would be dead.

The operator hurriedly called the telephone exchange in Ranrahirca and screamed her warning. The man at the other end ran frantically from his shack, shouted mad warnings to his blinking neighbors, climbed on a horse and galloped from the doomed area.

Six miles away Dr. Leonica Guzman heard the noise and lifted his head toward the mountain. "I saw a cloud forming and turning golden in the setting sun. When I saw that the cloud was actually flying downhill, I got into my car and drove as fast as I could to Ranrahirca, where my two children were guests at a birthday party."

The *huayco* (Indian for avalanche) rushed downward with such tremendous force that it lifted boulders weighing thousands of tons and sent them skipping ahead like giant marbles bouncing. As it multiplied its crushing forty-foot-thick mass, the avalanche spread out to a mile wide and gouged out earth and rock before it until its height was a hundred feet. The odd thing about the Huascarán avalanche was that instead of chunks of ice breaking off and falling, a huge slab of glacier the size of four Empire State Buildings had cracked away from the summit and plunged down the funnellike canyon leading to hapless Ranrahirca.

For most of the 2,456 residents of that town, there was no escape. The Indian and mestizo farmers and miners working on the mountain's slopes had no hope at all. They were flattened. One woman who lived above Ranrahirca, sixty-year-old Zoila Christina Angel, saw the *huayco* coming. "I saw it sweep by like a river, carrying away one farmer after another. Voices called, 'Run! Run!' but I could not run. I could not move. I could not speak. I just looked at that awful thing that came rushing at us like the end of the world." The avalanche's outer fringes missed her hut by only a few yards.

But it did not miss the town. The avalanche blotted out the town's red tile roofs, its unpaved streets, and its lovely orchards, burying everything before it. Dr. Guzman arrived in his car just as the *huayco* crunched into the edge of Ranrahirca and gave up what some later described as a "hellish roar."

"When I got there," Guzman later stated, "the town was already crumbling under the avalanche. I saw some children running out of the house where my two children were, and then everything went—vanished, like a nightmare."

How he and ninety-seven others in Ranrahirca survived is impossible to ascertain. None in the five villages below this town did and scores more in the next three hamlets perished as the avalanche tore through ten miles of the valley in seven minutes, hurtling its massive debris into the Santa River, smashing the dam there and sending bodies downstream to the seaport of Chimbote, a hundred miles away.

Alfonso Caballero, mayor of Ranrahirca, survived the rock and ice onslaught; hysterically he later described his town as "being wiped off the map. . . . I don't know why I didn't go mad." The area was nothing more than a jumble of debris under which were a pulverized cathedral, a city hall, and hundreds of homes.

More than 4,000 perished in the nine afflicted villages, and when rescuers finally arrived at obliterated Ranrahirca, Dr. Guzman only stared at them, saying, "There is really nothing to do; they are all dead."

(ALSO SEE: Alps; Kansu, China)

HURON

MARINE DISASTER
November 24, 1877

Dense fog closed in about the treacherous Oregon Inlet, North Carolina, on November 24, 1877. A howling gale swept the sloop of war USS *Huron* toward jagged reefs with her jib stay-sail already torn away. The ship, built in 1874 and first christened the *Alliance,* displaced 1,041 tons and was one of the newest naval vessels afloat. She was powered by steam, as well as sails, and was capable of ten and a half knots.

Rear Admiral Trenchard had ordered the *Huron* to sea on November 17, despite the Signal Service's warning that heavy gales were prevailing along the coast on the day of the ship's departure from the Brooklyn Navy Yard. The *Huron* was to proceed first to Fort Monroe, then to Havana, and subsequently to the West Indies on a surveying expedition. The northeaster changed all that as it drove the ship onto the rocks of the Oregon Inlet.

Hundreds from shore watched helplessly as the men on board the *Huron* vainly attempted to save themselves. Ten minutes after striking the reefs, the first cutter was swamped and sank with all hands. The wind then ripped away all remaining lifeboats from their davits. Terrified shouts from the crew to those on land became muffled wails in the blasting wind.

Captain George P. Ryan, one of the ablest seamen of his day, stood on the main deck, and instantly realized that there was but one avenue of escape for his more than 130 men: they would have to swim for it—a distance of close to two miles in the boiling surf. Ryan was not a man to lose his head. He had established a distinguished career as a fighting lieutenant on the Union's sloop of war *Sacramento* during her implacable blockade of Confederate ports during the Civil War. Following the war Ryan had served as a professor of chemistry and physics at Annapolis, and he was consid-

The USS *Huron* sank on November 24, 1877, off the coast of Oregon. More than 100 crewmen perished. *(Frank Leslie's Illustrated Newspaper)*

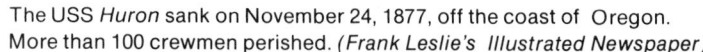

ered one of the best navigators in the navy. Navigation, however, became useless the moment the *Huron* smashed and lodged herself on the rocks at the Oregon Inlet.

Ryan shouted to his second-in-command, Lieutenant Lambert G. Palmer, son of a famous commodore, that the *Huron* was breaking up and that "we must swim for our lives."

The drenched crew was ordered to the main deck and then, in the absence of life preservers, told to hold on to wooden spars and debris torn from the *Huron* by the storm. Then Ryan ordered all overboard. He led one party of men, Palmer another. Those on shore saw the sailors dive from the railings of the *Huron,* which was fast splintering under the impact of the gale. The heads of the swimmers, appearing as black, bobbing corks in the wave washed sea, began to disappear in groups.

The crew vainly swam on until their arms ached and their legs stiffened, some gasping and shouting before sinking, others merely waving weak farewells before floating downward in the deep. About half a mile off shore the inward current began to aid the few remaining swimmers, and they drifted toward land. Of the *Huron's* star-crossed crew only thirty survived. Ryan, Palmer and a hundred others did not make it to land.

Though an investigation of the tragedy was held in Washington, the sinking of the *Huron* was ruled a "mishap." Admiral Trenchard's irresponsible order received critical murmurs by "those whose rank is high enough in the service to permit it" before the books on the doomed ship were phlegmatically closed forever.

HUSSAR — MARINE DISASTER, November 3, 1780

background: The twenty-eight-gun British frigate *Hussar,* a 114-foot-long pay ship with a 40-foot beam, attempted to flee possible capture during the American Revolution but ran aground at Pot Rock in the East River, New York, on November 3, 1780. Perishing were fifty American prisoners chained in the holds and a dozen British seamen; many attempts to salvage the from $2 to $4 million in silver and gold in her have failed.

When it was evident that the colonists under Washington would capture New York City, the snaring of valuable British vessels in its harbor became a threat. The spanking new British frigate, *Hussar,* a twenty-eight-gun pay ship loaded with between $2 and $4 million in gold and silver, was ordered to set sail to safer waters.

The *Hussar* got under way on November 3, after her captain, Charles Pole, ordered a Negro pilot, who argued against it, to sail up the East River to Long Island Sound and then up the Connecticut coast to join other British ships of the line. After sailing around Manhattan and past the narrows known as Great and Little Mill Rock, the *Hussar* came abreast of the treacherous shoals off Pot Rock, which offered only eight feet of passage. A strong wind pulled the frigate off course, and her side was caved in by a jutting reef. His ship sinking fast, Captain Pole ordered his men to abandon ship.

The *Hussar* settled within minutes and aboard her died a dozen English seamen; most of the British sailors escaped in lifeboats. As she went down the anguished cries of American prisoners chained hand and foot in her holds could be heard.

Much has been made of the *Hussar's* cargo, the only authenticated sunken treasure off Manhattan, but its recovery has proved impossible. The last attempt to get to the *Hussar's* reported millions in silver and gold occurred in 1937. Two men in their sixties, George Thomas and Simon Lake, used every modern underwater apparatus then available and still came up with nothing.

Since that time the sunken wreck has no doubt moved beneath shifting bodies of land. According to the *Treasure Diver's Guide,* "the wreck of the *Hussar* may lie between Locust Avenue and 134th streets, deep under the Riker's and North Brothers Island ferry, or under the Hell Gate power plant of the Consolidated Edison Company."

HYDERBAD, WEST PAKISTAN — STORM, June 13-14, 1964

Freak storms and floods struck the district of Hyderbad, West Pakistan, on the night of June 13, 1964. Hundreds of poorly constructed houses were toppled in the storm when raging floodwaters crashed down on their sleeping occupants. The town of Natli was hardest hit, with 115 dying in their huts. The nearby Thar Parkar district on the edge of the Thar Desert was also ravaged by the storm with more than 100 killed there. Total fatalities in both districts reached 332.

I

IBERIA AIRLINES — AIR CRASH
January 7, 1972

Iberia Airlines' Flight 602, returning to the Spanish mainland from Ibiza with Christmas revelers on board, smacked into the highest mountain on Ibiza Island on the afternoon of January 7, 1972. Not one of the ninety-eight passengers and nine crew members survived.

According to a farmer, Juan Ribas, the Caravelle jet piloted by Captain Jose Luis Ballester was departing Ibiza Airport "very low." He noted the time as being 12:10 P.M. Ballester could apparently not pull up his plane beyond the peaks of the Atalayasa range. Searching parties found burned bodies and wreckage scattered over a radius of almost a mile.

IDA — TYPHOON
September 27-28, 1958

The destructive typhoon called Ida came ashore at Izu Peninsula, seventy miles south of Tokyo, Japan, on September 27, 1958, slashing away 244 bridges, washing away 1,000 homes and creating 1,875 landslides. With winds bucking at 100 m.p.h. the typhoon killed more than 600 persons as it toppled buildings and caused muddy landslips and floods. Another 1,200 were missing, and thousands were injured.

Ida devastated a goodly share of Japan's rice crop, turning 120,000 acres of rice paddies into small lakes. The Kano and Arakawa rivers flooded some twenty inches and swept dozens of villages away. An estimated 10,000 persons were made homeless by the typhoon. Government relief was quick in coming but seemingly small with 40 million yen ($112,000) voted for aid.

I. G. FARBEN WORKS — EXPLOSION
July 28, 1948

background: The immense industrial complex of the I. G. Farben Works in Ludwigshafen, Germany, was partially destroyed by an explosion in the lacquer plant on July 28, 1948, while 22,000 persons were at work; 184 employees were killed, and more than 6,000 were treated for injuries. Causes for the blast were never determined, but most authorities attributed it to ignition of propulsion fluids for V-1 and V-2 rockets.

At 3:44 P.M. on the afternoon of July 28, 1948, a massive explosion ripped apart a large section of the eight-square-mile area encompassing the enormous chemical manufacturing center, the I. G. Farben Works in Ludwigshafen, Germany. The exact time of the blast was fixed by ex-Wermacht veteran and elevator operator Ernst Heuszler as the explosion threw him against a wall—"I felt as if I suddenly had wings."

Raging waters batter houses along the Meguro River swollen by typhoon Ida, which killed more than 600 persons on September 27 and 28, 1958. *(UPI)*

For an area of five miles window panes were smashed, and 3,500 persons outside of the main plant area were injured. As the 22,000-man work force streamed from the stricken area, great billowing clouds accompanied by jets of flame shot upward. Barrels of chemicals and, it was later discovered, fuel for rockets (first developed by the Nazis and then tested by the occupying French forces) rapidly exploded.

Three more explosions tore through the works as the methyl violet section ignited. More than 600 United States soldiers streamed in trucks and jeeps into the area to assist French troops. A United States Army medical

The devastating blast that nearly wiped out the I.G. Farben works in Ludwigshafen, Germany, on July 28, 1948, killed 184 employees. Another 6,000 were injured. *(UPI)*

team had just amputated a young man's leg to extricate him from fallen steel beams when a concrete pillar caved in and crushed him to death. One of the blasts sent a German youth through a second-story window to his death. Equally bizarre sights occurred by the hundreds. A worker was tossed head first into a tar vat and drowned.

Thirteen miles away in Heidelburg chimneys quivered and windows rattled under the impact of the explosion. Within hours dozens of bulldozers driven by United States military personnel ground into the Farben Works and began clearing away rubble so trapped victims could be removed. Fires spread wildly from one plant to another. One soldier, Bill McKee, was driving a bulldozer when he spotted six loaded gas tank cars near a fire and drove his machine through heavy smoke to drag them to safety.

Most of the residents in the area appeared to their occupiers shockingly indifferent to the catastrophe. Since its inception the Farben Works had been subject to repeated fires and explosions. In 1921 the Oppau plant section had exploded in a gigantic roar that claimed 565 lives. In 1943 another 73 workers had been torn to pieces in a chemical explosion. Hundreds had been killed by Allied bombs during the war.

Only minutes after the 1948 explosion inhabitants of Ludwigshafen stepped to their streets and laconically remarked, "So it is the factory again."

By nightfall more then 1,000 doctors and nurses were at the scene to treat the estimated 6,000 injured; they could do nothing for the 184 killed and 70 missing. Though rumor had it that sabotage had caused the explosion, it was ruled an accident by French authorities.

Damages were estimated in the millions of dollars with Laurence Wilkinson, the director of United States Military Government Economics, commenting, "The loss of the plant will require an entire recalculation of the industrial program for West Germany."

(ALSO SEE: Texas City, Texas)

IGOLKINO, RUSSIA — FIRE

March 12, 1929

Victor Seastrom's classic silent film, *The Wind,* was to be shown in the small Russian hamlet of Igolkino, 250 miles northeast of Moscow, Vladimir Province, on March 12, 1929. It was an anniversary celebration of the czar's abdication. The event became a nightmare only minutes after the movie began.

The film was shown in an 8-by-8-yard second-story room above a factory, which was jammed with 250 people, mostly adults. The factory manager had protested against the use of this room as unsafe. There was only one exit; the windows were small, and a few days earlier thirty gallons of gas had been spilled accidentally on the floor. (The *New York Times* report of this disaster stated that the factory operator's "real reason was that he feared the peasants would steal tools stored in the room.")

His warnings were useless, and the president of the village soviet told the manager, "If you will not allow the cinema in your factory I will have you arrested." The film commenced with a drunken projectionist named Bazarnof, who was swilling vodka from a large bottle, squatting in front of the only exit. Before him the projector was placed in such a way as to throw its image upon an opposite white wall. Half the people crammed into the small room were drunk, many oblivious to the movie and calling for music.

Bazarnof shouted to one of his friends, "You run the machine, and I will provide the music." With that he produced an accordion and began to play. Unskilled, the friend allowed the film to snake in heaps on the floor without affixing a takeup reel to the machine. Into this highly flammable nitrate film the drunken Bazarnof indifferently flipped a burning cigarette.

A ball of flame suddenly erupted, spreading across the gas-soaked floor and engulfing everyone. Bazarnof bolted through the wall of flame, fleeing to a neighboring village where he was later arrested. Those trapped inside the room clawed at the locked windows and cowered screaming in corners; 120 of them died by fire and smoke. Someone found a trap door, and about half of those in attendance escaped by that route.

Venting their anger the peasants of the village blamed the factory manager, stoned and beat him unconscious and then tossed him into the still flaming building, where he burned to death. A mass burial was held the next day following a ceremonial contribution of 15,000 rubles from the state executive to care for village children orphaned by the fire.

A local priest, using the mass burial to attack the regime, said, "This would never have happened in the old days when men feared God. This disaster is a judgment upon an unbelieving and profligate generation. . . . Our poor friends have perished in the flames, but they died quickly. What about the eternal flames of hell that await sinners and blasphemers and those who deny God's name?"

A Moscow newspaper was prompt to retort, "Drunken Bazarnof was arrested, but why should this provocative priest be allowed to remain at liberty?"

New York Times reporter Walter Duranty, then in Moscow, concluded, "The Russian people care little for human life. . . ."

ILLINOIS (and MIDWEST) — TORNADO

March 18, 1925

background: A massive tornado sweeping down the Ohio valley on March 18, 1925, cut a swath through 300 miles within five hours, killed 689 persons, and injured hundreds more in five states, Indiana, Missouri, Kentucky, Tennessee and, most notably, Illinois. More than $500 million in damages was done by this deadliest tornado in American history.

"A scientific truant," is how James C. Young of the *New York Times* described the monster tornado that devastated five Midwest states for five hours on March 18, 1925. Emanating from a massive storm rolling down the Ohio valley, the tornado let loose its full fury over Illinois, ripping apart the towns of De Soto, Griffen, Murphysboro and Annapolis.

In hard-hit De Soto 118 died under the twister's blast. Most of them were children who were crushed to death when the local schoolhouse literally exploded as the tornado struck it head-on. A brakeman leaning from a freight moving sluggishly outside the town gaped at the carnage and later described the storm as "a crash of thunder preceded by two blinding flashes of lightning after which there was nothing left." Bodies, looking as if they had either been cremated or butchered in a slaughterhouse, littered the entire hamlet. Some bodies were identified by rings on detached arms.

A De Soto mother, who had been lying in bed with her baby, looked up to see the ceiling collapse. Two giant timbers crossed themselves in such a fashion as to prevent the remaining debris from injuring the mother and child. A rescuer discovered the top of a baby's shoe protruding from a huge mound of debris and, tugging at it, discovered an infant girl, Becky Reed, a miner's daughter, alive and unhurt. Her family had disappeared.

It was the same story in Griffen. One particularly gruesome sight was nine bodies huddled about a coal stove in a grocery store; they had been cremated. There was no means to combat the many fires that broke out in Griffen, since the town's only fire engine had burned to twisted metal.

Princeton, Indiana, was hit by a gigantic tornado on March 18, 1925; 689 persons died as this twister rampaged through six states. *(UPI)*

In Murphysboro flames broke out following the twister's visit, and the residents slaved all night to erect a makeshift pumping system on top of their ruined water works to fight the fires.

The outskirts of Princeton, Indiana, appeared surrealistic. An upright barber's chair could be seen in an open field where it had been blown by the tornado, a distance of two miles from the wrecked shop where it had once been bolted to the floor. An intact victrola was in another field. Dozens of trees were coated with underwear swept from a women's shop.

In Princeton a seventeen-year-old boy thought quickly when he heard the tornado roar down his block. He huddled his two younger brothers and his mother beneath a heavy rug, and the shower of broken glass and debris that fell upon them when the roof gave way did not reach them.

Four miners approaching Princeton in a car were sucked out of the auto and survived. The car was flattened like a pancake. The town's $2 million Southern Railroad yard was a giant ruin of bent track and squashed freight cars, many of which were tossed like toys for hundreds of yards. Before the tornado struck the yard T. H. Phillips, a railroad employee sitting with a helper named Jim in a coal scale shop, looked out a window and said, "Guess it's gonna storm, Jim." Within a minute Phillips was hurled outside along with his office furniture, his head jammed into the mud. Pushing himself free Phillips found Jim buried alive under a pile of coal.

L. Montgomery, who lived near the Princeton schoolhouse, dove under the kitchen table when he heard the twister hit his home. The table broke the fall of crashing beams, and Montgomery was spared. His next-door neighbor, Mrs. George Wallace, fared worse. The twister hurtled her partly up her fireplace, killing her.

The tornado raced from town to town. Annapolis, Illinois, was broken and was set on fire. In Missouri the schoolhouse of Cape Giradeau was crushed to kindling; fortunately students had been dismissed ten minutes earlier, so no one died there.

Perhaps the strangest story to come out of this weird disaster was that of a Poplar Bluff, Missouri, man, W. E. Lemley. Lemley was seated in the local eatery, munching a piece of apple pie. "The roof went off first," he said, "and then all four sides were swept away. I was left sitting on the floor with nothing around me and a slab of apple pie in my hand. Then I got out."

The final official death count of this most destructive of tornadoes reached 689, but scores more were never found.

ILLINOIS (THROUGH MISSISSIPPI) — TORNADOES May 26-27, 1917

The Midwest, particularly Illinois, was overrun by a series of tornadoes beginning on May 26, 1917, that left 249 dead and damages of more than $5.5 million in seven states. One tornado had the longest continuous path on record—293 miles—as it traveled from Louisiana, Missouri, to Jennings County, Indiana. In Mattoon, Illinois, 101 persons were killed by a twister that tore up $2.5 million in buildings and property. Most of the northern section of town, a residential area two and a half miles long, was leveled.

Charleston, Illinois, where thirty-eight persons were killed by the tornado, lost 221 homes. Other states torn up by the flurry of tornadoes included Missouri, Kansas, Tennessee, Indiana, Kentucky, Alabama and Arkansas. Many of the twisters were freakish. In Andale, Kansas, a tornado raced down the main street and demolished everything in its path. When coming to the Catholic church directly in its path at the end of the street, it suddenly veered off, encircled the church and moved away, leaving the structure intact. In Konts, Indiana, a tornado lifted a large mansion bodily from its foundations and moved it a full block without so much as disturbing a windowsill.

IMPERIAL AIRLINES

AIR CRASH
November 8, 1961

background: A nonscheduled Imperial Airlines plane (formerly Regina Cargo Airlines) on November 8, 1961, with seventy-four Army recruits and a crew of five on board, malfunctioned while attempting to land at Richmond, Virginia, crashed into a swamp and exploded, killing seventy-seven persons. Imperial's shoddy performance record was cited by the press, and the armed services were criticized for employing the firm.

Penny-pinching, many said, caused the air crash deaths of seventy-seven persons on a failing, ancient four-engine Imperial Airlines Constellation over Richmond, Virginia, on November 8, 1961. Commercial air firms had pressured legislators to pass federal laws compelling the armed services to employ them to carry the military personnel over the continental United States. They argued that they needed the business. The critical result was that the lowest bids for military passenger contracts were universally accepted from small, nonscheduled air companies (in 1961, eleven such firms had snared most of these contracts). Imperial Airlines, despite a poor record and a "fleet" of only four planes, was one of these.

The record of this firm would make the most seasoned air traveler cringe, yet the United States Army and other branches of the military entrusted to its care scores of young recruits en route to training camps in the United States. In 1953 an Imperial DC-3 crashed outside of Centralia, California, killing nineteen soldiers and two crew members. In 1959 the Federal Aviation Agency fined the company $1,000 for transporting thirty marines in an "unworthy" C-46. In March, 1961, the FAA had taken away the licenses of three of Imperial's pilots for "flying their aircraft under conditions dangerous to servicemen aboard." Irrespective of such jittery performances the Army skin-flinted and used firms like Imperial; it was claimed that the savings amounted to about two dollars per ticket.

In the case of the Imperial Constellation, a 1946-model, one of the most ancient of its type still flying, that was reduced to twisted steel and burning debris outside of Richmond on November 11, the savings made by the Army on its seventy-four recruits on board amounted to $148. Ironically Imperial's severest critic, the FAA, had been satisfied only days before the crash with the

Asbestos-clothed rescuers grope their way through the flaming crash area of an Imperial Airlines plane near Richmond, Virginia, on November 8, 1961; 77 passengers were killed. *(UPI)*

company's safety regulations and had marked it qualified.

Imperial's nonscheduled Constellation began its shaky flight at Newark Airport, where twenty-six recruits boarded it. Thirty-one more youths got on at Wilkes-Barre, Pennsylvania, and another thirteen at Baltimore. While aiming for Fort Jackson near Columbia, South Carolina, pilot Ronald Conway began to have engine trouble. Number 3 and Number 4 engines were out when he radioed Byrd Airport at Richmond, Virginia, for an emergency landing. As he made his first pass over the field, Number 1 engine lost power. The pilot noted that the nose wheel of the landing gear would not lock. Conway began to circle the landing strip, but the huge plane lurched downward with a scream, smashed through a small forest, tore through a swamp and then exploded. Conway and flight engineer William Poythree, the only survivors, scrambled from the cockpit escape hatch.

Three other crew members and seventy-four recruits were reduced to mangled and charred bodies. This time the Army didn't count its change.

INDIA — FAMINE 1790-91

Lack of rain and ruined crops led to the Indian famine of 1790-91 that affected the province of Baroda and neighboring districts. Thousands perished. Suicide was widespread, and one historical account relates that "some killed their children and lived on their flesh."

INDIA — FAMINE 1833

The Guntoor district and adjoining provinces in the Madras presidency underwent a famine in 1833 that took the lives of more than 200,000 persons, a conservative estimate by most standards. According to Danvers, the English historian, this famine "was the most serious famine which has occurred since the British occupation. . . ." Deaths in the region were so enormous that the disaster was called the "Guntoor Famine."

INDIA — FAMINE 1866

Rain, ever so precious to the vital crops of India upon which millions of lives depend each season, was the cause of the Indian famine of 1866. Affected most were the lower provinces of Bengal, Orissa and Behar. According to one historian "much rain fell early in the season before the usual time for sowing, while the later rains, which are usually expected in the end of September and October, failed." As a result more than 1.5 million persons died of starvation and subsequent diseases.

INDIA — FAMINE 1876-1877

The Great Famine of 1876-77 was the most extensive on record and took a record number of six million lives, mostly in the Madras presidency and in the Bombay district of Poona. Between tax monies lost and aid monies given, the government lost ten million pounds sterling.

For two years, 1874 and 1875, the deficiency in rainfall and short monsoon seasons dwindled crop production, until in 1876 the Madras presidency was all but depleted of food. By October of that year nine districts of the Bombay Deccan were in the throes of famine. Coupled to this was widespread cholera, which took more than half the lives lost.

INDIA — FAMINE 1898

background: Southern and western India and the Punjab suffered a massive famine during 1898. It touched an area of 300,000 square miles and affected more than sixty-one million persons; more than a million died of this famine.

Scarcity of food for two years, the failure of major crops and an almost total absence of rain reduced great tracts of India to rampant famine during 1898. Starvation was everywhere, and the government was almost helpless to stem it. From southern India a missionary reported, "Poor emaciated women, clothed only in thin rags, came and fell down at our feet and said, 'Oh, sir, we can not live, we can not keep from starving on two and a half cents a day, with grain so high priced, and breaking stones [for money] is such hard work.' "

In the first few months of that year a population equal of that of Ireland was on India's relief rolls. Poorhouses, which specialized in near-slave labor, prostitution and criminal activities, flourished. One indignant English woman wrote home, "Bad men, immoral women, pure young girls and innocent children were freely mixing [in the poorhouses]. Many were suffering from leprosy and other unmentionable diseases. God help the young girls who are obliged to go to the relief camps and poorhouses."

Thousands of children were deserted or orphaned, mainly because their parents fell dead of starvation. All of western and southern India and most of the Punjab crawled with destitute armies of citizens searching for work. Some walked hundreds of miles for work that offered only a few days' labor at three cents. Most died before they reached such unpromising destinations. Millions were reduced to eating berries, roots, thorny cactus and grass seed. This was followed in some places by cannibalism.

In a fund-raising appeal the Reverend J. Sinclair Stevenson wrote from hard-hit Parantij, Gujarat, "My chief work was to take care of orphans. Already I have between seventy and eighty, and they have doubled in the last ten days. But often you get them out just in time to fill your cemetery. Even here things are not as bad as in native states, where much of the relief exists only on paper, and from one of which I saw a letter the other day, containing the following: 'To go out every morning and whenever we see a child lying beside its dead mother, we, of course, take it back with us. Yesterday morning, within two hundred yards of our house, I saw sixteen corpses; today, within the same distance, ten.' Must people really *see* ribs and skeletons to make them give?"

The death toll of this Indian famine topped one million.

INDIA — EARTHQUAKE
March 4, 1905

Northern India was struck by a series of sharp earthquakes on March 4, 1905, with extensive damage to places like Lahore and Calcutta and Debra Dun and Rajpur districts. Eleven distinct shocks, starting at 6:10 A.M., were recorded in Mussooree.

In Lahore many historical buildings were dashed to ruins. The towers of the Golden Mosque were toppled, and the Wazir Khan Mosque was severely cracked. Scores of native houses fell in several cities; hundreds were killed, and thousands were injured.

INDIA (and PAKISTAN) — MONSOONS
October 7-12, 1955

Standing in a ruined square of Orissa Prime Minister Nehru looked at the pathetic crowds around him and noted several males nearby almost in tears as they babbled incoherent descriptions of the monsoons that had flooded their district and killed more than 1,700 persons. "Why do you behave like women?" Nehru asked them with a frown and then, noting females in the crowd, said softly, "Excuse me, sisters."

The shock of male and female alike in India, particularly in the coastal state of Orissa, 200 miles southwest of Calcutta, and in Pakistan was the result of the most deadly monsoons to hit these regions since the shattering floods of 1871. Eight rivers in the Orissa section had overrun their banks, swamping thirty-five hundred square miles of cropland that was, ironically, all but dead from drought. More than 300,000 persons were evacuated by Indian paratroopers from this region alone, and 10,000 villages were completely wiped out of existence by the rushing floodwaters. (Dr. Francois Daubenton of the International Red Cross, estimating that 28,000 villages were wiped out, commented, "In my 35 years of public health experience in Europe, Africa and Asia, I have never seen a disaster of the extent of that. . . borne by India and Pakistan. . . .")

It took days for thousands of persons clinging to trees in which cobras and other wild beasts also had sought safety to be rescued. The United States, which had only recently been devastated along its eastern seaboard by hurricane Diane, sent 10,000 tons of wheat to India for emergency relief.

To some in India the best way to control the huge death tolls taken annually by the monsoons was to decrease the population. In the wake of the devastating October, 1955, monsoons, Health Minister Rajkumari Amrit Kaur proposed that women be given sets of beads to aid them in using the rhythm method of birth control. Green beads meant infertile days, black beads meant fertile days. Tens of thousands of the beaded necklaces were distributed, but women thought they were identical to the ones worn by their cows or became convinced that they held evil charms against conception. The program failed, and the monsoons went on claiming their immense human harvests. The Indian people, for the most part committed to thinking of monsoons as a violent but lovely time for courtship, continued to chant the love sonnets of such poets as Amaru (A.D. seventh century), while the rains came and the rivers flooded:

> The summer sun, who robbed the pleasant nights,
> And plundered all the water of the rivers,
> And burned the earth, and scorched the forest-trees,
> Is now in hiding; and the rain clouds,
> Spread thick across the sky to track him down,
> Hunt for the criminal with lightning-flashes.
>
> Where are you going in the dead of night?
> 'To meet my lover who is life and death to me.'
> And are you not afraid to walk alone?
> 'How can I be alone? Love keeps me company.'

INDIA — FLOODS-LANDSLIDES
October 1-4, 1968

For four days in early October, 1968, India's three northeastern states of West Bengal, Bihar and Assam were hit by floods and landslides that killed an estimated 1,000 persons. The cities of Darjeeling and Jalpaiguri lost many inhabitants when scores of native homes collapsed and were without electricity and drinking water for weeks.

When the Tista River outside of Jalpaiguri overflowed, the town was submerged in ten feet of water (250 were drowned), which prevented helicopters from landing to rescue people. Landslides and floods washed out roadways and railway beds and destroyed much of the 500-mile oil pipeline between Assam and Bihar states.

INDIA — DROUGHT

May, 1972

A heat wave combined with drought roasted fourteen Indian states during May, 1972. More than 800 persons throughout the country were killed, and 50 million more were affected. Sugar cane and jute crops were destroyed with a loss of $400 million. For almost a full month the beleaguered Indians sweltered in temperatures hovering at about 110 degrees while waiting for the belated monsoons.

INDIANA (and MIDWEST) — TORNADOES

April 11, 1965

background: In approximately twelve hours on April 11, 1965, thirty-five tornadoes and about fifty thunderstorms tearing through the Midwest killed 271 persons, injured thousands and caused damages to $235 million. Hardest hit was Indiana, where 130 were killed in Elkhart, Goshen, Marion, Kokomo and Lebanon. Other states affected were Wisconsin, Illinois, Ohio and Michigan. Damaging floods followed in Minnesota, Wisconsin, Iowa, Illinois, Missouri, North Dakota and Montana. It was the worst tornado outbreak in the Midwest since 1936.

Though $430 million was allocated by the federal government each year up to 1965 on all atmospheric science and services, only $5 million went to "weather modification," none of which was ever spent on detecting or forestalling storms, particularly the most unpredictable of all, tornadoes. (Plaguing officials to this day is the memory of two government-sponsored scientists who "seeded" a hurricane with dry ice in 1947. This storm then turned inland and created widespread damage.) Controlling twisters, especially in the epidemic proportions reached by those racing up Tornado Alley on April 11, 1965, remains scientific theory. Unlike the self-contained storm mass of a hurricane, there is simply too much weather to control in handling tornadoes.

In the first week of April, 1965, cool, dry air raced down from western Canada and collided with warm, moist air from the Gulf of Mexico, creating squall lines in Texas and Oklahoma. The storms then moved northward and eastward across the Midwest along the path known as Tornado Alley.

The warm air at 7,000 feet drifting upward met the cold air mass pressing down from ten thousand feet and contracted into ugly tornado spouts, wicked spirals of air moving at 200 m.p.h. The first twister touched down at Dubuque, Iowa, at 1:30 P.M. on April 11. Weather bureaus in the next few hours were deluged with calls from observers sighting whole "families" of twisters, dozens at a time, in six Midwest states.

Six tornadoes swept through Watertown and Monroe, Wisconsin, smashing buildings and crushing three persons. Outside Toledo, Ohio, a family of four riding in their car suddenly found their auto in a creek. Their two young sons were dead. Twisters hopped and dodged and

A double-funneled tornado approaches Elkhart, Indiana, on April 11, 1965, one of a series of twisters that killed 271 persons. *(Wide World)*

danced along the Ohio-Michigan expressway, scooping up dozens of cars and hurtling them into ditches; four were killed and eight injured that way. A twister descended on Strongville, Ohio, and caught a woman tending her baby next to an open window. The rush of air sucked the wedding ring off the mother's hand, and the baby, still in its bassinet, was sent flying to its death.

Crystal Lake, Illinois, where a shopping center and subdivision were destroyed, was ringed by tornadoes. Insurance agent Charles Swanson was caught taking a shower. The twister sucked him out of his crumbling house stark naked. "The next thing I knew," Swanson later told a *Newsweek* reporter, "I was sliding out into the street with no clothes on. I got up and there was no house left and I could hear my wife hollering from the basement that she was all right but couldn't get out." A neighbor ran to the rescue with a pair of old pants, which Swanson quickly donned, and then both men proceeded to dig out Mrs. Swanson. Five others in Crystal Lake were not so lucky—they were dead, pierced by hurtled steel shaped like thistles in the twister's wind.

A tornado touching down in Cleveland lifted Dan Avins, seventeen, out of his bed and sent him across the street into a neighbor's yard, the bedding still tucked neatly about him. Other people over six states were moved about abruptly, almost mysteriously surviving the freakish twisters. Earl Dove, fifty-six, of Grand Rapids, was closing the shutters of his home when he suddenly found himself sitting atop a pile of splinters, a neighbor's house, a hundred feet from his own home.

Indiana suffered most, with clusters of tornadoes swooshing down viciously on Kokomo, Lebanon, Marion, Fort Wayne, Elkhart, Dunlap and Goshen. The house of James Petro, Jr., eight months old, was collapsed by a descending twister crashing through Dunlap, but the child was miraculously saved, sucked 150 feet from the falling building and receiving only a black eye. A few miles to the east, in Goshen, Indiana, where a score of twisters struck, the loss of life was appalling.

"God, what a sight," exclaimed Elkhart County Sheriff Woody Caton when he came upon a trailer park that had been directly in line with a tornado's path. He described the scene to a *Time* reporter, "It was an unbelievable mess. Ninety-two trailers had been completely leveled. Another dozen were upended. Trailers were ripped from their frames, squashed and twisted. Some were tossed onto the highway. Everyone I saw was covered with blood. There wasn't a thing left to the paved sidewalks, trees or hedges. Power lines were down. It looked like a giant auto-crushing machine had simply chewed the place up. There were several people dead. So we stacked them over here, and we stacked them over there."

The grisly work of the sheriff's rescue squads was interrupted by the appearance of yet another tornado. Said Caton, "It looked as if it was coming right for us. It looked very big. It didn't have that kind of corkscrew-type spiral. This one looked like the stem off the ugliest kind of mushroom I'd ever want to see."

When this twister veered off, Caton leaped behind the wheel of his car and raced after it, siren blaring. He chased the tornado to a subdivision two miles distant. Here he found "trees . . . twisted and twisted again and then ripped in half. The tornadoes seared paint off cars, squeezed them together like accordions, or exploded them as if by dynamite."

Indiana was a wreck six hours later, a dozen towns ripped apart, 130 persons killed and hundreds injured. President Lyndon Johnson strolled through the rubble of Dunlap, Indiana, a few days later, angrily kicking debris aside and muttering, "Terrible, it's just terrible."

But the onslaught of tornadoes in the Midwest was but the first of a one-two disaster punch to that broken section of land. Dozens more were to die in Minnesota, Wisconsin, Illinois and Iowa when the Mississippi and several tributaries flooded, due to massive rainfalls. In St. Paul the Mighty Miss rose 27 feet, in Minneapolis 21 feet as homes by the hundreds went under water. The Red Cross set up more first aid and relief stations next to straining levees.

INDIANA-OHIO — TORNADOES
March 28, 1920

The first of a series of tornadoes to strike through Indiana and Ohio on March 28, 1920, bringing about the deaths of seventy-one people and causing almost $3 million in damages, hit Wells County, Indiana, about 5:30 P.M. It slashed through Wayne and Lucas counties, killing thirteen, and then veered into Ohio, where it killed ten more.

A second twister blasted through West Liberty, Indiana, a half-hour later, devastating that hamlet and hopping into Ohio to destroy the village of Van Wert. A third tornado roared through the outskirts of Fort Wayne, and it too moved into Ohio, striking just south of Lima.

INDIANAPOLIS, INDIANA — EXPLOSION
October 1, 1869

More than 15,000 people attending the state fair in Indianapolis, Indiana, on October 1, 1869, were sent into a flying, trampling stampede when a steam boiler connected to a portable saw mill on exhibit exploded. One large fragment of the boiler was sent hurtling out of the fair site. Twenty-seven persons were killed, mostly women and children who were crushed under the heels of the panicked crowd. Another 56 were injured.

INDIANOLA, TEXAS

HURRICANE
August 19, 1886

Unlike stubborn Galveston, Texas, the small town of Indianola, following repeated attacks on it by violent hurricanes, succumbed to a massive storm that moved from the Gulf angling between Lavaca and Matagorda bays, on August 19, 1886. Pushed by 72 m.p.h. winds, the hurricane raced inland and smacked Indianola at its center. An estimated 176 persons were either instantly drowned or crushed by buildings toppled by the storm.

Weather observer I. A. Reed ran for his life when the Signal Building collapsed, but a huge flying timber hurtling through the air caught up with him and decapitated him. The *Monthly Weather Review* (August, 1886) described the thorough destruction of Indianola: "The appearance of the town after the storm was one of universal wreck. Not a house remained uninjured, and most of those that were left standing were in an unsafe condition. Many were washed away completely and scattered over the plains back of the town; others were lifted from their foundations and moved bodily over considerable distances. Over all this strip of low ground, as far as could be seen, were the wrecks of houses, carriages, personal property of all kinds and a great many dead animals. Very few people were able to save anything whatever, and as the houses which were left were scarcely habitable the town was deserted as fast as possible."

Indianola to this day remains a ghost town, never rebuilt, a stumpy reminder of the savage hurricane of 1886.

INEZ

HURRICANE
September 24-30, 1966

Caribbean-born hurricane Inez lashed at the Dominican Republic, Haiti and Cuba for five days in September, 1966, with winds gusting up to 160 m.p.h. The French island of Guadeloupe was hit by these terrific winds; forty persons were killed in crashing homes or swept out to sea, and another fifty, mostly fishermen, vanished. The island's $20 million banana crop was wiped out.

Inez overran the Dominican Republic, where she killed 200 and injured another 1,000 persons. General

This roofless church in Jacmal, Haiti, was typical of the destruction brought about by hurricane Inez in September 1966. *(Wide World)*

Enrique Perez, head of the country's armed forces, stated that all crops in the republic were destroyed, that the Juancho area was a wreck and that the only building left standing after the storm's onslaught on Oviedo was the city hall.

Haiti, then under the domination of Francois "Papa Doc" Duvalier, suffered the most at Inez's fury. The dead piled up so high in the deep gorge flanked by mountain ranges running through the country that the area became known as "the valley of death." More than 1,100 corpses were ultimately recovered, but hundreds more were never found. The town of Jacmel on Haiti's southwest coast lost 1,000 persons alone.

The destruction Inez caused in Cuba was much less severe than what hurricane Flora did in 1963 when that country lost 1,000 to the storm, but hundreds did die and 150,000 persons were evacuated from low-lying river and coastal areas.

(ALSO SEE: Flora)

INTERFLUG ILYUSHIN 62 — AIR CRASH
August 14, 1972

Conflicting reports added to the unsolved mystery of the East German Ilyushin 62 that crashed six miles outside of East Berlin's Schönefeld Airport on takeoff on August 14, 1972. The jetliner, capable of cruising at about 520 m.p.h., belonged to Interflug, the East German state airline. All 148 passengers and 8 crew members were killed in the crash near Konigs Wusterhausen.

En route to the Bulgarian Black Sea resort of Burgas, the plane never went higher than an estimated altitude of 100 feet, according to one witness. He claimed that the pilot apparently attempted to raise the nose of the plane but that it exploded as it dipped toward earth. He said there had been flames, but another witness stated there was only an explosion.

West Berlin officials then claimed that several of its citizens had been on board. East Berlin authorities insisted that all on board had been residents of their sector.

IOLAIRE — MARINE DISASTER
January 1, 1919

Built in 1902, the 362-ton British steam yacht *Iolaire* had once been the proud possession of Sir Donald Currie. He turned the vessel over to the British navy for the purpose of training young seamen. While sailing near Stornoway, Scotland, on January 1, 1919, with 300 Australian seamen and heading for holiday resorts, the *Iolaire* was swept off course by a gale and struck the ship-crushing rocks known by mariners as "The Beasts of Helm."

The ship was instantly wrecked and broke up within minutes. Only 30 men out of 300 managed to swim to shore, and these were gashed bloody by the reef.

The smoldering wreckage of an East German Ilyushin 62 contained the bodies of all 156 passengers and crew members on board when the plane crashed outside of East Berlin on August 14, 1972. *(Wide World)*

IRAN — EARTHQUAKE
September 2, 1962

background: Beginning at 10:52 P.M. on September 1, 1962, an earthquake ravaged 8,000 square miles of Iran. Leveling thirty-one villages, it hit hardest at Dan-Isfahan; the quake killed 10,000 persons, injured another 10,000 and left 25,000 homeless. The shocks lasted about one minute and were thought to have begun thirty miles beneath the surface of the earth.

Not since 1775, when 40,000 persons were crushed to death, did Iran experience an earthquake of similar magnitude. In one minute a series of earthquakes reduced an area sixty miles long and twenty-five miles wide to blood-smeared rubble. "The earth went wild with wrath," said Sayid Abdullah Hussein, a teacher in the village of Buin. "Then, suddenly, the roaring ended and there was silence amidst the darkness and dust. I called again and again for my wife and family. But there was no answer."

There was no answer from 10,000 others who had died inside their homes and in mosques. The age-old custom of building mud-brick houses with thick walls prone to collapse instantly under earth tremors contributed greatly to the death count. Only a few dozen houses remained standing in thirty-one villages and in the town of Dan-Isfahan, only the mud mosque survived destruction.

Had the epicenter of the quake been ninety miles from teeming Teheran, scientists later estimated, more than a million would have died. Only 1,300 in Dan-Isfahan, a town of 4,500, were still alive following the tremor. The *mullah* there lamented, "We have brought this evil on ourselves. It is God's vengeance for our sins."

The following day the Shah of Iran, Mohammed Reza Pahlevi, toured several of the devastated villages with his ministers. In the obliterated town of Buin the Shah stood on the hood of an army truck and made lists of the victims' needs. He cried great tears as he scribbled down requests for bread and water (for the *ganats,* the underground water conduits, had broken).

A woman approached the Shah and told him that her two children lay dead under debris. She took note of his weeping and said, "I have no tears left in my eyes."

Beyond the meager aid Iran could afford its own people, forty-three United States planes flying in from Ramstein AFB, Germany, brought 1.14 million pounds of supplies and equipment. CARE shipped 11 million tons of food to Iran and raised $100,000 in aid. Even Turkey and Russia, also hit by earth tremors that caused much damage, sent Iran aid.

As bizarre and unpredictable as the quake itself, one warped individual posing as a police official panicked all Teheran when his false report of an impending quake in the jammed city was broadcast. He, like hundreds of the quake's victims, was never located.

(ALSO SEE: Agadir, Morrocco; Erzincan, Turkey)

Nothing but rubble remained of this woman's home minutes after an earthquake ravaged 8,000 square miles of Iran on September 2, 1962. *(UPI)*

IRELAND — FAMINE 1845-1850

background: For four years, beginning in 1845, the potato crop in Ireland was destroyed by blight (as it was throughout Europe). Since potatoes were the staple food of the Irish people, famine set in along with typhoid, typhus and scurvy, killing 1,029,552 and causing 1,180,409 to emigrate, mostly to America, thus reducing the population of Ireland by one-fourth. Other sources of food—corn, wheat, and cattle—were plentiful, but most of it, under unjust British commerce and navigation laws, was shipped to England, whose leaders were held responsible by most historians for the staggering deaths. The loss of the potato crop for four years was placed at 16 million pounds, about $500 million by today's standards.

From 1800 and all through the Napoleonic era, Ireland prospered in a wartime economy, but when Wellington's forces, more than a third of which were Irish, were disbanded in 1815, tens of thousands glutted the labor market. Coupled to this economic strain were the strict British Corn Laws that imposed impossible tariffs on small landowners in Ireland. All of the country's rich produce, corn, wheat, oats and rye, and herds of cattle were channeled to England, leaving the burgeoning Irish peasantry with one crop and food staple, the potato.

While the population exploded—there were more than five million people in 1800, exceeding the population of the United States—the country was systematically raped of its harvests, and conditions worsened until it became a nation in tattered rags. In 1817 the Irish novelist William Carleton prophetically described his country as "one vast lazarhouse, filled with famine, disease and death."

High-minded, lofty-toned Englishmen toured the stricken country and wrung their hands over the brutal poverty and the semistarvation prior to 1845. They came as sightseers. Wincing their ways through charnal houses they were bloated with empathy and appeared to be wreaking humane thoughts as they stared from polished carriages and peered through the new glass panes of elegant inns at the wretched, the starving and the dying before them.

The English poet Shelley: "The poor of Dublin are assuredly the meanest and most miserable of all. . . . thousands are huddled together—one mass of animated filth. The rich grind the poor into abjectness, then complain that they are abject. They goad them to famine, and hang them if they steal a loaf."

The English poet Keats: ". . . the rags, the dirt and the misery of the poor common Irish. A Scotch cottage is a palace to the Irish one."

The English essayist Carlyle: "Never saw such begging in the world . . . Often get in a rage at it . . . [beggars] storming round you, like ravenous dogs round carrion

. . . [Kildare was] one of the wretchedest wild villages I ever saw; full of ragged beggars . . . exotic altogether like 'a village in Dahomey.' . . . But human pity dies away into stony misery and disgust at the excess of such scenes . . . the whole country figures in my mind like a ragged coat; one huge beggar's gaberdine, not patched or patchable any longer."

Two years before the outbreak of the "Great Famine" England sent the Devon Commission to study conditions in Ireland. Its 1843 report stated, "It would be impossible adequately to describe the privations which they [the Irish] habitually and silently endure . . . in many districts their only food is the potato, their only beverage water . . . their cabins are seldom a protection against the weather . . . a bed or a blanket is a rare luxury . . . and nearly in all, their pig and manure heap constitute their only property."

And after all the reports, essays and poems had been written of this vast human disaster, the visitors left, satiated with compassion but impervious to change. On the edge of destruction for twenty years, the Irish subsisted on the poorest type of potato, called "lumpers," a gray tuber used for pig fodder in all other parts of the world. The Irish people, then 8.2 million in population (half that of England, which feared its numbers), became even more empty-bellied in 1845. The potato crop was blighted, and practically all available food ceased to exist.

Tens of thousands died in their hovels, along the roadways, their faces stained with nettles they had attempted to eat. The Cromwellian subjugation of Ireland had done its work. Instead of revolting against English landowners, who demanded rents in the form of all wheat raised and then shipped it off to England, more than a million Irish over a period of four years lay down and died on their rich earth. There was little consolation and even less realization of the true problem from the *London Times,* which editorialized the Irish as "suffering a real though artificial famine. Nature does her duty; the land is fruitful enough, nor can it be fairly said that man is wanting. The Irishman is disposed to work; in fact man and nature together do produce abundantly. The island is full and overflowing with human food. But something ever intervenes between the hungry mouth and the ample banquet."

That "something" was the British government, which refused to dispense aid to the populace (although half-hearted measures limped along for years) or return some of the foodstuffs pouring cornucopia-like from Ireland to England. As the country was reduced to a giant coffin of poking ribs and cannibalism, its people watched, according to Irish writer John Mitchel, "immense herds of cattle, sheep and hogs . . . floating off on every tide, out of every one of our thirteen seaports, bound for England; and the landlords were receiving their rents, and going to England to spend them. . . ."

The British government did institute work projects, mostly roadways that led nowhere but into bogs and swamps, ending like those who worked them, pathetically unfinished and dead. No railroads or public buildings were built as the famine ground on from one year to the next, until, as John Mitchel wrote in his *Jail Journal,* "a calm, still horror was over all the land. Go where you would, in the heart of the town or in the church, on the mountain side or on the level plain, there was the stillness and heavy pall-like feeling of the chamber of death. You stood in the presence of a dread, silent, vast dissolution. An unseen ruin was creeping round you. . . . You could weep, but the rising curse died unspoken within your heart, like a profanity. Human passion there was none but unhuman and unearthly quiet. Children met you, toiling heavily on stoneheaps, but their burning eyes were senseless, and their faces cramped and weasened like stunted old men. Gangs worked, but without a murmur, or a whistle, or a laugh, ghostly, like voiceless shadows to the eye. . . . The very dogs hairless . . . the vertebrae of the back protruding like the saw of a bone, glared at you from the ditchside with a wolfish avid eye, and then slunk away scowling and cowardly. . . . It seemed as if the 'anima mundi,' the soul of the land, was faint and dying, and that the faintness and the death had crept into all things of earth and heaven."

Everywhere the land crawled with shabby clots of people bearing coffins, and as many died of cholera, dysentery and typhus, an equal number began to flee Ireland for England, where they for the most part perished in squalid cellars and hovels months later, or for America, more than a million, half to die on immigrant "death ships" or in the Irish ghettos of Boston, New York and Baltimore.

When the peasants ran out of wheat and other crops with which to pay their rent, their landlords evicted them by the thousands, pregnant women physically hurled into the snow of winter, half-dressed children thrust screaming into freezing temperatures that would claim their lives in a matter of hours. None was more barbaric than the Earl of Lucan in County Mayo, who threw more than 40,000 peasants from their miserable hovels when they failed to pay their rents, an act that made him as despised by the Irish as his irresponsible blundering later in the Crimea and his part in the murderous "Charge of the Light Brigade" against Balaclava Heights shocked and disgusted the British, the idiotically hawkish Lord Tennyson notwithstanding.

Lucan's senseless mass eviction was endorsed by the *London Times* correspondent in Ireland, the Reverend

Sidney Godolphin Osborne, described as "philanthropic." Osborne sided with most British leaders in thinking that the overpopulation of Ireland was a threat to England and that Lucan's vile measures considerably aided the reduction of a potentially menacing nationality. An admirer of Lucan's feats in the Crimea, Tennyson advocated open genocide to rid England of the Irish problem. "Kelts are all made furious fools," he bellowed. "They live in a horrible island and have no history of their own worth the least notice. . . . Could not anyone blow up that horrible island with dynamite and carry it off in pieces—a long way off?"

The British Census Report for 1851 submitted to the prime minister, obviously prepared by an official ever-mindful of British alarm over Irish population, stated that more than two million people had disappeared from the island, obsequiously concluding, "we feel it will be gratifying to your Excellency to find that, although the population has been diminished in so remarkable a manner, by famine, disease and emigration, and has since been decreasing, the results of the Irish Census are, on the whole, satisfactory."

Few English statesmen bothered with Ireland's plight. Indifferent to the famine, Disraeli flippantly remarked, "One day the Pope, the next day potatoes." Lord Salisbury later complained, when prime minister, that the Irish were nothing more than "Hottentots" incapable of self-rule, not to mention self-survival. (No British historians of note, including T. S. Ashton, James Froude, and Winston Churchill, took conscionable time to document the near destruction of the Irish people during the famine.)

One indignant voice, that of Lord John Russell, in the House of Lords made itself heard if not heeded on March 23, 1846: "We have made Ireland, I speak it deliberately—we have made it the most degraded and most miserable country in the world. . . . All the world is crying shame upon us; but we are equally callous to our ignominy and to the results of our misgovernment."

In Ireland the dying went on endlessly. "The roads were literally black with funerals," wrote William Carleton in *The Black Prophet,* "and as you passed from parish to parish, the deathbells were pealing forth in slow but gloomy tones, the triumph which pestilence was achieving over the face of our devoted country—a country that was every day filled with darker desolation and deeper mourning."

Irish graveyards became so overcrowded that the dead were buried alongside the roadways and often as not gravediggers were so weak from hunger that they were compelled to bury coffins only a foot beneath the earth. Hordes of emaciated, starving dogs howled in the distance, waiting until the gravesites became deserted before digging up the coffins, smashing through them, and consuming the dead. Carleton wrote: "In one place, lay a mangled arm, in another a half-eaten head, in another a leg that had been partially pulled from the earth. In a corner by the wall a wolfish hound lay undisturbed making his meal off the features of a head held calmly between his paws."

Such was Ireland during the famine, a grotesque nightmare. She would have her revenge against England's economic tyranny through rebellion and partial freedom decades later, but for that frustrating, hopeless era, its people's anguished voice spoke through such enraged poets as Oscar Wilde's mother, Lady Wilde, who secretly submitted her verses to the insurgent publication The *Nation,* under the name "Speranza." One such poem, "The Famine Year," ended with:

Now is your hour of pleasure—bask ye in the world's caress;
But our whitening bones against ye will rise as witnesses,
From the cabins and the ditches in their charred, uncoffined masses,
For the Angel of the Trumpet will know them as he passes.
A ghastly spectral army, before great God we'll stand,
And arraign ye as our murderers, O spoilers of our land!

IROQUOIS THEATER — FIRE

December 30, 1903

background: At 3:20 P.M. on December 30, 1903, the thirty-eight-day old Iroquois Theater in Chicago caught fire in the fly area of the stage. This spread through the 17,500-square-foot theater area; when performers escaped through an emergency exit backstage, a forceful draft blew into the auditorium under a partially descended curtain; the cause of the fire, which took 602 lives, mostly women and children, was sparks or hot particles from the carbons of an electric arc lamp on a perch used as a floodlight; these sparks ignited cloth borders used as scenery backdrops. Investigation proved the theater wholly unsafe and without protective fire devices. Several persons were found responsible, but all lawsuits were eventually dropped. This disaster, the worst theater fire in United States history, led to a stricter fire code for public places in Chicago.

"Absolutely fireproof." These words greeted the 2,105 persons who jammed the elegant, new Iroquois Theater in Chicago on the afternoon of December 30, 1903. The words were printed in large, bold letters in the left-hand corner on page one of the day's program announcing the musical farce, *Mr. Bluebeard,* featuring the popular song-and-dance comic Eddie Foy. The Iroquois, with its imposing granite, Bedford stone and glass facade gleaming on Randolph and Dearborn streets, was anything but fireproof.

In the custom of the day the entire theater was draped with heavy plush drapes covering all thirty fire exits (all but three exits were locked, and several of these were backed by padlocked iron grates). Electric arc lamps were not properly enclosed, the ventilating system was not in working order, there were no fire hydrants, buckets, hand pumps or cutting hooks on stage or in the auditorium. The elaborate sprinkler system was not completed, and there were no fire extinguishers, save six power devices that subsequently proved useless. In addition the staff had no idea what to do in the eventuality of a fire or panic; no fire drills were ever practiced, and fire instructions were ignored. Although a firehouse was down the block, the Iroquois management had no direct telephone line to it. It was later claimed that the theater possessed a fire curtain on stage, but no such asbestos curtain had ever been installed (a stagehand later insisted that only three of Chicago's many theaters had asbestos curtains, and none were in working order).

Everything in the theater was flammable. The heavy scenery and drapes used in the cast-bloated show, carpeting throughout the theater and the plush covered seats stuffed with hemp belied the pompous program statement. There was no attempt to restrict the number of patrons to the 1,602 seats in the new Iroquois, though a score of theaters had been closed by mayoral order in 1898 for overloading the theater and other offenses. A check of tickets sold for the matinee performance indicated that 1,830 persons were in attendance, more than 200 spectators standing in aisles and near exits.

Before the play's opening, the throngs of people—mostly women and children dressed heavily against the bone-chilling Chicago winds and driving snow in long dresses, flowing coats, mufflers, large, furry hats—marveled at "the most perfect theater in America," oohing and ahing at the magnificent foyer, the Indian red and spring green interior color scheme and the stunning marble staircases.

The staircases, which hours later would be coated with splattered blood and flesh, were poorly designed. The main balcony and gallery exits fed into one corridor and one series of staircases. It was in this passage that most of those now gaily entering the theater would meet death.

When the first act ended, a double octet, eight men and eight women, sang the lyrical number "In The Pale Moonlight." The lighting for this tune, accordingly a pale blue, was thrown from a floodlight high on a perch that jutted outside of the stage and slightly into the auditorium with wires extending from it and trailing behind stage.

Only a few bars of the tune had been sung when the floodlight began to give off sparks, which quickly ignited a small portion of the heavy scenery. Two stagehands climbed to the perch. One attempted to extinguish the tiny flame with his hands. The other foolishly grabbed a stick and tried to knock it out, which only succeeded in fanning the fire higher. A man whose job it was to handle just such unruly blazes rushed up to the perch with one of the six powder extinguishers and sprayed the area, but as one of the performers later complained, "The stuff was useless. One good bucket of water would have stopped the whole fire."

The assistant electrician, William McMullen, ordered his aide up to the perch. "Put the fire out," he ordered, thinking it a minor disturbance.

"All right," the assistant said, using his hands as if to clasp it.

"Put it out! Put it out!" McMullen bellowed.

"I am! I am!" The assistant threw out the powder from the useless extinguisher and still tried to suffocate the flames between his hands.

Other stagehands looked up and yelled, "Look at that fire! Can't you see you're on fire up there! Put it out!"

"God dammit, I'm trying to," the stagehand screamed.

The performers on stage noted the blaze, but intrepidly kept on singing and dancing, assured from the wings by stagehands that the blaze would soon be brought under control. Some persons in the audience saw the sparks and small flame, but did not become immediately aroused. A small boy glimpsing it stood up in the gallery and weakly cried out, "Look, a fire." A man behind him jovially clamped his bowler hat over the youth's head and said, "Be quiet, laddy, do you want to start a panic? Sit down and enjoy the play like a good little fellow." The boy sat down.

Half made up as a comic elephant, the show's star, Eddie Foy, was in his dressing room when he heard the first commotion. He thought it was another fight. The supers and stagehands had had a donnybrook a few days before over responsibilities behind stage. When the noise swelled in volume, Foy became frightened and ran half-dressed from his room. His six-year-old son, Bryan, was sitting in the wings watching the performance; there was not a single seat in the auditorium available to him.

When Foy reached the stage the octet members were trembling and stumbling, their mouths moving automatically in their song but their eyes riveted to the mounting flames. Foy pushed through their ranks and stood by the footlights. Before he could speak, one of the dancers, Edith Williams, fainted. She had been dancing with Jack Strause. "I can't stand it," she half whispered to him. "I'm going to faint." Strause held her tighter and told her to "Brace up, My God, brace up, there's a thousand children out there." When she collapsed Strause immediately picked her up and took her from the theater. The performers closed ranks and Foy shouted in stentorian

Fire gutted the orchestra section of the Iroquois Theater where 602 persons lost their lives on December 30, 1903.

tones, "Don't get excited! There's no danger! Take it easy!" He told them to remain seated.

By this time the audience was near panic. Most of those in the orchestra began to file calmly out toward the main exits. In the balconies and gallery more than a thousand persons leaned forward, staring wide-eyed at the flames above and behind the stage, swaying as one person in a near swoon.

Foy noticed that the orchestra had stopped playing and shouted down to the director, Herbert Dillea, "Play! Start an overture—anything! But play!" Dillea led his orchestra in wobbling music. Foy had already told a stagehand to "take out my boy," and Bryan Foy had been carried out the backstage door to safety. Though the octet had already bolted, along with most of the 275 players, crew and staff, Foy remained on the burning stage. He shouted to the wings, "The asbestos curtain! For God's sake, doesn't anyone know how to lower the curtain!" But there was no asbestos curtain. A stagehand began to lower a regular dropcurtain painted with an autumn scene. Emma Schweitzler, a painter, had studied this curtain before the play and later stated angrily, "The 'autumn scene' was done in heavy red, and in order to get some of the effects, the artist had used great daubs of paint, smearing it on pretty thick in some places. I am certain that the backing was common canvas and if this was so it must have been covered with wax before the paint was put on. This same curtain came down after the first act, so I had plenty of time to know it. . . . The 'autumn scene,' with its highly flammable paint, came down, and it was like pouring fire into the people's faces. It was a great piece of bungling—far worse than if no curtain had been lowered at all."

When the mobbed-up stage performers and some musicians escaped via the rear entrance, a tremendous gust of wind rushed into the theater and this blew the now enormous stage fire under the partially lowered curtain, which was about four or five feet above the stage at one end and higher on the other. It was held up by wires from the floodlight. The opening served as a tremendous draft to the raging inferno, and a giant ball of fire shot out into the auditorium. Foy's hairpiece was smoldering. The violin, cello and bass fiddle instruments in the orchestra pit were on fire. According to one musician, Antonio Frosolono, the musical director was surrounded by flames and then he "went out like a shot out of a gun; he went over the stand and everything. He went under the stage." Foy remembered a lone musician who stayed behind, "that brave, fat little violinist . . . still fiddling alone and furiously." Foy kept shouting to the now panicked crowds beginning to crunch their way toward the pitifully jumbled exits. "Don't be frightened, folks!

Go slow! No danger!" He then shouted to the few remaining stagehands in the wings, "Cut the wire, cut it, cut it!" No one did.

The draft created by the opened backstage door and the partially lowered curtain bulged the curtain out like a balloon. Next came a cyclonic blast of flame as the rest of the massive scenery ignited and the flame swept out into the auditorium in a huge tongue, past and over Foy. It sought out the only completed ventilator, one in the back of the theater high in the crammed gallery.

Weeping in anguish, Foy, his costume smoking, fell to his knees and in a glance saw "the upper tiers [where] they were in a mad, animal-like stampede—their screams, groans and snarls, the scuffle of thousands of feet and bodies grinding against bodies merging into a crescendo that was half-wail, half-roar—the most dreadful sound that ever assailed human ears."

The "brave, fat little violinist," Antonio Frosolono finally stopped playing. "I saw people rushing out, some jumping over, hallooing and screaming; then I turned around at the instant to my right and saw the instruments on fire . . . and then I went out."

Getting out of the Iroquois was a paramount horror. Its seats, carpets, and drapes were now blazing; the stage, from which Foy had crept on hands and knees to safety, was a furnace. Of the more than 1,800 persons in the auditorium only a few hundred from the orchestra section managed to escape through ground-floor exits.

The gallery, packed with hundreds of small children, had gone mad. Women attempted to drag out as many as four or five youngsters at a time, frequently losing them to the thrusting, clawing crowds. Little girls and boys were knocked down and trampled to death. A crowd of sixty persons raced from the balcony down an unmarked hall leading to the women's rest room and a locked exit and were trapped there, later found in terrible heaps, burned and suffocated to death.

Even the orchestra panicked. Mrs. Charles B. Gibson rose from her seat, moved into the aisle, and then someone stepped on her long dress. As she fell men, women and children trampled on her. "From the place where I fell, I crawled on my hands and knees to the entrance. When I got to the rear, the curtain was all burned away."

Mrs. William Mueller, Jr., who had taken her two children, Florence, five, and Belle, three, to the play, had stepped with her daughters into a rest room. As she was about to return to her seat, she saw flames dancing through the windows of the room. Racing over to an attendant she demanded her children's wraps.

The maid absent-mindedly replied, "Oh, that's all right. I won't give you those things now. I'll go and see what is the matter."

Mrs. Mueller demanded the coats.

"Not now," said the attendant and went off to look at the fire in the theater. Mrs. Mueller, after trying several exits and finding them locked, collapsed. Her daughter Florence then fainted. Following the holocaust Mrs. Mueller miraculously found both daughters safe in a barber shop.

Caught up in the stampede in the balcony, Mrs. W. F. Hanson was nonplussed about her survival. "I cannot tell how I got out of the theater. I remember starting for one of the aisles when the panic was at its height. I was separated from my friends. We had a row of seats in the second balcony. Suddenly, someone seized me, and I was tossed and dragged along the aisle, and I lost consciousness. When I came to my senses I was in a store across the street."

Escapes were astounding, considering the hundreds who died at the exits, in the balconies and galleries and on the lone, horrible marble staircase. Winnie Gallagher, eleven years old, was sitting with her aunt in the orchestra, almost directly under the stage, when the fire burst into the auditorium. Separated from her aunt, Winnie was knocked down and trampled so badly that almost all her clothing was torn off. Somehow she managed to stand up and clamber over seats and find her way to the street. A Western Union messenger boy ran up to her, threw his overcoat about her, and then took her to Central Station, where he gave her 50 cents and sent her home to 4925 S. Michigan Avenue.

The fire transfixed many who remained. Helen Dickinson had been holding hands with her fiancé, Kenneth Collins. "I was sitting in the fifth seat from the aisle," she later stated, "but the fire, which was bursting out from both sides of the stage, had such a fascination for me."

Unconsciously stroking what had once been a long, white beard and was now a singed ruin, D. W. Dimmick, seventy, remembered standing in the upper gallery, where most of the deaths occurred. He numbly recalled the shrieks of "Fire!" coming from all sections of the theater before he slipped out onto the stairway and hugged the wall. "When we got down to the platform," he all but whispered, "where the first balcony opens, it seemed to me that people were stacked up like cordwood. There were men, women and children in the lot. At the same time there were some people who I thought must be actors, who came running out from somewhere in the interior of the house, and whose wigs and clothes were on fire. We tried to beat out the flames as we went along. By crowding out to the wall we managed to squeeze past the mass of people who were writhing on the floor and practically blocking the entrance so far as the people still in the gallery were concerned."

When he reached the bottom landing Dimmick spied a woman struggling vainly to escape from a mass of bodies on top of her. He pulled her out, and she ran screaming out the front entrance of the theater. "I tried to rescue a man who was also caught by the feet," Dimmick said, "but, although I braced myself against the stairs, I was unable to move him. . . . I came in from Apple River to see the sights in Chicago and I have seen all I can stand, ever."

At the base of the marble staircase scores of people began to pile up one on another. The squirming, screaming mass of humanity spilled out into the lobby ten, then twenty, bodies deep, scores dying as life was crushed out by the sheer weight of struggling flesh. John C. Galvin, who was passing by the theater when the fire broke out, saw dozens of persons running wildly to escape. He stepped inside the foyer as people fought frantically to get past him through the only two open doors. He tried another section of glass-paneled doors. They, like most of the theater exits, were locked. A fat woman fell, rose and then was tripped by her own trailing skirt and fell again in front of Galvin. People fell on top of her until she was unconscious. Scores of persons who had already escaped realized that they had left their children and dove back into the theater, creating yet another furious jam at the narrow entrance.

Galvin saw a bolt locking the west section of entrance doors and attempted to release it. He could not. Smoke was curling hideously throughout the foyer. Galvin threw back a crowd around him and quickly kicked out six glass panels in the doors. People dove through the open areas to safety, carrying John Galvin with them. Outside police and firemen had begun to arrive at the nightmarish scene, having received the first alarm thirteen minutes after the fire broke out at 3:33 P.M. Galvin could do nothing more. "I then went across the street and watched the destruction of the theater."

The heroism displayed by Galvin was repeated dozens of times. Behind the stage pandemonium was in control. Six open tiers running along the side of one wall and reachable only by elevator had begun to burn, and along these walks, which led to the dancers' dressing rooms, frantic, costume-bedecked women raced screaming. The young elevator boy, Robert Smith, would not desert his post. He ran his elevator a dozen times to the sixth tier, removing unconscious dancers and delivering his brimming, hysterical cargoes to the stage level, where a few courageous stagehands led by J. R. O'Mally, Arthur Hart and William Price had formed a human chain. As the women left the elevator they ran wildly about, but the men grabbed them and literally tossed them down the line until they reached the backstage entrance. Several times Smith was almost overcome by smoke. He could barely see as he jerked his elevator up and down the burning wooden tiers. On his last trip he entered each burning dressing room on each tier and dragged half a dozen unconscious women to the elevator. By then the wooden elevator was also on fire. The control box was blazing and Smith gritted his teeth and then thrust his hand into the flames to grab the operating lever that would bring him down. He clutched the burning lever as the flames gnawed away his flesh. He and the women were taken from the elevator at the bottom level moments before it was consumed by flames. Smith was permanently crippled from his injuries.

Three baseball players, William "Smiling" Corbett, Frank Houseman and Charley Dexter, were in the audience when the fire erupted. They had purchased seats in an upper box. After the fire broke out Houseman and Dexter led several people from upper box seats down the balcony stairway. They were met by a mob of people attempting to get through a locked doorway leading to an alley. Houseman and Dexter shoved the crowd back and broke down the door.

Corbett had gotten to the main lobby and was met by frantic firemen pouring into the theater. A woman ran to him and begged him to save her children. "They're in the gallery!" The baseball hero ran for the stairs.

"Don't go up there," a fireman yelled at Corbett. "You'll get hemmed in."

"To hell with that," Corbett replied and took the stairs two at a time, leaping over scores of fallen, crushed bodies. Upward he ran until the dense smoke forced him to grope his way forward. He finally reached the gallery entrance and reeled back in shock. "There they were," he later moaned to reporters, crying great tears. "Positively the most sickening spectacle I ever saw. They were piled up in bunches, in all manner of disarray. I grabbed for the topmost body, a little girl of about six years old, I would say. Catching her by the wrist, I felt the flesh curl up under my grasp. I hurried down with the little one, then back again, each time with the body of a child, all dead, all the little ones dead. There was no one to save, really, in that awful gallery." But Corbett kept running back and forth with the small, limp, charred bodies until a burly fireman stopped him and told him it was no use. He realized that "everybody was stark dead. I turned away and fled. . . . I never again want to go near that place."

Families became separated in the rush to the exits. Young Verma Goss held tightly to the hand of her five-year-old sister, Helen, and led her to safety. She thought her mother was immediately behind her, but her mother had already fallen with the mass on the balcony staircase and was crushed to death. One woman was pinned to a wall in the hall leading to the alley exit mobbed with people. She cried out for anyone to save her child. A man wedged his way to her side, picked up her child and called to other men in front of him and then the child was thrown hand to hand over the heads of the roaring people to the alley, landing on the pavement outside with only minor bruises. Her mother perished. The man who had rescued her child, a stranger, also suffocated next to her, shielding the woman with his own body before dying.

Children looked after children. Twelve-year-old Willie Dee was seated with the family nurse and his brothers, Allerton and Edward, six and seven, along with a two-and-a-half-year-old baby. When he first noticed the small fire on stage, Willie told the nurse to take the family outside. She smiled and told Willie it was part of the play. "No, it isn't," Willie stubbornly said as he grabbed the brother nearest to him, Allerton, and led the crying child, who was angry at missing the play, down the balcony stairs and outside to survival. His other brother, Edward, was found burned to death in his seat. The nurse was later found crushed to death at the first landing, the baby still in her arms. The infant was revived, but it died the following morning at the Goss home on Cottage Grove Avenue.

A man named Chester made his way to the fire escape from the lower balcony, going through one of the few open exit doors. Flames licked at his coat and the clothes worn by his wife and two daughters. Fire raced up the stairs of the fire escape from below. Having no other choice he dropped his daughters and wife to the pavement below, a distance of ten feet, and then jumped himself; all were saved. W. G. Smith, whose firm, the Chicago Teaming Company, was next door at 37 North Dearborn Street, rushed into the alley to see the Chester family landing on the pavement. Behind them Smith noted a throng of hatless, screaming women, their faces already scorched by the flames dancing about them.

"Wait a moment," he called to them. "Firemen are coming."

One woman, her hair on fire, jumped and was killed. Two of Smith's employees, Morris Eckstrom and M. J. Tierney, ran beneath the smoking fire escape. Eckstrom cupped his hands to be heard above the wails and shouted, "Jump one by one, and we'll catch you." He and Tierney, holding a long blanket, caught more than twenty frantic women as they leaped from the fire escape, but the fire eventually closed off that avenue of escape. "I saw a dozen women and children and some men," Eckstrom later lamented, "through the open door to the fire escape fall back into the flames."

The more than 900 persons in the first and second balconies were berserk with rage, frustration and fear. In

Bodies, mostly of children, were dragged out and covered in front of the burned-out theater. Panic, barred exits, and an irresponsible theater staff caused the staggering loss of life.

their efforts to escape people tore away the iron guard railings from the balconies so they could drop on the people below them, but most of these people died. Among the throngs many families dropped to their knees and prayed. As people blistered to death, several ghouls, under the pretext of being rescuers, ran into the theater to rob the victims; many of them also perished in the flames. (Firemen and policemen ultimately recovered ten bushel baskets of money and jewelry from the dead as four bodies per minute were removed from the devastated theater for almost three hours.) Tons of human weight half in and out of death welled up at doorways, narrow aisles, the staircase landings, hallways, down to the main foyer.

All in the first balcony managed to get out of their seats and work their ways up the slanted aisles to the level aisles above, where they fought violently to survive. They fell, hardly singed, in grotesque piles; those on top burned to a crisp, charred, unrecognizable.

A Chicago Board of Trade clerk, James M. Strong, was lucky enough to flee the doomed gallery where he had been standing with his wife, his mother, Mrs. B. K. Strong and his sixteen-year-old niece, Vera, of Americus, Georgia. The Strongs ran along a passageway leading to the front end of the theater. A locked door greeted them. Strong smashed a glass transom and climbed through it. As hundreds behind the door pleaded with him to open the door, Strong, crazed by the sobbing voices of his own family on the other side, grabbed a piece of timber and beat at the door, but it would not budge. Hands appeared at the transom, but no one succeeded in climbing through; the fire caught them and burned all to death. Strong staggered down the stairs to the main lobby.

Some of the exits leading to what was later termed "Death Alley" were broken open by the crowds in the top balcony and the gallery. Ruth Michel, a schoolgirl sitting in the upper balcony with four friends, arose when the fire started. "A man rose and said he would knock our heads off if we got out," she later stated, "so we sat there." When the fire burst into the auditorium Ruth bolted with the rest for an exit. Four floors up she found herself on a fire escape. "I got down two or three steps, and we were driven back by flames below us. The heat came up just like a furnace, and I went up two or three steps, and then I got under the railing and dropped to the alley. I lit on my toes and a man caught me at the same time, so I was not hurt . . . Men in the alley called to me not to jump, but I knew I had to jump or else burn up, because the flames were coming up so right behind me." Her four friends were later found roasted on the fire escape.

Across from the western exit of the balcony on the alley side was the Northwestern University building. Painters working here saw the exit door fly open and a crowd of terrified persons swaying in smoke, trapped by flames from behind and below. They quickly threw open windows and pushed planks to the fire escape. A man on his hands and knees attempted to cross and fell into the alley. On top of his body a dozen more men, women and children fell to their deaths while trying to cross the planks. Those few who fell and showed signs of life were crushed for the most part by scores more jumping from other fire escapes.

Six persons, the last of which was a Chicago school teacher, Alice Kilroy, did make it across the planks to the building. Firemen in the alley threw up a weak spray of water while she waited to cross on hands and knees. "I did not see very much because I held a collarette up to my face to protect it from the hot air, which was unutterably awful," she said. "The crowd behind us that had been fighting and pushing so hard seemed to die away and collapse all in an instant. The scrambling and pushing ceased. This crowd was at the entrance to the door. Something happened to them and they did not have any life, because they did not push when I turned back. . . . Part of them fell on the floor and part outside on the fire escape platform. I think I was the last to escape alive over the planks across the alley. I was terribly burned." Miss Kilroy turned to a newsman interviewing her. "You can see by the bandages that I don't dare to take off yet."

Throughout the theater the voracious flames licked at humans and destroyed everything in their path. Within fifteen minutes the Iroquois was a burned-out shell. Mounds of humans were found everywhere, especially at the exits, where two piles almost six feet deep were jammed against two ground-level exit doors that had been pried open, but the iron-barred grates on the other side of these were padlocked. (One of the few ushers who did not immediately flee the theater at the first alarm stood passively guarding one of the gates and refusing to open it with a key he claimed to have in his pocket.)

As the crowds of firemen and policemen moved into the theater, led by Chief O'Neill and Assistant Chief Schuettler and Fire Marshal William Musham, a bevy of reporters and sketch artists from Chicago's sensation-seeking newspapers appeared. The appalling sights before their eyes startled even the most hardened of the lot. O'Neill bounded up the stairs to the landing of the first balcony. For a moment he turned his head away from the twisted, gnarled mass of humanity before him and then shouted, "Look out for the living, boys! Try to find those who are still alive!"

There was a faint moan.

"Someone alive here, boys! Quick!" With that cry reporters and artists joined scores of policemen and firemen in dragging away bodies from the first heap to get to a woman whose head protruded from the mass.

A policeman grunted, "We can't do it, chief. We can't untangle them."

"We must take these bodies out of the way to get down to those who are alive," O'Neill barked back. He grabbed the legs of a twisted body. "This man here is dead. Lay hold, now, boys! Pull him out."

Two large firemen took the body by the shoulders and yanked it free. Then another and another. The moans from the woman kept coming. O'Neill was almost beside himself. "For God's sake, hurry! Get to the one who's alive down there." A policeman finally succeeded in withdrawing the woman, later identified as a Mrs. Harbaugh, yelling, "I've got her, chief, she's alive all right!" The woman was removed to John R. Thompson's restaurant next door, which had been transformed into a hospital/morgue, and revived.

A hundred policemen and firemen moving rapidly down the stairs with their grisly burdens placed the bodies outside the theater in long rows. As they were clearing away the dead a burly fireman appeared from the balcony, moving swiftly down the stairs. "Out of the way, men, let me out!" he shouted as he carried a small still form in his arms, its blond hair unsinged and its pink face unmarred, its eyes closed and its lips quivering. "The kid's alive."

But this was the exception. All were dead in the gallery; most were dead in the balconies. The men worked with flashlights, the theater lights having gone out during the fire, making the disaster all the more horrendous. Forty arc lamps were set up to illuminate the still smoking theater. Firemen crawled over the human debris, mostly the bodies of children. Hundreds of children were dead in their seats where they had remained, choking to death on smoke. Many had fallen forward, with their heads resting on the seat ahead of them, as though in prayer.

Under the eerie light of arc lamps Chief Musham saw one of his giant firemen holding the lifeless form of a little girl.

"Give that girl to someone else and get back there," he ordered, pointing to a mound of bodies jamming an exit.

The fireman said nothing.

"Did you hear me?" Musham said. "Hand that girl to someone else."

The fireman turned, red-eyed, and even in the dim light Musham could see his blackened cheeks crossed with rivers of tears. "No, I won't do that, chief," the fireman said. "I won't hand her to someone else."

"What?"

"I'm going to carry her out myself. I got a little girl like this at home, just like this, and I'm carrying her out."

Musham bent his head forward so that his large fireman's hat shaded his own eyes. "Yes, of course," he choked, "go ahead, son."

A police lieutenant, his hands bloody from carrying the dead, slid down against a wall in the lobby dazedly muttering, "The children, the children, the children." A man, whose own child was later found safe, wandered through the gutted theater until stopped and taken away. He was carrying a fireman's axe and was in search of the theater manager, Harry J. Powers, who was later arrested for manslaughter. "I was going to kill the murdering bastard," the man later told a reporter.

The dead came blistered, burned, charred, relatively untouched, some almost peaceful. One woman's face was stamped with a boot heel. A couple had clung to each other so tightly in the fire the blaze had welded them together, and they were carried away inseparable. Little boys held the cinders of what had once been programs. Little girls still grasped dolls and tiny purses.

By 6:00 P.M. it was thought that no one else would be found alive. Emerging from the balcony a fireman carried the lifeless form of another girl who appeared to be about sixteen years old.

"Isn't that girl alive?" Assistant Chief Schuettler asked the fireman.

"No, the poor darlin'," responded the fireman in a thick Irish accent. "She's dead, God rest her soul." As the fireman moved down the stairway, picking his way through the bodies at his feet, Schuettler saw the girl's arms go weakly into a clasp about the fireman. "She's alive, Paddy, alive! Run!"

The fireman bolted forward, shouting hoarsely, "Gang way, boys, gang way! She's alive! She's alive!" The fireman raced into Thompson's Restaurant, now a charnal house, with the last survivor of the Great Iroquois Fire. Dr. E. E. Vaughan, who had been working to revive hundreds as they lay on the dinner tables all afternoon, saw the fireman and directed him to a table.

"She's the last one, doctor," the fireman blurted. "You pull her through."

Vaughan looked at the exhausted man and told him to get some coffee.

"I'll do that when she comes around. You must save her."

Vaughan applied the resuscitator to the girl's mouth. "I'll do my best," he promised. "But it's really God's work."

"You and God, then," the fireman said, not moving from Vaughan's side. "She must live, you know. She's the last one left. They're all dead back there."

In moments the girl's eyes fluttered open. The fireman took her small hand in his massive paw, kissed it and said, "There's a grand darlin'," and strode outside.

Rows of dead lined the walls of Thompson's, and clots of survivors and relatives moved along searching for their own. An odd man, John Maynard Harlan, walked along, staring at the victims, weirdly commenting later, "I was profoundly impressed by the expressions on the faces of many of the dead. Perhaps it was only a fancy, but it seemed to me that the faces of those having the higher order of intelligence showed less horror and more resignation. Some of these seemed to have passed away almost with a smile of faith, so serene were their countenances. But the faces of the less intelligent were uniformly struck with suffering to a terrible degree." Harlan didn't bother to explain how he knew the degrees of mentality possessed by the deceased.

Arthur E. Hull found his wife and children in Thompson's, all dead. "It is too terrible to contemplate," he groaned as he sank to his knees and pressed his head in his hands. "I can never go to my home again. To look at the playthings left by the children just where they put them, to see how my dear dead wife arranged all the details of her home so carefully, the very walls ring with the names of my dear dead ones. I can never go there again."

James Blackburn escaped the fire and returned to find his teen-age girl on the staircase. She was horribly burned. He wrapped the dead child in his overcoat and carried her to the street. There he hailed a cab, got inside and asked to be driven to the Northwestern Station. He boarded a train with the body and rode home to Glenview.

A frantic Mrs. Lulu Bennett searched for her daughter, Gertrude, for hours after the fire. She went home and friends later bore the body of a sixteen-year-old girl, her daughter's age, to her residence. Mrs. Bennett took one look at the body and screamed, "That's not my Gertrude. Take it away, take it away." Her daughter was later found in a morgue.

Relatives searching for loved ones turned Thompson's into bedlam. Louis Wolff, Jr., staggered among the crowds searching for his sister and two nephews. One hysterical woman shrieked, "Have you found Miss Helen McGaughan? She's from the Yale apartments, and—." Another cried out, "I'm looking for a Miss Errett. She's a nurse." A man turned Dr. Vaughan from his sweat-dripping labors, "My little boy, Charles Hennings, have you seen him, doctor?" Appeals and questions swept the restaurant and ran along Randolph Street. "Please go back for my little girl," one woman whose face and hands were almost burned away pleaded with a policeman before she collapsed and was taken to a hospital. "Oh, where's my little Annie?" sobbed another woman supported by two policemen into the restaurant. As she spoke she fell dead.

It took two days for charwomen to sweep up the brains, broken skulls, burned flesh, and human hair from the floors of Thompson's Restaurant. By then 602 Iroquois fire victims were buried, many in common graves. The only member of the show troupe who died in the blaze was Nellie Reed, leader of the Flying Ballet—one of the wires used by this group prevented the curtain from dropping at the fire's onset. Long files of relatives trailed into the police storeroom at 58 Dearborn Street the following Sunday. Here were the effects of the dead waiting to be claimed by relatives.

One woman pointed out a singed prayer book. "There. That's my little boy's."

A well-dressed young man strolled along the wall where dresses and furs of the deceased were hung. Suddenly he grabbed a fur boa and kissed it. "It was hers," he said solemnly. "May I take it with me?"

The Iroquois disaster brought about the arrest of Harry Powers, the manager. Arthur Hull, who lost his wife and three children in the blaze, swore out a warrant for his arrest on manslaughter. Powers was later released, and there was never a trial. Indicted and ordered held for a grand jury were Will J. Davis, president and general manager of the Iroquois; Carter H. Harrison, Chicago's mayor; George Williams, building commissioner; Edward Loughlin, building inspector; William Sallers, the Iroquois fireman; William McMullen, the stage electrician, and James E. Cummings. All, the coroner's jury thought, were responsible. None ever had a trial.

The Iroquois was eventually turned into a vaudeville house, but the stigma of the fire forever left its imprint on the theater. In 1913, writing for *Harper's Weekly,* Agnes Lee, a survivor of the inferno, penned the following maudlin yet memorable verse:

> By a new name they call the house today.
> The balconies of blood are gilded o'er.
> Tardy Precaution writes upon the curtain,
> And lights a beacon lamp at every door.
>
> Where are we? Who hath told us all these things?
> Dreaming with us, till we know and see?
> This is the Iroquois, the house of death.
> Here echoed one united agony,
> Muted how suddenly in char and ember,
> Here, in this very place. The walls remember.
>
> And bright the revel now, and loud the laughter.
> But what is yonder swaying, faltering host?
> Shall this gay vault give mirth alone hereafter?
> No! Hark,—the sobbing of a little ghost!
>
> House evermore to darken thought of man,
> Let some stern Azrael above thy portal
> Attest the sacrifice! Through all thine aisles
> Let stanzas ring, born sounding and immortal!—
> Ah, not the strident slang, the castanets!
> Ah, not the long cheap laughter that forgets!

Even more touching, or at least more chillingly prophetic, were the words of a *Chicago Sun* reporter who on February 13, 1875, twenty-eight years before the Iroquois blaze, predicted a terrible theater fire in Chicago to demonstrate the fire hazards prevalent in the city's theaters. In his futuristic tale the writer described the "smoking ruins down in the heart of the city—ruins of one of the finest theaters in Chicago, which fell prey to the devouring element last night. There are mourning households and rows of dead bodies at the morgue. . . ." A grim fancy in 1875, these words became a realistic epilog.

(ALSO SEE: Baquet, Brooklyn, and Ring Theaters)

IRVING, KANSAS — TORNADO
May 30, 1879

No sooner had the small frontier town of Irving, Kansas, been hit by a tornado at about 5:30 P.M. on May 30, 1879, than a colossal black mass about two miles wide with dozens of tornadoes swirling downward inside it passed over the reeling town. The second mass of twisters leveled every building in the town and killed almost fifty people, the exact number being undetermined.

Those who survived this nightmare described the sky as red and purple, that smoky sulfurous fumes emitted from the raging vortex, that the earth itself heaved about as if rattled by an earthquake, and that they thought, indeed, that "Judgment Day was at hand."

ITALY — EARTHQUAKE
September 8, 1905

background: Beginning at 2:55 A.M. an earthquake rumbled throughout Italy, toppling thousands of buildings and killing an estimated 5,000 persons on September 8, 1905; twenty-five villages were destroyed and ancient Mount Romboli was activated.

At the first moment of the earth's trembling in the predawn hours of September 8, 1905, the populace of southern Italy panicked. In the hardest-hit province of Calabria more than twenty-five villages were utterly destroyed. These included Piscopio, Tripapni, Zammaro, Bratico, Sanfeo, San Constantino and Conidoni. Death tolls soared. Martirano suffered 2,000 casualties. In Parghelia 800 were killed. Lappolo lost 200.

The widespread shocks, lasting an estimated eighteen seconds each, raced through Sicily to southern Italy, and were felt as far north as Naples and Florence. One report stated, "Scenes of indescribable terror ensued. Women roused from sleep rushed half-clothed into the streets screaming with fear. They carried babies, dragging along their other children, and called for help on the Madonna and the saints."

Mobs of berserk residents in a dozen cities ran crazily through the open-air cafes and inexplicably wrecked several of them. In Monte Leone, prisoners in the local jail staged a riot in which several persons were killed. Then the walls of the prison collapsed, burying scores under debris. Dozens more were killed on the island of St. Romboli when the ancient volcanic crater dominating the island was stirred into eruption by the quake. Romboli gave off a shower of stones and lava.

About 20,000 were made homeless by the quake. King Victor Emmanuel promised to send $24,000 in relief funds to the victims. Two days later the king and a large entourage departed Racconigi en route to Calabria to inspect the ruins and "interview" survivors. His train, complete with a gilt-edged private car specially equipped with bathtubs and luxurious dining and sleeping facilities, was forced to return when it was discovered that the quake had torn up a large section of track.

(ALSO SEE: Calabria)

ITAVIA AIRLINES — AIR CRASH
January 1, 1974

Originating in Cagliari, Sardinia, Flight 897 of Itavia Airlines, a twin-engine Fokker 28 jet, smashed into a dairy farm outside of Turin, Italy, on January 1, 1974, killing thirty-nine of the forty-two persons on board. It was never determined whether pilot error or instrument failure caused the crash.

Gianpaolo Sciarra, the flight engineer and a survivor, stated, "Our high precision radar was working regularly when we suddenly heard a heavy blast in the plane's tail. We lost altitude abruptly. . . . The commander tried in vain to regain control of the plane."

The effort proved hopeless. Dropping fast through dense fog, the Fokker lost power. "We were flying in absolute darkness," recalled bricklayer Enrico Isoni, another survivor, "when the fog suddenly scattered, and I saw trees very close to us. One moment later the plane hit a shed and lost a wing." Then the plane skidded more than five hundred yards, struck another building and burst into flames. Four persons stumbled out of the burning wreckage; one died a short time later.

IVANHOE, INDIANA — RAILWAY WRECK
June 22, 1918

background: A troop train of the Michigan Central Railroad, with engineer A. K. Sargent at the throttle, smashed into the rear of the Hagenbeck-Wallace Circus train as it stood in the train yard of Ivanhoe, Indiana, on June 22, 1918. The crash killed fifty-three circus performers. Sargent was accused of falling asleep at the throttle but was later tried and acquitted.

One of the great fears of train management and passengers alike is that an engineer might fall asleep at the

The wreck of the Hagenbeck-Wallace circus train in Ivanhoe, Indiana, June 22, 1918, took the lives of fifty-three performers. *(Chicago Historical Society)*

throttle. This is exactly what happened on the disastrous night of June 22, 1918, at Ivanhoe, Indiana.

Alonzo K. Sargent, an engineer for the Michigan Central Railroad, had been overworked. He had been shuttling troop trains across the country from Chicago to New York for three days.

After leaving a trainload of troops in New York, Sargent was barreling his empty train back to Chicago.

Just outside Ivanhoe, Indiana, the second section of the Hagenbeck-Wallace Circus train (performers and baggage only, the animals already having departed in the first section) was stalled on the tracks.

Over 300 clowns, acrobats, jugglers, animal trainers, dancers, strongmen, aerialists and roustabouts were sleeping in three-tier bunks on the circus train.

Red light signals were flashing all along the route for the awaited troop train to come to a stop.

But Sargent, who later stated at his trial that he had taken some "kidney pills" for a minor ailment, had fallen asleep, and his engine roared on through the train yard at top speed. His fireman, Gus Klauss, was busy feeding the boiler.

When he looked up he saw the rear of the circus train on their track. He threw himself immediately into the coal bin behind the engine.

Sargent awoke just before the impact. He applied the emergency brakes a moment before the collision.

"I was startled by a second crash," Sargent later said. "And then a third and fourth crash as my big engine ripped through coach after coach of the train ahead. I clung to my post, and then it was all over.

"I got down from the cab and looked over the scene."

Klauss jumped down and ran past the dazed and bleeding circus survivors. "He was asleep!" he yelled. "The engineer was asleep!" Fireman Klauss ran, screaming hysterically, into the nearby woods.

The survivors of the crash dazedly watched him go, and then staggered back to help others pinned beneath the crushed steel and splintered wooden coaches.

The next day saw the battered circus performers gather about a mass grave as fifty-three of their coworkers—only three identifiable—were buried.

A van filled with flowers arrived from the greatest showman of them all, George M. Cohan. Even more touching was a single rose and a card reading: "From a little girl who laughed at your show and now cries for you."

Still the show went on that night in Hammond with bandaged performers and talented stars who had rushed from other circuses to fill the void created by the tragedy.

J

JACOB'S CREEK, PENNSYLVANIA — MINE DISASTER December 19, 1907

background: At 11:30 A.M. on December 19, 1907, an explosion tearing through the Darr Mine of the Pittsburgh Coal Company was heard for several miles. Killed were 239 miners; one man escaped alive. The cause of the explosion, though never fully determined, was thought to be the projection of flame into a gaseous and dusty atmosphere by an open light or a blown-out shot.

Every miner of the 239-man crew that worked the Darr Mine at Jacob's Creek, Pennsylvania, was at work deep in the shaft, a distance of almost two miles, when an explosion shook the area on December 19, 1907, at exactly 11:30 A.M. Most of those immediately trapped inside were immigrant Italian and Greek miners, and their situation was hopeless from the beginning.

The mine, operated by the Pittsburgh Coal Company, was almost inaccessible at its mouth, making the work of rescuers doubly difficult. Getting to the mouth of the mine meant using the "sky ferry," a crude wooden basket in which the men pulled themselves, six at a time, from Jacob's Creek to the entrance across a jagged gorge. There had been numerous riots between the Greeks and Italians, shouting in their native languages, over who would use the sky ferry while getting to and from work. The local constabulary, at these times, had been called out with fixed bayonets to restore order.

Following the massive explosion, which was heralded by deep murmurs beneath the surface, there was never a need to argue over the sky ferry's use; all but one of the 239 miners were dead, either asphyxiated or crushed under fallen timbers.

Down in the ramshackle hodge-podge of buildings that made up the impoverished mining community, wives and children heard the explosion and instinctively raced for the mine. Many wives had heard their husbands complain of the pockets of gas hanging heavily in the shafts, and they had predicted just such a mishap.

Living only fifty yards from the mouth of the mine, Mrs. John Campbell, whose husband was the mine foreman, was all but resigned to the disaster. "About 11:30 o'clock," she told a correspondent, "there was a loud report and the dishes in my cupboard and on the table were rattled and knocked out of place, while the glass in the windows was shattered. . . . I knew what had happened. I have for a long time feared an explosion in the mine, for I knew it was gaseous. My husband and I had talked of it, and he often referred to the gas in the mine. My husband was just about due for his dinner when the loud report came, and I looked out the back door toward a manway from the mine, through which he always came to his meals. Instead of my husband I saw a great cloud of dust and smoke pouring out of the mouth of the mine through the manway. It floated upward and disappeared across the river."

As the giant cloud of black smoke rolled over the Youghlogheny River, scores of women and children rushed to the sky ferry and, desperate to reach their loved ones, fought as had their husbands, for use of the rickety basket. They were eventually calmed by the mine's supervisors, who promised to get the miners out quickly. But the only miner to get out quickly and alive was a pumper, Joseph Mapleton, who emerged cut and bruised from a side entry.

"I was near entry twenty-one," he stated later, "when I heard an awful rumbling. I started toward the entry, but the next instant I was blinded, and for a little time I did not know anything. Then I got to the side entry and worked my way out."

After his wounds were dressed, Mapleton joined mine superintendent William Kelvington and fifty others in a futile rescue attempt to get to those trapped below. The roof of the main shaft had collapsed 1,500 feet from the surface, and the fallen debris held up the desperately digging rescuers. When they did break through to the shaft beyond, they found bodies stacked up like cordwood. No one lived.

JAMAICA — FAMINE 1788

After a violent series of hurricanes swept Jamaica in 1788, the island's crops were in ruins. More than 200 of the 775 sugar estates were bankrupt. Scores more were abandoned, and country homes were left to rot in silence. With no work for the more than 25,000 slaves on the island, owners refused to feed them. Though they rioted and killed dozens of whites, the blacks began to die of starvation by the hundreds. One historian estimates that 15,000 black slaves perished in the ensuing six-month-long famine.

JAMESTOWN, VIRGINIA — FIRE-FAMINE 1608

Of the one hundred adventurous persons who established the first English settlement in Jamestown, Virginia, in 1607, sixty-two died of starvation following a devastating fire on January 7, 1607. It obliterated, in the words of Captain John Smith (who was being held prisoner by Indians at the fire's outbreak), "most of our apparel, lodging and private provision. . . . Many of our old men diseased, and our new, for want of lodging, perished."

The bitter winter to which the colony was exposed took dozens of lives as the threadbare settlers simply froze to death on empty stomachs.

JANET — HURRICANE September 22-28, 1955

background: Originating off Venezuela, Janet wrecked the Navy Station at Swan Island, moved on to Honduras where 200 were killed, and slashed across the Mexican coastal areas, killing another 300. Veracruz and Tampico were hardest hit by 114 m.p.h. winds. More than 60,000 persons were made homeless by this wide-ranging storm and unestimated millions of dollars in damages done. Janet finally dissipated in the Gulf of Mexico.

Pilot G. B. Windham, maneuvering his Navy Neptune plane only 700 feet above the swirling storm mass, was the first to describe the monster hurricane, Janet, on September 26, 1955. He, eight other crew men and two news photographers flew into the eye of the hurricane and sent back reports to Hurricane Hunter Squadron in Jacksonville, Florida. Early the next morning, caught in 150 m.p.h. winds in Janet's eyewall, all transmissions from the large plane ceased, and the nine disappeared forever, the first known victims of this hurricane.

Hours later, the Navy and United States Weather Bureau personnel based on tiny Swan Island off Cape Gracias a Dios found themselves directly in Janet's path. The hurricane pancaked every building on the island and snapped every one of its 10,000 cocoanut trees in half. The station was later evacuated.

From there Janet roared on to Honduras, demolishing the city of Corozal. An estimated 200 persons were killed. Hugging the coast and whipping winds at about 114 m.p.h., Janet next struck Mexico. Shaky huts with thatched roofs in the Yucatan, particularly in the ancient town of Chetumal, were thrown down by the thousands; the Quintana Roo district was awash, and after Veracruz had been struck by the hurricane, Janet drove wildly into

Chetumel City, Mexico, was only one of the regions destroyed by hurricane Janet in September 1955. The hurricane claimed 500 dead and made 60,000 homeless. *(UPI)*

Tampico and literally exploded countless houses, making 60,000 homeless, many of whom took to trees and the scant buildings that survived the storm's heavy seas. When the Tamesi and Panuco rivers flooded, jumbles of poisonous snakes were washed into village streets, and scores met death through snakebite.

Relief eventually came from the Mexican government, the United States Army and Air Force, the Salvation Army, and the Red Cross, but by then 509 persons were dead in the stricken areas, and hurricane Janet had blown herself out in the gulf.

JAPAN **TSUNAMI**
1737

An earthquake precipitated the *tsunami* that rushed inland along the Japanese coast from Yezo Island to the northern part of Kamchatka, destroying the town of Kamaishi, and killing thousands. In this 1737 *tsunami* one expert reported the height of the wave striking Cape Lopatka to be an unbelievable 210 feet.

JAPAN **EARTHQUAKE-TSUNAMI**
December 22, 1854

An earthquake striking central Honshu on December 22, 1854, utterly destroyed the cities of Tokaido, Shikoku and Osaka. About 60,000 buildings were toppled and more than 3,000 persons were killed. An enormous *tsunami* followed, the wave estimated to be between fifty and seventy-five feet high.

One of the first and most dramatic eyewitness reports of the *tsunami* came from an officer on board *La Diane,* a frigate anchored in Simoda Bay. The seaman wrote, "We feit the first shock at 9:15 A.M.; it was very strong, and it went on for two or three minutes. At ten o'clock a huge wave rushed into the bay, and within a few minutes the whole town was under water; the many ships at anchor were thrown against one another and seriously damaged—we immediately saw a great deal of debris floating. At the end of five minutes the water in the bay swelled and began boiling up, as if thousands of springs had suddenly broken out; the water was mixed with mud, straw, and every kind of rubbish, and it hurled itself upon the town and the land to either side with shocking force; all the houses were wiped out. At 11:15 the frigate dragged her anchors and lost one of them; presently she lost the other, and the ship was then whirled around and swept along with a strength that grew greater with the ever increasing speed of the water. At the same time thick clouds of vapor covered the site of the town, and the air was filled with sulfurous exhalations. The rise and fall of the water in this narrow bay was such that it caused several whirlpools, among which the frigate spun round with such force that everything on board was thrown down. Yet the frigate held her own in the midst of these gyrations; she turned clean around forty-three times, but not without sustaining serious damage. Until noon the rising up and the falling of the water in the bay did not cease; the level varied from eight to forty feet in height. Towards two o'clock the bottom of the sea rose again, and so violently that several times the frigate was laid over, and the anchor was seen in no more than four feet of water. At last the sea grew calm. The frigate floated in the middle of an inextricable tangle of her own rigging and twisted chains. The bay was nothing more than an expanse of ruins."

JAPAN **EARTHQUAKE**
October 28, 1891

In respect to land masses, Japan is considered one of the most unstable; the island chain has been plagued by earthquakes. Japanese historians, though sketchy on detail, over a period of nearly 1,500 years recorded a total of 223 destructive earthquakes. One of the most damaging occurred on October 28, 1891, in which an area of 243,000 square miles was shaken, encompassing three-fifths of Japan's entire area.

The stroke lasted only thirty seconds but 6,000 persons were killed outright, another 1,000 died of injuries in the following weeks, 17,000 more were seriously harmed, and 20,000 buildings (not the most sturdy constructions) were flattened.

JAPAN **TSUNAMI**
June 15, 1896

background: At about 8:30 P.M. on June 15, 1896, a seismic seawave (*tsunami*), following a minor earthquake by almost eight hours, struck the northeastern coast of Japan, hitting an area 170 miles long, and sweeping inland for almost 100 miles. The *tsunami* was estimated to be from thirty to a hundred feet in height, although three colossal waves were recorded. More than 28,000 were drowned, crushed by fallen structures, or pierced by debris driven by water estimated to be traveling at 500 m.p.h. Injured were about 50,000 persons, and tens of thousands of dwellings were destroyed; whole seacoast villages and towns in some instances were swept away.

The most feared phenomenon in Japan's long history of disasters is the *tsunami,* the enormous seawaves that are generated by seismic or underwater earthquakes and run beneath the surface of the oceans. One of the most violent and destructive of these seismic seawaves struck the Japanese coastal areas, particularly devastating the Sanriku district, on June 15, 1896.

A seacoast ceremony, known as the "Boy's Festival," was being held along the northeastern coast of Japan. Thousands of people gathered on the sandy shores to celebrate. At about noon, a distinct earthquake shock was felt trembling along the coast. Although the populace was conditioned to as many as three earth tremors a day in some years (more than 1,200 quakes had been recorded in this area in 1880 alone), most of the crowds dispersed, moving off to the nearby hills overlooking the ocean, which appeared calm. Quiet rain began to drizzle, and the sky blackened, but no great storm was unleashed. By dusk the sky cleared and thousands of persons marveled at the beautiful sunset as they moved back to the shores to complete the festival.

It was between 8:20 and 8:30 P.M. when the *tsunami* struck, catching more than 50,000 celebrants unaware. Of the 15,000 earthquakes along this coast, only 124 had been accompanied by seismic seawaves, and most of them had caused only minor damage. The 1896 *tsunami,* on the other hand, brought horror, destruction, and death.

At first the people on shore heard a large booming noise, as if an army of cannons was being fired simultaneously. Then came an eerie hissing sound. The water at the shore sucked back hundreds of yards into the ocean, and then emerged the roaring, crashing *tsunami,* the first wave coming inland at 500 m.p.h. like a giant water plow. As terrified thousands raced for the hills beyond, the water dashed forward, catching multitudes in its path. Nothing stopped the wave as it swallowed the earth for almost a hundred miles inland.

In distant Kobe the tail of the first wave slapped the steamers *Kawanoura Maru* and *Hozui Maru* together, sinking them and drowning 178 men aboard both ships. In the center of destruction one town after another was engulfed by the monster and obliterated. The seaside town of Kamaishi disappeared under thunderous thirty-foot waves, overpowering and killing 4,700 out of 6,557 people; only 143 buildings out of 4,223 remained partially standing.

Five miles farther north 600 persons died in the village of Futalshi; only 100 survived. At Yamada 3,000 out of 4,200 persons were killed. In Toni 1,103 out of 1,200 perished. The Kissen district lost one town and eleven villages; more than 6,000 were drowned and crushed. In the Iwate district one out of every three persons was either killed or injured. At Hashikami 400 died. At Quani Mura another 400 were killed. At Koldzumi 1,450 were lost to the waves. More than 600 vanished in Ctatsu.

Escapes were weird and miraculous. Scores of people swept out to sea in one area were thrown, alive, across the bay and onto the opposite beach. At the village of Hongo every person in the hamlet, 150 in all, was instantly killed under the *tsunami's* crush except for a group of old villagers playing the ancient Japanese game of "Go" high in a hilltop temple. Several people were torn from the Sanriku beaches and carried out to sea and deposited unharmed on an island.

People clung to timber or the debris of wrecked buildings and somehow managed to live. A father threw his six children onto the rafters of his home in Kuji as the water rushed through the building. One, the youngest, fell off and was swept away. The father swam desperately after the child, and both disappeared. The remaining five lived. In one area parents ran up a hill to deposit scores of children and then raced down again to save other children. All of the parents drowned, leaving the lonely peak crowned with naked, screaming orphans.

An old soldier in Washigami, so the story goes, when first hearing the booming voice of the onrushing *tsunami,* thought foreign troops were again invading the land from the sea and rushed to the beach sword in hand to repel them. He was later found on a small hill several miles inland. The wave had somehow wrenched the sword from his hand and driven it through him.

Ironically hundreds of fishing boats at sea when the *tsunami* struck the land were hardly disturbed. The fishermen later stated that they felt only a slight disturbance beneath their crafts, but that when they attempted to reach shore, huge waves drove them back. Hours later one fishermen spotted what he thought to be a large, dead fish floating near him. Coming upon it he discovered that it was a live baby floating on a mat. Dozens of children were rescued this way. One fisherman plucked his own sputtering son from the waters. But for most of the fishing fleets, there was the horror of discovering the dead, many times even the bodies of their own families, drifting out to meet the incoming boats.

For two days the living struggled with 170 miles of torn coastline, digging out bodies wedged beneath slivered debris. Houses were telescoped into each other, turned upside down, shattered. Wedged beneath and between rocks were the stinking carcasses of cattle and horses. Thousands wandered about aimlessly as if afflicted by mass aphasia, not even bothering to seek out their lost relatives. Bodies were piled in heaps and then mud was thrown over them. The bodies of men below the volcano Bandaisan collected in hideous mounds. They had been torn apart, limbs, torsos, heads rolling and awkwardly mingling with other pieces of torn flesh in the bloody waters. Though recovered only a few hours after the *tsunami* struck, the bodies appeared as though they had been decomposing for weeks.

According to one correspondent, "The wounds suffered by the survivors and shown by the bodies of the dead are of a shocking description. In some cases, the flesh is torn into shreds, exposing the bones beneath; in others the eyes are forced out of their sockets; in others the trunks seem to have been wrenched asunder by forces acting in opposite directions; in others the victim looks as though it had been plunged in boiling water and almost every body shows purple spots as if it had been fiercely pelted with fragments of stone or iron."

More than 28,000 people were dead, killed by the *tsunami* in the space of five terrible minutes. Had the festival-goers remained in the hills to which they originally retreated when they first felt the minor earth tremor, the immense loss of life would never have occurred. The historic reflex of the Japanese people to earthquakes, however, almost insured the slaughter. Months later Professor John Milne and others determined that the walls of the undersea crater known as the Tuscarora Deep (latitude: 44.50; longitude: 152.30), almost five and a half miles under the Pacific's surface, had collapsed and sent out the killer *tsunami* at jet speed beneath the waves while thousands looked out over the seemingly serene seas blessing their festival.

JAPAN — EARTHQUAKE-FIRE
September 1-3, 1923

background: Known as the Great Kwanto Earthquake, the shock registered 8.2 on several scales on September 1, 1923, and obliterated 600,000 houses in the Tokyo-Yokohama region, shaking the whole of the Great Eastern Plain. Preceded by a typhoon, the earthquake caused uncontrollable fires to break out, consuming vast areas of several cities. More than 143,000 persons were killed, mostly by fire, (although the first official death count released by the Japanese authorities listed 99,330); 200,000 were injured and a half million were made homeless.

It was precisely noon, Saturday, September 1, 1923, and most of the sprawling megalopolis of Yokohama-Tokyo was buzzing with activity. Tens of thousands of businessmen were at work in the almost endless three-story buildings housing their firms. Women in lightly built homes were lighting charcoal braziers to heat the noonday meal. Vacationers lined up at stalls and stations where trains began to take them aboard en route to seaside weekends. Then the tremors began.

The fluttering of instruments at Tokyo Imperial University did not, at first, alarm the watching seismologists. But as the seconds ticked off, the shocks increased until the machines went berserk and the scientists fell back in awe. The Great Kwanto Earthquake had commenced. Beyond Tokyo and Yokohama all points stretching across the Great Eastern Plain pitched and rolled like ocean water, the land, hills and mountains undulating crazily.

Millions of people, as they had been taught since childhood in this earthquake-prone land, rose as one and made for the streets, their homes and offices swaying frantically about them. Masses of people gathered and stared toward the Akasaka Palace where their emperor-god resided. Many among their numbers still believed that an unearthly catfish at the ocean floor beneath Japan had wriggled his enormous hump upon orders of the sun goddess, who was displeased with the reigning emperor, her deity son, in this case the sick, lame-duck Emperor Taisho whose twenty-three-year-old son, Hirohito, was regent. To many minds the Kwanto quake immediately called, as in times of antiquity, for the emperor's resignation in response to the sun goddess' displeasure of his rule. Hirohito was to bloody his hands in getting around that face-demolishing penance.

The sword-rattling Hirohito emerged from his earthquake-proof, two-story conference building of concrete and steel (built by the Shankland firm of Chicago) to see Tokyo toppling to the ground. Hordes of police rushed to encircle the imperial grounds to prevent screaming masses of people from entering the formal gardens in search of water for the great fire that had already begun.

Gone in the quake were Tokyo's tallest buildings. The recently constructed twelve-story Tokyo Tower broke like a matchstick and spilled all its occupants into the street. The Yokohama Club disintegrated. Monuments like the gigantic bronze Buddha standing fifty feet high in the fire-gutted seaside resort of Kamakura split at its base and fell forward. Fires fanned by a rainless typhoon that had been blowing all morning raced through the city, sending thousands sprinting directionless for safety.

A *Japan Chronicle* reporter watched the frantic residents attempt to escape the rising inferno engulfing both Yokohama and Tokyo. "Some had gained the streets and escaped the direct flames. Their bodies lay almost entire, but with cruel blisters. Theirs must have been a far greater agony than that of others whose remains are but charred fragments—perhaps just a bit of blackened skull visible amid piled-up bricks and twisted wire and shop goods. How many are buried in that tangled mass? No one will ever know. But already the stench is high, especially around the canal to which scores had run in vain hope of safety."

An American woman seeing friends off on the steamship *Empress of Australia* anchored in Yokohama harbor later related in the *Outlook:* "Suddenly the ground gave way with a violent crash. We were knocked against each other like ninepins. It was terrific. Both ends of the dock sank under water, leaving us stranded on a little island in the middle. Luckily, it was low tide and we managed to wade ashore. Fires were blazing everywhere and a dense pall of smoke was over everything. We saw the bottom coming up in places in the harbor. Half the breakwater had gone."

The center of Tokyo was in ruins following the earthquake that shook Japan's Great Eastern Plain; 143,000 officially died in the 1923 quake and resulting fires. *(Wide World)*

About to get under way, the *Empress of Australia* rose high in the bubbling waters. On deck Dr. T. D. A. Cockerell, a visiting professor of zoology from the University of Colorado, had noticed the colorful streamers connecting the departing passengers with their friends on the wharf. He looked to the wharf to see the waving handkerchiefs and hats as the quake erupted and the harbor rose. He felt "the great vessel violently shaken by some unseen force. At first simply bewildered, we realized what had happened when someone said 'Earthquake.' Looking toward the city, we saw clouds of dust; looking downward, the wharf had collapsed at either end, fortunately remaining in the middle, so that very few people were thrown into the water. The crowd below us did not seem at first to realize the magnitude of the disaster, but went on cheering and waving for a few moments, and then scattered, to make their way with difficulty along the half-submerged railings to the shore. The *Empress* made no attempt to leave; in fact, the propeller had got tangled up in the anchor chain of a merchant vessel just behind, and she was disabled. Soon fires were seen, and the wind, blowing from the shore, became exceedingly violent, so that before long the whole town [Yokohama] was ablaze."

Cockerell and the other passengers saw the wharves and warehouses along the waterfront burst into towering jets of fire. Crew men on the *Empress* broke out firehoses and sprayed the decks and sides of the ship onto which chirled huge firebrands and showers of sparks. Barges and hundreds of small ships were ablaze. The bay was suddenly full of thousands of swimmers escaping the heat and flames and calling for help. More than 2,000 were pulled aboard the *Empress*.

Following the earthquake, typhoon and fire, another calamity occurred at 4:00 P.M.: a snorting tornado ran down the Sumida River crushing the small boats laden with fire-singed survivors and cupping flames from the burning Higher Polytechnic School at Kuramaye and depositing balls of fire on the opposite shore, these feeding rapidly on the enormous flammable stores in the Military Clothing Depot, gulping up the stacks of uniforms with which Hirohito planned to dress his armies for world conquest.

Occupying several blocks, the depot was situated in the Honjo Ward, which had been relatively untouched by the fire to this time. More than 40,000 scrambling, panic-driven residents sought safety here. The fire trapped them in a cage of flames, and only a dozen or so blistered persons emerged from this oven hours later.

Seven Japanese prefectures were ripped wide by the quake, as fire tore through the area. The earth had actually somersaulted in many areas, flopped over as one would toss a pancake. Near the village of Chigasaki, a bridge built in A.D. 1182 and long since sunken in tons of mud emerged almost intact. Vegetables from carefully cultivated gardens were flung through windows by the quake. Landslides occurred, a whole forest in one instance shearing away from Mount Tanzawa at 60 m.p.h., sliding down a valley and steamrolling a village and a railway until the whole, shuddering mass of speeding human flesh and debris was deposited into Sagami Bay, changing to blood red for miles around.

At Nebukawa station a passenger train en route to Manazuru with 200 persons on board was slapped by a wall of mud and water, and the landslide, 200 yards wide and 50 feet deep, carried the train with all on board and the entire village into Sagami Bay; no one was ever seen again. Villages and hamlets by the score were buried under 100 feet of landsliding earth in many spots.

Henry W. Kinney, editor of the *Trans-Pacific* magazine, was caught by the quake and fire while waiting for a train in the Tokyo suburb of Omori. He managed to get across the Tamagawa River Bridge just before it collapsed in flames. While walking to safety he noticed large factories in ruins with feet, heads and hands jutting from the fire-torn ruins. In the large town of Kawasaki, Kinney saw every home in a shambles, heavy tile roofs, paper windows and wooden sides shredded and jumbled together. Outside of the village of Higashikanagawa, Kinney winced at the lethargy embodied in the quilt-padded survivors. Their expressionless faces and monolithic movements reminded him of the Japanese phrase *shikataganai* (it can't be helped). Kinney later described this awful resignation in the *Atlantic* magazine: "Men sat stolidly and watched fires creep onward, which they might in many cases have stopped with little effort. They might have saved entire blocks had they tried, had they had a little leadership. There was another conspicuous feature, the utter lack of leadership. The Japanese official, in ordinary life ubiquitous and often obnoxious with his fussy exactions, seemed to have vanished from the earth—even the police."

From a jagged ridge Kinney saw through hazy clouds of drifting smoke what was left of Yokohama. Where once a half million people resided, a pleasure-pot for foreigners, a magnificently tailored garden for wealthy Japanese businessmen, a glittering nighttime seaport that was the very essence of the exotic charm and bizarre adventure that the Orient offered, was gone.

Kinney related that "the lurid panorama lay outfolded before us—but it was meaningless . . . there were no landmarks, no familiar buildings from which one might determine locality. Yokohama . . . had become a vast plain of fire, of red, devouring sheets of flame which played and flickered. Here and there a remnant of a building, a few shattered walls, stood up like rocks above the expanse of flame, unrecognizable. There seemed to be nothing left to burn. It was as if the very earth were now burning. It presented exactly the aspect of a gigantic pudding over which the spirits were blazing, devouring everything."

On the ridge survived a small beershop and to this establishment, oddly enough still serving drinks as usual, staggered groups of businessmen, their expensive suits ripped and torn, holes in the knees from shoving their furniture out of the fire paths. As the flames from the city ate their way up the ridge, the exhausted men sipped beer and told of their experiences in the catastrophe that still had two days to play itself out.

One Japanese businessman described his entire office building as being tossed about by the quake like "a bucking horse," which hurled him fortuitously from his chair just as a massive safe smashed through the wall where he had been sitting. He and his employees vaulted down the stairs and escaped to the street only seconds before the earth opened up and the building disappeared with a grating crunch into a steaming fissure. The businessman shakily made his way down the street as two more heavy shakes tugged at his legs and sent him sprawling. But there was no street left, only ruins to scramble around and over "where, only two minutes before, had been our city, the town that I have seen grow into a modern city since I was a boy." This man, educated in Western universities and part of the international community that made up Yokohama, drank his beer and lamented, "And all over were people, people one knew, whom one had danced with, dined with, played bridge with, reduced in a moment, to the uttermost depth of despair, standing, crying wildly, by the ruins, clawing at them, desperately, to reach others caught under the bricks; and already, here and there, the flames were leaping forth, coming closer and closer, while the poor wretches were yelling for help."

In the low-lying waterfront and business districts of Yokohama, thousands were trapped by the fire. In one park area hundreds dove into pools and sat with only their heads above water. The burning debris that flew overhead was so thick that almost everyone's hair caught fire. To put out the blazes, people next to those afflicted slapped huge gobs of wet mud on their heads. Hundreds were crushed in Totsuka Station when trains toppled on them. In Yokohama Park 24,000 people fleeing the flames were surrounded by them and roasted to death. Those who dove into the vaporizing lagoon were boiled to death.

Tokyo and its citizens fared the same, although several buildings of more modern construction, the Mitsubishi Bank, the Russo-Asiatic Bank and the Imperial Hotel, the latter designed by the American architect, Frank Lloyd Wright, survived the holocaust. Wright had become earthquake-conscious following the San Francisco disaster and had insisted that the Imperial Hotel be constructed of steel frames connected to bedrock that would expand and contract, with diagonal supports to protect against lateral movement in the event of an earthquake. In effect his building floated on top of the quake. Wright's visionary precaution also included a large ornamental pool situated in front of the hotel. Ironically it was from this reservoir that much-needed water was pumped to save the Imperial and adjoining buildings from the flames.

The blaze did its worst damage at the waterfront, where thousands had fled to leap into the water and cling to debris and the sides of ships. For hours these survivors considered themselves fortunate. Then the nearby Standard Oil Building and the oil reserves near its base exploded. More than 100,000 tons of oil escaped into Yokohama Bay, catching fire and burning in great puddles that immolated thousands thrashing in the water.

When a swirling low-pressure front swept across Tokyo, clearing the city of smoke, 39,000 dead were found littering the streets and shelled buildings. Some of these were the 1,500 prisoners let out of Ichigaya Prison at the last moment. To guard against these and other potential looters, Hirohito and his staff had sent 500 carrier pigeons (the telegraph lines were out for two days) to Osaka and other areas requesting 35,000 troops to patrol the smashed, burned-out cities. There was little looting, however, since thieves quickly discovered that the cash and jewelry taken from the charred dead gave off a distinctively pungent odor that allowed authorities to track them down. Anyone found with such odorous valuables was arrested; some were killed on the spot.

Killing at the hands of police and the military under Hirohito's orders (as always, given indirectly through subordinates who fanatically assumed all responsibility) followed the Great Kwanto Earthquake. In his masterful study, *Japan's Imperial Conspiracy,* David Bergamini pointed out how, to absolve the throne of unworthy rule as deigned by superstition, Regent Hirohito declared martial law through General Masataro Fukuda, and then, incredible as it may seem to the Western mind but perfectly in keeping with the legend-fearing Japanese, explained that the much-hated Koreans and socialists "had offended the spirits before the earthquake and were taking advantage of the disaster by setting fires and pillaging shops." (In the September 19, 1923, edition of *The Outlook,* its editors, then as unsuspecting as most of the "informed" West, published a letter from an American woman in Yokohama during the disaster, a dupe and tool, really, for Hirohito's political pogrom, which read: "Late at night we got to the outskirts of the city . . . people were lying along the roadside in all conditions, dead, maimed, and stunned. A man screamed at us in English: 'The Koreans are looting!' ")

About 4,000 hapless Koreans were rounded up from the slums of Tokyo by the militaristic Black Dragon Society, and then, after mock street trials punctured by fanatical jeers and hootings, were beheaded in full view of the quake survivors, who may or may not have taken pleasurable vengeance in having living creatures to kill in mighty retort to an uncontrollable rampage of nature. Further, Bergamini discovered, a socialist orator, Osugi Sakae, who had encouraged terrified crowds to break through the police lines to avoid the fire and wade into the imperial pools of the palace by shouting "Remember Russia, and never lay down your arms!" was arrested with his wife and seven-year-old nephew and thrown into a secret police dungeon with the blessing of Hirohito, again using the disaster to eliminate a political foe. A sadistic police captain named Masahiko Amakasu strangled all three in their cells a few days later. Though his murders were unveiled, the killer was leniently sentenced to ten years in prison for infanticide, a sentence that through Hirohito was quietly reduced to three years; upon his release, Amakasu received funds from a "friend of the throne" and departed for Europe.

Japan's cool-headed scientists, however, knew that the causes of the quake and fire that killed more than 143,000 people emanated from less mythical regions than the legendary waters of sea monsters or the machinations of imaginary political foes. The Japanese coastal area about Kenasiyama had actually slid eight or more feet into the ocean at the instigation of an underwater quake. With the governmental establishment of the Earthquake Research Institute at the University of Tokyo immediately following the quake, its sponsor, Hirohito, privately made the same admission while publicly pointing a ridiculous, accusing finger at political scapegoats.

(ALSO SEE: Agadir, Morocco; San Francisco, Calif.)

JAPAN **LANDSLIDES-FLOODS**
July 18-19, 1964

Torrential rains followed a minor earthquake in Niigata, Japan, that devastated the five prefectures along the coast of the Sea of Japan on July 18-19, 1964. As rivers became swollen 150 bridges collapsed, and dikes that had held for fifty years broke in more than 200 places. Houses crumbled in Ishikawa, Toyamma, Niigata, Tottori and Shimane, 295 by police count.

Landslides abruptly destroyed several villages, and the death toll climbed to 108 persons, with 233 people injured and about 44,000 made homeless.

JAPAN **FLOODS-LANDSLIDES**
July 17, 1972

Heavy rains falling for close to a week deluged large sections of Japan and created floods in most of the provinces. The rushing waters eroded large sections of earth, and landslides by the dozens occurred, killing a known 370 persons, mostly in farming districts. Another 70 persons were never found, according to police officials who estimated $472 million in building and crop losses.

Jumbled debris is all that remained of Amakusa, Japan, one of the many towns in that country destroyed by landslides on July 17, 1972. *(UPI)*

JAPAN AIRLINES **AIR CRASH**
June 14, 1972

Approaching New Delhi's Palam International Airport on the night of June 14, 1972, a Japan Airlines DC-8 jet suddenly caught fire and crashed, splattering its seventy-eight passengers and eleven crew members and wreckage over two miles. According to terrified villagers the aircraft suddenly caught fire as the pilot was about to land and hurtled itself downward onto farmland next to the banks of the Jamuna River, which flows into New Delhi.

Rescuers found fourteen persons still alive when they arrived at the wreck, but eight died before they reached the hospital. The total count of dead was eighty-seven, and, although the Japanese officials sent to investigate the crash would not rule out sabotage (the crash followed by two weeks the massacre by Japanese terrorists of twenty-five persons in Tel Aviv's International Airport), no cause of the plane's breakup was ever officially filed.

Only a burned-out fragment of the fuselage remained of a Japan Airlines DC-8 jet that crashed near New Delhi, India, on June 14, 1972. Eighty-seven people were incinerated *(Wide World)*

JAVA **EARTHQUAKE**
1772

Early in 1772 the natives living in populous Papandayang on the slopes of a great mountain in Java began to hear and feel minor earth tremors. In spring the rumblings increased, and more than 2,000 persons were suddenly caught by a violent earthquake that split Papandayang Mountain and caused an area fifteen miles long and six miles wide to sink, forming a gigantic crater. The town was wiped out to a person and the mountain disappeared.

One historian, William A. Garesche, described the scene in graphic terms, "No day of judgment painted by Angelo or Dore could ever match that actual horror of the solid mountain sinking into the earth with human beings on its slopes—its huge bulk going down as a ship goes down into the deep."

JAY, FLORIDA

EXPLOSION
July 16, 1967

Poor safety regulations, along with poorer supervision, led to the deaths of thirty-seven inmates in the prison camp at Jay, Florida, on July 16, 1967. Two convicts got into a heated argument that led to a bloody fistfight. About fifty other prisoners gathered to view the slugfest, and according to one report guards did not interfere.

During the course of the brawl, the two men, hurtling themselves about, managed to break a gas line and a fluorescent lamp that ignited the gas and led to a terrific explosion that shattered the prison building and sent bodies flying a hundred yards.

JEREMIE, HAITI

HURRICANE-FLOOD
October 25, 1935

Following an enormous, sluggishly moving hurricane that smashed and crushed its way across Haiti, the province of Jeremie suffered widespread floods on October 25, 1935, as the Grande Anse, Voldrogue, and Roseau rivers sloshed over their banks. Dozens of small villages along the routes of these rivers were simply wiped out; hundreds of bodies floated along the estuaries to the sea never to be reclaimed.

The towns of Jeremie and Jacmel were severely struck by the onrushing floods, and these two valley cities were quickly inundated. More than 2,000 persons in these two towns and in other villages were estimated to be lost. A lone pilot flying above the racing floodwaters described the body-bloated rivers as "gripping fingers of watery death that reached out for anything living."

Immediate relief for almost 50,000 homeless storm victims was nonexistent except for the appearance of the hurricane-battered Standard Fruit steamer *Truxton* en route from Cuba, which managed to supply a little food and medicine.

The hurricane that struck Haiti had also rolled over Managua, Nicaragua and Tegucigalpa, Honduras, wiping out the banana crops and killing a score of field workers.

JESSORE, BANGLADESH

RAILWAY WRECK
June 4, 1972

Speeding from Khulna, a port town to the south, an express train loaded beyond its capacity with passengers barreled into the city of Jessore, Bangladesh, on June 4, 1972, carrying more than six hundred persons. Without

A gigantic explosion triggered during a fistfight between prisoners at the crudely-built prison camp at Jay, Florida, resulted in the deaths of thirty-seven inmates on July 16, 1967. *(Wide World)*

stopping, it smashed into another train standing still in the station. Striking the stopped train at full speed, the express broke to pieces, its locomotive and tender hurtling off the track, ten coaches telescoping into the other train.

Seventy-six passengers were immediately killed, and another five hundred on both trains received serious injuries. Upon investigation authorities discovered that the express had been directed onto the wrong track by a stationmaster.

JOELMA BANK BUILDING — FIRE
February 1, 1974

background: The newly completed (1973) twenty-five-story Joelma Bank Building housing the Crefisul Investment Bank in Sao Paulo, Brazil, caught fire on the twelfth floor on the morning of February 1, 1974, trapping about 500 office employees, killing 177, and injuring hundreds more; the cause of the fire was a short-circuit in an air-conditioning system.

"Most of the victims were cooked," sadly commented Sao Paulo's fire chief, Jonas Flores Ribeiro, Jr., while still looking at the smoking remains of the Joelma Bank Building on February 1, 1974. Dead at his feet were 177 persons cruelly trapped by the fire that broke out on the twelfth floor of the twenty-five-story building. It was caused by a short-circuit in an air-conditioning duct under repair.

A janitor, Edivaldo Almeida, was the first to spot the fire shooting out of the air-conditioning unit. "I grabbed a fire extinguisher, but it was too late," he told reporters later. "I ran down the stairs and I saw a desperate crowd running frantically trying to get out. Many people were trampled."

Of the more than 1,000 employees working regularly in the Joelma Bank Building, only 500 had arrived when the blaze started. With the first ten floors of the building occupied by automatic parking facilities, almost all the employees were trapped on the upper floors. For many there was no escape. Safety measures had been shunted aside in the building's construction; there was no fire escape and no landing pad for helicopters on the roof, deficiencies angrily decried by Sao Paulo Mayor Miguel Colasuonno. The mayor had, for weeks, openly criticized the use of flammable plastic materials in the building's construction, and it was this material, stacked high around the faulty air-conditioning unit, that caught and spread the fire.

Dozens of fire department units arrived at the burning building within minutes of the first alarm, but their efforts were impeded by the huge throng, estimated to be more than 10,000 curious spectators, filling the streets.

This towering inferno was the Joelma Building in downtown Sao Paulo, Brazil, on February 1, 1974. *(UPI)*

Fire department ladders were all but useless, reaching only to the seventh floor.

As terrified people crowded the large windows, moving out onto small ledges, shrieking and beating out flames on their clothes and in their hair, citizens and firemen below quickly made large signs and held them up. Some read: "Be Calm," "Don't Jump," "Danger Is Past." "Wait," "Firemen Here."

But the signs did not comfort those tortured and burning in the flames, forced half mad by the heat and tongues of fire that drove them farther and farther out on the small platforms. Some tried to lower themselves on sheets to the window platforms below and fell. One man fell on a ladder and knocked two firemen off. All three were killed. "People became desperate and jumped from the building," stated police colonel Teodore Cabete, "when they saw that our ladders could not reach them."

The street crowd groaned as a woman, her entire body blackened by smoke and flame, appeared at the fifteenth floor window with a baby in her arms. She leaped as flames roared at her back, and in her fall she held the child so that she absorbed the complete impact when hitting the street. The fall killed her, but the infant taken from her grasp was alive.

One of the lucky ones, Joao Alberto Moretti, found himself hemmed in by flames on the thirteenth floor. He looked down to see the ladder fully extended beneath him reaching only to the seventh floor. He let himself down by swinging inward by the arms to drop onto six window ledges until he reached the ladder and safety.

One of the 177 victims of the Joelma Building fire falls screaming to earth. *(UPI)*

About twenty-five persons took their chances by jumping several floors to the roof of an adjacent building. All were killed, several falling on top of others. Eighty persons made it to the roof of the Joelma Bank Building and stood pleading with hovering helicopters, ordered to lift them off by Brazilian state governor Laudo Natel. The smoke was so dense that the choppers could not land. Their pilots did drop containers of cold milk to those on the roof, shouting to them to drink as much as they could. (Firemen later pointed out that milk has detoxifying properties.)

The fire raged for four hours, gutting one floor after another, as groups of running employees sought shelter. Thirty-four persons locked themselves into a washroom and turned on the water taps, which soon dribbled out; later they were found suffocated. Scores had raced to the elevators and were burned to ashes. Their remains were later taken out in burial urns.

A giant Brazilian air force helicopter finally managed to set down on the fast-weakening roof and, in a series of quick takeoffs and landings, removed eighty-five people. The roof caved in only moments after the chopper took off the last ten persons.

The staggering death count of 177 persons (293 others were treated for serious burns) far surpassed Sao Paulo's Andraus Building blaze on February 24, 1972, in which 16 persons perished, and almost equaled in infamy the inferno that destroyed Brazil's Gran Circo Norte-Americano on December 17, 1961, when 323 people, mostly children, burned to death.

(ALSO SEE: Gran Circo Norte-Americano)

Five hundred office employees were trapped on the high ledges of the blazing Joelma Building. These men moments later fell to the street. *(UPI)*

JOHNSTOWN, PENNSYLVANIA — FLOOD — May 31, 1889

background: The famous Johnstown flood began at 3:00 P.M. on May 31, 1889, when the South Fork Reservoir, twelve miles above Johnstown, located in the western Pennsylvania mountains, broke through its dam (an earth dam approximately 1,000 feet long, 100 feet high, 90 feet thick at base and 20 feet thick at top) releasing through a 450-foot breach, at a peak rate of 400,000 cubic feet per second, 4.5 billion gallons of water weighing 20 million tons down the gorge, sweeping to ruins the towns of South Fork, Mineral Point, Woodvale, East Conemaugh, Gautier Mills (also known as Cambria, a borough of Johnstown) and Johnstown, traveling from an elevation of 400 feet above Johnstown. The number of deaths varies according to different reports; most place the dead at 2,500, but some claim that as many as 7,000 perished in the flash flood. Damage estimates ran beyond $17 million, a conservative figure.

The broken South Fork Dam as seen from inside the empty reservoir. *(Harper's Weekly)*

There was a running joke in the booming steel and wire city of Johnstown, Pennsylvania, which for several decades experienced minor floods of the Conemaugh River and its tributary, Stony Creek. At the first appearance of water in the streets, people echoed the same tired line, "The dam has busted—take to the hills!" And they laughed.

The dam at the top of the gorge, twelve miles distant, had always been a leaky, ludicrous affair. It held back Conemaugh Lake, placid waters stretching three and a half miles long, one and one-fourth miles wide and 100 feet deep. The lake was artificial and had been given over to the exclusive use of Pittsburgh millionaires belonging to the South Fork Hunting and Fishing Club. First proposed as a reservoir for the Pennsylvania Railroad's canal in 1836, the lake was completed in 1852. It was abandoned five years later at a loss of $240,000, the cost of building the original earth dam. The 500 acres of land and water lay waste until 1875, when Congressman John Reilly purchased the site; he turned it over to the country club five years later. The club consisted of three men, their leader being Colonel B.F. Ruff, a wealthy railroad and tunnel contractor. Under his orders the spillways for water runoffs were plugged up at the bottom to prevent catchable fish from escaping. This allowed the rising water to discharge only via a board flume over the top. Even an incompetent engineer could have told Ruff and his friends this was a lunacy that would result in disaster, but the financial sachem opted for economy, and no more than $17,000 was spent on the dam's reconstruction. Their savings, if not their stupidity, caused the deaths of unsuspecting thousands. (A corps of engineers inspected the broken dam following the disaster and cited "the lowering of the crest, the dishing, or central sag of the crest, the closing of the bottom culvert, and the obstruction of the spill-way" as major construction blunders.)

All in Conemaugh valley were oblivious to this Damocles' Sword except for a guest at the club, John G. Parke, an engineer who had curiously watched the reservoir rising for two days while constant rain beat down. On May 31 a cloudburst that began at noon and ended twenty minutes later added almost three inches of rain. Parke rounded up some of the club's workmen and directed them in digging new spillways around the dam for the runoff water. When he saw some of the ancient "rip-rap," small stone wedges, begin to fall away from the top of the dam he knew what would happen and jumped on a horse, racing two miles to South Fork, where he warned the residents that the dam would break. (There is mention of a man named Peyton spurring his steed all the way down the valley to Johnstown to warn citizens, à la Paul Revere, but the story is apocryphal.) Parke did send out two telegraph messages a few minutes after 3:00 P.M., one to Gautier Mills, also known as Cambria City because the great Cambria Iron Works with their 6,000 workers were located there, and one to Johnstown. Then he joined the more than 2,000 South Fork residents who, carrying what valuables they could handle, scaled up the steep inclines of the valley hills and waited.

No one in Gautier Mills or Johnstown received Parke's warning. Flooding had already occurred above and in both towns, and several downed telegraph poles cut off communication. In Johnstown flooding had reached the first floor of most buildings, and alarming as this might appear, residents had merely moved as usual to the second floor to wait out the inconvenience. The Western Union operator sent a cheerful message to her Pittsburgh superior, a man named Bender: "Had to move to second floor of office . . . water on first floor three feet deep." Bender tapped back asking her what was happening and she replied, "Same old thing, more flooding." The dam had not yet broken. When she noticed other houses filling up with water and heard the waters sloshing up the stairs, she wired, "I am frightened." Then the line went dead. "At 3:00," Bender later said, "the girl was there, and at 3:07 we might as well have asked the grave to answer us."

The deluge had not reached Johnstown when the telegraph line to Pittsburgh went dead, but the girl must have realized it was on its way and left her post; she was never seen again. The rip-rap at the dam was flying off in chunks that opened a 25-foot breach in the center. The resulting gush of water tore further at the aperture until almost 450 feet of dam gave way at once, sounding "louder than Niagara Falls," according to one witness at the dam. A wall of water 125 feet high rushed down the valley at about 50 m.p.h., and it obliterated every house in South Fork, which had fortunately been evacuated after engineer Parke's warning.

A mile farther down the steep gorge, the monster sprang upon Mineral Point. Forty houses were toppled. smashed, splintered and sent to shooting driftwood. Sixteen persons, the first dead attributed to the disaster, were counted as their bodies dashed by in the churning water. The Methodist Church was lifted bodily from its foundation by the onrush of waters. Its bell clanged wildly until it sank farther downstream.

A captured ghoul is protected by troopers against enraged Johnstown citizens. *(Harper's Weekly)*

The deluge rolled on to East Conemaugh. The first warning of the disaster here was not the roar and rush of waters but a piercing train whistle. A locomotive engineer who had been moving freightcars out of the sprawling Conemaugh yards a half mile out of town saw the floodwaters coming up swiftly behind him and raced the torrent to town, his whistle frantically crying disaster. Jumping from the still speeding locomotive, the engineer ran to his home, gathered up his family and climbed the hills to safety. His actions only puzzled scores of passengers sitting in the cars of two trains preparing to depart.

A conductor on one of these trains, John Barr, peered from the observation deck of the last car, saw the flash flood gurgling down the valley and then ran shouting through the cars for passengers to "get off and get up the hills . . . the dam is gone!" Out windows and down stairs at the ends of cars the excited passengers scrambled. Those in the second train had to crawl beneath the first train, no easy matter for women in the dresses of that day, to get to the slopes of the nearest hill. A ditch ten feet deep swallowed up nine women and girls. A man jumped the ditch and then looked back to see those trapped. One by one, he helped them out. All but one, an elderly woman set in her ways, escaped the waters. The old lady simply stated to her rescuer, "I will go this way," and with that walked steadily, cane-propped, down the track and into the raging floodwaters, where she disappeared.

From a steep hill Barr shouted at his passengers to hurry upward toward him. He saw the all-consuming floodwaters dash against one car that still contained at least twenty disbelieving passengers, engulf it and carry it along sideways, two men crawling from windows and clinging to the top until it sank with them still on top. Barr became goggle-eyed at the sheer force of the water as it struck the Conemaugh roundhouse, where thirty-seven locomotives, each weighing forty tons, were stored. All of the engines were swept away, none with sufficient weight to take them under the surface of the maelstrom. A baggage car was thrown out of the crashing flood tide and tossed fifty feet up the embankment like a twig.

One of Barr's passengers, a Miss Wayne from Altoona, managed to get to shore. The swift waters, she claimed, when found stark naked and lying on a hillside, had ripped off every stitch of clothing before depositing her on dry land. She gave rescuers a hair-curling story about how she pretended to be as dead as those corpses strewn about her while "foul-smelling, grunting Hungarians" rifled the dead. She said she saw through a squint, these "foreigners" slice off with "wicked knives" the fingers of women to obtain their wedding rings. Miss Wayne's lurid account so enraged a Conemaugh crowd that when they did discover a man looting the dead and holding a finger with a wedding band in his hand he was immediately beaten senseless and drowned. It was quick retribution by the mob, and, though the man had been a citizen born and raised in Conemaugh, convenient justification for Miss Wayne's xenophobia.

East Conemaugh was gone, totally submerged under rushing water, but the residents still doggedly fought against the monster. Two small sisters were roped from shore like steers and dragged sputtering to land. A floating house from Mineral Point crashed onto the side of a hill, and Conemaugh residents held onto it with hooks and hands until a family of five trapped on the roof jumped to safety.

Next in the flood's path was the town of Woodvale. Since this community was on a much steeper level than towns upstream, it was instantly overwhelmed by billions of tons of cascading water, and every one of its 800 buildings was uprooted and crushed. There were an estimated 5,000 persons living in Woodvale, and the dead here, never fully determined, accounted for at least half of those slain by the flood. Hundreds were seen hanging from pilings and rooftops as they were driven down the gorge.

Gautier Mills was equally unprepared, and when the floodwaters, almost a hundred feet high, dove into the walls of the Cambria Iron Works, everything collapsed, roofs, walls and machinery. The floodwaters flung tons of barbed wire manufactured there into midstream, ensnaring those struggling in the water, piercing their flesh, and causing thin shrieks to rise above the din. When the iron works were overcome, many stoves still burning floated downstream to later inflame debris while illuminating the most grisly sights of the disaster.

A woman was trapped all night near the shore, her body wedged between wreckage and a dozen corpses floating around her. The next day rescuers discovered that she had been driven mad by the hair of a dead woman which for hours had drifted across her face. One of the leaders of this community, a wealthy woman, was dragged from the bloated river at Gautier Mills to resignedly say, "My son Henry and his wife, my son Charles and my son-in-law were all drowned; my pastor and his wife and four nice little children were lost; there is not one brick of our good, big church left on top of another." She fumbled through the soggy handbag tied about her wrist and held up a shiny object. "And here is the key to that church, which alone remains." Then she closed her eyes and died.

Johnstown, the largest city in the valley with more than 12,000 people, was next, one end of its triangle of buildings pointing directly at the relentless waters. The suddenness with which this city was overtaken and swallowed by the flood continues to amaze historians and scientists. Buildings and their occupants were rolled up by the score, and then hundreds, in seconds. These were not the frame structures that had easily pancaked in the upper towns but great stone buildings that were battered down by the debris-carrying floodwaters. The enormous stone YMCA hall broke up. The German Lutheran Church, a mammoth structure, collapsed in a loud grinding of stone. All the municipal buildings fell down heavily in splashes of huge blocks of concrete and masonry. The finest hotel in Johnstown, the brick-built

Workmen dig out those trapped beneath the collapsed walls of the German Lutheran Church in Johnstown. *(Harper's Weekly)*

Hulbert House, came to ruin. The manager had just enough time to gather his kitchen help and bellboys to race about yelling for the residents to get to the roof before he and his staff escaped. Most of the startled guests, about sixty in all, were caught on the third set of stairs and drowned to a person.

The Reverend D. M. Miller and his wife were trapped in an upstairs bedroom. The clergyman looked out a window and saw houses and buildings reeling and spinning in the watery onslaught over orchards, stores, telephone poles and fences. Suddenly the water dashed against his house, spilling through the upstairs window and carrying the house off. Miller dove through the window, but his wife was cornered, floating on the bed. Water was already beyond the open part of the window, so Miller swung from the edge of the roof, kicked and punched out the upper portions of glass, severing an artery he later bound up, and dragged his wife out. They climbed to the roof and were joined by several children plucked from the waters as they coursed down the speeding river. They stayed floating for twenty-eight hours before they were rescued some thirty miles downstream.

The experience of Reverend David J. Beale, pastor of Johnstown's Presbyterian Church, was something out of *The Wizard of Oz.* At the first roar of the approaching floodwaters, Beale, his family and two visiting neighbors raced upstairs. When they reached the second floor they were already waist deep in water. At that moment a man shot through the window like a bullet by the tremendous force of the current.

"Where did you come from?" Beale asked.

"Woodvale," choked the man as he joined the Beales in working up to the third floor of the sturdy stone parsonage. He explained that he had ridden a rooftop "at a hundred miles an hour" until it collided with Beale's home and threw him through the window.

From the third floor of the parsonage, the Beales watched helplessly as people they knew, most of them drowning before their eyes, drifted by on pieces of houses. Two little children, almost naked, hung by their small arms to a roof and slipped under the water. Four young women holding each other tightly floated by. Captain A. N. Hart, his wife and two children floated to the parsonage on wreckage and climbed inside the second-story window. By then the building was near collapse.

"We must leave here now," Beale ordered, and after unsuccessful attempts to reach his church, which still stood, he decided that the fifteen persons in the parsonage should try to walk on the floating debris moving between his house and the strongest and largest building in Johnstown, the castlelike four-story Alma Hall, almost a block away.

Holding hands, they formed a chain and hopped and jumped onto the floating roofs of houses, the fixed tops of boxcars, slippery telephone poles, and fences that gave way under foot. They all made it to the hall, but one young woman was lagging. Like Lillian Gish's classic crossing of the ice-caked river in D. W. Griffith's *Way Down East* three decades later, this woman literally danced on debris, wildly stepping and sinking, striding and plunging. Almost reaching the building, she leaped onto a swirling wooden box and dropped from sight into the water, her long hair floating for only an instant. Captain Hart reached quickly from a window, grabbed her hair, and yanked her up to safety. The Beales found 260 other refugees in Alma Hall, all having made similarly harrowing escapes.

But none was more dramatic or hazardous than that of Horace W. Rose, a fifty-year-old lawyer, whose house

Death at the bridge, a dramatic sketch of the Johnstown flood. *(Harper's Weekly)*

was situated so that he could look up the Conemaugh valley for a mile. Rose had complained bitterly to his wife, two sons and daughter about the flooding of the first floor. He then went to shoot rats that were scampering wildly across floating debris in the yard. This was before the main attack of floodwaters. Suddenly he heard shouts, a steam whistle and clanging church bells. He gathered his family, and they hurried to the third floor of their home. From a window affording him a long view, Rose saw death looming. "I saw stretching from hill to hill, a great mass of timber, trees, roofs and debris of every sort, rapidly advancing, wrecking and carrying everything before it. It was then about the midst of what was known as the Gautier Works, a department of the Cambria Iron Works, which covered, perhaps, ten or eleven acres of ground. A dense cloud hung over the line of the rolling debris, which I then supposed was the steam and soot which had arisen from hundreds of fires in the

Gautier Works as the waves rolled over them. I stood and looked as the resistless tide moved on, and saw brick buildings crushed in an instant pass out of sight, while frame tenements were quickly crushed to atoms."

The waters would be on the Rose family in seconds. One of the Rose sons turned and asked, "Can't we escape?"

"No," Rose replied. "This means death to all of us."

"We have a big, strong house," Mrs. Rose said. "Won't it stand?"

"No, Maggie," Rose said glumly, watching the torrent approach. "No building can stand this awful jam. We are all lost."

Buildings of all kinds fell to pieces until the waters reached the Rose home. Just before they did Rose saw a building careen by and "at the attic windows. . .a number of ladies, one of whom held an infant in her arms; there was a crash, a sensation of falling, a consciousness that I was in the water, and all was dark. . . . A moment later I felt the press of a heavy shock, a sense of excruciating pain, involving my right breast, shoulder and arm. The thought came upon me that I was being crushed to death, that I could not long endure the agony I then suffered, and that death would come soon. I watched for the change, expecting in a moment to know the reality of eternity."

Rose heard his oldest son moan and thought he was dying. He could not help. He thought he heard his youngest son, Winter, beg for help. Next, Winter, a burly boy of twenty, was pushing him onto the floating roof of their house. His right side crushed, he could only watch as his daughter, June, rose out of the swirling water waist high and then sank beneath the waves and then his wife in similar manner rose and sank. Finally his youngest son reappeared, holding up both women. Rose spotted a young dentist, Harry Philips, swimming by. His own family—mother, niece, nephew and brother-in-law—had drowned before his eyes seconds before.

"Harry!" Rose called out. "For God's sake, Harry! Please help Winter save my wife and daughter. I'm helpless . . . my whole right side and arm are crushed."

The dentist swam with difficulty to the two women and the Rose boy and helped all of them up onto the roof. He then disappeared wordlessly into the waves. The Rose family rode the crest of the floodwaters for hours, each winding up on different fragments of the shredded roof. All survived, the oldest son returning thirty hours later.

At a stone bridge parallel to the floodwaters, a massive breakwater of debris, carcasses of animals, and bodies was formed. Inside of this half-mile long jam floundered and thrashed thousands of hapless persons who could not be reached by rope. Flames suddenly erupted in this giant jumble, and hundreds who had scrambled onto the debris in an effort to reach shore were trapped between the roaring waters and rising flames. More than 200 persons, according to one report, committed mass suicide by merely leaping headlong into the flames.

All night hundreds of stranded persons floated under downstream bridges. A raft carrying four women went sailing by; they were singing hymns. A small child on a roof was kneeling with her hands clasped in prayer. When someone threw her a rope from a bridge at Boliver, she ignored it and went down the river to her death. At Grubtown, a man on a swirling log caught in a whirlpool beneath a bridge told would-be rescuers exactly how he should be buried when his body was found. To his embarrassment he was suddenly thrown off the floating log and borne by the current to shore, where he coughed to back-slapping residents: "I was . . . only . . . joking . . . of course."

Fantastic rescues were performed by citizens from downstream towns who grabbed, roped, plucked, and snagged hundreds of Johnstown's residents as they were carried by the water. At Lockport Edward Deck swam through the torrent to save an old man dazedly clinging to a tree trunk. He swam out again and saved a Mrs. Adams and her small child by ripping through a tin roof until his hands bled to get to them. At Nineveh, a railroad employee, J. W. Esch, tied a rope around his waist and made a human breakwater out of his body, snaring sixteen people and saving all. C. W. Hoppenstall, a messenger on a fast-moving mail train running outside Boliver, saw a woman and baby struggling in the water. He dove from the train into the foaming torrent and pulled both to safety.

A partially wrecked house on which floated a crying five-month-old-baby arrived in Pittsburgh twenty-four hours after it had been uprooted in Johnstown, seventy-five miles away. Several babies were born prematurely during the calamity. One was named Moses; two were called Flood.

In the muddy thirty-acre backup of debris before the seventy-foot stone bridge in Johnstown that had withstood the flood, a beautiful young woman was hopelessly trapped even though she could reach out and

Militia and troops guard Johnstown's wrecked stores from would-be looters. *(Harper's Weekly)*

grasp the hands of rescuers. As fire approached her, they tugged violently to release her, but it was impossible. A clergyman named Trautwein grabbed an axe and said quietly to a man, "I think you'll have to chop off her leg, or she'll burn to death."

Just at that moment a young man jumped downward from the stone bridge, sank in the debris and swam underwater. He found a corpse wedged in wreckage below the surface. It was actually holding the woman's legs in a deathgrip. Unable to release the grasp, the young man surfaced, got a knife, and dove again, this time cutting away the desperate hands. The girl was saved only moments before the flames reached the spot. (This story was reported by the most reliable sources of the day.)

Floating all night on the raging waters, a machinist named Calliver, who had managed to save his entire family and had clutched them for fourteen hours, looked up in exhaustion to see a gleam in the east. "It's morning!" he shouted elatedly. "Morning!"

The great Johnstown flood was over, and anywhere from 2,500 to 7,000 persons were dead. It took three months for 7,500 workmen to clear away the debris and bury the bodies they found. After several weeks of prying them out with pitchforks from between rocks and under collapsed buildings, 800 were buried, unknown and unmarked, in one cemetery.

Interrupting this gruesome work were dozens of Johnstown citizens who stumbled about, their minds unbalanced. A preacher took to roaring drunks and attempted several suicides. A woman sat by the riverbank clutching a broken clock, her only possession, thinking it was the child she lost to the floodwaters.

The *New York World* printed an epilogue to this most remembered disaster: "Such an avalanche of horrors never slipped upon any American city. Horrors piled on horrors, woe augmenting woe; bankruptcy, orphanage, widowhood, childlessness, obliterated homesteads, gorged cemeteries and scenes so excruciating it is a marvel that anyone could look upon them and escape insanity."

(ALSO SEE: Ohio, 1913)

JOHNSTOWN, PENNSYLVANIA — **MINE DISASTER** **July 10, 1902**

Carelessness on the part of miners working the Rolling Mill Mine at Johnstown, Pennsylvania, was the cause of the explosion that took 112 lives on July 10, 1902. Several miners entered Number 2 room with open lamps flickering. These flames quickly ignited the gas known to exist in that part of the mine, and the explosion followed. Seven victims died of burns and blows from pulverizing timbers that fell on them. The remaining 105 miners were found dead of suffocation from afterdamp.

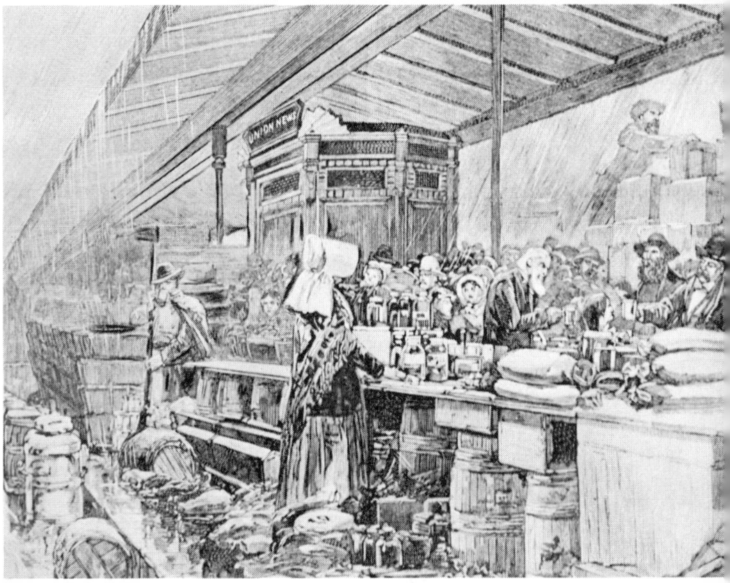

The dead were stacked in caskets next to emergency food rations handed out at Johnstown's railroad depot. *(Harper's Weekly)*

Since the explosion was not extensive, rescuers were able to make entry into the stricken shaft and pull out twenty-one men they managed to revive.

The miners knew the peril of using open lamps and yet repeatedly employed them in gaseous mine areas while the fire bosses looked the other way. A state safety inspector lamented: "I am expected to make suggestions which may aid in the prevention of such catastrophes . . . but . . . what can we do when a miner recklessly disregards safety and violates all laws and rules in the mine . . . where detection is no easy matter?"

JORULLO — **VOLCANIC ERUPTION** **September 28, 1759**

Born in the cultivated plain owned by Don Pedro de Jorullo in Michoacan Province, from which it takes its name, this volcano, located near Aguasarco, Mexico, burst into being September 28, 1759. Native reports claimed that this monster, boasting four cones—the highest reaching 1,300 feet—came into being in a single night with a horrendous blast that claimed the lives of several hundred farmers and their families.

One historian reports that "the first explosion blew out rocks, cinders, and other fragmental materials; clouds of steam and dust were emitted, and lava buried an entire plain where once there had been fields of sugar cane and indigo plants."

Owing to haphazard accounts, the exact number of deaths is uncertain, but the toll is estimated at a minimum of two hundred. Jorullo's eruptions continued for forty years before it became dormant.

K

K-13 — MARINE DISASTER
January 29, 1917

background: The *K-13,* capable of 23 knots, was accidentally flooded while surfacing on January 29, 1917, while performing initial tests at Gareloch before being commissioned. Of the eighty-one men on board, thirty-four were drowned. Later investigation proved a malfunctioning signal light to have caused the tragedy.

Just after completing her diving trials, the British submarine *K-13,* being readied for combat in World War I, made one further test that proved disastrous. Captain R. M. Herbert decided to take the sub down one more time. Checking the control panel, he noted that all the lights showed the proper green color that indicated that the ventilating doors were closed. He began his dive.

One light, however, malfunctioned and, though it showed green, the boiler room, which it represented, still had its ventilators open. As soon as the submarine dove, the aft compartments flooded and thirty-four seamen were instantly drowned. The sub settled in ten fathoms of water. Herbert and forty-seven others sat in near-airless compartments waiting for rescue.

During the night the sailors heard wires scraping along the sides of the sub and thought they had been located, but when hours passed they realized that they were still lost. Commander Herbert and a Commander Goodhart decided to attempt to reach the surface by equalizing the water and air pressure in the conning tower. They agreed that Goodhart would swim to the surface while Herbert would remain behind to stabilize the water and air pressure after he had gone.

Goodhart apparently neglected to remember that the K-class submarine had a steel roof over its conning tower and, swimming upward, hit his head and was killed. Herbert was dragged upward by the pressure and managed to get to the surface.

Personally directing a salvage crew, Herbert channeled air and food hoses to his trapped crew through the submarine's ammunition hoist. Relief came none too soon; the foul air coming up from the sub was almost the color of pitch. The ballast tanks were then blown full of air, and chain slings were affixed around the sub. In this manner the sub was hauled up, and the forty-six men still alive inside her hull were cut out with an acetylene torch. No sooner had the last man stepped from the sub than she sank again.

Weeks later the *K-13* was refloated, refitted, and then recommissioned the *K-22,* the number 13 apparently thought by authorities to be too risky.

KAGOSHIMA, JAPAN — TSUNAMI
January 12, 1914

Following an earthquake on January 12, 1914, which covered the city of Kagoshima, Japan, a *tsunami,* estimated to be approximately ten to fifteen feet in height, hurled itself against the waterfront area. Refugees escaping the earthquake area were caught by the wave in narrow dirt roads and landslips. The wave engulfed dozens of people, killing 35 and injuring another 112. Another 21 persons were lost during this disaster.

KAKANJ, YUGOSLAVIA — MINE DISASTER
June 7, 1965

Just outside of the small town of Sarajevo where, in 1914, the assassination of Archduke Francis Ferdinand by the youthful anarchist Gavrilo Princip set off World War I, Yugoslavia's most monstrous mine disaster occurred. More than 200 miners were at work in the various shafts of the Kakanj coal mines when an enormous explosion, caused by escaping methane gas, was set off.

Officials dug out only 21 men at first, bringing up small groups for hours following the explosion. Then they began to haul up the dead, 128 at the final count. Six months later a Belgrade court sentenced four of the mine's officials to seven and one-half years at hard labor for negligence and failure to observe safety rules.

KANGRA, INDIA — EARTHQUAKE
April 4, 1905

Almost as a warning, two distinct earth tremors were felt in the Indian district of Kangra in 1904, but these were far less destructive than the heart-pounding shocks that rent the district on the morning of April 4, 1905. Starting at 6:00 A.M., the second tremor registered 8.7 on the Richter scale and threw down hundreds of houses in Kangra, Dharmsala, Naggar, Sultenpur, Suket and Mandi, an estimated area of about 1.6 million square miles. The severe shocks of 1897 in this district spread out an additional 100,000 miles, but were far less devastating.

The majestic Bhowan Temple in Kangra, India, was reduced to rubble by a massive earthquake on April 4, 1905. *(Literary Digest)*

The city of Kangra was rocked to ruins in a matter of seconds, the Bhowan Temple, one of the oldest in the world, crumbling down on and killing 2,000 pilgrims, who were buried for days beneath the rubble. (The guru, or high priest, of the temple was the only one whose body was recovered. He was buried in a special shrine, while the fallen temple remained the permanent tomb of the pilgrims. More than 19,000 persons in the city were instantly crushed to death; most of them were sleeping.

Huge fissures opened up in the countryside. One peculiar side effect was that hundreds of springs were checked while hundreds more broke out in new places. The country people suffered equally with the city folk. One moving account was that of D. W. MacBean, owner of a sprawling tea estate outside Palampour: "When the second shock came, I sat up in bed and called out to my wife to come to the window. I had hardly done so when I saw the highest wall of our bedroom fall in like a torrent on my poor sleeping child; then all became dark with fearful dust from the falling walls. I felt suffocated, and pushed my hand through the panes of glass in the window into which I had crept; had I not done so I should have been killed by the wall that fell in on the head of my bed.

"I shall never forget those few moments that appeared like years—the noise of the falling masonry, smashing of beams, planks and slates. I had fully made up my mind that we should all perish. When the shock was over, I opened the window and dropped into the lower veranda, rushed out, and cried out for help. No one could be seen—all had fled to the villages to help their friends and relations. . . . All our houses (with the exception of the mali's hut) were leveled to the ground, including a magnificent factory built of cut stone, which my poor old father had lately built. All was still as death save for the wailing of a man who afterward turned out to be my head clerk."

MacBean rounded up several servants from his household, most of them still in a daze, and dug with his bare fingers at the limestone and plaster under which his only child was buried. He found her crushed to death. He made a coffin from the planks salvaged from the debris and buried her in a quiet spot on the estate. The tea

Kansas City, Kansas, was flooded after heavy rains in July 1951. *(Wide World)*

magnate ended his mournful narrative: "To look around the valley, nothing but desolation meets the eye. . . . The once pretty little villages with their bluish-white walls and slated roofs, mixed here and there with thatched buildings, all leveled to the ground . . . We have been ruined. . . ."

KANSAS **FLOODS**
May-June, 1903

Some of the worst floods experienced in Kansas occurred in May and June of 1903 after heavy rainfall and several tornadoes had already brought tragedy and death. The Saline River and several others broke over their banks and inundated farms and cities alike. Large sections of Topeka were flooded by May 31. On the following day the floods at Kansas City rose to thirty-five feet in height (more than $22 million in damage was done), only two feet less than that of the great Kansas flood of 1884.

The *Kansas City* [Mo.] *Times* reported that "hundreds were rescued from impending death, but late last night people standing on the West Bluff [of the Missouri River] could hear the agonizing cries for help from men and women in houses out on the wide expanse of water. . . ." All manner of wreckage accumulated in the Kansas River, including a great oil tank, and this debris, dozens of feet high, swept forward, surging against the double-decked Central Avenue bridge and tearing it in two "as if made of paper."

Five more bridges including the pipelines from the Kansas City waterworks were ripped apart, cutting off 200,000 persons from fresh water. More than 100 persons lost their lives in these disastrous Kansas floods.

KANSAS **FLOODS**
July, 1951

Following heavy rains the lower Kansas River bloated the Missouri River in July, 1951, leading to enormous flooding of areas about Topeka, Manhattan and Kansas City, Missouri. Close to 500,000 persons were made homeless and more than $1 billion in damages were done. Although only 50 persons lost their lives, these floods were considered the most damaging in the state's history. President Truman called on the Red Cross and other civilian agencies to handle the emergency.

KANSU, CHINA — **EARTHQUAKE-LANDSLIDES**
December 16, 1920

Beyond the earthquake that ripped apart Japan in 1923, the quakes that tore through China's remote Kansu Province on the bitterly cold night of December 16, 1920, were among the most devastating Asiatic tremors of the twentieth century. Hundreds of villages and their weakly constructed houses were immediately destroyed as the rolling quake registered, hundreds of miles distant, 8.6 on the Richter scale.

Huge rocks began to fall from towering bluffs in this mountainous region, and these in turn created immense landslides slicing downward into valleys. In hundreds of places the earth opened up with a "booming" sound, fissures swallowing anything above them. Roads vanished. Ten cities began to tumble into ruins, their ancient stone walls cracking and falling.

"Hills that walked" were described by the terrorized residents, many of whom lived in caves along the faces of the mountains that contained deep deposits of loess, a peculiar kind of extremely fine sand that would crumble and fall in a strong wind, let alone in Kansu's enormous earthquake. These deposits, which quickly fell from the sides of hills, formed most of the landslides.

National Geographic described the destruction of one area in Kansu: "At the junction of the valleys stands Swen Family Gap, a town of several thousand souls, in which one-tenth were killed by the collapse of buildings and cave dwellings; and the other nine-tenths were saved by the miraculous stoppage of two bodies of earth shaken loose from the mother hill and left hanging above the village, lacking only another half-second's tremor to send them down. A third avalanche, having flowed from the hills on the opposite side of the valley across the valley floor and the stream bed, is piled up in a young mountain, near enough to the village to overshadow the wall.

"In each case the earth which came down bore the appearance of having shaken loose, clod from clod, and grain from grain, and then cascaded like water, forming vortices, swirls, and all the convolutions into which a torrent might shape itself."

About 10,000 workers desperately destroyed dams of timber and rockslide created by the quake, to prevent floods. Close to 180,000 persons were killed outright by the Kansu quake, but another 20,000, scarred survivors of the nightmare who refused to build adequate housing because they feared more tremors, froze to death during the ensuing winter months.

(ALSO SEE: Japan, 1923)

Rescuers search frantically through the smoky ruins of the Katie Jane Nursing Home in Warrenton, Missouri, on February 17, 1957. Seventy-two persons died in the flash fire. *(Wide World)*

KASHMIR, INDIA — **EARTHQUAKES**
June-July, 1885

Dozens of earthquakes began to shake the Indian province of Kashmir in early June, 1885, first striking the city of Serinagur June 2, 1885, and then rippling throughout the province until July 8. Scores of cities, towns and hamlets were leveled by the quakes and close to 3,100 persons were killed. More than 5,000 were injured and whole herds of cattle disappeared into the yawning fissures that split the countryside.

KATIE JANE NURSING HOME — **FIRE**
February 17, 1957

The Katie Jane Nursing Home was only two years old when it burst into flames and roasted 72 patients to death at 3:45 P.M. on February 17, 1957. The fire began in a hallway of the main building, which was heated by steam from a powerhouse a block away in Warrenton, Missouri, while most of the 155 aged patients were at church services. A muffled explosion was heard after the fire started, but its true cause was never determined.

Mrs. F. H. Knigge, ironically the wife of the local coroner, heard the explosion and went to the nursing home. "I heard the screams and ran from my home to the building. By the time I got there ten or fifteen minutes later, it was all over."

The flash fire raced through the main two and one-half story building and an annex, once used by the Central Wesleyan College and closed in 1941. Several elderly persons, their ages ranging from fifty to ninety-nine years, jumped from the second floor of the building and were injured. Firemen arrived quickly, but were driven back by the intense flames; they resorted to pulling down the walls of the main building after the roof collapsed to rescue those who were inside.

Mrs. Woodrow O'Sullivan, wife of the owner, took

more than ten inmates out before being overcome by smoke. Firemen risked their lives repeatedly to carry out the bedridden, and they were joined by neighbors and passersby. One of these was John A. Berkholtz of St. Louis, who was driving past the burning building. "Flames were leaping sixty feet into the air," he later reported, "and when I got there the building was a total loss."

KAWACHI — MARINE DISASTER
July 12, 1918

The giant 21,420-ton Japanese battleship *Kawachi* was the pride of the Imperial fleet and was one of the best armed warships of her period. Built in 1912 in Kure, the *Kawachi* boasted twelve 12-inch guns, ten 6-inch guns and eight 4.7-inch guns, was 500 feet long and had an 84-foot beam. Unlike most dreadnoughts of that day, the *Kawachi* had also been fitted with five 18-inch torpedo tubes.

No one has ever explained what caused the violent explosion that tore the *Kawachi* in half on July 12, 1918, as she sailed majestically into Tokuyama Bay, 150 miles northeast of Nagasaki. The ship was suddenly and literally ripped to pieces by an enormous fireball that burst from below her decks. Of the 900 men on board the *Kawachi,* 500 were killed outright. One thought advanced on the disaster was that one of the battleship's lower-hold magazines ignited and set off a chain reaction.

KEELUNG, TAIWAN — MINE DISASTER
December 1, 1971

The Seven Star Mine at the eastern tip of Taiwan, near the town of Keelung, became the scene of the worst mine disaster in the island's history on December 1, 1971. An explosion rocked the coal mine, causing several shafts to collapse early in the day while a full crew was at work 7,260 feet below the surface.

The ignition of escaping gas by dynamiters was speculated upon, but the true case of the explosion was never established. Police dug out forty-one bodies. Seven more were never found.

KELUIT — VOLCANIC ERUPTION
1919

Another of Java's many volcanoes, Keluit, dormant since 1901, exploded in 1919, disgorging a crater lake that had been formed during the eighteen-year lull. The lake's waters, pouring into the neighboring valleys at a terrific speed, instantly drowned 5,500 persons.

To avoid a recurrence of this type of catastrophe, Javanese engineers dug a tunnel into the crater through which the lake now is drained constantly.

KEMMERER, WYOMING — MINE DISASTER
August 14, 1923

At 8:20 A.M. on August 14, 1923, with 135 men at work in the Frontier Number 1 Mine at Kemmerer, Wyoming, a fireboss who was restoring a wing brattice was suddenly standing in darkness. The area, he thought, had been cleared of coal gas, and he felt confident enough to light his flame safety lamp with a match. He was wrong. A great deal of gas was present in the area, and at the first spark of his match he and several others were blown to pieces.

The sound of the explosion panicked the miners, who left their working areas and ran quickly for the surface. In their wild attempt to reach the top of the mine, seventy men ran straight into the smoke and gas-filled areas and were overcome.

Twenty-nine others fled through alternate passageways only to be overcome by the fumes. A burly shot firer and a driver held a group of men back with sledge hammers and ordered them to barricade themselves in the working area. It was reported that they had to beat several men back to keep them in the area. Quickly a makeshift wall was constructed, and these men were found alive at 3:00 P.M. the same day when rescuers reached them with resuscitators.

The ninety-nine men who perished in this mine explosion need not, as was eventually proved, have died. The area in which they were at work was comparatively safe, though temporarily blocked off, and had they remained there, only a handful of them would have been killed.

KENDAL, JAMAICA — RAILWAY WRECK
September 1, 1957

background: A diesel-drawn twelve-car excursion train with about 1,500 vacationers on board at 11:15 P.M. on September 1, 1957, while traveling at high speeds around an S-curve about a mile from Kendal, Jamaica, suddenly uncoupled, sending nine cars plunging into a ravine, killing 175 persons and injuring another 750, making it the worst train wreck in the island's history. The wreck was attributed to the breaking of the coupling between the third and fourth cars of the train.

Organized by two American-born priests representing Catholic agencies, about 1,500 persons climbed aboard a Jamaican holiday train on September 1, 1957, for a weekend outing. The tourists traveled from Kingston to Montego Bay and were en route back to Kingston on a clear, warm night when tragedy struck. The train, then about a mile from Kendal and pulled by a diesel engine, was making fast time, too fast.

Rounding a wicked S-curve, where, in 1938, eighty

persons had been killed in a train accident, the holiday express jerked and jumped as the coupling between the third and fourth cars broke. As the diesel and the first three cars went forward, the remaining nine cars leaped from the tracks and tore down a steep ravine. Several cars went to the bottom of the ravine, their occupants screaming and jumping from windows. Others telescoped into these. One car actually climbed the embankment on the other side of the ravine, such was its momentum.

The *New York Times* reported that the engineer, ill-named Garnish Lurch, blamed the wreck on brake failure, stating that he had applied the brakes on the downgrade of the S-curve but that they had failed to respond. One of the more freakish episodes of this worst train wreck in Jamaican history occurred when one of the coaches was shorn of its ceiling and sides and sailed down the tracks for a quarter of a mile, some survivors clinging to its floor. Engineer Lurch and several passengers in the undamaged first three cars ran down into the ravine and helped scores up the embankment and into the remaining coaches. When filled with these bloody passengers, the train raced to Kendal for aid.

Rescuers labored for hours to remove 750 injured from the ravine; they took out 175 bodies. One survivor, a teenager named Pauline Donald, said, "They had trouble with the wheel on the way, and some men tightened it at Montego Bay, but it gave trouble again on the way back. We were going very fast and someone said, 'The wheel has slipped off!' Then, crash, smash and everything came off."

Hundreds came to view the scene of the massive train wreck outside of Kendal, Jamaica, on September 1, 1957. Nine cars derailed and plunged into a ravine; 175 passengers died. *(UPI)*

KENT — MARINE DISASTER
March 2, 1825

background: The British East Indiaman *Kent,* a 1,350-ton British troopship bound for Bengal and China, sailed from Downs, England, on February 19, 1825. While battling a gale in the Atlantic on February 28, the *Kent* caught fire and burned for two days while the brig *Cambria* and the *Caroline* took off 562 persons; 81 were killed, either in the explosion when the ship's magazines blew up or in the sea.

Major Duncan MacGregor, an officer of the Thirty-first Regiment, looked around at the howling Atlantic gale and the crackling flames leaping from the bow of the ship and hurriedly scribbled a message, jammed it into a bottle, corked it and threw it into the sea. His forlorn message read: "The ship, the Kent Indiaman, is on fire. Elizabeth, Joanna and myself commit our spirits into the hands of our blessed Redeemer whose grace enables us to be quite composed in the awful prospect of entering eternity."

MacGregor's attitude was shared by just about everyone on board the sinking troopship, except perhaps Captain Henry Cobb, who had given desperate orders to save his ship. That morning as a clawing gale hit his ship he had told his officers to check the holds and see that boxed goods were fastened down. An officer who was pitched forward when the ship lurched dropped his lantern and then spilled the contents of a whiskey keg, which quickly was ignited. Hearing of the accident Cobb ordered part of the *Kent's* lower decks flooded to keep the mounting flames from the powder magazines, located amidships.

Cobb's remedy worked for a while; the flames ate upward through the ship instead of toward the magazines, but the ship was soon waterlogged and her bow began to disappear into the waves. Death had already begun to strike down the magnificently disciplined passengers, 531 of whom were British soldiers en route to foreign garrisons. The rest were their wives and children. At least a dozen sick soldiers, unable to scurry updecks when the lower holds were flooded, drowned. About 600 persons were packed amidships or near the stern. Most of them were naked as they had rushed from their bunks at the first alarm. Almost as a way of illustrating the ship's hopeless situation, scores of troopers nonchalantly sat on the magazines.

The blazing East Indiaman *Kent* sinks with eighty-one on board, March 1, 1825.

Moments before Captain Cobb was to give the order to abandon ship, the tiny outward-bound brig *Cambria,* with a crew of eight, was sighted. She was answering the *Kent's* distress signals and sailing straight for the tower of smoke spewing from the ship's fires.

"We're saved, MacGregor," Cobb said. "Lower the boats." He then became puzzled as to who should leave the ship first.

MacGregor, who would live to be a lieutenant-general and write the stirring book, *The Loss of the Kent,* bluntly responded, "In funeral order, of course," signifying that women, children and youthful soldiers should go first. His superior, Colonel Fearson, clutched the hilt of his sword and said loudly, "See that any man is cut down who presumes to enter the boats before the means of escape are presented to the women and children." A dozen marines solemnly drew their blades from scabbards, but it was not necessary. Like those on the ill-fated *Birkenhead,* British soldiery showed its heralded mettle. Not a man panicked.

Entering a lowered boat, however, became as risky as staying with the ship. Giant swells engulfed the lifeboats several times.

The *Cambria* put over her own small lifeboats and rowed for the *Kent*'s swamped life craft, her sailors plucking women and children from the water. The troopship began to list so badly that it became impossible to lower more boats or take any more off the doomed ship other than those who, one by one, crawled to the end of the spanker boom at the stern and dropped themselves into the boats and struggled there against the gigantic waves.

The rescue process took hours, and about forty veteran soldiers, knowing they would be the last allowed to depart, climbed to the rigging. As the ship began to sink into the water, they cried out prayers.

All the crew members except four had left. One remaining sailor ran about the sea-swamped decks frantic with indecision. He had tied 400 sovereigns about his neck in a handkerchief and would not let go of his treasure.

"You'll sink with it then," Captain Cobb shouted to

him. He, Fearson and MacGregor were the last ones standing on the deck. The sailor suddenly rushed to the spanker boom, climbed out to its end, and, as he attempted to lower himself into a small lifeboat, fell and disappeared into the slapping waters. The officers shouted to the men in the rigging to come down, but fear froze them to their precarious perches. One man, trembling, finally climbed down and followed his superiors to the spanker boom and safety.

As the last lifeboat pulled away, another vessel, the *Caroline,* came into view. Cobb shouted to the men remaining on board the *Kent,* which was fast breaking up. None responded. From the deck of the *Cambria* Cobb watched two hours later as the *Kent*'s magazines, containing 500 barrels of gunpowder, blew skyward when the fires reached them. The sea shook with a terrific blast that disintegrated the troopship. Masts shot upward like catapulted trees. Cobb, clinging to the hope that some of the men in the rigging had survived, ordered still more boats lowered to search for them. Incredibly seventeen soldiers were found alive, clinging to the mizzenmast, but eighty-one—fifty-four soldiers, twenty children, one woman, one sailor, and five youths from the mess crew—were lost.

(*ALSO SEE:* Birkenhead)

KEY WEST, FLORIDA — HURRICANE

October 11-12, 1846

background: Originating in the Caribbean, a massive hurricane struck Cuba on October 10, 1846, sinking ninety-two vessels in various harbors and tearing through the Florida Keys the next two days, destroying about 600 buildings, causing $200,000 in damage and killing about forty persons. No accurate estimate of the speed of the blasting winds in this hurricane's eyewall was recorded, but the barometric reading fell to 27.06.

According to one historian, Colonel Walter C. Maloney, the hurricane that struck the Florida Keys on October 11-12, 1846, doing most of its damage at Key West, was "the most destructive of any that has ever visited these latitudes in the memory of man." After churning up the ports of Cuba and sinking all but twelve sturdy ships anchored in those harbors, the 1846 hurricane moved angrily up the Florida Keys.

On board a small vessel, the *Morris,* in Key West harbor was a Lieutenant Pease, who described how the vessel's anchor served to moor it rigidly in the path of the hurricane, which threatened to break it in two. He and thirty others managed to stay clear of the masts and rigging that were ripped out of their wooden sockets by the wild winds. "It was a narrow escape," he related. "The vessel continued to labor very heavily, and the sea made a complete breach over us. . . . At 4:00 P.M. the air was full of water, and no man could look windward for a second. Houses, lumber, and vessels drifted by us—some large sticks of lumber turned end over end by the force of the current, and the sea running so high and breaking over us brought lumber, casks, on board of us and across our decks. . . ."

Dozens of vessels in the harbor were wrecked by the hurricane, and at least forty persons were killed in Key West, fourteen when the lighthouse toppled. Another six persons were flattened by the storm's volcanic winds, and wharves in the harbor were washed away. The stone fort in the harbor was nothing more than rubble, and all the public buildings were destroyed.

KIANGYA — MARINE DISASTER

December 3, 1948

background: The ancient S.S. *Kiangya,* a Chinese coastal steamer displacing 2,100 tons and carrying more than 3,450 passengers and crew, struck a submerged Japanese mine on December 3, 1948, blew up and killed approximately 2,750 (an estimated 700 survived), making it the worst recorded marine disaster in history except for an unidentified Chinese troopship that foundered in November, 1947, while evacuating Nationalist troops from Manchuria. Six thousand were drowned in that accident.

Shanghai was a city of terror as Communist troops surrounding its outskirts began to close in. Almost anyone who could use his two legs headed for the harbor, laboring under the sweaty weight of children and heirlooms. The harbor area became a spectacle of fright and panic. The shoving, screaming horde welled up on wobbly piers, many of which collapsed under the impossible burden, dumping the teeming masses into the murky, brown waters. Tens of thousands of frantic citizens clogged the wharves, wails and shouts mingling and rippling along their fronts. Chaos was everywhere. In the midst of this human maelstrom rode the proud old coastal steamer, *Kiangya,* brown with rust, groaning beneath her massive cargo of more than 3,450 Chinese refugees.

The *Kiangya,* commissioned in the 1920's, was officially able to carry 1,186 persons. The additional 2,000-odd passengers gave the ship a weird, off-balance roll. Hundreds more were attempting to board her on December 3, 1948, as she was about to depart for Ningpo.

"Here! Here! Here!" shouted dozens of Chinese on board from portholes, throwing previously purchased tickets to their friends. Scuffles, bloody fights, even murder, resulted from the mad scramble for the tickets along the wharves. Many tickets fell into the deep water and dozens of yelling Chinese dove after them, disappearing in the scummy brine. Sampans and bobbing junks

Only the masts, funnel, and hurricane deck of the Chinese coastal steamer *Kiangya* remain after she struck an old mine, exploded, and sank off Shanghai on December 3, 1948. *(UPI)*

crashed against the *Kiangya*'s fantail as hundreds clawed at her filthy plates in attempts to board her.

About 2,250 people, all paying customers, had boarded the ship in Nanking. The additional 1,200 who managed to wedge their way on board past indifferent deck officers and a sad-eyed captain turned the open deck areas into a wriggling blanket of flaccid flesh. At 6:30 P.M. the *Kiangya* poked her battered nose into the Wangpoo River.

Just as the uncomfortable mass settled down for the long journey, a blinding, searing flash of light shot through the ship, instantly buckling plates and crushing bulkheads. Many thought it an attack by the Communists and pummeled their way to the top decks, for the *Kiangya* was already sinking into the riverbed, her lower decks awash, her compartments below the waterline already filled with rushing water, drowning hundreds. It was not the Communists but an old Japanese mine that had reared its gorgonlike head in the *Kiangya*'s sluggish path.

Only about 700 persons were able to reach the top deck. These nightmarish figures stood in waist-high water, bellowing for aid. There was precious little standing room and dozens of mostly aged people were rudely shoved across the railing into death splashes. Women, resigned to their fate in the churling waters of the Wangpoo, hurtled their infant children toward the shore only to watch them plop helplessly in the fast current and disappear.

One ship's officer, his tightly gold buttoned uniform sopped with water, drew a revolver and told several elderly women near him to "be of good cheer" before he sent bullets into their heads. As the water closed about him, he shot himself. Survivors noted his ornamented cap floating past them.

No messages from the stricken ship were possible. The radio shack had been destroyed by the explosion. The *Kiangya* settled for three hours, the river bubbling upward, inching toward those still on board. The tiny vessel *Hwafoo* then heaved into view and got off an SOS. The S.S. *Mouli* arrived first and attempted to come alongside the almost totally submerged *Kiangya*.

The captain of the rescue vessel was wary of the number of people clamoring to be saved, afraid the beseeching hundreds might swamp his ship. Their shrill cries unnerved his crew, but a *Kiangya* officer shouted at the mass, "Don't shout or they will think there are too many of us!" This quieted the survivors, and they were plucked by two's and three's from the settling ship.

As other vessels swarmed about, the grisly chore of gathering the bodies bloated with the brackish water of the Wangpoo began; more than 1,000 were recovered and taken back to Shanghai, where they were piled on the docks as streams of Chinese refugees scurried to small ships, still fleeing the Communists, who now were advancing on the waterfront. An estimated 2,750 souls died on the ill-fated *Kiangya,* the worst officially recorded marine disaster, but it mattered little in that year of the Chinese civil war in which millions perished and old ways of life ceased.

KINGSTON, JAMAICA — FIRE
December 13, 1882

The worst fire in Jamaican history occurred in Kingston's business quarter on the night of December 13, 1882, and quickly swept through lumberyards, warehouses, stores and wharves. More than 400 stores were gutted and at least two dozen persons burned to death. Damages were estimated to be a staggering $10 million. The fire, it was later determined, began inside piles of roof shingles in a lumberyard. Laws were immediately passed prohibiting the use of such shingles thereafter.

KINGSTON, JAMAICA — EARTHQUAKE
January 14, 1907

Not since Port Royal was destroyed in the earthquake of 1692 had Jamaica experienced a quake equal to the one that devastated Kingston at 3:30 P.M. on January 14, 1907. The earth moved vertically for thirty-six seconds, like a choppy sea, according to most reports. Objects literally jumped and hopped from the ground as huge fissures cracked open. Electric tram rails were twisted; pipes were bent. Every electric cable in town snapped, which cut off the city from the outside world for several days.

A seismic sea wave dashed inward on Anotta Bay and swept hundreds of houses out to sea with all their inhabitants. In Kingston hundreds of buildings were demolished, and those that survived the quake were soon aflame; the fires that broke out almost immediately following the tremor went uncontrolled since all the water mains were broken. More than twenty-five square blocks of the city were in ruins in a matter of seconds.

When the powerhouse was destroyed, scores of charged electric cables danced menacingly in the streets, and dozens of persons were killed outright when these coiling lines touched them. The death toll was staggering. A flimsily constructed cigar factory shuddered and its roof caved in, killing 125 workers. No place was safe in Kingston because of the fires, so the wounded were taken to ships in the bay. On one, the *Arno,* which had been converted into a hospital ship, seventy-nine amputations were performed by a single doctor. (Some observers later stated that the doctor had "gone crazy" during the quake and that many of these operations were unnecessary.)

The Jamaican governor, Sir Alexander Swettenham, first reported to the British Colonial office that 343 persons had been killed in the quake and that "a few bodies are still covered by the ruins." His estimate, however, was much too conservative. The final Kingston quake death count ran beyond 1,400.

KLM — AIR CRASH
July 16, 1957

Captain Bob de Roos, thirty-six-year-old pilot of a Lockheed Super Constellation belonging to the Royal Dutch Airlines (KLM), had just taken off from Biak Island in Dutch New Guinea and was heading on a routine flight to Amsterdam on July 16, 1957. On board were sixty-eight crew members and passengers, nineteen of which were children.

No sooner was the plane airborne than de Roos radioed that everything was normal. Then one of the plane's engines exploded and set fire to the remaining engines. Only five miles off Biak Island, the plane suddenly dipped into the sea, its tail section breaking off and floating, the rest of the fuselage sinking instantly and carrying with it to a watery death fifty-six persons. Only one child in the tail section survived, but he succumbed the next day to burns he had sustained, raising the death toll to fifty-seven. Those in the tail section were rescued by Papuan natives who took to their canoes and paddled to the crash area immediately.

A particular tragedy was that of Dirk Leuker, a missionary doctor who had been working among lepers for seven years. He lost his wife and four children in the crash, the cause of which was never determined by Dutch authorities.

KLM

AIR CRASH
August 14, 1958

Flight 607-E of the Royal Dutch Airlines (KLM), a Super Constellation, took off from Shannon Airport in Ireland at 11:05 P.M. on August 14, 1958, en route to New York's Idlewild Airport. On board were ninety-nine passengers and crew, eight of them children. Thirty-five minutes later the pilot radioed Shannon that he was proceeding without difficulty. The plane was then 130 miles west of Ireland over a dark Atlantic.

There was no more contact with the plane. It was later discovered that the KLM aircraft had encountered one of those unpredictable and violent electrical storms that sporadically erupt over the Atlantic Ocean. A study of the bodies recovered from the ocean the next day, authorities stated, revealed that a midair explosion had occurred, but they could not pinpoint the exact cause. All on board were dead. Mechanical failure, lightning and even sabotage were possibilities.

At Idlewild relatives of the passengers moaned with grief when told of the crash. One, Joseph Hawrys, a New York elevator operator, who was meeting his mother journeying from Poland for the first time, wept and said, "For fifteen years I've waited. We had a nice home in Poland, but the Russians took it. I sent her money every two weeks." In his hands he clutched red and white carnations he had bought for his mother and a pair of new shoes that would never be worn.

KÖBENHAVN

MARINE DISASTER
December 22, 1928

An ancient five-masted steel vessel, the *Köbenhavn* sailed for Melbourne on December 14, 1928, from the River Plate with a crew of seventy-five, sixty of whom were cadets in training. The last message the *Köbenhavn* sent out to her parent firm, the Danish East Asiatic Company, on December 22, 1928, gave her position as 900 miles off the island of Tristan da Cunha. Not a soul on board that ill-fated ship was ever heard from again.

The company sent out its best ship, the *Mexico,* in search of the *Köbenhavn,* but no trace, not even a life preserver, was ever found. Authorities later presumed that the ship had been trapped with all her sails unfurled in a violent storm and that the rigidity of the vessel had caused her to founder.

Most of the ninety-nine persons who were killed in a KLM crash off the coast of Ireland on August 14, 1958, were buried in a mass grave at Galway. *(Wide World)*

KRAKATOA — VOLCANIC ERUPTION
August 27, 1883

background: Krakatoa, a large volcanic island lying in the Sunda Strait between Sumatra and Java, was discovered in the sixteenth century. Its first recorded eruption was in 1680. Two hundred years later, when the island was covered with tropical vines, shrubs and trees and its volcano was thought to be extinct, the volcano erupted with such force on August 27, 1883, that its sides caved in, causing a 120-foot tidal wave that swept the Java coastal towns, killing more than 36,000 people. Krakatoa completely disgorged its giant magma (molten lava) chamber and flung five cubic miles of rocks and ash in arcs seventeen miles high. The shock wave created by Krakatoa's explosion encircled the earth seven times before dissipating. The 3,000-foot-high volcanic island disappeared into a basin of the ocean floor measuring five miles in width and 800 feet deep. In 1937 a new cone named Anak Krakatoa (Child of Krakatoa) rose from the old caldera (the bowl-shaped volcanic depression beneath the sea) to create a new volcanic island that is still active.

Nothing in recorded history equaled the volcanic explosion of Krakatoa on August 27, 1883. Although it was well known that the little, six-mile-square island between Java and Sumatra in the East Indies was volcanic, and that the entire island was the stump of an old volcano that might millions of years ago have been the largest and the tallest volcano in the world, no one suspected that it would erupt again.

Once a single island, Sumatra and Java were separated by a titanic earthquake and volcanic eruption in A.D. 1115 that left Krakatoa's 3,000-foot volcano intact and jutting between them. Prior to that time Krakatoa had been a towering volcano connecting both islands with a base estimated to have been twenty-five-miles wide, and supported a cone that no doubt mightily overshadowed the forty-nine other pygmy volcanoes (the highest of which was 12,000 feet) that clustered on Java and Sumatra, particularly the Kandangs range of volcanoes running along the southeast coast of Java. According to Sir Robert Ball, "That was the real volcano Krakatoa, after the work of its building up with lava layers had been completed, and before the phase of its self-destruction had begun."

Swollen to such proportions, the colossus first blew its top, then its shoulders and finally sent its body to ashes in 1680. Few details of this eruption are available, and the small but active base remaining on the island was soon forgotten. Though never inhabited Krakatoa was often visited by natives from Java, Sumatra and even Batavia, which was ninety-six miles away. They clambered over its rocks and picked luscious fruit in its verdant jungles.

The "basal wreck" of Krakatoa was dormant until September, 1880, when it gave off warning shocks, which quickly subsided. Then on May 20, 1883, Krakatoa began its ordeal by fire. On Batavia natives heard its first eruptions and described them "as booming sounds like the firing of artillery." A mail steamer passing through the Sunda Strait quivered as the shock waves passed beneath her, and her compass was violently agitated. The following day the German warship *Elisabeth* lay off Krakatoa. Her captain watched Krakatoa's initial upheaval with awe. He estimated the dust and steam column emitting from its cone to be almost 36,000 feet, or seven miles high.

By this time Krakatoa had three new craters rising next to the center cone, and all were in eruption. Far from fearing this smoldering giant, residents at Batavia were excited by the prospect of visiting the rumbling island, and a hundred or so persons, mostly Europeans, chartered an excursion boat and journeyed to the volcano, where they picnicked and played as fine showers of ash fell upon them. A few of the more adventuresome tourists climbed to the summit of the volcano to peer into its main crater. According to one account, "There they beheld a vast column of steam pouring forth with terrific noise from an opening about thirty yards in width."

The visitors, who arrived on May 27, estimated that the main crater, called Perboewatan, was disgorging a vapor tower of no less than 10,000 feet. Lumps of pumice were catapulted 600 feet upward. Deep underground explosions were occurring every five or ten minutes, and each eruption shot forth liquid lava. With each explosion the eerie glow from the lava lit up the overhanging steam column in colorful hues for a few seconds. This light show was considered "most entertaining" by the parasol-spinning visitors. A goodly number of this odd tour group would be dead three months later.

Subsiding for some weeks Krakatoa was again seen erupting from faraway Anjer on June 19. Its vapor column rose and its falling ash increased in density. Six days later another column of vapor was observed. The last human to set foot on the monster before its great paroxysm was a Captain Ferzenaar, chief of the Topographical Survey of Bantam. He stepped ashore onto the slightly quaking island on August 11, 1883, and was appalled to see Krakatoa's jungles leveled. Twenty inches of dust covered the entire island; three vapor columns were being thrown up, and a second crater, Danan, was almost as disruptive as the center crater, Perboewatan. Ferzenaar noted that eleven new eruptive foci were also emitting steam columns and dust. The constant rumbling unnerved the good captain, and he hastily departed after a few hours' visit.

Ten days of relative quiet followed. Then began the great eruption. Writing in England at the time, Sir Robert Ball solemnly commented: "It is indeed believed that in the annals of the earth, there has been no record of a volcanic eruption so vast as that which bears the name of this little island in the far Eastern seas, 10,000 miles from our shores."

On August 25 Batavians almost 100 miles away were kept awake all night by Krakatoa's subterranean rumblings. Avalanches of stone and ash began to erupt and fall. By morning natives at Batavia were prevented from reaching the Sunda Strait. All the bridges were down, and roads were sinking from sight. Fishermen discovered that the waters were sixty degrees hotter than usual, and on that day mountainous waves lashed the coast of Madua, 500 miles from the volcano.

Almost all the volcanoes on Java and Sumatra responded to Krakatoa. The first and largest, Maha-Meru, erupted, and then the most active volcano in the world at that time, Gunuung-guntur, followed, its four-mile diameter quaking as it vomited enormous streams of lava and sulfurous mud. Waterspouts by the scores leaped from the surrounding sea.

On the night of eruption Captain Thompson was on the deck of the *Medea,* which was sailing seventy-six miles northeast of Krakatoa. He watched a black mass of smoke he estimated to be seventeen miles high rising into the moonlit clouds. On another ship only forty miles away from the volcano, Captain Wooldridge thought, "Krakatoa was a terrifying glory . . . it looked like an immense wall, with bursts of forked lightning darting through it, and blazing serpents playing over it. These bursts of brilliancy were the regular uncoverings of the angry fires. As the hours passed, the sea gained an advantage through fresh breaks in the crater walls that offered new points of attack.

"The explosions became more and more frequent until about midnight they sounded to the people of Batavia and Buitentong like one continuous roar, the noise making it impossible for the inhabitants of these places to sleep."

In these towns the concussions of the volcano ripped apart stone walls, shattered lamps and tore gas meters from their sockets.

On August 27, 1883, Krakatoa erupted four times, tearing itself to pieces as its walls blew outward. The third eruption was the worst. As one historian related, "There came an explosion so loud, so violent, and with such far-reaching effects, that it made what had gone before seem as child's play in comparison, and made all other explosions known to the earth in historic times dwindle into insignificance." At Ishore people on the telephone (the lines included a mile-long submarine cable) heard reports like pistol shots. In Singapore, 500 miles away, many put receivers to their ears and heard a roar like a powerful waterfall.

The dust, pumice and vapor that filled the region were so dense that Anjer, at two o'clock in the afternoon, was "pitched into darkness." The sound of the explosions shot out to all points of the compass. Residents in St. Lucia Bay, Borneo, 1,116 miles away, heard it. Those in Tavoy, Burma, 1,478 miles away, listened to the roar. It was heard distinctly by startled people in Perth, Australia, 1,902 miles away; Alice Springs, Australia, 2,233 miles distant, at Diego Garcia in the Chagos Islands, 2,267 miles away; on the island of Rodriguez located on the opposite side of the Sunda Strait, a distance of 2,968 miles from Krakatoa. (There were even reports of hearing the explosion in the United States.)

James Wallis, chief of police in Rodriguez, filed a report in which he stated, "Several times during the night of August 26-27 reports were heard coming from the eastward like the distant roar of heavy guns. These reports continued at intervals of between three and four hours." It was later estimated that it took the sound of Krakatoa's titanic eruption four hours to reach Rodriguez. At St. Lucia Bay, Borneo, a tribe of headhunters was so alarmed at the thundering noise that they were driven mad with the belief that an avenging force was approaching or that an evil spirit was seeking revenge for the frightful murders they had committed. Dozens jumped off cliffs.

Government officials 3,351 miles from the volcano on the tiny island of Timor (made famous by Captain Bligh of the *Bounty,* when he and his loyal few reached the island in an open boat after having been set adrift by Fletcher Christian and his mutineers) became so alarmed that they ordered a steamer out of the harbor to discover the source of the disturbance.

Flocks of sheep stampeded at the sound of vociferous eruptions on the Victoria plains in West Australia, 1,700 miles away. People who lived in Daly Waters, South Australia, were awakened. Those closer to the source of the explosions responded first. Only 350 miles away at Carimon, Java, people pushed to sea in canoes, thinking the noise was that of a gunboat in distress and signaling with her cannons for help.

All the volcanoes in Java, including the fierce Papandayang, opened up with all their fury. Seven fissures opened up on Papandayang, hurtling steaming lava down the steep mountain slope. The entire Maylay Archipelago shuddered as sixty-five miles of the volcanic Kandangs range exploded and disappeared into the sea. Another fifty square miles of Java from Point Capucine to Negery Passoerang sank into the sea. Negery Babawang and Negery, towns with 15,000 inhabitants, disappeared under a colossal seismic sea wave that rushed from Krakatoa with its third and most destructive eruption. The wave was variously estimated to be 50, 90, even 135 feet high as it raced at 600 m.p.h. toward Java, Sumatra

An early Dutch lithograph depicts the volcanic island of Krakatoa before its doomsday eruption on August 27, 1883.

and other nearby areas. More than 300 towns were completely flooded and destroyed throughout the East Indies. Rolling above the *tsunami* were Krakatoa's ashes of powdery pumice stone, which darkened the sky for 275 miles around. Ships at sea as far as 1,600 miles away from the volcano had their decks coated with volcanic ash three days after the explosion.

The resultant *tsunami* was the real killer, rolling up before it the lives of 36,380 persons (although other authorities place the death toll as high as 80,000). N. van Sandick, the engineer of the ship *Loudon,* which was in the vicinity of Krakatoa's explosion, described the *tsunami* sweeping the Java coast. "Suddenly, we saw a gigantic wave of prodigious height advancing from the seashore with considerable speed," his account relates. "Immediately, the crew set to under great pressure and managed after a fashion to set sail in face of the imminent danger; the ship had just enough time to meet with the wave from the front. After a moment, full of anguish, we were lifted up with a dizzy rapidity. The ship made a formidable leap, and immediately afterwards we felt as though we had plunged into the abyss."

The captain had put the bow of his ship directly facing the huge wave, and she rode up almost vertically, the water pressure at the base of the wave shoving her higher and higher until she flipped over the crest and began a descent like a skate on ice at unheard of speeds.

"But the ship's blade went higher, and we were safe," van Sandick continued. "Like a high mountain, the monstrous wave precipitated its journey towards the land. Immediately afterwards another three waves of colossal size appeared. And before our eyes this terrifying upheaval of the sea, in a sweeping transit, consumed in one instant the ruin of the town; the lighthouse fell in one piece, and all the houses of the town were swept away in blow like a castle of cards. All was finished. There, where a few moments ago lived the town of Telok Betong, was nothing but the open sea. . . . We cannot find the words to describe the terrifying events which left us with the sight of such a cataclysm. The thunder-striking suddenness of the changing light, the unexpected devastation which was accomplished in an instant before our eyes, all this left us stupefied, without at first realizing what a disturbing phenomenon had taken place. . . ."

Merak Island and most of its inhabitants disappeared off Java, and those who managed to survive stared bug-eyed at the sea as fourteen new volcanic mountains rose like sea monsters, all gushing lava, steam and stone and forming a chain from St. Nicholas Point in Java to Hoga Point in Sumatra.

At Anjer and Batavia, also in the *tsunami's* path, 2,800 were washed away by the great seismic sea wave. At Bantam, 1,500 were instantly drowned. Serang Island disappeared beneath the waters—no one survived. Hundreds died at Cheribon, Java, as huge rocks and hot lava rained down on them.

The great temple of Boro-Buddor, the largest Buddhist temple in the East, was crushed to ruins by flying stones, rocks and showers of lava. The building was an architectural wonder, and for many it had no equal in the world. First erected about A.D. 790 on a mountain in a circular valley, it had a dome 140 feet high surrounded by seven smaller domes. On the platforms beneath these domes were 450 chapels cut out of granite, the walls exquisitely carved, each chapel with an elegant statue of Buddha. These beautifully chased bas-reliefs, over 4,000 in all, told the picture history of the Buddha. The great chapel beneath the central dome was reached by four enormous staircases, each 500 feet carved in marble. A European architect who visited the temple shortly before its destruction by Krakatoa's eruption said, "No other structure is comparable to it. A few may be even more splendid; but it was decidedly *sui generis.*"

Town by town in the islands was eradicated either by the *tsunami* or by tons of flaming rock and lava shooting across the countryside. Tamarang was engulfed by lava and burning stones that set every building on fire; 1,800 perished here. The island of Midah was covered and all there killed. Gone were the old islands of Steers, Calmeyer and Verlaten, covered with fourteen feet of water. The population of Sibuku and Sibesi islands was wiped out. All the lighthouses in Sunda Strait were snapped off and vanished. At Warlonge 900 were killed; at Talatoa 300 were buried beneath lava. Of the 2,500 persons working the stone quarry on Merak Island, which rose 150 feet above sea level, only two natives and a government bookkeeper survived the island's slow sinking and trembling as the sea plunged over it.

Lying off the Sumatra shore, the man-of-war *Berouw* was caught by the onrushing *tsunami,* then estimated to be fifty or more feet high, and hurled inland a mile and three-quarters, where it was deposited in a forest thirty feet above water.

The captain of the *Loudon,* having ridden out the *tsunami* and finding himself "livid with terror," made sail to Anjer to warn the Dutch fort. He found the entire garrison dead, except for one sailor who was wandering around the corpses that were strewn everywhere.

As Krakatoa sank into the sea, reducing itself to a lumpy rock of about sixteen square yards just barely sticking above the waves, its shock waves raced around the world seven times, four times one way, three the other. Every self-recording barometer in the world marked their passage, each circling the globe every thirty-six hours and traveling at about 700 m.p.h. According to Robert Ball in *Earth's Beginnings,* "every part of our atmosphere had been set into a tingle by the great eruption. In Great Britain the waves passed over our heads; the air in our streets, the air in our houses, trembled from the volcanic impulse. The oxygen supplying our lungs was responding also to the supreme convulsion that took place 10,000 miles away."

With the first atmospheric shock wave, the islands of Java and Sumatra experienced yet another horror. Whirlwinds and tornadoes swept high into the air the remaining rooftops, people and horses, running the death count ever higher.

As the world's barometers recorded this most momentous disaster, other scientists recorded the accompanying *tsunami* that raced across the oceans to Colombo, 1,760 miles away; to Bombay, 2,700 miles distant; to Cape Horn, 5,000 miles away, where the wave reached land traveling 350 m.p.h. and measured three feet.

The explosion of Krakatoa created one of the world's strangest natural phenomena; the fine dust from it remained in the upper atmosphere for more than two years, providing unequaled sunsets and skyglows. These skyglows were of such startling intensity that in such distant places as New Haven, Connecticut, fire engines more than once were called out to fight what were thought to be nearby fires. The Royal Society of London culled reports from all the world over. Weeks later at Seychelles the sun was "seen as through a fog at sunset, and there was a lurid glare all over the sky." At Mauritius: "Crimson dawn, sun red after rising, gorgeous sunset, first of the afterglows, sky and clouds yellow and red up to the zenith" At Natal: "Sky vivid red, fading into green and purple." The sun appeared blue in South America; in Panama it looked green. In Trinidad: "The sun looked like a blue ball, and after sunset the sky became so red that there was supposed to be a big fire." In Honolulu the sun set green for months.

Tennyson could not resist writing of the cosmic splendor that marked Krakatoa's fantastic end:

> Had the fierce ashes of some fiery peak
> Been hurled so high they ranged around the world,
> For day by day through many a blood-red eye
> The wrathful sunset glared.

For months the pumice shot off by Krakatoa settled, sometimes seven feet thick and floating on the sea, a definite hazard to navigation. The ash coated the Indian Ocean and covered beaches at Madagascar five months later.

Most geologists believe that the extreme suddenness and violence of Krakatoa's great explosion was due to the forming of a new cavity that allowed enormous volumes of ocean water to pour downward, meet with the heated strata beneath the earth's crust, and form ever-expanding steam pressure that created the force that blew the hole in the East Indies waters. Since that time Anak Krakatoa, born in the same spot as the old volcano, exploded in a minor way in 1928.

Krakatoa is not, however, dormant, and its occasional rumblings can be heard by neighboring natives. Some experts feel that this monster of all volcanoes, located in an area where the earth's crust is especially thin, could explode in the future the same way as it did in 1883.
(ALSO SEE: Cotopaxi, Etna, Tomboro, Vesuvius)

KREBS, OKLAHOMA — MINE DISASTER

January 7, 1892

background: Mine Number 11 owned and operated by the Osage Coal and Mining Company at Krebs, Oklahoma, rocked to pieces at 5:04 P.M. on January 7, 1892, when shot firers set off an overcharged blast that ignited the escaping gas, always plentiful and present in the main shafts. More than 500 miners were in the mine, and of these 100 were killed immediately or died later of injuries.

The Osage firm's Mine Number 11 at Krebs, Oklahoma, was usually seeping gas and dust. Supervisors felt they had overcome the danger by having shot firers do their blasting only after the shafts had been cleared of the 400 to 500 miners working below. Usually this meant that a crew of about six shot firers entered the mine and began blasting after 5:30 P.M.

On January 7, 1892, this crew was early and lethal. The mining crews were lined up at the bottom of the main shaft and were just being lifted to the surface in cages. Five cages had been raised, and about thirty men had stepped out of the entranceway at 5:04 P.M. At that moment, either in haste or stupidity, one of the shot firers set off a tremendous explosion heard for miles. As the last of six men stepped from the platform, the cage was sent fifty feet skyward through the roof of the mine tower. Flames and smoke carried it upward.

Hundreds of men at the base of the shaft were injured. They began to climb the shaft, some so badly burned that the flesh of their hands peeled off as they grasped the splintery ladders. One man scaled the 450-foot shaft with a broken leg. A father sent his son climbing upward while he looked for another son deep in the colliery; both were later found dead in each other's arms.

About 400 men managed to get out of the mine, which was then full of lethal gas. Another 100 were somewhere below. Thousands of miners in other shafts for a five-mile area stopped work and rushed to the scene to help. As the scores of rescuers descended slowly to the base of the main shaft, they reeled back in horror. Piles of dead, mutilated by the wall-collapsing explosion, jutted from the earth below. As one reporter stated, "Heads, arms, legs, hands and feet were in many instances torn from the trunks. Their clothes were either partially or entirely burned away . . . and in several instances the flames had literally roasted all the flesh on the body."

Bodies and pieces of bodies were hauled upward in baskets and taken to the blacksmith shop nearby where wailing relatives fumbled among the torn flesh. Those working below discovered "here a head, there a hand or leg protruding from the mass of fallen rock . . . A number of burned lamps, caps, [and] dinner buckets completed the desolation of the scene. The bodies were removed with all possible care, but this did not prevent an arm or leg, almost severed from the body, from being completely torn off when taken from under the wreckage."

A race riot almost erupted, according to the *New York Times,* when scores of blacks appeared and "assisted in the work in only a half-hearted way, and one of their number was heard to say that it served the miners right to have been killed." (The blacks had sought work in the Indian Territory mines for some time, but white miners had refused to work with them.) Hearing the remark, white miners turned on the blacks and began to beat them. A United States Deputy Marshal arrived with a posse to "drive the colored men from the place with Winchesters."

The final death count, although never fully determined because some bodies could not be identified, was estimated at 100.

L

L-24 — MARINE DISASTER
January 10, 1924

background: Completed in 1919 as part of England's war program, the *L-24* was one of the most modern submarines of her day with a displacement of 890 tons when surfaced and 1,070 when submerged. Essentially a minelayer with fourteen mine tubes and four torpedo tubes, the *L-24* was 238 feet, 6 inches long. Inexplicably the submarine surfaced abruptly in waters off Portland Bill, England, and was instantly rammed and sunk by the dreadnought *Resolution*. All forty-eight crew men in the sub were killed.

"It is feared that the *L-24* is gone with the loss of all hands" is the way the British admiralty announced the sinking of its then ultramodern submarine-minelayer, the *L-24*. Exactly what prompted Lieutenant Commander Eddis, captain of the *L-24*, to order the submarine to surface in the fatal path of the British battleship *Resolution* will never be known. The error cost Eddis his own life and those of forty-seven others who jammed the sub's compartments during maneuvers on January 10, 1924.

The *L-24* had joined the fleet for maneuvers just after two other subs, *K-2* and *K-12*, had collided, causing serious damage.

A minelayer carrying fourteen live mines, the *L-24* broke the surface in dense fog eleven miles off Portland. A lookout on the battleship *Resolution* spotted the submarine dead ahead. Though the *Resolution* was equipped with special hearing devices to detect the presence of submarines, she failed to locate the *L-24* until the ship reared up before her. The 25,750-ton battleship going 12 knots an hour was on the partly emerged submarine within seconds, and according to most reports, she "cut her in two."

The broken submarine sank in about thirty fathoms of water. At first there was hope that the forty-eight men on board might be saved, that perhaps there had been enough time for the crew to scramble behind watertight compartment doors. Salvage vessels rushed to the area, but they failed to uncover either bodies or wreckage.

The tragedy was further compounded because the *L-24* was carrying twice the usual number of crew members. Her compartments were filled with trainees. None of the forty-eight on board were ever found.

LA CANADA VALLEY, CALIFORNIA — FLOOD
January 1, 1934

Heavy rains in the San Gabriel range produced a New Year's Eve flood of great proportions that rolled rock, mud and debris into La Canada valley at dawn on January 1, 1934. Floodwaters, jagged with floating cars,

Britain's most modern submarine, the *L-24*, was rammed by the dreadnought *Resolution* off Portland Bill on January 10, 1924. All forty-four on board the sub perished. *(UPI)*

garages, torn bridges and splintered buildings, raced through the valley nestled outside of Los Angeles and converged on Verdugo Creek, swamping the main drainage canal and bloating all the surrounding tributaries that surged through Glendale. The flash flood destroyed 500 houses, caused $5 million in damages, and killed forty persons. Forty people were missing.

LA COUBRE — EXPLOSION

March 4, 1960

The Belgian munitions ship *La Coubre,* carrying seventy-six tons of arms and explosives in her holds, tied up at dockside in Havana harbor on March 4, 1960, as loaders and soldiers swarmed over her to take off her prized cargo. Just as longshoremen were swinging over the last of the grenade shipments at 3:00 P.M., the ship exploded, igniting the remaining cargo.

On *La Coubre*'s bridge was Don Chapman, who immediately jumped down to the next deck. He heard "exploding shells whistling all over the place." Chapman worked himself over the side and slid down two more decks. "Debris filled the air. The explosion blew out the entire aftersection, causing the ship to roll over in the water on its side."

Firemen rushed onto the dock—some were on the ship when she flopped over. One fireman, G. Delgado, was trapped in a rear hold. He was quoted as saying, "It looked like a scene from Dante's *Inferno.* Bodies and pieces of bodies were all over. God knows how I escaped. Bullets and shrapnel were flying all around me."

Above the flaming dock and sinking ship hovered a helicopter, and in it, Fidel Castro angrily gritted his teeth. He later charged the United States with sabotaging the ship. When some of his own officials pointed out that most of the 100 men who died in the accident were killed by grenade shrapnel that fell when a hoist broke, spilling its contents to the dock, Castro ordered an experiment. He had a plane drop two cases of grenades from 400 feet onto a baseball field; he later fulminated, "It is practically impossible for a grenade to explode when dropped."

Castro said nothing about the half-dozen persons who were killed or wounded when they attempted to pick up these grenades.

(ALSO SEE: Bone, Algeria)

LADY ELGIN — MARINE DISASTER

September 8, 1860

background: Built in Buffalo in 1851 by Bidwell & Banta for $96,000, the steam sidewheeler *Lady Elgin,* 300 feet long, sailed from Milwaukee to Chicago on September 7, 1860, and during the return excursion trip on September 8, 1860, at 2:30 A.M., the schooner *Augusta of Oswego,* running dark (the *Lady Elgin* was brightly lit), collided with the excursion steamer off Winnetka, Illinois. Of the 385 persons on board (300 members of the Union Guards, 50 regular passengers, and 35 officers and men of the crew), 287 persons were drowned when the ship foundered ten miles offshore in a hard gale, making this, next to the sinking of the *Eastland* in the Chicago River on July 24, 1915, the worst Great Lakes disaster ever. The captain of the *Augusta,* D. M. Malott, was arrested and tried but found not guilty of navigational negligence.

The sinking of the *Lady Elgin* on September 8, 1860, in Lake Michigan was to cause immense loss of life, years of bitterness and hatred and radical changes in the archaic maritime laws. The steam sidepaddler's end is almost the "classic" finish to a ship in distress—a jubilant, celebrating holiday crowd dancing in the salon in the middle of the night, ship's lights ablaze, the ramming by an ancient schooner without lights, and the abandonment of almost 400 terrorized souls in lake water churned furiously by a wild gale.

The *Lady Elgin,* owned by Gordon S. Hubbard and Company, was based in Chicago and carried passengers throughout the Great Lakes. The ship operated without mishap for four years. On September 7, 1860, the *Lady Elgin* stopped at Milwaukee to pick up 300 Chicago-bound members of the Union Guard club, who planned to form a volunteer unit to fight for the Union in the event of war with the South. The excursion trip to Chicago was really a fund-raising gala for that purpose.

The trip to Chicago was uneventful, but the return voyage to Milwaukee (with fifty additional passengers on board and a destination of Mackinac Island and other ports in Lake Superior) was a nightmare. All went well until about 2:00 A.M. on Saturday morning. Scores of Union Guard members and their sweethearts were dancing in the saloon. Captain John Wilson, an able and conscientious skipper, was at the helm of his ship, which was brightly lighted from bow to stern and making slow progress past Winnetka, Illinois, as the waves broken by the two side paddlewheels increased in height and a strong wind came up.

Ten minutes later the second mate of the *Augusta of Oswego,* which was southbound with a heavy load of lumber in her hold, spotted the tiny, flickering lights of the *Lady Elgin* in the distance. It appeared as if the two ships were on a collision course, but the mate only stared dreamily at the lights and, strangely, gave no orders. The *Augusta*'s captain, D. M. Malott, came forward and looked at the oncoming *Lady Elgin,* her lights looming larger. His own ship was dark, and Malott made no effort at all to signal his ship's approach. He was an old-school sailing master who knew "his rights," and the regulations at that time, stupid as they were, gave carte blanche right-of-way to any and all sailing vessels. They were not

The schooner *Augusta* limped into port after colliding with and sinking the *Lady Elgin* in Lake Michigan, September 1860.

required to show signal lights, and their arbitrary passage when encountering any steam ship was purely at the discretion of the skipper. The unwritten rule of the sea and lakes, however, was that Malott, from his position, should have passed the *Lady Elgin* from the larboard side. But that would have required special maneuvering, and he was apparently in no mood to expend the labor. He kept coming to starboard.

Moments before the two ships came together, rain began to fall, obscuring everyone's vision. Intense winds began to toss both ships about. Lightning fiercely brightened an otherwise pitch black night. Since the schooner was running dark, no one on board the *Lady Elgin* saw the *Augusta* racing forward until it was too late to take evasive action. A minute or two before the collision, Captain Malott, almost in an off-handed way, ordered his helm head up, but it was a useless gesture. The *Augusta,* lurching forward with the full weight of her cargo of lumber crammed in her bow holds, rammed into the *Lady Elgin,* gouging out a gaping hole in her side. The schooner then backed off and sailed alongside the *Lady Elgin,* whose Captain Wilson was already signaling the *Augusta* to give aid, which she did not. (At a subsequent inquiry Malott claimed he had hailed the steamer, shouting, "Do you need any help?" and, hearing no reply, sailed on to Chicago, where he casually informed port authorities that he had struck some sort of ship.)

Meanwhile the *Lady Elgin* was sinking fast in the full force of a gale. Captain Wilson lowered a lifeboat to check the damage, but this boat fell far astern of the steamer as it plowed through the waves. The more than 350 persons still on board rushed from the saloon and their staterooms.

As the freight in the steamer's holds began to shift violently, tipping her further into the water, Captain Wilson ordered his crew to hand out the life preservers—there were 400 of them on board, five-foot-long and eighteen-inch-wide planks with rope at each end to grasp—and lower the four remaining yawls and two lifeboats. The two lifeboats were lowered, filled with passengers, and quickly drifted off. The yawls were never launched. The *Lady Elgin* suddenly shifted into the water and dove for the bottom, her passengers and crew members leaping frantically into the swirling lake.

While the 18 persons in the lifeboats made for shore ten miles away, ignorant of the steamer's quick sinking, Captain Wilson and more than 300 others clung to a large, slippery piece of wreckage that was mostly submerged because so many people were trying to hang on to it. Wilson was a model of courage and stamina. He crawled upon this makeshift raft, shifting people about and constantly talking to them, encouraging them with loud promises of help to come.

One passenger who managed to survive the ordeal, a man named Bellman, was in this group and later recalled, "The raft was nearly under water from the weight of its living burden, and very few who clung to it . . . were above the waist in the turbulent sea. The captain was constantly on his feet, encouraging the crowd, and seems to have been the only man who dared to stir from his recumbent position, which was necessary to keep a secure hold upon the precarious raft. He carried a child, which he found in the arms of an exhausted and submerged woman, to an elevated portion of the raft, and left it in charge of a woman, but it was soon lost.

"He constantly exhorted the crowd to keep silent, and not only to make no noise, but to refrain from moving, in order that the frail framework might last longer."

Silently, with only John Wilson's strong voice and the whistling wind to break the quiet, dozens began to drown. The raft finally broke to pieces, and groups drifted off, trying to paddle somehow for shore. Wilson was last seen grabbing a floating door, lifting two women and a child upon it, and then sinking from sight. His body was found three days later.

A scant few survived the ten-mile swim to shore as they battled large combers crashing over and about them. Bellman, with two others, was thrown off a small raft about twenty times per hour for ten hours until, exhausted, he was washed ashore and picked up by Winnetka citizens.

A dozen students from the Garrett Biblical Institute and Northwestern University joined those on the Winnetka beaches, and these young men swam out into the foaming surf several times to make heroic rescues. One, Edward W. Spencer, who was studying to be a minister, became a ferocious rescuer, plunging over and over into the choppy lake waters, swimming great distances, and bringing back seventeen persons alive. He finally collapsed on the beach and, half-conscious, babbled through tears, "Did I do my best? Did I do my best?"

Spencer ruined his health for life in the rescue work, becoming so enfeebled by his heroism that he was forced to withdraw from college. He died many years later, at the age of eighty-one, a semi-invalid. "His was the real glory," a priest later eulogized.

Only 98 persons survived the sinking of the *Lady Elgin;* 287 died in the water. Captain Malott was arrested and tried but found not guilty of the ramming because the ancient maritime laws allowed sailing skippers complete freedom to navigate their ships at will, haphazardly or not. Because of this tragedy, however, new laws were soon established that compelled all classes of vessels to correspond to the same rules.

The *Augusta* became a hated ship, and once, though her color had been changed from black to white and her name had been changed to the *Colonel Cook,* she was almost burned by an angry Milwaukee mob of grieving relatives of the Union Guard members who perished in the calamity. The stigma of the disaster remained for thirty-four years. Sailors refused to ship on the schooner, and mishaps dotted her checkered career on the lakes. The *Colonel Cook* was finally smashed to splinters in a storm off Cleveland in 1894. The pig-headed Captain Malott was not aboard the schooner at that time. He quickly changed ships after the *Lady Elgin* ramming, but fate appeared to track him down. He and his original crew from the *Augusta* were all lost when their ship, the *Mahor,* sank in a storm.

(ALSO SEE: Eastland*)*

LAKE DENMARK, NEW JERSEY — EXPLOSION — July 19, 1926

background: During a massive storm on July 19, 1926, the Lake Denmark United States naval ammunition dump was struck by lightning. Dozens of warehouses exploded and sent out a shower of deadly shells, many of these falling on ten nearby towns and villages, which suffered extensive damage. Dead were 30 persons with another 400 seriously injured. Damage to the base and loss of material exceeded $85 million.

Several marines were doing kitchen police duty at the naval ammunition depot at Lake Denmark, New Jersey, on July 19, 1926, while a raging storm pounded the area. Most of the marines peeling potatoes thought themselves

United States Navy munitions warehouses burned and exploded at Lake Denmark, New Jersey, on July 19, 1926. Thirty were killed by flying bombs. *(UPI)*

lucky to be inside instead of slogging through the rain-drenched area on sentinel duty. Suddenly the mess building blew up; one marine flew fifteen feet through the air, literally hoisted clean out of his boots. He and others picked themselves up and ran for the hills as shells from the ammunition dump whistled overhead. After running three miles the shoeless marine realized he was barefoot. A companion ripped off his shirt and bound up his bloody, crippled feet. Then they ran on until they reached a highway and hitched a ride with a startled motorist. "We're all through with the Marine Corps, buddy," they told him and never bothered to explain that the arsenal had mysteriously blown up. They themselves did not know what had happened.

Lightning had struck one of the large buildings housing TNT on the base and had caused it to explode, creating a chain reaction that upended the entire base with explosions that took hours to subside. Machine gun bullets whined everywhere; heavy shells whizzed past and bombarded at least thirty towns.

Frances Feeney of Brooklyn happened to be driving by the base when the explosion took place. A shell landed on her moving car and blew it apart. It was noted that she wore a "blood-wet coat, one arm ripped off." Searchers found her husband's Elk's card in the coat. *Evening Post* reporters arrived while the explosions were still in progress, and one knelt down to pick up a souvenir shell. A sailor swung on him, knocked him down, and shouted angrily, "For God's sake, leave that alone! That can blow you to pieces, man."

Two hundred-twenty marines in gas masks and tin derbies arrived from Quantico and searched the shell-bursting hills for survivors. Civilians like Roger McCormick, a fruit huckster, helped. McCormick yanked a marine, Coasmer Kinzick, from the Rockaway River. He had been blown over 100 yards to the river and lived.

Reporters for the *New York American* found Dora Dowling, a refugee, in the home of friends in Glen Ridge. She had run a distance of eighteen miles to get there, and had been knocked down repeatedly by explosions. Her husband was Captain Otto G. Dowling, commandant of the shattered Lake Denmark base. "I was sitting with Captain Dowling in the sun parlor of our home watching the storm," she told the reporters. "Suddenly a livid streak of lightning flashed zigzag down the sky. He said to me, 'Wasn't that a wicked one?' " An orderly called the Dowlings seconds later to tell him the base was exploding. He dashed off into the storm, and his wife, knocked down by an exploding shell that hit the house, raced outside in time to avoid being crushed to death as the entire building collapsed.

She joined hundreds fleeing the exploding valley. A young pharmacist named Bernard Shackman, "with his lip torn half off and bleeding over his entire face," grabbed her as she fell again. He carried her for several miles.

Captain Dowling was injured by exploding shells as he drove up to the first exploding warehouse: his eyes were burned and his face was lacerated.

Henry Wadhams, a civilian bookkeeper who lived in a cottage on the base, was found wandering in the woods, cut behind the ear and bleeding. He insisted on returning to his house to look for his wife. Lieutenant William F. Jones and some others accompanied him. The Wadhams' cottage was a shambles. The marines poked about half-heartedly in the debris of broken dishes, records and women's clothing. Wadhams fell to his knees and began to claw at the debris.

"I'm sorry, old man," Lieutenant Jones said to him. "You know, I didn't want you to come . . ."

"But she's my wife," Wadhams wept back, "I loved her very much."

The party could hear the dull explosions still going on a quarter of a mile away. Wadhams pointed to a spot. "It was about here that the first explosion threw me on my face. I had run to the office, got the records. Had to get the records. I got up. I found myself alongside Building 23. Then the whole end of that building blew out. What do you know about that?"

The marines were motionless as they watched Wadhams scratching at the rubble, his words barely intelligible. He would stare up at them with a blank expression and then go on digging and talking. "Right in front of me—see?—the TNT cans stood exposed. 'They're going next,' I says to myself. I ran to the powerhouse. See over there—smokestack's all that's left. The third explosion lifted me up, jerked my hand off my neck, filled my eyes and ears with. . . . Just imagine, I was fifty feet away after that. I don't see how I flew there in the air. I was on my knees as if I were praying. Then I looked around for her. The noise frightened me. Shells made red flashes. So I got on my feet and ran. Three marines were yelling at me. A magazine blew up. They were gone. One minute I saw them plain as day. Then they—were gone. Can you beat that? Big shell fragments were falling at my feet. I was crazy with worry for my wife. I didn't know where to look. Everything was blown to hell." Henry Wadhams kept digging into the ruins of his cottage. "It's very strange," he moaned. "She ought to be around here somewhere."

Lieutenant Jones reached down and brought Wadhams up by the shoulders. "Come on, let's go back to Dover [the United States Naval Hospital]. We'll come back tomorrow, old man, okay?" They led Wadhams away. The body of his wife was found two hours later in a nearby woods where she had been blown.

Savage winds—estimated to be often at 500 m.p.h.—ripped across Florida in September 1928, creating $25 million in damage around Lake Okeechobee. More than 2,500 people were killed. *(Wide World)*

LAKE OKEECHOBEE, FLORIDA **HURRICANE September 10-16, 1928**

background: An Atlantic hurricane, swirling 500 m.p.h. at its eyewall, drove in a massive front more than 235 miles long at the Lesser Antilles, striking Guadeloupe, Montserrat, Nevis, St. Kitts, St. Croix, St. Thomas, Puerto Rico, part of the Dominican Republic, almost all the Bahama Islands, Florida, and the entire United States Atlantic coastline to Cape Hatteras, where it veered off into the ocean once again. Almost 5,000 persons were killed by this storm, and an estimated 350,000 were made homeless. This super hurricane caused damage estimated to be almost a half billion dollars; hardest hit was Florida's clear-water Lake Okeechobee, northwest of Palm Beach, where about 2,500 were killed and $25 million in damages was done.

Born somewhere off the African coast, a massive hurricane moved against Barbados on September 10, 1928, taking two days to reach Guadeloupe, where it flattened every building and left 600 dead. Puerto Rico was next hit by the relentless storm front, estimated by one authority to be about 230 miles in diameter. More than 1,000 persons died in Puerto Rico as a result of the storm, and a quarter of a million residents were left without shelter.

Of all the islands Puerto Rico was the most devastated. One figure given by Red Cross officials counted 284,000 persons made homeless by the killer storm. More than 1,000 would have been killed had it not been for a single girl, Felicia Cartegene, a telephone operator in Coamo, Puerto Rico, who stayed at her post and gave hundreds of warnings, calling for outside aid until the storm overwhelmed the small building in which she worked and killed her. News reports of the victims' plight in Puerto Rico were ghastly. A mother was found with a child in each arm, all three "almost cut in two" by flying sheets of roofing blown through the town of Cayey. Also in the same town, a storeowner, after having admitted several refugees to his shop, was blown freakishly through a window for hundreds of yards into a river, where he drowned. Fourteen churchgoers were found dead, kneeling at an altar that was still under construction. The dome collapsed on them as they prayed for deliverance from the storm.

With $50 million in damages done to Puerto Rico, the hurricane unraveled its fierce winds across the white beaches of the Florida coast, smashing with all its fury against West Palm Beach.

The twenty-one miles of mud dikes around Lake Okeechobee, a clear-water lake, were flattened, and the lake water was hurled upward to mesh with that of the hurricane, pounding Okeechobee buildings to ruins and killing the residents, mostly farmers who had come south during the Florida land boom two years earlier to cultivate the rich loam around the lake.

Belle Glade inhabitants, about 650 people in all, rushed for the safety of the two most sturdily-built shelters in town, the Glades Hotel and the Belle Glade Hotel. When the storm struck, the hurricane winds threw great walls of water over the entire area, crumbling all dikes, houses, and buildings, except the two hotels. Only those crammed into the hotels survived.

Every resident of Ritta Island and Pelican Bay was killed. In many swampy areas parents with children clinging to their backs climbed trees to escape the storm's wrath, but they were not alone. Hundreds of poisonous water moccasins also took refuge in the trees—many died from snakebite.

In two days National Guardsmen, Boy Scouts and other workers recovered about 2,500 bodies, many of which were so badly decomposed that they were unrecognizable. The bodies arrived in West Palm Beach by the truckload. In the swamps nauseated and angry would-be rescuers roped dozens of bodies together like rafts and floated the bloated corpses to shore for burial. In one West Palm Beach trench 700 bodies were covered with quicklime and buried quickly to prevent disease. When exhausted workers could not bury the dead fast enough, they built huge fires and tossed the corpses into the flames. These funeral pyres could be seen for miles away for two nights.

The failure of the dikes at Lake Okeechobee caused most of the deaths in Florida, and angry citizens lobbied for two years to acquire flood protection. In 1930 a $5 million bond issue supported by President Herbert Hoover enabled the building of a rock dike 85 miles long and 38 feet high to contain the 12,000 square miles of the Lake Okeechobee-Everglades water area. Sadly, like the people of Galveston, Florida residents had waited too long to build a hurricane-proof barrier. It took mounds of dead to warrant the construction.

LAKE VIEW SCHOOL

FIRE
March 4, 1908

background: The Lake View School in the Cleveland suburb of Collinwood, Ohio, had 325 students in attendance when it caught fire on March 4, 1908; the cause of the fire was never determined. Of the 325 children trapped in the school building, 176 perished in the flames along with two teachers who refused to desert them. Narrow halls, only one open entranceway (the rear door was locked) and doors that opened inward were blamed for the high death toll.

Three small girls were the first to spot the fire. Coming up from the basement of the Lake View School on March 4, 1908, they saw smoke curling out from beneath the bottom of the front staircase. "There's smoke over there," they chorused to Frank Herter, the janitor, and then climbed the stairs to their upper-floor classrooms and most probably their deaths. The grade school in the quiet suburb of Collinwood, ten miles from downtown Cleveland, was ripe for disaster. All of its classroom doors opened inward. Its front entrance door opened inward. Its boiler had been placed beneath the front hall stairways. For no apparent reason its back door was locked. The hallways in the school were extremely narrow.

Herter stopped sweeping the floor when the girls called out to him and looked up to see "a wisp of smoke." He ran to the fire alarm and pulled the gong. Then, according to his later testimony, he ran to the front and rear doors. "I can't remember what happened next," he later explained. It was obvious that he panicked, since rescuers who ran to the rear door of the school building found it bolted shut and were unable to either open it or break it down. In his terror Herter may have locked the door instead of opening it.

Though the children had had several fire drills throughout the year, most of them panicked at the first sound of the fire gong. Most of the teachers ran to a rear window of the schoolhouse and saved themselves. Among this group was the principal, Anna Moran, and two teachers, Miss Gollmar and Miss Rowley. Miss Gollmar led her class down the front stairs just after the alarm sounded, but the stairway was clotted with heaps of clawing, screaming children, and the flames walled up in front of her class. She told them to turn around and go back to the rear entrance. They became jammed up on the narrow stairway, and at this moment Miss Gollmar deserted her charges, working her way around them as they fought to escape, and making her way toward the rear stairways, explaining later, "The only thing for me to do was to get around to the rear door if possible and help those who were near the entrance." She claimed that she pulled at the children at the rear door, after climbing out of a window. How this was possible is unknown because the rear door was bolted shut. "I could not pull even one of them out," Miss Gollmar later stated. "Those behind pushed forward, and as I stood there, the little ones piled up on one another. Those who could stretched out their arms to me and cried for me to help them. I tried with all my might to pull them out and stayed there until the flames drove me away."

Minutes after the alarm was given, Mrs. Walter Kelly, whose home was near the school, ran to the building. By then the facade of the building was a mass of flames. The closed front door was blocked by an enormous mound of screaming, burning children whose agonized wails could be heard. Unable to open this door, Mrs. Kelly raced to the rear door, hoping to find it open. She had two children inside the school. A man passing by joined her and both of

Stunned parents and would-be rescuers mill helplessly about the Lake View School in Collingwood, Ohio, on March 4, 1908; 176 children died in the fire. *(UPI)*

them beat on the locked door until their fists were bloody. They then turned to the windows and began to smash them. When these were broken, dozens of small children appeared, and Mrs. Kelly and her companion began to take them out. Her own children died that day.

Another neighbor, Mrs. John Philits, was called to a window of her Poplar Street home by her four-year-old son, who pointed to the school, saying, "See the children playing on the fire escape." Mrs. Philits ran to the blazing schoolhouse and discovered her young daughter trapped inside the mass of struggling children behind the front door, which was then partially open. Mrs. Philits took hold of her daughter's hands, but she could not free her. "I reached in and stroked her head," the half-hysterical mother later said, "trying to keep the fire from burning her hair. I stayed there and pulled at her, and tried to keep the fire away from her till a heavy piece of glass fell on me, cutting my hand nearly off. Then I fell back and my girl died before my face."

Firemen from five station houses reached the school within minutes after the alarm was sounded, but they, too, could do nothing. They took what few children they could from the windows of the first floor, but their ladders would not reach the second and third floors. As more than 8,000 persons, almost every person in the suburb of Collinwood, surrounded the school, firemen were jeered and kicked when the pressure of their water hoses was insufficient to send a stream of water to the second and third floors.

Prior to their arrival, Henry Ellis, a real estate broker, and I. E. Cross, a train superintendent, saw the blaze and rushed together to the front door. Try as they might, like Mrs. Kelly and Mrs. Philits before them, they could not budge the inward-swinging door. "I could see the flames coming through the floor," Ellis said.

Both men ran to the rear door. They put their burly shoulders to it, and finally it gave way. They gasped at the sight of a huge mound of children piled there, roasted to death. Even more were screaming and piling up on the dead. Flames from the walls reached out, according to Ellis, to "catch first one and then another" child. "I saw one girl who could not have been more than ten or eleven years old protect her little brother, who was not more than six. He cried for help and clung to her hand. She encouraged him and covered his head with a shawl she had been wearing to keep the flames away. The fire caught them in a minute and both were killed." Cross and Ellis did manage to grab dozens of youngsters from the top of this awful heap of dying children. They worked furiously, literally tossing children out into the yard over their shoulders until their hands were so badly burned that the blackened skin fell off. One of those they hauled out from beneath the death heap was Pearl Lynn, a teacher who, while trying to stem the panic at the rear door, had been knocked down and buried by the bodies of the desperate children. She lived.

Courageous Laura Bodey, a fifth-grade teacher whose class was trapped on the third floor, threw herself across the door leading into the flaming hallway when seven or eight of her students cried to the rest in the class to run down the hall to the rear entranceway. Miss Bodey physically threw back her students who were about to follow this panicking group. Then she lined up the almost fifty remaining children and sent them in orderly file out the window and down the school's only fire escape to the ground. Miss Bodey waited for the seven or eight students who had bolted for the rear doors to return, but they never came back. Flames finally drove her out the window and down the fire escape.

On the first floor all was bedlam. Classmates already at the front door could not escape the flames as more and more children from the second floor fought to get out while they were fighting to get up the stairs. Ethel Rose, whose students were the youngest in the school, refused to let them into the first-floor hallway. She closed her classroom door, ran to a window and, finding it locked, smashed the glass with her hands. Clearing out the pane with a ruler, she lowered her pupils one by one to the ground. Three were lost in the flames and smoke, and Rose herself just barely escaped, carrying the two smallest children in her arms.

Another heroic teacher, Grace Fiske, died in the flames while desperately trying to save her children. Hers was the first classroom to be invaded by the fire, the first-grade room on the first floor that was very near the front entranceway, where the fire originated. In seconds the fire burst through the closed door of the room and Fiske cried out, "Children, the windows, get out the windows to the fire escape." She herself did not move toward the windows but began to gather up her startled students, shoving them toward the windows in groups. Most of those in her classroom survived; one little boy turned back and cried, seeing her engulfed in flames.

Another teacher, Katherine Weiler, also died while attempting to protect her pupils from the inferno. One of her students, Marie Whitman, asked Weiler if she could look for her little brother. "Go child, run," her teacher replied as she was dragging two unconscious children toward an open window. The Whitman girl ran through a burning hallway, rushed into her seven-year-old brother's classroom, and, dragging him by the hair, took him out a window. They fell into the arms of a fireman. Both were nearly asphyxiated by the smoke, but they survived.

Charles G. McIlrath, chief of the Collinwood police, arrived to see his son, Hugh, leading scores of younger students down the fire escape. A distance of about eight feet separated the bottom of the escape from the ground. Hugh McIlrath lowered several little children down when they would not jump. Noticing others afraid to make the jump, running back up the fire escape, he raced after them, saving a dozen from the fire. Flames were by then shooting from almost every window in the school and Police Chief McIlrath called to his son, "Jump, Hugh! Jump! Save yourself, boy!" Young Hugh McIlrath, his face already blackened by the fire, shouted back that there were still more children inside and he was going to get them. He ran inside the inferno as thousands watched and moaned. His body was later found on a stairway. In his arms were two small, dead children.

The throng outside agonized aloud at their inability to aid those trapped inside. They watched as small faces white with terror appeared at the windows. Arms shot upward in pleas. Then smoke and fire drew the children back and took them into death. They watched as three little girls, Mary Ridgeway, Anna Roth and Gertrude Davis, who had made their way to an attic window as they retreated before the fire, jumped three floors to their deaths. They watched as twelve-year-old Glenn Sanderson made a spectacular effort to save himself. Trapped on the third floor of the school auditorium, Sanderson saw that the flaming floor beneath him was about to give way and, swinging from one piece of stage drapery to another, he attempted to reach the fire escape. The brave lad had almost swung himself across the stage area when he missed a piece of the flimsy material and fell into the fire below.

In three hours it was all over. The fire abated, and the almost useless fire hoses were turned off. Stunned, the huge crowd stood silently staring at the gutted school until the sun went down. In the darkness under lantern light, they began to take away the small, charred bodies, most of which were unrecognizable. The first identified dead child was Nels Thompson, whose weeping mother recognized him by his suspender buckle. Fifteen-year-old Irene Davis was identified when her baby sister pointed to a fragment of her burned skirt. Little eight-year-old Dan Clark was recognized by a small pink handkerchief in which that morning, his father remembered, he had placed a new bright green marble. Deputy Coroner Harry McNeil shook his head bitterly as he pointed to the rows of dead. One hundred seventy-six there would be in all, lining the walls of the Lake Shore Depot, a makeshift morgue. Hundreds of anxious parents were lined up outside seeking information about their children. "What can I tell them?" McNeil, tears running down his cheeks, said to reporters with their heads bent, not looking at him or the dead. "What? I have portions of bodies and dozens of hands and feet which have been torn off and burned away. . . . How can identification be made? How?" The reporters had no answer.

Frank Herter, the janitor, was found that evening with his hands almost burned away. He had tried to help the children in the flames, he said. He sat and said in monotone, "I saw the flames shooting all about, and the little children running down through them screaming. Some fell at the rear entrance, and others stumbled over them. I saw my little Helen among them. I tried to pull her out, but the flames drove me back. I had to leave my little child to die."

County Coroner Burke called a news conference and almost drove his fist through the top of his desk as he shouted in anger, "The construction of this schoolhouse was an outrage. The hallways were narrow and there was practically only one mode of exit. Those children were caught like rats in a trap!" He called for prosecution of the builders, but action was never taken.

(ALSO SEE: Babb Switch School, Our Lady of the Angels School)

LAKI — VOLCANIC ERUPTION

June, 1783

The greatest flow of lava from any volcano in recorded history occurred when the more than one hundred craters of Laki on Iceland overflowed with lava for a period of six months, ending in June, 1783. Beginning at the Lakagigar, one of Laki's largest craters, lava alternately crept and raced over 123,500 acres of Iceland, killing an estimated 10,000 persons and destroying dozens of villages.

LAKONIA — MARINE DISASTER

December 22, 1963

After several refittings a Dutch ship, the *Johan van Oldenbarnevelt,* launched as a passenger vessel in 1930, was purchased by a Greek line and renamed the *Lakonia.* The ship departed Southampton on December 19, 1963, with about 1,200 passengers on board. Three days later, when the vessel was 180 miles off Madeira, Captain Mathios Zarbis, who proved, along with his officers, hopelessly incompetent to handle the impending crisis, was informed that a fire had broken out in the hairdressing salon.

Two stewards employing small extinguishers attempted to put out the blaze before the captain was informed, but by then it was out of control. After sending

On December 22, 1963, the *Lakonia* became a floating, smoking funeral crypt for 128 passengers. *(UPI)*

out an SOS, Zarbis ordered all the passengers to the restaurant, much to the puzzlement of everyone on board. The large dining room was three decks below the promenade deck and close to the raging fire. Only a few persons obeyed this command.

Realizing that the fire was beyond his control, at midnight Zarbis ordered everyone into the lifeboats, twenty-four davits that were perfectly capable of handling the entire passenger roster and crew. The davits, however, were not in good working order—much of the safety equipment had been neglected—and not all the boats got away to meet the four ships coming to the sinking liner's rescue. Ninety-five passengers and thirty-three crew members were left on board to either burn to death or drown in the sea. A Greek board of inquiry later attributed the 128 deaths to the improper organization and leadership of Zarbis and his officers.

LARCHMONT — MARINE DISASTER
February 12, 1907

The Long Island steamer *Larchmont* was a side-wheel steamer and sailing vessel plying between New York and Providence, Rhode Island. On the wintry night of February 12, 1907, the *Larchmont,* making her way almost blindly through heavy seas, was suddenly rammed by a large schooner, *Harry Knowlton,* which had been blown off course by the storm.

The *Larchmont* sank fast near Block Island, Rhode Island, with only 9 men, including her captain, George W. McVey, escaping to lifeboats; 332 (according to a belated 1950 report of Quartermaster James E. Staples) were lost, making this the worst marine disaster in New England history, topping the 303 persons who died on an ill-fated Dutch warship, the *Erfprinz,* which sank off Cape Cod in 1783.

The 9 survivors of the *Larchmont* disaster were rescued the following day by the Joy Line steamer *Kentucky* (*Larchmont*'s sister ship) and the fishing schooner *Elsie.*

LA SALLE HOTEL — FIRE
June 5, 1946

background: Chicago's La Salle Hotel, a twenty-two-story hostelry, built in 1909 and situated at Madison and LaSalle streets of the Loop's financial district, had 1,059 guests registered in 886 rooms and 108 employees on duty when fire broke out at 12:15 A.M. on June 5, 1946, in the Silver Grill Cocktail Lounge, beginning in the basement and working its way up through air shafts between wall partitions, elevator shafts and stairways. Dead were 61 hotel guests, most of whom died as a result of anoxia and carbon monoxide poisoning; some jumped from windows and were killed. More than 200 were treated for injuries. This was the worst hotel fire in United States history to that time, and damages reached $1 million (the hotel was insured for $2.3 million).

L. G. Harmsen, an ex-Marine, was one of those packed inside the La Salle Hotel's Silver Grill Cocktail Lounge on the night of June 4, 1946. It was a joyous group, many of whom were celebrating servicemen who had been with

An artist's rendering of the Long Island steamer *Larchmont* shows the hole in her side that caused her to sink after colliding with the *Harry Knowlton* on February 12, 1907. *(Frank Leslie's Illustrated Newspaper)*

the armies of occupation and were being mustered out. A few minutes after midnight, Harmsen complained to his date that his seat cushion was getting uncomfortably hot. He reached down and picked it up, and at that instant, flames shot upward and instantly ignited his clothing. The ex-Marine was up and running out of the cocktail lounge, flames shooting from him as he blazed his way into the expansive, walnut-paneled hotel lobby. As he moved, others caught fire and, screaming, dove for exits.

One of the worst hotel calamities in United States history had begun. Most of the hotel guests had retired by the time the fire began, originating in the basement and quickly moving up air shafts, behind wall partitions and elevator shafts. Those waiting for elevators in the lobby blinked as they saw the bright glow of mounting flames flickering across the dark varnished paneling above the elevator bank. Fire broke out in the lounge and the adjacent coffee shop. There were almost 1,200 people in the hotel at the time, and fear of panic led employees in the lounge to try putting out the fire themselves instead of calling the fire department. The bartender, a waitress and several patrons "joining in the fun" grabbed seltzer bottles and tried to "squirt out" the fire, not knowing it had already reached inferno proportions in other areas. The fire roared into the lobby and consumed the oriental rugs and the red-oak paneling. It moved so fast that several hotel cashiers stationed at the west end of the lobby who hurriedly attempted to gather up valuables were killed.

It would be twenty minutes from the onset of the fire until an engine company, one hook-and-ladder company, one squad, a battalion chief and one fire insurance patrol arrived at precisely 12:35 A.M. from the fire department (ultimately, hundreds of firemen—thirty-three engine companies, eight hook-and-ladder companies, ten squad companies, two water tower companies, two high pressure units, two light wagons, two ambulances and two fire insurance patrols—battled the blaze. Fire Commissioner Corrigan directed four fire department marshals and seven chiefs in the battle against the fire.)

Inside of those twenty minutes, 61 persons died and at least 200 more were injured. In the first five minutes of fire, marble tables were crumbled by the heat and flame; doorknobs were melted. Escape by elevator and stairs was blocked by the fire, and almost 800 persons were trapped in the twenty-two floors.

At the first alarm all the phone operators except Julia Barry, a forty-four-year-old hotel employee, ran from their positions. She shoved two rescuers away from her when they tried to carry her from her switchboard. She kept ringing rooms, calmly telling people to seek the fire escapes. She died at her post, overcome by smoke.

Escape was not immediately possible for most. Hallways had become roaring furnaces. Those who entered them were overcome by heat and smoke. Those who locked their doors opened their windows and began to throw down lamps, bric-a-brac, suitcases and anything that would attract attention on the deserted streets below. Many waved bedsheets and screamed. An eerie silence filled the streets. At one point, two parents holding their child were driven to the windows by flames that had poured into their room through an open transom. The terrified family looked down to a roof that joined the hotel several floors beneath. It was either the flames or the jump; they chose the latter. Two more persons in windows directly above them decided to do the same thing. All five, clad in half-burned away pajamas, were found crumpled in a grotesque death leap, the woman still clutching her four-year-old daughter.

By the time firemen arrived, the hotel's windows framed hundreds of frantic people yelling to be saved. The water sprays and ladders went up to meet them. An elderly man on the fifth floor dropped a note, which a police captain (755 policemen responded to the fire) picked up and read aloud: "I will kill myself if I am not saved." The policeman handed the note to a fire chief and pointed upward to a man standing on a window ledge. The chief ordered a ladder swung over, and the man was brought down over a fireman's shoulder within minutes.

Inside the rooms many people locked themselves in baths, turned on the water taps, dousing themselves or standing under showers. Others, smart enough to react intelligently, placed mattresses against their doors after sealing the transoms and soaking the bedding with bathroom water. Then they waited to be rescued.

A burly sailor roamed the upper halls, stopping several panic-gripped men. He wasted no time and knocked one after another unconscious, dragged them to the fire escape, and had others help them down to the street. He saved 20 persons that day.

The fire escapes were jammed with about 900 persons. Most of these carried what they could grab after learning of the fire; at least 100 were alerted by the selfless Julia Barry. In one instance there was much jostling and shoving. A stampede almost developed until a beautiful twenty-three-year-old blind woman, led by her seeing-eye dog, stepped delicately onto the escape. The fear-maddened crowd behind her suddenly grew calm and tolerant as the girl was slowly led downward, step by step, by the German shepherd to the street below.

Adding to the panic and confusion, the hotel lights went out about a half-hour after the fire began. Huge spotlights were trained on the hotel, and one picked up a man holding his wife at the end of several knotted sheets. The woman dangled helplessly several stories from the nearest roof. As his strength began to fail, the man shouted hoarsely for help to those below. The couple could not be reached, and the man desperately hauled up his wife, collapsing from sheer exhaustion just as she reached the window ledge and crawled inside.

Both heroic and despicable acts were performed during the fire. A tall, well-dressed gentleman went from room to room on the upper floors, taking out sleepy-eyed guests to the fire escapes. He saved scores, but his name remains unknown. One bellhop, only sixteen-years-old, carried a legless war veteran ten flights down a service stairway to safety.

Later, on an upper floor swarming with firemen and police detectives, two men were discovered leaning over a man who had died of asphyxiation. A detective watched them gently glide their hands over his body and deftly remove his wallet and valuables before stepping forward to arrest them. They both had two suitcases jammed with jewelry and money taken from the dead.

Army Major William Blake, his small son in his arms, cautiously led his pregnant wife down several flights on the fire escape. His calm voice rose to command those behind to "take it easy and we'll all make it." They did. Blake and his family survived to return to Bushnell, Illinois, where he planned to open a candy store.

Courageous firemen fought the flames as they entered the blazing lobby, using high-pressure streams of water to batter their way through. "They edged into the heart of the fire," *Time* reported, "heads down, coughing, while other firemen in the rear sent protective streams cascading over them."

A little less than four hours after answering the fire alarm, the firemen had put out the blaze. The grim chore of removing the bodies began. There would be sixty-one dead in all and damages to the hotel of more than $1 million. The old, elegant La Salle would never recover.

Forty-three charred bodies were taken to the lobby of the nearby City Hall, and blankets were placed over them. Upon the toes of their protruding bare feet hung coroner's tags. Above the silent row of dead was a sign: "Pay Water Taxes Here."

(ALSO SEE: Gulf Hotel, Winecoff Hotel)

LAST ISLAND, LOUISIANA — HURRICANE

August 13, 1856

Almost fourteen inches of rain fell for a week preceding the approach of a tropical hurricane that swept over Last Island off the Louisiana coast on August 13, 1856. Every house on the island was destroyed, and 137 persons were killed. Those who managed to reach the steamer *Star,* anchored in the bay and stripped by the winds to her hull and boilers, rode out the storm.

One survivor wrote the *New Orleans Picayune* four days later that the immense hurricane waves crested at 2:00 P.M. and that those who had reached the highest spot on the island no longer had "any doubt that the island would be submerged. The scene at this moment forbids description. Men, women, and children were seen running in every direction in search of some means of salvation. The violence of the wind, together with the rain, which fell like hail, and the sand blinded their eyes, prevented many from reaching the objects they aimed at."

Two hours later the island was totally under the gulf and bay waters, and the *Star*'s wildly bobbing wreckage was the only sign that there had once been an island on that spot.

LAUREL RUN, PENNSYLVANIA — RAILWAY WRECK

December 23, 1903

background: The Duquesne Limited's eastbound Number 23, a six-car train pulled by Engine Number 1465, of the Baltimore & Ohio, en route to Connellsville, Pennsylvania, from Pittsburgh, rounded a curve at 60 m.p.h. at Laurel Run, Pennsylvania, at 7:45 P.M. on December 23, 1903, and struck a pile of timbers that had fallen from the last freight car, Gondola Number 3087, a westbound freight of the Nickel Plate Railroad that had passed the spot fifteen minutes before. The engine, baggage car, smoker and a sleeper were derailed; sixty-four persons were killed, and nine were injured.

The fastest train on the B & O line, the Duquesne Limited, was living up to its reputation. Engineer William Thornley at the throttle of locomotive Number 1465, the road's heaviest, was pushing the passenger train at 60 m.p.h. The six-car train from Pittsburgh to Connellsville passed a slow-moving Nickel Plate freight about six miles from the hamlet of Laurel Run. The engineer of the freight gave a friendly wave. Unknown to him the last gondola car of his train had thrown off a pile of huge railroad ties hundreds of yards behind, and these timbers littered both tracks, blocking passage of the speeding Duquesne Limited.

Thornley had no time to apply the brakes. His train zipped around a curve and smashed headlong into the jumble of ties, throwing the engine immediately off the rails. The baggage car was tossed over an embankment and rode crazily down into the fast-swirling Youghiogheny River. As the baggage car twisted sideways before its descent, the smoker behind it rode upward and actually leaped the baggage car, landing on top of the engine and slicing off the steam dome. The boiler exploded, and the escaping water and steam horribly scalded the forty persons in this car. The sleeper twisted off the tracks and hung precariously over the embankment.

Another sleeper and a dining car also jumped the

tracks, but those inside were comparatively unhurt. Engineer Thornley and fireman Cook were pinned beneath their engine, and they cried out for help but went unheard. High above their own cries came the shrieks of those being miserably scalded to death in the upended smoker.

Benjamin Nicholas, a steward in the dining car, was knocked down upon impact, but he jumped to his feet and ran forward. As he did, he righted dozens of persons in their beds and chairs. Nicholas worked his way past the dead in the smoker until he was on top of the engine, struggling to avoid the searing steam and water. He took off his coat, ripped it to shreds and stuffed it into the open pipe—a very dangerous thing to do. Then he turned off the engine's boiler valve. The plucky steward returned to the smoker and grabbed one of the few men still moving there. He worked the man out through a window and placed him on the frozen ground. The wind puffed up and quickly covered the man's face with snow. Nicholas ran once again to the twisted metal and splintered wood frame of the smoker.

Louis Hilgot, conductor of the train, had been in the first sleeper when the crash came, and he found himself almost at the bottom of the embankment, to the puzzlement of porter D. W. Hills, who gaped down, open-mouthed, at him. How he was thrown such a great distance was never learned. Hilgot's face was all but burned away, and as he groped his way up the steep incline, he shouted to Hills, "I am scalded to death! For God's sake, some of you get a red lamp, and go and flag Number 49 or she will be on us!"

Hills could not leave the injured passengers in his car, but the intrepid baggagemaster, Thomas J. Baum, who had ridden the baggage car into the river and was himself seriously injured, heard the conductor. Baum, his head and body cut and bleeding profusely in several places, scrambled up the embankment and staggered down the track. The darkness and driving snow closed around him. In the distance he could see the small, yellow engine light of the eastbound Number 49 approaching. Desperately he looked about for something to wave, but realized he would not be seen. He reached into his pocket, withdrew a box of matches, took off his coat, and set it on fire, waving it frantically as it burned his hands. He collapsed, unconscious, but the engineer on Number 49 had seen his signal and brought his train to a stop just three feet from where Baum had fallen across the tracks.

Several trainmen and two detectives from this train ran forward to help the injured of the Duquesne Limited. The detectives promptly arrested several men who were looting the pockets of the dead. A detective became so incensed that he grabbed one of the thieves and broke his jaw.

Rescuers were aghast at the wreck. Five hundred yards of track on both roadbeds were ripped apart. The 7,000-gallon tank on the tender had been hurtled 100 feet ahead of the wreckage. Bodies, already stiffening, lined the embankment where Nicholas and Hills had placed them. Wails and cries punctured the silent night. Although it was later determined that every person on the train had been knocked unconscious at the time of the crash, it seemed peculiar that not one woman passenger was injured. Sixty-four men were dead, however, and nine more were injured. Most of them had been in the crowded smoker.

One of those killed was Harold B. Morrison, a sheet metal worker in Pittsburgh, who was returning to his wife after purchasing their first house (they were newlyweds). Edith Morrison was at the station waiting for the train but was told it would be late. After several hours she bought a paper and read that her husband had been killed.

Lillian Bennett, a blue-eyed girl from England, had just arrived on the *Cedric* after a particularly hazardous voyage. As she stepped from the liner, reporters told her that the man she had corresponded with for months and had planned to marry, Ambrose Good, an ironworker, had been killed in the crash at Laurel Run.

LAURIER PALACE THEATER — FIRE

January 9, 1927

background: The Laurier Palace Theater in Montreal (whose management had long neglected safety regulations) caught fire on the afternoon of January 9, 1927, with more than 800 persons, almost all children under the age of sixteen, in attendance. Several hundred small children were trapped in the balcony, and scores died on a narrow stairway leading to the main floor; 78 were killed, and 30 were injured.

The Laurier Palace Theater was a firetrap, and the Fire Prevention Bureau of the Montreal Fire Department knew it. The bureau had cited theater owners several times for "failure to observe the various provisions of the fire laws, such as those relating to the maintenance of unobstructed exits." The owner's license was revoked, but he continued to operate the theater. Political influence, no doubt, prevented authorities from closing the firetrap. The theater was situated directly across from a police station.

On the afternoon of January 9, 1927, more than 800 persons, mostly children under the age of sixteen, packed the theater to see a special matinee. About 500 were seated on the lower floor, and approximately 300 were in the balcony. Someone sitting in the center section of the balcony dropped a lighted cigarette (the employees often were found smoking in all parts of the theater). A blaze roared upward through the balcony in seconds.

All of those on the first floor filed out several exits. Three hundred youngsters in the balcony, unchaperoned and all at about age six or seven, were thrown into panic. The children poured down a single stairway forty-seven inches wide (at a sharp right angle turn at the bottom of the first landing, there was a doorway only thirty-seven inches wide). One child fell or was pushed down, and the pile-up began. Children were screaming and crawling to escape through the narrow doorway, where seconds before, a man had told them to return to their seats. There was no light in the stairway, which added further horror to the crush. Flames consumed the balcony in a little under two minutes. By then the projectionist had saved close to thirty children by throwing them two at a time through a window out onto the marquee and awnings over the sidewalk.

When firemen arrived they tried to break up the wedge eight bodies deep at the deathtrap stairway but could not. A dozen men tied a rope around one body and pulled, but they could not dislodge it. They finally cut a hole into the side wall of the stairway, entered and were able to save several children.

Dead were seventy-eight children—fifty-two killed by smoke asphyxiation, twenty-five crushed to death and one burned to death. Thirty more were taken injured to the hospital. The motion picture these youngsters had been watching that afternoon was entitled "Get 'Em Young."

(ALSO SEE: Iroquois Theater)

Two trains collided at Lebrija, Spain, on July 21, 1972, and seventy-six passengers were killed. *(Wide World)*

LAYLAND, WEST VIRGINIA — MINE DISASTER

March 2, 1915

The porter from the company store was passing the mouth of Mine Number 3 in Layland, West Virginia, at 8:30 A.M. on March 2, 1915, when a tremendous explosion bellowed out of the entranceway and hurled him a distance of 100 feet. He slammed against a post and was killed instantly. A dozen other men in the vicinity of the shaft entrance also were sent sprawling.

The apparent cause of the explosion was the use of black powder in blasting, which was recklessly packed with coal dust and bottom dirt. (The owners, the New River and Pocahontas Consolidated Coal Company, employed no firebosses to check on escaping gas and maintain safety regulations.)

When the blast came, 171 miners were below. Of these 114 men plus the porter were already dead when rescue parties fixed the broken fan in the entrance and started down the shaft. Scores of men found their way to the surface from all elevations of the mine—fifty-seven in all. Forty-two of the surviving group holed themselves up behind makeshift barricades on the tenth level of the mine. For four days they struggled here to stay alive. A young miner named John Whalen repeatedly talked them out of leaving before the gas in the passageways dissipated, and he is credited with saving every man in his group. Led by rescuers, these men emerged on March 6, 1915, to a tumultuous reception by relatives gathered on one side of the entrance. On the other side more than 100 newly-made pine coffins were stacked, waiting.

LEBRIJA, SPAIN — RAILWAY WRECK

July 21, 1972

The fast-moving Madrid-Cadiz Express, with more than 500 passengers jammed into its fourteen cars, collided head-on with a local four-coach train outside of Lebrija, Spain, on July 21, 1972, resulting in a tremendous derailment. The local train, which carried all of the seventy-six persons killed in the crash, apparently ran a red light and moved onto the single track on which the Express approached.

The dead were mostly Spanish sailors on leave at the height of the holiday season. The 103 persons injured were dug out of the wreck by scores of Spanish soldiers and American servicemen. The United States Polaris submarine base at nearby Rota sent teams of doctors and sailors by helicopter to the disaster site.

LEDUC CAMP BRITISH COLUMBIA, CANADA — AVALANCHE February 18, 1965

background: A copper mine, Leduc Camp, was at the edge of British Columbia's 3,000-foot Granduc Mountain. Operated by the Newmont Mining Company of New York, the camp at 9:57 A.M. on February 18, 1965, was obliterated by a powerful avalanche falling from the sheer snow cliffs of the mountain, trapping 70 of the 154 workers in the camp under tons of snow. Quick rescue operations caused 43 to be saved; 27 were killed, most outright upon impact.

Ever since a French prospector named Leduc discovered a rich copper vein in a British Columbia glacier in 1935, mining firms schemed mightily to unearth the hard-to-get-at ore. Leduc Camp was the outgrowth of a New York mining firm's dream of removing a half billion dollars' worth of copper from the frozen foothills of Granduc Mountain.

On February 18, 1965, twenty men went into the new mine shaft to work while 134 others busied themselves in the complex of buildings sprawling over a wide area. It was exactly 9:57 A.M., the time pinpointed by scores of men about to go to the coffee shack, when Granduc threw down a grinding, hissing avalanche of brick-hard snow that swept across the camp and crumpled to pieces the carpenter shop, cookhouse, coffee shack, garage and, at the mine shaft's entrance, the powerhouse and the machine shop.

Those in the mine were badly frightened but safe. The avalanche covered only a portion of the mine entrance, and the miners were able to dig themselves out after several hours. The plight of those in the wrecked buildings was considered hopeless. If the fifty men who were buried beneath the snow were alive, it would be all but impossible to locate them. The rush of snow had swept the buildings they were in far from their original locations. Only scattered splinters stuck from the heaps of snow.

The force of this avalanche was such that it bent steel beams, whittled giant timbers to sticks and crushed a large helicopter. Calls for help were sent to all points in western Canada and Alaska, and rescuers responded immediately by organizing relief parties to be flown in by helicopter. Even before they arrived people in the camp began digging.

The problem was that they did not know where to dig. It was not until some of the buried ones, like Salvatore Maglioti, tunneled their way up through thirty feet of snow with their bare hands that rescuers could estimate where most of the buildings had been carried. Using a bulldozer with a man riding on the blade to alert the driver if a human form appeared, the rescuers began to shear the caked snow away by inches.

The "white death," an avalanche, roared down upon Leduc Camp, British Columbia, on February 18, 1965, killing twenty-seven workers. *(UPI)*

Twenty-three men were slowly removed from their snowy tombs in this fashion, one of the last being the foreman, Oscar Louste. While the bulldozer was performing its grim work, carpenter Einar Myllyla felt its weight shifting above him. He had been swept away with the carpentry shop and buried far below the surface, sandwiched between huge slabs of plyboard which, no doubt, saved his life.

For four agonizing days of near coma and constant pressure (a helicopter port was directly over him and the in-coming aircraft landed and took off directly on top of him), the tough Finn survived. To their everlasting credit, rescuers refused to abandon their search until every man in the camp had been accounted for. As the bulldozer finally sliced into the helicopter port, a giant mound of snow slid away to reveal Myllyla, who looked up suddenly to see the bulldozer's blade only a few inches from his face. "Hey!" he shouted to the driver, Roger McPherson, "don't move me. I think my legs are frozen."

His was an impossible survival with an even more ironic ending. Myllyla was flown to the Ketchikan, Alaska, hospital where his legs were saved although he did lose the toes on one foot. Two years later the carpenter was crossing a Vancouver street when he was run over and killed by a cab.

Of the twenty-three miners killed in the Leduc Camp avalanche, according to medical reports, almost all died of an initial blow that either cracked their skulls or broke their necks. These sudden fatalities at the hands of the white death prompted avalanche expert Montgomery Atwater to remark, "Actually the avalanche was merciful, if such a word can be applied to a blind force."

LEUKERBAD, SWITZERLAND — AVALANCHE
January 17, 1718

The small Valais town of Leukerbad had been known throughout the world for centuries for two things. Its marvelous springs brought near-miraculous cures to the international rich. Its avalanches brought unexpected white death to its residents. The earliest recorded avalanche that wrecked Leukerbad occurred in 1518 when the Valais mountains hurled down tons of powdery snow. Almost all the buildings in the hamlet were destroyed, and the population was decimated, with sixty-one fatalities.

On January 17, 1718, a monstrous avalanche, recorded by a local scribe, Stephen Matter, struck the town and obliterated even those buildings especially reinforced to withstand such catastrophes. Following two weeks of intensive snows, a huge avalanche roared through the outskirts of the village and killed three young men. A large party using sounding rods made to detect bodies buried in snow found the corpses that evening. As this group returned to the village, another avalanche tore downward from the mountain slope and caught the entire town unaware.

Every house was destroyed a few minutes after 8:00 P.M. and fifty-two persons were killed. The three luxurious baths were wrecked, along with several quaint inns and the St. Laurentius Church. People were found in all manner of death poses. The Brunner family was wiped out—four children trapped in their house. One was sent flying dozens of yards in his bed, the blankets still tightly wrapped around him. The father and mother died in the chapel, where they were found kneeling in prayer.

One man, Stephen Roten, happened to be in a wine cellar looking for a bottle of his favorite wine when the avalanche hurtled over his house. He was trapped in the basement for eight days without food until rescued. He died of malnutrition and frostbite.

The village, after struggling to repair the baths and encourage its once opulent tourist trade, was struck by an avalanche in 1720 and again in 1758. These falls were far less severe in death and destruction than the previous avalanches.

LEYDEN, HOLLAND — FLOOD
October 1-2, 1574

An anecdotal story is told to illustrate the age-old battle the Dutch fight against their nemesis, the sea. Frederick the Great had cast a covetous eye upon the Netherlands and was attempting to intimidate the Dutch envoy at his court by displaying his power. In a special military review with the small Dutchman at his side, Frederick watched delightedly as his gargantuan grenadiers paraded past, each rank seemingly taller than the next, each company towering ever higher as the files reached the seven-foot level. As each company marched past, the wizened little envoy from the Netherlands coughed out the same words, "Very good, *but not tall enough.*" After he had repeated this several times, the towering Frederick turned angrily to the ambassador and demanded to know what he meant. "I mean," the Dutchman said softly, "*that we can flood our country twelve feet deep!*" Frederick's troopers kept clear of Holland.

Such was not the case in 1574, when Spanish troops occupied much of the lowlands in an attempt to subdue the Dutch upstart, William the Silent. The Spaniards besieged the large city of Leyden, a fortified town whose citizens were determined to hold out to the last man. As hundreds died of starvation, the inhabitants, according to historian A. H. Godbey, "were digging up every green thing, devouring roots of grass, old leather, offal, anything that could in the least aid to sustain life . . . so long as a dog barked in the city the Spaniards might know they held out."

The sea providentially came to the aid of the Dutch on the night of October 1-2, 1574, when miles beyond the encamped Spanish army, the dikes gave way during a fierce storm and flooded the lowlands, drowning an estimated 20,000 Spanish troops and lifting the siege of Leyden.

LEYTE — MARINE DISASTER
October 16, 1953

background: The U.S.S. *Leyte,* a huge American aircraft carrier with more than 1,400 officers and men in her crew, was in her berth in the Boston navy yard on October 16, 1953, when, at 3:15 P.M., the third deck, forward catapult room was ripped apart by a tremendous explosion, later attributed to "vaporized or atomized" hydraulic fluid, which killed 36 and injured 40 seamen.

"It sounded like the rumble of a subway train," said Captain Thomas A. Ahroon, after hearing the explosions on board his recently refitted ship. It was exactly 3:15 P.M., and almost all of the aircraft carrier *Leyte's* crew of 1,400 were on board, while the ship squatted in her giant Boston navy yard berth.

Through the open portholes and down the passageways on the portside and through the compartments stretching below decks, thick, billowing black smoke began to gush. Another explosion sent a blast of white heat and flame that withered everything before it. Osie Ward and ten others were trapped in the steward's compartment on the third deck.

"A big flame came down the hatchway to our compartment," Ward later recalled. "At first we didn't react, but a split second later the same thing happened again."

A seaman, who was about to step into a shower at the moment of the explosion, panicked and ran naked up a hatchway and into the searing flame. Ward and an ensign grabbed him and pulled him back into the compartment, but they were too late; he was dead; his body, a cinder. Someone was shouting and pounding on another hatchway, and several men in the steward's compartment opened it. His clothes aflame, an officer fell into the compartment.

Though still alive, Lieutenant Leonard M. De Rose's features were charred beyond recognition. The stewards wrapped him in blankets, and De Rose moved his lips slowly, "I am a Catholic. Get me a chaplain. My blood type is A."

"There's nothing we can do," Ward said. "We're all trapped in here."

"Morse code," De Rose said. "Tap it out on the bulkhead."

None of the stewards knew Morse code, but the heroic De Rose would not give up. He ordered the men to get a wrench and remain in the compartment, and he quietly instructed them how to tap out the SOS message. As two men frantically tapped at the bulkhead, De Rose said, "Let us pray." The stewards, sweating in the intense heat as the blaze turned the compartment to a furnace, began to say the Lord's Prayer.

Rescue workers swarmed throughout the ship only minutes after the initial explosion. They found the stewards and freed them within a half-hour. It was too late for Lieutenant De Rose, who died of his burns.

Though the FBI sifted the ruins of the ship in search of evidence to prove sabotage, the deaths of thirty-six sailors and the injuring of forty more were later attributed to hydraulic fluid used in the *Leyte*'s machinery. It exploded after becoming atomized.

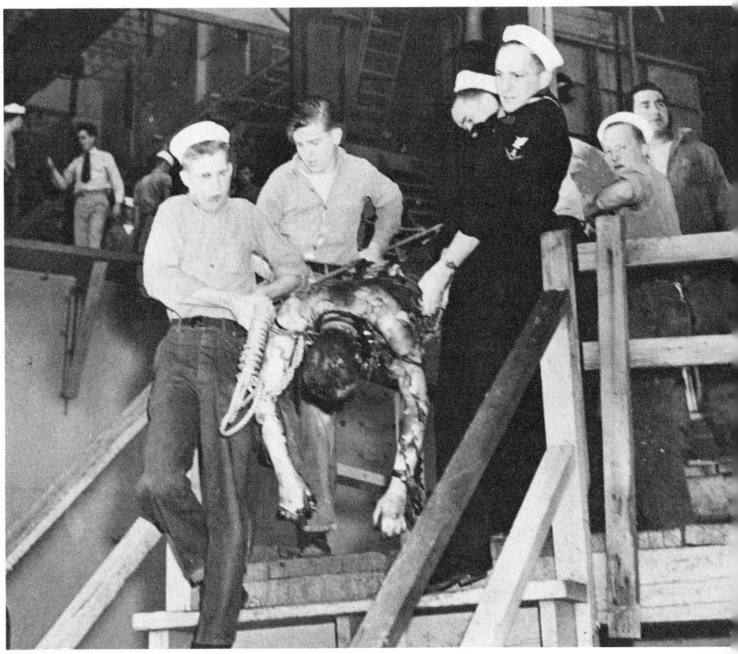

A seriously burned sailor is removed from the 27,000-ton United States aircraft carrier *Leyte*. Hydraulic fluid exploded on October 16, 1953, killing thirty-six men. *(UPI)*

A huge aircraft carrier *Leyte* burned at her berth in the Boston Navy Yard on October 16, 1953. *(Wide World)*

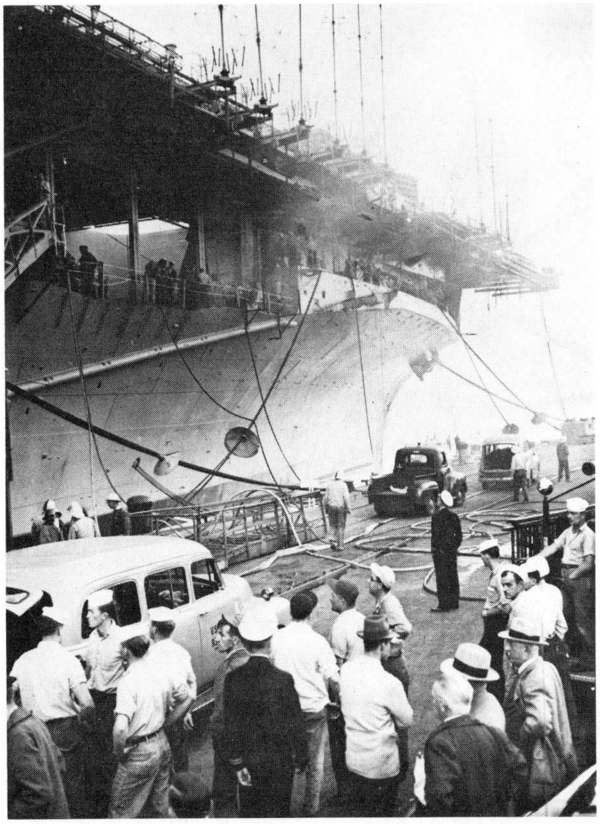

LIBAN — MARINE DISASTER

June 7, 1903

The French steamer *Liban,* carrying 240 persons, collided with the steamer *Insulaire* just off the Marseilles coast on June 7, 1903. Though the cause of this daytime collision was never determined, two pilot boats, the *Blechamp* and the *Balkan,* both nearby at the time of the crash, speedily recovered dozens of passengers. The *Liban* went to the bottom in seventeen minutes and took 150 people with her.

LIBERTÉ — MARINE DISASTER

September 25, 1911

Launched in 1905, the 14,865-ton French battleship *Liberté* became a victim of ancient powder in her magazines that blew up on September 25, 1911, a fate that had befallen other war vessels in pre-dreadnought days.

Fatalistic as it may seem today, such explosions were almost commonplace in the navies of the world before World War I. Defective "B" powder, which had decomposed and was highly combustible after long periods of storage, was also responsible for the explosion, which killed 120 men, on the *Liberté's* 12,052-ton sister ship *Jena,* while in Toulon harbor on March 12, 1907. The captain of the *Jena* complained to his superiors six months before the explosion that the "B" powder on board his ship was six years old and ought to be replaced.

Deteriorated explosives ignited and wrecked the *Mikasa,* one-time flagship of Japanese Admiral Togo, as she was lying in the Sasebo dockyard on September 10, 1905. On January 21, 1906, the Brazilian battleship *Aquidaban* blew up under similar circumstances. Faulty ammunition killed 788 men on board the British battleship *Bulwark,* which blew up off Sheerness on November 26, 1914. Twelve survived. More than 400 sailors, the entire crew, died when the British minelayer *Princess Irene,* at anchor at Port Victoria, was sent to the bottom in pieces after her magazines blew up on May 27, 1915. Spontaneous ignition of unstable powder was also responsible for the destruction of the German light cruiser *Karlsruhe* on November 4, 1914; the Russian *Empress Maria* on October 20, 1916; the Japanese cruiser *Tsukuba* on January 14, 1917; the huge battleship *Kawachi* on July 12, 1918; and the Italian battleships *Benedetto Brin* on September 27, 1915, and *Leonardo da Vinci* on September 27, 1915. Defective ammunition, not a mine as was then claimed, was also responsible for the destruction of the American battleship *Maine,* while she was anchored in Havana harbor on February 15, 1898, the comments of William Randolph Hearst notwithstanding.

The violent death of the *Liberté* was not a rarity and the marvel of the explosion was that it did not envelop the vessel's escort, the battleships *République* and *Democratic,* lying next to her in Toulon harbor. At 5:30 A.M. lookouts on these ships noticed flames erupting from the *Liberté's* foredeck. Her captain ordered the forward magazines flooded, but twenty-two minutes later the ship's forward magazines exploded with such force that half the battlewagon's armament, including huge guns, was hurtled to the shore, where extensive damage was caused. In all it was later determined that close to 5,000 shells exploded on the *Liberté,* ignited by badly decomposed "B" powder, which had been on board for five years. Out of a total crew of 717 (140 of whom were fortunately on shore leave), 235 men were killed outright, and several hundred more were injured.

Kaiser Wilhelm of Germany, prompt to respond to any military disaster, sent the following message: "Words fail me in endeavoring to find expression for my profound sympathy for France in the national misfortune. The families so terribly grieved may be consoled by the knowledge that the men of the *Liberté* have perished in the performance of their duty toward their country."

Many persons were crushed to death at the National Stadium in Lima, Peru, in a wild human stampede on May 25, 1964. *(UPI)*

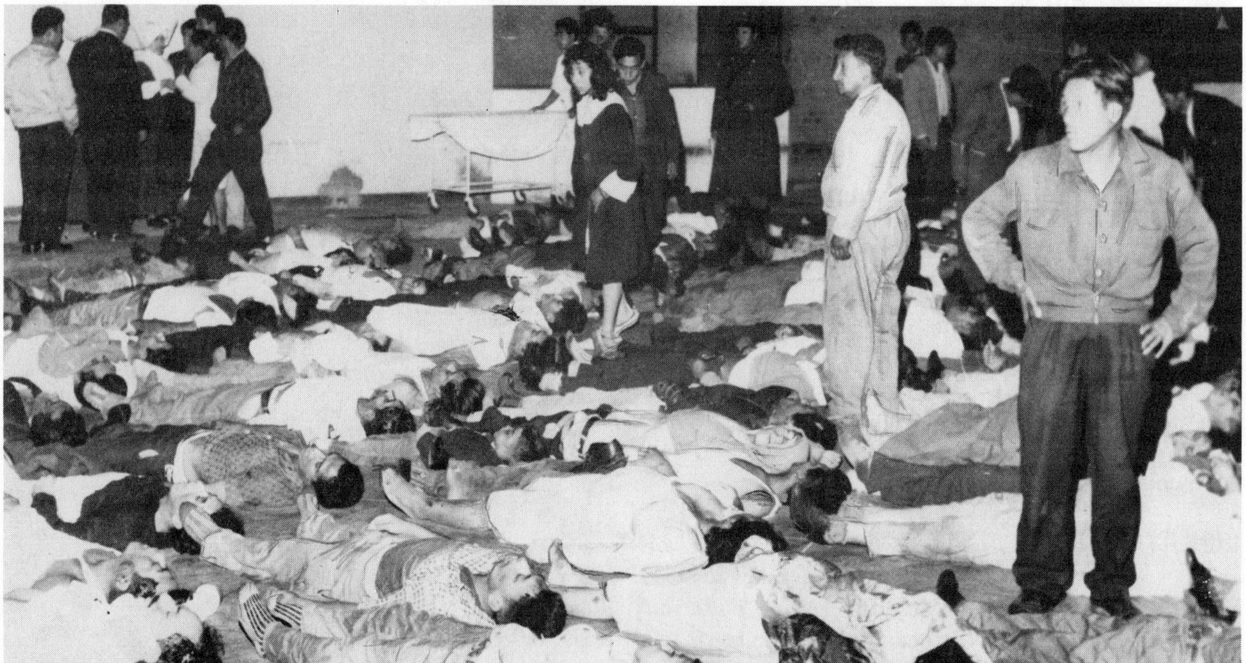

LIMA NATIONAL STADIUM — STAMPEDE
May 25, 1964

Peruvian spectators, enraged over the decisions of soccer referees, caused one of the most tragic disasters in modern sports history on May 25, 1964. The more than 45,000 soccer fans packing the National Stadium in Lima, Peru, were riveted to their seats as an Olympic qualifying game came down to its final minutes with Argentina one point ahead of Peru. When referees nullified the tying point made by Peru for rule violations, the crowd rioted by hurling bottles and other objects at the referees. As the audience began to tear down fences and wooden structures in the stadium, squads of tough riot police showed up.

Resorting to tear gas to quell the vicious mobs, the police suddenly had a stampede for the locked exits on their hands. (The exit gates were locked since the game was not officially over.) In panic to avoid the gas, thousands tore and pushed and shoved their way to these gates, and the pressure of their mounting weight broke them open. By that time 218 persons had been trampled and crushed to death, most of them children and women.

The huge L'Innovation Department Store in Brussels, Belgium, burned on May 22, 1967; 322 persons died. *(UPI)*

L'INNOVATION DEPARTMENT STORE — FIRE
May 22, 1967

background: The second-largest department store in Brussels, Belgium, L'Innovation, located on the rue Neuve, caught fire in three places (arson was suspected but never proved) on May 22, 1967, quickly consuming the five-story building. Of the estimated 3,000-4,000 persons in the building at the time of the fire—1,200 were store employees—322 were crushed, burned or leaped from windows to their deaths, the highest fatality toll of any store fire in history.

The five-story L'Innovation department store in Brussels was featuring a million-dollar showcase of American goods on July 22, 1967, and its walls were decorated with red, white and blue bunting and colorful United States travel posters. Flocking to the sale were about 2,500 Belgians. Serving this crowd were 1,200 store employees.

At noon, when the shopping rush was in full swing, those on the third floor craned their necks to the ceiling, where they could hear the thumping of many feet. The fire had started there, and panic broke out immediately. Blazes sprang up in two more places in the store, which was totally without adequate fire protection. There was no sprinkler system, and only two of the fifteen full-time firemen employed by the store responded to the alarm, furtively using two small hand extinguishers in a feeble attempt to put out the flames. They were quickly driven back by the smoke and heat and abandoned the fight, running for their lives like everyone else in the store.

The panic was complete; all 4,000 persons in the store raced for elevators and exits—clawing, kicking and punching their way forward. Dozens were trampled unconscious. Catherine Seydel, twenty-two, was swept along with the mob on the third floor the moment she emerged from a dressing room. The new garment she was trying on was ripped from her shoulders. She was fortunate to be carried by the human tide to a bank of windows, where she escaped by climbing out onto a ledge, after a man smashed the locked panes with his fists.

Located in the older part of the city, the store was difficult for the firemen to reach. Their engines were jammed in narrow, confining streets. It was ten minutes or more before the first fire contingent arrived, and by then scores were being driven off the window ledges by flames and smoke. They took their chances in jumping for the roofs of cars. Those who hit the parked autos lived but were injured. Dozens missed.

As the fire crackled through the floors of the building, hundreds of bottles of butane gas stored on the roof for eventual sale to campers were ignited, and this last explosive inferno completed the building's ruination. Damage finally was set at $23 million.

Those who clung to the window ledges as the fire increased had little choice but to jump. Fireman Jacques Mesmans, helpless in the street, watched as "one man was transformed into a living torch before my eyes as he hesitated to leap from a high window."

A total of 322 persons perished in this disaster, the most terrible store fire on record.

Lisbon, Portugal, was almost totally destroyed on November 1, 1755, by an earthquake and a seismic sea wave. *(From an old print)*

LISBON, PORTUGAL

EARTHQUAKE
November 1, 1755

background: On Saturday, November 1, 1755, beginning at 9:30 A.M., Lisbon, Portugal, was shaken by three distinct shocks (two more shocks at 11:00 A.M. and 1:00 P.M. were also severe, but those occurring before 10 A.M. did the most damage). The entire city was brought to ruins by this earthquake, which was followed by great fires and a tremendous sea wave, both of which destroyed the harbor, opening fissures that swallowed landmark buildings. An estimated 50,000 persons were crushed, drowned, or burned to death. Some authorities put the death toll as high as 100,000. This earthquake, the most violent in modern times, was felt over an area of 1.5 million square miles, throughout Europe and North Africa, especially in Fez and Mequinez, Morocco, where an estimated 10,000 persons were killed. Rough estimates of loss for harbor and merchant goods alone soared beyond $60 million, and historical losses such as the 70,000-book library in the king's palace, which included extensive incunabula, were inestimable. In addition more than 200 priceless paintings were lost.

It was All Saint's Day, Saturday, November 1, 1755. Thousands thronged the half-dozen magnificent cathedrals in the booming port city of Lisbon. Packed were the churches of Santa Catarina, Sao Paulo, Sao Vicente de Fora, the Basilica de Santa Maria and the Misericordia. In the Basilica of Sao Vicente de Fora, a huge structure where about 600 were at prayer, the priests of the choir had just begun to chant the words of the Introit (it was 9:30 A.M.) when the entire marble church began to roll and sway like a raft on a rough sea.

Church after church crumbled around its kneeling parishioners. Santa Catarina Church fell on 400 persons; the Church of Sao Paulo collapsed on 300. A huge fissure fifteen feet wide opened in the center of the city. More than 18,000 buildings—bricks, masonry, timbers—crashed into the streets, throwing up a billowing dust cloud. Thirty thousand persons were dead within two minutes.

Unlike previous earthquakes the Lisbon shocks were recorded by men of science, who soon determined that the tremors were caused by the sudden movement of a submarine fault off the coast (although there are no deep trenches in the ocean floor off Portugal). Minutes after the first two shocks, thousands of terrified residents fled to the docks, crowding onto the newly constructed Cays de Prada, a magnificent gray marble quay jutting out into the harbor. Another horror presented itself at this time in the form of a seismic sea wave estimated to have been from fifty to seventy feet high.

An English merchant named Davy survived the quake and the wave. He described the onrushing waters in a letter he sent to England, "On a sudden, I heard a general outcry: 'The sea is coming in, we are lost!' Turning my eyes toward the river, which at this place is nearly four miles broad, I could perceive it heaving and swelling in a most unaccountable manner, as no wind was stirring. In an instant there appeared, at some small distance, a large body of water, rising, as it were, like a mountain. It came on foaming and roaring, and rushed toward the shore with such impetuosity, that we all immediately ran for our lives, as fast as possible; many were actually swept away, and the rest were above their waists in water, at a good distance from the bank.

" . . . I had the narrowest escape, and should certainly have been lost, had I not grasped a large beam that lay on the ground, till the water returned to its channel, which it did with equal rapidity. As there now appeared at least as much danger from the sea as the land, and I scarce knew whether to retire for shelter, I took a sudden resolution of returning, with my clothes all dripping, to the area of St. Paul's. Here I stood some time, and observed the ships tumbling and tossing about as in a violent storm. Some had broken their cables and were carried to the other side of the Tagus; others were whirled around with incredible swiftness, several large boats were turned keel upward; and all this without any wind, which seemed the more astonishing."

Davy's survival was, indeed, remarkable. When the first quake struck, every floor in his four-story building collapsed into his first-floor quarters. He looked up from writing a letter to see through the dust of the debris a woman holding a baby only a few feet from him. He helped her from the building just as the walls fell inward, noticing that "the sky in a moment became so gloomy that I could now distinguish no particular object; it was an Egyptian darkness. . . ."

As Davy stumbled along the ruined streets, he found himself falling over the bodies of dead people and animals. There were countless persons "so bruised and wounded that they could not stir to help themselves . . . destruction appeared to me unavoidable . . . I only wished I might be made an end of at once, and not have my limbs broken, in which case I could expect nothing else but to be left upon the spot, lingering in misery, like those poor unhappy wretches, without receiving the least succor from any person."

Reaching St. Paul's Church (Sao Paulo), which was already in ruins and where scores had been crushed to death beneath its ponderous fallen concrete slabs, Davy fell on his knees in prayer. A second shock reverberated through the city, and those partially destroyed buildings then tumbled to pieces. Davy looked up the hill to where the towering Santa Catarina Church stood and saw it fall to ruins. "The consternation now became so universal, that the shrieks and cries of the frightened people could be distinctly heard from the top of St. Catherine's Hill, a considerable distance off, whither a vast number of the populace had likewise retreated. At the same time we could hear the fall of the parish church there, whereby many persons were killed on the spot, and others mortally wounded." Littering the hilly city of Lisbon were all manner of dead and debris following the second shock. Coaches had been crushed in mid-journey. Horses and riders had been crushed by falling buildings, scores anchored in their saddles. "Here, mothers with infants in their arms; there, ladies richly dressed, priests, friars, gentlemen, mechanics, either in the same condition or just expiring; some had their backs broken, others great stones on their breasts; some lay almost buried in the rubbish, and crying out in vain for succor, were left to perish with the rest."

One harrowing escape followed another during the quakes. An Englishman named Chase was quoted by *Blackwoods Magazine* in 1860, a century after the catastrophe (upon the discovery of a letter he had written his sister), as having survived the crashing of the old house in which he lived. From his bedroom on the fourth floor, Chase saw "the most horrid prospect that imagination can figure. . . . The house began to heave to that degree that to prevent being thrown down I was obliged to put my arm out of a window and support myself by the wall, every stone in the wall separating and grinding against each other (as did the walls of the other houses with variety of different motions) causing the most dreadful crunching, jumbling noise ears ever heard. I thought the whole city was sinking into the earth. I saw the tops of two pillars meet, and I saw no more." Chase was hurled to the ground from his perch. (His injuries left him permanently crippled.) As he crawled up the dust-clogged street, he saw "friends running from friends, fathers from their children, husbands from their wives, because everyone fled away from their habitations full of terror, confusion and distraction."

J. Latham was in a boat on the River Tagus, heading for a village three miles away when the disaster struck. "The boat made a noise as if on the shore or landing, though then in the middle of the water. I asked my companion if he knew what was the matter. He stared at me, and looking at Lisbon, we saw the houses falling, which made him say, 'God bless us, it is an earthquake!' About four or five minutes after, the boat made a noise as before, and we saw the houses tumble down on both sides of the river."

Latham and his friend, after climbing a nearby hill, could see nothing of the once magnificent new quay. It had vanished under 600 feet of water brought by the seismic seawave. They also spotted the beginning of the great Lisbon fire, which began about 11:30 A.M. "Indeed, every element seemed to conspire to our destruction, . . . fires broke out in three different parts of the city, occasioned by household goods and kitchen fires being jumbled together." A northeast wind fanned the flames, which gutted the central section of the city and most of the surrounding hills. The Carmo and Trindade convents went up in smoke. The magnificient new Opera House caught fire and became ashes; the flames tore up Castle Hill and devoured the king's royal palace. All of Lisbon's museums and libraries caught fire, including the palace of the Marques de Lourical, where more than 200 classic paintings by Rubens, Correggio and Titian, among others, were destroyed, along with 18,000 books. Many of these were irreplaceable volumes. A history written in the hand of Charles V burned. An herbal once owned by Hungarian King Matthias Hunyadi (1440-90) was incinerated. Maps and charts of the world made by Portuguese seamen over centuries of exploration were destroyed. Incunabula—those rare books published before 1500—were obliterated, and links with the past severed. Gone were the libraries of the king's palace, the Oratory (where an exclusive collection of Marian literature was housed), the Braganca Archive in the Palacio dos Duqes de Braganca, and the Dominican convent, which had recently been catalogued and opened to the public. The intellectual wealth along with the mercantile glory of Lisbon disappeared in smoke and flames as the fire consumed the city for an entire week.

The intellectual world would bemoan the loss of Lisbon for decades. Voltaire set Candide and Pangloss squarely in the debacle: "They had scarcely set foot in the town when they felt the earth tremble under their feet; the sea rose in foaming masses in the port and smashed the ships which rode at anchor. Whirlwinds of flame and ashes covered the streets and squares; the houses collapsed, and roofs were thrown upon the foundations; and the foundations were scattered. . . ."

Much later Oliver Wendell Holmes refreshed the world's memory of the disaster with a poem:

> There stood the stout old one-hoss-shay
> As fresh as on Lisbon-earthquake day . . .

Unlike the quake that had devastated Lisbon in 1531, killing countless thousands, this All Saint's Day quake produced dozens of shocks that continued during the weeks and months that followed the initial disaster. It was estimated that there were 500 aftershocks following the

Sao Vicente de Fora Cathedral in Lisbon was in ruins after the murderous earthquake that took the lives of 100,000 inhabitants.

first, prompting a Spanish nobleman to inquire of a visiting dignitary from Lisbon, "Will your earth never be quiet?"

The shocks themselves reached throughout Europe and into Africa, where almost 10,000 persons died in Fez and Mesquinez in Morocco. Algiers felt the shock and lost dozens of buildings to it. In the ports of Amsterdam and Rotterdam, ships' anchors were snapped. The quake dried up hot springs in Bohemia, almost 1,400 miles away. An ugly fissure occurred in Derbyshire, England. Another chasm gaped open for fifteen miles through the Pyrenees. Norway, Sweden, Germany, Switzerland, Corsica and the West Indies all felt the earth move. Mt. Vesuvius, then in eruption, suddenly ceased its bellowing. Cadiz, Spain, was elevated several feet by the quake. People on a ship in the West Indies were thrown up a foot by the seismic waves that hit there.

A sixty-foot seawave struck Cadiz, and a fifty-foot wave hit Cornwall, England, the Canaries, the Azores and Madeira. The wave traveled in less than an hour to Leyden, Holland, and reached the Gulf of Finland hours later. A "black wall of water," twenty-two feet high, roared against the Lesser Antilles. In Martinique and Barbados water rose to the roofs of houses and receded in seconds.

Scores of Portuguese cities and towns suffered destruction and casualties during the first three severe shocks, the most notable being Oporto. The quake, seawave and fire brought still another affliction to Lisbon. When the walls of the prison collapsed, hundreds of prisoners escaped and ran through the streets. The king, young Dom Joseph, ordered gallows erected the first day in a great circle about the city, elevated on the hilltops. Soldiers dragged several hundred persons to these gallows and hanged them in full view of the quake survivors, almost as a retribution for the disaster visited upon the city, an attempt to propitiate God, for Lisbon was a bastion of the Inquisition.

There were several "confessions" from the looters before their execution, in which they admitted setting fires to aid them in looting and to add to the confusion. One, a Moor, "confessed at the gallows that he had set fire to the king's palace with his own hand; at the same time glorying in the action, and declaring with his last breath, that he hoped to have burnt all the royal family."

But Dom Joseph and his family were not in the palace at the time of the quake. They were in residence at nearby Belem, and at the first shock the apprentice monarch was beseeched by a throng of priests "to intercede with the saints for forgiveness of the sins which had brought about this calamity." (Battalions of priests roved through the debris of Lisbon looking for heretics to burn, such as the previously mentioned Chase, who, to avoid their attention, pretended to be unconscious as he lay sprawled in the Terreiro de Paco; a Protestant minister was surrounded by a mob of Portuguese priests and forcibly baptized in admonishment of his obviously sinful instigation of the quake.)

The king was a practical man who brushed aside the frantic clerics and asked his secretary of state, the level-headed Marquis de Pombal, "What can be done?" His response has come down in history: "Sire, we must bury the dead and feed the living." This simple statement commited Pombal to a herculean chore. For five days he lived in his carriage, sipping only broth, as he gave orders for the rescue and restoration of Lisbon. The dead were, for the most part, found and buried within a week by the soldiers of the Marquis of Abrantes, who worked under Pombal's direction. Tons of food were brought from other provinces to feed the more than 200,000 survivors. Pombal also set about rebuilding the city, prescribing new streets "forty feet in width, with pavements on either side." His ambitious plans called for the elimination of slums.

Pombal was also a shrewd statesman who used the quake as an excuse to reduce foreign commercial influence and control in Lisbon, especially that flexed by Germany and England. Opposed to the Inquisition, Pombal, again employing the disaster as a political device, banished the Jesuits from Portugal four years later, citing their religious zeal as a cause of the quake chaos. It took fifteen years for the Marquis to rebuild the city. More importantly, this remarkable man was responsible for collecting the first hard data on the quake itself, gathering from each parish a report of its conduct and building an impressive archive of source material that scientists to this day consult.

(ALSO SEE: Calabria; Concepcion, Chile; San Francisco, 1906)

LITTLE FALLS, NEW YORK — RAILWAY WRECK, APRIL 19, 1940

background: The New York Central's Lakeshore Limited, a fifteen-car train pulled by a Hudson locomotive on its New York-Chicago run, exceeded the hazardous Gulf Curve speed limits of 45 m.p.h. by 14 m.p.h. at 11:30 P.M. in a driving rain as it approached Little Falls, New York, on April 19, 1940, and left the tracks. Nine cars were derailed along with the engine; thirty passengers were killed, another one hundred injured. The engineer, who failed to reduce speed, was blamed for the wreck.

The plush Lake Shore Limited was twenty minutes late as it left Albany, New York, and the engineer of the fifteen-car train, seventy-three-year-old Jesse Earl, tried to make up for lost time. He raced the train at 75 m.p.h., the top limit for the Mohawk Division, and as the train approached Little Falls, New York, it headed into a blinding rainstorm, moved on a steep downgrade and headed onto the dangerous Gulf Curve. Foreman Bayreuther warned Earl about the speed.

The old engineer momentarily appeared confused as he placed his hand on the throttle and mumbled something about taking orders. Earl jammed the throttle closed while the train, traveling at 59 m.p.h. (the speed restriction for this curve was 14 m.p.h. less), had entered the curve. The engine and the whole weight of the remaining train was thrown onto one rail and hung there for precarious seconds, until it left the tracks.

Incredibly the baggage car broke loose of the engine and the cars behind it as they sailed off the tracks into a stone abutment. The baggage car continued undamaged down the tracks. The engine bolted over two other sets of tracks and smashed into the stone wall, its boiler exploding. Earl was seriously injured; Bayreuther was thrown clear.

Passengers in the first two Pullman cars were mangled when cars crashed into one another and smacked into a stone wall. Seven more cars followed, snaking out and flopping to their sides. Rescuers found thirty dead and one hundred injured in the caved-in cars.

Ironically the last car behind the baggage car managed to stay on the tracks. Its passengers were thirty-five Chinese, totally unperturbed at the rescue operations going on. They were being deported.

New York Central's Lakeshore Ltd. derailed near Little Falls, New York, on April 19, 1940. Thirty passengers were crushed to death.

Train officials determined that Earl was to blame for the accident because he failed to reduce speed at the Gulf Curve. Jesse Earl never faced a reprimand. He died five minutes after he was dragged from the wrecked train.

LITTLEFIELD NURSING HOME — FIRE
March 29, 1953

"The flames swept over everything. We couldn't go back in. We heard screams and groans, but we couldn't help." With these words, Mabel Walter, a nurse at the Littlefield Nursing Home in Largo, Florida, explained the hopelessness of those trapped in the fire that gutted the 75-by-100-foot flimsy building on March 29, 1953.

The William Littlefields, owners of the home, were awakened at 3:00 A.M. by smoke drifting over them from a supply room. They attempted to put out the mounting fire with a small hand extinguisher. Mrs. Littlefield then had a heart attack, and her husband, assisted by nurse Aletha Herring, who had rushed across the street from her cottage when she spotted the blaze, carried the woman from the building. The two then dragged out six more persons.

Many of the sixty-five inmates at the home were dyspeptic and prone to depression (some were mentally ill) and refused to save themselves. When Littlefield aroused one elderly man, shouting at him, "Get up, the place is on fire," the man replied, "What for?" and held tightly to the posts of his bed, where he was later found burned to death.

Failing to reach the fire department in nearby Clearwater when her phone went dead, Mrs. Frank Parker, wife of the home's caretaker, drove at high speeds for three miles to contact the Largo police. The effort was useless. By the time firemen arrived, the building's sheet-metal roof had collapsed to its burned-out concrete foundation; metal beds and bodies melted into them were all that was left.

Retired Air Force Captain John Beecher, suffering from asthma, was sitting up in bed and reading when flames from the home broke through the walls of his adjoining cottage. He barely managed to drag his invalid wife from the cottage before it, too, was gutted.

In the ruins the cremated bodies of thirty-three persons, ages fifty-five to ninety-four, were found; one of them was Arthur Fields, the songwriter.

About thirty of the survivors were injured, and in the absence of ambulances, had to be driven to hospitals in private cars. Angus Smith and his wife, who noticed the blaze from the highway as they were driving by, took three badly burned patients in their car. Two blocks away from the still smoldering ruins, another car, driven by Feton Bennett, hit the Smith car broadside. The fire

The Littlefield Nursing Home in Largo, Florida, burned on March 29, 1953. Thirty-three died in the fire. *(UPI)*

survivors received no injuries in this accident, but Mrs. Smith was killed.

A seventy-year-old Forked River, New Jersey, banker, Thomas Clements, arrived at the nursing home at 6:00 A.M., three hours after the fire had started. His crippled wife was to have been released that day. She was among the ashes.

(ALSO SEE: Katie Jane Nursing Home, Little Sisters of the Poor Home)

LITTLE SISTERS OF THE POOR HOME — FIRE — July 24, 1931

background: Housing 213 men and women, all over sixty years of age, the Little Sisters of the Poor Home in Pittsburgh, Pennsylvania, caught fire at 10:00 P.M. on July 24, 1931, when combustible materials in the basement ignited. The six-alarm blaze brought twenty-two companies of firemen to the site and a number of passersby who performed heroic rescues. Killed were 48 residents; all of the survivors were injured. The building suffered a $50,000 loss, the worst institutional fire in Pittsburgh to that date.

Sister Agatha, mother superior of the little Sisters of the Poor Home in Pittsburgh, was awakened from a deep sleep by the sound of thumping canes pounding on the floor above her. Although she was eighty, she was still spry and alert. It took her little time to get up and race toward the disturbance. Through the smoke that filled the four floors of the nursing home, Sister Agatha and eighteen other nuns made their way, rousing scores of old and crippled inmates.

In the basement a roaring fire was in progress. (Initial reports indicated the fire had started in the men's infirmary of unknown causes; Fire Chief Smith later reported that the basement floors had been oiled and polished that night and an oil-soaked mop had caught fire.) It was a little after 10:00 P.M. on July 24, 1931, when the Pittsburgh Fire Department got the call. It was a six-alarm fire, and twenty-two companies of firemen drove siren-screaming engines toward the home at Penn and Aiken avenues, aiming their vehicles toward the glowing light in the distant night sky. Before their arrival scores of passersby spotted the blaze from the streets and ran to the gates of the home. Finding the high iron gates locked, many climbed the eight-foot brick walls surrounding the grounds and ran up the hill to the building where dozens of pale-faced old people were frantically signaling for help.

Several street-corner gangs and a mob of men from a nearby poolroom, among the first to see the fire, came on the run, joining in the rescue operations. Most afflicted were the 145 men trapped in the men's dormitory wing. Several men jumped from the second and third floors. Policemen rushed up and told those preparing to leap from windows to stay where they were until life nets could be brought by firemen.

To many trapped inside, the building was protected by God. John Hoffman, a city employee who ran to the rescue, placed a rickety ladder to the second floor of the burning men's wing and climbed to a window in which an old man sat with a rosary dangling from bony hands.

"C'mon, get down the ladder after me," Hoffman told the man.

"This place is under divine guidance," the man said softly. "It cannot burn." Another man standing nearby agreed and stepped forward, reaching through the window and pushing Hoffman down and off the ladder. Both men died in the flames that soon engulfed them.

Other rescuers found more cooperation. A neighbor, William Gaefke, spotted a man waving for help. He scaled the walls of the home and eventually led fifteen persons, most of them blind, to safety. Thomas Martin, eighteen, and a younger friend ran into the building and broke into the chapel. Half of the home's male population had taken refuge here. Flames surrounded them. Many refused to leave. Martin ran to the altar, removed the chalice and then led out twenty-one persons. His companion dove seven times through the flaming doorway, bringing out a person each time. He collapsed from smoke inhalation, and firemen carried him out.

In addition to ambulances a fleet of about forty cabs responded to the fire. The hackies had a rough time explaining their mission in some instances to roaming pickets who were striking against the taxi firms. One cabbie stopped by two strikers wielding clubs was quoted as saying, "Don't stop me now, buddy. I'm going out to haul some of the old people hurt in the fire at the home." The strikers hopped into the cab. All three men carried the injured from the blazing rest home.

When firemen finally battered down the locked gates of the home and rushed into the main building, they found Sister Agatha and ten other nuns shepherding forty-five people, mostly cripples in wheelchairs and blind persons jiggling white canes, toward the front door. Sister Agatha turned away from this group at the door and attempted to return to others still inside the building. Firemen forcibly restrained her, and she was taken away in an hysterical condition.

On the third floor Sister Pascaline compelled a dozen or so women to put their heads out the windows for fresh air. They ran from window to window doing so. One, seventy-five-year-old Margaret Connell, aided several others too feeble to move as they battled against suffocation and heat. Her stamina soon gave out. She recalled, "There were no lights and the heat on the floor was intense. I felt too weak to go on. I sank back on a bed, and a fireman carried me out."

Mary Kline, eighty, merely "got down on my knees and prayed to God . . . and then I was rescued."

Sarah Carlson also was taken out of the third floor trap as the flames swooped into the women's wing, but calling out her husband's name, she broke away from firemen and, to the astonishment of the firemen, almost sprinted back into the flames. Her husband was also an inmate of the same home. Both perished in the fire; their bodies were later found together.

Firemen had a hard time saving several men who refused to climb down ladders. They were saved by force as the ladders leaning against the burning window sills caught fire and went to ashes. Joining the firemen, policemen, nuns, and citizens of all stripes helped to evacuate the flaming home. There was little that could be done for those who remained behind in the incinerated chapel. Found there later were about thirty bodies, all men. Eighteen more inmates died in the hospital, bringing the death count to forty-eight. At least another hundred were seriously injured.

Relatives searched through the half-dozen Pittsburgh hospitals for those taken alive from the home. One of these was Patrolman Gabriel Voletto, whose mother had been a long-time resident of the home. He could not find her and glumly went to the morgue. Her body had not been recovered, he was told. At daybreak Voletto went back to another hospital, and as he shuffled red-eyed through a ward, a tiny voice cried out, "Gabriel." His white-haired mother smiled up at him from a hospital bed.

(ALSO SEE: Cleveland Clinic, Katie Jane Nursing Home)

LITTLETON, ALABAMA — MINE DISASTER

April 8, 1911

background: At 6:20 A.M. on April 8, 1911, the Banner Mine of the Pratt Consolidated Coal Company exploded, as a result of a careless miner exposing an open-flame lamp to safety powder while dynamiting. Of the 170 miners inside (90 percent of whom were black chain-gang prisoners), 128 were later found dead, all killed by poisonous black damp. The mine had been pronounced safe earlier that morning by firebosses.

Convict labor, mostly black chain-gang workers serving from ten days to two years hard labor, made up more than 90 percent of the work force in the Banner Mine operated by the Pratt Consolidated Coal Company outside of Littleton, Alabama.

Twenty minutes after the day crew of 170 men relieved the night shift, at approximately 6:20 A.M. on April 8, 1911, according to a mine foreman and chain-gang overseer who were sipping coffee at the mine's entrance at the time, a loud explosion was heard. Smoke mixed with a shower of gravel shot out of the mouth of the mine, and minutes later groups of coughing men emerged.

Although a night fireboss named Sparks had reported that the mine was safe, the shafts were, in fact, filled with gas and coal dust. The "black damp" was everywhere when the day crew went to work. When a careless foreman exposed his safety lamp to coal dust, an explosion took place, causing 128 men to be asphyxiated by the black damp that thickly rolled through many shafts in the mine.

Several convicts with mining experience knew that the damp was forming and spread the alarm. There was a race with death as scores of workers sped for the entrance, hooting and shouting in their panic. Forty-two survived the holocaust. Many men who were working in the third level hours after the explosion were startled to hear of the disaster. They vacated the mine via an alternate entrance.

The explosion tossed pit cars into walls and shattered massive timbers, causing cave-ins. As a group of men were running for the entrance, convict Charles Brown returned to the mine, penetrating it to the point where the damp was concentrated. He made repeated trips to help sixteen fellow convicts to safety.

Convict foreman O. W. Spradling was among those five white men killed in the Banner Mine explosion. His head had been crushed, but, mysteriously, there were no fallen timbers or debris near his body.

LONDON — MARINE DISASTER

January 11, 1866

background: Built in 1864 the *London* displaced 1,752 tons and was a combination steamship (with 800 horsepower) and sailing vessel. Owned by the Money Wigram and Sons firm, the ship was launched at Blackwell, England, and completed two successful trips to Melbourne, Australia, before foundering in a storm of near-hurricane proportions 200 miles southwest of Land's End, England, on January 11, 1866. More than 220 passengers and crew men drowned.

The *London's* last voyage was marked for tragedy at the outset. The ship sailed from Gravesend on December 30, 1865, and ran smack into a violent storm in the English Channel. The winds were so fierce that Captain Martin ordered the vessel into the harbor at St. Helen's Roads, where she sought shelter. From that point Martin ordered his ship, loaded with 236 passengers and crew, down the channel the next day.

A great gale of wind and pitching seas almost engulfed the ship near Plymouth. Upon reaching that port, an ominous event occurred; the pilot boat capsized when it put off, and the pilot drowned as those on board watched. Calm winds met the *London* as she sailed for Melbourne on January 5, 1866. Three days later gigantic winds swept the sea, and Captain Martin, to keep the ship on course, ordered the topsails reefed. The large steamship plodded through squalling seas under the power of her churning screws. Wind, the likes of which the crew had never seen before, tore at the *London* the following day, ripping away three masts and the jib boom. That night, one report said that "the sea was running mountains high" and carried away lifeboats. Still Martin kept his ship on course.

When the *London* reached a point approximately 200 miles southwest of Land's End, she was hit by wind and seas approaching hurricane velocity. Huge waves cascaded onto the ship, drenching the boiler-room fires. Passengers and crew men alike labored at the pumps and baled frantically with buckets, but Martin realized the effort was useless; the *London* was out of control and doomed. He called everyone on board to the giant saloon and told the exhausted crew and passengers that the ship would soon sink.

Water was now up to the ship's mainchains. One lifeboat lowered into the violent sea was instantly swamped; its five crew members were pulled from the sea with hooks.

While a clergyman led prayers in the saloon, sixteen members of the crew and three male passengers dashed for the only remaining lifeboat, the starboard cutter. Battling the storm, which knocked them down several times, these men managed to free the lifeboat by slashing the ropes holding it to the *London* and, as it crashed flat into the sea, jumped into it.

Engineer John Greenhill looked up from the lifeboat to the deck above to see Captain Martin staring solemnly down at him. Greenhill shouted for the captain to join them.

Martin shouted back, "No! I will go down with the passengers, but I wish you Godspeed, and safe to land."

The storm wrenched the small craft away from the *London,* and those in the lifeboat could only watch in horror as the vessel, five minutes later, slid beneath the waves, stern foremost. There was no panic among the 220 souls on board the *London.* Survivors later related that they could hear the unified murmur of men, women and

Going down off Land's End is the *London,* caught in a hurricane on January 11, 1866.

children calmly uttering prayers before they were gone.

For twenty hours the small cutter was driven wildly across the raging ocean like a flat rock skipping the surface of the water, once coming close to being swamped. Then the Italian bark, *Marianople,* commanded by Captain Carasa, plucked the half-dead survivors from the sea and returned them to Falmouth.

The sinking of the *London* in 1866 was one of the worst maritime disasters to that date.

LONDON, ENGLAND FOG

December, 1952

"The English Disease" has been known for centuries in Europe as a killer that strikes the lungs. The noxious fumes given off by tens of thousands of chimneys mix with fog, and when stalled warm-air masses collect over London, hundreds and sometimes thousands of persons, mostly the elderly, die.

The noted diarist, John Evelyn (1620-1706), lived far from London's poisonous air in country-squire luxury when he wrote, "London's inhabitants breathe nothing but an impure and thick mist accompanied with a fuliginous and filthy vapor, so that catharrs, phthisicks, coughs, and consumption are more in this city than the whole earth besides."

The most deadly fog experienced in London occurred in December, 1952, when a giant warm-air mass hovered over the metropolis like an inverted saucer, trapping a lethal compound of sulphur dioxide, coal smoke, gasoline and chemical fumes. The result was that more than 4,000 persons were killed by its effects and another 8,000 persons, according to Dr. Ernest T. Wilkins, chief of the Atmospheric Pollution Division of the Department of Scientific and Industrial Research, eventually perished from its prolonged effects.

The 1952 fog brought about England's Clean Air Act in 1956, the result of a four-year study by the Beaver Committee.

LONDON, ENGLAND FOG

December 3-7, 1962

Although the Clean Air Act of 1956 was in force, the pea-soup fog that blanketed London for three days and nights on December 3-7, 1962, combined with great quantities of sulphur dioxide and caused 136 persons (all over age fifty-five) to perish. An additional 1,000 persons were hospitalized for treatment, and the city of 12 million came to a complete standstill.

Robbers looted banks and jewelry shops almost at random, and police were powerless to pursue them. One

A thick, sooty fog blanketed London in December 1952. The polluted air killed more than 4,000 citizens. Shown here is the Antarctic exploration vessel *Discovery* anchored at the waterfront, an eerie sight in the deadly soup. *(UPI)*

man stole $28,000 and simply walked into the fog. He wore, as did most who ventured through the streets, a gauze facemask.

The city's 5,000 buses were ordered into garages after two double-deckers collided, injuring thirteen passengers. Scores of persons were run over by motorists. A train engineer was killed when, not knowing he was on a bridge, he stepped from his cab and disappeared into forty feet of water.

A reader of the *New Yorker* wrote to that magazine from London: "The fog floated visibly, like ectoplasm, into theatres, cinemas, and shops, where sales assistants stood around gossiping among the sparsely populated wastes of Christmas presents. In the evenings, the West End was as empty as on a night in the blitz, and nearly as dark in residential side streets, where street lamps cast the illumination of nursery nightlights. If you had felt the urge to do so, you could have danced in the eerie middle of Piccadilly in safety, if not in comfort."

Though the noxious fog fumes claimed lives, many scientists took advantage of its presence. The Ministry of Aviation tested a new blind-flying system, safely guiding a plane into London Airport. United States scientist and pollution expert Dr. Richard Prindle flew to London and took samples of the deadly air. He commented: "There are not many smogs like this one! It sets off a beautiful cough!"

LONG BEACH, CALIFORNIA — EARTHQUAKE
March 10, 1933

background: Though measuring only 6.3 on many scales, the earthquake that struck densely populated Long Beach, California, on March 10, 1933, took 120 lives and caused damage estimated to be $50 million. The number of deaths and extensive damage were attributed to panic and poor building construction.

The destructive earthquake that struck Long Beach, California, on March 10, 1933, was heralded fully thirteen years earlier when minor shocks began to emanate from a fault. Minor tremors continued until March, 1933, when the shocks increased. In the late afternoon of March 10, the earth seizure happened, doing much damage to Long Beach's flimsily constructed school buildings. It was fortunate, however, that classes were through for the day and many lives were spared.

It was later determined that the epicenter of the quake was in an offshore fault about three miles southwest of Newport Beach. The 6.3 shock wave quickly destroyed about $50 million worth of property, crumbling myriad buildings constructed on sand and water-soaked alluvium. The heavily jammed highways undulated and caused autos to careen crazily into each other.

One driver remembered that "cars zigzagged on the road. Tall ornamental light standards along Anaheim began breaking off and showering the car with debris. I continued along toward Long Beach and had almost reached a tank farm when a series of gas tanks exploded. A transformer station went out at almost the same time with a dazzling pyrotechnic display."

The expansion joints of the Balboa Island Bridge tore loose, pinging from their moorings, and the cliffs around it gave way in hurtling slabs of crusted earth and rock. People went screaming down streets. Fantastic rumors were shouted. One related that Catalina Channel had sunk almost 400 feet, another that the earth all around Long Beach had been wrenched violently thirty feet from the mainland.

The shock raced through the entire Los Angeles basin, but did its worst damage to Long Beach and Compton. Hours later 120 dead persons were taken off the streets and dug out from beneath the rubble. Hundreds more were injured.

(ALSO SEE: San Francisco, Calif.)

LONG ISLAND, NEW YORK — HURRICANE
September 17-21, 1938

background: The hurricane that wrecked Long Island, New York, and southern New England on September 17-21, 1938, killed 494 persons (with 100 more missing and presumed dead; 1,754 people were injured) and destroyed 13,898 houses, business buildings and summer homes; it sank more than 2,500 boats in various harbors. The estimated 186 m.p.h. winds created damages that soared beyond $400 million. (Winds measured at Blue Hill Observatory in Massachusetts were 183 m.p.h.; barometric readings taken measured 27.94 inches.)

The killer storm of 1938, since called the "Great New England Hurricane," was first sighted by a ship steaming 600 miles east-northeast of Puerto Rico on September 17. After frightening Florida residents for several days, the tropical storm veered up the Atlantic coastline, but did no damage to the shore. Suddenly at 8:30 A.M. on September 21, 1938, the hurricane turned at Cape Hatteras, its 186 m.p.h. winds tearing for shore. A weather plane was caught in the hurricane's eyewall where the wind velocity was estimated to be 140 m.p.h. Neither the pilot nor the copilot could control the craft, and the crew said their good-byes over the radio. Miraculously the plane did not crash into the sea, but returned to base. It was literally in shreds, 150 rivets having been sheared from one wing alone.

Forecasts from New Jersey to Maine that day only warned of a "broad trough of low pressure." By 3:30 P.M., the whole force of the hurricane smashed against Long Island, New York. The Empire State Building was lost to sight as swirling silver-sheeted clouds driven by 120

Scores of elegant homes were demolished by the hurricane that swept over Long Island, New York, on September 21, 1938. *(Wide World)*

m.p.h. winds engulfed and swayed it to and fro. Because most radio stations were broadcasting a shrieking bombast of an Adolf Hitler state speech when the hurricane drove ashore, they neglected to give weather reports. As the throbbing, pounding waves of the hurricane lashed ashore, the seismographic needles at Fordham University fluttered in much the same way that they might respond to a minor earth tremor. An eighteen-foot wave roared ashore at Long Island and drowned several swimmers.

Then the lights, phones and everything else went off. Like an arcing club swung by a giant, the hurricane leveled one town after another—Bridgehampton, Brentwood, Southampton, Sagg Pond. At Sag Harbor the historic Presbyterian Church steeple was snapped off in an instant. Houses by the hundreds fell like cards, burying their startled occupants. Only 6 buildings out of 150 in Westhampton were still standing after the monster passed.

The vortex of the storm swept up Connecticut, slashing into New Haven and Hartford. It skipped up the twenty-mile channel of Narragansett Bay and ate through several Rhode Island towns. In one hotel there, great waves poured through doors and windows and drowned every person lounging among the potted palms. At Hartford 1,000 men ran from the Colt arms factory to the Connecticut River to hurriedly throw up a sandbag dike against the rising waters.

Land-borne, the storm jerked its massive front through Massachusetts, where it wiped out Worcester, and then on to New Hampshire, Vermont and Maine. (At the Mount Washington Observatory in New Hampshire, elevated at 6,000 feet, gusts of the hurricane's winds were measured at 190 m.p.h., the greatest ever estimated in that area of the United States.) Most of the storm blew itself up the St. Lawrence valley, vanishing somewhere in Canada's arctic regions.

The damage left in its wake was appalling—almost $400 million. And the dead were everywhere, 494 persons by rough count, and another 100 were never found.

One blessing amidst the mammoth tragedy was that thousands of unemployed men, then suffering through the depression, were employed to repair the damage to the almost 14,000 homes and offices demolished and the telephone lines knocked down (one estimate being 72 million feet of wire).

In recorded history this was the ninth serious hurricane to affect New England, but it was thought to be a freak until a similar hurricane struck almost the same area and followed the same path during September 8-16, 1944, in which 390 persons were killed, and $100 million in damage was done.

LORAIN, OHIO

TORNADO
June 28, 1924

background: A tornado originating in Sandusky, Ohio, at 4:35 P.M., where it killed 8 persons, injured 100 and destroyed 125 office and residential buildings at a $1 million loss, moved out into Lake Erie for twenty-five miles and again struck the shore at Lorain at 5:14 P.M. where it killed 78, injured 1,200, and totally wrecked the business district, damaging 200 offices and stores and demolishing 500 homes at a cost of $11 million.

After touching down on a one-half mile killing spree in Sandusky, Ohio, on June 28, 1924, a tornado skipped across Lake Erie before it moved inland. Taking the form of a "queer yellow cloud," according to one report, it struck Lorain, Ohio, at 5:14 P.M. The twister was a mile wide when it touched down, and it gradually diminished until it contracted to a width of 500 feet. By then it had swept through the city and wrecked it.

Bodies, cars, trees, trucks and debris were hurled down the street. Members of one office were blown out windows they had run to, thinking that a low-flying airplane was about to crash. They were sent more than sixty feet down the street. The State Theater was heavily damaged while a horde of viewers fled from the quaking building, dodging falling bricks, beams and concrete ceilings. One man was reported to have stood outside the theater holding his young son. "I've found him!" he shouted to dazed passers-by. "I've found my boy. He was in the theater and he ain't hurt a bit!"

But 78 others were dead and about 1,200 were seriously injured. One man was crushed to death when a freight car was blown off its tracks and against another car on the tracks running next to it. The dead littered the streets within five minutes after the storm passed. Arranged in the middle of Broadway was a jumble of wrecked autos, dead horses and crumpled corpses. The chief of police held up a megaphone and hollered, "We've found some men robbing bodies. From now on I'm giving orders to shoot to kill anybody found looting the dead."

The twister caught Mrs. Charles Newsome and her four small children just as they were headed for Lake View Park. Hearing the approaching twister, Mrs. Newsome herded her children back into the house and then into the basement. "But the basement started to fill with water, so we had to come upstairs again," she explained. The tornado blew straight through her house, taking every piece of furniture, every picture and every drapery with it. The family survived with only minor scratches.

Their destination, Lake View Park, looked like a battlefield. Trees were uprooted and splintered. In other trees that the wind had spared, all manner of objects were dangling and flapping—an exquisite Persian rug, a pink evening gown, and bolts of cloth. A fragile statue of Venus survived undamaged.

One man who had retired early jumped from bed when he heard the tornado's roar. From his window he saw his neighbor's house slip down the street, and he felt his own home quaking. He leaped out the window, and while the wild winds stripped his pajamas away, he clung to a hitching post.

Mrs. Jack Stewart stopped her car to avoid a falling tree and couldn't get it started again. She got out of the car and began to run. "All of a sudden I felt just like a giant hand was scrubbing my face with mud," she later remembered. "Then I was hurled to the ground, and I slid without any power to stop myself across the roadway. As I got to the other side, I grabbed at the steps of a porch and the porch and house were snatched from my grasp."

Mrs. C. C. Smith was upstairs at home with her daughters when the storm bellowed in from the lake. She leaned out a second-story window to see "the sky and earth touch. I looked out and in the sky there seemed to be a streak of white about a foot wide; it was swirling in a circle and the rest of the sky was a terrible blue-black. I screamed to the girls to run downstairs, 'My God, something terrible is going to happen. Run for your lives!' By the time we reached the first floor, the roof and upper stories of the building were swept away, and there was a horrible sound of splintering and crashing in the air."

James Robbins of the *New York World* was at the scene as rescue operations commenced. He wrote of one

The heart of the business district in Lorain, Ohio, was wrecked by a tornado on June 28, 1924. The twister killed seventy-eight people. *(UPI)*

"tireless man [who] dug into the ruins of a building. Hour after hour passed. Relief workers assisting him tired and were replaced by fresh men. But the man worked on. Following the removal of an immense heap of mortar and crumbled cement, the search ended. The man dropped to his knees beside a crumpled body, then fell in a merciful faint."

Lorain had been leveled as if by an enormous buzz saw. The national director of the Red Cross disaster relief program, Henry M. Baker, described the carnage as "the most complete" he had ever witnessed.

LOS ANGELES CALIFORNIA — RAILWAY WRECK — January 22, 1956

The failure of the Santa Fe line to detect the epileptic condition of one of its engineers was the vital factor that sent one of its two-car trains off the tracks near Los Angeles on January 22, 1956. The R.D.C. multiple unit built by the Budd Company was jammed with 161 passengers as it rounded a curve four miles from the station.

The speed on this curve was restricted to 55 m.p.h., yet the engineer, who was not harmed in the accident, allowed the train to take the curve at 72 m.p.h. He later revealed that he had suffered a seizure. The fireman claimed to have warned him of the upcoming curve while the train was still a thousand feet from the approach, but the engineer did not respond in time.

As the train hit the curve, where the outside rail was elevated higher than the inside one, the train merely lifted from its tracks and careened over the outside rail. Both cars flopped on their sides and slid violently along the tracks for more than 500 feet.

Thirty passengers were killed when they flew through broken coach windows, slid beneath the cars, and were crushed as the cars slid along the tracks. None of the crew members were hurt.

LOS ANGELES, CALIFORNIA — LANDSLIDES — January 18-26, 1969

background: Southern California was inundated by ten inches of rain from a subtropical storm sweeping in from Hawaii that began on January 18, 1969, and continued for nine days; the heavy rains caused immense landslides, chiefly in the Los Angeles area. Death came to ninety-five persons, and damage was estimated at $138 million.

Ten inches of rain fell as a result of a Hawaiian storm that swept over the Los Angeles area during January 18-26, 1969. Thousands of people whose exclusive homes precariously perched on the hillsides of the San Gabriel and Santa Monica mountains lived through some of the worst mudslides in the history of "Tinseltown." Homes in Mandeville Canyon were hardest hit, and dozens of volunteer groups manned shovels in an attempt to turn back the house-crunching landslides.

The ninety-five people killed in the landslides included poor and rich alike. One company president was buried as his $100,000 home collapsed around him. Rainbow Drive in scenic Glendora was swamped by running yellow mud on January 22. The landslide was half mud and half water, turning into a torrential flood that in a few seconds dove into the home of Lorin Rimers and demolished it. Rimers barely managed to escape by jumping through a window.

In the Highland Park area on El Paso Drive, the home of John Gonzales was covered by mud. Mrs. Gonzales was trapped in the mud, which had pushed her home into the street. "My babies are in the front room," she desperately cried to a neighbor, but they were beyond aid; three hours later, two small, dead boys were dug out.

Santiago Creek was perilously close to overflowing its banks and flooding Santa Ana. About 5,000 volunteer workers arrived, most from the black community of Watts, and slaved for hours to hold back the creek. To make a unique stopgap, Marine helicopters carried wrecked cars from junkyards to the breached banks, and these were used to build a barrier.

The Twentieth-Century Fox sets for Charleton Heston's movie *Planet of the Apes* were wrecked by the mudslides in the nearby Santa Monica mountains. More than one hundred boats were sunk at Ventura and Santa Barbara; Carpinteria and Montecito were also badly damaged. The cost of the disaster leaped to $138 million. President Richard Nixon declared the site a disaster area and sent $3 million in relief funds.

LOUISIANA — HURRICANE — August 19, 1812

A furious hurricane, one of the first recorded in the Louisiana area, struck west of the Mississippi River and ran the length of the river through the state, in what weather-watchers have determined is a traditional path for gulf-tracked hurricanes. Beginning about noon on August 19, 1812, the hurricane slashed through New Orleans, damaging buildings and flooding streets. The historic Market House with its huge twenty-four-inch diameter columns was blown down by the winds.

Severe damage was suffered by towns and hamlets farther up the Mississippi, notably at Fort St. Philip, where a contingent of American volunteers awaited British forces who were then at war with the United States. Havoc spread here; the fort was flooded and many of its sturdy buildings were splintered by the howling winds. Most of those sheltered in the fort took refuge in the thick log barracks and survived, but forty-five died in the fort and at upstream Grand Prairie.

One account agonized: "John Dennis and his wife, Sylvan Dennis, and his five children are all drowned and a number more. Oh!—the afflicting, heart-wounding sight to behold thirty-two persons committed to the earth in one common grave."

Along the river, where undetermined scores perished, fifty-three ships were smashed and sunk, "crushed to atoms," as one writer reported.

LOUISIANA — HURRICANE
October 1, 1893

An unusually small but severe hurricane brought violent winds and heavy rains from the gulf into Louisiana on October 1, 1893, striking between New Orleans and Port Eads. A tidal wave that was ten or twelve feet high was reported here; its unexpected arrival caught thousands of residents off guard, killing, according to one report, 2,000 persons.

Millions of dollars' worth of goods and ships were lost in this storm that ran through all the South Atlantic states before moving off to sea.

LOUISIANA — HURRICANE
September 1, 1918

Winds up to 100 m.p.h., meshed with dense cloud and rain formations inside a hurricane, tore at the Louisiana shores on September 1, 1918. First sighted at Barbados, this storm did considerable damage to Jamaica before crossing the gulf, flattening scores of homes, and killing thirty-four persons, chiefly in the Lake Charles area. Damage was estimated at more than $5 million in Louisiana alone.

LOUISIANA, MISSISSIPPI, and ALABAMA — HURRICANE
September 10-20, 1909

A ponderous storm front ripped through the Leeward Islands on September 10, 1909, and developed that day into a full-fledged hurricane that growled westward across the Caribbean. Nicking the western edges of Cuba on September 17, the hurricane moved against Louisiana and struck the coast about fifty miles west of New Orleans on September 20.

Dikes and barriers in the mouth of the Mississippi gave way as 60 to 70 m.p.h. winds lashed the coast. The Mississippi rose an unprecedented three feet, and Lake Borgne's waters overflowed to meet the onrushing waves of the gulf. New Orleans was awash, and every wire in the city was swept away by the onslaught. The broad front of the hurricane encompassed Louisiana, Mississippi, Alabama and parts of Florida.

At Pensacola the giant steamer *Romanoff* turned turtle with dozens of other ships in the harbor, and scores of people drowned. To the west the towns of Warrington and Woolsey were utterly flattened, and dozens were crushed or drowned in the debris that was hurtled forward by the water, rain and wind.

More than $5 million in damage was done in Louisiana and Mississippi, and the two states sustained the loss of an estimated 350 persons.

LOUISVILLE, KENTUCKY — TORNADO
March 27, 1890

background: A wild tornado struck Louisville, Kentucky, then a city of 200,000, and the surrounding area on March 27, 1890, at about 8:00 P.M. moving at about 40 m.p.h. in a 300-yard path. The twister, moving northeast, took 106 lives, injured another 235, and did $3.5 million in damage (which would be four times that amount today). The tornado traveled a distance of seventy-five miles and did extensive damage in nearby Jeffersonville, Indiana.

Beginning about eight miles outside Louisville, Kentucky, on the night of March 27, 1890, a monstrous twister set down and worked its way into the town in a northeasterly direction. An early observer described it as "balloon-shaped, twisting an attenuated tail to the earth. It emitted a constant fusillade of lightning and seemed to be composed of a lurid, snake-like mass of electric currents whose light would sometimes be extinguished for a few moments, making an almost intolerable darkness. It was accompanied by a fearful roar, like that of a thousand trains crossing the big bridge [across the Ohio River] at once. It could be seen to strike Louisville, and then, with incredible rapidity, it leaped the river, churning it into white foam as it went toward the Indiana shore."

Stores and residences where about 10,000 persons waited were directly in the tornado's path. Its huge base never touched the ground, but tore off almost every roof within its scope of 300 yards. The suburb of Parkland was wrecked. This twister jogged about, devouring Louisville almost block by block and, in many instances, doubling back to buildings that had already escaped its erratic stalking. It sidestepped the city hall and then, almost as if it suddenly recollected something, turned around the block on Market Street, smashed into the city hall, and ground it into timber. The monster raced down five blocks on Main Street and headed right for the sprawling Louisville Hotel, in which hundreds of guests were lodged. The twister came almost to the entranceway and then abruptly turned and drove through a small three-story building that housed a saloon on the first floor and apartments for the hotel's employees on the second and third. It brought the structure down "with not a timber left a dozen feet higher than the ground," according to an Associated Press correspondent. All the employees in this building were killed.

An artist's re-creation shows the devastation that befell Louisville, Kentucky, when a tornado raged through the community, taking 106 lives on March 27, 1890.

Hopping about, looking for a second "course," the tornado then moved north toward the river, devouring the Union Depot on its way. Fortunately only one person was killed. Crossing the river, the twister gnawed away a section of Jeffersonville's Front Street, recrossed the river about four miles from where it had left Kentucky, and ground down the Louisville Pumping Works. The storm then cut along the Kentucky shore for forty miles until it reached Eminence, Kentucky, where it did some additional damage. Finally it was off again, moving into Carroll County, where it dissipated.

The storm had left Louisville at about 8:50 P.M., and by then the city was breaking into flames as several small fires from overturned kerosene lamps, gas mains and other combustible materials had ignited. The flames joined and raced through splintered buildings. The city hall had been packed with people, many attending various social club meetings. James Hassen, one of the first rescuers to reach the hall, dug through the debris and found his wife, who had been attending a meeting. She died minutes later in his arms. Hassen then dug out nine women; all were dead, clasped in each other's arms. What had been a dancing room where classes were being conducted just before the twister struck was a jumble of brick and broken beams. One woman, who died a few hours later, was taken out of this debris. Her three children were found unconscious, but they lived. Before any more victims could be rescued, fire broke out in the smashed building, and rescuers were driven off as they listened to "the groans of the imprisoned" that "changed to fearful shrieks, while the watchers, helpless to render aid, screamed and ran wildly about with anxiety and horror."

The badly bruised volunteer fire department arrived and sprayed the giant pile of burning debris with four hoses, but it took an hour to put out the fires, and by then many had burned to death. Others caught beneath the weight of the fallen hotel were asphyxiated by gas escaping from broken pipes. Rescuers worked for three more hours, removing bodies and survivors until midnight. About fifty persons were killed in the city hall.

A youth who had been at dancing class told of his experience, "I was dancing when a flash of lightning, followed by a crash, made me think that the lightning had struck some part of the rear of the building. The next moment, the big doors that enter into the big hall in front flew open. I continued dancing, and cried to some of the boys to close the doors. They did so, and were bolting them when they were again forced open with such force as to knock down everyone around them. Then the window sashes were blown in, and the building commenced rocking. I saw that the hall was about to fall, and I hallooed: 'The walls will go next!' I ran to the dressing-room, and I think most of the girls followed me. I got under a table and held fast to the legs, thinking that I might be saved in that way. Then the walls began crumbling, and the lights went out, and the floor descended like an elevator. The crash stunned me for a moment, but finally a flash of lightning showed me a hole in the debris, through which I might have crawled had not my leg been pinioned between some timbers. There were people all around me, and they were crying for help; but there was no one to aid us. I tugged and strained, but I could not get loose. Finally, I heard my father's voice, and answered him, and directly he crawled down the hole. It took him three quarters of an hour to extricate me, and then we both crawled out."

In the building adjoining the Louisville Hotel, many of the hotel's servants met death when they were thrown down into the cellar as the walls and floors collapsed. Five laundry girls were found there, one sitting upright, another lying on her back, hands thrust upward as if to push away the debris hurled down on her, another sitting, dust covering open eyes, and two lying face down. One purple-prose writer of the day lamented, "Poor laundry girls! Let their dead dust be mentioned with reverence. Had they been spoiled daughters of wealth and fashion, press reporters would have waxed eloquent of their birth, their history, their beauty, their accomplishments, their heritage. We should have heard in detail the names of their wealthy and mourning friends, and of their impressive obsequies. Magnificent monuments would have risen to mark their sleeping dust. These five laundry girls were taken up tenderly, and two or three days later, together borne without pomp to humble graves. But is not honest industry in useful avocation toiling for bread a more royal thing than silks and diamonds, bedizzening frivolity and idleness? Is there not in America many a haughty heiress, less worthy of our tears, than these?"

The tornado caught most of the town by surprise. The pastor of St. John's Episcopal Church and his four-year-old son were crushed to death when the rectory came down on their heads, yet next door, a few yards away, a group of eleven card players continued their game undisturbed. A man named Tierney, who ran a saloon at Eleventh and Main, survived when he jumped into a large icebox with four of his patrons when the twister struck. The complex of Catholic buildings at Seventeenth and Broadway was wrecked. Elmer Barnes was actually chased by the tornado down Market Street. He bounded into Eckerle's Saloon, and the building promptly fell down on him. He died two hours after being yanked from the ruins. Three men in a grocery store at Sixteenth and Magazine streets were dumped into a basement when the tornado flecked the building. A lone candle set the debris on fire, and the men, trapped beneath, were slowly cremated as horrified, helpless people stood nearby listening to their calls for help.

Others were lucky. Eleven men sitting in the barbershop at 1803 Broadway heard the tornado roaring down the street and dove through windows to safety. A group of persons on Market Street saw the twister turn a corner and come toward them. They tried to enter a store, but even with the clerk inside pushing and four men pulling the door, the wind made it impossible. The building was struck down, but the men at the door survived except, as one report states, "a Negro who had a hole knocked in his skull larger than a silver dollar, and was used up generally."

(ALSO SEE: Gainesville, Georgia, 1936)

LUCILLE

TYPHOON
May 22, 1960

In a double cataclysmic attack the Philippines suffered a seismic sea wave and a tropical typhoon named Lucille almost simultaneously. The seismic wave was the result of Chilean earthquakes; its wall of water struck the main island of Luzon, killing thirteen people.

Hours later on May 22, 1960, Lucille, a typhoon accompanied by torrential rains and winds gusting up to 70 m.p.h., slashed across the island, deluging the capital city of Manila and sending its two million residents scurrying to the rickety second floors of their homes. For several days most of the city was under water, and within a week one hundred persons were found dead, most having drowned when the typhoon first sent her deadly waters inland.

A street in Manila quickly filled with water as typhoon Lucille ripped through the city. The dead horse still in harness in foreground was electrocuted. *(UPI)*

LUZON ISLAND, PHILIPPINES — TYPHOON
December 17-18, 1944

background: In what was considered the most violent typhoon in the region of the Philippines, a storm that lasted through December 17-18, 1944, Admiral William F. Halsey's Third Fleet was caught in violent seas, and three destroyers, the *Monahan, Spence,* and *Hull,* sank. The total fatalities in the disaster numbered 790 killed or missing. Another twenty-eight ships were crippled, and 156 airplanes were lost.

After assisting General Douglas MacArthur's troop landings on the main island of Luzon in the Philippines in early December, 1944, Admiral Halsey sailed his Third Fleet to waters off to the east to refuel. Here the worst typhoon yet experienced by American seamen boiled up on December 17-18.

Blasting winds created canyons of roaring green water with sucking troughs into which the ships plummeted. Winds were estimated at 100 to 150 m.p.h. The typhoon itself was initially undetected by Halsey, who relied upon Weather Central in far-off Honolulu for information, but those in Hawaii were too distant to detect the massive 300-mile-wide typhoon that embraced the Third Fleet.

The smaller ships, for the most part battered destroyers that had fought all through the war from Pearl Harbor days, were easy victims of the storm. Immense waves slapped them back and forth, and for almost twenty-four hours they remained half-submerged under crashing combers while their crews locked themselves in steel compartments and prayed.

Naval historian Hanson Baldwin remembered "the cacophony of the ships—the racked and groaning ships, the creaking of the bulkheads, the working of the stanchions, the play of rivets, the hum of blowers, the slide and tear and roar of chairs and books adrift, of wreckage slipping from bulkhead to bulkhead . . ."

As soup-thick rain reduced visibility to zero and the sea punched upward with huge watery fists that knocked ships of all sizes about like corks, the fleet broke up and slid away; all command was lost, and each craft was on her own to seek survival. It was a nightmare that every survivor would long remember.

But only six people on board the *Monahan* (DD 354), a destroyer that proudly displayed twelve battle stars on her bridge, lived to remember the typhoon. This tired ship, in service since the beginning of the war, was simply too old and too worn out to live through the monstrous typhoon. She lasted through the first night of the storm and then only scanty messages were heard coming from her bridge. "I am unable to come to base course. . . . Have tried full speed but it will not work. . . . Am dead in water . . . Bearing is 225,—1,400 yards . . ."

Sometime in that fog-and-rain vortex, with waves at least 100 feet high pounding at her, the 1,500-ton *Monahan* was driven consistently over and onto her side until she sank with 256 officers and crew men on board. This ship was never seen again; 6 survived.

In short order the *Spence* (DD 512) and the *Hull* (DD 350) followed the *Monahan.* The *Spence,* a heavier ship of 2,000 tons, was sent down into a water trough and rolled over to 72 degrees. Miraculously Lieutenant Al Krauchunas, who was trapped in the captain's cabin, escaped by crawling along the walls of a passageway and then reaching topside before the ship went under. He was the only officer to escape. Seventy enlisted men joined him in the churling waters and were subsequently picked up.

The *Hull* flipped up and down the mountains of water at crazy angles without any water ballast. Her captain, Lieutenant Commander James A. Marks, tried "every possible combination of rudder and engines," but the vessel was thoroughly out of control. Marks watched a gigantic curtain of water close over the ship, and as it rolled up and whipped downward, every officer on the bridge was catapulted from his station. "I had served in destroyers," Marks said later, "in some of the worst storms of the North Atlantic and believed that no wind could be worse than that I had just witnessed."

The wind, like an unseen hand, hammered forward at an estimated 110 knots, pressing the *Hull* onto her side and keeping her there, flattened on the pitching water. The entire ship flooded as water dashed into cabins, the bridge and the pilot house. Marks and a few others simply stepped "off his capsized ship" into a sea so violent that it wrenched the lifejackets off those lucky enough to swim away from the sinking destroyer.

By December 19, Halsey's once-magnificent Third Fleet was a shambles. Three destroyers were lost along with 790 men, and twenty-eight other ships were damaged. Ripped from aircraft carriers and also lost were 156 vital planes. The disaster was the worst ever experienced by the United States Navy in a storm, and led thankfully to the establishment of another Weather Central control station at Guam that could more accurately determine upcoming typhoons in that part of the world.

LZ-18 — AIR CRASH
October 17, 1913

background: Built in the summer of 1913 for the German Navy, the dirigible *LZ-18* (also known as the *L.2)* was 518 feet, 2 inches in length, powered by four 165-horsepower Maybach engines mounted in two gondolas, and had a hydrogen gas capacity of 953,000 cubic feet. While taking part in maneuvers during her tenth flight, the *LZ-18,* with twenty-eight crew members, zeppelin and admiralty officers on board, caught fire, exploded, and crashed in a flaming wreck over Johannisthal, Germany, killing everyone on board. The dirigible's predecessor and sister ship, *L.1,* had been destroyed in a violent storm over the Atlantic on September 9, 1913, and only six of her twenty crew members had survived.

The largest airship of her day, the dirigible *LZ-18* was designed specifically for the German Navy by Felix Pietzker, a student of Count Ferdinand von Zeppelin, who constructed Germany's first dirigible, the *LZ-1 (Luftschiff Zeppelin Number 1)* in 1900. Pietzker's modifications of standard zeppelin construction included the closer fitting of the gondolas to the hull of the ship and innovative windscreens affixed to the bows. These windscreens became points of contention with other engineers, who warned that their close proximity to the hydrogen-bloated hull was extremely dangerous. Pietzker pooh-poohed these notions, and building continued according to his plans.

On September 9, 1913, the *LZ-18* made her maiden voyage to Friedrichshafen, the same day that her sister ship, the *L.1,* was clutched by a terrific storm above Heligoland and smashed into the sea, killing fourteen of her crew members.

Undaunted, Pietzker and twenty-eight others—crew, admiralty officers and zeppelin consultants—took off at Johannisthal, Germany, on October 17, 1913. The dirigible rose to a height of 1,500 feet. It was a warm morning, and the heat of the sun caused the airship's hydrogen to expand the hull, making the craft extremely light. Gliding across the field in a complete arc, the *LZ-18* was then powered by her four 165-horsepower Maybach engines toward the west.

Cries erupted from the throats of dozens of ground spectators as a flame shot forth from the forward engine gondola. A streamer of fire then snaked its way along the bottom of the ship's hull to the rear gondola engines and these, too, blazed upward. Observers could see some of the officers in the gondolas gesturing frantically in an apparent attempt to lower the dirigible, but the flames by then were shooting into and about the aircraft's hull. Totally engulfed by fire the great ship descended, nose first, her gas tanks spitting red and white jets of flame.

Crunching to the ground, the *LZ-18,* in a matter of minutes, had been reduced to a glowing skeleton, her steel ribs gleaming with white heat. Several explosions occurred as the ship crashed, these being the remaining gas cells. A great black cloud mushroomed upward into the clear sky.

Many soldiers and civilians tried to get into the flaming debris. They assumed the formation of the flying wedge of early football days, as the point of the group desperately threw dirt onto the sizzling fire as they moved, but they were driven back. A half-hour passed before rescuers managed to extract from the heat-twisted girders, three passengers who were incredibly still alive, although their faces had been burned away. Agonizing hours later, these three perished. No one on board, including the designer Pietzker, survived the crash; twenty-eight fatalities were the highest death toll to date of any air crash.

Solemn engineers, who had warned against Pietzker's innovations, sat on a board of inquiry later and determined that the windscreens at the bows of the ship had helped to form a vacuum through which the burning hydrogen gas, escaping from the hull, managed to reach the gondolas and explode the engines there.

(ALSO SEE: Akron, Dixmude, Hindenburg, Roma, Shenandoah)

M

MAGHAGHA FERRY **MARINE DISASTER**
May 4, 1963

A double-decked ferry at Maghagha, Egypt, about 200 miles upriver from Cairo, sank while transporting more than 200 Moslems returning from a pilgrimage on May 4, 1963. Only 15 persons survived. The conductor of the ferry, Asmed Abdel Hadi, one of those who escaped the disaster, later explained that his small vessel was able to carry only 80 persons and that, when reaching the eastern bank of the Nile, his little craft was swamped by "a multitude. . . .There must have been more than 200 on board."

Swarming onto the ancient craft, the Moslem pilgrims returning from the traditional four-day Kurban Bairam (Feast of Sacrifice) merely pushed conductor Hadi aside. He busied himself collecting fares (by his own count he took thirty-two fares before the ship sank) and complaining about the large crowd. When the ferry was a few hundred yards from the eastern shore, she foundered in the muddy, two-mile stretch of the Nile.

Few persons reached the shore, which even a weak swimmer should have been able to do. The reason for the mass drowning was that Egyptians seldom learn to swim.

A fireman in Maghagha, Abdel Rehim Mohamed, rushed to the shore as the ferry hooted an alarm. The first body he recovered from the river was that of his wife. The successive bodies he pulled to shore were those of his three brothers, three children and two grandchildren: his entire family.

MAHBUBNAGAR, INDIA **RAILWAY WRECK**
September 2, 1956

A ten-car train of India's Central Railway fell victim to a shaky bridge above a monsoon-swollen river on September 2, 1956. About midnight, as the train approached Mahbubnagar between Secunderbad and Dhone in the province of Hyderabad, all passengers were either in their berths or preparing for bed.

The engine crossed the twenty-foot, single span bridge, which appeared unstable. Beneath it, at the bottom of a steep gorge, a normally small stream had been transformed by three days of torrential rains into a charging river. Just as the engine reached the other side of the bridge, its supports gave way and sent the tender and first two cars hurtling downward.

None of those in the two passenger cars, an estimated 112 persons, survived the death dive. A shower of steel bridge fragments fell on top of the plunging cars. Eighty-five bodies were found days later in a pond two miles downstream where the river had carried them. Authorities thought that these passengers had somehow managed to break out through the train windows underwater and had attempted to swim to the surface.

The bridge guard on duty that night was a mile away checking on another faulty bridge. He returned in time to help the twenty-nine injured into the hamlet of Mahbubnagar.

MANCHESTER, NEW YORK **RAILWAY WRECK**
August 25, 1911

A particularly poignant tragedy and one of the most serious ever involving a broken rail occurred when a fourteen-car Lehigh Valley Line train, carrying Grand Army of the Republic veterans and their families, was derailed near Manchester, New York, on August 25, 1911. The eastbound train, pulled by two engines, was packed with the Civil War veterans returning to their New Jersey and Pennsylvania homes after attending their annual convention in Rochester, New York.

As the train raced across a steel girder bridge arching the Canadaigua River, a rail broke (into seventeen pieces, it was later determined) just after the locomotives and the first five cars had crossed. The seventh car hurtled off the track, and it plunged forty feet downward into the river bed, killing twenty-eight passengers outright. Dozens more were injured.

MANILA, PHILIPPINES **EARTHQUAKE**
July 3, 1863

background: Two enormous shocks all but destroyed the city of Manila in the Philippines at 7:30 P.M. on July 3, 1863, bringing to the ground almost all government buildings, hospitals and historic churches. The death toll reached 1,000, according to most reliable sources, and damages to the city's main export, tobacco, and its warehouses amounted to more than $2 million.

The earthquake that struck Manila in the early evening of July 3, 1863, was the most devastating in the Philippines' history up to that time, and it brought to ruin the elegant buildings in the main part of the city. The great loss of life, a minimum of 1,000, rendered by the quake's two shocks was attributed to the fact that at 7:30 P.M., when the earth trembled and opened, most of the residents were either in the main square markets shopping or in the numerous cathedrals for vespers.

At first the people heard only slight underground rumblings. Then the shocks, lasting only a minute, brought the great buildings down on their heads. The Church of St. Domingo crashed, as did the Binondo Cathedral. The convents of St. Clara, St. Rosa and St. Catalina were reduced to debris in seconds, burying Dominican nuns and friars.

Under the giant dome of the Binondo Cathedral, hundreds were trapped; only seven priests escaped by standing beneath an arch. Dozens of canons and choristers were buried near the altar. The bodies of parishioners—legs, arms, heads—protruded from the dust-emitting rubble. Several priests were recognized as they called for help from beneath tons of fallen masonry. Rescuers heard them call for water, and they improvised a channel to carry water to the trapped by jamming a pipe from the church organ deep into the debris. It did no good. When the debris was finally cleared away, all were dead.

In one section of the church where at least 100 were crushed, a crew of street loungers worked feverishly to clear away the rubble. The stench of death was already thick in the air and caused the correspondent of the *Illustrated London News,* who arrived to sketch the disaster, to complain, "The smell while I was drawing was very offensive, and has since become so strong that the labors which were going on in search of church property have had to be suspended." The hard-working diggers were not attempting to save those who might be alive under the collapsed walls and ceilings, but were trying to locate a cache of diamonds, gold, and silver plate known to be secreted beneath the ruins.

All along the banks of the Pampanga River, there was much destruction and death. The banks of the river had caved inward, taking with them to deep water scores of office buildings, and warehouses containing about $2 million in tobacco, Manila's economic lifeblood. The ocean near Manila Bay gave off shock waves, and captains saw from their ships what was described as "a brilliant halo of what appeared to be phosphoric light over the city." They "felt a shock which resembled the sensation caused by a ship striking the bottom."

In the distance the great volcanoes, Taal, Albay and Arayat, began to smoke, awakened by the earthquake. Fissures opened in many parts of the city, and these chasms swallowed people and animals alike as they fled in hysteria. One well-groomed English merchant had just

Dozens were killed when the roof of Manila's St. Domingo Church collapsed during a devastating earthquake on July 3, 1863. *(Illustrated London News)*

The exquisite tower of Binondo Cathedral was in ruins after the earthquake. *(Illustrated London News)*

Survivors of the quake file past the ruins of the once resplendant Danish Consulate. *(Illustrated London News)*

finished dinner in an elegant mansion and was enjoying a cigar and brandy as he and his friends took in a magnificent view of Manila at sunset from a hillside veranda. When the shocks came, the servants clearing away the dinner dishes were crushed to death as the ceiling caved in. Their pampered masters on the veranda were more fortunate. The merchant clung "to the balustrade in total darkness, hearing the infernal din of the falling houses round us and expecting every instant to lose the ground on which we had found refuge." One frock-coated gentleman panicked and bolted the terrace wall. He ran several feet until the earth opened before him and he fell screaming into a fissure that quickly closed up again, crushing him into his permanent grave.

A Swiss businessman was suffering from fever at the time of the quake. When his enormous mansion began to sway, he leaped from his canopied bed, ran down stairs that collapsed after him, through marble halls that crumbled just as he passed, and out onto his terrace, his shredded nightshirt flapping. The terrace gave way and carried the terrified man and crashing debris that followed him into his stables. He was deposited on top of a manure pile. He not only survived, but was cured of the fever. One wagging friend mused, "Or, at least, he has never felt it since."

The governor of Manila and his son escaped injury while riding in the nearby hills. They hardly felt the quake at all. In the governor-general's palace, his wife, daughter and the servants sat stupefied as the quake brought the elegant building to ruin around them. Walls, rafters and huge tiles pounded down about them, but somehow they were not struck. The ladies, hours later, greeted the governor on the steps of the mansion, gutted behind them, with dinner-laden plates. The governor complained that the food was cold.

Rent-gouging was rampant following the Manila quake since most buildings had been destroyed. Thatched huts built by Indians and owned for the most part by the gentry, which previously had been available for about $4 a month, soared to $30 to $40 a week. It was considered a fair price to pay by those who had escaped the disaster.

MANILA, PHILIPPINES — RAINSTORM-FLOOD
July 19, 1972

Rain beat down on the main island of Luzon in the Philippines for thirty hours, flooding the largest city, Manila, and the provinces of Bulacan, Pampanga, Pangasinan, Nueva Ecija and Tarlac. It resulted in powerful floods, which peaked on July 19, 1972. According to subsequent reports 289 persons were killed, most of them drowned.

In the province of Tarlac alone, 45,000 persons were left homeless. The most devastated area was that of

Manila, where vast stores of food were wiped out. A week after the disaster, President Ferdinand E. Marcos ordered troops into the city to search for rice that was being hoarded by merchants who expected the price to rise as starvation set in.

MARCINELLE, BELGIUM MINE DISASTER August 8, 1956

background: The short-circuiting of an electric cable in the Bois du Cazier coal pit at Marcinelle, Belgium, at 8:15 A.M. on August 8, 1956, caused far-reaching fires to engulf most of the shafts. Of the 276 miners in the various shafts at the time of the fire, only 6 managed to escape.

For a decade following World War II, Belgium suffered from the ravages of war: its manpower was depleted and its citizens, wary of its ancient collieries, compelled mine owners to use foreign labor to work its mines. At first German prisoners were put to work, but when they were repatriated, calls to destitute European countries went out. Italy, terribly burdened with an unemployed population, provided legions of impoverished men to work Belgian mines. (Half of the 90,000 miners working the shafts up to 1956 were Italian.)

The bulk of the morning work crew of 276 miners who entered the prophetically named Bitter Heart Mine at Marcinelle on the morning of August 8, 1956, were Italians. Shortly after 8:00 A.M. a coal car leaped from its tracks and smashed into a ventilating shaft. An electric cable snapped in two, and the resulting short circuit immediately caused far-reaching fires to break out.

Only six men were able to grope their way through the smoke to the elevator before it made its last upward surge to the surface. As these men jumped from the car, a blast of intense heat burned away its cables, and the car rattled backward down the shaft, crashing into pieces.

Engineers quickly went to work. They found that a passage with 30 men trapped inside it would have to be sealed off to prevent the fire from spreading to other chambers a half-mile below in order to save the 240 men taking refuge there. A dozen workers lowered themselves down the main entranceway, their oxygen tanks bumping the walls, and carefully rammed spun-glass fiber shields across the upper mine shaft openings in hope of suffocating the fires. The 30 men in these shafts, the authorities knew, would suffocate. But they were expendable in the light of saving the greater number of men.

An injured miner is removed from the collapsed mine in Marcinelle, Belgium, where 270 workers perished on August 8, 1956. *(Wide World)*

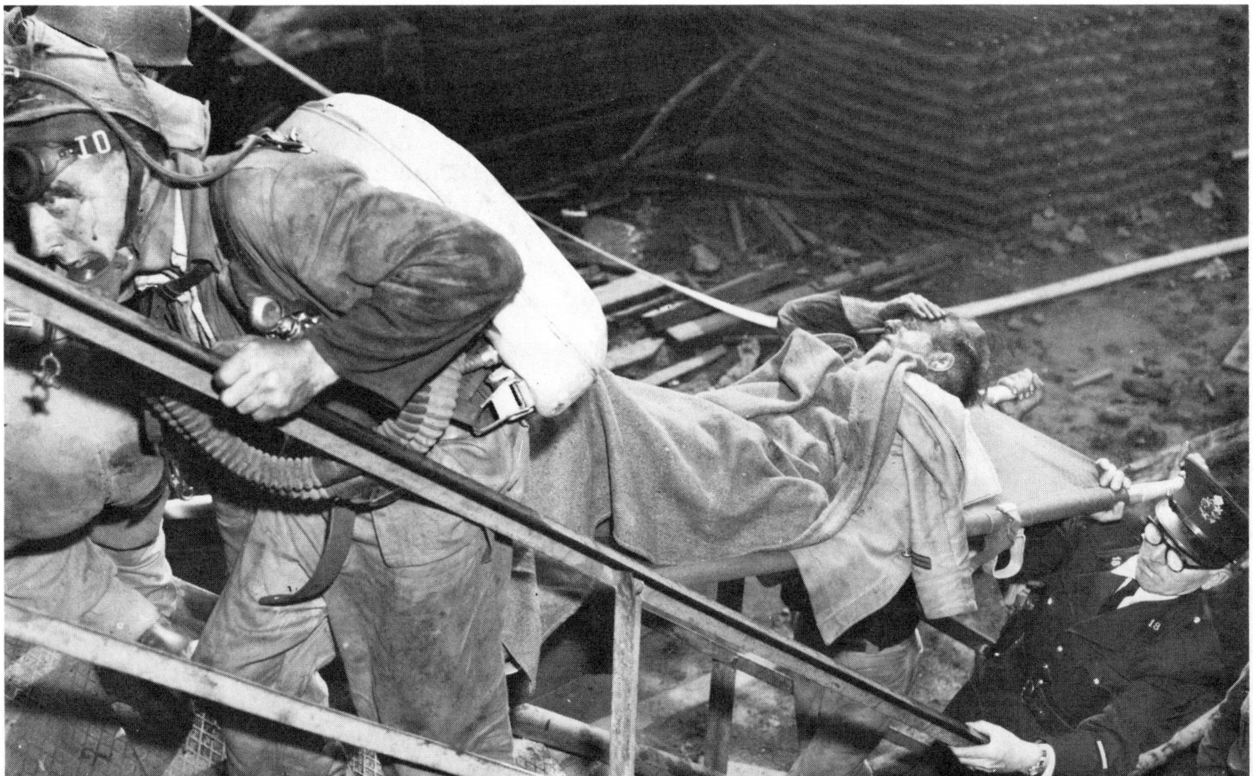

Unable to penetrate the 3,000 feet to the 270 men below, officials waited for them to emerge, but as the hours went by only scurrying rats and moles were seen fleeing the mine. Flames did penetrate the lower shafts, and within forty-eight hours rescuers lowered in swaying buckets found everyone in the mine dead, all 270 men.

Rene Albert, one of the lucky miners who escaped the mass deaths, could not take his eyes from the hundreds of white-knuckled hands clutching the steel fence surrounding the mine works. Unable to do anything else, he walked slowly along pressing the hands of the stunned relatives. He did not speak but pressed hand after hand after hand.

MARIANNA, PENNSYLVANIA — MINE DISASTER, November 28, 1908

Statistics show that the year 1907 was a horrendous year of mine disasters; 3,125 men were killed in separate coal mine explosions throughout the United States, a death rate of 4.86 per 1,000 men employed. Despite an enraged public, hortatory newspaper attacks and many moratoriums and inquiries, the safety standards were not upheld in the mines, and men continued to die in appalling numbers the following year.

On November 28, 1908, at 10:45 A.M., every man inside the Rachel and Agnes Mine at Marianna, Pennsylvania, except one (who was literally blown a hundred feet out of the mouth of the mine) was killed when a careless miner exposed his flaming lamp to coal dust in the Number 3 shaft and caused a terrific explosion. A second explosion destroyed the entire mine, splintering every timber and dislodging ceilings that had been bricked up.

Wrecked machinery outside the main shaft of the mine at Mather, Pennsylvania, marks the place where 195 miners died. *(Leslie's)*

The ventilating system was thoroughly wrecked, and it took rescuers hours to restore the fan to working order. By then all inside were dead, either killed by the concussion of the explosion or suffocated by the afterdamp. Dust produced by cutting, blasting and hauling, it was long known, was never properly watered down in this mine. Safety inspectors knew that the water system was ineffective, and yet they had approved the mine for work, an approval that turned out to be a sanction for the deaths of 154 miners.

At a later inquiry a chief mine inspector blamed "foreigners" employed at the mine for the accident, exhorting "the Commonwealth of Pennsylvania to teach the foreign miners the language of the country and how to mine coal with safety to themselves and to others."

MARSHFIELD, MISSOURI — TORNADO, April 18, 1880

A fierce tornado with an estimated mile-wide base tore through Marshfield, Missouri, on April 18, 1880, and literally wiped the town off the face of the earth. Killed outright were 101 persons, with another 600 persons seriously injured. Every structure in the town was ripped to pieces as this tornado joined another almost in the middle of the community. The storm traversed four counties and caused, even in the then sparsely populated region, almost $2 million in damages.

MARTINIQUE — HURRICANE, August 18, 1881

A devastating hurricane struck Martinique on August 18, 1881. Though it lasted but four hours in the early evening and its front was relatively small, damage was widespread. More then 700 people lost their lives in the killer winds and heavy waves. A staggering $10 million in damages was recorded.

MATAMOROS, MEXICO — HURRICANE, August 4, 1844

A violent hurricane moving across the Gulf of Mexico struck the Rio Grande coastal area and did extensive damage to Matamoros, Mexico, on August 4, 1844. Cutting inland at about 10:00 P.M., tremendous winds and huge waves toppled every building in the town except a new church and two haciendas. Officials reported seventy persons killed by the blow.

MATHER, PENNSYLVANIA — MINE DISASTER, May 19, 1928

One of the most severe mining mishaps in this century occurred at Mather, Pennsylvania, on May 19, 1928, at 4:07 P.M., when about 400 men were changing shifts. (The mine employed 750 men around the clock every day of the year, their output being one million tons of high-grade coking coal a year.) Inspectors later reported that at the time, with 209 men still in the mine, an accumulation of bituminous coal gas was ignited by an arc from a "non-permissible" storage-battery locomotive.

The shock of the explosion and the afterdamp killed 193 men on the spot; 2 more men who were rescued later died, bringing the total deaths to 195. Rescuers searched the many shafts of the mine for almost three days in the hope of finding survivors. As a method of spotting noxious gases, the rescue groups used more than 100 canaries, sending them down mine shafts to test the air. Fourteen men were finally saved, the last being Frank Bucsha, who for three days had successfully barricaded himself from the escaping gases.

(ALSO SEE; Dawson, New Mexico)

MATTOON, ILLINOIS — TORNADO
May 26, 1917

Mattoon, Illinois, had had its share of tornadoes, the two most violent occurring in 1864 and in 1877. These were mere preliminaries to the one that struck on May 26, 1917. Described as two giant blue-black masses of clouds, one moving from the north and the other from the south, the storms clashed over Mattoon and shredded 500 houses, damaged another 175 and killed fifty-three persons. Total loss in Mattoon alone was $1.2 million.

This untraditional twister became a monster that swept across 293 miles in the longest continuous tornado path ever recorded. Charleston, Illinois, was also wrecked by this tornado, and another 38 persons were killed. Fatalities in these two and surrounding towns soared to 101, and damages were over $2 million.

MAYON — VOLCANIC ERUPTIONS
1616-1928

background: Six miles from the Albay Gulf on southeastern Luzon Island, the Philippines, towers the 8,000-foot volcano Mayon. The earliest record of an eruption was in 1616. A lengthy record describes an eruption in 1766 when hundreds were killed. Its most destructive eruption was on February 1, 1814, when 2,200 Filipinos were killed. Since that time to 1928, twenty-eight major eruptions have been recorded, the most serious ones being in 1825, 1853, 1888, 1897, 1914 and 1928.

Rising from a broad plain that spreads behind the peaceful Albay Gulf at Luzon Island in the Philippines, the majestic volcano Mayon, considered to be one of the most beautifully contoured volcanoes in the world, has been belching death and causing widespread damage for centuries. Like those of Etna, Mayon's lavas are feldspathic and doleritic, and also like Etna, the symmetrical cone, misleadingly placid, is an active menace even today.

A century after Columbus sailed with hopes and doubts to the New Land, Spanish galleons, heavy with looted silver from Mexico, steered through dark seas lit by Mayon's guiding, spurting fires. Luzon's superstitious people long had believed an evil spirit within the fire mountain periodically showered upon them, in wrath, great globs of flaming lava, searing ash and rocks the size of churches. It took the bravery of a Franciscan, Estaban Solis, to convince them otherwise.

Solis, in 1592, gathered thousands of people from scores of villages to the foot of the volcano, and in their presence scaled Mayon almost to the summit, to prove that no devils lurked within its crater. His climb dispelled the image of devils but brought about his own death. Solis apparently inhaled great quantities of the sulfurous gases escaping through Mayon's many fissures. He fell ill and died within a year. Before that time Filipinos flocked to his churches for baptism and conversion to Christianity.

A little more than two decades later, in 1616, Mayon erupted with great force, causing terrible destruction. Its falling rocks and rivers of lava destroyed scores of villages, and few lived to tell of the disaster, let alone to describe its upheaval in detail.

The eruption of October 23, 1766, lasted for six days. It threw forth a stream of lava 100 feet wide that rushed down the eastern slopes for two days, overwhelming the town of Malinao and several other villages. The dead were numbered in the hundreds. Many of these were killed when Mayon vomited great quantities of water that flowed into rushing rivers 80 to 200 feet wide. The force of these rivers was so great that when they reached the shoreline, the tide was turned back. Everything in the water's path was washed away—roads, villages, livestock and humans. (It was thought at the time that Mayon's several lakes were sent pouring down on those below during its subterranean explosions.)

During this prolonged eruption communities within a radius of twenty miles of the mountain suffered terribly. Cagsauga, then called Daraga, was utterly ruined by the hurtling rocks, ash and cataracts of water. On the other side of Mayon, the towns of Camalig and Tobaco were destroyed. For two months the volcano incessantly hurled out lava and ash.

Figures of death among the populace vary, but at least 2,000 perished in Mayon's onslaught. Most of the dead were caught in the onrush of floods and landslips, similar to the ancient explosion of Java's Galung Gung. Volcanologist T. A. Jaggar explained the catastrophic proportions, saying: "The gulches on such a symmetrical cone fill with unbalanced heavy masses of high-level lava flows capable of sliding down with debris below. Possibly this combination of landslip erosion and basal accumulation about an overweighted steep summit, occasions the beautiful cone curve [of Mayon]."

The volcano was comparatively inactive after the 1766 eruption, but subterranean noises were heard again in the early part of 1811. The rumblings continued for three years, and on February 1, 1814, Mayon went on an unparalleled killing spree. A torrent of fire, stones, ashes and lava gushed from its bowels with terrifying force. All of northern Luzon was darkened by the giant clouds issuing from the volcano. Beginning at 8:00 A.M. great shocks, like those of an earthquake, preceded the blast that suddenly sent columns of burning stones, sand and ashes to great heights. The bombardment went on all day. Thousands of nearby residents fled from their villages and towns. Cagsauga, Badiao and two other towns were squashed beneath a shower of stones so thick that no building escaped destruction. The depth of accumulated stones from the explosion was 30 feet in some places. Cocoa palm trees were buried to their tops, and observers estimated that Mayon had blown away more than 100 feet of its top. A local priest, Father Aragoneses, took the death count in the area: over 2,200.

For the remainder of the nineteenth century, Mayon was in constant activity. In 1825 landslips of mud and rock caused by eruption destroyed a half-dozen villages and killed 1,500. Another 35 persons were boiled alive in an onrush of Mayon's lava in 1853.

Mayon shuddered through the next three decades with minor eruptions of lava and ash, but in 1886 the giant once again began to stir in epic proportions. A correspondent for *Nature Magazine* ascended the lofty volcano in that year, but he could manage to reach only the 5,000-foot level. "Incandescent stones and ashes obliged me to come quickly down," he later wrote. "I crossed a patch of forest half burned and covered with ashes. The sight was magnificent. I never saw anything like it as a sublime scene of devastation—ashes and stones and smoke everywhere, and fearful noise like heavy artillery all around. . . ."

On July 9, 1888, Mayon heaved up an ash-and-stone storm from its crater that partially destroyed the towns of Libog and Legaspi. Rich and sprawling plantations around the villages of Bigao and Bonco were demolished, and at least 500 buffaloes and oxen were killed. About two dozen persons lost their lives.

Prior to Mayon's last great eruption on June 23, 1897, Professor Samuel Kneeland, who later wrote *Volcanoes and Earthquakes,* observed the volcano from the sea in its preliminary stages. On a steamer bound for Iloilo, Kneeland gaped at "its pillar of cloud by day and its pillar of fire by night." He would later see "pieces of lava six feet in diameter . . . thrown from the crater to a distance of five miles."

For five months the volcano simmered and threw its lava, which offered Kneeland a scenic dessert: "At night the scene was truly magnificent and unique. At the date of my visit the volcano had poured out . . . a stream of lava on the Legaspi side from the very summit. The viscid mass bubbled quietly but grandly, and overran the border of the crater, descending several hundred feet in a glowing wave, like red-hot iron. Gradually fading as the upper surface cooled, it changed to a thousand sparkling rills among the crevices, and, as it passed beyond the line of complete vision behind the woods near the base, the fires twinkled like stars, or the scintillations of a dying conflagration. More than half of the mountain height was thus illuminated."

On June 23, 1897, Mayon began its most prolonged eruption in recorded history, a series of almost ceaseless titanic explosions that lasted for seven days. Showers of stones and ashes, burning white, fell like rain within a radius of twenty miles. Thousands of tons of stones were hurtled outward, burying the town of Tobaco. The entire province was pitched into darkness, and in some places the volcano's thundering caused the earth to open and close with hissing fissures.

Lava gushed from the summit and flowed seven miles eastward from Mayon. The sky was laden with ashes for almost one hundred miles by the fourth day of eruption. Village after village succumbed to the fiery attack. In Libog 100 residents were burned to death. Another 150 hapless inhabitants of San Roque, Misericordia and Santo Nino perished under the falling stones and from incredibly hot blasts of air shot in their direction. The village of Bacacay vanished beneath fifty feet of falling stones and lava. A total of 400 persons died during this holocaust.

There have been two more large eruptions: one in 1914 when the town of Cagsauga was obliterated and hundreds were killed, and another on July 1, 1928, when 200 were killed in several villages. These almost approached the scale of Mayon's gigantic upheavals of 1766 and 1897, though fewer people were killed.

(ALSO SEE: Cotopaxi, Etna, Krakatoa, Taal, Tomboro)

MAYS LANDING, NEW JERSEY — RAILWAY WRECK, August 11, 1880

A two-train excursion party of 1,500 parishioners of Philadelphia's St. Anne's Church met with disaster on August 11, 1880, when the second train, during a heavy thunderstorm, ploughed into the rear of the first train at Mays Landing, New Jersey. All 23 passengers riding in the last car of the first train were killed in the collision.

Officials of the West Jersey and Atlantic Railroad later determined that the engineer of the second train did not maintain the customary five-minute interval between the first train and his own. Other factors contributing to the accident were slippery rails, a steep downgrade leading into Mays Landing, a severe curve obscured by the storm and the unusual length of the first train.

Maintenance of the traditional five-minute interval was usually conducted not only by engineers, but also by station agents, track foremen and crossing watchmen, none of whom were apparently in their prescribed positions when the excursion trains collided.

MEDUSA

MARINE DISASTER
July 1, 1816

background: The French frigate *Medusa* sailed for Senegal on June 17, 1816, with about 250 persons on board. Through carelessness on the captain's part, the ship struck the Arguin reefs off Africa on July 1, 1816, and was abandoned. There were 155 fatalities.

Flotsam of Napoleon's wrecked armies, following his ignoble defeat at Waterloo, searched throughout the world for a place and an identity. Nowhere was the predicament of his once-glorious campfollowers more tragic than on board the ill-starred *Medusa,* a frigate that set sail for Senegal to reinstitute the French colony there, a gesture permitted by the victorious British as a sop to French pride.

The *Medusa*'s captain, de Chaumareys, was less than an incompetent skipper; he was, in the words of naval historian Ralph D. Paine, "a most indifferent seaman and a worse master of men and emergencies." The French captain was also a drunken sot who preferred handling a bottle to the wheel of his ship. For ten days after leaving Rochefort, the *Medusa* blundered about, de Chaumareys ultimately discovering that his ship was thirty degrees off her course for Senegal, which was situated on the west coast of Africa between Cape Blanco and the Gambia River. This failed to alarm the drunken captain, who fatuously ignored the advice of his officers and unconcernedly managed to lose the three smaller escort vessels that had departed with the *Medusa.*

When the ship crossed the Tropic of Cancer, de Chaumareys used the event to institute an on-board holiday of singing, dancing, and naturally, drinking. Before the revels the captain turned over the ship to one M. Richefort, a citizen who claimed to have had some naval experience. Almost all of the 250 passengers and crew members joined in a wild party. As the officers sat in the wardroom sipping wine, they spoke nervously about Richefort's ability to handle the ship "while the crew performed the fantastic ceremonies usual on such occasions although the frigate was surrounded by all the unseen perils of the ocean."

The party began on the morning of July 1, 1816, and by late afternoon, thanks to the ridiculous efforts of Richefort, the *Medusa* was hung up on the labyrinthian reefs, then called the Arguin, curling out from the coast of Africa. Alarm expressed by the crew was cavalierly waved away by Richefort, who insisted he knew what he was doing and that the ship was sailing with a hundred fathoms of water under her keel. (In reality there were only ten fathoms of water under the vessel.) The musicians continued to play, and the ship's crew went on guzzling rum and wine.

A terrified survivor of the foundered French frigate *Medusa* is whipped about by fierce seas. *(From an old print)*

When the *Medusa* smashed onto a reef, everyone in her felt a spar-crunching shock that ripped masts away and permanently grounded the ship. Though in a calm, sunny sea, the captain suddenly became fearful that winds would come up and destroy the vessel. He ran wildly about the ship giving the order to abandon ship and then disappeared momentarily below decks.

Panic ensued, with drunken sailors saving their own skins first, jumping into the five lifeboats, and rowing crazily away from the still intact *Medusa.* About 170 persons, mostly women and children, were left aboard the ship to fend for themselves. Soldiers and sailors stranded with them hastily pieced together a sixty-five by twenty foot raft of broken timbers. Without even a thought of taking aboard supplies and navigational equipment, they shoved off, with 150 persons precariously balancing themselves on the small raft.

De Chaumareys suddenly appeared at a porthole and ordered one of the lifeboats back. "The last glimpse of him," one account relates, "was framed in the porthole while his ship was still crowded with terrified castaways for whom there were no boats. He was a feather-brained poltroon who, by accident, happened to be a Frenchman." The five lifeboats reached African shores days later.

Seventeen men remained on board the *Medusa*, all too drunk to save themselves. They retired to the wine room and proceeded to drink themselves into stupors. Of these only three were discovered alive when the *Medusa* was found fifty-two days later, her upper works still above water. The survivors were, by then, quite insane. "They lived in separate corners of the hulk and never met but to run at each other with drawn knives."

For those confined to the bobbing, narrow raft, it was much worse. Sailors in the longboats, it was understood, would tow the raft, but none of those in the boats would take lines thrown to them. The raft soon drifted out of sight, with those on board consigned to death. They were adrift for twelve days and nights of storms, mutiny and murder. Many sailors went mad and tried to throw the women and children overboard. Other sailors who had spirited rum on board the raft became permanently drunk and simply rolled into the sea.

M. Savigny, one of the nine survivors from the raft, later wrote chillingly of those who lost their senses after a week without food. "Firmly persuaded that they were all on the point of being drowned, both soldiers and sailors resolved to soothe their last moments by drinking until they lost their reason. Excited by the fumes acting on empty stomachs and heads already disordered by danger, they now became deaf to the voice of reason and boldly declared their intention to murder their officers and then cut the ropes which bound the raft together. One of them, seizing an axe, actually began the dreadful work. This was the signal for revolt. The officers rushed forward to quell the tumult and the mutineer with the axe was the first to fall, his head split by a sabre. . . . One fellow, detected secretly cutting the ropes, was immediately flung overboard."

The maddened mutineers destroyed the raft's sail and mast, then turned and seized an infantry captain who had fought at Waterloo, broke his thigh and threw him into the sea. He was rescued by other officers. The insurrection calmed down, and half-delirious, the crazed men wept and begged for mercy from their officers, pleading on their knees. They were spared, but at 1:00 A.M. in a high-pitching sea, the revolt broke out again.

"The mutineers," Savigny continued, "ran upon the officers like madmen, each having a knife or sabre in his hand, and such was the fury of the assailants that they tore with their teeth at the flesh and even the clothing of their adversaries. There was no time for hesitation, a general slaughter took place, and the raft was strewn with dead bodies."

The battle on the raft only hastened the deaths of many who would have, no doubt, died in the sea. Several storms capsized the raft, and one by one, men, women and children began to die, slipping away in the huge combers. One twelve-year-old boy named Leon "died like a lamp which ceases to burn for want of aliment. . . . Whilst he had strength to move he ran incessantly from one side to the other, loudly calling for his mother, for water and for food. He trod upon the feet and legs of his wounded companions who in their turn uttered cries of anguish, but these were rarely mingled with threats or reproaches. They freely pardoned all that the poor little lad caused them to suffer."

Only sixteen persons were alive, more dead than alive really, when the French sloop *Argus*, sent by the alarmed governor of Senegal, arrived to take them aboard. Seven died en route to hospitals, and the remaining nine were scarred on face and limb for the remainder of their lives.

MERAPI — VOLCANIC ERUPTION

December 13-28, 1931

The giant volcano Merapi in Java, long active, had its most destructive eruption in modern times on December 13-28, 1931. For almost three weeks the mountain belched a lava stream four miles in length, two hundred yards wide, and more than eighty feet high. Its rain of ashes, blown laterally from the flanks of its cumulo-dome (Merapi builds continuous plug domes that are destroyed by explosions and thus collapse), coated half the island. More than 1,300 natives lost their lives in this eruption.

MERCY HOSPITAL — FIRE

January 7, 1950

background: Mercy Hospital in Davenport, Iowa, caught fire at 10:00 P.M. on January 7, 1950, the flames consuming the three-story mental ward. The building was gutted in minutes, and thirty-nine patients and a nurse died in the fire. The sixty-year-old building was hopelessly in need of fire safety devices and rescue efforts were thwarted by bars on windows.

"I've seen horror. I've seen tragedy. I thought I had seen just everything—until I saw that fire this morning. It was just plain hell." Thus Lieutenant Alex Koranda of the Davenport, Iowa, fire department described the inferno that consumed Mercy Hospital's mental ward at 2:00 A.M. on January 8, 1950. Before Koranda and his men arrived in fourteen-degree weather, the three-story wing of the hospital, which housed sixty-five women and three men, all of them either mentally ill or senile, was ablaze from basement to rooftop. The fire began on the first floor and leaped up a dumbwaiter shaft, eating its way into every floor.

The flash fire caught most of the nurses off guard, but fifty-five-year-old Anna Neal intrepidly raced through the women's ward cajoling, pleading and threatening patients to flee for their lives. She managed to bring out a score of hysterical people. The three men escaped the blaze by breaking through first-story windows.

Neal sprang back into the fire after depositing her charges on the frozen lawns of the hospital. She was never seen again. When firemen arrived, they were met by terrified, screaming women clad in skimpy nightgowns, tearing and pulling at the wire mesh and iron bars covering the windows of their rooms. With crowbars and shovels the firemen desperately attempted to bend back the steel and extricate the trapped females, many of whom unintelligibly screeched out their pain and then disappeared inside fast-climbing walls of fire. Firemen and other rescuers struggled to free more than a dozen but gave up the others, as the intense heat and flames crackled backward on them in their helpless retreat.

Two hours after the fire abated, a smoke-besmirched fireman lumbered into a women's ward to discover, astonished, one patient still alive. She was sitting calmly in a chair, her clothes burned away, bodies all about her. Her legs were coated with ice, water from the hoses that had frozen on the spot.

"Are you all right?" the fireman asked her.

"I think so," she said. "Of course, I have my rosary."

"This way." He led her slowly to a ladder, since the stairs had been burned away.

Twenty-eight survivors walked like zombies across the bleak grounds as policemen led them to shelter. Patrolman Richard Fee shook his head. "Some of them were like animals who had something new happening to them and didn't know what to do."

Forty persons, including nurse Neal, were dead inside the sixty-year-old hospital building. Authorities had warned that it was not adequately protected against fire. Fire Chief Lester Schick was in a rage, when he told reporters, "Last spring we recommended that a sprinkler system be installed in all the Mercy Hospital buildings, but nothing was done. . . . There are no teeth in our state fire laws."

Incredibly this fire was almost an exact duplicate of the much-publicized blaze that killed nine women, including Zelda Fitzgerald, the wife of the author F. Scott Fitzgerald, at Highland Hospital in South Carolina on March 11, 1948. The South Carolina fire started on the first floor, shot up a dumbwaiter, igniting each floor as it reached for the roof, and trapping inmates on the third floor. Firemen arriving at this blaze were hampered from reaching the patients by locked doors and barred windows. And, as in the Davenport fire, there was no sprinkler system.

(ALSO SEE: Cleveland Clinic, Katie Jane Nursing Home, Littlefield Nursing Home)

A cauldron of fire consumes thirty-nine patients trapped in Mercy Hospital in Davenport, Iowa, on January 7, 1950. *(Wide World)*

MESSINA, SICILY

EARTHQUAKE
December 28, 1908

background: The Sicilian city of Messina, then the eighth largest Italian port and a popular tourist area, was obliterated by a series of earthquakes registering 7.5 on the Strasbourg scale on December 28, 1908, occurring between 5:25 and 6:00 A.M., destroying 98 percent of the city. A seismic sea wave estimated to be thirty-five to fifty feet high added further damage to Messina and Reggio di Calabria, the port city opposite on the mainland. Enormous fires raged in Messina despite heavy rains following the quakes, and this added to the damage and death. Other towns and villages either wrecked or wiped out in the 120-mile radius of the quakes included Castroreale, Catania, Palmi, Casano, Cosenza, Bagbara, Riposto, Seminaria, San Giovanni, Scylla, Lazzaro, Cannitella, Floridia, Noto, Chiaramonto, Vittoria, Paterno, Terranova, Marianopoli, Naro, Mineo, Augusta, Patti and Caltanissetta. Of the 147,000 population in Messina, about 80,000 persons were killed. Of the 34,000 population of Reggio di Calabria, 25,000 people were killed. Together with other stricken towns, the death toll soared to well over 160,000.

Millions of carrion crows and ravens vigorously flapped and cawed above Messina, Sicily, by noon of December 28, 1908, swooping vengefully earthward to pluck the eyes of the dead scattered everywhere in the town that would be known the world over as *La Citta Morta.* Messina truly was a "dead city," utterly reduced to rubble as was its sister port Reggio di Calabria, across the Straits of Messina, by the worst earthquake in its history.

Messina had suffered earthquakes and extensive damage and loss of life for hundreds of years. Underwater quakes in the Straits of Messina had long devastated Reggio di Calabria and Messina. In 1783 a quake shook Calabria and almost wiped out Messina, which lost 60,000 citizens. The Sicilian city had been plagued by dozens of minor shocks before 1908. Rebuilding old quake-cracked structures to massive proportions was an ongoing activity. All were of stone, however, great stone cornices, heavy stone overhanging the eaves of buildings, a city of a thousand pyramids of stone that would topple to ruins in the 1908 disaster.

Shortly before dawn at 5:25 A.M. on December 28, with most of the city's inhabitants asleep, Messina and Reggio di Calabria began to feel a quake that lasted about two or three seconds, this preliminary shock racing from the epicenter in the middle of the straits (it was a wonder to scientists that the underwater cable laid in 1881 between Sicily and the mainland had not snapped violently under the constant submarine upheavals through the decades). A second shock, this one lasting almost ten seconds, much longer according to many people caught in Messina, rattled the entire area. This was followed by an erratic series of exceedingly violent tremors moving from northeast to southwest, the undulations lasting thirty-five or forty seconds. It was during this last barrage that Messina fell.

In a matter of seconds, people in the tens of thousands tumbled streetward with mortar, bricks, masonry, chimneys, roofs and walls, all blending and meshing in one stupendous crash as the city gave way under the convul-

This photo shows the Straits of Messina only days before an underwater quake, originating here, took place and killed more than 100,000 persons.

sion. Great crevices and ditches yawned open and swallowed animals and humans alike. Water mains exploded, gas pipes snapped and caught fire. All reservoirs broke, flooding vast sections of the city. The near hurricane winds and pelting rain that incongruously slashed across Messina failed to quench the towering fires that leaped up to the raging skies. The sea, from which the killer quake emanated, drew back for several blocks, first at Messina on one side of the straits and then at Calabria at the other, pounding back with a forty-foot seismic sea wave that raced three blocks inland at about 500 m.p.h., sweeping over docks and sea frontage, destroying anything left to be destroyed. Thousands were drowned at the seaside.

Messina's lush tourist hotels, the Trinacria, the France, the Metropole and the Victoria, crashed to ruins with their occupants trapped inside. The Victor Emanuele and Munizione theaters crumbled, architectual wonders gone to dust. Vanished, too, was the great Sicilian cathedral, Annunziata dei Catalani, a Norman structure that had been a vast storehouse of art treasures. Only one wall with ancient Gothic carvings was left standing. Alexander Hood, staggered at the Duomo's destruction, later lamented, "The monster monoliths of granite with gilded capitals, which once were the columns of Neptune's Temple at Faro, lie half or wholly covered by the painted woodwork and debris of the roof, among which are fragments of marble tombs and inlaid altars, golden figures of angels and sculptured saints—a mountain of ruined masonry many feet high and open to the sky. The beautiful carved pulpit has been hurled to the ground, together with the pillar which supported it, with the mosaic and frescoes, with the arches and cornices which had made the Duomo so rich a treasure house of art. One thing alone remains of this ancient glory—the colossal figure of Christ in mosaic in the dome of the apse at the east end. It is still there with serene countenance and hand uplifted in the act of blessing as for five hundred years or more it has remained, gazing benignly on the passing generation of worshippers. The calmness of that majestic life-like figure was startling!"

Gone was the convent of San Gregorio and with it Antonella de Messina's exquisite triptych of the Madonna, dating back to 1463. Urbina's classic collection of majolica vases dating back to 1568 was no more. The twenty-six room Castel Durante fell, burying the numismatic and prehistoric artifact collections it held. Montorsoli's majestic Neptune Fountain survived, one of the few structures to do so, along with a cracked statue of Don Juan of Austria, but the Bank of Italy with Messina's total savings of $2 million was a shambles, and the American consulate was rubble. The seaward fronts of the university and Palazzo Municipale survived, but were mere shells after their roofs caved inward. The various army barracks in and about the city, especially the sprawling Santelia complex, collapsed, killing almost all the soldiers therein and leaving the city prey to the 750 convicts who escaped when the walls of the archaic Cappuccini Prison fell outward.

At the beginning puzzlement and incredulity preceded horror.

A London ship broker, Constantine Doresa, went to sleep in the Trinacria Hotel; his traveling companion, naval architect Charles Caiger, was asleep in the adjoining room. "I was awakened without warning at 5:25 A.M.," Doresa later remembered. "The bed first rose up and then rocked violently. I clutched the sides of the bed, which seemed to be falling through the space of ages. [Everyone's bed that night in Messina fell; one soldier in the Santelia Barracks rode his bed downward through five consecutively collapsing floors; he survived.]

"Afterwards," Doresa stated, "I estimated the time to be ten seconds. Then came a series of awful crashes, the roof falling all around me. I was smothered in brick and plaster. I knew it was an earthquake. I had been in one before in Athens. Then followed terrific crashes, mingled with a continuous roar."

Caiger called out to Doresa from the next room, asking him if he could make his way there. Doresa said yes and dangled his feet over the bed as he lit a match. "I was horrified to find my bed on the side of an abyss." In the darkness Doresa had not known that the hotel walls had been sheared away; there was nothing for five floors on the left side of his bed but open space. He quickly swung over to the other side of the bed, found footing and joined Caiger. Together, using knotted bedsheets and draperies, they lowered a Swedish family they found in the next room and then escaped. They returned with ropes supplied by Captain Owen of the *Afonwen,* which was anchored in the harbor.

Close to 100 persons were buried in the ruins, but still more clung to the sliced-away rooms, high, shaky perches threatening to give way at any moment. Captain Owen, his second mate Read, and several sailors helped Caiger and Doresa rescue many terrified tourists.

They spotted two children on a high balcony as the building shuddered and swayed. Captain Owen shouted to them to lower a piece of string with a rock tied to it. This they did, and then Read, who had placed a ladder against a wall that led to a small balcony, turned to a sailor and said, "Now then, Smith."

Doresa continued: "I shuddered. It seemed like certain death. Smith turned his quid in his mouth, and without a word went up the ladder to the first balcony. Then, to the string which had been let down by the children, he attached a light line, which the children hauled up and placed around one of the standards at the top of the

The death and destruction at Messina, Sicily, on December 28, 1908, was recorded by an artist who survived the horrendous earthquake.

balcony. By this means Smith hauled up a two-and-one-eighth-inch manila rope. He then took off his boots and in a trice was shinning up the rope beside the crazy ruin. I held my breath. I have read of many brave deeds, but I never heard of one braver than Smith's."

Smith reached the high perch and then leaned over and shouted: "Why, there's a ton of them up here. I can't manage all of them myself." Read went up next, and the two seamen lowered ten children with the rope. A stout, elderly woman was next, and then came a man who seemed dumbfounded. Smith threatened to throw him down unless he helped to lower the woman. He helped.

Among his adventures while wandering through the ruins—almost everyone, dead or alive, was somehow buried beneath the rubble—Doresa saw "panic-stricken fugitives and escaped prisoners, the latter looting. I saw wretches hacking off the fingers of the dead to get their rings." He followed a cluster of convicts and watched in awe as they drunkenly smashed out the windows of a women's dress shop and emerged crazily adorned with the latest Paris and London creations. Madness was spreading.

As the day wore on—Doresa swore he felt at least thirty shocks during the morning—hungry crowds broke into warehouses and fought for morsels of food. A refugee aboard the British steamer *Ebro,* about to sail to safety with passengers everywhere on her decks, looked at the shore and saw a maddened mob break into the customs house. Many were naked, others half clothed; all were mud spattered and appeared half-demented.

Bleeding and injured, "bands of famished individuals," the refugee later claimed, "were groping among the debris in the hope of discovering food. The first of the searchers who were successful were attacked by others with revolvers and knives, and were obliged to defend their finds literally with their lives. . . . The struggle was fierce. The famished men threw themselves upon each other like wolves, and several fell disemboweled in defending a handful of dry beans or a few ounces of flour. One of the unfortunates was pinned to a plank with a knife, while clinging to his hand was a little child, for whom he had sought food."

Revolver shots echoed in hollow reverberations as a few loyal troopers attempted to quell the mobs, but they were overcome, beaten senseless and thrown into the sea to drown. The chief of police was dead in his home; a timber had crushed his head. Most of the civilian authorities were dead. Only about 5,000 persons were upright and wandering through the ruins. Everyone else was either dead or trapped beneath the immense rubble.

Bodies by the hundreds floated along the shoreline, all victims of the giant seismic sea wave.

An officer on board the torpedo boat *Sappho,* anchored in the harbor before the quake, described the wave. "At 5:30 in the morning the sea suddenly became terribly agitated, seeming literally to pick up our boat and shake it. Other craft were similarly treated, and the ships looked like bits of cork bobbing about in a tempest. Almost immediately a tidal wave [really a *tsunami*], of huge proportions, swept across the straits, mounting the coasts and carrying everything before it. Scores of ships were damaged, and the Hungarian mail boat *Andrassy* parted her anchors and went crashing into other vessels. Messina Bay was wiped out, and the sea was soon covered with masses of wreckage, which was carried off in the arms of the receding waters."

Captain Owen of the Welsh steamer *Afonwen,* who later helped Doresa to rescue those trapped at the Trinacria Hotel, was on the deck of his vessel in the harbor when the wave struck. "Suddenly the *Afonwen* gave a terrific leap," he said. "That is the only word I can use. The ship seemed to rise up from the surface of the water as though lifted bodily by some mighty power underneath. The anchor chains snapped and we started to drift shoreward very fast. . . . From the land came sounds of tremendous crashing and falling of buildings. The low, muttering thunder which I first heard now became a roar of destruction. All the lights along the shore went out in an instant. The darkness was intense . . . the sea became . . . tremendously agitated with waves and walls of water rising on every side. The ship listed to her beam ends. The deck heeled over to an angle of twenty-five degrees, so that we scarcely could keep our feet. For thirty-five minutes it was touch and go . . . a great wall of water struck us with such violence that I thought all was over. . . . It was a cyclone from all points of the compass. The wind howled and the waves battered and swept the decks. Amazing and terrifying things were happening all around us. Great holes opened in the sea itself and seemed to reach down twenty to thirty feet, and some at lesser depths . . . The water at first appeared to grow livid and then became white with foam. . . . As soon as the worst of the wave had passed, I tried to see what had befallen the town of Messina as the first faint streaks of daylight appeared, but nothing was visible . . . I could see at first only the outline of the hills and a vast eddying cloud of dust which speedily enveloped everything and settled down over the ship like a fog."

The ferryboat that worked between Messina and Reggio di Calabria was caught broadside by the wave. The sea opened almost to its bottom, and the boat slid downward, engulfed. A druggist named Pulco, one of the few survivors on the ferry, held onto a railing in terror as the boat slid first downward and then up to the top of the succeeding wave. Hundreds were swept away, but Pulco and a few others managed to float ashore clinging to the wrecked boat.

Jabez Larkin, a seaman on board the *Drake,* also anchored in Messina Bay, rode out the seismic seawave, watching the thousands who had jumped, run, and scrambled from falling buildings to seek safety on the broad avenues facing the sea. Larkin watched the wall of water close over these unfortunate wretches. "Then, suddenly," he recalled, "the cries from the shore ceased, so I expect the people who had lined the quayside had been washed away as all the boats in the harbor were carried out by the wave."

For most it was a matter of digging out. Francesco Missiano, a cobbler, urged his large family to run from their home at the first shock. Fires leaped up everywhere as they ran; buildings tumbled down nearby. Missiano heard groans from a nearby pile of stones and, upon investigating, found two small girls dying, one with her skull open to the bone, another with her chest caved in. The cobbler picked up a baby, but it died in his arms. Another man raced back into a falling house after the wave struck to retrieve his infant son from the third floor only to find his son missing and his bed full of fish.

A German cotton dealer woke at the first shock. He lit the lamp next to his bed, but when all became quiet he went back to sleep. "Suddenly," he later narrated, "fresh shocks occurred in violent and terrific repetition. I rose, but the house was swaying and my door jammed. I tore sheets from the bed and made a rope and lowered myself from the window to the street. An Italian family of five persons escaped from the house with the aid of my rope." No sooner was he in the street than the house collapsed. "All day I wandered the wrecked streets. No food could be got, and I had only a few nuts to eat."

Cries came incessantly from the ruins. An actress named Flora Parini was half-buried in debris. As she struggled to free herself, she heard the voice of an army lieutenant who recognized her. He was buried much deeper than she.

"Signorina," he cried, "save me! Call someone to rescue us. Don't leave me. I was at the theater last night, and I applauded your singing. I have a mother . . . don't leave me to die."

When rescuers finally dug out the actress, she directed them to where the army officer was buried and he, too, was taken out. Some remained buried for days. The wife of Nicolo Fulci, a deputy in parliament, was imprisoned for four days before being extricated. She and her niece kept themselves alive by munching cookies. The niece later died.

An infant clad only in a torn nightshirt also survived for four days beneath a square yard of flooring in a house that was otherwise completely wrecked. Taken alive from the rubble of his palace was the Archbishop of Messina. The Marquis de Semmola was trapped in the wine cellar of his home. Colonel Minicci and his daughter were dug out from the ruins of their home by the Mother Superior of St. Vincent Military Hospital. The nun had seen the house collapse on the two and went to work immediately.

Victims died appalling, agonized deaths. Bodies were later found self-mutilated. According to one report, "Several died gnawing their arms and hands, evidently delirious from pain and hunger. Other bodies had parts of shawls and clothing in their mouths. One woman's teeth were firmly fixed in the leg of a dead babe."

Madame Karalech, the Hungarian prima donna who had given a magnificent performance in *Aida* the night before, jumped from her second-story suite in the Trinacria Hotel and broke both her arms, but she managed to get up and run with other frightened refugees to the quayside and somehow to survive the wave that swept ashore there. Naval officers conducted her to the Italian cruiser *Piemonte* the following day, and she was taken to Palermo to give another performance a week later. She sang with her arms in casts.

The British vice-consul, A. J. Ogston, fled his tumbling home at the first tremors with his wife and daughter. "As we were passing a building a balcony fell and killed my wife. By a miracle the child escaped unhurt."

Arms and legs frantically signaled for help from the ruins. The city hall collapsed, killing scores. Forty-one customs agents out of 200 survived the destruction of their quarters. Only 8 out of 280 employees at the railroad station survived.

One Englishman, Edward Ellis, was thrown from his second-story hotel room, landing in a massive pile of mattresses, clothing and furniture. "Right in front of me in the black darkness," he later stated, "I heard moaning. I put out my hand and touched something horrible. When I drew it back my hand was colored crimson. Someone was dying there, but I was unable to afford any help." With the earth heaving and rolling underfoot, Ellis groped his way through the darkness, hearing screams all about him. Men rushed by and knocked him down. A mud-splattered form rose up before him, a policeman gone insane, and tried to strangle him for no apparent reason. He had to fight to break away. "I felt that I was constantly treading on bodies, and perhaps on living persons. Once the body of a woman fell down on me from somewhere overhead." He continued until he was surrounded by fire. Ellis fell to his knees and prayed. A building then toppled and suffocated the flames in one area, through which he made an escape. He trudged through the incredible nightmare until he slipped and began rolling uncontrollably downward. Then he splashed into the sea, but was rescued by fishermen.

There were numerous suicides. A soldier who had been fortunate enough to escape the destruction of the barracks staggered to his home to find it demolished and his family crushed. He yelled his anger at the skies and then sent a bullet through his brain.

As night settled bodies came to life and somehow managed to emerge from the ruins with the help of the more conscientious survivors who were not off hunting food. Others slowly perished. Packs of wild dogs and pigs and droves of rats began to feed off the dead and molest the wounded.

The Marquis di Ruvolito arrived in Messina that night, having traveled from hard-hit Catania down the coast through dozens of destroyed villages and towns. On seeing Messina in flames, the marquis exclaimed, "The spectacle that greets the eye here is beyond the imagination of Jules Verne." He spotted an entire family, all naked, sitting beneath an umbrella and asked them to come along with him. They refused, telling him they preferred to die among the ruins of their own home. A naked female artist from the Pelolo Theater rushed up to the marquis and demanded a pair of shoes. He found his friend, the Baron di Scotti, in a large square. "He was covered with mud. He wore only a pair of white undergarments, an opera hat, and wooden sabots." A wealthy young man named Bonanno, carrying the body of a dead child, walked up to the marquis. He "appeared to have lost his reason."

By dawn sleek gray battleships of the Russian Navy, the *Slava, Tsaritsa* and the armored battle cruiser, *Admiral Makiroff,* raced through the straits to Messina from Agoata, where its commander had received word of the enormous disaster. Looking through his telescope, the captain saw "nothing but a heap of ruins." Six hundred armed Russian sailors began the job of organizing rescue parties. They also established an open-air hospital, where more than 1,000 were treated in the first hour of operation.

When they found looters, Russian sailors, under orders from their captain, lined them up in groups of a dozen and shot them. Methodically they hunted down the escaped convicts and either put them in chains or to work digging out those still trapped. Two hours later, at 1:00 P.M. on December 29, a British fleet, comprised of the *Exmouth, Duncan, Euryalus, Canopus* and *Sutlej,* steamed into Messina Bay and Admiral A. G. Curzon-Howe sent ashore swarms of bluejackets to set up soup kitchens and aid in search and rescue. American vessels did not appear.

When the American warships *Indiana, Whipple* and

Messina was destroyed in the earthquake of 1783. *(From an old print)*

Missouri had gone to help stricken Kingston, Jamaica, after an earthquake on January 14, 1907, the governor, Sir Alexander Swettenham, violently anti-American, had objected. The American fleet in the Red Sea at the time of the Messina disaster refused to sail for Messina unless their presence was requested by King Victor Emmanuel. American aid in the form of supplies worth millions, however, was soon dispatched.

The king and queen, who arrived in Messina to inspect the carnage, were more than grateful to the British and Russian fleet commanders who took it upon themselves to bring order out of the city's chaos. Victor Emmanuel was an uplifting sight to the Messina survivors, who wept at his appearance. He personally spent hours digging in the ruins, and according to one report, "he personally extricated several injured persons pinned under the ruins. . . . The queen rescued with her own hands a little boy three years old, bleeding from many cuts and wounds, and herself carried him to the deck [of the battleship *Vittoria-Emmanuel*]."

But there was very little the king could do immediately to relieve the suffering except to order huge relief supplies to be sent to Messina and all other stricken towns. (His mission was accented by the grotesque when he saw an elderly man dancing at the quayside. This dazed resident held a dead child in his arms; he was quite mad and chanted in his dance of death how nothing had really happened in Messina, that there had been no earthquake, no fires, no seawave, no hurricane, indeed, how happy he was.)

Only one house, reinforced with concrete and iron and built by a merchant who had been considered eccentric, was left intact at Messina. Fifty structures survived the devastation that befell Reggio di Calabria, but the death and damage were almost equal to Messina's.

In Calabria the prison also collapsed, but no convicts escaped; 180 were killed outright. Reggio College was leveled, and all students inside were killed. Twelve miles of railway had been ripped up. Convents, churches and government houses had been gutted. When ruffians and hoodlums began to patrol the streets in search of booty, Lieutenant General Fiera Di Cossatto pronounced martial law and ordered out soldiers to keep order.

The earth behaved in Reggio as it had on Sicily, where four mountain towns had been swallowed by gaping fissures. In Reggio a chasm eighty feet wide opened, and into this maw hundreds of fleeing victims fell to their deaths as the earth closed and opened repeatedly like huge jaws. Geysers of hot water shot forth, scalding those nearby. As in Messina and other Sicilian towns, the dead of Reggio were heaped in funeral pyres and burned to avoid pestilence. These fires were the only signals that survivors remained in the coastal towns along the straits. They were eerie beacons flashing not signs of life but signs of the gruesome disaster that killed at least 160,000. (Professor Rioco of the Mount Etna Observatory placed the death figure at 250,000.)

A navy lieutenant who had set out to get help in a torpedo boat traveled along the coastline of Sicily and southern Italy, noticing the funeral fires, racing close to shore to discover the towns and cities in ruins. He almost wrecked his boat at Reggio, when he ran it too far into shore where the coastline was submerged for blocks and would remain so for weeks.

The lieutenant went on his way, realizing the futility of his actions. "I obtained a rowboat and crossed under a beating rain with death in its soul, the sinister strait, still agitated by the horrible crime it had committed."

MEXICO — HURRICANE
August 27, 1909

In a hurricane-punctured 1909, the most intense storm of that year began east of the Windward Islands on August 20. Two days later it reached Puerto Rico, and on August 23 Haiti was struck full force by the hurricane, which flattened St. Nicholas, Haiti. The following day Cuba was battered by the hurricane's 60 m.p.h. winds. As the storm moved through the Yucatan Channel, its winds roared upwards of 100 m.p.h. After sideswiping the Texas coast, the hurricane passed inland over Mexico, devastating the northeastern provinces and creating flash floods that took the lives of about 1,500 persons.

MEXICO — EARTHQUAKE
September 29, 1973

The worst rain-and-flood season in thirty years was capped by an earthquake that registered 6.5 on the Richter scale and made a shambles of 300 miles of southeastern Mexico on September 29, 1973. At least twenty-four cities, towns and villages in the provinces of Veracruz and Puebla in the Sierra Madre mountain range were ravaged by the quake, and more than 700 persons were killed.

Damage was widespread in the cities of Orizaba, Tehuacan, and Ciudad Serdan, thought to be the center of the quake, where more than 100 died. Scores of sixteenth- and seventeenth-century churches were felled by the quake. In many areas gaping fissures opened, especially about the extinct volcano Pico de Orizaba, where many destroyed villages were cut off without power for days.

The tremor occurred at 3:51 A.M., catching most people in bed. The plight of the Martinez family in Tehuacan was typical. "It was before dawn when the earthquake began," Santiago Martinez, sixty-seven, later told a newsman. "I thought it was going to be the end of the world. So I ran out of my home with my wife, and both of us knelt and started praying. . . . But my son, I couldn't wake him up, and when I looked back at our house, it had collapsed. . . . Later, me and other friends pulled out his body."

For days in the same city, cars with loudspeakers crawled through the rubble-strewn streets, blaring, "We need your help to save the lives of our brothers in misfortune," and asking for blood, clothing and food.

In the beer-brewing center of Orizaba, most of the eighty deaths occurred when a five-story building was shattered by the quake, killing almost all of the twenty families residing inside.

Tens of thousands were left homeless in this quake, the worst since July 28, 1957, when seventy persons were killed in a quake centering about Mexico City. Adding to the misery of survivors were vicious floods throughout Guanajuato province, Mexico's fertile breadbasket.

MEXICO CITY, MEXICO — FLOOD
May 3, 1972

Violent thunderstorms over Mexico City, Mexico, caused the San Buenaventura River to break out of its banks on May 3, 1972, and cascade down from the hills into the city of eight million inhabitants. Mudslides mixed with rocks and trees ripped apart more than 500 houses, killed thirty-seven persons and injured another seventy.

Winds tore the roofs from another 4,000 houses, leaving 100,000 homeless. Many cars were either blown by the winds or torn off the roads by sudden landslides. An accompanying hailstorm did further damage.

MINATITLAN, MEXICO — LANDSLIDES
October 29. 1959

Heavy rains caused massive landslides about the hill-surrounded Mexican town of Minatitlan on the night of October 29, 1959. More than 800 persons were trapped in their beds by the swiftly moving landslides that all but obliterated their community. Another 200 residents died later, as a result of snake, scorpion and tarantula bites, when swarms of these creatures were unearthed by the landslides and sent slithering through the wrecked town. Frantic requests for serums were wired to Mexico City hospitals.

Minatitlan was only one of the dozen towns along the Pacific coast of Mexico wiped out. Another 1,000 persons in other villages and towns perished under the onslaught of mud and rock. The town of Zacoalpan in northern Colima state was leveled first by landslides and then flooded so deeply that a pilot flying over the stricken area noted only the church steeple protruding from the swirling waters.

A seismic sea wave also apparently rushed forward against the Mexican coast and sank ten small freighters, including the passenger-freighter *Sinola,* which went down with twenty-seven on board. In all, more than 5,000 persons met death during this disaster.

MINERVE

MARINE DISASTER
January 27, 1968

The 850-ton French submarine *Minerve,* named after the Roman goddess of wisdom, was approaching her home port of Toulon on January 27, 1968, when she radioed to a French plane passing overhead that she was running smoothly beneath the surface at a depth of forty feet. At that point the submarine was about twenty-five miles from her berth and functioning well. Then radio contact was broken off, and the *Minerve* disappeared in the Mediterranean.

Wide-scale rescue operations were set in motion, and the French searched the area by sea and air for almost a week. It was then concluded that the entire crew of fifty-two was dead; oxygen reserves were adequate for only four days. If the ship sank below the 1,000-foot level—the sea is at least a mile deep in that area—the hull would certainly have burst under the pressure. A *Time* writer envisioned "the doomed men" dying "in the particularly horrible ways that threaten those who go under the sea in ships. If death came quickly, they either drowned or were crushed when massive undersea pressure wrenched the vessel's steel hull. If the . . . submarine somehow remained intact, the trapped crew men slowly suffocated."

The disappearance of the *Minerve* came only forty-eight hours after the Israeli submarine *Dakar* vanished 1,500 miles away on the other side of the Mediterranean. *(ALSO SEE:* Dakar)

MINNESOTA

FIRE
October 12, 1918

background: Following an extremely dry summer, the underbrush in northern Minnesota caught fire, and on October 12, 1918, a 60 m.p.h. wind caused vast tracts within a 2,000-square-mile area, stretching north from Duluth, to burst into flames; twenty-six towns and villages were destroyed by the fires, an estimated 800 persons were killed, and 13,000 left homeless. More than $175 million in damage was done.

For six months in the summer of 1918, the thick underbrush and peat lands in northern Minnesota smoldered with a fire that slowly ate away at tree roots. No attempt was made to extinguish these fires, which were considered normal in the dry season. The area had only recently been opened to settlers, who for the most part had little or no knowledge of such underground fires. At about 1:00 P.M. on October 12 a gale of 60 m.p.h. wind suddenly swept across the smoldering area, causing the bogs and forests to crackle into towering flames that advanced rapidly.

The entire area affected ranged from Bemidji to Two Harbors, a 175-mile stretch of land, and from the Mesaba Range in the north to a midway point between Duluth and Minneapolis. For those caught in this blazing inferno, it became an ashen nightmare. First struck by the fire was the small hamlet of Brookston. Adequate warning was given to allow the safe evacuation of every inhabitant by trains, which raced 30 miles east to Duluth even as flames licked at the railroad ties.

Another massive and amazing evacuation was that of Cloquet, a sprawling lumber town of almost 10,000 citizens, where not a soul was lost, thanks to the quick action of railroad authorities who herded everyone onto box cars, flat cars and passenger cars. "They were hanging from the sides and tops of the cars like birds," one trainman remarked. "And they all lived." The entire population was first taken to the small town of Carlton, about six miles away, but the fires roared into the village behind them. The trains again pulled out with every Carlton resident on board, eventually reaching safety in Superior, another small town twenty miles away.

Those living in the resort area of Moose Lake, however, were not as fortunate. The town was completely surrounded by walls of fire that burned every building to the ground within minutes and literally roasted to death the entire population, about 400 persons. The fire reached such intensity at Moose Lake that it funneled down a thirty-foot well where a family had taken refuge and burned them all to death.

The fire utterly devastated the summer-cottage region to the north of Duluth. Although this area is dotted with lakes, the fire leaped across the small expanses of water, searing everything in its path. Residents waded into the lakes, but dozens were overcome by the smoke and scorching flames that lashed out across the placid surface of the bone-chilling water. Scores of persons were killed trying to row across Pike Lake. In their panic they capsized their overcrowded boats and drowned. An eight-year-old boy waded into this lake with three brothers and three sisters in tow. He ducked the heads of the smaller children beneath the water and thus saved them. The dead bodies of his parents were floating nearby. About 400 more persons perished in this lake region.

More people would have died, but almost a thousand persons took to their autos and drove crazily down the smoke-clogged roads leading into Duluth. There were countless pile-ups, traffic jams and crashes. Those cars unable to continue were abandoned on the spot, their occupants hurriedly crawling into other cars and then speeding on toward the metropolis.

Duluth itself was threatened by a great wall of fire that roared forth. Bells and horns signaled its approach. The mayor, standing in a church steeple, wept at the impending menace. A raging inferno approached from the west and threatened to join the fires racing down from the north, where one suburb, including an elegant country club, had already been reduced to cinders. Just as the flames were working their way into the city, the fierce, cyclonic wind shifted and caused the fires to veer off; the city was saved.

Though an estimated 800 persons were killed in this 200-mile-broad forest fire, Frank J. Bruno, of the American Red Cross, was astounded that thousands had not perished. Writing later in the *Survey,* Bruno pointed out that "this calamity, which is the greatest the state of Minnesota has ever suffered . . . is not without its benefits. A forest station will, without doubt, be given a chance by the interest which it has evoked; fire protection and the treatment of the peat bogs, the ever-present menace, will be more carefully studied. Agriculturally, it will probably be a distinct gain."

(ALSO SEE: Peshtigo, Wisconsin)

MINOTAUR — MARINE DISASTER
December 22, 1810

The British frigate *Minotaur,* laden with seventy-four cannons and weighty cargo, was caught in a hurricane off Holland on the night of December 22, 1810, and driven onto sand reefs near the entrance of the Texel River. By 2:00 A.M. the ship began to break up quickly, waves shooting across her main decks. The 680 persons on board, realizing the vessel was sinking, made for the lifeboats. Only two were intact. These were lowered and filled to the gunwales with 110 persons who survived. The remaining 570 persons ran crazily about the *Minotaur's* deck in search of any debris that would float, but the ship sank so fast that none escaped the closing waters.

MISSISSIPPI (LOUISIANA and TENNESSEE) — TORNADOES
February 21, 1971

More than fifty tornadoes struck through the Mississippi delta in mid-February, 1971, crisscrossing Mississippi and some parts of Louisiana and Tennessee. The death toll came to 110, and thousands were left homeless. Mississippi suffered the most; towns such as Inverness were violently wrenched off the map.

Inverness, with a population of 1,119, lost 90 percent of all its structures when a monumental tornado slashed through the heart of town. Eyewitness Skipper Campbell was caught by the twister just as he drove into the town. It appeared to be "a big, black funnel, about 75 yards wide at the ground and 500 feet high. . . . I pulled down

The British frigate *Minotaur,* her masts snapped away by a pounding gale, turns over off Holland on December 22, 1810. Only 110 survived out of 680 passengers. *(From an old print)*

the window and heard a drone like a million bumblebees come at me." The tornado passed over Campbell's car, bouncing it up and down like a ball.

"I could detect all sorts of things swirling around me. At one point I thought I saw a human body fly past. I could see right through the storm. I suddenly realized that I was in the eye of the storm. One house suddenly came apart like a dollhouse. . . . The roof flew up, the walls spread out, and I could see two elderly persons, colored folks, crouched inside. Then everything sprang right back on top of them, and they disappeared."

As is common in most tornadoes, the pressure of the storm against the unequal pressure contained in the closed house caused the building to simply explode. Campbell waited until the storm passed, then dove into the debris of the house, and dug out the elderly couple, who had survived by hiding beneath a strong oak table.

Another Inverness resident, Adie Thorton, saw her home "torn to bits. I was in a corner, and all of a sudden a great big piece of concrete flew in and then flew out. I screamed, and that's all I remember."

Seventeen citizens of Inverness were killed by this savage twister, which capriciously destroyed all the black business and housing areas.

Campbell drove home to nearby Rayville that night, stating to reporters before leaving: "I think I'm a miracle."

(ALSO SEE: Gainesville, Georgia, 1936)

MISSISSIPPI RIVER — FLOODS
April, 1874

The Mississippi River, bloated by rains and melting snow in early April, 1874, broke over its banks at hundreds of places throughout the Mississippi valley, inundating tens of thousands of acres. Louisiana and Mississippi were the hardest hit. This was the first seriously noted flood of the river, but few details were made available then, since most of the stricken areas were rural and communication feeble, if not nonexistent. An estimated 200 to 300 persons were drowned by the floodwaters.

MISSISSIPPI RIVER — FLOODS
January-April, 1890

background: Aided by severe rains and sudden snow meltings, the Mississippi River, from Cairo, Illinois, south to New Orleans, flooded drastically on January 4, 1890, breaking down dikes in dozens of places, inundating 5,000 square miles, leaving 50,000 persons homeless and killing at least 100.

After the Mississippi flash floods in 1882, extensive building of dikes and levees along vulnerable sections of the river was begun, but eight years later in January the waterway again broke through its banks in several places.

A stranded telegraph operator sends out last signals from flooded Morganza Bend when the Mississippi burst its banks on April 24, 1890.

The United States Signal Service had warned Mississippi valley residents that floodwaters could be expected after the massive snowfalls that had occurred in the Ohio region. On January 1, 1890, authorities in Cairo, Illinois, sent out an alarm that the river was at eighteen feet and rising rapidly. The floodwaters rose one and three-eighths feet a day after that.

By the end of February almost all the southern cities—Memphis, Shreveport, Vicksburg and New Orleans—were threatened. In March the Mississippi began to spill over its dikes into Phillips County, Arkansas. Within hours 500 persons were forced to flee their homes, which were swept away. At Arkansas City and Memphis, on March 28, the river raged over and through barriers and swept eastward to the Yazoo River, drowning dozens and enveloping thousands of acres of land.

Greenville, Mississippi, was an angry lake by April 3. Most of its 10,000 residents scurried to safety onto nearby ridges, where they awaited rescue or famine. Telephone lines were cut, but messages for aid filtered down the valley from Greenville. One contradictory report imperiously stated, "There is no destitution here that home people can not relieve. If the Negroes want to wait for government rations and refuse from $1.50 to $2.50 per day to work on levees, their starving arouses no sympathy. While all these sensational reports of destitution are traveling about, the steamboats are running into Memphis and Vicksburg begging for levee hands, and the native Negro is sitting on the levee fishing."

This old print shows a burial of one of the dozens drowned by the Mississippi floodwaters of 1890.

For three weeks in April residents of Madison Parish Front, Louisiana, fought the rising waters, building dikes higher and higher. They won. But those persons battling the rising river at the ever-widening Morganza Bend failed to drive the river back. A fierce storm added turmoil to the rising river, and heavy, leaden skies shadowed by dull, slate-black clouds poured down menacing rain. The gale whipped the Missisippi at the Morganza Bend into ribs of foam that sloshed increasingly over the sandbags.

Hundreds of persons held torches while others piled up more sandbags. A wealthy plantation owner later wrote that "planters' wives and daughters stood ankle-deep in mud, filling sacks and helping to lift them upon the shoulders of the men who were carrying them to the levee. Two bold Creoles stood at one weak place, though they felt the levee dissolving beneath their feet. They sank to their knees in the mud and water, but they stood stubbornly on the sinking dike, piling sacks in the breach, though again and again the flood seemed to be in the very act of overpowering and sweeping them away in the very center of a crevasse."

The effort was useless. The waters pressuring the Morganza Bend suddenly gushed over the walls, tearing away 400 feet of artificial embankment and sending thousands running for their homes in vain efforts to save belongings. The levee gave way to Bayou Sara, and waters roared across the flat lowlands, drenching everything. Massive breaks in dikes near Atchafalaya caused the surging waters to unite behind the barricades and race forcefully one hundred miles to the sea. Then on April 24 the waters won everywhere. The dikes and barriers at Pointe Coupee, Concordia Parish, Nita and Baton Rouge collapsed. Three thousand square miles of land in Louisiana alone, albeit much was swamp and bayou, were under water. More than 50,000 persons throughout the Mississippi valley had no homes; many a man could not even locate the spot on which his house had rested.

Thanks to the Signal Service warning, great loss of life was prevented; however, at least 100 did perish in the watery avalanches. One homeowner who lost everything and who had navigated paddlewheelers up and down the great Mississippi for three decades helplessly said, "I have lived on the river for thirty years, and I have studied it, for it was my business to do so. I have been steamboating all that time. I am now certain that I don't know anything about it, or about what ought to be done to it."

(ALSO SEE: Johnstown, Pennsylvania)

MISSISSIPPI RIVER — FLOODS

April, 1912

Due to late and heavy snowfalls that melted suddenly, the Mississippi's tributaries, particularly in the Mississippi valley, caused the river to swell, breaking its banks in thousands of places in early April, 1912. On April 2 the river broke through dikes manned by troops in Cairo, Illinois, and the rushing floodwaters quickly inundated the Mobile & Ohio train yards. Three days later the Realfoot Lake district went under water when the levee west of Hickman, Kentucky, gave way.

The floods were the worst in Mississippi, peaking on April 20 around Benoit, where fifteen persons were drowned when a dike gave way. Beulah, Mississippi, was under water, and all of Bolivar County became a small deadly sea in which 200 lost their lives. The death toll from the April flooding reached 250 throughout several states, 30,000 were homeless, and $10 million (a conservative estimate) in damage was done to the 2,000 square miles of flooded territory.

MISSISSIPPI RIVER **FLOODS**
April, 1927

From Cairo, Illinois, south the Mississippi River rampaged over its boundaries in early April, 1927, in the greatest flood of its history. Heavy rains up to twenty-four inches caused the swollen river to burst through its banks and levees in dozens of places, which put more than eighteen million acres of farm land under water. Drowned or killed by water-rushing debris were 313 persons; 700,000 were left homeless. A staggering $300 million in damages was incurred.

At the requests of their governors, six states were sent aid under a program developed by Herbert Hoover, then secretary of commerce.

Aid was quick in coming to the stricken residents of the Mississippi valley. A nationwide Red Cross drive yielded $15 million in relief funds. Through the government, the Rockefeller Foundation established a sanitation fund of $1 million. The United States Chamber of Commerce provided $10 million for low-rate loans; "every cent of which was paid back," Hoover carefully pointed out. "But those were days when citizens expected to take care of one another in time of disaster and it had not occurred to them that the Federal Government should do it."

The massive job of rehabilitation following the destruction brought about by the flooding Mississippi was described by Hoover in his *Memoirs:* "For rescue work we took over some 40 river steamers and attached to each of them a flotilla of small boats under the direction of Coast Guardsmen. As the motor boats we could assemble proved insufficient, the sawmills up and down the river made me 1,000 rough boats in ten days. I rented 1,000 outboard motors from the manufacturers, which we were to return. . . . We established great towns of tents on the high ground. We built wooden platforms for the tents, laid sewers, put in electric lights, and installed huge kitchens and feeding halls. And each tent town had a hospital. As the flood receded, we rehabilitated the people on their farms and homes, providing tents to the needy and building material, tools, seed, animals, furniture, and what not to start them going again. We established sanitary measures to put down malaria, typhoid, pellagra and generally [prevent the spread] of contagious disease, all of which we continued after the flood."

MIYI-YAMA **VOLCANIC ERUPTION**
1793

The tremendous eruption of the volcano Miyi-Yama on the island of Kiousiou off Java was that of a mud and water explosion that inundated all neighboring plains. Historical details are not available, but historian Kampfer estimates 53,000 people were killed in the blast.

MOBILE, ALABAMA **HURRICANE**
July 27-28, 1819

background: A small but intense hurricane struck Mobile Bay on July 27 and 28, 1819, veering from east-southeast to northeast, destroying scores of houses and commercial buildings in Mobile and adjoining towns. Also hit were Pensacola, Biloxi and New Orleans. More than 200 persons were thought to be killed by this storm and several ships were sunk.

Though its radius was small, the hurricane that lashed Mobile Bay, beginning about 8:00 P.M. on July 27, 1819, was one of the most savage to strike the American coast in the nineteenth century. Writing in *De Bow's Review* almost forty years later, bay resident J. C. Moret considered the storm "the most severe and strongest that ever blew on this coast since I came to it."

For about four hours the hurricane raced up the bay and through Mobile, which acted as a funnel for its brutal winds. The eye of the hurricane passed over the area at midnight, and then the wind increased from the southwest "twice as hard as it had blown from any other point." Though New Orleans and other cities experienced some pummeling by the storm, the brunt of its attack was borne by the towns along the bay.

Herds of cattle were engulfed and swept away by rushing waters at Lake Pontchartrain and Lake Borgne. Winds and waves toppled scores of buildings at Bay St. Louis and Pass of Christian. Water six feet deep swirled through Bay St. Louis, undermining the weakly built homes there. Only three buildings were left standing at Pass of Christian. Dozens of bodies rose and disappeared in the churning waters all along the coast.

At the height of the storm, early on July 28, the streets of Mobile were strewn with giant turtles and snapping alligators. Tides rose so high that many ships anchored in the bay were tossed into the city; a large brig was found later at Dauphin and Water streets. Scores of vessels were either driven ashore or capsized, the crews killed instantly. Moret, on board the schooner *Peacock of Pearl River,* was saved when the ship took anchor and escaped up the Pearl River, where she rode out the storm. The *Favorite*'s hull was splintered when she was thrown by the storm onto reefs at Henderson Point. Her master and crew survived. It was a different story for the man-of-war schooner *Firebrand* and her eighty United States sailors commanded by Lieutenant Cunningham.

Cunningham and seven others had left the ship before the storm on a mission to New Orleans; they were the only survivors of the *Firebrand*'s crew. The ship was discovered capsized on July 29, her hull jutting from the sandy shoal known then as "The Square Handkerchief," a patch of land between the Louisiana and Mississippi shores, west of Cat Island. One report stated, "The greater number of her crew were supposed to have been confined in her hull, as she lay with her bottom upward and for a considerable length of time emitted great stench, and but few of the bodies were found."

Pensacola was also much damaged by the storm, but details of the death and destruction there were skimpy. The city was then in Spanish hands, and no official reports were made public until a newly established American newspaper printed some facts of the storm's devastation in 1821.

MODANE, FRANCE — RAILWAY WRECK
December 12, 1917

One of the most devastating train wrecks in world history occurred in the southeastern corner of France, near the town of Modane on December 12, 1917. A troop train laden with more than 1,200 soldiers returning from the western front on Christmas vacation rushed through the Mount Cenis Tunnel and tore down a steep grade that had a wooden bridge and an extremely sharp curve at the bottom.

The overweighted train shot off the curve, its derailed cars piling up on each other in a deep gorge. The entire train then burst into flames. The engineer miraculously survived, although his life had been directly threatened only hours before the train was under way. He had become alarmed at the perilously overcrowded train and refused to move it. A French staff officer leaped into his cab and told him he would be courtmartialed unless he moved the train. Again he refused, pointing out that the train was unsafe with so many soldiers packed on board. The officer produced a pistol and threatened to have the engineer executed for failing to obey wartime orders. Under duress, the engineer of the train finally raced it off on its death route.

The fire engulfing the wrecked train certainly claimed more than the 543 official deaths subsequently admitted to by French officials (who also listed 243 others as being injured). Responsible authorities insist that at least 1,000 were killed and that no more than a handful could have possibly survived the monstrous crash and flames.

The Modane disaster occurred at a time when the fortunes of war scowled on France, and the morale of the *polus* was at its nadir. It was for this reason, officials later mumbled, that news of the disaster and its details was suppressed for fifteen years. Even in 1932 the French still rankled at the mere mention of the Modane wreck, cringing from the total irresponsibility of the army that had brought it about.

(ALSO SEE: Cuartla, Mexico)

MONONGAH, WEST VIRGINIA — MINE DISASTER
December 6, 1907

background: At 10:28 A.M. on December 6, 1907, a massive explosion tore to pieces the two main shafts of Number 6 and Number 8 mines of the Fairmont Coal Company outside of Monongah, West Virginia. At the time of the explosion, 367 miners were at work. Of these, 362 were killed, their bodies taken out weeks after rescue operations began. The cause of the explosion was never fully determined, but consensus has it that it resulted from dust accumulated from a trip of coal cars that broke away and crashed.

In mine Number 6, which connected with mine Number 8 in the Monongah coal works, an eighteen-year-old miner was operating a train load (or "trip") of coal cars up the shaft to the processing plant when a coupling broke and sent the cars rumbling backward down the sloping mine. The miner ran ahead to cut the electric circuits in the mine, but he was too late. The cars slammed into a wall, severing electric cables that ignited the resulting dust cloud, it later was staunchly maintained, and caused an explosion so massive that it crumbled almost every wall and ceiling in both mines, instantly killing 362 men working below.

The train operator survived when he was blown straight out of the entranceway. Another miner, close to the entrance of Number 8, received a splinter in one eye (he lost use of it). He felt for the fingers of one hand but realized that several were missing. Almost all of the 3,000 persons living in the mining town came on the run and ultimately stood in rain and snow and darkness for days, waiting for the bodies of their loved ones to be brought to the surface.

Four men escaped from an outcrop opening above mine Number 8 hours later, groggy, bleeding, their clothes singed. They were the only survivors. It took five days for struggling rescue parties, shoring up walls and ceilings as they dug downward, to locate the bodies of the trapped miners. Many were burned to death, apparently caught in the path of the igniting methane gas;

others had suffocated under tons of fallen timber and dirt. One man was found with a half-eaten sandwich in his mouth; probably he had been hungry early and decided to eat his lunch just as the blast went off.

It took five days to bring out 337 bodies. Another week went by and 17 more were recovered. Eight more dead miners were removed around the first of the year, bringing the death toll to 362. One dead man was not a miner but an industrious businessman who had been moving among the miners in Number 8, groping his way through the dark, almost airless tunnels, handing out cigars and waving sheaves of paper, as he shouted above the din of work. He was selling the miners life insurance.

MORADABAD, INDIA — HAIL STORM

April 30, 1888

Hail storms of gigantic proportions have historically plagued India and often have been killers. In one province in 1853, an enormous hail storm killed 3,000 cattle and literally beat to death eighty-four persons; this count was verified by authorities. In 1855 hailstones weighing an average of one and one-half pounds fell in Naini Tal and killed dozens.

This country's worst hail storm occurred on April 30, 1888, in Moradabad, when hailstones as large as "goose eggs and oranges" dropped to earth, destroying windows, glass doors and light roofs. About 230 persons, mostly men working in the fields, were killed, although some estimates place the death figure closer to 250.

One chilling account of this storm, by an Englishman living in the area, relates, "The verandas were blown away by the wind. A great part of the roof fell in, and the massive pucca portico was blown down. The walls shook. It was nearly dark outside, and hailstones of enormous sizes were dashed down with a force which I have never seen anything to equal. . . . There were long ridges of hail one or two feet in depth. . . . Not a house in the civil station that did not receive the most serious injury. . . . Men caught in the open and without shelter were simply pounded to death by the hail."

(ALSO SEE: Chartres, France)

MORGAN COUNTY, KENTUCKY — FLOODS

May 29-30, 1927

One of the most severe floods in Kentucky's history occurred on May 29-30, 1927, when the Kentucky River, bloated by torrential rains, overflowed its banks in dozens of places, crashed through barriers, and swamped Morgan County. Harlan County, in the southern part of the state, was hit hard. Damages to homes and crops soared to more than $7 million. Eighty-nine persons were drowned in the rapid waters and about 12,000 were homeless.

MORRO CASTLE — MARINE DISASTER

September 8, 1934

background: The 11,520-ton passenger liner *Morro Castle,* a twin-screw turbo-electric vessel, operated by the New York & Cuba Mail S.S. Co., a subsidiary of the Ward Line, was first launched on March 5, 1930, at Newport News, Virginia. She caught fire during a voyage between Havanna, Cuba, and New York on September 8, 1934, six miles off the New Jersey coastline, and burned to a gutted shell. Of the 455 passengers and crew members on board, 133 persons, mostly passengers, were either drowned or burned to death. Acting Captain W. F. Warms was tried, convicted and sentenced to two years in prison for negligence, but this ruling was later overturned. This disaster, fraught with mystery, intrigue and possible intentional arson (the board of inquiry attributed the wreck to "an act of God") remains an enigma to this day.

For those who served in high and low capacities on board the ill-fated *Morro Castle,* the swank, top-of-the-line luxury ship of the Ward Line carrying tourists between New York and Havana, there was an air of fear if not outright terror from the outset of her voyage. This vessel's scenario was one of mystery, mutiny and unknown evil.

The fact that such a pleasure ship was operating at all during the depression incited its polyglot crew to near mutiny over starvation wages. Labor problems had reached a violent stage with the antiunion Ward Line in the early 1930 s. The crews demanded not only better pay but, more importantly, decent food. "It was slop, awful slop," one sailor aboard the *Morro Castle* remembered. Captain Robert R. Wilmott was once accosted on his bridge by a member of the black gang that stoked the boilers. This sooty, irate seaman had run up from below carrying a plate of rotten eggs, his breakfast. He held it under the captain's nose and shouted, "Would you eat this?"

Wilmott could hardly argue with the man after just having breakfasted with passengers who could choose from several juices, ten hot or cold cereals, meat and fish, eggs made to order, several kinds of rolls and a host of beverages. He grimaced, ordered the stoker below, and brushed out the creases of his white tropical captain's uniform. There were problems on the *Morro Castle* more important than the miserable food fed to her crew.

Smuggling was rampant. Wilmott was a one-man army ferreting out illegal caches from secreted spots throughout the ship. Narcotics were hidden everywhere, and Wilmott would conduct tedious daily searches of the holds and the crew's quarters, sometimes turning up heroin and cocaine in small sacks that had been brought aboard at Cuba, then a way station receiving tremendous amounts of dope from Europe, the Middle East, the Orient and Latin America. Try as he might, Wilmott could not suppress the narcotics smuggling. It was simply too profitable for seamen, many of whom, according to authorities, bought their jobs for high prices in order to pass dope.

Cuban rum was also smuggled into New York in large quantities. Wilmott found several kegs on one cruise hidden at the bottom of an elevator shaft. He had them thrown overboard in front of his crew.

The *Morro Castle* also was a veritable haven for political refugees and illegal aliens attempting to sneak into the United States. Fleeing a purge of the Cuban dictator Machado, General Julio Herrera escaped Cuba in 1932 by paying a sailor $5,000 and secreting himself in the *Morro Castle*'s wine cellar; he was eventually offered asylum in the United States. To supplement their monthly salaries, crew members and officers alike smuggled scores of Chinese aboard the ship and into the United States. The indefatigable Wilmott had discovered several clusters of terrified aliens and had put them off the ship at a port before leaving Cuban waters.

Nothing on board the *Morro Castle* ran smoothly for the captain. Gambling was everywhere, and when an engineer complained to Wilmott that he had lost all his wages in a fixed game, the captain ran to the crew's quarters to discover a small casino operating, roulette wheel and all. He gathered up the gaming equipment, lugged it topside and hurled it into the sea.

Wilmott not only faced an angry, resentful crew on the last voyage of the *Morro Castle,* but he also had to contend with officers he distrusted and feared and who, in return, thought he was an ill-tempered, sickly, unbalanced man. The captain was inexplicably afraid of chief radioman George Rogers, stating to another officer as the obese, six foot, two inch wireless operator sauntered by on deck, "There goes a very bad man." Rogers, in the decades to come, would prove to be just that. The junior radio operator, George Alagna, was referred to as a communist by Wilmott after Alagna had attempted to organize a union aboard the *Morro Castle* and throughout the Ward Line. Wilmott had repeatedly asked Line authorities to remove Alagna from the ship.

Chief mate William F. Warms was a curious specimen. Though he had his master's papers, Warms had shown himself in the past to vacillate at moments of crucial decision. He was wishy-washy, and oftentimes appeared confused as to his duties. Captain Wilmott, who bossed the ship from stem to stern, did not apparently alleviate Warms's feeling of insecurity.

The chief mate's license was once suspended for eighteen months for failing to hold fire drills on a freighter operated by the Ward Line. This rebuke no doubt created the penchant Warms displayed for fire exercises. He would roust the crew from their quarters, sometimes battering down bolted doors to get them moving. Most of them drilled slowly. The majority were drunkards who consumed huge quantities of hidden liquor each day and slept in a stupor at night.

On the last night of the cruise returning from Havana on September 7, 1934, drunkenness spread not only among the crew but also the passengers, 138 of which belonged to the German-American Concordia Singing Society, a Brooklyn group of wealthy businessmen. The travelers had been treated to exotic Havana tours where they were driven by limousine through sultry streets guarded by Machado's machine-gun-carrying mercenaries to drink at Havana's famed watering holes. There was the sensation of the unreal for the *Morro Castle* passengers who fell asleep at night in their luxurious hotels listening to the subtle stacatto of rapid-firing weapons in far away parts of the city where insurrection was seething. Perhaps this surrealistic experience caused many passengers to act strangely on the return trip to New York.

The first sign of the unusual that last night at sea occurred when the normally garrulous Captain Wilmott declined to dine with his guests at the captain's table. This was a nightly ritual that Wilmott never missed. He loved food and he loved conversation. When he failed to appear, several officers became alarmed. Wilmott ordered steak and vegetables sent to his cabin, where he dined alone. About 7:00 P.M. he called the ship's doctor, DeWitt Van Zile, and asked him to bring up an enema. The doctor hurried to the captain's quarters and found him sprawled halfway into his bathtub, dead of what Van Zile and several other physicians on board who were also consulted termed a heart attack.

A junior officer walked up to the captain's door and was stopped by Chief Officer Warms. The younger officer wanted to pay his "last respects" to the captain, but Warms curtly told him, "No. He looks awful. His face is all blue." With that Warms went to the bridge and wired the home office and informed them of Wilmott's death. "Tell everyone I'm in command of the ship," Warms told an officer, but as events would prove, he most certainly was not.

Bad luck accumulated for the *Morro Castle* hour by hour as she made her way up the Atlantic coastline at about 18 knots, running into a howling gale that sent huge breakers over her bow. Warms, nervous, his hands fidgeting over jittery instruments on the bridge, peered into the swirling storm. Guests in the dining room moved to the grand ballroom to consume potent mixed drinks. Others retired to their staterooms for brandy. Crew men below began to slip into boozy conditions.

Returning from the captain's quarters where he had put Wilmott's body into bed, Dr. Van Zile joined several officers in the purser's office. Drinks were poured and Van Zile raised his glass. "Here's to death," he said laconically, adding a cryptic note, "Which one of us will be next?"

As the storm increased throughout the night, passengers became ill and staggered to their cabins. As many as six women overcelebrated and were carried dead drunk to their rooms. A group of men, also drunk, sat in the writing room and flipped lighted cigarettes into a basket to amuse themselves. After starting a small fire on a rug, the group was upbraided by watchman Art Bagley. He quickly put out the fire and inspected the writing room for more damage. There was none, although almost everything on board the *Morro Castle* was highly flammable, even her steel plates, which were caked with no less than fourteen coats of paint. Throughout the cabins, dining room, ballroom, saloon and writing room were overstuffed chairs, carpets and thick wooden paneling.

Foghorn blasts from the ship bounded off the swirling storm clouds sweeping by the vessel as jazz dribbled from the ballroom where a girl was limply playing. It was about 2:15 A.M. when passenger Paul Arneth, dressed only in bathrobe and pajamas, went looking for his roommate. He stumbled into the writing room and noticed billowing smoke rushing from beneath the double doors of an immense locker where 150 extra blankets were stored. The blankets, highly combustible because of the fluids used to clean them, rested against a wall that faced one of the smokestacks which, it was later deduced, were hot enough from overheating to become the source of the great fire that was to gut the liner.

Before breaking a fire alarm box, Arneth summoned a steward who threw open the locker doors. A giant wall of flames leaped outward, instantly igniting the wooden paneling, carpets and furniture in the writing room. Some officers and crew members came running with a hose a few minutes later, but there was little pressure and only a trickle of water came out. This was because Warms, when hearing of the fire, had ordered all the hydrants on board opened up, thus lessening the individual pressure of each. Warms himself was so preoccupied by the hurricane battering his ship that he did not notice smoke drifting out of a small ventilator on the bridge until another officer pointed it out. He then became dumbfounded and acted like a man who had lost his senses.

As the fire spread rapidly through the ship, orders were given and then countermanded. Passengers were alerted and told to stand by, but Warms was suddenly a man without direction. Though asked several times by Alagna if Rogers should send out an SOS, he did not reply; he merely ordered the ship to continue at top speed with the screaming wind, which forced the fire to the stern. The smoke became so thick on the decks that no one could see more than a few feet. People were burning to death in their cabins, their shrieks, for the most part, ignored by crew members scurrying topside to save their own lives.

A junior officer named Hansen reached the bridge and insisted that Warms make for shore. According to writer Hal Burton, Warms told Hansen that the *Morro Castle* could make New York harbor, and Hansen, who knew the ship's only chance for survival was to be beached on the New Jersey shore, exploded and yelled, "You damned fool! That's forty miles away! We've got to stop this ship. We won't last that long."

With that Hansen struck Warms under the eye and knocked him down. A seaman rushed onto the bridge and asked, "Where's Warms?"

"The bastard's on the deck," Hansen replied.

Warms got unsteadily to his feet. Several men asked him what he was going to do. His voice was hollow as he muttered, "Drop the hook." With some difficulty inexperienced crew men dropped the anchor.

In the radio shack Alagna, who had finally wrenched an okay from Warms to send out an SOS, sat with Rogers, their feet propped high above the hot steel plates beneath their chairs, wet towels wrapped around their heads to keep them from fainting, sending out distress signals. Several ships picked up the signals and immediately responded.

At the time the anchor was dropped, the ship was about six or seven miles off Atlantic City. Warms gave the order to abandon ship with blasts from the foghorn. It was then that the wholesale desertion of the crew took place. Within the running, shoving, hollering ordeal to man the lifeboats, the crew displayed gross cowardice, jumping into several lifeboats and swinging out the davits to save themselves.

The chief engineer, Eban S. Abbot, never once joined his belowdecks crew when the fire erupted, but ordered them by phone to stay at their posts and then ran for a lifeboat. His behavior was typical of the crew. In one lifeboat that reached shore, there were thirty-one crew members and one passenger. In another nineteen crew members and one passenger rowed to the sandy beaches of Atlantic City. Many hardy passengers had to swim miles to save themselves.

The debacle was complete when the *Morro Castle* drifted to shore later that morning, thousands lining the beaches to view her awful gutted hulk, smoke still streaming from her burning holds, 133 persons dead, either still on board and charred beyond recognition, or in deathfloats somewhere in the violent sea.

Warms was charged, along with four others, including Abbott, with negligence, and he was subsequently found guilty and sentenced to jail for two years; Abbott got four years. These sentences were reversed by higher courts, and none of those responsible for the disaster ever served a day in jail.

One man not charged eventually did go to jail. In his superbly detailed book, *Fire at Sea,* Thomas Gallagher looked into the background of Rogers, the chief radioman, and discovered a long criminal history. Rogers, first hailed as one of the rare heroic figures on board the *Morro Castle,* was responsible, Gallagher claimed, not only for setting the ship on fire in retaliation for rebukes from Wilmott but for poisoning the captain as well. There was no evidence other than Rogers's sordid background, however, to indicate that he indeed did start the tragic blaze that ended the *Morro Castle* that storm-tossed night in 1934. He was later involved in several murders and went to prison.

Because of the lax fire regulations and improper safety precautions prevalent on board the *Morro Castle,* strong new marine laws governing fire hazards were enacted along with modern fireproofing systems.

MUD RUN, PENNSYLVANIA — RAILWAY WRECK — October 10, 1888

background: Eight excursion trains were allocated to the Total Abstinence Union of Wilkes-Barre, Pennsylvania, on October 10, 1888, each running up to picnic areas near Hazelton in the morning and returning that night and each separated by ten-minute intervals. The sixth excursion train with about 500 persons on board was halted at Mud Run. The seventh train was erroneously signaled at this station to come ahead. It then telescoped into the last car of the sixth train, which then telescoped through half of the next car. Dead in one of the worst United States railway accidents were 64 persons; 100 more were injured.

It was no mystery to those who lived through the pioneering railroad days of the nineteenth century that most of the fatalities in railway wrecks resulted from cars' telescoping into one another. The disaster that overtook and killed sixty-four persons at Mud Run, Pennsylvania, on the brisk fall day of October 10, 1888, was sadly typical.

Earlier that day, hundreds of basket-toting picnickers from Wilkes-Barre, all members of the Total Abstinence Union, were on board eight special excursion trains of the Lehigh Valley Line to campgrounds in the hills near Hazelton. The day was uneventful except for an altercation between a rowdy minority and a tongue-clucking and finger-wagging majority that excoriated backsliding. Ironically these "wayward souls" wound up in the last car of the sixth train that evening as it made its way back to Wilkes-Barre. Halted at Mud Run, the engineer of this train inched his load 170 feet beyond the stationmaster's house.

Hannigan, the rear brakeman for the sixth train, walked back to the far side of the station platform, approximately 400 feet from his train, and held out a warning lantern. He apparently considered the responsibility routine and spent most of his time talking to people on the platform, instead of watching for the seventh train.

As the sixth train waited to be cleared, the seventh train—one of the largest, pulled by two engines—approached at about 20 m.p.h., although Henry Cook, the engineer of the first engine, Number 452, later stated that his speed was between 12 and 14 m.p.h. as he approached the stop.

The Lehigh Railway Line had taken what it thought to be every precaution to safeguard the passengers on these trains, its superintendent, Mitchell, issuing special orders that instructed all engineers to maintain a ten-minute interval between trains rather than the normal five-minute span. Officials also posted two specially assigned brakemen in the cab of each leading engine as lookouts. "Watch the rear of your trains, " Mitchell had warned.

As the seventh section approached Mud Run, several factors conspired to create tragedy. The first engine on the seventh train had only steam brakes. The engine behind it, Number 466, with engineer Major at the throttle, controlled the train brakes and he would apply these only if he heard a warning whistle, the only means of communication, from the first engineer, Henry Cook. The station house at Mud Run was also hard to spot since there was a long curve leading into the station. Brakeman Pohl saw that the order-board signal at Mud Run was white, or all clear, and reported this to Cook in the first locomotive's cab. As the train rushed forward, Gallagher, Cook's fireman, saw the tiny red light held by rear brakeman Hannigan on the station platform.

About five telegraph poles from the station, Hannigan came to his senses and began to frantically wave his lantern.

"Oh, my God! Stop her, Henry!" Gallagher shouted to his engineer. Cook applied the steam brakes and yanked the warning whistle to tell Major, in the second engine, to apply the train brakes, but it was too late. Engine 452 plowed into the rear of the sixth train with the whole weight of the seventh train hurtling behind it.

The last car of the sixth train, with its lot of sorry drunks in their singing revels, was telescoped for twenty feet. It then plowed half way through the next car. Both cars, containing about 200 persons, were totally wrecked and 64 persons, most of whom were in the last car of the sixth train, were killed instantly. Dozens more were rendered limbless. Others were crippled, blinded and scalded.

None of the crew members of the seventh train was

even scratched. For a moment the only noise penetrating the eerie silence was the hiss of steam from the engines. Then came the screams, the groans and the pitiful cries for help.

Gallagher worked his way down from Number 452's cab through the wrecked cars.

"I'm gonna back her out," Cook called to him.

"No, no, Henry, you better not," came Gallagher's voice from the dark shambles of the wreck. "It'll do more harm than good. There's folks here twisted all around and under the wreckage. If you move the train it might collapse on them." He paused. "There's folks under your wheels . . . "

In addition to the dead, about 100 other passengers had been seriously injured, and it took hours to extricate them from the splintered wooden coaches.

The Mud Run disaster was one of the first thoroughly investigated train wrecks in American history and the board of inquiry placed the blame on the two engineers, Cook and Major, the rear brakeman, Hannigan, and the two brakemen who had been riding in the first engine of the seventh excursion train. All were arrested and charged with manslaughter. They were subsequently freed, due to the confusion between the station's order-board signal lights and the lackadaisical signal given by the rear brakeman.

This calamity was commemorated a year later in a book that bewailed the wreck in what now seem to be archaic tones: "Oh! What tongue can tell, or what pen picture this most dreadful calamity. The roasting, scalding engine under which were crushed those poor, young children, and the car ahead being telescoped and the lives crushed out of those who but a few moments since were full of life. Oh, God, why visit upon your unhappy children such a death."

(ALSO SEE: Camp Hill, Pennsylvania; Chatsworth, Illinois)

Sixty-four persons perished in the telescoped cars of the Mud Run, Pennsylvania, train disaster of November 10, 1888.

A Murphysboro, Illinois, schoolhouse was ripped apart by a tornado that killed 689 persons in three states it traversed. *(UPI)*

MURPHYSBORO, ILLINOIS TORNADO March 18, 1925

background: Following an almost straight path for 219 miles, the tornado that utterly devastated Murphysboro, Illinois, traveled east-northeast from Reynolds County, Missouri, where it originated at 1:00 P.M. on March 18, 1925, moved through Illinois and dissipated outside Princeton, Indiana, at 4:15 P.M. Overall deaths in three states were 689; 1,980 were injured and $16.6 million in damages were recorded.

There was no warning whatever of the coming of the worst tornado in American history. No Weather Bureau alarms were sent out, and as the mammoth tornado, moving along a path from a half to one mile wide, destroyed one town after another, those surviving the holocaust apparently lost all presence of mind and failed to warn neighboring cities.

This tornado, one of eight that whipped through midwestern states on that date, displayed none of the usual characteristics of the ominous funnel clouds: it did not skip or hop or rise and fall on the land; it stayed level, a mass of boiling air and cloud. No survivor described a funnel-shaped vortex. One man saw only a "rolling fog" shooting at him.

The state of Missouri suffered an overall death rate of 11; 141 were injured, and there was $560,000 in damages. The first town to be struck was Annapolis, Missouri.

When the tornado left the state of its birth, its speed accelerated to almost 60 m.p.h. as it smashed through Illinois, striking and all but obliterating the towns of DeSoto, Gorham, Parrish and Murphysboro. The latter received the full brunt of the storm, which went right through the heart of the town, unraveling 1,200 houses, office buildings and industrial structures for 152 blocks—over 60 percent of the community. The tornado killed 234 persons outright and seriously injured more than 800 others. Property damage was conservatively estimated at $10 million, which, no doubt, would be four times more today. Eight thousand residents were homeless; the tornado had so completely destroyed the business and manufacturing areas that 2,000 workers were jobless for months.

"It was an incredible sight," one dazed Murphysboro citizen exclaimed later. "The storm came right up the street, peeling up houses, cement, people, poles, anything and everything, peeling it all up like you would peel a potato. I don't know how I got out, how I lived at all."

The largest city to be struck by the storm was West Frankfort, Illinois, and here the tornado knocked over 925 houses, killed 127, and wounded 450 persons. The storm sliced through the northwest part of town, a residential area, touching sixty-four blocks and wiping out thirteen that later appeared as if they had been flattened by a giant steamroller.

DeSoto, Illinois, was next; seventy-two people were killed here. At Gorham, Illinois, another thirty-four joined the fatality list.

When the tornado crossed the Indiana line, moving at almost 70 m.p.h., it slapped Griffin, killing thirty-four, and then raced on to Princeton, where another twenty persons met death.

(ALSO SEE: Gainesville, Georgia, 1936)

N

NAGA CITY, PHILIPPINES — **BRIDGE COLLAPSE** — **September 16, 1972**

The ancient, shaky bridge spanning the Bicol River in Naga City, the Philippines, 160 miles southeast of Manila, had a history of mishaps. For the superstitious or fanatically religious it was the scene of the annual Catholic Penafranca Fluvial festival. In the late 1940's, the bridge, then at least 100 years old, collapsed and killed thirty residents.

This did not prevent hundreds of Naga City citizens from crowding onto the 18-foot-wide, 130-foot-long bridge on September 16, 1972, to await the statue of the Virgin of Penafranca that was to sail beneath them on a boat in celebration of the religious holiday. The rickety bridge had been repaired only two weeks before, but under the weight of the throng its timbers gave way, hurling hundreds of celebrants downward. Dead or missing were 100 persons; another 200 were injured. All the victims were women and children.

NAPERVILLE, ILLINOIS — **RAILWAY WRECK** — **April 25, 1946**

background: The thirteen-car westbound Number 11 of the Burlington line was stopped to inspect possible damage in Naperville, Illinois, on April 25, 1946, when train Number 39 roared up behind it at more than 80 m.p.h., despite warning signals along the track. Killed were forty-five persons, almost everyone on the stopped train. The engineer of Number 39 was held for manslaughter, but was later released.

Few times in American railroading has such near-criminal negligence been demonstrated as in the horrendous crash that took the lives of forty-five persons, mostly passengers, at Naperville, Illinois, at 1:00 P.M. on April 25, 1946. The irony of this wreck was that the engineer, who apparently caused the accident, had no explanation for it.

The thirteen-car Advance Flyer, Burlington's Number 11, was speeding westward when it was signaled to stop at Naperville by a brakeman who thought he saw a large object shoot from beneath the train as it raced over the tracks. While the train was being inspected, the rear brakeman, James Tagney, jumped from the train with a large red flag in his hand and ran back down the tracks for a distance of 800 feet. Though the track was level and straight and the weather clear and sunny, Tagney conscientiously waved the flag back and forth.

His efforts, though mandatory according to regulation, were only supplementary since the entire route was marked by signal lights, all of which were red while Number 11 was in the Naperville station. Yet, Tagney could see in the distance the fast-approaching Exposition Flyer, Burlington's speedy Number 39. At the throttle of this train was sixty-eight-year-old M. A. Blaine, an experienced engineer.

When Number 39 appeared not to slow down, Tagney's actions became frenzied. He jumped up and

Death on a sunny afternoon—a rear-end collision between two Burlington trains at Naperville, Illinois, on April 25, 1946, took the lives of forty-five passengers. *(Wide World)*

down and shouted. The Exposition Flyer kept coming, its speed later estimated at between 80 and 86 m.p.h. All along its route approach signals blinked red, but Blaine either did not see them or, more inexplicably, refused to acknowledge them. Train personnel on board Number 39 later testified that they did feel a slight decrease in speed as if the service brakes had been applied, but the reduction was negligible.

With a wild shriek Tagney leaped out of Number 39's path at the last moment. He saw its fireman hop down the stairs from the cab, swing outward for a moment while holding a safety bar and then, moments before Number 39 smashed into the rear of the vulnerable Advance Flyer, leap for his life. His body hurtled outward from the speeding train, and he was killed when he hit the ground.

Number 39 screeched sickeningly into Number 11, its weighty diesel engine eating three-quarters of the way into car thirteen, which weighed 170,000 pounds. Car twelve, which weighed as much as car thirteen, was only slightly damaged, but the racing weight of Number 39 buckled the eleventh car, the diner, which had a light metal construction, into a U. Almost everyone inside was killed.

Blaine had stayed in his cab at the moment of impact and somehow survived. He was called before a board of inquiry, but he could give no satisfactory explanation why he had not stopped Number 39 in time. He was later charged with manslaughter, but he was not indicted by a county grand jury due to insufficient evidence. His advanced age may have been a factor that prevented prosecution. The disaster in Naperville remains an enigma to this day.

NARVAEZ EXPEDITION — MARINE DISASTER
September 22, 1528

One of the earliest Spanish excursions sailing from already settled Hispaniola to visit Florida was the Narvaez expedition. Members of this discovery party explored what are now the Tampa and Tallahassee areas and then departed from Apalache Bay on the gulf, when they were caught in a sudden hurricane and all of their ships were torn to pieces or capsized. Of the 400 soldiers and sailors on board, only 20, according to historian Woodbury Lowery, survived.

NASHVILLE, TENNESSEE — RAILWAY WRECK
July 9, 1918

The railway disaster taking the highest toll in human life in America occurred on the Nashville, Chattanooga & St. Louis line shortly after 7:00 A.M. on July 9, 1918. The staggering death toll was 101, and at least another 100 were injured. Either because there was very little drama in telling of the massive civilian death during wartime, or there was little mystery or excitement in the development of the accident, newspapers gave the event little space. Perhaps it was because most of the 87 civilian victims—14 more fatalities were crew members—were black. This disaster occurred during a time of widespread racial hatred—the violent racial riots of 1919 were only months away.

Engineer Kennedy of train Number 1, which was carrying Negro workers to nearby munition plants, apparently was to blame for the disastrous head-on collision that occurred between the Harding and Shops stations outside Nashville. He had standing orders to stop at Shops and allow the faster Number 4 express train to pass him on the double tracks before proceeding on the single track to Harding. After watching an engine with several freight cars flit by, Kennedy pulled out Number 1 and at 50 m.p.h. headed for Harding.

Number 4 came down the same single track toward Shops at an identical speed, and the resulting head-on collision completely destroyed both engines and tenders and threw several cars sideways off the tracks. The first two wooden cars of Number 1 went completely to pieces, killing everyone inside. Had these cars been made of metal, many authorities agree, the fatalities would have been considerably less.

The reason for Kennedy's blatant error was never learned; this experienced, usually alert engineer died in the crash. The only plausible explanation was that he was daydreaming when the freight went past his train, and he thought it was the express. None of the crew men aboard Number 1 warned Kennedy that it was a freight and not Number 4 that had gone by, since all were new; it was, ironically, their first day on the job.

NASIRABAD, BANGLADESH — TORNADO
April 2, 1972

Tornadoes raged through the Mymensingh district north of Dacca, Bangladesh, on April 2, 1972, killing about 200 persons and making 25,000 homeless, when their flimsy homes were shredded by the storm. The town most devastated by the tornadoes was Nasirabad, which lost 35 residents; 96 others there were hurt.

This rash of tornadoes covered an immense area, about 800 square miles, and winds around the vortex of some of the storms were estimated to be between 150 and 160 m.p.h.

NATCHEZ, MISSISSIPPI — TORNADO
May 7, 1840

Moving up the Mississippi River about ten miles south of Natchez, Mississippi, a vicious tornado struck the city about 2:00 P.M. on May 7, 1840. The barometer reading at the time of the storm's arrival was 29.37, and parts of the riverfront and residential areas behind it were completely destroyed. As happens in many tornadoes, a great number of houses were exploded by the opposing pressures of the storm's vortex and that within the buildings. An estimated 317 persons were killed in this tornado; 109 persons were seriously injured.

Winds whipped about by the tornado took only five minutes to tear through the city. Sheets of tin were found twenty miles from where they had been torn away from buildings. Some windows were carried thirty miles from Natchez. Property damage was enormous—more than $1.26 million.

Most of the deaths in the storm occurred on the river when two large steamers and sixty flatboats were sunk, all turning turtle at the same time, like flapjacks being flipped. Adding to the misery, nine inches of rain mixed with enormous hailstones pelted the area.

This storm was one of the first for which a tornado's freak accidents were recorded. In one office, a huge desk tightly fastened with three locks was blown open as the air within it expanded.

In nearby New Brunswick, also struck by the storm, another curious accident occurred. According to one historical report, "A towel hanging on the wall was found apparently blown nearly through it. The expanding air had driven the towel in a large crevice which opened in the wall behind it; and the crevice closed as the storm passed on, holding the towel to puzzle the neighborhood."

Natchez was visited by another violent tornado on June 16, 1842, in which an estimated 500 persons met death, but the destruction wrought by this twister was not half of that brought about by the tornado two years earlier.

NAUTILUS — MARINE DISASTER

November 19, 1803

The British sailing ship *Nautilus* was ground to splinters in a violent storm near Macao on November 19, 1803. Twenty-seven of the crew members, including the captain and chief mate, were killed; nineteen others survived. A survivor's vivid account of the destruction of the *Nautilus* appeared anonymously almost a year later in the *London Times*. It read in part: "At eight o'clock at night, the squall increasing, and dismal-looking weather [approaching], we handed our top-sails and courses, and lay to under the mizzen stay-sail, heaving the lead throughout the night, at midnight, blowing hard, with rain, the wind about North East.

"At three o'clock the next morning, wore ship to the Southward and Eastward, blowing furiously, and a tremendous sea. At four o'clock wore ship again. At daylight saw an island under our lee [Macao]; let go both the bower anchors; but at that time, the wind being so very violent, the anchors had no effect on the ship, and she drove bodily on the island, and went to pieces shortly after she struck . . . The hardships we suffered are almost indescribable . . . Seven of the crew [of the nineteen who made land] perished for want of food."

NEBRASKA — FLOODS

May-July, 1950

One of the worst deluges of Nebraska's history was the flooding of southeast Nebraska, which began with a monstrous rainfall of fourteen inches on May 8, 1950. For almost three months, until the end of July, a series of floods never before witnessed by most residents emanated from a veritable conspiracy of rivers—Big Blue, Loup, Beaver, Little Nemaha and Salt Creek. Officially twenty-three persons lost their lives, but scores of others disappeared in the flash floods. In the swamped 60,000 acres of Nebraska land lay the ruins valued at more than $60 million.

NEFFS, OHIO — MINE DISASTER

March 16, 1940

No firebosses were employed at the Willow Grove Mines at Neffs, Ohio, which, no doubt, accounted for the massive explosion that occurred in Number 10 shaft on the morning of March 16, 1940. An excessive amount of blast powder was used at about 11:00 A.M. It ignited coal dust and sent roaring, shooting flames through the shaft. Several dozen men were killed almost immediately by burns and gas. Miners called to the surface for help, and officials outside heard over the phone the men die, one by one, of asphyxiation.

A motorman driving a trip of cars to the surface began to black out as the gas caught up to his small train, but he had the presence of mind to put the controller on full before lapsing into unconsciousness. It did him no good; the train came out of the shaft, smashed into the trolley pole and then coasted 900 feet back into the lethal mine. The motorman died, along with 71 others.

Wearing gas masks, squads of rescue teams took out 104 survivors hours later.

NEPAL — FLOODS-LANDSLIDES

August 7, 1972

Following particularly destructive monsoon rains, a series of floods throughout Nepal created scores of landslides. An estimated 105 persons were drowned or buried during the black day of August 7, 1972.

NEW ALBANY, INDIANA — TORNADO
March 23, 1917

The complete north side of New Albany, Indiana, was ground to pieces by a savage tornado that tore into the city a little after 3:00 P.M. on March 23, 1917. Before it crossed the Ohio River into Kentucky and devastated Harrods Creek, more than 300 New Albany houses were demolished by the twister. Forty-five residents, most of whom had been trapped inside, were killed by the storm. Overall damages went beyond $2 million.

NEW CASTLE, COLORADO — MINE DISASTER
February 18, 1896

On the morning of February 18, 1896, a shuddering explosion tore through the Vulcan Mine at New Castle, Colorado, instantly killing all forty-nine miners who were digging in the shaft. Though adequate safety measures had been taken in this mine (according to a state mine inspector's report), careless blasting had caused the explosion.

The official report of the disaster laconically read: "Explosive placed on a lump of coal blocking the chute and covered with a small quantity of dust and slack . . . set off gas and an explosion resulted. . . . The ingredients were dust and gas."

NEW DELHI, INDIA — MASS POISONING
January 23, 1972

Of the several hundred persons attending a wedding in one of New Delhi's many hut-camps, at least one hundred died on January 23, 1972, from a mass poisoning. Those who perished, authorities later determined, had consumed large quantities of liquor that contained wood alcohol and varnish. Police tracked down the bootlegger who had sold the liquor to the wedding sponsors. They found him in a slum populated by street cleaners and cobblers. The man and his mother and brother were dead. They, too, had attended the wedding and had drunk their own deadly spirits.

NEW ENGLAND — FLOODS
November 3-4, 1927

Following a tropical storm that swept over Cuba at the end of October, 1927, New England was ravaged by some of the most severe flooding in its history. Massive rains bloated streams and broad waterways, chiefly the Winooski, Ottauquechee and Lamoille rivers, which broke their banks and inundated dozens of towns. Vermont's Winooski and White valleys suffered tragically; eighty-four lives were lost. At least twice that number of deaths occurred from Vermont to Connecticut where more than $40 million in damages was done.

In the words of one weather authority, the 1927 New England floods created "tragedy . . . upon tragedy in such rapid succession that the people were stunned and helpless for a time, and the losses of life and property were staggering for an area comparatively so small."

NEW ENGLAND — HURRICANE
September 8-16, 1944

background: The monster hurricane first spotted in the West Indies on September 8, 1944, moved sluggishly across a 500-mile front, grazing the Bahamas and Florida Keys and then moving along the Atlantic seaboard, striking inland at North Carolina and then on to New Jersey, New York, and particularly New England on September 14, wreaking $50 million in damages throughout several states and killing 389. Thanks to adequate weather warnings, loss of life was kept to a minimum. Winds of this hurricane were measured up to 140 m.p.h.

Following almost the identical path of the hurricane that devastated Long Island and New England on September 21, 1938, a killer storm swirled into existence off the West Indies in the Caribbean, moving northward at approximately 15 m.p.h. on a 500-mile front that flicked at Puerto Rico, the Bahamas, and some of the Florida Keys from September 8 to 14, 1944.

Just before the storm inexplicably turned inland along the North Carolina coast, Colonel Lloyd B. Wood, thirty-six-year-old deputy chief of the Army Air Force's Weather Division, took off in an A-20 Havoc light bomber from Washington to survey the hurricane.

His was one of the first detailed advance reports of any oncoming hurricane threatening United States territory, "The storm was like a giant upright funnel with the top of about 40,000 feet. Winds were twisting counterclockwise. Our course was laid to reach the eye of the gale. We bore into it. There was a heavy rain and black clouds. Occasionally, we could see ocean spray which must have been several hundred feet above the sea's surface. We flew about one hundred miles farther along. At 5,000 feet, I cut the power. The clouds thinned and through a thin mist we could see the sun. We were just at the edge of the hurricane's eye."

It was Wood's chillingly accurate report on the hurricane's progress that allowed United States Weather Bureau experts to predict the storm's destructive march once it came inland—it was "the best charted hurricane in history," according to authorities at that time—unraveling 140 m.p.h. winds across the Carolinas, Maryland, Delaware and New Jersey.

Warnings blared through loudspeakers and soundtrucks on the streets and over hundreds of radio stations from Delaware to Maine, a furious activity that reminded one graphically inspired writer to compare the frantic

A hurricane with 140 m.p.h. winds smashed New England in September 1944, killing 389 people. Here New Yorkers battle the raging winds on the first night of the mammoth storm. *(Wide World)*

scene to "pygmies running ahead of a mad elephant."

Atlantic City was one of the hardest-hit areas; the famous Boardwalk was splintered; Heinz Pier was cut in two; 200 feet of Asbury Park's municipal fishing pier was washed away. At Sea Isle City, New Jersey, 400 of the hamlet's 700 homes were severely damaged; 50 houses were flattened. Traveling through New York on September 14, rains whipped by 95 m.p.h. gusts of wind rocked the skyscrapers of Manhattan before the storm ripped its way up the New England coastline, covering a total area of almost 1,000 miles.

The New England states suffered heavy damages, but there were few killed on land; the majority of deaths came at sea. The 1,850-ton Navy destroyer *Warrington* foundered in the storm along with two Coast Guard vessels. Before the hurricane raged off and disappeared in the mists of Nova Scotia, there was $50 million in damages, mostly to tobacco and fruit crops, and 389 persons were dead.

Tens of thousands of ancient, beautiful trees were down throughout New England, forcing many a homeowner in the storm's path to chop his or her way out. More than 300,000 telephones were out of service, when hundreds of miles of telephone poles were felled in the storm, and electricity also was unavailable.

Gertrude Springer, a correspondent for the *Survey Graphic,* described the scene of devastation in Cape Cod where the storm had torn the land.

"Daylight revealed the extent of the shambles. All the big trees are gone. About half our trees are uprooted—the rest are broken off ten or fifteen feet up . . . [Houses are] covered with gray salt spray mixed with tree siftings and dirt. All the shrubs and flowers . . . are blackened and blasted by the spray. . . . Lots of trees are down in the village [Osterville] and the steeple is off the Baptist Church . . . cottages and bath houses gone . . . the big houses along Long Beach tossed off their pins . . . the bridge at Parker River, West Yarmouth way, gone . . . all the waterfront houses at Hyannis and Hyannisport badly mauled . . . the Oyster Harbor bridge unusable . . . the Crosby shipyards a tangle, with big cruisers tossed up on the docks. . . . The unique beauty of this part of the Cape—the tall pines—is gone forever. Well, anyway, the Germans didn't do it with bombs, and we're winning the war."

(ALSO SEE: Long Island, New York)

NEWFOUNDLAND, CANADA HURRICANE
September 9, 1775

The roaring hurricane that swept across Newfoundland on September 9, 1775, was either the same storm that had wrecked North Carolina towns six days earlier or a new storm formed out of the dissipating "Independence Hurricane." In either case the storm caught hundreds of fishing boats off Newfoundland shores and the Grand Banks and capsized many of them.

Reported killed were 4,000 sailors, almost every available fisherman in the area. Losses of ships, merchandise and buildings on land were estimated to be around £140,000, a staggering sum. One report stated: "On land roofs were torn off, chimneys crumbled, and houses collapsed from the force of the wind."

(ALSO SEE: Bar, North Carolina)

NEWFOUNDLAND, CANADA HURRICANE
August 25, 1935

One of the five vicious hurricanes in 1935 that struck the American continent, the storm that raged from the West Indies through the Atlantic to strike Newfoundland on August 25 followed much the same course taken by the great Nova Scotia hurricane of 1873. Sighted seven days earlier, the storm almost described a huge S as it curved through the Atlantic waters, barely missing Bermuda.

The fishing fleets in Newfoundland harbors were wrecked almost beyond repair when the storm charged inland and killed dozens of villagers and fishermen.

NEWHALL HOUSE FIRE
January 10, 1883

background: Built in 1857, the six-story, 300-room Newhall House Hotel in Milwaukee, Wisconsin, was almost totally constructed of wood. It provided guests with only two fire escapes, a factor that assured the deaths of seventy-one persons on the morning of January 10, 1883, when fire broke out and raced up an elevator shaft, igniting most of the building; because of its dangerous construction, all local insurance agents had refused to provide coverage.

The site of the most elegant hostelry in Milwaukee, Wisconsin, the Newhall House, was the scene of repeated fire disasters. The structure preceding the Newhall House's construction was the lavish, rambling United States Hotel, which was gutted by a blaze in 1854. Three years later, the town's leading financier, Daniel Newhall, ordered the building of what he thought would be the most impressive hotel in the Midwest. The result was Newhall House, a six-story building of cream-colored bricks that offered rooms for 300 guests. Milwaukee was partial to cream-colored bricks; they were used for its streets and buildings, ergo the early sobriquet "Cream City."

Though handsomely carpeted and brandishing thick oak paneling and gold accouterments, the hotel, according to one person, was "a regular tinder box." The myriad partitions that created a maze of hallways were not filled in with bricks, the woodwork was "exceedingly dry," and only two fire escapes—almost wholly inaccessible—were provided. When a fire started in the kitchen and raced to the hotel roof on January 10, 1880, almost $7,000 in damage was done to the top north section of the hotel, causing insurance agents to refuse to insure the building thereafter.

Ironically three years to the day after the first Newhall House fire, a blaze began about 3:30 A.M. at the bottom of one of the hotel's elevator shafts, all of which were unprotected. The flames raced upward to the roof. At first the 300 guests and most of the 40 maids and stewards were not alerted. The owner had given strict instructions not to arouse the guests in the event of another fire; the 1880 blaze had created considerable panic. This policy eventually led to the fire's high mortality.

An alarm to the fire department was thus delayed until after 4:00 A.M., and by that time the entire six stories were fully aflame. When firemen, accompanied by enormous, shouting crowds, arrived at the burning hotel, there was little they could do to aid the trapped guests who cried out from burning windows. Telegraph wires thickly strung around the entire hotel impeded rescue work and served as fateful snares for those either brave enough or mad enough to jump.

Leslie's described the holocaust: "A scene of the wildest confusion ensued. The unfortunate inmates were in many cases only aroused from their slumbers by the noise of the flames, and found their escape already cut off. Men, women, and children rushed up and down the halls in the dense suffocating smoke, missing in their frantic efforts the stairways and windows leading to the fire-escapes. In despair many leaped from the windows of their rooms to the pavement several stories below, although such a leap meant death or shattered limbs. A few leaped upon an outstretched canvas held by citizens, but only to receive fatal injuries. The maze of telegraph wires encircling the building on the south and east sides played sad havoc with those who made the frightful leap for life. Several of the bodies were cut deep into by the wires and then the torn and bleeding forms dropped to the ground. Others struck the wires crosswise, rebounded, and were hurled to the ground with a dreadful crash."

As the mangled bodies of terrified guests began to form grotesque heaps before the helpless, rage-filled firemen and citizens, several dozen hotel employees, almost all "waiter-girls" who occupied rooms on the top floor, appeared at the burning roof, pleading for help.

Before the flames engulfed them, many dove downward into an alley. Here rescuers found an ugly mound of writhing, broken-limbed female servants who all died within minutes. More than a dozen women were trapped in a wing on the sixth floor, and their plight seemed hopeless until two heroic firemen, Edward Ryemer and Herman Strauss, appeared on the roof of the bank building opposite the hotel and servants' quarters.

Both firemen had tried to reach the upper floors with an extension ladder brought to the scene by their fire company, but the ladder could not be extended to that height, and they took it upon themselves to race up the stairs of a nearby bank building to the roof and attempt rescue from that position. Strauss later stated that he almost went mad hearing the "shrieking and calling for help." He and Ryemer threw up a ladder they carried with them, but the unwieldy thing spun in midair before crashing into a window of the hotel.

Strauss scrambled across this shaky bridge. Below him, thousands witnessed his raw heroism and wildly cheered. While Ryemer held the ladder steady, Strauss loaded a woman on his back and crawled slowly across the ladder to the bank's roof. He made twelve trips across the ladder spanning the alley, each time bringing out a woman dressed in badly singed nightclothes.

A particularly harrowing experience occurred when the last woman fainted as Strauss was halfway across the ladder, one end of which was already burning. As the woman slipped off his back and began to fall, Strauss reached out and caught her by an ankle. She dangled there in midair as bug-eyed spectators gasped. With what must be considered a herculean effort, the fireman pulled her up to the quaking ladder bridge and dragged her to safety. Strauss had performed one of the bravest feats ever accomplished by any fireman and would receive honors and awards for years to come.

Fire Company Number 1 had many heroes that day. A fireman named Van Haag dashed into the hotel and ran to the top floors, knowing the danger was most acute there. As clusters of terrified guests groped their ways through the smoke and mazelike hallways, Van Haag appeared, shouting, "Here! Here! This way!"

When confused guests questioned his ability to get them out, he yelled, "If you value your lives, you'll follow me." Scores did, and he led them to the almost hidden fire escapes. It was Van Haag who was credited with saving the lives of General Tom Thumb and his wife. The celebrated midget, P. T. Barnum's star, was staying at the Newhall that night preparing for a show with his troupe.

Van Haag burst into the performer's suite and swept up both him and his wife. The fireman ran down a burning hallway with the little figures tucked under each arm until he reached a fire escape where others took the celebrities to safety (one performer in the group suffocated).

Milwaukee's Newhall House burned on January 10, 1883. Telegraph wires around the hotel served as deathtraps for those who jumped from upper floors. *(Frank Leslie's Illustrated Newspaper)*

Milwaukee fireman Herman Strauss performed stupendous acts of heroism in the Newhall House blaze of 1883. He is shown here saving one of twelve chambermaids trapped on the roof of the burning hotel. *(From an old print)*

For almost two hours while the entire building was slowly eaten away by flames, Van Haag continued his rescue work until he died in the blaze. His end was spectacular. In full view of the many gaping thousands lining the surrounding streets, a wall of the hotel gave way and the fireman rode it downward, a screeching child held high in his arms. As the brick and plaster and timber toppled into the telegraph wires, Van Haag somehow had the presence of mind to toss the child into an outstretched canvas held by his fellow firemen and the child was saved. He became hopelessly entangled in the wires. As he struggled to get free, two telegraph poles collapsed, crashing directly on top of him and killing this courageous father of nine.

Seventy others lost their lives in this inferno, including Milwaukee business leader Allen Johnson and his wife, who leaped to their deaths from their third-floor rooms; New York capitalist Thomas E. Van Leon; James Vose, a distinguished government engineer; and Mrs. John Gilbert, of Tom Thumb's Madison Square traveling group.

The destruction of the Newhall House was no surprise to William E. Cramer, editor of the *Wisconsin* newspaper. Cramer, severely burned in the fire, had once written that the hotel was "doomed if it ever got on fire in the night."

The tragedy was captioned by the following bit of doggerel, later sold as part of a bizarre souvenir pamphlet:

Milwaukee was excited as it never was before,
On learning that the fire bells all around
Were ringing to eternity a hundred souls or more,
And the Newhall House was burning to the ground.

(ALSO SEE: La Salle Hotel; Winecoff Hotel)

NEW ORLEANS, LOUISIANA — **HURRICANE**, **September 11, 1723**

A violent tropical storm drove inland against New Orleans on September 11, 1723, killing two dozen citizens and obliterating thirty buildings, including a church, most of which were crude wooden structures. Three sailing vessels anchored in the river were quickly sunk by the waves and wind of the gale.

The devastating hurricane did little to improve the lot of the early dwellers in the fledgling city. Historian Charles Gayarre offered an interesting description of the town following the hurricane: "The whole city was surrounded by a large ditch, and fenced in with sharp stakes wedged close together. For the purposes of draining, a ditch ran along the four sides of every square in the city, and every lot in every square was also ditched all round, causing New Orleans to look very much like a microscopic caricature of Venice. Mosquitoes buzzed and enormous frogs croaked incessantly in concert with other indescribable sounds; tall reeds, and grass of every variety, grew in the streets and in the yards, so as to interrupt all communication, and offered a safe retreat and places of concealment to venomous reptiles, wild beasts, and malefactors, who, protected by these impenetrable jungles, committed with impunity all sorts of evil deeds."

NEW ORLEANS, LOUISIANA — **FIRE**, **March 21, 1788**

The exact number of persons killed in the raging fire that swept through New Orleans on the night of March 21, 1788, was never determined although scores were thought to have perished. The conflagration began small: a candle on the altar in the chapel of the home of Don Vincente Nuñez, the military treasurer of the province, was knocked over and set fire to heavy draperies. The house was soon enveloped in flames that spread to nearby buildings, fanned by a strong south wind.

For five hours the fire went unchecked through the heart of the city, gutting 856 buildings, all the stores and homes, except a few along the waterfront. The arsenal blew up. The town hall crumbled into ashes, as did the church, the Capuchin convent and the prison. Matters were intolerable for the citizens of New Orleans because they were caught in their homes without warning; local priests refused to allow the church bells to be rung as an alert because it was Good Friday.

NEW ORLEANS, LOUISIANA — **HURRICANE**, **September 29, 1915**

In the particularly severe hurricane season of 1915, a large storm originating in the Cape Verde region passed the Windward Islands on September 22 and moved onto the Louisiana coast after slicing through the Yucatan Channel. A widespread monster, the storm caused barometers at New Orleans to descend to 28.11 inches at about 7:00 P.M., September 29, 1915, a record low for the United States up to that date. Ninety percent of all buildings at Leeville and along Lake Ponchartrain, and those on the Mississippi below New Orleans were simply blown flat by titanic winds estimated to be between 130 and 140 m.p.h.

New Orleans and its surrounding areas suffered staggering property damage of more than $13 million. Thanks to the extensive warnings of the approaching storm by the United States Weather Bureau, the final death count in the area was limited to 275, but hundreds more were injured at the height of the storm by flying debris.

NEW YORK — MARINE DISASTER
September 6-7, 1846

En route to New Orleans from Galveston, her regular run, the steamer *New York* was caught in the northwestern Gulf of Mexico by a small but extremely violent tropical hurricane and was almost split in two. Of those on board during the storm-lashed night of September 6-7, 1846, an estimated twenty-one persons drowned when the ship foundered.

NEW YORK, NEW YORK — COLLAPSING BUILDING
December 12, 1946

background: An unused ice-manufacturing plant caught fire early on December 12, 1946, and its concrete roof and thirty-six-inch wall collapsed on the rear of an adjoining six-story tenement building at 2515 Amsterdam Avenue at 1:19 A.M., trapping ninety-four residents and killing thirty-seven.

Two young boys started a fire "for fun" early in the evening of December 11, 1946, on the roof of an abandoned icehouse on New York's Amsterdam Avenue, but this blaze was quickly put out. Another fire, beginning in a pipe shaft at the east end of the icehouse, caused rotting wooden timbers supporting the roof to catch fire at about midnight and burn undetected for almost an hour.

The second blaze was discovered by Pasquale Fucci, who lived on the fifth floor of the adjoining tenement at 2515 Amsterdam Avenue. He had smelled smoke as he made his way upstairs, but he did nothing about it and went off to have a cup of coffee with his sister Rose.

The blaze ate its way through the wooden beams supporting the heavy concrete ceiling, which gave way a few minutes after 1:00 A.M., causing the collapse of the thirty-six-inch brick wall, six stories high, which in turn toppled onto and crushed the rear portion of the tenement at 2515 Amsterdam, sending the residents in twelve apartments hurtling downward. Almost one hundred persons were buried under a three-story mound of smoking debris.

Scores of firemen quickly arrived, but they found the job of removing those pinned beneath the rubble almost impossible. Half of the building had been sheared away, revealing kitchen tables set with breakfast dishes. Moans of the trapped occupants in the shattered apartments could be heard from deep beneath the mound of rubble.

One of the first survivors dug out was Paul de Gastani, who was treated at Jewish Memorial Hospital for a compound fracture of the leg, multiple injuries and shock. He told reporters, "All I know now is that flames came shooting up, and it seemed as if lightning had struck us. I fell six stories to the ground and went unconscious. When I came to there was an awful lot of rubbish around me. Some firemen pulled me out."

Edith De Rico was wedged beneath the debris for several hours with a broken leg, but she refused to give up hope of rescue. Near her was her five-year-old daughter Margaret, who cried loudly. As firemen attempted to dig down to her, they heard her repeatedly call out to her daughter, "Keep praying, Margaret. God will take care of us." To a neighbor, Elizabeth Biancardi, trapped nearby in the debris, Mrs. De Rico called out comfort, "Keep up your courage. We'll be all right."

Hours later, thirty-seven-year-old Mrs. Biancardi, mother of six, called back weakly, "I am dying." Nothing was heard from her again. Firemen later recovered her crushed body. Next to her, also dead, was little Lucille Biancardi, her daughter. The child was

Part of a tenement building in New York City collapsed on December 12, 1946, killing thirty-seven persons. *(Wide World)*

clutching a gaily wrapped Christmas present she had saved, a carton of cigarettes intended for her uncle. Edith De Rico and her daughter survived.

Deep in the heap of ruins was a 265-pound chef, Joe Origo, age sixty-five. Firemen heard him calling and began tunneling toward him, shoring up their way as would miners building a mine shaft. Voice contact was maintained with Origo for several hours.

For almost an entire day the race to reach the entombed chef went on. As his moans grew fainter, a Catholic priest, Father Charles Carroll, crawled through the tunnel to a point only six feet from the trapped man. Here he administered Extreme Unction, a rite of the Catholic Church performed when death is close as hand. That night part of the tunnel began to give way and Origo was given up as lost.

In all thirty-seven residents were dead. It had been impossible to reach them before the tons of brick and timber squeezed the life from them.

NEW YORK TELEPHONE COMPANY — EXPLOSION October 3, 1962

background: At 12:07 A.M. on October 3, 1962, a steam boiler exploded in a two-story, yellow-brick and cinder-block building, operated by the New York Telephone Company at 213th Street and Broadway. It hurtled through several walls and a ceiling, killing twenty-three office workers, mostly women, and injuring another ninety-four persons. New York Fire Commissioner Edward Thompson attributed the explosion to overheating "due to the automatic devices which regulate the high and low water level." It was the first time the boiler had been used during a time when the conversion from air conditioning to heat was being made.

"I was sitting at my desk. I heard a big noise. I couldn't breathe. There was steam all over the place. The girls began screaming. We didn't know how to get out. Then we heard a man yell, 'Is anyone there?' " The boiler beneath Dolores Broff's desk in the New York Telephone Company building in mid-Manhattan had exploded, and the one-ton boiler had rocketed through a wall into a cafeteria, where at least 100 workers were eating lunch. It shot upward, punching a twenty-by-twelve-foot hole in the ceiling, slammed downward, and then crashed through another wall into a filing room. Miss Broff was one of the lucky office workers who was not thrown, desk and all, down the hole into the cafeteria.

Hurriedly several men who were phone installers rushed into the office above the cafeteria, calling out to Miss Broff and others. "We started yelling," she said. "He [an installer] told us to grab hands and make a chain. In this way we groped through the steam. One of the girls fell through the floor. Some of the other girls climbed through the windows."

Diane Gerstel, who had been working at the desk next to Miss Broff's, was also one of the fortunate survivors. She explained, "There was a terrific gush of steam. You couldn't see anything. People screamed. The men calmed us down, told us to take it easy. We grabbed one another's arms. We followed the installers out."

Outside the building men were rushing down the streets to the smoking structure. George Haddock, the janitor of a nearby tenement, was sweeping a sidewalk when he heard the terrific roar and looked up to see "lots of smoke, and there were girls jumping from the second floor." He dropped his broom and dashed forward. Running, too, was Robert Roth, an off-duty fireman who had heard of the explosion. His fiancée, Margaret Meyer, was an office worker in the building. She was dead before he got to the front door.

A subway employee, Joe Bartholomew, ran to the building as soon as he heard the roar. Going through the Tenth Avenue entrance, he came upon a grisly scene in the obliterated cafeteria, and he related, "There was tables on top of girls and men and women. We tried to help as many as we could. Four other fellows from the subway were with me." The subway men carried out several girls. They returned to the building, but were driven outside by the mounting heat and smoke.

In the accounting section Raymond Guggolz, a commercial representative for the phone company, stood talking with George T. Forve. Moments after the explosion, he rushed into the stricken area. "Bing, it happened just like that," Guggolz said later. "The place was covered with girls."

He looked down briefly through the jagged hole in the floor to see a grotesque mound of splintered desks jumbled with crushed bodies.

Pat Talbot, a nearby apartment dweller, heard the explosion and thought it sounded like 100,000 back-fires." Talbot ran downstairs and outside to see girls at broken windows "hollering and crying." One girl jumped to the pavement. "She was hurt pretty bad . . . she just lay there on the sidewalk."

Responding to the alarm were massive groups of police and firemen. About 240 policemen and 200 firemen arrived within minutes to aid in rescue operations. It was an hour and a half later, 1:30 P.M., before the fires in the building were brought under control. By then almost 100 persons had been taken to hospitals for treatment; 23 persons were dead. Nineteen of them were women.

The Red Cross responded immediately by sending 107 pints of whole blood to the various hospitals treating the injured.

Twenty-three persons who worked in the offices of a New York Telephone Company building were killed when a boiler blew up. *(Wide World)*

NIOBE — MARINE DISASTER

July 26, 1932

The German naval-training ship *Niobe* was mysteriously lost while on an exercise off Kiel, Germany, on July 26, 1932. Formerly a Norwegian vessel named *Thyholm,* the four-masted sailing ship was capsized by a sudden and extremely violent squall.

So fast did the *Niobe* founder that her skipper never had time to order the lifeboats put over. Fortunately the schooner sank in heavy shipping lanes, and forty sailors were eventually saved; sixty-nine drowned.

(ALSO SEE: Eurydice, *1878)*

NIUAFOU — VOLCANIC ERUPTION

June 24, 1853

Nestled between Samoa and Fiji in the warm waters of the Australian shelf is an odd-looking island made up of the 6,000-foot volcano, Niuafou. Most of the volcano is underwater, and the upper ridges of its crater form a near-perfect ring. It is on this ring that the native Tongans, a Polynesian tribe, live and reap an extraordinarily rich harvest of cocoanuts. The spot is also called Tin Can Island, named for the swimmers who once met the mailboats and towed mail to shore in soldered tin cans. The practice was stopped when one native was attacked and killed by a shark.

Niuafou has been a known source of volcanic activity since 1814, when records were first kept. Dozens of eruptions have been noted, but the volcano's most lethal blast occurred on June 24, 1853. Tribal legend relates that the leader of a dissatisfied faction called upon the gods to destroy his enemies. He resettled his people in the village of Ahua rather than permit them to live under the dictates and taxation of the high chief of Angaha, ruler of the island's main faction.

His prayers were answered on June 24, 1853, when, as one dramatic report states, "The ground opened, and lava spouted up directly under the village headman's house. There were earthquakes and rumblings. The crack extended lengthwise down the village street, and the fiery slag spouted up and flowed down to the sea. Presumably, the eruption was at night, for the headman and many of the natives were trapped and burned. The village was destroyed, and two-thirds of its population were killed."

The death toll caused by lava that flowed at an amazingly fast speed reached seventy. Survivors took refuge on the trembling peaks of the island, which reached upward to 800 feet.

Other notable eruptions on Niuafou include the eighteen-day quakes, beginning on August 31, 1886, which caused much damage but killed no one, and the massive blasts of 1919, 1929 and 1943, which utterly devastated the island but caused few deaths.

(ALSO SEE: Tomboro)

NORGE — MARINE DISASTER

June 28, 1904

The 3,318-ton Danish steamer *Norge,* bound for New York from Copenhagen with 780 immigrant passengers and crew members on board, came to disaster at 7:45 A.M. on June 28, 1904. The captain ran her onto the deadly shoals of Rockall, Scotland, and then compounded his navigational error by ordering his engines reversed. The *Norge* had been severely damaged by the rocks. The skipper should have realized this, but the ship was backed off nevertheless. She quickly filled with water.

The manner of death aboard the sinking *Norge* was a mass drowning for 651 persons, most of whom were panic-stricken immigrants. Most of the crew members behaved badly and took to the lifeboats almost at once, giving no heed to the screaming passengers. Nearby vessels *Energie, Silvia* and *Cervona* picked up 129 survivors.

NORONIC — MARINE DISASTER

September 17, 1949

background: The Great Lakes steamer *Noronic* of the Canada Steamship Lines, Ltd., built in 1913, was a five-deck, 6,905-ton passenger ship. She caught fire at dockside, at Pier Nine in Toronto, Canada, a stopover anchorage, on September 17, 1919. Of the 695 persons on board the ship at the time, 118 perished. (The official death count is 104, with 14 listed as missing two months later.) The cost of the ship, which was totally ruined, was $3.5 million.

The inland passenger steamers, *Noronic, Hamonic,* and *Huronic,* all sister ships operated by the Canada Steamship Lines, were familiar sights on the Great Lakes. First to succumb to disaster was the *Hamonic,* which was destroyed at dock by fire at Point Edward, Ontario, on July 17, 1945. The ship's combustible construction was amply illustrated by the flames that quickly gutted the vessel. Miraculously only one of the 360 passengers and crew members aboard the *Hamonic* was killed. Such was not the fate of those sailing on the *Noronic* four years later.

Though the *Noronic* was a steel-hulled ship with steel decks supported by steel stanchions, she was still a floating tinder box. All of her stateroom partitions were heavily painted plywood on wood studs. There was no sprinkler system on board, and the firefighting equipment had not been checked and maintained. The crew members were slack and had little idea of what to do in case of a fire. Crew members, from first officer on down, were merely given a card telling them how to blow the ship's whistle—one long, three short, one long—in the event of a fire emergency. The 362-foot vessel had no vertical fire bulkheads. Most of the decks were wooden planks; ceilings were covered with either canvas or masonite, and combustible furniture and fixtures cluttered every public room on the ship. There were no automatic fire-detection or fire-alarm devices on the *Noronic,* and, in the words of the *NFPA Quarterly,* "The small congested cabins provided a 'forest' of timber within the steel shell and between the steel decks." In addition long, narrow promenade walks on four decks and a large, open-well area running downward through all decks provided draft funnels that whipped the fire along, accompanied by a 12 m.p.h. southwest wind. Obviously the *Noronic* met few if any of the fire prevention standards then regulating ships.

In 1949 the passenger vessel was running between Windsor, Ontario, and Detroit, Michigan, to Duluth, Minnesota. This route was abandoned for a seven-day excursion tour to the Thousand Islands and Prescott, Ontario, which was to end in Detroit in September. At 6:00 P.M., on September 16, the *Noronic* arrived at Toronto, a layover port, and docked at Pier Nine. Most of the 171 crew members went ashore, including the captain, William Taylor; the majority of the 524 passengers remained on board, where several parties were being held.

At about 1:30 A.M. on the seventeenth, a passenger named Church stepped out on C deck for some air. He noticed a haze accumulating in the aft part of the starboard corridor. He walked toward the haze and realized at once that smoke was coming from the sides and top of a linen locker adjacent to the women's washroom. The locker contained towels, bed linen and soap and brushes used by the cleaning women. There was also a large carton inside where paper rubbish was dumped. On many occasions, maids had been observed smoking cigarettes in this closet, but they had never been reprimanded.

Church attempted to open the locker, a mistake made aboard so many other ships destroyed by fire. (It is always preferable to contain the fire and not allow it to feed on air and spread by opening compartments already on fire.) Church tugged violently at the linen locker doors, but they would not open, so he ran shouting for help. The ship's head bellboy, O'Neill, answered his call, and together they ran back to the locker and forced it open. Using two small fire extinguishers, they attempted to douse the flames, which were shooting outward and igniting the wooden decks and window casements. Oddly neither man thought to rouse the ship's fifteen-man fire squad until it was too late.

Running aft, Church and O'Neill yanked a hose from a hydrant and rushed forward to the fast-spreading flames. When Church opened the valve to the hose, no water came out. He threw down the hose and said to O'Neill, "This fire is out of control." With that, he departed.

It was a full eight minutes after his discovery of the blaze before it occurred to O'Neill to send out the alarm to crew members and officers. He broke the fire-alarm glass at approximately 1:30 A.M. The Toronto Fire Department was immediately notified. It rushed units to Pier Nine, and called in a fire boat located about a mile and a half away.

The passengers, most of whom were asleep in their cabins, had yet to be aroused. This was done haphazardly by crew members, who acted more or less on their own, without official guidance. As startled passengers ran to the bow and stern of the burning ship, Captain Taylor arrived. He had been ashore celebrating with a passenger, and many of the frightened tourists, watching his erratic actions, later claimed that he was drunk. This was never proved, although the skipper did admit to having had "one drink" while ashore.

Taylor's actions were, at least, suspicious. He failed to arouse passengers or to organize an orderly evacuation of the ship. Instead, according to some witnesses, he ran around the decks, smashing in windows with standpipe hoses and shouting incoherently. Authorities later concluded that "in doing so, he acted more as a crew member than as the Master of the vessel."

Passengers scrambled either to safety or to death on their own. One passenger, hearing a racket in the hall, jumped from his berth, in his pajamas, and opened the door. The hallway was filled with smoke, and shouting and crying passengers were streaming past him. He turned for a moment to snatch up some clothing before stepping into the hall. In those few seconds the corridor had become a blazing inferno, filled with collapsed, agonized people whose clothes were aflame. The man slammed his stateroom door and smashed out a porthole, escaping with only minor cuts.

Many people were jumping from the decks into the water. Others jumped onto the dock, breaking and cracking ankles and legs. The fire department had drawn up several ladders at District Chief Stevens's orders. Firemen could see the brightly illuminated decks awash with flames and through them the silhouettes of passengers running. A group of passengers knotted at the bow and a long, wooden ladder was thrown up to them. A woman and five men began to scramble downward. Halfway down the woman faltered; the men jammed up on top of her, and the ladder broke, spilling all of them into the water. Using other ladders and hooks, firemen pulled them out.

Chief Stevens ordered a steel aerial to be placed about ninety feet off the bow of the ship, and using this as a ladder, firemen clambered up to take off dozens of stunned passengers. A fireboat came alongside the sizzling *Noronic* and began to pump tons of water into her. On the dock a dozen powerful hoses sprayed the ship, but she was beyond saving.

So intense was the fire that the steamers *Kingston* and *Cayuga,* also docked at Pier Nine, had to be moved so that they would not catch fire. The 115 firemen and 9 officers fought the blaze for two hours, but their progress was impeded by cars parked near the pier. They poured 1.7 million gallons of water on the flames, but it was useless. The *Noronic* was gone by sunrise.

It became the grisly chore of firemen to search the cinders for bodies. One hundred four corpses, reduced almost to sludge by the searing fire, were shoveled up and taken off. Another 14 persons were never found, bringing the count of fatalities in this near-criminal disaster to 118. Scores were seriously burned.

As in the case of the *Morro Castle,* the *Noronic* disaster led to a stiffening of fire regulations and safety measures aboard ships that sailed the Great Lakes.

(ALSO SEE: Morro Castle)

NORTH AFRICA — EARTHQUAKE

June, 217 B.C.

North Africa suffered what most historians describe as "the greatest shaking recorded in her history" when a massive earthquake rattled the northern rim of the continent. This happened in early June, 217 B.C., at about the same time that the Carthaginian general, Hannibal, was exterminating the Roman legions of Gaius Flaminius at Trasimeno Lake.

More than 100 cities in North Africa were smashed, and about 50,000 to 75,000 persons were killed outright. Several cities in Italy, where "lakes and streams tumbled from their beds," were also affected by the quake, but loss of life was minimal.

NORTH CAROLINA — HURRICANE

September 16-17, 1713

One of the earliest hurricanes recorded in North Carolina was the storm that sliced inland, accompanied by massive winds, on September 16-17, 1713. Extensive damage was done at Charleston and throughout the Cape Fear area. Port Royal was also touched by the storm.

An early chronicler, Mark Catesby, wrote in that year, "Some low-situated houses [in Charleston] not far from the sea were undermined and carried away with the inhabitants; ships were drove from their anchors far within land, particularly a sloop in North Carolina was drove three miles over marshes into the woods."

Catesby, traveling in the Bahamas some years later, discovered a large boat jammed ten feet up in a tree and attributed this to the 1713 hurricane.

The sheer force of this hurricane is demonstrated in a report telling of an eighty-foot lighthouse on Sullivan's Island that was snapped in two by the gale.

In this sparsely settled colonial area, the number of deaths caused by the storm was considered enormous; an estimated seventy persons, a conservative figure, were drowned.

NORTHEAST AIRLINES — AIR CRASH
February 1, 1957

background: Northeast Airlines Flight 823, a DC-6A, was Miami-bound on the afternoon of February 1, 1957. It took off from La Guardia Airport in snow and fog, and minutes later it crashed into Rikers Island, which housed the New York City Penitentiary. Of the 101 on board at the time, 22 persons were killed and the remainder escaped with injuries. The crash was attributed to pilot error.

After waiting three hours to take off from La Guardia Airport, which was enveloped in snow and fog, Flight 823 of Northeast Airlines was finally given a go-ahead to proceed. At the controls of the Miami-bound DC-6A was Captain Alva V. Marsh, who had been with the airlines for nineteen years.

The passengers had become jittery during the long wait. One woman had cried to Stewardess Doris Steele, "I want to get off the plane. I'll go to Florida some other time."

Miss Steele responded by quietly telling the woman, who was more exasperated than frightened, "Of course, that's your privilege, but it will mean taking off baggage and delaying the flight even more." The woman was pacified.

Night fell before Runway Four could be cleared. It was 5:45 P.M. when Flight 823 began to taxi down the runway.

Air Traffic Control radioed, "Flight 823, you are cleared to Bellmead. Maintain 7,000 feet." Captain Marsh and his copilot, Basil Dixwell, raced the engines and were soon on the runway and in the air at 125 m.p.h. As the plane climbed, Marsh went over the instruments. At that time both pilots thought the craft was at 300 feet. Moments later Dixwell saw what appeared to be trees or telephone poles in the plane's path and shouted to Marsh, "Al, the ground!"

On a previous occasion Marsh had slammed into the treacherous night waters of the East River in a small Convair 240 (all passengers survived). This time such was his confusion that he saw the trees and poles and thought he was about to crash somewhere in the Bronx. In reality the lurching DC-6A was heading downward onto Rikers Island, the stark buildings of the New York City Penitentiary looming in the distance.

Prison guards saw the plane's lights flickering and watched open-mouthed as it crashed to earth, its wings sheared away by trees and poles, its flaming fuselage sliding sickeningly forward. Angel Corbea, an inmate guard, and trustee, saw the plane's left wing rip away and explode, leaving a jagged hole in the side of the burning plane. "The whole sky, even through the snow, was lighted," Corbea recalled. "We saw the people tumbling out of that ship—they were all lighted, too, by the flames. We saw them and their shadows. We saw them stumble. We saw some fall, we saw some just jump out, land on their hands and knees, and then get up and run. They slipped on the snow. They beat at themselves because maybe their clothes were burning. Some just ran a few feet from the plane and rolled in the snow, as they were trying to smother the fire on their clothes."

On impact Stewardess Catherine Virchow, who was to be married soon and was on her last flight, was standing midway in the aircraft. She noticed that passengers still had their seat belts fastened (which, no doubt, contributed to the great number of survivors). She was hurtled forward suddenly as the plane crunched to a stop. In the darkness, pierced only by the light of the flaming engines, Virchow heard another stewardess, Doris Steele, call out, "Over here! Over here! This way, folks!" Steele had coolly groped her way to an emergency exit and forced open the door. Dozens of bruised and bleeding passengers ran forward, including Selma and Kenneth Kronen. They were carrying their two sons, Rickie and Mark.

When the plane crashed six-week-old Mark Kronen was thrown out of his father's arms, but, in spite of the darkness, Kronen quickly retrieved his son. His wife scooped up two-year-old Rickie, and the family tried to squeeze through a window that had been smashed, but the opening was too small. As flames began to close in on them, Kronen heard Steele's voice, and he led his family to the emergency door.

The brave stewardess, with flames at her back, stood calmly at the open door, directing terrified passengers with a confident "This way out." The Kronens reached the door, flames jetting all about them. "I threw Mark out into the snow," Kronen later told reporters through his face bandages, "while my wife got out with Rickie. When I jumped, my hair and hands were on fire. I rolled in the snow and I think that saved me."

Those who had gathered at the main entrance found that the door had jammed, crumpled by the buckled body of the plane. Many turned away from this door, but one passenger, Abraham Ball, was so crazed by the fires and his flaming clothes that he savagely kicked the door out and dove into a snowbank. A prison guard dragged him away from the wreck.

Captain Marsh, Dixwell and the flight engineer battered out a window in the cockpit and let themselves down into the snow. They were all unharmed. Quickly they ran to the aid of passengers who were jumping through the jagged hole in the side of the plane.

Relatives of those on board the ill-fated plane gathered at the Marine Air Terminal and bombarded officials with questions about their loved ones. Robert Selmonsky begged sailors en route to Rikers Island to allow him aboard their cutter, but he was refused. It would be several hours of agonized waiting before he learned that his wife, Sandra, and two-year-old son, Gary, had miraculously survived the crash.

It was a different story for the twenty-two other passengers who had been burned to death or killed on impact. Seventy-nine others lived. Captain Marsh was ultimately held responsible for the crash.

Stewardess Virchow, who had escaped through an emergency door, sighed heavily when reporters questioned her just after the crash and then said, "I don't think I'll want to keep flying."

NORTHEAST AIRLINES — AIR CRASH

August 15, 1958

To the thirty-three passengers and crew members of the twin-engine Convair, Flight 258 of Northeast Airlines, the landing at Nantucket Island, on August 15, 1958, was routine. Everyone, including Gordon Dean, former chairman of the Atomic Energy Commission, were vacation-bound to the sunny Atlantic-swept holiday island. Dean had been commuting every two weeks to be with his wife at their summer home.

Preparatory to landing, Pilot John Burnham banked the plane slightly to the left, as he had done dozens of times before. But there was fog rolling thickly over the area, and the airport was ringed by dense forests of scrub pine. Burnham somehow missed the airstrip and went into the trees. The Convair furrowed through the trees for 500 feet and then burst into flames. The fuselage cracked open, and the passengers were scattered.

Brooklyn attorney Paul Kozinn knew something was wrong when the plane descended rapidly and he "felt something scraping on the bottom of the plane. It felt like a rough landing strip. . . . Next thing I knew I was on the ground, ten feet from the plane . . . I heard people moaning and women calling for help."

Help came in the persons of Thomas Gibson, who was Nantucket's airport manager, and several ground crew members who rushed to the scene. "I can still hear their screams," Gibson later remembered, "like they had been through hell." Using cranes, rescuers quickly began to lift heavy chunks of debris from three trapped persons. One woman upon whom a burned out engine rested screamed, "Why don't you kill me?" She survived along with eight others, but Dean, Harvey Schwamm (the Wall Street broker) and twenty-two others were dead. Investigation of this crash proved fruitless, and the pilot's misdirection was attributed to a lack of communication. The control tower had warned Burnham about the fog, but he had failed to respond by radio, indicating an apparent malfunction of equipment.

NORTHFLEET — MARINE DISASTER

January 22, 1873

A series of mishaps dogged the British passenger frigate *Northfleet,* which had been constructed in 1853, for Far East service. On June 13, 1862, the vessel was caught by large waves that washed away several of her crew members. On many occasions, water had gushed through weak areas of the hull and ruined the cargo.

The ship's bad luck tragically returned on January 22, 1873, while she was enroute to Tasmania with a large number of immigrants. Off Dungeness the Spanish steamer *Murillo* collided with the *Northfleet,* which broke up almost immediately, sending the captain, Knowles, and 299 others to their watery deaths.

NORTHWEST AIRLINES — AIR CRASH

June 24, 1950

The downpour of rain was heavy as thirty-five-year-old Captain Robert Lind piloted a Northwest Airlines DC-4 across Lake Michigan, on June 24, 1950. His flight had begun in New York, and he had just passed over Battle Creek, Michigan. His destination, and that of fifty-five passengers and two other crew members, was Seattle with a layover in Minneapolis.

As the storm closed in, Lind asked a ground station if he might be allowed to drop to 2,500 feet from his present altitude of 3,500 feet. The answer was negative. There was too much traffic at that altitude.

Lind then told ground control that he was leaving the shoreline near South Haven, Michigan. It was the last message ever received from the plane. In hours hundreds of planes and ships were searching frantically for the lost Northwest flight. The destroyer escort *Daniel A. Joy* finally located floating debris and an oil slick.

Almost a week later, a Milwaukee diver, Jack Browne, descended at the spot where the oil slick had been sighted and brought up the first of the fifty-eight bodies from the plane's watery grave.

The cause of the crash, the most disastrous in commercial aviation to that date, was never determined.

NORTHWEST AIRLINES — AIR CRASH
March 17, 1960

On March 17, 1960, Northwest Airlines Flight 710, from Chicago to Miami, became another victim of the weak wing structures of Lockheed's turboprop Electra class. At about 3:15 A.M., as the plane droned its way over Tell City, Indiana, at 18,000 feet, farmer Albert Harper looked skyward. He thought he had heard shotgun blasts.

One of the wings had torn away, and the prop had exploded, sending the luxury airliner in a straight death plunge to earth, at a speed of 600 m.p.h. From his back porch, farmer Theodore Wilson saw the plane plummet. He knew no one could have lived through such a dive or through the subsequent explosion, which created a deep crater in the middle of a field.

All sixty-three persons on board were killed instantly. Their bodies were hardly recognizable to those who rushed vainly to the rescue. The passenger list of Flight 710 was impressive. Among the dead were R. L. Oare, the millionaire, and Chicago Superior Court Judge John A. Sbarbaro, whose funeral home had once held services for notorious gangsters of the 1920's, such as Dion O'Bannion, Earl "Hymie" Weiss, and Vincent "The Schemer" Drucci. Also on board were Mrs. Morris Chalfen, the wife of the producer of *Holiday on Ice,* her children, and Andy Frain's wife, Dolly.

A gaping, steaming hole in the ground at Tell City, Indiana, marks the place where an American Airlines Electra crashed on March 17, 1960, taking the lives of all sixty-three persons on board. *(Wide World)*

It would be long months before Lockheed would discover that its Electras had wings that broke under certain types of flight vibrations. More Electras, like Flight 710, would crash before that knowledge surfaced.

NORTHWEST AIRLINES — AIR CRASH
September 17, 1961

The crew and passengers on board a Northwest Airlines Electra that crashed in Chicago, Illinois, on September 17, 1961, hardly knew what hit them. The plane, having made twenty-nine scheduled flights in two months, was structurally weak; an aileron safety cable had worked itself slowly out of place with each flight. Mechanics of several ground crews neglected to check the gradually weakening boost assembly; their collective excuse at subsequent hearings was that they had no Electra manuals telling them to fix the part.

The flight crew of five and the thirty-two passengers took off in Chicago and rose to an altitude of 200 feet. When the pilot began a severe bank, the plane drastically lost altitude, slashed a power line, dove into a railway embankment, and then horribly cartwheeled forward, exploding into fiery pieces—all in less then three minutes. Everyone on board died instantly.

Experts later studied a garbled tape that had been retrieved from the wreckage. The tape proved that, though the crew had fought for their lives, there had been no time to prevent the crash. A high-pitched voice on the tape, probably the captain's, said, "We're in trouble—uh and all units holding this is Northwest alert—I still don't have release—right turn—in no control—CAN YOU?—HAVE YOU? . . ."

NORTHWEST AIRLINES — AIR CRASH
February 12, 1963

Departing from Miami, at 1:35 P.M. on February 12, 1963, a Northwest Orient Airlines flight ran into heavy turbulence from stormy weather. The pilot reported that the weather looked "pretty bad" as he climbed through buffeting winds to 17,500 feet.

Fourteen minutes later this aircraft and all forty-three persons on board crashed in a flaming mass in the Everglades National Park, about forty miles from Miami International Airport. The subsequent inquiry into the crash became what one expert termed, "an investigator's nightmare."

After studying the wreck and the violent weather conditions of that day, authorities lamely blamed the disaster on "man-machine environment." This ambiguity meant that the pilot had fought his aircraft, which

Only fragments remain of a Northwest Airlines plane which crashed in the Everglades on February 12, 1963. Forty-three persons died. *(Wide World)*

was being directed by the storm, instead of "swinging with the blows." It was surmised that he had forced the nose of the aircraft down against a violent updraft in order to maintain his altitude, an act that caused him to go into an uncontrollable crash dive.

NORTHWEST AIRLINES — AIR CRASH
June 3, 1963

It was 10:06 A.M. on June 3, 1963, when Captain Albert F. Olsen, pilot of a military-chartered flight of Northwest Airlines, radioed the air station at Sandspit, British Columbia. He asked the air station, located on the east coast of Graham Island, for permission to change altitude—from 14,000 to 18,000 feet. Sandspit told Captain Olsen to stand by while clearance was okayed by Elmendorf Air Force Base in Anchorage, Alaska, the piston-engined DC-7's destination.

A Pacific Northern Airlines plane, Flight 5, was already at 18,000 feet, headed north on the same route, and only five minutes behind Olsen. When Sandspit went on the air again, to okay an altitude of 16,000 feet, there was no answer. Sandspit tried again and again, even asking the Pacific Northern Airlines plane to try to contact the Northwest craft. Nothing.

While this was going on, a period of four or five minutes, a fishing boat off Anchorage had picked up a sputtering, static-crossed message, that was probably Olsen's voice, saying, "This is DC-7—emergency!" That was all.

Planes and ships began a frantic search for the Northwest plane that had left McChord Air Force Base in Washington at 7:30 that morning carrying ninety-five military passengers, including dependents, and a crew of six. Twelve United States planes, six Coast Guard cutters, and three Royal Canadian Air Force planes scoured the area. One of the Canadian planes reported sighting uninflated life rafts, floating seats, torn pillows, suitcases and other wreckage off Graham Island, but there was no sign of life.

Authorities held out hope and rushed Coast Guard vessels to the site. Other amazing rescues had been achieved when planes had gone down in the sea. All 57 passengers on a flight that crashed in the Pacific in July, 1960, had been saved. Another Northwest military charter plane, a DC-7C, had ditched in the Pacific near Sitka on October 22, 1962, and cutters arrived before the plane sank and rescued all 102 persons on board.

This kind of near-miraculous rescue, however, was not to occur for the 1963 flight. The cutters that arrived to search the area for survivors were hampered by increasing darkness, mist and fog, and a running sea whipped by 55-knot winds. The futile search was soon given up, and the 101 persons on board the Northwest flight were considered lost forever.

NOTRE DAME DU LAC, CANADA — FIRE
December 2, 1969

A nursing home in tiny Notre Dame du Lac, Canada, (population 2,200, fifteen miles from the northernmost tip of Maine) suddenly caught fire on the night of December 2, 1969. Unknown causes were blamed for the destruction of the three-story, all wooden structure, built as a school in 1894. About seventy elderly men and women, twenty of whom were too crippled to escape the flames without help, were trapped.

The fire alarm was set off at 6:00 A.M., but when Fire Chief Joe Gagnon arrived minutes later, the heat was so intense that he had to park his car several hundred feet away from the flaming building. "When I got there," he later recalled, "it was already too late. We could hear screams and moans."

Staggering down the hilly lawn was seventy-six-year-old August Blanchard. He had tried but failed to save an old woman who struggled free and ran back into the blaze. "She wanted to get her money, but I don't think she made it out. The place was filled with smoke. I got out by the fire escape."

The entire population of the town turned out to aid those trapped inside the ancient nursing home, but it was already hopeless just minutes after the fire began. Marjorie Bergeron, who lived near the home, ran to the scene after she had been awakened by frantic calls for help. "They were yelling, 'My God, they're trapped! Good God, do something!' "

"They had no chance," reported a Catholic priest, the Reverend Fortunat Blanchet.

There were twenty-nine badly burned survivors; thirty-eight died in the fire. At least that was the number of bodies finally found in the ashes of the leveled nursing home.

(ALSO SEE: Cleveland Clinic)

NOVA SCOTIA, CANADA — HURRICANE
August 24-25, 1873

Known as the Great Nova Scotia Hurricane, the storm that ravaged the ports in this province of Canada had taken a great toll of shipping and of seamen's lives before it ever turned inland. In its wake 190 vessels of all types were lost, either by foundering or by simply being ripped in half.

The hurricane swept inland and up the Gulf of St. Lawrence on August 24-25, 1873. It utterly destroyed the harbors of Nova Scotia, Cape Breton and Newfoundland. In these ports, 1,032 ships, of which only 35 were small fishing schooners, were demolished. Property damage alone reached $5 million, and a conservative death toll estimated 600 lives lost. Most of these were ships' crew members.

NOVEDADES THEATER — FIRE
September 22, 1928

background: The ornate, wooden Novedades Theater, the largest in Madrid, was built in 1860 and had a seating capacity of 3,200. It caught fire on the night of September 22, 1928, when flammable scenery was ignited; 110 persons burned and suffocated and another 350 people were injured. Damage was total, estimated at a million pesatas (about $165,000), a fourth of which was covered by insurance.

The Novedades Theater, the most popular theater in Madrid, Spain, had been standing for seventy-eight years when a flash fire raced through its ancient, rotting scenery and set it ablaze on the evening of September 22, 1928. The theater was almost filled to its 3,200-seat capacity, but fortunately most of the orchestra patrons were promenading at the time of the fire's outbreak.

Those in the upper galleries, all working-class spectators, suffered the most. They were in their seats when a short circuit near the ceiling and next to flammable scenery created fire in the wooden rafters. Seeing the flash of flames, the gallery audience began to panic. Men, women and children spilled over the railings and dropped to their deaths on the floor below.

A report from a *New York Times* correspondent said that "many persons mad with terror tried to fight their way out stabbing with knives right and left or biting, scratching or shoving aside weaker persons in their way." These were fathers insane with the desire to save their children. But for most, such barbaric action was fruitless. The two narrow stairways leading from the gallery were soon choked with people struggling and unable to move, their bodies wedged between the burning wooden walls.

It was only a matter of minutes before the entire inside of the theater was afire, but the performing troupe, changing costumes for the next act of the light opera, were saved by exiting, half-dressed, from their dressing rooms.

There were repeated acts of bravery to offset the cowardice and, in some cases, outright barbarity of the panicking crowd. An elderly man was seen turning back to lead out several children before he himself perished in the flames. Other men held children aloft and sent them to safety over the heads of those on the stairways. An usherette kept a flashlight shining on one of the few exits, enabling scores to flee; she was enveloped in flames and was found later dead, still holding the flashlight.

Rescuers and firemen arrived at the scene only minutes after the blaze had begun, but their mission was hopeless. The old theater was a firetrap, and its creaking, dry timbers and wooden walls burned in seconds. There was nothing to do but wait for the fire to go out. Streets surrounding the theater were so narrow that no ladders could be raised to those who had managed to reach the

Police and firemen search for the remains of 110 persons who burned to death in the Novedades Theater in Madrid, September 22, 1928. *(Wide World)*

upper-story windows. Here, scores yelled for help and, driven senseless as the flames licked at them, dove headlong into the street and to their deaths.

When firemen did work their way into the smoldering ruins, they found pitiful heaps of dead. Groups of twenty and thirty persons, almost welded together by the intensely hot fire, were found beneath collapsed stairways, and others were discovered in front of fire exits that had been jammed by bodies.

Spanish dictator Primo de Rivera visited the scene three times, directing the removal of the 110 bodies found in the gutted theater and of the 350 severely injured persons saved from the blaze. At each visit he was overcome by the staggering loss of life, which forced him, repeatedly, to retreat to an auto parked nearby, where he plied himself with wine.

Morgue scenes found relatives frantically attempting to identify dozens of bodies, most of which were charred beyond recognition. One young man, his clothes all but burned away, sorrowfully identified the bodies of his wife and six children.

(ALSO SEE: Igolkino, Russia; Iroquois Theater; Laurier Palace Theater)

NUESTRA SEÑORA DE LA CONCEPCION — MARINE DISASTER — November 1, 1643

The *Nuestra Señora de la Concepcion,* flagship of the Spanish silver fleet, departed from Havana for Spain on September 13, 1643. A week or so later, the ship, with 514 passengers and crew members aboard, was caught in a shuddering hurricane north of Hispaniola. The lumbering galleon, heavily laden with casks of silver, had trouble with a rotting hull even before the storm. Her weak timbers were quickly snapped by the winds and waves, and on November 1, the ship was eventually driven onto the treacherous coral heads of the Ambrosian Banks. The Spanish had named these reefs, which extended from the Bahamas, *Los Abreojos*—the shoals of "Watch Out."

The *Nuestra Señora* quickly settled, bow first, to the bottom. Her crew members and captain scurried for longboats into which they threw much of the silver treasure. Of those on board the doomed vessel, 324 perished in the waters churling about the reefs while squads of soldiers were dragged to the bottom by their heavy armor.

O

O-9

MARINE DISASTER
June 16, 1941

background: On the morning of June 16, 1941, the 480-ton, 172-foot United States Navy submarine, *O-9,* built in 1918, submerged with two sister submarines while on maneuvers east of Portsmouth, New Hampshire, but failed to resurface. Divers discovered the vessel three days later, and the thirty-three-man crew was then given up for lost. The cause of this sinking was never determined.

An inside view of the United States Navy's *O-9;* all thirty-three men aboard died when the aging submarine failed to resurface after test dives near Portsmouth, New Hampshire, on June 16, 1941. *(Wide World)*

It was dangerous duty, and the thirty-three-member crew on board the ancient, leak-spouting United States submarine, *O-9,* knew it. Originally designed for duty in World War I, the sub and several others of her type, the smallest and oldest class made, had been taken out of moth balls in the Philadelphia navy yard, where they had rested in their berths from 1930 to 1940, and had been recommissioned. The threat of war was close at hand for the United States, and finding its depleted navy wanting, the government resurrected every derelict that could float.

In the *O-9's* first shallow water test dive, the relic groaned and creaked. "Everything went wrong," Seaman Charles L. Eagleton wrote to his father. Another test provoked Seaman Francis Golden to write home, describing the nineteen leaks breaking through the old sub's hull: "Water poured into her right away."

In the company of two other submarines, the *O-8* and *O-10,* the *O-9* gave off her throaty huff and slid beneath the blue-black waves glistening beneath the sun. They were fifteen miles southeast of the naval station at Portsmouth, New Hampshire, on June 16, 1941. Final diving tests for the three subs began at 8:36 A.M., and for the *O-9* ended forever three days later. The sub ran downward beyond the eight reefs that jut out from the Isle of Shoals. Exactly two hours later the *O-8* and *O-10* broke the surface, their sister sub still somewhere below. Four minutes after the deadline an urgent wire was sent to headquarters that the *O-9* was in trouble.

Even after repeated signals, no answer came from the sub's commander, Lieutenant Howard J. Abbott, an officer with four years' experience. A Navy flotilla of subs, destroyers, and tugs raced out of Boston's Squantum Naval Base. Squadrons of naval planes flew sorties over the watery place where the two other submarines waited. The diving bell, which had gone to aid the stricken *Squalus* two years before and had managed to save thirty-three sailors, was rushed from the New London navy yard.

Dozens of ships assembled in the area. Night fell, and scores of searchlights played eerily about the pitching waters. By that time there seemed to be little hope. The rescue tender *Falcon* had already picked up strange debris floating to the surface—painted cork from the sub's inner walls and gratings of her deck. An oil slick and air bubbles were spotted, and these were thought to have emanated from a depth of 67 fathoms. It was then that naval officials concluded that their task was hopeless. The *Squalus* rescue of 1939 had been achieved at 240 feet, but 67 fathoms was a depth of 402 feet, 152 feet below the maximum pressure that the *O-9* was built to withstand.

But there had been a miscalculation. Hours later the *O-9* was found at 73 fathoms, 440 feet down, where the 200-pounds-per-square-inch pressure could only mean one thing. As one writer said, "The old *O-9* must have folded bow to stern, like an accordion."

The Navy continued its fruitless attempts to reach the sub. Diver George Crocker almost died. As he was sliding down a grapnel line to 370 feet, his special mixture of helium and oxygen, which kept nitrogen out of the bloodstream and forestalled the bends, began to fail him.

Two more divers descended to the bottom where they could see, just barely, the crumpled form of the sub resting in the murky deep. On June 18 the Navy gave up hope of bringing the *O-9* to the surface and Admiral Stark, Chief of Naval Operations, announced, "The decision must be to accept the situation as loss of naval personnel at sea, who can best be honored as men still at their station of duty. Not one of them would expect or wish another naval man to risk his life to provide another final resting place."

In front of the reporters who had gathered in a sleepless vigil in the press room at the Portsmouth base, a Navy officer threw the ship's file onto a table, grimaced, and said, "Well, boys, that's the end of the *O-9*."

(ALSO SEE: Squalus*)*

OAKLAND COUNTY, MICHIGAN — TORNADO

May 25, 1896

A devastating tornado, moving along a half-mile path, struck eastward across Oakland County, Michigan, at about 6:00 P.M. on May 25, 1896. Ortonville was demolished along with the hamlets of Oakwood and Thomas; the twister barely missed striking the outskirts of Detroit. Forty-seven died, the highest death toll caused by a tornado up to that time, and the record of damage stood until funnel clouds appeared over Port Huron, Michigan, almost six decades later. (The Port Huron twister would be the state's most destructive, creating $2.5 million in damages.)

Hundreds of houses were smashed to pieces. One was blown several hundred yards from its foundation. The force of the wind was such that a piano was torn from a building and sent flying some blocks away. It was later found with grass driven through it like nails. The twister caused more than $400,000 in damages, a sum that would approximate at least $1 million today.

OAKLEY PRISON FARM — FIRE

July 21, 1913

Twenty miles outside of Jackson, Mississippi, squatted the crudely constructed, hazard-ridden Oakley Prison Farm. There, thirty-five black convicts, locked up in a fire trap, roasted to death during a blazing fire on the night of July 21, 1913. The rotting lumber used to construct the two-story jailhouse had been taken from a discarded penitentiary in 1903.

The ground floor of the building contained highly flammable materials. The prisoners, who slept on the floorboards of the second story, were trapped at the fire's outset when the only stairway leading to the first floor flamed up. As the fire consumed the jail, the convicts, shouting for help, tore wildly at the prison bars covering the upstairs windows. It was to no purpose.

As one report all too vividly described, "Their screams brought guards and other prison attachés, but the flames drove back members of the rescue party each time they attempted to liberate the Negroes, who one by one fell back into the flames and perished."

Farmers from miles around came to witness the event. They stood in the flickering glare of the crackling flames as the convicts, used as slave labor in the cotton fields, died. "Among them were some desperate criminals," concluded the *New York Times.*

(ALSO SEE: Ohio State Penitentiary)

OAXACA, MEXICO — EARTHQUAKE

May 11-12, 1870

One of the most severe earthquakes in Mexico's quake-plagued nineteenth century occurred around the city of Oaxaca on the night of May 11, 1870. Minor shocks continued until dawn of the following day. Half the town was razed, and more than 100 persons were crushed under falling buildings.

OCEAN MONARCH — MARINE DISASTER

August 28, 1848

The overcrowded immigrant ship *Ocean Monarch,* typical of a day when mariners trafficked in cheap human freight, set sail from Liverpool to New York on August 28, 1848. The vessel, with 396 passengers and crew members aboard, never got beyond the River Mersey.

Fire broke out on the *Ocean Monarch* a few miles down river, and the flames soon burned away the topsails. Flaming canvas and falling masts crashed downward, sending terrified passengers overboard to quick drownings. As the ship began to settle, it became evident that no boats could be lowered because the main decks were on fire. Several vessels in the area appeared and took off scores of people, but 178 persons had by then been drowned or roasted to death.

OCRACOKE BAR, NORTH CAROLINA — HURRICANE
September 1-3, 1772

After mauling the western Florida coastline, a ponderous hurricane moved across Florida on September 1-3, 1772. It stalked the eastern seaboard, where many early colonial settlements were located, striking hard near Edenton, North Carolina, and doing its worst damage off Ocracoke Bar. Here fourteen or fifteen ships, many of them large frigates, were lifted bodily from their anchorages and hurled inland for several miles. A conservative estimate placed the death count at fifty persons, most of whom were sailors.

OERAEFA JÖKULL — VOLCANIC ERUPTION
A.D. 1362

Little is known about the pre-eighteenth-century eruptions of the many volcanoes on Iceland. The population was sparse then, and there were few inhabitants, mostly farmers, who cared to record, let alone witness, such murderous outbreaks. It is known, however, that Iceland's loftiest peak, Oeraefa Jökull, exploded with monstrous force sometime in 1362, and the resulting flash floods of melted ice and snow swept away forty to fifty farms and large herds of livestock. Loss of life was estimated to be about 200.

OGDEN, UTAH — RAILWAY WRECK
December 31, 1944

background: A two-part train, the Pacific Limited of the Southern Pacific line, crashed outside of Ogden, Utah, early on the morning of December 31, 1944. The second twenty-car section rear-ended the first eighteen-car section, which had slowed down for a stalled freight; fifty persons were killed, and eighty were injured.

It was almost dawn on the last day of December, 1944, and the first part of the Southern Pacific's Pacific Limited was racing for San Francisco. Its eighteen cars were jammed with citizens and troops on furlough. A little after 6:00 A.M., about twenty miles west of Ogden, Utah, a freight train signaled the express that it was having difficulty, and the passenger train halted. Its brakeman ran back down the line and set several flares.

These warning flares, however, were difficult to see in the swells of morning fog that drifted across the marshes surrounding the Great Salt Lake. Minutes after the flares were lit, James McDonald, engineer of the second section of the Pacific Limited, raced his twenty mail and express cars down the same track at 65 m.p.h.

McDonald failed to see the flares through the thick mist. His train quickly overtook the first section of the Limited, which was just getting under way. His fireman

One section of the Pacific Ltd. ran into the second section on the shores of the Great Salt Lake near Ogden, Utah, on December 31, 1944. Fifty passengers were killed. *(Wide World)*

did see one flare and shouted to the engineer to stop, but McDonald's movements appeared "sluggish," and he did not apply the brakes until a few seconds before his engine slammed into the rear of the first section of the train.

The last car of the first section practically disintegrated at impact, shooting off the track. The Pullman next in line escaped serious damage, but the next two cars were thrown off the seven-foot-high roadbed and sent hissing and screeching into the marshes.

Of the fifty persons killed in the crash, twenty-nine were soldiers who had been in the last car. An entire family, LeRoy Porter, his wife, and two daughters, was killed. Rescue efforts to aid the eighty persons injured in the rear-end collision were impeded by the marshes, but fortunately, two undamaged Army hospital cars were attached to the train, and medical attention was at hand.

A quick, subsequent investigation put the blame for the accident on engineer McDonald, but he was not present to answer charges. The sixty-four-year-old trainman was dead. Apparently aware of his miscalculation, the engineer had suffered a heart attack moments before the crash.

OHIO — FLOOD
January, 1937

A distance of more than 1,000 miles along the entire Ohio River basin was flooded in late January, 1937, when the Scioto and Ohio rivers broke through their dikes and barriers. Cities between Pittsburgh, Pennsylvania, and Cairo, Illinois, suffered, and approximately $418 million in damages was done. The Mississippi valley area was not as severely afflicted as the Ohio region.

Most of Cincinnati was under about ten feet of water for several days. Louisville, Kentucky, was also hard hit. A unique problem arose in Cincinnati. Though most of the town was under water, the fire department still found that, because of broken mains, there was little water pressure available to fight fires. Drinking water in that city was also affected when the pumping station was flooded.

Fire Chief Barney Houston solved both problems by commandeering several 1,000-gallon trucks, filling them with clean water, and escaping before the floodwaters hit. All available fire extinguishers were filled, and these were used with considerable effect on the many fires that broke out in the submerged city. The Cincinnati Fire Department was also credited with having saved hundreds of lives while patrolling the water-filled streets.

No fewer than twenty cities sent firefighting equipment to Louisville, Kentucky, when numerous fires broke out there after the deadly flood.

Ironically it was not the vast flooding that took most of the 137 lives in this disaster. The floodwaters moved slowly; there was no torrent sweeping away houses. Most of the deaths occurred in fires and explosions. The Louisville Varnish Company caught fire on January 26, causing $500,000 of damage. Gas explosions in Louisville continued for almost two weeks. Ten persons were killed at one of these on February 5. Others were killed in Ironton, Ohio, when gas mains blew up.

One estimate stated that 165 billion tons of water in twenty-five days of rainfall caused the Ohio and its tributaries to flood. The flooding spread across 182 counties in 12 states. The Red Cross reported that over one million persons were caught in the floodwaters that surged over 204,000 square miles.

The Red Cross undertook the mammoth burden of rescue and relief. Through its auspices 5,400 boats were used to take persons off crumbling houses, 300 emergency hospitals were organized, and 3,600 nurses attended the injured. The Red Cross raised more than $25 million in relief funds.

OHIO (INDIANA and ILLINOIS) — FLOOD
March 25, 1913

background: Great floods in late March, 1913, inundated large tracts of land in Illinois, Indiana, and particularly in Ohio, where the cities of Dayton, Middleton, Hamilton, Piqua, Xenia, and Zanesville suffered great damage and loss of life. Heavy rains bloated the Scioto, Mad, Miami, and Muskingum rivers. More than 500 lost their lives in the waters; hundreds more were missing, and more than $47 million in damage was done.

Mass flooding through southern Illinois, Indiana, and Ohio began in late March, 1913. Heavy rains had inflated rivers that smashed over their banks and swept through towns that had been safe for decades from such calamities. On March 25, the Miami River above Dayton broke across its dikes, and a half dozen rivers elsewhere followed suit.

In minutes Dayton, Ohio, was a watery wreck, flooded to a depth of seven to twelve feet. Buildings collapsed by the scores, and the city's predicament was unknown to the outside world for hours, because its last link, a single telephone wire, snapped under the pressure of the water. Dayton's 125,000 residents were sent scurrying to rooftops and up quaking trees as the Mad River, which joined the Miami near the city, also broke across its banks.

One citizen was quoted as saying, "Daytonians had never dreamed of such a flood menace. The levees were considered by them to be among the strongest and finest in the country, not even those of the Mississippi excepted. It is incredible to me that these substantially built levees should give way."

The amount of rain, almost six inches, that fell on the

Flood survivors are pulled to high ground in Dayton, Ohio, during the disastrous flood of March 25, 1913.

previous day was enough to force the already weakened levees. As a writer from the *Cleveland Leader* then wrote, "Six inches of rain throughout Ohio means about 575 million cubic feet of water. That is equivalent to a lake ten feet deep, eighty miles long and twenty-five miles in average width. It would make a lake twenty feet deep, forty miles long and twenty-five miles wide, throughout its length. . . . The weight of such a mass of water is monstrous . . . the rain which has come down in Ohio in three days means about 18 billion tons."

When this avalanche of water smashed into Dayton, its citizens, who were wholly unprepared, were swept down streets and out of their homes and offices. The suburbs of Riverdale, West Side, and North Dayton were totally submerged at once. Before the phone lines were torn down by the floodwaters, two telephone operators flashed word of the catastrophe to nearby Lebanon.

The towns of Troy and Tadmore were completely under water. Angry rivers throughout the Ohio River basin burst in unison on March 25. The Scioto River, which enters the Ohio River at Portsmouth, was rising in the central watershed of Ohio. It slashed through Portsmouth, as well as Columbus, Circleville, and Chillicothe. The Wabash River in Indiana tore through Terre Haute and partially submerged Lafayette. The White River, also in Indiana, caused great damage and loss of life in the western suburbs of Indianapolis.

One of the last wire messages from Dayton was a desperate one: "Dayton is a lost city. . . . It is completely separated from the rest of the world. . . . Its isolation is almost primeval. . . . Only one telephone wire is working. . . . The city government is completely imprisoned by water. . . ."

About 100 bodies floated and spun grotesquely in the churning waters as citizens performed heroic rescues of trapped persons. The seventy-year-old president of the National Cash Register Company, John H. Patterson, was barefooted and half-dressed as he rowed a boat through the streets, plucking gasping victims from the floodwaters. The flood had made 70,000 persons instantly homeless, and many people floundered in the water awaiting rescue. Boats of all kinds sloshed about, the oarsmen rescuing people from the water.

Withstanding the flood in Dayton were ancient buildings such as the Arcade, the Conover Building, the Kuhns Building, the Calahan Bank, and the United Bretheren Publishing Company. About 7,000 persons had sought shelter in these places. The National Cash Register plant was converted by the Red Cross into a hospital and relief center.

Thousands in North Dayton were imprisoned in their attics by the floodwater. One of these, Lisa Matiny, hailed a passing rescue boat and put her mother and two sisters into it. The rescuers told her they would come back for her, but the boat disappeared, and she later found her family dead in the National Cash Register Building. Lisa Matiny rode a floating door to safety and took charge of refugees at the Van Cleveland School. She could do nothing, however, for an elderly woman who had lost her senses and kept repeating, "Where's Billy, where's Billy?"

The violent waters took many innocent victims. Two women, part of the throng taking refuge in the Longfellow School, gave premature birth to babies, one of whom died.

Freakish incidents occurred in the wild flood. A horse was swept through the broken doors of the First National Bank and was later found dead, standing behind a teller's cage. A dead sow was found in the lingerie department on the second floor of a large clothing store.

Ben Hecht of the *Chicago Journal,* then only an eighteen-year-old cub reporter, was the first outside newspaperman to reach Dayton and report the disaster. He had taken the train from Chicago as far as it would go, marched through heavy snows, then fast-talked two trainmen into letting him pump a hand-car to the stricken town. Militiamen and deputies, ordered to patrol against looters, took several shots at him and narrowly missed.

His first cable to his newspaper, sent from the stricken town of Miami Junction, described the twelve gritty telegraph operators who sat at their posts for thirty hours: "Among the heroes of the flood are the telegraph operators. They have sent tens of thousands of messages and have stuck to their jobs day and night. Some have dropped from exhaustion. The Western Union men, who were the first to break into the city, haven't slept since Tuesday. 'Safe,' 'safe,' the monotonous words of rescue and death have jammed the wires since the first one was opened." None of these operators knew, of course, whether their own families were safe.

Hecht recalled his adventure in Dayton in his nostalgic *Child of the Century,* remembering how he "spent the day in a canoe, paddling through flooded Dayton, interviewing other boatmen and gathering data on the catastrophe. Toward evening I had fallen asleep in the canoe. Rescuers had found me and taken me to the National Cash Register plant where the Red Cross had set up its headquarters. I woke up on a refugee cot, in a strange nightgown, with a tag around my neck. I began yelling for my clothes and brought a nurse down on me. She insisted I was one of the victims of the flood and refused to 'discharge' me until I was examined by a doctor. I answered [that] I was a newspaperman, a staff correspondent for the *Chicago Journal* and had a story to file for the first edition. Humiliation robbed my voice of conviction. I stood yelling in my skimpy refugee's nightgown, as unlike a journalist as could be imagined."

During the flood, some of the stranded Dayton residents were taken aboard boats built by the National Cash Register Company.

As the flood in Dayton began to subside, the generous citizens of Dayton offered free clothing from their stores; signs appeared everywhere offering free food to the victims.

Howard Lowrey, who had been separated from his family in the first onrush of water, stood knee-deep in a mudhole on River Street, anxiously watching refugees stream by, tearfully looking for his family. Finally a woman in tatters, who was holding a small child, staggered along. Lowrey leaped from his mudhole and embraced his wife. They laughed at the fact that they had survived. The little family moved off in smiles and tears, unconcerned that their house had been obliterated.

Most of Ohio was about as hard hit by the torrent as Dayton. Passengers on a train that ran through Ohio on a high embankment witnessed in awe the flooded destruction outside Toledo, where men were poling their way through choppy waters. Passenger Perry Hollister, whose reaction was less than compassionate, supposed these waterways "were once streets. Some of them [the victims] appealed to the engineer of our train. . . to stop and take them aboard, and he complied. These people were brought to Toledo. All they did was moan and weep about their losses. The wind was raw, too, and some of them were nearly frozen when we took them aboard. . . . Toledo was struck badly. The lower part of the city was under water."

The New York-Chicago Special was at times in danger of being thrown from its tracks by the rushing water. It reached Chicago's Union Station safely, but was many hours behind schedule. Henrietta Lama of Pittsburgh told reporters at the station, "Our ride on the train was a long period of awful suspense. Every moment we feared the train would be wrecked."

This possibility was real. The engineer could see that the tracks were covered with water in many places. He had to stop the train several times to get out, walk ahead, and inspect the stability of the track before continuing. Many times, moments after the train passed, the tracks were washed away.

Another passenger on this train, J. F. Holmes of Fargo, North Dakota, saw, near Lima, Ohio, "hundreds of persons walking on the tracks, knee-deep in water, carrying with them the most precious of their household effects. The women were in tears. Many families were in small boats, which were so heavily loaded they appeared in momentary danger of overturning."

George B. Dodge of Boston, another passenger, remembered passing through Fort Wayne, Indiana, and seeing "water which had risen to the second [floor] windows of homes. Several homes had been demolished and were floating about in the streets. Temporary platforms were built to allow passengers to get on and off the trains. There were not many who got off, however."

Florence Wyman, an art instructor at Wesleyan University in Delaware, Ohio, watched the flood from a rooftop. She reported, "It was like a horrible nightmare. The water crept up slowly, but, oh, so steadily and relentlessly. First it was six inches deep in some of the lower streets; then a foot deep, and at last it had covered all the lower part[s] of town and was lapping at the foot of the hills, while the houses in the flooded portion stood, many of them, with only the upper stories and roofs visible. And on nearly every house there was a family, or what was left of the family, clinging to the ridgepole and chimneys and praying for deliverance."

University students at Delaware performed countless acts of heroism. One unnamed student, who swam into the raging current tirelessly, rescued thirty persons. A boatload of students rowed against the charging waters to save a woman and her three children who were dangling from a railroad bridge. The family dropped, one by one, into the students' boat.

A seventy-five-year-old man was seen on top of a floating house. He was holding his lifeless wife. Suddenly the old man lifted the woman in his arms, carried her to a chimney hole, and let her down into it. When rescuers reached him and took him off, someone asked him about the strange act.

"She was my wife and she is dead," he replied. "She died two hours ago, and I was afraid to let her lie on the roof because the water would carry her away."

The Ohio town of Piqua was saved from starvation when four carloads of provisions arrived from Lima. Doctors in half-demolished Piqua operated on injured flood victims who were laid on top of pool tables in the local poolhall. These were the only "beds" available.

In Prospect, Ohio, a minister borrowed a boat from a farmer. With the aid of a newspaperman from Marion, he busily went about saving more than a dozen women and children, taking two at a time because the boat was small. In the afternoon the farmer appeared on the ridge and demanded the return of his boat.

"Are you crazy?" the newspaperman said. "We need it to save lives."

"I got business on the other side of the river," the farmer said laconically. "I want my boat."

The minister pleaded with him and promised to take him across the swiftly moving river if he could keep the boat to continue his rescue efforts. Grudgingly the farmer accepted, and with great difficulty the newspaperman and the minister rowed him across the river. As they were returning to the other side, the vicious current spun the small boat around so violently that it capsized,

Downtown Dayton, Ohio, was flooded and on fire on March 25, 1913; a wireless operator tapped out: "Its isolation is almost primeval. . ."

and both men inside were drowned. The farmer called them "fools," and went about his business.

In flood-stricken Zanesville, Ohio, where the waters in the streets had risen to fifteen feet, a woman rushed into the train depot, which was being used as a refugee center. She pulled frantically at her hair and clothes as she looked at the rows of injured lining the walls. With a shriek she rushed to a man covered in a wet blanket.

"Jim!" she yelled. "That's you, ain't it, Jim? It's you—you ain't dead, are you, Jim? Say you ain't dead!"

Without opening his eyes, the woman's half-conscious husband said, "I ain't dead."

There was insanity, too. Martin Ellis and his wife took refuge in Dayton's Algonquin Hotel. Its front doors were blocked by a team of horses that had become wedged there. From a second-story window, the Ellis couple witnessed one scene of horror after another as the floodwaters engulfed scores of people and animals. Mrs. Ellis began to wail about her four children and the fact that the youngsters, at home in the flooded district, were probably all drowned. Her husband tried to calm her, but the hysterical woman jumped into the water and was swept away to her death. This occurred at about 8:50 A.M. when the Lewiston Reservoir broke above Dayton. In the words of Mr. Ellis, "The water traveled like a sheet to the east, passing over the city. A panic followed. People ran to the tops of buildings and were brushed off like flies. My four children were home. We lived on North Main Street. We saw the top of our house burn. . . . My wife couldn't stand it. . . . She jumped. . . ."

Miss Flossie Lester, a stenographer, leaped onto a horse-drawn van that was racing down a street in Edgemont. The van was just ahead of the pursuing floodwaters. When the water caught up to the dashing van and overturned it, the horses broke free, and swam down the street. Miss Lester grabbed a dangling strap and pulled herself onto the back of one of the horses. The animal carried her a mile and a half to a levee near a farmhouse where she was saved.

Eight huge elephants were strange victims of the floodwaters encircling Peru, Indiana. They belonged to the Wallace-Hagenbeck Circus that wintered in Peru. The keepers, fearing that the elephants might stampede through the town if released, kept the snorting pachyderms chained to their posts, and the animals were drowned as the torrent poured over them.

There were those who stubbornly refused rescue, such as Mr. and Mrs. Walter C. Howard and Cordelia A. Carrager. These elderly people insisted on staying with their floating home in flooded Columbus, Ohio. "We have enough provisions to ride this out," Howard called to Wilber Morris, who vainly encouraged them to get into his boat. Days later Morris found all three dead.

The George Roller family, also of Columbus, used a unique ploy to make sure that they would not starve. Seeing the flood approaching their home, they somehow coaxed the family cow into the kitchen and upstairs, where it was given its own room. They also raced upstairs with plenty of hay and corn. They had ample milk for themselves and neighbors for the five days until the flood receded.

Doctors in Columbus were very busy certifying victims as dead and ordering their immediate burial in order to prevent plague. A small boy was standing before a row of dead victims about to be buried in Greenlawn Cemetery, when he noticed a slight motion. "Hey, hey," he shouted as a body was being lowered in a grave, "that man there moved."

"Hush," his mother said.

The boy began to cry. "I saw him move. He moved!"

Diggers began to throw dirt down on the body. The boy yelled so loudly that a doctor walked over to him to ask what was wrong.

"The man in the hole there. I saw him move. He's alive and you're covering him up."

The doctor jumped into the freshly dug grave and lifted the body out. Working with restoratives, the doctor was able to revive C.A. Turney of Glenwood Avenue.

Miraculous rescues were common in this wide-ranging flood. Charles M. Adams of Riverdale, near Dayton, managed to get his wife and ten-month-old twin daughters into a skiff just before the torrent burst upon his house and tore the roof away. He rowed against the powerful current to a neighbor's home. Just then that home gave way, causing the skiff to capsize. Adams managed to swim a few feet in the icy water before farmers in another boat picked him up. He looked back once before passing out and saw his wife go down for the third time and his little girls swept away.

When Adams awoke in an attic, his wife was beside him. A Boy Scout had swum out to save her, bringing her back to life with artificial respiration. As Adams stood up, his mind filled with the horrible thought of his drowning daughters, a grinning farmer walked up the attic stairs with a child under each arm. "Dangdest thing," the farmer said, handing over the crying girls, "my house was going along with the water when I see these two young ones stickin' inna tree. I just reached down and took 'em off like pickin' apples. Ain't that the dangdest thing?"

This was the third worst flood of the twentieth century. More than 1,000 miles of the Ohio River basin had been flooded, and approximately 500 persons had been killed. In Ohio 150 were drowned in Dayton, 64 in Columbus, 50 in Hamilton, 50 in Miamisburg; the highest death toll in Indiana was at Peru where 20 deaths were recorded. More than 175,000 persons in Ohio were left homeless, and $147 million in damage was done to the entire region.

Massive relief supplies, clothing and funds were provided by the Red Cross and citizens throughout the country. The wife of a Dr. McGrudder in Baltimore read of the disaster and ordered her maid to pack up several boxes of old clothing for the survivors. She sent the boxes to the Red Cross in Washington, D.C. A week later General Devine of the Washington, D.C., Red Cross received a letter from the wealthy Mrs. McGrudder. Her maid, she explained, had accidentally packed her $1,000 seal-skin coat in the relief parcels, and she wanted it returned. The coat was never found.

(ALSO SEE: Johnstown, Pennsylvania; Mississippi River)

OHIO STATE PENITENTIARY — FIRE — April 21, 1930

background: At 5:30 P.M. on April 21, 1930, the antiquated prison buildings of the Ohio State Penitentiary caught fire. The fire started in a scaffold next to a six-story cell block that was being expanded. Soon the fire spread through the tiers, where locked-in prisoners went berserk. There were 322 convicts killed by the fire and fumes; some committed suicide. Another 230 injured inmates were hospitalized. Warden Preston E. Thomas blamed the fire on arson. Although three men were convicted of this act, the crime was never proved, and most authorities consider the blaze accidental.

The Ohio State Penitentiary was a grim and ancient jumble of grey cell blocks squatting almost in the center of Columbus, Ohio. It had a notorious reputation on two counts; it had housed some of the most celebrated criminals in United States history, and it was a known firetrap. It had no safety devices or regulations to combat even the smallest of blazes.

Its most famous inmate was a bank teller named William Sydney Porter, who embezzled money to begin a literary journal. He was discovered and fled to Honduras, only to return and be arrested at his wife's deathbed. Porter spent three years (1898 to 1901) in the Ohio State Penitentiary before his release. He walked out the gates and into the arms of fame, for in those three years of confinement he had churned out dozens of stories that had made him the most popular writer of his day. His pseudonym was O. Henry.

Less rehabilitated inmates included Harry Pierpont and Charles Makley, notorious members of the lethal

John Dillinger gang. In September, 1934, they attempted to duplicate Dillinger's infamous Crown Point, Indiana, escape (he had used a wooden gun to bluff his way to freedom). They fashioned pistols out of soap bars, but their ruse was uncovered, and they were shot full of holes.

Makley was killed outright, but Pierpont was nursed back to health only to sit down in the penitentiary's electric chair for the killing of Lima, Ohio, Sheriff Jess Sarber on October 12, 1933, while freeing Dillinger from custody. The electric chair that executed handsome Harry Pierpont had been designed by another Ohio Penitentiary inmate, Charles Justice, who developed the chair after the state discarded hanging. Justice himself was electrocuted in the very chair he had helped to build.

The Ohio State Penitentiary was also infamous for its total lack of fire equipment and firefighting systems and its staff's compassionless disregard of fire drills. Constructed on twenty acres of barren ground, most of the buildings were more than a century old and were originally intended to house no more than 1,500 prisoners. In April, 1930, the cell blocks were bloated with 4,500 inmates, all crowded into cramped, almost unlivable cells. Warden Thomas's hardline attitude did little to relieve the situation. During one jailbreak attempt, the warden personally grabbed a shotgun and blasted four convicts in the backs with buckshot, knocking them all to the ground in one charge.

Discontent turned to outrage, and as the prisoners were on the verge of full-scale rioting, authorities gave in and ordered the cell blocks expanded. This minimal operation was under way, and wooden scaffolding scaled the walls of the six-story tiers of cells like misshapen vines when the disaster occurred.

Smoke began to snake through the wooden scaffolding at about 5:30 P.M. on April 21, 1930. A convict, Barry Sholkey, spotted it first. Sholkey was known as "a great kidder," and his shouts to guards only brought laughter. According to an Associated Press report, "They refused to become excited. But a few minutes later, with the roaring flames spreading under a stiff wind, they saw the fire and mighty screams were sent up."

Trapped, the prisoners began shouting all at once. Guards were unsure of what to do. Inmates pounded on their cell doors with chairs and cups, yelling to be released into the corridors. Columbus residents heard the roar of agonized voices, and dozens scurried to the prison to see flames leaping skyward and huge, ugly pillars of black smoke curling upward.

The prison was thought to be fireproof, but as the flames seared their way through cell block after cell block, this assumption was proved tragically false. Warden Thomas thought the fire was an attempt by inmates to escape, and at first he refused to open their cells. He listened resolutely as they "rattled their bars and screamed with terror as snake-like coils of heavy black smoke crawled into the cells through ventilators."

Squads of firemen arrived minutes after receiving the alarm, but their chiefs refused to allow them to go into the prison until armed protection arrived. This necessitated calling out the local National Guard of Columbus, a delay that took precious minutes and many prisoners' lives.

Those in the upper tiers of the cell blocks were the first to succumb. Dense smoke and unbearable heat accumulated there. Guard Thomas Watkinson, keeper of the master set of keys, shouted to inmates and other guards that he could not open the cells because his superior, Captain John Hall, had given him strict orders to keep all cells locked even in such an emergency. Warden Thomas and Captain Hall later denied ever having given these

Firemen battle a blaze inside the ancient Ohio Penitentiary on April 21, 1930, where 322 convicts burned to death. *(Wide World)*

unconscionable commands; Thomas later suspended Watkinson for making such claims.

As the convicts went mad with panic and pain, two guards, Little and Baldwin, grabbed the truculent Watkinson and wrestled the keys away from him. Running down the smoke-crammed corridors, they unlocked as many cells as possible before they both fell unconscious, overcome by smoke.

Fire raced through the upper tiers, burning away the wooden floors, killing many prisoners. Rather than be overcome by smoke, several prisoners plunged their scorched faces into wash basins, committing suicide. Suddenly the keys were lost. Guards and freed prisoners grabbed sledgehammers and axes and began hacking away at the steel doors behind which other prisoners were suffocating to death. A. H. Roberts of the *Cleveland News* later wrote: "Two of the dead men had cut their throats, driven to suicide by the terror that grew on them as the flames mowed down their prison mates."

Contrary to Warden Thomas's fears, the prisoners made no attempt to escape. Many turned back into the burning cell blocks to aid cornered inmates. A lifer, the notorious Cleveland bank robber Big Jim Morton, was able to free scores of prisoners before collapsing with smoke-filled lungs (his sentence was later commuted for this heroism). One-time gunman "Wild Bill" Donovan proved to be another selfless hero that day. (He was named after the adventuresome man who led the old Sixty-ninth New York Irish regiment when it distinguished itself in France in World War I and who later was head of the OSS.) Donovan dashed back and forth from the burning tiers, carrying unconscious convicts into the yard. He saved twelve men before he died in the flames.

By the time firemen appeared in the prison yard, guarded by 600 rifle-bearing troopers from Fort Hayes, their hoses played on an inferno that was hopelessly out of control. Death on a massive scale had occurred in the prison. Swinging grotesquely from an upper tier, his corpse jerked about by the high-pressure streams from the hoses, was an inmate whom fellow prisoners had tried to lower to safety by rope. He had slipped, and the rope had whipped about awkwardly, looped around his neck in a noose and hanged him.

Firemen winced as they heard other prisoners calling from the upper tier cells where they were being roasted alive. They begged guards to shoot them. The ancient wooden roof caught fire, soon blazed up, and within minutes collapsed upon the wretched, pleading figures beneath it. "Frantic men suffocated like vermin behind their steel bars," the *Ohio State Journal* reported. It went on to quote a guard who said, "I saw faces at the windows wreathed in smoke that poured through the broken glass. With others I tried to get at them, but we could not move the bars. Soon flames broke into the cellroom, and the convicts dropped to the floor. They were literally burned alive before our eyes."

Only one prisoner, Michael Dorn, took advantage of the blaze to make a break. Dorn, a prisoner barber dressed in white, simply joined a line of medical stretcher bearers who were attending the fire and escaped in an ambulance. After a week's freedom, Dorn voluntarily returned to the penitentiary.

For almost two hours firemen fought the blaze, but a strong wind hampered their efforts. By 8:00 P.M. the fire was all but out, and firemen, using acetylene torches, broke into the burned-out shells of the cell blocks. They discovered 322 dead prisoners. Another 230 inmates were removed to the hospital with serious burns.

The senseless catastrophe aroused the national press to word-lashing anger. "The responsibility for the holocaust rests squarely upon the State," shouted the *Columbus Evening Dispatch*. "For many years successive legislatures have dawdled over the prison problem . . . while defenseless human lives remained in jeopardy."

Warden Thomas pinned the blame on three prisoners. Although proof was almost nonexistent, they were quickly convicted of arson and second-degree murder. Two of them later committed suicide. Gilbert Bettman, Ohio's attorney general, insisted that Governor Myers Y. Cooper remove Thomas, but the state's chief executive refused, and the warden stayed in his position, stubbornly commenting, "If I was to blame for anything, I'd like to know it. I did three things: called the fire department, ordered release of the men from their cells [this was hardly in evidence when guards had to battle other guards for the keys to those cells], and sought the protection of the public. Those things I had in mind when the fire began, and those I attempted to carry out."

But it was the *Cleveland Plain Dealer* that had the last word, echoing genuine public reaction to the Easter Monday tragedy made possible by neglect, indifference and insane regulations: "The cries of men behind steel bars, held in a vise for creeping flames to devour, are ringing in Ohio ears. The State is more cruel than we believe if the cries are unanswered."

(ALSO SEE: Jay, Florida)

OIL CITY, PENNSYLVANIA — FLOOD-FIRE, June 4, 1892

Fires that occur during flooding are almost always caused by oil storage tanks that are torn from their foundations or by oil lines and pipes that are ruptured. This is exactly what happened in Oil City, Pennsylvania, on June 4, 1892, when floodwaters submerged that town and neighboring Titusville.

Oil from broken pipes coated the floodwaters and was soon ignited, creating a blazing lake that incinerated 130 people and burned every structure in the city to the waterline. Those who survived the searing heat and flames perished minutes later by drowning as they feebly attempted to escape.

OKLAHOMA (ARKANSAS and MISSOURI) **TORNADOES April 12, 1945**

Large stretches of Oklahoma, long a hotbed of tornadoes, were savagely ripped apart by a series of twisters on April 12, 1945. First and hardest hit was the town of Antlers, where 3,000 residents felt the terrible impact of the storm. All power was wiped out, and scores of houses along several residential blocks were flattened or exploded. Sixty-three persons were killed, and hundreds were injured.

Tornadoes set down at Muskogee, killing eleven, and at Hulbert, where three died; they sliced through the southeast corner of Oklahoma City, killing four, and tore through Greenwood Junction, Boggy, Red Oak, and Rowland. A total of eighty-five persons died in the tornado blasts across the state.

Arkansas was also besieged by families of tornadoes, and 21 persons died in Marble, Jamestown, McKendree, Dora and other towns. In the Missouri Ozarks 6 persons were killed. The final death toll in all three states reached 112 with damages running into the hundreds of thousands of dollars.

Identification of the dead in Antlers, Oklahoma, was a tedious affair that took several days. The owners of the only funeral parlor had been killed, and bodies had to be removed to other towns for burial. This prevented immediate identification by the victim's relatives.

OKLAHOMA CITY, OKLAHOMA **TORNADO June 12, 1942**

Records show that no other city in the United States has been struck by as many tornadoes as Oklahoma City. A particularly vicious twister set down on the city on the night of June 12, 1942, and tore up about one hundred weakly built homes in a residential district. Thirty-five citizens were killed outright. Another thirty persons were hospitalized. Damage was estimated to be more than $300,000.

OKLAHOMA STATE HOSPITAL **FIRE April 13, 1918**

Patients sleeping in the Oklahoma State Hospital for the Insane in Norman never had a chance to escape the flash fire that swept through the asylum's decrepit wooden buildings in the early morning of April 13, 1918. The fire, which was caused by defective wiring, started in a linen closet. It burst through the dry timbers of Ward 14 at 3:00 A.M. and quickly enveloped the two-story frame structure.

For some reason, unknown to this day, the fire alarm was not turned in immediately, and thirty-three inmates were burned to death in their beds. In Ward 10 staff members brawled with eighty unbalanced Negro inmates, and only after bloody battles did they manage to rescue their charges.

Three of the four wooden buildings of the hospital were leveled by the fire. The total death count reached thirty-eight. Several inmates managed to escape during the fire but were recaptured. Credit for saving many crippled patients went to female nurses who repeatedly risked their lives to rescue those in the burning buildings.

(ALSO SEE: Cleveland Clinic, Mercy Hospital)

OMAHA, NEBRASKA **TORNADO March 23, 1913**

background: The most devastating tornado to occur in Omaha, Nebraska, struck at about 6:00 P.M. on March 23, 1913. In about twelve minutes it moved in a northeasterly direction, on a five-mile-long and one-fourth-of-a-mile-wide path. More than 600 homes were utterly destroyed; another 1,110 were seriously damaged with losses mounting to more than $3.5 million. There were 115 victims.

It was Easter Sunday, a balmy spring day, and the sun peeped tantalizingly through rolling clouds that threatened rain. Long considered "tornado-proof" because of the surrounding hills that barricaded the city, Omaha, Nebraska, in the gentle evening of March 23, 1913, was

"The noise was like ten million bees," one resident of Omaha, Nebraska, said of the tornado that slashed through the center of the city on March 23, 1913.

The twister smashed the Idlewild Poolhall (left of the laundry) at Twenty-fourth and Grant streets in Omaha, where dozens were killed.

The fashionable home of J. H. Driscoll was flattened by the Omaha tornado of 1913. Driscoll's young daughter was pulled alive from the debris at right.

wholly unprepared for what one writer of the era termed "the wind demon" that "came careening over the prairies."

A little before 6:00 P.M., as the entire population was sitting down to dinner, a gigantic tornado, its pendant funnel-shaped cloud roaring, dropped down at Forty-fourth and Frances streets and began its murderous northeastern march through the city. Heralding its approach was a giant barn roof that flapped in the cyclonic winds like a huge preying crow.

Four Omaha businessmen who were on a hike saw the cloud first and jumped into a ditch as it passed them, headed for the city. A boy on horseback raced up and asked one of them, H. F. Neely of the Equitable Life Insurance Company, if he knew where there was a phone. Neely directed him to a tavern at Concordia Park.

Galloping wildly, like some latter-day Paul Revere, the boy rode to the tavern and shouted to the innkeeper, "Can you get Omaha on the phone?" Blood was streaming down the boy's face from a head wound, but he ignored it. "Father is in the ruins, and the house is on fire! I want the fire department! I want the fire department and some men with axes!"

But there were to be no phone calls to Omaha. Pole after telephone pole snapped and crashed as the twister ground into the city at Center Street. The fashionable mansions in West Farnam began to disintegrate. It uprooted the dead in West Lawn cemetery, draping cadavers and bones over tombstones, sending skeletons eerily flying about its eyewall. Hail, sleet and rain accompanied the storm, lashing at the gesticulating forms running before it.

A man named Kreidmer, a foreigner who spoke only a few words of English, came staggering down a hillside from his house, which the twister had freakishly tipped on its foundation.

According to one reporter, "The cottage had the rakish, debonnaire tilt of a new hat on the head of a drunken man." To confused passers-by, Kreidmer pointed to his wrecked home, at Forty-ninth and William streets, and sobbed hysterically. He had built it with his own hands. He asked about his family, but no one knew where his wife and children could be located.

Kreidmer was unconsolable, and he soon flung himself into the mud of the street, bemoaning the loss of his family and his fine house. Others, too, became crazed by the brutality of the storm.

L. F. Stover, returning from work, found his house on Poppleton Avenue gone and his wife and three children vanished. He discovered them hours later in the county hospital, all uninjured. C. K. Walsh was about to enter his home on South Forty-eighth Street when the winds of the twister caught him, his wife, and his baby boy and sent them rolling furiously down three city blocks. They survived with only minor cuts and bruises.

Residents died in their homes. The John Hanson family of Mayberry Avenue was found crushed to death over their dinner plates. A month-old baby and a three-year-old boy were the only survivors of the Fred Nash family on Leavenworth Street.

At Forty-eighth and Leavenworth streets, a streetcar tried to outrace the twister. When the motorman realized it was hopeless, he jumped off, abandoning his passengers. L. F. Stover, who had yet to discover his home and family missing, leaped on the car and tried to operate it by running it into a cut across the railroad tracks farther up a hill. Before the car reached this haven, the tornado struck it broadside and turned it over. Stover was sent flying. An infant in the streetcar died of glass cuts in his father's arms.

To many, this brutish twister was a visual wonder. Milton Tabor of the *Topeka Daily Capital,* who was picnicking with friends, described the storm, "The tornado . . . whirled furiously over our heads. We looked up into what appeared to be an enormous hollow cylinder, bright inside with lightning flashes, but black as blackest night all around. The noise was like ten million bees, plus a roar that beggars description."

Thomas Herbert, historian, recalled that "a terrible, but beautiful spectacle accompanied the crossing of the lake, when the twister sucked the water high into the air."

Though more than 600 houses had been destroyed, Omaha's business section escaped with only minor damage. The Bemis Park District, the most beautiful in Omaha, had been greatly damaged. A pretentious Edwardian mansion known as the "Joslyn Castle" was a shambles. Its roof was twisted off, its windows were punctured and its great stones were torn away and littered the millionaire-owner's uprooted lawns.

The Nebraska governor, J. H. Morehead, hearing of the disaster, ordered a special train to take him from Lincoln to Omaha. At first sight of the ruined city, Morehead moaned, "It's awful, it's awful." He said to reporters, "It's miraculous how so many, many men and women escaped with their lives. I cannot conceive how a storm so disastrous permitted a single person to live. It doesn't appear possible to me that anyone went through this awful thing and lived."

Morehead then led a group of sightseers, high-ranking politicos, through the devastated city, stepping gingerly over broken telephone poles, the carcasses of dead horses and even a few bodies. At Twenty-fourth and Grant streets, Morehead was shown the shambles of what had once been the Idlewild Poolhall. Still sticking awkwardly from the jumble of collapsed brick walls were the arms and legs of twenty Negroes, all of whom had been crushed to death.

"Poor souls," commented the governor.

"If they had been home with their families instead of in a place like that—" added another politician.

The group came to the shattered home of Clifford Daniels, a postman. He, his wife and two small children had been killed when their home, which was in the direct path of the tornado at Twentieth and Ohio streets, exploded. Morehead was informed that the eighteen-year-old Daniels boy had lived; he had not been on the premises when the storm hit.

The governor jutted his jaw and said, "I would not be surprised if he was to lose his reason."

On Twenty-fourth Street, a politician spotted a shadowy figure going through the ruins of a house. He waved over one of the many troopers sent to the area to

The Sacred Heart Convent in Omaha was destroyed by the tornado.

guard against looters. "Fire a shot at that man. An obvious ghoul. We want none of that here. This is no Galveston."

The soldier prudently shouted at the man in the ruins, who was seen slinking away into the night.

Morehead finally had enough. "I can't stand any more," he said. "Let's go back to the hotel. I have seen more destruction than I believed possible.

A few days later, a local minister gripped the rail of his pulpit and in a stentorian voice sermonized, "When the light of day had brought the ghastly magnitude of the horror beneath the eyes of the surviving citizens of the metropolis, it was realized that the torrential downpour which followed the cyclonic demon had saved the city from annihilation by fire.

"Thus, even in the face of such deep distress, the brave Omahans have seen a true resurrection in this fateful Easter Sunday; have taken countenance of the saving grace which fell upon them, and are even now deeply engrossed in the sturdy work of erecting a new and greater residential district from the splinters and ashes of that gruesome path of ruins. . . . Sweet charity is at every hand . . ."

(ALSO SEE: Flint, Michigan; Gainesville, Georgia, 1936; Illinois and the Midwest, 1925; Indiana and the Midwest, 1965; Lorain, Ohio; Murpheysboro, Illinois)

ONAWA, MAINE — RAILWAY WRECK
December 20, 1919

Confusing multiple orders from a train dispatcher helped to create the head-on collision of two Canadian Pacific trains outside Onawa, Maine, on December 20, 1919.

The engineer of an eastbound freight, Number 78, was given a series of orders that cited different stops where he was to pull to sidings and allow three sections of a westbound passenger train, Number 39, to pass. Each one of these sections consisted of a long line of passenger cars, and all of them were behind schedule by several hours. The freight engineer, Bagley, as was often the case with freight engineers, attempted to make up lost time. He misread the confusing train orders and advanced down the single track, thinking that the passenger train was far up the track and long delayed.

The third section of Number 39 was loaded with British immigrants and Canadian soldiers returning from the Army of Occupation in Germany. It was late. The two trains, both going at high speeds, met head on, on a forty-degree curve that angled around a mountain near Onawa.

Both engines were destroyed, and the firemen and engineers were killed on impact. The baggage car of the passenger train was demolished, and it crashed through the next two cars, crushing nineteen passengers to death. The death toll came to twenty-three.

ONDINE — MARINE DISASTER
October 4, 1928

The 787-ton French submarine *Ondine,* with forty-three officers and crew men aboard, vanished on the night of October 4, 1928. She was making her maiden voyage from Cherbourg to Toulon. The submarine was running on the surface at night, so she ran the risk, as do all small vessels, of being run down by larger ships. Apparently, this is what occurred to the *Ondine* off Vigo, Spain. The Greek freighter *Aikoterini M. Goulandris* later reported striking "wreckage" near this point.

(ALSO SEE: K-13, L-24, O-9*)*

ONEIDA — MARINE DISASTER
January 23, 1870

background: The United States frigate *Oneida,* having been on duty in Yokohama, Japan, was returning home on the night of January 23, 1870, when she was accidentally rammed by the British steamer *Bombay* twenty miles off Yokohama. Of the 176 officers and crew men aboard, 120 perished. Charges were later made against the skipper of the *Bombay* for gross navigational error and negligence.

One of the strangest marine disasters befalling a vessel of the United States fleet involved the frigate *Oneida.* For three years the ship had conducted a cruise of Chinese and Japanese ports. Setting out for America on the night of January 23, 1870, she was only about twenty miles from Yokohama when the large British steamer *Bombay* rammed her. The British ship was captained by the eccentric Arthur Wellesley Eyre. Though lights on the *Oneida* burned brightly, the British ship approached and struck the American ship on her starboard quarter, cutting away the poop deck and shearing away the entire stern.

Startled American officers hailed the *Bombay* three times with, "Ship ahoy!" "Stand by!" "You've cut us down!" No reply came from the *Bombay,* which began backing off.

A United States wheelman was knocked overboard at impact. Lieutenant Commander W. L. Stewart and an Ensign Adams rushed to the captain's deck, intent on firing the warning guns, but the man who had been swept into the sea had the keys to the magazine. Stewart and Adams broke into the locker and fired three shots as a signal to the fast-retreating *Bombay* that the *Oneida* was sinking and in need of aid. Officers all over the American ship blew their whistles, but still there was no response from Captain Eyre or any of his crew.

Captain Williams stood on his bridge and looked silently at the British ship. She had all but disappeared in the mist that rolled about the *Oneida.* His worst fears had become reality: the American ship was a deathtrap. All but three of her lifeboats had been wrecked in a typhoon

Commander E. H. Williams heroically went down with the crippled *Oneida*. *(Harper's Weekly)*

weeks before. Oddly enough, when Williams had asked American authorities in Yokohama to replenish his small boats, his request was refused. Now he had only two small boats in which to take off 176 sailors, many of whom were sick. The third boat had been reduced to splinters in the crash.

Lieutenant Commander A. W. Muldaur ran up to the captain and shouted, "Sir, this ship is sinking. We must abandon her."

Captain Williams shook his head and said, "I know it, but what can I do? I asked for more boats, and they were not allowed me." He ordered the men in sickbay to be brought topside, placed in the two small boats, and taken ashore. Many of the bedridden sailors, however, could not be moved. The ship began to sink stern first. An officer called to Ensign Charles A. Copp, who was attending the invalids below, that the ship was going under and that he should save himself.

Copp, who had served in the Union Navy during the Civil War, as had Captain Williams and many others on board the *Oneida*, shouted back an answer that is still a legend in the United States Navy: "No! I am stationed here and can not come until relieved!"

With water swirling across the decks, an officer named Yates ran to the captain and pulled hard at his arm. "Get off the vessel, sir," Yates yelled.

Captain Williams jerked his arm away and said, "No. This is my place, and here I remain. I go down with my ship." He did.

Using the two small boats, 56 survivors managed to cling to the sides and oars until they reached shore. Going under with the ship were 120 men. The first word of the disaster was brought by the ship's surgeon, Frothingham, who reached Yokohama with 15 gaunt-looking men the next day. Captain Eyre of the British ship had not reported a collision when he arrived in the port the previous night.

A board of inquiry brought flickering light to the English captain's actions. He repeatedly stated that he knew of no collision, but he thought he had detected a "mere graze" against some object. When asked if he had heard the whistles, shouts and warning shots coming from the *Oneida*, Eyre said no. Yet these shots were heard by many in Yokohama twenty miles away. When quizzed about this, Eyre, obviously annoyed at the insinuation that he would leave innocent men to drown, stated that perhaps he was prevented from hearing the distress shouts and signals because there was a strong breeze.

The *Bombay*'s steward later testified that his vessel had "run down a ship and cut her into the water's edge . . ." and that he "could see the men carrying some person on deck."

A Lieutenant Clemens of the British ship *Ocean* testified to Captain Eyre's accidental ramming and intentional desertion of the *Oneida*'s crew, as well as his rampant anti-Americanism. Clemens said Eyre had boasted to him on the evening of his arrival in the Japanese port that "he had cut the whole quarter off a damned Yankee frigate and served her bloody right well."

Beyond this testimony, there was no more proof of Eyre's culpability in the catastrophe. He received a reprimand, but he kept his master's papers.

(ALSO SEE: Cimbria*)*

The United States frigate *Oneida* (right) was cut in half by the British steamer *Bombay* on January 23, 1870. The *Oneida* sank with 120 men aboard. *(Illustrated London News)*

OPERA COMIQUE THEATER — FIRE
May 25, 1887

background: The Opera Comique Theater in Paris, France, was an old brick and wooden structure with thick wooden trim and filigree. It was ignited into a flash fire by gaslights on the stage, which inflamed scenery on the night of May 25, 1887. Failure to drop the iron fire curtain, open locked exit doors, and the ensuing panic caused the deaths of 200; another 200 were seriously injured.

The burning of the elegant Opera Comique Theater on May 25, 1887, was unfortunately to set a pattern in theater fires for the next twenty years and more. Uncontrollable flames, no safety regulations and panic would add up to gruesome fatality figures. Several hundred Parisians were in attendance on the night of the fire. The first act of *Mignon* had begun, and M. Taskin was singing. Suddenly the gas jets that illuminated the stage flickered up and the flames caught nearby scenery, igniting the flimsy fabric into a large blaze.

Patrons of the Opera Comique Theatre were driven to the windows by the blaze that took the lives of 200 on May 25, 1887. *(Illustrated London News)*

Taskin and another singer named Soulacroix immediately stepped forward, as Kate Claxton and others had done in the Brooklyn Theater fire a decade before, and attempted to calm the excited, shouting audience. It did no good; the audience panicked immediately and mad dashes were made for exits. Women in long gowns and men in evening dress frantically elbowed each other, clambering to get outside.

The flames quickly engulfed the stage, and the actors bolted through side exits, escaping into the Rue Favart. Not one of the many stage hands had the sense to lower the iron curtain that separated the stage from the audience. This curtain instantly would have averted the mass tragedy.

As the fire quickly spread, those in the upper gallery shoved and fought their ways down narrow staircases. They jammed and were unable to move on staircase landings and at locked exits. Those in the foyer, the stalls and the dress boxes fared no better. In most instances their paths were blocked by obstructions, and they found it impossible to reach the exit doors. Many found their way to the top of the building and ran across the roof, which also began to crackle into flames.

Below, in the broad place Boïeldieu, the Paris firemen, called *pompiers,* assembled and began to pump water onto the fire, which was already out of control and enveloping the entire ancient structure. Firemen threw up ladders, but these failed to reach most of the people trapped on the roof.

Men, praying and shouting farewells to their families and the world, began jumping from the windows and the roof. Firemen managed to rescue two unconscious women who were draped over windowsills. These two were never revived. They died on the counters of a nearby druggist's shop, adorned in ornate jewelry and velvet dresses.

The apartments above the theater, the dressing rooms where hundreds of flammable garments blazed, and the priceless library, filled with papers, plays, books and music sheets, roared into flames. By 11:00 P.M. the burning wooden roof had collapsed. Those standing on it, pleading for rescue, hurtled downward to fiery deaths. The *pompiers* did bravely rescue a man and woman who were sitting on a brick rooftop cornice. They took the man off by ladder and lowered the unconscious woman via a rope. These were the last ones to come out alive from the burning shell.

The firemen fought the blaze, however, until dawn of the next day and, upon entering, sifted through the ashes and debris to discover 200 bodies, most of them crammed together on staircases and exits under fallen sections of burned roof. Eighteen women were found in a burned heap, practically welded together by the intense flames. They had been crushed to death in the panic. Most of the deaths were attributed to asphyxiation, but those near the blocked and locked exits had certainly roasted alive. *(ALSO SEE: Baquet Theater; Brooklyn Theater; Exeter Theater; Iroquois Theater; Opera House, Nice, France)*

OPERA HOUSE, NICE, FRANCE — FIRE, March 23, 1881

Gaslights were a constant danger in the nineteenth century. They were the cause of a theater fire that killed seventy patrons of the Opera House in Nice, France, on the night of March 23, 1881. Jets of flames from the lamps that lit the stage either exploded or caused scenery to ignite during the performance. How the gaslights caused the fire was never fully determined. There was widespread panic in the audience, and the lack of a sufficient number of exits, coupled with the ushers' adherence to the archaic code of "one way out," assured disaster.

An ill-contrived, ancient building, the Opera House in Nice was a "mantrap" with narrow corridors and massive doors that, as a later investigation revealed, remained bolted during the fire. The fact that more of the theatergoers were not killed was attributed to the valor of American sailors and French naval cadets from Villefranche. They saw the flames shooting from the structure, raced to the site and pulled scores from the flames.

One eyewitness, with the cool Mediterranean at his back and the blazing fire before him, later said, "From the beach the sight was a magnificent one, though singularly awful. The brilliant tongues of flame shooting up clear into the dark sky, an immense cloud of smoke and sparks extending far towards the southwest, the vast crowd, backed by the dark sea, fringed with flame-colored foam, formed a picture not soon to be forgotten, in spite of the fearful tragedy being enacted inside—a tragedy felt to be going on, and yet unseen, the mystery of which only added to its horror."
(ALSO SEE: Baquet Theater, Opera Comique Theater)

"Fringed with flame-colored foam . . . a picture not soon to be forgotten," is how one eyewitness described the blaze that consumed the Opera House at Nice. *(Frank Leslie's Illustrated Newspaper)*

The burning of the Opera House in Nice on March 23, 1881, snuffed out seventy lives. *(Harper's Weekly)*

ORISKANY

MARINE DISASTER
October 26, 1966

background: The 42,000-ton United States carrier *Oriskany* caught fire at sea in the Gulf of Tonkin at 7:18 A.M. on October 26, 1966. Magnesium parachute flares in a locker had ignited and quickly spread a searing blaze inside the hangar bay and through the quarters below. Killed were forty-three men, of whom thirty-four were officers (twenty-four of these being combat pilots who had flown many missions over Vietnam).

The United States carrier *Oriskany,* her bow northward toward the wind, had just begun to launch a dawn strike of A-4E Skyhawk jet bombers against North Vietnamese military installations on October 26, 1966. The sun was already filling the broad reaches of the Gulf of Tonkin when a sailor, shouting incoherently, burst from a locker that contained stacks of hissing Mark-24 magnesium parachute flares. The seaman dogged down the locker hatch and sprinted for the telephone on the flight deck.

At 7:21 A.M. a red light blinked on in Damage Control Central, located many decks below. A sailor picked up the phone and, seconds after receiving the report from the hangar bay, rang up the bridge. He reported: "I have a fire alarm indication for Alpha 107 Mike." Captain John Iarrobino immediately realized the seriousness of this alarm. "Alpha" meant that fire had broken out at the forward part of the carrier, "107" meant that the blaze was on the starboard side of the hangar deck, and "Mike" meant the worst—a magazine full of explosives.

Klaxon horns blurted, bells rang, and loud-speakers throughout the ship blared: "Fire, fire, fire in frame 42! This is no drill! This is no drill!"

The 700 flares in the locker, located in the enormous Hangar Bay Number 1, began to explode in loud thuds, their magnesium heating the steel bulkheads of the locker to 7,000 degrees F. Naval firefighters, pumping hundreds of gallons of water on the locker, gaped as the steel bulkheads began to expand, buckle, and balloon outward.

"Get back, back!" one seaman shouted to the firefighters. "She's gonna go!" With a terrific blast, the steel hatch shot forth and a great gout of flame followed it, searing nearby sailors who ducked as rocketing fireballs passed over their heads. *Oriskany*'s fire marshal, Lieutenant Robert Williamson, led scores of sailors toward the locker. They carried a dozen high-pressure hoses, but the magnesium-fed flames could not be quenched by water.

Smoke spews from the forward hangar deck of the U.S. aircraft carrier *Oriskany,* October 26, 1966; 43 sailors died in the blaze. *(Wide World)*

Williamson knew this, but he intended to spray water on the entire area to keep other lockers, planes loaded with bombs, and nearby stacks of bombs and rockets from exploding.

Magnesium fireballs rocketed along the ceiling, knocking down sailors but, astonishingly, not injuring them. Burning magnesium from the ceiling showered down on Williamson and set his prematurely gray hair on fire, but he continued to direct firefighting operations. Two helicopters began to burn and then exploded. Hoses were trained on the wrecks to keep the flames away from other planes, which were hurriedly hand-pushed onto the hangar's elevator and taken topside to the flight deck. Countless feats of heroism were performed each second. "There were too many acts of heroism to number," Captain Iarrobino later commented. "There were literally hundreds. If there hadn't been, God only knows what the toll and the damage might have been."

One junior officer had an inkling of what might have happened. He had seen the two-man jettison teams struggle with dozens of 500-pound bombs, carrying them to the rails and dumping them into the sea. "If the bombs had gone off," he later remarked, "we would have lost the ship." One unforgettable sight among these scurrying bomb carriers was a petty officer who calmly hosed an immovable 1,000-pound bomb. The bomb was so hot that the water from his hose caused clouds of steam to rise.

If the job of the firefighters seemed impossible, that of sailors in Damage Control, far below decks, was twice as nerve-racking. The phone monitors and operators located there knew that they were directly beneath the fire. Tons of water were being pumped against the flames. The water began to seep belowdecks and trickle onto the steel bulkheads in Damage Control. The operators worriedly looked up. A report was received that a man was overboard and one monitor asked nervously, "Are they abandoning ship?" Another asked, "What the hell's going on up there?"

Lieutenant Commander Mel Berg, in charge of Damage Control, glanced at the sailors and quietly said, "Okay, now, settle down, boys."

The number of the firefighters dwindled—five sailors had been burned alive, and dozens more had succumbed to the unbearable heat. In addition, scores of officers were trapped in their bunks in the forecastle. Many of these men were pilots, exhausted from flying combat missions over Vietnam. The dense, dirty smoke that poured into their quarters quickly overcame them. Of the 3,400-man crew aboard the heaving *Oriskany,* the officers suffered the most casualties. Thirty-four of them died.

When smoke began to billow into their compartment, pilots James Harmon and Gordon Smith threw open the door. On hands and knees, they crawled through several rooms, pulling limp bodies from bunks and dragging them out onto the flight deck, not knowing whether these men were living or dead. After putting on oxygen breathing apparatus, these two men repeatedly went back to save more of their fellow pilots who had been overcome with smoke.

David Willis, a quartermaster, was trapped in a compartment with ten young sailors who began to panic as smoke gushed through a ventilator. Willis yanked an extension cord from the wall and ordered the sailors to hold onto it and crawl on their knees. He led them through the black smoke to the safety of the flight deck.

Escape seemed impossible for Commander Richard M. Bellinger, a large, 205-pound jet pilot, who had won the Silver Star. His room was full of suffocating black smoke. So he threw open the porthole and stuck his head outside, gasping for air. He could hear the flames shooting down the corridor. His door was turning red hot. Taking off all his clothes, Bellinger attempted the impossible. He began to squeeze his large frame through the small porthole. For minutes he struggled to get his shoulders through, then he got stuck at the hips. A sailor, looking down over the side of the ship, spotted him and lowered a cable. The steel frame of the porthole scraped his skin, and the fire behind him singed his feet. With a final, desperate jerk, he freed himself and was hauled stark naked to safety.

To Lieutenant Commander Marvin Reynolds, such an escape seemed unlikely, so he decided to battle the smoke and fire in his room. Breathing what fresh air he could get through his porthole, Reynolds constantly ran to his sink, dousing blankets and sheets with water and throwing them over his body. Jets of fire slivered through the louvers of his stateroom door. The walls grew burning hot to the touch. Reynolds thought he would soon be incinerated.

As he once more took fresh air, Reynolds was spotted by Boatswain's Mate Noel Hartford.

"What are you doing?" Hartford called to Reynolds.

The question struck Reynolds as totally absurd, and he answered sarcastically, "Well, right now, I'm burning up."

"Hold on," Hartford yelled and disappeared. Minutes later he returned and dropped an oxygen mask and a small hose. Donning the mask, Reynolds turned the hose on the advancing fire and beat it back. For three hours this imprisoned officer battled the flames and smoke, alternately turning the water from the hose on the menacing fire and then on himself. He was finally saved from the sizzling-hot compartment.

An effort to preserve himself and fifteen others was equally hazardous to Commander Charles A. L. Swanson (the L. stood for Lindbergh), executive officer of one of *Oriskany*'s fighter squadrons. Finding no escape route from the officers' quarters, Swanson led his men into a dead-end shaft that ran seven decks downward. He had taken with him an injured officer who had bounced off of the searing walls of a corridor. The officer was badly burned, and a wicked gash in his forehead spouted a river of blood.

Bosun's Mate Jerry Robinson caught the officer, who shouted, "I am dying, sailor." Swanson helped Robinson and the stricken officer into the shaft. The pilots and sailors clung to a single ladder. Some gathered on small platforms. One man who lost his grip and fell several decks was knocked unconscious when he landed. Closing the hatch after him, Swanson knew they were risking suffocation. He also knew that if the carrier were to go down they would be trapped several decks downward, without any way of abandoning ship.

Swanson and his men broke into storage lockers for more air and found a rusty phone set. Swanson plugged it in and shouted, "Can anyone hear me? Anyone there?" There was no response.

Realizing that his men would soon be without air, Swanson led them up the ladder and along smoke-filled corridors. He lost them three times. After hours of bullying, cajoling, and ordering, he managed to lead his men to the fresh air of the flight deck. All the while, he had carried the wounded officer.

Perhaps the most horrifying experience was endured by Claude Harper, a fireman trapped in Number One Pumping Station at the very bottom of the ship, nine decks downward. Alone in his small quarters, Harper was in phone contact with those above. He told them that smoke was seeping into his cramped area. An hour and a half after the fire broke out, he was still trapped and was getting weaker from inhaling smoke.

Harper got Machinist's Mate First Class J. B. Tupper on the phone. By then Harper had covered himself with sheets that he had soaked in a water basin. He told Tupper that it was difficult to breathe. The bosun's mate had been talking to Harper on and off for about an hour, and was trying to get a rescue team down to him.

"I don't know what you guys are doing," Harper, understandably upset, shouted into the phone, "but if you'll get me an O.B.A., I'll be okay down here."

"I'll try, really," Tupper promised. But he knew that saving Harper was questionable. Thousands of tons of water from the firefighters' hoses had gushed downward, flooding several compartments in the decks over Harper's quarters. There seemed to be no way to reach him.

Tupper located some scuba equipment, and found diver Bob Davis. The two men worked their way downward to the fifth level. Water had filled the compartments here, and Davis asked Tupper if he thought all the compartments below were also flooded. Tupper did not know. Davis, donning the scuba gear, began his descent. Harper had tried to get out of his trap several times. Opening a hatch, he had attempted to swim upward against the tons of water that drove down on him from the eighth level. He had been forced back, fortunate to be able to again close the hatch.

After four hours Harper simply stretched out under wet sheets and awaited death. Smoke soon made him semi-conscious. He vaguely heard a rush of water, the clanging of steel against steel, and then Bob Davis's voice shouting triumphantly up to Tupper, "He's alive! The guy's alive!"

Forty-three men died on the *Oriskany*.

(*ALSO SEE:* Bennington, Forrestal)

ORPHEUS — MARINE DISASTER

February 7, 1863

The 1,706-ton British steam corvette *Orpheus* met her doom on the morning of February 7, 1863. The twenty-one-gun warship carried a crew of 260 men. She was trying to navigate the treacherous reefs off Manukau Harbor on the west coast of New Zealand.

Commodore Burnett, considered an excellent seaman, brought his ship too close to the eight-mile-long Manukau Bar, which at low tide was approximately thirty feet high. At the time the *Orpheus* was under sail. Just after she struck the bar, Burnett ordered her backed off under steam, but the engines would not move.

Great combers rolled over the vessel's decks and hatchways popped open, water gushing into the bowels of the ship. Quickly filling with water, the *Orpheus* was a doomed ship, and Commodore Burnett knew it. Then the captain, perhaps thinking there was enough time to allow his men to be saved by boats from shore, ordered the large cutter lowered and filled it with records and valuable papers, which were taken ashore. Minutes later he ordered Lieutenant Hill to take another boat to Manukau Harbor and arouse those on board the *Harrier,* another British ship that was in port. Hill asked this vessel to send out her lifeboats to take off the *Orpheus*'s crew.

The launch returned with forty of the *Orpheus'* sailors and attempted to reach the stricken vessel, which was now breaking up quickly in an increasing turbulent sea. The launch was caught up by huge waves, capsized, and all in her drowned. The small steamer *Wonga Wonga* had chugged out from port and attempted to reach the *Orpheus,* which, except for her rigging, was clear under

The British warship *Orpheus* sank at Manukau Bar, New Zealand, February 7, 1863; 190 seamen went down with her. *(Harper's Weekly)*

water. Dozens of seamen, including Commodore Burnett, had climbed into the rigging. Rescue efforts continued until 9:00 P.M. Those on the *Wonga Wonga,* unable to get close to the wrecked *Orpheus,* watched as one mast after another snapped off, sending the sailors who had perched in them into the foaming sea. One report states: "The people in the tops were heard cheering and encouraging each other as they fell."

At this time a seaman named Johnson distinguished himself by repeatedly swimming along the reef, through thunderous waves, to rescue four drowning sailors. His efforts and those of others proved insufficient; 190 men of the *Orpheus* went to watery graves before midnight.

(ALSO SEE: Birkenhead*)*

OSAKA, JAPAN — TYPHOON

September 21, 1934

The people of Osaka had a long history of escaping most of the major disasters that plagued them. Perhaps, this was why Osaka authorities had allowed the construction of flimsy buildings unsupported by strong foundations.

These buildings included many schools and hospitals and were the first to disintegrate under the 125 m.p.h. winds of the typhoon that ravaged Osaka on September 21, 1934. It also sliced through the western cities of Kyoto and Kobe. Tokyo and Yokohama also were brushed by the storm, but their winds were only about 50 m.p.h. Damage was minor, and no deaths occurred.

The death toll in Osaka, however, was staggering. The schools, none of them reinforced with more than fragile timber, were especially vulnerable. Eighty-seven schools were utterly demolished by the typhoon. First their roof shingles were ripped away, and then their walls and ceilings collapsed. Four hundred twenty children were killed while studying; another 1,000 were seriously injured by flying debris.

Osaka's Sorojima Leper Hospital was shattered in the storm, and 200 of its 560 inmates were simply blown away to death. The insane asylum was crushed, and 50 patients were killed outright. The city's flourishing textile industry was wrecked for years when 3,082 factories were blown to pieces, and hundreds were killed at their jobs. (The industrial loss of these plants alone was estimated to be 300 million yen.)

By 10:00 P.M. the same day, Osaka's police had counted by candlelight 1,067 bodies lying in the streets of the shattered town. (Osaka, Kyoto, and Kobe were all pitched into darkness when all of their power lines were torn down.) The toll mounted to more than 4,000 the following day. Most of these victims were residents of Osaka. The Osaka Municipal Assembly appropriated 10 million yen for reconstruction work, but this would only cover a fraction of the damage wrought by the typhoon.

OTAY VALLEY, CALIFORNIA — FLOOD — January, 1916

During the middle and near the end of January, 1916, the Otay valley and neighboring areas in California experienced massive rainfalls that measured up to 395 cubic feet per second per square mile. These storms quickly bloated the Otay, San Diego, Cottonwood, Sweetwater, and other rivers. The Otay Dam broke in several places, sending an avalanche of water downward into the valley.

Unprepared residents were caught in their homes and on the low-lying fields. Twenty-two persons were instantly drowned. The Otay valley area alone suffered more than $10 million in damages to crops and houses.

(ALSO SEE: Johnstown, Pennsylvania)

OUR LADY OF THE ANGELS SCHOOL — FIRE — December 1, 1958

background: With 1,515 children in attendance, Our Lady of the Angels Grade School, run by the Sisters of Charity in Chicago, caught fire when rubbish in the basement ignited. Fire raced through the building. Although passers-by, firemen and the teaching staff rescued more than 1,000 children and several classes safely exited, 90 students and 3 nuns were killed.

It was about 2:30 P.M. on December 1, 1958, when thick smoke began to curl upward out of a pile of rubbish in the basement of Our Lady of the Angels School in Chicago. In another half-hour the 1,500 students would have been dismissed and sent home. Instead scores would go to the morgue.

Parents and neighbors wait for news of children caught in the murderous blaze that consumed Chicago's Our Lady of the Angels School on December 1, 1958. *(Wide World)*

A teacher on the first floor of the school was alerted when two of her students returned to class and reported the smoke. She quickly conferred with a teacher across the hall, and the two decided to take their classes out of the school. They did this promptly. The fire alarm, however, was not sounded at that time. Meanwhile flames licked their way up the high walls, eating into the heavy wooden trim.

As he entered the school, a janitor spotted the blaze. He shouted down a hall, asking the parish housekeeper to turn in the alarm. It was then 2:42 P.M. Incredibly none of the teachers in the rambling two-story building were notified of the blaze. Second-floor classes were not alerted until they saw and smelled the smoke. By then teachers had emptied the first floor in an orderly fire drill.

Five minutes later dozens of children were screaming for help from the second-story windows. Firemen arrived. They began to spray the building, and they threw up ladders. One cool-headed nun ordered her children out into the smoke-filled second-floor corridor and told them to crawl under the heavy smoke. Then she literally rolled them down the staircase, an act that saved them.

Using her wits, another teacher barricaded her room with books and furniture against the fire and then conducted a prayer session. Firemen soon appeared at the windows and evacuated them. The teacher went down the ladder last; she lost one child to the fire.

Most of the children on the second floor panicked. Historian Donald Robinson described the horrific scene: "Regardless of the nuns' directions, they ran insanely up and down the corridors or scrambled around the classrooms. Many jumped out of the windows to their death."

Priests, passers-by, and policemen aided the firemen in dozens of heroic rescues. A man who had already led out four trapped children turned and began to go back into the burning school. A fireman grabbed his arm and told him to stay out. He yanked free and shouted, "There may be more kids in there, and I'm going inside!" He and another man found an entire class huddled in their room and shepherded the children outside. A priest was seen carrying out three children. A nun carried two. A policeman piggybacked four youngsters to safety.

As hundreds of terrified citizens and parents lined the streets, the first of the children jumped from the windows, crashed on the pavement below and died.

Ten-year-old Juanita Murphy later sobbed, "Everybody was jumping. The smoke was terrible. Everybody was screaming. Everybody was trying to get on the firemen's ladders at the same time."

Firemen raced up and down ladders with their arms full of gasping students. They caught some jumping students in midair. Some reached out from partially extended ladders and grabbed jumping students by the

A fireman surveys a second-floor classroom in the gutted Our Lady of the Angels School. Ninety students were killed in the fire. *(Wide World)*

arms, the legs, and the hair, but it was not enough. Firemen shouted for others to stay in their classes until they could be rescued. (Twenty-four students did sit patiently at their desks and were found later in that placid position, all dead.) One petrified girl could not bring herself to jump and waited for the firemen. As she clung to a windowsill, she watched her classmates hurl themselves into space. "Some of the boys jumped out the window. When we looked down, we saw them lying still on the ground. We stayed, and the firemen saved us."

In a short time, the old building was a mass of flames, and there was little more the firemen could do. Had the school been equipped with a sprinkler system, it is quite probable that many of the ninety students and three nuns who perished could have been saved. As it was, their deaths only served once again to frighten authorities into establishing stricter safety regulations, a lesson they should have learned from the gutted remains of the Lake View School fifty years earlier.

(ALSO SEE: Babb Switch School, Cleveland Rural Grade School, Lake View School)

P

PAKISTAN INTERNATIONAL AIRWAYS — AIR CRASH, May 20, 1965

A lack of landing aids, for which Cairo Airport had long been notorious, contributed greatly to the flaming crash of a Pakistan International Airlines 707 on the night of May 20, 1965. One hundred twenty-four persons perished. The airport, which was always difficult to approach, was accused of inadequate lighting for the night approaches. One runway was particularly dangerous. To land on it, a pilot had to drop his plane almost one thousand feet and then fast-break. (This runway was a downhill affair.)

In addition, one report indicated that crash equipment was all but unavailable. Although the airport possessed modern equipment, it inexplicably had held it in mothballs for years.

Conditions in Cairo were so shabby that the International Pilots' Association had refused to make night landings unless improvements were made. New facilities and equipment were made available, but they were too late for those killed in the 1965 wreck.

As a United States Air Force plane circles, survivors from the sunken German training ship *Pamir* signal they are alive, September 22, 1957. *(Wide World)*

PALOS, ALABAMA — MINE DISASTER, May 5, 1910

The blast that tore apart the Palos Number 3 Mine outside of Palos, Alabama, on May 5, 1910, was inevitable, due to the shoddy safety measures employed by the owners. The coal was mined with picks, but "permissible" explosives were used to blast. Conditions were anything but safe in this mine. Large amounts of fine, dry coal dust and pockets of methane gas were very evident.

Miners were allowed to wear open lamps, their flames exposed to the dust and gas. On May 5, a miner in a large group headed into a shaft of Number 3 exposed his open lamp to a pocket of methane gas. The resulting explosion blew eighty-three miners to pieces. Another miner, standing at the mouth of the shaft, was hit by the impact of the explosion as it rolled outward to the surface and was hurtled skyward. He was killed by the fall.

PAMIR — MARINE DISASTER, September 22, 1957

background: The sailing vessel *Pamir,* used for training cadets in the German Mercantile Marine, was caught in a violent gale southwest of the Azores on September 22, 1957, and broke up. Of the eighty-six crew members and trainees on board, only five cadets survived.

The German training ship *Pamir,* once part of the proud windjammer fleet operated by Gustav Erikson, set sail from South America with eighty-six on board and a perilously stowed cargo of grain. Because of a stevedore strike, hundreds of grain sacks had been loaded on the *Pamir* by inefficient soldiers. This cargo would prove lethal to Captain Johann Diebitsch of the German Mercantile Marine.

Entrusted to his care were fifty-six young naval cadets, between ages sixteen and eighteen. These novices ultimately were caught in a freakish, powerful storm that was moving through the Atlantic when the *Pamir* set sail from the River Plate in mid-September, 1957.

The sailing ship ran into this gale, which soon developed into a full-scale hurricane, whipping the ship wildly about as she approached the Azores on September 22. The poorly-stowed grain sacks began to shift crazily in the holds of the ship, threatening to capsize her.

Diebitsch ordered several SOS signals sent out, but there were few ships in the vicinity of the menaced *Pamir*. The American freighter *President Taylor,* nearest to the threemaster, stoked up her fires and made top speed in the *Pamir's* direction.

Radio operators on other distant vessels clearly heard the *Pamir's* last message as she was breaking up in the storm: "Lost all sails. Beginning to list badly. Need help."

By the time the *President Taylor* arrived in the dead of night, there was nothing to be seen at the location last reported. By dawn the American ship was joined by scores of other merchant vessels, but a wide search revealed only several of the *Pamir's* drifting lifeboats, all empty. Toward dusk a lookout on the *Saxon,* another American vessel, picked out a lone lifeboat. The *Saxon* steamed over to find five frantically waving German naval cadets, the only survivors from the *Pamir.* They animatedly described how the ship had rolled over and how they had managed to splash their way into a boat and cut it adrift before it was dragged to the bottom with the sailing ship. Eighty-one others were never found.

(ALSO SEE: Eurydice, *1878;* Niobe*)*

PAN AMERICAN AIRLINES

AIR CRASH
April 11, 1952

A New York-bound Pan American DC 4 took off from the San Juan, Puerto Rico, airport on April 11, 1952, and was in flight for about nine minutes when one of the engines failed and the plane began to descend rapidly.

The pilot realized that he was only four or five miles offshore and decided to try his chances in the water rather than turn about and make for the airport in San Juan. Although a radio report of the ditching was repeatedly sent out, the passengers, it was later determined, were not informed as to the location of life jackets (one behind each seat) or rubber rafts.

After the plane crashed into the sea, and was bobbing up and down on fifteen-foot waves, the crew apparently opened the wrong doors while herding passengers out, and these openings allowed great amounts of water to enter the aircraft, which hastened its sinking. Confused passengers emerged on a wing, many without life jackets. Dozens of the sixty-nine aboard would not leave their seats and the captain threw several of them out before the plane began to sink.

Only one raft was inflated and carrying seven, it quickly drifted away. The captain and a handful of passengers stayed on the plane's wing until the ship sank, only three minutes after the crash. Vessels steamed to the rescue, but those who survived spent as long as an hour in the shark-infested water.

The fifty-two fatalities of this crash, authorities stated, could have been saved had the crew had the presence of mind to remove all the rubber rafts stored behind the captain's cabin.

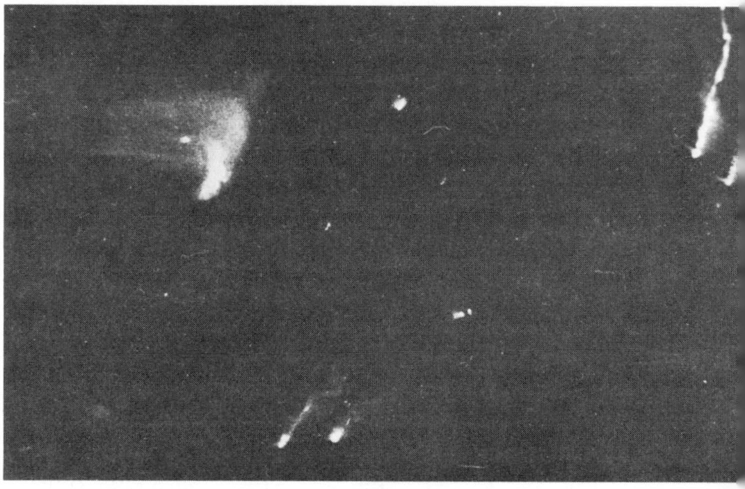

This photo, taken by a University of Delaware student through the window of his dormitory, shows the flaming fragments of a Pan American plane a moment after it exploded near Elkton, Maryland, December 8, 1963. All eighty-one on board died. *(Wide World)*

PAN AMERICAN AIRLINES

AIR CRASH
December 8, 1963

The use of the inexpensive "wide-cut gasoline," known better as JP-4, that was mixed with kerosene, was determined to be the cause of the Pan American Airlines crash over Elkton, Maryland, on December 8, 1963. The big Boeing 707, carrying eighty-one passengers and crew members, was struck by lightning that ignited the fuel-air mixture in a fuel tank, the Civil Aeronautics Board later concluded.

This explosion caused the port wing to shear off and send the plane into a spiral downward, crashing and killing everyone on board.

Also using this highly volatile fuel mixture for a short time were Trans World Airlines, K.L.M., Air Canada, Japan Air Lines and Sabena. Subsequent crashes would cause all of the airlines using JP-4 to change to a safer fuel mixture. Interestingly enough, following the Maryland crash, JP-4 was discreetly banned for use in the United States Presidential fleet. It was replaced by what was then considered the safest of all aviation fuels—JP-5.

(ALSO SEE: Trans World Airlines, November, 1964)

PAN AMERICAN AIRLINES — AIR CRASH
January 31, 1974

background: A Pan American Boeing 707, Flight 806, crashed just before landing at Pago Pago Airport on Samoa on January 31, 1974. The flight originated at Auckland, New Zealand, and was destined for Honolulu. Ten persons among the 101 on board were rescued from the flaming wreckage, but several later died, bringing the total death count to 96.

Flight 806 of Pan American Airlines was approaching the landing strip at Pago Pago, Samoa, at 12:52 A.M. during a thunderstorm on January 31, 1974. Pilot Leroy Peterson radioed Tutuila Airport that he was battling a wing-tugging squall and a fire on board his ship.

As the plane made its approach, the raging storm suddenly forced it downward, and about a mile from the runway, Flight 806 slammed into a 400-foot hill. In flames, with much of its metal sheared away, the plane plowed through the dense jungle for almost 200 feet, setting everything around it on fire.

Of the 101 persons on board the Pan American craft bound for Honolulu, only 10 were found alive by rescue teams, who speedily arrived at the burning wreckage. Rescuers ran onto one wing and began pulling out as many passengers as they could grab before the flames and heat became too intense for such efforts. The remaining passengers stayed in the funeral pyre that Flight 806 had become. The director of Samoa's modern hospital, Dr. Peter Veales, grimly commented that "most of the dead fried in the plane."

Ten survivors, with burns covering more than 50 percent of their bodies, were not expected to live. Five of them died hours later. An unnamed survivor said, "We all tried to get out and jammed the exits. I managed to get out over a wing, but most of those aboard did not."

The cause of the 707's quick fire and crash was never fully determined. It remained as much a mystery as the Pan American Boeing 707 that crashed July 23, 1973, shortly after it had taken off from Papeete, Tahiti. In that crash seventy-eight passengers and crew members perished, leaving one survivor.

PAPANDAYAN — VOLCANIC ERUPTION
1772

For centuries the natives on Java considered the towering volcano, Papandayan, approximately 8,750 feet high, a peaceful giant. They marveled at the colorful emissions of steam and smoke from its green sulfur deposits. Since

A Pan American 707 crashed and burned near Pago Pago on Samoa, January 31, 1974. Ninety-six passengers died. *(Wide World)*

A.D. 1500 great geysers had been thrown off by Papandayan, and without warning, in 1772 the entire mountain blew its contents outward in an eruption that sent out more fragmentary material than that of Krakatoa a century later.

Forty villages, several towns, 3,000 people, herds of cattle, and rich plantations located on its slopes disappeared as the volcano sank into a bubbling, lethal lake of lava. Papandayan lost almost 4,000 feet of its original height.

One historic report noted, "The area that was sunk down was fifteen miles long and six broad. No day of judgement painted by Angelo or Dore could ever match that actual horror of the solid mountain sinking into the earth with human beings on its slopes—its huge bulk going down as a ship goes down into the deep."

(ALSO SEE: Krakatoa)

PARDUBICE, CZECHOSLOVAKIA — RAILWAY WRECK — November 14, 1960

Only sketchy details are available of the head-on collision of two trains, both traveling at excessive speeds, outside of Pardubice, Czechoslovakia, on November 14, 1960. A monitoring of the broadcasts behind the Iron Curtain determined that the engineers of both trains ignored traffic regulations.

Both passenger trains met head-on at about 6:00 P.M. only a few miles from Pardubice, sixty-eight miles east of Prague. One hundred ten people were killed outright, and another 106 injured passengers were taken to hospitals. Whether or not any of the injured later perished is not known.

PARNASSUS, PENNSYLVANIA — MINE DISASTER — March 21, 1929

background: At 7:25 A.M. on March 21, 1929, the Kinlock Mine in Parnassus, Pennsylvania, exploded violently when a conveyor broke. The resulting dust was ignited by an electric arc from equipment in the shaft. Of the 258 men then working in the various mine shafts, 46 were killed and dozens more were injured.

The Kinlock Mine outside of Parnassus, Pennsylvania, was an extension of the old Valley Camp shafts worked in decades previous to the one in which a massive explosion took the lives of forty-six miners. The disaster occurred during the early morning of March 21, 1929. Kinlock was a comparatively safe mine. The accident that set off the disaster was not the fault of workers, but of equipment. A five-foot-wide conveyor, used to haul coal up the main shaft of 300 feet, was running at high speed and suddenly snapped, unraveling downward and creating great clouds of dust.

An electric arc on open electric equipment ignited the coal dust and some gas, and the explosion that followed was, according to mine inspector J. J. Forbes, "violent, traveling up the slope where it destroyed the conveyor structure and part of the tipple by force and fire and damaged the fan dust; traveling into the mine, the explosion destroyed doors, stoppings, overcasts and all equipment through about half the mine."

The tremendous blast hurled miners several feet through the air and slammed them, already dead, into the walls of the shafts. Others of the full working crew of 258 men were asphyxiated by billowing gas, and still others were burned alive by great gouts of flame that shot through the passageways.

The five-man crew on the tipple was blown flat by the upheaval; jets of flame closed over them and ignited their clothes. Four badly-burned men managed to roll into the dirt and extinguish the flames, thus saving themselves. One of this crew was immolated. Forty-five miners deep in the shafts and close to the explosion were dead minutes after the blast.

Rescuers arrived in minutes and, donning oxygen equipment, went into the mine, battling large fires as the men slowly moved forward. After extinguishing five fires, rescuers were suprised to find only a few stragglers to save. By then several intrepid foremen, at serious risk to themselves, had raced through many shafts and collected the bulk of the work force. They led 212 miners into the old workings of the abandoned Camp Valley shafts. The mass escape was hard-going, but all in this group survived. For almost a half-mile, they had to dig through collapsed walls, shore up rotten timbers and wade through icy water that swirled about them waist high.

An assistant foreman had the presence of mind to prevent his section of sixteen men from entering a shaft area where deadly pockets of gas had gathered. He threatened to "beat their brains out" with a pick unless they immediately threw up a barricade around a small room. He saved them until rescuers broke through to tell them the gas had dissipated. A lone miner working in a pillar section also barricaded himself for twenty-four hours against the gas. When he was rescued, his sanity was shattered.

PELAGIA — MARINE DISASTER — September 15, 1956

The 7,282-ton American freighter *Pelagia,* launched in 1943 and owned by Eastern Seaways Corporation, was bound for Baltimore from Narvik, Norway, with a full load of iron ore. On September 15, 1956, the ship was engulfed by high seas. The gale quickly closed over the vessel, and she foundered; only five members of the thirty-eight member crew survived.

PELÉE

VOLCANIC ERUPTION
May 8, 1902

background: In April, 1902, the 4,430-foot volcano Pelée at the northern point of the island of Martinique began to throw out clouds of ashes over the city of St. Pierre and neighboring villages. The volcano took up 50 square miles of land on the 400-square-mile island. By May 5 steam emissions from the volcano's lake mixed with ashes; liquid mud and lava began to flow downward. On May 8 at 7:50 A.M. the mountain gave off a gigantic explosion that blew out its side, the slope facing St. Pierre, and sent out a blast of stone, sand and noxious gases. In an estimated three minutes, the entire city of St. Pierre and other villages were completely engulfed in flames and from 30,000 to 36,000 persons were annihilated; only 30 persons survived, 4 in St. Pierre. The shockwave went around the world and the explosion was heard 300 miles distant. The blast, estimated to be at 300 m.p.h., carried temperatures from 450 to 1000 degrees. Also wiped out were the towns of Le Precheur, which had between 3,500 to 4,000 persons, Manceau and St. Philomène, which had populations half that number. Sixteen vessels in St. Pierre harbor were sunk with all hands on board and ten square miles of country incinerated. The volcano erupted again in September, 1929, but did little damage.

This sketch of the volcano Pelée, its sides blown open in a great eruption, was drawn by an eyewitness to the 1902 catastrophe who watched from a ship at sea.

Of all the lush, soft islands in the Lesser Antilles, Martinique, at the turn of the century, had come to symbolize a happy amalgamation of Western and native cultures, with 189,599 inhabitants (according to its last census before the doomsday of Pelée) living peacefully and cooperatively together. Its many sugar plantations, factories and 118 rum distilleries provided excellent livelihoods and above-average incomes. The capital, Fort de France (once Fort Royal), was small (population 17,274) compared with the bustling, architecturally elegant St. Pierre. With between 30,000 and 32,000 residents, St. Pierre, located north of Fort de France, boasted the largest community on the island.

St. Pierre was a verdant dream world of the past. Progress intruded only by sea in the form of iron steamers that took the riches of Martinique to the concrete capitals of the world. Lafcadio Hearn visited the city before its volcanic obliteration and later wrote a vivid, unforgettable description, calling it "the quaintest, queerest, and the prettiest withal, among West Indian cities; all stone-built and stone-flagged, with very narrow streets, wooden or zinc awnings, and peaked roofs of red tile, pierced by gable dormers. Most of the buildings are painted in a clear yellow tone, which contrasts delightfully with the burning blue ribbon of tropical sky above; and no street is absolutely level; nearly all of them climb hills, descend into hollows, curve, twist, describe sudden angles. There is everywhere a loud murmur of running water, pouring through the deep gutters contrived between the paved thoroughfare and the absurd little sidewalks, varying in width from one to three feet. The architecture is that of the seventeenth century, and reminds one of the antiquated quarter of New Orleans. All the tints, the forms, the vistas would seem to have been especially elected or designed for aquarelle studies."

That violent death and utter disaster could penetrate such a paradise was inconceivable to Martinique's inhabitants. The island previously had tasted natural catastrophes, but these outbreaks were nothing compared to the holocaust of 1902. Long after Columbus discovered the island, there had been several sketchily recorded volcanic outbursts. The earliest known eruption of Pelée occurred in 1727. In 1767 an earthquake rattled the island and killed 16,000 persons. Another quake in 1772 destroyed Martinique's military fortifications, but the loss of life was minimal.

Pelée erupted again in 1851 and in August, 1856, but little damage was done. Tourists were told more about Napoleon's Empress Josephine, who was raised in Martinique, than they were about the lofty, jungle-covered volcano.

On April 23, much to the surprise of St. Pierre's citizens, Pelée began to throw off showers of fine ash.

United States Consul to St. Pierre Thomas T. Prentis, his wife, and two daughters. Prentis knew that Pelée would eventually destroy St. Pierre and told a friend that he "did not expect to leave the island alive."

These showers increased in intensity, drifting down over the city, which was five miles away from Pelée's water-filled crater. Days later the top of the mountain began to hiss and give off clouds of vapor as its lake was set boiling by the intense heat of the magma beneath it. The quiet little streams that flowed downward from the mountain and through St. Pierre were transformed into raging rivers. The populace became further alarmed.

For several days even at high noon the sky was dark with dense showers of ash. Residents, fearful of the mountain for the first time in fifty years, began to pack belongings and move to other sections of the island or to distant shores. The United States consul's wife, Mrs. Thomas T. Prentis, wrote a letter to a sister in Boston from St. Pierre expressing her apprehensions: "My husband assures me that there is no immediate danger, and when there is the least particle of danger, we will leave the place. There is an American schooner in the harbor, the *R. J. Morse,* and she will remain here for at least two weeks. If the volcano becomes very bad, we shall embark at once and go out to sea."

The United States Consul, Prentis, apparently kept his real feelings from his wife and two daughters, for he told a visitor some months before the disaster that he "did not expect to leave the island alive."

Others weren't waiting for their own destruction and began to leave the city as torrential rains poured down from the heated sky, now black and full of thunder; the rains flooded the streams and villages were swamped, huts and humans sent on watery sheets to the sea. The local paper, *Les Colonies,* reported that "the exodus from St. Pierre is steadily increasing. From morning to evening and through the whole night, one sees only hurrying people carrying packages, trunks, and children." The St. Pierre newspaper attempted to coax its readers into returning by interviewing Professor Landes, a so-called authority on the volcano, who told citizens, "Pelée presents no more danger to the inhabitants of St. Pierre than does Vesuvius to those of Naples." *Les Colonies'* editor then added, "We cannot understand this panic. Where could one be better than at St. Pierre? Do those who invade Fort de France believe that they will be better off there than here should the earth begin to quake? This is a foolish error against which the populace should be warned."

Finding no suitable homes in other parts of the island, many of St. Pierre's residents returned. Their number was bloated by inhabitants of villages located on the high slopes of the volcano, some only 2,000 feet from the summit. Still the mountain increased its violent eruptions, its quakes rumbling around the clock. On May 5, 1902, new craters had formed on Pelée's sides, and these gave off showers of ash mixed with small stones. Streams of liquid mud ran from these craters, and one engulfed the Guerin sugar factory. Sulfur fumes were so thick in St. Pierre that those compelled to go out in the streets wore handkerchiefs about their faces. "The smell of sulfur is so strong," one letter writer reported, "that horses on the streets stop and snort. Some of them are obliged to give up, drop in their harness, and die from suffocation."

Letters sent to the United States in the last few days of St. Pierre's existence reflect a sense of foreboding, doom and death. One writer stated: "I write under the gloomiest impressions, though I hope I exaggerate the situation. This unchaining of the forces of nature is horrible. Since last month I have wished myself far from this place. My husband laughs, but I see he is full of anxiety and is trying to show a brave face in order to raise my courage. He tells me to go. How can I go alone?"

Another described St. Pierre as "a city sprinkled with gray snow, a winter scene without cold. . . . The inhab-

The fiery blast of lethal gas that spread through the streets of St. Pierre annihilated 36,000 people when Pelée erupted on May 8, 1902.

itants of the neighborhood are abandoning their houses, villas, and cottages, and are flocking to the city. It is a big, curious pellmell of women, children, and bare-footed peasants, big, black fellows, loaded with household goods. The air is oppressive, your nose burns. Are we going to die asphyxiated? What has tomorrow in store for us? A flow of lava, rain of stones, or a cataclysm from the sea? Who can tell? Will give you my last thought if I must die."

Another wrote: "If death awaits us, there will be a numerous company to leave the world. Will it be by fire or asphyxia? It will be what God wills. You will have our last thoughts. Tell brother Robert that we are still alive. This will, perhaps, be no longer true when this letter reaches you."

Martinique's governor, M. L. Mouttet, not the most intelligent of men, told the inhabitants of the island that there was no danger whatever of Pelée erupting. He sent 1,500 troops into St. Pierre to forcibly detain any residents from leaving the city, thinking that such stringent measures would avert panic. As it was, the action assured the deaths of thousands, including the governor, who, with his wife, had moved from Fort de France to St. Pierre. This show of confidence took place only hours before Pelée exploded.

In hindsight many reacted as lunatics. A fellow named Rivette led a group of European sightseers up the slopes of the lethal mountain only twenty-four hours before the end came. They wished to view the emissions of ash, vapor and lava, considering it a "novel spectacle." Children in Fort de France, comfortably distant from the volcano, frolicked in the falling ashes from Pélee. Pretending it was snow, they shouted, "Iceland! Iceland!"

Though many small sailing vessels had left St. Pierre's beautiful harbor, eighteen large ships, most of them British and American, stayed at anchor. One merchantman who took his ship from the doomed port commented, "The captains evidently thought that if the eruption grew dangerous they could hoist anchor and sail off. But those vessels will not sail away again in this world."

Only a few days before the eruption, the editor of *Les Colonies,* blithefully ignorant to the last, was attempting to form an "exploratory party" to ascend the volcano and picnic near its summit.

A wealthy planter, Fernard Clerc, had no such silly notions as he lay awake throughout the night of May 7, 1902, listening to the sullen detonations of the mountain. He rose early and immediately studied his barometer. His eyes popped as the needle frantically jiggled. Hardly bothering to dress, Clerc gathered his family and servants and jumped into a carriage. As he drove his horses at top speed through the streets of St. Pierre, some of his acquaintances saw him speed past and laughed, waving delicate lace handkerchiefs at him. It was 7:00 A.M., and it took Clerc fifty minutes to reach the hill known as Mont Parnasse, a mile outside St. Pierre. The moment he alighted from his carriage, Clerc looked down on the city; then he jerked his head upward toward Pelée as the volcano gave off a powerful cracking explosion that seemed to split the sky.

A mountain of flame shot upward out of its main crater, and at the same instant the entire side of the volcano blew open, stone, lava, ash and a tornadic whirlwind of fire lashing downward on St. Pierre. With enormous speed black clouds shot out after the fireballs. They engulfed the city within an estimated three minutes, and then rose to 13,000 feet. One narrative recorded, "It was as if the other three rocky sides of Pelée formed the mouth of a gigantic cannon from which shot a bolt of superheated vapor, gas, and white-hot fragments of molten rock."

This hurricane of fire, gas and smoke roared down the slopes of Pelée. The gases inside the volcano were exploding like bombs. Passing through the city, the blast of smoke and gas and stone fanned out into the sea, igniting the ships at anchor and raising a twelve-foot-high tidal wave that rolled toward Fort de France. Those on board the ship *Pouyer-Quertier,* six miles at sea, turned in the direction of a tremendous blast and saw that "light appeared in the direction of St. Pierre. . . thirty seconds later the binoculars showed the town to be in flames. The whole flank of the mountain on the side towards St. Pierre was glowing red."

All but two of the ships in the harbor were immediately capsized by the blast. Their crews were dumped into the steaming water, where they were literally boiled alive. Surviving were the steamers *Roddam* and the *Roraima.* The latter was almost totally wrecked. Her steel masts were snapped off two feet above the deck, and her bridge, boats and funnel were ripped away as if by a giant, unseen scythe. Half of the *Roraima's* crew and all but two of her passengers on deck were instantly burned to death by the blast of heat and gas.

Captain Freeman of the *Roddam* quickly ordered up-anchor as he watched the vast black cloud shoot down on St. Pierre. He watched thousands of casks of rum stored on the quays explode. The burning rum then rushed through the angling streets and down into the bay. The *Roddam,* 120 tons of ash coating her burning decks, got under way and limped out of the steaming harbor.

On board the *Roraima,* Assistant Purser Thompson viewed the entire destruction of the city and later wrote, "I saw St. Pierre destroyed. The city was blotted out by one great flash of fire. Nearly 30,000 people were all killed at once. Out of eighteen vessels lying in the roads, only one, the British steamship *Roddam,* escaped, and she, I hear, lost more than half of those on board. It was a dying crew that took her out. Our boat, the *Roraima,* arrived at St. Pierre early Thursday morning. For hours before we entered the roadstead we could see flames and smoke rising from Mt. Pelée. No one on board had any idea of danger. Captain [G. T.] Muggah was on the bridge, and all hands got on deck to see the show. The spectacle was magnificent. As we approached St. Pierre, we could distinguish the rolling and leaping of the red flames that belched from the mountain in huge volumes and gushed high into the sky. Enormous clouds of black smoke hung over the volcano. There was a constant muffled roar. It was like the biggest oil refinery in the world burning up on

The first relief party entered devastated St. Pierre while smoke still filled the streets. The man at left center holds a handkerchief to his face to counteract the stench of the dead.

the mountain top. There was a tremendous explosion about 7:45, soon after we got in. The mountain was blown to pieces. There was no warning. The side of the volcano was ripped out and there was hurled toward us a solid wall of flames. It sounded like thousands of cannon.

"The wave of fire was on us and over us like a lightning flash. It was like a hurricane of fire. I saw it strike the cable steamship *Grappler* broadside on, and capsize her. From end to end she burst into flames and then sank. The fire rolled in mass straight down upon St. Pierre and the ships in the harbor. The town vanished before our eyes.

"The air grew stifling hot, and we were in the thick of it. Wherever the mass of fire struck the sea, the water boiled and sent up vast clouds of steam. The sea was torn into huge whirlpools that careened toward the open sea. One of these horrible, hot whirlpools swung under the *Roraima* and pulled her down on her beam end with the suction. She careened way over to port, and then the fire hurricane from the volcano smashed her, and over she went on the opposite side. The fire wave swept off the masts and smokestacks as if they were cut with a knife."

Captain Muggah was the only man on the ship's deck to survive the initial blast of searing gas and flames sweeping over the vessel. His clothes were burned away and his lungs were burned so badly that he dove, half-mad, into the sea, holding on to a lifeline and then disappearing.

In St. Pierre there were two or three minutes of excruciating pain and madness as thousands attempted to flee, but were caught in mid-flight by the whirlwind. To take one breath was to die, the lungs shriveling instantly. Thousands were stopped as the flaming hurricane trapped them at the docks, where they collapsed at once in heaps. Before the *Roddam* put to sea, the United States vice-consul at St. Pierre, Amedee Testart, reached the ship by diving off a dock and swimming alongside. When he was halfway up the side, the flames caught him and he fell open-mouthed, silently gasping for air, back into the water, his death mingled with thousands of others.

Following the initial blast, which killed every living soul except four in St. Pierre, came torrential rains that mixed with ash and formed a pastelike substance that covered many houses to the rooftops. The *Roraima*'s First Officer, Ellery S. Scott, later reported: "After the stones came a rain of hot mud, lava apparently mixed with water, of the consistency of very thin cement. Wherever it fell it formed a coating, clinging like glue, so that those who wore no caps it coated, making a complete cement mask right over their heads."

One of St. Pierre's four survivors (she and two others died later as a result of injuries) was a native girl, Harvira Da Ifrile. She had left the cathedral that morning, and at her mother's orders, had traveled to her aunt's cottage to deliver a message. The cottage was situated near St. Pierre's cemetery, up the slope near an old crater called the Corkscrew. She later told her rescuers, French seamen from the cruiser *Suchet,* "I had hardly gone more than three steps when I felt a hot wind from the Corkscrew. Thinking that something must be on fire, I ran to the top of the path, and there I saw the bottom of the pit all red, like boiling, with little blue flames shooting up from it. There were two guides leading a woman up the path and hurrying as fast as they could run. I saw a puff of blue smoke seem to hit the party, and they fell as if killed."

The girl watched, transfixed in horror, as the lava spurted from the crater below her and slithered down on the three persons in its path until it completely covered them. Screaming in terror, she ran down the slope, ignoring her own family at prayer in the cathedral—it was the vigil of Ascension—and raced toward the waterfront.

"Just as I got to the main street, I saw this boiling stuff burst from the top of the Corkscrew and run down the side of the hill. It followed the road first, but then, as the stream got bigger, it ate up the houses on both sides of the road. Then I saw that a boiling red river was coming from another part of the hill and cutting off the escape of the people who were running out of the houses."

Harvira made it to the stone wharf, where her brother's boat was tied. It was ready with sail set, and she jumped into it. She heard a loud cry and then saw her brother "run toward me. But he was too late, and I heard him scream as the stream first touched and then swallowed him." Cutting the rope that held the boat to the wharf, the girl covered herself with canvas. Fireballs passed over her. The boat was driven seaward by the tidal wave, and though severely burned, she paddled to a small cave where she had often played. She stayed there until the French cruiser picked her up.

There was only one other survivor to relate to the outside world the horrors that befell the obliterated city and its dumbfounded citizens. He was a convicted murderer, Raoul Sarteret (alias Peleno), who had been sitting in a deep dungeon of the St. Pierre city prison when the fiery hurricane struck the town. His view was confined to the small grated window of his cell. He stood on a table to peer out. Before being overcome by noxious gases, Sarteret witnessed one of the most colossal disasters ever seen by human eyes. It was to be his last vision of anything; he survived but was blinded. His amazing account, embellished no doubt by purple-prose scribes who first wrote it down, reads thus: "I was just eating my breakfast that morning when the rumbling which I had heard beneath my cell for three or four days previously stopped suddenly. I do not know why, but I felt frightened, as though something fearful were to happen. Then the whole place became black.

"I could not help feeling that there was a disaster near, and I screamed to the jailers to come and unlock my cell, but I could not make anyone hear. The little window in my cell looked out on the back of the convent, where 200 girls and a large number of nuns frequently stayed, but there was a high wall between my cell and the convent.

"The violet darkness grew blacker and blacker until it was almost as dark as though it were night, and then suddenly the whole place was lighted up with a curious glow, sometimes red, sometimes green, but generally red. I put my little table against the cell window and, hanging on by the bars, attempted to look out, but could not see anything because of the brick wall in front of me.

"While I looked, however, a huge red-hot stone crashed down just in front of my window, right on the top of the wall, knocking it down. The heat from this stone was most intense and made my post at the window fearful to endure, but the sight was such that I could not turn away.

"Right in front of me where the brick wall had stood I saw the large convent, and I could see that molten matter had come down the hill and had run into the grounds of the convent. I realized then that there must have been an eruption of Mt. Pelée. To my horror, I discovered that the lava had completely encircled the convent with its first rush and that all the girls and sisters who were in the building were doomed.

"While I looked, I saw another stone, even larger than the one which had fallen near my cell window and broken down the wall, strike on the convent roof and crash through its three stories, evidently plunging through to the ground. I had not seen any of the sisters until that time, and I suppose they had depended for safety on the building, seeking shelter from the rain of hot ashes which I could see falling.

"In an instant after this huge stone crashed through, I saw the poor girls flocking out in the utmost terror. Their actions looked as though they were screaming in an agony of fright, but I could not hear a sound owing to the hissing of the lava and the roar of the volcanic discharge. As the girls came running out I saw that they carried with them bodies of those who had been injured by the crashing stone through the building. Some they carried out were dead, while I could see that others were only injured.

"The sisters came running out, too, bringing appliances for helping the injured, but those who had hurried out of the building were driven in again by the blinding ashes and the fumes which I could see rise from the lava.

"A pit had been dug on the inside of the wall in order that none of the girls should be able to climb up from the inside [a typical measure of girls' convents in that era to prevent any tampering with chastity], and this acted as a sort of moat, in which the lava floated, and thus made a complete circle round the convent, rendering escape impossible, even if it had been possible to live in the rain of hot stones and ashes from the mountain.

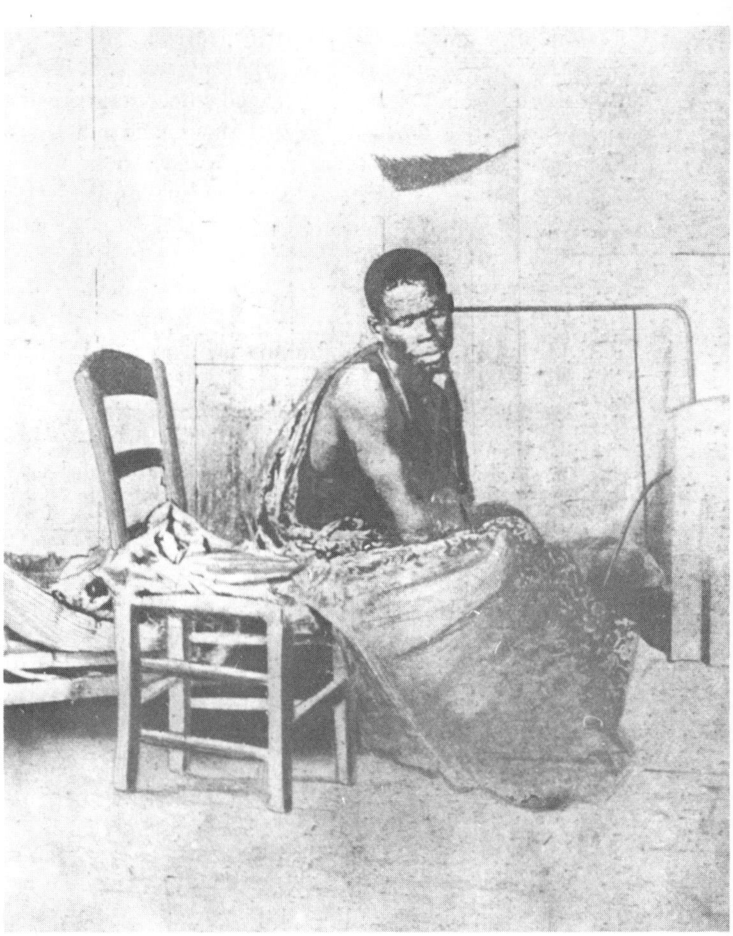

The only survivor of the St. Pierre disaster was a murderer, Raoul Sarteret, who later became a missionary.

"Again as I looked I saw another stone fall upon the building, and this time many more of the girls rushed out. This time there were far fewer. A part of them broke down one of the doors, and holding this over their heads, they tried to run for the gate, but were amazed to find their escape cut off by the river of lava.

"The lava gradually rose and rose, and I could see the huddled group of girls growing smaller and smaller, as first one and then others succumbed to the poisonous fumes and the fearful heat of the surrounding lava. And as the group got smaller, the lava rose and rose, until there was but a small piece of land around the building where the ground was not a heaving, swelling mass of molten matter.

"Then with one great burst, it seemed to me, a fresh stream of lava flowed into the moat and overswept the building and the little island on which the girls were standing a moment before. I turned away my eyes in horror, and when next I looked nothing was to be seen of the convent but a heap of calcined stone, and here and there the blackened corpses of those who but a few moments before had been full of life and hope.

"I could not see what was happening in the town for the reason that the window of my cell was so small and besides there was a pall of blackness over all the scene. I could, however, see here and there as the smoke lifted, that the lava had extended clear down to the sea and that but a few of the larger buildings had successfully withstood the attack of the volcanic eruption.

"While I was looking from my cell window, my eyes almost seared out of my head by the heat pouring through the narrow orifice, I noticed a thin blue smoke curl along the ground, and, caught by some eddying gust of wind, the fumes struck straight into my cell window, and I remember no more."

Sarteret had been in a state of semiconsciousness for almost four days before rescuers responded to his moans. When found, the blinded prisoner went momentarily mad and raced about his cell shouting. Somehow he managed to get down a corridor and stumble through the ruined town, where he was tripped by some sprawled bodies and recaptured. As the last survivor of doomed St. Pierre, Sarteret was pardoned. He later performed commendable missionary work.

French sailors, armed to repel looters and ghouls flocking into devastated St. Pierre from the surrounding countryside, arrived off the cruiser *Suchet* only three and a half hours after Pelée's monstrous outburst. The captain of the French ship had responded to a cable received from Fort de France that read: "St. Pierre is infested with pillagers who are forcing safes and stealing money, and valuable books and papers."

The sailors arrested twenty-seven men and three women for looting. None of the looters had been in the city at the time of the eruption. Two men found rummaging through the clothes of the dead were shot on sight.

The heat that radiated from the burning city blocked passage for the French sailors and for those who arrived on the rescue ship *Marin,* which had steamed from Fort de France. What these men found gave them nightmares for a lifetime. Incinerated bodies were sprawled in heaps. Thousands, many in collapsed buildings, were found with their hands at their throats. The swirling blast of sulfuric gas and fumes had withered their lungs; they had been asphyxiated by a type of poison gas somewhat

Ghouls and looters, depicted here in an artist's sketch, infested the city of St. Pierre following the eruption of Pelée.

similar to fire-damp found in the coal mines. Identification was impossible in many cases.

With Herculean power the blast had mowed down three-foot-thick walls and sent ten-foot-long iron siege guns flying for blocks. A three-ton statue of the Virgin Mary was hurled fifty feet from its pedestal. Heavy trees, some a hundred years old, were uplifted, roots and all, and thrown like sticks into the harbor. The constantly exploding and expanding gas of the eruption had carbonized fruits and flesh and melted glass in an estimated temperature of 1000° C. This type of eruption was ever after known as a Peléean Eruption, especially when the outbreak is at the side and not at the top of a volcano.

The disposal of the entire citizenry of St. Pierre, more than 30,000 bodies and maybe thousands more, was a mammoth chore. It took months, and all the while the monster volcano spat out ash stone and lava, imperiling the lives of the gravediggers. The mountain erupted again on August 30, 1902, and killed an additional 2,000 persons, most of whom were rescuers, engineers and mariners bringing relief supplies to the island.

Working along the devastated streets, policemen from Fort de France, soldiers, and sailors found mass burials impossible. They began to scoop up the scattered remnants of bodies and burn them on huge pyres. The stench was so overwhelming that many passed out. The sweetly sickening odor of burning flesh lingered over a portion of the island for months.

The dead were found in every conceivable position, most of them either carbonized or roasted. In many cases the abdomens had been burst open by the intense heat. The disaster had played freakish tricks. A woman completely charred was found still holding a silk handkerchief to her lips; the cloth was undamaged. A family of nine was found seated around a breakfast table, their arms locked, their faces unrecognizable. Young girls were found burned to a crisp, but their shoes were untouched. The features of the dead were twisted in fright and agony. Most of the dead were naked, their clothes having been burned away.

The Italian consul at Barbados, M. Paravicino, arrived at St. Pierre and began to systematically search for the body of his daughter, who had been visiting in the city when the eruption took place. He found her in the ruined cathedral, among hundreds of other bodies. He calmly supervised the spraying of her body with disinfectant before she was removed for burial. The man who believed he would never leave St. Pierre alive, United States consul Thomas T. Prentis, was found dead, along with his wife, both charred, sitting in chairs and facing a window that opened toward fuming Pelée. The bodies of the Prentis girls were never located in the gutted consulate.

Rising in grotesque triumph out of Pelée's central crater, during the grim weeks when funeral pyres fed by petroleum dotted the dead city, was an immense, chimneylike column of hardened lava which was later to be called the Tower of Pelée or Pelée's Spine. This ugly pillar continued to rise to about 1,000 feet before it disintegrated a year later. It was thought by some to be extremely viscous lava forming a neck that was literally squeezed upward by the ever closing mouth of the crater. Some vulcanologists thought the spine "was an enormous plug of solid lava which had solidified in the throat of the volcano" following an ancient outbreak and was then forced upward by the accumulated gases and magma that had set off the 1902 explosion.

Writing two years after the outbreak and after having visited the monster, volcano expert Angelo Heilprin stated, "There remains little doubt in my mind that the tower of Pelée was merely the ancient core of the volcano that had been forced from the position of rest in which solidification had left it. . . . The power to lift, or even sustain so gigantic a structure as this tower, with a cubical content equal to that of the Great Pyramid of Egypt, must have been prodigious." In 1903 Heilprin got about 700 feet away from the still steaming tower and took a famous picture, about which he later remarked, "The aspect of the tower from this point, with the steam and ash puffs and blue sulfur fumes playing about its base, was one of great magnificence . . . extraordinary obelisk of lava like a veritable Tower of Babel."

(ALSO SEE: Krakatoa, Soufriere)

PESHTIGO, WISCONSIN — FIRE
October 8, 1871

background: A series of small logging and settler fires were whipped together by a fierce wind on October 8, 1871, and raced through eastern Wisconsin. Within a single day they wiped out the town of Peshtigo and nearly all of its population, as well as hundreds in nearby communities. More than four million acres of timber and prairie land were burned, and 1,500 Wisconsin residents were killed. In Peshtigo more than $3 million in damage was done, most of which was suffered by lumber mill owner William B. Ogden, whose losses during the Chicago Fire were also great.

The year 1871, particularly during the October week of the Chicago Fire, was studded with massive outbreaks of fire throughout the simmering drought-blighted plains. It had not rained for three months, and humidity was almost nonexistent. The gale wind that blew the Chicago blaze to such fury also raced across seven states.

Searing holocausts hit the towns of Peshtigo, Manistee and Glen Haven in Wisconsin, as well as towns in the states of Iowa, Minnesota, Illinois, Indiana and the Dakotas. The blazing fires literally dropped from the heavens in hurricanes of flame in Wisconsin, encompass-

People and livestock sought refuge in the river during the burning holocaust of Peshtigo, October 8, 1871. *(Peshtigo Times)*

ing nine towns and 400 square miles. The suffocating cloud instantly killed 750 people, and another 750 residents were burned to death.

Peshtigo was wiped out. On the same night that Chicago went up in flames, Peshtigo met its doom, and half of its inhabitants were killed outright. The town was surrounded by swamps giving off methane gas, and when the tornado of fire hit the small community, this gas went off like an atom bomb. Houses actually exploded.

An eyewitness who managed to escape wrote, "In one awful instant a great flame shot up in the western heavens, and, in countless fiery tongues, struck downward into the village, piercing every object that stood in the town like a red-hot bolt. A deafening roar, mingled with blasts of electric flame, filled the air and paralyzed every soul in the place. There was no beginning to the work of ruin; the flaming whirlwind swirled in an instant through the town.

"All heard the first inexplicable roar; some aver that the earth shook, while a few avow that the heavens opened and the fire rained down from above. The tornado was but momentary, but was succeeded by maelstroms of fire, smoke, cinders and red-hot sand that blistered the flesh."

Survivors staggered toward the nearby Peshtigo River holding their breaths. To inhale the red-hot air was to die from scorched lungs. Peshtigo firemen watched their houses burn to ashes. One house, raised one hundred feet into the air by violent winds, exploded into flames above the fleeing throng.

A correspondent for the *New York Tribune,* who wrote from the scene of the Peshtigo horror on October

20, stated: ". . . the mad horde saw the bridge in flames in a score of places, and, turning sharply to the left, with one accord, plunged into the water. Three hundred people wedged themselves in between the rolling booms, swayed to and fro by the current, where they roasted in the hot breath of flame that hovered above them and singed the hair on each head momentarily exposed above the water."

Those in the river struggled to remain afloat, beating back others who crowded the waters and kicking frantically at frenzied animals who thrashingly joined them.

Others, rushing toward the river, were mowed down by blasts of fire that raced across the waters.

Those who survived this wave of fire were horribly disfigured in seconds, but continued to crawl in agony acorss the pebbly flats beneath the billowing flames toward the river. Upon reaching the river, several merely put their heads beneath the water and drowned as the exposed portions of their bodies burned. Particles of burning sand were shot as if by cannon across the open spaces of the town, and these pierced the flesh of the running citizens. Such was the force of the flaming whirlwind that holes were later found in iron plows.

Those who managed to dive through a wall of flames at the edge of the town ran into a clearing and pressed their faces into sand. They were found the next day, roasted to cinders. Not everyone ran from their homes. One man named Hansen, with his wife and four children, believed that "Judgment Day" had come, and there was nothing he could do about it. He refused to evacuate his wife and four children from their house, and "while the fire rained down, he began to walk composedly up and down his parlor with his family about him." The Hansens were never seen again.

Inside one home was a man sick with fever. Hearing this, a lumberjack dashed through the burning structure, scooped him up, and carried him outside. Furiously the woodman dug a pit at the side of the house, where it was protected somewhat from the wind and rain of fire. He placed the ill man inside and covered him with his own body. The lumberjack was burned to death, but the fever victim was found alive the next day.

Tradesmen and merchants, in an effort to save valuables, threw goods down all of the many wells within the community. Minutes later, scores of women and children were lowered into these wells by husbands and fathers who sought to save them. The goods in the wells, however, caught fire and roasted everyone who sought refuge there. One observer related how he "looked into every well in the ash-covered clearing, and there is no possibility that a living thing could have endured the flames that boiled and seethed in them."

About one hundred men, all workers in William B. Ogden's sawmill and lumber company (ironically, Ogden's interests were also wiped out in Chicago during the Great Fire a day before Peshtigo went to ashes) were trapped in a huge warehouse, and all were found dead. They had refused to leave what they thought to be the safest building the town had and, "trusting to the stout walls of the company's building, perished *en masse*."

When the fire died the next day, the survivors were horrified at the destruction. Peshtigo was gone, and so were 1,152 of its citizens.

One mother who burned to death had been caught in the center of town when the fire struck. She dug a small hole in the ground and placed her baby in it to shield the child from the flames. But the infant was found suffocated to death under its mother's body. A farmer and his family were trapped by four solid walls of flame. The man took out his pistol and shot his family and then himself.

Help did not come to Peshtigo and other destroyed towns in Wisconsin and Michigan for weeks. Aid was first directed to Chicago.

Chicago was rebuilt and the only reminder of the Great Fire on its hundredth anniversary was the well-maintained Water Tower. But Peshtigo remains ghostly with barren wastelands greeting the visitor to this day.
(ALSO SEE: Chicago, Illinois, 1871)

PHENIX — MARINE DISASTER
June 15, 1939

The French submarine *Phenix,* with seventy-one crew members on board, was navigating the deep waters in Cam Ranh Bay off what was then French Indochina on June 15, 1939, when she disappeared forever. In a mock battle attack against her sister ship *L'Espoir,* the *Phenix* submerged and attempted to maneuver against the cruiser *Lamotte-Picquet.*

When the submarine failed to resurface, a flotilla of ships and scores of French warplanes searched the area, which plunged to a depth of 375 feet. The *Phenix's* hull had been made to withstand pressure down to 330 feet. Consequently, after the sub was submerged close to two days, authorities reasoned that the vessel's hull had burst and all in her were dead.

All submarines in the French Navy at the time, including the *Phenix,* lacked escape diving bells or "lungs" that were in use in American and English submarines. The French had planned to purchase four such bells from the United States only weeks earlier.

Days later oil slicks in the area of the sinking confirmed the loss of the *Phenix.*

Among the wires of condolence sent to the French was a message from Adolf Hitler. French President Albert Lebrun did not respond.
(ALSO SEE: Squalus, Thetis*)*

PHILADELPHIA, PENNSYLVANIA — FIRE, July 9, 1850

A fire that created an immense amount of property damage occurred in Philadelphia, Pennsylvania, on the afternoon of July 9, 1850. About 4:00 P.M. a blaze sprang up in a store on Delaware Avenue. In minutes adjacent buildings were set afire. Reaching the cellar of the store where it had begun, the fire ignited explosives that went off with terrific reports and sent flaming objects flying through the street. Several hundred people from the slum districts gathered to watch firemen battle the flames.

Then a third and more violent explosion occurred, and the entire street shook as buildings collapsed, firemen were sent scurrying, and thirty spectators were instantly killed. One report stated: "This . . . caused a panic among the firemen and spectators, and in the efforts of all to escape from the danger, many were trampled upon and injured [about one hundred persons]. Some were thrown into the Delaware [River], and others jumped in to get away from the falling bricks and beams sent up from the burning building by the explosion." Nine more persons, mostly children, drowned in the river.

The uncontrollable fire swept through the most densely populated area of the city and destroyed more than 400 buildings, almost all in the slum districts. Damages were estimated to be more than $1 million.

(ALSO SEE: Baltimore, Maryland; Chicago, Illinois)

PHILADELPHIA, PENNSYLVANIA — FIRE, February 8, 1865

Sitting on an open lot on Philadelphia's Washington Street, near Ninth Street, were 2,000 barrels of coal oil, wholly unprotected from the elements. These caught fire early on the morning of February 8, 1865. They quickly exploded, and set fire to several buildings in the district. Firemen were helpless as the burning coal oil slithered onto Ninth Street, and then onto Federal Street. A huge column of flames and smoke was sent up. Residents of the area, slipping and sliding in the snow and slush in their nightclothes, attempted to flee. "People leaving their blazing homes," one report states, "hoping to reach a place of safety, were roasted to death."

Fifty buildings in a three-square-block area were completely ruined. The loss amounted to $500,000. An estimated twenty persons perished in the blaze.

(ALSO SEE: Philadelphia, Pennsylvania, 1850)

PHILIPPINES — TYPHOONS, October 14-15, 1970

Almost 1,500 persons were killed, and a half-million more were made homeless, by the three typhoons that crisscrossed the Philippine Islands on October 14-15, 1970. Winds up to 100 m.p.h. sent waves and torrents over southern Luzon, Mindanao and smaller islands; the nonstop storms obliterated 90,000 homes in twenty-four provinces. Damages to crops, small cities and homes soared into the millions. Under Red Cross direction relief supplies quickly were made available by the United States. Medicine, food and clothing also were sent to the stricken islands from Singapore, Canada and the Soviet Union.

PHOENIX — MARINE DISASTER, October 3-4, 1780

background: The forty-four-gun British frigate *Phoenix,* commanded by Captain Sir Hyde Parker, in company with the *Badger,* set out from Montego Bay on October 2, 1780, to patrol the Spanish Main. They were caught by the massive Savanna-la-Mar hurricane, and were carried north. The *Phoenix* was wrecked on the shoals of Cabo de la Cruz, Cuba, on October 4, 1780, with a loss of about 200 sailors. Only a handful survived. Twelve British ships sank in the storm; more than 3,000 sailors perished.

In the gritty annals of sailing one of the most stirring first-hand accounts of a shipwreck during a hurricane was that written by an officer who was aboard the ill-fated British frigate *Phoenix,* which was destroyed by the infamous Savanna-la-Mar hurricane that overpowered several fleets in the Caribbean on October 3-5, 1780. Completely overwhelmed was the British squadron under the command of Sir Hyde Parker. Departing the tranquil waters of Montego Bay in late September and early October, the *Victor, Barbadoes* and *Scarborough* were never seen again; the *Badger* and the flagship *Phoenix,* a gleaming forty-four-gun frigate, were driven across the violent seas and reduced to splinters on the rocks near Cuba.

The hurricane first struck the ancient Spanish port of Savanna-la-Mar, Jamaica, destroying it, and then raked Montego Bay just after the British squadron had departed. Pursuing these ships on its relentless course, the hurricane overtook the vessels one by one, and then moved on to gouge Cuba.

Lieutenant Archer on the *Phoenix,* in a long and graphic letter to his mother, recounted in a blow-by-blow narrative the devastating storm that engulfed his ship. It remains a classic to this day.

At eleven at night it began to snuffle, with a monstrous heavy appearance from the eastward. Close-reefed the topsails. Sir Hyde sent for me.

"What sort of weather have we, Archer?"

"It blows a little and has a very ugly look."

"Don't hoist the topsails till it clears a little, there is no trusting any country."

At eight in the morning I came up again, found it blowing hard from the east-northeast with close-reefed

The British ship *Phoenix* capsized in 1780.

topsails upon the ship, and heavy squalls at times. Sir Hyde came upon deck.

"Well, Archer, what do you think of it?"

"Oh, sir, it is only a hurricane in the Indies, and the beginning of it has much the same appearance as this; so take in the topsails; we have plenty of sea-room."

At twelve, the gale still increasing, wore ship, to keep as near mid-channel, between Jamaica and Cuba, as possible; at one the gale increasing still; at two harder yet; it still blows harder. In the evening no sign of the weather taking off, but every appearance of the storm increasing, prepared for a proper gale of wind; secured all the sails with spare gaskets; good rolling tackles upon the yards; squared the booms; saw the boats all made fast; new lashed the guns; double-breeched the lower deckers; saw that the carpenters had the tarpaulins and battens all ready for hatchways; got the top-gallant-mast down upon the deck; jim-boom and spirtsailyard fore and aft; in fact, everything we could think of to make a snug ship.

The poor devils of birds now began to find the uproar in the elements, for numbers, both of sea and land kinds, came on board of us. When they came over the ship they dashed themselves down upon the deck, without attempting to stir till picked up, and when let go again, they would not leave the ship, but endeavoured to hide themselves from the wind.

At eight o'clock a hurricane; the sea roaring, but the wind still steady to a point; did not ship a spoonful of water. However, got the hatchways all secured, expecting what would be the consequences should the wind shift; placed the carpenters by the mainmast with broad-axes, knowing from experience that at the moment you may want to cut it away to save the ship, an axe may not be found. Went to supper; bread, cheese, and porter. The purser frightened out of his wits about his bread bags, the two marine officers as white as sheets, not understanding the ship's working and groaning in every timber, and the noise of the lower deck guns which by this time made a pretty screeching and straining to people not used to it. It seemed as if the whole ship's side was going at each roll. Old "Woodenhead," our carpenter, was all this time smoking his pipe and laughing at the doctor; the second lieutenant upon deck, and the third in his hammock.

At ten o'clock I thought to get a little sleep; came to look into my cot; it was full of water, for every seam, by the straining of the ship had begun to leak and the sea was also flooding through the closed gun-ports. I stretched myself, therefore, upon the deck between two chests and left orders to be called, should the least thing happen. At twelve a midshipman came up to me:

"Mr. Archer, we are just going to wear ship, sir."

"Oh, very well, I'll be up directly. What sort of weather have you got?"

"It blows a hurricane, sir, and I think we shall lose the ship."

Went upon deck and found Sir Hyde there. Said he:

"It blows damned hard, Archer."

"It does indeed, sir."

"I don't know that I ever remember it blowing so hard before, Archer, but the ship makes a very good weather of it upon this tack as she bows the sea; but we must wear her, as the wind has shifted to the south-east and we are drawing right down upon Cuba. So do you go forward and have some hands stand by; loose the lee yardarm of the foresail and when she is right before the wind, whip the clewgarnet close up and roll up the sail."

"Sir, there is no canvas that can stand against this a moment. If we attempt to loose him he will fly into ribands in an instant, and we lose three or four of our people. She will wear by manning the fore shrouds."

"No, I don't think she will, Archer."

"I'll answer for it, sir. I have seen it tried several times on the coast of America with success."

"We'll try it."

This was a great condescension from such a man as Sir Hyde. However, by sending about two hundred people into the fore-rigging, after a hard struggle, she wore; as the sea began to run across, she had not time to rise from one sea before another lashed against her. My God! To think that the wind could have such force.

At this point, sounds from below decks increased, the racket strongly suggesting to Archer and his shipmates that one of the heavy guns had broken away from its moorings and, shifting about in the storm, was battering a hole in the ship.

Archer went into the gloom below and encountered a marine officer who shouted above the din: "Mr. Archer, we are sinking! The water is up to the bottom of my cot. All the cabins are awash and the people flooded out!"

". . .as long as it is not over your mouth you are well off. What the devil are you making all this noise about?"

The lieutenant noticed the creeping water, and ordered several men to turn to at the pumps.

"Come pump away, my lads! Will you twiddle your thumbs while she drowns the lot of you? Carpenters, get the weather chain-pump rigged."

"Already, sir."

"Then man it, and keep both pumps going. The ship is so distressed that she merely comes up for air now and then. Everything is swept clean but the quarterdeck."

The ship was fast breaking up and after seeing to several leaks below, Archer returned to the storm-swept deck.

Who can attempt to describe the appearance of things upon deck? If I were to write forever, I could not give you an idea of it—a total darkness all above; the sea on fire, running as it were in Alps or Peaks of Teneriffe (mountains are too common an idea); the wind roaring louder than thunder, the whole made more terrible if possible, by a very uncommon kind of blue lightning; the poor ship very much pressed, yet doing what she could, shaking her sides and groaning at every stroke. Sir Hyde was lashed upon the deck to windward, and I soon lashed myself alongside of him and told him the state of affairs below, saying that the ship did not make more water than might be expected in such infernal weather and that I was only afraid of a gun breaking loose.

"I am not in the least afraid of that," said the captain. "I have commanded her for six years, and have had many a gale of wind in her, so that her ironwork, which always gives way first, is pretty well tried. Holdfast, Archer, that was an ugly sea! We must lower the yards, for the ship is much pressed."

"If we attempt it, sir, we shall lose them, for a man aloft can do nothing; besides, their being down would ease the ship very little; the mainmast is a sprung mast; I wish it were overboard without carrying everything with it, but that can soon be done. The gale cannot last forever. 'Twill soon be daylight now."

Found by the master's watch that it was five o'clock, glad it was so near dawn and looked for it with much anxiety. Cuba, thou are much in our way! Send a midshipman to fetch news from the pumps. The ship was filling with water despite all their labor. The sea broke halfway up the quarterdeck, filled one of the cutters upon the booms and tore her all to fragments. The ship lying almost upon her beam ends and not attempting to right again. Word from below that the water had gained so fast they could no longer stand to the pumps. I said to Sir Hyde:

"This is no time, sir, to think of saving the masts. Shall we cut away?"

"Aye, Archer, as fast as you can."

I accordingly went into the chains with a pole-axe to cut away the lanyards; the boatswain went to leeward, and the carpenters stood by the mast. We were already when a very violent sea broke right on board of us, carried everything upon deck away, filled the ship with water, the main and mizen-masts went, the ship righted, but was in the last struggle under us. As soon as we could shake our heads above water Sir Hyde exclaimed:

"We are gone at last, Archer—foundered at sea!"

"Yes, sir. And the Lord have mercy on us!"

I thought I heard the ship thump and grinding under our feet; it was so.

"Sir, the ship is ashore."

The *Phoenix* had crashed onto the Cuban reefs known as Cabo de la Cruz, but only a skeleton crew remained, about 200 perishing when the ship broke up. When Hyde Parker returned to Montego Bay he faced a court martial for losing his frigate but was acquitted. He, Archer, and a handful of others had lived through one of the worst hurricanes on record in a wooden sailing ship that was the best their century had to offer.

(ALSO SEE: Capitanas, Centaur*)*

PIEDMONT AIRLINES — AIR CRASH
July 19, 1967

"I could see bodies falling like confetti," one witness said, as he described the destruction of a Piedmont Airline 727 jet and a Cessna 310 moments after they collided near Hendersonville, North Carolina, on July 19, 1967. The bodies—all eighty-two on board both planes—plummeted everywhere; one crashed through the roof of a house, and another fell in a service station. Corpses were draped in trees and scattered along highways.

Only minutes before the crash the Piedmont Boeing had made a perfect takeoff from the Asheville-Henderson Airport and was on course. The Cessna 310 was twelve miles off its run. David Addison, a veteran pilot, and two businessmen from Missouri were on board. Airport officials instructed Addison to turn north, but he apparently failed to do so and, moments later, crashed into the large passenger plane. The twin-engined Cessna vanished in a ball of yellow flames, and the crippled Piedmont jet, struck in the forward fuselage, lumbered along for a minute or so before it exploded, sending its grisly cargo earthward.

John McNaughton and his wife were killed. McNaughton, one of Robert McNamara's "whiz kids," was a Naval Secretary-designate, scheduled to be sworn into office a week later.

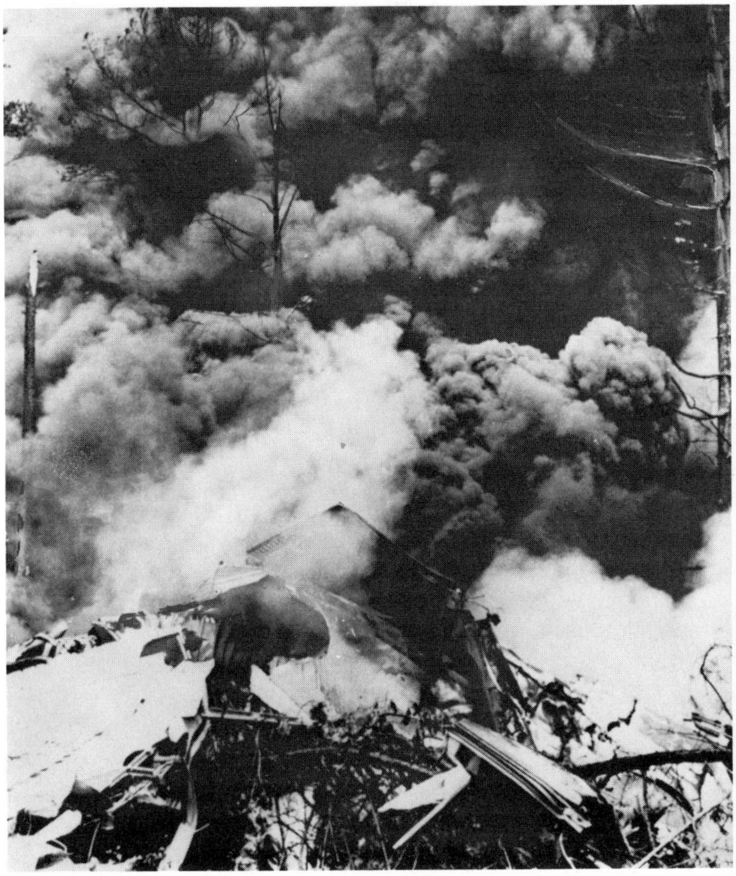

Black smoke rises from the wreckage of a Piedmont Boeing 727 which crashed in a patch of woods near Hendersonville, North Carolina, on July 19, 1967. *(Wide World)*

PITTSBURGH, PENNSYLVANIA — RAILWAY WRECK
October 9, 1880

The rear-ending of a Pennsylvania train in Pittsburgh, Pennsylvania, on the night of October 9, 1880, was due to overcrowding and slack observation of safety rules. Following a massive downtown Democrat parade, commuters jammed Union Depot so thickly that two trains in separate sections were quickly added on one run. The first train, according to one report, had "passengers standing in the aisles, hanging on the railings, and perched everywhere a foothold could be obtained."

At least a dozen passengers stood on the observation platform of the last car, and when the first train stopped at the Twenty-eighth Street Station, the travelers' bodies obscured the rear signal lights. In addition the rear brakeman, instead of getting off the train and protecting it with a lantern signal, as was the rule, kept collecting tickets.

Julian Huey, engineer of the second section, compounded these gross errors by either failing to see or ignoring the signal outside the Twenty-eighth Street Station. It indicated that the first train was stopped there. Huey shot his train into the depot area at about 16 m.p.h. Seconds before his engine telescoped into the rear of the first section, Huey jumped screaming from his train (he survived). As the second train struck the first, its boiler valves were snapped, and live steam scalded the already dead and dying victims in the last car of the first train. Thirty-two persons died. Huey was not reprimanded.

PLAYTOWN CABARET — FIRE — May 13, 1972

background: The Playtown Cabaret, situated atop the Sennichi Department Store in Osaka, Japan, caught fire on the night of May 13, 1972. Panic and blocked exits assured the high death toll of 118 persons. The cause of the blaze was attributed to faulty electric wires ignited by flaming, oil-soaked rags.

An electrician, Keiji Kewashima, working on the third floor of the sprawling Sennichi Department Store in downtown Osaka, Japan, was suddenly surrounded by flames on the evening of May 13, 1972. He ran down the aisles shouting the alarm, but the store, which comprised the first five stories of the seven-story building, was deserted. Scores of festive people, who were celebrating in the Playtown Cabaret that occupied the top floor of the building, remained unaware of the flames creeping up toward them.

Their clothes and flesh burned, several nightclub employees climb down a fire ladder from the charred Playtown Cabaret in Osaka, Japan, on May 13, 1972. The fire killed 118 persons. *(Wide World)*

When the blaze burst into the nightclub, everyone panicked and desperately sought emergency exits. Unfortunately sofas and drapes obscured the exits from the yelling, shoving throng. An emergency escape chute was discovered, and twenty persons hurriedly began to descend to street level, but the chute collapsed and sent them all crashing to their deaths.

Those lucky enough to reach the building's elevators also found themselves trapped. The power cables controlling the elevators had been severed by the fire raging up the shafts. Wielding tables and chairs, the lung-seared nightclubbers smashed out windows and, to avoid suffocation, began to leap earthward. Others climbed out the windows and inched themselves to the roof, but they were trapped there, too, by the flames. They began to hurtle themselves, half-mad with the heat, into space and down to death.

One survivor later said, "I broke a window pane and waited for rescue. I watched several people fall to their deaths. So I decided not to climb outside, although I really wanted to."

Death leaps continued even after firemen arrived. With scantily-clad hostesses leading the way, 19 persons attempted to jump to an adjacent roof. All missed. By the time firemen worked their way into the nightclub, 118 persons had either suffocated or perished in falls. Thirty-eight persons were injured, and 48 were rescued. The dead were found huddled together in heaps, most in the corners of the charred nightclub. Firemen reasoned that they had died trying to locate the hidden fire exits.
(ALSO SEE: Coconut Grove)

PLYMOUTH, PENNSYLVANIA — MINE DISASTER — September 6, 1869

The Avondale coal mine, operated by the Lackawanna and Western Railroad and located outside Plymouth, Pennsylvania, caught fire on the morning of September 6, 1869. Two hundred miners were trapped in the many shafts, the deepest of which was 237 feet. To create a draft for fresh air, the crude custom in early mining, a furnace was kept burning deep in the mine. Sparks from this furnace ignited nearby timbers and adjacent dry scantlings, causing sections of the roof to collapse.

In the words of a *Harper's Weekly* reporter, "Whatever fresh air there was in the mine went to feed the fierce flame, while the sulfurous gases, having no longer an outlet, were forced back into the chambers and galleries of the colliery."

As black smoke billowed from the mine entrance, hundreds of Plymouth citizens arrived, and rescue squads were organized. Before the rescue squads descended, however, a dog with a lantern hung around its neck was lowered by rope into the mine. He was brought up alive, and the lantern was still lit, indicating a safe passage for rescuers. About eighty men were taken out of the mine; most were unconscious. One hundred ten miners were asyphyxiated.

POCAHONTAS, VIRGINIA — MINE DISASTER

March 13, 1884

background: The Laurel Mine in Pocahontas, Virginia, owned by the Western Railroad Company and operated by the Southwest Virginia Improvement Company, exploded at 1:00 A.M. on March 13, 1884, when afterdamp was ignited by an open lamp. On orders of Colonel George Dodds and others, the shafts were sealed to put out the raging blaze. Though 112 miners were officially listed as dead, most reports listed a total of 150 workers killed out of the usual 500-600 man work force.

The blast that ripped apart the Laurel Mine in Pocahontas, Virginia, at 1:00 A.M. on March 13, 1884, was probably the most devastating in American history and one of the most controversial. The mine owners practiced few safety precautions. The shafts were extremely dry and dusty. Gas hung in pockets deep inside the mine, and ventilation was poor. Excessive amounts of black blasting powder were commonly used, and danger existed on a minute-to-minute basis.

Worked mostly by Hungarian and German immigrants and blacks, the mine contained from 112 to 150 men at the time of the explosion. The direct cause of the explosion was never fully determined, but improper blasting was cited as the cause by more than one authority. The roar of the explosion was heard for twenty miles and every living thing in the paths of the fireballs was obliterated. The fan used for pumping fresh air into the shafts was crazily bent. Pieces from this machine were blown 200 feet from the mine's entranceway. Shot out of the shaft like a bullet out of a rifle was the little dummy engine and several cars loaded with coal. At least two workmen at the mouth of the colliery were crushed as the careening engine ran over them.

The train's engineer was blown to his death one hundred feet beyond the mouth of the shaft. His body, horribly mutilated, was found hours later. Six more miners, standing at the mouth of the main entrance, were decapitated instantly by the blast, their heads sent flying hundreds of feet distant, and these had to be found before body identifications could be made. Mixed with the grotesque bodies were ten shredded carcasses of mules.

The force of the blast tore through every exitway of the mine, searing, burning and killing anything before it. A *New York Times* correspondent wrote: "On the topmost summit, 400 yards from the mouth

This melodramatic sketch shows a wife discovering the body of her husband, blown out of the mouth of the Pocahontas mine. *(Frank Leslie's Illustrated Newspaper)*

Laurel Mine in Pocahontas, Virginia, blew up on March 13, 1884. The inset shows dead miners arrayed in a local blacksmith shop. *(Frank Leslie's Illustrated Newspaper)*

of the ill-fated shaft, a mule's head and a child's foot were picked up . . ." Scores of miners' cottages in the explosion's path had been demolished, crushed to splinters, and all in them were buried by debris. "The very trees on the mountains, which have withstood the beating storms of ages, were shriveled, torn and blasted, their branches scattered in every conceivable direction." Steel, wood and flesh were blown as far as a mile. "Even the coal dust was blown over the mountain, and covered the earth on the opposite side to a half of an inch."

A writer for *Leslie's* arrived at the scene of horror to discover "fragments of human bodies lodged in tree-tops and on the roofs of houses and sheds."

At first the citizens of the small Virginia hamlet in Tazewell County ran hysterically in front of the blazing entrance to the mine. "Screams, lamentations and wild manifestations of grief, terror, supplication and despair on the part of both men and women were heard and seen everywhere. Dazed people ran aimlessly to and fro . . . seeking friends and relatives, and no one seemed to have any idea of what could or ought to be done."

Knots of miners, with soaked blankets thrown about them, attempted to enter the mine shafts several times, but the fierce fires drove them back and injured many. Organization appeared hours later with the arrival of several mining engineers led by Colonel George Dodds. Seeing the flames still shooting out of the mine exits, Dodds ordered every entrance sealed, believing this to be the only way to put out the fire. The fate of any miners who might still have possibly been alive in the shafts was thus decided. Barricades were quickly thrown up. Hoses were inserted, and the systematic flooding of the mine commenced.

Two weeks later investigators cautiously made their way into the pits and counted 112 bodies, some of whom had been drowned.

Publications around the country criticized the owners for their apparent disregard for safety. Conditions at this mine, however, as well as in those across the mining states, improved little during the next five decades.

(ALSO SEE: Crested Butte, Colorado)

POPLAR BLUFF, MISSOURI — TORNADO — May 9, 1927

On May 9, 1927, a series of storms originating in Arkansas quickly fanned out over Oklahoma, Texas, Kansas and Missouri. Poplar Bluff, Missouri, was hit the hardest when a tornado traveling at about 50 m.p.h. completely uprooted the three square blocks making up the center of the town's business district at 3:15 P.M.

The East Side School was devastated, and several children caught inside were killed; many more were injured. Main and Broadway streets, at the heart of the city, bore the brunt of the twister's devastation. The Harris Hotel caught fire and threatened to burn what was left of the business area, but rain squalls that followed the tornado quenched the fire. The Drucker Hotel, a four-story brick building, completely collapsed, and all of its occupants were buried. Some waited hours to be rescued. This also was the case for those trapped in the nearby and newly built Melbourne Hotel.

Governor Sam Baker ordered troops to Poplar Bluff to protect against looting and ghouls, but no incidents occurred. A trainload of medical supplies, doctors and nurses rushed from nearby Dexter, but by the time relief arrived, ninety-two persons were dead in the city, and more than $1 million in damage had been done. Another fifty persons died in other states.

PORTAGE, PENNSYLVANIA — MINE DISASTER — July 15, 1940

An explosion rent the Sonman E. Mine at Portage, Pennsylvania, at 10:40 A.M. on July 15, 1940. Three hundred fifty men were inside the shafts at the time. Although the mine had been empty for two days, the fireboss pronounced the mine clear of lethal gas. The explosion had not been heard on the outside. Word of the detonation came when an underground superintendent called on the phone to a foreman above, told him the air had been reversed, and said that miners were being asphyxiated. The foreman collected a crew and descended.

Checking the ventilating system as they went, this group found that the airlock doors were out of order. They repaired several of these at many stations. Smoke and dust stopped them at Shaft 18. Another group of rescuers brought in oxygen tanks to help in exploring the area. Following footprints in the dust, this group found clumps of men, all dead of afterdamp, behind a partially built barricade.

Many men did manage to escape the explosion, which was thought to have been caused by a collapsing roof. However, the pocket of methane gas released by the collapse killed sixty-three miners within seconds.

(ALSO SEE: Primero, Colorado)

PORT CHICAGO, CALIFORNIA — EXPLOSION — July 17, 1944

On San Francisco Bay squatted the small shipping town of Port Chicago, a hub of Liberty Ship activities during World War II and a chief loading area of munition bound for the Pacific fronts. Late on the night of July 17, 1944, two ships, the *Quinault Victory* and the *E. A. Bryan,* were taking aboard vast quantities of TNT and cordite.

Just as most of the 1,500 residents of Port Chicago were going to bed, an explosion cracked the silence with a

Splintered wharves and wrecked cars and equipment testify to the devastating reach of the explosion of two munitions ships at Port Chicago, California, on July 17, 1944. Three hundred were killed. *(Wide World)*

deafening roar, blowing the two ships and the wharves near them to splinters. The citizens of Oakland, San Francisco and Alameda felt the earth tremble like a quake; such was the force of the explosion. Flame could be seen shooting skyward fifty miles away. Every home in Port Chicago was damaged, and windows were cracked and broken in buildings twenty miles from the explosion. Not until dawn did anyone begin to look for the 321 men on the ships and docks. They had simply disappeared; only shreds of their bodies were left as evidence of their existence.

The cause of the explosion was never determined, but some authorities blamed faulty, ancient ammunition left over from World War I.

(ALSO SEE: Bone, Algeria; Texas City, Texas)

PORTER, INDIANA — RAILWAY WRECK
February 27, 1921

background: The New York Central's Interstate Express, traveling westbound, and the Michigan Central's Canadian collided at Porter, Indiana, on the night of February 27, 1921; a coach and an engine were totally demolished, and thirty-seven persons were killed. The blame for the accident went to the engineer and fireman of the Michigan Central train.

Good block signals and a control tower at the crossing did not prevent the collision of two trains near Porter, Indiana, on February 27, 1921. On that evening, the New York Central's Interstate Express, approaching Chicago, and the Michigan Central's Canadian, going east, were about equidistant from the crossing at Porter. The New York Central, Number 151, hit the signal circuit first, ringing the annunciator bell in the tower. The train was given the green light to proceed across the intersection.

Block signals facing Michigan Central's Number 20 showed red, or stop, but they were not seen by Engineer Long as he approached the crossing, according to his later testimony. He did see what he thought was the caution light at the crossing about a mile away, and he reduced his speed to 10 m.p.h. His fireman, a man named Block, leaned slightly out the cab window as they got closer. Then he shouted, "All the way!" as he continued to shovel more coal.

Long opened the throttle, and Number 20 increased its speed to about 55 m.p.h. The stop signal was still showing as the Michigan Central train shot ahead, but Long stated he did not see it because of a slight curve and the fact that there was a great deal of steam coming from a freight at a siding as he passed. The crew from the engine of the saw the signal, however, and became almost hysterical when they spotted the Canadian racing toward the red light. They shouted and waved lanterns for Long to stop, but he sped on. Since these men were on either side of Number 20, it was a wonder that Long never saw them.

As the Michigan Central made the crossing, Long's engine somehow managed to stay on the tracks, even though the switch had been set for the New York Central train to pass. However, Number 20's nine passenger cars which followed Long's engine were derailed. The first car, a wooden coach, came to a halt and sat directly in the path of the oncoming New York Central train. Number 151, traveling at about 50 m.p.h., smashed into the wooden coach, was derailed, and sent the Canadian's coach flying about seventy-five feet, killing thirty-five passengers. The two-man engine crew in the Interstate Express was killed when the engine flopped on its side.

Long denied responsibility for the accident, insisting that his view of the signals was blocked by the curve and the steam. He had also been "misled" by his fireman, he claimed. However, he could offer no reason for why he did not respond to the signals from the freight crew standing next to his speeding train. Nor could he explain why, when the absolute top speed at this most dangerous crossing was 40 m.p.h., according to Michigan Central regulations, he had overshot it by fifteen miles.

PORT ROYAL, JAMAICA — EARTHQUAKE June 7, 1692

background: At 11:40 A.M. on June 7, 1692, the thriving Jamaican city of Port Royal was hit by an earthquake—three tremors in all—that created giant fissures and several seismic seawaves that submerged most of the lower city and killed or drowned approximately 1,600 persons. About 1,300 buildings were destroyed.

The city of Port Royal, founded by General Brayne in 1657, after the British had wrested Jamaica from the Spanish, soon became a haven for buccaneers and "rapidly acquired a notoriety in the West Indies as a carousing Gomorrah," according to historian David Niddrie. The pirate Morgan and other adventurers often visited the port to relax and refit their ships. In forty-five years the city had changed from a peaceful sandy beach lined with native huts to a bustling port with more than 2,000 buildings and a population approaching 4,000. Yet in 1692, just before it was visited by the most powerful earthquake known to the Western Hemisphere, one Rector Heath announced to the world that the city's morality was as shabby as ever, labeling its inhabitants "a most ungodly debauched people."

The sun spread through a clear blue sky on the morning of June 7, 1692, a tranquil day with merchants doing business as usual and seamen leisurely performing their chores. This aura of serenity was shattered at 11:40 A.M., when a large earth tremor knocked over mugs in taverns, crockery in homes, and sent signs and lamps swaying. The streets soon filled with citizens who had fled their houses. In minutes, another, more violent, tremor knocked down almost every inhabitant, and then a third tremor, which lasted almost a full minute, broke the brick, plaster and wattle of the two- and three-story buildings throughout the town, tumbling them into the streets and onto the heads of the staring people. At the same time the quakes hit, seismic seawaves raced ashore and submerged half the town in three or four fathoms of water; the remaining buildings collapsed, and approximately 1,600 persons, a third of the population, were either drowned or crushed beneath the weight of collapsing walls. The entire cataclysm took only two minutes, but afterwards, Port Royal was finished forever as a major Jamaican city.

In one strange incident, the frigate *Swan,* lying on her side in a slipway at the eastern end of town as her sailors scraped barnacles from her, was suddenly thrust up by a huge seismic seawave. She sailed crazily through the city at unheard-of speeds, skimming over the submerged part of the city. As they thrashed about in the water, the people fortunate enough to have survived the instant flooding grabbed at the many life lines dangling from the *Swan.* Many were thus saved. They were yanked from the water by the ship as she sailed wildly forward. The ship finally beached on top of a partially sunken building.

A miraculous survival was experienced by one citizen, a merchant, Lewis Galdy. Galdy was walking toward a warehouse when the second tremor struck, causing a large fissure to open before him. He fell into it, and the fissure closed rapidly, trapping him in water and sand. A minute later, the third and strongest shock combined with the third seismic seawave to force open the fissure, and the water swirling above it forced the still-living Galdy upward, like a cork shooting from a bottle. Galdy lived to become one of the island's leading citizens; he died forty-seven years later of old age.

The Reverend Emmanuel Heath, rector of St. Paul's Church, was lunching with the president of the town council when the quake struck and sent plates, wine glasses, and chandeliers flying. He and the president ran out of the house and, as he later stated in a letter to a friend, they "made towards Morgan's Fort, which being a wide open place, I thought there to be more secure from the falling houses; but as I made towards it, I saw the earth open and swallow up a multitude of people, and [I saw] the sea mounting in upon us over the fortifications.

"I then laid aside all thoughts of escaping, and

resolved to make toward my own lodging, there to meet death in as good a posture as I could. From the place where I was, I was forced to cross and run through two and three very narrow streets. The houses and walls fell on each side of me; some bricks came rolling over my shoes, but none hurt me. When I came to my lodging, I found all things in the order I had left them."

The Reverend Heath was encouraged to paddle a canoe to the merchant ship *Siam,* which had ridden out the seismic waves. Days later he returned to the ruined city. He exclaimed, "It is a sad sight to see this harbor, one of the fairest I ever saw, covered with the dead bodies of people of all conditions, floating up and down without burial; for our burying place was destroyed by the earthquake whick shook to pieces the tombs, and the sea washed the carcasses of those who had been buried out of their graves. We have had other accounts from several parts of this island, but none suffered like Port Royal, where whole streets with their inhabitants, were swallowed up with the opening of the earth, which when it shut upon them, squeezed the people to death. And in that manner, several are left with their heads above ground; only some heads the dogs have eaten; others are covered with dust and earth, by the people who yet remain in the place, to avoid the stench."

The quake, its epicenter some distance to the north of the island and under water, had caused two mountains to slide nearly a mile from their original positions. The house and dozens of acres of one plantation were sliced off horizontally, like the top crust of a pie, and were sent sliding across flooded land for a mile.

This beautiful port, which would require centuries to rebuild as a small hamlet, was transformed in minutes to a sad charnal house, and for months—some people even say years—after the disaster, the rotting corpses of the hundreds of people trapped in the fissures and cracks throughout the island gave off "offensive odors."

PORT ROYAL, JAMAICA — HURRICANE, August 28, 1722

Thirty years after the earthquake that devastated Port Royal, the town was struck broadside by a severe hurricane on August 28, 1722. The depleted population once again was ravaged by nature, and in addition to the twenty-six merchant ships that were sunk and crushed by the storm's forceful winds, 400 Port Royal residents were killed.

One bizarre account by William Gerard de Brahm states: "A heavy gale of wind from the northeast so greatly impeded the current of the Gulf Stream that the water forced, at the same time, in the Gulf of Mexico by the trade winds, rose to such a height that not only the Tortugas and other islands disappeared, but the highest trees were covered on the Peninsula of Larga, and at this time, the *Litbury,* John Lorrain, master, being caught in the gale, came to an anchor, as the master supposed, in Hawke Channel, but to his great surprise found his vessel the next day high and dry on Elliott's Island and his anchor suspended in the boughs of a tree."

POTGIETERSRUS, SOUTH AFRICA — RAILWAY WRECK, March 30, 1972

A diesel locomotive pulling nine heavily packed passenger cars through the remote stretches of northern Transvaal in South Africa suddenly plunged off a railroad trestle near Potgietersrus and dove into a riverbed. Killed were 38 persons; another 179 were injured. Though "signs of sabotage" were rumored to have been found, investigators found nothing to support such a theory. The train was loaded with blacks, most of whom were members of a large African independent church en route to Pietersburg.

A train derailed and plunged into a gorge near Potgietersrus, South Africa, on March 30, 1972. Thirty-eight persons were killed. *(Wide World)*

PO VALLEY, ITALY — FLOODS

November, 1951

After completion of hydraulically controlled dikes and canals in the 1930's, many felt that the Po Valley in Italy finally was secure from flooding. The torrential rains of November, 1951, shattered that belief. The low-lying Po plains were inundated by rampaging rivers that crashed over dikes and levees, and virtually entrapped tens of thousands of people. More than one hundred lives were lost to the waters. Thirty thousand cattle were destroyed, and crop damage ran into the millions.

PRIMERO, COLORADO — MINE DISASTER

January 31, 1910

The Primero Mine in Colorado was extremely dusty and usually full of gas, a veritable death trap for the 110-man shifts that worked it. Few safety measures were taken. The bad conditions led to the explosion that occurred at 4:30 P.M. on January 31, 1910. About 35 men had come out of the mine, another 72 were still at work, and 4 men were standing at the mouth of the main entrance when a violent explosion took place. The 4 men at the tunnel's mouth were hurled forward and slammed into a moving row of cars; all of them were killed.

Days later, rescue teams dared to penetrate the main 5,000-foot shaft. They found one man alive; he had barricaded himself in a room. Three and a half months later, on May 19, 1910, the bodies of the seventy-one remaining miners were removed from the lethal mine. The death toll was set at seventy-five.

The cause of the explosion was never fully determined, but a federal inspector, G. S. Rice, theorized that part of the roof in one shaft had fallen, and the collapse had caused the thick dust in the air to ignite and explode nearby pockets of gas.

PRINCESS ALICE — MARINE DISASTER

September 3, 1878

background: While returning from Gravesend, the excursion ship *Princess Alice,* with more than 700 passengers and crew members on board, sank in the Thames after colliding with the steam collier *Bywell Castle* on the evening of September 3, 1878. An estimated 645 passengers drowned.

The London Steam Packet Company possessed one of the finest excursion ships in all of England, the elegantly appointed *Princess Alice,* a giant vessel with a passenger capacity of almost 800. On the warm summer morning of September 3, 1878, the excursion ship left London Bridge with more than 700 festive vacationers on board. She headed for Gravesend and Sheerness.

On the deck a band played parasol-spinning airs, and the women and children who made up the majority of the passenger list amused themselves in the many parlors of the *Princess Alice.* The few husbands and fathers on board sought refuge in the large saloon. After a pleasant outing the ship returned to the Thames about 6:00 P.M. and began heading for her berth at North Woolwich pier. In order to make better time, Captain William Grinstead hugged the south side of the river to avoid the two-knot ebb.

Coming toward the *Princess Alice* was the steam collier *Bywell Castle,* whose pilot spotted the excursion steamer's red warning light on the port side. At that time there were no regulations governing how ships were to pass each other except that passenger ships were given leeway, so the *Bywell Castle* accordingly moved to port to give the *Princess Alice* room to pass. Grinstead kept hugging the shore, however, and this put him on a collision course with the collier.

Shouts, frantic waving of lanterns and blasts on horns did nothing to avert the disaster. The collier slammed into the midsection of the *Princess Alice* and literally ripped the vessel in two. Hundreds of screaming children and women were dumped into the fast-moving river, none of whom had life preservers. All the available lines on the *Bywell Castle* were thrown over the side, but few of the passengers from the excursion ship had the strength to hold on to these lines or pull themselves on board the fast-moving collier.

It was all over in approximately two minutes. An estimated 645 persons, almost all women and children, had drowned. A board of inquiry placed the responsibility for the accident on Captain Grinstead for "improper starboarding." A subsequent hearing put the blame on both ships.

(ALSO SEE: Eastland; General Slocum*)*

PRINCESS SOPHIA — MARINE DISASTER

October 27, 1912

The Canadian steamer *Princess Sophia,* which departed Skagway for Vancouver on October 25, 1912, with 346 persons on board, was engulfed by a violent snowstorm and was driven off course, striking the Vanderbilt Reef the following day. For almost two days the steamer was hemmed in by the storm, which offered no escape for the people on board. Her anchors failed to grapple the rocky bed, and the ship finally slipped from the reef and quickly sank, disappearing with all her crew and passengers on board.

PRINCESS VICTORIA — MARINE DISASTER

January 31, 1953

background: Launched in 1946, the channel ferry *Princess Victoria,* with 174 passengers and crew members on board, capsized and sank near Mew Island, off Belfast, Ireland, in the late afternoon of January 31, 1953. The vessel was trapped by a severe gale early in the morning while she tried to reach Ireland, and her stern doors, used for loading cars, were thrown open; the ship subsequently foundered. Drowned were 121 persons.

The *Princess Victoria,* a ferry with a capacity of 1,515 passengers plus cars, shuttled between Scotland and Ireland. She was caught in a fierce gale that swept across the Irish Sea on the morning of January 31, 1953. The stern doors of the ferry, which were used to load cars, were ripped open by the storm at approximately 9:00 A.M. The stanchions supporting these doors buckled, and the doors, therefore, could not be closed, despite the desperate efforts of most of the forty-nine crew members.

Captain Ferguson sent out a call for help at 9:45 A.M. The message read: "Hove to off mouth Loch Ryan. Vessel not under command. Urgent assistance of tug required." No tugs were available in the immediate area, and valuable time was lost before the Navy sent the H.M.S. *Contest* into the storm to seek out the stricken ferry.

About forty-five minutes later, authorities received another SOS from the *Princess Victoria:* "Car deck flooded. Heavy list to starboard. Require immediate assistance. Ship not under command." While awaiting rescue passengers and crew members used buckets to bail out water that had seeped into the lounge areas. Captain Ferguson then ordered the passengers to don their life jackets, told them that several ships were steaming to their rescue, and instructed them to assemble on the promenade deck.

The list had increased to such an extent that to reach this deck the passengers had to pull themselves up life lines. They waited on the B deck through the storm as the wireless operator continued to send out frantic SOS signals. No help arrived by 1:30 P.M., and the forty-five-degree list of *Princess Victoria* assured that she would founder. Ferguson had waited too long to give the order to abandon ship, and the list of the vessel prevented the passengers and crew from using the lifeboats on the starboard side. These were useless because they could not be lowered without being immediately swamped with water. One boat on the port side was filled with children and women and lowered, only to capsize. Its occupants spilled into the raging sea and quickly drowned.

When the ferry turned over, several persons on board ran up her bottom, and several seamen managed to free one of the overturned lifeboats.

The *Contest* was delayed by the storm in reaching the area designated by the wireless operator of the *Princess Victoria.* Several other ships joined the *Contest,* and they plucked small groups of survivors, who floated aimlessly in some of the ferry's lifeboats and on several rafts, from the sea. Captain Ferguson and three-fourths of those aboard the ferry were never found.

PRINCIPE DE ASTURIAS — MARINE DISASTER — March 5, 1914

An uneventful Atlantic crossing marked the voyage of the *Principe de Asturias* from Barcelona en route to Buenos Aires. Aboard this modern 8,371-ton vessel, considered one of the finest of her day, were 588 passengers and crew members. Off Brazil the ship moved into a dense fog, but her captain continued sailing at top speed and at 4:00 A.M. on March 5, 1914, the Spanish ship struck the jagged reefs along the Brazilian coast at Ponta Boi.

The ship hit so hard that her boilers exploded, and she nearly broke in half. Because she was sinking quickly in about twenty fathoms of water, there was little time to lower lifeboats. The French steamer *Vega* picked up the survivors, but 445 persons had drowned.

PRINCIPESSA MAFALDA — MARINE DISASTER — October 25, 1927

background: The 9,210-ton Italian passenger steamer *Principessa Mafalda,* built in 1908, was bound for Rio de Janeiro from the Cape Verde Islands, with 971 passengers and 288 crew members, when she sank ninety miles off Brazil after her port propeller shaft broke and her boilers burst. Killed were 314 passengers and crew members; the remainder were saved by ships steaming to the rescue.

The *Principessa Mafalda,* the pride of the Navigazione Generale Italiana line, had every one of her luxuriously appointed cabins filled when she left the Cape Verde Islands for Rio de Janeiro on October 8, 1927. Two weeks later, she and her 971 passengers ran into trouble. On the afternoon of October 25 the *Mafalda* steamed past the Blue Star liner *Empire Star;* both ships were then about ninety miles off Abrolhos Island, Brazil.

Captain C. R. Cooper, skipper of the *Empire Star,* was handed a radio message ten minutes later. From the *Mafalda,* it was an SOS warning of: "Danger to engines." Cooper ordered his 7,199-ton vessel to head at top speed for the stricken Italian ship.

The liner was dead in the water. Inexplicably the ship's port propeller shaft had snapped, and thousands of gallons of sea water had poured through a gaping hole into the boiler rooms. At first the passengers were informed that there was some slight damage to the ship, and crew members, as a safety precaution, swung lifeboats out on their davits. There was an orderly queuing up of the passengers, who donned their life jackets, thinking that the exercise was a mere drill. Then came a violent roar from the bowels of the ship as the swirling sea water overcame and drowned the black gang below and filled up the boilers, which exploded.

What had been an orderly rescue drill turned into a rout of murderous panic. Passengers dove into the lifeboats. Some missed and splashed into the sea, where they quickly drowned. When the *Empire Star* arrived Cooper and his men could see sailors on board the *Mafalda* battling with passengers in useless attempts to calm them down. The Italian liner was sinking quickly when Cooper ordered his own lifeboats rowed over to the *Mafalda.* He watched helplessly as berserk passengers lowered two of the Italian lifeboats so quickly that they capsized, sending their human cargo to watery graves.

Other ships began to arrive in response to the *Mafalda*'s SOS. They began putting over lifeboats. Joining the *Empire Star* were the French ships *Mosella* and *Formose,* the British vessels *King Frederick, Avelona* and *Rossetti,* and the German ship *Alhena.*

While the *Mafalda* lingered more than four hours in her death throes, 945 of her passengers and crew members were rescued. It was a wonder that more than 314 deaths did not occur during the prolonged panic.

PROSPECT, PENNSYLVANIA — RAILWAY WRECK

December 24, 1872

A flyer of the Buff, Corry & Pittsburgh line broke a wheel while crossing a trestle bridge near Prospect, Pennsylvania, on December 24, 1872. While the five-car train was extended on the long span, the long-neglected wooden timbers of the bridge gave way and sent all the coaches plummeting to the frozen riverbed below. Stoves in the cars quickly exploded and set the wreck on fire. Twenty-five persons were killed, about half in the crash and the remainder in the subsequent blaze.

(ALSO SEE: Angola, New York; Ashtabula, Ohio)

PUEBLO, COLORADO — FLOOD

June 2-3, 1921

In one of the worst flood years in United States history, the most devastating single flood occurred near Pueblo, Colorado, on June 2-3, 1921, when the Arkansas River went wild and spilled over its levees, cascading at a speed of 1,000 cubic feet per second per square mile through the area. Killed were 120 persons, most of whom were caught totally unprepared by the flash flood. A conservative estimate of damage was placed at $25 million.

PUERTO RICO — HURRICANE

July 26-August 31, 1533

Three devastating hurricanes struck Spanish settlements on Puerto Rico in 1533; the first on July 26, the second on August 23, and the last on August 31. Killed were hordes of black slaves used by the Spanish to work the rich cane fields. One estimate of the number of slaves who died during the savage storms is about 2,000. With their work force depleted, the Spanish had to suspend their cane field operations and plead with the crown for more slaves in order to continue working the plantations.

PUERTO RICO — HURRICANE

July 26, 1825

The killer hurricane known as "Santa Ana," that struck Puerto Rico on July 26, 1825, after ravaging Guadeloupe, was one of the most severe storms ever experienced by inhabitants of that storm-torn island. Hurricane winds knocked down more than 7,000 buildings throughout the length of the island and took the lives of 374 persons, most of whom were crushed under falling walls and ceilings. Almost 1,200 were left homeless.

PUERTO RICO — HURRICANE

August 8, 1899

The greatest hurricane of the nineteenth century (or any other, for that matter) was the storm that moved directly over the entire length of Puerto Rico on August 8, 1899. Known as the "San Ciriaco," the storm first struck Arroyo at about 8:00 A.M. The port of Humacao was inundated by tidal waves, and Aguadilla, a town of considerable size, was all but wiped out by winds gusting to 125 m.p.h. Only San Juan escaped the more brutal punishment of the storm. By the time the hurricane reached this city, its winds had slackened to 90 m.p.h.

One account reported that "there was no escape. The wind would rise to a hundred miles an hour, and you could not stand up before them. You couldn't see, either. The roofs would come off tile by tile and plank by plank and go whizzing through the air. Plates and metal strips soared through the streets like giant razor blades, cutting and slicing, decapitating, amputating, maiming, killing."

More than 3,000 persons were slain by this monster, which also destroyed $20 million in property.

PUERTO RICO — HURRICANE

September 26, 1932

Known as the "San Ciprian" hurricane, the storm that passed over Puerto Rico on September 26, 1932, rolled over Ceiba at about 10:00 P.M. The steamer *Jean,* anchored at Ensenada Honda, recorded a barometric reading of 27.70. The winds of this hurricane were incredible; they measured from 120 to 150 m.p.h. (The wind instrument tower at San Juan was blown over.) Before dissipating into Mexico, the storm claimed the lives of 225 Puerto Ricans, injured another 3,000 residents, stripped bare the homes of 75,000, and inflicted $30 million in damages.

Q

QIR VALLEY, IRAN

EARTHQUAKE
April 10, 1972

"I was saying my prayers when a slight tremor shook me. I had hardly finished when the whole roof collapsed with a shock like a bomb explosion." When Safar Keshtar turned around, he saw that his wife and four young children had been crushed to death. It was that way for most persons in Iran's Qir valley, in the early morning of April 10, 1972.

The earthquake began at 5:38 A.M., and within seconds fifty-eight villages were wiped out. The 5,044 dead far outnumbered the 1,336 injured. Measuring 7.0 on the Richter scale, the shocks were certainly less deadly than those that struck Iran in 1968, killing 12,000, but the tremors were enough for the Shah of Iran to declare a national emergency and to call upon all the resources of the Red Lion and Sun (Iran's Red Cross) to aid the stricken.

The event grimly reminded residents of historian Jellal As-Soyuti's description of an apocalyptic quake that raced through ancient Persia: "The earth vomited up the bones of the dead, and a village with its inhabitants was suspended between heaven and earth during half a day; then it was swallowed up."

A villager, Roghieh Salari, who gave birth to a child during the 1972 shock waves, aptly named her newborn son Zelzelleh, which means earthquake.

An Iranian man lugs his possessions on his back through the ruined village of Ghir, one of dozens of communities utterly demolished by the earthquake that ripped apart the Qir Valley in Iran on April 10, 1972. *(Wide World)*

QUEEN CHARLOTTE — MARINE DISASTER
March 17, 1800

The enormous British frigate *Queen Charlotte* caught fire while sailing off Leghorn, Italy, on March 17, 1800, and was soon a mass of flames. A report to the *London Times,* received on April 5, 1800, stated that the fire "was occasioned by some hay which was lying under the half deck, having been set on fire by a match in a tub, which was usually kept there for signal guns."

A Lieutenant Dundras valiantly attempted to control the fire by taking several squads of men below decks to work the pumps, but the fire quickly ate through the canvas sails and a wooden deck, causing the heavy cannons to fall through to the next deck, where Dundras and others were at work. The ship foundered and sank quickly, drowning most of her crew, approximately 700 British seamen. A handful survived. They were picked up by an unnamed American ship.

QUETTA — MARINE DISASTER
March 1, 1890

The 2,254-ton steamship *Quetta,* built in 1881, was owned by the British Indian Steamship Company. While en route to Queensland via the Torres Straits, a treacherous stretch of water, she struck reefs off Cape York, Australia, and quickly foundered on March 1, 1890. Of the 282 persons on board, 146 were known to have perished.

Traveling first class in those days, as the following report clearly indicates, not only had its privileges, but a fair guarantee of survival: "Saved were the captain, three of the officers, the purser, and five saloon passengers, one of them a lady . . . about forty steerage passengers with children perished as did some fifty Lascars and Javanese. . . ."

The ironically named *Albatross,* an Australian steamer, rescued 136 persons.

QUINCY, MASSACHUSETTS — RAILWAY WRECK
August 19, 1890

background: A five-car passenger train on the Vineyard, Nantucket & Hyannis line, heading for Boston, was derailed on August 19, 1890, by a heavy jack left wedged beneath a track by a road gang that had made repairs on the track. Twenty-three passengers in the fourth coach were killed; a dozen more persons were injured. Responsibility was placed on the gang foreman.

Number 182 was heading down the line toward Quincy, Massachusetts, en route to Boston, on August 19, 1890, as a road gang several miles away was adding ballast to the west side of a track. The five-car train, with engine and tender, was run by veteran D. C. Babcock. He had no knowledge of the roadwork being done ahead. Section Master Joseph Welch, however, knew full well that the Vineyard, Nantucket & Hyannis Express (also known as the Old Colony Road) was due any moment, and yet he casually allowed his workmen to continue raising one side of the track.

The crew had finished a leisurely lunch and was back working at 1:00 P.M. Michael Hartney, an inexperienced section hand, was struggling with a heavy jack that was wedged beneath one track, and his boss, Welch, was some

The British steamship *Quetta* was lost on the reefs of Cape York, Australia, on March 1, 1890. *(Illustrated London News)*

distance down the line to the south, standing beneath a bridge and sighting down the track. Inexplicably the foreman had neglected to set up signal flags or station a signal man farther down the track to warn Number 182, the arrival of which he knew to be imminent.

A freight crunched slowly down the opposite rails, and this sound, Welch later explained, drowned out any noise from the approaching express, which he claimed he would normally have heard. As Babcock's engine turned a curve, the engineer spotted the cluster of workers, and he yanked his warning whistle several times. The work crew scattered, except for Hartney, who looked up, swore profusely, and continued to struggle with the jack, which was hopelessly wedged under the track. The train bore down on him, 350 feet . . . 250 feet, running about 40 m.p.h. At the last moment Hartney jumped clear, and Babcock, leaning from his cab window, spotted the jack, applied the brakes, and prayed.

The engine derailed immediately after striking the jack and soared over the embankment, its end jutting up slightly across the track. The next two cars were also derailed with slight damage and only one casualty: B. F. Benson, a parlor car conductor, was hurled through a window.

The last two cars of the train stayed on the embankment, but the fourth car caught the edge of the engine, which caused it to be raked down the side of the embankment. Some quick-footed passengers managed to jump to the other side of the car, but twenty-three persons were killed; some were crushed by the sideswipe and others were scalded to death when steam pipes in their car burst.

Engineer Babcock survived. He was found unconscious, lying atop his smashed engine. Welch, the section foreman, was "severely criticized" for his carelessness. He went back to work the following week.

QUITO, ECUADOR — EARTHQUAKE
February 4, 1797

One of the victims of the giant earthquake that shivered through many South American countries on February 4, 1797, was Quito, Ecuador. The city and the surrounding countryside were completely changed by the upheaval; landmarks, mountains and rivers were moved and changed in the space of a few seconds. Most of the population at that time, about 40,000 persons, was killed in this colossal quake.

One report stated: "During this tremendous scene the ground opened in all directions, vomiting sulfur, mud, and water." This quake also widely damaged the cities of Cotocollao, Nono, Pomasqui, San Antonio and others. The cataclysm activated the monster volcanoes Cotopaxi and Chimborazo, which rained down death in the form of shooting lava and stones upon the town of Ambato.

A view of Quito, Ecuador, before its ruination by an earthquake on March 22, 1859, which killed 5,000 citizens. *(Illustrated London News)*

QUITO, ECUADOR — EARTHQUAKE
March 22, 1859

The Ecuadorian city of Quito, perched on its 10,000-foot plateau, was rattled by a powerful earthquake on March 22, 1859, which brought down most of its historic monuments and buildings. Beginning at 8:30 A.M. and continuing for six minutes, the prolonged tremors razed the city's great cathedral, the Chapel of El Sagrario, the Temple of the Augustines, the Temple of the Catalines, the Temple of the Dominicans, the Church of Our Lady del Carmen, the Temple of Santa Clara, the Temple of La Merced, the Temple of San Francisco, the Temple of St. Roque, the two churches of St. John the Evangelist, and the Church of Recoleta de Dominicos.

All of these religious structures—Quito, with such a plethora of churches and temples, was certainly one of the most devout cities in South America—suffered more than the government buildings, but the architectural wonders, the Government Palace and the Archepiscopal Palace, were also brought to ruins.

About 5,000 inhabitants of Quito died under the fall of this heavy masonry.

QUITO, ECUADOR — TRAFFIC ACCIDENT
August 28, 1972

One of the worst bus accidents on record happened near Quito, Ecuador, on August 28, 1972. An overcrowded bus, destined for the city, went out of control and plunged down a 150-foot ravine. Nineteen persons were killed on impact.

R

R.38 **AIR CRASH**
August 24, 1921

Built for the United States, the dirigible *R.38,* after a few trials, was being put through her most rigorous trials on August 24, 1921 with a British crew on board. The airship, 699 feet long with an 85.5-foot diameter and a capacity of 2,750,000 cubic feet, had an estimated range of 3,000 miles and could stay aloft for 211 hours. Her six 350-horsepower Sunbeam Cossack engines, located in three twin gondolas, could boost the *R.38's* maximum speed up to 70 m.p.h., but her normal cruising speed was 65 m.p.h. The dirigible was considered one of the finest built to date, but her designer, C. I. Campbell, had some misgivings about her structure's ability to withstand certain stress.

Campbell's fears were realized at dusk on August 24. The ship had stayed aloft all night, due to her failure to locate her destination, the Pulham, England, base, which was closed over by pea-soup fog. Coming in from her perch over the North Sea the following day and heading for Howden, the *R.38,* under the command of Lieutenant A. H. Wann, was put through a series of yawning exercises, her motors going full blast and slipping the airship along at 69 m.p.h.

At approximately 5:40 P.M., when the dirigible was over Hull, the ship suddenly split in half, her gondolas spilling out her forty-nine crew members and observers. Designer Campbell was on board; he fell to his death as did forty-three others, including a United States Navy observer. Lieutenant Wann and four others rode their gondola to earth and somehow managed to survive.

The enormous dirigible *R. 38* (or *ZR-2*) crashed into the Humber River on August 24, 1921. Forty-four crew members were killed. *(Wide World)*

Only the giant skeleton of broken and twisted girders remained of the *R. 101* dirigible after she crashed and burned near Beauvais, France, on October 4, 1930. Here French police and soldiers inspect the ruins. *(UPI)*

R.101

AIR CRASH
October 4, 1930

background: The *R.101* and her sister ship the *R.100* were gigantic dirigibles built by the British Airship Guarantee Company. Each had a capacity of five million cubic feet, which allowed them to lift 150 tons with accommodations for 100 passengers. Powered by six Rolls-Royce Condor engines, the *R.101,* completed first, had her initial five and one-half hour flight on October 1, 1929. On a flight to India, on October 4, 1930, the ship was caught in a storm and crashed, her 777-foot-long hulk splitting in two and exploding near Beauvais, France. Killed were 48 crew members and high ranking observers; 6 survived.

Britain's entries for the dirigible passenger sweepstakes in the late 1920's were two monster airships, the *R.100* and the *R.101*. The *R.101* was completed first and undertook her maiden voyage on October 14, 1929. Right from the beginning there was trouble with this ship. The engines malfunctioned, and the airship's envelope was of unsound construction. (The fabric on top of the envelope would eventually tear away and doom the ship.) Still, Britain pushed for an aerial triumph and prematurely scheduled the dirigible for an extended flight to India. (The *R.100* had proven herself in a round-trip voyage across the Atlantic in July, 1930.)

The *R.101* was released from her mooring mast at her Cardington base on October 4, 1930, Lieutenant H. C. Irwin in command. On board were forty-two crew members and twelve observers, including Lord Thomson, who had insisted on the flight against the warnings that the ship might not be able to handle the radical temperature variations encountered during the flight.

Trouble was present even before the airship went aloft. Somehow four tons of water were accidentally dumped while the dirigible was at her mooring. Then a gusty rainstorm closed in on the ship just after she moved off toward the channel at 6:40 P.M. At about 1,000 feet the *R.101* was inside the storm, her controls unresponsive. She pitched about crazily like a cork on a choppy sea. Her alarmed passengers were sent slamming against the walls of the gondolas. An engine stopped. Yet the ship limped across the channel, her altitude unsteady; at times the dirigible maintained her 1,000-foot level, other times she dipped towards the water, plummeting to 700 feet.

One of the few men on board not upset by the hazardous movement of the ship was her commander, Lieutenant Irwin. Even though the *R.101* was being buffeted by 35-knot winds, Irwin radiated confidence. His radio message to Cardington was incredibly nonchalant in the light of the punishment his ship was taking: "After an excellent supper our distinguished passengers smoked a final cigar and, having sighted the French coast, have now gone to rest after the excitement of the leave-taking."

Only a few crew members were on duty by the time the dirigible crossed over the French coast; the others had taken to their hammocklike beds and were blithely sleeping through the storm. The *R.101,* at times, was almost on the ground. When she passed over Poix, the dirigible was only at about 250 feet. This was at 1:00 A.M.

Citizens of the small town of Beauvais, fifty miles from Paris, were awakened an hour later by the drone of the dirigible's engines. They stepped into streets to see the giant struggling through the storm, plunging and then jerking upward. Inside the control gondola the coxswain found the ship was not responding, and he helplessly watched as the ship slid downward in a shallow movement.

At first it appeared that the *R.101* would manage a soft landing as she nosed her way across a gentle sloping meadow, but suddenly she struck a steep ridge. Just before the dirigible came to a fabric-shredding stop, her occupants battered out windows and prepared to jump for their lives. There was a good chance all would survive. But when the ship hit the hill, she burst into flames, her hydrogen exploding in a red ball of fire. Only six crew members managed to scramble to safety; forty-eight others, including Lord Thomson, perished in the fire.

Airship historian Robert Jackson considered the air crash of the *R.101* "a burnt-out testimony to bungling, mismanagement and crass governmental stupidity which, fortunately, has had few parallels in the history of aviation."

(ALSO SEE: Akron, Dixmude, Hindenburg, LZ-18, Shenandoah*)*

RAPID CITY, SOUTH DAKOTA — FLOOD — June 9, 1972

background: Beginning at 9:00 P.M., torrential rains flooded the dams and creeks in and around Rapid City, South Dakota, on June 9, 1972; rainwaters accumulated in some areas to ten inches. More than $100 million in damage was done to the devastated city with 1,200 homes destroyed, another 2,500 damaged and 5,000 autos wrecked. Of the 43,000 residents, 236 were killed; some of these were tourists and citizens of nearby Keystone, a hamlet of about 500. Hundreds were injured, and President Richard M. Nixon officially declared the city a national disaster area, ordering $1 million in relief supplies immediately dispatched to Rapid City. The Red Cross set up three medical and food areas.

It had been a pleasantly cool week in Rapid City, South Dakota, and the tourists swarmed into the town nestled at the foot of the Black Hills. They gaped at the huge granite faces of four presidents on the wall of Mount Rushmore and moved merrily into the hills to camp, hike and fish. Rapid City merchants were doing a brisk business as they had every year since the gold dust thinned out and the vacationing hordes thickened.

On the night of June 9, 1972, rain began to fall until it accumulated to six inches, then ten inches. Rapid Creek, a mountain stream running down from the Black Hills and through the heart of Rapid City, swelled from 20 feet to more than 400 feet wide by 9:00 P.M. The city was under the attack of a deluge as deadly as the flood that swept through Johnstown, Pennsylvania, eighty-three years earlier.

Houses began to crumble and were swept away; autos floated through the streets; telephone poles snapped, and live wires crackled, jumping above the surface of the waters. The radio stations lost their power and could not warn residents. They switched to civil defense bands later, ominously blaring: "If you find a body, do not touch it, call. . . . Stay in your homes and do not impede emergency vehicle traffic. . . . Don't drink the water . . . boats are needed immediately. . . ."

The onslaught of water caught most Rapid City citizens in bed or otherwise totally unprepared. Sam Lee, a reporter for station KIMM, saw it coming just in time. "I was looking out a window when I saw the water come over the creek bank. I grabbed my wife, and we got out of there."

Another reporter, Harold Higgins, lived in a basement apartment near the exploding creek. He walked outside and was awestruck by the sight before him. "I was standing in the middle of the road when a four-foot bank of water came down the creek." He watched a large trailer race along with the floodwaters. Later, amidst the debris of the wrecked city, he told the *New York Times,* "It's like a war zone. There are fires all over the place, and nothing can be done about it because the city has been cut in half by the flooding of Rapid Creek." Higgins's editor, Jerry Mashek, of the *Rapid City Journal,* heard the noise of the flash flood and thought it "sounded like a freight train in the night."

The city's fire department ignored all but the major fires, its members busying themselves with rescue operations. Immense floodwaters cutting off all routes in and out of the city prevented neighboring fire departments from coming to Rapid City's rescue. When the dams at Canyon Lake and Deerfield burst, flooding occurred around the city for sixty miles from north to south and fifty miles from east to west. The nearby village of Keystone, with its 500 residents, was completely inundated; every one of its buildings was torn down by the rushing waters.

As people clung to rooftops, shimmied up trees, and jumped onto the tops of floating cars and houses, 1,800 National Guardsmen from Camp Rapid on the western edge of the city moved in trucks through still-passable streets and plucked victims from the waters. One young soldier, reaching for a dying child, lost his grip on a door, plunged into the churning water, and was drowned.

A fifty-one-year-old mailman, Roger Pryor, who lived with his mother in the West Boulevard Trailer Court, watched horrified as every mobile home in the court (200 in number) except his own, was swept away with screaming occupants. "My mother and I just got out with the clothes on our backs."

John Clark's house collapsed to its foundation as the waters drove in on it; he barely managed to flee. Hearing the cry of a neighbor, Clark tried to help, but a mountain of water embraced him and sent him in a mad toss down the street. He stated later that he thought at that time, "I've lived for thirty-seven years, and now it's time to die."

For days the city struggled to survive. Bloated bodies were everywhere, floating in the receding waters, slumped and drowned to death in overturned cars, hanging from the smashed windows of buildings. Skip Johnson found nothing left of his house the day after the flood except the roof, which had been thrown four blocks away. Looking up, he moaned as he saw a ninety-year-old woman, dead, hanging like a lifeless doll from a tree.

Malcolm MacPherson of *Newsweek* arrived and was told by one sobbing victim how "our daughter just floated away. She tried holding on to a tree, but she just floated away."

Refrigerator trucks were used to pick up and store the bodies found in the streets. Hoses in the three emergency morgues were used to wash away the thickly caked silt covering the corpses so that the long lines of waiting citizens seeking relatives could made identification.

Rapid City was a ruin: 1,200 houses were totally wrecked, another 2,500 shattered; there was more than $100 million in damages. The Red Cross worked feverishly to set up three first-aid shelters, and President Richard M. Nixon declared the city a disaster area, ordering immediate federal relief sent. Hundreds had

A once-busy downtown Rapid City, South Dakota, intersection was converted into a surging river as floodwaters took over the town on June 9, 1972. *(UPI)*

been injured; the death count took months to finalize. Thousands of tourists were camping in the Black Hills when the flash flood broke. Ron Stephenson, a rescue director, said, "They'll be picking them up out there all summer." He was correct. A total of 236 persons died in one of the worst floods in recent history.

(ALSO SEE: Johnstown, Pennsylvania, 1889)

RAVENNA, OHIO — RAILWAY WRECK
July 3, 1891

The rear-end collision between a passenger train and a freight of the Erie Railroad on July 3, 1891, was a simple matter of disregarding strict timetables. The eastbound Number 8 passenger train was stopped at Ravenna, Ohio. Its engineer, Pendergast, ignoring his timetable, took time to walk out on the running board from his cabin to fix his train whistle, which was not working.

Engineer Halman, whose freight train consisted of twenty-four refrigerator cars, also ignored the timetable that morning and left Kent, a station seven miles away from Ravenna, ahead of schedule by several minutes. He thought the passenger train on the same track would be far ahead of him. Halman raced his freight into the Ravenna yard while the passenger train limply waited for the impact.

Signalman Barney Dyer walked out of the Ravenna station at that moment, blinking at the bright sunrise. He saw the freight bearing down upon the passenger train and, according to his later testimony (quoted by train historian Robert Shaw), provided what would become a legendary cliche: "Says I to myself, says I, this is a hell of a way to run a railroad."

Halman's freight tore into the last three cars of Number 8 at a speed of about 30 m.p.h. The old-fashioned day coaches, made entirely of wood, broke up like matchsticks, and twenty-five persons were crushed to death as one car telescoped into another.

Minutes after the accident, Pendergast, the laconic engineer of Number 8, uncoupled the last three cars and took his train down the track to its destination while station employees were left to cart the bodies to the morgue.

RED ASH, WEST VIRGINIA — MINE DISASTER
March 6, 1900

Known to generate a lot of gas, the Red Ash mine was a dangerous pit that had to be constantly checked by firebosses each day before the miners entered. The fireboss was apparently late on the morning of March 6, 1900, and the miners entered the shaft after refusing to wait beyond 7:15 A.M. for him to appear. This was in direct violation of the mining law, which dictated: "No workman shall enter or be permitted to enter any mine or part of a mine generating firedamp until it has been examined by the fireboss and reported by him to be safe."

A minute after the morning shift entered the Red Ash mine, one of the open lamps the miners wore ignited a pocket of gas. The resulting explosion killed forty-six men.

This very same mine was to be the scene of two more explosions on March 18-19, 1905; the first was a result of careless blasting, and the second was caused when miners attempting to rescue victims of the first explosion walked into an area thick with gas and ignited it with their open lamps. A total of twenty-four were killed in these blasts.

RED CANYON, WYOMING — MINE DISASTER
March 20, 1895

A blown-out shot igniting coal dust caused the monstrous explosion in Mine Number 5 of the Red Canyon, Wyoming, works on March 20, 1895. It occurred at 5:45 P.M. when most of the 150 miners employed in the shafts were leaving for their homes and dinner. Some of these men, already out of the shaft, were injured when they were struck by flying debris from the hoisting apparatus, which was splintered by the explosion.

Workers had often complained that "due precaution had not been exercised" in this gassy, unsafe mine. Black powder was used any time during the shifts to blast, and this was always hazardous. All fifty-eight men still in the mine when the explosion occurred were killed. Four others just stepping from the mouth of the shaft were also killed, bringing the death toll to sixty-two.

The Red Canyon mine was totally wrecked by the blast, which tore apart timbers and supports, cracked and crashed down walls and ceilings. It was more than a year later before the mine was again opened in May, 1896.

REINA DEL PACIFICO — MARINE DISASTER
September 11, 1947

Having been used as a troopship during World War II, the *Reina Del Pacifico* now was being refitted for passenger duty. On September 11, 1947, the ship was being tested in the Irish Sea when overheating caused the captain to stop the port outer engine. When the engines were again started, a crankcase explosion in the vessel's boiler room ripped her apart, killing twenty-five persons, mostly black gang members. Twenty-one people were injured.

REINA REGENTA — MARINE DISASTER
March 11, 1895

The 5,000-ton Spanish cruiser *Reina Regenta,* after carrying ambassadors to Morocco in early March, 1895, was en route to Cadiz from Tangier on March 11, 1895, when she was suddenly enveloped by a withering storm.

As she sailed into the Bay of Trafalgar, the cruiser was hit by the full force of the gale. Her captain got off one message before the storm capsized the ship: "No hope of being saved. Twelve miles from Bajos d'Aceitunois. Segond—Cruiser *Reina Regenta.*"

It was a month before the wrecked ship was found by the *Isla de Luzon* lying in a depth of 109 fathoms. Her entire crew of 402 had perished with her.

REVERE, MASSACHUSETTS — RAILWAY WRECK — August 26, 1871

background: At 8:30 P.M. on the night of August 26, 1871, the Bangor Express, traveling at about 10 m.p.h., struck the rear car of a local train while the local was stopped outside Revere, Massachusetts. Both trains belonged to the Eastern Railroad Company. Thirty persons were killed; another thirty-two passengers, injured. Poor safety standards on the part of management were the overriding factors in the crash.

The Eastern Railroad Company was something out of a bygone era. Even for 1871 its management was fossilized in its approach to modern train methods and measures of safety for its badly-treated passengers. Although almost every depot operated by the company was equipped with telegraph offices, Eastern's crusty superintendent, Jeremiah Prescott, refused to allow such "new-fangled" instruments for dispatching trains and stuck to the old way of using a printed timetable. Prescott insisted that the telegraph housed in his depots be used for cash-paying customers only.

Such archaic and deadly thinking carried over to the technical side of Eastern's train operations. Just as Prescott and the line's president, Samuel Browne, disdained the use of the telegraph, they dismissed the idea of using air brakes on their trains. Coupled with that was their insistence on the time-interval system, which sometimes threw their overcrowded trains hours behind schedule.

The "terribly dramatic" disaster, as Charles Francis Adams, Jr., described the Revere wreck, was brought about by these arch-conservative methods, and it was justly pointed out later that Prescott and Browne were the real culprits responsible for the crash.

On the mist-shrouded evening of August 26, 1871, one of the most confusing mixups in Eastern's history occurred when three local trains fell far behind schedule as unusually large crowds crammed onto them. A fourth train, the fast Bangor Express, was compelled to wait until all local passengers had boarded and their trains had slowly pulled out of Boston, heading for their whistle-stop destinations. Prescott's policy was to sell tickets to everyone and if conductors ran out of seats, the passengers could stand in the aisles, which is what occurred on the three locals this night.

The rear-end collision of two trains at Revere, Massachusetts, on August 26, 1871, killed thirty-two passengers. *(Frank Leslie's Illustrated Newspaper)*

Two of the local trains were destined for Saugus via a branch line that forked at Everett. A third train, bound for Beverly, which normally followed the Saugus locals, somehow got wedged between the first and second Saugus-bound trains. The Bangor Express followed all three, waiting to get past Everett, where it could open up.

All four trains, however, were held at Everett until a south-bound Saugus local—the Saugus branch was a single track—was cleared. This train was almost an hour late, and by the time it went through Everett, the passengers were loudly complaining (which did them no good at all); the conductors were frantic, and the engineers on all four northbound trains were exasperated.

Ashbel Brown, the engineer of the Bangor Express, thought the Beverly local, which ran on the main track as did the Express, was where it was supposed to be—directly behind the two Saugus locals. The first Saugus train pulled onto the branch line and disappeared. The second train, actually the Beverly-bound local, found itself out of timetable order and pulled onto the main line, heading for Revere station. When the second Saugus local pulled onto the branch line and disappeared, Ashbel thought this was the Beverly-bound train. He waited a proper interval and then began to get up steam, racing up the main line at close to 30 m.p.h.

The Beverly local, stopped at Revere for minor repairs, took on more passengers. Conductor John Nolan was busy checking tickets. In the cabin of the Express engineer Brown kept looking for signals from the poles that would indicate either a stop or all clear at Revere. Fog clouded his vision, and he averted his eyes from the road too long while attempting to spot these old-fashioned overhead signals. He may not have seen the two signal lights of the local in time anyway—the fog was thick and rolling along the tracks.

"Suddenly," Brown later told questioners, "I saw two lights looking me in the face. I immediately reversed my engine and whistled for brakes." But he knew it would do no good. The brakes had to be applied manually, and at that distance it would have made no difference. His train did slow to about 10 m.p.h., but by then Brown was no longer in the cab. He had jumped like a man springing from a diving board.

Conductor Nolan heard the sound of the oncoming *Express* at the same time a man standing on the Revere station platform shouted, "Here comes a train!" Nolan spun about, grabbed a lantern, and desperately waved it a few paces from the rear of his own local. He was signaling a ghost; there was no one at the Express's throttle. Leaping aside moments before the Express ran him down, Nolan watched in horror as it rammed into the last car of the local, telescoping half way through it and grinding most of the passengers to death. Its smokestack sheared away and its boiler cut wide, the engine let off jets of searing steam in all directions, scalding trapped victims.

The crash caused the kerosene lamps in the local's cars to crash and explode into flames that ate rapidly through the last three wooden coaches. Passengers dove through windows to safety.

Thirty passengers were killed; another thirty-two were seriously injured. Almost all of these were in the last local car. Among the fatalities was the Reverend Ezra Gannett, a fire-and-brimstone preacher and pastor of the Arlington Street Church in Boston. His death, more than any other factor—and there was enough contemptible recklessness to suffice—created one of the loudest outcries against "the evils of railroading" in America to that date.

Members of Reverend Gannett's congregation exploded in wrath over the disaster: they organized torchlight marches and a barrage of petitions to politicians, decrying the lack of telegraph communications on Eastern's line. Thousands took up the cause and more than $500,000 in damage suits hammered away at the railroad company. At first the imperious Prescott ignored the commotion, but the wave of public disgust continued. He finally resigned, as did President Browne, grumbling into crotchety retirement. Under new, progressive management, Eastern immediately set in motion a series of improvements, such as air brakes, modern road signals and, the routing of trains by telegraph.

(ALSO SEE: Chicago, Illinois; Dugald, Ontario, Canada; Harrow-Wealdstone, England; Ivanhoe, Indiana; Jessore, Bangladesh; Mays Landing, New Jersey; Mud Run, Pennsylvania; Naperville, Illinois.)

RHONE (WYE and OTHERS) — MARINE DISASTER, October 29, 1867

background: A powerful hurricane of small diameter, considered to be one of the great hurricanes of the century, crashed over the Virgin Islands on October 29, 1867, destroying much of the housing at St. Thomas (where the barometer fell to 27.95 inches) and moving off to level the city of Caguas in Puerto Rico, where the hurricane was called "San Narciso." Particular damage was done to the mail ship *Rhone* and sixty other vessels; most of the 600 deaths in this storm occurred at sea.

About sixty vessels, most of them belonging to the Royal Mail Fleet, were anchored throughout the Virgin Islands when a vicious hurricane descended upon them from a north-northwesterly direction at 11:00 A.M. on October 29, 1867. Lying at anchor off Peter Island was the 2,738-ton liner *Rhone,* under the command of Captain F. Woolley. Anchored close by was the paddle steamship *Conway,* also belonging to the same line. As the skies darkened above the bobbing ships, Captain Woolley checked the barometer. It had fallen to a startling 27.95 inches.

Woolley then saw the black shape of a hurricane approaching from the northwest and ordered his engines to steam full speed to the ship's anchors. The 129 crew members and passengers sought safety below decks as the storm passed overhead, lashing at the vessel. It snapped off a spar from aloft, sending it deckward. This struck the first officer, Topper, and killed him instantly.

A lull then came upon the sea, and Woolley decided to outrace the storm. He pulled up anchors and got under way. He had steamed through several island channels, and thought he was clear of the storm, when the edge of the violent hurricane caught up with the *Rhone.* The full blast of the storm lifted the liner from the sea and hurled her onto the rocks of Salt Island, where she broke in half and foundered. Woolley and 122 others perished; 21 crew members and a passenger, an Italian immigrant, survived.

Dozens of other ships belonging to the Royal Mail Steam Packet Company suffered just about the same fate. The 819-ton *Wye,* at anchor in the harbor of St. Thomas, got under way immediately as the storm approached. Her first officer, Hodgson, was in command (the captain was visiting the master of another ship, the *Tyne*). The little steamship, with sixty-nine crew members on board, could not, like her big sister *Rhone,* outrun the storm.

Off Buck Island the full weight of the hurricane pounded the *Wye* to pieces, ripping away her masts and binnacle. The ship was carried by mountainous waves onto the island, where she broke up. Forty-one sailors drowned in the raging surf. Hodgson survived with a broken arm and so bitter a memory of the angry sea that he retired.

The *Tyne,* with the *Wye's* skipper aboard, managed to survive, but was wrecked, as was the *Solent.* The *Derwent* was ripped from her moorings by the storm and many aboard her died. Only two vessels out of the sixty at anchor in and about the Virgin Islands remained intact after the hurricane passed. More than 600 persons, mostly sailors on these vessels, lost their lives.

RHYTHM NIGHT CLUB — FIRE, April 23, 1940

Once an old church, the Rhythm Night Club in Natchez, Mississippi, on St. Catherine Street, was a decrepit building of rotting wood. Only one exit was available to the hordes of blacks who jammed into its small confines to dance and listen to nationally known jazz bands. On the night of April 23, 1940, more than 250 Negroes were inside the club when fire broke out in the highly flammable Spanish moss that decorated the overhead beams.

A stampede toward the front door ensued. It was the only way out. The windows of the old church had been solidly boarded up, and though dozens of patrons wildly flailed at the boards with their fists, they could not escape. About forty persons, mostly men, did manage to dash through the roaring flames covering the front door. All were badly burned. The rest were driven back toward the bandstand, and they died there in heaps, roasted to death. R. E. Smith, managing editor of the *Natchez Democrat,* arrived to inspect the inside of the ruined building. He winced at the sight of burned bodies.

The death toll was 198 persons. All of those who were lucky enough to escape the blaze had to be treated for injuries.

For 198 persons attending the dance at the Rhythm Night Club in Natchez, Mississippi, on the night of April 23, 1940, the music ended forever when a roaring fire consumed the highly flammable building in minutes. *(Wide World)*

RICHMOND HILL, LONG ISLAND

RAILWAY WRECK
November 22, 1950

background: The Babylon Express, eight months after a similar crash, smashed into the rear of the Hempstead commuter train stalled at Richmond Hill, Long Island, at 6:26 P.M. on November 22, 1950, killing 79 persons and injuring another 363 passengers. The conductor of the Express, who was killed, was charged with disregarding signals.

The Long Island Railroad was having more than its share of woes in 1950. On February 17, two of its trains had met in a side collision at Rockville Center, Long Island, and thirty-one people had been killed. What occurred eight months later at Richmond Hill made the first wreck a gory prelude to the worst accident in the line's history. (The parent of the Long Island Line is the Pennsylvania Railroad.)

William Murphy, motorman for the Hempstead train, which consisted of twelve cars jammed with rush-hour passengers, was approaching Metropolitan Avenue in Richmond Hill when he slowed his train to 15 m.p.h. in obedience to warning signals. The brakes, however, began to grab, as he later explained (subsequent investigations failed to find any fault with the brakes), and the train came to an abrupt stop between stations.

Also, according to instructions, the rear car flagman, Bertram Biggam, of the Hempstead train, jumped from the last car carrying a red lamp. He walked a few paces down the track, prepared to wave off any oncoming train. His actions were sufficient to maintain safety ordinarily, but the stop between stations was irregular enough so that he should also have placed torpedoes or flares. This he did not do.

Motorman Murphy got a go-ahead signal from the overhead board to his front but could not move his train. The sound of the motors indicated to Biggam that his train was about to depart, so he walked back to the rear car and got on. The Hempstead train, however, did not move. Seconds later, its glaring white light filling the last car of the Hempstead train, the Babylon Express, with fifty-five-year-old Benjamin Pokorney at the controls, came roaring up the same track from behind.

The rear-end collision was inevitable. Pokorney could not reduce speed in time to prevent the accident. He was going almost 40 m.p.h. only seconds before impact.

Death was assured for almost all of those passengers in the last car of the Hempstead train and the first car of the Babylon Express, which was also a twelve-car train.

Fred Mergi, a passenger on the Hempstead train, was one of the lucky few in the last car to survive. He saw Biggam reboard the train after Murphy attempted to

One car of the Babylon Express rides the top of a coach of the Hempstead commuter train after a rear-end collision at Richmond Hill, Long Island, on November 22, 1950, killed seventy-nine passengers. *(UPI)*

start it, and then he saw the white light from the Babylon Express. "This big white light flooded the car," he later said. Mergi dove for the floor as the crash occurred. The first car of the Babylon Express dove under the last car of the Hempstead train, lifting it into the air. Mergi slid down the aisle as his car was thrown upward. That movement saved his life. "The lights went out and glass crashed. Everybody was yelling and screaming. A chandelier came down on my head."

For most of the 79 persons killed, it was a quick death. Motorman Pokorney was killed instantly, but his body was wedged for hours beneath debris. Another 363 seriously injured persons were taken from the scene of twisted steel to hospitals.

Apparently, as investigators later reconstructed the disaster, Pokorney had been following the overhead signals, and had not seen the Hempstead train around a bend. He saw the same "go ahead" signal that Murphy had attempted to respond to, however, and interpreted it as a directive to the Babylon Express. (He obviously assumed that the Hempstead train was far up the line.)

The staggering death toll and muster of wounded caused a great public outcry against the Long Island Line. New York's Mayor Vincent Impelitteri went so far as to brand it a "disgraceful common carrier."

After paying out $11 million in damage suits, the line readily agreed to and set in motion radical improvements in its signal system.

(ALSO SEE: Chicago, Illinois; Ivanhoe, Indiana; Naperville, Illinois)

RICHMOND, VIRGINIA — FLOOD — May 27, 1771

The worst flood in the history of Virginia remains to date the one that emanated from the James River, which reached astounding heights on May 27, 1771, and caught citizens totally unprepared. The Geological Survey reported that 150 persons drowned in this flash flood, following heavy rains.

RICHMOND, VIRGINIA — MINE DISASTER — March 18, 1839

The explosion that took place in the Black Heath Mine outside Richmond, Virginia, on March 18, 1839, is one of the earliest on record in the United States, although several undocumented explosions in mine shafts had occurred previously. Virginia historian Henry Howes provided details on the Black Heath explosion in his book, *Virginia, Its History and Antiquities.*

There were fifty-four men in the mine at the time of the explosion, and three more miners were descending into the shaft in a basket. What touched off the terrific explosion is not known. The blast roared in flames out of the mouth of the mine shaft, and only two men were able to take refuge in small crevices to avoid the searing blaze.

The basket containing the three miners "was blown nearly one hundred feet into the air. Two fell out and were crushed to death, and the third remained in, and with the basket, was thrown some seventy or eighty feet from the shaft, breaking both his legs and arms."

Most of the fifty-three miners killed in this blast died of gas fumes. Their bodies found later were untouched by the flames.

RIDERWOOD, MARYLAND — RAILWAY WRECK — July 4, 1854

On July 4, 1854, a joyous political outing of the Know-Nothing Party turned into a bloody disaster when the second train of a three-train convoy returning to Baltimore from Riders Grove, Maryland, ten miles away, was involved in a head-on collision with the afternoon train from York.

The mixup occurred when the York train, waiting for the excursion trains to pass it on the main track at Relay Station, prematurely took to the main track again. Somehow the conductor of this train thought there was only one excursion train instead of three, and when the first passed, he thought the main track was clear. (How this came about is puzzling; officials for the Baltimore and Susquehanna Line knew full well that 5,000 people made up the excursion and that the line had provided three trains for their use. A dispatcher had distinctly ordered the York train to stand down for the excursion *trains.*)

Moving at top speed, the York train rounded a bend near Riderwood at 5:20 P.M. and immediately plowed into the second excursion train headed in the opposite direction on the same track. For some unknown reason this excursion train was being backed into Baltimore. Its engine was at the rear, and eight gondola cars and two passenger cars were in front. The York train smashed into the first two passenger cars, splintering the wooden coaches to pieces, and killing thirty-four persons.

The conductor of the York train was blamed for the accident. He was charged with disregarding orders.

RING THEATER — FIRE — December 8, 1881

background: The Ring Theater of Vienna, Austria, built by the Imperial Government in 1873, caught fire on stage a few minutes before 7:00 P.M. on December 8, 1881, as the result of a careless lamplighter. Hundreds were trapped in the balconies and of these, 850 perished; hundreds more were injured while trying to escape the blaze.

Vienna's mammoth, ornate Ring Theater, named for the circlelike plaza it stood in, was originally intended to

Vienna's marvelous Ring Theatre was ablaze on the night of December 8, 1881; 850 persons in the audience burned to death while thousands watched helpless outside. *(Illustrated London News)*

house comic opera, but soon after its completion in 1873, the building was competing with the Grand Opera House in presenting the world's leading talents in music and theater. Madame Patti's Italian opera company performed there to much acclaim. So too did Signor Salvini's dramatic troupe, the Meiningers, and the incomparable Sara Bernhardt. Unlike the Grand Opera House with its stiff-backed seats, the Ring Theater was designed for comfort. It was soon the preferred theater in Vienna.

On December 7, 1881, Offenbach's opera *Les Contes de Hoffman* was performed for the first time and received unstinting praise from the city's critics. The reviews drew hordes of theatergoers the following evening. Professors, bank directors, clerks, railway directors, merchants, students, concierges, brokers, servants, knights, actors from other theaters (more than 200 actors, dancers, and musicians were thrown out of work following the Ring Theater disaster), and countless others flocked to the theater, most arriving before 7:00 P.M.

By 6:50 P.M. the balconies were all jammed, but most of the lower boxes and stalls were still empty, their blue-blooded occupants yet to arrive. At this time a stage lamplighter moved behind the drawn curtain, lighting the upper row of gas jets. Just above the stage lights were low-hanging pieces of scenery, clouds made of highly flammable canvas. Somehow the lamplighter's torch brushed this scenery, and it burst into flames. The curtains were next; they were so quickly ignited that the blaze blew them outward toward the audience. A heavy draft from the stage area abetted the fire.

The stagehands immediately panicked. They made no attempt to lower the protective iron curtain onto the stage, a simple act that would certainly have averted the tragedy that followed. When the curtain bulged outward into the auditorium, those few in the orchestra and the mobs of spectators in the two balconies, about 1,000 persons in all, rose, screaming hysterically, "Fire! Fire! Fire!"

The occupants of the boxes and stalls made an orderly retreat to the street, where hundreds of other theatergoers, mostly those of the wealthy class who were habitually late, were just arriving. Bedlam ruled the balconies. To add further trauma to the widespread panic, a stagehand foolishly turned off the gas, pitching the entire theater into darkness. (The act was later explained as an attempt to prevent the gas in the lamps from exploding and further increasing the fire. Ironically, no one thought to drop the iron curtain; the fire alarm bell to summon the fire brigade was not rung, and the water hose on stage was ignored.)

Fire soon swept into the theater, crawling up the walls and shooting across the ceiling. By this grim glare hundreds struggled to escape. A woman fell screeching to her death from the upper balcony. She landed on two people and killed them also. Scores of people, mostly children, were trampled to death in the mad flight. Dozens of people choked the narrow balcony aisles, corridors and exits. There they died, shrieking in their agony as the fire closed in on them. A reporter stated, "These were consumed in one mass, as a huge furnace, while the house continued to burn."

Outside, the fire brigades arrived with gongs banging. Ladders were hurriedly thrown onto shoulders, and lines of men dashed into the theater. Women in long, bustled evening gowns, men in top hats and greatcoats used their theater glasses to view the fire, which had replaced their originally scheduled amusement. Firemen inside the theater attempted to throw up their ladders to the balconies, but they did not reach. Frantically firemen searched through the burning theater for tapestries, drapes, anything they could stretch out as a net for those trapped above to jump onto. None were available; all by then were burned.

People began to jump screaming from the first balcony; many died, more survived with crippling injuries. Firemen finally managed to locate a large cloth, which they spread out. A fire captain shouted up to the yelling throng, "Jump onto this cloth, one at a time! Hear me! One at a time!" As the fire crackled about them and overhead, an eerie silence permeated the hundreds in the balconies.

One man, a towering figure, his dress coat burned half away, raised both arms and turned from the first balcony to the one above. "Children first! Help the little ones first! Then the women! Any man who jumps before them I will deal with!" The children began to jump, initially from the first balcony, then the second. All the while there were shouts and moans as the fire ate its way into the milling, waiting throngs. When the women began to jump onto the cloth held by the firemen, several were on fire, their bodies leaving a bizarre trail of smoke as they descended. Then some of the men began to jump, and by that time the entire theater was ablaze. In this fashion the Viennese firemen saved 112 persons; many of these suffered broken arms and legs, but they did survive the great holocaust.

Outside, firemen, militiamen and theatergoers worked frantically at fire pumps, but the pressure of their hoses was puny and failed to reach the lofty towers and roof of the theater. As the magnificent structure was all but consumed, Austrian royalty and political figures arrived by coach to witness the fiery spectacle. Gilded carriages carrying the five Austrian archdukes dashed into the plaza. These resplendently-attired young men, William, Albrecht, Eugene, Salvatore and Charles, all grandnephews of Franz Joseph, who was to succeed to a war-shaken throne in 1916 as the last emperor of Austria, gazed at the burning theater. They dipped into their purses to begin the collection of relief funds for victims.

At the height of the fire, the screams of the dying piercing the night and bodies tumbling from the cathedrallike windows onto the pavement below, another coach arrived, pulled by eight black horses. From it stepped the ill-starred Crown Prince Rudolf of Austria, who, eight years later, on January 30, 1889, would join his mistress, Baroness Maria Vetsera, in suicide at Mayerling, the site of the royal hunting lodge. His suicide was prompted by the order of his father, Emperor Franz Joseph, to end the affair. Rudolf watched the human carnage for some minutes, was seen to weep openly, and then turned away from the burning theater. There was nothing anyone could do but keep a gloomy deathwatch.

Days later, sifting through the gutted remains of the Ring Theater, firemen counted the charred bodies of 850 persons, the highest number of fatalities ever recorded in a theater fire.

(ALSO SEE: Baquet Theater; Brooklyn Theater; Exeter Theater; Iroquois Theater; Laurier Palace Theater; Opera Comique; Opera House, Nice)

RINGLING BROTHERS and BARNUM & BAILEY CIRCUS — FIRE — July 6, 1944

background: During a matinee of the Ringling Brothers and Barnum & Bailey Circus in Hartford, Connecticut, on July 6, 1944, a small blaze ignited the twenty-ton big top tent, which was 550 feet long, 250 feet wide, and 75 feet high. More than 6,000 of the tent's 12,000 seats were filled when the fire broke out. One hundred sixty-eight persons were burned to death; another 250 spectators were injured. Five circus officials were indicted for manslaughter. The tent had been treated for rainproofing with a highly flammable chemical.

Since their inception in 1790, American circuses have been plagued by many catastrophes. Fires, storms, stampedes and accidents have destroyed the big tops and killed spectators and performers alike. After scores of wild animals were killed when P. T. Barnum's menagerie burned in 1887, it became all but impossible to insure most circuses for the next three decades.

Of the more than 1,000 circuses traversing the country during the big-top heyday, the largest was the Ringling Brothers and Barnum & Bailey Circus, known the world over as "The Greatest Show on Earth." This mammoth exhibition of talent had known its share of tragedy. Ringling Brothers lost their enormous tent on August 22, 1912, in Sterling, Illinois, when the canvas caught fire from a barn burning nearby. No one, fortunately, was in the tent at the time, and the big top was replaced so quickly that the circus moved on the next day to Kewanee, Illinois. In 1938 the show failed to go on—the only time in its history—when a workers' strike closed the big top in Scranton, Pennsylvania. Death came to the Ringling circus late in the 1941 season as, one by one, ten of their elephants died. Veterinarians suspected arsenic poisoning, and the police finally tracked down a half-lunatic ex-employee of the circus's roustabout gang who had poisoned the animals as revenge for being fired. On August 4 of the following year, the Ringling menagerie tent caught fire in Cleveland, Ohio, and forty wild animals either died from the smoke or were shot by animal trainers as they escaped from their cages. Three circus employees were injured in that fire.

All of these incidents paled before the disaster that

struck the huge Ringling circus as it was encamped on the dry grasslands outside Hartford, Connecticut, on July 6, 1944. The temperature soared to 90 degrees before noon, and makeup freshly applied to the faces of such internationally known clowns as Emmett Kelly and Felix Adler melted into colored rivulets that coursed down their cheeks. The previous evening's performance had drawn raves from the *Hartford Courant,* which described the circus as "bigger, better, and smarter than ever." As a result almost 6,000 persons flocked to the matinee the following day, most of them children.

It was wartime, and many parents who would otherwise have escorted their youngsters to the Ringling circus were at work in defense plants. Aging grandparents, uncles and teen-agers became baby sitters under the big top.

The war had deprived the circus of necessary equipment. Prewar fireproof hemp ropes, so vital to the construction of the big tent, had been replaced by ones of inferior quality. The tent itself—said to be the largest in the world—was in bad shape. Patches covered rips and tears. The tent had been waterproofed with paraffin, which had been thinned with gasoline. While this might have worked as waterproofing, it made the tent a firetrap.

The big top would also serve as fuel for controversy. Some would imply that Hartford's fire marshal had been pressured not to check the volatile canvas. Explaining that the fire marshal for the District of Columbia had refused to be pressured by congressmen into overlooking safety hazards of other circuses, Paul W. Kearney angrily wrote in 1952: "What a pity that Hartford's fire marshal wasn't in the same enviable position eight years ago! For then six of the big show's top hired hands would not have been sentenced to from two to seven years in prison for involuntary manslaughter; John Ringling North would have avoided having to scrape up ten or fifteen million dollars to settle the damage claims which nearly bankrupted the show; 168 men, women and children would still be alive. . . ."

As the throng took their places under the big tent, band conductor Merle Evans put his spirited musicians through their warm-up paces. Of the six entrances into the gigantic tent, four had become almost totally blocked after the crowds entered the wooden tiers. First performers blocked them during the grand parade, and then were blocked by the cages used in Albert Court's lion-and-tiger act. (Following the grand parade around the tent, most of the performers had retired to their tents and began changing for their individual acts.)

Court entered the arena and worked his beasts in a large circular cage for twelve suspenseful minutes, riveting spectators to their seats. Following "a tremendous applause," as one eyewitness later wrote, "led by shrieking, whistling children who seemed to line the front of the rising tiers of seats forming a continuous oval around the walls of the tent, the lion tamer took his bows and departed."

Bright spotlights shot upward and played on a thin wire stretched between two perches fifty feet above the center ring. Smiling and waving to the crowd were the "Flying Wallendas," the incredible high-wire performers. Their silken tights bedecked with spangles glittered down at the hushed crowd. In the darkness below, roustabouts began to clear away the apparatus of Court's act, in order to prepare for the three-ring performances that were to follow.

Helen and Henrietta Wallenda stood on one high platform; Joe Wallenda stood on another. Herman and Karl Wallenda began to move toward each other on bicycles from opposite platforms, riding the high wire. Meeting over the center ring, they backed away, advanced, backed away. Suddenly Herman Wallenda glanced downward to a small spot of canvas. He saw a flame about the size of a clenched fist. Quickly it ate its way up the side of the tent toward the roof. The Wallendas quickly backed their bikes to the platforms.

Merle Evans saw the flame, too, and ordered his band to play "The Stars and Stripes Forever," the traditional disaster signal among circus folk. Some roustabouts ran for the elephant quarters and picked up buckets of water from which the pachyderms were guzzling. Inside the performers' tent Felix Adler, known as "The King of Clowns," was putting on a false nose when he heard the disaster signal and raced for the big top to look for his sixteen-year-old daughter Muriel. Flames crept through the opening of Adler's tent as he retrieved his daughter and led her to safety. "Then I thought of my pet pig," Adler later remembered, "and went back to get him."

Emmett Kelly heard the signaling music, too, and then he "heard what sounded like laughter at first, and then it turned into a terrible scream—they all sounded like beaten dogs. . . ."

Roller skating stars called The Four Macs were greasing their skates when, as one said, "the music stopped so suddenly . . . the air crackled like gunfire for a few minutes and then there were screams pitched high above a steady roar. . . ."

Fear gripped the thousands inside the big top as the flames raced rapidly up the side of the tent, grew into a wall of fire, and ate into the roof, creating an ever-widening hole that let in the bright sunlight. People sitting in folding chairs around the rings jumped up excitedly when they first saw the blaze. Thomas E. Murphy, an editorial writer for the *Hartford Courant,* was attending the circus with his five-year-old son. He turned abruptly in his seat when he "heard a woman gasp—'look—fire!' There near the main entrance to the tent, a tiny tongue of flame crept up the side wall." As the terror grew, men could be heard shouting, "Take it easy, take it easy! Walk out quietly!"

Through megaphones several ringmasters shouted, "Let's all sing! Sing!" Merle Evans led the band into "Old Black Joe," but the crowd would have none of it. From tier to rising tier the panic shivered and line after line of spectators rose and stampeded toward the six exits, four of which were still blocked. Flames shot through the sawdust of the three rings and up the center poles. The countless ropes strung from the big top's ceiling lit up. The crowd was uncontrollable. Men, women and children shoved, kicked, and pushed screaming toward the exits.

Scores stumbled and fell over the chutes that were used to bring the wild animals into the tent. Murphy, holding his small son, ran with one mob to an exit partially blocked by two three-foot-high steel runways. He turned back to view the pandemonium in the wooden seats. "All semblance of order was gone now. Women screamed, children cried. I saw one woman in the top row take her flaxen-haired little girl in one arm, grab a rope in the other and slide to the ground. Her arm was raw and red. But there was little time now for observation."

Murphy reached the barrier. Next to him, a struggling woman tried to climb over it, but she fell back, slumping to the ground. A powerfully built roustabout stood before her and held back the crowd, trying to give her enough time to regain her feet, but it was hopeless. He was knocked over by the advancing mob, and both he and the woman were trampled. Murphy was slammed into the animal chutes, but he managed to lift his son up and throw him over the barrier. Overhead were the flames; the heat was almost unbearable. Murphy crawled over the barrier, retrieved his son and ran outside.

As the big top burns, terrified customers flee the Ringling Brothers and Barnum & Bailey circus in Hartford on July 6, 1944; 168 burned to death in the inferno. *(UPI)*

"I looked back as I left the tent," he recalled, "and saw people still struggling madly to get over the barrier. Outside children were running around crying. Men and women had the vacant look of shock. Some were just sitting on the grass staring into space. I would say that it was less than forty-five seconds from the time the first sign of fire appeared until the top of the tent had been consumed."

As the fire raced up the walls of the tent, people were jolted into desperation, and from the top of the wooden tier, they began to throw their children down to those on ground level, hoping someone would save them. Many on the ground did exactly that, but some children were hurled into the fleeing mass and trampled to death.

Billowing black smoke, caused by the paraffin and gasoline on the canvas, added to the misery of the victims. Merle Evans and the courageous musicians were choking on the smoke, but they continued sputtering out tunes. "None of them looked like they had a chance of ever getting out of that place," one observer remarked. (The band did escape without serious injuries.)

Herman Wallenda wanted to save his bike from the fire, but Carl pulled him down from a platform. Herman looked down at the yelling, terrified audience. It was a sight he would remember the rest of his life. "I can never look down at a crowd again without smelling the flames and the burning flesh." Carl Wallenda dragged Herman down a rope, and The Flying Wallendas fled in the direction of the animal cages. They crawled over these and ran outside to safety. Helen Wallenda was separated from the troupe and carried along with one mob. Just as she emerged from the burning tent, people behind her began wild shoving and pushing.

"I fell," she said, "and they stepped on me. I could feel them over me, and I thought I was going to be trampled to death."

One of the thousands of little girls who had seen the aerialist perform saw the coral fluff of Helen's costume. "I heard her yell as she covered me with her little body. 'The bright flying lady; help her!'" An usher dashed forward and used a broom sideways to hold back the crowd long enough for others to pick up the little girl and Helen Wallenda and drag them to safety.

Heroism rose above cowardice and panic. The circus midgets worked feverishly to retrieve scores of children. These brave men repeatedly risked their lives crawling back and forth under the tent flap, bringing more and more people out, until their clothes were smoking.

Clown Emmett Kelly, attired in his tattered costume, found it hard to move in his oversized shoes. He first tried to douse the fire by lugging single buckets of water, but it was a useless, pathetic gesture. Then he joined the Wallendas and others in directing the fleeing spectators to points of safety. He and the Wallendas began to carry out bodies piling up at the entranceways. He later recalled that he would never forget the crumpled dead forms "of the kids who have earned my living for so many years . . . the little ones who laughed at me. . . ." Next to Kelly worked the clown Felix Adler, carrying out the bodies of more children, his false nose burned away.

Ten minutes had gone by, and hundreds were still trapped in the inferno. A small teen-ager with a deformed foot led a group of little children to one of the few tent walls not in flames. Taking out a Boy Scout knife, he frantically slashed a large hole in the canvas. More than 300 people escaped through this opening. A teen-ager and a wounded serviceman managed to work one tent flap free and held it up while scores dashed to safety as the veteran shouted, "Don't panic!"

Desperate parents separated from their children were beside themselves as they searched through the milling crowds outside the burning tent. Murphy remembered seeing one woman "standing, moaning and saying, 'My four children, my four children. Where are they?' Then she spied a six-year-old coming to her, crying, and she ran and threw her arms around him. Then another, then another. Finally she had all four, ages six, seven, eight, and nine. They were all crying and embracing each other. The woman was shouting, 'Thank God, thank God.'"

At one exit, which was comparatively free of obstruction, the crowd emerged in fair order, but signs of panic began to develop. A roustabout, one of his hands badly burned, held up a pistol used by the lion tamers and fired two shots into the air. "I'll shoot the first man who stampedes here," he threatened. This group maintained order. The pistol contained blanks.

There was no time at all to put the three water trucks into action or to hook up hoses to stifle the blaze. Hydrants for most of the hoses were too distant to be of any use. Hartford firemen, Red Cross workers, and civil defense wardens arrived at a scene one described as a "flaming forest of canvas," but the fire was hopelessly out of control by then.

Emmett Kelly was weeping, his sad clown's face for once in true character. A little girl came to him sobbing, and asked for her mother. "Listen, honey," he softly said to her. "Listen to the old man! You go way over there to the 'victory garden' and wait for your mommy. She'll come along soon."

Whole families had been trapped inside the burning big top and had perished, huddled together. Near the center ring more than 100 bodies were later found, most of these charred beyond recognition, their identity ultimately determined through dental records. Morgues filled up and in the National Guard armory about eighty children were stretched out under olive green blankets "from which little feet," a reporter wrote, "some of them bare, some in the well scuffed shoes of active little boys and party shoes of good little girls, protruded." It would take days to discover the exact number of dead, 168 in all.

More than 250 persons were taken to three of Hartford's hospitals. Their injuries were severe. Psychologically, some would never recover.

A newspaperman found Herman Wallenda nervously knotting and unknotting his colorful red, white, and blue tie. The aerialist told his story of carrying out bodies. "I went back for more the last time," Wallenda said in a tired monotone, "when a man called to me and asked me to help him pull out his child. He called from the grandstand, and I reached up toward him. Then he fell back into the fire." Wallenda could not continue.

Pat Waldo, director of performer personnel for the circus, walked about the body-littered grounds as the smoke from the devastated big top rose behind him. He was like a man sleepwalking. "I don't know," he murmured. "I don't understand it . . . we made so many people happy . . . so many kids laugh . . . and now they are all dead."

Dr. Albert Ostermaier, prince of the horse act, stared angrily at the horrifying scene and blurted: "I loved the circus always. Now I almost hate it, because there are so many, many dead."

As reporters swarmed into the fire-charred area, they carefully examined the remnants of the big top. It had burned so thoroughly that they could not find a piece of canvas left that was more than three square inches. The entire tent had sizzled to nothing in fifteen minutes. It was then that suspicions were aroused.

When Hartford's state's attorney, Hugh M. Alcorn, Jr., charged that the tent had been treated with paraffin that had been thinned with gasoline ("enough to make it highly flammable"), the Ringling people fought back. People at the circus headquarters in Sarasota, Florida, announced that the big top had definitely been treated to resist fire, and that, being canvas, it could not be made fireproof. In Evanston, Illinois, Robert Ringling, president of the circus, issued this statement: "Every test we put that tent through showed that it would resist fire; a fire might endanger some of the equipment, but would never endanger human life."

How the fire started, whether by a carelessly tossed cigarette or a match, was never determined, but five circus officials were initially arraigned in Hartford's police court and charged with involuntary manslaughter. These were J. A. Haley, vice-president; George W. Smith, general manager; Leonard Aylesworth, boss canvas man; Edward Versteig, chief electrician, and David Blanchfield, chief wagon man. Following a lengthy investigation and trial, several of the circus's top people went to jail to serve long sentences.

The Ringling Brothers disaster in Hartford remains the worst circus tragedy in United States history, and is exceeded only by the burning of the Gran Circo Norte-Americano in Niteroi, Brazil, on December 17, 1961.

A haunting postscript to the Hartford blaze was a small newspaper dispatch that appeared the following day. The report told how the Dailey Brothers' circus, then appearing in Sheboygan, Wisconsin, "was unaffected by news of the Ringling circus disaster. . . . The main tent was crowded to capacity at the night performance. Members of the audience smoked freely."

(ALSO SEE: Gran Circo Norte-Americano; Ivanhoe, Indiana)

RIO DE JANEIRO — MARINE DISASTER

February 22, 1901

background: The Pacific Mail Steamship Company's ship *Rio de Janeiro,* built at the Roach shipyard and launched on March 6, 1878, struck rocks off the Golden Gate in San Francisco Bay at approximately 4:30 A.M. on February 22, 1901. She sank within fifteen minutes. Of the 208 persons on board, mostly immigrants, 131 drowned. The ship, valued between $800,000 and $900,000, was a total loss. She carried cargo worth $200,000, and insurance coverage was about twice that amount.

As the first great ocean disaster of the twentieth century, the foundering of the mail steamship *Rio de Janeiro* off the Golden Gate in San Francisco Bay on February 22, 1901, was a study in puzzling ineptitude. Sailing from Hong Kong and Honolulu, the steamer carried 208 passengers and crew members. Most of the passengers were Chinese immigrants who throughout the long voyage were kept continuously in the steerage holds, where the men sat comatose in opium stupors, the children swung humorlessly in hammocks, and the women silently padded in small steps, their feet still bound in the ancient fashion, around their sprawled families. These quiet victims would come to watery deaths because of irresponsible seamen.

At about 4:00 A.M. on February 22, the *Rio,* which had been anchored mid-channel off the entrance to San Francisco Bay, proceeded northeast at an estimated speed of 9 m.p.h. At first, as the ship edged into the bay, the weather was clear, but a fog bank soon rolled out and engulfed the ship. Whistles and foghorn were of little use against the rocks off Point Fort near Mile Rock, toward which the *Rio* was headed.

The immigrant liner *Rio de Janeiro* sank off San Francisco's Golden Gate on February 22, 1901. The captain locked himself in his cabin and 131 passengers drowned. *(Frank Leslie's Illustrated Newspaper)*

Most of the passengers and crew members were asleep. Captain Ward was not on deck; his duties were assumed by First Mate Coghlan. Quartermaster Lindstrom was in the wheelhouse, and try as he might, he could see nothing in the dense fog through which the *Rio* sliced like a phantom, smoke billowing from her single track, her sails set full and blown forward.

Coghlan inexplicably had not positioned a line man to take soundings. There was no real excuse for ignoring this mandatory precaution. He later testified before a board of inquiry: "You could not take soundings with the hand line, and it would have done no good anyhow . . . you couldn't find the bottom with a thousand fathoms of line." This was a ridiculous statement in that the deepest spot in the San Francisco Bay channel was, at that time, 63 fathoms, and the *Rio* was equipped with a modern lead, a patent sounding machine invented by Lord Kelvin, which operated to a depth of 300 fathoms (1,800 feet). The depth of water over which the *Rio* passed was no more than 30 fathoms. Officials on the board of inquiry, unfamiliar with nautical terms and devices, however, accepted Coghlan's absurd statement without blinking an eye or finding any negligence on his part.

As the 3,548-ton steamer moved by Point Fort, Quartermaster Lindstrom saw a red flash, which he thought was a light from the fort, "overhead and in front." Moments later the *Rio* jolted upon the rocks, and gaping holes were torn in her bow. An officer ran to Captain Ward's cabin and banged on his door loudly.

"What is it?" Ward asked.

"We've struck the rocks, Captain . . . we're sinking fast."

"Yes, I heard."

"We're taking on a great amount of water, sir."

"That's too bad."

"Won't you open the door, sir?"

"No." With that, Captain Ward approached the door and slammed the bolt-lock into place, shutting himself off forever from his crew and passengers. His actions were far less understandable than the actions of the Chinese immigrants, who, upon hearing the crash and seeing water gushing into the holds, panicked and fled on deck with wild shrieking. Some brandished knives and threatened crew men. They screamed for the lifeboats, but there was simply no time to swing the boats over.

The *Rio,* unlike more modern ships of her day, was not equipped with watertight bulkheads, a deficiency that hastened her end. The Chinese hurled themselves into the fog-bound waters and sank in thrashing clusters. Sailors abandoned passengers and, clutching deck chairs or other wooden items that would float, let themselves over the sides by ropes and swam away.

Consul-General Wildman of Hong Kong and his wife and two children were abandoned, left standing on deck as the ship hurried downward. The entire family drowned; 131 in all perished. Most of the crew, except for the locked-up Captain Ward, survived.

The sinking of the *Rio* was the twenty-first loss of the Pacific Mail Steamship Company in a fifty-year span. Its most serious marine disaster had been the foundering of the *Golden Gate* off Mexico on July 27, 1862. The sinking of the *Rio* was a loss that need not have happened, incurred through stupidity and indifference.
(ALSO SEE: Golden Gate*)*

RIO DE JANEIRO, BRAZIL

LANDSLIDES
January 11-13, 1966 and February 17-20, 1967

Rio de Janeiro's verdant mountains, ringing one of the most beautiful harbors in the world, have always seemed exquisitely picturesque to tourists, but to the Brazilians of Rio in early 1966, they became towers of death. Between January 11-13, 1966, following torrential rains, the illegal shanty towns surrounding the city on its highest hills, known as the notorious *favelados* to residents, were inundated by floods and house-crunching mudslides.

Hundreds were injured as their homes in the districts of Santa Teresa, Copacabana and Ipanema were destroyed;

239 slum-dwellers were killed. All of these deaths and most of the injuries could have been averted, authorities later claimed, if the *favelados* had been restrained from cutting away all the foliage that held the soil in place and had been compelled to shore up house foundations on exposed slopes with protective walls. There was, however, an almost criminal carelessness on the part of most of Rio's officials with regard to these safety measures. Rio's Governor Francisco Negrao de Lima echoed the general lack of concern by blithely stating: "Rains like this happen only once in a century."

Slightly more than a year later, an eleven-inch rainfall again swamped the slum sections, and houses again began to topple, trapping hundreds beneath them. A particularly dramatic event was the death of a beautiful nineteen-year-old girl, Berenice Marahao, who was visible to rescuers but unreachable; she died after seventeen hours of painful pleading while debris from her apartment building slowly crushed her lifeless.

This time not only the *favelados* suffered, but the white-suited executives of Rio's social upper crust. The mudslides welled up and over the city's three power plants and cut Rio's electrical supply down to 40 percent. This, in turn, eliminated all of the city's air-conditioning during the hottest hours of the day, and businessmen, because of malfunctioning elevators, were compelled to climb the stairs of Rio's white skyscrapers. Many became cardiac victims in the 100-degree heat. A total of 224 persons were killed or died indirectly because of the landslides.

An army of geologists surveyed the three mountain ranges surrounding Rio and their warnings were dire. They insisted that, unless immediate concrete shorings were put up on the exposed slopes and vegetation was allowed to grow, the hills of Rio would topple completely and crush the city. Governor Negrao de Lima reacted with surprising alacrity. He forbade more construction in and about the hills, set up a geological "police force" to patrol the mountains, instituted new laws to prevent the destruction of vegetation, and sent out military helicopters to enforce his edicts. The once indifferent population complied, and Rio, at this writing, has yet to endure another killing landslide like those of 1966 and 1967.

RIO GRANDE — FLOOD

June 24-30, 1954

background: Following several days of heavy rains, the Pecos and Devil rivers caused the Rio Grande to crest at a record sixty-two feet at Laredo, Texas, in late June, 1954, creating more than $5 million in damages and killing fifty-five Americans in Ozona, Laredo and other small towns; an estimated 130 Mexican residents of Pedras Negras also perished.

The surging waters of the flooded Rio Grande swept into Laredo, Texas, on June 27, 1954. *(UPI)*

The Rio Grande has never been as high as it was in the soggy days at the end of June, 1954. Its main tributaries, the Devil and Pecos rivers, were swollen by tremendous rains. Cloudbursts caused arroyos and streams such as Johnson's Draw to burst their banks with deadly flooding. By June 27 the Rio Grande wildly jumped its banks near Laredo, tearing away five bridges at three points. At Laredo proper the railroad bridge and United States approach to the international highway bridge were swept away. The Pecos River bridge collapsed.

In the greatest flood of its history, the Rio Grande dashed through Ozona, Texas, wiping it out and killing 13 residents. Ciudad Acuna in Mexico, was inundated, and 15,000 citizens were made homeless within a few hours. A Southern Pacific passenger train was halted by the raging river outside Langtree, Texas, once the lair of the notorious Old West curmudgeon Judge Roy Bean. Travelers found themselves hopelessly stranded on the high railroad bed as the surrounding waters inched upward. Army helicopters swarmed to the rescue and evacuated the entire train in a frenzied airlift.

The twin towns of Del Rio, on the American side of the Rio Grande, and Piedras Negras, on the Mexican side, were struck by tremendous floodwaters that reached halfway up the first floor of every building. Although warned repeatedly by border patrolmen and officials that the flooding was imminent, citizens in both towns did little to prepare against the flood. Del Rio authorities did compel residents to take some precautionary action, however, and when the flood came, no lives were lost. Unfortunately, this was not the case in Piedras Negras, where the mayor and other officials dismissed the danger as paltry, and only a small detachment of Mexican soldiers made any attempt to thwart the disaster by building several sandbag dikes.

These barriers failed to hold back the floodwaters, and the Coahuilan town was completely swamped; an estimated 130 deaths occurred. The city's water became polluted, and typhoid broke out. From either small-town pride or sheer stupidity, the local Mexican officials flatly refused aid from the Red Cross and other agencies until formal requests were made. This may have caused the deaths of several citizens. The Red Cross finally was allowed to send in $50,000 in supplies and medicines.

President Dwight Eisenhower declared the southwest Texas region a disaster area and dispatched $350,000 in initial relief funds.

RISING SUN — MARINE DISASTER

September 3, 1700

In the ill-documented hurricane of September 3, 1700, the city of Charleston, South Carolina, was severely swamped. One historian laconically stated that the storm "was very severe, overthrowing many houses and overflowing the town." The exact number of fatalities is not known, but 97 of 112 persons were drowned on board the Scottish frigate *Rising Sun,* which was anchored off the bar at Charleston harbor.

The ship, in convoy with the *Duke of Hamilton,* had recently evacuated a Scottish colony from Darien in Panama. Fifteen crew members had gone ashore before the storm struck to seek fresh provisions. The ships planned to return to Scotland. The hurricane intervened, however, and the *Rising Sun* was hurled by tremendous winds and seas onto the rough beaches near Charleston. She immediately broke up. Only three on board, plus those already ashore, survived. The *Duke of Hamilton* and other ships standing off the port were thoroughly wrecked, but suffered no deaths.

RIVIERA (FRANCE AND ITALY) — EARTHQUAKE

February 23, 1887

background: A severe earthquake rattled the entire French and Italian Rivieras, as well as southern France, Italy and parts of Switzerland with several shocks that were registered shortly after 6:00 A.M. on February 23, 1887. Hundreds of buildings, including historic structures, were thrown down, and more than 2,000 persons were killed. The distance of the quake was from Leghorn, Italy, to Lyons, France, and seismoscopes in Washington, D.C., recorded shock waves traveling more than 500 m.p.h.

It was the morning of Ash Wednesday, following the Mardi Gras of Shrove Tuesday, and for rich and poor alike along the warmly lethargic Riviera it was a time of celebration, of gay dances, parties and masked balls that would last until dawn. Royalty, in its last pompous heyday, was represented in the elegant hotels and villas all along the Mediterranean coast. The Prince of Wales was at Cannes. The Duke of Chartres and others of the Orleans family were at Nice. Financier Baron Rothschild and his family were in the area. The king and queen of Wurtenburg were at their winter home, an extravagant villa in Nice.

Everywhere the lights were lit, the music played, and party-goers reveled in wild costumes and grotesque masks. Thousands, joyfully malingering, were returning home, their wine-soaked throats still full of song and their steps happily unsure when the earthquake struck. It was 6:02 A.M., and with death came a splendid dawn.

The first of five shocks shivered through Nice. The Comtesse Lina Araldi, who had just taken to bed after celebrating all night, was thrown across the floor when her home at Number 7, rue Paganini began to crash about her. The comtesse's leg was broken in three places. She was fortunate. Thousands of celebrants caught on the streets, still in costume, were struck by falling buildings

Panic and terror raged in the streets of Nice, France, as a violent earthquake interrupted the celebrants of Mardi Gras on February 23, 1887. *(Illustrated London News)*

and flying debris. Crowds on the avenue de la Gare in Nice went berserk with fear as the quake rumbled through the area.

One eyewitness described the scene in Nice as pure havoc: "People ran shrieking from many of the houses at the second shock, which brought down some buildings already shaken by the first; and in a few minutes every open space in the town, the Jardin Public, the place Massena, place de la Liberté, and other places were full of an excited, frightened mob of women and children."

The quake offered two more tremendous shocks following the first and then two slightly less volatile shocks some time later. The entire Mediterranean coast undulated, cracked, and broke. Lyons, France, felt the quake; so did Leghorn, Italy, and many cities and towns deep into Switzerland were affected by the tremors.

Worst hit was the Italian Riviera di Ponente. Towns along this scenic water frontage fell in heaps, killing hundreds. The 1,500 residents of Bajardo ran to the local church to seek refuge. A priest found it impossible to keep order so he led his terrified congregation in prayers that were more like baleful howls as the tremors continued to rattle the town. A massive shock suddenly cracked the thick masonry of the church, and the walls momentarily bulged and then collapsed; the ceiling crashed in one swoop, killing all in the church, about 300 people.

In Bussano, a town of about 800, every house was razed with the first tremor. Beneath the rubble were more than 300 dead. The celebrants of Mardi Gras in the town of Diano Marino were still dancing in one hall when the quake struck, causing the ballroom to collapse, crushing more than 250 dancers to death. Their exotic dresses and harlequin costumes were shredded and splotched with blood.

Horror continued to ripple down the French and Italian Rivieras with the earth-wrenching quake. The railway was ripped to pieces at Savona. The exquisite Ducal Palace at Genoa was rent with ugly cracks. Turin's fabulous cathedrals were damaged, some beyond repair. Mentone lost dozens of citizens and half its buildings. More than 300 were killed by falling buildings or disappeared into gaping fissures at Cervo. The shock waves tore through the towns of Oneglia, Noli, Pavia, Lucca, Cuneo, Albissola and Porto Maurizio.

At Oneglia there was a large penitentiary; its prisoners, hysterical with fear, were herded by their jailors

American and British tourists lived in tents after the earthquake drove them from shattered hotels all along the Riviera. *(Illustrated London News)*

into a courtyard and then were removed to Genoa when the quake leveled the prison. At St. Étienne the École Maternelle was brought to ruins. Carried downward to death was the much respected school mistress, Madam Cheylon.

Foreigners, who had flocked to the Riviera in previous weeks, were sent in fear to the heights of the Cimiès, where they pitched tents, and in the words of one, "awaited the end of the world." These were mostly wealthy American, English and Russian tourists. Several thousand more departed, still attired in their ballroom costumes, on whatever trains would speed them to Paris.

Colonel A. F. Bingham Wright, who was in Mentone when the quake struck, gave this eyewitness account of the quake: "Just as the day was breaking on Ash Wednesday, we were roused from our sleep by a fearful noise, and by the violent shaking of the room, with the crash of falling masonry and breaking glass and china. There was, of course, no doubt about the cause: it was an earthquake shock and one of the most violent I ever experienced; and I expected every moment to find the house falling with us. We dragged our little boy out of his bed, fortunately untouched by the falling rubbish, and rushed for the stairs just as we were, for there seemed no time to spare if we wished to get down alive.

"Having got the child down in safety, we returned to aid our friends, and found a gentleman and his little girl were both buried under the debris in rooms close to ours. With frantic exertions, they were both recovered; the father much hurt, but the child, most providentially, quite uninjured; she was completely covered, not merely by loose rubbish, but by masses of stonework, so heavy that the ladies who were trying to rescue her had not strength to move it. I helped them with all my might, and we were fortunate to get at the right spot to find her, and to get her out before she had suffered from want of air; while we were doing so another severe shock came, but, fortunately, not enough to add much more to the ruin; and in a short time all were out of doors.

"During the day and night there were frequent shocks, but, as a rule, diminishing in force. I noticed that a wave of disturbance came on about every three hours; but there were other shocks as well. Hardly anyone on the west side of Mentone slept in a house that night. We lay on mattresses under the orange trees in the garden of the Hotel de Venise, close by; some under an improvised tent. Though but little mention had been made of Mentone, I believe it has suffered more than any other place on this part of the coast. I have, since the occurrence, passed in daylight along all the Riviera from there to Marseilles, spending some hours at Nice; and nowhere is there a twentieth part of the damage visible. Mentone, in fact, has much the appearance of having undergone a bombardment; it is sad, indeed, to see this lovely place reduced to such a state."

In all more than 2,000 people perished in this quake, most of whom were permanent residents of the Riviera. None of the royal tourists were scratched, and many, like the king and queen of Wurtenburg, sat in silk pajamas, sipping coffee on their veranda as they watched the chaos. (The Wurtenburg monarchs did contribute relief funds out of their own purses.)

Ruins of the École Maternelle in St. Étienne.

As trains pulled into the Paris stations from the devastated Riviera, swarms of wealthy persons emerged from the jammed cars, most still wearing their colorful Shrove Tuesday costumes. Furs and coats failed to hide bright evening gowns and ballroom slippers. A dispatch from Paris, which appeared days later in the *Illustrated London News,* reported that the earthquakes had "caused a certain joy, because they have sent back to Paris some hundreds of people of leisure whose presence is desirable in the interests of luxury and elegance of life."
(ALSO SEE: Lisbon, Portugal; Messina, Sicily)

ROBINSON, NEW MEXICO — RAILWAY WRECK — September 5, 1956

The head-on collision at Robinson, New Mexico, was simply a matter of confusion in addition to the violation of a long-standing rule of the Sante Fe Railroad. A westbound passenger train, Number 19, consisting of a four-unit diesel with fourteen passenger cars, was heading out of Raton, New Mexico, on the morning of September 5, 1956. Eastbound from Las Vegas was Sante Fe's Number 8, also powered by a four-unit diesel and pulling sixteen passenger cars. Both trains were to meet at Robinson at 2:45 A.M.; and Number 8 had been given instructions to take to the siding and allow Number 19 to keep to the main track. The engineers of both trains had been given this explicit order.

The engineer of Number 8 dutifully pulled onto the siding at Robinson to await Number 19. His fireman went to a switch and admitted the eastbound train to the siding. The fireman then went to the far end of the siding and carelessly opened the lock. In doing so he was violating train rule 104A, which expressly forbade any employee against unlocking the main track switch.

When he saw Number 19 approaching, the engineer of Number 8 let loose several short blasts from his horn and the fireman at the switch, obviously confused, dashed across the tracks and opened the switch leading into the siding. The westbound Number 19, barreling along at 63 m.p.h., then raced into the siding area and struck Number 8 head-on, demolishing Number 8's engine and killing the engineer. Number 19's employee car, where two dozen off-duty waiters sat, was broken to pieces, and nineteen waiters were instantly killed.

ROCKFISH, VIRGINIA — RAILWAY WRECK — July 7, 1903

Misinterpretation of orders led to the head-on collision that destroyed a Southern Railway freight train and passenger train Number 35 at Rockfish, Virginia, on July 7, 1903. The freight conductor was told that Number 35 would be twenty minutes late. He was apparently in a hurry and only glanced at this order, for he told the engineer that the passenger train would be "an hour and twenty minutes late." The engineer, against standing orders, did not ask to read the dispatcher's communication, but instead, accepted the conductor's statement.

After waiting for what he thought to be the proper amount of time, the freight engineer brought his train onto the main track and began racing northward. Number 35, moving at full steam, met the freight outside Rockfish, and both trains were demolished. Nineteen passengers were killed in the first coach of Number 35 and four crew workers from both trains were crushed to death as the two trains telescoped into one another.

ROCK SPRINGS, TEXAS — TORNADO — April 12, 1927

A vicious tornado set down on Rock Springs, Texas, an isolated town of 800 souls in the heart of the sheep-and-cattle belt, at 8:30 P.M. on April 12, 1927. The small town, situated on the Edwards Plateau at an elevation of 2,400 feet, had no protection from the two-mile-wide twister.

Smashing through the very heart of the town, the tornado either threw down or exploded every building except the stone courthouse and five homes, creating over $1.2 million in damage. At first all communication with the city was cut off. Vague reports had it that 200 people had been killed and twice that number injured.

So remote was Rock Springs that a detachment of cavalry from Fort Clark at Brackettville was sent out to inspect the wreckage. A lineman for the Southern Pacific Railroad climbed a telephone pole some miles from the town of Del Rio, seventy miles from Rock Springs. The dispatcher in Del Rio responded to the lineman's inquiry by dramatically signaling back: "Rock Springs was hit by a tornado that slapped the town flat, hit as if by a gigantic hand."

Seventy-two persons in the town and two on the outskirts were killed outright in their homes or trapped in the town's dusty streets by the twister. More than 100 were injured.

ROKATINDA — VOLCANIC ERUPTION — August 4-5, 1928

The highly volcanic island of Paloeweh, north of Flores in the Netherlands East Indies, had no record of volcanic outbreaks before 1928, when its towering volcano, Rokatinda, began to set off serious tremors on July 25. On the night of August 4-5, Rokatinda blew its top, shooting out pumice, ash and gigantic lava blocks. Natives in the southern villages abandoned their homes and ran through the night to the north end of the island, but the shower of rocks and lava blocks caught up with many of them and literally pulverized them, killing 98. Another 128 persons were caught by sudden floodwaves which resulted from two huge landslides on the south and southeast ends of the island. This brought the total of fatalities to 226.

As Rokatinda exploded, residents on the island of Flores could clearly see the red-hot lava blocks shooting into the air. Most were the size of a man's head. These blocks ignited the dry grasslands on the southern end of the island and set that entire region on fire. The volcano sprouted three new craters, one 500 meters around.

For two days distant Java and Bali received showers of ashes from Paloeweh. Steam clouds hung menacingly over the island for weeks as Rokatinda continued its eruptions until September 25. Four villages were obliterated; two more were damaged, and the southern end of the island completely reshaped as one beach disappeared and the earth was uplifted in another area to create steep bluffs.

(ALSO SEE: Krakatoa, Tomboro)

ROMA

AIR CRASH
February 21, 1922

In the dreamy days of the dirigibles, Italy's first significant contribution to such aircraft was its *Roma,* an ill-constructed ship that crashed only a few months after her completion, and thus gave the Italians a poor reputation in the field. The truth is, however, that the ship was built by American engineers, even though she had been designed by an Italian named Usuelli. American engineers had little faith in the *Roma*'s six Ansaldo engines and substituted two for two 240 horsepower Liberty engines.

Though the American-made engines managed to save the *Roma* from destruction once, on December 21, 1921, during her first long-distance flight from Langley Field to Washington, D.C., when all of the Italian-made engines failed, the Liberty engines put too much stress on the semirigid ship. This was the cause given for the *Roma*'s end, when on February 21, 1922, the dirigible crashed into a hillside after dropping from 1,000 feet (where high-speed tests were being performed) at Hampton Roads.

Thirty-four passengers and crew members were killed, most of them roasted to death when the airship's hydrogen exploded. Eleven survived.

Italian designers of dirigibles were vindicated, however, when the *N.1,* created by Colonel Umberto Nobile, became the first dirigible to fly over the North Pole in 1926.

(ALSO SEE: Akron, Dixmude, Shenandoah*)*

ROSE

TYPHOON
August 17, 1971

Furious typhoon Rose struck Hong Kong on August 17, 1971, devastating harbor shipping and overturning a ferryboat in which about eighty persons drowned. Winds estimated upward of 130 m.p.h. whipped the

Engulfed in flames and black smoke the dirigible *Roma* burns to her metal frame on February 21, 1922. *(UPI)*

storm along and created huge sea waves that, in turn, crashed ashore and caused severe mudslides that buried another dozen residents.

The ferryboat, running between Macao and Hong Kong, sought shelter off the northeast tip of an outlying island, but the full force of the storm struck her and flipped her over like a spinning flapjack. All on board were crew members, and helicopters hovering over the area later saw no survivors. Twenty-six ships in Hong Kong harbor were lifted up and hurled ashore by typhoon Rose. Among these was the United States Navy supply ship *Regulus.* Six of her 270-man crew were injured.

Hundreds in Hong Kong proper and along the coast were injured by the storm, and 2,000 became homeless as their thatched huts were blown flat. Rains up to twelve inches poured down during Rose's sweep and flooded the countryside. Total dead: 130.

(ALSO SEE: Hong Kong, China, 1841, 1906)

ROSE IN BLOOM — MARINE DISASTER — August 23, 1806

The United States coastal vessel *Rose in Bloom* was caught by the great coastal hurricane of 1806 on the morning of August 23 and torn to pieces. The ship foundered near Barnegat Inlet, New Jersey, and only twenty-eight of the forty-nine persons on board survived the sinking.

ROSLYN, WASHINGTON — MINE DISASTER — May 10, 1892

The terrific explosion that ripped apart the Roslyn Mine in Roslyn, Washington, on the afternoon of May 10, 1892, was caused by exposing naked lamps to gathering gas and coal dust. A crosscut from the airway to the slope was being drilled, and this quickly filled with gas (the mine was highly gaseous and dust-ridden, and was seldom checked by firebosses). Forty-five miners were blown apart when the gas was ignited by one of the naked lamps the workers were wearing.

ROUMANIA — MARINE DISASTER — October 27, 1892

Bound for Bombay, India, from Liverpool, England, the British steamer *Roumania* was caught by a ferocious storm off the Portuguese coast on the evening of October 27, 1892. Captain W. S. Young and sixty-seven crew members could see the flickering lights of Peniche, fifty miles north of Lisbon, through the rain-swept sea, but the ship was unable to make port. Hurricane winds ripped the vessel to pieces. Perishing in the deadly waters were Young and his entire crew, along with forty-six passengers, most of whom were English missionaries or staff officers and their families destined for Indian posts.

The steam-and-sail vessel *Roumania* was destroyed by a hurricane off Portugal, October 27, 1892. *(Illustrated London News)*

The survival of Captain G. F. D. Hamilton of the Bengal Lancers was particularly tragic since his new wife was one of the victims. Her body, along with most of the other 113 dead, washed ashore on Portuguese beaches for weeks following the sinking.

ROYAL CHARTER — MARINE DISASTER — October 25, 1859

background: The 2,719-ton *Royal Charter* was a combination steam-and-sail ship (with a 326-foot length and 41-foot beam) owned by Gibbs, Bright & Company. She was caught in a gale while approaching Liverpool on October 25, 1859, and sank after crashing on the Moelfre rocks. Drowned were 438 passengers and crew members; 34 survived.

The *Royal Charter* was one of the first steam-and-sail iron ships to be built. She had a capacity of 500 passengers and crew members. She was the pride of Gibbs, Bright & Company, and her long voyage from Melbourne, Australia, in September, 1859, to Liverpool, England, a journey that took close to two months (neither the Suez nor Panama canal was then available), was considered routine. The ship approached the Irish coast

British auxiliary ship *Royal Charter* dashed herself to pieces in Moelfre Bay, October 25, 1859, killing 459 passengers.

on October 24, 1859, and the passengers gave Captain Taylor a festive testimonial in the vessel's saloon.

When the *Royal Charter* came alongside Holyhead Island, her engine producing a nine-knot speed, 360 passengers lined the rails to see the *Great Eastern,* one of the largest iron ships afloat, docked in Holyhead harbor. From there the ship sailed past the Skerries as a heavy wind came up. Only hours from Liverpool, but not quite into the more placid waters of the Irish Sea, the vessel was slowed considerably by winds approaching gale proportions.

Captain Taylor ordered the anchors lowered, and he decided to ride out the storm rather than attempt to outrace it. It was a fatal decision. The wind fast developed into a sea cyclone, and its winds at one point exceeded 100 m.p.h. As passengers and most crew members huddled belowdecks or in their cramped, unheated staterooms, Taylor ordered the masts to be cut, and this was done with great haste. One anchor cable snapped, then another. The ship jerked forward, as if punched by a colossal fist, and rocketed toward shore, striking the shoals and breaking in half.

The loss of life was staggering and instantaneous. Every child, woman and officer on board perished. Only 3 first-class passengers, 13 second- and third-class passengers, and 18 crew members survived; 438 persons plunged to their deaths in the deep.

A board of inquiry determined that the loss of the *Royal Charter* was attributable to many factors: iron bulkheads not sufficiently watertight, an engine too weak to hold position against a powerful wind, and the use of full-set sails, which increased the stress against the anchor chains.

ROYAL GEORGE

MARINE DISASTER
August 29, 1792

The foundering of England's prize battle frigate, *Royal George,* which had carried the flags of some of that country's most distinguished admirals, was a calamity not quickly forgotten. The 100-gun battleship was at Spithead while repairs were being made. Workers had careened the ship to replace a small pipe only a few feet beneath the waterline, but in so doing they had brought

The British freighter *Royston Grange* burned after her collision with the Liberian freighter *Tien Chee* in the River Plate near Montevideo, Uruguay, on May 11, 1972. *(Wide World)*

the port side of the ship dangerously near the water. The *Royal George*'s port gunports were open, and when a stiff wind momentarily buffeted the vessel, tons of water poured into her, abruptly sinking her like a lead weight.

Incredibly there were more than 1,300 persons on board the giant ship—workers, sailors and hundreds of merchants. This mass of humanity suddenly found itself thrashing in water that sucked it down in whirlpool fashion with the ship, which rested quickly on the shallow bottom. Her giant masts stuck grimly above the waves. More than 900 bodies gurgled to the surface within minutes, making this one of the worst marine disasters in history.

ROYALTON, ILLINOIS — MINE DISASTER, October 17, 1914

The mine explosion in Number 1 mine at Royalton, Illinois, at 7:25 A.M. on October 17, 1914, was another in the seemingly endless blasts caused by an exposed lamp in a highly dangerous shaft. The mineowners again were negligent in providing safety standards. The mine was always dust-ridden, and no attempt to water down the dust was made. The shaft was constantly gaseous, and ventilation to clear it was hopelessly inadequate.

On the day of the explosion, 357 men were at work. The mine manager was just about to step into a cage at the surface to be lowered when a blast of dust rumbled up the shaft. He immediately reversed the fan, causing the air to force back the gas in the hoisting shaft and provide enough oxygen to enable 90 miners, then waiting to be lifted, to crawl to the surface.

Another 220 workers, toiling in other sections of the mine, were not injured by the original blast and were called up. Twenty men were killed in the first blast; another 32 succumbed to afterdamp. It took days to bring out the bodies.

The first blast was set off by a miner's open lamp as he moved into a gas-filled area. The second blast occurred when kegs of black powder, carelessly stored nearby, were ignited.

ROYSTON GRANGE (and TIEN CHEE) — MARINE DISASTER, May 11, 1972

Approaching each other in a narrow channel of the River Plate, seven miles from the port of Montevideo, Uruguay, two freighters collided on May 11, 1972. A violent explosion devastated both ships and killed eighty-four persons. Destroyed were the *Royston Grange,* a British cargo ship carrying grains and refrigerated meat to London, and the Liberian flag tanker *Tien Chee* carrying 20,000 tons of crude petroleum.

How the collision came about was never determined; all aboard the *Royston Grange,* ten passengers and sixty-three crew members, were killed; ten on the *Tien Chee* were never found. The ships locked bows, and the Liberian ship's holds were ruptured, causing tons of oil to spill into the Plate and spread out for miles onto the Uruguayan beaches. Fire then erupted, and the oil-coated water was soon aflame.

No time was available for either ship to lower lifeboats, and only thirty-one of the Chinese crew on the *Tien Chee* managed to jump overboard and swim through the fiery waters before the two ships disappeared in a titanic explosion. One of the desperate swimmers was so badly burned that he died only minutes after being dragged from the flaming water.

RUTH — MARINE DISASTER, August 3, 1863

The Mississippi paddlewheeler *Ruth,* in the service of the Union Army during the Civil War, fell victim to fire just off Island Number 1 on August 3, 1863, after leaving St. Louis for Vicksburg. Flames were discovered raging between decks. The captain steered the vessel to the Missouri shore, while 200 passengers, mostly Union troops, made for land. Thirty men were burned to death as the steamboat blazed to the water line; at least fifty more were seriously burned. A Major Feliger, in charge of a huge sum of money intended for Grant's army at Vicksburg, managed to save the Union payroll.

Completed in 1866 after the war, the second *Ruth,* an elegant four-stacker with a capacity of 1,600 passengers, met the same fate on March 13, 1869, when she was gutted by fire off Pawpaw Island above Vicksburg. There were no fatalities.

Heading for the Missouri shore near Island Number 1, the side-paddle-wheeler *Ruth* caught fire and sank on August 3, 1863. *(Harper's Weekly)*

S

S-4 MARINE DISASTER
December 17, 1927

The United States submarine *S-4* was rammed and sunk by a coastguard destroyer off Provincetown, Massachusetts, on December 17, 1927, with the resulting loss of every crew member, forty men in all. The sub, though broken up somewhat, was in comparatively shallow water, and a few crew members remained alive in a forward compartment. Relief ships and divers soon arrived, but they had to abandon rescue efforts when a wild gale threatened to capsize their ships. Another collision a short time later between the liner, *City of Rome,* and the *S-51* (off Block Island, Rhode Island; thirty-four submariners perished) caused the Navy to quickly develop such life saving gear as the McCann rescue bell and the Momsen diving lung, which saw service in retrieving the almost hopeless victims of the United States submarine *Squalus* eleven years later.

SABINE, TEXAS HURRICANE
October 12, 1886

In the violent hurricane season of 1886, four storms ravaged the coastal cities of Texas. Sabine, Texas, was inundated in a June hurricane; Indianola and San Antonio were wrecked in an August storm, and Brownsville was wrecked in a September hurricane. The worst of the

Forty U.S. sailors died when the submarine *S-4* was rammed by a destroyer. Here is a view of the inside of the *S-4* after it was refloated. *(Wide World)*

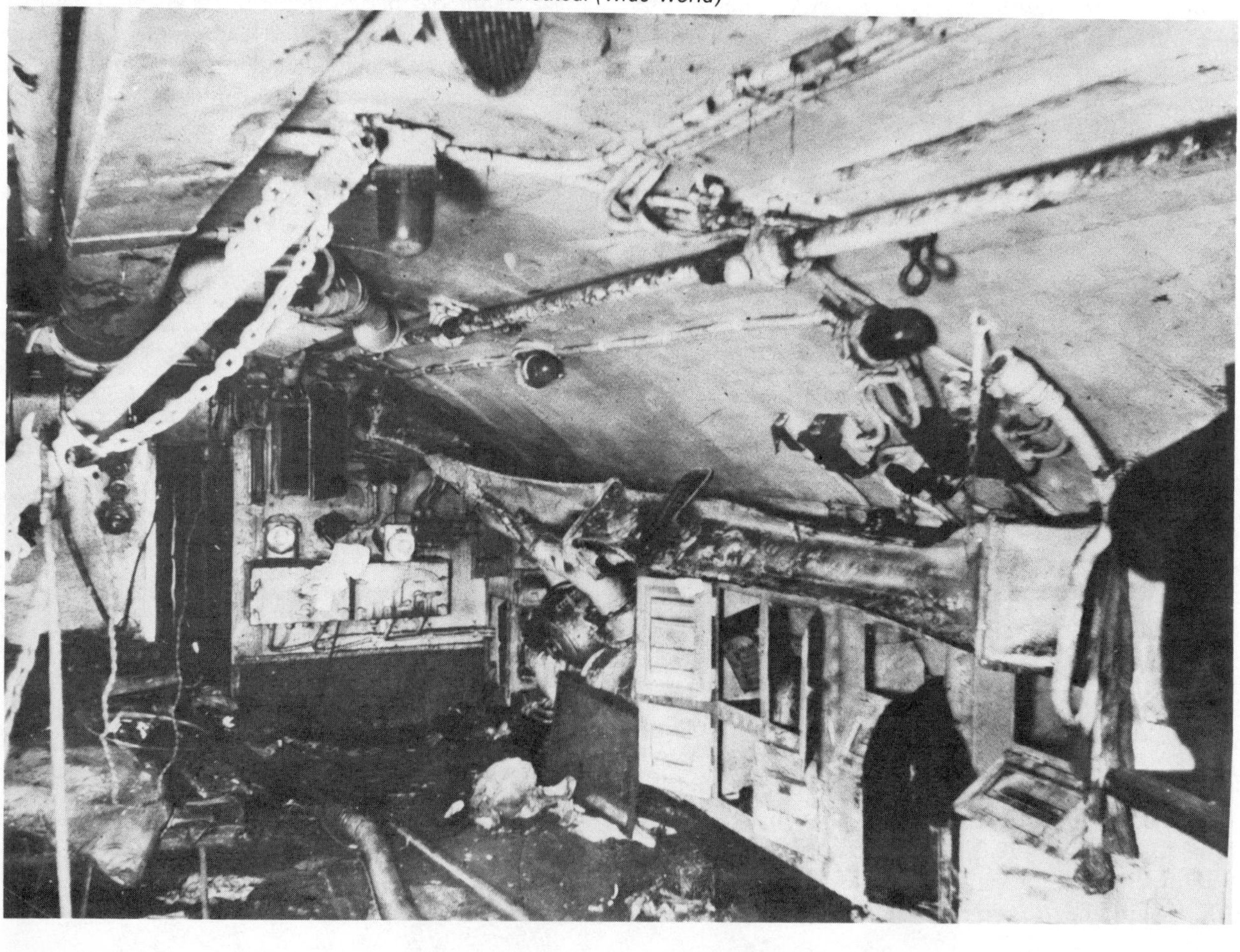

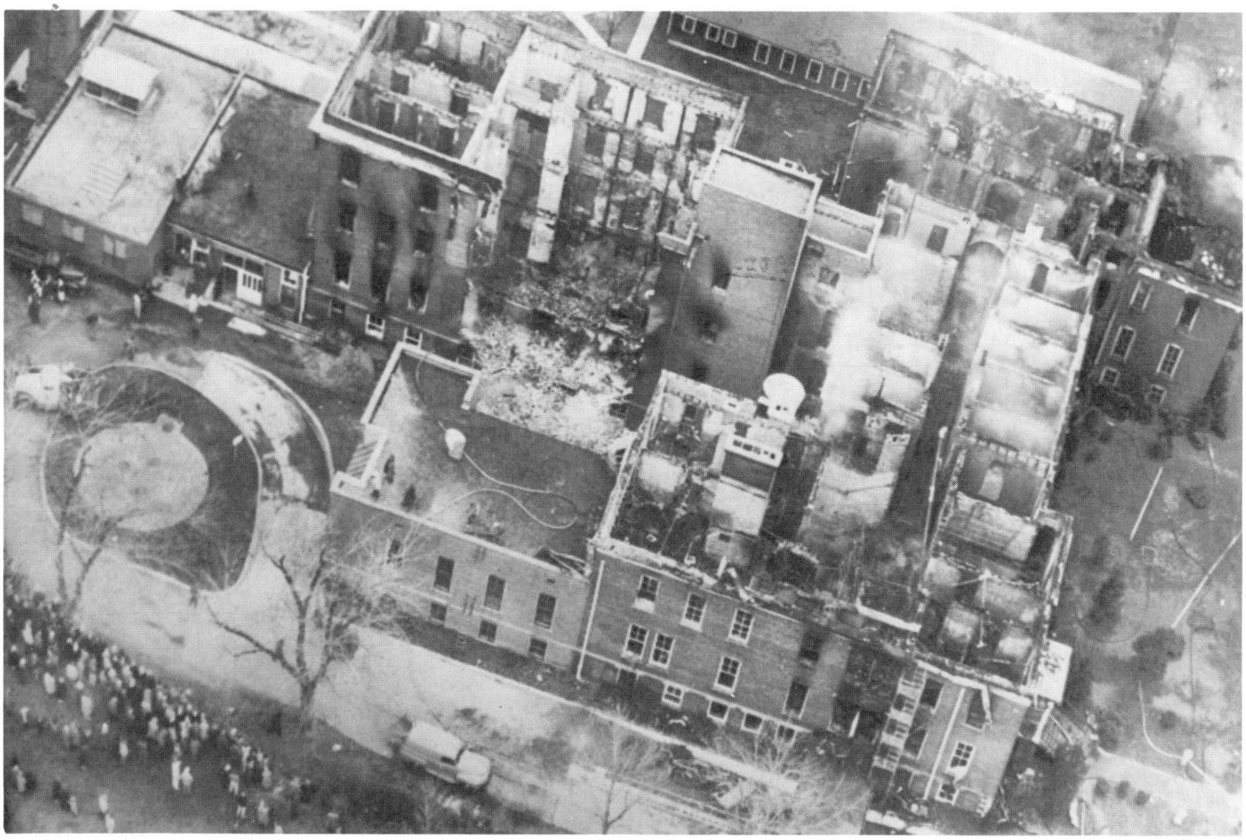

The fire that swept St. Anthony's hospital in Effingham, Illinois, on April 5, 1949, burned out most of the three-story building, as this aerial photo shows, and killed seventy-seven patients, mostly infants. *(Wide World)*

lot was the storm that raged ashore at Sabine on October 12, 1886. Every building in the city was blown down by tremendous winds, and an area twenty miles around the town was completely flooded. Most of the 150 persons killed in this storm drowned in flash floods.

ST. ANTHONY'S HOSPITAL — FIRE — April 5, 1949

background: St. Anthony's Hospital, a 125-bed institution in Effingham, Illinois, caught fire at 11:50 P.M. on April 5, 1949. Despite repeated warnings of the blaze, little was done to stem the flames. Seventy-seven patients, a score of which were newly-born babies, burned to death.

Nothing went right. Everyone was confused, indifferent or incompetent in the roaring inferno that engulfed and gutted St. Anthony's Hospital in Effingham, Illinois, on April 5, 1949. A visitor approached the hospital's head night nurse and said he was certain he smelled smoke.

"It's nothing," he was told, and the visitor forgot about it. Some minutes later the man was back at the desk. He reported seeing smoke in a corridor. The head nurse told the visitor that the janitor, Frank Reis, would take care of it. The visitor left the hospital, and Frank Reis appeared briefly in a smoke-filled corridor, carrying one of the hospital's twenty-eight fire extinguishers. Apparently, when he realized the entire "fireproof" wing was on fire, he ran about looking for his wife, a practical nurse who had already escaped from the burning building by diving through a window.

An expectant mother, Mrs. Arnold Adderman, thought she smelled smoke and reported her fears to a nun on duty. "Oh, that's my rubber gloves you smell," the sister replied. A minute later the hospital corridor outside Mrs. Adderman's room was dense with smoke; tongues of flame were shooting down the passageway. The pregnant woman, half mad with fright, kicked out a screen, and crawled onto a porch. She spied a ladder and feebly climbed down. Two hours later, in her own home, Mrs. Adderman gave birth to an eight-pound boy.

Others were not as fortunate. In a delivery room annex, Mrs. Wenton Sidner, who was alone, smelled smoke and panicked. She managed to reach a second-story window, but by then flames were racing up from behind her, licking at her nightgown. She leaped screaming from the window and broke her back and right arm. Her child was born dead an hour later.

The hospital staff appeared as if in a daze. Only two persons even attempted to use the fire extinguishers, and their attempts were ineffectual. The fire, which had begun in a basement laundry chute, quickly raced upward through walls and floors until the entire three-story brick building was infested with flames. A room full of newborn infants was guarded by one nun who inexplicably did not attempt to save any of them, or even to place them on an available fire escape; it is quite extraordinary to note that none of the building's many fire escapes, all of which were accessible, were used. Twelve babies and the nun perished in the infant room (the story that this nun took too much time in administering baptismal rites before attempting to rescue the children is wholly apocryphal).

The inability of the staff to deal with the emergency, however, was evident when several nurses and nuns could not free those patients in tractions. Many of these pitiably died in their beds screaming for help that never arrived.

Sister Anastasia, who was at the switchboard, did call the volunteer fire department in Effingham, and it did arrive—all *two men* who found, once their hose was hooked up to a nearby hydrant, that there was not enough pressure to throw out an appreciable stream of life saving water.

Worse were the crowds of gawkers who arrived and did little or nothing to save the patients yelling for help from the windows. As writer Paul W. Kearney aptly pointed out, "Numerous press photographs show dozens of able-bodied citizens gaping at the spectacle without any effort at rescue work."

Inside, human beings were roasting to death. Either incomprehensive or indifferent to this fact, scores of people including policemen loitered about the streets, and merely watched. As one woman spectator put it: "People were standing in the windows and screaming. I turned away."

The result of the holocaust was seventy-seven deaths, most of which might have been averted had someone, *anyone* had the presence of mind and the courage, and, maybe, more importantly, the conscience, to have properly organized systematic rescue efforts.

(ALSO SEE: Cleveland Clinic, Mercy Hospital)

ST. GEORGE (and DEFENCE) — MARINE DISASTER, December 24, 1811

Admiral Reynolds of the British Navy had been ordered to leave the Baltic station with his flotilla in November, 1811, but poor weather delayed the sailing. When Reynolds eventually did order his ships to sail for England on December 17, they were met by a series of storms that mounted to hurricanes by the time they staggered into Wingo Sound.

Here the ships *St. George* and *Defence* were utterly stripped of their masts and equipment. In a few hours the ships went to the bottom. Parts of their hulls resurfaced later, bringing with them the eerie sight of more than 500 men, including Admiral Reynolds and Captain Ginon, sprawled lifeless on deck. The *Cressy,* which had been part of the flotilla, managed to escape, but was badly damaged. The loss of life from both the *St. George* and the *Defence* was well over 2,000; only 14 men lived to remember this horror at sea.

ST. GERVAIS, SWITZERLAND — AVALANCHE, July 12, 1892

For the 150 residents of the resort towns of St. Gervais and La Fayet in Switzerland, the coming of the White Death was unheralded by sound or motion until the last fatal second. Nestling in the shadow of Mont Blanc, St. Gervais had long attracted tourists to its elegant hotel and sulfur springs baths. The village was crowded with visitors on the night of July 11, 1892, as was neighboring La Fayet, located a few miles down the sloping valley.

At 2:00 A.M. the following morning, the overhanging glacier called the Tete Rousse, which was suspended on the brink of a gorge above the glacier de Bionnassay on the western side of Mont Blanc, suddenly broke off. The accumulated waters there cascaded downward with blocks of snow and thundered directly on top of sleeping St. Gervais. None had time to rise from their beds. The hundreds of tons of debris and snow and water tore through the hamlet and crushed every building before it, including heavy stone structures such as the local church and the hotel. The avalanche rolled onward down the valley and flattened La Fayet, too, in both towns killing about 140 persons.

ST. HILAIRE, CANADA — RAILWAY WRECK, June 29, 1864

The most deadly bridge disaster on the American continent occurred near St. Hilaire, Canada, on June 29, 1864, when an eleven-car train of the Grand Trunk Railway plunged through an open drawbridge and into a canal about forty-five feet below. Though company regulations demanded that trains running along this route come to a complete stop before this bridge, rules became so relaxed that engineers merely slowed their trains in order to prevent having to get up more steam when proceeding.

The crash happened when the engineer tore through the bridge area only seconds after it had been opened to allow a six-barge flotilla to pass through. The cars, one after another, followed the engine downward, which crashed through one barge while the cars flopped onto other barges. Only the last three cars sustained minor damage. Out of the 354 passengers on board, mostly German and Norwegian immigrants who had recently reached Quebec, about 90 were killed.

Astonishingly the engineer survived this monstrous wreck when he was thrown into the ten-foot-deep canal. Thomas Finn, the conductor who was later held responsible for the accident, was killed as the train went over the bridge embankment.

ST. JAMES — MARINE DISASTER
Spring, 1586

The Portuguese ship *St. James,* with more than 500 persons on board, rounded the Cape of Good Hope in the spring of 1586. Running before a heavy wind, the ship crashed off Madagascar close to midnight on jagged rocks and was held fast while she began to break up. The captain of the ship stubbornly refused to listen to passengers who had begged him not to sail with full canvas at night in such dangerous waters. The captain, Admiral Fernando Mendoza, and a score of others were the first to leap into one of the *St. James*'s lifeboats. They rowed for shore, promising that they would send back help. No one returned, and no help was sent to the hundreds left aboard.

About seventy more persons managed to repair a damaged lifeboat and work their way free of the scores who attempted to board it. The pinnace was so overcrowded that those in the boat, fearing that people swimming after it and trying to climb on board would cause it to capsize, took out hatchets, knives and sabers and hacked away at the helpless, floundering souls in the water.

As the boat made for shore some fifty miles away, it became obvious that there were still too many in the boat. A Portuguese nobleman was appointed the leader, and this aristocrat merely pointed wordlessly at those who appeared too weak to him to carry out duties. These pitiable persons were summarily tossed into the sea. One man agreed to drop himself overboard, but asked for some wine first. He was allowed to drink his fill, and he then slipped into the water on his own.

When the nobleman singled out an elderly carpenter, the carpenter's younger brother insisted that he be put overboard instead. Although those in the boat admired the unselfish act, they put the younger brother into the sea anyway. He was a plucky lad, however, and swam energetically after the pinnace. One account relates how the youth kept pace with the boat for six hours: "making incessant efforts to get on board, sometimes on one side, sometimes on the other, while those who had thrown him over endeavored to keep him off with their swords. But that which appeared likely to accelerate his end proved his preservation. The young man snatched at a sword, seized it by the blade, and neither the pain, nor the exertions made by him who held it, could make him quit his grasp. The others, admiring his resolution, and moved with the proof of fraternal affection which he had displayed, unanimously agreed to permit him to enter the pinnace."

After twenty days at sea, those in the pinnace went ashore at Africa and discovered the captain and his party. Hostile natives captured these survivors, tortured and killed some, and allowed others to depart. Some reached Mozambique. The captain was allowed to command another vessel, which he sailed with the same abandon. He destroyed a ship and himself some years later.

Only an estimated 60 persons survived the ordeal; 450 men, women and children died on the deserted *St. James.* *(ALSO SEE:* Medusa*)*

ST. JO, FLORIDA — HURRICANE
September, 1841

One of the many early boom towns of Florida, St. Jo was a thriving community of more than 4,000 persons in 1841, so thriving that local preachers on horseback labeled it a "hellhole" of wickedness and predicted its end by fire or flood. In September of that year, the latter occurred, created by a colossal hurricane that swept in from the Gulf of Mexico. Within hours St. Jo was obliterated; almost every person in town was washed away to death and every structure destroyed. Only a few unkempt gravesites now mark the spot where the town once stood on a deep-water bayou a few miles distant from Apalachiola on the Apalachiola River.

ST. JOHN — MARINE DISASTER
October 6, 1849

Caught in the coastal hurricane that swept New England during the first week of October in 1849 was the brig *St. John,* which was loaded with Irish immigrants from Galway, Ireland. The ship, tossed wildly about by huge combers, was dashed against the rocks of Cohasset and fast broke up on October 6. Killed were twenty-seven persons. Their bodies and the wreckage of the ship drifted to shore the next day, where it was spotted by the celebrated philosophical hermit, Henry David Thoreau.

Visiting Cohasset, Thoreau watched as scores of townspeople flocked toward the beach. He moved along with them. "As we passed the graveyard we saw a large hole, like a cellar, freshly dug there, and, just before reaching the shore . . . we met several hayriggings and farm-wagons coming away toward the meeting-house, each loaded with three large, rough deal boxes. We did not need to ask what was in them."

Thoreau wrote in *Cape Cod:* "Many horses in carriages were fastened to the fences near the shore, and, for a mile or more, up and down, the beach was covered with people looking out for bodies, and examining the fragments of the wreck. . . . There were eighteen or twenty of the same large boxes that I have mentioned, lying on a green hillside, a few rods from the water, and surrounded by a crowd. . . . Some were rapidly nailing down the lids, others were carting the boxes away, and others were lifting the lids, which were yet loose, and peeping under the cloths, for each body, with such rags as still adhered to it, was covered loosely with a white sheet.

". . .I saw many marble feet and matted heads as the cloths were raised, and one livid, swollen, and mangled body of a drowned girl,—who probably had intended to go out to service in some American family,—to which some rags still adhered, with a string, half concealed by the flesh, about its swollen neck; the coiled-up wreck of a human hulk, gashed by the rocks or fishes, so that the bone and muscle were exposed, but quite bloodless,—merely red and white,—with wide-open and staring eyes, yet lustreless, dead-lights; or like the cabin windows of a stranded vessel, filled with sand. Sometimes there were two or more children, or a parent and child, in the same box, and on the lid would perhaps be written with red chalk, "Bridget such-a-one, and sister's child."

ST. LOUIS, MISSOURI — TORNADO, May 27, 1896

background: Entering the western limits of St. Louis at 6:10 P.M. on May 27, 1896, a tornado raced through six miles of densely populated area, crossing the Missouri River twenty minutes later. Lafayette Park was particularly hard hit; more than $12 million in damage was done. Killed were 306 persons, some of these in East St. Louis, Illinois, and 2,500 injured. This twister destroyed more property than any other tornado up to that date.

The tornado that destroyed a great section of St. Louis, Missouri, on the evening of May 27, 1896, was not particularly large, but its violence was something never seen before by residents habitually exposed to twisters. Shortly before 5:00 P.M., one of the most stupendous electrical storms ever witnessed by St. Louis citizens took place.

An official of the United States Weather Bureau, who observed the gathering storm, wrote: "The electrical display during the storm was of exceeding brilliancy. It was first observed at 5:00 P.M., an hour before the tornado occurred. This continued with short intermissions until 5:45 P.M., when it became almost continuous and extended more into the west and north. At 6:00 P.M., when the tornado occurred, the whole west and northwest sky was in a continuous blaze of light. Intensely vivid flashes of forked lightning were frequent, being outlined in green, blue, purple, and bright yellow colors against the dull yellow background of the never ceasing sheet lightning."

For twenty minutes after touching down, the twister stalked through major sections of St. Louis. The winds around the vortex of the tornado were unheard of, impossible. One weather expert, Frank H. Bigelow, estimated the speeds to be in excess of 250 meters per second, or 560 m.p.h.

In addition to demolishing hundreds of structures and creating more than $12 million in damages, the force of the wind did incredible things. Though there was no pendant, funnel-shaped cloud, the boiling mass of wind-driven clouds rushed forward with such velocity that, according to Willis L. Moore, chief of the United States Weather Bureau, who visited St. Louis the day after the tornado struck, "the writer saw a two-by-four pine scantling shot through five-eighths [of an inch] of solid iron side of the roadway, exemplifying the old principle of shooting a candle through a board. He saw a six-by-eight piece of timber driven four feet almost straight down into the hard, compact soil, a gardener's spade shot six inches into the tough body of a tree, a chip driven through the limb of a tree, and wheat straws forced into the body of a tree to the depth of over half an inch. Such was the fearful velocity of the wind as it gyrated about the small center of the tornado—a velocity exceeding that of any rifle bullet."

This factor, no doubt, contributed to the awesome number of deaths in the St. Louis tornado, 306 in all. Another 2,500 persons were seriously injured in the twenty minutes it took the twister to traverse the city.

ST. LOUIS, MISSOURI — TORNADO, September 29, 1927

background: At 1:05 P.M. on September 29, 1927, St. Louis was struck by a tornado that destroyed 210 blocks in its southwest section, killing 85 persons and injuring another 1,300. Damages were between $10 and $100 million. Other areas devastated included East St. Louis, and a cluster of Illinois towns—Granite City, Madison and Venice. More than 1,800 homes were demolished in this storm, but relief forces of the Red Cross, National Guard, American Legion and Boy Scouts moved quickly into action and prevented outbreaks of fires and looting. They quickly administered aid to victims.

The twister that tore through St. Louis, Missouri, at 1:05 P.M. on September 29, 1927, lasted less than five minutes, of eighty-five persons and vast destruction to a major portion of the city amounting to more than an estimated $100 million. The tornado struck through the heart of the city, slicing through the southwest sections, flattening and exploding more than 1,800 family dwellings as it churned up the earth.

Minutes before its touchdown, residents noticed how thick the air had become. There was a continuous low rumbling of thunder and lightning flashed everywhere. Suddenly the telltale black clouds of the twister rolled forward. Glass began to crack and smash. The air was dark with dust and flying debris as chimneys fell and houses crashed. Still a mystery, scores of observers swear that "sheets of flame" appeared, swept past them and quickly dissipated against a tree, a wall, a house.

A correspondent for the *New York Evening Post* watched as "automobiles moved crazily about, overturning and wrecking themselves like playthings of children. Everywhere the thud of falling walls and the tearing sound of piazzas being wrenched from their foundations filled the air." The *St. Louis Star* later reported "houses broken, twisted, distorted. Roofs at crazy angles like a futuristic picture. Men and women running about, searching frantically for a lost loved one or some missing valuable. An ambulance clanging its way through the traffic with a load of injured. Policemen bawling orders."

Along one quiet street the twister sliced off the roofs of every house as if it were a giant carving knife. On another street telephone poles were evenly tilted to form a menacing arch festooned with dangerous hanging wires. Everywhere the streets were totally littered, the pavement plastered with newspaper, roofing, clothing and posters. Block after block of stores in the downtown district, with their windows smashed and gone, stared grotesquely at the scene like old men with empty eye sockets. Hundreds of cars were crushed and tumbled together at curbs, on lawns, and even inside the display windows of department stores. Streetcars were empty, many having been crushed by falling trees. Their wires dangled uselessly. Everywhere wires were waist-high, creating a hundred barriers. Men rushed forward with planks taken from ruined houses to prop them up.

A large factor in saving the lives of many of the 1,300 injured was the prompt action of several radio stations, chiefly stations KFVE and KMOX (station KFWF was powerless; its antenna was torn down by the twister). KFVE's Thomas Patrick Convey reported the wild event from the top of the Chase Hotel. George Junkin of KMOX fought through debris-packed streets to reach the KMOX offices in the Coronado Hotel to relay the news. Both stations, in keeping with a plan developed two years earlier by the local Disaster Committee, went on the air, directing units of the Red Cross, National Guard, American Legion and hundreds of well-organized Boy Scouts to disaster sites, where some victims were instantly treated for injuries and others were dug out of homes. The stations were the real heroes of the storm.

A vivid example of their service was recounted by Captain G. F. Schwartz, commander of the Seventh Battalion of United States Naval Reserves in the St. Louis area. "It seemed almost a hopeless task," Captain Schwartz remembered, "as I looked out of the armory windows down there at the foot of Ferry Street and saw that twister cross over into Illinois, scattering lumber and debris in every direction and wrecking part of one of the armory buildings. It looked worse when I rode away from the armory in an automobile and found myself jammed on all sides by fallen wires and wrecked automobiles and debris piled high. Then I went back to the armory, and I found the phone was O.K. and [so I] called Commander Veatch. Veatch called Station KMOX, and in a few minutes the boys commenced to arrive, all out of breath and intent on action; and all I can say is, it worked. Those boys got down to the armory; some right away and some, crawling through the wreckage, far into the night, and we took up our station where Chief Clark of the Police Department assigned us in North St. Louis."

The radio broadcasters worked around the clock, begging for relief supplies and money. Through their efforts, food, clothing, medical attention and tens of thousands of dollars arrived within hours to aid the stricken and to help rebuild the city.

ST. LOUIS THEATER — FIRE, June 12, 1846

The rather plain, small (80-by-40 feet) St. Louis Theater in Quebec, Canada, was filled to capacity with more than 300 patrons on the evening of June 12, 1846. The crowd was attentive as a man named Harrison demonstrated a series of illuminated dioramas portraying the city of Ramesses, Orleans Cathedral, the city of Jerusalem and the Crucifixion.

The show was over at 10:00 P.M., and the patrons began filing out. About 240 persons had already left the theater when someone exiting from one of the box sections knocked over a large camphine lamp used by Harrison in his show. Flames quickly spread to the stage and ignited the exhibits, which were chemically treated. They shot up the thick, highly flammable drapes. About fifty people exiting from the box section panicked, and although several avenues of escape were available, all chose a narrow stairway. One person fell, then another. At once the stairway was filled with helplessly enmeshed persons, thrashing wildly about and yelling for help.

They were impossible to reach, and fire soon closed in on them. Such was their desperation that some men feared to go to their aid lest they be grabbed and drawn into the trapped throng. One witness told the *Quebec Mercury:* "One foot was interposed between the hapless crowd and eternity, and on that space, we, with five or six others, stood, the fierce flames playing around us, and the dense smoke repelling all efforts to extricate.

"As far back as we could see, there was a sea of heads, of writhing bodies and outstretched arms. Noise there was none—but few moans escaped the doomed. At the extreme end in view, there were faces calm and resigned; persons, who, from the funereal veil of smoke which gradually enshrouded them, appeared calmly to drop into eternal sleep. By our side was one brother striving to extricate another, but abandonment was unavoidable. One poor creature at our feet offered his entire worldly wealth for his rescue; the agonizing expression of the faces before us can never be effaced from our memory."

How this witness, so entrapped, escaped to tell his ghastly tale is not known. Forty-five persons perished when the theater's roof caved in and flames rained downward.

(ALSO SEE: Iroquois Theater, Ring Theater)

ST. PETERSBURG, RUSSIA — FLOOD
November 19, 1824

In the worst flood of the River Neva's history, St. Petersburg, Russia, then the winter home of the czar, was flooded on November 19, 1824. The river suddenly rose to the first story of almost every house in the city. One report has it that "carriages and horses were swept away, and a regiment of Carabineers, who had climbed to the roof of their barracks, were drowned."

Nearby Kronstadt was also inundated, and a 100-gun ship of the line was left by the floodwaters in the middle of the market place. In both cities more than 10,000 persons lost their lives to the charging waters of the Neva. Damage to property amounted to many millions of roubles.

ST. SIMON ISLAND (GEORGIA) — HURRICANE
September 15, 1824

A savage hurricane lashed the Georgia coast on September 15, 1824, wrecking in particular all the plantations and structures on St. Simon Island. The fierce storm, driving in from the southeast, sent overflowing waters across the entire island. Eighty-three persons, mostly slaves, drowned. One report stated that "whole families [were] separated and crushed amidst the ruins of buildings, or drowned in the water thrown up by the sea."

ST. THOMAS — EARTHQUAKE/CYCLONE
August 2, 1837

The mistress of West Indian commerce and considered the most beautiful island of the Virgin Islands, St. Thomas turned ugly in a single day as it came under attacks from a flurry of raging elements. On the morning of August 2, 1837, a powerful hurricane swept over the island and through its whitewashed towns. Ships began to rock at anchor; rooftiles flew away and clattered down streets. For six hours the hurricane pummeled inhabitants.

Buildings began to disintegrate under the roaring winds of the storm, and the heavy guns of the fort reportedly were blown away from their moorings and sent flying into the once lovely bay. Here, ship after ship sank, and sailors thrashed about pathetically in the boiling waters as they attempted to swim to shore.

At about 6:00 P.M. the earth began to undulate, and fissures cracked open as an earthquake began. Almost every building in St. Thomas that had not been wrecked by the storm tumbled to the ground under this second onslaught. Fires broke out within the rubble, and those wedged beneath the tons of debris burned to death. Sailors who managed to reach shore were thrown back into the sea when a seismic sea wave raced in and dragged them out. Those residents fortunate enough to have reached the street minutes before the quake did its worst destruction fled to the twin mountains above St. Thomas. There they watched, horror-struck, as their town was consumed by fire, flood and quake. The multiple disaster caused the deaths of at least 500 and injured four times as many. Not a single vessel was left afloat the following day. Splintered masts protruded above waters that returned to tranquility as the bodies of sailors washed ashore. Damages were never fully estimated, but millions of dollars of goods, crops and houses were destroyed.

SAKURAJIMA — VOLCANIC ERUPTION
December-January 1779-1780

During a series of earthquakes the 3,506-foot volcano Sakurajima came to life in December, 1779, and exploded with great force, sending out showers of ash and huge quantities of mud. Those living on the island at the southernmost point of Japan could not tell day from night as the eruptions continued. Village after village, about twenty in all, became quagmires of mud and quickly settled out of sight, taking many of their inhabitants with them. Deaths were never exactly totaled, but one estimate placed fatalities at about 300.

SALEM, MICHIGAN — RAILWAY WRECK
July 20, 1907

The destruction of two trains of the Pere Marquette Line at Salem, Michigan, on July 20, 1907, resulted from a misinterpretation of orders. This was a frequent and tragic happening in the early days of railroading. An eleven-car excursion train, eastbound from Ionia to Detroit, was jammed with railroad employees and their families. The engineer and conductor of a long freight train heading west had been ordered to wait for the excursion train, but they misread the directives, thinking that the holiday special would go through Salem, Michigan, at 9:25 A.M. The dispatcher had specified, however, that the excursion would go through Salem at 9:10 A.M. The freight train crew simply mistook another town and time—Plymouth at 9:25 A.M.—for the Salem go-through and, as a result, started down the single track ahead of the excursion train.

Both trains met in a thunderous head-on collision outside Salem. The engines of both trains were hurtled off the tracks side-by-side and six cars of the passenger train followed the engine down an embankment, thoroughly wrecking themselves as they piled atop one another. Experts later marveled at the fact that though the excursion train, its coaches made of wood, was demolished there were but thirty deaths in this wreck.

SALERNO, ITALY — MASS ASPHYXIATION
March 2, 1944

One of the most disastrous accidents to occur in European railroad history happened outside Salerno, Italy, on March 2, 1944. A train packed with military and civilian passengers somehow stalled in a long tunnel a short distance from the city and within seconds, the crew was overcome by fumes from the engine. They were unable to warn passengers to flee the tunnel. The fumes quickly engulfed all the cars, and almost all 426 travelers on the train died of asphyxiation in their seats.

(ALSO SEE: Modane, France)

SAN ANTONIO, TEXAS — EXPLOSION
March 18, 1912

Mechanics for the Southern Pacific Railroad in San Antonio, Texas, were hard at work repairing one of the line's huge locomotives on March 18, 1912, when something went wrong. As steam pressure was being raised in the locomotive's boiler and a worker was hurriedly setting safety valves, a terrific explosion occurred. The boiler burst into fragmentary chunks and went flying every-which-way. One 1,600-pound piece of the boiler was sent sailing more than 1,200 feet. A 900-pound chunk was hurtled more than 2,000 feet and sheared the side of a frame house, killing all inside. Twenty-six yardworkers and residents were killed in this accident, and another thirty-two were seriously injured.

SAN ANTONIO, TEXAS — FLOOD
September 7-11, 1921

Following the heaviest single rainfall ever recorded in the United States (23.11 inches at Taylor, Texas), resulting from a broad-fronted hurricane that swept through the Gulf of Mexico and Mexico, San Antonio, Texas, was totally awash. The floodwaters came on so rapidly, that by September 9, 1921, residents were at one moment driving down dry streets; at another they were swimming for their lives. Every auto in the city was instantly abandoned as drivers climbed onto buildings to save themselves.

One report stated that from "five to nine feet of water stood in the large hotels, theaters and stores." Fifty-one persons were killed or drowned in this flood. Damages soared to $5 million.

SAN BERNARDINO, CALIFORNIA — FLOOD
February 27, 1938

Heavy rains lasting over several days in February, 1938, created massive flooding in the San Bernardino area. The Santa Ana, San Gabriel and Mojave rivers overran their banks, and vast tracts of land were under water by February 27. Killed were eighty-seven persons and damage to property was estimated to be almost $79 million.

SAN FRANCISCO — MARINE DISASTER
January 14, 1854

background: The steampacket *San Francisco,* a 3,000-ton paddlewheel-and-steamship with a capacity for 1,600 persons (350 cabin passengers and steerage berths for 1,000), a keel length of 280 feet and a 41-foot beam, was built by the W. H. Aspinwall Company for the Pacific Mail Steamship Company in 1853 at a cost of $350,000. Departing on December 21, 1853, and carrying a regiment of artillery, dependents and crew members numbering about 750, the ship was struck and wrecked by a violent hurricane on her maiden voyage to California from New York. One wave carried about 150 men overboard. She lingered for days while the ships *Three Bells* and *Antarctic* took off 450 survivors before the vessel sank. An estimated 300 died.

The huge, spanking-new *San Francisco,* pride of the Pacific Mail Steamship Company, was completed in late 1853 and immediately pressed into service without any trial runs, a gross oversight that would eventually cost the lives of 300 soldiers, sailors, women and children. The transcontinental railroad had yet to be completed, so the Third Regiment of the United States Artillery was shipped on the *San Francisco* to assume duties in California. Sailing on the huge ship from New York on December 21, 1853, were about 700 persons, eight companies of troops comprising 500 men, 200 dependents, and a crew of 50.

On the second day of the voyage the ship encountered a storm off Cape Hatteras that grew to hurricane proportions by early evening. The *San Francisco*'s two 1,000-horsepower engines and full sails did little to combat the gale; it was later determined that the ship's paddle wheels were too deeply immersed in the water, which made the ship sluggish and unmaneuverable.

More than 150 troopers joined sailors in clearing away the debris of fallen sails and broken masts during the storm. These men became the first victims of the disaster when, at 8:00 P.M., according to the vivid account of Lieutenant William A. Winder, a gigantic comber breached the ship—the wave was thought to be more than thirty feet high—and carried away with it almost everyone above deck. It also swept the decks clean of lifeboats and rafts.

The engines had already given out, and Winder described how the "sea broke over our starboard wheel house, and with mightful force dashed against the after cabin, carrying away all of the cabin and about 150 people, including Colonel J. M. Washington, Major George Taylor and his wife, Captain H. B. Field and Lieutenant Smith . . . were swept off . . . I had gone below but a few moments before this terrible crash, and was lying at the foot of the stops at the time. I never experienced such a sensation as when the water came pouring into the cabin, together with the debris of the upper cabin, down upon my head and breast. I was swept across the cabin with terrible force, but after three attempts succeeded in regaining my feet. I supposed that the ship had broken in half, and that we were fast sinking. I followed after some I saw going on deck, and on reaching it my blood ran cold at the sight of the poor fellows struggling among the fragments in the sea; the waves were, to my eyes, frightful; we could render no assistance whatever, and, in fact, expected outselves that we should go down every minute."

Winder bumped into the ship's skipper, Commodore Watkins. "What are our chances?" he asked.

Watkins surveyed the situation of broken spars, torn decks and drowned bodies eddying about the railings and laconically stated: "Good."

For several days the artillerymen labored at the pumps and bucket lines, but the *San Francisco* was a mortally wounded ship. Morale among the troops flagged so deeply that many despaired of ever surviving the journey. Cholera broke out unexpectedly, and deaths mounted. Troopers and sailors, who thought themselves doomed, broke into the commissary and gorged themselves on preserves, cakes, sweetmeats and other dainties, and then, according to one report, "repaired to the spirit room, where they washed down their repasts with copious and undiluted draughts [of rum]."

As a result scores of these men were felled by violent attacks of cramps and diarrhea. After the ships *Three Bells* and *Antarctic* came alongside the stricken *San Francisco* to take off survivors, scores of these "debauchees died in less than ten hours." In all 60 men, who, out of uncontrollable fear, filled their bellies to bursting, succumbed. An estimated 300 persons lost their lives before the *San Francisco* broke apart and settled in fragments to the deep on January 14, 1854.

(ALSO SEE: Rio de Janeiro*)*

SAN FRANCISCO, CALIFORNIA — FIRE — May 3, 1851

The most destructive fire experienced in San Francisco, before it was torn apart by the ripping earthquake of 1906, was the blaze that reared up at 11:00 P.M. on May 3, 1851. The fire began in a paint shop on the west side of Portsmouth Square, next to the American House. Although the fire engines arrived, the entire block was ablaze within five minutes, and firemen found it impossible to contain the flames.

San Francisco then was built almost entirely of wood, and whole neighborhoods, such as those in the Chicago Fire twenty years later, blazed up while tens of thousands of people wildly fled. Fire ate its way up Kearney Street and down Clay Street. The fire department finally gave up hope of trying to put the fire out and merely attempted to slow it down. Hundreds of citizens joined in the firefighting effort, and the roaring inferno was finally stopped on the north side at Depont Street. The fire had its way everywhere else, and it stopped only at the water's edge, devastating even the piers that jutted out into the bay.

Shipping was saved only by the heroic efforts of scores of dockworkers who chopped away burning wharves. When the fire went out, 2,500 buildings, including the Custom House, 7 hotels, the post office and dozens of important office buildings, had been destroyed, a loss estimated to exceed $3.5 million. About thirty persons, mostly those who had joined efforts with the firemen, were killed.

Another fire attacked the city on June 22 of that year and burned an additional 500 buildings to the ground for a $3 million loss. No lives were lost in this later fire.

(ALSO SEE: Baltimore, Maryland; Boston, Massachusetts; Chicago, Illinois, 1871)

SAN FRANCISCO, CALIFORNIA — EARTHQUAKE-FIRE — April 18, 1906

background: At 5:13 A.M. on April 18, 1906, an earthquake emanating from the 600-mile-long San Andreas Fault struck San Francisco, Santa Rosa, San Jose and Stanford University. The quake registered 8.3 on the Richter scale (the jolt was, surprisingly, both horizontal and vertical) at the Lick Observatory on Mt. Hamilton, 50 miles away. It lasted approximately seventy-five seconds (the first jolt was forty seconds long; followed by a ten-second calm, and then a second tremor lasting twenty-five seconds). Thousands of cheaply constructed buildings, erected on land-fill areas of the city, were thrown down by the quake, huge fissures opened and closed, and most of the city's gas and water mains ruptured. Noteworthy buildings that were destroyed by the quake included the Valencia Hotel, the ornate city hall, and the Sonoma Wine Company, where 15 million gallons of wine were destroyed. Fires broke out shortly after the quake, and the inferno went unchecked for three days, consuming 3,000 acres, or about 4.7 square miles containing 520 city blocks and 28,188 buildings, half of which were homes. More than 700 persons were killed in the quake and fire. Damages ranged upward to an estimated $500 million. About 70 percent of this amount was paid to claimants by insurance firms, some of which went bankrupt because of the disaster.

"San Francisco has violated all underwriting traditions and principles by not burning up. That it has not done so is largely due to the vigilance and efficiency of the Fire Department, which cannot be relied upon to stave off this indefinitely." This prophecy of doom was made by the National Board of Fire Underwriters in October, 1905, just six months before its calculated prediction came true. Most of San Francisco might have been saved by one of the most courageous, inventive fire chiefs in America, Dennis T. Sullivan, if it had not been for the collapse of a mammoth chimney and sheer exhaustion that made him go limp with sleep two hours before catastrophe stalked into his city.

Fire Chief Sullivan had energetically mapped out a detailed firefighting plan in the event that San Francisco was threatened by a massive blaze. His plan, though elaborate, called for stopping the fire at various "breaks" with dynamite. The explosives were not to be used indiscriminately. Sullivan, twenty-six years with the fire department, had fought corrupt legislators at every turn and had demanded more funds to establish an auxiliary saltwater supply system for fire engines. He

The once majestic $6 million City Hall was in ruins moments after the quake struck. *(California Historical Society)*

Union Street's cobblestones and trolley tracks were ripped up during the 1906 earthquake. *(Wells Fargo Bank History Room)*

insisted on reactivating scores of long-sealed cisterns for use in a general conflagration. Sullivan had many other ideas for preventing the destruction of his city by fire, but he never got the chance to put them into action when they were desperately needed.

On the morning of April 18, 1906, two fires broke out, a small blaze on Market Street and a flare-up in a wire factory in North Beach. Sullivan had attended both fires and had worked tirelessly with his men. He had been at a social gathering and rushed, with his wife, to these outbreaks. It was 3:00 A.M. before the final cinders died out, and the Sullivans, rather than drive the long distance home, went to the fire station next to the ten-story California Hotel on Bush Street, where they went to sleep in separate bedrooms on the third floor.

Two hours later, racing in from a point 200 miles north out in the sea, the quake descended upon the sleeping city. It sliced away sea cliffs, remade shorelines, and toppled five hundred-year-old giant redwood trees. While making his rounds at Washington and Davis streets, Sergeant Jesse Cook, who was later to become police commissioner, talked leisurely with a producer named Al Levy. A pink dawn filled the skies. Suddenly a hundred conversations of early risers went silent. Dray horses and livestock whinnied and snorted. Cook heard a "deep rumbling." The officer had that rarest of experiences with no time for terror; he literally watched the earthquake come at him down Washington Street.

"The whole street was undulating. It was as if the waves of the ocean were coming toward me, and billowing as they came."

On the top floor of the fire station, Chief Sullivan heard the first racket of the disaster and sleepily jumped from his bed. Masonry was crashing all about him; he thought of his wife in the next room. Sullivan lumbered forward, pitching and rolling with the quaking building. The door leading to the other bedroom was out of plumb, and he had to bash it down. After diving through the opening, Sullivan abruptly dropped three stories through a gigantic hole made by a collapsing three-story chimney that had toppled from the California Hotel next door. His skull, legs and arms were fractured, and he was taken to a hospital in a coma. Sullivan never regained consciousness; he died some hours later.

The man to whom Sullivan's fire-fighting duties fell was San Francisco's Mayor Eugene Schmitz, a one-time fiddler in the orchestra of the Columbia Theater who had been put into office by a grafter named Abe Ruef. Since 1901, Schmitz and Ruef had looted the city treasury, which was, no doubt, the reason why the mayor consistently refused to endorse the appropriation of additional funds for Chief Sullivan's expensive safety measures. Schmitz feared any action that might reveal his plundering.

(In reality Ruef was mayor of San Francisco, controlling Schmitz on every decision. This arrangement was natural to Schmitz, who later admitted, "From boyhood, I had ever heard: Make money, no matter how. People will never ask how you made it, only get it." He and Ruef not only looted the city coffers, but also received tremendous kickbacks from scores of opium, gambling and prostitution dens in Chinatown and along the Barbary Coast, which they allowed to operate around the clock.)

Just as policeman Cook was thrown off balance and sent tumbling by the quake that rolled beneath his feet, John Barrett, news editor for the *San Francisco Examiner,* peered incredulously out a window of his office to see buildings everywhere "dancing." They jiggled like jelly, bending, swaying and bulging. Barrett slid uncontrollably across his office floor. "It was as though the earth was slipping quietly away from under our feet. There was a sickening sway, and we were all flat on our faces."

From the city's most fashionable hotels, to the homes of frugal Italian fishermen, to the Chinatown dwellings of Oriental immigrants, the quake took everyone by surprise. Enrico Caruso, who had opened in *Carmen* the night before, was jostled from bed in his expansive suite in the Palace Hotel (Number 622, which had once been occupied by Civil War hero General William T. Sherman). Spilling to the floor in the first terrifying seconds of the tremor, the great tenor yelled wildly for his valet and hurriedly dressed as he nervously fumbled through several trunks containing tens of thousands of dollars worth of clothes and jewelry. He plucked a photograph of the President of the United States from a drawer. It was inscribed: "To Enrico Caruso. From Theodore Roosevelt." Clutching this single item to his bosom, Caruso lunged about his suite in terror, while chandeliers crashed to the floor, huge glass windows popped and spattered, and the screams of the panicking guests assailed his ears in notes higher than any Caruso had ever reached. On his arrival in San Francisco the previous day, the tenor had heard that Vesuvius was erupting over his native Naples, and he remarked, "Maybe it was God's will that, after all, I should come this far." He now feared that the quake had ruined his vocal cords.

Alfred Hertz, Caruso's conductor, rushed into Caruso's suite to discover the tenor frozen in silence, eyes bulging, his large hands tearing at his shirt. Hertz ordered the tenor to sing, and he did. His voice pierced the cacophony hammering down the street outside. People in nightgowns, a woman running and holding a baby by the legs, men with shaving lather on their faces who had poured into the street suddenly stopped, looked upward at Caruso's Palace Hotel rooms, and were comforted. One guest, hearing the magnificent voice, considered this Caruso's "bravest and best" performance, "an attempt on the singer's part to show the world that at least he had not been scared." But though his voice rose above the clamor of calamity, terror would continue to grip Caruso by the throat for several desperate hours to come.

One floor above Caruso's suite in the Palace Hotel, Albert H. Gould of Chicago was also thrown out of bed and hurtled half-way across his room. Hitching up his pajamas, Gould ran to the ornate stairs, which were cluttered with plaster chips and broken masonry, and made his way down seven flights. He ran into the main lobby.

"I was the first guest to appear," he later remembered. "The clerks and hotel employees were running about as if they were mad. Within two minutes after I had appeared, other guests began to flock into the corridor. Few if any of them wore other than their night clothing. Men, women, and children with blanched faces stood as if fixed. Children and women cried, and men were little less affected."

Moments later Gould ran up the seven flights of stairs and got dressed; then he set out for the Western Union office, some blocks away, to wire his wife the news of his survival in the great quake.

Huge sections of the majestic Palace Hotel had skidded into the street. Walls tilted forward and buckled inward, and debris from its towering structure was scattered for blocks.

People began to flee. Los Angeles millionaire John Singleton and his family hurriedly dressed and raced from the doomed hotel. In their rooms they left $3,000 worth of personal effects. It would take the Singletons three days to escape from San Francisco, and, en route, the four-member family would have only one meal. The gougers had taken over by then. "We paid $1 apiece for eggs and $2 for a loaf of bread."

Another millionaire, C. C. Kendall of Omaha, had arrived in the city only hours before the quake and had immediately gone to sleep in his room in the Palace Annex. He was shaken from his slumber at 5:13 A.M.; his entire room had tilted and rolled him out of bed. He ran to a window and looked out to see "houses reeling and tumbling like playthings. I hurried on clothing and ran into the street. Here I saw many dead, and the debris was piled up along Market Street. I went to the office of the Palace Hotel, and there men, women, and children were rushing about, crazed and frantic, in their night clothes." Though the first shock lasted only forty seconds, it seemed to Kendall as if it were "two hours." The second shock, which came after a ten-second lull, was according to the businessman "light, compared with the first, but it brought to the ground many of the buildings that the first shock had unsettled."

Kendall, like almost everyone else in San Francisco that dreadful morning, thought of only one thing:

General Funston's troops take over. Soldiers direct civilians to line up for food and clothing. *(California Historical Society)*

escape. He recalled, "Fires were breaking out in every direction. Market Street had sunk at least four feet. I started for the ferry. It is only a few blocks from the Palace Annex to the ferry, but it took me from 6:00 A.M. to 10:15 A.M. to cover the space. . . . Men and women fought about the entrance of the ferry like a band of infuriated animals. I made my escape—I do not remember how, for I was as desperate as any of them. As the boat pulled over the bay, the smoke and flame rose sky high, and the roar of falling buildings and cries of the people rent the air."

Huge sections of the city, especially areas that had been reclaimed from the bay by the cheap use of land fill, which was really sand, and occupied by massive jumbles of poorly constructed wooden-frame buildings, came to a splintering collapse. At Ninth and Brannon streets, an entire half-block was leveled by the quake, and dozens of people were crushed to death when ancient, rotted timbers gave way in scores of rooming houses and homes. Buildings along Dore Street, south of Market Street, teetered in and out and then set themselves at crazy angles on the buckled street. Writer William Bronson thought they looked "like a row of tottering drunks."

The wholesale district was a vast ruin, with tons of bricks and beams piled fifteen feet high in the streets, from which protruded the stiffened legs of dead horses and the heads of produce men. Almost all of the hundreds of shanties along the waterfront, the Barbary Coast, were flattened in the quake, and huge steamers at dock were on their sides. They looked as if they had been flicked over by a giant, unseen finger.

One of the few San Francisco water mains not broken in the quake allows firemen to fight a fire that broke out in some ruins. *(California Historical Society)*

The single most destructive occurrence during the quake in terms of human life was the collapse of the Valencia Hotel in the Mission District. The four-story wooden building skidded out into the street, and one floor after another broke off from the bottom with a sickening, screeching noise. Timbers separated, and 100,000 rusty nails snapped, broke and twisted. Only the top floor remained, resting upon the flattened lower floors and crushing the life out of the hotel's eighty occupants.

The pride of San Francisco, the city hall at McAllister and Larkin streets near Market Street, was gone. This mammoth $6 million building, which took twenty years to complete, was a lofty mass of cast iron and stone columns grouped around a steel-framed dome. It tumbled into the streets; its columns were thrown forward, crushing several passers-by. Spires, ceilings and walls fell in almost all the churches; only rubble remained of St. Patrick's in Menlo Park, and St. James's, St. Bridget's, St. Dominick's and St. Patrick's churches and the Church of the Holy Cross in San Jose were all destroyed.

The elaborately constructed hotels, with their imposing rococo cornices and pillars, fell by the scores. Gone were such grand inns as the Denver, the Cosmopolitan and the Brunswick. The Palace Hotel, which had cost $1.26 million and was the finest in the city, was completely wrecked. The Fairmont cracked and splintered with damages amounting to $200,000. The elegant St. Francis, valued at almost a million dollars, was a shambles, although its main structure was still standing.

To Sam Wolfe, who ran wildly from the disintegrating Grand Hotel at the moment of the quake, "The street seemed to move like waves of water. On my way down Market Street the whole side of a building fell out and come so near me that I was covered and blinded by the dust. Then I saw the first dead come by. They were piled up in an automobile like carcasses in a butcher's wagon, all over blood, with crushed skulls, and broken limbs, and bloody faces. A man cried out to me, 'Look out for that live wire!' I had just time to sidestep certain death."

People found themselves doing the oddest things. W. H. Saunders, a government geological engineer, was almost too punctilious for his own good. When the St. Francis Hotel began to sway and splinter, Saunders methodically "made [his] toilet and then packed [his] grip." He was the last guest to step from the hotel. In the lobby he stopped a frantic clerk.

"See here, young fellow," Saunders said quietly. "I want to pay my bill. I'm leaving."

The clerk looked at him, dumbfounded: "Are you

Fire eats its way up Sacramento Street while hundreds stand in the rubble-strewn street watching its smoky approach. This photo, taken by Arnold Genthe, is considered to be one of the ten best news photos of all time. *(California Historical Society)*

mad? This is no time for settlement!" With that the clerk broke away and dashed into an office to retrieve valuable records. Saunders marched into the office after him.

"I'm going to have to insist," Saunders said, and he offered payment.

The clerk stared at Saunders. "You *are* mad. But, here." He took the money, patiently made out a receipt and only then did Saunders leave the building, quietly stepping over rubble in the lobby and the bodies of dead horses just outside.

James Hopper, a reporter for the *San Francisco Call,* was awakened not by the earthquake, but by the sound of gas escaping from a main outside his bedroom window. He hurried to the street, noticing the awful carnage and the strange silence of hundreds of people shuffling down the streets.

Hopper automatically reverted to his role as reporter and slowly worked his way toward the *Call* Building, which was relatively undamaged by the quake due to its all steel-and-concrete structure. As he went, Hopper began to record the destruction of each building that he passed, carefully writing down descriptions of the cornices fallen, the walls separated, the roofs caved in, along with the addresses of each ruined structure. After several minutes he realized the folly of his microscopic endeavor among the enormous ruins of San Francisco. He suddenly threw down his writing pad, looked about, and shouted, "Good Lord! I'm not going to take a list of *all* the buildings in the city!"

In a mad flight from his hotel room moments after the quake struck, Dr. Taggart of Los Angeles ran up the steps to a small hospital at Page and Baker streets. The second tremor caught him on the stairs, and he stumbled and pitched forward. A pistol that he was carrying inside his coat pocket (it was not uncommon for citizens to be armed in such a rowdy city as San Francisco) discharged, and the bullet entered near his heart. Staggering to his feet, the doctor cried out, "I am dying!" then spun around, and fell into the arms of another physician who was entering the building. In an instant Taggart was dead.

The St. Louis brewer Adolphus Busch and his family were in the St. Francis Hotel, which the beer magnate later described as "swaying from south to north like a tall poplar in a storm; furniture, even pianos, was

The incredible panorama of San Francisco on fire as seen from Russian Hill. The two young girls captured in this Arnold Genthe photo smile in spite of the holocaust. *(California Historical Society)*

overturned, and people [were] thrown from their beds." The Busch family escaped the building and made their way through Jefferson Square, which was clogged with thousands of wailing, bleeding refugees, and from there they made a long, agonizing trek up Nob Hill. Hours later Busch watched from this promontory of the rich as the "indescribable drama" of San Francisco's utter destruction unfolded before him. "Block after block was devastated. Fires blazed like volcanoes, and all the business houses, hotels, theaters—in fact, the entire business portion—lay in ruins, and two thirds of the residences."

People with money had little trouble leaving the scene of disaster. Multimillionaire Hermann Oelrichs, of New York, also a guest at the St. Francis Hotel, escaped with his valet, traveling by ferry to Oakland and there boarding the next train east. He did not have a dime in his pockets, but he had remembered to retrieve a scrap of paper from his debris-littered room. He held this up to a conductor who demanded fares. It read: "Pass Hermann Oelrichs and servant to Chicago upon all lines. This paper to serve in lieu of tickets.—E. H. Harriman." Edward Harriman, president of the Southern Pacific Railroad, to his credit subsequently offered free service to all refugees leaving San Francisco.

Unlike the millionaires and grand dames of society who fled the St. Francis, John Barrymore, then a young actor appearing in Richard Harding Davis's play *The Dictator,* at the Columbia Theater on Powell Street, appeared nonchalant about the entire nightmare. He had been up all night entertaining the fiancée of another man in his suite and emerged, still wearing his evening clothes, after the first tremor. He approached a hotel waiter, Larry Lewis, and calmly stated, "I need a drink." Lewis explained that the liquor was either locked up or destroyed in the maze of broken bottles behind the many bars in the St. Francis.

Barrymore hurriedly walked outside, adjusting his dinner jacket and brushing off his tails. Gingerly he moved through the debris, apparently indifferent to the yelling throngs that fled past him. As he moved by the crowds who were in near-pandemonium in front of the Palace Hotel, he spotted Enrico Caruso sitting atop a horsecart with broken wheels. Caruso had wept bitterly at not being able to escape the disaster; he had shown his autographed picture of President Roosevelt, thinking that it would serve as his letter of transit, to any and all policemen and firemen. A kindly police captain had placed Caruso and his suitcase in a broken-down peddler's cart; he was temporarily out of harm's way. But nothing seemed to shake the great tenor's deep depression nor stop the flow of tears across his florid face.

"Hello, old boy," Barrymore said to him, according to one story. "Rather dumpy about the whole thing, eh?"

Caruso peered down at the actor, whom he knew, taking in Barrymore's formal evening dress, the winged collar, precise black tie, diamond-studded shirt, cummerbund, jacket with tails, pressed satin-striped pants and patent-leather evening shoes. The singer's face slowly cracked into a weak smile, then broadened into an even wider grin. He realized, for the first time since the quake had throttled him into a stupor of fear, the complete absurdity of the situation.

"Mr. Barrymore," Caruso said laughingly, "you

know, you're the only man in San Francisco"—he had to stop a moment to choke back laughter—"the only man *in the world,* who would dress for an earthquake!"

Barrymore gave a little salute and walked off toward the Bohemia Club, where he wangled a bottle of brandy. He then proceeded to get drunk, and drunk he was for two days. At the end of his binge, the actor sat down and penned a ridiculous account of the earthquake he never witnessed. He hoped to sell the report for $100 to a New York magazine. In part, it read: "What I had seen in those harrowing days and what I myself had been through—people shot in the street, spiked on bayonets and other horrors so great that the imagination was almost blunt from contemplating them." Barrymore's disappearance while drunk was also calculated to prevent his sailing for Australia to continue the tour of *The Dictator.* He knew that the acting troupe would believe him to be a victim of the disaster and would sail without him, which they did. The disaster, therefore, became Barrymore's excuse for dropping a play he hated and for not sailing to a country that held little interest for him. All of this he would smilingly admit twenty years later when John Barrymore, "lovable rogue," was as famous as the quake he endured without benefit of sobriety.

For most people there was little humor in the catastrophe. During the second tremor one man grabbed his two babies, yelled to his wife to flee, and ran outside. With a child tucked under each arm, he turned to see his wife crushed by the falling walls of their home. Seizing two suitcases, the traumatized father placed an infant in each and then raced toward the ferry. Not until he reached Oakland hours later did the dazed father open the valises to discover that his children had suffocated. In an instant he became violently insane and had to be restrained by a straitjacket.

Chicagoan John H. Ryan and his wife escaped from their hotel in their nightclothes and then returned to dress, while the walls of their room literally swayed back and forth. They found a man in another room as they were leaving and rescued him from a mound of fallen masonry. He begged them to look for his wife and child. "We looked and finally found them dead." In the streets, moving over and around buckled slabs of concrete, ripped cobblestones and twisted trolley tracks, the Ryans "saw ambulances and undertakers' wagons by the score. . . . They were filled with the bodies of the injured and in many cases with dead. The injured were piled into the wagons indiscriminately without respect for any consequences in the future of the patients."

Agnes Zink was awakened in time to see the entire rear half of her rooming house crack and collapse, carrying the landlady and thirty of her boarders to their deaths. She scrambled naked across the remaining portion of the roof and then let herself down a drainpipe. A policeman with a blood-smeared face ran up to her and arrested her for indecent exposure.

J. P. Anthony, who had been walking on Market Street, watched with horror as the second quake shook the huge Emporium Building. Hundreds who had fled at the first tremor were paralyzed with fear, and some were too dazed to flee any more. Anthony himself was frozen in his tracks. He looked up, expecting to die any moment, as "the walls of the building swayed a distance of three feet . . . but another tremor seemed to restore the big building to its natural position."

J. R. Hand, president of a Los Angeles fruit company, missed death by inches. "The Grand Hotel tossed like a ship at sea," he later reported. "There was a wavelike motion accompanied by a severe up-and-down shake. The shock was accompanied by a terrific roar that is indescribable. An upright beam came through the floor of my room, and the walls bulged in. I thought I should not get out alive." Hand kept the key to his room, Number 249, as a life-long souvenir.

It was the same story at the Terminus Hotel. "It did not go down at the first shock," remembered F. O. Popenie, editor of the *Pacific Monthly.* "We were sleeping on the third floor when the quake came. The walls of the hotel began falling, but the guests had time to run outside before the building fell in." The six-story Terminus, a building of stone and brick, crashed to

Danger was everywhere. Here a burned-out building collapses while startled troops and civilians watch. *(California Historical Society)*

rubble seconds after Popenie ran outside and started for San Jose on foot.

A native Californian, Dr. Ernest W. Fleming was an old hand at surviving earthquakes, but never in his long life had he endured such a shock as the 1906 rip. "An earthquake in San Francisco was no new sensation to me. . . . I was there in 1868, a boy ten years old, when the first great earthquake came. But that was a gentle rocking of a cradle [compared] to the one of Wednesday. . . . I awoke [in a third-floor hotel room] to the groaning of timbers, the grinding, creaking sound, then came the roaring street. Plastering and wall decorations fell. The sensation was as if the buildings were stretching and writhing like a snake. The darkness was intense. Shrieks of women, higher, shriller than that of the creaking timbers, cut the air. I tumbled from the bed and crawled, scrambling toward the door. The twisting and writhing appeared to increase. The air was oppressive. I seemed to be saying to myself, will it never, never stop? I wrenched the lock, the door of the room swung back against my shoulder. Just then the building seemed to breathe, stagger and right itself.

"But I fled from that building as from a falling wall. I could not believe that it could endure such a shock and still stand. The next I remember, I was standing in the street, laughing at the unholy appearance of a half a hundred men clad in pajamas—and less.

"The women were in their night robes; they made a better appearance than the men.

"The street was a rainbow of colors in the early morning light. There was every stripe and hue of raiment never to be seen outside the boudoir.

Dynamite is used to demolish a burned-out building on Market Street (the Kamm Building, gutted, its ornate dome still intact, can be seen to the right). Troops handled the explosives ineptly, causing more fires. *(Insurance Library of Chicago)*

"I looked at a man at my side; he was laughing at me. Then for the first time I became aware that I was in pajamas myself. I turned and fled back to my room."

The two great shocks that brought down huge areas of San Francisco, mostly the shanty structures in the landfill areas, brought equal destruction to Stanford University, San Jose, Santa Rosa and other areas. The sixty-four-year-old philosopher and psychologist William James had traveled to California from the academic serenity of Harvard to experience "a touch of earthquake." While staying at Stanford, James got much more than he had anticipated. Jarred from his sleep, James wasted no time in analyzing his own reactions to the disaster.

"When I felt the bed begin to waggle my first consciousness was one of gleeful recognition of the nature of the movement. . . . Sitting up involuntarily, and taking a kneeling position, I was thrown down on my face as it went *fortior* shaking the room exactly as a terrier shakes a rat. Then anything that was on anything else slid off to the floor, over went bureau and chiffonier with a crash, as the *fortissimo* was reached; plaster cracked, an awful roaring noise seemed to fill the outer air, and in an instant all was still again, save the soft babble of human voices from far and near that soon began to make itself heard, as the inhabitants in costumes *negliges* in various degrees sought the greater safety of the street and yielded to the passionate desire for sympathetic communication. . . .

"The emotion consisted wholly of glee and admiration; glee at the vividness which such an abstract idea or verbal term as 'earthquake' could put on when translated into sensible reality and verified concretely; and admiration at the way in which the little wooden house could hold itself together in spite of such a shaking. I felt no trace whatever of fear; it was pure delight and welcome. 'Go it,' I almost cried, 'and go it stronger!' I ran to my wife's room, and found that she, although wakened from sound sleep, had felt no fear either. As soon as I could think, I discerned retrospectively certain peculiar ways in which my consciousness had taken in the phenomenon. These ways were quite spontaneous, and so to speak, inevitable and irresistible.

"First, I personified the earthquake as a permanent individual entity, which had been lying low, and holding itself back during all these intervening months in order to invade my room. It came moreover directly to me. It stole in behind my back, had me all to itself, and could manifest itself convincingly. Animus and intent were never more present in any human action, nor did any human action ever more definitely point back to a living agent as its source and origin."

Whereas the quake amused and titillated the psyche of

In the hills beyond the city limits, thousands stood and helplessly watched San Francisco burn. *(California Historical Society)*

William James, it pushed the inmates of Agnews Insane Asylum into hysteria. The San Jose institution, which housed 1,100 certified lunatics, was a state-run hospital of rambling five-story brick buildings. It was also nothing less than a jail, with heavy bars on the windows and numerous padded cells. The mentally disturbed, in accordance with the archaic custom of the era, were treated like criminals, and many were trapped in their barred rooms when ceilings and walls gave way around them. The quake ran directly beneath the asylum's buildings and brought them to instant rubble, killing eighty-seven patients, eleven nurses, the superintendent and his wife.

Hundreds of mad people fled through the broken walls; fifty or sixty of them ran across the grounds and into the nearby woods where they made good their directionless escape. It would be two weeks before they were rounded up. Newspaper photographer Harry C. Carr drove past the asylum a few hours after the quake had demolished most of the buildings. "Scores were lying dead stretched on the lawns," he said later, "and others were walking about hideously wounded. Amid this scene an insane woman was wandering, blithely singing little songs of her own improvision about the earthquake and the killing. One giant maniac had broken his shackles and rescued one of the guards from the building. He had just one sane moment; long enough to be a hero. Then he fled howling into the hills."

Los Angeles Sheriff William White happened to be in San Jose when the quake struck. He reached the mental institution about 7:00 A.M. in time to help remove the crushed body of Dr. Kelly, an assistant superintendent; Kelly had been pulverized when four floors of a building fell in on him. White reported, "A nurse who was also taken out of the ruins by me died a little later."

About one hundred students from Santa Clara College arrived. They helped to solve the dilemma of the escaped patients. All the padded cells had been smashed; there was no place for the mentally disturbed to be housed. Sheriff Ross of San Jose, twenty armed deputies and the students watched bug-eyed as the patients attempted to escape. Ross said, "They were wild, and rushed to and fro, attacking everyone who came in their path. The question of what to do with them arose. There was no building nearby in which they could be confined, and as they were violent, it was necessary to restrain them in some way. A doctor suggested that they be tied to trees."

Ropes were brought, and hundreds of inmates were then bound hand and foot by the lawmen and students to sturdy trees that had not been uprooted by the tremor. The patients remained in these grotesque positions, fed baby fashion by nurses, for many hours before they could be removed. From the mouth of one patient struggling against the ropes came the words: "Jesus of Nazareth is passing." From another demented

San Francisco's corrupt Mayor Eugene E. Schmitz ordered execution squads to kill all those caught looting.

Brigadier General Frederick Funston, shown here with his wife, declared martial law in San Francisco without civil approval, an unconstitutional act for which he was never criticized.

James D. Phelan, a former San Francisco mayor, was a leader in efforts to rebuild the ruined city, giving more than $1 million of his own funds to citizens.

soul, the shouted belief that "I'm going to heaven in a chariot of fire! Don't you hear the rumbling of the chariot wheels!"

North of Market Street, perched atop Nob Hill on the lawn of his towering mansion, Brigadier General Frederick Funston peered through field glasses to see several fires breaking out in the most quake-devastated area of the city. Moving toward him and his resplendent home, he noted, were trudging columns of the homeless and destitute. Reports came to him by the minute telling how hordes of hoodlums and thugs had poured forth from the ruined buildings of the Barbary Coast and were wildly looting and killing anyone who opposed them.

Without consulting any other civil authority, Funston ordered out the troops from the nearby Presidio garrison. He had always been a man of action and the great San Francisco quake and fire would not stop a man who had once failed at West Point but had "redeemed" himself in wild adventures in the Yukon, Death Valley, Central America, and who had fought twenty-three pitched battles with the insurgents against the Spanish in Cuba in 1896-97. This was a man who had fought again, this time with the United States Army, in the Philippines and earned the Medal of Honor and the rank of brigadier general before he was thirty-five. Indeed, Freddie Funston would not be intimidated by holocaust. Using troops with fixed bayonets, Funston declared San Francisco under martial law.

Lieutenant Long of Funston's staff first went to Fort Mason and awakened Captain M. L. Walker from his slumber. A company of engineers, laden with high explosives, was soon on the march toward the now burning center of town with instructions to stop the fire by dynamiting whole blocks, if necessary. When Lieutenant Long arrived at the Presidio to instruct Colonel Charles Morris, the acting commander, to order his troops into the city, the nightgowned colonel rubbed sleep from his eyes and then angrily stated before returning to bed: "Go back and tell that newspaperman [Funston had once done a stint as a journalist] that he had better look up his army regulations, and there he will find that nobody but the President of the United States in person can order regular troops into any city!"

Waiting until Morris had gone back to bed, Long, ever obedient to his chief's orders, had the bugler sound assembly, and within minutes he marched the entire garrison out of the Presidio and on to the streets of San Francisco. Squads of troops with rifles held shoulder high prowled after looters, whom they had been ordered to shoot on sight. They entered the city around 7:00 A.M.

But the shooting had already begun. Sol Allenberg, a New York bookmaker who had escaped from the ruins of the Randolph Hotel, was making his way from the fires on Market Street past the St. Katherine Hotel. There he saw, deep beneath wreckage, the arms and bloody head of a trapped man "with a great iron girder across his chest. . . . He could not be saved from the flames that were sweeping toward him, and begged a policeman to shoot him."

The cop took careful aim, but his hand shook and when he fired, the bullet missed its mark. "That was my last slug. I used the rest up on pilferers." The policeman apparently had had enough of execution, for he took out a large knife and handed it to an elderly man, A. W. Hussey. "Here. Cut the veins in his wrists." Without pausing the old man climbed over brick and masonry and slashed both arms of the doomed man. Swearing, he threw down the knife and staggered off the pile of debris. (Hussey worked his way through and around the mounting fires for hours to later reach the Hall of Justice, where he confessed the mercy killing to a haggard police sergeant, only to be told, "Go home, old man, all of San Francisco is dying this day and it no longer matters how.")

Allenberg looked grimly upon the killing but said nothing, only remembering how "the crowd hurried on and left him to die alone."

Chuck Connors, one of many prisoners released from jail to dig graves (at the gunpoint of policemen, and later soldiers), remembered seeing a man who had been trapped in the wreckage of a large house for hours. His legs were crushed. The fire was creeping toward him also, and he kept shouting, "'Shoot me, for God's sake, shoot me,' and crying like a kid. A policeman came up and shot him twice but didn't hit him properly because he just kept on yelling. Then a young fellow snatched the cop's revolver and held it to the trapped man's head and blew out his brains."

Even Enrico Caruso aimed a pistol on that first day of the calamity. Thinking that four Chinese were about to steal his belongings, he produced a small weapon and waved it in their faces. "You give me my trunk or I'll shoot! I'll shoot!" Caruso's valet raced up to tell him that the Chinese were taking his trunk to safety at his instructions. Caruso grimaced, pocketed the pistol and then, taking only a sketch pad under one arm and the signed portrait of Theodore Roosevelt under the other, he joined the exodus away from the searing fires that were forming a titanic wall of flame. Caruso headed toward Nob Hill, where he was later seen calmly sketching the sweeping disaster.

Looters rummage through broken bank safes. Scores of thugs from the Barbary Coast were shot by troopers, police and vigilantes. *(California Historical Society)*

Survivors eat their fill at a hot food station in Union Square two days after the quake. *(California Historical Society)*

Eugene Schmitz, upon hearing that Funston's troops had entered the city, pretended that the general had his tacit approval to declare martial law and issued a proclamation that read in part: "The federal troops, the members of the regular police force, and all special police officers have been authorized by me to KILL any and all persons found engaged in looting or in the commission of any other crime."

Abe Ruef, Schmitz's partner in crime, did not appear at any of the mayor's special disaster meetings. He merely watched the fires destroy the city he had so expertly mulcted. He stared in wonder as the Palace Hotel went up in flames. (Ruef lost an estimated $750,000 in personal property in the fire. Both he and Schmitz were later sent to jail for extortion. The mayor died in 1928. Ruef died in 1936, an obscure, penniless bankrupt, who, only days before his death, had seen Clark Gable and Jeanette MacDonald in the motion picture *San Francisco,* watching his city shudder and burn all over again.)

Newspaper czar William Randolph Hearst, who had been born and raised in San Francisco and who owned the *San Francisco Examiner,* was asleep in his ornate New York apartment when a phone call awakened him. The city editor of his *New York American* informed him that San Francisco had been ripped wide open by a quake and was in the process of burning up. The editor asked how the *American* should handle the story, and Hearst reportedly replied, "Don't overplay it. They have earthquakes often in California." The *American,* in typical Hearstian-style journalism, dug up a photo of buildings being consumed in the Baltimore fire of 1904, doctored it, and ran this picture on its front page as a portrait of the San Francisco holocaust. Rival newspapers promptly exposed it as a fake.

Once he understood the magnitude of the disaster, Hearst, to his credit, did his utmost to aid the stricken city. Through his many newspapers he organized relief trains that rolled out of New York, Chicago and Los Angeles packed with supplies, physicians and nurses. Further, as a congressman, Hearst quickly went to Washington to introduce a bill calling for a $4.5 million appropriation to aid San Francisco in rebuilding its public buildings. He then collected more than $200,000 in cash that his newspapers had raised to aid the injured and headed west to personally distribute these funds. The money was tucked away in a single valise. In the words of his biographer, W. A. Swanberg: "This was one of the occasions when even his enemies must have wished that his greatness in action, in getting things done, was not marred by so many grievous flaws."

Hearst's mother, Phoebe, had lost her gew-gaw filled

mansion in the fire that crackled through San Francisco, eating up one block after another. At first the Barbary Coast was gone; then Chinatown, the last large section, was gutted.

When the dives and brothels of the Barbary Coast flared up, hundreds of villainous toughs went on a rampage of looting. They broke into bars and quickly became intoxicated. Then they smashed store windows and helped themselves to merchandise. They broke down the doors of banks and scooped up currency.

At one point the rowdy mobs attempted to loot the United States Mint building, but a small army of armed clerks, policemen and vigilantes, later joined by regular troops, turned them back with a hail of gunfire. In their attempt to steal the $39 million in currency, gold and silver housed in the Mint, thirty-four white men were shot to death.

By the evening of the first day, hundreds of vandals could be seen in the flamelight, squatting on corners in drunken stupors, casks of wine at their sides and plunder scattered all about them. According to one report they "exulted in [the] unhindered joy of doing evil. . . . They toasted chunks of sausage over the dying coals of the cooling ruins even as they drank, and their songs of revelry were echoed from wall to wall down in the burnt Mission district."

Prostitutes staggered through smoke and rubble carting champagne, and drunkenly toasting the inferno. Other prostitutes quickly set up tents just ahead of the fire and continued doing "business as usual." One notorious madam wearing a pink silk slip and high heeled satin slippers walked the length of what had once been Natoma Street, carrying a bucket of water. From this she ladled out deep drinks of water to those dazed wretches huddled next to their salvaged household goods.

"Let them drink and be happy," she said, "water tastes better than beer to them now."

The efforts of the city's 585-man fire department were frustrated because the water mains were thoroughly smashed throughout San Francisco. Though water was not available to the Italian community around Telegraph Hill, the residents resorted to what was available in their wine cellars. Families also brought keg after keg of wine from storage areas, about 1,000 gallons in all, and used this to hold back the encroaching flames. "The barrel heads were smashed in, and the bucket brigade turned from water to wine," said one eyewitness. "Sacks were dipped in the wine and used for beating out the fire. Beds were stripped of their blankets, and these were soaked in the wine and hung over the exposed portions of the cottages, and men on the roofs drenched the shingles and sides of the house with wine."

EXTRA THE DAILY NEWS EXTRA

HUNDREDS DEAD!

Fire Follows Earthquake, Laying Downtown Section in Ruins--City Seems Doomed For Lack of Water

CHICAGO AMERICAN

SOLDIERS TO BE RE-ENFORCED IN FRISCO TO STOP RIOTS!

EXTRA Oakland Tribune.

PEOPLE SHOT DOWN BY SOLDIERS IN STREETS OF SAN FRANCISCO

PEOPLE BURNED ALIVE

ST. FRANCIS HOTEL DESTROYE

Sunday Mercury and Herald

PLAGUE IS NOW THREATENING THE HOMELES

The front pages of California and other U.S. newspapers tell the three-day tragedy of San Francisco's earthquake and fire, April 18 to April 20, 1906.

This hastily-published sheet music appeared shortly after the San Francisco disaster. *(Bancroft Library)*

The cover of the magazine *Judge* portrayed the San Francisco earthquake with off-beat (and somewhat unpopular) humor. *(Bancroft Library)*

Silent squads of soldiers moved just ahead of the fire, ushering bewildered people out of the reach of the flames. Many were so dazed that they would only move at bayonet point. Looters, and some innocent persons thought to be looters, were shot on sight with no questions asked. R. F. Lund of Canal Dover, Ohio, who had broken out of the ruins of his hotel by smashing his 230 pounds against doors and walls that had entrapped him, was making his way down a narrow alley behind the Emporium when he spotted his first ghoul.

"A rough fellow, evidently a south of Market Street thug, was bending over the unconscious form of a woman. She was clothed in a kimono and lay upon the sidewalk near the curb. His back was toward me. He was trying to wrench a ring from her finger, and he held her right wrist in his left hand. A soldier suddenly approached. He held a rifle thrust forward, and his eyes were on the wretch.

"Involuntarily I stopped and involuntarily my hand went to my hip pocket. I remember only this, that it seemed in that moment a good thing to me to take a life. The soldier's rifle came to his shoulder. There was a sharp report, and I saw the smoke spurt from the muzzle. The thug straightened up with a wrench, he shot his right arm above his head and pitched forward across the body of the woman. He died with her wrist in his grasp. It may sound murderous, but the feeling I experienced was one of disappointment. I wanted to kill him myself."

At Third and Market streets, a Los Angeles man, Jack Spencer, saw "a man attempting to cut the fingers from the hand of a dead woman in order to secure the rings. Three soldiers witnessed the deed at the same time and ordered the man to throw up his hands. Instead of obeying he drew a revolver from his pocket and began to fire without warning.

"The three soldiers, reinforced by a half-dozen uniformed patrolmen, raised their rifles to their shoulders and fired. With the first shots the man fell, and when the soldiers went to the body to dump it into an alley, eleven bullets were found to have entered it."

Bessie Tannehill, an actress at the Tivoli Theater, saw "many looters and pickpockets at work. On Mason Street a gang of thieves was at work. They were pursued by troops, but escaped in an auto."

J. C. Gill and his wife, trudging toward the ferry, passed through scenes that were "sickening and indescribable . . . scores of men, wharf rats, who had looted wholesale liquor houses and were maudlin drunk, were burned to death without being the wiser, because of their condition."

Vigilantes roamed through the streets just ahead of the moving lines of soldiers. They, too, summarily shot anyone suspected of looting. Oliver Posey, Jr., was with a crowd outside the Palace Hotel, and he and others "discovered a miscreant in the act of robbing a corpse of its jewels. Without delay, he was seized, a rope was procured and he was immediately strung up to a beam which was left standing in the ruined entrance of the Palace Hotel.

"No sooner had he been hoisted up and a hitch taken in the rope than one of his fellow criminals was captured. Stopping only to secure a few yards of hemp, a knot was quickly tied and the wretch was soon adorning the hotel entrance by the side of the other dastard."

It was noon on the first day of the disaster before Mayor Schmitz was told that wholesale executions were going on in his city. He was unmoved, and gave his complete support to the shootings and lynchings of looters. Three men were dragged from a Stockton Street basement when they were caught rummaging through scattered belongings. They were lined up against a wall within seconds and executed by a squad of Funston's troops. Photographer Moshe Cohen discovered five bodies shot by troopers. "They'd been shot and left to die there."

Squads of troopers loaded down with high explosives moved with the fire, trying to set charges beneath buildings that would stop the flames. They proved inept at their job, however, and created more fires than they put out. One demolition squad at Clay and Kearney streets attempted to blow up a drugstore. They used too much powder and tore half the block away; burning mattresses sent hurling into Chinatown ignited that hodgepodge of ancient buildings at 6:30 P.M.

That evening W. W. Overton witnessed the destruction of San Francisco's old Chinatown district. It had always been a forbidding place, rampant with opium dens and miserable cribs where white and yellow slavery flourished, a nether world of insidious earthen tunnels where the Chinese kept their slaves of sex and narcotics. Overton's remarkable narrative of the destruction of Chinatown is vividly memorable and self-revealing as it describes his own fears and prejudices:

"No heap of smoking ruins marks the site of the wooden warrens where the slant-eyed men of the orient dwelt in thousands. The place is pitted with deep holes and seared with dark passageways, from whose depths come smoke wreaths. All the wood has gone and the winds are streaking the ashes. Men, white men, never knew the depth of Chinatown's underground city. They often talked of these subterranean runways. And many of them had gone beneath the street levels, two and three stories. But now that Chinatown has been unmasked, for the destroyed buildings were only a mask, men from the hillside have looked on where its inner secrets lay. In places they can see passages 100 feet deep.

"The fire swept this Mongolian section clean. It left no shred of the painted wooden fabric. It ate down to the bare ground and this lies stark, for the breezes have taken away the light ashes. Joss houses and mission schools, grocery stores and opium dens, gambling hells and theaters—all of them went. The buildings blazed up like tissue-paper lanterns. . . .

"From this place, I, following the fire, saw hundreds of crazed yellow men flee. In their arms they bore their opium pipes, their money bags, their silks, and their children. Beside them ran the baggy trousered women, and some of them hobbled painfully [Chinese women were still binding their feet].

"These were the men and women of the surface. Far beneath the street levels in those cellars and passageways were many others. Women who never saw the day from their darkened prisons and their blinking jailors were caught like rats in a huge trap. Their bones were eaten by the flames.

"And now there remains only the holes. They pit the hillside like a multitude of ground swallow nests. They go to depths which the police never penetrated. The secrets of those burrows will never be known, for into them the hungry fire first sifted its red coals and then licked eagerly in tongues of creeping flames, finally obliterating everything except the earth itself."

On the heels of Chinatown's residents came swarms of brown, black, red and gray rats, most of them infected with bubonic plague carried from the Orient. It had been present in Chinatown since 1900, but this was hushed up by Mayor Schmitz and others. Though concentrated in the unsanitary Chinatown district, rats by the thousands squealed in clawing packs upward in all parts of the city where the quake had heaved up the earth and broken wide the sewer system. Master photographer Arnold Genthe, who watched Chinatown being destroyed, was attracted to an overturned cupola around which scores of rats were concentrating. Upon investigating, Genthe found two Chinese crushed to death beneath the cupola. The rats were gnawing the protruding arms and legs of the dead Chinese while others frantically tried to claw their way beneath the fallen dome to get at the trunks. With a shudder, Genthe reeled away down the street.

The bubonic plague could not be covered up by Schmitz and others now. Within a year more than 150 cases broke out. Most rat-bite victims died.

Everywhere the fire burned. Half the city was in flames. San Francisco's population of 383,000 got through the night and had to face the dawn of a second day of calamity. They gravitated toward the pockets of unburned houses on some of the hills—Russian, Nob, Telegraph—with flames and flying cinders at their backs. They moved as if drugged into Golden Gate Park and into the Presidio, where they collapsed and fitfully slept body on body. Clusters of homeless people clutched

A tent camp for quake survivors was established at Fort Mason. *(California Historical Society)*

strange artifacts from their ruined city. Some held desperately to clocks that had smashed mechanisms. Others held washboards, dead pets, torn portraits. Soldiers found two women breast-feeding their children. Both infants were dead. Only at gunpoint would the torporous mothers allow the dead infants to be taken away for burial.

Soldiers blew up more and more buildings, working furiously and mostly failing to stop the fire. The explosions went on all night and the next day, streets shuddering to collapse. On the night of the second day, Dr. Fleming had almost reached Golden Gate Park. "All the while we were moving onward with the crowd. Cinders were falling about us. At times our clothing caught fire, just little embers that smoked and went out. The cinders burned our faces, and we used our handkerchiefs for veils." He arrived in the park as darkness was setting in. Behind him San Francisco was engulfed in flames. "It was a weird twilight. The glare from the burning city threw a kind of red flame and shadow about us. It seemed uncanny; the figures about us moved like ghosts. The wind and fog blew chill from the ocean, and we walked about to keep warm. Thousands were walking about, too, but there was no disturbance. . . . The streets, walks, and lawns were wiggling with little parties, one or two families in each. . . .

"The cinders still kept falling. They seemed at times to come down right against the wind. They stung my face and made me restless. All night we moved about the hills. Thousands were moving with us. As the night wore on, the crowds grew. Near daylight the soldiers came to the park. They were still moving in front of the fire."

Albert Gould, who had fled the crumbling Palace Hotel in the quake, had walked barefooted to the telegraph office and spent hours picking glass from his feet. Not until the following night did he reach the ferry that would take him to safety in Oakland. He would forever remember the glut of terrified humanity attempting to board the boat. "People by the thousands and seemingly devoid of reason were crowded around the ferry station. At the iron gates they clawed with their hands as so many maniacs. They sought to break the bars, and failing in that, turned upon each other. Fighting my way to the gate like the others, the thought came into my mind of what rats in a trap were. Had I not been a strong man I should certainly have been killed.

"When the ferry drew up to the slip, and the gates were thrown open, the rush to safety was tremendous. The people flowed through the passageway like a mountain torrent that, meeting rocks in its path, dashes over them. Those who fell saved themselves as best they could."

From the ferry Gould barely could make out the city, hidden as it was by a pall of smoke. "The cloud was five miles in height and at its top changed into a milk white."

Adventurer and saga-spinner Jack London, the literary roaring boy of the era, found himself in the middle of the city's ordeal by fire. He took bittersweet notes as he walked toward Union Square "through miles and miles of magnificent buildings and towering skyscrapers. There was no water. The dynamite was giving out. And at right angles two different conflagrations were sweeping down. I knew it was all doomed."

The fire was six blocks away, a raging inferno roaring toward London as he stood at Kearney and Market streets in the very heart of the city. Only some mounted cavalrymen were nearby in the deserted streets. "That was all. Not another person was in sight. In the intense heat of the city, two troopers sat on their horses and watched. Surrender was complete." Union Square, London went on to describe for *Collier's,* was choked with refugees. "Thousands of them had gone to bed on the grass. Government tents had been set up. Supper was being cooked, and the refugees were lining up for free meals."

London spotted an injured man nearby and struck up a conversation. "He was old and on crutches. Said he, 'Today is my birthday. Last night I was worth thirty thousand dollars. I bought five bottles of wine, some delicate fish and other things for my birthday dinner, and all I own now are these two crutches.'"

Gougers on horseback were the last costermongers of the catastrophe, the last grim reminder of human avarice thriving in the midst of tragedy. Draymen charged as much as $1,000 to carry a load of furniture a dozen blocks. Drivers of autos charged half as much to carry injured people to makeshift hospitals. An army sergeant learned of a baker who was gouging customers. The trooper ran into the bakery, where he discovered loaves of bread being sold for seventy-five cents each instead of the usual ten cents. The sergeant aimed his rifle at the baker's head.

"What's the price of your bread?"

The wide-eyed baker tore down his seventy-five cent sign and threw it to the floor. He stuttered, "A nickel a loaf, sir."

"Keep it that way until this is all over, or there will be one less baker in the world tomorrow."

In other areas gougers were charging fifty cents for a glass of water.

As troops moved forward they took axes and broke open warehouses where food was stored. This was distributed to the starving throngs.

The exodus continued for another day. More than 75,000 made their way to Oakland across the bay and to Berkeley, Alameda and Benicia. Tens of thousands more moved into the hills just outside San Francisco's city limits.

The fire was finally stopped on the broad expanse of Van Ness Avenue, where dynamiters finally managed to create several successful backfires. But most of San Francisco was by then in ashes. It was a city financially gutted, too. Almost all the bankers had left their complete funds inside the banks, including all important papers. These burned to cinders—even the vaults melted under the fire's incredible heat. Only Amadeo Giannini had had the presence of mind to flee with the capital of the small Bank of Italy, about $80,000 in sacks, guarded by rifle-bearing relatives. Shortly after the fire he set a plank across two empty barrels and opened his bank for business. He loaned money to one and all who wished to rebuild San Francisco. This single act was the beginning of the mighty Bank of America.

There was a lot to rebuild. More than 500 blocks had been obliterated. The dead were numbered from 500 to 700, and hundreds more were missing. Thousands were injured, and the whole population was starving. The financial loss was estimated at $350 to $500 million, and many insurance companies defaulted on their payments. Some insurance firms, such as Aetna of Hartford, paid all claims in full. And one of the most stirring—and reassuring—wires received by San Francisco authorities was the telegraph message that read: "The Continental Insurance Company sold fire insurance and will deliver the goods undamaged. Henry Evans, President." Continental offered a "dollar-for-dollar" payment for losses, one of the most heroic and ethical stances ever taken by an American business.

There was little that anyone could do, however, in bringing back the glamorous past of the city. As long-time native and local scribe, Will Irwin, wrote shortly after the holocaust, "The old San Francisco is dead . . . those who have known that peculiar city by the Golden Gate, who have caught the flavor of the Arabian Nights, feel that it can never be the same. It is as though a pretty, frivolous woman had passed through a great tragedy. She survives, but she is sobered and different. If it rises out of the ashes it must be a modern city much like other cities and without its old atmosphere."

Poet Lawrence Harris gave the old San Francisco its most eloquent epitaph:

Put me somewhere west of East Street where there's nothin' left but dust,
Where the lads are all abustlin' and where everything's gone bust,
Where the buildings that are standin' sort of blink and blindly stare
At the damnest finest ruins ever gazed on anywhere.

A break in the St. Francis Dam allowed the San Francisquito Valley to be flooded in March, 1928. *(Wide World)*

SAN FRANCISQUITO VALLEY, CALIFORNIA — **FLOOD**
March 12-13, 1928

Heavy rains placed tremendous pressure on the St. Francis Dam above the San Francisquito valley on the night of March 12-13, 1928. At midnight the structure broke in several places, sending 38,000 acre-feet of water into the valley. The flood wave moved at an overwhelming 500,000 cubic feet per second, and 350 persons were instantly drowned. More than $15 million in damage was done.

SAN JUAN CAPISTRANO, CALIFORNIA — **EARTHQUAKE**
December, 1812

Reports of the quake that shuddered through San Juan Capistrano, California, are sketchy, but it is known that in December, 1812, the tremor completely shattered the town's church. Forty Indians attending Mass were killed when the roof collapsed. Other churches wrecked by this wide-running quake included those in Purisima, Santa Inez, Santa Barbara, San Buenaventura and San Gabriel.

SANRIKU, JAPAN — **TSUNAMI**
March 3, 1933

An undersea earthquake measuring 8.6 on several scales caused an enormous *tsunami* to rush inland at Sanriku, Japan, on March 3, 1933. Witnesses later recalled the front of the gigantic wave approaching the shore as having been as bright as a searchlight, giving vent to sea dragon superstition. It was speculated that the 500 m.p.h.

seismic seawave had unearthed phosphorescent ocean creatures and rolled them in its onrush. This was said to create the spectacular visual phenomenon.

The *tsunami,* which came ashore more than thirty feet high at Sanriku, sank 8,000 ships, most of them small fishing vessels. It ripped away more than 10,000 homes, and killed about 3,000 persons.

(ALSO SEE: Japan, June 15, 1896)

SAN SALVADOR — EARTHQUAKES 1854-78

Long a center of earthquake activity, San Salvador, capital of the republic of San Salvador, was built to withstand severe shocks. Most of its houses were one-story, thick-walled structures. In the homes of the upper classes, courtyards with firmly planted trees were traditional. These spacious courtyards offered safety to hundreds of residents during the violent quake of April 16, 1854. San Salvador was reduced to ruins, with only a few public buildings and private dwellings left standing. More than 5,000 persons perished. A premonitory shock before the great one warned inhabitants, so that many escaped to their courtyards before their homes fell down upon them.

Another murderous quake raked San Salvador in October, 1878. The city of San Salvador was not alone in this disaster; the towns of Santiago de Marie, Guadeloupe and Incuapa were also destroyed, with thousands losing their lives. One account of this quake states: "The shock causing the most damage had at first a kind of oscillatory movement lasting over forty seconds and ending in a general upheaval of the earth; the result being that solid walls, arches, and strongly braced roofs were broken and severed like pipe-stems. In the vicinity of Incuapa a number of villages disappeared entirely."

Survivors of the 1854 earthquake in San Salvador save what they can from the ruins.

SANTA MARIA — VOLCANIC ERUPTION October 24, 1902

Towering above the rich coffee lands of western Guatemala is the volcano Santa Maria, rising 12,361 feet. This belching giant had its most famous eruption on October 24, 1902, when its ashes covered more than 125,000 square miles. Pumice stone and ashes accumulated to a depth of eight inches.

Hundreds of farmhouses were flattened by Santa Maria's shower of rock debris. An estimated 6,000 persons perished, most of them crushed to death by stones while they nestled in their houses next to the volcano. The entire side of the mountain blew away.

Santa Maria's eruption cloud shot upward to a distance of 18 miles and was heard even in Costa Rica, more than 500 miles away.

Another less violent eruption occurred in 1929.

SANTA CRUZ DEL SUR, CUBA — HURRICANE November 9, 1932

The hurricane that leveled the city of Santa Cruz del Sur in Cuba on November 9, 1932, was accompanied by a sea wave and winds up to and beyond 210 m.p.h. (A ship's captain at sea estimated the hurricane as force 12, the highest number on the Beaufort scale; winds were so furious that he merely reported "winds infinite.")

Of a population of more than 4,000, about 2,500 residents of Santa Cruz del Sur were killed, most drowned when a huge wave came ashore.

SANTA DOMINGO — HURRICANE September 23, 1834

Thousands of Santa Domingo's inhabitants were killed by a fierce hurricane that swept across the island of Dominica, where 200 died. The storm struck Dominica on September 20, 1834, and three days later broadly moved across Santa Domingo just when a much-respected local priest was being buried. Henceforth, this storm was known as the "Padre Ruiz Hurricane." The storm did great damage to forests and crops all along the Ozama River. Scores of vessels on the river sank with all of their crews.

Santo Domingo was in ruins following the hurricane of September 3, 1930. More than 10,000 buildings were blown down. *(Wide World)*

SANTO DOMINGO, DOMINICAN REPUBLIC

HURRICANE
September 3, 1930

background: After striking Dominica, a powerful hurricane dove upon Santo Domingo, capital of the Dominican Republic. A four-hour blast, the storm killed 4,000 persons, injured another 5,000 and obliterated all but 400 of the city's 10,000 buildings. About $40 million in damage was done.

The city of Santo Domingo was the prime target for the devastating hurricane that struck the Dominican Republic on the afternoon of September 3, 1930. Winds estimated in excess of 200 m.p.h. slashed through the city, crumbling almost every wooden building, about 10,000 structures. The storm front was almost twenty-five miles broad, but it dissipated after striking the mountain range outside Santo Domingo.

E. F. White, a pilot for Pan American Airlines who had landed two hours before the hurricane struck, later gave this account: "Four other men and myself took refuge in a hotel when the storm began. About noon the skylights blew off, and the shutters crashed in. From then on the wind and rain increased. It was apparent that the center of the storm passed over Santo Domingo. At about 2:30 P.M. the wind reached its highest velocity. Then there was thirty minutes of dead calm. The skies brightened a little, and I thought the sun was going to come out.

"About three o'clock the wind changed from the north to the opposite direction. The second blow was not as severe as the first. Destruction in the city was terrific. None of the buildings, except those made of concrete, stood up. Many of the buildings still standing are badly damaged. Water, light and telephone service was paralyzed.

"After the storm subsided, dead and injured were seen on every hand. It was horrible, but I saw no signs of great hysteria or excitement. The people seemed dazed. Bodies were laid out on the streets for possible identification. Many are being burned on huge funeral pyres. Prisoners in the jail were put to work helping the natives. Martial law was declared, and food supplies were put under guard."

Rafael Trujillo, dictator of the tiny island, barely escaped with his life. His executive offices were wrecked. As the eye of the storm passed over the city, he and his retinue ran wildly through the streets toward refuge in the ancient Fort Ozama. Undamaged was the city's monolithic cathedral, which reputedly holds the tomb of Columbus and hundreds of colonial artifacts.

Deaths ultimately mounted to 4,000. Many of these were victims of typhoid fever that resulted from contaminated water; the city's water system was completely destroyed by the storm.

SATENA AIRLINES — AIR CRASH

January 10, 1974

Only minutes after a Satena Airlines two-engine turboprop had taken off from Florencia, Colombia, en route to Bogotá, fire broke out in the passenger section, and the plane quickly went out of control. It crashed, January 10, 1974, on an Andean foothill not far from Florencia, and all forty persons on board were killed.

SAUGUS, MONTANA — RAILWAY WRECK

June 19, 1938

background: An eleven-car, Milwaukee Railroad passenger train, the *Olympian,* was wrecked at 12:35 A.M. on June 19, 1938, when a steel trestle over Custer Creek near Saugus, Montana, weakened and collapsed under waters from a flash flood. Officially, forty-seven persons were killed.

The bridge spanning Custer Creek, a tributary of the Yellowstone River, just outside of Saugus, Montana, was made of steel and was heavily reinforced with concrete. The 180-foot-long span was considered to be one of the safest railroad trestles along the Milwaukee Railroad line, even though it was twenty-five years old. No warning of this bridge's collapse under a heavy flash flood came to the engineer of the *Olympian,* an eleven-car passenger train running westbound on the night of June 19, 1938.

Though heavy rains had swollen waters beneath the bridge to about seven feet, the trestle remained intact. A sudden cloudburst to the north, however, caused a twenty-foot wall of water to crash through the girders of the bridge at the same moment the *Olympian* began to cross the trestle.

As the bridge started to sag, the first five cars followed the engine and made it safely to the far bank, but the next two cars, which were sleepers, were wrenched away from the other cars and thrown into the raging creek. It was never fully determined how many persons drowned; 47 bodies were later recovered (out of 193 passengers on board) from the flooded Yellowstone River, but more deaths were thought to have occurred. Some of the corpses were found as far as fifty miles downstream.

SAYRETON, ALABAMA — MINE DISASTER

August 28-29, 1943

Coal dust and methane gas were set off in a reverberating explosion in the Sayreton Mine at 10:10 P.M. on August 28, 1943, while 107 miners worked in the shaft. An arc from a cable-reel locomotive set off the blast, which killed fourteen nearby workers (the engineer survived). When a rescue team of seventeen men probed the ninth level of the mine, another blast occurred after midnight. Two more men were killed, and fifteen were injured. Twelve more died of injuries. The death toll from the two explosions was twenty-eight.

The Milwaukee Road's *Olympian* crashed into Custer Creek near Saugus, Montana, on June 19, 1938, killing forty-seven passengers. Floodwaters had weakened a steel trestle. *(Wide World)*

SCANDINAVIAN AIRLINES — AIR CRASH January 19, 1960

The crash of a Scandinavian Airlines Caravelle, while attempting to land at Esenboga Airport in Ankara, Turkey, on January 19, 1960, was simply a pilot's error, a mistake that cost the lives of the forty-two persons on board.

Due to a heavy snowstorm, Esenboga Airport authorities instructed the Scandinavian pilot to "circle" just after he had dropped to an altitude of 6,500 feet and was preparing to land. It was during the renewed "checklist operations" that the captain, according to experts, misread his altimeter (the plane was equipped with three altimeters, including a new drum-type device) within the span of thirty seconds. Thinking he was safely above the field, the pilot came in too short of the runway and crashed. (An identical misreading of the drum-type altimeter was made by the pilot of a South African Boeing 707, which crashed at Windhock, South Africa, on April 20, 1968. One hundred twenty-three on board died.)

SCHOOL OF THE SACRED HEART — FIRE January 22, 1974

background: A Roman Catholic institution, the School of the Sacred Heart near Heusden, Belgium, caught fire on the night of January 22, 1974, on the top floor of a three-story building constructed in 1926. Out of a total of 225 boys in the orphanage, 25 children were burned to death. Thirty-eight boys escaped the blaze in the building.

"Of course, there had been talk of the need of fire drills," lamented the Reverend Filibert Coenen of the School of the Sacred Heart near Heusden, Belgium, "but none were staged. That I know. After the catastrophe, it is very regrettable, but it is like with sin—contrition comes afterwards."

The fire that raced through a forty-year-old, three-story dormitory, which housed sixty-three boys from ages twelve to fifteen, began on the roof of the building at 11:00 P.M. on January 22, 1974. It was at least twenty minutes before the fire department in the nearby hamlet of Heusden, forty-five miles northeast of Brussels, was alerted.

Boys on the third floor of the building awoke when dense smoke gushed through their ward. One fast-thinking orphan later told authorities: "There was smoke all around me, and I heard the noise of burning wood. I grabbed my pants and started running. I don't know how I made it."

The Reverend Albert Lerno and other priests were in the recreation lounge when the fire erupted. Lerno's first reaction was to get to the trapped boys. "We all ran up there as fast as we could, but the smoke was getting very thick as we reached the dormitory. I tried to get in anyhow, but the smoke was overpowering and my hair started singeing from the heat. I think if I had gone further, I would have collapsed."

Lieutenant Joseph Daniels led firemen into the burning wing of the main building (the other wings remained undamaged), but he and his men were driven back by the overwhelming smoke. The heat was so intense, one fireman said, that it was "like breathing fire."

The boys trapped inside dove madly for the exits and windows. Some made it down a narrow stairway, but one exit, police angrily pointed out later, was completely blocked by a row of iron beds. Twenty-five bodies were later found in the charred ward. Most of them were unrecognizable and were in heaps near an exit and at windows that would not open. Cubicles of plywood and fiberboard served to feed the flames. Some of the orphans were trapped inside these. Thirty-eight children escaped death, but most were seriously burned.

Lieutenant Daniels concluded: "The emergency exit possibilities were absolutely inadequate. . . . There was only one door that really served as an exit and entrance at the same time." It was this door that flamed up first.

(ALSO SEE: Babb Switch School, Lakeview School, Our Lady of the Angels School)

SCIO, TURKEY — EARTHQUAKE April 3, 1881

background: Three sharp tremors on April 3, 1881, brought ruin to forty-four villages and towns on Scio, an island in the Grecian Archipelago then controlled by Turkey. The quake completely leveled many towns, and from 5,000 to 7,000 persons were killed. Another 20,000 were injured (out of a total population of 80,000). The thirty-two-mile-long, eighteen-mile-wide island suffered mostly at its southern end.

The island of Scio, a small dot in the Aegean Sea, fifty-three miles west of Smyrna and five miles from Cape Blanco in Asia Minor, was a long bloodied isle before it was visited by an awesome earthquake on April 3, 1881. The Genoese took the island by force in the Middle Ages. The Turks invaded Scio in the sixteenth century and controlled it until a Greek expedition landed in 1822 and, aided by many of the inhabitants, overpowered the garrison at the citadel. In retaliation a massive Turkish army again stormed upon the island, massacred half the population and dragged off thousands into slavery. Scio remained in Turkish hands until the 1881 earthquake. (One of the island's insistent claims is that it was the birthplace of Homer; Lord Byron's poem "Childe Harold" states, in reference to Homer, "The blind old man of Scio's rocky isle.")

Visiting the island a day after the quake, a correspondent for the *London Times* reported: "The town [Scio] looks as if it had been subjected to a terrible bombardment; hundreds of houses have been transformed into a shapeless mass of ruins, under which lie buried an unknown number of victims. A majority of the remaining houses, already cracked and roofless, may fall at any moment. . . . The unhappy inhabitants wander about, anxious to search for missing relatives and lost property, but afraid to risk their lives in the perilous work of clearing away the rubbish. Many who are willing to expose themselves to the danger are prevented by their friends or the police. Fear, grief, and despair are depicted in nearly every face, and all have some sad or tragic tale to tell."

Of the 80,000 natives on the island, the dead from the quake were estimated as high as 7,000. Nearly 25 percent of the total population were injured. Forty-four villages and towns were almost wiped out. The type of buildings dominating the island contributed largely to this mass devastation. Most were lofty stone structures without wooden beam supports and with little mortar. They fell by the thousands at the first tremor, burying all occupants. Ten villages in the southern district of Kampos were leveled. The extent of damage was revealed in the statistics of one village, Kalimasia, which was the largest. Of a population of about 1,000, those killed numbered 670. More than 150 were injured.

There was the remarkable escape of a pregnant woman who was buried beneath several tons of debris from her collapsed stone house. Trapped for fifty-two hours, the woman gave birth to a child, delivering the infant herself while entombed. The child perished just as rescuers dug down to the pair, but the woman survived.

The large town of Castro in southern Scio was one of forty-four towns wiped out by a shattering earthquake on April 3, 1881.

Out of the 3,000 buildings in the seaport town of Castro, only 100 were left standing when the quake subsided. A behemoth structure built on the slope of a towering cliff, the Convent of Neamonti, crumbled at the start of the quake and tumbled downward into the sea, taking with it in its rolling stone rubble all of the scores of nuns living there. Only one sister survived.

An English merchant visiting Castro had just finished dinner and was preparing to take a nap when the quake began to rattle the town. He later wrote to the *Illustrated London News:* "There was an awful booming sound and feeling the house, which was one-story high beginning to shake, I placed myself in a doorway. The walls fell down, and the roof, which was a flat terrace, opened and through the cloud of dust which rose I dimly saw the open heavens above. . . . Disengaging myself from the stones and mortar, which reached nearly to my knees, I clambered up onto the top of the ruins of the dwelling.

"No sooner had I emerged than a girl called to me: 'Come, sir, do come, and help me save my mother!' Yielding to the entreaties of the girl, who rushed in over the ruins of the next house, I followed her and saw the mother with her feet fastened down, her head covered with dust and dirt, and feebly moving her hand in an effort to rise. Telling the girl to take her mother's hand, I disengaged the feet, and, together we dragged her out. Washing her face, revealed frightful bruises.

"While waiting upon her, a father came up with his two children, one of whom was dead and the other apparently so, though a little cold water dashed on his face brought him to his senses. All this happened in ten minutes from the first shock. A second booming sound was heard, and the downfall of other houses and walls, tottering in consequence to the first shock, was seen."

The merchant raced to the Quarantine Office, running up and over piles of ruins in the streets that reached ten or twelve feet. Along the foot-slashing route he met only one other fugitive, a man who had gone completely mad. A third shock came when he reached the Quarantine Office, and he quickly made his escape from the island by a small steamer. At sea he watched dumbfounded as "the awful roaring continued, and for a few minutes a cloud of smoke burst from the slope at the back of the town."

The captain of a Greek tug was caught by the quake in the Custom House. He described the buildings "as veering first to one side and then the other, and then [he] felt a violent upheaving of the ground." The captain sprinted toward the sea, pausing to watch a balcony of enormous proportions crash on top of a woman and child attempting to flee. Everywhere he could hear the shrill voices of those trapped in the ruins: "Save me! Save me! I am not dead!" But no one bothered to stop in the undulating town of Castro. They ran toward the seashore,

where they leaped into small fishing boats and rowed frantically away from the crumbling town. Those running toward the outskirts of the town and the hills beyond were deaf to the many hundreds in the ruins. These refugees literally ran over the stone-encased bodies of their relatives and friends, many of whom were still alive, crushing scores to death with their own jittery feet.
(ALSO SEE: Messina, Sicily)

SCOFIELD, UTAH — MINE DISASTER
May 1, 1900

Although no explosive gases were present before or after the blast that tore apart mine shafts Number 1 and Number 4, which connected at the Scofield, Utah, coal works, careless storage of blasting powder was enough to assure the deaths of 200 miners on the morning of May 1, 1900. The explosion occurred first in the Number 4 shaft, and moments later more explosions took place in Number 1.

About thirty kegs of black blasting powder had been carelessly stored in the Number 4 shaft, and whether by windy or blown-out shot (it was never determined which) these were ignited at 10:25 A.M., setting off a series of explosions so violent that men were hurled from the entranceways of both shafts. The dust in Number 1 was damp, but 60 miners in this shaft were still smothered to death by the afterdamp. The 140 other fatalities occurred in the more seriously damaged Number 4. Almost all of these men were blown to pieces by the explosion.

SCORPION — MARINE DISASTER
May 21, 1968

background: The 3,075-ton United States submarine *Scorpion,* launched in 1960 as an attack sub of the Skipjack class, sank and disappeared off the Azores on May 21, 1968, with her complete crew of ninety-nine officers and men. In November, 1968, the sub was located by the search ship *Mizar* by dragging cameras along the ocean floor. The cause of the sinking of the 252-foot-long vessel was listed as faulty pipe joints.

Like the *Squalus* and *Thresher* before her, the United States submarine *Scorpion* and her entire crew of ninety-nine men met death at the bottom of the ocean floor. The sub cracked like an egg shell hit with a sledge hammer under the impossible pressure at the bottom of the ocean. En route to her berth in Norfolk, Virginia, the *Scorpion* left the Mediterranean waters and was last heard from on May 21, 1968, when she sent the terse message: "Posit 35:07 north; 41:42 west; speed 18 knots; course 290." At that moment the ship was running beneath the water and taking it easy. The sub had a 35-knot capability beneath the waves and could submerge safely to a depth of 1,000 feet.

Ten thousand feet beneath the surface of the Atlantic Ocean, an underwater camera records the resting place of the U.S. submarine *Scorpion* in which ninety-nine crew members were entombed. *(Wide World)*

The Annapolis-trained captain, thirty-six-year-old Commander Francis A. Slattery, did not signal any problems with the ship or underwater navigation, but these both were possible problems that apparently became more real days after the vessel disappeared. When the *Scorpion* failed to appear at her Norfolk berth on the appointed hour on May 27, 1968, the Navy immediately launched a massive search. At the peak of the quest, fifty-five major vessels and twenty-seven aircraft were employed to scan the ocean, particularly in and about the Azores.

Several false sightings of debris and a yellow buoy marker (the sub, like all others in the United States Navy, was equipped with two radio buoys that could be sent to the surface to send out the ominous message, "SOS—sub sunk," for six hours) only served to further frustrate rescue efforts. Days, then weeks elapsed, and still nothing was found of the *Scorpion.* Yet, the navy refused to ring the death knell for the ship and merely posted her as "missing." If she had not sunk below the 2,000-foot level where her hull would be crushed by pressure at the bottom of the ocean, officials were careful to point out, the nuclear-powered sub could survive, and the men inside the *Scorpion* were equipped with enough provisions and oxygen to stay alive for a maximum of seventy days.

Sudden discovery of a 250-foot-long steel hulk lying in 180 feet of water off Cape Henry, Virginia, raised hopes, but a probe indicated that this submarine was a relic of World War II (which had sunk with all of her hands on board). Another startling interlude in the search was a radio message reading: "Any station this network. . . . This is Brandywine . . ." Brandywine was the secret code name for the *Scorpion.* But the discovery that six or seven other ships bore this name, operating in the same area where the sub disappeared and signaling on bands used by the navy, caused authorities to discount the message (one even labeled it a "cruel hoax").

The navy finally gave up the search, and the $40 million ship and her ninety-nine crew members were written off. The cause of the ship's sinking, however, was debated hotly for months. Some stated that the *Scorpion* had smashed into a seamount—the top of an underwater mountain, many of which populate the vast, uncharted deeps of the Atlantic. One-time submariner, retired Captain Charlie N. G. Hendrix, then a professor of oceanography at the Naval Academy, felt that such a collision might have accounted for the ship's fate. (Hendrix, ironically, had authored a book entitled *The Depths of Ignorance,* which was published shortly after the sub's disappearance.)

Hendrix pointed out that the great depths to which the Atlantic trenches plunged were inestimable, and he likened a subsurface voyage to that of "a pilot flying over the Rocky Mountains without knowing how high the highest peaks are, where they are or even if they exist. The great-circle track in the vicinity of the Azores has never been systematically surveyed in detail."

Even if the vessel hit a seamount less than 2,000 feet below the surface, her maximum depth, there was little the navy could have done to save the crew below 1,300 feet. Its equipment at that time, such as the McCann Chamber, was hopelessly inadequate for such rescue operations. The navy's chief of the Deep Submergence Systems, Captain W. M. Nicholson, sounded the swan song for the *Scorpion* when he told reporters: "We all recognize that if a submarine is lost in deep water, there is nothing that can be done about it."

One of the ship's crew men, who was sick and had been left ashore in Spain, later insisted that the submarine had been leaking hydraulic fluid around her periscope section and that the ship was, indeed, having navigation problems. Another report came in that the *Scorpion* had a serious oil leak near her propeller shaft.

Scientific instruments finally settled the riddle. Experts of the navy's Antisubmarine Warfare Division (ASW) consulted the secret and elaborate underwater listening devices on the ocean floor known as the SOSUS system. They discovered a jagged line of ink on a tape made by the system on May 21, 1968. It registered a heavy underwater implosion at about 2,000 feet, 400 miles southwest of the island of Sao Miguel in the Azores and almost exactly where the *Scorpion* should have gone down.

Next the scientifically equipped search ship *Mizar* was sent to the area to methodically scan the ocean floor by dragging 35mm cameras. At almost 10,000 feet, in the murky depths of the Atlantic, the cameras photographed several huge steel fragments, which were immediately identified as the remains of the crushed *Scorpion.* Study of the fragments revealed that the sub sank due to faulty pipe joints and an inadequate deballasting system.

The sinking of the *Scorpion* further hastened the completion of the navy's $300 million program in developing special mother subs of reinforced steel. When completed, they would be capable of descending deeper than all other rescue devices; they could also rescue twenty-four more people at one time than previous ships had handled.

(ALSO SEE: Squalus, Thresher*)*

SEABIRD — MARINE DISASTER — April 9, 1868

A Great Lakes sidewheeler, the *Seabird,* a 638-ton passenger steamer, was gutted to the water line by fire on April 9, 1868, while en route to Chicago from Milwaukee. The disaster, which took between 68 and 103 lives (passenger manifests were lost), was caused by a steward ignorant of basic sailing rules; he dumped hot ashes from stoves used to heat the salon and staterooms to the windward side of the ship.

Moments after the steward threw the ashes overboard, they flew back into open holds and ignited straw packing around new bathtubs, which had been thickly coated with varnish. The tubs burst into flames, and only two crew members attempted to put out the fire. Almost all the passengers were asleep in their bunks when the fire started, and they were not warned in time to save their lives.

The ship's captain, John Morris, lashed the *Seabird*'s wheel and joined others in attempting to arouse the sleeping passengers. As the ship steamed around in a

This lithograph depicts the burning sidewheeler *Seabird* moments before it took seventy-two passengers to the bottom of Lake Michigan.

large circle, about twenty passengers jumped overboard. Most sank immediately, and a few floundered about in the night waters for some time before drowning. One man, James H. Leonard, who was in excellent physical condition, swam more than fifteen miles to the shore at Evanston, Illinois.

Two more men, C. A. Chamberlain and Edwin Hanneberry, were rescued by the schooner *Cordelia,* which came alongside the sinking *Seabird* and waited until she had burned to the water line and all passengers were presumed dead before heading for shore.

SEISTAN — MARINE DISASTER

February 19, 1958

The 7,400-ton cargo motorship *Seistan,* owned by the Strick Line, caught fire in the Persian Gulf on February 17, 1958. Captain W. A. Chappell, knowing that the explosives, fuses and detonators in his ship's holds might ignite any moment, had the lifeboats swung out and steamed rapidly for port, attempting to suffocate the flames with steam in the holds that did not contain explosives.

Reaching Bahrein, the *Seistan* docked, and most of the explosives were removed. The fire was kept under control for two days and was thought to be almost out. Flames were confined to holds that carried less flammable cargo, but it was discovered too late that among these shipments were several cases of toe puff, then not known to be explosive. This material was used to form toecaps in shoes and boots and contained cotton or wool mixed with solvent, dye, rosin and cellulose nitrate.

At about 9:00 P.M. on February 19, 1958, flames reached these cases, and a terrific explosion occurred. The blast snapped the *Seistan* in half and killed fifty-seven seamen, most of whom were Indian workers. Captain Chappell died with his ship.

(ALSO SEE: Bone, Algeria; Port Chicago, California)

SENECA, MICHIGAN — RAILWAY WRECK

November 27, 1901

When two passenger trains on the Wabash Line were late on the night of November 27, 1901, a dispatcher's order redirected the engineers of both trains to meet in Seneca, Michigan, instead of the usual stop at Sand Creek. Though the conductor of Number 3 read the order to his engineer and had the engineer read it back to him, this train failed to stop and instead raced on to Sand Creek.

A few miles east of Seneca, Number 3 met Number 13 as both trains rounded a sharp curve on a single track. A terrible head-on collision resulted. Killed were twenty passengers, most of whom were immigrants. The engineer of Number 3 was held responsible for the accident.

SHENANDOAH — AIR CRASH

September 3, 1925

background: The *ZR-1* dirigible known as the *Shenandoah* made her first one-hour flight on September 4, 1923, under the command of Commander F. R. McCrary. The $2 million airship, patterned after the German *L-49,* was constructed in 1919. Her 680-foot hull was made of Duralumin, an aluminum alloy; her tanks were filled with helium, making her the first dirigible to use this gas. Leaving her hangar at Lakehurst, New Jersey, on October 7, 1924, the *Shenandoah* crossed the country, completing a 9,317-mile journey in nineteen days. The much-criticized flight of September 2-3, 1925, commanded by Lieutenant-Commander Zachary Lansdowne, ended in disaster when the ship was caught in a violent updraft. She broke in two over Ava, Ohio. Fourteen members of her crew were killed. Twenty-eight survived.

"Daughter of the stars" was the Indian meaning of the name *Shenandoah* which was painted on the gleaming hull of the first great United States dirigible. This helium-filled child of early American aeronautics would, like the *Akron* after her, fall from the grace of the skies into a death plunge on September 3, 1925, an air crash later shrouded in volatile criticism, anger and embitterment. The $2 million craft (her hangar cost again as much) was first constructed in 1919, and her short life was flecked with harrowing near disasters.

Weather alone had made the *Shenandoah* and her sisters pariahs of the air. In the words of pioneer aviator Laurence La Tourette Driggs: "When the heavy winds blew, she could neither leave nor enter her hangar. When ordinary storms broke about her, she was in peril. When no mooring mast was handy, she required 500 men to catch her and hold her to earth. When rain drops clung to her envelope, she feared to attempt landing under their weight until they evaporated. When every condition was favorable, she sailed through the skies majestically—*but to what purpose?"*

The purpose, it seemed, was to convince the public that the shaky experiments of the Zeppelin engineers had value, and that the giants of the sky could provide some safe mode of transportation on a mass level, and also gather important scientific information on weather conditions. Concern for safety caused the engineers to fill the *Shenandoah* with helium, a less flammable gas than the conventional hydrogen, but this slowed the dirigible's maneuverability in flight, and especially hindered her ability to climb out of deadly storms.

The first scare came on January 16, 1924. Berthed at a newly designed mooring mast at Lakehurst, New Jersey, the ship was suddenly engulfed in a massive weather front with winter winds of 65 m.p.h. ripping at her. The

Shenandoah suddenly broke loose, and the rigid airship began to perilously drift toward a row of pine trees, their tops slicing the ship's hull like lances. The skeleton crew was trapped on board. Led by Lieutenant Commander M. R. Pierce and Captain Anton Heinen, a German constructor and pilot of dirigibles, the crew managed to save the craft. Though the two forward gas bags had been ripped apart as the ship tore from her mooring mast, Heinen and Pierce dove for the controls and managed to steady the ship. Fuel and ballast loads were quickly redistributed, and the dirigible's engines were started only seconds before reaching the trees. She pulled upward and the crew kept her aloft until dawn, when they managed to steer the *Shenandoah* back to her berth.

A long-distance flight was scheduled later that year. This exploit, a voyage of 9,317 miles back and forth across the United States, was designed by the navy to demonstrate the durability of its prize airship. Lieutenant Commander Zachary Lansdowne, considered the most experienced dirigible pilot the United States had to offer, captained the flight. Born on December 1, 1888, Lansdowne had graduated from the United States Naval Academy in 1909. He began a stellar aviation career in 1916 at the Pensacola Air Station and received instruction in dirigibles in England during World War I. Lansdowne was aboard the British rigid ship *R-34* when she made her historic Atlantic crossing on July 2, 1919. It was Lansdowne who had piloted all of the *Shenandoah*'s memorable flights, and he was therefore the logical person to captain the ship on her transcontinental journey from Lakehurst to Los Angeles and back in a record nineteen days and nineteen hours. (The proudest moment in the life of Mrs. Elizabeth Lansdowne was seeing her son fly over the family home in Greenville, Ohio, on his way to California in the lofty leviathan.)

There had been minor mishaps on this trip, but the weather had been favorable throughout the journey. The *Shenandoah* sliced through southerly winds as she sailed the southwestern routes. The scheduled flight that would take the ship across the Midwest in the following year was another matter. The weather was known to be poor, and Lansdowne more than once had remarked to his wife that he was being "forced" to make the trip by naval authorities "for political purposes."

Shortly after the *Shenandoah*'s tragic end, one of Lansdowne's fellow officers bitterly remarked, "There's a string of country fairs through the Middle West right now, and all the politicians have been pulling wires to have the *Shenandoah* fly over their home towns as part of the circus."

Despite his misgivings, Commander Lansdowne ordered the ship away from her Lakehurst mooring on September 2, 1925, and the dirigible proceeded steadily west toward death. It was 4:00 A.M. the next day when fierce headwinds began to buffet the *Shenandoah*. Though all five of the ship's engines were running, the craft made little headway. Lansdowne ordered the engines opened up to full capacity and directed the ship's bow to be nosed downward at eighteen degrees. Her rudder hard over and elevators hard down failed to stop the ship from shooting from 2,000 to almost 7,000 feet. In her rapid ascent the craft began to shred to pieces. When desperate officers and crew finally managed to check the upward surge, the ship, then much too heavy for the altitude, plunged earthward.

Lansdowne shouted heroically to his crew: "Let every man stick to his post regardless!" (These words, the last to be heard from the skipper's lips during the raging storm, were likened by one much moved editorialist to those of American patriots: "They were brave words, great words, fit to rank with Lawrence's 'Don't Give Up the Ship.' ") The commander ordered the jettisoning of tons of water ballast, but the giant aircraft, moving at an estimated 1,400 feet per minute, was diving too fast. Two engines stopped—they were useless. Heavy equipment, fuel tanks, anything that could be stripped from the dirigible and dumped was thrown overboard.

Lieutenant Commander Charles E. Rosendahl was in charge of the operation. Oddly, this forlorn gentleman, when he climbed white-lipped into the ship's control cabin before the flight, had loudly stated, "I hope I get killed!" Rosendahl's fiancée, it was learned later, had died in an auto accident near Princeton, New Jersey, and her death had left him depressed. He vowed to a friend at the girl's funeral that he would "join the most dangerous branch of the air service. . . . I don't care what becomes of me."

Now this executive officer calmly scrambled into the keel of the ship. Using a hand valve, he released great quantities of helium. Six other men worked frantically alongside of him. "At this moment there was a crash," he remembered later, having survived against his wish. "I heard the struts breaking and saw the nose of the ship parting from the control compartment. A second later I heard another crash, which must have been the control compartment hitting the ground. It was in this compartment that Commander Lansdowne and the [ten] others were killed."

The ship broke in two. The nose, with Rosendahl and the other six men hanging precariously from its struts, sailed off at a speed of 25 m.p.h. It shot upward to almost 10,000 feet, but Rosendahl and his men managed to release more helium and the 200-foot-long bow section gradually drifted to earth. "We handled the nose as if it were a free balloon and landed safely at Sharon [Ohio]. . . ."

Looking like a beached whale, the after section of the dirigible *Shenandoah* rests in a meadow near Ava, Ohio. Hundreds of curious spectators inspect the ruined airship. *(Wide World)*

This was about twelve miles from where Lansdowne and the others fell to their deaths, within sight of the skipper's birthplace. Chief Machinist's Mate Shine S. Halliburton, who rode the nose portion down with Rosendahl, recalled that he "was just reaching for pliers to cut the stay-wires on the [fuel] tanks and let them drop out of the ship when she parted. Then she began to drop. When I got to the ground, I borrowed a shotgun from a farmer and shot holes in the helium bags to let it out so the hulk wouldn't drift around in the wind."

Ernest Nichols, a farmer, watched as the nose portion of the *Shenandoah* drifted downward on his land. A neighbor had telephoned to tell him that an airship had broken up, and that it appeared to be headed for Nichols's house. The farmer ran outside. Later he recalled, ". . .and here it came right through our orchard, headed straight for the house. I looked up, and there was my oldest boy—I have six boys and one girl—sticking his head out the upstairs window. I knew I had to stop that thing or the house would be smashed and my kids would be killed."

From the shunting bow section, Nichols could hear Rosendahl and the others yelling, "Grab hold! Grab hold! Turn her south!" Nichols jumped up and grabbed a cable dangling from the hulk and quickly wrapped it around a fence post. The post snapped away. Nichols again clutched the cable and looped it around the large stump of a maple tree. "The stump had two prongs on it, and I thought sure it would hold, but it didn't. By that time the nose was so close to the ground, the underside had me backed up against a fence, and I had to run." Scooting violently just above the ground, the hulk tore off the top of a grape arbor, ripped away a roof from a shed, splintered the wheel on a well. Doggedly Nichols held on to the cable and managed to wrap it around a sturdy tree. "All that time I didn't know what the thing was. I didn't know it was so big. . . . Why, it's over 190 feet long. . . . Soon my kids came running out and we helped to tie it up. Then the men began climbing out. Even then it didn't stay where it was, for we had to tie it again several times during the day, and the men borrowed my shotgun and punctured the gasbags."

The after-section of the *Shenandoah* had also floated free like a balloon with twenty-five men still clinging to it. One of these was crew man Ralph Joneson, on duty in Engine Car 3. When the ship broke in half, this sailor told himself, "'Well, Jones, you might as well sit here and let it happen; you can't do any good by moving away.' So I sat tight by the engine and closed my eyes. First thing you know, I was walking around on the ground. Then she blew away again, and there I was alone in the field."

His incredible escape was repeated over and over by others. Crew member Frederic J. Tobin had just awakened and rolled out of his wildly swinging hammock as the storm ripped away at the dirigible. He started for the control car and was only a few feet from it when it disappeared downward into space. "The first thing I knew," he later excitedly blurted to reporters, "was that where I started to step for the control car was space, 7,000 feet of it. I crawled back to the catwalk, aft of the break. Soon the silver cover was ripped off, and I stood there, thousands of feet in the air holding on to a slim brace. I thought I might as well look down. I did, and I've never seen trees rush so in my life. They seemed to be rushing straight for me. When I could see the green of them, I got ready to jump, but the section I was in bumped once and rose again to drift another half a mile. When I did get out, I saw nothing but twisted steel."

The last man to leave the control car was Lieutenant J. B. Anderson. His survival was, perhaps, the most incredible of all. Anderson's casual step was so close to death that, in one second, the car practically dropped from beneath his feet. "Commander Lansdowne told me to release 800 gallons of gas," he said later, "to lighten her, and that was when I started for the ladder. After I reached the catwalk, she dropped dizzily to 2,500 feet, groaned in every girder and fell apart."

Anderson felt himself falling; he dove for a strut and held on, dangling in space. Lieutenant R. C. Mayer, who was in the bow section with Rosendahl, saw Anderson about to fall and grabbed a rope and, although never schooled in the ways of the cowboy, he threw the rope "with the accuracy of a plainsman" and lassoed Anderson just as he began to fall. Anderson shot downward and was then jerked upward by the rope held by several men who hauled him to safety.

Another officer, Lieutenant W. L. Richardson, on board to make a photographic record of the flight, rode the aft section to earth. He enacted an overhand trapeze movement to save his life. Richardson left nothing out of his dramatic story: "I got out of bed at about 4:00 A.M. yesterday and went for a drink of water. I intended to go forward to the control-car, which was in the front end of the ship, to see if weather conditions would be right for making pictures. After getting a drink, however, I looked at my watch and saw it was too early, so I decided to go back to bed.

"This decision undoubtedly saved my life. Instead of entering the control car, I returned to my berth. The control car dropped clear of the ship and dropped through space like a comet, killing all who were in her.

"After I returned to my berth, the pitching of the ship became more violent, and it started nosing down. Suddenly a cool gust of wind came down from the keel of the ship, probably caused by its sudden rise from 3,000 to 7,000 feet. What is called a twister line squall caused the sudden rise. It also caused a drop back to the 2,500-foot altitude a few seconds later.

"Then the ship started straight up again and broke in two. One section, the forward part, carrying the control car, shot straight up. The other section, on which we were, dropped rapidly downward. It seemed to flutter down like a falling leaf. First the point end, then the rear end, would be on top. A part of our section was torn away before we finally landed. I managed to save myself from sliding off into space by grabbing wires and girders near my berth. Then as soon as possible I started to the after part of the section.

"I got hold of a gasoline tank, but it broke loose from its moorings, and I caught some girders again. Through an open hatch I could see trees speeding under us a few feet away. Then I saw the ground. I started down a folding ladder that had been used by an after engine car, which had been carried away [and in it three men who were killed, bringing the total dead in the disaster to fourteen]. Both of my hands were caught in an angle, and I broke them loose, tearing my fingers slightly.

"Then I dropped to the ground and a wire caught around my leg, dragging me down hill under the end of the ship. I finally got loose and ran up the hill out of the way of the rolling bag."

Cook John J. Hahn had no time for such maneuvering; he hardly noticed what happened. The *New York Herald Tribune* later quoted him as saying: "I was in frame 105 getting breakfast for the boys. I was turning down the flame under the boiling coffee, when oil-cans began to rain about my head. I thought: 'This won't do,' and turned and saw Allenly hanging on the frame supports. Then I felt a long sickening drop. Allenly fell off. Then I stepped out on the ground, got a car from a fellow and went to a town, where I sent the telegram."

Hahn's direct telegram to naval authorities was the first word of the disaster, and the *Shenandoah*'s end was soon flashed across the country, provoking a storm of angry statements. Zeppelin captain Anton Heinen, pointing out that certain automatic valves had been removed from the airship, went so far as to label the disaster "murder." A fiery prophet of flight, Colonel Billy Mitchell, charged that the *Shenandoah*'s last and fatal voyage was nothing but a propaganda trip. Mrs. Lansdowne was quoted as saying "that her husband was compelled to make the flight." "He had to go because the

Secretary of the Navy wanted to play politics by sending the ship over the Middle-Western cities. . . . My husband was very much opposed to making the flight at this time because of the weather conditions he knew so well. He asked officials at Washington to delay the flight until a better season."

A court of inquiry ignored the vitriolic criticism and concluded that the *Shenandoah* had broken apart and crashed because of "large, unbalanced, external, aerodynamic forces arising from high velocity air currents." A telling probe of the accident was hampered by souvenir hounds, who swarmed over the remains of the once-great dirigible, picking her clean of dead men's effects, as well as parts of her wrecked structure. This material was never made available for examination. The Ohio American Legion finally sent out armed detachments to guard the remains of the ship. Souvenir hunters became so bold at one point that the legionnaires had to fire at them to drive them off. Lamented the *Chicago Evening Post:* "The sole complaint that we lodge against the legionnaires is that they did not shoot straight."

(ALSO SEE: Akron, Dixmude, Hindenberg)

SHIGATSE, TIBET — FLOOD
August 10, 1954

Shigatse (population 20,000), the second largest city in the Chinese province of Tibet, played host to a monastic trade center in early August, 1954. Previous months of torrential rains had swollen the Nyang Chu River to overflowing and on August 10 hundreds of tons of water bloated Lake Takri Tsoma to the point of bursting. Barriers around the lake gave way, and foaming cataracts of water burst down upon Shigatse (elevation: 12,800 feet), cascading into the Palace of the Western Paradise. Here the revered sixteen-year-old Panchen Lama, religious leader of three million Tibetans who considered him the reincarnation of the Buddha of Boundless Light, resided.

The avalanche of water crushed the walls of the palace and leveled it in most areas, instantly drowning scores of Buddhist monks in prayer. A nearby barracks housing the Lama's Communist household troops collapsed, killing all of them. Though the Lama escaped injury, between 500 and 1,000 persons lost their lives in the flash flood.

SHINNSTON, WEST VIRGINIA (and PENNSYLVANIA) — TORNADOES
June 23, 1944

After a serious hot spell, violent storms broke over West Virginia and Pennsylvania on the evening of June 23, 1944. A flurry of tornadoes touched down erratically at Boothsville, Joetown, Oakdale, Flemington, Meadville, Pleasant Hill, Montrose and Thomas in West Virginia, and many towns and cities along the Monongahela valley in Pennsylvania were hit, including Pittsburgh and Chartiers, the latter extremely hard hit.

The area around Shinnston and Pleasant Hill, West Virginia, was utterly devastated by a monstrous twister moving across the land and plowing up a 300-yard path that appeared, according to one account, as if "an army of bulldozers had streaked through the valley," smashing trees, fences and houses. In Pleasant Hill the tornado touched down at 8:51 P.M. It was a long funnel cloud which witnesses described as "white to greasy green in color." The twister trailed a long cloud of smoke and roared like an express train. Fifteen of the twenty-five houses in the town were completely leveled. Their occupants died instantly.

Near Shinnston, which was devastated, stood a high radio tower operated by the West Virginia State Police. Next to the tower squatted a one-story concrete building from which State Trooper G. F. Randall watched the tornado. "As it got closer," he said later, "I could see it was filled with wood, trees and outhouses. It seemed to be coming directly toward me. I was so damned interested I never moved." The tornado hit the tower head-on and bent the pyramid of steel to an inverted V-shape. Randall, inside the concrete blockhouse, survived without injuries, which made him a rare human in that area visited by the twister. Scores were injured at Boothsville as a tornado literally picked up a $250,000 pumping station *en masse* and slammed it into a hillside. There were fifty-eight dead in the Shinnston disaster, making it the worst in West Virginia's history.

Pennsylvania was badly mauled by other tornadoes. The worst touched down at Chartiers. A soldier from Chartiers, Private John Barnish, had arrived home on special leave to bury his father, who had died a week before. After the twister swirled away from his town, his mother and twelve-year-old sister also were dead.

A total of 151 persons perished in both states—103 in West Virginia. A total estimate of damage ranged upward to $2 million.

SHOEMAKERSVILLE, PENNSYLVANIA — RAILWAY WRECK
September 19, 1890

A 150-car coal train was southbound on the Reading Line on September 19, 1890, when part of the train separated, and both sections came to a jerky stop. The freight was just outside Shoemakersville, Pennsylvania, and the train crew worked quickly to couple the cars and proceed. During the ten-minute delay the flagman failed to place flares in front of or behind the train, and another coal train came up speedily from behind and slammed into the first freight, creating minor damage.

This accident further delayed the large freight from taking to a siding on the single track so northbound traffic could pass through. A speeding passenger train en route to Pottsville from Philadelphia rounded a curve and then hit the large freight head-on. Five of its cars and the engine caromed off the track and spilled crazily into the Schuykill River. Twenty-three passengers were killed; many were trapped as the cars slid beneath the river waters.

SHOHOLA, PENNSYLVANIA — RAILWAY WRECK

July 15, 1864

A Union troop train, carrying hundreds of Confederate prisoners in eighteen cars, met a fifty-car coal train on a wicked reverse curve outside Shohola, Pennsylvania. One of the most disastrous head-on collisions in history resulted. The prisoner train was scheduled to leave Jersey City at 4:30 A.M. on July 15, 1864, destined for the prison camp at Elmira, New York. This Erie train was delayed, however, because three Confederate prisoners hid themselves on the boat that had transported them to Jersey City. They had to be found while the train was held. The troop train did not depart from Jersey City until 6:00 P.M.

By that time the control operator at Lackawaxen Station telegraphed ahead to the enormous coal train that the tracks were clear and it should proceed on the single track. The coal train did, but outside Shohola, it rounded a curve at considerable speed and smacked head-on into the prisoner train. Both engines were derailed, and several cars of the prisoner train telescoped into one another. Seventy-four persons—fifty-one prisoners, nineteen guards and four engine crew members—were killed in the collision.

SIERRA PACIFIC AIRLINES — AIR CRASH

March 13, 1974

A twin-engine Convair, chartered from Sierra Pacific Airlines, crashed on March 13, 1974, only minutes after takeoff from the airport at Bishop, California. Its destination was Burbank. All of the thirty-six persons on board were killed, including thirty-one members of the "Primal Man" television series, one of which was Janos Prohaska. He had played a comic bear on the Andy Williams show. The film crew had been working in the Mammoth Lakes area to complete the third show in the "Primal Man" series.

Taking off at 8:24 P.M., the plane suddenly lost altitude and slammed into a 7,000-foot ridge in the Forest Service land some seven miles away from Bishop. An Inyo County deputy sheriff saw it explode "into a ball of flame."

A helicopter pilot, Mike Antonio, who flew aeronautic experts to the crash site to investigate, described how "the plane smacked hard into the ridge and spread wreckage for 300 feet. . . . There wasn't much left to the plane, only the tail section, part of an engine and not much else. All of it was burning."

SILVER CREEK, NEW YORK — RAILWAY WRECK

September 14, 1886

Confusion of orders led to the destruction of a Nickel Plate Road train on September 14, 1886, outside Silver Creek, New York. The fourteen-car train, crowded with members of the Methodist Church of Erie, Pennsylvania, on a special excursion, was instructed to meet Number 29, a westbound freight, at Silver Creek. It was given priority to go through while the freight train waited on the siding.

Number 29, however, did not take to the siding. Instead, it came upon another freight, Number 41, which was disabled, and pushed it into the yard at Silver Creek, remaining on the main track. Contrary to orders from a dispatcher, it then continued down the main track. The excursion train met the freight head-on as both rounded a wide curve, and the smoker of the passenger train was telescoped by the baggage car. Twenty men were killed (ladies were not then, fortunately for those on the excursion, allowed in the smokers). The conductor and engineer of the excursion train were indicted for manslaughter and thrown into jail. The engineer, a man named Brewer, went crazy.

SIRIO — MARINE DISASTER

August 4, 1906

Built in 1883, the 2,401-ton Italian liner *Sirio,* sailing from Genoa to Montevideo and Buenos Aires and carrying about 690 passengers and crew members, attempted to navigate the straits of the Hormigas Islands off Cape Palos along the Spanish coast. However, she was smashed against the treacherous rocks there on August 4, 1906. Panic ensued, and many passengers fought among themselves and with crew members for places in the few undamaged lifeboats. Several people were murdered with knives and pistols as those on board the fast-settling *Sirio* tried to save themselves, and 422 persons were drowned when the ship flopped minutes later to her starboard side and sank stern first.

SKAPTAR JOKUL — VOLCANIC ERUPTION

June 11-August 3, 1783

background: Preceded by seismic eruptions of the sea around Iceland for several weeks, the volcano Skaptar Jokul erupted on June 11, 1783. It continued to emit tremendous volumes of lava (perhaps the greatest volumes on record—an estimated twenty cubic miles) until August 3, 1783. Twenty villages were destroyed, and 9,000 persons were killed out of a population of 50,000.

The eruption of Skaptar Jokul on Iceland from June 11 to August 3, 1783, has been considered one of the most prodigious ever in the annals of volcanic explosions. For several weeks prior to the volcano's awakening, the seas around Iceland were greatly disturbed by seismic upheavals, huge geysers, wide whirlpools and towering water spouts shooting skyward and drawing the water away and then toward the island's shores. Iceland's 50,000 inhabitants, mostly rural, grew so fear-ridden that they refused to leave their homes. Their apprehensions burst into reality on June 11, 1783, when Skaptar Jokul vomited forth streams of burning lava.

These enormous flows gushed from a fifteen-mile-long fissure, welled up and dove into the broad River Skapta. They dried up the river in hours, displacing the water in a rocky gorge from 400 to 600 feet deep with lava that spread 200 feet wide and moved seaward. Ashes were so thick in ensuing eruptions that grasslands for fifty miles around were poisoned, and vast herds of cattle and sheep suffocated. One report states: "The hills were dotted with the decaying carcasses. The air was filled with horrible stench. The ashes fell in such volumes into the ocean that the fish deserted the coast. The flying clouds of dust spread to Europe. The appalling horror of the scene can hardly be imagined. Death stalked abroad in his most repulsive form."

Village after village—twenty in all—was engulfed by the quickly moving lava streams, and whole populations were cut off from escape and either drowned in the sea, roasted to death by lava or asphyxiated by noxious vapors. More than 9,000 persons died during the almost two-month eruption of Skaptar Jokul. Hundreds of these perished when basic sources of food disappeared. Crops were utterly wiped out, and fish, on which the residents depended, entirely deserted the coastal areas of Iceland.

The enormity of the lava flows from this eruption is hard to conceive, even by standards of more modern upheavals. Two streams of running lava, forty and fifty miles long respectively, reached widths of fifteen and seven miles and an average depth of one hundred feet.

According to one scientific estimate, "These two principal streams were, then, sufficient to cover 1,000 square miles to a depth of 150 feet." In contrast to Skaptar Jokul's titanic eruption, the greatest of Vesuvian eruptions (twenty million cubic meters) covered a square mile to a depth of 25 feet. Vesuvius then produced only .006 as much lava as that thrown off by Skaptar Jokul.

Professor Bischoff, an early vulcanologist, called this eruption, in quantity, "the greatest eruption of the world—the lava, piled, having been estimated as of greater volume than is Mont Blanc."

(ALSO SEE: Krakatoa, Tomboro)

SOCIETY ISLANDS — TSUNAMI
January 13, 1903

After days of fierce pounding by hurricanes, the Society Islands were visited on January 13, 1903, by what can best be described as a wave of the *tsunami* classification. The tiny group of South Pacific islands was struck by many abnormally large waves that day and, toward evening, a monstrous wave, estimated to be at least forty feet high, swept over every island. It almost obliterated them and killed 1,000 persons; hundreds more were listed as missing.

SOUFRIERE — VOLCANIC ERUPTIONS
1718-1902

background: Also known as Morne Garou, the volcano Soufriere (sulfur pit), on the island of St. Vincent, had been in eruption long before Columbus discovered the island in 1498, when he subdued the Carib Indians (for whom the Caribbean Sea is named). Its first recorded upheaval was in 1718, when hundreds were killed as enormous lava flows engulfed them. The volcano burst open in 1785 and on April 27, 1812, when 1,000 or more residents were killed. Soufriere's most titanic outburst was, almost in unison with that of Pelée on Martinique, on May 6-7, 1902, when 3,000 persons, mostly Carib Indians, were killed.

In 1498 when Columbus stumbled ashore at St. Vincent, he was met by a wide-eyed tribe of people known as the Caribs. The explorer promptly named the Caribbean Sea after this tiny Indian nation. It took him only a few hours to discover that the Caribs were ruled by fear and superstition as they shakily pointed to the towering Soufriere volcano belching clouds of sulfuric smoke. The mountain then towered thousands of feet above a 4,000-foot range of dense woods and rocks made up of previous flows of lava. Columbus learned from the gesturing natives that they considered themselves doomed, and that all of them, down to the last babe, would eventually be sacrificed to the fire god they worshipped daily. The prophecy amused the discoverer, but it was fulfilled with a vengeance over the next 400 years.

A member of the Windward Islands of the West Indies, St. Vincent was 17 miles long and approximately 10 miles wide; it had an area of 132 square miles, and the rich loam of its valleys was more than conducive to the raising of arrowroot, coffee, indigo, maize and sugar, and yet it was

177 years after Columbus's visit before the island was settled. (No doubt, Columbus preferred to forget the ominous volcano, sailing away to less lethal lands.) In 1675 African slaves en route to America were shipwrecked off the island. They established the towns of Kingston, Georgetown and Richmond.

St. Vincent then became the object of a four-power struggle between Spain (to which the island had been granted by decree of the Pope), France, England and Holland. The early sixteenth century saw the island as the hub of the Spanish Main around which swirled "the scene of many a battle and of the exploits of Drake and Hawkins." France ceded the island to England in 1763, but the pirate-enmeshed Carib Indians rebelled against their British masters (they were particularly agitated when the British prohibited their worship of Soufriere), and with French aid they almost succeeded in overthrowing the government. The Caribs were subdued in 1785 after committing barbaric attacks on English settlements, at which time they vivisected and cannibalized their victims. Their chief, Black Bulia, was captured by British troops and his followers were compelled to watch as he was gibbeted alive in chains. The British further retaliated by transferring part of the tribe to the island of Rattan in the Bay of Honduras. The remaining Indians were compelled to live in the shadow of Soufriere, at the very base of the volcano, thus insuring their fiery deaths in years to come.

The first significant blast came in 1718 before the Caribs were partitioned; about 200 natives at Wallibu, trapped in a spider web of speeding lava streams, died miserably. A less fatal eruption was recorded in 1785 when scores of Indians perished. In 1812 the natives on St. Vincent, chiefly the Caribs, felt the full fury of Soufriere

Gıeat convulsions gripped all the continental southern coastal shores sliding into the Caribbean for two years prior to the 1812 outbreak. On March 26, 1812, the coast of Venezuela shook violently, and 12,000 persons in the city of Caracas were crushed to death as the city fell down upon them. For a month subterranean upheavals shuddered beneath the sea, seeking an outlet along a line of least resistance. That outlet was Soufriere on St. Vincent.

An old legend records that on the morning of April 27, 1812, an Indian boy tending cattle grazing on the slopes of the volcano was pelted by small stones. Thinking that boys concealed behind rocks were throwing the stones, the boy picked up the hot pebbles and hurled them upward at his unseen antagonists. Only when a large shower of burning stones, dust and ashes fell

The lake-filled crater of the giant volcano Soufriere on the island of St. Vincent was depicted by an artist just before its deadly eruption in 1902.

about him did the boy realize that he had been battling the volcano itself and run down the side of the mountain to save his life.

Towering columns of inky smoke slipped upward from Soufriere's crater, the enormous flange of Morne Garou, and one writer states, "A roar, or, rather, a series of explosions and roars, continued through several hours, and were heard in Venezuela and Barbados. [English troops on Barbados, 100 miles distant, thought the noise signaled cannonades of a distant naval battle and prepared themselves to repel invaders.] The imprisoned gases broke through the rocky side of the mountain with inconceivable fury and hurled into the heavens a cloud of shattered rocks, dust, and black volumes of smoke that for three days thereafter covered the island with the darkness of night."

Barbados was attacked all right—by ashes. The constant explosions of Soufriere threw out an enormous amount of sooty ash, which blanketed Barbados to a depth of five inches. The black pall blotted out the day and "turned the brilliant sunlight of the tropics into darkness." Strong trade winds buffeted the volcano's sinister-looking smoke, which had billowed to 16,000 feet, to Barbados and beyond.

On St. Vincent the ash turned to a light gray and in many places accumulated to a depth of several feet. All vegetation was incinerated as the volcano spewed forth its rock and ash for three days. Carib Indians living directly beneath Soufriere in Morne Rond fled to Kingston, abandoning their homes, which were burned to cinders by the showers of blazing stones and subsequent lava flows.

On the third day of the 1812 outburst, Soufriere sent a massive stream of lava over its northwest cliff, and this racing river of molten rock soon engulfed many villages, setting houses afire and killing about 1,000 natives.

Following this eruption the sulfur pit was transformed into a lovely blue lake shored up by 800-foot cliffs, an aesthetic marvel that tourists traveled to see for half a century. Soufriere once again ceased to be beautiful in 1902.

In union with the colossal eruption of Pelée on nearby Martinique, which wiped out the city of St. Pierre and its 36,000 inhabitants in a single blow, Soufriere began to emit gigantic clouds of ash and steam on May 6, 1902. The Caribs on the northwest side of the island, incredibly, made no attempt to flee. "They seemed to be hypnotized," said one writer. On the following day the volcano burst wide through seven new craters, sending forth gushing streams of lava. Terrified Indians attempted to escape, but scores were swallowed up by the flaming liquid. Fearful lightning played about the top of the mountain, shooting downward into the ruptured valleys to strike fleeing natives. Dozens were killed by these flashing bolts.

Rivers of lava split again and again until a half dozen villages and towns were completely surrounded. The streams then rejoined and trapped hundreds of natives, burning them alive. Fresh water streams dried up, everything blazed—huts, trees, the smallest of shrubbery. Offshore the steamship *Wear* of the Royal Mail Service was held fast by blocks of floating ash. The population of St. Lucia watched in horror that night as Soufriere sent up immense, lurid flames into the skies.

By dawn Kingston was surrounded by lava flows, one river of lava halting only 100 yards from the town. Its streets were filled with ashes two inches deep, and flying stones from the crater fifteen miles away continually pelted its hysterical citizens who, for the most part, knelt upon the cobblestones and prayed for deliverance.

Still the lava kept coming, racing forward like bloated springtime brooks. It surrounded the village of Chateau Belaire and reduced it to burning debris, killing all of its dwellers. Wallibu and Richmond were obliterated. No one survived in these hamlets. Many of the island's 2,500 Europeans living in this district mounted fast horses and raced the lava floods to Georgetown and safety. One Englishman later wrote home describing the grim sights he encountered in his flight to Georgetown: "The first place we stopped at was the overseer's house in Langley Park. Thirty-seven bodies were found. They had already been buried, but many dead animals, the working stock, lay scattered about, and the stench was unbearable.

"At every step we encountered fresh scenes and horrors. Here and there a band of men who had been at work from the early morning were dragging corpses to the trench. There was only one way in which their work could be performed. One of the men, having first tied a handkerchief saturated with carbolic acid over his face, would rush into the ruins and slip a noose around an ankle of one of the corpses; then the other men would drag the body by a long rope to the trench, in which it was rapidly covered over with quicklime. In the schoolroom twenty-four bodies had been found, and had been buried in a trench close by. A few oxen, more or less uninjured, were wandering about in search of water. Death was everywhere—death in its worst form. As we went along mounds were pointed out to us which contained fifteen, thirty, or more bodies. In one shop forty persons had taken refuge, and all had perished.

"The following day [May 11], old Soufriere seemed less angry, and the fear-burdened hearts began to hope the end of its fury had come. Still the lava did not cease. All the plantations were seen to be buried beneath volcanic matter. Everywhere were dead bodies, some partially buried, others covered with lava."

More than 5,000 survivors staggered into Georgetown to collapse and half-sank into the ash-covered streets. On May 13 the volcano again gave off tremendous explosions. Wrote a strangely detached Charles Morris in *The Volcano's Deadly Work:* "For this great tragedy the setting was wonderful. Soufriere literally rocked in its agony. From its summit a majestic column of smoke reached skyward. The craters were vomiting incandescent matter that gave forth prismatic lights as it rolled away toward the sea. Great waves of fire seemed to hedge about the mountain top. Such thunder as has seldom been heard by man cracked and rolled through the heavens. From the earth came tremendous detonations. These joined with the thunder, all merged in an incessant roar that added to the panic of fleeing inhabitants. This lasted through the night and the day and night following . . . a huge column so black that it had the appearance of ebony arose to an estimated height of eight miles from the top of the volcano. Ashes and rock, as well as lava, were carried skyward in this column to deluge the island and the ocean for miles around. Gradually the column mushroomed at the top and spread out into dense clouds that descended to bring night at noontime."

It was then that the thick sulfuric fumes from the explosive crater gushed down upon the northwest end of the island, overwhelming hundreds of natives who suffocated to death before they were even touched by burning stones or lava. The district encompassing the villages of the Carib Indians was entirely gutted, coated over with lava. Every one of the Caribs disappeared, and only a few survivors turned up much later.

On May 13 Sir Robert Llewelyn, governor of the Windward Islands, arrived on St. Vincent. His dispatch to the colonial office, following a frightening inspection of conditions, read: "The country on the east coast, between Robin Rock and Georgetown, apparently was struck and devastated in a manner similar to that in which St. Pierre was destroyed, and I fear that practically all living things in that radius were killed." Llewelyn figured at least 1,600 were dead, but the total number reached well over 3,000.

An American businessman, writing to friends in Chicago on May 14, stated: "The burial parties are having the greatest difficulty. In some instances rough coffins are being made to receive the remains of the victims. The hospital is filled with dying people. Fifty injured persons are lying on the floor of that building, as there are no beds for their accommodation, though cots are being rapidly constructed of boards. This and similar work has been in progress since immediately after the disaster. Two days elapsed before there were any burials. . . . Often the bodies found are buried with dust so deeply that they are not found until walked on by the rescue parties. Bodies have been discovered in houses in lifelike attitudes, presenting gruesome spectacles. There are decomposed bodies in many houses, and in order to guard against disease it probably will be necessary for the authorities to burn these dwellings. Owing to the many difficulties in the way of those who have the matter in hand, hundreds of bodies have not yet been interred. . . . The injured persons were horribly burned by the hot grit which was driven along with tremendous velocity. Twenty-six persons who sought refuge in a room ten feet by twelve were all killed. One person was brained by a huge stone thrown nine miles from the crater."

So it went in St. Vincent, as choking rescuers for weeks stumbled through the ruined villages and farmhouses, peering into the remains of buildings to view the dead, dust-covered and silent as they sat with bulging, staring eyes. The ancient Carib prophecy had come to pass. The tribe was no more, and the fire god went on.

(ALSO SEE: Pelée)

SOUTH NORWALK, CONNECTICUT — RAILWAY WRECK, May 6, 1853

background: An express train of the New York and New Haven Line traveling at speeds estimated to be between 30 and 50 m.p.h. failed to stop at a drawbridge then open at 10:30 A.M. on May 6, 1853, though a warning signal was in effect, and its locomotive, tender, two baggage cars, the second containing a smoker, and two passenger cars and a part of a third dove headlong into the Norwalk River at South Norwalk. Killed were forty-six persons, all passengers, with another twenty-five injured. This was the worst railway accident in United States history to that date.

Edward Tucker was a man besieged by misfortune. His career before joining the New York and New Haven Railroad as an engineer was solely that of a handyman, and he obtained his railroad job, some said, by "talking his way into it" without the benefit of experience. Tucker was hired by the railroad in 1849, the year it began operation, and he was involved in the railroad's first major wreck in January, 1851. At that time he was running a train toward New Haven. Against his own judgment he raced through Mamaroneck at the insistence of the conductor, who informed him that a down train scheduled to approach them on the single track would not appear. A few miles further on at Greenwich, the down train roared around a sharp curve and a head-on collision resulted, in which Tucker was horribly injured.

The railroad was extremely generous with Tucker. It gave him a large cash settlement, which he promptly squandered by traveling to California to try his hand in the gold fields. A year later he arrived in New York,

The New York and New Haven express plunged into the Norwalk River on May 6, 1853. Forty-six passengers were killed.

pockets empty and begging for a job from the railroad. The railroad's superintendent, George Washington Whistler, brother of the painter, put Tucker back to work as a relief engineer, which meant he was not really required to pilot any train. Such preferential treatment of Tucker, was, no doubt, prompted by his previous injury, but some reports had it that he was being bribed to keep his mouth shut regarding the reckless orders of the conductor responsible for the Greenwich disaster, a conductor still employed by the railroad.

How Tucker came to be the engineer of the Boston-bound express out of New York on May 6, 1853, remains a nagging mystery to most railroaders to the present. The disaster only two and a half hours ahead of him as he pulled out of the Canal Street station in Manhattan at 8:00 A.M. that day was attributed, according to one writer, to the fact that "he might still have been suffering some after-effects of the first accident at the time of the second." His express consisted of a locomotive, tender, two baggage cars and five passenger coaches.

Thirty doctors who had been attending an AMA convention in New York just barely managed to find seats in the crowded train when it departed, a few of them sitting in the half-smoker that took up part of the second baggage car. It was a bright and clear May morning, and the trip was uneventful until the train reached Norwalk. Tucker had strict instructions to be careful just after going through this station (only locals stopped here). A dispatcher had told him repeatedly: "Watch out for the red ball at the Norwalk bridge."

This bridge, a wooden span with two sixty-foot draws that pivoted on a central pier, had long been a hazard, for it was opened irregularly for the heavy river traffic on the Norwalk River. A red ball two feet in diameter hung from a forty-foot tower next to the bridge to indicate a safe passage for trains across the bridge. At night a light was placed inside the ball. The absence of the red ball on the tower indicated that river traffic was moving through and the draw was open. At such times engineers were required to brake their trains and await the hoisting of the red ball to signal the go-ahead. The required speed when approaching this bridge was 10 m.p.h.

Tucker later told a coroner's jury that severely censured him, "I am [as] familiar with the road as I am with my ABC's." Yet he raced his express through Norwalk, according to most passengers and those on the station platform, at better than 35 m.p.h. (A strong rumor following the accident noted that the conductor of this train, Charles H. Comstock, had instructed Tucker to "go like hell through Norwalk.")

About twenty minutes before the express came roaring down the single track, a small steamer, the *Pacific,* was allowed to go through the drawbridge, which was swung wide into the river. The vessel had just cleared the bridge when the New Haven train arrived. Tucker adamantly insisted later that the red ball was on the tower, and that he thought it was safe to proceed as he neared the bridge; his testimony was wholly refuted by a score of observers on the *Pacific* and near the bridge, who stated the ball had been removed.

Though approaching trains had a clear vision of the tower for more than 3,000 feet, no one on board the express bothered to look for the ball. Conductor Comstock was too absorbed in a conversation with a passenger to notice. Fireman George Elmer never looked once for the signal from his position in the cab next to Tucker. ("It's not my duty to look for it," he lamely volunteered later.)

Tucker's train was already past South Norwalk and about 370 feet from the open drawbridge when Tucker saw the sixty-foot gap to his front. Frantically he signaled for "down brakes" by sounding two short blasts of his whistle. But the brakemen in the five passenger coaches, who were to apply hand brakes at this signal, all looked out, saw the approaching expanse of water, and without a word of warning to passengers, leaped for their lives. Conductor Comstock let out a yell and jumped. He suffered only bruises. Fireman Elmer jumped, too, bouncing unharmed in high grass.

Engineer Tucker saw no reason to stay in his cab and leaped at the last second before the train dove head-long into the river. He landed hard and received a broken leg. It was another matter for those trapped inside the coaches.

The shooting train rushed forward into space. The engine actually leaped the sixty-foot expanse and slammed into the center pier (which indicates the high speed the train was then traveling). It immediately sank into the twelve-foot waters, dragging down with it the tender, the two baggage cars, two more coaches and a part of a third, which was ripped in half when passengers in the last two cars jumped for the handbrakes and then jerked back, bringing the two cars to a whining halt.

A resident of South Norwalk was standing only a few yards from the open drawbridge when the train leaped forward. He watched bug-eyed as "the third passenger car snapped like a match, the flooring, the sides, and the foremost end flying forward, with a jerk, half across the draw. Many of the seats and the dislodged window sashes, with a crowd of timber fragments, were propelled, some of them, fully across the gulf, and two of the passengers, who were seated just at the spot where the car snapped asunder, were thrown [a] full twenty feet forward and pitched with frightful force upon the ruins of the second and first cars." This terror-struck witness then "heard the crash of breaking timbers and one scream, uttered simultaneously by many voices. Then, for a second or two, all was still as death. Then I heard the gurgling of the waters as they rushed into the cars, forming eddies or little whirlpools on the surface. In another moment shrieks from those in the rear cars and in the hind part of the third passenger car filled the air, and in the next instant there was but one scene of indescribable confusion."

Those in the smoking compartment at the rear of the second baggage car were fortunate. Their car had piled on top of the first baggage car and tender and had remained above the swirling river waters. All eight men inside managed to crawl to safety through the splintered wreckage. Those in the first and second coaches, however, were hopelessly trapped; most drowned in seconds.

One man in the second coach, Thomas Hicks, a young artist, managed an incredible escape. Traveling with his fiancee, a Miss King, Hicks was sitting near the back of the second passenger car when the train took its fatal plunge. His car broke to pieces as it dashed itself onto the top of the first coach. He lived to tell reporters how he "beheld the front part of the car rushing toward me in fragments, the passengers being tossed in the air like chaff, dashed up against the top of the car, and thrown about in a hurricane of destruction."

As the car quickly filled with water, Hicks desperately thrashed about in search of Miss King, diving repeatedly downward into the murky, debris-clogged water but only bumping into dead bodies. His fiancee was gone. With his last drams of energy, the fledgling painter wriggled through a small crack in the top of the car. Before it sank he gripped the wooden top of the coach, shouting wildly for Miss King. The steamboat *Pacific,* which was put full astern the moment her captain witnessed the train going into its death splash, came alongside the sinking car to pluck Hicks from the fast-disappearing rooftop.

Sobbing at the loss of his future wife, Hicks suddenly gaped upward to the track. There stood an unperturbed Miss King smoothing down her long dress. She had been one of the first to escape the wreck. Hicks climbed the embankment and embraced her; he then turned, startled to see an angry throng of South Norwalk citizens surround engineer Tucker, who was propped upon a pile of railroad ties holding his shattered leg, grimacing and waving away the volatile crowd.

One man in the mob carried a thick rope. "You murdering fiend," he cried. "We're gonna lynch you!"

Another man intervened as he withdrew a pistol. "No. That takes up too much time. We'll shoot him and then throw him into the river with the rest of them he's killed."

An argument then developed as to whether Tucker should be hanged or shot. Fortunately for Tucker, the debate consumed enough time to allow constables from South Norwalk to arrive and escort the injured engineer to town. (One in this vigilante group later wrote the *New York Herald:* "It would have been a good effect if the engineers, switch tenders and some of the directors of our railroads were occasionally made to feel the force of lynch law.")

Anger seethed through the coroner's jury hastily gotten together that very afternoon in South Norwalk, while the splintered remains of the train, along with forty-six bodies, were still settling at the bottom of the river. Jurors lost no time in finding Tucker guilty of extreme negligence in not recognizing that the red ball signal was not in effect and taking the curve leading to the bridge "at such a rapid rate, and under such circumstances that we think him guilty of the most criminal recklessness." He was, however, let off with a censure, and the bulk of the jury's wrath was vented on the directors of the railroad, particularly George Washington Whistler for rehiring Tucker.

The highly publicized findings further shocked the country when fireman Elmer's testimony revealed that most of the New Haven's engineers read newspapers during their fastest runs. This and Tucker's obvious attempt to whitewash himself caused the nation's press to let loose heavy salvos at the railroad. An editorial writer for the *Railroad Record* blasted away: "Public feeling has been grossly outraged by these reckless sacrifices of life on railroads. Indignation meetings have been called, and several legislatures have taken action upon the matter. We sincerely trust they will continue to agitate the matter until some remedy shall be applied to this great evil. Corporations have no souls, but they have pockets, and if they cannot be reached in any other way, heavy damages should be required of them in every instance where loss of life was the result of carelessness."

Stunned officials of the New York and New Haven Line quickly ordered all their trains to come to a full stop before any and all drawbridges. The Connecticut legislature also acted promptly, setting up the state's first Board of Railroad Commissioners, which was required to investigate all railroad accidents involving the loss of life. It turned out to be an ineffective commision, but nevertheless, it led to stricter safety rules on the rails.

An ironic fillip to the disaster was the disappearance the following year of the New Haven's esteemed president Robert Schuyler, grandson of the Revolutionary general. Schuyler had issued phony shares of stock on his own company, pocketed a fortune, and fled to Europe, where he lived in luxury to the end of his days. Engineer Edward Tucker died in obscurity, broke.

SOUTH AMERICA — EARTHQUAKES
August 13, 1868

Almost the entire continent of South America was rattled by a series of earthquakes beginning on August 13, 1868, and extending from Ibarra on the northwestern border of Ecuador to Cabija on the coast of Bolivia, a distance of approximately 1,400 miles. The most severe shocks were felt along the Peruvian coast. Here the towns of Arica, Iquique, Tacna, Port Ilay, Arequipa, Pisco and many others were utterly destroyed. In Ibarra, Ecuador, almost the entire town was thrown down, and almost every inhabitant was buried beneath the rubble. The Ecuadorian town of Cotocachi was wiped out and replaced by a lake now called by the same name. More than 20,000 South Americans lost their lives in these heavy tremors.

SOUTH CAROLINA (and SOUTHERN UNITED STATES) — TORNADOES
February 19, 1884

One of the largest and most devastating series of tornadoes to invade South Carolina and most of the southern states occurred on February 19, 1884, when more than sixty tornadoes touched down. More than 800 people died in South Carolina and six other states. Whole towns, such as Davisboro, Georgia, were obliterated by twisters can best be illustrated by the example of W. A. down, leaving 10,000 homeless. The ferocity of the twisters can best be illustrated by the example of W.A. Miller of Blountsville, Georgia. Miller's entire house was "blown to atoms," according to *Frank Leslie's Illustrated Newspaper*. His wife and three children were crushed to death in seconds when the twister hit, and his infant boy was carried off by the tornado, never to be found again.

SOUTH CAROLINA (and SOUTHERN UNITED STATES) — TORNADOES
April 29-30, 1924

Seven states in the South, chiefly South Carolina, were badly mauled by twenty-two tornadoes that set down on April 29-30, 1924. The storms took the lives of 115 and caused over $4.3 million in property damage. The South Carolina towns of Riverside Mill, Walnut Grove, Florence, Horrell Mill, Sumter and Spartanburg were wrecked by separate twisters. At Riverside Mill a huge tornado flattened half the houses and the entire business district. A $500,000 mill was reduced to splinters in seconds, leaving 1,500 homeless.

In all twenty-six towns were demolished in South Carolina, Georgia, Alabama, Arkansas, Louisiana, North Carolina and Mississippi. The storms created more than $10 million in damage, a minimal estimate.

SOUTH KOREA — FLOODS-LANDSLIDES

August 19, 1972

The worst rains in South Korea's modern history struck the central portion of the country on August 19, 1972, and subsequent floods in Kyonggi, Kangwon and North Chungchong provinces created massive landslides. (The rains in Seoul measured, according to the central weather bureau, 17.8 inches, the greatest rainfall since 1907, when the country's first modern meteorological station was established.) More than 150,000 persons were made homeless by the house-crunching landslides and floods. Refugees were housed in schools and factories. Of these 127,000 alone were in Seoul, where 180 persons were killed and another 158 injured, with 34 residents missing. Thirteen landslides in this city were responsible for 175 deaths.

An ancient city wall, once built to repel invading armies, fell down in Suwon, crushing several houses and killing all inside. The 17,000 persons living in Yongwol, ninety miles southeast of Seoul, fled in panic as their city was quickly submerged. Weeks later, authorities counted 463 dead.

SOVIET AEROFLOT — AIR CRASH

February 17, 1966

The Soviet Union never releases information regarding air crashes involving its planes unless foreigners have been killed. This, no doubt, is the reason why even sketchy details were permitted to filter out of the country following the crash of a TU-114 on February 17, 1966, moments after it took off from the airport in Moscow. Then the world's largest airplane with a seating capacity of 170, the TU-114 was a smoldering wreck before any rescuers could reach the crash site.

Russian officials at first insisted that six passengers and a crew of seven died in the crash, a total of thirteen deaths. They gave no cause for the disaster. Reliable sources later placed the true death count at forty-eight.

SPANISH ARMADA — MARINE DISASTER

August-October, 1588

background: In an attempt to invade England, Philip II of Spain sent 127 ships, sailing from Lisbon on May 28, 1588, with almost 30,000 sailors and soldiers on board. Following four huge sea battles in July along the English Channel, the Armada sailed northward into the North Sea and attempted to circumnavigate Scotland and Ireland. However, it was caught in vicious storms of hurricane proportions and many of the vessels, nineteen in all, were wrecked upon the Scottish and Irish coasts. From August 8-10, 1588, another thirty-five ships were lost. Loss of life from the wrecked Armada is estimated to have been between 4,000 and 10,000 men.

In league with Pope Pius V, who had excommunicated Queen Elizabeth I of England, and declared that her subjects owed allegiance only to the Roman Catholic Church, Philip II of Spain, the most powerful monarch in Europe, ordered his vast Spanish Armada of 127 ships and 30,000 sailors and men-at-arms to invade England in late May, 1588. Commanding this unwieldy flotilla was Don Alonzo Perez de Guzman, Duke of Medina Sidonia, who protested his appointment on the grounds that he knew nothing of navigation and little of naval warfare. Furthermore, he informed his king that his one previous ocean voyage had produced only a single memory—his violent seasickness.

Philip merely shrugged and told the duke to do his duty. The Armada sailed into the English Channel and was promptly out-gunned: four of its ships were lost in four consecutive battles. Following the last of these encounters, at Gravelines, Medina Sidonia ordered his fleet up the channel and into the North Sea. He had lost the chance to invade England and decided to return to Spain by sailing around Scotland and Ireland. It proved to be one of the most disastrous decisions in naval history.

The first fatality of the already stricken Armada was the *Gran Grifon,* the *capitanas* of the fleet, which was driven onto the rocks of the Fair Isle. Though Captain Juan Gomez de Medina and part of his crew managed to clamber onto the rocky shoals of the island, at least 1,000 seamen and soldiers perished in this single sinking.

The fleet sailed on, many ships leaking so severely that seamen labored to exhaustion to patch up the holes torn through the hulls of the twenty-five hulks (loaded down with horses, artillery, mules and stores), the nineteen cutters, thirteen coasters, four galleys and four galleasses. The galleasses were twice the size of the largest galley, and to supplement the sails, they were oared by 1,000 galley slaves, who were mostly captured British seamen.

Medina Sidonia turned south at the Hebrides, confiding to his diary as savage headwinds from the southwest engulfed his battered flotilla: "God has seen fit to direct the course of events other than we would have wished." His own flagship, the *San Martin de Portugal,* was holed in several places and barely remained afloat. In early August, with water running low due to poorly made barrels, and food molding, the duke ordered every animal on board his ships flung into the ocean (had he the presence of mind, he would have slaughtered the horses and mules and used them to feed his men, all of whom would suffer miserably from hunger before the month was out).

The next major disaster to befall the Armada as it made its sluggish way toward Spain was the sinking of the *Santa Maria de la Rosa,* a huge galley and vice-flagship of the fleet captained by Martin de Villafranca. This ship was thoroughly rent by cannonballs shot from the English ships of Drake, Hawkins, Howard and other British buccaneers at Gravelines, some of them still wedged into her hull. She took on massive amounts of water as she lurched forward. Her sails were in tatters, and her masts were splintered. Disease had reduced the *Santa Maria*'s crew to half her usual number, and one report of conditions on this miserable vessel described seamen as having to strain the water they drank through their teeth to filter it because it was filled with foreign objects.

Off the coast of Ireland on September 29, Villafranca realized his ship was slowly sinking, and he made for land, hoping to find a suitable harbor off Kerry. Wild winds drove him ashore near Dunmore Head between Great Blasket Island and Beginish where two other Spanish ships, the *San Juan de Portugal* and the *San Juan,* had already taken refuge. Both of these vessels were also near sinking and could offer no assistance to the *Santa Maria* as she tossed into the bay ahead of near hurricane winds and tremendous combers.

The commander of the *San Juan,* Marcos de Aramburu, who was also a fleet paymaster, witnessed the end of the galley: "At midday the ship *Santa Maria de la Rosa,* of Martin de Villafranca, came in by another entrance nearer the land, towards the northwest, and on coming in, fired a gun, as if seeking help, and another when further in. [Both ships at anchor, having only one good lifeboat between them, could lend no assistance.] She had all her sails torn to ribbons, except the foresail. She anchored with a single anchor, as she had no more. And as the tide, which was coming in from the southeast, beat against her, she held on till two o'clock, when it began to ebb, and at turn she commenced drifting, about two splices of cable from us, and we with her; and in an instant we saw she was going to the bottom while trying to hoist the foresail and immediately she went down with the whole crew, not a soul escaping—a most extraordinary and terrible occurrence."

Going down on the *Santa Maria* were 300 soldiers and sailors. The only survivor was a Genoese seaman, Giovanni de Monana, who rode a board to shore. After interrogating Monana, an English official, James Trant, reported to his superiors in elation: "In the flagship there is left but twenty-five pipes of wine and but very little bread, and no water but what they brought out of Spain, which stinketh marvellously, and the flesh meat they cannot eat, the drouth is so great."

Armed men from the *San Juan de Portugal,* under the command of Juan Martinez de Recalde, vice-admiral of the Armada, raided the small hamlets for food and water. British soldiers captured a few of Recalde's men, but fresh provisions were taken aboard the *San Juan de Portugal,* and the lumbering galleon moved down the Irish coast, losing an average of two to three men a day to thirst and starvation. By the time she reached Spain, 200 men had died on board.

The greatest privations were reserved, however, for the giant of the fleet, the galleass *Girona,* which had been wrecked by several storms and, along with two sister ships, sought safe harbor at Killybegs. The *Girona,* much damaged by the storms, managed to get into port; the other two ships were hurled to splintered wrecks in the harbor as they made their entrance. For days the *Girona* drifted about the harbor until Admiral Alonso Martinez de Reyva arrived on a litter, carried overland from the seacoast wrecks of two other ships he had commanded. These were the *Santa Ana,* destroyed in a hurricane in Loughros Bay, Donegal, and the monster merchant ship, *La Rata Santa Maria Encoronada,* loaded to the gunnels with heavy guns, which was wrecked and subsequently burned by the admiral after he had taken off her wealth and stores in Blacksod Bay, Mayo. De Reyva organized the remaining crew men into work parties. The English, who knew that the Spanish captain and his crews were somewhere about, searched the coast with armed companies. Though sorely injured, the Spanish captain managed to take advantage of the great amount of wreckage in Killybegs Bay to rebuild the *Girona* before the British could arrive. He ordered his scavenger crews to strip "the great store of timber of wrecked ships as was in that place . . . more than would have built five of the greatest ships I ever saw, besides mighty great boats, cables and other cordage answerable thereunto, and some such masts for bigness and length, as in mine own judgement I never saw any two could make the like."

The *Girona* was a ship reborn, patched and refitted from the settling hulks of her sister ships, and onto her de Reyva carried the riches, cannon and stores of four other ships, as well as all those who survived the previous wrecks, almost 1,300 men. He then set sail on October 26, 1588, thinking to go again north to Scotland and back down the channel. Whether or not it occurred to him that the British fleet would still be waiting for any Spanish ships escaping in that direction is not known. His plan, however, was futile.

Yet another savage storm engulfed the *Girona* on October 27, and her rudder, which had been broken in the first storm, again splintered, and she soon sank off what later became known as Port-na-Spagna. (The wreck and some of its great treasure was discovered there in 1967 by Robert Stenuit.) To a man, the 1,300 aboard the stricken *Girona,* including the enterprising Admiral de Reyva, perished with the ship.

Of the once invincible Spanish Armada, only sixty-four ships returned to Spain; sixty-three vessels were

missing or sunk along the Scottish and Irish coasts. Philip II was as laconic about his staggering loss as he was in appointing the incompetent Medina Sidonia to command his fleet. "I sent my ships to fight against the English," he is quoted as saying, "and not against the wind and waves. Praise be to God!"
(ALSO SEE: Capitanas, Nuestra Senora de la Concepcion*)*

SPANTAX AIRLINES — AIR CRASH

December 3, 1972

A takeoff from Santa Cruz in the Canary Islands of a four-engine Convair 990-A Coronado belonging to the Spantax Airlines quickly developed into a fiery disaster on December 3, 1972. The plane, chartered from a Spanish firm by a group of Germans who were members of a Bavarian bus operators' federation, took off from Los Rodeos Airport without difficulty, but when it reached 1,000 feet, one of the engines caught fire. Moments later the craft plunged earthward, crashing onto the island of Tenerife, one of the seven islands in the Canary group off the African coast in the Atlantic.

Civilians and soldiers from a nearby military base rushed to the burning plane, which exploded upon impact, but found only one of the 155 persons—148 passengers and 7 crew members—still alive. The woman found was severely burned and repeatedly mumbled: "Save me, save me." She died hours later in the fourth worst air crash up to that time.

SPARROWHAWK — MARINE DISASTER

August 15, 1654

En route from Formosa to Japan, the small Dutch vessel *Sparrowhawk* was caught in a typhoon off the Korean coast and quickly broke to pieces beneath the climbing waves and lashing winds. One survivor, Hendrick Hamel, who was aboard the ship, vividly described the storm that struck the *Sparrowhawk* on August 15, 1654: "The wind blew so boisterously that we could not hear one another speak, nor durst we let fly an inch of sail. And, to add to our misfortunes, the ship took in so much water that there was no mastering of it. Besides, the waves every moment broke in upon us in such manner that we expected to perish every minute.

"That night our boat and the greatest part of our gallery were carried away, which shook our boltsprit and made us fear we should lost our prow. All possible means were used to repair the damage sustained and prevent the ill consequences it might produce. But in vain, for the gusts of wind were too violent and came too close one upon another, besides the breaking of the waves which were ready to sink us every moment. At length finding there was no way to save ourselves but by abandoning the vessel and the company's goods, we resolved to loose a foretopsail the better to avoid the greater surges.

"Whilst we were thus employed, a wave coming over our stern had like to have washed away all the seamen that were upon the deck. It filled the ship so full of water that the master [Captain Egbertz of Amsterdam] cried out, 'My mates, cut down the mast by the board immediately and recommend yourselves to the mercy of God! For if one or two such waves return, we are all lost and all our skill and labor will not save us.' ".

At that moment crew members sighted land, one sailor "adding that we were not above a musketshot from it, the darkness of the night and the rain having obstructed our discovering it sooner." This was the rocky, barren island of Quelpaert, some fifteen miles distant from mainland Korea. The crew attempted to anchor the *Sparrowhawk* in the storm, but no bottom could be found. Then three successive waves of immense size swept over the vessel, and a gaping hole in her hull was made so quickly "that those who were in the hold were drowned before they could get out. Some of those that were on the deck leaped overboard, and the rest were carried away in the sea."

Seaman Hamel and fourteen others managed to reach the rocky shore of the island and were joined by twenty-one more of the crew the following day; twenty-eight of the crew perished, including Captain Egbertz. His crew found him later "stretched out in the sand, ten or twelve fathoms from the water, with his arm under his head."

The crew of the *Sparrowhawk* were to undergo extreme hardships as captives of the Korean islanders. They were not released until 1668, after fourteen years in slavery.
(ALSO SEE: Medusa*)*

SPARTA — EARTHQUAKE

464 B.C.

The first earthquake of which careful historic mention is made was that which occurred in ancient Sparta in 464 B.C. In that year during the reign of Archidamus, a cataclysmic quake rolled throughout Greece, most violently destroying Sparta so that not five houses were standing in the entire country following the quake. More than 20,000 persons perished by the shock, and according to one account, "the flower of the Spartan youth was overwhelmed by the fall of those buildings in which they were exercising and developing themselves into physical perfection."

Another early report states that "in several places the country was entirely swallowed up. Taygetus and other mountains were shaken to their foundations, many of their summits, being torn away, came tumbling down, and the whole city [Ithome] was laid in ruins. To heighten the calamity, the Helots, who were slaves to the Cacedemonians [and descendants of the enslaved Messenians], looking upon this as a favorable opportunity to recover their liberty, pervaded every part of the city, to murder such as had escaped the earthquake."

The Helots were to control Ithome through a ten-year siege by the Spartans, who invited the Athenians to aid them. The Spartans subsequently dismissed their allies with such rudeness that the seeds of the Peloponnesian War were sown.

SPRING HILL, NOVA SCOTIA

MINE DISASTER
October 23, 1958

Disaster came to the Cumberland Rail and Coal Company outside Spring Hill, Nova Scotia, on October 23, 1958, when a seam of coal suddenly shifted, creating massive cave-ins. Trapped in Number 2 mine at about a mile's depth were 173 miners, 80 of whom were rescued within three hours.

Rescue teams, however, found it rough going to get to the remaining workers. They were forced to tunnel through great stretches of collapsed mine shaft. In a sealed-off room nineteen survivors stretched out on the floor and breathed quietly, waiting for rescue. Since it was miner Garnet Clark's birthday, several miners made a cake out of a sandwich and pretended to have a party.

For almost nine days this group held out, rationing the food in their lunch buckets. When that ran out, they chewed slivers of wood from support timbers; some even gnawed on coal. Late in the night of the eighth day, rescuers finally shoveled their way through to this group. Twelve of these workers were still alive.

Seventy-four men were killed in this mine disaster.

SQUALUS

MARINE DISASTER
May 23, 1939

The first crash dive of the United States submarine *Squalus,* on May 23, 1939, twelve miles off Portsmouth, New Hampshire, almost proved fatal for all the fifty-nine crew members aboard. As was the case with the British sub *K-13* in 1917, the electric control panel, which indicated the condition of all the hatches, failed, and while the sub was diving, a huge amount of water poured into the ship through an open air inlet valve in the conning tower. The malfunctioning indicator panel had signaled green, indicating that this opening was closed.

Within a few minutes the sub sank to about forty fathoms—approximately 240 feet—which was consid-

Friends and relatives of trapped miners wait to hear word of rescue in Spring Hill, Nova Scotia. Seventy-four workers were killed in massive cave-ins. *(Wide World)*

The ill-fated United States submarine *Squalus* is raised from her Davy Jones berth; twenty-six dead men were on board. Thirty-three men managed to escape in the newly-developed McCann rescue bell. *(Wide World)*

ered a safe rescue depth. Captain Naquin of the *Squalus* ordered his men to stay quiet and conserve air. He informed them that the salvage ship *Falcon,* equipped with the new McCann rescue bell, was only 150 miles to the south in New London, Connecticut, and should arrive in about twenty-four hours. His calculations proved amazingly accurate.

The *Falcon* arrived above the stricken *Squalus* the following day in company with the *Squalus*'s sister ship, *Sculpin,* which located the other submarine. Divers quickly descended with the McCann rescue bell, which was placed over an escape hatch. In four trips thirty-three men, including Lieutenant Naquin, were hoisted slowly to the surface. Twenty-six others were dead and remained entombed in the ship for 113 days, until the submarine was refloated and water pumped from her hull in the Portsmouth Navy Yard.

Rescuing the thirty-three sailors off the *Squalus* proved to be one of the first major life-saving feats involving United States submarines. Conditions, however, were ideal at that time, the submarine having sunk to a minimal depth where strong tidal currents were not present. Such was not the case with the British submarine *Thetis,* when rescue attempts off the Great Ormes Head ended in failure and tragedy two weeks after the *Squalus* sank.

(ALSO SEE: K-13, Thetis*)*

STALHEIM HOTEL — FIRE

June 23, 1959

The Stalheim Hotel in the exclusive Norwegian resort of the same name was long considered one of the finest inns in Europe. It was a favorite of royalty. Among its celebrated guests was Kaiser Wilhelm II of Germany, who stayed at the hotel with his entire family and massive retinue just before World War I. The Stalheim, an impressive wooden building erected in 1885 and situated on a rock about 400 yards up a sloping mountain, caught fire at 3:00 A.M. on June 23, 1959, and burned to its foundation in a matter of minutes.

Harris Waldwell, a tourist from Georgia, first noticed

the blaze and began to race through hallways, alerting the 147 guests (130 of whom were Americans) and the inn's staff. "I ran down the corridors," he told reporters hours later, "and screamed all I could and continued down to the lobby, where one of the hotel employees came running and helped to set the fire alarm working." Caldwell, his wife and another man were the only fully dressed guests to escape the flaming hotel, and they wound up sharing their garments with half-naked survivors.

By the time firemen arrived from the village, which was located eighty-seven miles north of Bergen, the hotel was gone, and inside its charred remains were thirty-four bodies. Another thirty-five persons were injured in the blaze.

STARKVILLE, COLORADO — MINE DISASTER — October 8, 1910

The explosion in the Starkville Mine at 10:00 P.M. on October 8, 1910, which took the lives of fifty-six miners, was caused by the derailment of a heavily laden coal car train. The cars crashed into timber that was coated with fine coal dust; this ignited and created the blast.

STATE OF CALIFORNIA — MARINE DISASTER — August 17, 1913

Attempting to navigate the inlets of Gambier Bay, ninety miles off Juneau, Alaska, the 2,266-ton steamship *State of California* slammed onto a rocky shoal and sank within three minutes. The $400,000 vessel of the Pacific Coast Steamship Company, of all iron construction, was holed in several places, and her captain, Thomas H. Cann, Jr., knew the situation was hopeless. He ordered what few lifeboats were available put over and made quick signals to a passing ship, which turned out to be the *Jefferson,* on her regular run for the Alaska Steamship Company and headed for Juneau.

Captain Nord of the *Jefferson* immediately ordered his vessel to put about in the direction of the *State of California,* but he was too late to save forty persons—thirty-three passengers and seven crew members—who went down with the ship. He did manage to bring aboard about eighty others who were clinging to the sides of two small lifeboats.

STAUNTON, ILLINOIS — RAILWAY WRECK — October 4, 1910

Less than a month after a disastrous collision of two interurban electric cars on the Fort Wayne and Wabash Valley Line at Kingsland, Indiana, which took thirty-four lives, the Illinois Traction System experienced an even worse calamity on October 4, 1910, outside Staunton, Illinois. Following its orders, a northbound local waited for a southbound express at Staunton. However, the engineer either forgot or ignored instructions pointing out that the southbound train was running in two sections. After the first electric car went by, the engineer raced his car down the track and promptly collided at a sharp curve with the second section of the southbound train.

The engineers and conductors on both cars jumped from the two cars only moments before the collision and received minor injuries. Thirty-six passengers, most on board the southbound train en route to a St. Louis celebration of the Veiled Prophets, were killed instantly as the cars telescoped each other.

STELLA — MARINE DISASTER — March 30, 1899

background: The 1,059-ton channel boat *Stella,* built in 1890 by the J. & G. Thompson Company for the London and Southwestern Railway Company, struck rocks off the French coast in a thick fog after sailing from Southampton. She sank with about 100 persons still on board.

The *Stella* was a large channel ferry. She had seen only nine years of service when she sank on March 30, 1899, after leaving Southampton for France at 11:30 A.M. (regular packet boats departed England at night, but this was a special Easter excursion trip). On board were approximately 200 persons, including a crew of 40.

Thick fog set in about an hour after the *Stella*'s departure and late in the afternoon, the boat's speed having been drastically reduced by Captain Reeks, the rocky shoals of the Casquets suddenly loomed up. The boat struck the dreaded Black Rock, and her hull was split wide open. Within ten minutes the ship foundered and sank. Splendid discipline was maintained by the crew and the passengers. As would be the accepted rule on board the sinking *Titanic* thirteen years later, women and children entered the six lifeboats first.

Ships from several English and French ports put out to sea when the *Stella* failed to arrive at her appointed hour. But the fog was so dense that it was almost seventeen hours before lifeboats were spotted by the *Lynx* and the first group of survivors was rescued. The *Vera* next found several lifeboats and pulled sixty-two persons to safety. French ships picked up others; one tug almost ran down an overturned lifeboat which had capsized moments before. All who had been in this boat were saved; they were found floating nearby.

Though the passenger list was lost with the ship, reliable sources estimated the loss of life in the *Stella* disaster at 100, mostly males who heroically gave up their seats in the lifeboats to women and children.

(*ALSO SEE:* Kiangya)

The clipper ship *Strathmore,* sketched by her carpenter who survived her sinking, approaches the rocky shoals of the Crozet Islands.

Marooned *Strathmore* crew members are rescued from Crozet Island. *(Spencer Joslen)*

STOCKTON, GEORGIA — RAILWAY WRECK

August 4, 1944

A speeding passenger train of the Atlantic Coast Line was passing through Stockton, Georgia, on August 4, 1944, when a rail slipped from its position and derailed the ninth and tenth cars of the express. The ninth car was a Pullman full of sleeping occupants, but it was little damaged and no one in this car was injured. The car behind it, however, was full of Negro railroad workers, forty-seven of whom were killed when the car smashed against a freight train and was literally sliced in half lengthwise.

STRATHMORE — MARINE DISASTER

June 30, 1875

background: The iron clipper ship *Strathmore* sailed from Gravesend, England, to New Zealand on April 19, 1875, with eighty-eight persons on board. She was wrecked on the rocky shoals of the Crozet Islands; forty-four persons took to the lifeboats and escaped to a nearby island, where they lived for six months before being rescued by an American whaling ship. Five of the survivors died on the island, bringing the death toll to forty-nine.

The British sailing ship, the *Strathmore,* an iron-hulled vessel carrying eighty-eight passengers and crew, was badly navigated through the Crozet Islands in the Indian Ocean, about 700 miles southeast of the Cape of Good Hope. On the night of June 30, 1875, the ship lumbered onto the rocks of a tiny island about three miles long and a half-mile wide. The *Strathmore* began to sink slowly, breaking up as passengers and crew scrambled for the lifeboats. Only forty-four people managed to draw away from the sinking vessel before she went down.

Reaching the small island nearby, the survivors climbed the rocky cliffs in a bone-chilling rainstorm and took refuge under a small boat they managed to drag up after them. The remaining boats were dashed to pieces in the storm. For six months, from July 1 to January 21, the survivors lived on the barren rock. To keep warm, they burned what few pieces of driftwood they could snatch from the water while hanging from the rocky bluffs, there being no beach on the island. They later burned the skins of dead birds after eating them, in order to keep warm.

According to one survivor, Spencer Joslen, whose brother Percy was drowned when the *Strathmore* went down: "During the time we were on the island, we were miraculously provided with food. Though sometimes it seemed as if there was not another bird on the island, we always managed to catch a few to keep us alive until they got more plentiful. We also ate a sort of herb, the top of which resembles carrot tops. Our firewood lasted a month. Five of our number died on the island." Three of these were persons who "complained of sore feet" after making their escape from the sinking *Strathmore*. Their toes were frostbitten, and for want of proper care, they died, "parts of the toes having rotted clean away." A little boy, the last of the survivors to perish, died on Christmas Day.

During their stay on the island, the marooned survivors, which included one woman, a Mrs. Wordsworth, saw four ships pass the island. They tried frantically to signal them, but the vessels were too far at sea to spot them. On January 21, 1876, the weakened survivors managed to attract the attention of Captain D. I. Gifford, skipper of the American whaling ship *Young Phoenix*. Gifford put about and stood by while his lifeboats brought the thirty-nine persons on board his ship. He then met the *Sierra Morena,* and this vessel took the *Strathmore* survivors to Ceylon and, eventually, to England.

STUART, WEST VIRGINIA — MINE DISASTER, January 29, 1907

A mine in Stuart, West Virginia, completely collapsed after a monstrous explosion on January 29, 1907, when a miner entered a room wearing an open light that ignited a body of gas and coal dust. Two cageloads of workers had just that moment gone to the surface, but eighty-four workers were still at work in the mine when the explosion occurred. All of the workers were killed instantly.

Stuart company officials were later indicted and charged with allowing more men to work the small shaft than were legally permitted.

SULLIVAN, INDIANA — MINE DISASTER, February 20, 1925

The igniting of coal dust by the open lights worn on miner's caps has been the reason for so many mine explosions. It was the cause of the blast that ripped apart the City Mine at Sullivan, Indiana, at 10:45 A.M. on February 20, 1925. Of the 106 miners at work in the main shaft at the time, half quickly escaped through an air shaft. Fifty-two men died.

SULPHUR SPRINGS, MISSOURI — RAILWAY WRECK, August 5, 1922

Number 32 of the Missouri Pacific Line was halted at Sulphur Springs, Missouri, taking on water on August 5, 1922, when an express going about 40 m.p.h. crashed into its rear. The last two cars of the local, all-wooden coaches, were ripped from the tracks and sent flying down an embankment. Thirty-two St. Louis-bound passengers were killed when the coaches splintered to pieces and fell into a fast-moving stream. Many were drowned. Two more fatalities brought the death toll in this wreck to thirty-four.

The engineer of the express, Number 4, seeing his train about to crash into the local, jumped clear seconds before impact and was impaled on railroad spikes. The other death was curiously ironic. A thief had broken into the railroad area and was in the act of stealing material when the two cars roared down the embankment on top of him.

SULTANA — MARINE DISASTER, April 26-27, 1865

background: The 1,720-ton Mississippi sidewheeler *Sultana* had a total capacity of 376 for passengers and crew. While en route from New Orleans to Cincinnati, she stopped at Vicksburg, Mississippi, on April 25, 1865, where she took aboard approximately 2,400 Union soldiers, mostly prisoners of war recently released from Confederate internment camps. After stopping in Memphis, Tennessee, on the evening of April 26, 1865, the *Sultana,* while passing the Hens and Chickens islands, caught fire following the explosion of one of her boilers and burned to the water line. Although many reports are contradictory as to the number of persons on board at the time of the disaster, reliable sources confirm 1,547 deaths, which makes this sinking one of the greatest marine disasters in history, 30 fatalities above that lost on the *Titanic.*

They came to Vicksburg in broken-down carts, their legs dangling lifelessly over the sides, on small clanking trains, scores lying on the rooftops, on foot, hobbling, old bloody bandages yellowing. They leaned on each other for support. Some were blind, some were armless, some were legless; all were scarecrow-thin, emaciated, starved. The great American Civil War was over, gone more than a week with Appomattox, all the battles and the dead, the causes eternal, slipped into sullen silent history, and those Union troops stumbling toward the teetering docks of Vicksburg had only the acid memories of Confederate prison camps at Catawba and the cesspool that had been Andersonville. These thousands of men in tattered blue uniforms welled up like lemmings on the docks, waiting for steamboats to carry them north.

"They are like the dead walking home," one payclerk remarked to his sergeant.

"You needn't worry," the noncom replied. "They'll most of them be dead before they get there."

As thousands of the ragged troops waited on the docks, small steamboats began to appear, and the expatriated soldiers calmly filed on board to standing-room-only spaces. The *Henry Ames* took aboard 1,300 men and paddled upstream. More than 700 soldiers crammed themselves onto the small *Olive Branch,* and that steamboat, too, moved north. Then the *Sultana* appeared. Though a comparatively new boat, the vessel had trouble as soon as she departed New Orleans on April 21, with her boiler plant in need of much repair. Engineers hurriedly went to work on one boiler as men from once-proud Michigan, Indiana and Ohio regiments wordlessly crossed the gangplank to the *Sultana.*

The question of how many persons this ship could actually hold has been debated by many authorities. On leaving New Orleans, the 1,720-ton side paddlewheeler already had 100 civilian passengers in her first-class cabins. In addition there was a crew of 80 men, a bulging cargo of sugar, 100 horses, mules and hogs, and a ten-foot alligator. Her official capacity was 376, but that number was surpassed quickly as hundreds of soldiers began to fill up the decks.

Overloading the *Sultana* by the transportation officer was, at least, suspect, especially since two other large riverboats had pulled to the docks to take on troops and remained empty. A board of inquiry later determined that this Union officer had been charging the owners of one steamboat line $1 per head to put soldiers on its boats and when this was discovered, making for near-mutinous cries from the sweating ranks, the nervous officer merely ordered every man remaining on the docks onto the creaking *Sultana* to dispel any idea of collusion.

Exactly how many troopers jammed themselves aboard the steamboat is debated to this day. Loading officers at first regulated the number boarding the *Sultana,* making accurate rolls and assigning Ohio men to the hurricane deck, Michigan troops to the main deck and Indiana soldiers to the promenade deck. This soon got out of hand when the officer in charge ordered *everyone* on board the boat. Men then broke rank and swarmed onto the vessel in fast-moving groups, throwing planks over to the boat and crossing on their own. The pandemonium made an accurate check of passengers impossible.

As the *Sultana* cleared the Vicksburg wharf on April 25, 1865, she was very low in the water, steaming toward Cincinnati. A clerk on board reported hours later to an officer that by his count there were 2,400 soldiers on board and 180 civilians, in addition to the animals and cargo. "If this vessel reaches Cairo, Illinois," he said in a prosaic tone, "the *Sultana* will have made Mississippi riverboat history. It will have carried the greatest passenger load since travel on the river began. However," he prophetically added, "it is my belief that the vessel will never make Cairo."

Huddled everywhere on the open decks of the *Sultana,* the troops broke into animated conversations, songs, the first signs of spirit they had shown in the years since their misery in prison camps began. There was a pluck of banjo and tweet of harmonicas. Rippling through the ranks ran "Swing Low, Sweet Chariot," and "When Johnny Comes Marching Home." Feeble as they were, there were jokes.

The Mississippi riverboat *Sultana* is engulfed by flames after one of her boilers burst; 1,547 men, Union troops being mustered out, perished in one of the greatest marine disasters in history. *(Mariners Museum)*

Men took off their knapsacks and shared the rations they had been given in Vicksburg. Some even fed the alligator yawning in his wooden cage. Others gambled with the large amounts of back pay they had been given at Vicksburg. The river seemed quiet and rolled easy under them as the *Sultana*'s paddle wheels methodically churned.

Eighteen hours after leaving Vicksburg, the steamboat berthed in Memphis. It was 7:00 P.M., April 26, and the *Sultana* had seven more hours to live. Scores of men left the boat in Memphis to visit an alley lined with fourteen saloons known as "Whiskey Chute." Some of these soldiers got abysmally drunk and passed out before they could return to the boat. Years later they would thank the cheap alcohol that had blotted out their minds.

The *Sultana* crossed the river to a barge and took on bunker coal while engineers continued to labor over one of her malfunctioning boilers. While taking on fuel, the steamboat regained one of her saloon-visiting passengers. A soldier appeared in a skiff rowed by a Negro. He had paid the ex-slave $2 to get him back on board the vessel before she departed.

Captain W. S. Friesner of an Ohio regiment, who had watched the wharf gangs unload the ship's sugar cargo, saw the lone soldier arrive at the steamboat and climb aboard, telling his companions how "lucky" he was not to have missed her. Friesner went to his stateroom and, fully dressed, fell exhausted into his bunk.

Her coal bins full, the *Sultana* moved back out into the middle of the Mississippi as troops watched the distant lights of Memphis flicker into oblivion. One of these, a cavalryman named Perry Summerville from Indiana, turned away and found room on deck to sprawl, going to sleep as darkness engulfed the steamboat. It was midnight.

At 2:00 A.M., the steamboat was moving sluggishly through a stubby group of islands called the Hens and Chickens. Spring floods had swollen the river at this point, and half of the islets were submerged, the tops of their trees streaming with the forceful flow of the river.

Coming downstream, headed for Memphis, was the large new sidewheeler *Bostona*. In her wheelhouse was young Loftus Keating. Next to him stood the captain, John Watson. Piercing the darkness ahead, Keating suddenly saw a bright flash that turned the blue-black sky a lurid red. "That must be some man's cotton gin going up," he told Watson.

On board the *Sultana,* Captain Friesner was jarred from his sleep by what he first thought to be a riot among the soldiers. He bolted for his stateroom door, ready to reprimand the quarrelling soldiers. Steam, smoke and huge tongues of fire met him on deck. Panic screamed lustily through the ranks of soldiers as they hurled themselves into the river. The *Sultana* was sinking, and for a fearful moment as he stood at the guard rail, Captain Friesner remembered he could not swim.

Private Summerville had no such problems. He awoke to find himself already in the water, blown there by a tremendous blast. As he thrashed about, he saw the *Sultana* become a mass of flames. Everywhere about him, hundreds of men called out for help.

Seconds before, the malfunctioning boiler in the steamboat's bowels had exploded with such velocity that it ripped apart the hurricane deck, sending splinters, steel shards and hundreds of sleeping bodies high into the air. Many fell into the river; many more, some only in bloody pieces, rained back down upon the already flaming ship. Those below fared little better. The flame-belching explosion collapsed the wheelhouse, the texas, and one of the smokestacks. This weighty, blazing debris showered down on hundreds of sleeping troopers, scalding and burning them to death.

The fire did the rest. Flames, beginning about one-third of the distance from the bow, were driven toward the stern by downstream winds. Fires ate their way upward to the staterooms and promenade deck, forcing soldiers to jump. Many of these were amputees who had no hope of surviving the water. Throughout the ship one vast horror unfolded as men attempted to save themselves.

Soldiers crawled wildly over their companions, friends who had been burned and scalded and pleaded for help. Screams of agony surmounted the roar of the flames. "I couldn't stand it," said one man later, "the stench of burning flesh was intolerable." In mad scrambles motley groups of men raced from stern to bow, and back again, always met by the flames and trampling others underfoot. "They jumped overboard as fast as they could," one report states, "tumbling into the river upon each other and going down into the deep by the hundreds."

Captain Friesner was one of these, but he took the precaution of ripping off his stateroom door and diving into the river, with the door tucked beneath him. He used the door as a raft and paddled away from the mobs of drowning men who were floundering and taking strong swimmers to the bottom with them in death grasps.

The *Bostona* appeared in the distance. At her wheel Keating pointed out the wildly burning *Sultana.* "Why, just look at the cattle jumping into the water," he shouted to Captain Watson.

Watson leaned forward, peering. "My God, them ain't cattle. They're people! Holler down to the engineer. We must get there as soon as we can. Why, just look at them jumping!"

Private Summerville saw the *Bostona* coming downstream, but by then he had already secured two planks, and holding one between his legs and the other under his arms, he paddled for shore. All about him men were coughing and dying. He saw a horse swim by with ten men trying to hold on to it. They went under *en masse.* A friend sitting on a barrel and using his feet as oars, splashed by him. The man's face had been burned away; his eyes were gone. Summerville drifted with the current for an hour, sliding with the river back to Memphis, where he was plucked from the river by a Negro. Once in the skiff, Summerville realized that almost every rib in his body was cracked.

A large slab of the boiler deck, which had been sheared away from the *Sultana* in the blast, was still intact. A dozen men, who had been sleeping on it, used it as a raft to sail to Memphis; none were injured. For an hour close to 700 soldiers took refuge on the steamboat's bow as the fire consumed the aft portion of the *Sultana.* The wind then shifted, and the blaze was swept toward them. In one agonized rush, it swept the men from the bow of the boat and into the water where hundreds perished.

The *Bostona* bore down on the flaming wreck, its fires lighting up the river for miles and illuminating the hundreds of bobbing heads in the water. Watson ordered the yawl lowered, and scores of men soon were picked up. Captain Friesner simply paddled his door to the side of the steamboat and was dragged upward to her cargo deck by a roustabout using a gaffhook.

The sidewheeler burned for an hour and a half. When survivors began drifting into Memphis, the *Essex* and *Tyler,* along with a half-dozen smaller boats, got up steam and put into the river in search of more soldiers. More than 600 persons were brought into Memphis, but almost 200, the flesh of their bodies burned away, died in makeshift hospitals. For days steamboats and barges edged along the riverbanks, finding bodies wedged in thickets and piled on sandbars. All of the public buildings in Memphis were opened and used as charnal houses.

The enormous disaster received little publicity. The *New York Times* gave the calamity only five inches of coverage, and its information was sketchy. The final count of the dead remained long in debate. An army board of review sought to minimize the disaster and claimed that only 1,238 men had been killed. This figure was refuted, however, by Memphis courts holding open hearings; the death toll was placed much higher. Officially the United States Customs Service at Memphis finally released the total death count: 1,547. This number represents to date one of the worst marine disasters in the world and exceeds by 30 the fatalities on board the star-crossed *Titanic.*

For years after the disaster, members of the *Sultana* Survivors' Society met annually, members reminiscing over the disaster and marveling at their own escapes. At one session someone remembered the alligator that had been on board. Everyone felt sure that the beast had certainly survived. Then an Ohio man stepped forward and sheepishly confessed that the alligator died with the *Sultana.* Of this he was positive. He admitted rather sorrowfully that during the raging fire, he became a beast himself, stabbing the alligator to death, taking its wooden box and using it to float to safety.

(ALSO SEE: America, General Slocum*)*

SUNDERLAND, ENGLAND — MINE DISASTER, August 17, 1880

background: The Seaham Colliery near the town of Sunderland, England, opened in 1840 in the richest coal fields of Durham County. On August 17, 1880, one of its two main shafts exploded at 2:30 A.M., while 246 miners (out of an entire work force of about 1,600) were at work. Following sixteen hours of digging by rescue teams, 85 miners were rescued; the bodies of 161 workers were later found.

An enormous coal mine, the Seaham Colliery near Sunderland, England, had been relatively free of mishaps for forty years, though its two main shafts, it was learned later, contained extreme amounts of dust and lethal gases. Its massive crew of 1,600 miners worked the mine in three shifts. In the early morning hours on August 17, 1880, the crew inside the shafts consisted of 246 workers. This was a "weak shift"; many of its number had worked the previous shift in order to attend a nearby public flower show scheduled later that day, an event that, no doubt, saved the lives of hundreds of miners. (It was austerely noted by the *Illustrated London News* that Lord Londonderry would distribute prizes to the miners with the most attractive flowers at the show and that "the cultivation of gardens and flowers is a favorite pastime with the colliers of that neighborhood and is wisely and kindly encouraged by their social superiors.")

About 2:30 A.M. a thunderous explosion rattled the main tunnel, originating in the lowest seams and causing the ceilings and walls to collapse. Many of the miners who were not killed immediately by the explosion, caused by the ignition of afterdamp with an open light from a miner's cap, were trapped in pockets or rooms sealed by the fall-ins. Ralph Marley and eighteen others were one of these groups. Only moments before the explosion, Marley felt a "rush of wind." He shouted, "There's something up!" Then came the blast. Marley, who had survived three previous explosions, led the other eighteen men to a caved-in wall and quickly dug through it. They followed the shaft about a quarter of a mile. At one point they found "a deputy overman named Wardle lying insensible, with his face covered with blood, and here they met the afterdamp." Up to this point the group had fresh air, but now they stumbled along, holding cloths to their faces, crouching low to stay beneath the layer of gas.

As this group made its way out of the shaft, they saw the twisted, broken bodies of other miners, piles of dead and the immense debris scattered about, all created by the explosion. They arrived at the cage in the shaft by which they ordinarily reached the surface. It was badly damaged and hung precariously above them, halfway to the surface. Looking down the shaft to lower levels, the miners witnessed the absolute destruction of everything below them.

Air filtered down from above, but they could not see the surface. The area about them was somewhat befouled by gas, and it made the room smoky. Marley told them there was nothing to do but await rescue, so the 19 men made a small fire, brought out a pot and made tea. They continued shouting up the shaft, and they traveled in couples to investigate other shafts. Almost all of the shafts were quickly filling with gas, and bodies were sprawled every-which-way. Their biggest fear at this time was a second explosion, but it never came. It was to be almost three hours, until approximately 5:00 A.M., before they heard voices above them. Someone shouted down that rescuers were "digging down." Marley and his followers began to pray. At 1:00 P.M., the owner of the mine, Mr. Stratton, appeared with ten others and took the 19 men out to safety through the shaft that housed the cage. It was several more hours before another 61 trapped miners were saved. The removal of the 161 dead workers killed by the blast and subsequent gases required several days.

One of the bodies was that of a man named Hindson, a member of the Seaham Harbor Volunteer Artillery Corps, which had taken high prizes during annual competition. Hindson was to have been awarded a gold cup by Lord Londonderry on the day of the explosion for his performance. Hindson's "corpse was found in burned fragments, the head and both legs torn off and thrown several yards apart." The miner had a wife and four daughters, one of whom was to be married to another miner that week. And that young man lost his life, too, in the great colliery explosion of 1880.

SURF, CALIFORNIA — RAILWAY WRECK
May 11, 1907

The second section of a northbound Southern Pacific train, jammed with convention-bound Shriners, was derailed at Surf, California, on May 11, 1907. A switch was thrown to allow the train to pass, but the rails slipped as the locomotive and tender drove safely through. The next two cars, one of them a diner, were hurled from the tracks and crashed down an embankment to a sandy beach. The diner flopped on top of the first car and almost all of those lunching—it was 1:00 P.M.—thirty-three persons, were killed. Most were scalded to death by steam. The cooks in the small galley, however, survived.

SWITCHBACK, WEST VIRGINIA — MINE DISASTER
December 29, 1908

The gas-free Lick Branch mine at Switchback, West Virginia, had an almost perfect safety record until December 29, 1908, when it was rocked by an ear-shattering explosion. Miners were blasting, and they used an excessive amount of black powder, a strict violation of company regulations as well as the law. This ignited coal dust. Fifty miners in the vicinity of the blast were killed outright.

T

TAAL **VOLCANIC ERUPTIONS 1591-1965**

background: Taal volcano, forty miles south of Manila on Luzon in the Philippine Islands, was active long before its first recorded outbreak in 1591, when thousands were killed. Its next serious eruptions were in 1754, when hundreds died, 1911, when 1,335 died, and in 1965, when 200 natives were killed.

The gigantic volcano Taal sits in the middle of a small volcanic island in Lake Taal, south of Manila in the Philippines and, like its sister volcano, Mayon, the mountain has been belching death for centuries. Taal's first recorded eruption was in 1591, although the volcano had been active for several centuries before that. In the 1591 outbreak there was a great loss of life, many thousands perishing not from lava flows but from asphyxiation. As on Martinique when Pelée burst, victims were quickly overwhelmed by lethal fumes shot quickly from the mouth and side of the mountain. On May 13, 1754, the volcano again erupted with great damage, and for seven months it sent out great showers of pumice, rock and flames, destroying four villages and killing hundreds.

In modern times Taal's most devastating eruption occurred on January 30, 1911. It was preceded by earthquakes that rattled the surrounding countryside for 100 miles at 8:00 P.M. on January 27. These tremors continued for twenty-four hours, and during the night of January 27-28, Taal began to give off a great column of black smoke.

A party of United States engineers encamped at Bayuyungan were awakened from their sleep on January 28, stepping from their tents, which were situated about a quarter of a mile from Lake Taal (or Bombon Lake). One of the engineers, a man named Couch, described the upheavals: "About 3:00 A.M. severe detonations and an electrical display occurred. Crater smoke was carried off southward, and this condition lasted about three minutes. Earthquakes were felt at daylight, January 28, and ashes fell at camp all day. This continued, and at 4:00 P.M., January 29, a violent quake occurred, another at 11:00 P.M. and one about 1:00 A.M. On January 30, I was awakened by a loud rumbling noise. The explosions resembled heavy artillery. There was electrical display in great volumes of black smoke at the crater, and the smoke drifted over our camp with a light fall of ash. The explosions ceased and we went to sleep until the great explosion of 2:20 A.M., January 30.

"Loud rumbling noise was again heard, and before I could get out of bed an explosion of indescribable severity took place. Smoke came out of the crater in dense clouds. The rumbling noise grew louder and louder, and then came a heavy report. I then saw the mud issuing from the crater as a cloud. In a few seconds I saw this cloud drifting across the lake toward our camp. Our camp was then swept by a heavy wind which broke the tent ropes and threw the tent into the air. This atmospheric disturbance threw me a distance of about fifteen feet. A rain of ashes fell about eight inches deep, the air was oppressive, and we gasped for breath for twenty seconds. For half a minute there was light warm rain, then cold rain for fifteen minutes. A tidal wave from the lake reached the camp a quarter mile back from the shore. We took refuge on higher ground, everything was washed away at the camp, one of the party was slightly burned about the arms with hot ashes, but otherwise we did not suffer injuries."

Couch and his fellow engineers were more fortunate than natives dwelling closer to the volcano. Thirteen villages and towns were obliterated by the blast of hot mud mixed with sulfuric acid, flaming stones and rocks and searing ash. One villager was awakened by the thunderous roar, but before he could rise his son ran to the door. The boy dropped dead, coated with a thin layer of scalding mud. The villager's entire hut was covered with burning ashes and mud that had been driven through every available opening by a cyclonic wind accompanying the eruption. Another villager in Tabla looked up from his bed to see scalding mud pouring through his roof. He barely managed, badly burned as he was, to run to the lake, dive in and swim for his life.

Mud, ashes and gases moved in a whirlwind sheet outward from Taal as it vomited. Everything in the path of this volcanic hurricane was flattened. Trees were cut down to stubby, splintered stumps. Plants were carbonized for a distance of six miles. Every blade of grass within ten miles was destroyed. Nothing lived three miles east and nine miles to the west of the crater.

Burning mud rained down on the town of Guilot and incinerated it. A wave of gas and heat swept through the village of Bugaan and killed all there. Almost six miles from the volcano, the volume of mud reached thirty-one inches in depth.

Forty miles away the sprawling city of Manila was thrown into panic. Taal's abrupt roar was heard 310 miles away, and its immense black clouds could be seen from a distance of 250 miles. The wind created about the volcanic island and over the waters of Lake Taal was so forceful that it squashed every hut in a dozen villages; it knocked down hundreds of fleeing natives. The eruption created an atmospheric depression recorded 186 miles away.

The 2:20 A.M. outbreak was actually a double explosion that ripped away the volcano's lake-covered floor, and as great electrical storms played about Taal's summit, huge fissures opened and fire and lethal gases escaped. The town of San Jose, about fourteen miles from the crater, was wiped out, half its population asphyxiated by the sulfuric fumes sweeping over them.

During a lull from 3:00 to 3:45 P.M. on January 30, geologist W. E. Pratt and a photographer climbed close to the crater to take pictures. Fifteen minutes after they departed, the volcano, as if on cue, once again exploded with killing force. They later said, "No animal life could have lived on that island. Not a blade of grass escaped. Trees eight inches in diameter were broken, leaving stumps one to two feet high with ends shredded in splinters by the sand and small stones driven by the force of the eruption. A 600-pound boulder fell on top of the highest ridge. A breadcrust bomb of augite andesite was found, one meter in diameter."

This eruption took the lives of 1,335 people and severely injured another 199. Most of those caught in the death zone either succumbed to sulfur dioxide in the escaping steam or were simply splattered to death with scalding mud—there was no flow of lava. Taal's burning mud and ashes covered an area of 2,000 square kilometers, but its steam eruption ceased shortly after it began.

This was the case when its next outbreak was recorded at 2:00 A.M. on September 28, 1965. Ironically scientific observers had measured the temperatures of Lake Taal only hours before and found conditions to be safe; villagers were not warned and, as a result, when Taal exploded, more than 200 perished. Vulcanologists later reasoned that the volcano had erupted when lake waters surrounding the crater seeped into one of its many underground fissures. The waters reached the volcano's magma (from the Greek word meaning "underground water" or "a well"), created steam and subsequent pressure, like an overloaded boiler, which caused Taal's solid magma plug to be disgorged, throwing up its titanic clouds (which reached ten miles high) of ash, dust, gas and mud.

(ALSO SEE: Mayon)

TABSO AIRWAYS — AIR CRASH
November 24, 1966

On its regular flight from Sofia to Budapest and Prague, a Soviet-built Ilyushin-18 plane belonging to Tabso Airways crashed near Bratislava, Czechoslovakia, on the night of November 24, 1966. The four-engine turboprop, carrying eighty-two passengers and crew members, had just taken off from Bratislava airport after an unscheduled stop. Snow began to fall. This was a contributing factor of the crash, as the pilot was apparently blinded and crashed into the steeply rising Carpathian Mountains surrounding the Czech capital on the Danube. All on board the plane were killed. Passengers included the Bulgarian opera singer, Katya Popova.

TACOMA, WASHINGTON — STREETCAR WRECK
July 4, 1900

A streetcar packed with Independence Day celebrants went out of control while descending a steeply graded street in Tacoma, Washington, on July 4, 1900. A dozen people jumped wildly from the speeding streetcar as it plummeted down the hill, and those trapped inside and unable to reach a platform tossed their children from the windows. The motorman leaped from the car a moment before it catapulted into the air, turned over and landed upside down, its heavy wheels crashing through the floor and crushing a dozen people to death. Forty-one persons, including some of those who jumped or were thrown from the hurtling car, were killed in this streetcar wreck.

(ALSO SEE: Chicago, Illinois, 1950)

TACONA — VOLCANIC ERUPTION
April 18, 1902

Preceding the killer eruption of Pelée on Martinique by three weeks, the volcano Tacona in Guatemala let loose a furious outpouring of rocks and lava on April 18, 1902, that showered down upon the city of Retalbulen, situated at the foot of the mountain. Enormous quantities of lava, stones and ashes covered the town and surrounding countryside, and 1,000 inhabitants were killed.

One account states: "For weeks a black pall of smoke hung over its summit, and the glare from the crater frequently illuminated the sky. Many of the inhabitants of Retalbulen fled from their homes to places of safety. . . . When the eruption at last broke forth in its full fury, showers of lava, ashes and stones were ejected and covered the country for miles around. The Bay of Champanico was a mass of floating pumice and ashes."

(ALSO SEE: Pelée)

A helicopter hovers next to the blazing Taeyunkak Hotel in Seoul, South Korea, December 25, 1971; 163 persons perished in the raging fire. *(Wide World)*

TAEYUNKAK HOTEL **FIRE**
December 25, 1971

The twenty-one-story Taeyunkak Hotel in downtown Seoul, South Korea, blazed into a towering inferno on December 25, 1971, at 10:00 A.M. The fire started in a second-floor coffee shop, where propane gas used for cooking burst into flames. Fortunately the luxurious 222-room hotel was half empty at the time of the fire, and many business offices in the building were vacant. Many of the 187 guests and 130 employees, however, were hopelessly trapped by the flames.

Scores of terrified persons attempted to find fire escapes, but the few available were cut off by smoke and flames. Firemen arrived, but when guests shouting from the windows realized that their ladders reached only to the fourth floor and their hoses were capable only of sending water to the ninth, they panicked and began to jump to the pavement below. Twenty-six bodies fell together in an ugly clump of dying humanity.

Thirteen helicopters then hovered about the building, attempting to pluck guests from window ledges (the roof was not safe as a landing area). Though they did manage to rescue a handful of people, two more persons slipped from the helicopter ladders and fell to their deaths.

The most determined effort at rescue was that of Sydney Sien-yung Yu, the sixty-four-year-old Minister of the Chinese Embassy, who was trapped in his smoke-filled room on the eleventh floor of the hotel. Special Forces members of the Korean Army tried to climb the building and failed. A circus troupe of acrobats then attempted to get a rope to the diplomat by using a series of interconnected bamboo poles. Everything failed. When the fire went out four hours later, two Seoul policemen simply climbed the charred stairs and carried the minister out alive. The fire took the lives of 163 persons and dozens more were seriously injured. Three days later, Korean authorities arrested 8 persons and charged them with negligence. These included the hotel owner, Kim Yong San, and 4 other hotel officials, plus 2 former city officials and a fire officer.

(ALSO SEE: Gulf Hotel, LaSalle Hotel, Newhall House, Stalheim Hotel, Winecoff Hotel)

TAITO, FORMOSA **TYPHOON**
September 16, 1912

The typhoon that struck Taito, Formosa, on September 16, 1912, killed 107 persons and injured another 293. It was one of the worst ever experienced in that hemisphere. When the barometer was at 28.05 inches, the temperature increased almost twenty degrees. Wind velocities shot well over 200 m.p.h., and these fierce winds were responsible for the destruction of 200,000 houses.

TAMPA BAY, FLORIDA **MARINE DISASTER**
August 20, 1559

A Spanish expedition seeking to colonize Florida set sail from Veracruz, Mexico, in July, 1559. Fifteen hundred men were crammed into thirteen lumbering caravels. After two weeks of easy navigation under the command of Don Tristan de Luna, the flota entered the Bay of Miruelo, now Tampa Bay, and was overwhelmed by a powerful hurricane on August 20, 1559. Every ship was either broken apart or hurled onto land by the fury of the storm. About 600 Spaniards, mostly soldiers, perished with the fleet. One caravel, according to a report, was found perched upon a towering bluff, carried there intact by the fierce hurricane winds. All aboard her were dead at their stations.

TAMPICO, MEXICO — HURRICANE

September 24, 1933

Crossing the southwestern Gulf of Mexico, a wild hurricane jumped inland at Tampico, Mexico, on September 24, 1933. This was the second hurricane to visit the city within the space of ten days, and its punishing winds and flooding waters created more than $5 million in damage. An exact number of fatalities is unknown since thousands of unemployed vagrants at the height of the Depression had settled in the city. It was estimated that hundreds of these displaced persons, unable to find refuge from the storm, were killed.

TAYLEUR — MARINE DISASTER

January 20, 1854

background: The 1,997-ton iron sailing vessel, *Tayleur,* designed and built for immigrant crossings by Charles Moore & Company, sank on her maiden voyage on January 20, 1854, a day after leaving Liverpool, as she struck the rocks of Lambay Island. Drowned were 349 passengers and crew members.

One of the first huge ocean-going passenger ships of the newly organized White Star Line, the same ship company that would suffer the *Titanic* disaster in 1912, was the iron vessel *Tayleur.* Her ship-broker owners, Henry Wilson and John Pilkington, claimed she was the "perfect immigrant ship." They publicly claimed that the *Tayleur* would "undoubtedly prove the fastest of the Australian fleet, as she has been constructed expressly with the object of attaining the highest rate of speed."

The owners neglected to inform the 500-plus passengers and crew members who boarded the *Tayleur* at Liverpool on January 19, 1854, that the vessel was embarking without any trial runs whatsoever and that she was a perilously unbalanced ship. Her captain, John Noble, discovered this hazardous fact when at sea only one day. He found it impossible to compel the ship to respond to her helm, so he reduced speed to about one knot.

Most of the immigrant passengers, en route to the gold fields of Australia, were unaware of the navigational difficulties and enjoyed a rather calm first day as the ship edged down the Irish Sea. On the second day a sudden gale rose, and the ship was in serious trouble off Lambay Island, about ten miles north of Dublin. Noble attempted all sorts of maneuvers, but the ship failed to respond properly, so he ordered his anchors dropped. The cables of both anchors snapped in the storm, and the ship was thrown sideways onto the jagged shoals of Lambay Island. Quickly holed, the *Tayleur* drifted out to sea some distance, but crew members managed to get a line ashore, and as the ship began to sink, passengers tried to grapple the line and pull themselves to land. About 230 managed to get to shore this way, but 349 persons drowned as the ship slipped beneath the waves. About 250 of the dead were women and children. They included the wife and child of the ship's doctor, Cunningham, who attempted to bring his family to shore over the line. A large wave drove the Cunninghams under in agonizing view of those shouting encouragement from shore.

TEMPLETON & SONS — FIRE

June 17, 1876

Nothing is known of the cause of the great fire that gutted the massive Templeton & Sons manufacturing company in Ayr, England, except that it began in the teasing department at noon on June 17, 1876. Most of the employees of the woolen and carpet company were young girls, ranging in age from eleven to twenty-five, such were the compassionless work laws of the era. The entire work force was trapped when the blaze broke out; most were on the second and third floors of the main building.

About twenty girls ran screaming down one gangway in search of an escape route, but were blocked by roaring flames. One girl jumped three floors and, miraculously, was unhurt. This, in turn, prompted several more girls to leap to the cobblestones; all of them died, their bodies "forming a mound of quivering flesh."

The fire soon spread to that portion of the building called the new mill and engulfed the single staircase by which at least twenty more girls tried to escape. Met by the flames, they raced to the windows. As they called out

Crowds collect outside the manufacturing plant in Ayr, England, owned by Templeton & Sons, after it caught fire on June 17, 1876. *(Illustrated London News)*

for help to those gathered below, they realized that no firefighting equipment was on the way and that they were left to their fate. Someone below shouted up to them that the only way to survive was to jump. One terrified girl did and was killed. The others found a lower roof and let themselves down to it and safety. In all twenty-nine persons, mostly female employees, perished in the fire. Templeton & Sons estimated their loss at £100,000.

TEXANITA (and OSWEGO GUARDIAN) — MARINE DISASTER — August 21, 1972

In heavy fog on August 21, 1972, two Liberian tankers, the 43,339-ton *Texanita* and the 48,300-ton *Oswego Guardian,* collided fifty miles off Cape Agulhas, South Africa. The *Texanita,* which had emptied her cargo of oil, had in her empty tanks what one official called "easily ignited and terribly explosive fumes." Only moments after the collision, the *Texanita* "had her guts ripped out," according to her captain, Juorios Salvuardos, who managed to be blown clear of the ship. He survived with two other crew members. The vessel sank in four minutes, and forty-seven of her fifty men went down with her.

This towering funnel-shaped tornado of April 9, 1947, proved to be the most destructive in the history of the Texas Panhandle. It killed 169 people. Damages were estimated at $15 million. *(Wide World)*

TEXAS — FLOODS — December 1-5, 1913

Heavy rains bloated the Brazos, Guadalupe, Little and Colorado rivers in Texas, December 1-5, 1913. Sudden overflows quickly inundated farms and caught the mostly rural population by surprise. Drowned were 177 people. More than $9 million in damage was done.

TEXAS — FLOODS — July 1, 1936

The San Antonio and Guadalupe rivers in Texas were sent to floodtide on July 1, 1936, following torrential cloudbursts. The rampaging rivers soon overwhelmed the towns of Kyle, Bunt Branch, Uhland and several more communities. Lost in the floodwaters were twenty-six persons. Approximately $2 million in damage was done.

TEXAS (COAST) — HURRICANE — July 21, 1909

The coastal cities of Texas were lashed by a ponderous hurricane that drove sluggishly out of the Yucatan Channel but vented its full fury against Bay City, Galveston and Velasco, as well as a score of smaller towns, on July 21, 1909. This savage storm created a ten-foot tide at Galveston, wrecked Bay City and, at its center, utterly flattened Velasco. Killed along the coast were forty-one Texans, and damage from the storm soared to $2 million.

TEXAS (and OKLAHOMA) — TORNADOES — March 13, 1953

The most destructive of a series of tornadoes that set down on March 13, 1953, was the one that swept through Knox City and O'Brien, Texas. Killed were seventeen Texans, and twenty-five others were injured. More than $1.5 million in property damage was done by this single storm.

Oklahoma also suffered from a flurry of six tornadoes on this day in which three more persons were killed; losses reached $500,000.

TEXAS (OKLAHOMA and KANSAS) — TORNADO — April 9, 1947

> **background:** The most destructive tornado in Texas Panhandle history struck White Deer, Texas, on the evening of April 9, 1947, and moved in the widest path ever known—one and a half miles—into Oklahoma, and then Kansas, striking down a dozen towns, killing 169 in Texas and Oklahoma, and creating more than $15 million in damage. The twister moved a distance of 221 miles from White Deer, Texas, to St. Leo, Kansas.

The thick humidity and eerie silence that pervaded the flatlands near Amarillo, Texas, on the evening of April 9, 1947, soon boiled over into an exploding tornado, one of the wildest twisters to ever stomp through the Panhandle. H. W. Holmes, a stockman living in the small Texas town of White Deer (population 500), stepped from his back door and grimaced as he spotted the tornado poking its black snout over the horizon. He remained petrified on the threshold of his home as he watched the twisting, clutching, plowing tornado growl forward. Its low rumble sounded to him like "a fast freight train." This funnel did strike a freight train just as it entered White Deer, derailing nineteen cars and two cabooses.

Holmes stated that as he watched the monster grind toward him, "debris filled the air as far as I could see." He saw a house uprooted and jerked into the air. It "hung there, and shook like a fish net being dipped out of the water." Though only three people were hurt in the town, White Deer was half destroyed by the twister, which suddenly lifted and dashed off to the northeast.

Its next victim was Glazier, Texas, and it marched through this town with what must have seemed vengeance to its 125 residents. Two of these, C. S. Wright and Art Beebe, saw the tornado coming and quickly hung up a closed sign in their filling station. They raced to Wright's home and dove into the basement of the two-story masonry building. Bracing themselves against a wall, the men felt the full impact of the twister as it struck the house. Up went Beebe, 30 feet into the air. The tornado bore him aloft for 200 yards and dropped him on a pile of debris. The 240-pound Wright was yanked into the purple mass and sent flying more than 300 yards before he was deposited on a plum thicket. When he struggled out of the thicket, Wright could see scores of cattle all about him bellowing in agony, boards and sticks driven into their sides.

Glazier was finished, completely leveled with only a small schoolhouse to testify that the town had been there. Sixteen of its residents were dead.

Fifteen miles away the tornado ground into Higgins, Texas (population 750), flattening every building save three and killing 45 persons. Though torrential rains and golfball-sized hailstones fell in the twister's wake, Higgins burned furiously when fires were ignited in its debris.

At the Oklahoma border the town of Shattuck was wiped out, and then the tornado plunged into Oklahoma, its destructive force gathering and increasing rather than dissipating.

Woodward, Oklahoma, a town of 5,500, received the tornado's most destructive blow. It was exactly 8:42 P.M., remembered Clyde Grim, a fifty-seven-year-old mechanic. He had just finished dinner with his wife when the kitchen door was ripped from its hinges by the wind. "It blew us outside on the ground," he recalled. "There were cars in the air, some blowing straight up. People were screaming. It was awful. There was a hissing and a popping sound, and through it all I could hear my wife praying." Grim's wife and 94 others would be dead before the twister relented. Almost a third of the town, about 100 blocks, was utterly devastated.

White Horse, Oklahoma, received a glancing blow as the tornado ripped its way northeast into Kansas, where it created $200,000 in damage but killed no one. It died outside St. Leo. In all 169 persons lost their lives to this monster twister.

(ALSO SEE: Gainesville, Georgia; Lorain, Ohio; Omaha, Nebraska)

TEXAS CITY, TEXAS — EXPLOSION-FIRE — April 16-18, 1947

background: The community of Texas City, Texas, ten miles north of Galveston on Galveston Bay, was rocked by a colossal explosion at 9:12 A.M. on April 16, 1947, when more than 2,300 tons of fertilizer made with highly combustible ammonium nitrate caught fire in Number 4 hold of the 10,419-ton, former Liberty Ship, *Grandcamp*. The sprawling Monsanto chemical plant, which occupied fifty acres along the waterfront, and next to which the ship was berthed, was obliterated by the blast. Most in the vicinity were killed or so seriously injured that death came shortly thereafter. A total of 552 persons died, with 3,000 injured and 200 missing. Damage exceeded $100 million. The explosion on April 17, 1947, of the 6,214-ton *Highflyer,* which was carrying sulfur and ammonium nitrate and was berthed near the *Grandcamp,* further added to the calamity by setting fire to and exploding bulk sulfur in a nearby terminal warehouse. These fires spread through Texas City, destroying fully a third of the buildings. It was the worst harbor explosion in American history.

It was called "The Port of Opportunity." Springing up during World War I, Texas City, Texas, mushroomed from 5,000 to 15,000 people during World War II. Ideally located as a deep-water port ten miles across Galveston Bay from Galveston, Texas City was a bustling boom town and one of the country's leading oil refinery centers. It also provided an enormous amount of synthetic rubber through vast styrene plants like that operated by the Monsanto Company. The government had pumped more than $18 million into Texas City's styrene production alone. Cheap Mexican and Negro laborers made up half of the work force that worked along the city's docks constantly loading and unloading the seemingly endless stream of Liberty Ships that steamed into the harbor. Through the flat, marshy plain edging the bay stretched honeycombs of oil and gas tanks. Prosperous as Texas City might have been, it was, like Halifax, Nova Scotia, during World War I, an immense tinderbox storing just about every conceivable product that could explode.

On April 12, 1947, the French-converted Liberty Ship *Grandcamp* entered the harbor and tied up next to the quay adjoining the huge Monsanto complex, only 700 feet from the main plant. The ship's giant holds were slowly filled by grunting stevedores with sacks of fertilizer to be taken to the war-ravaged farms of France. The fertilizer was a highly flammable composite of nitrate and ammonium. Four days later, at 8:00 A.M. on April 16, ship's carpenter, Julien Gueril, entered Number 4 hold and smelled smoke. Moving a few of the sacks (made of extremely dangerous plasticized paper despite laws prohibiting such packaging), Gueril saw that a few fertilizer bags were on fire. He called for some buckets of water from other crew members, and these were passed down to him. The fire increased. The carpenter next seized a fire extinguisher and began spraying the cargo, but he made little headway.

Becoming nervous, Gueril called up to shipmates to pass down a hose. Just as the hose was being lowered, the *Grandcamp*'s skipper, Captain Charles de Guillebon, appeared above the hatchway and shouted down: "Stop! Don't put water on that cargo! You'll ruin it. [Destroying that cargo would have meant a loss of only $400 to $500.] Come up out of there, and we'll turn on the steam system." Gueril climbed out of the hatch, which was then battened down. Steam jets were turned on to suffocate the fire, a standard firefighting measure practiced by seamen for decades. The ammonium nitrate, however, reacted in a most unpredictable way. It was later learned that its critical decomposition point is 350 degrees Fahrenheit, and the steam soon brought it over that.

As the *Grandcamp* billowed smoke from her hold, hundreds of curious dockworkers, businessmen and passers-by stood on the pier gawking at the smoky spectacle. A camera fan showed up and began to film the fire. Two weeks later when receiving the film and showing it for friends she would faint at what suddenly appeared on the screen.

On board the *Highflyer,* berthed nearby, second mate Ken Lapham watched the *Grandcamp*'s crew abandon ship when Captain de Guillebon realized that the fire had been sent out of control through his use of steam. Texas City's entire small fire department appeared and began spraying the ship. Said a lucky Lapham later: "Everybody on our ship was standing around watching them fight it. The Number 4 [hold] had nitrate fertilizer in it, and there were rumors that the Number 5 had ammunition." Lapham did not know that in 1921, workers in Oppau, Germany, used explosives to destroy a dump of ammonium nitrate and blew up themselves, as well as 1,500 other persons and most of Oppau. Nobody warned the almost 300 spectators watching the *Grandcamp* fire that a similar explosion was probable. Ammonium nitrate was the same white sugary chemical that went into the making of TNT.

Only thirty-six hours earlier, at a National Maritime Union meeting in New York, James Gavin stood before members and told them that he didn't "like the looks of a Gulf port named Texas City, where inadequate safety precautions made the harbor a 'natural' for a major explosion disaster."

By 9:00 A.M. the firemen had made little progress against the mounting fire. Volunteer fireman and the president of the Texas City Terminal Company, Henry J. Mikeska, called Galveston for tugboats to pull the *Grandcamp* out into the bay. The tugboats never appeared.

It was 9:12 A.M., and scores of children out of school joined gapers on the wharf. Their observations became a "vision of hell," as one writer put it. In one of the most devastating thunderclap explosions on the North American continent, the *Grandcamp* exploded into nothing; Captain de Guillebon and 32 of his sailors were blown to pieces (there were 10 surviving crew members). Those lining the wharf were mowed down *en masse,* 227 people, including six-year-old Ken Adams, whose father had reluctantly allowed him to tag along to work with him to "see the fire."

The force of the blast is almost impossible to conceive to this day. Some have likened it to a low-yield atomic bomb; one expert thought of it as "the detonation of 250 five-ton blockbusters going off at once."

The roar was heard 160 miles away. Every window in Texas City shattered, as well as half of those in Galveston 10 miles distant. Fragments of the *Grandcamp* blew skyward for a distance of almost 3 miles and landed as far as 5 miles away from her berth. A one-ton piece of her propeller shaft was found later 13,000 feet from the wharf, imbedded 6 feet in someone's driveway. Twenty blocks of Texas City's waterfront and twelve blocks inland were obliterated in a second. Two planes circling 1,000 feet overhead were caught by the blast and blown apart, their four occupants falling crazily to earth in bloody chunks.

All the surrounding buildings and oil and gas tanks erupted into towering flames—including not only the huge Monsanto complex, but also the tanks owned by the Humble, Stone and Republic oil companies. More than 3,300 dwellings were smashed to splinters and 600 cars were flattened. But the carnage in human life was most appalling, traumatic and utterly terrifying.

A moment after the blast a Negro worker, Frank Taylor, crawled through a hole blown through one of the Monsanto plants and fell into the bay. He swam a mile to his home and found his house all but leveled. Stupid with fear and exhaustion, Taylor found a hammer and nails and began to rebuild the structure on the spot while the city burned around him.

Explosive oblivion for Texas City, Texas, came when the cargo ship *Grandcamp* blew up in her berth and ignited oil dumps nearby. *(Wide World)*

The first blast sent a 100-pound metal fragment through the windshield of Hollie O. Youngman's auto, and both he and his wife were decapitated. Eight persons, four of them brothers, were crushed lifeless by a railroad flatcar that flew from its tracks. A baby was blown out of its mother's grasp and disappeared forever. Another baby in the arms of its mother was dead, a splinter of glass driven into its brain. Refusing to give up her infant the dazed mother wandered down Sixth Street with the baby still in her arms.

All the telephone lines except one were down in Texas City, and over this wire a frantic operator screamed to anybody: "For God's sake, send the Red Cross—thousands are dying!"

For two miles down Dock Street, Texas City flamed, bright orange tongues licking skyward. Sightseers on board a ferryboat in the bay gasped as a tremendous waterspout went up, and they continued to gasp as, one after another, gas tanks blew up in orange-yellow mushrooms.

Inside the Monsanto plant all was chaos. Dr. W. H. Lane, a research chemist, reported "looking out of the window at the burning ship. All of a sudden there was a frightful explosion. The ship literally blew into bits. The walls were crashing as we scrambled for the door." A worker raced from the plant, yelling at the top of his lungs to a friend, "Hey, Harry! Look at me! Ain't I lucky? I didn't even get scratched!" He jumped onto a bicycle and pedaled furiously for 200 yards before toppling over dead. The back of his skull had been blown away.

The 800 workers in the Monsanto plant raced as the ceilings and walls began to cave in. One worker was blown through a fifth-floor window and survived with only a broken ankle. A man with a wooden leg, who had been watching the fire on the wharf, was blown several hundred feet away and escaped unharmed. His wooden leg was found a block away sticking in the ground. Monsanto warehouse worker Philip Flores also miraculously survived and later reported, "I was working in a warehouse twenty-five yards away from the ship when it blew up. I crawled over to some flour sacks and buried my head under them. Then a few seconds later there was another explosion. The roof and walls of the warehouse were coming down around me. I helped pull the bodies out of the wreckage. One man with a leg blown off was screaming with pain. I couldn't tell you how he looked because he didn't have much face left."

The blast tore through the black ghetto, which was only 4,000 feet from the docks. It pancaked hundreds of homes. Classes in an elementary school were abruptly halted as all the windows in the building went to pieces in the detonation and slashed the faces of almost all the 900 children inside. Traumatized and then panicked, the children bounded screaming past their teachers in wild searches for their parents.

Almost everything in Texas City was destroyed. The water mains ruptured, and there was no water to fight the raging fires. All electric lines and all telephone lines except one were down.

Confusion was rampant in police headquarters. The chief of police and his dispatcher reacted to the blast by running into the toilet and remaining there for a full minute. "I never have figured out why [I did that]," he later said.

Across the bay in Galveston, a Red Cross doctor saw the mighty explosion. He dove for his phone and began calling doctors, nurses and ambulances. Police and fire department teams were alerted, and they left Galveston, Fort Worth, Houston, Dallas, Beaumont, Port Arthur and San Antonio to aid burning Texas City. Red Cross units across the country boarded airplanes and were en route to the stricken city within minutes.

Bodies or pieces of bodies littered the streets. One man picked up a glove and found a single severed finger inside. A dockworker fainted as he looked down to see that he was slipping on gory intestines tangled about his feet.

People were running about naked, but no one noticed. A woman wearing only a corset raced from a lingerie shop when its windows blew out. A man who had been near the wharf watching the fire managed to scoot beneath his auto just as the ship blew up. Steel splinters ruptured the gas tank, and the gas spilled down on him, burning his flesh. He got up and ran, but the friction of the cloth increased his pain. First he took off his pants, then his shorts, and finally, he ran all the way home, a distance of two miles, naked from the waist down. "Nobody gave a damn," he stated later. "In fact, nobody even saw me because they were all so busy going someplace else."

Uptown, a mile distant from the blast, the manager of the White House department store was picked up by an unseen force and hurled through the post office door. Windows and doors of the First State Bank blew out, and money flew crazily over the floor and out windows. Nobody attempted to retrieve the cash. Everyone was busy scurrying for cover.

In the composition room of the *Texas City Sun*, pressman Jay Cohen blinked incredulously as linotype machines weighing many tons jumped several inches from the floor. Jeweler Louis Alexander looked up at the first second of the blast as his front door tore away from its hinges and flew directly at him. The explosive force mashed autos in the business area and collapsed buildings like closing accordions.

Staggering away from the blast, dockworker Juan Torres found his home leveled. Gone were his brother, father and sister-in-law. He plopped down onto the rubble and wept.

Many people inside buildings several miles distant were tossed about wildly. One woman, Mrs. Tena Lide, was lifted up and carried out of a second-story window by the rush of air.

There were feats of unthinkable bravery. A warehouse worker with half his foot blown away revived eight unconscious workers and led them down to the fifth floor of a burning building where flames blocked the way. The man then climbed five stories down a drain pipe, tearing the flesh from both arms as he moved, to alert rescuers to the plight of those still inside. When rescuers saved these eight men, they found the injured worker sitting on a pile of rubble. Offered medical aid, he told them to attend to others and took a long swig of whiskey from a bottle he carried. The man then began to cut off the dangling part of his foot with a pocket knife "to ease the pain."

Everything burned along the waterfront. The fires went unchecked into a half-dozen residential districts. The huge Texas Terminal Railway building blazed up, and seconds later a man emerged carrying a bedsheet. Inside he had tossed $10 million in insurance policies that he turned over to the police.

By noon Texas City was a billowing inferno of hundreds of fires converging on each other. The dead and dying were everywhere. City hall was immediately converted into a hospital, and Red Cross doctors and nurses ushered thousands of injured inside. A group of Texas Rangers wearing pearl-handled pistols kept order. The medical teams were overwhelmed. One nurse could not believe it: "All of a sudden the casualties poured in on us, by foot, automobiles, trucks, ambulances, commandeered school buses. There were thousands of them, cut and bleeding. Litter bearers with dying patients couldn't get in the doors, the crowds were so dense."

Hundreds of volunteers were ordered to pick up the human debris scattered throughout the city. One dockworker thought he had been stumbling over hunks of meat on the wharf where the *Grandcamp* had been; he thought it was part of the cargo. He was falling over dismembered bodies of the ship's crew. Another volunteer went about the dock area, avoiding the flames, plucking human gore from the debris. "I carried out pieces of bodies all afternoon," he later told newsmen, "but for all that work I don't believe they added up to two people."

By night Texas City was acrawl with National Guardsmen warding off looters from ruined buildings. Regular troops arrived by plane and began to unload blankets, plasma and C-rations. President Truman ordered all federal agencies to send direct aid to Texas City. Firemen from other cities refitted water mains and were, by dawn, successfully driving back the fires.

On board the *Highflyer,* which had somehow escaped the initial blast, Lieutenant W. L. Gregg of the navy received orders to withdraw his team from the ship. The *Highflyer* had caught fire on the morning after the disaster, and several attempts had been made to put out these flames. Tugs arrived and tried to pull the *Highflyer* into the bay, but she had been smashed into the nearby *Wilson B. Keene* by the initial blast, and the ships were hopelessly locked together. The tugs gave up, and Lieutenant Gregg ordered his men off the *Highflyer.* (Controversy later surrounded the fate of the *Highflyer.* Deputy Mayor John Hill was to state: "We asked the tugboats to pull the *Highflyer* out to midstream. They refused. They heard she was carrying ammunition. The ship drifted free and then exploded.")

Moments before this second titanic blast at 1:10 P.M. on April 17, Lieutenant Gregg had remarked to one of his men: "I'll have to tell my wife I'm safe." A second later Lieutenant Gregg was blown off the bridge, his right leg sliced away.

The *Highflyer*'s explosive cargo went up with an earsplitting blast, demolishing the ship and the *Keene* next to her. Captain Vulney J. Shown of the Houston police department watched horrified as fifty men combating the waterfront blazes "were cut down like wheat before a sickle." The fires inland raged anew, and the firefighters were driven back in the second day of the holocaust. Hundreds more perished in the second fire and shock wave. All that night Texas City burned while a wild evacuation of terrified residents was under way. The lurid fires, roughing the grim faces of those fighting them, blazed up mightily. By 2:00 A.M. Galveston County constable Herbert Whitmore turned to a newsman and lamented: "All of Texas City is liable to go if the wind turns back to the south."

But the wind did not turn and what was left of Texas City was spared more devastation by fire. Its mayor, J. C. Trahan, a war veteran who had been exposed to all kinds of horrors in the European theater of operations (World War II) stood on the stairs of city hall, stairs blotched with the blood of his fellow citizens. Peering toward the waterfront and the billowing black smoke towering upward, he said: "I got the Purple Heart for

Rows of corpses await identification in the Danforth School gymnasium after the Texas City fire; 552 people were killed. *(UPI)*

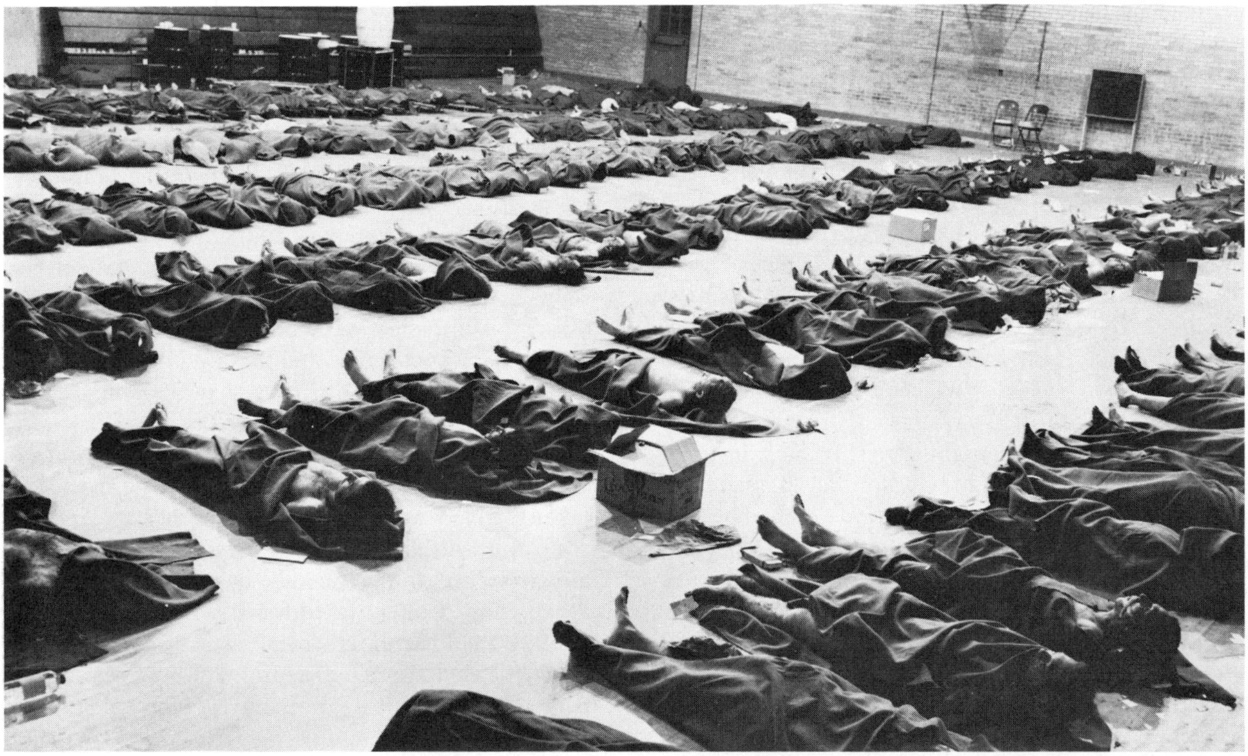

buzz-bomb wounds in Belgium. No buzz bomb could ever compare with what happened here. . . . It is such a terrific tragedy that the people have not been able to realize what happened."

He was right. The stunned residents of Texas City had been worked over by personal trauma and insanity (three persons were adjudged hopelessly insane following the explosion). One man, a leading citizen, was seen walking directly into the waterfront fires on April 18, muttering: "I've got to get some sleep." Another man sat in tattered clothes in his home, five miles from the fire, staring at the handle of a coffee cup that had encircled his finger for two days. He was lifting a cup of coffee to his lips in a downtown restaurant at the moment of the explosion. He remembered nothing else, not even how he managed to get home.

Scores of faithful filled a Presbyterian church. A hollow-eyed man entered and stood for a moment in the aisle. He then screamed: "It's going to blow!" The entire congregation stampeded outside only to discover that nothing had happened and nothing was about to happen. The alarmist had disappeared.

Panic and terror lurked everywhere on the last day of the disaster. Soot-covered rescue teams collapsed in sleep in front of city hall. With the crash of a crumbling wall in a burned-out building nearby, the rescue teams leaped up and began running with no destination in mind. Rumors were whispered along the ranks of rescue workers that tanks were seeping chlorine gas and poisonous nitrogen dioxide. When a mortician entered a supply room and asked for a gas mask for his embalming chores, a worker shouted, "Hey, get me a gas mask!" The cry caused everyone present to momentarily abandon reason and scramble for gas masks. These groups ran to the street wearing their masks and incited further panic.

The storing and embalming of bodies was grisly and unending work. Many corpses brought in were so rent with splinters and steel slivers that the bodies would not hold embalming fluid. Texas City's largest repair shop, McGar's Garage, was turned into a temporary morgue. This morgue became a place of horror, a charnal house a foot deep with blood to which 552 bodies or pieces of bodies were brought.

As bodies were brought into McGar's, each was covered with a blanket, and a yellow tag was tied around each person's toe. The identification tags had been borrowed from the nearby Port Arthur Police Department, and they bore the printed line: "You have violated a traffic law."

But most of the corpses brought into the morgue were impossible to identify. One person was identified by only his right hand. Nothing else was left. The hand was fingerprinted and the prints revealed his identity. (The identities of 200 were never determined.) Several persons were identified after pathologists examined their stomachs and analyzed the contents. Relatives were then asked what the deceased ate for breakfast on the morning of the explosion, so the identification could be made.

One gruesome identification was made when a torso, minus head, arms and legs, was brought to the morgue. Buried in its chest was a car key. A woman thought the key looked familiar and asked to see it. An attendant dug out the key and the woman took it to her family car and inserted it into the ignition. The car started; the torso was her husband.

The identification of the dead went on for days; people collapsed in grief or became violent when they recognized a loved one. A woman who finally found her husband after hours of rummaging through the rows of dead laughed in wild hysteria. Another wife stared a long time at the half-obliterated face of one corpse and then shook her head. Just before she turned to go, she glanced at the feet and let out a piercing scream. It was her husband. The night before the explosion she had, in a moment of bizarre caprice, painted his toenails with bright-red fingernail polish.

(ALSO SEE: Bone, Algeria; Halifax, Nova Scotia)

THETIS — MARINE DISASTER

June 1, 1939

background: The British submarine *Thetis,* on her first diving trial fifteen miles north of Great Ormes Head, submerged too quickly because of malfunctioning equipment and sank bow first in shallow water. Although salvage and rescue attempts to save the crew trapped inside were repeatedly made, the *Thetis* slipped from grappling lines and disappeared. Dead from asphyxiation were ninety-nine crew members and observers; four men escaped.

Taking her trial diving runs in the Irish Sea, the British submarine *Thetis,* with Lieutenant-Commander Sam Bolus in charge, began to slowly submerge fifteen miles from land in shallow water on June 1, 1939. The tugboat *Grebecock* was close at hand to ward off other ships. As the *Thetis* began the slow process of flooding, Lieutenant Coltart, an observer on board the *Grebecock,* was startled to see the vessel suddenly plunge beneath the waves. Unknown to him at the time, the submarine had taken on too much water, causing her to go out of control during her dive. The *Thetis* did not resurface along the prearranged course covered by the tug, and at 4:00 P.M., Coltart wired for help in locating the sub.

More than two hours later, a small flotilla began to sweep the area. Night fell before a thorough search could be organized, and it was not until the following morning at 7:30 that the destroyer *Brazen* found the stern of the submarine jutting from the water. Before the destroyer could put men into a long boat, two heads bobbed to the surface, those of Captain H. P. K. Oram, who commanded the submarine flota to which the *Thetis* was assigned, and Lieutenant Woods. They explained that part of the sub was flooded and that many men had collapsed for lack of air. *Thetis*'s skipper had made the mistake of keeping his men busy while they awaited rescue instead of having them remain quiet to conserve oxygen. Woods and Oram had escaped from one of the two escape chambers located forward and aft in the ship. These were air lock chambers that were flooded after the escaping men had put on special breathing apparatus. When the water pressure in the chamber was equal to that outside, the outer hatch was opened, and the men swam slowly to the surface. It wasn't until 10:00 A.M. that another team of men, Frank Shaw, an engine fitter, and a stoker named Arnold, appeared.

These two men explained that panic had seized one crew member when he and three others had entered the air chamber. After the escape chamber had been closed, the four men had attempted to open the outer hatch but found it stuck. One of them became so frenzied that he pulled off his oxygen mask and those of the others. All four drowned, and it took those still conscious in the sub almost an hour to drain the escape hatch and yank out the bodies. The powerfully built Arnold wrenched free the difficult outer door, and Arnold and Shaw then made their escape.

Even while the escapees were narrating their horror stories, salvage ships arrived and slipped cables around the *Thetis*, which was sinking fast. A crew using acetylene attempted to cut open a piece of the sub's hull, but the vessel suddenly lurched forward and quickly escaped the restraining cables, going to the bottom with ninety-nine crew members and naval observers still on board. The ship was brought to the surface weeks later by the cargo ship *Zelo*, and the bodies were removed.

The *Thetis* was eventually refitted and sent back to service as the *Thunderbolt*. She saw heavy action during World War II until she was sunk by the Italian warship *Cigogna*, which depth-bombed her out of existence on March 14, 1943.

(ALSO SEE: Squalus)

THRESHER — MARINE DISASTER

April 10, 1963

The huge 4,300-ton United States submarine *Thresher*, the first of her class, was launched in July, 1960, and the nuclear vessel conducted several routine missions before she came to disaster on the morning of April 10, 1963. Accompanied by the *Skylark*, a sub rescue ship, the *Thresher* began a series of test dives 220 miles east of Cape Cod. At 9:13 A.M. the *Skylark* received an inexplicable message: "Have position up angle attempting to blow up ballast tanks." Moments later the *Thresher* again signaled, but the message was garbled by what appeared to be the sound of a ship breaking up.

The *Thresher* and the 129 persons on board (34 more persons than the regular crew, including 17 civilian technicians) were never seen again. The ship went down in an estimated 1,400 fathoms where the pressure of 3,700 pounds per square inch would certainly have crushed her to pulp.

(ALSO SEE: Affray, Duplinar*)*

TIME GO-GO CLUB — FIRE

November 2, 1974

The Time Go-Go Club in the Dawang Building in the eastern part of Seoul, Korea, burst into flames in the early morning hours of November 2, 1974. The building contained a hotel and offices as well as the club, which was situated on the sixth floor. There were 350 people in the building at the time. While flames shot up from an undetermined source, patrons coughed and gasped their ways to windows that they smashed open with their fists. Not waiting for firefighters, a half-dozen people jumped, screaming, to their deaths six floors below.

When the fire alarm was set off in the building, many club patrons raced for the doors and escaped. Management personnel, one report stated, barred the doors because they thought the alarm was a ruse by customers to avoid paying their bills. This possibly contributed to the high death count of seventy-eight charred bodies. Another forty persons were injured in the blaze.

(ALSO SEE: Joelma Building)

TIPTON FORD, MISSOURI — RAILWAY WRECK

August 5, 1914

The first railway wreck involving a "doodlebug"—an all-electric, single suburban rail car—occurred outside Tipton Ford, Missouri, on August 5, 1914. A seven-car passenger train, which belonged to the Kansas City Southern Railway and ran on Missouri & North Arkansas tracks, met the suburban car head-on as both trains were making about 35 m.p.h. The doodlebug, carrying about 100 gallons of gasoline, exploded as it was driven backward down the track more than 600 feet from the point of impact. Its three-person crew and forty-four passengers were instantly cremated. The blame was placed upon the dead crew of the doodlebug for disregarding orders that instructed them to wait for Kansas City Southern's Number 56 to pass at Tipton Ford.

TITANIC

MARINE DISASTER
April 14, 1912

background: Built during 1910-12 with her sister ship, the *Olympic,* at Harland and Wolff's shipbuilding works in Belfast, Ireland, for the British White Star Line, the S.S. *Titanic* was a super luxury liner 882.5 feet long, 92.5 feet broad, and displacing 45,000 tons. The *Titanic* possessed a crew of 700 and was capable of providing accommodations for more than 1,500 passengers. Her tragic deficiency in lifeboats led to the loss of 1,517 passengers and crew members (out of 2,207) when she sank on the fifth day of her maiden voyage from Queenstown en route to New York after striking an iceberg off the Grand Banks. The date was April 14, 1912.

The *Titanic,* pride of the British White Star Line, though much publicized as the "greatest ship on the seas," was not unique. Her sister ship, the *Olympic,* was an exact duplicate. Both ships were 882.5 feet long and luxurious. Both displaced 45,000 tons.

Both were launched from Harland and Wolff's shipbuilding works in Belfast, Ireland. When the *Titanic* sent out her desperate SOS, her sister ship, more than 500 miles away and heading in the opposite direction, heroically turned about, her boilers heated to the bursting point, and plowed frantically through the north Atlantic toward the *Titanic.*

The sinking of the *Titanic* was the kind of tragedy and drama seldom found even in the best of fiction. But the real tragedy is that the sinking of the ocean colossus need not have happened.

Tragedy could not have been further from the mind of Captain E. J. Smith on April 13, 1912, as the *Titanic* sailed through a tranquil Atlantic on her maiden voyage to America. The white-bearded, kind-eyed captain had been with the White Star Line for thirty-eight years and was its most experienced officer.

He was happy with this crossing. His job of late had been simple. He commanded all new White Star Line ships on their maiden voyages, a job given to him out of respect for his service. The crossing of the *Titanic* was going to be his last act for White Star. Captain Smith planned to retire after this trip.

Much has been blamed on this hapless man who, according to the ancient tradition of the sea, went down with his ship and thus could not defend himself at several boards of inquiry. For years people believed that Captain Smith was a grandstander out to make his last voyage spectacular—that he was determined to set a record in speed and that it was because of speed that the ship sank.

Untrue. The *Titanic,* capable of almost thirty knots, a great speed even today, was under orders from White Star owners to proceed slowly. This was a company

The *Titanic* being launched. The 45,000-ton liner was 882½ feet long, 92½ feet broad.

policy for every new ship, and Captain Smith obeyed. The *Titanic* steamed along at a conservative twenty-two knots.

Smith walked on *Titanic*'s proud decks, listening to her triple screws turning and the humming of her two powerful sets of four-cylinder reciprocating engines. She was a beauty, and Smith knew it as well as her other 2,206 passengers and crew did.

But everything was against the *Titanic,* even nature. That winter had been the mildest in recent years. It was well known that more icebergs than ever before had broken away from the polar caps and come down with the Labrador current into the Atlantic.

White Star officials knew this and purposely charted a southerly course for the *Titanic.* According to all information on icebergs, this should have put the great ship on a free course.

When the *Titanic* crossed the Grand Banks on Sunday night, April 14, 1912, neither Captain Smith nor anyone else had any idea that the icebergs had slipped much farther south and that the *Titanic* was sailing at twenty-two knots (forty-five nautical miles every two hours) right into them.

Reports of several sightings of icebergs did come over the wireless, but since the closest reported one was 250 miles away and posed no danger to the *Titanic*'s path, Smith saw no reason to alter her course.

Five days out of Queenstown and headed for New York, the *Titanic* rode a beautiful, quiet sea on April 14. First officer Murdock and second officer Lightoller, watching the water that night from the bridge, remarked that it looked like glass.

The whole, broad expanse of ocean before them was moonless, but it was brightly lit by dozens of star clusters. It was 10:00 P.M. and Murdock was relieving Lightoller.

The second officer was amazed at the brightness of the stars. The horizon was a knife's edge, and the stars went down and through it shooting half-light in slivers across the water.

Murdock and Lightoller knew there was always a possibility of icebergs; extra seamen had been posted as lookouts.

"It's a pity that the wind hasn't kept up while we are going through the ice region," Lightoller said. His wish was a simple one. If there had been wind that night, the iceberg that struck the *Titanic* would have been spotted earlier. The wind would have created a wash from its breakers that could have been seen by lookouts. But there was hardly any wind at all.

Shortly before, at 9:40 P.M., John George Phillips, the first officer in the Marconi wireless room on board the *Titanic,* had received a message from the *Mesaba,* which was sailing directly in front of the *Titanic.*

White Star Line's elaborate brochures advertised the *Titanic*'s elegant entrance hall and grand staircase (top); spacious writing room (bottom) where millionaires and cabin boys silently sat and waited for the water to close above their heads.

The *Mesaba* ominously warned of the location of icebergs and repeated: "Saw much heavy pack ice and great number large icebergs. Also field ice. Weather good, clear."

Phillips did not deliver this message to the bridge. He was swamped with messages to be sent to New York by the *Titanic*'s wealthy passengers making arrangements to be met at docking time. Besides he had received iceberg warnings all day, and they had become routine.

In addition, Phillips was unaware of the *Titanic*'s navigational position and he could not interpret the iceberg locations as being anywhere near the *Titanic.* He placed the *Mesaba* message on the desk next to him and continued sending passenger messages. He decided to deliver it when he had time.

That time would never come. Situations and fate were stacking up fast against the *Titanic.*

By 11:30 P.M. first officer Murdock had taken a

position next to the forward rail, sixty feet above the sea. He was exceptionally watchful that night. He had even ordered a lamp-trimmer named Hemmings to shut the forescuttle hatch since a dim light coming from there affected his vision.

Seaman Frederick Fleet was in the crow's nest, eyes straining. Suddenly he saw it, a giant menacing hulk of ice looming up forty to fifty feet from the flat surface of the sea. Quickly he lunged for the warning bell and rang it three times—object dead ahead.

Fleet grabbed the phone to the bridge and shouted: "Iceberg, right ahead!"

"Jesus, Mary," Murdock whispered prayerfully and dove for the telegraphs. He yanked them over to "Stop!" Wheeling about, Murdock yelled at wheelman Robert Hitchens, "Hard-a-starboard!"

Hitchens threw his entire weight against the wheel and glanced at the clock on the bridge, which read 11:40 P.M. He saw the berg about a quarter of a mile away. The *Titanic* slipped slowly to port, still doing twenty-two knots.

Then the berg drifted rapidly toward the *Titanic*, coming up fast to starboard. Hitchens felt the wheel stop. "Wheel hard over!" he called to Murdock.

"Hard-a-port!" Murdock yelled back.

Then they felt a slight tremor begin forward of the foremast and continue alongside the ship. Unseen, a spur of the iceberg sticking out like a razor on an underwater shelf caught the ship as she threw her entire weight against it. It ripped the *Titanic* like a can opener cutting tin.

It was only ten seconds before the ship disengaged, but the iceberg had cut into her on a line of over 300 feet. The gash tore through three large holds and two boiler rooms.

At first passengers were not alarmed: first-class passengers watched, amused, as the iceberg slipped past them. It was an adventure. Second-class passengers were more aroused—the iceberg brushed so close to the ship that hunks of ice fell through open portholes.

Steerage passengers, mostly immigrants, felt the full impact of the collision and were tossed about wildly. They panicked.

Thomas Andrews, the designer and builder of the *Titanic*, was on board. When he heard the faint noise of the collision from his cabin, he went to the bridge. Someone remarked that the grinding noise sounded as if someone were "tearing a long, long strip of calico."

Andrews raced below decks to inspect the damage with the ship's carpenter. Although all the watertight doors had been closed upon impact, Andrews soon reported that the situation was hopeless. The ocean water was fourteen feet above keel level, and there were holes in no fewer than six compartments along the starboard side.

The *Titanic*, pride of the White Star Line and the British Empire, the "unsinkable ship," was doomed.

Only Captain Smith, Andrews and the carpenter knew this, however, and even the crew and officers were kept in the dark about the extent of the *Titanic*'s damage.

Smith ordered "all hands on deck," and men poured out onto the boat decks. The 325 men working in the holds and boiler rooms, who would later die at their stations, plus 50 officers throughout the ship, remained at their posts.

The *Titanic* had been sailing with a full head of steam, and when she was abruptly halted, the steam roared off at all four exhausts. The sound was like blast-furnace explosions, and when the passengers heard it for the first time, terror began to creep into their minds. Was it possible? Could the *Titanic* actually sink?

Except for the steerage passengers, who were in pandemonium in the lower decks, the first-, second- and third-class passengers had no idea what was happening. They were politely asked to leave their cabins by soft-spoken stewards: "And bring your life preservers, please."

Hundreds of people came out on deck in sweaters, bathrobes, fur coats and evening dress. There was no panic. The decks felt solid, and only the roar of steam from the four giant funnels gave any cause for alarm.

The stewards were amazingly breezy about it. "It's only temporary," they said when asked why the *Titanic* was dead in the water. "In a few hours we'll be on our way again. Minor repairs."

The passengers on the *Titanic*'s many decks looked apprehensively at the sixteen wooden boats and the four canvas collapsibles known as Englehardts. They did not know that the twenty available lifecraft, if filled to capacity, could carry only 1,178 people. And there were 2,207 on board.

Captain Smith hurried to the wireless shack and ordered Phillips to send out the distress signal—CQD—to any and all ships in the vicinity. Phillips leapt to the wireless and tapped out frantically: "CQD MGY *(TITANIC)* I REQUIRE ASSISTANCE IMMEDIATELY STRUCK BY ICEBERG IN POSITION 41 46 N 50 14 W."

It was a message that shocked the world.

The Atlantic was loaded with ships that night, but many either failed to pick up the *Titanic*'s signal or were too far away to give assistance. Even though the great ship *Olympic* turned around 500 miles away, she would arrive far too late.

The old Cunard liner, *Carpathia*, however, picked up the *Titanic*'s signal. *Carpathia*'s captain, Arthur Rostron, was awakened in his cabin by his wireless operator, who read the distress signal.

The *Titanic*'s captain, E. J. Smith, went down with his ship. He was later criticized for making too much speed through the ice packs.

Valiant Major Archibald Butt threatened "to shoot the first man who made for the lifeboats" before women and children were taken off the sinking *Titanic.* He went to the bottom singing a hymn.

A hero of the *Titanic* disaster was Captain Arthur Rostron, who all but wrecked his vessel, the *Carpathia,* in steaming to the rescue.

Bruce Ismay, general director of the White Star Line, survived to live in shame. Ismay jumped into the last lifeboat being lowered, taking the place of a woman.

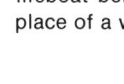

New York millionaire Isidor Straus remained with the men on the liner and bravely went to his death.

Colonel John Jacob Astor (inset) and his wife were aboard the *Titanic.* Astor refused to enter a lifeboat until all the women and children had abandoned ship. He died on the liner; his wife survived.

"The *Titanic,*" he said. "That's impossible. She's the greatest ship afloat. How could she be in trouble?"

The wireless operator checked back with Phillips. It was true. Rostron ordered the *Carpathia* about.

Phillips was desperately sending out his CQDs when the *Carpathia* answered: "WE ARE COMING TO YOUR ASSISTANCE."

The *Olympic* broke in wanting to know the *Titanic*'s position. Phillips answered with: "*TITANIC* TO *OLYMPIC.* WE ARE PUTTING THE WOMEN OFF IN BOATS."

"Off in boats," *Olympic*'s captain groaned. "My God, she's going down!"

"*OLYMPIC* TO *TITANIC.* WE ARE LIGHTING UP EVERY BOILER AND MAKING FOR YOU AS FAST AS WE CAN."

But it would be the rusty old *Carpathia,* her boilers next to exploding, her frame shuddering with a speed she had not known in years, that would be first to the scene of the disaster.

As second officer Lightoller, the only officer to survive, tried to enforce the rule of women and children only into the lifeboats, Phillips sent out the new code distress signal. "SOS, SOS, SOS, *TITANIC* SINKING HARD BY THE BOW . . . SOS. . . ." The *Titanic* was the first ship in history to send out an SOS.

All the available lifeboats, carrying 711 women, children and seamen (with a few men disguised as women), rowed away from the sinking ship. The ship's band played ragtime music on deck, and then switched to "Londonderry Air" and the hymn, "Autumn."

About 1,500 persons, mostly men, stood helpless on the decks, watching their wives and children disappear in the little boats into the ice field. The *Titanic* fired off all her rockets in hopes that passing ships might see her.

One did, the *Californian,* but her Captain Lord mistook the white and red flares for a party on board the luxury liner. Only five miles away he ignored the signals and went to sleep—an act which would make him infamous forever.

Artist Willy Stoewer envisioned the nightmarish sinking of the *Titanic* days after the great ship sank.

The old *Carpathia* was up to twenty-four knots, a speed she never reached in her prime years. She was only an hour away. Entering the ice field, Captain Rostron refused to reduce speed. The *Carpathia* twisted and dodged one iceberg after another. There was ice on all sides, but the *Carpathia* turned desperately at full speed like a broken field runner in her mad dash toward the *Titanic*.

It was 2:15 A.M. Phillips sent out his last message. "*TITANIC* TO ALL SHIPS. ENGINE ROOM FULL UP TO THE BOILERS . . . CQD-CQD-SOS-SOS. . . ."

Suddenly, the *Titanic* gave a great shudder as her boilers exploded, left their beds and thundered through the length of the ship. She rose to an angle almost perpendicular to the sea; her passengers were slung like confetti into the sea and slipped fast into it as she went down, down.

Those in the lifeboats watched her go, and the roaring din she made echoed in their ears.

Millionaires and immigrants died together, all common people at the end. A great bubble of water rose in the *Titanic*'s wake as she raced and roared to the bottom. One lifeboat passenger said later, "I heard her going down through the water . . . it sounded like a long freight train leaving its tracks."

She was gone.

In an hour the *Carpathia* steamed into view, firing her rockets to signal that she was coming. This valiant little ship, which was to save 711 survivors, performed one of the most courageous acts ever witnessed on the high seas, risking her own safety to do so.

There was much courage that night—and some cowardice. Most of the men on board accepted their fate heroically, including Captain Smith, who wrapped his flag and slipped it into his pocket and then stood resolutely on the bridge to go down with his ship.

But the general director of the White Star Line, Bruce Ismay, did not display courage. In desperation he jumped into the last boat as it was lowered and lived for the rest of his days with the shame of saving his own skin.

There were many melodramatic and moving stories connected with the sinking of the *Titanic*. One was that a French man named Navatril smuggled his two small sons on board the ship before sailing without telling his wife, who remained in Paris. Though he went nobly down with the ship after assisting several women into boats, his sons were saved, but no one knew who they were. Newspapers all over the world ran their photos, and their mother, living in Paris and not knowing where their father had taken them, identified the boys. They were reunited with their mother weeks later.

Another story dealt with one Gus Cohen, whose

Titanic survivors were taken on board the *Carpathia* only hours after the great ship went down.

This photo of the Navatril children appeared in newspapers throughout the world as authorities sought to identify them. Their father had sailed with them secretly on the *Titanic* and was drowned, but his children were saved. Their mother recognized them, and they were returned to France.

friends later called him "The Cat" because he seemed to have nine lives. Cohen not only survived the *Titanic* sinking, but also a head wound in World War I and near-miss bombing in World War II. Nearly fifty years later, Cohen was riding a train to a television station in England when he fell off and was hit by a car. He survived that, too.

There was also a report that the captain's safe contained a mysterious "Black Buddha" statue, encrusted with rare gems and worth millions. The story goes that the statue had been stolen from a temple in Peking and that it carried a curse that had caused the disaster.

True and yet most unbelievable is the fact that the *Titanic* disaster had been predicted in detail fourteen years before the sinking.

Morgan Robertson, a popular novelist, wrote a novel called *Titan* in 1898. The author wrote of a great luxury liner—an unsinkable ship—loaded with wealthy passengers that hit an iceberg in the month of April and sank in the Atlantic with almost all on board lost.

The fictional *Titan* did not have enough lifeboats to accommodate passengers—and this was true of the *Titanic*. The *Titan* had only twenty-four lifeboats—and the *Titanic* had only twenty.

Robertson's imagined liner was 800 feet long. The *Titanic* was 882.5 feet long.

And the fictional *Titan* sank on her maiden voyage.

Some occult experts claimed that this was a perfect example of "promnesia," a memory of the future. Perhaps it was.

"Everything was against us, everything," young officer Lightoller said later.

It was a correct statement of the disaster, which could be attributed to the mildest winter ever recorded, no wind, a careless wireless operator, an underwater spur that should not have been there, a black Buddha and a strange vision of the future that went unheeded.

TJAEREBORG AIRLINES — AIR CRASH

March 14, 1972

A Tjaereborg twin-engine Caravelle, en route from Colombo, Ceylon, to Copenhagen, Denmark, signaled Dubai Airport on the Persian Gulf that it required an emergency landing to refuel on March 14, 1972. The plane, with 106 passengers and 6 crew members on board, was about forty miles north of Dubai. It was purposely off its scheduled course because of bad weather. No further word from the plane was heard by ground control, and hours later the wreckage of the Caravelle was reported scattered over the slope of a nearby mountain. All on board were killed, and the cause of the crash was never determined.

TOKYO, JAPAN — EARTHQUAKE-FIRE

March 21, 1857

Following a massive earthquake that shook most of the provinces ringing Tokyo, Japan, fires broke out on March 21, 1857, and spread rapidly through the cheaply constructed buildings that made up the bulk of the metropolis. Though the quake had killed thousands, the fire, as would be proved again in San Francisco five decades later, was the greater hazard, destroying large sections of the city and causing most of the 107,000 fatalities in the disaster. Cyclonic winds of 60 m.p.h. greatly aided the blaze.

TOKYO, JAPAN — TYPHOON

September 30, 1918

background: A severe typhoon raged in from the Philippines to the south and struck Tokyo, Japan, on September 30, 1918, devastating the city and surrounding areas. Killed in collapsing houses or drowned by heavy waves were 1,619 persons; 2,400 people were homeless. Almost all the neighboring fishing fleets, about 2,000 boats, were destroyed. Damage soared into countless millions of yen.

September is the typical storm month for Japan, with heavy gales and even typhoons sometimes sweeping up from the Philippines; winds in these storms usually reach 70 m.p.h. The high pressure storm that struck Tokyo, Japan, at 9:00 P.M. on September 30, 1918, eased its way onto the mainland, causing the inhabitants to think it no more than the average heavy rainstorm. By midnight, however, the gale had developed into a full-fledged typhoon, one of the worst ever to strike Tokyo and the Tokaido region, as well as the provinces of Kanagawa, Chiba and Ibaraki.

The city's sleeping residents were rattled from their slumber by winds and rains traveling at more than 100 m.p.h. In the words of Y. Shima, writing for *Japan Magazine:* "A furious hurricane was blowing, the rain coming against the windows like buckshot and the houses rocking and swaying as though the next blast would undo them. By 3:00 A.M. the wind was at its height, and the cottages of the poor were tumbling over their heads and killing them in various parts of the city."

Though the maximum velocity of the storm lasted only an hour, more than 600 people in Tokyo were killed. The weak structures of the working classes gave way first, then even such solid buildings as the Ebisu Brewery and the Seiyoken Hotel collapsed. To foreign visitors in Japan, the typhoon was an unbelievable nightmare. Shima stated, "Even those in the strong, foreign-built houses sat up all night, the roofs rocking over their heads, and the rain streaming down through the ceilings where tiles were blown off, expecting every move of the houses to be the last. Here and there windows burst out with a sudden explosion as in a cyclone, and shutters and roofs were lifted into the air and disappeared."

Those living along the waterfront suffered most, especially when the winds slapped down their feeble dwellings and drove them out into a storm that had caused giant waves to sweep inland, flooding neighborhoods like Kasai and Sunamura in nine feet of water. Whole families, suddenly caught waist-deep in rushing waters, were swept away. Dozens of children were dragged from the arms of their parents and sent to watery graves.

The following day found Tokyo in ruins. Miles of electrical wires were in mammoth, tangled masses. Millions of pieces of broken roof tiles littered every street and byway. Every fence, wall and lamppost were torn away. Clumps of ancient pines that had withstood typhoons for hundreds of years were uprooted and splintered. Parts of bodies stuck out from beneath crushed houses.

In Tokyo 629 people died. Another 990 deaths occurred outside of the city. Hundreds were missing and 139,000 persons were made homeless when 200,000 houses fell in the storm (45,000 in Tokyo alone).

To partially defray the millions of yen in damages, the emperor sent out his imperial chamberlain with 100,000 yen to give the poor along the wrecked waterfront. The government announced that the army and civilian technicians would rebuild the entire city in a short time. So thorough was this propaganda that it produced a kind of dazed cheerfulness among the residents, as Shima pointed out: "Men, women and children might be seen wandering around among the wrecked houses, gazing at the debris of their former belongings without any sign of despair on their smiling faces, evidently persuaded that all would come right.

"Thousands flocked from other parts to see the scenes of destruction, some preferring to witness the devastated regions by moonlight, as being more impressive and picturesque. As the fury of the gale abated near dawn, the full moon peeped brightly through the clouds; some of the people remarking that it did so innocently, not knowing what ill the wind-god had wrought upon the inhabitants."

TOMBORO — VOLCANIC ERUPTION

April 5, 1815

background: The ancient 13,000-foot volcano, Tomboro, on the island of Sumbawa, the third island east of Java, erupted with colossal violence beginning on April 5, 1815, and culminating with an eruption on April 11-12, 1815, that hurled an estimated thirty-six cubic miles of matter into the air. This exceeded all known volcanic eruptions. Only 26 natives on Sumbawa, out of a population of well over 12,000, survived the steamblast. An estimated 37,000 more people on neighboring islands died of starvation, an indirect result of the eruption.

Long thought extinct, the towering volcano of Tomboro on the lush island of Sumbawa, situated east of Java, began to show signs of life in late 1814, when thin showers of ash were thrown off. Residents took little notice of the activity until the night of April 5, 1815. According to one account, the deep-cratered explosions so resembled "the firing of heavy cannon at a distance that the people of many vessels at sea supposed there was a great naval engagement within hearing, but could not imagine what nations were engaged." Several English forts throughout the islands were strengthened, and commanders ordered some ships to sea to repel invaders or pirates.

All through the Indian Ocean, Tomboro's outbreaks could be heard. The volcano's blasting could be heard in Java, Sumatra, Borneo, the Moluccas, the Celebes and for 1,000 miles.

The quantity of ash thrown out by Tomboro was incredible. It darkened an area of 400 miles for three days. The blackness at midday on Java was so intense that "one could not see one's hand in front of one's face." The ejection of material from Tomboro changed from ash to huge, glowing stones as the eruption advanced into its most deadly stage on the evening of April 10-11, 1815.

By then hundreds of homes on Sumbawa and neighboring Bima, forty miles away, had been crushed by the sheer weight of ash on rooftops. The English governor on Java, Sir Stamford Raffles, recorded Tomboro's historic outbreak: "In a short time, the whole mountain appeared like a body of liquid fire, extending itself in every direction. The fire and columns of flame continued to rage with unabated fury, until the darkness caused by the quantity of falling matter obscured it about 8:00 P.M. Stones at this time fell very thick at Sangir, some of them as large as two fists, but generally not larger than walnuts. Between 9:00 and 10:00 P.M. ashes began to fall, and soon after a violent whirlwind ensued which blew down nearly every house of Sangir, carrying the roofs and light parts away with it."

The whirlwind, in a radius of fifty miles, sucked up cattle, houses, horses and people and carried them to death in the air. An enormous wave, estimated to be between twelve and thirty feet in height, moved outward from the island, like Krakatoa's devastating wave in 1883, raced ashore on neighboring islands and drowned hundreds.

Tomboro began to disintegrate under its own upheavals. It blew away its top and part of its sides so that in two

Rescue ambulances (bottom left) arrive at the pit head of the mine in Tonypandy, Wales, on May 17, 1965, only minutes after an explosion shattered the colliery. Thirty-one miners required hearses. *(Wide World)*

months it shrunk from 13,000 to 9,000 feet. The towns of Tomboro, Tempo and Pekate on Sumbawa vanished in the April 11-12 blast. Gone with these thriving towns were more than 12,000 people; only 26 badly burned inhabitants managed to paddle their scorched canoes to neighboring islands and survive.

The ejection of material by Tomboro was the greatest ever recorded. Ash, rock and debris from the half fragmentized Sumbawa littered the ocean for 500 miles. Ships' captains found it impossible to navigate their vessels; many thought the immense floating debris was land and lowered boats to investigate. Had all the ash given off by Tomboro been gathered, Raffles estimated, it would have made "three mountains the size of Mont Blanc, the highest of the Alps, and if spread over the surface of Germany, would have covered the whole of it two feet deep."

More than three feet of ash completely coated the island of Tombock, 100 miles distant from the erupting Tomboro, and everything growing on this island died. With all vegetation gone, the natives of Tombock, an estimated 37,000 people, perished by starvation. When this number is added to the 12,000 who were killed on Sumbawa, the Tomboro eruption becomes the most deadly volcanic outbreak in recorded history.

The blast produced more than ash and flying, burning rocks. Huge lava streams curled away from the decomposing mountain and raced to the sea. The rush of this lava was so fast that it was likened to "a running mountain stream," and it caught within its flow hundreds of fleeing persons.

To picture the amount of material thrown off by Tomboro—a volume of thirty-six cubic miles—historian Hendrik Willem Van Loon used this illustration. Imagine the world population of 3.3 billion gathered together in one spot. Allowing forty cubic feet per person, the space occupied would be less than a cubic mile. The whole human race could be comfortably placed into one thirty-sixth of the space that Tomboro occupied with the debris from its titanic eruption.

(ALSO SEE: Krakatoa, Pelée)

TONYPANDY, WALES — MINE DISASTER
May 17, 1965

Britain's most highly mechanized mine in Tonypandy, Wales, the government-owned Cabrian Colliery, exploded on May 17, 1965, killing thirty-one miners. The blast—the cause of which was never determined—occurred 850 feet beneath the Thondda valley. An entire crew was entombed in the shaft, which was not more than two feet, eight inches high; the gallery was not much higher.

A spokesman for the company stated: "The men working in that area had little chance." Twelve workers were brought to the surface hours after the explosion; all of them suffered from shock and injuries. Ironically, this mine was scheduled to be closed permanently.

This heavy mining area was the location used in Richard Llewellyn's poignant novel, *How Green Was My Valley,* the bittersweet tale of a mining family's struggle to elude the poverty and hazards inherent in the collieries.

TORONTO, ONTARIO — RAILWAY WRECK
January 2, 1884

A head-on collision between a suburban passenger train and a freight outside of Toronto, Ontario, on January 2, 1884, resulted in the deaths of thirty persons. Both were Grand Trunk trains. The suburban passenger train was made up of a small engine and three cars carrying workers to a nearby factory. The engineer of the freight failed to wait for this passenger train to pass and struck it head-on at high speed. The engine of the passenger train was telescoped. Half of the sixty workers on this train were killed. The freight's crew members jumped to safety just before the collision.

TOYO MARU **MARINE DISASTER**
September 26, 1954

While attempting to navigate the Taugaru Strait during a typhoon on September 26, 1954, the Japanese ferry *Toyo Maru* capsized in the storm and was swept ashore and demolished on the rocks near Hakodate. Although 196 persons managed to save themselves, the death toll was a staggering 794 people.

TRANS-AFRICAN AIRLINES **AIR CRASH**
March 4, 1962

A Caledonian DC-7 crashed on takeoff from the airport at Douala on the west coast of Africa on March 4, 1962, killing all 111 persons on board. The chartered plane, operated by the Trans-African Air Coach Company of London, was going from the Portuguese colony of Mozambique in East Africa to Luxembourg by way of Lisbon, Portugal and Douala in Cameroon. The four-engine craft was only aloft for about two minutes before it crashed under mysterious circumstances. Its smoldering wreckage was found one and a half miles from the end of the runway.

TRANS-CANADA AIRLINES **AIR CRASH**
April 8, 1954

A Royal Canadian Air Force training plane being tested in the clear skies over Moose Jaw, Saskatchewan, on April 8, 1954, suddenly went out of control and shot into a passing Trans-Canada plane carrying thirty-five passengers and crew. Both planes disintegrated, falling in large, flaming chunks to earth. All of those on board the North Star passenger plane died before they struck the earth. What remained of the Harvard training plane and its dead British pilot slammed onto a golf course. Debris from the passenger plane knifed through several houses in northeastern Moose Jaw, setting some on fire. A cleaning woman in one home was killed when a piece of the plane tore through a living room. Her death and that of the air force pilot brought the fatality count in this disaster to thirty-seven.

TRANS-CANADA AIRLINES **AIR CRASH**
December 9, 1956

Captain Allan J. Clarke watched the control panel in his North Star Canadair, a plane similar to the United States' DC-4, and quickly realized that one of his four engines was malfunctioning. It was 7:00 P.M., December 9, 1956, a little over an hour after the excursion plane had taken off from Vancouver, British Columbia, en route to Calgary, Alberta.

Clarke radioed Vancouver that he had feathered (stopped) an engine that apparently had caught fire and was returning to Vancouver, then 100 miles away. He asked for permission to drop from his 19,000-foot position to an altitude of 8,000 feet. Permission was granted. At Vancouver International Airport ambulances and fire trucks were alerted, and the vehicles edged up to a runway. Twenty-five minutes later search planes took off to look for the stricken North Star. Snow storms and fog shrouded the wilderness landscape, and the search planes, which swelled to an air armada of seventeen, came up with nothing after many hours of flying.

It was some time before the debris of the Trans-Canada Tourist Flight Number 810 was spotted near Chilliwack, British Columbia. It had crashed in the rugged wilds in the blinding storm and all sixty-two persons (fifty-nine passengers and a crew of three) perished with the plane. Killed were some players of the Saskatchewan Roughriders football team and their wives. Also among the dead passengers was Russell S. Stratton, a worldwide authority on teletype machines.

TRANS-CANADA AIRLINES **AIR CRASH**
November 29, 1963

A Trans-Canada DC-8F attempting to take off from Montreal Airport on November 29, 1963, suddenly crashed and burned so quickly that not one of the 118 passengers and crew members escaped death. A board of inquiry placed the blame on a faulty vertical gyro warning system inside the plane. Authorities further pointed out that an instrument indicating the plane's horizontal stabilizer position was needed to prevent such accidents from recurring.

The site of a Trans-Canada DC-8F crash near the Montreal airport on November 29, 1963, looked like a bombed-out area in wartime. *(Wide World)*

This TWA Boeing 707 crashed into a steamroller at the end of a runway at Fiumicino Airport in Rome; fifty-one persons were killed in the resulting explosion. *(Wide World)*

TRANS WORLD AIRLINES AIR CRASH November 23, 1964

A Boeing 707, operated by TWA, attempted to take off from the Rome airport on November 23, 1964, but due to mechanical difficulties, the flight was aborted just before liftoff. The plane, which was carrying seventy-three passengers and crew members, lunged into a construction company's steamroller parked at the end of the runway; several explosions occurred. Although forty-four persons managed to escape from the plane, fifteen of them, plus the twenty-nine remaining in the plane, were killed, a total of forty-four fatalities.

A team of Italian aviation investigators later reported that seats blocked wing exits on the TWA plane and that escape chutes were not brought out with enough speed to allow the passengers to flee. It was also pointed out that use of kerosene in the jet engines, instead of the highly flammable JP4 liquid then employed, would have caused the flames from the explosions to spread at a slower rate and would have improved chances for survival.

TRANS WORLD AIRLINES AIR CRASH March 9, 1967

A midair collision over Dayton, Ohio, on March 9, 1967, involved a Trans World Airlines Douglas DC-9 and a Beech B-55 Baron owned by the Tann Company of Detroit. The TWA flight was preparing to land at Dayton when the Beech, en route to the airport at Springfield, Ohio, struck the passenger plane. All twenty-six occupants of both planes were killed in the collision. A subsequent hearing determined that the TWA plane was exceeding the terminal area speed limit and that Dayton Radar traffic control had notified the passenger plane only fourteen seconds before the crash that the private plane was in the area.

TRANS WORLD AIRLINES AIR CRASH November 20, 1967

background: Trans World Airlines Flight 128, a four-jet Convair 880 en route from Los Angeles, crashed while attempting to land at the Greater Cincinnati Airport on November 20, 1967. Killed were sixty-eight persons; fourteen survived. Charges were made that the airport approach was unsafe.

Captain Charles Cochran, 45, with 14,000 hours flying time, was more than familiar with the approach to the Greater Cincinnati Airport outside Hebron, Kentucky. Yet the runway he would use to land his TWA Convair 880 on a snowy November 20, 1967, had a record of curious mishaps. An American Airlines Boeing 727 had crashed about a mile from Runway 18 on a rain-swept November 8, 1965, while making its approach. Fifty-eight persons died in that accident. This same runway was the sight of the crash of a DC-4 belonging to Zantop Airlines on November 14, 1961 (the two crew members of this freighter managed to escape before the plane exploded).

As Cochran brought the Convair into its landing path,

Stewardess Eleanor Kurtock was heard to remark: "I sure hate to land in Cincinnati." Passenger Robert Cooley looked out a window. "I thought we were coming in for a normal landing," he later told newsmen. Instead he had found himself 200 feet from the burning wreckage of the plane. George Brokaw saw sparks emanating from the plane's nose and quickly put his head between his knees, remembering the card instructions of what to do in case of a crash. It saved his life.

For some arcane reason, Captain Cochran nosed his plane down too quickly, and the Convair was soon slicing off the tops of saplings along a ridge over the Ohio River. The plane made the bluff on its belly; its nose burrowed into the earth and created the sparks Brokaw spotted. It then ripped through heavy woods and halted in an apple orchard, where flames engulfed the whole front of the plane and incinerated Cochran. Residents and volunteer firemen came on the run, reaching the wreck, which was 7,050 feet short of Runway 18, just as survivors began to stagger through the smoke.

Fifty feet from the plane, resident Ed Walton saw "this man standing . . . leaning over a fence. 'My eyeballs are burned,' he screamed. 'I can't see! Don't leave me here!' "

Another survivor lumbered through the flames and smoke that lit up the night. Walton approached him.

"Is the plane taking off?" the man asked Walton.

"What?"

"The plane, the plane," he said dazedly. "Is the plane taking off?"

"No, it was landing."

"Oh," yelled the man, "my wife. Thank God, she's safe. I was going to meet her."

Paul Dickman came running up to the flaming debris. He saw a man emerge with all of his hair and half his face burned away; his flesh was hanging from hands that gripped a small child. He looked at Dickman and shouted: "Get to someone who needs help." Then he and the child collapsed into Dickman's arms.

Many did need help, for unlike the history of such crashes, there were three children and fifteen adults still alive. Though four adults would later die, the survival of fourteen persons out of the eighty-two passengers on board was largely due to the quick help administered by residents. The surviving children included a fifteen-month-old baby and Chris and Eileen Haile, ages five and two, orphaned by the crash.

The Civil Aeronautics Board conducted an inquiry into the flaming finish of TWA's Flight 128, but found no outstanding irregularities, other than the fact that Runway 18 was being lengthened at the time of the crash and that Cincinnati's electronic glide slope indicator had been out of service for more than two months (a fact that all pilots had been made aware of). Yet Ohio Governor James A. Rhodes ordered the runway closed. He stated that the approach to the north-south strip was hazardous because winds rolling over the hills of Hebron caused severe buffeting of any plane attempting to land, and the peculiar terrain along this approach caused an optical illusion, which convinced pilots that they were at a much higher altitude than they actually were.

TRANS WORLD AIRLINES (and UNITED AIRLINES) — AIR CRASH, June 30, 1956

background: A TWA Super-Constellation, Flight 2, en route from Los Angeles to Kansas City, Missouri, and a United Airlines DC-7, Flight 718, also originating from Los Angeles but destined for Chicago, crashed in a midair collision at 10:31 A.M. 21,000 feet over the Painted Desert of the Grand Canyon on June 30, 1956. All on board both planes, a total of 128 passengers and crew members, were killed in America's worst air crash to date. The causes of the collision were never fully determined.

In 1956 air controllers were swamped with work, and in the opinion of many of them, their collective ability to handle air traffic was a maximum capacity of 20,000 airborne planes out of the 100,000 aircraft aloft. Indeed it was more than a crowded sky. It was "standing room only."

The overloading caused an average of four near misses each day, four near collisions in midair averted only at the last second by pilots relying upon their own vision to spot an approaching plane. These ugly facts were not known to the general public, and certainly most of the 128 persons who climbed aboard a TWA plane and a United craft on June 30, 1956, were totally unaware of the degree of this daily hazard.

TWA Flight 2, captained by Jack Gandy, took off from Los Angeles International Airport at 9:00 A.M., about a half-hour late, and headed for Kansas City. Gandy's assigned altitude was 19,000 feet. Three minutes later United Air Lines Flight 718 took off from the same airport with instructions to fly at 21,000 feet. The United Airlines flight was headed for Chicago. Neither plane would arrive at its destination.

Twenty minutes after he had powered his TWA Super-Connie into the sky and headed for Salt Lake, Gandy radioed Los Angeles Air Route Traffic Control and requested permission to climb from 19,000 to 21,000 feet, which would allow for a smoother flight above the clouds. The air controller contacted Salt Lake.

Salt Lake responded by telling Los Angeles that United Airlines Flight 718 was already at 21,000 feet and that "their courses cross and they are right together."

Los Angeles ground control informed TWA ground control, who informed Gandy to maintain his scheduled altitude. Gandy then asked for "1,000 on top." This, in essence, meant permission to climb 1,000 feet above the clouds. Incredibly Los Angeles ground control approved this request, which would put the TWA flight, once Gandy had edged his plane above the cloud banks, exactly at 21,000 feet, the very altitude that, moments before, was denied.

Now both the TWA and United planes were at the same altitude. Gandy in the TWA plane had been informed of the United plane's presence, but Captain Robert Shirley in the United DC-7 had somehow remained ignorant of the Constellation's change in altitude. Further, to appease the passenger's appetite for a sightseeing view of the Grand Canyon, both planes would soon be on a collision course.

As both planes moved over the Grand Canyon, the pilots maneuvered their crafts to afford their passengers snapshot views of the Painted Desert. A thundercloud began to obscure vision, and soon both planes were flying blind on parallel courses that, at 10:30 A.M., became only inches apart.

Suddenly the air controller who knew that both planes were at the same altitude and would appear over the Painted Desert at the same time, heard a shouted message that sent terror through him. Crackling over the radio came the shouts: "Salt Lake! United 718! We're going in!" Then, another voice, later thought to be that of a different crew member, broke in with the terse command, "Up! Up!" Then silence.

Just before that moment the United and TWA planes had collided. The Constellation was destroyed in an instant, most of its fuselage disintegrating as the United plane ripped it open. It spilled downward in pieces, its passengers and crew members in deadfalls. Later speculation indicated that all on board the TWA flight were dead before they splattered in bits on the ground; the fast decompression of air caused death. The United plane rode downward in a crash dive, sending out its fatal message, and then hurtling to earth to break up. Its steel frame and human cargo slammed into Chuar Butte, not far from the prophetically-named Cape Final. The remains of the craft showered down on Temple Butte.

All was silent on the Painted Desert for hours, until rescue planes arrived over the crash scene. Noting the pieces of wreckage, the pilots of the rescue planes radioed for helicopters to work their way into the desolate area. The choppers descended many hours later, but rescuers found no one alive to rescue. They got out rubber blankets and began to gather up pieces of bodies. Of the 128 persons killed on both planes, not one body was found intact. The largest human fragment was "half of a woman." Dr. D. R. Hunter, who had experienced years of grim fatalities, moaned to newsmen: "It was a sight I don't want to see again." What was found of the TWA people were charred remains. All on board had been cremated. There was little more remaining of the fifty-eight persons who rode the United plane to death. Half of them were buried in a common grave, as was the case with those who died on the TWA flight.

Scattered among the rocks of the Grand Canyon was the twisted debris of a TWA Super Constellation and a United Airlines DC-7. The two planes collided over the Painted Desert on June 30, 1956. All 128 passengers and crew members on both planes were killed. *(Wide World)*

Grim reminders of this needless crash popped up months later as tourists and prospectors came to authorities with pieces of mummified bodies, clothing, coins and rings. A year after the midair crash, a prospector appeared in Phoenix, Arizona, where he turned over two diamond rings he had taken from the severed hand of TWA passenger Mildred Hatcher, who had been near the tail section of the Constellation, an incongruous, sand-burnished, and gleaming monolith in the Painted Desert.

TRENTON (and VANDALIA, NIPSIC, ADLER, EBER)

MARINE DISASTER
March 16, 1889

background: The U.S.S. *Trenton,* a 3,900-ton, wooden corvette built in 1873 with 2,414 horsepower and capable of twelve knots, along with several other ships of the British and German navies, was overwhelmed by a typhoon on March 16, 1889, while anchored off Apia Upolu in the Samoan Islands. Although only 1 fatality was recorded on this ship, the storm killed a total of 147 sailors through the separate fleets.

Ever since the Dutch discovered the Samoan Islands in 1722, the ten principal islands and several uninhabited ones in the 350-mile-long chain have been hotly contested by many nations. In 1889 the particularly fertile, volcanic islands of Savaii, Upolu, Apolima and Manono became the object of British, German, and United States contention. War ships of all three countries steamed into the harbor of Apia Upolu and anchored; this display of power developed into a military staredown.

On March 16 heavy seas rose, and following this a full-scale typhoon soon roared into the harbor. The three United States ships and four German vessels did not, as would be expected, pull anchor and sail out into the storm to avoid being trapped in the harbor, thereby running the risk of being driven onto dangerous reefs.

The lone British ship, the 2,770-ton *Calliope,* commanded by Captain Kane, got under way, but the seas were so volatile that it took her almost an hour to travel a half-mile. She precariously wended her way through and about the still-anchored German and United States ships. The admirals of the other flotillas refused to leave port, each fearing that the other would quickly land forces and lay claim to the islands. This imperialistic stance soon would cause the deaths of 147 seamen in the two fleets.

As the storm approached its most violent stage, around 5:00 A.M., the German ship *Eber,* a 550-ton gunboat, went out of control. Her anchors were ripped away and she was sent flying onto a jagged reef that quickly holed the ship. The *Eber* sank instantly. Going down with her were seventy-six sailors; only five managed to swim to shore.

As a purple dawn edged behind the raging typhoon, the U.S.S. *Nipsic,* a 1,375-ton vessel, also broke from her moorings. Her captain, Commander D. W. Mullen, immediately decided to allow his ship to sink in order to save his crew. He aimed the vessel for the beach and ordered his sailors into lifeboats. One of the lifeboats capsized in the turbulent waters, and seven men drowned.

Next it was the turn of the 884-ton *Adler,* a German gunboat. A titanic wave hit this ship broadside at 8:00 A.M. and hurled her literally over the water and onto a shoal. She quickly broke up, and twenty sailors fell into the sea and drowned.

Huge combers began to climb over the 981-ton *Vandalia,* a United States gunboat. It soon appeared to Captain C. M. Schoonmaker that his ship was going to the bottom; he ordered his boats lowered. Schoonmaker was too late. His ship foundered, and forty-three of his crew members died struggling in the heavy seas.

That left only the flagships of the German and American fleets, the 2,169-ton *Olga,* commanded by Captain von Ehrhardt, and the United States corvette *Trenton,* under the command of Rear Admiral Kimberley.

The *Trenton* had been struck a glancing blow by the British ship *Calliope* as she made her sluggish escape into the open sea. She was taking a terrific beating from the storm, and Kimberley knew that saving his ship was a hopeless task, but he had been ordered not to yield the harbor to the Germans. He was determined to carry out his instructions. Von Ehrhardt was steadfast to similar directives. As the two flagships pitched and rolled, the German vessel suddenly got up enough steam to move ominously toward the *Trenton.* It appeared that the German vessel was out of control, but Kimberley soon realized that the two damaging blows against the *Trenton* by the *Olga* were intentional rammings.

Anchors snapped and with her crew of 450 men holding on for life, the *Trenton* swung sharply about in the typhoon and was quickly driven to shore. Rear Admiral Kimberley personally directed the well-ordered evacuation of his ship, and lost only one man in the sea. Standing on the shore, the American crew watched as the *Trenton* slipped off a reef and went to the bottom.

The rammings had all but wrecked the *Olga* too, and this ship, the last to go down, was also wildly driven onto a reef. Her crew and Captain Ehrhardt waded ashore in soggy uniforms. The Americans greeted them with ironic pomp. Rear Admiral Kimberley ordered his band to play "The Star Spangled Banner" as the Germans fell exhausted on the beach.

A United States officer marched up to Captain von Ehrhardt, who was still coughing up ocean water and, as the hurricane roared about them, screamed in his ear: "Welcome to American Samoa!"

TRIANGLE SHIRTWAIST FACTORY — FIRE — March 25, 1911

background: The Triangle Shirtwaist Factory, occupying the eighth, ninth and tenth floors of the Asch Building on the corner of Washington Place and Greene Street in New York, caught fire at 4:45 P.M. on March 25, 1911. The building was gutted in eighteen minutes; 145 employees, mostly young females, were killed. Safety regulations and devices were all but nonexistent. Indicted for manslaughter were factory owners Max Blanck and Isaac Harris, who were later acquitted.

Bodies were falling. Excited, terrified knots of people on the sidewalk held up hands and in trauma pushed the air as if attempting to ward the hordes of screaming, burning girls at the flame-licked windows of the Asch Building's ninth floor back into the fiery rooms they were trying to escape. Of all the horror-gripped building fires in history, the burning of the Triangle Shirtwaist Factory on March 25, 1911—a sunny Saturday afternoon—remains one of the most vivid in gruesome memory. It was slaughter on high ledges, death in space and through glass and onto concrete, and it was all so terribly public.

If there was a single aspect of their lives that Max Blanck and Isaac Harris insisted remain private, it was their business: the unsafe, unsanitary and inhumane sweatshops they operated and owned on the eighth, ninth and tenth floors of Manhattan's Asch Building at the corner of Washington Place and Greene Street. The Triangle factory was like that of so many other loft works in New York, where scores of underpaid Italian and Jewish girls, mostly immigrants who spoke little English, labored long hours to earn about $5 each six-day week to support their families.

Firemen unsuccessfully fight the inferno that blazed through the Triangle Shirtwaist Factory in the Asch Building on March 25, 1911. Many employees jumped from the windows, and their bodies littered the street. *(Wide World)*

The Triangle fitted shirt, like most other fitted shirts manufactured in the country at the time, was a popular item. It was worn with skirts by American females from all walks of life. The workers who made them, however, found them too expensive, and a few of the ragged sweatshop workers stole them. The pilfering was minor, but Blanck and Harris felt compelled to screen their employees by installing narrow exits through which only one employee at a time could leave the premises while being scrutinized. This made for a humiliatingly slow departure for home after working hours. It also placed employees in great jeopardy in the event a speedy exit was necessary in case of fire.

Coupled with this single-file egress that led into halls was only one fire escape, and that, an iron fixture located at the rear of the building, reached down only to the second floor. For some reason the building planners did not complete the fire escape. It ended hazardously over an open concrete courtyard. The reason, no doubt, was money. The architect had skimped on the Asch Building at every corner. He argued that a sprinkler system would have cost an additional and prohibitive $5,000 when the structure was completed in 1901. (Asch later paid $400,000 for the job.)

Further, building planners had skimped on construction codes, which required that every building have three complete staircases. The staircase on Greene Street was the only roof-to-street passage. The Washington Place flights ran only to the tenth floor. The incomplete fire escape, reasoned the architect, functioned as the third mandatory staircase.

It was originally thought to build the Asch Building 150 feet high, but building codes required that structures of that height provide expensive metal trim, metal windows and stone or concrete floors. The building was therefore built to a height of 135 feet with wooden trim, windows and floors that were within the law.

All of these factors came into play when the fire broke out just before closing time in a heap of oil-soaked rags in the cutting department on the eighth floor. Many Triangle employees were either on the way out or preparing to leave. Someone spotted the flash fire and yelled. A male employee attempted to put out the flames, but they soon spread throughout the department and a general panic ensued. Scores of women raced into the halls and tumbled down staircases. Some, apparently trying to reach the roof, ran thoughtlessly up the Washington Place staircase and were trapped on the incomplete staircase at the tenth floor. Others clawed madly at a single elevator door, which finally opened. By jamming together and diving on top of a dozen girls already in the elevator, about thirty girls were able to ride the jerking conveyance down to safety, shrieking in panic.

Dinah Lifschitz, an employee on the eighth floor, used the telephone to warn those working on the tenth floor. But after repeated attempts to contact those on the ninth, she was compelled by the encroaching flames to run for her life. Like those before her, she found it difficult to navigate the narrow passageway from the shop to the outer hall. It was through this confining space that the girls had to leave the premises while security guard Joseph Wexler checked their purses to make sure they were not stealing any shirtwaists.

The production manager for the firm, Samuel Bernstein, was one of the last to leave the flaming eighth-floor working area, which by then had been almost wholly consumed by flames. He knew that no one on the ninth floor had been warned, so he raced up the smoke-filled Greene Street staircase, but a large oil drum on the floor above exploded in flames, and he was driven back. Only seconds before, Bernstein had tried to douse the flames on the eighth floor with a rotting hose brought in from a hall by a machinist, but there was no pressure, no water at all; the machinist burned to death before Bernstein's eyes.

The fire department received word of the fire a minute after it began, but the flames spread so rapidly that by the time they arrived the blaze was beyond their control. The tenth floor was quickly evacuated, since most of the girls, along with Blanck and Harris, had fled to the roof. All but one of the seventy workers survived.

Blanck, who was stupefied by the fire, had been trapped in the middle of the shop area on the tenth floor, gripping the hands of his two small, terrified daughters who had come to visit his office. An employee, Edward Markowitz, who was just about to leave, turned and saw Blanck and his children. He ran back, scooped up the youngest child, and led his catatonic employer into the hall and up the stairs to the roof.

The fatality on the tenth floor was shopgirl Clotilda Terdanova. Bernstein, who was helping Harris direct employees to the roof, saw Miss Terdanova go mad with fear. "She tore her hair and ran from window to window until finally, before anyone could stop her, she jumped out. She was young and very pretty. She was to leave us next Saturday to be married three weeks later," he said. She was the first to jump to her death.

Author Leon Stein in his exhaustive work on the fire interviewed Joseph Fletcher, an assistant cashier of the Triangle firm who managed to reach the roof. He ran to the edge and gaped in horror at what was occurring below. "I looked down the whole height of the building," Fletcher told Stein. "My people were sticking out of the windows [on the ninth floor]. I saw my girls, my pretty ones, going down through the air. They hit the sidewalk, spread-out and still."

When flames erupted in the ninth floor, the work force there, all 250 persons, bolted for a single door leading to the Washington Place staircase. The door was locked. (It would be later claimed by those prosecuting Blanck and Harris for manslaughter that they purposely locked this door to prevent employees from leaving the premises until they had been checked to see if they were smuggling out shirtwaists.) Most of the employees here raced to the windows and screamed to those below for help.

But there was little the people on the ground could do. Several fire department squads were cursing ladders that would only reach to the sixth floor. They were frustrated and in agony that the streams from their hoses could not reach to those now climbing out onto window ledges as flames licked at them.

Some women managed to gain the ninth floor hallway, and like lemmings, they crammed themselves into a single elevator. They were the last to descend. When the elevator went down, a half-dozen panicking girls leaped onto its top. More followed. As the elevator moved downward, more and more girls jumped down on top of it, landing on the prostrate and unconscious bodies of their fellow workers. The elevator shaft became a bloody death pit piled high with corpses.

The fire escape at the rear of the building was suddenly crawling with shrieking employees pouring out from the ninth floor. They tumbled down the rickety affair from flight to flight, crawling over each other. Fire shot from all the floors of the building by then, darting out and setting clothes and hair on fire. In a mad rush the mob made its way to the bottom of the fire escape, which abruptly ended at the second floor. Beneath it was an open courtyard. Nearby was a glass skylight of a first-floor extension.

Those at the bottom of the fire escape held back. The fall, they knew, would kill them. The heat grew so intense that the very iron fire escape to which at least one hundred persons clung began to separate from the side of the building. The metal was so hot that it melted in places. Bolts and rivets popped loose. The structure became a bending, billowing, ballooning nightmare of iron that threatened to collapse at any moment. As sections of the fire escape began to swing away from the building, many people jumped, crashing grotesquely through the glass

The ninth floor of the Asch Building was where 250 Triangle workers were trapped. It was from these windows that most of the 145 victims jumped. *(Wide World)*

skylight to their deaths. More and more jumped, only to die in blood-splattered piles in the concrete courtyard below. In one buckling swing, the fire escape jerked outward and jolted a large group of workers off their sizzling perches, sending them downward in screaming groups.

The situation was no better on Washington Place. By the time the first of the thirty-five fire units to respond to the fire arrived, bodies were already falling all over the street. The horrified crowds lining the street shouted in unison to the firemen, "Raise your ladders! Raise your ladders!"

On one of the ninth-floor window ledges, a young woman frantically waved a handkerchief at a mechanized fire unit, one of the first of its kind in New York, as if to direct its ladder to her position. The ladder went up and up and then stopped at its full length at the sixth floor, three floors below the girl, whose skirt had caught on fire. She leaped to the ladder thirty feet below her. She missed and plummeted downward, her entire body aflame. The fire consumed her before she hit the sidewalk.

Soon all the window ledges along the ninth floor were jammed with workers; great gouts of fire hunted them out from inside. A United Press reporter, Bill Shepherd, arrived at this moment, and with a clear vision of the ensuing carnage, described the awful scene over the phone to his editor: "Thud—dead! Thud—dead! Thud—dead! I call them that because the sound and the thought of death came to me each time at the same instant." In all Shepherd would count sixty-two bodies hurtling downward to the concrete, sixty-two ghastly deaths. He took poignant note of the humanity displayed upon the ledges above him, even witnessing "a love affair in the midst of all the horror."

"A young man helped a girl to the windowsill on the ninth floor. Then he held her out deliberately, away from the building, and let her drop. He held out a second girl the same way and let her drop. He held out a third girl, who did not resist. I noticed that. They were all as unresisting as if he were helping them into a street car instead of into eternity. He saw that a terrible death awaited them in the flames, and his was only a terrible chivalry. . . . He brought another girl to the window. I saw her put her arms around him and kiss him. Then he held her into space—and dropped her.

"Quick as a flash, he was on the windowsill himself. His coat fluttered upwards—the air filled his trouser legs as he came down. I could see he wore tan shoes. Together they went into eternity. Later I saw his face. You could see he was a real man. He had done his best. We found later that in the room in which he stood, many girls were burning to death. He chose the easiest way and was brave enough to help the girl he loved to an easier death."

Shepherd noted that those still clinging to windowsills glued their eyes to those who jumped, watching them "every inch of the way down," before they themselves leaped into space. The attitudes of each fall became separate studies by the reporter, who narrated his shocking story with steely descriptions. "I watched one girl falling," he illustrated. "She waved her arms, trying to keep her body upright until the very instant she struck the sidewalk."

Those below tried every means in attempting to catch the girls. It was impossible. Fire Captain Howard Ruch later estimated that the bodies fell with a force of 11,000 pounds each, and there was no conceivable way to catch them. But the firemen tried. They stretched out canvas and netting, gripping these white knuckled, and bodies fell into them with such force that the firemen were somersaulted forward, many knocked unconscious. Bodies crashed straight through the nets, tearing them wide open. Bodies crashed through plate-glass slabs in the sidewalk. Bodies so densely covered the fire hoses that the water pressure was shut off by their collective weight. Squads of firemen were kept busy removing the corpses so that water streams could again, though ineffectively, be played upon the flame-roaring building.

Fire Battalion Chief Edward Worth watched it all happening and wept openly in bitter agony at his inability to save the falling girls dashed to death at his feet. He knew the life nets were useless. "Life nets? What good were they? The little ones went through life nets, pavement, and all. I thought they would come down one at a time. I didn't know they would come down with arms entwined—three and even four together."

One net with fifteen burly firemen stretching it wide seemed to hold for a moment as a girl landed. The net dipped quickly to the sidewalk but did not tear. Chief Worth pulled her upward. She blinked and said nothing as he told her to " 'go right across the street.' She walked ten feet—and dropped. She died in one minute."

On Greene Street the story was the same. Most of the shopgirls preferred to die together, jumping nine floors to their deaths while holding on to each other in large groups, sometimes five at a time. Bill Shepherd walked among the crushed forms littering the street and saw how "the floods of water from the firemen's hoses that ran into the gutter were actually red with blood. I looked upon the heap of dead bodies, and I remembered these girls were the shirtwaist makers. I remembered their great strike of last year, in which these same girls had demanded more sanitary conditions and more safety precautions in the shops. These dead bodies were the answer."

There were 145 answers, to be exact, one of the worst death counts ever mounted in a building fire that, amazingly, lasted only eighteen minutes before firemen managed to bring it under control. Outrage on the part of the public and press brought about the trials of Max Blanck and Isaac Harris on charges of first- and second-degree manslaughter. They were exonerated on the specific charge that they had locked their employees in to prevent pilfering of their goods. Harris admitted on the stand that the total loss to the firm in stolen goods over the years had amounted to no more than $25.

One of the jurors announced, "After this I have no faith in jury trials." He recalled how survivors had described the horrible burning death of only one victim, Margaret Schwartz, who was visible through the plate-glass window of the locked door. She clawed and screamed to be saved while the fire consumed her in front of her helpless fellow workers. Yet other jurors felt the door might have been accidentally locked by one of the panicked girls. Some thought that state factory inspectors should have been on trial instead of Blanck and Harris.

The normally conservative *New York Tribune* reacted to the verdict by thundering: "The monstrous conclusion of the law is that the slaughter was no one's fault, that it couldn't be helped, or perhaps even that, in the fine legal phrase which is big enough to cover a multitude of defects of justice, it was 'an act of God!' This conclusion is revolting to the moral sense of the community." The paper went on to add that the responsibility for the

Firemen search for bodies that crashed through the skylights of cellars. *(UPI)*

145 deaths extended further than Blanck and Harris; it included "city and state inspectors, superintendents, and those who passed on plans and licenses, all the personnel engaged in the empty farce of protecting lives in workshops."

Eventually much good would come from this horrible calamity, but it would take years before stricter safety regulations and devices were instituted. The strengthening of the International Ladies Garment Workers Union, a direct result of the fire, would help mightily to change conditions.

But in that winged-collar and cane-wielding time of 1911, the great Triangle fire did not immediately effect vital changes on behalf of the misery-encompassed workers. It was still the age of the totemic boss, and almost no one took issue with the legally correct Joseph J. Asch, who coldly stated to reporters following the fire: "I have obeyed the law to the letter. There was not one detail of the construction of my building that was not submitted to the building and fire departments. Every detail was approved, and the fire marshal congratulated me."

Then there was a safety expert, H. F. Porter, who had contacted the Triangle owners to institute fire drills—operations never begun. "The neglect of factory owners in the matter of safety of the employees is absolutely criminal," Porter told the *New York Times*. "One man whom I advised to install a fire drill replied to me: 'Let 'em burn. They're a lot of cattle, anyway.' " And in 1911 almost no one took issue with that, either.

TRINACRIA — MARINE DISASTER

February 8, 1893

The 2,107-ton Anchor Line steamer *Trinacria* departed from Greenock on February 2, 1893, with four female passengers and a crew of thirty-seven, bound for Gibraltar. The women missionaries intended to provide spiritual inspiration for the garrison based upon the rock. The small ship immediately encountered heavy gales as she plowed her way down the Irish Sea and across the Bay of Biscay.

At 6:00 A.M. on February 8, 1893, the *Trinacria* was rolling before a storm of hurricane proportions off Cape Vilano, Spain, when she struck outlying rocks and rapidly began to sink. Captain S. Murray ordered the four women passengers put into a lifeboat. As soon as this boat was lowered, she capsized. Only the strongest of the women, Mrs. John Rust, managed to swim to shore.

In the same instant a tremendous wave engulfed the entire ship, collapsing her funnel and ventilators, which crashed into the bowels of the ship. Six crew members dove overboard just before the wave hit, and they and Mrs. Rust were the only survivors; thirty-four persons, including Captain Murray, drowned.

TRUCULENT — MARINE DISASTER

January 12, 1950

During trials on January 12, 1950, the British submarine *Truculent* was run down by the Swedish tanker *Divina*. The freighter collided with the submarine while the latter was running on the surface of the Thames. Those in the *Truculent*'s conning tower were hurled into the water upon impact, and the submarine was sent to the bottom. Crew members did not wait the prescribed time for rescue vessels to reach them; they began to use escape chambers beneath the submarine, bobbing up to the surface in the middle of the night. What these men thought was the sound of rescue vessels was actually the propellers of passing ships, which were unaware of the sinking. Of the seventy men on board the sub when she was sent to the bottom, only fifteen survived in the freezing water.

Bodies were found far out to sea days later. A board of inquiry investigating the ramming held officers of the *Truculent* mostly to blame for the accident, since the *Divina* had been showing the proper red warning lights during her voyage.

(ALSO SEE: Affray, Squalus, Thetis, Thresher*)*

TRURO, MASSACHUSETTS — HURRICANE

October 3, 1841

Racing in from the mid-Atlantic on October 3, 1841, a monstrous hurricane caught a fishing fleet of seven ships from Truro, Massachusetts, while they were returning to the harbor. Since known as the "October Gale," this storm sideswiped the vessels as they were attempting to turn toward Cape Cod, and, in the words of hurricane expert David M. Ludlum, "They were either overwhelmed and submerged by the gigantic seas or were dashed to pieces in the cruel breakers along the beaches." Fifty-seven seamen, all from the hamlet of Truro, perished in the storm.

TRUXTON (and POLLUX) — MARINE DISASTER

February 18, 1942

background: The 1,193-ton United States destroyer *Truxton,* while accompanying the 6,085-ton supply ship *Pollux,* ran aground near St. Lawrence, Newfoundland, on February 18, 1942. Both ships foundered and broke up in a gale that drove them ashore in 60 m.p.h. winds. Killed were 189 sailors from both vessels.

Built just after World War I, the United States destroyer *Truxton* was an old ship no longer capable of weathering the kind of storm that engulfed her and her companion, the new supply ship *Pollux,* as they attempted to make their way into the mouth of the St. Lawrence harbor off Newfoundland on February 18, 1942. (The *Truxton*'s sister ship, the *Reuben James,* had been torpedoed and sunk in the Atlantic earlier.) The *Pollux,* on the other hand, was virtually a new ship, afloat for only a year before the catastrophe.

Driven before near-hurricane winds, the two ships became bottled up in the St. Lawrence harbor, where waters are particularly treacherous in winter. As the ships began to break apart, ramming repeatedly onto rocks, residents from St. Lawrence gathered at the edges of high cliffs and attempted to catch ropes thrown from the ships. Once the ropes were secured, scores of sailors attempted to reach land by pulling themselves hand over hand along the ropes. Dozens fell into the water and were drowned in full view of the civilians. Most of the ropes were coated with oil, and the sailors found it impossible to hold on to them.

Next the civilians lowered a small fishing boat over the edge of one cliff, but she capsized when she struck the swirling waters and her seven occupants were thrown into the sea. They were quickly hauled up the cliffs to safety by rope.

A bosun's chair was rigged and lowered to those in the water. One by one, more than 100 seamen were lifted to safety, but several men slipped off this precarious perch and sank beneath the waves. Lost were 189 men, including the skipper of the *Truxton,* Lieutenant Commander Ralph Hickox.

TUBARAO, BRAZIL — FLOOD

March 24, 1974

During March, 1974, early autumn in South America, torrential rains created enormous floods in Brazil. The mighty Tubarao River reached flood stage on March 24, 1974, and completely overwhelmed the city of the same name, causing more than 100,000 people to flee to high ground. At least 200 persons lost their lives to the floodwaters that also destroyed the mainstay crops of rice, potatoes, corn and cassava. More than 8,000 head of cattle drowned, and overall property damage soared to $250 million.

The town of Tubarao squats at a curve in the river. When the river crested, water poured over the curve at amazingly high speeds, crushing to death fifty persons in two houses alone in the suburb of Sao Joao.

TUNISIA — FLOODS

September-October, 1969

background: A shift in high-pressure areas off the Azores coupled with cold-air masses from Russia caused thirty-eight consecutive days of rain over Tunisia that, in turn, created the worst floods in that country's history in September and October, 1969. More than 80 percent of the country

Housewives in Tubarao, Brazil, await the distribution of foodstuffs. Massive floods in March 1974 drowned 200 persons and obliterated crops. *(Wide World)*

was flooded, and 542 persons were killed. In addition 1 million livestock drowned and 10,000 olive trees were uprooted. More than 100,000 people were left homeless, and $200 million in damage resulted.

Tunisia had never before experienced the overwhelming floodtides that covered the countryside when more than a month of incessant rain bloated every river, especially the Zeroud and the Marguelil, in September and October, 1969. Tunisia's foreign minister, Habib Bourguiba, Jr., ironically quipped, "We were three days short of a Biblical record." But the thirty-eight days of torrential downpour and subsequent floods from the Gulf of Tunis to the Gulf of Bou Grara, covering 80 percent of the country, produced no sardonic laughter from inhabitants, especially the relatives of the 542 persons who lost their lives to the rampaging waters that swept away dozens of villages and inundated scores of towns and cities.

Following the rains, the floods leaped forward without warning. One peasant farmer remembered, "It was very dark, and there was thunder and lightning. It was like the end of the world. Some of us snatched children and made for higher ground."

The rivers, cresting thirty-six feet above normal, tore away thirty-five major bridges; the jabbing thrusts of the waters were so forceful that 100-ton concrete slabs that anchored the spans were torn away. In six hours a $7 million irrigation project was wiped out. Millions of tons of rich farming loam was sent swirling into the Mediterranean.

Eight miles wide in some areas, the floodwaters engulfed 100,000 cattle, goats and other livestock, carrying dead herds many miles and littering the high ground with their bloated carcasses. One Red Crescent (the equivalent to the Red Cross) worker remarked, "Peasants are stunned. The water, which they had always considered more precious than gold, behaved like a demon."

So did many peasants driven half-mad by starvation and thirst. When United States Air Force Major Robert McDougal landed his craft, which was part of a seventeen-helicopter contingent flying in supplies to isolated villages, the door of his helicopter was ripped off its hinges by crazed villagers. They tore like wild beasts at the food parcels inside and then clawed each other for the contents. None of them had eaten in weeks.

The only benefit brought by the floods occurred on the Kairouan Plain where three feet of earth was sheared away by the raging flood waters to reveal a long-buried Roman village an invaluable archaeological find. Coastal towns, which brought in more than $40 million each year from tourists, were spared damage. The catastrophe left 100,000 homeless and sent a quarter of a million people fleeing the waters.

Tunisia's plight was aided immediately by a host of nations. One diplomat commented: "We had a sort of competition in charitable deeds." The United States led the way with loans totaling $4 million. West Germany gave $2.5 million. France, Belgium, the Netherlands and Spain loaned Tunisia regiments of engineers to rebuild bridges. A Jewish group, the American Joint Distribution Committee, sent a check for $250,000. The Congo sent one for $96,000. Russia donated $20,000 in blankets and food. Eighty nations came to the rescue, but all this meant little to teen-ager Ahmed Fredj, who looked up from the ruins of his home in the hamlet of Sidi-el-Hani, remembered the dead and lamented, "You hear women crying every night."

TURKISH AIRLINES — AIR CRASH
January 26, 1974

Departing Cumaovasi Airport at Izmir, Turkey, en route to Istanbul, 200 miles distant, a Turkish Airlines twin-jet Fokker F-28 crashed on takeoff on January 26, 1974. Of the seventy-three persons on board, only ten—one of them an infant wrapped in a blanket, who was dragged from the wreckage immediately after the plane went down and survived with only a few bruises—lived through the crash and flames.

Hamid Tig, another passenger, received only scratches. "As soon as the plane took off, it veered to the left, and I felt a great wave of heat," he said. "Then the plane struck the ground. I managed to throw myself out and succeeded in dragging a few burning passengers with me."

The airplane rose only about 450 feet off the runway before it suddenly crashed back onto the strip. Engine trouble or a locked left wheel were offered as reasons for the crash.

This was the second crash in 1974 involving an F-28 jet, the first being the smash-up of an Itavia craft that crashed while landing at Turin, Italy, on January 1, 1974. (All but four of forty-three persons involved were killed.)

TURKISH AIRLINES — AIR CRASH
March 3, 1974

background: Flight 981 of Turkish Airlines, a $20 million DC-10 McDonell Douglas (181 feet long, seating eight persons abreast), crashed at 12:40 P.M. on March 3, 1974, from an altitude of 12,500 feet, after taking off from Orly Airport in Paris, France, destined for London. Traveling at 475 m.p.h., all 346 persons on board were killed when the plane crashed in the Ermenonville Forest near Mortefontaine, France. It was the worst crash in the history of aviation. A subsequent investigation proved that the plane's cargo door blew open and caused sudden decompression in the plane. The FAA on July 14, 1975, ordered a complete technical overhaul of all DC-10s, 747s and other similarly built craft.

Stupidity and indifference were the real reasons why Flight 981 of Turkish Airlines crashed in the picnic area of Ermenonville Forest, France, on March 3, 1974. Three hundred forty-six persons were killed. Some critics even suggested criminal negligence. The three-engine jumbo jet, crammed to capacity because an engineers' strike had reduced the number of flights between France and Britain, took off from Orly Airport at 12:31 P.M. and quickly rose to an altitude of 12,500 feet. Nine minutes later, at 12:40 P.M., the door of the lower cargo hold blew open. With a rush of air the cargo hold began to lose its baggage. The sudden decompression caused a floor above to buckle and six passengers, while still strapped in their seats, were sucked out through the hole in the floor and the sprung cargo door and sent earthward to their deaths.

The Turkish plane went into a steep dive as the crew members babbled about their helpless state.

Ground control heard someone shout: "What happened?"

"The cargo door!" another voice responded.

"Are you sure?"

"Pull a nosedive!"

"[Probably the captain.] I can't very well. It doesn't respond."

"We're going to hit the ground."

No matter what the pilot had attempted, there was no way he could have prevented the crash of his plane or the deaths of his passengers and crew. When the cargo door flew open, causing the floor above to buckle and break open, all the cables operating the tail, engine and flying controls had been severed. Flight 981's back was broken because a cargo door had not been fastened properly, even though it appeared from the outside to have been locked.

Maurice Lhote, control tower official at Le Bourget Airport where Lindbergh had once joyously landed in 1927 to instill forever in mankind the belief in transcontinental flight, saw the Turkish jet above him as he strolled during his lunch hour through the Ermenonville Forest with his wife and dog. He heard a "booming noise" and glanced skyward to see the jumbo jet begin its crash dive. "It went down very rapidly," he remembered. "I was attracted by the noise of this big thing. I looked up and it was going straight down and very fast. I lost it as it went behind some trees. Then there was this big ball of fire. We didn't hear anything. And we didn't see any smoke. I called the control tower at Le Bourget, and they said that was the first news they had of the crash. Then my wife and I went over to look."

A farmer in a field saw the plane go out of control. He saw something falling toward him. "I didn't know it was a dead body. . . . I thought it was something else falling from the explosion. . . . It was a woman, although I could not be sure that it was a woman because she was completely smashed, completely broken. . . . Her head

The worst crash in aviation history: All 346 persons on board a Turkish Airlines DC-10 jumbo jet perished when it crashed into Ermenonville Forest north of Paris on March 3, 1974. *(Wide World)*

French firemen carry away bodies after the Turkish Airlines crash, an accident that could have been prevented. *(UPI)*

was here, her brains were here. . . . Then I ran to another one, and I saw the other woman. . . . One breast had been torn off. She was dead, too, and completely broken."

Picnickers came dashing from the woods as the plane sliced into 150-year-old oak trees, cutting them down to stumps as it gouged a black, burnt path in the earth. The jet exploded as it went, cracking every window in houses on the edge of Mortefontaine, several miles away. Shards of metal, pieces of bodies, bits of clothing were thrown over a wide area as the plane disintegrated. A man approached Lhote and his wife shouting: "God, go back, go back. My God, the blood!"

Police and firemen began to arrive. One fireman took a look at the crash site and shook his head. "When we got there, we started looking for survivors. Forget it, I said to myself. In a minute you knew that there was nothing but pieces."

A police official approached one of his units waiting near the still-burning debris and ordered his men forward to retrieve what was left of the bodies. He told them to take blankets and paper bags. One policeman fainted. Another sighed, "Oh, Mother of God," gritted his teeth, and stooped to pluck the human gore.

"Through the smoke, I saw blood, blood everywhere," one witness jabbered as the police worked methodically, bobbing up and down to gather the remains of the passengers and crew members of Flight 981.

The English National Rugby Team had survived by a stroke of fate; its members had earlier switched to another plane. On the polyglot death list were Wayne Wilcox, cultural attaché of the United States Embassy in London, his wife, and two children (two younger children had remained in London). More than 200 British travelers were on board the ill-fated plane. One was Esther Collin, an attractive twenty-year-old soon to be married. Her parents suffered like all the rest who had relatives on the Turkish jet, plagued for weeks afterward to provide officials with grim details of their daughter's height weight, teeth. Turkish officials eventually called to inform them that they were sure their daughter was dead: they had "identified half of her head."

Hours after the crash, a Buddhist priest led fifty relatives of the forty-nine Japanese who had perished in the crash through the grisly section of forest littered with the ruins of the plane. Relatives prayed, scattered flowers about and scooped up blood-flecked handfuls of earth to carry home with them.

Only four bodies were found intact, about three miles from the site of the crash. Everything else was fragment. Pieces of bodies dangled from trees, as did raincoats, suit jackets, socks. A Turkish dictionary was found on top of a rock. Someone else found a book in Chinese. A Red Cross worker discovered a hand clutching a Paris restaurant guide. One searcher, Pierre Guyermat, found in a tree a passport belonging to a British businessman, Trevor Vincent Dangerfield. "Born: 1936."

For weeks these grim artifacts were gently unearthed and categorized while the seemingly endless process of identification continued. Yet the cause of the crash remained more a mystery than the identities of those lost in it. Then began the investigation of the faulty cargo door. Even though an identical crash involving an American Airlines DC-10 had occurred at Windsor, Ontario, on June 6, 1972, almost two years before the Paris crash, little or nothing was done to make the proper safety adjustments. In that instance the cables were not severed, and the pilot crash-landed safely. Instead of grounding all DC-10s and similar planes until safety mechanisms could be installed to insure that the baggage doors were locked from the inside, the FAA and McDonell-Douglas postponed corrections. Some planes with this very same problem were still operating eighteen months after the Windsor crash. Further, two DC-10s were manufactured and sold by McDonnell-Douglas two years following the Windsor crash without the corrected safety adjustments for the cargo door. One of these was Flight 981.

TURTLE MOUNTAIN, ALBERTA, CANADA — LANDSLIDE, April 29, 1903

The 3,100-foot Turtle Mountain in Alberta, coated with heavy rains, suddenly unleashed almost a half-mile-square slab of its side on the morning of April 29, 1903. This gigantic mass slid down into the valley at express-train speeds, pulverizing everything in its path. Smashed to rubble was the village of Frank, where seventy persons were crushed to death. Almost 7,000 feet of Crow's Nest Railway track was splintered as the land mass roared up the other side of the valley for three miles.

TYROL — AVALANCHES, 1915-1918

During World War I while thousands of Austrian and Italian troops fought in the mountains of Tyrol, avalanches killed a staggering number—between 40,000 and 80,000 soldiers—over a four-year span. In one instance following two weeks of steady snow, an avalanche swept over the town of Marmolada, wiping out 253 men inside their barracks. According to Matthias Zdarsky, who was skiing instructor for the Austrian army, "The mountains in winter were more dangerous than the Italians."

U

UDALL, KANSAS

TORNADO
May 25, 1955

background: Following a record total of 110 tornadoes in Texas, Kansas, Oklahoma, Missouri, Nebraska and Iowa in a three-day period, a monstrous twister struck Udall, Kansas, at 10:30 P.M. on May 25, 1955, after pummeling Blackwell, Oklahoma, where it killed 19 persons. Udall was obliterated, with only one building left standing and 82 persons killed out of a population of 612.

The month of May in 1955 was a killer as dozens of tornadoes whipped through six states, their combined fury creating millions of dollars in damage and causing the deaths of 114 citizens and injuring 700 more. A tornado in Texas actually reached out and snatched a passing B-36 bomber from the skies over Sterling, pulverizing the craft and killing its 15-man crew.

In Blackwell, Oklahoma, it was 9:22 P.M., and Pearl Peckham was standing on her front porch. Huge hailstones began to fall, and Pearl's boyfriend kneeled to pick up some out of curiosity. The youth suddenly looked across the prairie and dove for Pearl, grabbing her. "C'mon!" he yelled. "My God, it's a tornado!"

Before they ran inside Pearl's house, the girl turned for one terrible look. "There it was," she recalled later, "right on top of us. It was dark, but this thing was much darker than the night. We ran into the house and got down on the floor and prayed."

The twister growled and whined through Blackwell, tearing up 500 houses and injuring 493 persons as it passed through the center of the community. Dead were 19 residents. Gone was the $500,000 Hazel-Atlas glass plant, the town's mainstay employer. One man working

Gone with the wind was Udall, Kansas, after a tornado pulverized the town on May 25, 1955. Eighty-two persons out of a population of 612 were killed by the twister. *(Wide World)*

the night shift inside the factory would never forget "that awful roaring noise, and the building just kind of shuddered and went down." Blackwell had $10 million in damage, but the population of 10,000 fared far better than the hamlet of Udall, Kansas, just across the state line and twenty-five miles away.

A farmer three miles south of Udall spotted the twister howling over the landscape. "It sounded like a bunch of jets and looked black as an oil slush pond. I didn't look long. I lit out for the cellar."

It was an unforgettable sight to Udall's mayor, Earl Rowe. "I was standing at the front door. There was lightning and just a little rain. Then it hit. My house just floated away. I don't know where it is. My wife and three children were in the house—they lived, but one of the boys had a bad gash. I had two cars in the driveway. Nobody's found them yet. I was knocked out . . . got an eight-penny nail driven through my leg."

The twister that tore up Udall performed weird feats. It sucked Fred Dye, a retired railroad worker who was outdoors, out of his shoes and sent him up a tree where he sat out the storm unharmed. Kneeling in fright in a back bedroom, William Sweet and his wife emerged minutes after the storm passed to find that the rest of their house had disappeared. Harry Norris, a barber, was thrown from his bed out a window and into the street while he still slept.

The twister also killed. A telephone operator, Mary Taylor, was crushed when her phone exchange collapsed. Edward, her son, was killed along with six other pool players when the pool hall he owned was flattened. Eighty-two persons were slain by the tornado that wiped out Udall, leaving only one building still standing. Three churches, the grade school and the new $250,000 high school were all in ruins. It was the worst disaster to happen to the town; in fact, it was the apparent end of the town.

Irony, as usual, could be seen everywhere, but none so devastating as with the man who insisted that policeman Lester Thompson help him save his television set while his home went to splinters. The console was saved, but there was not an electric socket to plug it into within thirty miles.

UNCLE JOSEPH — MARINE DISASTER

November 24, 1880

The immigrant ship *Uncle Joseph,* a German vessel carrying 305 persons and 800 tons of merchandise to Buenos Aires, was rammed at sea by the Genoese ship *Ortiga* while both ships were off La Spezia, Italy, on the moonlit night of November 24, 1880.

No cause was ever given as to why the *Ortiga* blundered into the immigrant ship, but the number of fatalities was alarming in light of the fact that the Italian vessel could have easily rescued more than the 55 floundering sailors and passengers who held on to her bow as she backed away from the stricken *Uncle Joseph,* which had been struck amidships. As the Italian ship went astern, tons of water poured into the German vessel, and she sank within eight minutes, taking with her 250 persons, including Captain Dacombe. The *Ortiga* did manage to lower one lifeboat and pick up a few survivors.

UNION TRANSPORTS AFRICAIN — AIR CRASH

October 2, 1964

A French-owned Union Transports Africain DC-6, on its way to Mauritania, West Africa, from Palma on Majorca, crashed into the Mediterranean on October 2, 1964, with seventy-three passengers and seven crew members aboard. The piston-powered aircraft disappeared soon after takeoff from Palma and was sighted by several ships as it dove into the sea off the Spanish mainland. Although the crash area was searched by Spanish, French, British and Italian ships, neither survivors nor even wreckage of the doomed plane was ever discovered.

UNITED AIRLINES — AIR CRASH

October 24, 1947

background: A United Airlines DC-6, bound for New York from Los Angeles, caught fire while in flight on October 24, 1947, and crashed at Bryce Canyon, Utah. All fifty-two persons on board died. The cause of the crash was later discovered to be a gas leak in the cargo hatch.

It was a clear day, and the peaks jutting up from Bryce Canyon, Utah, appeared orange, red and gold, a brilliant array of colors that spread beauty through the national park. Above it and beyond caring about its grandeur was Captain E. L. MacMillen, who was piloting a big Douglas DC-6, two hours out of Los Angeles on October 24, 1947. MacMillen's voice echoed his alarm as he radioed air control at Salt Lake City.

"We have baggage fire aboard," MacMillen said. "We are coming to Bryce Canyon. We have smoke-filled plane. Unable to put out fire yet."

It was another five minutes before MacMillen's voice again came on the air. "The tail fire is going out. We may get down and we may not. Best place we can . . ." Another minute ticked away while Bryce Canyon airport officials were alerted for the crash landing. The pilot's voice cracked once more through the air waves: "We may make it. Think we have a chance now. Approaching the strip."

Observers at Bryce Canyon saw nothing. There was a last shout from MacMillen: "The tail is gone!" And so was the DC-6 and all of its fifty-two occupants. From the

Bryce Canyon airport tower, controllers spotted a fire burning at the lip of the runway. By the time crash vehicles arrived, it was too late to save anyone. Bodies and parts of the burning plane were strewn all over a gentle slope. The United plane had crashed just fifty feet short of the runway; had MacMillen been able to keep his craft aloft for only a few seconds more, the DC-6 would have cleared the top of the small hill. It was a matter of five feet.

Exploding upon impact, the four engines of the plane had scudded across the hillside as far as 300 feet. The forty-seven passengers, including two small children, were sprawled, burned and broken, for another 100 feet, the five crew members incinerated with the fuselage. Searchers found burly Jeff Burkett, professional football star, dead. They found Clement D. Ryan, ex-president of Montgomery Ward & Company, dead, too. Also among the bodies was Jack Guenther, managing editor of *Look* magazine.

The fire on board the United plane was duplicated only a few weeks later when an American Airlines DC-6 caught fire in its baggage hold. The captain managed an emergency landing at Gallup, New Mexico, before anyone was killed. Investigators of the Civil Aeronautics Board (CAB) thoroughly checked this plane and found gas stains from a fuel vent leak. The vent had been dangerously positioned only ten feet from the air scoop, and the gas leaking from it had splashed into the air scoop and then exploded in the heater, the same cause of the fire on board the ill-fated United plane.

Unlike the lethargic attitude prevalent in remedying the faulty cargo doors of the DC-10s in 1972-74, which caused the world's worst air crash in Paris on March 3, 1974, CAB ordered all DC-6s grounded. The vents were repositioned and many lives were saved.

(ALSO SEE: Turkish Airlines, March 3, 1974)

UNITED AIRLINES — AIR CRASH — December 8, 1972

Attempting to abort a landing at Chicago's Midway Airport on December 8, 1972, a United Airlines Boeing 727 suddenly pancaked into a row of houses near the airport. Dead were forty-five persons—forty passengers, all three members of the cockpit crew and two neighborhood residents. Among those killed on the plane was Mrs. E. Howard Hunt, wife of a conspirator in the Watergate break-ins. Found next to Mrs. Hunt's body was $10,000 in $100 bills, thought by many to be "hush money."

United Airlines paid record claims of over $4 million in January, 1974, to the families of seven of the passengers who died on the aircraft. The claimants charged that the pilot had failed to maintain 55 percent power during icing conditions as the plane approached the airport, thus violating one of the airline's own rules. Also, the copilot was cited for not obeying the pilot's command to change the angle of the flaps after receiving orders from Midway controllers to abort the landing and make another approach to the field.

UNITED AIRLINES (and TWA) — AIR CRASH — December 16, 1960

background: A United Airlines DC-8 and a TWA Constellation crashed in a midair collision over Staten Island, New York, on December 16, 1960, after the former aircraft had flown off course. Killed in the crash were 128 passengers and crew members; 8 others on the ground, who were struck by parts of the disintegrating plane, were also killed.

In Chicago, Illinois, and Dayton, Ohio, two giant airliners were taking on passengers for New York. One, United Airlines Flight 826, was headed for Idlewild (now called Kennedy) Airport. The other, TWA Flight 266, was on its way to LaGuardia Field. Both were destined to become flaming coffins amidst the Christmas decorations in the streets of New York. It was December 16, 1960.

Captain David Wollam and copilot Dean Bowen were in the cockpit of the TWA Constellation, which was one of the most reliable planes in the air.

The United Airlines DC-8, an equally dependable plane, was flown by Captain R. H. Sawyer. First Officer R. W. Fiebing sat beside him.

The pilots of these two powerful planes approached New York at approximately the same time. There were seventy-seven passengers on the DC-8. The Connie carried fifty-one. Most passengers, coming home for Christmas, were loaded with colorfully wrapped gifts.

As the Connie approached LaGuardia, Captain Wollam radioed to the ground controller. He reported his position at 10:28 A.M.

The controller shot back, "Trans World 266, LaGuardia approach control. Roger Solbert at 28. Maintain 9,000, report 101 Robbinsville. ILS Runway 4, landing Runway 4; no delay expected."

Wollam listened as the controller droned on: "The wind is northeast at 15, the altimeter 29.65, LaGuardia weather—measured 500 overcast visibility one mile, light snow. Stand by."

Wollam acknowledged, happy that he would not be stacked up in the soupy mists above New York.

The ground controller broke in, telling Wollam to lose altitude. "Continue descent to five."

"266 to 5,000," Wollam responded.

Suddenly the ground controller noticed something on his radar scope. Another blip had come onto the screen. Obviously it was another plane, but this didn't upset him.

The wing of a United Airlines DC-8 occupies a street in Brooklyn after a mid-air collision with a TWA plane. One hundred twenty-eight passengers and crew members and eight persons on the ground were killed. *(Wide World)*

He knew that the holding patterns for both LaGuardia and Idlewild were only five miles apart—but it was sufficient for safety's sake.

The controller took no chances, however, and radioed Wollam, "Trans World 266, traffic at 2:30. Six miles. Northeast bound."

Wollam was heading southeast, and the report wasn't alarming. The strange blip continued to gradually veer toward the Connie. Three-dimensional radar was not employed in 1960, so there was no way the controller could tell how much altitude separated the two planes. He only hoped.

The two blips were now separated by only a few thousand feet of air, and the controller broke in again, this time sounding somewhat tense, "There appears to be jet traffic off your right wing. Now at three o'clock. Northeast bound."

Sweat broke out on the controller's forehead as he watched the blips come even closer. He waited for an answer from Flight 266. There was none. Suddenly the mike opened up as if a message was coming over, but nothing was said. The mike went dead. The controller nervously called for the Connie.

Meanwhile the DC-8 had been carrying on a similar dialogue with its ground controller at Idlewild. Captain Sawyer radioed: "Idlewild Approach Control, United 826 approaching Preston [New Jersey] at 5,000."

"Roger, 826," ground control replied. "And hold at 5,000."

Suddenly the communication between the DC-8 and Idlewild ground control went dead. The controller tried again and again to reach Sawyer. Nothing.

A frantic controller called Idlewild from LaGuardia. "I think we have trouble here with a Connie! There's something wrong. He's not moving or anything! He might have got hit by—by another plane!"

LaGuardia asked Idlewild, "Is that your traffic at, uh, Flatbush?"

"No, it's not our traffic, LaGuardia."

"Well, now, he's—" LaGuardia broke off, then shot back on again at Idlewild. "We lost communication with an aircraft and, uh, something may be wrong with him."

Incredibly the two giant airports discovered that their planes had merged on their radar screens at the same time. Their frantic conversation raced on.

Someone in the control tower at Idlewild yelled: "Just a minute! Wait a minute! LaGuardia. It could be ours on approach control."

"Well, what kind of airplane is it?"

"A DC-8, United," Idlewild responded.

"And what—what's his altitude?" LaGuardia demanded.

"Five thousand feet."

"Oh, God. We had one at five too!"

When the blips joined on the radar scope, the DC-8 and the Constellation had collided. The United plane tore into the cabin of the Connie. Its Number 4 jet engine, sucking air from its compressor, gulped the debris and human bodies from the TWA plane.

The DC-8's wing was sheared off, and it fell with the Connie, which plummeted toward the frozen earth of Staten Island.

Mrs. Edward Brody watched horror-stricken as the Constellation crashed onto Miller Army Field. All the TWA passengers were killed instantly, but fortunately this was not the case on the ground, where dazed spectators watched. No one on the ground was hurt by the Staten Island crash.

The DC-8 lumbered through the overcast sky. It was off its course, and it was the culprit for the massive collision. Captain Sawyer fought hard to land the crippled plane.

With his Number 4 jet engine and a piece of wing gone, Sawyer managed to fly the DC-8 over the waterway outside the New York skyline.

The ground came up fast as the DC-8 groaned forward, desperately attempting to reach LaGuardia. Those who watched from the crowded streets below knew it was hopeless.

It was a scene of terror in the streets of Brooklyn as pedestrians saw hunks of the DC-8 rain down on them. Mrs. Ann Carretta couldn't believe her eyes as she saw an airplane coming down the street straight at her after she stepped from a shop.

The bakery truck driven by Julius Lehman was almost overtaken by the burning wreckage that slid after it. The DC-8's massive tail section slid down the street right for Ray Rothenburg's truck.

Powerless, Rothenburg watched it come at him. It stopped with its tip only a few feet from his truck.

Part of the fuselage smashed into another section of Brooklyn a block away. The racket of the explosions as the debris crunched parked cars was like a heavy artillery bombardment. This section contained some of the DC-8's passengers, now engulfed in flames.

"Those people are burning to death!" a teen-aged boy yelled, running down the street with his face bleeding.

Huge chunks of the DC-8 were falling everywhere. Apparently the plane disintegrated as it fell to earth. One hunk fell into a funeral parlor, throwing embalmed corpses into the air and onto the street.

The Pillar of Fire Church, ironically named, was hit and set ablaze. Fires were breaking out all over Brooklyn.

Another section of the DC-8's fuselage smashed down, and James and Anthony Troiano rushed to it only to see horribly mutilated bodies burning in the wreckage. In the snow a few feet away, they found the still-breathing body of an eleven-year-old boy, Steven Baltz, alive on a snowbank. His father was William Baltz of the Admiral Corporation.

Troiano and a patrolman reached the boy at the same time and quickly put out the flames shooting from his clothes. They wrapped him in a blanket and wept as they listened to him cry, "Mommy! Daddy!"

Both his legs were broken, but worse still, this only survivor had breathed in the flames of the diving plane, and his lungs were terribly seared.

The boy was taken to Methodist Hospital, where a team of ten of the city's finest doctors fought to save his life. The nation clung to the hope that this child would survive one of the worst air calamities in history to that time.

Steven fought death courageously for twenty-six hours; his father, mother and sister were at his side. Then his father sadly had to announce to the press: "Our Stevie passed away about 1:00 P.M. Stevie tried awfully hard [to live] because my son was a wonderful boy. God bless you for your prayers."

Now there were no survivors. Between the two air giants 128 persons were killed; another 8 persons were killed on the ground when the DC-8 crashed in Brooklyn, making a total of 136 dead.

Investigations dragged on into the cause of the accident, and it was the off-course DC-8 that shouldered most of the responsibility.

But it didn't seem to matter any more. TWA's Flight 266 and United's Flight 826 ceased to exist. And no amount of investigation could bring them back.

(ALSO SEE: Trans World Airlines, June 30, 1956)

UNITED STATES AIR FORCE C-119

AIR CRASH
November 14, 1952

Forty-four servicemen, a crew of seven and thirty-seven soldiers returning to Korea after rest and recuperation leave, went to their deaths when the United States Air Force C-119, a flying boxcar in which they were flying, crashed against a steep hilltop outside of Seoul, Korea, on November 14, 1952. There was no communication with the plane's pilot, and reasons for the crash remain a mystery.

Searchers going through the debris of the crash discovered Christmas presents the GIs had purchased in Japan for friends and relatives. Strewn among the dead bodies was a woman's wristwatch, satin slippers and a pair of child's pink pajamas.

UNITED STATES AIR FORCE C-124 — AIR CRASH — December 20, 1952

The cause of the crash of the United States Air Force C-124 Globemaster shortly after takeoff at Larson Air Force Base in the state of Washington on December 20, 1952, long baffled experts. Nothing was apparently wrong with the pilot or craft as it taxied down a 10,000-foot runway with 131 soldiers and crew members aboard the double-decker. But two minutes later, the huge plane lumbered downward out of shallow altitude and smacked onto the snow-filled plain at the end of the strip, breaking up in a dozen explosions.

A dispatcher, Sergeant Gerald Wright, had watched the plane rise and then blinked as the Globemaster wavered and plummeted downward, vibrating the earth with its crash and sending up flames in the predawn snow-covered desert. Wright lunged for a field phone and shouted to crash crews standing by in their vehicles: "Flight 0100 crashed at E between nine and ten. . . . Flight 0100 crashed at E between nine and ten."

Men wearing asbestos suits and hoods with plexiglass windows were soon stomping through the flames and yanking out survivors from the still-intact tail section of the fuselage. They ignored the incinerated bodies in the front part of the plane, which had been reduced to bits. They did find the flight engineer horribly injured and carried him away as he shouted deliriously: "Myra! I checked the power!"

Teams of medical experts struggled for days to save the scores dragged from the crash site; some of the men required as much as twelve pints of blood. In the end eighty-seven died and forty-four survived, some crippled for life.

Fortunately for Air Force investigators, when the locking gear of the huge plane was found intact, it was easily determined that the pilot of the plane had been responsible for the crash. Quite simply, he had neglected to move a knob on the throttle pedestal to the third and fourth notches, which would have freed the rudder and elevators from the plane's locking device. The knob was found at the second notch, allowing the Globemaster to take off, its throttles and ailerons free, but incapable of maneuvering once it was airborne until the knob was thrown down two more notches. The pilot had apparently been preoccupied, and by the time he reached for the all-important knob, the Globemaster was in its death dive.

A Globemaster crashed at Larson Air Force Base on December 20, 1952; eighty-seven servicemen perished. *(Wide World)*

UNITED STATES AIR FORCE C-124 — AIR CRASH — June 18, 1953

Carrying 129 military passengers and crew members, a United States Air Force C-124 Globemaster had just taken off from Tachikawa air base outside Tokyo on June 18, 1953, en route to Korea. Four minutes later, the pilot came over the radio to announce: "One engine out. . . . Returning to field." Four minutes later, the four-engine double-decker troop transport was a burning wreck in a rice paddy, crashing in full view of amazed farmers, its debris a smoldering funeral pyre for all 129 persons on board.

Though Far East Air Force Command ordered all C-124s grounded to determine the cause of the crash, the reason for the disaster was never fully unearthed.

UNITED STATES AIR FORCE C-131 — AIR CRASH — December 17, 1960

Carrying thirteen United States military service dependents to London for Christmas celebrations, a C-131 took off from Munich-Riem Airport in Germany on December 17, 1960, only to develop engine trouble four minutes after takeoff. The Convair hovered through the fog as Munich's fire brigades roared forth into the snowy streets, their horns blaring. Then the plane hurled down into the city.

Horrified onlookers watched as the C-131 nosed

A crushed and incinerated trolley car in Munich, Germany, smolders after it was struck by a United States Air Force C-131 on December 17, 1960. Fifty-three fatalities occurred. *(Wide World)*

earthward, banked sharply to avoid one building and struck St. Paul's Church a glancing blow, slicing off its steeple. It then dove into the Bayerstrasse, a main thoroughfare, and slammed into a moving streetcar. The plane exploded upon impact, and flames from it spread to buildings on both sides of the street. The rear of the still-moving car became a wall of fire. Trapped behind electric doors that no longer worked, shoppers with armfuls of Christmas presents were immolated.

A second streetcar behind the plane and first car barely missed the explosion. Its driver stared bug-eyed at the holocaust. "The coach was blazing," he told reporters. "I could hear screams and see people inside, but there was a mass of flames and nothing could be done."

All twenty persons on board the United States C-131 were dead, and another thirty-three people on the ground perished in the blaze—a total of fifty-three fatalities.

UNITED STATES ARMY AIR FORCE — AIR CRASH, July 28, 1945

background: A United States Army B-25 Mitchell bomber, en route to Newark Airport, New Jersey, crashed into the 102-story Empire State Building in New York City at the 78th and 79th floors, at 9:50 A.M., on Saturday, July 28, 1945. All in the plane and some workers in the 1,250-foot building were killed; a total of fourteen died. More than $500,000 damage was done to what was the world's tallest building at that time.

The nightmare envisioned by many pilots and civilians alike, that of a low-flying airplane crashing into one of the skyscrapers of New York, became a reality on the morning of July 28, 1945, when a Mitchell bomber, piloted by Lieutenant Colonel William F. Smith, Jr., smacked into the Empire State Building. The odds against just such a disaster happening had been computed as 10,000 to 1, but the weather helped to inch up the handicap.

Smith, twenty-seven, a West Point graduate, had flown for two years in Europe as a combat pilot, amassing 1,000 hours of flying time and earning the Distinguished Flying Cross, Air Medal and the *Croix de Guerre* for his wartime service. Flying from New Bedford, Massachusetts, Smith first attempted to land at LaGuardia Airport in New York, but dense fog had compelled him to try for the runway at Newark.

LaGuardia control center told Smith that the ceiling was almost zero in New York and that forward visibility was approximately three miles. The operator added ominously: "The top of the Empire State Building is not visible." Smith flew on, and startled pedestrians looked up at 9:48 A.M. to see his twin-engine bomber appear briefly at 500 feet and just barely miss the towering Rockefeller Center. The plane zoomed up sharply and disappeared into the heavy, swirling fogbanks above.

Normally there would have been 15,000 people at work in the world's tallest building and, perhaps, another 35,000 persons visiting the proud structure on business, but this was Saturday and most of the offices were empty and silent. War, however, was a full-time job, and some workers in the seventy-ninth-floor offices of the War Relief Services of the National Catholic Welfare Conference were busy at their desks.

The Mitchell droned on, and experts speculated later, Smith saw a curling river below him through a break in the clouds. Mistaking the Hudson for the East River, he descended for his landing at Newark. *Old John Feather Merchant*—the name was painted in bright letters on Smith's Mitchell—soared through foggy space at 225 m.p.h., and within seconds the plane was upon the Empire State Building. For a split second Smith tried to veer away, but there was no room to maneuver. The aircraft crashed into the north side of the seventy-ninth and seventy-eighth floors, ripping open an eighteen by twenty-foot hole through the structure's steel and masonry and sending a roar that shivered all the way down the building's steel ribs.

Gaping pedestrians looked quickly up to see flames jet from the windows at the 913-foot level. The deafening explosion was heard two miles away. Flames and dense clouds of smoke obscured the top of the building. A section of the plane's wing flew a block east onto Madison Avenue. Luckily no one was injured. The walls of nearby buildings were studded with fragments of hot metal. One of the motors skidded through seven crumbling walls and came out the south side of the building, flying over Thirty-third Street and crashing through the skylight of a penthouse atop a twelve-story building owned by Vincent Astor. There it started a $78,000 fire in the studio of sculptor Henry Hering. The other motor, also in flames, screeched through the door of an elevator shaft, fell eighty floors and sheared away the cables of another elevator in which a woman was riding. She was sent downward at terrifying speeds in the plummeting cab, but automatic braking devices prevented a basement crash; however, the top of the elevator caved in, and the woman was trapped in darkness.

The Mitchell's fuselage disintegrated inside the offices on the seventy-ninth and seventy-eighth floors and tore to shreds Smith; his crew chief, Staff Sergeant Christopher Demitrovich; and Albert Perna, a sailor who had hitched a ride from New Bedford. Those working in the war relief offices were gouged by flying metal and then burned to death by shooting flames from the exploding remnants of the plane buried in the building. The body of one man who was hurled out a window was later found on a seventy-second-story ledge; he was charred beyond recognition.

In the street hundreds were frozen in terror, but one quick-thinking passer-by, Donald Maloney, a Coast Guard hospital apprentice, acted immediately. Sprinting to a drugstore, he ordered a clerk to give him hypodermic needles, drugs and other medical supplies. He then raced into the building. Minutes later rescuers battered a hole in the elevator containing the unconscious woman. Maloney squeezed himself into the hole and lowered himself down into the cab's maw. He brought the woman out, gave her a shot of morphine and is credited with saving her life, a cool-minded act of heroism for which he would be long remembered.

Arriving firemen raced up the building in working elevators and soon got the fires under control by pouring tons of water into the flames. Streams of water mixed with red gasoline ran down the side of the building. It was all but miraculous that only fourteen people had been killed and another twenty-five badly injured. And it was a marvel that the top of the Empire State still stood, but the building had been constructed well and could withstand even the battering of a ten-ton airplane.

More than $500,000 in damage was done to the building. This amount was whittled down by the army to $288,901.90 before it was paid. The New York Telephone Company itemized the equipment it lost in the crash and demanded $1,869.67. It was paid immediately without haggling. Childs Restaurant at 200 Fifth Avenue claimed a broken plate-glass window and asked for $365. The army paid. Henry Hering, the sculptor, told the army his life's work had been demolished and asked for $137,000. The army offered him $25,000—period. So much for art.

UNITED STATES (EAST) BLIZZARD

March 11-14, 1888

background: Record snowfalls—20.9 inches—were created in the great blizzard of 1888, beginning on March 11 and continuing for three days throughout the New England and eastern seaboard states. More than 400 persons either froze to death or died later from the effects of the storm. Scores of ships and fishing boats were destroyed in the storm by waves and winds averaging 60 m.p.h. Property damage exceeded $7 million.

A thriving metropolis by the late 1880s, New York had never experienced a storm as severe as the one that lashed it for four days beginning on March 11, 1888. The entire eastern seaboard was blanketed with snow in one of the most furious blizzards in American history, a storm that claimed the lives of 400 persons from Maine to Maryland.

New Yorkers who received the brunt of the blizzard first reacted with amusement, then curiosity, finally fear. Winds from the west and north conspired against the city and blew walls of snow with wind gusts up to 100 m.p.h. At 4:00 P.M. on the first day of the blizzard, according to one account, "The snow came so fast that five minutes sufficed to obliterate the footprints of a man or a horse in the streets." Horse-drawn streetcars came to a halt as huge mounds of snow stopped their passage. The elevated trains were blocked. A collision on the Third Avenue elevated resulted in the death of an engineer, the first fatality of the storm.

Snowdrifts quickly rose to six, seven, ten feet by midnight. All along the east coast, cities were cut off, all wires were blown down, and communication between cities ceased to exist. Boston, New Haven, New York, Washington, Philadelphia, Newark and Baltimore were isolated. Furthermore, fire-alarm systems in these cities, particularly in New York, no longer functioned, thus leaving helpless those hundreds whose homes and businesses caught fire during the storm.

By the second day of the unabating blizzard, people began to die while attempting to walk home; their bodies were found frozen stiff under hillocks of snow days later. Manhattan hansom drivers still able to urge their half-frozen horses down partially opened streets gouged their customers. *Harper's Weekly* indignantly reported: "Twenty dollars was paid for a conveyance from the Astor House to Madison Square, and forty dollars for a cab from Wall Street to the Fifth Avenue Hotel. The hotels ran over. The corridors of the Astor House were changed into sleeping rooms, and 400 applicants for lodgings had been turned away at 5:00 P.M. [of the first day]."

New York began to shut down. The Custom House, the Clearing House, the Stock Exchange, the sub-Treasury and all other exchanges were closed. Only 95 persons out of a 1,700 membership of the Produce Exchange appeared on the floor by the second day of the storm. Barnum's freak show played to a house of fewer than 100 the first night of the storm, and German theater star Ludwig Barnay walked off the stage at the Academy of Music after counting only 12 persons in the audience.

George D. Baremore, a prominent businessman in New York, told his clerks that the blizzard didn't frighten him and that he would walk home. He was found days later beneath a towering snowdrift, dead; he was only one block from his house. Political boss Roscoe Conkling, who fancied himself "an athlete," shrugged off the dangers of the blizzard and strode into the storm at 6:00 P.M., starting at Wall Street and heading for The New York Club at Twenty-fifth Street. He walked tilted against hurricane winds and along the snow-clogged great boulevards that were pitched into darkness when the city's entire electrical system failed. For two miles Conkling drove against the howling wind and snow, and finally he managed to reach Union Square. It was unlighted, and as Conkling tried to cross it, he sank to his armpits in snow. Using every ounce of strength, the political sachem managed to free himself in twenty minutes. He reached his club four hours later, exhausted and collapsing in a soggy heap in the foyer.

A street scene in Printing House Square, New York City, during the great blizzard of March 1888. *(Leslie's)*

Members ran from a cheery fire to administer brandy to Conkling. He choked it down and through blue lips sputtered, "It's death out there. . . . People are dying everywhere. . . . I saw bodies sticking from the snow. . . . I was almost in their number."

The numbers grew, drastic scores, sometimes whole families succumbing to the storm. Nine families in Brooklyn sat in frozen resignation after the roofs of their homes blew away. *Leslie's* announced: "Of the hundreds who were overcome, but taken to places of shelter, a

Firemen found it impossible to get to fires reported during the great blizzard. Snowdrifts reached twenty feet in height.

number died from the effects of exposure. The hospitals and station-houses were filled with sufferers from frost-bites or broken limbs."

The storm struck wildly in Delaware, overwhelming dozens of fishing boats in the harbor at Lewes, where twenty-two persons drowned. Three-dozen schooners and barks were driven ashore by the snow gale in a half-dozen ports, and scores more were drowned while trying to make land. The fate of the *Harold C. Beecher* was typical. Her skipper, Captain Elverett, ordered his crew of seven men to lower a boat and escape to the shore of Long Island. He and the others were half way to land when the boat was lifted by fierce winds and capsized; all were drowned except one sailor who managed to swim to shore. The ice had to be chipped from his frozen limbs.

An ice bridge formed over the East River, and many New Yorkers tried to scurry across it on March 13. It broke "with the turn of the tide," and scores were swept into the waters to drown. Tugs sliced through the ice floes and picked up a few lucky ones.

On March 14, when the snow turned to a powdery shower, thousands of merchants and homeowners began to build bonfires, thus melting the snow into small lakes as New York's sewers struggled to send the millions of tons of water to the sea. The blizzard was over, and in the words of one grateful scribe, "The sun was a splendid and efficacious ally. The horse-cars broke into Park Row, and the gutters sang merrily. On Friday, the cross-town cars were running, and some of the snow heaps were not more than five and a half feet high."

UNITED STATES (EAST) — HURRICANE
September 14, 1944

For six days in September, 1944, a hurricane worked its way up and across the Atlantic, moving at a ponderous 15 m.p.h. from Puerto Rico. The storm struck New Jersey, Long Island, and the New England coast on September 14, 1944; the 140 m.p.h. gale lining its core also slashed into Maryland, Delaware and New Jersey. The famed Steel Pier at Atlantic City was torn apart by furious winds and waves.

The center of the storm vented its wrath upon Long Island and along the coasts of the New England states. Off shore, the 1,850-ton United States destroyer *Warrington* and two Coast Guard vessels were caught by savage winds and capsized by gigantic waves; many lives were lost. Though twenty-seven lives were lost at sea and on land and $50 million in damage was done to private homes, businesses and utilities, this storm paled before the hurricane of 1938, which destroyed $500,000 in property and killed hundreds.

(ALSO SEE: Long Island, 1938)

UNITED STATES (NORTHEAST) — HURRICANE
October 5, 1869

A savage hurricane struck the northeastern coast of the United States on October 5, 1869, with the greatest loss of life and damage occurring in Massachusetts. Almost fifty vessels were smashed to pieces in many bays along the coast, and twenty-seven ships were lost in Rumney Bay alone. This hurricane, known as Sexby's Gale, took the lives of fifty people. Damage was estimated to be more than $1 million, a staggering sum at that time.

UNITED STATES (NORTHEAST) — BLIZZARD
February 15-16, 1958

background: The northeastern United States was blanketed by snow during the great blizzard of February 15-16, 1958, which dumped record snowfalls in many cities, including some in the Midwest and South. Temperatures were also at record lows in a half-dozen states, and an estimated 500 persons were killed in the storm. Millions of dollars in damage was done to crops and millions more to property.

The 8.5 inches of snow that fell on New York during the blizzard of February 15-16, 1958, which swept through the northeastern United States, nowhere approached the record 25.8-inch snowfall that buried Manhattan in 1947 or the 20.9 inches of snow in the historic storm of 1888. But the outcome of the 1958 storm was just as drastic as that of the other two. As in previous storms this blizzard all but closed down the city, even though it was then equipped with new snow-fighting equipment. So clogged were New York streets and outlying highways throughout the state that dairy farmers had to dump more than $1 million in milk that could not be delivered.

It was the same story in Boston, which was coated with 19 inches of snow. Washington, D.C., which received 14 inches of snow, came to a standstill. More than 80 percent of all government employees failed to go to work on the second day of the storm. Nerve centers of the American defense system—the Pentagon Building, the National Security Agency, the Atomic Energy Commission—were all but closed down. A janitor answered desperate phone calls made to the United States Weather Bureau.

One Washingtonian commented: "It makes you wonder why the Soviets should ever bother to attack Washington with an H-bomb. It would be cheaper for them to buy a few sacks of dry ice and seed the clouds of the United States capital on some winter's day to create a snowstorm. The turmoil would be almost as bad."

President Dwight D. Eisenhower fled the storm that was blasting into Washington by flying to Thomasville, Georgia, to play golf in the sun. But there was no sun in Georgia, only cold and the state's first measurable snowfall in forty-six years. The president was compelled to play bridge by a roaring fireside as the northeastern part of the United States endured the great two-day blizzard. (Those who stayed in Washington got home on foot the first day of the storm, including Supreme Court Justice Earl Warren, whose car stalled, compelling him to trudge home through snowdrifts.)

The furious storm buried Lebanon, New Hampshire, under 60 inches of snow. Michigan City, Indiana, disappeared beneath 54 inches of snow. Temperatures plummeted and snared scores of rural victims who died of frostbite. It was 48 degrees below zero in Wisconsin and 26 degrees below zero at Bismarck, North Dakota. Lake Erie froze solid, as did the Chicago River, where ice blocks eight feet thick closed the locks at Lake Michigan for the first time.

Two trucks that jackknifed in the storm on the new superhighway outside Baltimore halted thousands of cars. Some of those stranded there died of frostbite. More than 4,000 horse-racing fans were trapped at Bowie Racetrack between Washington and Baltimore when the storm hit. An army of state troopers driving jeeps and half-tracks opened a road to the track, but the gale winds closed it minutes later behind them so that they, too, became trapped there. Emergency trains of the Pennsylvania Railroad bulldozed their way through the fifteen-foot drifts after twenty-four hours and evacuated the shivering, miserable handicappers.

In all, the blizzard killed more than 500 persons, making it the worst killer snowstorm in United States history.

UNSEN — EARTHQUAKES-VOLCANIC ERUPTION

April 1, 1793

Between 1780 and 1800, unusual volcanic and quake activity was present throughout the islands of Japan. On one of the islands, the volcano called Unsen blew up on April 1, 1793. The island itself disappeared in a titanic upheaval of combined earthquakes and volcanic eruptions that took the lives of an estimated 53,000 people.

Dozens of islands were formed by the outbreak in the Satsuma Sea. The great volcano Sakurajima reportedly "blew out so much pumice material that it was possible to walk a distance of twenty-three miles upon the floating debris in the sea." The belching volcano Asama "ejected many blocks of stone—one of which is said to have been forty-two feet in diameter—and a lava-stream" 425 miles in length.

URYU-JIMA, JAPAN — TSUNAMI

September 4, 1596

An island known as Uryu-Jima, approximately twenty-five miles wide and thirteen miles long, just off the mainland of Japan, suffered a minor earthquake on the morning of September 4, 1596. Few of the island's 5,000 inhabitants were alarmed at the small fissures that opened up on the island. Following the tremor, a deadly calm settled in. Shortly afterward, a *tsunami,* a great wall of water estimated to be fifty feet high, raced ashore. Half the island was instantly inundated, and 700 persons were drowned on the spot. The island began to sink slowly into thirty fathoms of water, but the surviving population managed to reach the mainland by crowding into fishing boats. Nothing remains of Uryu-Jima today.

UTOPIA — MARINE DISASTER

March 17, 1891

Loaded with more than 800 Italian immigrants on their way to New York, the British steamer *Utopia* of the Anchor Line was caught in a violent gale while attempting to clear the harbor at Gibraltar on March 17, 1891, and was sent flying into the iron bow of the British

Masts and funnel of the *Utopia* poke ominously from the waters of Gibraltar Harbor. The steamer was rammed by another ship during a gale and sank on March 17, 1891; 576 persons died in the disaster. *(Illustrated London News)*

battleship *Anson.* Quickly holed, the steamer began to sink while hundreds of wild-eyed immigrants leaped into the storm-whipped waters.

A half-dozen ships, including the Swedish vessel *Freya,* the *Rodney,* the *Anson* and the *Immortalité,* steamed to the rescue and picked up hundreds of thrashing victims. Scores of these wretched homeless died later from exhaustion, ballooning the overall death count to 576 persons, half of whom were crew members on board the *Utopia.*

UTTAR PRADESH, INDIA — FLOOD

October 24, 1956

In a land of constant flooding, the inhabitants of the Punjab and Bengal in India thought little of the average twelve inches of rain that fell each day during the third week of October in 1956. But alarm quickly spread as the mighty Jumna River suddenly broke from its banks on the twenty-fourth and raced across the wide farmlands and rickety hamlets in the province of Uttar Pradesh. The floodwaters were so quick and overwhelming that fifty persons were immediately drowned, 300,000 homes were smashed flat, and $30 million in crops were destroyed.

V

VALPARAISO, CHILE

EARTHQUAKE
August 16, 1906

An earthquake of great magnitude shook the entire length of Chile on August 16, 1906. Its epicenter was at Valparaiso, where 1,500 were killed and hundreds of millions of dollars in damage was done. More than 100,000 were made homeless by this shattering tremor, which occurred only four months after the quake that devastated San Francisco. According to seismologists, however, there was no connection between the two disasters.

VALS, SWITZERLAND

AVALANCHES
January 20, 1951

background: A series of heavy avalanches buried a dozen towns in Switzerland, Austria, and Italy as Alpine snows gave way following heavy rains; a total of 240 persons were killed in those three countries. Hardest hit was the 4,100-foot-high village of Vals in central Switzerland, where 19 died, in a single avalanche.

Feared more than any other raging element, the "white death" is a constant, haunting specter to those who reside permanently in the majestic Alps. The worst destruction ever by avalanche occurred on December 13, 1916, when thousands of Italian and Austrian troops fighting for Alpine passes were overcome and buried by 105 avalanches. Such massive killing by avalanches was almost equaled on January 20, 1951. There had been little snow in December 1950, and tourists were promised by natives that much more snow would soon arrive. It did, but it was mixed with rain. This wet snow coated the earlier powdery snow, which had little time to find a firm hold on the craggy mountaintops.

The snow turned to rain on January 20, and suddenly whole mountainsides of snow broke loose. The over-burdened masses of snow let go with a roar in a dozen places. The white death came at night over Vals, Switzerland. The entire town was buried, crushed by a torrent of snow mixed with broken timber and rocks. Fourteen of the nineteen dead in Vals were children.

Anton Casanova's story was typical. He lost his wife and two children. The local schoolteacher, Phillip Peng, lost his two baby sons to the avalanche. He himself perished while trying to get home. Rescuers later found Peng's babies, "their lifeless bodies looking like wax dolls as they nestled together on their bed."

Andermatt, also in Switzerland, was ripped apart by six successive avalanches in the space of an hour; thirteen were crushed to death there. The guests of a small hotel in Oberalspee were crushed in their sleep as the white death engulfed the building and buried it for weeks. At Davos, Zermatt, Arosa and St. Moritz—winter playgrounds of the rich—the story was the same. The avalanches came without warning and killed just about everyone in their paths.

The only signal the avalanches gave was the sound of hurricanelike winds that preceded the rush of millions of tons of snow, which quickly snapped off the thousands of trees that had been planted to prevent just such an occurrence.

The St. Gotthard rail line between Switzerland and central Europe was blocked for a week, and most Alpine towns in Austria and Italy were equally isolated as avalanches cut their communication with the outside world. More than 45,000 people in the Austrian provinces of Tyrol, Salzkammergut and Styria were isolated for weeks.

As weary consolation, the Swiss Avalanche Institute at Davos, the only research organization of its kind in the world, announced that the avalanches could have been worse. Those that fell, institute spokesmen explained, had been *Grundlawinen* (ground avalanches), in which snow masses slide down valleys intact from the snow's surface to the ground. Had it been a *Staublawine,* they added, deaths certainly would have been higher. *Staublawinen* heave up enormous clouds as they race down a mountain; even those surviving the impact of this type of avalanche are guaranteed to die of suffocation as fine snow particles clog the lungs.

The total death count raced upward to 240 as more and more bodies were dug out of the heavy snows. In Vals and in Andermatt, common graves were dug and mass funerals were held. At the graveside stood Johann Lutz. When the first avalanche cascaded down on Andermatt, he had climbed to his roof to sweep off the snow, lest his roof cave in. Then came another avalanche and another, five in all, while he clung to his roof. Inside his house his wife and two-year-old son were crushed to death by the snow that crunched through the windows and doors.

VANGUARD **MARINE DISASTER**
July 9, 1917

The *Vanguard* was the second ship of that name in the British Navy; the first one sank in 1870. Built in 1910, the second *Vanguard,* a St. Vincent-type dreadnought, fought, but she went undamaged in the battle of Jutland, which decisively saw the end of the German fleet. While lying in the Scapa Flow on the night of July 9, 1917, the battleship was suddenly lifted half out of the water by a tremendous explosion that sent the ship swiftly to the bottom. It was thought that her magazines had accidentally been ignited. The *Vanguard* sank so quickly that the entire crew of 806 men were caught by surprise; only two sailors managed to survive.
(ALSO SEE: Liberté*)*

VARIG AIRLINES **AIR CRASH**
November 27, 1962

A Varig Airlines Boeing 707 jet with ninety-seven passengers and crew members on board was about to land in Lima, Peru, on November 27, 1962, when the pilot began to have trouble with his craft. At 5:30 P.M. the control tower at Lima received a distress signal from the pilot, and then transmission suddenly broke off.

Search aircraft found the smashed 707 on the side of an Andes mountain some eight hours later. All on board had been killed. The airliner was on a routine flight from Brazil to Los Angeles. Among the dead was Fidel Castro's economic adviser, Raul Bonilla. No reason for the crash was discovered.

VASA **MARINE DISASTER**
August, 1628

The sinking of the Swedish flagship *Vasa* was due simply to improper construction and abject stupidity. Involved in the Thirty Years' War, Sweden ordered an enormous vessel with sixty-four guns, which were set in two tiers. When the ornate ship first slid into the water, her prow bedecked with a gilded lion with spreading claws and gleaming fangs, all the gunports remained open to display the heavy bronze cannon to the cheering throngs.

The *Vasa* set sail before thousands of Swedes, but the galleon never cleared the Stockholm harbor. Not more than a mile from land, the great ship suddenly began to founder. All 400 crew members dove for the bronze guns on the port side and attempted to drag them to starboard, but water was already pouring into the lower tier through the open gunports. The ship went down almost immediately, taking with her fifty of the crew.

VERA **TYPHOON**
September 26-27, 1959

background: The worst typhoon in Japan's history occurred on September 26, 1959, striking at central Honshu and devastating several provinces. Named Vera, the typhoon all but wrecked the city of Nagoya, Japan's third-largest city, with a population of 1.3 million. The death toll went beyond 5,000; three times that number were injured. Most of the fatalities were in Nagoya. Another 400,000 were made homeless, and $750 million in damage was done by the storm.

Japan averages from fifteen to twenty-five typhoons a year. But the inhabitants, despite thorough, advanced warnings, have a tendency to take as ritual, storm alerts, because most of the monster storms veer off from the main islands and spend themselves across lonely seas. But on September 26, 1959, one storm, called Vera, hailed by weathermen as a "super typhoon," did not veer off, but drove with her full weight and fury against the central part of Honshu, Japan, bringing more destruction and death than any previous typhoon on record.

The storm drove inland on the night of September 26, 1959, at high tide, creating seventeen-foot-high waves that inundated the shoreline from Nagoya to Tokyo. The megalopolis of Yokohama-Tokyo received blasting winds of 92 m.p.h., and hundreds of streets were flooded. At the height of the storm there, twenty-two trains, including seven express trains, were canceled between Osaka and Tokyo. All airplanes were instantly grounded.

Rushing across central Honshu, the storm turned at a right angle and followed the island to its northern tip, devastating the provinces of Toyama, Yamagata, Akita and Niigata. But the main force of the storm was vented against the city of Nagoya, then celebrating its seventieth anniversary. As a herald of the hell to come, the 7,412-ton British-owned freighter *Changsha* was hurled from the ocean onto Nagoya's beaches. In front of and behind the stricken vessel swirled titanic combers driven forward by 135 m.p.h. winds.

Logs were ripped loose from piles in the Nagoya lumber yards and sent racing down the water-churned streets. The logs acted like battering rams, tearing down fragile buildings and breaking open shutters and heavy doors on commercial buildings. Torn from their moorings were the golden dolphins that had been placed on Nagoya's 350-year-old castle to commemorate the city's anniversary.

Hundreds of people were swept out of their houses as the floodwaters raced inside. More than 5,800 homes were destroyed within minutes. One apartment house, a sturdy, modern structure, collapsed at the height of the typhoon, pinning eighty people in the wreckage. Many of these died before rescuers, hampered by the rising waters and fierce winds, could reach them.

The following day found 25,000 people in Nagoya clinging in fright to the rooftops of their rickety homes. Swarms of helicopters arrived to remove these survivors, but by then the city was in chaos. To survive, male members of families had taken to diving into the polluted waters, swimming to small gardens under water and retrieving, perhaps, a single sweet potato. Bodies floated everywhere. Thieves were so numerous that they attempted to steal valuables from houses still occupied. It took a special police force of 1,100 men, many of whom had lost their own families to the typhoon, to drive off the ghouls.

Disease spread rapidly in Nagoya, and soon hundreds were suffering from tetanus, gas gangrene and dysentery. It took days to evacuate the flooded sections of the city; one United States pilot commented as he gulped coffee between runs, "Somebody should have cried wolf."

Vera's statistics were gruesome: 5,000 or more people were dead, 2,000 more missing, 10,000 injured, and 400,000 homeless. Damage to property was a staggering $750 million. The United States contributed large amounts of relief goods.

The aid seemed of little use to the mayor of Nangyo, who officiated over the peaceful little suburb five miles from Nagoya. He looked about his ruined domain, hardly able to distinguish rooftops above the cataracts of water, and wailed: "I feel as if my arms and legs had been cut off. All I can see is the whole town submerged under a sea and filled with dead."

VERSAILLES, FRANCE — RAILWAY WRECK

May 8, 1842

When it was announced that a huge celebration in honor of the French king's birthday would be held at Versailles on May 8, 1842, thousands of Parisians journeyed there by train to view the magnificent fountains. Only minutes after the ceremonies were concluded at 5:30 P.M., there was a rush to get to the waiting trains returning to Paris. The first of these moved down the track perilously overburdened.

A few miles outside of Versailles, the axle of the first of two locomotives pulling one train broke, sending the engine downward with a crash onto the tracks. The second engine climbed onto the back of the first, and the following three coaches, all flimsy wooden affairs, were shattered. Few were killed in this initial crash, but fire quickly spread, and scores were trapped in the derailed cars. The wooden coaches roared into flames and passengers began to roast to death, having no way out of the cars since it was then the custom at that time to lock all coaches before departure and unlock them only upon arrival.

Though the death count of this first major railway wreck in the world was given as fifty-four, the number of fatalities was probably much higher, perhaps even one hundred or more. Most of the victims could not be recognized in the charred ruins of the train, and dozens of passengers actually melted or disappeared in the blaze.

VESTRIS — MARINE DISASTER

November 12, 1928

background: Launched in 1912, the *Vestris,* a passenger ship only capable of fifteen knots and belonging to the Lamport and Holt Line, foundered in the Atlantic on November 12, 1928, while en route to Buenos Aires. Drowned were 110 persons, mostly passengers and of these mostly women and children. Though partially exonerated by a board of inquiry, Captain W. J. Carey, through inexplicable acts, appeared largely responsible for the disaster.

The *Vestris* was a slack ship, and her captain, W. J. Carey, for all of his experience with the sea, proved incompetent and indecisive on her last voyage. These factors pointedly led to the vessel's foundering 350 miles off Chesapeake Bay while she was sailing from New York to Buenos Aires with 128 passengers on board. The sixteen-year-old ship left port with more freight than was safe to carry, but it had long been a practice of Sanderson & Company, American agents for the Lamport and Holt Line, to overload the ship. When she sailed on her fatal voyage, her holds were crammed to the ceilings. Eighty tons of coal in excess of the standard 2,769 tons was on board, causing the *Vestris* to sail almost a foot over draft.

Leaks were present from the beginning of the voyage on November 10, 1928. Before the Statue of Liberty was out of sight, water was discovered pouring through the starboard ash-ejector discharge. Then someone found water streaming through a coal chute door in the stokehold. A five-inch pipe, a sanitary discharge funnel, also let in great amounts of seawater, but this leak was not discovered until the ship began to sink two days later.

A strong northeast wind came up, and the *Vestris* began to battle through heavy seas, but gale conditions were never reached. Yet Captain Carey acted as if his ship were caught in the sweep of a hurricane. He wired his managers that he was "lying hove-to" against the storm. This meant, of course, that he was meeting the heavy seas bow first with engines stopped, yet Carey actually called for full power and his ship's maximum speed of fifteen knots. Many naval authorities believe that his proper course of action should have been to bring the ship about so that her stern faced the wind. But Carey did not adopt this standard sailing procedure. The already water-soaked coal in the hold began to shift, along with cargo in the holds, which broke loose, and this shifting weight caused the *Vestris* to develop a critical list to starboard.

Though pumps were working, leaks seemed to spring everywhere, and the water was inching toward the starboard boiler. In one stokehold the water was knee-deep. The passengers, however, were uninformed of conditions; Carey did not want to alarm them.

One passenger, T. E. Mack, from Wyoming, who was later picked up by the *Berlin* as his lifeboat bobbed in a choppy sea, remembered that "most of the passengers were awake all night Sunday because of the storm, and we realized that something serious was wrong early Monday morning, when the ship heeled over and furniture began to slide and crash down to the right. . . . At 6:00 A.M. on Monday morning the sea suddenly became calmer, and I thought that the ship might get straightened up all right. But at 10:00 A.M. the list was more pronounced, and finally, the captain ordered the lifeboats to be launched. . . . I was in No. 8; when it was being lowered, it crashed against the side of the *Vestris* and spilled everybody out." Fortunately for Mack, he was able to climb back aboard the sinking liner and find a berth in No. 13 lifeboat, which was successfully launched from the port side.

It is a wonder that any of the boats were launched at all. Carey, up to the last minute, refused to believe that his ship was in serious danger. He kept saying that the pumps would "make the ship come right again," but the job of the pumps had long been overwhelmed by tons of seawater that filled the ship's holds.

The captain's attitude might have been explained by the Lamport and Holt general instruction to its skippers: "In the case of a serious disaster happening to one of the vessels of this Line, whilst at sea, the master must in the first instance carefully consider the actual amount of peril there may be for the lives of those under his charge and then judge whether he will be justified or not, in fighting his own way *unaided* [italics added] to the nearest port. His being able to succeed in this will always be considered a matter of high recommendation to him as a master."

Carey also delayed sending out an emergency message, and it was not until two hours before the ship sank that he authorized the radio operator to transmit a "CQ" alarm to all ships at sea. (The "CQ" signal being a British maritime signal.) Forty-five minutes before the ship sank, he thought of using an "SOS" ("Save Our Ship") signal, which had long been adopted as the universal maritime signal for disaster.

Also at the last moment, Carey ordered the port lifeboats to be made ready for lowering, placing all the women and children—forty-nine in all—in the weather boats, but refusing to lower them. He thought that rescue vessels would arrive before such action was necessary. These port boats were high in the air and doubly difficult to lower. Why a man of Carey's alleged seamanship did not first lower the starboard boats that were much closer to the water has never been explained. The port boats either smashed up and spilled out their occupants when they were lowered or stayed with the ship and went to the bottom with her. Only eight women, no children at all, survived the sinking.

Though ships did steam to the rescue—the United States battleship *Wyoming,* the *Berlin,* the *American Shipper* and the *Myriam*—the *Vestris* was nowhere in the area. She had already sunk. Only eight boats, loaded with mostly male passengers and crew members, were found. These survivors were picked up, but the wonder of the entire disaster was that any of the 110 victims died at all; the *Vestris* was equipped with enough boats to accommodate 800 people and only half that number were on board. The death toll was due simply to more of Carey's bungling (although a court of inquiry placed little fault with the skipper). The captain, however, would never have to face an accusing finger.

Carey was last seen sloshing through heavy water on a port deck. He wore no life preserver and looked like a man sleepwalking. He was seen to walk directly into the sea, exclaiming to a stoker who was about to dive overboard: "My God, my God, I am not to blame for this!"

VESUVIUS — VOLCANIC ERUPTIONS A.D. 79-1944

background: The 4,000-foot-high volcano Vesuvius, towering above present-day Naples, has been active since before the time of Greek colonialization. Its first recorded eruption in historic times was in A.D. 79, when it covered dozens of villages and the cities of Stabiae, Herculaneum and Pompeii with great showers of ash, steam, water, sand and noxious vapors that killed approximately 16,000 persons. The volcano's most serious eruptions were then in 203; 472, when hundreds were killed; 512; 685; 993; 1036; 1049; 1139; 1198; 1302; 1306; 1500; 1538; 1631, its deadliest outbreak, in which 18,000 lost their lives; 1707, in which hundreds died; 1737; 1760; 1766; 1779; 1793-94; 1822; 1855; 1872; 1879; 1900; 1903; 1905-06, a tremendous blast with great lava flows; 1929, and 1944.

The graceful slopes of the volcano Vesuvius dominated the beautiful Bay of Naples long before recorded history. The mountain is probably the best known volcano in the world. Long known in legend, writers from Pliny to E. Bulwer-Lytton have depicted the mountain as a giant of terror wreaking wrathful vengeance upon the wayward populations dwelling at its feet. And it is a grim fact that Vesuvius is the most consistently lethal volcano on earth.

Roman colonists who had taken over the area around the mountain from the Greeks, long after that civilization had perished by its own top-heavy aristocracy in a corrupt republic, did not believe Vesuvius alive, or that it would ever erupt again. That was solely a thing of decadent Greek mythology. The Romans thought the volcano dormant and crowned its summit with a temple of Jupiter. The Roman historian Strabo wrote of Vesuvius in A.D. 25: "About these places rises Vesuvius, well cultivated and inhabited all round, except at its top, which is for the most part level and entirely barren, ashy to the view, displaying cavernous hollows in cineritious rocks, which look as if they had been eaten by fire; so that we may suppose this spot to have been a volcano formerly, with burning craters, now extinguished for want of fuel."

But Strabo and those who came to live in the white cities of Herculaneum, Stabiae and Pompeii and inside the luxurious Roman villas of the rich overlooking the sea from craggy perches were to have their world blotted out and their lives ended purely because they refused to believe Vesuvius could return to life, volcanic life that had never quit its bowels. (One of the opulent Romans dwelling near Vesuvius was Servilia, the favorite mistress of Julius Caesar and the mother of Brutus, who slew Caesar; Cicero, the great orator and member of the Roman Senate, also maintained a villa above Pompeii.) A forerunner of things to come occurred during the reign of Nero, on February 5, A.D. 63, when a violent earthquake threw down half the buildings of Herculaneum and Pompeii. Vesuvius, however, remained quiet, and as the inhabitants quickly rebuilt their cities, they continued to believe the volcano dead, merely "a cone-shaped mountain with a flat top, on which was a circular valley filled with vines and grass, and surrounded by high precipices."

To the slopes of this sleeping killer came the gladiator, Spartacus, who led a slave revolt against Rome from an encampment high on the mountain. He was defeated here by Roman legions in A.D. 72, only seven years before the first great eruption of Vesuvius blasted into reality.

The outbreak at 1:00 P.M. on August 24, A.D. 79, was abrupt; none of the 50,000 inhabitants living under the volcano's shadow had any warning. The eruptions lasted for eight days, and the populations of Stabiae, Herculaneum and Pompeii were decimated. Thousands unable, somehow, to believe that the mountain would kill them, refused to flee. The first vivid account of any Vesuvian eruption or detailed, firsthand observation of any volcanic eruption up to that time was presented by Pliny the Younger, a wealthy, young Roman. His eyewitness account, related in two letters to the historian Tacitus, remains as a classic of disaster literature.

Pliny wrote: "Your request that I would send you an

This street in Pompeii was buried beneath ash, stone, and lava in the A.D. 79 eruption of Vesuvius.

account of my uncle's death [Pliny the Elder], in order to transmit a more exact relation of it to posterity, merits my acknowledgements; for should the calamity be celebrated by your pen, its memory, I feel assured, will be rendered imperishable. He was at that time, with the fleet under his command at Misenum . . . my mother desired him to observe a cloud which seemed of unusual shape and dimensions. He had just returned from taking the benefit of the sun, and after a cold water bath and a slight repast, had retired to his study. He immediately arose, and proceeded to a rising ground, from whence he might more distinctly mark this very uncommon appearance.

"At that distance it would not be clearly perceived from what mountain the cloud issued, but it was afterward ascertained to proceed from Mount Vesuvius. I cannot better describe its figure than by comparing it to that of a pine tree, for it shot up to a great height like a trunk, and extended itself at the top into a kind of branches; occasioned, I imagine, either by a sudden gust of air that impelled it, the force of which decreased as it advanced upward, or by the expansion of the cloud itself, when pressed back again by its own weight. Sometimes it appeared bright, and sometimes dark and spotted, as it became more or less impregnated with earth and cinders. This extraordinary phenomenon excited my uncle's philosophical curiosity to inquire into it more closely. He ordered a light vessel to be got ready for him, and invited me to accompany him if I pleased. I replied that I would rather continue my studies.

"As he was leaving the house, a note was brought to him from Rectina, the wife of Bassus, who was in the utmost alarm at the imminent peril which threatened her; for her villa was situated at the foot of Mount Vesuvius, the only mode of escape was by the sea. She earnestly entreated him, therefore, to hasten to her assistance. He accordingly changed his first design, and what he began out of curiosity now continued out of heroism. Ordering the galleys to put to sea, he went on board, with an intention of assisting not only Rectina, but several others, for the villas are very numerous along that beautiful shore. Hastening to the very place which other people were abandoning in terror, he steered directly toward the point of danger, and with so much composure of mind that he was able to make and to dictate his observations on the changes and aspects of that dreadful scene.

This citizen of Pompeii was buried and preserved for centuries by the volcanic material.

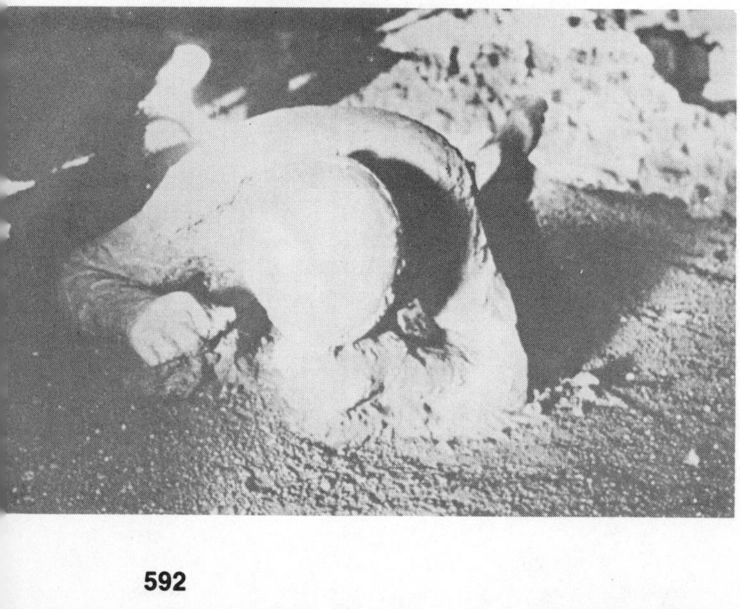

"He was now so nigh the mountain that the cinders, which grew thicker and hotter the nearer he approached, fell into the vessel, together with pumice-stones and black pieces of burning rock; and now the sudden ebb of the sea, and vast fragments rolling from the mountain, obstructed their nearer approach to the shore. Pausing to consider whether he should turn back again, to which he was advised by his pilot, he exclaimed, 'Fortune befriends the brave: carry me to Pomponianus.'

"Pomponianus was then at Stabiae, separated by a gulf which the sea, after several windings, forms upon the shore. He had already sent his baggage on board; for though not at that time in actual danger, yet being within prospect of it, he was determined, if it drew nearer, to put to sea as soon as the wind should change. The wind was favorable, however, for carrying my uncle to Pomponianus, whom he found in the greatest consternation. He embraced him tenderly, encouraging and counselling him to keep up his spirits; and still better to dissipate his alarm, he ordered, with an air of unconcern, the baths to be got ready. After having bathed, he sat down to supper with great cheerfulness, or what was equally courageous, with all the semblance of it.

"Meanwhile, the eruption from Mount Vesuvius broke forth in several places with great violence, and the darkness of the night contributed to render it still more visible and dreadful. But my uncle, to soothe the anxieties of his friend, declared it was only the burning of the villages, which the country people had abandoned to the flames. After this, he retired to rest; and it is certain he was so little decomposed as to fall into a deep sleep; for being somewhat corpulent, and breathing hard, those who attended without actually heard him snore.

"The court which led to his apartment being nearly filled with stones and ashes, it would have been impossible for him, had he continued there longer, to have made his way out; it was thought proper, therefore, to awaken him. He got up and joined Pomponianus and the rest of his company who were not unconcerned enough to think of going to bed. They consulted together which course would be the more prudent: to trust to the houses, which

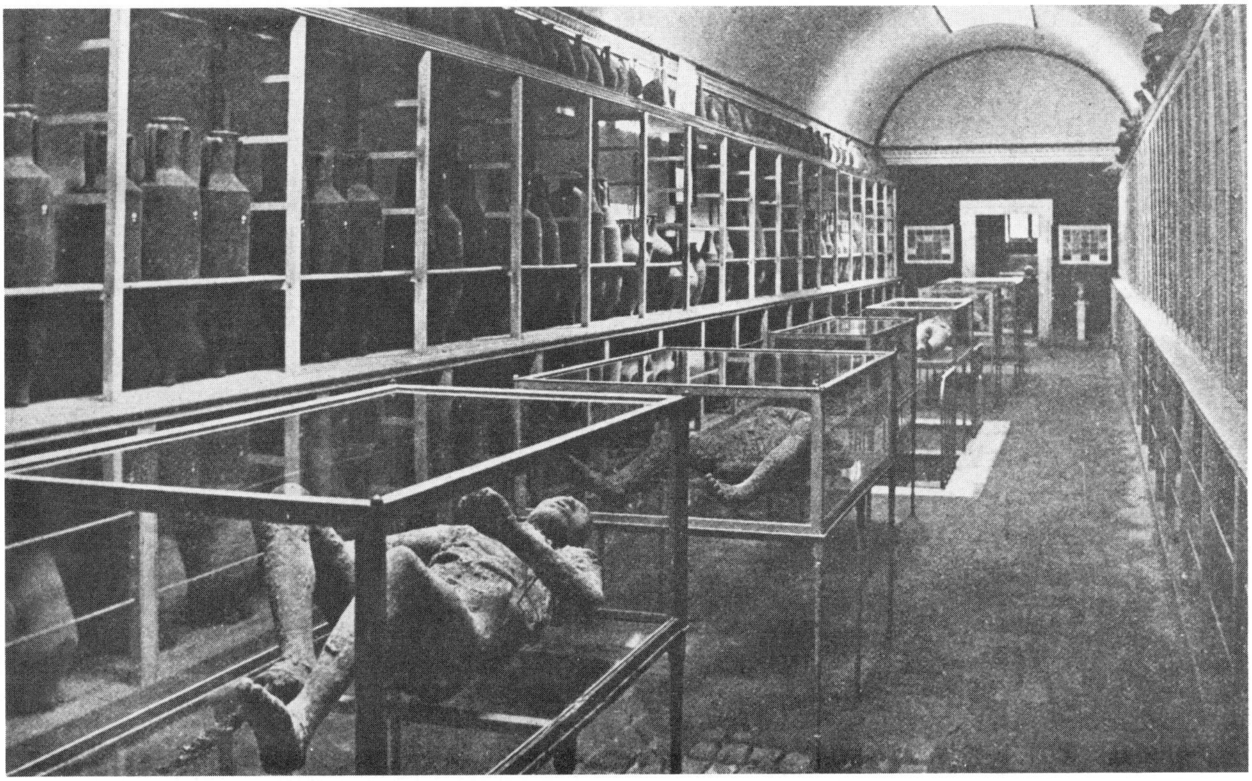

Petrified humans from Pompeii rest in museum cases. The jugs and jars, also unearthed from Pompeii, contained eatable figs and olives and drinkable wine, sealed for centuries.

now shook from side to side with frequent and violent concussions; or to escape to the open country, where the calcined stones and cinders fell in such quantities, as notwithstanding their lightness, to threaten destruction. In this dilemma they decided on the open country, as offering the greater chance of safety; a resolution which, while the rest of the company hastily adopted it through their fears, my uncle embraced only after cool and deliberate consideration. Then they went forth, having pillows tied upon their heads with napkins; and this was their sole defense against the storm of stones that fell around them.

"It was now day everywhere else, but there a deeper darkness prevailed than in the obscurest night, though it was in some degree dissipated by torches and lights of various kinds. They thought proper to go down further upon the shore, to ascertain whether they might safely put out to sea; but found the waves still extremely high and boisterous. There my uncle, having drunk a draught or two of cold water, flung himself down upon a cloth which was spread for him, when immediately the flames and their precursor, a strong stench of sulphur, dispersed the rest of the company, and compelled him to rise. He raised himself with the assistance of two of the servants, but instantly fell down dead, suffocated, I imagine, by some gross and noxious vapor. As soon as it was light again, which was not until the third day after this melancholy accident, his body was found entire, and free from any sign of violence, exactly in the same posture that he fell, so that he looked more like one asleep than dead."

Pliny the Younger then related his own experiences in a second letter to Tacitus while still at Misenum. He wrote: "Day was rapidly breaking, but the light was exceedingly faint and languid; the buildings all around us tottered; and though we stood upon open ground, yet, as the area was narrow and confined, we could not remain without certain and formidable peril, and we therefore resolved to quit the town. The people followed us in a panic of alarm, and, as to a mind distracted with terror every suggestion seems more prudent than its own, pressed in great crowds about us in our way out.

"As soon as we had reached a convenient distance from the houses, we stood still, in the midst of a perilous and most dreadful scene. The chariots which we had ordered to be drawn out oscillated so violently, though upon level ground, that we could not keep them steady, even by supporting them with large stones. The sea seemed to roll back upon itself, and to be driven from its strands by the earth's convulsive throes [no doubt a seismic sea wave]; it is certain, at least, that the shore was considerably enlarged, and that several marine animals were left upon it. On the other side, a black and terrible cloud, bursting with an igneous serpentine vapor, darted out a long train of fire, resembling but much larger than the flashes of lightning [St. Elmo's Fire].

"Soon after the black cloud seemed to descend and enshroud the whole ocean; as, in truth, it entirely concealed the island of Caprea [now Capri] and the headland of Misenum. The ashes now began to fall upon us, though in no considerable quantity. Turning my head, I perceived behind us a dense smoke, which came rolling in our track like a torrent. I proposed, while there was yet some light, to diverge from the highroad, lest my mother should be crushed to death in the dark by the crowd that followed us. Scarcely had we stepped aside when darkness overspread us; not the darkness of a cloudy night, or when there is no moon, but that of a chamber which is close shut, with all the lights extinct.

"And then nothing could be heard but the shrieks of women, the cries of children, and the exclamations of men. Some called aloud for their little ones, others for their parents, others for their husbands, being only able to distinguish persons by their voices; this man lamented his own fate, that man the fate of his family; not a few wished to die out of very fear of death; many lifted their hands to the gods; but most imagined the last eternal night was come, which should destroy the world and the gods together.

This old print depicts an eruption of Vesuvius in 1754.

"At length, a glimmer of light appeared, which we imagined to be rather the foretoken of an approaching burst of flames, as in truth it was, than the return of day. The fire, however, having fallen at a distance from us, we were again immersed in dense darkness, and a heavy shower of ashes fell upon us, which we were compelled at times to shake off—otherwise we should have been crushed and buried in the heap.

"After a while, this dreadful darkness gradually disappeared like a cloud of smoke; the actual day returned, and with it the sun, though very faintly, and as when an eclipse is coming on. Every object that presented itself to our eyes (which were extremely weakened) seemed changed, being covered with a crust of white ashes, like a deep layer of snow. We returned to Misenum, where we refreshed ourselves as well as we could, and passed an anxious night between hope and fear, though, indeed, with a much larger share of the latter; for the earthquake still continued, while several excited individuals ran up and down, augmenting their own and their friends' calamities by terrible predictions."

The devastation that befell Herculaneum and Pompeii was much worse than experienced by either Pliny the Elder or Pliny the Younger. Contrary to what Dion Cassius wrote a century and a half after the eruption of A.D. 79, which influenced E. Bulwer-Lytton's *The Last Days of Pompeii,* the population of Pompeii was not totally overwhelmed in a moment by Vesuvius. In addition, the residents were not all gathered in an amphitheater and killed while they sat in their seats. The city, along with Herculaneum, had ample warning to evacuate the area. Thousands out of a population of 20,000 in Pompeii did depart. At least 6,000 others in Pompeii and Herculaneum refused to escape, believing they would somehow survive the catastrophe.

For seven days it rained pumice stone, hot lava blocks (there was, oddly enough, no flow of lava) and millions of tons of ash. Coupled to this, on the last day, were enormous quantities of steam and vapor, which proved to be noxious, forming a poisonous cloud that spread and killed everyone present. Then came a great flood of water, dashing down the mountainside. The water, mud and ashes mixed rapidly into a volcanic paste. This liquid quickly covered the cities, preserving for centuries buildings and inhabitants alike.

The excavation of the two cities began almost immediately, but not in the cause of science; Emperor Alexander Severus dug out huge slabs of marble, columns and statues, which he used to decorate his buildings in Rome. Coins, jewelry and items of gold and silver were also removed from the buried cities, but archeological examination would not begin in earnest until the middle of the eighteenth century.

During the construction of an aqueduct in 1592, some foundations were uncovered but ignored by workers. Almost a hundred years later, workers found several buildings bearing the inscription "Pompeii." These were also ignored. Then, hearing that great treasures were buried in subterranean passages within Pompeii and Herculaneum, a Spanish colonel of engineers named Alcubierre obtained permission from the King of Naples to dig out the ruins.

In 1748 Alcubierre found "a picture eleven palms long by four and one-half high, containing festoons of eggs, fruits and flowers, the head of a man, large and in good style, a helmet, an owl, various small birds and other objects." Then a man's skeleton was unearthed. An amphitheater was dug up, and the bodies of what appeared to be gladiators slain in the arena at the time of the volcano's final eruption had been preserved in the volcanic paste. The city of Pompeii had been, so to speak, hermetically sealed; its continued excavation proved that thousands had died swiftly in the city.

Carbonized loaves of bread were found in ovens; vials containing the solidified fluids to be dispensed by apothecarists were unearthed. There were vases with olives still swimming in oil, fruit retaining its flavor, wines, still drinkable, in sealed jugs, shelves laden with raisins, figs, chestnuts. Two Roman soldiers who were apparently being punished at the moment of the eruption were found intact, locked in stocks.

The excavations went on for centuries, and the wonders never ceased. The Temple of Isis was unearthed. On a pedestal was a statue of the goddess, draped in purple and gold. In the next room was the body of a priest holding an axe in his hand. Another priest was found in an adjoining room sitting at his dinner. Many other priests were found in other rooms, and historians have speculated that they had fled to the temple thinking that Isis would protect them against the wrath of Vesuvius. A skeleton was found lying next to the main gate of the prison, and in his hand was a fistful of silver coins. Nearby, according to one report, "in his narrow niche, a Roman sentry stood, fully armed; observing to the last, stern, unflinching obedience to superior powers, who neglected to relieve him in the terror of the time."

At the suburban villa of Diomed, eighteen adults were found in a vault, along with a boy and an infant; all were preserved in volcanic paste. "To the skulls of the children cling their long, blonde hair." Near the villa's gate were found two skeletons, one holding a bunch of keys and a large sum of money, the other grasping silver vases. It was surmised that while the family had sought shelter in the cellar of the villa, two servants had attempted to make off with their wealth.

One historian described how "in the house of the Faun stood the skeleton of a woman, her hands raised over her head. Her scattered jewels lay about the floor. Endeavoring at length to leave the house, she found the doorway blocked with ashes. The flooring of the upper rooms began to fall, and she lifted her arms in vain attempt to stay the crumbling roof. Thus she was found." Another woman was found in the garden of the same house, seven feet below the earth. She had died while trying to get over the wall. She was petrified in volcanic mud.

Greed met the diggers at one spot where a man was found in an upright position, sword still in hand. His foot rested on a pile of great silver and gold he had obviously been protecting. Scattered about him were five other bodies, most likely would-be looters he had killed.

In one house two completely preserved bodies were found. They were thought to be mother and daughter. "The former lay outstretched and tranquil; the young girl of fifteen, in an attitude expressive of frightful agony. Her legs were drawn up, her hands clenched. With one hand she had drawn a veil about her head, to screen herself from the ashes and smoke. The form and texture of her dress are clearly seen; and through its rents the fair young skin appears like polished marble."

Although only 700 bodies and skeletons were found, it is estimated that at least 16,000 persons died in the three cities and many villages overcome in the A.D. 79 eruption.

The next serious eruption was in 203, after which a long period of calm set in, and Vesuvius once again became overgrown with brushwood and a forest of tall trees. Its plugged basin for 200 years was a favorite Roman hunting area for wild boars. In 472 the mountain erupted again with great violence. According to one account, "The clouds of ashes spread over the entire adjacent region. Houses toppled down miles away. Scores of people were suffocated. The ashes fell in showers at Constantinople and Tripoli."

As in the Pompeiian upheaval no streams of molten lava poured forth in any of the destructive outbreaks occurring before A.D. 1000. But in 1036 Vesuvius gave up enormous quantities of lava, and rivers of the molten liquid ran wide and swift to the sea, killing scores in their paths. It was the same in 1049. The 1198 eruption was so great that it activated the neighboring crater of Solfatara Lake. Ischia, dormant for more than 1,400 years, was activated by the Vesuvius eruption in 1302.

On September 29, 1538, an eruption at the foot of the mountain gave forth great vomitings of smoke, fire, stones and mud made of ashes. One narrative has it that "stones and masses of pumice larger than an ox were thrown out. . . . The large stones were thrown about as high as a crossbow would carry, and then fell, sometimes into the lake." The town of Pozzuoli on the Bay of Baiae was almost totally destroyed, and scores were killed.

Most of the outbreaks up to the eruption of 1631 were feeble, but in that year on December 12, began Vesuvius's most destructive tremors. Bracini, who observed the volcano in 1631, wrote that "the crater was about five miles in circumference and about a thousand feet deep; its sides were covered with brushwood, and at the bottom was a plain on which cattle grazed. . . . In one part of the plain, covered with ashes, were three small pools; one filled with hot and bitter water, another saltier than the sea, and a third hot but tasteless." Vesuvius looked in 1631 almost exactly as it had in A.D. 78 before it destroyed Pompeii; it is truly one of the most deceptive volcanic killers in the world.

All of the vines, woodlands and pastures inside the enormous crater were once again annihilated when the mountain erupted for a month, sending down huge streams of molten rock that spilled over the lip of the crater and poured in seven rivers of fire down the southern slopes. The flows were likened to that of guttering candles, and these fast-rushing streams soon engulfed the towns on Torre dell' Annunziata, Torre del Greco, Portici and the large town of Resina, which had been built on the site of the long-buried Herculaneum.

Cinder showers, millions of tons of ashes, coated the southern areas; more than 18,000 persons were killed in this greatest of Vesuvian outbreaks. Since that time the volcano has been in constant activity. Notable eruptions occurred in 1707, when hundreds were killed in Naples as lava welled up against the gates of the city, and in 1737, when a stream containing 300 million cubic feet of lava burst from the mountain's side. The scientist Breislak estimated the outpouring was enough to cover a square mile twelve and a half feet in depth.

The prolonged eruption of 1793-94 began in February and lasted until the following July; at one point staggering amounts of lava forming fifteen rivers from the crater of the mountain to its base poured continuously for fifteen hours, causing the sea to boil for 100 yards outward. The English ambassador to Italy, Sir William Hamilton, witnessed on many occasions this six-month upheaval, which covered half the mountain with fire.

Hamilton was agog at the "huge masses of white smoke [that] were vomited forth by the disturbed mountain, and formed themselves at a height of many thousands of feet above the crater into a huge, ever-moving canopy, through which, from time to time, were hurled pitch-black jets of volcanic dust, and dense vapors, mixed with cascades of red-hot rocks and scoriae. The rain from the cloud canopy was scalding hot.

"As the lava rushed forth from its imprisonment, it streamed a liquid, white and brilliantly pure river, which burned for itself a smooth channel through a great arched chasm in the side of the mountain. It flowed with the clearness of honey in regular channels, cut finer than art can imitate and glowing with all the splendor of the sun."

The lava in one of the fifteen streams was estimated to be from 12 to 40 feet thick and flowed 380 feet to the sea. Again the town of Torre del Greco was utterly destroyed, and at least fifty persons were killed.

Fanatic to reclaim the land, the natives of Torre del Greco rebuilt their city on the same spot Vesuvius had twice devastated. This caused the smug, untouched citizens of Naples to jest: "Naples sins, and Torre is punished."

The eruption of April 24, 1872, was spectacular, if not lethal, to more than two dozen trapped natives. The mountain was described by a Professor Palmieri as "sweating fire." Blocks of stone 45 feet in circumference were hurled down the mountain, and two lava floods rushed down the volcano's slopes on two sides. An estimated 20 million cubic feet of lava were ejected in a single day.

This display paled in comparison to the eruptions of 1905-06, when enormous red-hot stones shot upward to 1,600 feet above the cone and dropped down the flanks of the mountain with deafening sounds. These were dubbed "lava bombs." One of these bombs weighed more than two tons. Seismologists had climbed partway up the mountain, and their instruments recorded 1,844 violent explosions in a single day. (The great tenor Enrico Caruso, absent from his native Naples, considered himself lucky when he heard the news that Vesuvius was once again in eruption; he was subsequently trapped in the San Francisco earthquake of 1906.) The steam-and-dust cloud above the volcano towered to eight miles. Frank A. Perret, after witnessing the volcano's massive outbreak, wrote in 1906: "Strongest of impressions was . . . that of an infinite dignity in every manifestation of this stupendous releasing of energy. No words can describe the majesty of its unfolding." Again dozens were killed.

The 1929 eruption of Vesuvius was less dramatic, but its lava streams and outpourings of ashes caused damage to a dozen villages and killed more than 100 persons. At least that number perished in Vesuvius's last great eruption, which began on March 18, 1944, and continued for a week.

Allied armies were then battling Nazi divisions in the area, but the eruption ceased hostilities. Awestruck, tens of thousands of soldiers sat back and marveled at the raging mountain. War correspondent Milton Bracker wrote for the *New York Times:* "Those who watched Vesuvius in action this morning will never forget it. The crater, from which alternately oozed or spurted the fiery volcanic matter, was forgotten in the presence of one prong of lava 100 yards wide and actually 30 feet deep. It was like the monstrous paw of an even more monstrous lion, slowly inching forward toward his prey.

"The lava was white-hot; it was orange-gold, with occasional black patches, undulating like waves. As the stream advanced, great boulders cracked off and tumbled down, setting fire to small fruit trees and causing onlookers to leap back in alarm. The general sound was like that of an infinite number of clinkers rolling out of a furnace, but sometimes a great chunk of rock bent rather than broke. Its effect was like that of the devil's own taffy being pulled and twisted to suit his taste. . . . At one side stood a peasant whose weathered face turned tawny in the glow. *'Guerra, fame, distruzione'* ["war, hunger, destruction"], he repeated, shaking his head. *'Guerra, fame, distruzione!'*

"But there was humor, too. An American corporal from Indiana squatted at a safe distance and muttered: 'Gosh, wait till I tell 'em about this in Muncie!' "

(ALSO SEE: Etna)

VICTORIA — MARINE DISASTER

June 22, 1893

background: While on maneuvers ten miles off Tripoli and preparing to anchor, the flagship of the British fleet, *Victoria,* and the battleship *Camperdown* collided at 3:43 P.M. on June 22, 1893. The *Victoria* sank in thirteen minutes and took 358 men with her, including the commander of the fleet, Vice-Admiral Sir George Tryon, who was later held responsible for the disaster.

"His brain must have failed him." With these words Admiral Sir Reginald Bacon evaluated the mental condition of the British Navy's much-esteemed Vice-Admiral Sir George Tryon, the man most responsible for the disastrous collision between his flagship, *Victoria,* and the battleship *Camperdown.* The accident occurred while the British Mediterranean fleet sailed toward anchorage in Tripoli on June 22, 1893. The ramming of the *Victoria* is still considered one of the most embarrassing events in British military history.

Tryon was a stern disciplinarian who prided himself on his clever sea tactics. He was forever creating difficult maneuvers for his fleet to perform and watching such arduous operations from the bridge of his flagship in wordless fascination, much as one might observe a million dominoes crashing in predesigned patterns.

Sailing from Beirut at 10:00 A.M. on June 22, 1893, and bound for Tripoli, the fleet under Tryon's command consisted of eight battleships and five cruisers; the *Victoria* was in the lead. All went well until the ships were about ten miles off Tripoli. At that time Tryon announced to his officers that he wanted a special maneuver before entering port and ordered the fleet to change to columns of divisions.

The operation was complex; it first called for the eight battleships to line up in two columns, the *Victoria* leading one, the *Camperdown* the other. Next the ships were to turn inward upon each column in a half turn that would thus bring the fleet into port with the *Victoria,* the flagship, in first position to anchor. The maneuver was delicate, and the space Tryon allowed between the two columns before the hazardous turning-inward movement was shallow, too small a space, as it proved, to provide proper navigation.

The error made by the commander-in-chief, experts have since put forward, was prosaic. Tryon had confused the radius of the turning circle with the diameter. At 3:28 P.M. Tryon ordered the following instructions to his fleet to be run up in signal pennants: "Second division alter course in succession sixteen points to starboard, preserving the order of the fleet. First division alter course in succession sixteen points to port, preserving the order of the fleet."

The *Victoria* and *Camperdown* began to turn inward toward each other. The *Camperdown,* with Rear Admiral Albert Hastings Markham on board and in command of the second division, began her turn in a much wider arc than the *Victoria.* As the ships proceeded toward each other, Captain Archibald Bourke, skipper of the *Victoria,* approached Tryon, who was standing at the aft-end of the chart house deck, looking intently astern at the battleship *Nile.*

Bourke pointed to the approaching *Camperdown* and nervously said to Tryon: "We had better do something, sir. We shall be too close to that ship."

Tryon was like a man mesmerized. He did not respond, but only peered at the *Nile* as she battled the *Victoria*'s wake.

Again Bourke said loudly to the vice-admiral: "We

The huge British battleship *Victoria* was the victim of zany navy maneuvers and a collision with her sister ship *Camperdown.*

Frantic British sailors leap from the stern of the sinking *Victoria* on June 22, 1893.

had better do something, sir. We shall be very close to the *Camperdown.*"

Tryon did not reply.

"We are getting too close, sir! We must do something, sir!"

The *Camperdown* bore down on the *Victoria,* and still Tryon did not respond. Three times Captain Bourke almost shouted the question: "May I go astern with the port screw?"

With a casual air Tryon turned from his position and saw the *Camperdown* coming on. "Yes, go astern," he said quietly.

Bourke ordered both screws full speed astern, but the measure was hopelessly late. Collision was inevitable, and all watertight doors were ordered shut and the collision mat was positioned.

The *Camperdown* bore down on her sister ship with 14,000 horsepower engines going full tilt. As the ship drew near, Tryon cupped his hands and shouted to Rear Admiral Markham, who, along with his staff, was visible on the bridge: "Go astern! Go astern!"

As the *Camperdown* crunched for nine feet into the *Victoria,* crew members in the mess hall and seamen's quarters scrambled madly for the deck. Scores were knocked senseless, yet no water poured inside the ship. All of the watertight doors had not been closed and, because of the steaming hot day, almost every hatch and port in the *Victoria* had been opened wide. At that moment Tryon made another fatal error. Seizing a megaphone, he ordered the *Camperdown* to go immediately astern. She did, and moments later tons of sea water poured in through the nine-foot hole that was twelve feet below the waterline.

Fortunately Bourke had had the presence of mind to order most of the *Victoria*'s crew, almost 600 men, lined up on the port side of the ship's deck to prepare for ramming. The bluejackets, long after the collision, stoically held their positions four ranks deep. The ship was already low in the sea, and still more tons of water gushed through the many open portholes and hatchways. In thirteen minutes the ship sank bow first, her screws still churning wildly in the air as the stern lifted up. (Thinking that his flagship would never sink, Tryon had ordered the *Dreadnought* to pull back the lifeboats she had lowered. This order proved fatal to hundreds of nonswimmers of his crew who were eventually catapulted into the water.)

Steel-eyed, heavy-bearded Vice-Admiral Tryon refused to leave the chart bridge, calling out to a sixteen-year-old midshipman awaiting orders on a lower bridge, "Don't stay there, youngster. Go to a boat." Tryon was last seen standing implacably at the bridge, his white-gloved hands gripping the railing, his demeanor calm. He went down with his ship, along with 21 other officers and 336 seamen. It was one of the worst disasters ever suffered by the British Navy.

One of the survivors was Commander John Jellicoe, the future naval hero of World War I. Jellicoe raced to the deck of the fast-sinking *Victoria,* jumped into the sea and swam like mad to avoid the suction created by the sinking vessel. Luckily he avoided the flesh-slashing screws that ground dozens of other sailors to death.

One account of those caught at the stern of the ship when she went down reported: "A new horror was visited upon the struggling men. The powerful engine, deep down in the heart of the ship and enclosed in the watertight compartments, kept throbbing and working, and the formidable steel flanges of the twin screws whirled round and round, at first high up in space, and then gradually came nearer and nearer to the surface of the water until the ship descended in the midst of the mass of human beings struggling for life, and then as it disappeared the suction increased until it became a perfect maelstrom, at the bottom of which these deadly screws were moving like circular knives, gashing and killing the poor creatures who had battled vainly for life.

"Then came the scene that caused the officers on the decks of the remaining vessels of the fleet to turn sick. Shrieks were heard, and then the waves and the foam were reddened by the blood of the hundreds of victims. Arms, legs wrenched from bodies, headless trunks were tossed out of the vortex to linger on the surface for a few moments and then disappear."

Admiral of the Fleet Sir Geoffrey Phipps Hornby read this story and branded it a lie in a lengthy article for the *Review* in which he quoted "a mature officer of the *Victoria*" who went unnamed. "As for me," Hornby quoted, "when she gave the lurch, I clutched the fore-and-aft chain, and I felt the ship turn over on top of me. I know little more, except when I came to the surface there were very many round me, and large quantities of wreckage and breakers [small casks for holding water or provisions] and gear to get hold of. I saw the stern of the poor old ship, the screws still going round, for a second, and she sank. There must have been many men now left swimming over the spot; there is much evidence to show this. Then came a terrible explosion from the ship below water—I suppose the boilers. This threw up a huge hummock of water, like a torpedo; and this it was, I think, that drowned very, very many of the poor fellows."

A short time later, Jellicoe, the future admiral, wired his father, a retired sea captain living on the Isle of Wight: "Jack Saved. An awful affair. Thank God."

VICTORIA, BRITISH COLUMBIA — STREETCAR WRECK — May 26, 1896

In honor of Queen Victoria's birthday, a mammoth celebration had been scheduled in Victoria, British Columbia, on May 26, 1896. Thousands jammed themselves onto trolley cars and headed for the site of the gala. One of these electric trolleys attempted to cross an iron bridge spanning a gorge. The structure was ancient and had originally been designed for wagon service. The sheer weight of the overcrowded car caused the bridge to collapse, and the occupants were thrown seventy-five feet downward to their deaths. Of the eighty passengers on board the trolley, fifty-four were killed and all the rest injured. Those who survived managed to do so by riding on top of other passengers who broke their fall.

VICTORIA HALL — STAMPEDE — June 16, 1883

Victoria Hall, the largest building for popular entertainment and meetings in Sunderland, England, became a bloody scene of disaster when 1,200 children stampeded on June 16, 1883. More than 200 of them were crushed to death in a narrow staircase and a half-opened door leading to the stage.

A. Fay and his wife were giving a special children's performance of "conjuring, moving and speaking wax-figures and marionettes, and other diverting illusions and mock spectres," and almost all of the city's children were in attendance, with only a few parents, almost all women, as chaperones. About 1,500 children crammed into Victoria Hall; most of these were occupying the gallery.

At the end of Fay's performance, toys and other prizes were to be distributed, so the children eagerly pushed forward down a lone staircase to get to the stage. The children ran from the gallery down the narrow staircase. At the bottom of the staircase was a door fixed so that only one child at a time could pass; the width of the opening was about twenty to twenty-four inches. The management had jammed the door in this manner in order to assure that each child had purchased a ticket. This situation created a deathtrap, for when the first child became jammed there, the next one piled up on top until the bodies were twenty deep. Those on the bottom of the gruesome heap were crushed to death as those behind continued to stampede.

The caretaker, Frederick Graham, tried to untangle the squirming, shrieking mass, but found the weight too much to lift. He then ran up another staircase and led approximately 600 children to safety by another exit.

A number of adults ran forward and began to lift the children from the bloody heap. One man cursed the owners of the theater as he tore the locked door from its hinges. It was too late for about 200 children who were already under the weight of their companions. Mass funerals were held in Sunderland the following day.

VIERZY, FRANCE — RAILWAY WRECK — June 16, 1972

Two trains entered the ancient and crumbling Vierzy tunnel, one from the south, the other from the north, at the same moment on June 16, 1972. The tunnel, sixty miles northeast of Paris, had collapsed only moments

The ancient train tunnel at Vierzy, France, collapsed and trapped two trains on June 16, 1972, killing 107 persons. Here rescue workers search through the debris. *(Wide World)*

before. Parts of its ceiling at the center had fallen in when rotting timbers gave way.

Both trains, speeding at about sixty m.p.h., hit the rockfall at the same time, and the debris catapulted them up through the ceiling, causing the rear cars to telescope into those in front. For three days rescuers worked with handsaws to free those pinned in the wrecked cars. They feared that electric saws might ignite diesel fumes and cause the entire wreck to explode. Ninety persons, 40 of them badly injured, were taken from the tunnel alive. Police and rescue teams carried out 107 bodies some time later.

VIETNAM (and JAPAN) — TYPHOON
September 25, 1953

More than 1,300 inhabitants of central Vietnam were killed on September 25, 1953, when a typhoon swept across a ninety-mile section of the central coast. Most of the deaths and destruction occurred in and about the old capital of Hue, 325 miles north of Saigon. The entire rice crop was demolished as two provinces were inundated and tens of thousands of straw huts were blown down, leaving 100,000 homeless.

This typhoon also struck Japan; it pounded 100 towns and villages throughout Honshu and killed twenty-nine persons. The storm caused $1.9 million in damage to the United States Air Force base at Otsu.

VIRGINIA CITY, ALABAMA — MINE DISASTER
March 23, 1905

The use of too much dynamite in blasting a section of the Virginia City Mine at Virginia City, Alabama, was given as the cause of 112 deaths on March 23, 1905. Every man working the coal mine at the time lost his life. A state mine inspector examined the shaft following the lethal explosion and found coal dust present. It was the element, his report stated, that was ignited by a "windy shot" on the reckless part of one of the blasters. (Most of the mines in Alabama were then worked by convicts, and gross negligence of safety standards, such as the use of short fuses, was rampant.)

VOLKLINGEN, GERMANY — MINE DISASTER
February 7, 1962

Of all the coal mine works in the heavy industrial area of the Saarland, the Luisenthal pit at Volklingen, Germany, was thought to be one of the safest and most modern. That reputation was shattered at 8:00 A.M. on February 7, 1962, when escaping methane gas somehow ignited on the second level of the main shaft, and roaring flames hunted out the 480 miners in the works at the time.

The flames shot down two levels and created another violent explosion at the 1,800-foot level. Coal gas erupted almost every inch of the way. Killed were 298 men. They suffocated; their lungs were punctured, and they were crushed to death as tunnel walls gave in. A surviving miner, George Kneip, helped to bring several men to the surface.

To reporters, he coughed: "They [bodies] arrived piled on cars from deeper inside the gallery. One body was headless. The injured looked terrible. Some looked completely black. Many cried in agony."

The Volklingen disaster was the second worst mine calamity in German history, the most destructive having been the explosion at the Kamen works in 1946, when 402 miners were killed. Both of these catastrophes paled by comparison to the disaster that occurred in a blast in Honkeiko, Manchuria, in 1942, when 1,549 miners perished.

VOLLAND, KANSAS — RAILWAY WRECK
January 2, 1907

John Lynes, an operator for the Rock Island Line who was stationed in Volland, Kansas, had loved trains since he was a lad. At the first opportunity he obtained a job where he could be close to his beloved iron behemoths. His ambition, however, was far beyond his ability to direct trains. Lynes told his Rock Island employers that he was twenty-two years old and that he had six years' experience as a railroad telegraph operator and station manager. He was really eighteen and had no experience at all. Yet the Rock Island hired him. After three days on the job, his boyhood fascination brought him tragedy.

On January 2, 1907, as Lynes sat in the small station house at Volland, Kansas, a dispatcher signaled over the wire to hold the westbound California fast mail train, Number 29, so that a northbound passenger train, Number 14, could maintain the single track. This Lynes did. But moments after Number 14 went through, the dispatcher was back on the wire asking if Number 29 was still at the station. Lynes replied in the affirmative. The dispatcher then asked Lynes further to hold Number 29 so that another passenger train, eastbound Number 30, could go through. Lynes replied affirmatively.

Looking out the station window, Lynes saw Number 29 move onto the main track, but he thought the engineer was only edging up to the water tower. He fumbled with the lever of the train order board to give Number 29's engineer the new instructions to wait for Number 30. But the train had already passed the order board and slowly was heading west. Lynes leaped from his chair, grabbed a lantern, ran alongside the train and waved his lamp frantically. So wildly did Lynes signal that the light went out. He grabbed a pumping house lantern and swung that to and fro, but the train was by then far out of the station and the engineer oblivious to his signals.

Moments later, as Number 29 rounded a curve at a crawling speed of 10 m.p.h., Number 30 met it head-on. Thirty-one Mexican workers sitting in the smoker of Number 29 were killed when their old wooden car broke to splinters as the baggage car telescoped into it. Only one man, a hobo secreted in the baggage car, was killed on Number 30, bringing the total fatalities of the crash to thirty-two.

John Lynes was nowhere to be found following the wreck. He had run away minutes after Number 29 disappeared from his gaze, knowing a head-on collision was inevitable. Apprehended later, he was jailed but let go.

VOLTURNO — MARINE DISASTER, October 9, 1913

background: The small 3,600-ton liner *Volturno* of the Royal Line, with 600 immigrant passengers and 57 crew members, en route from Rotterdam to New York, caught fire in the mid-Atlantic. But before she sank, no fewer than eighteen large ships responded to her SOS and took off 521 people; 136 persons perished, these being in three lifeboats the stricken ship had lowered.

Carrying a highly combustible cargo of chemicals, oil, burlap, peat moss, rope and gin, the Royal Line's passenger ship *Volturno,* an immigrant vessel loaded down with 600 people and a crew of 57, left Rotterdam for the United States on October 2, 1913. Seven days later, while the ship was in mid-Atlantic, a blaze broke out in one of the cargo holds. The ship's skipper, a Captain Inch, was faced with double hazard. At that moment a fierce gale was raging, making the successful launching of lifeboats perilous.

Inch lost no time and sent out an SOS signal to all ships at sea. Only one year before, the *Titanic* disaster had shocked the world, and Captain Inch was determined to prevent his vessel from turning into a similar catastrophe. As the fires raged below in sealed holds, Inch, in spite of his great doubts, ordered some of the lifeboats lowered, while expressing great anxiety about the high-swelling waves.

Number 2 lifeboat was swung out on the davits and sent downward with twenty-five people in it. The boat slapped onto the angry surface of the sea and immediately capsized. Three officers managed to turn the boat over and climb inside. They were last seen clawing frantically with oars, trying to rescue those who were barely keeping their heads above water. The boat and the people thrashing and sputtering in the huge waves drifted away and were never seen again. On board the *Volturno* the fires were moving upward to the main deck. Inch still thought his passengers' chances were better in the sea and ordered Number 6 lifeboat over the side. This boat managed to stay afloat, and the immigrants on board waved confidently to the hundreds of grim faces at the liner's rails. Lifeboat Number 6 was never seen again.

Seventy-five miles distant from the sinking *Volturno* was the elegant Cunard steamship, *Carmania.* When Captain Barr of the *Carmania* was handed the *Volturno*'s SOS, he instantly ordered his ship about and steamed at full power to *Volturno*'s position. A host of other ships—American vessels *Kroonland* and *Minneapolis* of the Atlantic Transport Line, the *Rappahannock,* the German ships *Seydlitz* and *Grosser Kurfürst*—turned from their courses without question and made quickly for the *Volturno*'s radioed longitude and latitude.

The Royal Line's immigrant vessel *Volturno* caught fire in mid-Atlantic on October 9, 1913; 136 persons died on board the ill-fated ship. *(UPI)*

This immigrant family was taken on board the *Seydlitz,* one of the flotilla of ships that came to the *Volturno's* aid and rescued 521 passengers. *(UPI)*

Captain Inch was still taking his chances with the ocean, and seeing Number 6 lifeboat successfully lowered, he ordered Number 7 swung out. This boat, jammed with crew members and immigrants, made it to the sea, but a series of waves swept her quickly astern. The churning propellers of the liner sucked the boat under, grinding her to pieces. All in the small boat drowned in full view of Inch and the other officers who had run to the stern to witness the destruction.

More vessels along the Atlantic shipping lines responded to the distress signals from the *Volturno* as her intrepid radio operator incessantly crackled out an SOS. The French liner *La Touraine,* the Russian steamer *Tsar,* the *Asian,* the *Devonian,* even the large oil tanker *Narragansett,* set their courses for the sinking ship. The tanker, though arriving late, was the most important vessel of the international rescue flotilla.

A short time after Inch had ordered Lifeboat Number 7 into the water, he was faced with a new problem. A large group of the black gang burst upon the main deck, shouting that the fires were getting close to the boiler rooms and stokeholds, that the metal walls had become unbearable under the "white heat."

Captain Inch and a few officers backed the grime-smeared stokers toward the ladders leading down to the boiler rooms. A surly giant of a man would not budge. "Captain, we're not going back down there. It's death."

"There are still more than five hundred souls on board this ship," Inch said. Wasting no time, he drew his revolver and pointed it at the black gang. "Go below and do your duty." The stokers stared defiantly. "I'll shoot the first man who breaks for the boats." Grumbling, the stokers went slowly down the ladders to their stations.

When the word spread through the tense immigrant ranks that the captain would lower no more boats, a group of panicky seamen, joined by some of the immigrants, let over a boat without orders. These men came to tragedy in seconds as the boat twisted crazily out from the davits halfway to the water and tossed all the occupants into the sea. They drowned while begging to be saved. Before lines could be thrown to them, they had disappeared beneath the waves.

Just when all on board were preparing to meet the same fate, the Cunard steamer *Carmania* arrived. Those on the *Volturno* cheered, but their joy was premature. The sea was so choppy that boats from the *Carmania* could not reach the stricken ship. Helplessly, Captain Barr of the Cunarder watched as flames began to appear at the stern of the immigrant vessel. The *Grosser Kurfürst,* the *Minneapolis,* the *Tsar,* the *Devonian* and many others steamed over the horizon. But try as they might—they put over lifeboats that had to turn back in the violent sea—the rescue ships could not reach the crowds of praying, screaming people on the *Volturno*'s burning decks.

The decks began to buckle under the intense heat from the flaming cargo holds below. The fire reached the bridge, and flares, Coston lights, rockets and all sorts of explosive devices used to signal distress at sea exploded in a mighty bang. Captain Inch's hair, most of his resplendent uniform and pieces of his shoes were blown away. Badly burned, Inch bravely continued to keep his passengers and remaining crew members from panicking.

As hope diminished, Inch told his crew members that if any one of them wanted to jump overboard before the entire ship blew up, he was free to do so. Many did and were picked up by lifeboats from the international flotilla sailing in great circles about the *Volturno.* Others stayed and displayed enviable courage in calming the passengers.

In a minute-to-midnight drama, the huge oil tanker *Narragansett* arrived. Her captain shrewdly ordered an oil slick created around the *Volturno,* and the released oil caused the seas to remain calm and diminished the waves. All the rescue vessels then put over lifeboats, and sailors rowed like madmen to the immigrant ship, now burning at both bow and stern. It was a race against time.

Inch ordered all the men behind a rope that was stretched across the main deck. It was to be women and children first, as it had been on the *Titanic* and in the great tradition of the sea. Some of the men bolted and tried to join their wives and children, but they were turned back by Inch and some of his officers.

The lifeboats arrived alongside and speedily took off all the women and children. Then the men were allowed to the railing, and one by one, they were saved. Captain Inch was the last man to leave his ship, now entirely engulfed in flames. His clothes in tatters, Inch was the storybook seamaster. Under one arm he carried his ship's log; under the other he held the squirming small dog who served as the ship's mascot. He sat down in a lifeboat, staring wide-eyed at the blazing *Volturno.*

"Don't look at it, Captain," someone advised.

"No matter," Inch replied. "I can't see it. I was blinded in the explosion." He remained blind for several days. Saved were 521 grateful passengers and crew men. Gone down to the sea were 136 persons who had taken their chances in the *Volturno*'s lifeboats.

To the surprise of everyone, the burning ship did not sink. Not until October 17, 1913, did she go under. A Dutch work crew from the tanker *Charlois* boarded the dead ship as she lurched through the seas. They knocked open the sea-cocks, and the liner quickly settled, a burned-out derelict reluctant to quit her dark passage.

W

WACO, TEXAS — **TORNADO**
May 11, 1953

background: A huge tornado struck central Texas on the afternoon of May 11, 1953, first hitting San Angelo, where ten persons were killed and seventy-two were hospitalized; the twister then hit the center of Waco (population 84,000), driving through the city southwest to northeast on a five-block-wide path. Five miles of the city was destroyed, and 114 persons were killed, another 500 injured, and $50 million in damage done. This was the most destructive tornado known in Texas up to that time.

John Anderson, a farmer who lived just outside San Angelo, Texas, heard radio warnings of possible tornadoes in his area and drove home at top speeds to warn his wife. The woman thought him an alarmist and challenged: "How do you know where the tornado might hit?" When the twister gouged its way through San Angelo early on the afternoon of May 11, 1953, she was caught still sitting in her kitchen and became one of the area's seventy-two injured people, fortunate enough not to have been counted with the ten killed by the tornado as it ground its way across the Texas flatlands.

In the city of Waco heavy rains fell from a purple-black sky for several hours that day. There were warnings of a tornado, but many residents scoffed at the idea. Waco had never been struck by a twister, and not a few of the inhabitants placed their solid belief in an old Huaco Indian legend that insisted that the 104-year-old city was immune to twisters.

From 3:00 P.M. to 4:45 P.M., the height of the rush hour in the business district, broadcasters told Waco's 84,000 citizens to take cover. But many were in offices and stores and did not hear the reports; they heard only the angry skies thundering above and the heavy drumming of the rain. Then the howling vortex of the storm set down on the city's southwest side, on the lip of the business district, and began its fearful march northeast, straight through the most congested section of Waco. One business building after another began to topple, to flatten, to explode—eighty-three buildings in all.

Two men driving home suddenly realized that their car was aloft, almost two stories in the air. As they blinked in wonder, they saw a man sail by and shoot above them. He was holding on to his hat. Seconds later their car was set gently down upon the street again without a scratch. "Look," the driver said to his friend and pointed to the front of the car. The badly mangled body of a woman was draped over the hood.

Ira J. Baden was caught as the twister passed directly over him. He dove onto the sidewalk and clung to a steel rail "to avoid being sucked into the vortex." He later told the *Saturday Evening Post:* "I saw the tornado's incredible forty-five second thrust through the business heart of the city. I saw the fronts and the walls of the buildings explode outward and roofs collapse into their own basements. I saw roofs pop up like corks from champagne bottles and burst apart, while their supporting walls remained intact. I saw automobiles—some unoccupied, others bearing passengers—crushed like bugs and buried out of sight under great mounds of brick, timber, steel and glass. I saw one car, an old model, leap upward and disappear into the air as if by magic.

"I saw blocks of stone and timbers blown horizontally through the atmosphere at unbelievable speed, and razor-sharp chunks of steel and glass flew toward me as though shot from rifles—only to change their course at the instant before impact and leave me unharmed. Others may have witnessed what I saw. But, so far as I know, nobody else who saw as much of the storm as I, lived to tell of it."

Baden also witnessed the ruin of the Dennis Department Store, a five-story edifice the twister hit head on, crushing it to a pile of rubble two stories high. Many people, thinking the building was of steel construction and the basement was the safest place to be, took refuge in the basement only moments before the tornado struck. It became a deathtrap as the old building collapsed.

A saleswoman in the store somehow survived. "I just happened to look and I said, 'Oh, look up there at the front! It's as black as ink. What's the matter? There is coming a cyclone!' The wind went ooo-ooo-ooo, and you looked up toward the front, looked like windows coming toward you. And when you looked up you could hear popping and squeaking and all kinds of noises, and those walls seemed to be leaning, coming right toward you.

"The furniture was up in the air, blowing, half of it, seemed to me like, up, the tables and things all scattered, was up where they shouldn't be. . . . Everywhere you looked, you see the building coming toward you, the sides were caving in and the front, the wind just mourning, making the awfullest noise you ever heard." The woman was so mesmerized by the twister that she was unaware she had been severely slashed by flying debris. Then she noticed that she "was lacking . . . I was covered with water, till my arm, I went to, to move myself, and the arm was hanging and then I knew, I put my hand . . . I said 'Oh, Lord, my arm's cut or something, here, lookit, blood's a-pouring out of it."

The Torrance Recreation Hall, which was located directly behind the Dennis Department Store, was also squashed to ruins. Rescuers, scrambling through the debris of this building minutes after the twister roared off toward the northeast, saw a man crawl from beneath a jumble of bricks.

"How many others are trapped in there?" he was asked.

"It's a miracle!" the half-mad survivor yelled.

"How many more in there?"

"A miracle, a miracle," he stammered almost incoherently.

"How many?"

He came to his senses for a second. "Everybody's dead in there but me! A miracle, I tell you, a miracle!" He skipped away as a small child might do, skipped, laughing, through the ugly rubble of the alley.

There would be no miracle for the 114 residents of Waco whose lives had been snuffed out by this bizarre shrug of nature. Another 500 persons were dug out alive from the ruins. All through the night and into the next day, rescue teams, Red Cross units, doctors, nurses, policemen and rangers dug and dug. A loudspeaker system was quickly rigged throughout the business district. Every few minutes a voice would blare: "Silence! Silence!" The cranes, plows, power tools and tractors would promptly grind to a halt. Thousands of diggers would then stand in stony silence, listening, listening. Then would come the thin sound of human voices calling out for help from beneath the rubble. The diggers would locate the sound, and the cacophony of excavation would resume.

(ALSO SEE: Gainesville, Georgia, 1936; Omaha, Nebraska)

A tornado left downtown Waco, Texas, a shambles and 114 persons dead on the afternoon of May 11, 1953. *(Wide World)*

WAIOURI, NEW ZEALAND RAILWAY WRECK
December 24, 1953

New Zealand's worst railway disaster occurred late on Christmas Eve, December 24, 1953, when a nine-car passenger train jammed with hundreds of native passengers en route to welcome Queen Elizabeth II crashed through the Tangiwai Bridge into the River Wangaehu. The bridge had been substantially weakened by a flash flood, which resulted when millions of gallons of water were released in a minor volcanic eruption of the nearby 9,000-foot Mount Ruapehu.

As the train crossed the bridge, situated near the town of Waiouri, the underpinnings, already weakened by the surging river, sagged and buckled. The first six cars and the engine of the Wellington-Auckland Express tumbled off the broken bridge and sank in the river. The occupants desperately and belatedly attempted to climb from the windows. One car went somersaulting down the river for two and a half miles as its passengers screamed and hooted for help. Killed were 155 persons.

WANDA TYPHOON
August 2, 1956

Typhoon Wanda, following a heat wave unprecedented for a century in the Yangtze area from Shanghai to Wuhan, struck the China coast on a wider front than any other typhoon in recent history; she ravaged the provinces of Kiangsu, Chekiang and Anhwei. When widespread warnings of the approaching typhoon went out, peasants around Shanghai hurriedly began to harvest their precious rice crops. But the storm was upon the mainland sooner than expected, and one-third of the rice crops of the three provinces was wiped out, along with 40 percent of the cotton crop.

More than 38,000 homes (most of them river huts) were blown down, and 1,960 persons were killed; another 1,200 people were injured.

WANKIE, RHODESIA MINE DISASTER
June 6, 1972

As if fired from a cannon, a cable car shot out of the mouth of the Wankie Colliery in Rhodesia on June 6, 1972, to testify to the terrific force of the blast that crumbled the walls of Number 2 shaft, in which 464 miners were instantly trapped. Almost every inhabitant of Wankie (population 20,000) came on the run to begin digging for survivors. Lethal methane fumes drove back several rescue parties, and penetration into the coal mine, Rhodesia's largest, was halted for several hours.

Thirty-seven men, most of whom had been in separate rooms and were able to barricade themselves in until rescuers reached them, survived the blast, the cause of which was never determined. The bodies of 427 men were recovered within a week. Sir Keith Acutt, chairman of the Anglo-American Company of South Africa, which owned and operated the mine, told the hundreds of relatives who had kept a constant vigil at the pit: "Indications are that the men died instantly and were not aware of what happened."

WANSTEAD, ONTARIO RAILWAY WRECK
December 6, 1902

In one of the first rail accidents involving a telephone, confusion over a telephone dispatcher's line led the station operator to permit a freight standing by for clearance in Wyoming, Ontario, to proceed down the track on December 6, 1902. The operator thought he had been instructed to let the freight proceed when the dispatcher had merely stated: "I *may* bust that order."

The result was a head-on collision between the freight and a Grand Trunk passenger train, which met at high speeds outside Wanstead, Ontario. Twenty-eight persons, most of them in the forward section, died.

WAPPINGER'S CREEK, NEW YORK RAILWAY WRECK
February 6, 1871

The crew of a New York Central freight, halted on the small, rickety wooden bridge spanning Wappinger's Creek, New York, outside New Hamburg, were attempting to recouple a car in the middle of their train on the snow-swept night of February 6, 1871. The Pacific Express approached from the south and, without proper red warning lights to halt it, smashed into the freight. The collision ignited a flatcar carrying two enormous vats of unrefined petroleum, and the blaze quickly spread to the passenger train. Twenty-one persons were killed; most of them burned to death.

Charles Francis Adams described the remarkable scene in his book, *Notes on Railroad Accidents:* "Dante himself could not have imagined a greater complication of horrors than then ensued: liquid fire and solid frost combined to make the work of destruction perfect. The shock of the collision broke in pieces the oil car, igniting its contents and flinging them about in every direction. In an instant bridge, river, locomotive, cars and the glittering surface of the ice were wrapped in a sheet of flame.

"At the same time the strain proved too severe for the trestle-work, which gave way, precipitating the locomotive, tender, baggage cars and one passenger car onto the ice, through which they instantly crashed and sank deep out of sight beneath the water. Of the remaining seven cars of the passenger train, two, besides several of the freight train, were destroyed by fire, and shortly, as the supports of the remaining portions of the bridge burned away, the superstructure fell on the half-submerged cars in the water and buried them from view."

WARATAH — MARINE DISASTER — July 28, 1909

background: The 9,339-ton *Waratah,* built and launched by Barclay and Curle & Company for the Blue Anchor Line in 1908, was 465 feet long and capable of a speed of thirteen knots. Sailing from Durban to Capetown on July 26, 1909, with 211 passengers and crew members on board, the *Waratah* vanished; the ship was considered sunk in an ocean gale on July 28, 1909, with a loss of all on board.

The Blue Anchor Line's immigrant vessel *Waratah* was a dangerous ship from her inception, a ship that badly frightened William Bragg. This professor of physics at the University of Leeds was on the *Waratah*'s maiden voyage from London to Australia in November 1908, with 154 crew members and 689 immigrants in dormitory accommodations, which were rearranged as cargo holds on the return voyage. Bragg, on that trip, had been one of the 67 cabin passengers, and he remembered being "very alarmed. My impression was that the metacenter was just slightly below the ship's center of gravity when she was upright; then as she heeled over to either side she came to a position of equilibrium."

Bragg was not alone in his fear of the *Waratah*'s instability. Numerous times, Chief Engineer Hodder, who eventually disappeared with the ship, grumbled to his father: "I am not going back in her after this trip. She's top-heavy, father, she's top-heavy."

Before her last voyage from London to Durban and then to Capetown, the ship was examined in dry dock by Lloyd's surveyors, and she was pronounced seaworthy. Yet the trip, beginning in London and pausing in its second leg of the journey at Durban after visiting Australian ports, was one of constant terror for passenger Claude G. Sawyer, who had booked passage from Sydney to Cape Town. He was so frightened of the ship's movements that he got off the vessel at Durban. Sawyer had overheard the third mate tell another seaman that "the ship was top-heavy and that he would leave her if to leave her did not mean that he must also leave the company, and hence his prospects."

For three successive nights, as the *Waratah* pitched and rolled her way toward Durban, Sawyer had the same nightmare as he fitfully tossed in his bunk. He dreamed of seeing a man adorned in blood-smeared armor, an ugly apparition wielding a sword and calling out his name. Along with this premonition of death, Sawyer was driven half crazy by the vessel's "sickening motion, as if the ship were uncertain what her next move might be and was tired of trying to remain upright." Outside Melbourne Sawyer realized that the *Waratah* "had a slow roll and bad. When she rolled she would often remain a long time on her side, and recover all too slowly. Then she would come up again with a jerk. Several passengers had had falls because of this jerk."

A nervous wreck by the time the ship reached Durban, Sawyer quickly packed his bags and forfeited the money for the remainder of his passage by angrily stomping down the gangplank. Some of the ship's officers and passengers laughed loudly at his jittery departure. The ship sailed on to Cape Town and oblivion.

Early in the morning of July 27, a crew member of the tramp *Harlow* saw the *Waratah* as she sailed her coastwise passage. The last human to see the liner while at sea later that day was the captain of the steamer *Clan Macintyre.* He later described the ship's motion as "neither to have a list nor to be rolling excessively, but to be proceeding in an exceedingly steady manner."

This same skipper was appalled at the roaring seas that engulfed his own ship the next day, July 28. "We experienced a great storm," he later narrated. "I never met with anything as bad on this coast during my thirteen years in the trade. The wind seemed to tear the water up and was of quite exceptional fierceness and power, rising at times to hurricane force. There was a tremendous sea." It was inside this storm, a fatal ocean hurricane for all of her 211 passengers, most authorities conclude, that the *Waratah* spent her last moments.

Author Alan Villiers imagined the vessel's end with: "Perhaps in the awful tumult of the dreadful storm, she was flung violently about and then suddenly she lurched and rolled far over, and did not come back. She hung there for a frightful second, swung helpless into the trough of the sea, was struck by a great sea, and, as if she were sick of it all, rolled right on over. With a crashing of the five steel boilers breaking from their beds and a roar of steam stifled upon the instant by the inrush of the cold sea, quickly she went on down before her startled passengers had time to scream. Then the sea boiled over the place where she had been."

W. A. SCHOLTEN — MARINE DISASTER — November 19, 1887

background: The 3,300-ton *W. A. Scholten,* owned and operated by the Netherlands-American Steam Navigation Company of Rotterdam, collided with the steam collier *Rosa Mary* at 10:30 P.M. on November 19, 1887, while both ships were attempting to navigate the English Channel near Dover. Drowned were 134 people, mostly Dutch, German and British immigrants en route to New York; 87 were saved. No one on board the *Rosa Mary* was killed.

The immigrant vessel *W. A. Scholten,* while sailing for New York with 221 passengers and crew members on the night of November 19, 1887, suddenly found herself surrounded by thick fog, a strung-out necklace of fog that choked the English Channel and caused dozens of ships that night to slice haphazardly through waters while their captains blindly groped for ports. One of these was the *Rosa Mary,* a large steam collier that had ridden at anchor for twenty-four hours while her captain, T. Webster, impatiently waited for the fog to lift. Webster got his ship under way and headed in the direction he thought would bring him to the harbor at Dover.

A lookout in the forecastle head saw a dim light through the mist in front of the bow. It became bright a point and a half off the starboard bow. He then saw a green light from the same vessel, the standard signal from a passing ship. The *Rosa Mary*'s chief mate joined the lookout, and the two of them went to the upper bridge. Again they spotted the white and green lights. Suddenly the green light disappeared, and a red one took its place. A moment after the red light glared through the fog, there was a terrific crash of bows. The *Rosa Mary* had collided almost bow-to-bow with the *W. A. Scholten.*

As the *Rosa Mary* backed off, a gaping eight-foot hole in the *W. A. Scholten's* port bow could be clearly seen. Through this metal wound poured tons of seawater.

On board the immigrant ship, Captain J. H. Taat sent up rockets and blue lights as signals of distress. It was instantly apparent to Taat that his ship was going to sink—fast. The fog, almost as if realizing it had completed its diabolical work, then lifted completely, and the *Scholten* could be seen to list severely to port. The *Rosa Mary* was badly holed also and did not put over a lifeboat to aid those then jumping into the sea from the *Scholten,* but sluggishly made her way to Dover.

In response to the rockets, the steamer *Ebro* and several smaller boats arrived, and lines were thrown aboard the sinking *Scholten.* Eighty-seven sailors and passengers swarmed across these lifelines to safety, but the ship abruptly went down headforemost and took with her 134 people, including Captain Taat and most of his officers.

For several days bodies floated with flotsam into Dover from the *Scholten.* To commemorate the tragedy, a poet created the following lament:

> And the sea yawned around her like a hell;
> And down she sucked with her the whirling wave,
> Like one who grapples with his enemy,
> And strives to strangle him before he die.
> And first, one universal shriek there rushed,
> Louder than the wild ocean, like a crash
> Of echoing thunder; and then, all was hushed
> Save the wild wind and the remorseless dash
> Of billows; but at intervals there gushed,
> Accompanied with a convulsive splash,
> A solitary shriek, the bubbling cry
> Of some strong swimmer in his agony.

WASHINGTON — MARINE DISASTER
September 17, 1821

The schooner *Washington,* attempting to ride out a hurricane on September 17, 1821, sought safety in the Bay St. Louis on the Mississippi coast. Fierce winds buffeted the ship about during the night, and she was eventually driven close to shore. At dawn searchers discovered the ship "bottom upwards, with her bows open from her deck to her keel, lying about 50 or 60 yards from the water." All on board the *Washington,* an estimated twenty persons, were killed.

WASHINGTON, D.C. — RAILWAY WRECK
December 30, 1906

A three-car excursion train and an empty passenger train, both belonging to the Baltimore & Ohio Line, crashed outside of Washington, D.C., on the fog-bound night of December 30, 1906. The excursion train, stopped momentarily outside Washington, was hit from behind by the passenger train, then being used to carry railway equipment. The second train's engineer, Harry Hildebrand, insisted to one and all that he had been given a double green light (caution light) to proceed down the track by several operators at different stations.

Hildebrand barreled his train along at 60 m.p.h., knowing that the excursion train was somewhere up front. This speed hardly permitted him to come to a safe stop when he spotted the stationary excursion train directly ahead. The resulting crash killed forty-three people. Authorities, no doubt because the accident occurred outside the nation's capital, held full-scale inquiries. Hildebrand and others were charged with manslaughter, but were acquitted a year later because of conflicting testimony.

The wreck did serve, however, to increase the Interstate Commerce Commission's authority over railroad safety standards.

WASHOE, MONTANA — MINE DISASTER
February 27, 1943

More than 3,700 feet down in the Smith Mine in Washoe, Montana, seventy-seven men were entombed when an explosion went off at 9:30 A.M. on February 27, 1943. Thirty men were killed instantly, and the other miners moved off into separate shafts as they looked for an escape route. Three miners were quickly removed from the entrance of the mine, but the remainder, seventy-four in all, died of asphyxiation within two hours. This time was fixed by the notes they left to their loved ones just before dying. One read: "It's almost 11 A.M.—time to go."

The mine was operated on a slipshod basis. Although firebosses found large quantities of gas and afterdamp each day, little or nothing was done about it. And though electric lights were available, many of the miners still employed the open lamps that had created so many mine explosions in the past. Also, according to a mine inspector's report, "smoking was practiced," which is to say, suicide was rehearsed.

WELLINGTON, WASHINGTON — AVALANCHE, March 1, 1910

Heavy snows had trapped a packed passenger train, a mail train and several locomotives in the mountain way station of Wellington, Washington, for nine days in February, 1910. As anxious travelers peered from their compartment windows, they agonized over the massive buildup of snow, the blizzard that was producing an incredible foot of snow per hour. In one day eleven feet of snow fell.

Try as they might, Great Northern railroaders in Wellington found it impossible to clear away the tracks with their plows. Above Wellington loomed the huge and menacing peaks of the towering Cascade mountain range. Those permanent residents of Wellington knew how perilous conditions were. The sides of the cliffs above them had been swept bare of thousands of trees by a hungry fire the previous fall. Those trees had been the only natural barriers against an inevitable avalanche.

Late on February 28 the snow stopped, and rain accompanied by warm winds ran over the mountains shrouding Wellington. At 1:20 A.M. on March 1, 1910, a great slab of snow more than twenty feet deep, a half-mile long and a quarter-mile wide suddenly broke free and raced down the mountainside, heading directly for the small town.

Crashing at a terrific speed into the passenger train, still loaded with more than 100 people, several locomotives, a snow plow, an engine house, a water tower and several boxcars, the rush of snow swept everything into a 150-foot gorge. The hotel, where several trainmen lived, was narrowly missed, and the residents ran outside with shovels and immediately began digging for survivors.

People were located by muffled shouts from beneath the snow. In other instances a lone hand or leg, weakly waving or kicking, brought rescuers. Twenty-two persons were dug out, but ninety-six people, almost all those who had been traveling and living in the passenger train, perished. Many of the bodies and cars were not discovered until late spring brought thaws that melted the icy snow and revealed its grisly contents. The Wellington disaster was the worst single avalanche in United States history.

More than ninety persons were crushed to death near Wellington, Washington, March 1, 1910, when a train was almost completely buried by an avalanche. *(Wide World)*

WENELA AIRLINES

AIR CRASH
April 4, 1974

Eighty black goldminers and a white flight crew of two crashed in a propeller-driven DC-4 Skymaster just after takeoff from the remote airstrip at Francistown, Botswana. Six miners and the flight engineer were thrown clear of the wreckage immediately upon impact. The plane then went up in flames. Dr. J. S. Moeti from the Francistown Hospital was among the fifty rescuers who rushed to the burning craft. "It was like a real inferno," Moeti stated to the press. "It was really blazing away."

Officials of Wenela Airlines (an acronym of the Witwatersrand Native Labor Association), who operated the plane that shuttled miners to gold mines and then back to distant homes, could offer no explanation for the crash. Seventy-seven passengers were killed in the wreck.

WEST FRANKFORT, ILLINOIS

MINE DISASTER
December 21, 1951

The 119 miners who were killed in the blast that tore apart the New Orient Mine Number 2 outside West Frankfort, Illinois, on December 21, 1951, need not have died, according to most experts. The mine, owned by the Chicago firm Wilmington & Franklin Coal Company, was thoroughly checked by two federal mine inspectors in July, 1951. They strongly urged that abandoned workings in the New Orient Mine Number 2 be either sealed off or ventilated separately from those areas of the mine still being worked.

Mine Superintendent John R. Foster declared the federal recommendations "controversial," adding that he was under no legal obligation to follow such advice. The Illinois Mining Code did not ban the reuse of air, fouled or not by methane gas. It was this very gas that exploded on December 21, 1951, at 8:30 P.M., while 281 miners were at work in the shaft.

One survivor inside the mine described the explosion as "so terrific that it knocked cars weighing several tons off the tracks and brought down overhead timbers."

That night a basketball game in West Frankfort's gym was interrupted, and the gym was quickly converted to a temporary morgue, where the bodies of 119 miners were placed in sad rows. Many of these men were the fathers of boys who, minutes before, had been playing ball on the court.

Angrily Governor Adlai Stevenson told reporters that he had pushed to no avail to have a modern mine-safety code adopted in Illinois. "I presented such a code, the

Rescue squads remove some of the 119 bodies of miners killed in an explosion in the New Orient Mine, West Frankfort, on December 21, 1951. *(Wide World)*

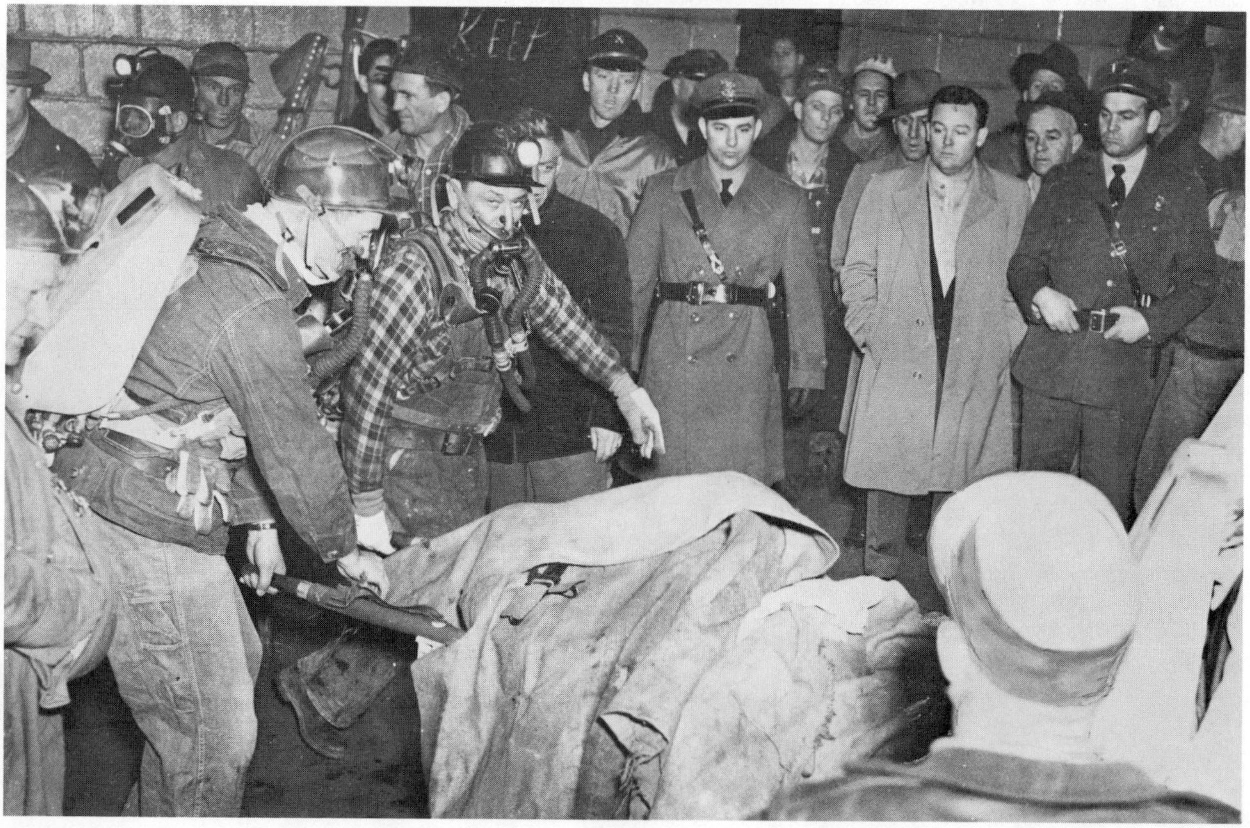

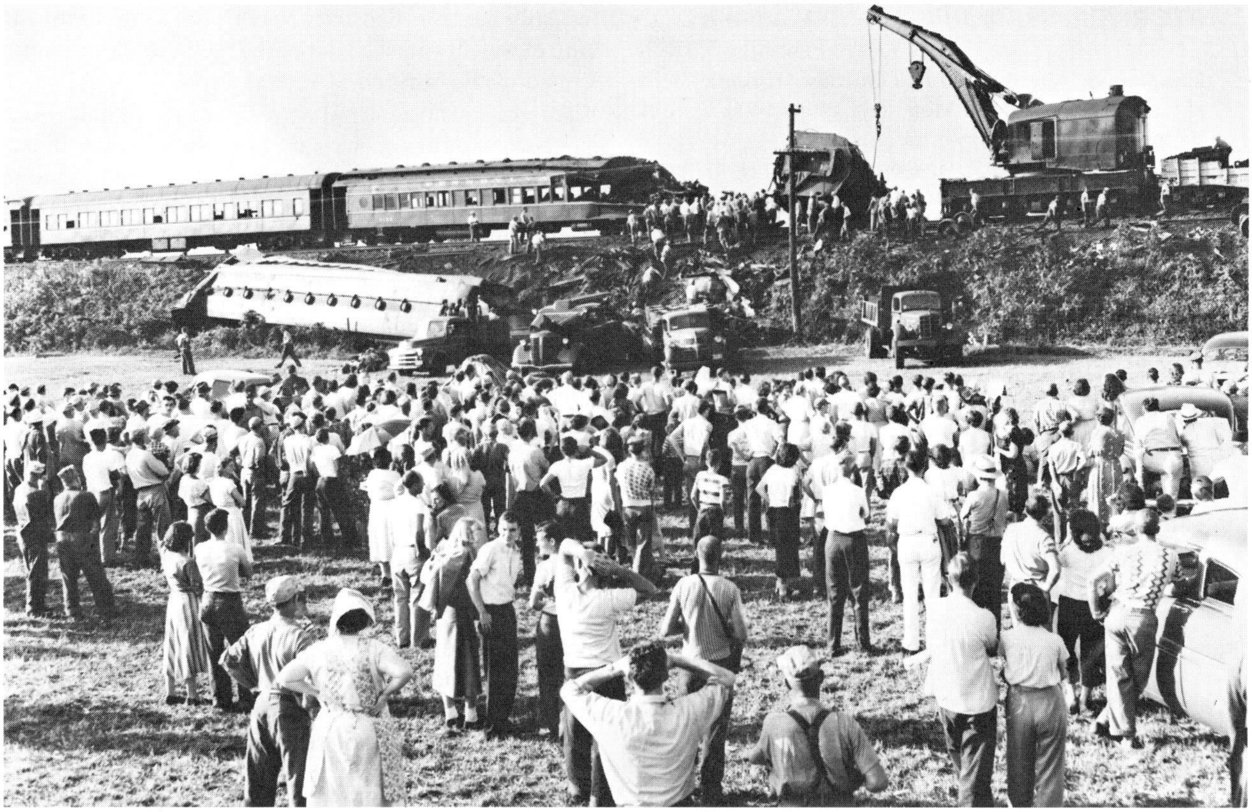

A railroad crane lifts a car of a troop train back onto the track. This train was hit by the crack Spirit of St. Louis near West Lafayette, Ohio, and forty-two persons were killed. *(Wide World)*

work of many months, at the last session of the legislature, but neither the union, the operators, nor the senators from Southern Illinois would support it."

The West Frankfort explosion was the worst mine disaster since 1928. The staggering loss of life prompted the *Nation* to thunder: "Once again tragedy has struck at a mining community because profits were placed above safety. . . . We hope that the West Frankfort tragedy will move Congress to action before more blood is smeared on our coal."

WEST LAFAYETTE, OHIO — RAILWAY WRECK
September 11, 1950

A westbound twenty-car troop train packed with soldiers of the twenty-eighth National Guard Division, en route to Camp Atterbury as part of the Korean War mobilization, came to an emergency stop at West Lafayette, Ohio, on the morning of September 11, 1950. The air-and-steam connections in the last two cars were malfunctioning. As they were being checked, the flagman walked back down the line to set flares.

Following the troop train, Pennsylvania's Spirit of St. Louis, Number 31, had halted when the military train broke down a half-hour before. The sixty-eight-year-old engineer of Number 31, William Eller, was thus informed of the troop train's presence on the tracks in front of his own train and aware of its trouble. Yet after the first stop, Eller came on again throttling the Spirit of St. Louis at 70 m.p.h. (He later testified that he did not heed any of the warning signals along the track, including those flares placed by the troop train's flagman.)

As Number 31 roared down the tracks, the flagman protecting the troop train frantically waved his flares. When the speeding passenger train failed to slow down, he hurled his flares in frustration at the approaching train. These bounced off the windshield of Eller's cab. But the express did not halt; it smashed into the rear of the troop train.

In the rear car Captain F. R. Brannan looked up and saw the other train approaching. "The red flares were out on the track at the time, and we couldn't figure what was happening," he reported after the accident, in which thirty-three of his soldiers died. "I dashed through the train yelling to the men to fall on the floor. I pulled a lot of them down with me. But it happened so fast we couldn't prevent casualties from happening. Lots of men were pinned inside. It was amazing how orderly the boys behaved."

WHITE RIVER, VERMONT RAILWAY WRECK

February 5, 1887

background: A broken 200-foot rail caused the derailment of the six-car Boston and Montreal Express of the Central Vermont Railroad just as it was crossing the bridge spanning White River at 2:20 A.M. on February 5, 1887. Four cars of the express fell into the fifty-foot opening, and fires resulting from exploding stoves and lamps caused most of the thirty-two deaths.

The railroad shops in St. Albans, Vermont, were beehives of activity in 1881 as more and more rail track was demanded by roads spreading weblike through the country. In that year one of the shops accepted a shipment of unfinished steel from Scotland; this was rolled into the track. One 200-foot rail found its way to the tracks just before the White River Bridge outside White River Junction, Vermont. For more than six years, this flawed piece of steel somehow supported regular heavy freight and passenger trains. It survived six bitter winters, but in the early hours of February 5, 1887, its tolerance for any kind of weight vanished under the pressure of the Central Vermont's Boston and Montreal Express.

The Montreal Express crashed through the White River Bridge on February 5, 1887, and burned on the ice while scores crawled from the splintered coaches. *(Leslie's)*

An ice carnival at Montreal attracted ninety-one passengers onto the six-car train. Many were taking advantage of the reduced fares the railroad offered in conjunction with the event. Two of these were Dartmouth students Albin Veazey and Edward Dillon, who got on the train at White River Junction after attending a dance. They took bunks in the sleeper, the second to the last car, and were deep in slumber some minutes later.

It was a few seconds before 2:20 A.M.—a passenger remembered looking at his watch—when people in the six cars "felt sudden jolts and knew the cars were off the track. Each individual tie was felt as the wheels rolled over it, indicating a speed of about ten miles an hour." This was a *Harper's Weekly* estimate based upon first-hand interviews with survivors. To brakeman George Parker, it seemed as if the train was going much slower.

Upon hearing the commotion, Parker grabbed a lantern and stepped out onto the platform of the first car, leaning out and looking back down the line. Sparks flew outward from the tracks into the clear, freezing night air. He looked to the front of the train and, to his horror, saw that the express was just about to cross the wooden 650-foot-long White River Bridge. Fifty feet beneath this span the White River lay frozen solid and crusted with snow.

Parker jumped from the first car, thinking to signal engineer Charles E. Pierce in the 45-ton locomotive, Baker, to bring the train to a halt. "We were going about seven miles an hour," Parker told reporters, "and I thought that I should land all right on my feet." He fell, however, into a snow bank on the lip of the gentle slope leading to the river and, shouting vainly for Pierce to halt, slid all the way down to the river bank. He glanced up to see the last car of the train, the sleeper Pilgrim, screech halfway off the tracks while the train was fully on the bridge.

By this time engineer Pierce was alerted to the derailment as conductor Smith Sturtevant, a Civil War veteran, furiously rang the alarm bell. Pierce jumped for the air brakes. After applying them, he stuck his head out of the cab window to gape in terror as he "saw the hind end of the Boston sleeper swinging off the bridge to the right. As that went off, it pulled the Springfield sleeper, then the Springfield Coach, then the Boston Coach."

The locomotive and part of the mail car directly behind it remained on the bridge. The other cars, having fallen fifty feet onto the unbroken ice of the White River, were in splinters. The stoves and lamps in all the cars instantly ignited the broken wood of the wreck. Dozens of people, shrieking out for help, were trapped.

Only the wheels and steel couplings of the wooden coaches remained after the fires at White River were out. *(Harper's Weekly)*

Albin Veazey remembered "being thrown from side to side" as the car in which he and his friend Dillon were riding hurtled downward onto the river. "Then the car, bottom up, struck the ice with a tremendous crash."

Veazey looked about in the dim light and realized that he was lying on the ceiling of the lower berth. His friend Dillon, who had taken the upper, was now pinned below him. Veazey could not move and called out to Dillon, "Ed, are you hurt?"

"Yes," Dillon responded in a weak voice, "badly." Fires were now beginning to break out in the cars because of exploding stoves. Fire ironically aided Veazey in freeing his legs from some timbers as it ate the wooden beams in half. Leaping out of a hole, Veazey grabbed a nearby axe and began to chop away at the spot where he thought his friend Dillon was trapped.

Only moments earlier, brakeman Parker had scrambled up the snowy embankment, run to a farm house and convinced a sleepy farmer to hitch up his team of horses. Whipping the team, Parker and the farmer rode madly through the snowy road to White River Junction to spread the word of the disaster and bring a relief train back to the bridge.

Inside the first coach a lecturer named Henry Tewksbury found himself trapped, unable to move an inch. He screamed for help, but no one seemed to hear him. Craning his neck, Tewksbury watched bug-eyed and helpless as a fire from the stove at the other end of the car broke out and began working its way toward him.

"It was a time of mental torture," he later recalled, "but I still could not help noticing an old couple who had sat a few seats behind me. They were hopelessly tied down by heavy seats, and the flames were approaching them with frightful rapidity. I could do nothing for them. Before the smoke shut them from sight, I saw them locked in each other's arms."

Similar scenes occurred throughout the burning wrecks of the four shattered cars. A French Canadian traveling on the express with his young son was pinned in the wreck of the last car. His boy had managed to crawl out of the debris, but realized that his father, whose head and arms jutted from the wreck, was trapped. The boy began to tug wildly at his father, trying to free him before the flames closed in.

"Pull, boy, pull," the father said. "Pull me out if you have to break my legs."

The youngster, weeping and shouting for help, put all his strength against the pinned-down body of his father, but it was useless. Seeing the flames only a few feet away, the father reached up, embraced his son, kissed him and said: "God love you, boy. Now go!" He threw the youth backward on the ice only a moment before the flames surrounded him.

Tewksbury was prepared to die in the same way. He pulled his cap low over his eyes so he would not have to look at the flames about to roast his flesh. Just then he heard voices beyond the debris and tore his cap off to see engineer Pierce, his fireman, the baggagemaster, two mail agents and an expressman trying to chop passengers free. All of these men had grabbed shovels and axes just after the four cars hurled onto the ice and had run down the embankment to save as many as possible.

"Here! Here!" Tewksbury shouted to them from a small opening in the wreck.

Pierce turned and motioned his fireman over. "Take

This editorial cartoon in *Harper's Weekly* indicted all railroads that used stoves, the very kind that led to the killing fires of the White River disaster.

hold," the engineer told the fireman. "Perhaps we can save him."

Their feet braced against the timbers, both men, each powerfully built, yanked away, pulling on Tewksbury's arms. His feet were permanently stuck, it seemed.

"We'll have to leave you," Pierce sighed, "there's others to get out."

"No, don't, don't!" cried the lecturer. "Try, for God's sake, to save me. Try again!"

Again the two men pulled with all their strength. Tewksbury's body remained fixed in the flaming debris.

"It's no use," Pierce grunted.

"Once more, please, once more," begged the lecturer. "Pull my leg off if you have to, but for God's sake, don't let me burn!"

The two men tried once more. This time Tewksbury felt a slight loosening of the timbers pinning him down. "Pull! Pull! Pull!" he yelled. They were inching him from beneath the pile of splintered timbers. "Oh, with what a joyous feeling did I feel my feet gradually slipping from my shoes. I cried out that I was moving . . . I felt one of my legs break, but I was released. To do it, they had to haul me over the debris by the collar."

The two men were about to go to another trapped passenger when Tewksbury called after them: "Draw me back farther! I shall burn here!" Pierce and the fireman pulled the lecturer back another twenty-five feet and returned to the wreck, hacking like crazy men at the debris. Tewksbury was looking heavenward to thank God for his deliverance when he noticed that the bridge directly above him had caught fire from the blazing wreckage and that it would only be a matter of minutes before it would collapse.

Albin Veazey, unable to save his friend Dillon, who burned to death before his eyes, smashed a small hole into one of the cars and dragged out Mrs. W. S. Bryden, who had been returning to her home in Montreal. Veazey wrapped her badly burned body in a blanket. He then raced off to help Pierce and the others.

Mrs. Bryden realized that she was still too close to the fire, which was then shooting out tongues of flame as gas lamps exploded inside the wrecked coaches. A man came staggering out of the wreck with his clothes smoking. Mrs. Bryden held up a feeble hand and begged him to move her away from the fire. He looked about vacantly for a moment. Then he noticed that the ice was strewn with bananas, apples and oranges, the contents of a buffet that had spilled out when the train crashed. He picked up an apple and handed it to the near-hysterical woman.

"Here," the dazed man said in a monotone. "Eat this. It's supposed to be good for you." He staggered away and collapsed in the snow.

Mrs. Bryden was later picked up by men riding to the rescue in the relief train from White River Junction, but she would always remember the shrieks of the dying. "From the car, I could hear the most terrible cries, piercing my soul. One voice still rings in my ears. It was that of another woman, who kept crying, 'Won't someone let me out?' "

Pierce returned to Tewksbury and noticed the bridge above about to collapse. He pulled the lecturer to a safe spot and then ran up the embankment and drove his engine across to safety just moments before the flaming wooden span tumbled down onto the ice.

Rescuers began pouring from the relief train as it pulled up to the place where the White River Bridge had once been; they scurried down the snowy embankments to help fifteen more people from the flaming wreckage. One of the last persons saved was the conductor Sturtevant, who could be seen staggering through one of the wrecked cars, his clothing on fire. As he lurched toward a window, several men grabbed him and rolled him into the snow to put out the flames crackling along his back. Sturtevant was taken to a farm house, where he died of his burns some hours later.

Dead in this soon-to-become-notorious railway wreck were thirty-two persons, with almost twice that number seriously injured. *Harper's Weekly* unleashed its editorial bombast against the use of stoves in rail cars (which, in fact, had caused at least half of the deaths in railway accidents to that date): "It is not the number of people who happen to be burned in any one case that makes up the case against the deadly lamp and stove. It is the monotonous regularity with which the event recurs that impresses travelers with the belief that when *their* accident comes, torture to death may be their fate, if perchance they escape crushing."

Five years later, the White River horror having been a large contributing factor, the Railway Appliances Act came into being, the first national legislation to establish strict safety codes, regulations that cut railway fatalities by more than 50 percent.

(ALSO SEE: Angola, New York; Ashtabula, Ohio; Hamilton, Ontario)

WIDECOMBE-IN-THE-MOOR, ENGLAND — TORNADO — October 21, 1638

The little English hamlet of Widecombe-in-the-Moor, at the southern part of Dartmoor, was hit broadside by a violent tornado on Sunday morning, October 21, 1638, while its entire population was in church. A violent wind smashed the church's windows just as the vicar was about to begin services, and everything went black.

Stone and masonry showered down on the hundreds gathered inside as the roof and tower began to collapse. A fireball, or so it was described, shot through the church and out a window. According to an old tract, the fireball "so much affrightened the whole congregation that the most part of them fell downe into their seates, and some upon their knees, some on their faces, and some one upon another, with a great cry of burning and scalding, they all giving up themselves for dead."

Dozens of men and women were bowled over by the storm and the lightning ball of fire, which sometimes accompanies severe tornadoes. Yanked screaming from their pews, parishioners were swirled about in the church; a yelping dog was thrown to the rafters above. One man's head was "cloven, his skull rent into three pieces, and his brans throwne upon the ground whole, and the haire of his head through the violence of the blow at first given him, did sticke fast unto the pillar or wall of the church; so that he perished there most lamentably.

About fifty persons were killed in the church when the storm struck and another dozen were injured, including the Mistress Ditford who had "her gowne, two wast-coates, and linnen next to her body burned cleane off." The pious ascribed the tornado to the work of the devil, and for centuries the twister's legend was to taint Widecombe as "the Evil One's residency."

WILBURTON, OKLAHOMA — MINE DISASTER

January 13, 1926

Two firebosses had pronounced Number 21 Mine in Wilburton, Oklahoma, free of gas on the morning of January 13, 1926. An hour later at 8:15 A.M., a violent explosion caused "the timbers in the hoisting shaft to be blown out." Trapped were 101 miners. Ten men were quickly brought out through the air shaft by rescue teams, but 92 others, many of them young boys (state laws permitted them to work), were killed by the after-damp as they stumbled over fallen beams and pushed through caved-in walls in attempts to work their way toward the air shaft.

Mine inspector W. W. Fleming reported laconically: "Had the men stayed in their places, many would have been saved."

WINDSOR HOTEL — FIRE

March 17, 1899

The devastating fire that took the lives of ninety-two persons in New York's Windsor Hotel on March 17, 1899, could probably have been brought under control within minutes and countless lives saved had it not been for a stubborn cop. The disaster occurred during a fes-

Firemen battled the Windsor Hotel fire on March 17, 1899, but, as the second photo shows, were unsuccessful. The front wall collapsed. Ninety-two people died in the holocaust. *(Harper's Weekly)*

tive St. Patrick's Day parade, when marchers bedecked in green were passing the hotel on Fifth Avenue.

More than 300 persons swelled the crowd of 250 guests already in the hotel. The visiting people wanted only to get a better view of the parade than that of those thousands lining the curbs outside. One of the spectators in the hotel lit a cigar while watching the marchers beneath and absent-mindedly threw the still-burning match out a window facing Forty-Sixth Street.

A startled headwaiter saw the match ignite a delicate curtain, and he quickly attempted to put out the blaze. He could not. The waiter told a porter to inform the manager that the flames were out of control. He then dashed down the stairs to turn in the alarm. The alarm box was across the street. The waiter fought his way through the dense crowd watching the parade, seven ranks deep. A policeman saw him and grabbed his arm. "No jostling now, or I'll run ya in!"

Frantically the headwaiter tried to explain that the Windsor Hotel was on fire and that he must cross in front of the marchers to get to the fire alarm box. Ignoring his pleas, the policeman shoved him back into the crowd. Again the waiter tried to cross the street, and again the cop refused to let him pass. Minutes later the crowds on the street turned in horror and shouted, "The Windsor's on fire!" The obstinate cop ran across the street and broke the window on the fire alarm box, but the delay was a costly one. By the time police could move the crowds out of the way in an orderly manner for the many fire units that arrived, fourteen guests had jumped from flaming rooms to their deaths and another seventy-eight persons had either burned to death or had been asphyxiated in the seven-story hotel, which was reduced to its chimneys and part of an outer wall. More than $1 million in damage was suffered by the hotel, and an additional $750,000 was lost in personal effects owned by the guests.

(ALSO SEE: Gulf Hotel, LaSalle Hotel, Newhall House, Winecoff Hotel)

WINECOFF HOTEL — FIRE

December 7, 1946

background: The fifteen-story Winecoff Hotel in Atlanta, Georgia, with 285 guests crowding its 194 rooms, caught fire at 3:15 A.M. on December 7, 1946. The thirty-three-year-old brick-and-cement hotel was gutted after a roaring six-hour inferno that took the lives of 119 guests and injured another 90, making it the worst hotel fire in United States history.

"Her nightgown shone white against the flames behind her as she stood on the window ledge, high above the street. Then it, too, caught fire. She jumped. But she missed the net stretched by firemen. She landed astride overhead wires. There she hung in flames. Finally, her body broke loose and toppled to the ground."

This is how a reporter described one of the victims of the worst hotel fire in American history, the burning of the Winecoff Hotel in Atlanta, Georgia, on December 7, 1946. Located at Peachtree and Ellis streets, the Winecoff Hotel was built by W. Frank Winecoff in 1913. Like most hotels in Atlanta it had no outside fire escapes or sprinkler systems and had a central staircase winding around an enclosed bank of elevators. This staircase was the only exit other than the elevators. Yet this building had been classified as "fireproof," and only a short time before the fire, the hotel had been inspected by the city's fire marshal, who had pronounced it safe. (Oddly enough, Atlanta's Terminal Hotel had burned almost to the ground eight years before, on May 16, 1938, a blaze in which thirty-eight trapped guests were incinerated. The Terminal, like the Winecoff, had neither outside fire escapes nor a sprinkler system.)

It was 3:30 A.M. when the Winecoff's night clerk, Comer Rowan, who was sitting in for his wife, noticed the switchboard light of Room 510 begin to blink. The gentleman wanted some ice and ginger ale. Rowan rang for Bill Mobley, the only night bellhop on duty. Mobley, juggling the ice and ginger ale in the elevator, was joined by the night engineer, who was making his routine nightly check. They had to wait for three minutes outside Room 510 while the guest finished taking his bath. The elevator girl started down slowly. By the time she reached the third floor, she smelled smoke and took her elevator to the basement. From there she ran up to the main floor and warned Rowan. He told her to go to the fifth floor and get the bellhop and the engineer. Leaping over his desk, Rowan raced up the stairs to the mezzanine and saw flames reflected there in a mirror. In a shot he was at his switchboard calling the fire department. It was 3:42 A.M., and within a few seconds three ladder and four pumper companies swung out from their station only two blocks away.

On the fifth floor Mobley and the engineer emerged from Room 510, where they had spent a few minutes talking to the night-owl guest. As they opened the door, flames and dense clouds of black smoke met them. They slammed the door.

Rowan plugged in every guest phone as fast as his hands could move, shouting "Fire! Fire! Fire!" Then the switchboard went dead. The 285 guests within the 194 rooms of the fifteen-story hotel were then on their own. By the time the rushing companies of firemen arrived at the hotel, the facade of the building was crawling with frenzied people. Some had already begun to jump.

"Don't jump! Don't jump!" the firemen yelled out, but the hotel from the third to the fifteenth floor was a blistering inferno. The firemen were faced with the dilemma of either fighting the blaze or saving those frantic persons shrieking from window ledges above them. They chose their ladders and sent them up. More fire brigades began to arrive, until the city's complete sixty-piece fire department was arrayed before the flame-encased hotel. Their ladders, though they reached to the tenth floor, could not be elevated fast enough.

Everything had burned in the hotel—drapes, wooden trim on the windows, bedding. With no sprinkler system to douse the blaze, scavenger flames united in hallways and blasted like flamethrowers up the main staircase and elevator shafts, where tremendous drafts were created. Most of the rooms had transoms, which were open, as were room windows—more drafts to feed the flames.

The intensity of the fire—the heat was estimated to be in excess of 1,500 degrees Fahrenheit—drove guests to the windows in frantic clusters. One woman appeared on a seventh-story ledge holding her two children. A ladder shot up to meet her, but before it came within reach, she threw her small son into space and then her smaller daughter. A moment later, her nightgown on fire, she leaped to join her dead children.

A fireman reached one woman on the fifth floor just as her grasp on the window ledge failed. He swung her around on the ladder and onto his back. As he backed downward with the unconscious woman, another woman jumped from some floors above. She struck the fireman and his burden, and all three were sent plunging to death.

Though firemen and spectators cried out to those on the ledges not to move, scores of bedsheets tied together suddenly wiggled at the windows, and half-crazed guests began to lower themselves. One girl crawled two floors downward on just such a makeshift rope. A fire ladder swung over to get her. Holding on to the sheets with one hand, she lunged for the ladder, but a split second before, one of the knotted sheets gave way and she crashed to the pavement.

Firemen and spectators held nets out and tried to catch the falling bodies. One man missed a net by inches after jumping 200 feet.

On the eighth floor a woman stood on a window ledge and called out for someone, anyone, to save her four-year-old son. As a great tongue of flame shot up her back, she hurled the boy outward into space. "My God," said a spectator, who noticed no firemen beneath the child's line of fall and raced to the spot. Miraculously he caught the boy in midair; the child was saved without injury. The mother came down seconds later, killing herself in the fall.

Seeing others jump to their deaths, the fatalistic action spread as would a mania. Others began to leap toward the cement and certain death, preferring that end to being immolated by the raging fires scouring their rooms. A girl dove for a ladder two floors below as searchlights flooded her face, a face distorted by terror. She groped in the lurid light for the ladder, blinded, it seemed, by the light, and missed. Her body fell crazily and smashed through the hotel's marquee. A cold-hearted type among the watching crowd said in a detached tone: "I knew she'd hit that marquee."

Another woman climbed out onto one of the make-shift ropes of knotted bedding and began to let herself downward. She appeared as if she would reach a nearby ladder. Suddenly another woman crawled onto the dangling sheets from the thirteenth floor. The combined weight of both women broke the rope, and they were sent hurtling downward.

Many, however, were saved by the nets spread out below, yet others died when their bodies hit the nets with such force that the nets were ripped from the firemen's hands.

A girl on the seventh floor had been patiently standing on a ledge as the flames crept up behind her. A net was finally arranged beneath her. Observers heard her shout: "I hope I live! I hope I live!" Then she jumped, feet first (as did everyone else). She did live, suffering a broken hip, arm and leg.

One man was burned alive on the ledge of his hotel room window, but even in death his grip held his charred body to the face of the building. He had to be pried off the wall hours later. Firemen saw a man on the fifth floor throw out a sheet rope and then go back into his room. He never appeared again. Another man above this sheet was caught in a panel of flame, and he died inside the blaze while his head rolled from side to side. Deadly gas, smoke and flames urged scores of guests onto the window ledges. After the first twenty had either fallen or leaped to their deaths, those still on the ledges waited. They were saved by the swiftly moving firemen (twenty-five of whom were overcome by smoke).

Inside the lobby a section of firemen began battling their ways up the burning main staircase from the second floor, their hoses blasting the flames into hissing steam. They could hear the wails and screams of trapped guests burning to death in the rooms above. One man tried to seal off his room, taking his family into the bathroom. He turned on all the taps but the flames converted the water into steam. The toilet exploded (as did many others). He was found later asphyxiated with his head in the shower; his wife, holding on to their children, lay next to him. All were dead.

One couple on the fourteenth floor were determined to live. As flames shot over the transom of their door and ignited their room, they crawled along the window ledge to the next room and saw that its transom was closed. The couple there were trying to barricade the door. The man and woman on the ledge crawled into this room, and the two couples jammed a mattress against the door, soaking it constantly with water from the bathroom. For two hours they soaked the mattress as the room changed into a steam bath. But they lived.

Behind another door were Major Jake Cahill and his wife. He had sealed the transom and then anxiously waited until a ladder reached his seventh-story perch. Down the hall on the same floor was Cahill's elderly mother. Climbing down the ladder to safety after his wife, Cahill immediately rushed into the neighboring Mortgage Guarantee Building and ran up the stairs. Somehow obtaining a long plank, Major Cahill went from window to window until he spotted his mother's room directly across an alley. He extended the plank, crawled across it, and led his mother back over the quaking board to safety.

Another military officer, Major General P. W. Baade, who had commanded the 35th Division in Europe during World War II, escaped along the route created by Major Cahill, crawling along the board with his wife to the business building across the alley.

For six hours the firemen fought their way, floor by floor, up into the fire, extinguishing the blazes on each floor and then proceeding upward again. None of them had ever experienced such a holocaust, and as they broke into one room after another, they found the scenes were excruciating. Brass doorknobs and phones had melted. Furniture crumbled under the slightest touch. Five people had died in one room, but a live canary sang in the midst of the smoke.

The dead were everywhere. Bodies sprawled along the hallways with the telltale signs of asphyxiation, trickles of hardened blood from the nose and mouth. A woman was found cradling her head at an open window, as though asleep. In her dead hand she clutched a purse. Room after room contained dead people in bed who appeared as if in deep slumber.

Outside his tenth-floor suite was the seventy-year-old W. Frank Winecoff, dead, asphyxiated. Though he had sold the hotel in 1937, he lived on in his own building rent-free, a building he insisted until the day he died was completely "fireproof."

When the pale winter sun rose that day in Atlanta, crowds assembled in great numbers and watched the firemen take away 119 corpses. Another 90 persons were carried on stretchers to the hospital. The worst hotel fire in American history was over.

Major Cahill stood in the middle of Peachtree Street for a long time, staring up at the gutted Winecoff Hotel. He then gathered up his wife and mother and began to walk away. He found his coat, which he had dropped moments after getting off the ladder and before saving his mother's life. Cahill snuggled into it and then reached into his pockets and grimaced. Someone had stolen his travelers' checks and fountain pen.

(ALSO SEE: Gulf Hotel, LaSalle Hotel, Newhall House, Windsor Hotel)

A Filipino farmer transports an electrocuted water buffalo through the flooded streets of Manila, one of the oddities of hurricane Winnie's devastation, June 1964. *(Wide World)*

WINNIE — TYPHOON
June 30, 1964

Typhoon Winnie first struck Hong Kong on May 28, 1964, with 70-m.p.h. winds that tore ships from their moorings in the harbor. Forty-one persons were injured, and thousands were left homeless. This was but the preliminary blow of Winnie's wrath, for the typhoon swept across the Philippines two days later, devastating chiefly the main island of Luzon. Her 80-m.p.h. winds ripped away all telephone, telegraph and electrical wires, which plunged Manila into a terrifying blackout. Its two million people were sent running for their lives as building after building collapsed. Forty-three persons died here, and 373,000 were left homeless. The official death count would certainly have been higher if the bodies of at least 200 missing persons had been found.

WOLLASTON STATION, MASSACHUSETTS — RAILWAY WRECK
October 8, 1878

A misplaced switch caused an Old Colony excursion train to derail at Wollaston Station, Massachusetts, on October 8, 1878. The wreck was one of the worst pile-ups of cars, twenty-one in all, ever witnessed; some of the passenger coaches climbed on top of each other until they were three deep. Resulting fires from exploding stoves killed most of the twenty-one passengers who died in the crash.

Eerie lights and grim-faced onlookers collect around the derailed Broker on February 6, 1951. Eighty-four died when the train jumped the tracks, slid onto an embankment, and cars telescoped into one another. *(Wide World)*

WOODBRIDGE, NEW JERSEY — RAILWAY WRECK February 6, 1951

background: At 5:43 P.M. on February 6, 1951, Pennsylvania's Number 733, the Broker, derailed at Woodbridge, New Jersey, the locomotive and the next seven cars of the eleven-car train going off the track. Most of the eighty-four persons killed in the crash occupied the first four cars. The engineer was held responsible for approaching a dangerous curve at excessive speeds.

The Broker was the Pennsylvania's deluxe commuter train, running from Newark to Red Bank and making stops at the upper-middle-class havens along the New Jersey shore, where many of its business executive passengers resided. Number 733 also had the further distinction of being one of the last important trains in the United States to maintain a steam locomotive. This image of quality and charm in railroading came to a gruesome end on the evening of February 6, 1951.

At that time a new railway bridge over the New Jersey Turnpike was being built. While its construction was under way, the Broker was to use a bypass that involved a lazy S-curve—a five-degree turn as it swung right, a short tangent of track and then a sharp curve to the left. Engineer Joseph H. Fitzsimmons, a forty-seven-year-old Pennsylvania employee with a long and commendable record with the line, received the following general order on February 6, 1951:

PERTH AMBOY AND WOODBRIDGE BRANCH
WOODBRIDGE—GENASCO
Number 2 main track and catenary moved 50 feet northward between a point 1,000 feet west of Woodbridge Station and a point 4,000 feet west of Woodbridge Station. Trains and engines must not exceed a speed of 25 miles per hour between these points.

Conductor "Honest John" Bishop and Fitzsimmons talked about the "slow" order before the trains' departure from Jersey City, a conversation Bishop was to recall later at an inquiry. (The conductor wasn't called "Honest John" for nothing; he had once returned to a passenger a satchel containing $25,000, which he found in Grand Central Station.)

Though the old steam engine Fitzsimmons was piloting had no speed indicator, the engineer, for all his years of service, would certainly have known whether he was traveling much above the restricted 25-m.p.h. limit The fact was that Fitzsimmons was fairly racing his train onto the perilous bypass (the railroad had also demanded that the Broker make its thirty-five mile run in a forty-four minute schedule).

Conductor Bishop realized the train was moving onto the bypass at excessive speed and tried to push his way through a crowded car to get to the emergency signal cord, but he was too late. Number 733 swung sharply onto the first five-degree turn, roared down the straight track, and then, at speeds later estimated to be between 50 and 60 m.p.h., attempted to make the second curve. The speed was too much.

With a screech of grinding metal, the locomotive left the tracks, sailed over an embankment and landed on its side with a loud crash. Fitzsimmons was thrown clear with only minor scratches. His fireman, A. M. Dunn, was mortally injured.

Following the engine, the next seven cars left the track and flopped onto their sides. Although these cars were of all-steel construction, they were severely damaged. Bedlam broke out in these cars as, according to one eyewitness, unhinged passengers went berserk in their efforts to get out. They punched each other; they kicked each other: "They were like a bunch of wild animals trying to get out of overturned cages, clawing each other to get clear." The chaos was the second nightmare of the crash; the inside of the first four coaches looked to arriving rescuers as if they had been blown apart by grenades. Bodies were everywhere, jammed beneath seats, in luggage racks; pieces of bodies and blotches of blood smeared the walls and remaining windows.

Dozens were so crazed by the crash that they mistook Fulton Street, glistening beneath streetlights, for a river, and as they stumbled from the wreck they dove from the embankment onto the concrete, further injuring themselves.

The accident, which claimed the lives of eighty-three passengers and that of fireman Dunn (who lived for only three hours and could therefore not testify against his engineer), was clearly the responsibility of Joseph Fitzsimmons. He was interrogated by Benjamin Van Tine, New Jersey's deputy attorney general, but he insisted that he was not going more than 25 m.p.h., as per the general order he had received that morning, when the Broker entered the bypass.

Conductor Bishop and scores of passengers refuted his statements, and a board of inquiry later determined his speed at a little more than 50 m.p.h. Fitzsimmons then stated that he was looking through a thin fog for a warning light even though he knew that the general order obviated the use of any such light. Finally Fitzsimmons, near collapse, admitted he could have been going 50 m.p.h. His testimony then trailed off into a dull, witless monotone as he repeated: "I kept looking for a yellow light, a yellow light, a yellow light . . ."

WOODVILLE, INDIANA — RAILWAY WRECK

November 12, 1906

A blinding snowstorm on the night of November 12, 1906, led to the head-on collision of two Baltimore & Ohio trains, one a freight waiting at a siding, the other a speeding passenger train in two sections. The first section went by in the storm with its green lights and signal flags unseen, signals that meant another passenger train was directly behind the first train. Ignorant of the second section, the freight pulled out onto the main track and collided with the second section outside Woodville, Indiana.

Thoroughly demolished, the second section, Number 47, caught fire. The entire train burned to ashes in a matter of minutes, incinerating forty-three people, all but two of whom were Rumanian, Serbian and Polish immigrants going west to establish new lives.

WOODWARD, OKLAHOMA — TORNADO

April 6, 1947

The most destructive tornado ever to strike its area reduced Woodward, Oklahoma, to ruins on April 6, 1947. The twister raced over a path of 221 miles from White Deer, Texas, to Woodward, Kansas.

Woodward was struck dead center by the tornado, which killed 95 residents and injured 723 others. Damages here alone soared beyond $6 million.

WORCHESTER, MASSACHUSETTS — TORNADO

June 9, 1953

Setting down outside Worchester, Massachusetts, on June 9, 1953, at 5:00 P.M., the most severe tornado ever to howl through any New England state crushed the life from 90 persons, 62 in Worchester alone, where another 738 were injured. The twister moved about 36 m.p.h. in its forward movement and dug out a path of forty-six miles that encompassed Holden, Shrewsbury, and particularly Worchester.

Property damage was a record high—$52 million—perhaps the highest ever recorded in the United States from tornado devastation. More than 4,000 buildings were demolished by this tornado, which became fused with another twister just before converging on Worchester.

Canard or not, the story is often told of the Worchester man who rushed home from work minutes after the

Assumption College stood in ruins after a tornado gouged its way through Worchester on June 9, 1953. *(Wide World)*

tornado had passed. He found his brother standing in the ruins of his house.

"What happened, Harry?" he asked his brother. "What happened? Who did we lose?"

"Well, we lost Ma."

"What about Pa?"

"Well, Pa is in the hospital in rough shape."

"What about my wife?"

"I don't know . . . And I lost my head completely."

WORLD — DELUGE-EARTHQUAKE 2400 B.C.

The great deluge, or flood, accompanied by worldwide earthquakes, has some basis in fact beyond the words of Genesis. Though vague, ancient tracts refer to "immense earthquakes and floods that shook and covered all southern Europe and Asia Minor, opening an outlet for the Black Sea, which had before been entirely inland." In the 2400 B.C. convulsion of the seas, we are told that "almost all the people of Greece and Asia Minor perished."

Chinese reports tell of an immense earthquake, occurring at the same time, that "raised the bottom of the Great Northern Sea, pouring its waters out upon all North China and drowning the people." Where the great sea once was, Chinese legend has it, is now the great Mongolian Desert.

The island of Atlantis, which was described to Plato by Egyptian priests as lying off the coast of North Africa, is supposed to have sunk into the sea at this time. One scientist speculated: "It would seem that a great sea once extended northeastward from the present basin of the Caspian over the deserts of Central Asia; and that an awful upheaval of this basin was the chief factor in the flood. . . . Isthmuses were torn asunder, vast oceans hurled their gigantic waves over the continents and over islands engulfed forever. The extraordinary evaporation from the unusual expanse of water, the sudden chilling of the atmosphere, produced torrents of rain [Noah's rain, perhaps]."

Chinese literature records that "the same day were all the fountains of the great deep broken up, and the windows of heaven were open."

X

XENIA, OHIO **TORNADO**
April 3, 1974

background: Of the more than sixty tornadoes that swept through eleven states in early April 1974, the most devastating was the one that struck Xenia, Ohio (population 27,000), at 4:45 P.M. on April 3, 1974, when 34 persons were killed and 585 persons were injured. In five minutes the twister sliced through three miles of the city on a half-mile-wide path. The total dead in an eleven-state area went over 300, and the damages, the worst in United States history, were well over $500 million.

"We had about thirty seconds' warning before it hit," one Xenia, Ohio, resident said about the twister that devastated the little town on April 3, 1974. "All you could hear was wind, the crashes and the people praying."

The tornado, one of sixty that struck eleven states that day, crunched down at 4:45 P.M. at the southeast corner of Xenia's city limits. In moments it roared through three miles of the town, utterly destroying 40 percent of the houses and buildings and creating $100 million in damage.

In fifteen minutes the town had been all but obliterated. The twister caught Ron Anderson and his family at supper. He barely had enough time to gather his children together before the tornado struck his house. He and his wife threw their bodies over the children as the roof spun

This massive black tornado moved through Xenia, Ohio, on April 3, 1974. It left thirty-four persons dead and a third of the city in ruins. *(Wide World)*

away, the furniture flew out and even the carpet upon which they were lying was sucked from beneath them. They survived with bruises and cuts. "I'm happy we're alive," Anderson told newsmen.

An elderly woman whose entire house was blown away was left sitting in a rocking chair in the middle of the debris. She would talk to no one minutes after the twister roared away. For hours policemen begged her to leave, but she merely stared blankly and shook her head.

Mrs. Peggy Schmidt heard the rumbling of the tornado and stepped to her front porch with her daughter Michele. They could see the tornado coming across the land, carving through houses.

"It looks like it's full of birds," Michele said.

"Those aren't birds," Mrs. Schmidt said ominously. "It's debris."

Mrs. Schmidt and her daughter went inside. She later stated, "We went into the downstairs bedroom and opened the sliding glass door, like they said to do so there wouldn't be any suction. Then we laid between the two beds. At the last moment we pulled a cover over us."

The wind at that moment blew apart the glass doors and sent a shower of deadly glass through the air. The Schmidts thought themselves lucky, escaping with only a few broken windows. When they stepped outside, they discovered the entire second story of their home had blown away.

Nothing was left of Victor Gregory's home—nothing, that is, but a case of unbroken eggs, a hall mirror and a box of Christmas ornaments.

Half of Xenia's residents were in Gregory's fix; the town had been shattered. Six of the city's twelve schools were rubble; five of its seven supermarkets no longer existed. The twister's 300-m.p.h. winds had crushed scores of cars, flattened school buses and overturned a fifteen-car freight train.

Minutes after the storm passed, a police broadcast announced to anyone listening that "we are begging for all kinds of medical assistance, manpower and other help."

Ohio Governor John J. Gilligan immediately declared Xenia a disaster area, ordered 250 National Guardsmen to patrol the streets and give aid and then went to the stricken town in person.

After it was over, a battle-hardened National Guard sergeant picked up a little eight-year-old girl wandering in the ruins. She could not tell him where her parents were, only that "my house came down and crushed my dolly . . . Who was that? The bogieman?"

(ALSO SEE: Waco, Texas)

Y

YARMOUTH CASTLE — MARINE DISASTER

November 13, 1965

background: The 5,000-ton cruise ship *Yarmouth Castle,* built in 1938 and flying the Panamanian flag, was sailing between Miami and the Bahamas and caught fire sixty miles northeast of Nassau on the morning of November 13, 1965. Of the 370 passengers and 175 crew members, 89 were lost. Safety standards of the ship were slipshod, as hearings later pointed out.

Almost three months before the obviously unsafe cruise ship *Yarmouth Castle* sank with eighty-nine on board (only two of which were crew members), California Congressman William S. Mailliard, a member of the House Subcommittee on Merchant Marine and Fisheries, labeled the vessel a "shining example of a ship that was not in proper condition to engage in cruise trade."

The thirty-eight-year-old ship had flown the United States flag as a troop carrier during World War II, the Liberian flag, and lastly, the Panamanian flag. The latter, critics argued, was flown so that her owners would not have to maintain the vessel according to American safety standards, even though the bulk of her passengers were American tourists.

The *Yarmouth Castle*—loaded down with highly combustible furniture, thick wooden paneling in the staterooms, carpets, drapes—was a floating tinderbox, yet hordes of tourists believed trade blurbs describing her as a safe "fun ship" bound for "exotic, glamorous Nassau." Her fatal voyage began on November 12, 1965, when she departed for the Bahamas. There was enough dancing and partying that first (and last) night at sea to make even the heartiest of the ship's 370 passengers weary. Most of them were asleep in their staterooms by 2:00 A.M. when fire broke out in the unoccupied room 610.

Crew members saw sparks shooting through the louvers of the room's door and quickly kicked it open. Flames leaped out at them. Returning with fire extinguishers, crew men found they could not control the flames. The ship's captain, thirty-three-year-old Byron Voutsinas, who held a Liberian master's license, appeared briefly and then raced for the bridge. The flames followed him down the hallway and up the ladders.

Recently widowed, Mrs. Mary J. Hamilton opened her door to see "fire all over the place." She fainted.

Mrs. M. Herman heard a racket in the hall and opened her door. Running past her was a naked woman shrieking: "My baby! My baby!" Another naked woman was stopped by tourist Lloyd Lamm, who gave her his shirt.

Los Angeles salesman Arthur Gordon was awakened by the shouting. "I thought it was just a couple of drunks, but after the shouts continued I went out to the lobby. I was surrounded by flames."

Cruising about forty minutes behind the *Yarmouth Castle* was the pleasure ship *Bahama Star.* Her captain, Carl Brown, saw the orange glow in the sky ahead. He thought "at first it was the illuminated stack of a Cunard—it was the same sort of orange." Brown ordered full speed to investigate further.

The Finnish motorship *Finnpulp,* which was sailing just ahead of the *Yarmouth Castle,* noticed the blaze shooting up into the clear, bright night and put about.

Everywhere on board the cruise ship, passengers were having difficulty saving themselves. "They didn't have any life preservers in the cabin," Gerald McDonnell later complained. He went to the deck and found that "the ropes had been painted, and they couldn't lower the boats. . . . There were no life rings on deck."

Tourists George and Viola Brown managed to climb into a lifeboat, but Brown angrily remembered, "They couldn't lower it. The winch wouldn't work. We went aft to another boat, but there were no oarlocks on it."

Most of the passengers were near the stern of the ship, and many of the lifeboats there never made it into the water. One was lowered and crammed with fifty passengers and crew members. Malcolm Philbrook, a police sergeant from Miami Beach, was jostled into the water. He noticed the unmistakable appearance of the fins of sharks. "There were sharks all around the boat. I was clinging to an oar. They finally got me into the boat before the sharks noticed me, I guess."

As the *Bahama Star* and the *Finnpulp* arrived on the scene, Captain Voutsinas stepped into a lifeboat with several crew members and rowed away. The *Yarmouth Castle*'s second mate, José Ramos, who was helping passengers at the stern to enter lifeboats, spotted the captain leaving. Ramos cupped his hands and shouted to

Voutsinas, "Come back and help passengers! Remember the penalty for this!"

Voutsinas and his crew men pulled alongside the *Finnpulp,* only to be told to go back to their own ship and aid passengers. Voutsinas informed the captain that all he wanted to do was tell him to inform the Coast Guard of the fire. "We've already done that," came the terse reply. As the *Finnpulp* put over her own boats, Voutsinas and the others rowed back to the *Yarmouth Castle,* which was now blazing almost from stem to stern.

Captain Brown of the *Bahama Star* brought his ship so close to the sinking liner that the paint on his vessel's stack blistered. To those lining the rails of the stricken ship, he shouted through an electric bullhorn, "Listen to me. Our boats are coming to you. Go down the ropes hanging over the side or jump into the water. Be careful that you don't land on other people."

The *Bahama Star* took off most of the ship's passengers. Eighty-seven passengers and two crew members were lost when the ship went down at 6:05 A.M. Brown watched as "she listed more and more to port, then went stern first in a cloud of steam. It was a very sad sight to see."

The "fun ship" was gone.

(ALSO SEE: Morro Castle*)*

YARMOUTH, ENGLAND — MASS DROWNING

April 10, 1845

Hundreds of handbills were passed for days through the streets of Yarmouth, England, announcing that one Nelson, a clown traveling with a local circus, would be pulled up the Bure River beneath the north quay suspension bridge at the entrance to the town. The stunt was designed to entice the people of Yarmouth, chiefly the children, to attend the circus.

From the suspension bridge they would view Nelson in a clown's boat being pulled by four large geese. The clown never appeared, for Nelson's little boat capsized at the mouth of the river, where he was pulled to shore. The huge throng from Yarmouth, however, continued to wait for him, about 330 citizens and their children standing on the suspension bridge. Just as someone joyously shouted, "Here come the geese!" the bridge gave way on one side, then the chains gave way one after another and spilled all on the bridge into the swiftly moving river.

One account recalls the "fearful splash, and a few gurgling struggles only recognize the spot which had swallowed such a mass of human life."

One man clung to the broken bridge, and a woman somehow managed to clutch his ankles. "Hold tight!" he shouted to her. "Hold tight till the boats come!" The

The collapse of the suspension bridge at Yarmouth, England, on April 10, 1845, caused the deaths of 250 persons. *(Illustrated London News)*

This aerial view of the dikes at Yuba City, California, in January 1956 was taken just before high water broke through the dikes and flooded the area. *(Wide World)*

boats did come, about twenty-five of them, furiously rowed by local fishermen. They were able to save the woman and about 50 more people, but at least 250 persons died in the mass drowning. Most of the victims were small children whose mothers could find no way to save them. One woman clutched her children even in death: "She had in her arms an infant, and in one hand a little girl, three or four years old, and her firm hold had not been broken by the struggles of death, for it was with difficulty they were separated. . . . They were all corpses and very stiff."
(ALSO SEE: Ebro River)

YOLANDE, ALABAMA — MINE DISASTER

December 16, 1907

Although water lines and hoses were installed in Mine Number 1 at Yolande, Alabama, no sprinkling was done to hold down the coal dust before eighty-seven miners went to work on the morning of December 16, 1907. The coal dust present throughout the mine was predictably ignited by one of the miner's open lamps, and the explosion that wrecked the mine at 10:25 A.M. took the lives of fifty-seven men; thirty workers escaped from the shaft some hours later through another entrance.

YUBA CITY, CALIFORNIA — FLOODS

January, 1956

Tropical air freakishly carried by the jetstream from Hawaii to northern California created horrendous downpours—as much as 31.5 inches of rain by December 6, 1955—which, in turn, melted the snow in the Sierra Nevada. The melted snowcaps bloated the mountain streams, "which burst out of the woods like furious brown snakes," according to one reporter.

By the first week in January, 1956, the Feather River was running wild. It broke its banks and caused the Yuba River to flood. First Marysville was evacuated, and refugees fled to Yuba City, but the dikes there failed. The entire area was flooded. Ironically the dikes at Marysville held.

United States helicopters raced in and plucked about 150 persons from precarious rooftop perches. Another 74 were already dead, drowned in the floodwaters that would have been held back if a proposed $400 million concrete dam at Oroville had been built.

Z

ZAGREB, YUGOSLAVIA

RAILWAY WRECK
August 30, 1974

A passenger train traveling between 49 and 55 m.p.h. slammed into the station at Zagreb, Yugoslavia, on the night of August 30, 1974, causing several cars to turn onto their sides. It took hours to extricate more than 50 persons trapped beneath the wreckage. Among the 150 passengers killed outright were at least two dozen who were electrocuted by power cables knocked down during the crash.

The two engineers of the train, Nikola Knezevic and Stjepan Varga, were accused of running the train too fast and were initially arrested on charges of being drunk. The destruction of the Belgrade to Dortmund Express was the worst rail accident in Yugoslav history.

ZAMALEK STADIUM

STAMPEDE
February 17, 1974

Thousands of Egyptian soccer fans stampeded in Cairo's Zamalek Stadium while attempting to get inside to watch a game on February 17, 1974. The match was originally scheduled to be held at Cairo Stadium, which holds 100,000. The event had been sold out, but the 100,000 ticketholders went berserk when they learned that the game was to be held in Zamalek Stadium, which has only a 45,000 seating capacity. Following the disaster, the promoters limply explained the switch by saying that it had been done "to ensure the comfort of the spectators." Forty-nine fans were killed in the wild stampede.

A rescue worker stands near one of the cars of a train that crashed into the station at Zagreb, Yugoslavia, on August 30, 1974; 150 died in the derailment. *(Wide World)*

The waterfront of Zante was a scene of devastation following an earthquake on February 8, 1893. *(Illustrated London News)*

ZANTE — EARTHQUAKE

February 8, 1893

The earthquake that shook Zante, the most southerly of the Ionian islands off the western coast of Greece, killed hundreds of citizens and created more than $2 million in damages. About 2,000 were made homeless when their houses were pitched to the ground at 6:00 A.M. on February 8, 1893.

Bringing relief some days later was the British battleship *Camperdown.* British sailors distributed huts, tents, blankets and food to the sufferers. The *Camperdown* would herself be involved in calamity four months later when she would accidentally ram and sink the British flagship *Victoria* while on maneuvers off Tripoli.

ZANZIBAR — HURRICANE

April 15, 1872

In the search for Dr. Livingston, an expedition led by Royal Army Lieutenant Llewellyn Dawson and Royal Navy Lieutenant W. Henn was almost wiped out at Zanzibar by a powerful hurricane that began at 6:00 A.M. on April 15, 1872. The storm soon destroyed almost 150 ships in the harbor, including 6 of the sultan's private vessels, among which was the *Sea King,* formerly the Confederate raider *Shenandoah.* About 200 natives were killed in the storm, according to Dawson's dispatch to the *Illustrated London News.*

The report described how "all the trees were torn, mangled, or uprooted; the beach was strewn with wrecked and damaged merchandise; the streets were blocked with rubbish of all kinds, and almost every large house was more or less damaged. This is the first hurricane known at Zanzibar in the memory of the present generation."

Army tents supplied by the British Navy housed some of Zante's 2,000 homeless. *(Illustrated London News)*

The violent hurricane of April 15, 1872, totally wrecked the Zanzibar waterfront and sank 150 ships in the harbor. *(Illustrated London News)*

The once beautiful town of Zug, Switzerland, was destroyed by a flash flood when a dam broke on July 10, 1887.

ZARAND, IRAN **TRAFFIC ACCIDENT**
August 8, 1972

In probably one of the most devastating traffic accidents in world history, thirty-nine persons were killed outside of Zarand, Iran, when two buses collided on a narrow highway. Another forty persons were hospitalized.

ZIEGLER, ILLINOIS **MINE DISASTER**
April 3, 1905

The Ziegler mine had not been examined by safety inspectors for two weeks (and the fan had been shut off for four days) prior to the explosion that ripped apart the main shaft at 7:10 A.M. on April 3, 1905. An open lamp was given as the source that ignited coal dust. The forty-nine persons killed in this explosion included a district mine inspector and two others who were part of a rescue team that was overcome by afterdamp.

ZUG, SWITZERLAND **BROKEN DAM**
July 10, 1887

A new $80,000 dam at Zug, Switzerland, gave way on the morning of July 10, 1887; about eighty feet of concrete broke loose and sent tons of water from Lake Zug into the town. One report has it that "a dozen people rushed out from a neighboring cafe and were drowned . . . two boats proceeding to the rescue were swallowed up; one boatman rose to the surface, the other was seen no more."

A boatman's hut was washed into the swirling waters, and though three small children cried out for help from the windows, no one could save them. The death toll reached 70 before evening. More than 600 persons were made homeless, and damage was estimated at over a million francs. Toward morning someone found a live child in a cradle floating upon the floodwaters.

Major Air Crashes

(† indicates entries profiled in General Narrative. Airplane crashes are listed under name of airline, dirigibles are listed under name.)

Date		Place	Deaths	Description
†1913	**Oct. 17**	**Johannisthal, Germany**	28	The *LZ-18*, German Naval dirigible, caught fire and crashed.
1918	**Apr. 7**	**Straits of Otranto**	23	The zeppelin *l-59* exploded.
†1921	**Aug. 24**	**Hull, England**	44	British dirigible *R-38* cracked in two.
†1922	**Feb. 21**	**Hampton Roads**	34	Airship *Roma* wrecked; many injured.
†1923	**Dec. 21**	**Mediterranean or Sahara Desert**	52	French dirigible *Dixmude* disappeared.
†1925	**Sept. 23**	**Ava, Ohio**	14	U.S. Army dirigible *Shenandoah* broke apart.
†1930	**Oct. 5**	**Beauvais, France**	48	British dirigible *R-101* crashed.
†1933	**Apr. 14**	**New Jersey Coast**	73	United States dirigible *Akron* crashed.
1935	**May 18**	**U.S.S.R.**	27	Stunt pilot crashed into giant plane *Maxim Gorki.*
†1937	**May 6**	**Lakehurst, New Jersey**	36	German zeppelin *Hindenburg* exploded at mooring. (SEE *Hindenburg*)
†1938	**July 24**	**Bogota, Colombia**	53	Colombian military stunt plane smashed into grandstand.
	July 14	**Tyrrhenian Sea**	20	Rome-Cagliari Airliner I-Volo crashed.
	Dec. 2	**Chunking, China**	20	Soviet plane containing military experts crashed.
1942	**Sept. 27**	**El Affroun, Algiers**	25	Passenger plane crashed outside city.
	Oct. 2	**Coamo, Puerto Rico**	22	U.S. Army transport plane crashed near island.
1943	**Jan. 18**	**South Atlantic**	26	Army transport plane disappeared over Atlantic.
	July 29	**Trammel, Ky.**	20	American Airlines plane exploded after crash landing; 2 survived.
	Sept. 20	**Maxton, N.C.**	25	Army transport plane crashed carrying all soldiers.
1944	**Feb. 11**	**Memphis, Tenn.**	24	American Airlines transport crashed into Missssissippi River.
	Aug. 4	**Atkinson, Neb.**	28	C-47 Army transport crashed outside city.
	Aug. 23	**Freckelton, England**	76	United States bomber crashed into school; deaths included on ground and in buildings.
	Nov. 4	**Hanford, Calif.**	24	Transcontinental & Western Air transport crashed.
1945	**Feb. 2**	**Rome, Italy**	23	U.S. Army transport crashed into mountain 60 mi. from city.
	Feb. 13	**San Francisco Bay, Calif.**	24	Navy transport plunged into Bay 13 minutes after taking off from Oakland.
	†July 28	**New York City**	14	U.S. bomber (B-25) smashed into Empire State Building.
1946	**Dec. 25**	**Near Shanghai**	71	Three China Air Transport planes crashed in fog.
1947	**Feb. 15**	**Bogota, Colombia**	53	Avianca DC-4 crashed into Mount Tablazo.
	Feb. 21	**Chungking, China**	21	Chinese Air Force C-47 crashed near city.
	May 29	**New York City**	43	United Airlines DC-4 crashed on takeoff due to sudden wind; pilot and 6 others survived.
	May 29	**Tokyo, Japan**	40	U.S. Army C-54 hit mountain near city.
	May 29	**Iceland**	25	Icelandic Airways DC-3 crashed in the north.
	May 30	**Ft. Deposit, Md.**	53	Eastern Airlines DC-4 crashed near city on way to Miami; damaged tail assembly was responsible.
	June 13	**Leesburg, Virginia**	50	Pennsylvania Central DC-4 crashed into mountain during rainstorm; low flying blamed for crash. On board Dr. Courtney Smith; Red Cross Medical Director.
	June 13	**Melbourne, Florida**	21	A converted DC-3 chartered flight crashed into coastal swamp.
	†Oct. 24	**Bryce Canyon, Utah**	52	United DC-6 crashed into hillside.
	Nov. 18	**Ravello, Italy**	20	Swedish Airliner returning ferry pilots crashed near city; 5 survivors.
	Dec. 11	**Goose Bay, Labrador**	23	Air Transport Command C-54 crashed near city; 6 survived.
	Dec. 11	**Memphis, Tenn.**	20	Army C-47 crashed at airport.
1948	**Jan. 12**	**Between Santiago & Barahona, D.R.**	31	Dominican DC-3 crashed with entire Santiago baseball team.
	Jan. 28	**Coalinga, Calif.**	32	Immigration Service DC-3 exploded and crashed.
	Jan. 30	**Atlantic Ocean**	32	British South American Airways disappeared betweeen Azores and Bermuda; killed Air Marshal Sir Arthur Coningham who commanded the 2d Tactical Air Force in Normandy invasion.
	Mar. 12	**Mt. Sanford, Alaska**	30	Northwest Airlines DC-4 crashed 200 miles northeast of Anchorage.
	Mar. 15	**Shannon, Ireland**	30	Pan American World Airways Constellation hit a 3-ft. stone wall on landing; 1 survivor.
	June 17	**Mt. Carmel, Pa.**	43	United Airlines DC-6 crashed while making a forced landing. Notables on board: Vanities showman Earl Carroll, actress Beryl Wallace and Mrs. Venith Varden Oakie, divorced wife of actor Jack Oakie.
	July 4	**London, England**	39	Swedish DC-6 collided with an RAF 4-engine York Transport as both were circling during rain storm preparing to land.
	July 16	**Between Macao & Hong Kong**	25	Flying Boat crashed between two cities.
	Aug. 1	**Atlantic Ocean**	53	A 6-engine, 73-ton French Latecoere 631 Flying Boat disappeared between Martinique and French West Africa.
	Aug. 29	**Winona, Minnesota**	37	Northwest Airlines Martin 202 crashed on Wisconsin bank of Mississippi River; 1 survived.

Date	Place	Deaths

Oct. 21 **Prestwick, Scotland** 39
KLM Royal Dutch Constellation crashed while making a radar guided landing.

Dec. 15 **Bogota, Colombia** 30
Lansa Airways plane crashed shortly after takeoff.

Dec. 21 **Hong Kong, China** 35
China National Airlines C-54 Skymaster crashed on Basalt Island near city. On board was Quentin Roosevelt, grandson of Pres. Theodore Roosevelt.

Dec. 22 **Greece** 24
Czechoslovak Airlines plane crashed in southern part of country.

Dec. 23 **Tarragona, Spain** 27
Two-engine Iberian transport crashed 40 miles from city.

1949 **Jan. 17** **Loch Goil, Scotland** 20
B-29 Superfortress crashed into mountain 30 miles northwest of Glasgow.

Jan. 17 **Caribbean** 20
British South American Airways Tudor IV, the Star Ariel, missing en route to Jamaica.

Feb. 8 **Sweden** 28
Scandinavian Airlines British-made Viking crashed off coast.

Feb. 24 **Hong Kong Island** 23
Cathay Pacific plane from Manila crashed and burned.

Feb. 24 **Cuzco** 22
Peruvian Air Force transport burst into flames on takeoff; 4 survived.

June 6 **Florianopolis, Brazil** 27
Brazilian Army transport crashed shortly after takeoff.

June 6 **Athens, Greece** 22
Greek Airlines Dakota crashed 17 miles from city. On board was Maj. Gen. George Kotsalos, military governor of Kavella.

June 7 **Puerto Rico** 55
United States Strato Freight plunged into water; 27 rescued.

June 23 **Bari Harbor** 32
Dutch Constellation Airliner crashed in flames off Italian Coast.

July 12 **Bombay, India** 35
Dutch KLM Constellation with 13 newsmen crashed into a hill near city during blinding snowstorm. Among the victims were 2 Pulitzer Prize winners: S. Burton Heath, winner for his domestic reporting in 1939, and Hobert Renfro Knickerbocker, winner in 1931 for his foreign reporting.

July 12 **Simi Mountains, Calif.** 35
Non-scheduled Standard Airlines 2-engine transport crashed 30 miles north of Los Angeles. The airline had been ordered out of business by July 20 for violation of CAB rules.

Aug. 13 **Bojaca, Colombia** 31
Colombian airliner crashed near city.

Aug. 19 **Manchester, England** 24
British European Airways DC-3 crashed near city; 8 injured.

Aug. 21 **Northern Manitoba, Canada** 21
Royal Canadian Air Force amphibious plane crashed; carried 8 polio-stricken Eskimos.

Sept. 9 **St. Joachim, Quebec, Canada** 23
Quebec Airways DC-3 crashed on mountainside near city.

Sept. 26 **Popocateptl Volcano, Mexico** 25
Compania Mexicana de Aviacion DC-3 crashed in heavy fog.

Oct. 28 **Sao Miguel Island, Azores** 48
Air France Constellation crashed into a mountain; one of the victims was Marcel Cerdan, former world middleweight boxing champion.

†Nov. 1 **Washington, D.C.** 55
Eastern DC-4 rammed by Bolivian P-38 over airport.

Nov. 20 **Oslo, Norway** 27
Aero Holland DC-3 crashed on a wooded hill 20 miles southwest of city. Victims included 27 Jewish refugee children; 1 survived.

Nov. 29 **Dallas, Texas** 28
American Airlines DC-6 crash landed and burned; 26 persons survived; Swiss violinist Julio Cochard killed.

Dec. 1 **Ribeirao, Brazil** 20
Real Airline DC-3 crashed in rainstorm; 2 survived.

†1950 **Mar. 12** **Cardiff, Wales** 80
Chartered British Avro Tudor V crashed near Llandow Airport.

Apr. 21 **Tokyo, Japan** 35
U.S. Air Force C-54 en route to Manila crashed outside city.

May 24 **Pasto, Colombia** 25
Lansa Airways DC-3 crashed into volcano; girl, 10 survived.

June 5 **Bahamas** 28
Westair Transport C-46 crashed north of islands; 37 survivors picked up next day.

June 12 **Bahrein, Persian Gulf** 47
Air France DC-4 Skymaster crashed near island; 5 survived.

June 12 **Bahrein, Persian Gulf** 40
A 2nd Air France DC-4 crashed in the same area, the same night; 13 survived. Both planes were on regular Saigon-to-Paris flights.

†June 24 **Lake Michigan** 58
Northwest Airlines DC-4 crashed in storm near South Haven, Michigan.

June 30 **Pusan, Korea** 23
U.S. Army C-54 transport plane crashed near city.

July 9 **Casablanca** 21
French Aigle-Azur (Blue Eagle) DC-3 crashed shortly after takeoff; 9 survived.

July 17 **Pathankot, India** 22
Indian DC-3 crashed into Kashmir Mountains.

July 23 **Myrtle Beach, S.C.** 39
Air Force C-46 carrying Air National Guardsmen crashed after takeoff.

July 27 **Tokyo, Japan** 26
U.S. C-47 transport plane crashed at sea south of city. On board included James O. Supple of the *Chicago Sun-Times.*

Aug. 31 **Cairo, Egypt** 55
TWA Constellation crashed and burned near city.

Sept. 19 **Kwajalein, Marshall Isalnds** 26
Four-engine Navy transport, carrying all U.S. Navy personnel, crashed off island.

Oct. 17 **Mill Hill, England** 28
British European Airways Dakota crashed in mist; 1 survived.

Nov. 7 **Butte, Montana** 22
Northwest Airlines Martin 202 crashed into peak.

†Nov. 13 **Grenoble, France** 58
Canadian Curtiss-Reid Airtours, Ltd. crashed; all aboard were pilgrims.

Nov. 21 **Northwest Wyoming** 21
DC-3, owned by the New Tribes Mission, crashed into Mt. Moran; victims included 8 children.

Dec. 9 **Bangui, French Equatorial Africa** 37
French DC-4 crashed carrying all Senegalese soldiers.

Date		Place	Deaths
	Dec. 14	**Nilgiri Hills, India**	**21**
	Air India transport crashed.		
	Dec. 15	**Trujillo, Venezuela**	**31**
	Venezuelan DC-4 crashed near city.		
	Dec. 18	**Tourane, Indo-China**	**30**
	Collision of 2 Junkers containing mostly French officers.		
	Dec. 19	**Northern Philippines**	**37**
	USAF C-54 disappeared in Western Pacific and off islands.		
1951	**Mar. 11**	**Hong Kong Island**	**24**
	Thai Skymaster crashed into Parker Mountain.		
	Mar. 21	**Hato Nuevo, Colombia**	**27**
	Lansa Airline DC-3 crashed near city.		
	Mar. 23	**North Atlantic**	**53**
	U.S. Air Force C-124 wreckage found off Ireland.		
	Apr. 6	**Goleta, California**	**22**
	Southwest Airlines DC-3 crashed into Santa Ynez Mountains.		
	Apr. 8	**Charleston, West Virginia**	**20**
	Air Force C-47 crashed while trying to land in fog.		
	Apr. 25	**Key West, Fla.**	**43**
	Cuban airliner collided with U.S. Navy plane near city.		
	May 6	**Kirkland A.F. Base, New Mexico**	**23**
	A.F. B-36 bomber crashed and burned while landing in a sandstorm.		
	June 22	**Sanoye, Liberia**	**40**
	Pan American 4-engine Constellation crashed 4 mi. southwest of city.		
	June 30	**Rocky Mountain Nat'l Park, Col.**	**50**
	United DC-6 crashed into park.		
	July 12	**Aracaju, Brazil**	**28**
	Paulista Airlines plane crashed killing 5 Brazilian government officials.		
	July 21	**Gulf of Alaska**	**38**
	Canadian Pacific Airlines DC-4, bound for Tokyo, vanished.		
	Aug. 24	**Decoto, California**	**50**
	United DC-6B crashed near city.		
	Oct. 27	**Flores, Guatemala**	**28**
	Guatemalan C-47 crashed into the Peten jungles.		
	Nov. 13	**France**	**36**
	U.S. Air Force C-82 "Flying Boxcar" crashed on Mt. Dore.		
	Dec. 16	**Elizabeth, New Jersey**	**56**
	Non-scheduled Miami Airlines C-46 plunged into river after takeoff.		
	Dec. 29	**Salamanca, New York**	**26**
	Non-scheduled Continental Charters, Inc., C-46 crashed; 14 survived.		
	Dec. 29	**Phoenix, Arizona**	**28**
	USAF C-47 crashed on Armer Mountain northeast of city. On board were 19 West Point cadets on Christmas leave.		
1952	**Jan. 10**	**Wales**	**23**
	Aer Lingus DC-3 crashed into 2,860-foot Moel Siabod (Mt.).		
	Jan. 19	**British Columbia**	**36**
	Commercial DC-4 crashed into Pacific Ocean while attempting an emergency landing at Sandspit Airport; 4 survived.		
	†Jan. 22	**Elizabeth, New Jersey**	**23**
	American Airlines Convair crashed; victims included those on ground; on board was former War Secy. Robert Porter Patterson.		
	Feb. 11	**Elizabeth, New Jersey**	**33**
	National Airlines DC-6, marked third crash in two months.		
	Feb. 16	**Burgio, Sicily**	**34**
	Twin-engine British Viking crashed into 4,600-foot Monte Rosa.		
	Mar. 3	**Nice, France**	**37**
	Air France 4-engine Languedoc plane crashed; one of the victims, ballet dancer Harriet Toby of Brooklyn, N.Y.		
	Mar. 22	**Frankfurt, Germany**	**45**
	Royal Dutch Airlines DC-6 crashed in bad weather trying to land; 2 survived.		
	Mar. 27	**Moscow**	**70**
	Two Soviet planes collided over Tula Airport.		
	†Apr. 11	**San Juan, Puerto Rico**	**52**
	Pan Am DC-4 crashed.		
	Apr. 29	**Brazil**	**50**
	Pan Am Stratocruiser crashed in jungle to the north.		
	†Nov. 14	**Seoul, Korea**	**44**
	U.S. Air Force C-119 Flying Boxcar crashed into mountain 20 mi. east of city.		
	Nov. 23	**Alaska**	**52**
	U.S. Air Force plane crashed near Elmendorf Air Force Base.		
	Nov. 28	**Tacoma, Wash.**	**37**
	USAF C-54 crashed south of city trying to land blind in fog.		
	Dec. 6	**Bermuda**	**37**
	Cuban DC-4 crashed into Atlantic Ocean 2 mi. off coast; 4 survived.		
	†Dec. 20	**Moses Lake, Wash.**	**87**
	U.S. Air Force C-124 fell after takeoff and burned near city.		
	Dec. 25	**Teheran, Iran**	**23**
	Iranian Airways C-47 crashed while landing in fog.		
1953	**Jan. 5**	**Belfast, Ireland**	**27**
	British European Airways Viking Airliner struck a beacon pylon line and crashed while landing at Nutt's Corner; 8 survived.		
	Jan. 7	**Logan, Utah**	**40**
	Army chartered C-46 crashed into the Wasatch Mts.		
	Jan. 15	**Malta**	**25**
	Two RAF planes collided in the air over Mediterranean.		
	Feb. 2	**Gander, Newfoundland**	**39**
	Four-engine British York troop plane fell into sea.		
	Feb. 10	**Middle East**	**29**
	Egyptian C-46 crashed during sandstorm between Cairo and Suez Canal Zone.		
	Feb. 14	**Mobile, Ala.**	**45**
	Natl. Airlines DC-6 crashed into Gulf of Mexico southeast of city.		
	†Mar. 3	**Karachi, Pakistan**	**11**
	Canadian Pacific Comet Jet; first commercial jet to crash.		
	Mar. 18	**Newfoundland**	**33**
	USAF RG-36 and a USAF B-29 carrying all military personnel crashed.		
	Mar. 20	**Oakland, Calif.**	**35**
	Non-scheduled Transocean Airlines DC-4 crashed near city.		
	May 2	**Calcutta, India**	**45**
	BOAC Comet crashed during storm 30 mi. from city.		
	†June 18	**Tokyo, Japan**	**129**
	U.S. Air Force C-124 crashed and burned near city.		
	July 12	**Wake Island**	**58**
	Non-scheduled Transocean Airlines DC-6B crashed in ocean east of island.		
	Sept. 1	**McChord Air Force Base, Wash.**	**21**
	Regina Airlines DC-3 crashed on mountainside 25 mi. from base.		

Date		Place	Deaths	Description
	Sept. 16	**Albany, New York**	28	American Airlines Convair struck 2 transmission towers of radio station, crashed and burned.
	Sept. 28	**Louisville, Kentucky**	23	Army chartered Resort Airlines C-46 crashed at Standiford Field.
	Oct. 14	**Frankfort, Germany**	44	Belgian Sabena Airlines Convair crashed on takeoff at Rhein Main Airport.
	Oct. 29	**San Francisco, Calif.**	19	British Commonwealth Pacific Airlines DC-6 carrying concert pianist William Kapell, crashed killing all.
	Nov. 3	**Tarabuco, Bolivia**	28	Lloyd Aereo Boliviano Airliner crashed near city.
	Nov. 12	**Mugueta, Argentina**	20	Two Argentine AF planes collided in flight over city.
	Dec. 4	**Mt. Cabellero La Nueva, Spain**	23	Spanish Airline Bristol plane crashed on mountain 60 mi. north of Madrid; 10 survived.
1954	**Jan. 10**	**Elba & Monte Cristo Islands**	35	BOAC Comet jet airliner exploded in midair west of Italy.
	Jan. 11	**Manizales, Colombia**	23	Avianca Airliner crashed and burned in bad weather.
	Feb. 1	**Hokkaido, Japan**	85	AF C-46, carrying all servicemen, crashed into sea.
	Mar. 4	**French Alps**	20	AF C-47 crashed 9 miles from St. Etienne-de-Tinee.
	Mar. 13	**Singapore**	33	BOAC Constellation crashed and burned at airport.
	Apr. 8	**Mediterranean**	21	BOAC Comet jet airliner fell into sea near Capri.
	†Apr. 8	**Saskatchewan, Canada**	37	Trans Canada North Star and RCAF trainer collided over Moose Jaw.
	Apr. 23	**Vilgo Mtns., Argentina**	25	Argentine Airlines crashed into northwest mountains.
	July 2	**Salvador, Brazil**	24	Brazilian AF plane crashed in city.
	Aug. 9	**Terceira Island, Azores**	30	Colombian Avianca Constellation crashed into mountain.
	Aug. 27	**Ellsworth AFB, South Dakota**	24	Ten-engine B-36 bomber crashed while landing outside Rapid City.
	Sept. 5	**Shannon Airport, Ireland**	28	KLM Royal Dutch Super Constellation crashed into Shannon; 2 survived.
	Sept. 25	**Bittburg, West Germany**	29	Jet-plane fuel tank exploded near U.S. guided missile base.
	Oct. 31	**Between Md. and Azores**	42	U.S. Navy Super Constellation disappeared.
	Dec. 19	**New York City**	26	Italian Airlines DC-6B crashed while landing into Jamaica Bay; 6 survived.
	Dec. 24	**Prestwick, Scotland**	28	BOAC Stratocruiser crashed and burned at airport.
1955	**Feb. 13**	**Rome, Italy**	29	Belgian Sabena Airliner DC-6 disappeared in foggy weather.
	Mar. 8	**Puerto Vallarta, Mex.**	26	Compania Mexicana DC-3 crashed near town.
	Mar. 22	**Honolulu, Hawaii**	66	U.S. Navy DC-6 smashed into cliff near city.
	July 14	**Oaxaca State, Mex.**	22	Mexican Airlines DC-3 caught fire in air and crashed in mountains.
	July 17	**Chicago, Illinois**	22	Convair Braniff Airways plane crashed while making an instrument landing.
	Aug. 4	**Ft. Leonard Wood, Mo.**	30	Amer. Airlines Convair caught fire in flight and crashed during emergency landing.
	Aug. 6	**Voronezh, USSR**	25	Airliner carrying 10 women members of Norwegian Parliament crashed.
	Aug. 11	**Edelweiler, West Germany**	66	Two USAF Flying Boxcars collided; killed all G.I.s aboard.
	Oct. 6	**Laramie, Wyoming**	66	United DC-4 crashed into mountain west of city.
	Nov. 1	**Longmont, Colorado**	44	United Airlines DC-6B exploded and crashed; disaster caused by bomb planted by John G. Graham to collect insurance money on mother.
	Nov. 18	**Seattle, Wash.**	27	Non-scheduled Peninsula Air Transport DC-4 crashed and burned near city; 46 survived.
1956	**Jan. 18**	**Tatra Mts., Czechoslovakia**	22	Czech airliner crashed in mts. near Torysky; 4 injured.
	Feb. 17	**Miles, California**	40	Marine R5D crashed carrying marines.
	Feb. 18	**Valetta, Malta**	50	British Lancaster bomber crashed.
	Feb. 20	**Cairo, Egypt**	52	Transport Aeriens Intercontinentaux DC-6B crashed near city.
	Apr. 1	**Pittsburgh, Pa.**	22	TWA Martin 404 crashed and burned after takeoff.
	Apr. 15	**Prachuabkhiri Khan, Thailand**	30	Royal Thai AF plane accidentally dropped bomb into crowd.
	May 15	**Katmando, Nepal**	21	Indian Airlines DC-3 crashed into canyon while taking off.
	May 24	**Sierra de las Minas, Guatemala**	31	Guatemalan DC-3 crashed into mountains.
	June 20	**Asbury Park, New Jersey**	74	Venezuelan Super Constellation crashed in Atlantic south of New York City.
	June 24	**Kano Airport, Nigeria**	32	BOAC Argonaut crashed in rainstorm after takeoff 500 mi. north of Lagos.
	†June 30	**Grand Canyon, Arizona**	128	Trans World Airlines Super Constellation and United DC-7 collided in midair over canyon.
	July 13	**Fort Dix, New Jersey**	46	Military Air Transport C-118 crashed into wooded area during rainstorm. Plane believed to have been caught in a down-draft.
	Oct. 10	**Atlantic Ocean**	59	Military Air Transport C-118 disappeared in ocean 150 miles north of Azores.
	Nov. 15	**Salinda Grande, Nicaragua**	24	Aerovias Guest (Mexican) Airliner crashed near town.
	†Dec. 9	**Vancouver, Canada**	62	Trans-Canada North Star crashed in mountains near city.
†1957	**Feb. 1**	**La Guardia Airport, N.Y.**	22	Northeast Airlines DC-6A crashed on Rikers Island after taking off in snowstorm.
	Mar. 14	**Manchester, England**	22	British European Airways Viscount overshot runway at Ringway Airport; crashed into housing development and killed mother and child in one of 3 houses wrecked.

Date		Place	Deaths
	Mar. 17	**Mt. Bago, Philippines**	**26**
	C-47 twin-engine transport plane fell into mountain on fire, 22 mi. north of Cebu City. The Philippines President Ramon Magsaysay, 49, was a victim.		
	Mar. 21	**Pacific Ocean**	**67**
	United States Air Force Air Transport C-97 disappeared over sea.		
	Apr. 7	**Bage, Brazil**	**40**
	Brazilian Varig Airliner crashed outside city.		
	Apr. 8	**Biskra, Algeria**	**35**
	Air France DC-3 crashed shortly after takeoff.		
	Apr. 17	**Agaba, Jordan**	**27**
	RAF 2-engine Valetta transport crashed after takeoff.		
	May 1	**Blackbushe, England**	**32**
	Twin-engine Viking transport plane crashed.		
	May 9	**Madrid, Spain**	**37**
	Spanish Avianco plane crashed and burned at Barajas Airport.		
	July 1	**Chittagang to Dacca**	**24**
	Pakistani 2-engine Dakota Airliner disappeared.		
	†July 16	**Netherlands New Guinea**	**57**
	KLM Super Constellation plunged into sea.		
	Aug. 11	**Quebec, Canada**	**79**
	Maritime Central Airways DC-4 crashed outside city.		
	Aug. 15	**Copenhagen Harbor**	**23**
	Two-engine Ilyushin-14 plane struck a power station and crashed into harbor.		
	Oct. 3	**Mediterranean Sea**	**31**
	Lebanese C-46 Airliner caught fire and crashed 20 mi. southwest of Beirut.		
	Oct. 28	**Madrid, Spain**	**21**
	Spanish Airlines plane en route from Tangiers crashed.		
	Nov. 8	**Pacific Ocean**	**44**
	Pan American World Airways Stratocruiser vanished after passing point of no return between San Francisco and Honolulu.		
	Nov. 15	**Isle of Wight**	**43**
	British Aguilla Airways Solent Flying Boat crashed in flames; 15 survived.		
	Dec. 8	**Bolivar, Argentina**	**62**
	Aerolineas Argentina DC-4 crashed near city.		
1958	**Feb. 1**	**Los Angeles, California**	**48**
	MATS C-118 collided with USN P2V Neptune over city.		
	Feb. 6	**Munich, Germany**	**21**
	BEA twin-engine Elizabethan plane crashed and burned at airport; on board were 7 members of the Manchester United British championship soccer team.		
	Feb. 27	**Winter Hill, England**	**35**
	Bristol Wayfarer chartered plane crashed in fog; 7 survived.		
	Mar. 7	**Okinawa**	**25**
	Air collision of U.S. Marine Corps transport and Marine jet fighter.		
	Mar. 24	**Katmandu, Nepal**	**20**
	Indian Airlines DC-3 crashed near city.		
	Apr. 6	**Midland, Mich.**	**47**
	Capital Airlines Viscount plane crashed on landing at Tri-City Airport.		
	Apr. 7	**Guayaguil to Quito**	**32**
	Ecuadorean DC-3 crashed in jungle		
	Apr. 21	**Las Vegas, Nevada**	**49**
	United Airlines DC-7 collided with USAF jet outside city.		
	May 15	**New Delhi**	**20**
	Pakistan National Airways Convair plane crashed and burned after takeoff.		
	May 18	**Casablanca, Morocco**	**65**
	Belgian Sabena DC-6B crashed.		
	June 2	**Guadalajara**	**65**
	Four-engine Lockheed Constellation crashed in mountains during rainstorm.		
	June 16	**Curitiba, Parana State, Brazil**	**21**
	Brazilian Airliner crashed in storm; killed was Sen. Nerev Ramos, 69, acting president of Brazil in 1955-56.		
	Aug. 9	**Benghazi, Libya**	**35**
	Central African Airways Viscount plane crashed; 15 survived, 8 seriously injured.		
	†Aug. 14	**Atlantic Ocean**	**99**
	KLM Super Constellation plunged into sea 130 mi. west of Ireland.		
	†Aug. 15	**Nantucket, Mass.**	**24**
	Northeast Airlines Convair crashed on landing at airport; 9 survived. On board, dead, Gordon Dean, ex-chairman of the U.S. Atomic Energy Commission.		
	Oct. 15	**Venezuela**	**23**
	Venezuelan Airlines Super Constellation crashed 50 mi. northwest of Maracaibo.		
	Oct. 17	**Kanash, USSR**	**75**
	Soviet TU-104 jetliner crashed 400 miles northeast of Moscow.		
	Oct. 22	**Nettuno, Italy**	**31**
	Collision between British Super Viscount Airliner and Italian AF Saberjet fighter; the jet's pilot parachuted and was saved in sea.		
	Dec. 4	**Madrid, Spain**	**31**
	Spanish Avianco 4-engine plane crashed in heavy rain outside city.		
1959	**Jan. 11**	**Rio de Janeiro, Brazil**	**36**
	Lufthansa Super Constellation crashed 2 mi. from Galeo Airport; 3 survived.		
	Jan. 16	**Mar del Plata, Argentina**	**51**
	Two-engine Austrial Airlines Curtis Commando crashed before landing in a storm; 1 survived.		
	†Feb. 3	**New York City**	**66**
	American Lockheed Electra crashed into East River near city.		
	Mar. 10	**Para State, Brazil**	**23**
	Brazilian AF Catalina Flying Boat crashed in Amazon jungle.		
	Mar. 29	**Hailakandi, India**	**24**
	Indian Airlines DC-3 crashed northeast of city.		
	Apr. 17	**Guayamas, Gulf of California**	**26**
	Mexican twin-engine C-46 exploded in midair and crashed in small fishing village. One victim was an infant born 1½ hrs. before crash.		
	Apr. 29	**Cuenca, Spain**	**28**
	Spanish airliner crashed near city.		
	May 13	**Baltimore, Md.**	**31**
	Viscount turboprop plane crashed near city during storm.		
	June 26	**Milan, Italy**	**68**
	TWA Super Constellation exploded in storm near city.		
	Aug. 19	**Montseny Mt., Spain**	**32**
	British Transair 2-engine DC-3 crashed into mountain near Barcelona.		
	Sept. 23	**Sao Paulo, Brazil**	**20**
	Two-engine Brazilian Scandia crashed shortly after takeoff.		
	Sept. 24	**Paris, France**	**53**
	French 4-engine DC-7 of Transport Aeriens Intercontinentaux crashed and burned at takeoff from Bordeaux Airport; 12 survived.		
	Sept. 29	**Buffalo, Texas**	**34**
	Braniff Airways Electra exploded in midair.		
	Oct. 30	**Blue Ridge Mts., Va.**	**26**
	Piedmont Airlines DC-3 crashed into Mt. Afton; 1 survived.		

Date		Place	Deaths	
	Nov. 16	**Gulf of Mexico**	**42**	National Airlines DC-7B crashed 107 mi. southeast of New Orleans.
	Nov. 21	**Beirut, Lebanon**	**24**	Four-engine Ariana Airlines crashed at airport after takeoff.
	Dec. 1	**Bald Eagle Mt., Pa.**	**25**	Allegheny Airlines 2-engine plane crashed during snowstorm; 1 survived.
	Dec. 8	**Cartagena, Colombia**	**46**	C-46 Curtiss Commando of the private Sociedad Aeronautica Medellin line disappeared on way from San Andres Island.
	Dec. 13	**Tashkent to Kabul, Afghanistan**	**29**	Soviet 2-engine Ilyushin-14 disappeared.
1960	**Jan. 6**	**Wilmington, North Carolina**	**34**	National DC-6B exploded near city; bomb suspected.
	Jan. 18	**Richmond, Virginia**	**50**	Capital Viscount crashed into swampy ravine near city.
	†Jan. 19	**Ankara, Turkey**	**42**	Scandinavian Airlines French built 2-jet Caravelle crashed into hilltop near airport; 1 survived.
	Jan. 21	**Montego Bay, Jamaica**	**37**	Colombian Avianca Airliner exploded while landing; victims burned.
	Feb. 5	**La Paz, Bolivia**	**59**	Lloyd Aereo Boliviano DC-4 crashed near city.
	Feb. 25	**Rio de Janeiro, Brazil**	**61**	U.S. Navy transport collided in air with REAL DC-3 near city.
	Feb. 25	**Shannon, Ireland**	**33**	Alitalia 4-engine DC-7C airliner crashed just after takeoff; 19 survived.
	†Mar. 17	**Tell City, Indiana**	**63**	Northwest Airlines Lockheed Electra exploded in midair over city. Among dead was Chicago Superior Court Judge John A. Sbarbaro.
	Mar. 19	**Monteria, Colombia**	**25**	Sociedad Aeronautica de Medellin Airways DC-4 crashed on landing; 1 survived.
	Apr. 19	**Bogota, Colombia**	**33**	Colombian Lloyd Aereo plane crash landed at Eldorado Airport; 17 survived.
	Apr. 22	**Congo**	**35**	Belgian Sobelair DC-4 airliner crashed and burned on a mountaintop in the northwest.
	June 10	**MacKay, Queenland, Australia**	**29**	Trans-Australian airliner crashed; one victim was John F. O'Grady, U.S. Consul for Queenland.
	June 24	**Guanabara Bay, Brazil**	**51**	Brazilian Real Airlines Convair crashed in heavy fog.
	July 20	**Goma, Congo**	**34**	Belgian C-119, flying reinforcements to Congo, crashed and burned; 7 survived.
	July 27	**Chicago, Illinois**	**13**	First crash of a commercial helicopter; a Sikorsky S-58 crashed in suburbs outside city.
	Aug. 18	**Casablanca**	**27**	French naval bomber caught fire and exploded 100 mi. from city.
	Aug. 19	**Guam**	**78**	World Airways flight crashed shortly after takeoff.
	Aug. 29	**Dakar, Senegal**	**63**	Air France Super Constellation crashed into sea.
	Sept. 7	**Uruguay**	**31**	Argentine Airline plane en route to Asuncion, Paraguay, exploded in air and crashed.
	Sept. 19	**Agafia, Guam**	**78**	World DC-6B exploded.
	Sept. 22	**Pacific Ocean**	**29**	U.S. Marine Corps DC-6 transport crashed in ocean 180 mi. south of Okinawa.
	Sept. 26	**Moscow**	**31**	Austrian National Airlines Vickers Viscount crashed on landing at airport; 6 survived.
	†Oct. 4	**Boston, Massachusetts**	**61**	Eastern Electra crashed after takeoff into harbor.
	Nov. 7	**Quito, Ecuador**	**37**	Ecuadorian airliner crashed into mountain 45 mi. from city. On board Ecuadorian Congress Deputies Pedro Isais and Carlos Luis Perez.
	Nov. 24	**Mindoro Island, Philippines**	**33**	Philippine Airlines DC-3 crashed into mountain.
	Dec. 11	**San Andres de Giles, Argentina**	**32**	Argentine Air Ministry airliner exploded and burned.
	†Dec. 16	**New York City**	**136**	United DC-8 and TWA Super Constellation collided in midair over Staten Island; 6 persons on ground were also killed.
	†Dec. 17	**Munich, Germany**	**53**	U.S. Air Force C-131 Convair crashed into street car also killing pedestrians.
	Dec. 22	**Manila, Philippines**	**28**	Philippine Airlines plane crashed shortly after takeoff. Pres. Carlos P. Garcia ordered all night flights suspended.
1961	**Jan. 3**	**Vassa, Finland**	**25**	Finnair DC-3 Airliner crashed on way to Helsinki.
	Feb. 15	**Berg, Belgium**	**73**	Sabena Airlines Boeing 707 crashed killing 18 American figure skaters and civilians on ground.
	Mar. 28	**Nuremburg, West Germany**	**52**	Czechoslovak Ilyushin-18 crashed.
	May 10	**Ghadames, Libya**	**79**	Air France Starliner crashed in Sahara Desert.
	May 30	**Lisbon, Portugal**	**62**	Royal Dutch KLM crashed shortly after takeoff.
	†July 12	**Casablanca**	**72**	Czechoslovak Ilyushin-18 crashed after hitting power line.
	July 19	**Azul, Brazil**	**67**	Argentine Airlines DC-6 crashed.
	Aug. 9	**North Sea**	**39**	Cunard Eagle Airways Viking with 34 English school boys crashed off Norway.
	Sept. 1	**Hinsdale, Illinois**	**78**	TWA Constellation crashed in field near Chicago.
	Sept. 10	**Shannon, Ireland**	**83**	President Airlines DC-6 charter crashed.
	Sept. 12	**Rabat, Morocco**	**77**	Air France Caravelle crashed.
	†Sept. 17	**Chicago, Illinois**	**37**	Northwest Electra struck high tension line and crashed.
	Nov. 1	**Recife, Brazil**	**49**	Brazilian Panair Do Brasil DC-7C Airliner crashed and burned after hitting hillside outside city.
	†Nov. 8	**Richmond, Virginia**	**77**	Imperial Airlines Constellation carrying 74 Army recruits crashed in woods outside city.
	Nov. 23	**Sao Paulo, Brazil**	**52**	Argentine Comet jetliner crashed 4 mi. after takeoff from Viracopos Airport.
	Dec. 19	**Seville, Spain**	**30**	A photo plane crashed into crowd after hitting high tension wire.
	Dec. 22	**Ankara, Turkey**	**27**	British European Airways Comet 4B Jetliner exploded and burned 4 minutes after takeoff; 7 survived.

Date | **Place** | **Deaths**

1962

Feb. 27 — Margarita Island, Caribbean — 22
Avensa Airlines F-27 crashed into mountain on island.

Mar. 1 — New York City — 95
American Boeing 707 crashed after takeoff into Jamaica Bay.

†Mar. 4 — Doula, Cameroon — 111
Trans-African British Caledonian DC-7C crashed in jungle.

Mar. 16 — Pacific Ocean — 107
Flying Tiger Super Constellation charter vanished.

May 22 — Centerville, Iowa — 45
Continental Boeing 707 exploded in flight.

†June 3 — Paris, France — 130
Air France Boeing 707 crashed after takeoff.

†June 22 — Guadeloupe, West Indies — 113
Air France Boeing 707 crashed during storm.

July 7 — Bombay, India — 94
Alitalia DC-8 crashed in storm 50 mi. northeast of city.

July 19 — Thailand — 26
United Arab Airline Comet IV jet crashed into a teakwood forest 50 mi. north of Bangkok.

July 23 — Honolulu, Hawaii — 27
Canadian Pacific Britannia Airliner crashed in flames on return for propeller repairs after takeoff 20 minutes earlier.

Sept. 10 — Mount Kit Carson, Wash. — 44
Strategic Air Command KC-135 crashed into canyon 25 mi. northeast of Spokane.

Nov. 26 — Paraibuna, Brazil — 27
Viacao Aeren de Sao Paulo collided with private plane over mountainous area 60 mi. northeast of Sao Paulo.

†Nov. 27 — Lima, Peru — 97
Varig Airlines Boeing 707 crashed and burned.

Dec. 14 — Brazil — 50
Panair Do Brasil Constellation crashed in Amazon jungle.

1963

Feb. 1 — Ankara, Turkey — 95
Turkish Air Force C-47 and Lebanese Viscount collided and crashed.

†Feb. 12 — Everglades, Florida — 43
Northwest Boeing 720-B crashed.

Mar. 2 — Malalag, Mindanao — 27
Philippine DC-3 Airliner crashed on a mountain slope south of city.

Mar. 15 — Mount Tacora, Chile — 40
Lloyd Aero Boliviano DC-6 crashed on slope 60 mi. northeast of Arica.

May 3 — Sao Paulo, Brazil — 41
Cruzeiro do Sul Airline Convair crashed into residential district minutes after takeoff. (A fire truck killed 4 pedestrians on way to disaster); 8 survived.

May 5 — Mount Cameroon, Cameroon — 54
Four-engine Air Afrique DC-6 airliner crashed half-way up 13,000-foot mountain; 1 survived.

May 12 — Nawa Village, Nile Delta — 34
United Arab Airlines DC-3 crashed shortly after takeoff from Cairo Airport.

†June 3 — Pacific Ocean — 101
Northwest DC-7 charter crashed off Alaska.

June 16 — Southeast Hungary — 31
Rumanian Ilyushin-14 crashed near villages of Tokomlos and Bekessamson.

June 26 — Sennelager, West Germany — 38
Belgian transport plane crashed; 9 parachuted to safety.

July 28 — Bombay, India — 62
United Arab Comet wreckage found near city.

Sept. 2 — Zurich, Switzerland — 80
Swissair Caravelle crashed after takeoff.

Date | **Place** | **Deaths**

Sept. 12 — Perpignan, France — 40
Two-engine French Viking Airliner crashed in the Pyrenees.

†Nov. 29 — Montreal, Canada — 118
Trans World Airlines DC-8F crashed after takeoff.

†Dec. 8 — Elkton, Maryland — 81
Pan Am Boeing 707 crashed into field near city.

1964

Jan. 9 — Zarate, Argentina — 28
Argentine Ala Airlines DC-3 crashed 6 mi. east of city; 3 survived.

Feb. 25 — New Orleans, Louisiana — 58
Eastern DC-8 crashed into Lake Pontchartrain.

†Feb. 29 — Innsbruck, Austria — 83
British Eagle International Britannia turboprop crashed near city.

Mar. 1 — Lake Tahoe, California — 85
Paradise Airlines Constellation crashed in snowstorm.

Apr. 17 — Santa Rosa, Peru — 46
Argentine Military DC-4 crashed into a sand dune.

May 7 — Concord, California — 44
Pacific F-27 crashed near city; a tape recording indicated pilot was shot.

May 8 — Persian Gulf — 49
Middle-East Airlines Caravelle crashed during sandstorm.

May 11 — Philippines — 75
U.S. MATS C-135 Stratolifter crashed at Clark AFB; 8 survived.

June 20 — Fengyuan, Taiwan — 57
Chinese Civil Air Patrol plane crashed outside city.

July 9 — Newport, Tennessee — 39
United Viscount crashed near city.

Sept. 4 — Nova Caledonia Mt., Brazil — 39
Four-engine Viscount VASP crashed into mountain during rainstorm 60 mi. northeast of Rio.

†Oct. 2 — Granada, Spain — 80
Union Transports Africain DC-6 crashed near city.

†Nov. 23 — Rome, Italy — 44
Trans World Airlines Boeing 707 crashed.

1965

Jan. 16 — Wichita, Kansas — 30
Military plane crashed into homes.

†Feb. 6 — Chile — 87
Chilean Linea Aerea Nacionale DC-6B crashed into Andes Mountains.

†Feb. 8 — Atlantic Ocean — 84
Eastern DC-7B crashed near New York's Kennedy Airport.

Mar. 31 — Straits of Gibraltar — 50
Iberia Convair charter crashed.

Apr. 10 — Damascus — 54
Royal Jordanian plane crashed outside city.

Apr. 14 — Jersey, Channel Islands — 26
Jersey Airlines DC-3 crashed into trees while attempting to land in fog; 1 survived.

May 5 — Santa Cruz de Tenerife, Canary Islands — 23
Iberian Airlines Super Constellation crashed while landing in thick fog at Los Rodeos Airport; 26 survived.

†May 20 — Cairo, Egypt — 124
Pakistan International Boeing 707 crashed at airport.

June 25 — El Toro, California — 84
U.S. Air Force C-135 hit mountain and crashed after takeoff from Los Angeles.

July 6 — Oxford, England — 41
British Royal Air Force Hastings transport plane crashed into field 5 mi. outside city.

July 8 — 100 Mile House, British Columbia — 52
Canadian Pacific DC-6B crashed.

Aug. 16 — Lake Michigan — 30
United Boeing 727 plunged into lake near Chicago.

Date		Place	Deaths
	Aug. 24	**Hong Kong**	**58**
	U.S. Marine Corps transport crashed after takeoff.		
	Sept. 7	**Montserrat, West Indies**	**30**
	Pan American Airways Airliner crashed and burned on island.		
	Sept. 16	**Quangngai, South Vietnam**	**39**
	Air Vietnam Dakota Airliner crashed and exploded.		
	Oct. 27	**London, England**	**36**
	British European Airways Airliner crashed on landing at London Airport.		
	Nov. 8	**Cincinnati, Ohio**	**58**
	American Airlines Boeing 727 crashed in storm near city. (SEE TWA, Nov. 20, 1967)		
	Nov. 11	**Salt Lake City, Utah**	**42**
	United Boeing 727 crashed and burned while landing.		
1966	**Jan. 14**	**Caribbean**	**51**
	Colombian DC-4 crashed into sea minutes after takeoff from Cartenga Airport; 10 survived.		
	Jan. 22	**Haiti's Dutchiti Region**	**30**
	Haitian airliner crashed en route to Les Cayes.		
	†Jan. 24	**French Alps, Switzerland**	**117**
	Air India Boeing 707 crashed into Mont Blanc.		
	†Feb. 4	**Tokyo, Japan**	**133**
	All-Nippon Boeing 727 plunged into Tokyo Bay.		
	Feb. 7	**Himalayas Banihal Pass, Kashmir**	**37**
	Indian F-27 crashed en route to New Delhi.		
	†Feb. 17	**Moscow**	**48**
	Soviet Aeroflot TU-114 crashed on takeoff from Moscow's International Airport after skidding on snowbank.		
	†Mar. 4	**Tokyo, Japan**	**64**
	Canadian Pacific DC-8 crashed on landing.		
	†Mar. 5	**Mount Fuji, Japan**	**124**
	BOAC Boeing 707 caught fire and crashed into mountain near Honshu.		
	Apr. 22	**Ardmore, Oklahoma**	**82**
	Military chartered Electra crashed during storm.		
	Apr. 27	**Andes Mountains, Peru**	**49**
	Lansa Constellation crashed in mountains.		
	Aug. 6	**Falls City, Nebraska**	**42**
	Braniff BAC-III jetliner crashed near city.		
	†Sept. 1	**Ljubljana, Yugoslavia**	**97**
	Britannia Airways Ltd. 102 turboprop crashed during landing.		
	Nov. 13	**Shikoku, Japan**	**50**
	Japanese All-Nippon YS-11 crashed into Inland Sea while landing.		
	Nov. 21	**South Arabian Desert**	**28**
	Aden DC-1 Dakota crashed 130 miles east of Aden.		
	†Nov. 24	**Bratislava, Czechoslovakia**	**82**
	TABSO Bulgarian Ilyushin-18 crashed in Carpathian Mountains.		
	Dec. 24	**South Vietnam**	**129**
	U.S. military chartered CL-44 crashed into village; many villagers also killed.		
1967	**Feb. 16**	**Celebes, Indonesia**	**21**
	Garuda Indonesian Electra exploded minutes after landing; 9 survived.		
	Mar. 5	**Monrovia, Liberia**	**48**
	Brazilian Varig DC-8 crashed into a house while landing during heavy fog; 53 survived.		
	Mar. 5	**Kenton, Ohio**	**38**
	Lake Airlines Convair 580 crashed in storm near city.		
	†Mar. 9	**Dayton, Ohio**	**26**
	Trans World Airlines DC-9 and twin-engine Beechcraft collided in air.		
	Mar. 30	**New Orleans, Louisiana**	**18**
	Delta Airlines DC-8 crashed into motel.		
	Apr. 8	**Seoul, Korea**	**55**
	South Korean Air Force C-47 struck church dome and crashed into slum section; 41 persons on ground perished.		
	Apr. 20	**Nicosia, Cyprus**	**126**
	Swiss Globe Britannia turboprop charter crashed while landing.		
	June 3	**French Pyrenees**	**88**
	British Air Ferry Ltd. DC-6 charter crashed into Mont Canigou.		
	†June 4	**Stockport, England**	**72**
	British Midland charter DC-4 crashed.		
	June 23	**Camp Le Jeune**	**22**
	Two U.S. Marine helicopters collided.		
	June 23	**Blossburg, Pennsylvania**	**34**
	Mohawk Airlines BAC-111 crashed near city.		
	June 30	**Hong Kong**	**24**
	Thai International Caravelle jet crashed into Kowloon Bay during heavy rainstorm; 56 survived.		
	†July 19	**Hendersonville, North Carolina**	**82**
	Piedmont Boeing 727 collided with Cessna 310 outside city.		
	July 19	**Tananarive, Malagasy**	**41**
	Air Madagascar DC-4 crashed after takeoff from Ivato Airport.		
	Sept. 5	**Gander, Newfoundland**	**34**
	Soviet-built Ilyushin 18 Czech crashed minutes after takeoff; 35 survived.		
	†Oct. 12	**Turkey**	**66**
	British European Cypriot Mark IV Comet crashed into sea off coast.		
	Nov. 4	**Fernhurst, England**	**37**
	Iberia Caravelle crashed during rainstorm 40 mi. southwest of London.		
	†Nov. 20	**Cincinnati, Ohio**	**68**
	Trans World Airlines Convair 880 crashed outside city during snowstorm.		
	Dec. 8	**Huanuco, Peru**	**68**
	Peruvian Faucett DC-4 crashed outside city.		
1968	**Feb. 16**	**Taipei, Taiwan**	**22**
	Civil Air Transport 727 crashed into tea plantation. Pilots of plane faced manslaughter charges; first time commercial pilots were ever charged.		
	Mar. 5	**Guadeloupe, West Indies**	**63**
	Air France Boeing 707 crashed.		
	Mar. 24	**Atlantic Ocean**	**61**
	Irish International Viscount crashed off Wales.		
	Apr. 8	**Aysen Province, Chile**	**36**
	Chilean DC-3 crashed into forest.		
	†Apr. 20	**Windhock, South-West Africa**	**123**
	South African Boeing 707 crashed outside city. (SEE Scandinavian Airlines)		
	†May 3	**Dawson, Texas**	**88**
	Braniff International Electra crashed during storm.		
	May 22	**Paramount, California**	**23**
	Los Angeles Airways helicopter, coming from Disneyland, crashed.		
	Aug. 9	**Pfaffenhofen, Germany**	**48**
	British Eagles Airways Viscount crashed on West Germany Autobahn.		
	Aug. 10	**Charleston, West Virginia**	**35**
	Piedmont Airlines turboprop crash landed just short of runway; 2 survived.		
	Aug. 14	**Compton, California**	**21**
	Second crash of L.A. helicopter shuttling Disneyland visitors.		
	Sept. 3	**Burgas, Bulgaria**	**50**
	Bulair Ilyushin-18 crashed.		

Date		Place	Deaths
	Sept. 11	**Nice, France**	**95**
	Air France Caravelle crashed off French Riviera.		
	Sept. 28	**Nigeria**	**57**
	Nigerian DC-4 crashed between Lagos and Port Harcourt.		
	Oct. 21	**Central Highlands, Vietnam**	**24**
	U.S. C-47 crashed 175 mi. northeast of Saigon.		
	Oct. 25	**Moose Mt., New Hampshire**	**32**
	Northeast Airlines crashed and burned on mt.; 10 survived.		
	Dec. 2	**Anchorage, Alaska**	**39**
	Wien Consolidated Airliner crashed southwest after takeoff.		
	Dec. 12	**Caracas, Venezuela**	**51**
	Pan Am Boeing 707 crashed.		
	Dec. 24	**Bradford, Pa.**	**20**
	Allegheny Airlines propjet crashed while landing; 27 survived.		
	Dec. 27	**Chicago, Illinois**	**26**
	Two-engine Convair of North Central Airlines crashed into a hangar at O'Hare. Eight on ground hurt; 27 survived.		
1969	**Jan. 2**	**Southern Taiwan**	**24**
	China Airlines DC-3 crashed into mountain.		
	Jan. 5	**Gatwick, England**	**50**
	Ariana Afghan Boeing 727 crashed.		
	Jan. 18	**Los Angeles, Calif.**	**38**
	United Airlines B-727 crashed shortly after takeoff.		
	Mar. 16	**La Coruba, Venezuela**	**155**
	Venezuelan DC-9 crashed into nearby suburb of Maracaibo after takeoff; tape recording indicated pilot had been shot.		
	Mar. 20	**Aswan, Egypt**	**91**
	United Arab IL-18 crashed while landing.		
	Apr. 3	**Zawoja, Poland**	**53**
	Polish Airlines plane crashed outside city.		
	Apr. 16	**Kinshasa, Congo**	**45**
	Congolese Air Force plane crashed while attempting emergency landing at Ndjiii Airport.		
	Apr. 21	**Khulna, East Pakistan**	**44**
	Indian Airlines Fokker Friendship crashed during storm.		
	June 4	**Monterrey, Mexico**	**79**
	Mexican Airways Boeing 727 crashed into mountain near city.		
	July 11	**Katmandu**	**35**
	Royal Nepal DC-3 crashed after takeoff.		
	July 26	**Algerian Desert**	**35**
	Chartered twin-jet Caravelle crashed 200 mi. south of Algiers; 2 survived.		
	†Aug. 9	**Indianapolis, Indiana**	**83**
	Allegheny DC-9 collided with a student's plane outside city near Shelbyville, Indiana.		
	Sept. 9	**Eastern Colombia**	**32**
	Twin-engine C-47 military transport crashed in mountainous area.		
	Sept. 12	**Manila, Philippines**	**45**
	Philippine jetliner crashed outside city.		
	Sept. 14	**Andes Mountains**	**20**
	Twin-engine Otter Aircraft disappeared 560 mi. south of Santiago, Chile.		
	Sept. 20	**Danang, Vietnam**	**77**
	Air Vietnam DC-4 crashed outside city.		
	Sept. 21	**Mexico City, Mexico**	**27**
	Mexicana Boeing 727 jet crash landed in rain; 60 survived.		
	Sept. 26	**La Paz, Bolivia**	**74**
	Lloyd Aereo Boliviano DC-6 crashed in the Andes outside city.		
	Nov. 20	**Iju, Nigeria**	**87**
	Nigerian DC-10 crashed near city.		
	Dec. 3	**Caracas, Venezuela**	**62**
	Air France Boeing 707 crashed shortly after takeoff.		
	Dec. 8	**Athens, Greece**	**92**
	Olympia Airways DC-6B crashed during storm outside city.		
1970	**Jan. 12**	**Athens, Greece**	**23**
	Greek Army transport crashed into mountain 43 mi. from city.		
	Jan. 13	**Western Samoa**	**30**
	Polynesian Airlines DC-3 crashed after takeoff from Faleolo Airport.		
	Jan. 13	**Lima, Peru**	**28**
	Faucett DC-3 crashed into mountain north of city.		
	Feb. 4	**Asuncion, Paraguay**	**38**
	Argentine Airlines plane crashed en route to Buenos Aires.		
	Feb. 15	**Santo Domingo, Caribbean**	**102**
	Dominican DC-9 crashed into sea after takeoff.		
	Apr. 1	**Casablanca, Morocco**	**61**
	Royal Air Force Maroc Caravelle jetliner crashed.		
	May 2	**Virgin Islands**	**23**
	Dutch Antilles jetliner ditched in heavy rain; 35 hospitalized.		
	†July 3	**Barcelona, Spain**	**112**
	Dan-Air British charter Comet jet crashed while landing.		
	†July 5	**Toronto, Canada**	**108**
	Air Canada DC-8 crashed north of airport.		
	July 18	**Iceland**	**23**
	Soviet Antonov An-22 disappeared off coast.		
	Aug. 6	**Islamabad, Pakistan**	**30**
	Pakistan turboprop crashed on takeoff.		
	Aug. 9	**Cuzco, Peru**	**100**
	Peruvian Electra crashed into a hill after takeoff.		
	Aug. 31	**Assam State, India**	**39**
	Indian Airlines Fokker Friendship wreckage was found; no survivors.		
	Oct. 2	**Silver Plume, Colorado**	**30**
	Martin 404 crashed into Rocky Mountains; on board were part of Wichita State football team.		
	Oct. 8	**Formosa**	**43**
	Wreckage of U.S. Air Force Hercules transport found.		
	Nov. 14	**Huntington, West Virginia**	**75**
	Southern Airways DC-9 crashed into mountains while landing; on board was the Marshall University football team.		
	Nov. 27	**Anchorage, Alaska**	**47**
	DC-8 troop carrier, heading for Vietnam, crashed during takeoff.		
	Dec. 31	**Leningrad**	**99**
	Soviet Aeroflot Ilyushin-18 crashed on takeoff.		
1971	**Jan. 1**	**Algiers**	**30**
	French Nord 262 crashed in Mediterranean.		
	Jan. 20	**Lima, Peru**	**31**
	Peruvian Air Force C-46 crashed into mountainside 100 miles east of city.		
	Jan. 21	**Privas, France**	**21**
	French Nord 202 crashed in snowstorm west of city.		
	Apr. 15	**Basa Air Field, Philippines**	**39**
	Philippine military plane crashed shortly after takeoff; 3-year-old child sole survivor.		
	May 23	**Belgrade, Yugoslavia**	**78**
	Yugoslavian civil Tupolex-134A crashed on landing at Rijeka Airport.		
	June 6	**San Gabriel Mountains, Calif.**	**50**
	Hughes Air West CD-9 collided with Marine Phantom F-4 fighter jet; jet's pilot parachuted to safety.		
	June 7	**Tweed-New Haven, Connecticut**	**28**
	Allegheny Convair 880 crashed on landing; 3 survived.		

Date | Place | Deaths

July 3 | **Hakodate, Japan** | **68**
Japanese airliner crash landed in fog on a mountainside near city.

†July 30 | **Morioka, Japanese Alps** | **162**
All-Nippon Boeing 727 collided with Japanese Air Force F-86. Pilot of F-86 parachuted to safety.

Aug. 11 | **Irkutsk** | **97**
Soviet Aeroflot Tupolev-104 crashed at Irkutsk Airport.

Aug. 18 | **Pegnitz, West Germany** | **37**
U.S. Army Chinook helicopter exploded in air.

†Sept. 4 | **Juneau, Alaska** | **109**
Alaska Airlines Boeing 727 crashed into mountain near city.

Oct. 2 | **Ghent, Belgium** | **63**
British European Airways Vanguard exploded.

†Nov. 9 | **Ligurian Sea** | **51**
British Royal Air Force C-130 Hercules crashed near Leghorn, Italy.

Dec. 21 | **Sofia, Bulgaria** | **28**
Bulgarian airliner crashed shortly after takeoff.

Dec. 24 | **Peru** | **91**
Peruvian airliner crashed in jungle; 1 survived.

1972 **Jan. 6** | **Yucatan Peninsula, Mexico** | **23**
Mexican DC-6 exploded while attempting an emergency landing in jungle near Bacalar.

†Jan. 7 | **Ibiza, Spain** | **107**
Iberia Caravelle jet crashed into mountainside while approaching Ibiza Airport.

Jan. 21 | **Andes Mountains, No. Colombia** | **35**
Satena DC-3 crashed and burned in mountains.

Jan. 21 | **Bogota, Colombia** | **20**
Uraca turboprop crashed on takeoff in rainstorm.

Jan. 26 | **Czechoslovakia** | **26**
Yugoslav airliner exploded. Sabotage believed reason because Premier Dsemal Bijedic was thought to be on plane; 1 survived.

†Mar. 14 | **Kalba, Arabia** | **112**
Tjaereborg Airlines charter exploded to bits 60 mi. east of Dubai.

Mar. 18 | **Aden, S. Yemen** | **21**
Yugoslav DC-9 crashed into mountain near city.

Apr. 18 | **Addis Ababa, Ethiopia** | **41**
East Africa Airways VC-10 struck a farm house. The cause still remains a complete mystery; 66 survived.

†May 5 | **Palermo, Italy** | **115**
Alitalia DC-8 jetliner struck a mountainside outside city.

May 18 | **Kharkov, USSR** | **108**
Soviet plane crashed in Ukraine.

May 21 | **Lonbito, Angola** | **20**
Angola airliner crashed while attempting to land.

†June 14 | **New Delhi, India** | **87**
Japan Airlines DC-6 caught fire in midair as it attempted landing at Palam Airport; 6 survived.

†June 15 | **Central Highlands, Vietnam** | **81**
Cathay Pacific jetliner crashed in mountains.

†June 18 | **London, England** | **118**
British European Trident Airways airliner crashed into field minutes after takeoff from Heathrow Airport; Britain's worst crash to this date.

July 29 | **Las Palomas Mts., Colombia** | **38**
Two Colombian airliners collided in midair.

Aug. 12 | **Mekong Delta, Vietnam** | **30**
U.S. transport plane crashed while taking off from Soctrang Airport.

†Aug. 14 | **East Berlin, Germany** | **156**
Ilyushin-62 chartered by Interflug, the East German state airline, exploded after takeoff from Schonefeld Airport.

Aug. 18 | **Bay of Bengal, Nepal** | **25**
Burma Airlines plane crashed.

Aug. 27 | **Canaima, Venezuela** | **24**
DC-3 excursion flight crashed 190 mi. southwest of Caracas.

Sept. 13 | **Dkulikhel, Nepal** | **31**
Nepalese paratroop plane crashed.

Sept. 24 | **Sacramento, California** | **22**
Korean war vintage F-86 Supersabre jet skidded on takeoff from the Executive Airport and smashed into an ice cream parlor. In the parlor were 100 birthday celebrants; 22 were killed. A few weeks earlier the plane was judged unflyable; pilot lived.

Oct. 4 | **Sochi, USSR** | **100**
Ilyushin-18 plane crashed near Black Sea resort.

Oct. 13 | **Andes Mountains, Chile** | **29**
Plane carrying 45 people vanished in mountains; 16 survivors were found Dec. 22-23 and 8 others died in an avalanche.

Oct. 14 | **Kranaya Polyana, USSR** | **176**
Aeroflot Ilyushin-62 airliner crashed while landing in heavy rain three mi. from Sheremeteo Airport. Worst air disaster in history to this date. (Russians refused to confirm information.)

Oct. 21 | **Athens, Greece** | **34**
Olympic Airways crashed into sea minutes before landing; 19 survived.

Oct. 28 | **Clermont-Ferrand, France** | **48**
French domestic airliner crashed into hill 38 mi. outside city; 20 survived.

Oct. 30 | **Bari, Italy** | **27**
Aero Transporti Italiani Airliner crashed 12 mi. west of city.

Nov. 4 | **Ploudiv, Bulgaria** | **34**
Bulgarian Airlines, Russian-made Ilyushin-14 crashed into mountainside.

Nov. 20 | **North Pescadores Is.** | **25**
Taiwan airliner crashed.

†Dec. 3 | **Santa Cruz de Tenerite, Canary Islds.** | **155**
Spantax Airlines Convair 990-A Coronado exploded and burst into flames shortly after takeoff from Los Rodeos Airport.

†Dec. 8 | **Chicago, Illinois** | **45**
United Airlines Boeing 737 jet crashed into a row of houses 1 mile from Midway Airport. Among the dead was Mrs. E. Howard Hunt, wife of a defendant in the Watergate bugging case; 16 survived.

Dec. 8 | **Himalayas** | **33**
Pakistani International Airlines plane crashed into the foothills of mountains.

Dec. 29 | **Florida Everglades** | **99**
Eastern Airlines L-1011 Tri-Star jetliner crashed 17 mi. west of Miami. First crash of jumbo jet; 77 survived.

1973 **Jan. 22** | **Kano, Nigeria** | **176**
Boeing 707 jet returning 200 Nigerian Moslems from a pilgrimage to Mecca, crashed and exploded in thick fog; 24 survived.

Jan. 29 | **Kyrenia Mountains, N. Cyprus** | **38**
Egyptian Airlines Ilyushin-18 jet crashed.

Feb. 19 | **Prague, Czechoslovakia** | **66**
Soviet Tupolev 154 jetliner crashed about 200 feet short of runway at Prague Int. Airport; 34 survived.

Mar. 3 | **Aden, Southern Yemen** | **25**
Twenty-five Southern Yemen diplomats, including Foreign Minister Mohammed Saleh Aulagi, were killed when plane crashed 300 miles north of Yemen.

Mar. 5 | **Moscow** | **25**
Soviet built Ilyushin-18 owned by Bulgaria's Balkan Airlines crashed while landing at Sderemetyvo Airport.

Date		Place	Deaths
	Mar. 19	**Central Highlands, Vietnam**	**62**
	Air Vietnam passenger plane crashed while approaching Ban Me Thout Airport.		
	Apr. 10	**Basel, Switzerland**	**104**
	British airliner crashed in heavy snowstorm while attempting to land. Plane's wing tip struck a tree; 39 survived.		
	Apr. 30	**Nantes, West France**	**68**
	DC-9 Iberia Airliner collided in midair with another Spanish plane.		
	May 25	**Southern Siberia**	**40**
	Soviet airliner crashed near China border. Gunfight with would-be hijacker was blamed.		
	May 31	**Palam, New Delhi**	**48**
	Indian Airlines jet crashed and burned while approaching airport; 17 survived.		
	June 1	**Sao Luiz, Brazil**	**23**
	Brazilian Caravelle jetliner crashed and burned on landing.		
	June 20	**Mexico's Pacific Coast**	**27**
	Mexican DC-9 hit a mountain peak and exploded.		
	July 11	**Paris, France**	**122**
	Brazilian Boeing 707 airliner on fire attempted to land at Orly Field but crashed and burned. Most dead suffocated from smoke; 12 survived.		
	July 23	**St. Louis, Missouri**	**38**
	Ozark Airlines jet crash landed during thunderstorm. One survivor believed lightning had struck plane; 6 survived.		
	July 23	**Papeete, Tahiti**	**78**
	Pan American World Airways Boeing 707 jetliner crashed within 90 seconds after taking off; 1 survived.		
	†July 31	**Boston, Massachusetts**	**88**
	Delta Airlines flight 723 crashed on landing at fog-bound Logan Airport; 1 survived.		
	Dec. 23	**Mt. Mallaytine, Tangiers**	**106**
	Belgian Caravelle struck mt.		
†1974	**Jan. 1**	**Turin, Italy**	**39**
	Itavia Airline twin-engine airliner crashed on landing; 4 survived.		
	†Jan. 10	**Florevcia, Colombia**	**40**
	Satena turboprop caught fire and crashed on an Andean foothill.		
	†Jan. 26	**Izmir, Turkey**	**63**
	Turkish Fokker F-28 crashed on takeoff from Cumaovasi Airport.		
	†Jan. 31	**Pago, Pago, Samoa**	**96**
	Pan American World Airways crashed on landing.		
	†Mar. 3	**Paris, France**	**346**
	Turkish DC-10 crashed shortly after takeoff from Orly Airport; largest air crash in aviation history.		
	†Mar. 13	**Bishop, Calif.**	**36**
	Sierra Pacific twin-engine Convair crashed minutes after takeoff.		
	†Apr. 4	**Francistown, Botswana**	**77**
	Wenela DC-4 Skymaster crashed immediately after takeoff.		
	Apr. 27	**Bali, Indonesia**	**107**
	Pan American 707 jet crashed while landing.		
	Apr. 27	**Leningrad, Russia**	**108**
	Soviet Ilyushin-18 crashed shortly after takeoff.		
	May 2	**Andes Mountains**	**22**
	Ecuadorean airliner crashed on a local flight.		
	June 28	**Cambodia**	**20**
	Civilian passenger plane crashed on takeoff.		
	June 9	**Cucuta, Colombia**	**43**
	Colombian aircraft crashed into mountain.		
	Aug. 13	**Upper Volta**	**47**
	Air Mali airliner crashed on highway after running out of gas.		
	Aug. 14	**Maragatita, Caribbean**	**49**
	Venezuelan aircraft crashed from violent winds.		
	Sept. 7	**Sumatra**	**35**
	Indonesia Airways crashed on runway in a storm.		
	Sept. 8	**Ionian Sea**	**88**
	Trans World Airlines crashed off Greece.		
	Sept. 11	**Charlotte, N.C.**	**71**
	Eastern DC-9 crashed into woods.		
	Sept. 18	**Ponta Pora, Brazil**	**21**
	Brazilian Air Force transport plane exploded.		
	Oct. 29	**Melville Island, Canada**	**32**
	Panarctic Oils Ltd. Lockheed Electra crashed short of runway.		
	Dec. 4	**Colombo, Sri Lanka**	**191**
	Dutch DC-8 crashed while landing.		
	Dec. 22	**Maturin, Caracas**	**77**
	Venezuelan airliner exploded in midair.		
	Dec. 28	**Mayan Mts.**	**23**
	Lockheed Lodestar crashed into mt.		
1975	**Jan. 4**	**Lotru Mts.**	**33**
	Tarom Airliner crashed in mts.		
	Jan. 8	**Neiva, Colombia**	**20**
	Satena Airlines C-47 crashed near city.		
	Jan. 30	**Istanbul, Turkey**	**41**
	Turkish Airlines F-28 crashed into Marmara Sea; airport was blacked out due to city-wide power failure.		
	Feb. 2	**Manila, Philippines**	**32**
	Philippine Airliner lost 1 of 2 engines; crashed near city.		
	Feb. 9	**Crete, Greece**	**42**
	West German military transport crashed in snowstorm.		
	Mar. 16	**Santa Carlos de Bariloche**	**52**
	Argentine Foker-26 crashed.		
	Apr. 4	**Saigon, So. Vietnam**	**172**
	USAF Galaxy C-58 crashed on takeoff while airlifting 2,000 orphans to U.S.A.		
	June 24	**New York City**	**113**
	Eastern Airlines Boeing 727 crashed in thunderstorm at Kennedy Airport.		
	July 31	**Taipei, Taiwan**	**27**
	Far Eastern Air Transport crashed near city.		
	Aug. 3	**Imzizen, Morocco**	**188**
	Alia Boeing 707 crashed 30 mi. northeast of Agadir while landing.		
	Sept. 1	**Leipzig, Germany**	**26**
	East German TU-134 crashed on flight from Stuttgart.		
	Sept. 29	**Beirut, Lebanon**	**60**
	Malev TU-154 crashed in Mediterranean en route to Budapest.		
	Oct. 27	**Andes Mts.**	**55**
	Bolivian Air Force Convair-440 crashed.		
	Oct. 30	**Prague, Czechoslovakia**	**74**
	Czechoslovakian DC-9 crashed while landing at airport.		

Major Avalanches and Landslides

(† indicates entries profiled in General Narrative)

Date		Place	Deaths	Description
†218 B.C.		Alps	18,000	Avalanches devastated Hannibal's army; in the crossing he lost 2,000 horses and many elephants.
A.D. 1440		Davos, Switzerland	11	Avalanche destroyed 2 houses; one survivor was dug out after being buried 24 hours.
1459		Disentis, Switzerland	16	Avalanche destroyed the Church of Saint Placidus which had stood for 655 years.
1478		St. Gotthard Pass, Switzerland	60	Avalanche devoured Milanese soldiers.
1499		Great St. Bernard Pass, Switzerland	400	Avalanche surprised mercenary army on way to attack the Milanese.
1518		Leukerbad, Switzerland	61	Avalanches ravaged little village famous for its medicinal baths.
1598		Graubunden, Switzerland	100	Avalanche in the Eastern Canton.
1606	Jan. 16	Davos-Frauenkirch, Switzerland	100	Three weeks of continued snow caused avalanche which destroyed 70 buildings; 5 people were rescued alive after a 36-hr. search.
1609	Mar. 13	Davos-Dorf, Switzerland	26	Ash Wednesday avalanche caught victims at breakfast.
†1618	Sept. 4	Chiavenna, Italy	2,427	Landslide from mts. surrounding valley.
1689		Montafon Valley, Austria	300	Avalanche accounted from the famous *Montafon Letter.*
	Jan. 25	Calmur, Switzerland	16	Avalanche on Saint Paul's Conversion day.
	Jan. 25	Saas, Switzerland	57	Avalanche at midday knocked down 155 buildings.
†1718	Jan. 17	Leukerbad, Switzerland	61	Avalanche destroyed St. Laurentius Chapel, all the inns and 50 houses.
1720		Obergesteln, Thone Valley, Alps	88	The much-feared Galen avalanche let loose and destroyed 400 cattle and 120 buildings.
		Ftan, Lower Engadine, Alps	32	Avalanche destroyed house filled with young people gathered to sing.
		Rueras, Tavetsch Valley, Alps	100	Avalanche destroyed 237 head of cattle and 60 houses; the disaster was a rare case when the villagers seriously contemplated total abandonment of town.
		Brig, Alps	40	Avalanche swept down on town.
		Great St. Bernard, Alps	23	Avalanche buried victims.
1755		German, French & Italian Alps	200	Avalanches took heavy toll in Savoie, Nice, and Aosta.
1799	Oct. 5	Panixer Pass, Switzerland	100s	Avalanche from heavy snowfall destroyed Russian Army and 300 pack animals.
1800	May	Great St. Bernard Pass, Switzerland	56	Avalanche struck Napoleon's army on its way to the Battle of Marengo.
	Nov.	Splugen Pass, Switzerland	30	Avalanche buried the Army of the Brisons.
†1806	Sept. 2	Goldau Valley, Switzerland	800	Landslide of Rossberg Peak wiped out 4 villages.
†1825		Philippines	1,500	Landslips of mud & rock caused by eruption of Mayon. (SEE Mayon)
1827		Biel, Switzerland	88	Avalanche wiped out half the village in the Upper Valais.
†1869		Biel, Switzerland	27	Flash avalanche devastated village in seconds.
1880	Sept. 18	Himalayas, India	230	Naini, a sanitary station, was destroyed by the descent of a mountain.
†1881	Sept. 11	Elm, Switzerland	150	Thirty houses swept away.
†1892	July 12	St. Gervais, Switzerland	140	Avalanche of muddy torrent carried away 30 houses.
1893	May 18	North Trondhjem, England	113	Thirty buildings destroyed at Vaerdalem.
1896	Oct. 17	Macon & Aix-les-Bains, England	48	Landslip buried a train of railway workmen.
1889	Sept. 21	Quebec, Canada	30	Landslip below the citadel, 7 dwellings fell.
1899	Sept. 23-24	Darjeeling, India	310	Landslip caused by a storm. 10 European children lost.
†1903	Apr. 29	Turtle Mt., Alberta, Canada	70	Landslide stunned small town.
1905	Aug. 14	Spence's Bridge, Canada	30	Vast landslide hit village on the Canadian Pacific Railway. Victims chiefly Indians.
1906	Jan. 9	Haverstram, New York	22	Eight houses buried by landslide.
	Feb. 21	Isa Fiord, Iceland	23	Avalanche overwhelmed Hnifsdal.
	Feb. 27	Wallace, Idaho	75	Avalanche buried inhabitants.
	Feb. 29	Mace, Colorado	60	Avalanche wiped out entire town.
	Mar. 6	Rogers Pass, Canada	62	Snow-slide buried a snow train including 37 Japanese.
	Mar. 7	Lofoden Isles, Switzerland	21	Avalanche injured 39.
	Mar. 17	Rio de Janeiro, Brazil	20	Landslide left many injured.
	Mar. 17	Petropolis	50	Twelve landslides inundated village; many injured.
†1910	Mar. 1	Wellington, Washington	96	Avalanche swept two trains into canyon.
	Mar. 11	Virginia, Minnesota	26	Landslide buried workers in the Norman open-pit mine.
†1915-1918		Tyrol	40,000-80,000	Avalanches in mountains terrorized Austrian & Italian troops over a 4-yr. span.
1915	Mar. 23	Vancouver, British Columbia	50	Avalanche descended on miners; many injured.
1916	Mar. 12	Cuneo, Italy	25	Avalanche buried Agordo district.
	†Dec. 12	Marmolada, Switzerland	253	Avalanche swept away whole barracks of the Austrian Army. (SEE Tyrol)
†1920	Dec. 16	Kansu, China	180,000	Great landslides caused by massive quake which registered 8.6 on the Richter Scale.
1922	Jan. 11	San Fratello, Sicily	100s	Landslide wiped out town.
	Feb. 5	Japan	110	Avalanche buried railroad train.
1925	Mar. 27	Irkutzsk, Siberia	22	Avalanche buried train near city; 30 hurt.
1926	July 17	Serajevo, Bosnia	117	Landslide trapped train near city.

Date		Place	Deaths
	Nov. 5	Pereira, Colombia	100
	Landslide blocked River Otun and flooded village; 60 injured.		
	Nov. 24	Rocque Billierre, Switzerland	24
	Series of avalanches laid village to waste.		
1928	Mar. 10	Mt. Serrat, Brazil	92
	Avalanche evacuated area; many houses crushed.		
1929	Mar. 6	Madeira Island	40
	Landslide injured many in Valley of St. Vincent.		
	June 18	Seville, Colombia	40
	Landslide caused Quilcace River to change course and flood city.		
	July 22	Northern Anatolia, Turkey	1,000
	Landslides and earthquakes caused mass destruction.		
1930	Nov. 18	Manizales, Colombia	32
	Landslide dammed Augacatal River.		
1931	Jan. 28	Bardonecchia, Italy	21
	Avalanche struck soldiers; 9 starving survivors reached Rochemolles Valley.		
	Feb. 14	Huigra, Ecuador	190
	Landslide buried track workers along the Guayaquil and Quito Railroad.		
	Oct. 20	Jeypore, India	30
	Landslide near city.		
1932	May 8	Lyons, France	27
	Landslide destroyed 2 apartment houses.		
	Aug. 8	Sharlin, Korea	22
	Landslide struck small village.		
1933	Apr. 13	Chiclayo, Peru	20
	Landslide leveled city.		
1934	Feb. 5	Ortiperio, Corsica	39
	Avalanche destroyed 10 houses.		
	Mar. 20	Banyitsa, Yugoslavia	30
	Landslide in the Batignole quarry.		
	Apr. 7	Norway	100s
	Cliff fell into fjord; engulfed 2 towns.		
	May 23-24	Kwantung Province, China	500
	Landslides raped area for 2 days.		
1935	Aug. 8	Balongon, P.I.	50
	Town buried by landslide.		
	Dec. 8	Kirovsk, U.S.S.R.	88
	Town swept by ice; 44 hurt.		
1936	Sept. 13	Loen, Norway	21
	Series of slides caused mass damage; 50 injured.		
	Dec. 3	Nueva, Ecija	20
	Landslide entombed miners.		
1937	Feb. 2	Italian Alps	23
	Avalanche surprised skiers.		
	May 27	Tlalpujahua, Mexico	70
	Landslide destroyed El Carmen and Somosa ranches.		
1940	Feb. 6	Fuentes de Cesna, Spain	21
	Landslide destroyed many buildings.		
1942	Dec. 22	Aliquippa, Pa.	25
	Rockslide crushed passenger bus.		
1946	Apr. 18	Betania, Colombia	20
	Landslide in Providence of Antigua destroyed homes and suspended rapid transportation.		
1948	Jan. 14	Tanganyika, Africa	21
	Landslide left 15 injured.		
	Sept. 18	Assam, India	500
	Landslide caused severe damage in the North.		
	Nov. 1	Posillipo, Italy	25
	Sudden landslide buried victims.		
1949	Feb. 15	Sondondo, India	70
	Landslide buried 200 houses.		
	Nov. 17	Goa, India	40
	Landslide inundated village.		
1950	Oct. 22	Santa River, Peru	34
	Landslide wrecked public works project.		
1951	Jan. 4	Andes Mt., Peru	132
	Planned construction explosion caused avalanche.		
	†Jan. 20	Vals, Switzerland	240
	Many villages in northern Italy and Austria buried; disaster called worst in Alps history.		
	Feb. 13	Switzerland	21
	Rock and snow slides buried many.		
	July 10	Kyushu and Ijuin, Japan	28
	Sudden landslides trapped many.		
1952	Feb. 11-13	Melkoede, Austria	78
	Series of avalanches in 3-day period.		
	Mar. 24	West Java, Indonesia	28
	Landslide near Lembang.		
	June 23	Kyushu, Japan	20
	Heavy rain caused landslide.		
	Dec. 23	Langen, Austria	23
	Avalanche buried bus with 11 British tourists.		
1953	July 26	Tokyo, Japan	25
	Landslide outside city.		
1954	Jan. 11-14	Alps	145
	Snow avalanches in Germany, Italy, Austria, and Switzerland.		
	Feb. 27	Manchil, Kashmir	35
	Avalanche buried Himalayan village.		
	July 12	Andes Mt., Colombia	140
	Landslides near Medelin left real death count a mystery.		
	Oct. 22	Berly, Haiti	262
	Landslide wiped out town.		
	Dec. 28	El Carmen, Colombia	47
	Landslides ruined town.		
1955	Apr. 16	Sasebo, Japan	67
	Landslide of coal slag at mining community. Blame was placed on heavy rains.		
	Oct. 18	Atenguigue, Mexico	100
	Town buried by landslide.		
1956	Feb. 9	Toyama, Japan	40
	Avalanche buried construction workers.		
	Mar. 2	South Korea	79
	Snowslide on Eastern Front left 36 injured, 24 missing and 90 barracks, tents and huts destroyed.		
	Mar. 7	Lofoten Islands, Norway	26
	Sudden slides destroyed many homes.		
	Mar. 25	Santos, Brazil	36
	Landslide caused by heavy rains.		
	Oct. 20	Bampan, India	23
	Landslide in the Garwhal district.		
1958	Jan. 19	Pachaco, Andes Mts.	100
	Landslide buried town.		
	June 7	Lohit Region, India	52
	Landslide devastated northeastern region.		
	Aug. 13	Andes Mt., Colombia	30
	Landslide gutted mt. road.		
†1959	Oct.29	Minatitlan, Mexico	5,000
	Landslides caused by heavy rains left area ruined.		
	Dec. 16	Lowari Pass, Pakistan	48
	Avalanche was reported 2 weeks later in Rawalpindi.		
1960	Jan. 22	Mindanao Island, Philippines	40
	Landslide buried 40 children alive in their school in the mountain town of Dimatiling.		
1961	Feb. 3	Fleron, Belgium	20
	Rain-soaked rock pile near a coal mine slid onto several houses.		
	Mar. 13	Kiev, Ukraine	145
	Mud slide at a reclamation project in the Babi Yary destroyed many homes and public buildings.		
	July 1	Japan	80
	Landslide in the central part of country left 650 hurt.		
	July 5	Kerala State, India	73
	Landslide took a heavy toll.		

Major Avalanches and Landslides

Date		Place	Deaths	
†1962	**Jan. 10**	**Huascaran, Peru**	**4,000**	Peruvian avalanche devastated 6 villages; largest single avalanche disaster.
	Feb. 28	**Conchucos, Peru**	**60**	Mud slide caused by heavy rains buried the Andean village.
	Mar. 10	**Pensilvania, Colombia**	**23**	Landslide caused by heavy rains struck city in the department of Caldas.
	Mar. 15	**Oroya, Peru**	**41**	Landslide caused by heavy rains gutted the U.S.-owned workers' camp of Cerro de Pasco; most of the victims were women and children.
1963	**Mar. 3**	**Tampayaeta**	**300**	Landslide, in southern Andes, caused by heavy rains.
	June 24-25	**Koje Island, South Korea**	**116**	Landslides in Pusan and Kimhai County.
	Aug. 10	**Trisuli River, Nepal**	**150**	Landslide destroyed Manigram, Pairogram, and Danragram.
	Oct. 9	**Belluno, Italy**	**2,000**	Landslide with heavy rains turned Piave River Valley into artificial lake.
	Nov. 19	**Grand Riviare du Nord, Haiti**	**500**	Landslide destroyed all crops in island's richest section.
1964	**Apr. 24**	**Lobato, Brazil**	**40**	Landslide destroyed 100 homes.
	†**July 18-19**	**Japan**	**108**	Landslides caused by torrential rains on W. coast; many missing.
†1965	**Feb 18**	**Leduc Camp, British Columbia**	**27**	Avalanche struck Newmont Mining Co's copper ore mine.
	June 26	**Kawasaki, Japan**	**55**	Landslide buried many near Tokyo.
	Aug. 11	**Portillo, Chile**	**42**	Rock and snow avalanches caused severe damage.
	Aug. 30	**Saas-Almagell**	**88**	Avalanche in Swiss Alps caught workers.
	Nov. 27	**Manizales, Colombia**	**32**	Landslide hit small village.
†1966	**Jan. 11-13**	**Rio de Janeiro, Brazil**	**239**	Landslide caused by 9-inch rainfall damaged districts of Santa Teresa, Copacabana and Ipanema.
	May 14	**Quito, Ecuador**	**52**	Landslide occurred 50 mi. southeast of city.
	†**Oct. 21**	**Aberfan, Wales**	**145**	Avalanche of coal waste buried schoolhouse, farm and 13 homes; victims mostly children.
†1967	**Feb. 17-20**	**Rio de Janeiro, Brazil**	**224**	Landslide caused by 11-inch rainfall caused heavy damage in city's slum.
	Mar. 19	**Sao Paulo, Brazil**	**160**	Rock and landslides buried Caraguatatuba and Paraibuna.
1968	**Jan. 27-28**	**Swiss Alps**	**20**	Avalanche at the Davos sports center.
	Mar. 8	**Luhonga, Congo**	**150**	Avalanche of mud from a loose section of Mandwe Mountain.
	Mar. 20	**Sniezka, Poland**	**21**	Avalanche caught Soviet tourists in the Sudeten Mountains.
	Aug. 18	**Gifu, Japan**	**102**	Landslide swept 2 buses into river.
	†**Oct. 1-4**	**Bihar & W. Bengal, India**	**1,000**	Landslide following rains raped area.
	Dec. 30	**Rio de Janeiro, Brazil**	**50**	Landslide left many missing.
†1969	**Jan. 18-26**	**Los Angeles, Calif.**	**95**	Landslides caused by heavy rains; $138 million damage.
	Apr. 6	**Azerbaijan, Iran**	**20**	Landslide caused by torrential rains.
1970	**Jan. 31**	**Northern Iran**	**43**	Avalanches along the Amoz Maraz highway caused motorists to freeze to death.
	Feb. 10	**Val d'Isere, France**	**42**	Worst avalanche in French history left 37 injured.
	Feb. 24	**Reckingen, Switzerland**	**30**	Giant avalanche buried Swiss army camp.
	Apr. 16	**Plateau D'Assy, France**	**72**	Giant landslide crashed into children's TB sanitarium. Most victims were between the ages of 5 and 15.
1970	**Oct. 25**	**Medellin, Colombia**	**25**	Series of avalanches buried city.
	Dec. 12	**Cauca Valley, Colombia**	**100**	Avalanche gutted 10 miles of winding road near Bogota.
	Dec. 30	**Neot Hakakir, Israel**	**23**	Rockslide buried mess hall.
1971	**Feb. 19**	**Lima, Peru**	**600**	Avalanche in the Andes Mt. devastated town.
	Mar. 8	**Quito & Auayaquil, Ecuador**	**20**	Landslide buried cars, buses on highway between cities.
	Mar. 19	**Chungar, Peru**	**259**	Andean Mountain avalanche struck mining camp 60 mi. north of Lima.
	May 21	**West Sepik, New Guinea**	**100**	Landslide buried village in Star Mountains.
	July 30	**Khinjan Pass, Afghanistan**	**100**	Landslide destroyed village in Hindu Kush Mts.
1972	**Jan. 26**	**San Josecito, Colombia**	**70**	Landslide burried village and 14 houses near Bogota.
	Feb. 13	**Northwest Iran**	**60**	Avalanches caused by heaviest snowfall in 10 years.
	June 6-19	**Hong Kong**	**100s**	Landslides swept away squatters' village; many missing.
	July 17	**Japan**	**370**	Landslides caused by heavy rains; $472 million in damage.
	Aug. 7	**Nepal**	**105**	Landslides followed monsoon rains.
	Aug. 19	**South Korea**	**463**	Landslides brought on by massive rains engulfed country.
	Dec. 21	**Central Sri Lanka**	**50**	Landslide took heavy toll.
1973	**Apr. 25**	**Peruvian Andes**	**500**	Landslips triggered by torrential rains.
	Apr. 26	**Quito, Ecuador**	**25**	Avalanche of mud forced 2,000 to leave their homes.
	June 28	**Colombia**	**200**	Landslides on highway 95 mi. E. Bogota.
	July 27	**Colombo, Fri Lanka**	**27**	Landslide swept tea estate 100 mi. from city.
	Sept. 20	**Choloma, Honduras**	**2,800**	Giant mud slides caused by hurricane Fifi.
	Sept. 29	**Thailand**	**75**	Landslide buried small village in the north.
	Oct. 6	**Medellin, Colombia**	**90**	Landslide hit shantytown.
	Oct. 23	**Sal Tome**	**30**	Landslide on Portuguese Island.
1975	**Jan. 27**	**Philippines**	**scores**	Tropical storm set off series of landslides.
	Apr. 6	**Swiss Alps**	**scores**	Heavy snowfall left many missing in the Ticino & Grisons regions.
	Aug. 11	**Katmandy, Nepal**	**60**	Landslides caused by weeks of monsoon rains.
	Aug. 22	**Shikoku, Japan**	**56**	Landslides followed fifth typhoon of year; damage over $30 million.

Major Earthquakes

(† indicates entries profiled in General Narrative)

Date		Place	Deaths
1450 B.C		Italy (Central)	1,000s
	Quake swallowed cities and Lake Cimunus appeared in their place.		
†464		Sparta	20,000
	Massive quake also ruined Laconia.		
426		Euboea, Greece	1,000s
	City reduced to an island.		
†373		Greece	1,000s
	Helas and Bura consumed by quake.		
345		Campania and Greece	1,000s
	Duras buried; 12 other cities destroyed.		
283		Lysimachia	1,000s
	Quake buried city.		
224		Rhodes	1,000s
	The Colossus overthrown by quake.		
†217	June	North Africa	50,000-75,000
	Quakes smashed more than 100 cities.		
33		Palestine	30,000
	City overwhelmed by quake.		
A.D. 17		Ephesus	1,000s
	Many cities devastated by quake.		
19		Syria	120,000
	Country overturned by quake.		
33		Palestine and Bythia	30,000
	On the occasion of the Crucifixion the city of Nicaea was inundated.		
79		Pompei	1,000s
	Quake accompanied eruption of Mt. Vesuvius. (SEE Vesuvius)		
105		Eastern Europe & Asia	1,000s
	Four cities in Asia, 2 in Greece & 2 in Galatia were overturned.		
†115		Antioch, Syria	1,000s
	City destroyed by quake.		
126		Nicomedia, Asia Minor	1,000s
	Caesarea and Nicea also destroyed.		
157		Pontius and Macedonia, Asia	1,000s
	Vicious quake destroyed both cities; 150 other cities and towns badly damaged.		
358		Nicomedia, Asia Minor	1,000s
	City again destroyed; all inhabitants buried and 100 other cities shaken.		
359		Nicomedia, Bythynia	100s
	City leveled.		
†365	July 21	Alexandria, Egypt	50,000
	Quake destroyed city & the 4th Wonder of the Ancient World—a 600-ft. lighthouse.		
494		Asiatic Turkey	1,000s
	Laodicea, Hierapolis and Tripoli destroyed.		
†526	May 26	Antioch, Syria	250,000
	City buried with all inhabitants.		
551		Beyrout	1,000s
	Destroyed by quake.		
557		Constantinople	1,000s
	City buried; many principal edifices destroyed.		
560		Africa & Egypt	1,000s
	Scores of cities devastated.		
681		Tosa, Japan	1,000s
	Quake submerged 3-sq.-mi. area.		
742		Syria & Palestine	10,000
	More than 500 towns destroyed.		
778		Trivisia, Italy	1,000s
	Heavy damage throughout city.		
801		Europe	1,000s
	France, Germany and Italy badly shaken.		
856	Dec.	Corinth, Greece	45,000
	Massive quake wrecked city.		
869		Japan	1,000s
	Quake followed by *tsunamis* on Sanriku Coast.		
893		India	180,000
	Quake swallowed country.		
936		Constantinople	1,000s
	City destroyed and Greece shaken.		
1007		Deinar, Turkey	10,000
	Quake buried 1,000s in ruins.		
1029		Damascus, Asiatic Turkey	1,000s
	Quake destroyed half of city.		
1038		Shansi, China	23,000
	Quake destroyed city.		
1040		Tabriz, Persia	50,000
	Quake left city in ruins.		
1057		Chihli (Hopei), China	25,000
	City destroyed.		
1114		Syria	1,000s
	Antioch, Aleppo, Jerusalem and many other cities destroyed.		
1137		Catania, Sicily	15,000
	Quake accompanied eruption of Mt. Etna. (SEE Etna)		
1139		Gansana, Persia	10,000
	All inhabitants of city buried.		
1158		Syria	20,000
	Massive quake destroyed many towns.		
†1169		Calabria, Sicily	15,000
	Cathedral and city in ruins; quake accompanied eruption of Mt. Etna. (SEE Etna)		
1170		Sicily	15,000
	Entire country wrecked by quake.		
1186	Sept.	Calabria	1,000s
	City and all inhabitants overwhelmed in the Adriatic Sea.		
1218		France	5,000
	Mount Franche Comté opened and engulfed populace.		
1268		Cieilia, Asia Minor	60,000
	City devastated.		
1274		Glastonbury, England	100s
	City destroyed; shocks felt throughout country.		
1290	Sept. 27	Chihli, China	100,000
	Quake buried city.		
1293	May 20	Kamakura, Japan	30,000
	Quake devastated city.		
1318	Nov. 14	England	100s
	Greatest quake in British Isles to this date.		
1353		Borgo-Sansepolero, Italy	2,000
	Violent quake shook country.		
1361		Koty, Japan	1,000s
	Quake destroyed city.		
1456	Dec. 5	Naples, Italy	35,000
	City left in ruins.		
1491		Cos, Grecian Archipelago	5,000
	Quake caused severe damage.		
1504		Agra, India	1,000s
	Quake leveled every tall building.		
1505		Cabul, India	1,000s
	Dreadful quake left city in ruins.		
1509	Sept. 14	Constantinople	1,000s
	Killer quake wrecked city.		

Major Earthquakes

Date		Place	Deaths	
1531	Jan. 26	**Lisbon, Portugal**	30,000	City in ruins after mammoth quake; 1500 houses leveled.
†1556	Feb. 2	**China**	830,000	Largest death toll by quake in history.
1596	Sept. 1	**Bungo Funai, Japan**	700	City wiped out by quake.
1596	Sept. 4	**Japan**	2,000	Towns of Yamashiro, Settsu, Izumi struck; Fushimi Castle destroyed; giant Buddha statue at Hokeiji wrecked.
1602		**Port Royal, Jamaica**	100s	City nearly destroyed.
1605	Jan. 31	**Japan**	5,000	Quake ran down Pacific Coast from Kyushu to Boshu.
1611	Sept. 27	**Aizu, Japan**	3,700	City destroyed; land area at Inawashiro submerged and became lake.
	Dec. 2	**Sanrokw, Japan**	1,783	Quake, followed by *tsunami,* wiped out Ezo Coast.
1614	Nov. 26	**Echigo, Takata, Japan**	1,000s	*Tsunami* followed by quake wrecked cities.
1626	July 30	**Naples, Italy**	70,000	Quake destroyed city; 30 villages devastated.
1633	Mar. 1	**Odawa, Japan**	150	Sudden quake shook city.
1638		**Calabria**	100s	Terrible quake; 180 towns and villages ruined.
1645		**Manila, Philippines**	600	Quake devastated city; 1,172 buildings damaged; 2,000 injured.
1659	Apr. 21	**Aizu, Japan**	39	Slight shock; 400 buildings destroyed.
1662	June 16	**Kenai & Kinki, Japan**	500	Twin cities destroyed; 5,500 buildings destroyed.
	Oct. 30	**Hyoga, Osumi, Japan**	100s	*Tsunami* accompanied by quake destroyed 2,500 buildings.
1665		**Manila, Philippines**	100s	Quake of high intensity.
1666	Feb. 2	**Echigo, Takata, Japan**	1,500	Quake left city in ruins.
1667	Apr. 6	**Ragusa**	5,000	City devastated by quake.
	May-June	**Shemaka, Caucasia**	80,000	Series of quakes lasted months.
1672	Apr. 14	**Rimini, Italy**	1,500	Quake leveled city.
1676	July 12	**Iwami Tsuwana, Japan**	24	Quake smashed 133 buildings.
1683		**Manila, Philippines**	400	Quake damaged over 1,000 structures.
†1690	Apr. 6	**St. Eustatius**	100s	Quake tore main town in half and threw it into the sea in the Lesser Antilles.
†1692	June 7	**Port Royal, Jamaica**	1,600	Quake left West Indies paradise in ruins; houses were submerged 40 fathoms deep.
1693		**Naples, Italy**	93,000	Immense damage by sudden quake.
	†Sept.	**Cantania, Italy**	18,000	Quake buried city and all inhabitants. (SEE Etna)
	Jan. 9-11	**Sicily**	100,000	Fifty-four cities and 300 villages lost to quake.
1694	June 19	**Bugo Noshiro, Japan**	394	Quake struck large area in the south destroying 2,760 buildings.
1703	Feb. 2	**Aguila, Italy**	5,000	City ruined by quake.
	Dec. 30	**Edo (Tokyo), Japan**	200,000	Quake destroyed present capital.
	Dec. 31	**Japan**	5,233	*Tsunami* followed quake which destroyed 20,162 buildings at Mugashi, Sagami, Awa, and Kazusa.
1704	May 27	**Noshiro, Japan**	58	Quake swallowed 1,314 buildings.
1706	Nov. 3	**Naples, Italy**	15,000	Quake demolished city.
1707	Oct. 28	**Japan**	4,900	*Tsunami* following quake hit the Pacific Coast from Hyuga to Izu damaging 29,000 buildings.
1711	Mar. 19	**Japan**	4	Quake hit villages of Minasaka, Inabe, and Hoki damaging 500 buildings.
1714	Apr. 28	**Japan**	56	Quake destroyed 300 buildings at Shinano, Matushiro, and Omachi.
1716	May-June	**Algeria**	20,000	Country left in ruins by massive quake.
1720	June-July	**Old Delhi, India**	100s	Quakes continued for a month.
1726	Sept. 1	**Palermo, Italy**	6,000	Quake caused great loss of life.
1727		**Tabriz, Persia**	77,000	Quake overwhelmed city.
1729	Aug. 1	**Noto, Sado, Japan**	5	Quake destroyed 791 buildings.
1731	Nov. 30	**Pekin, China**	100,000	All inhabitants swallowed up by quake.
1732	Nov. 29	**Naples, Italy**	1,940	Quake destroyed city.
†1737		**Japan**	1,000s	Quake precipitated *tsunami;* town of Kamaishi destroyed.
	Oct. 11	**Calcutta, India**	300,000	Quake ruined mass area.
1746	Oct. 28	**Lima & Callao**	18,000	Violent quake left only 21 of 3,000 dwellings standing.
1750		**Cerigo, Ionian Islands**	2,000	Quake devastated island.
1751	May 20	**Takata, Japan**	1,700	Quake destroyed 9,100 buildings.
	May 24	**Concepcion, Chile**	10,000	Quake destroyed city.
	Nov. 21	**Port-Au-Prince, St. Domingo**	1,000s	Island destroyed by quake.
1752	July 29	**Adreanople, Turkey**	1,000s	City almost inundated.
1754		**Philippines**	100s	Quake followed eruption of Taal.
	Sept.	**Cairo, Egypt**	40,000	Quake destroyed half the houses in city.
†1755		**Portugal**	1,000s	Quake destroyed cities of Coimbra, Oporto, Braga, and St. Nebes. (SEE Etna)
		Archipelago, Island of Metelene	100s	Quake destroyed 2,000 houses.
	Apr.	**Quito, Ecuador**	1,000s	Quake wiped out city.
	June 7	**Kaschan, Persia**	40,000	Killer quake struck throughout North.
	†Nov. 1	**Lisbon, Portugal**	50,000-100,000	The most violent quake in modern times. Shocks felt in area of 1½ million sq. mi.
†1757		**Concepcion, Chile**	5,000	Quake & seismic waves inundated city.
1759	Oct. 30	**Baalbek, Syria**	20,000	Quake affected 10,000 sq. mi. of country.

Date		Place	Deaths
1766	Mar. 8	Hirosaki, Japan	1,335
	Tsunamis followed quake and leveled 7,500 buildings.		
†1767	Aug.	Martinique	16,000
	Quake wiped out 1/5 of populace. (SEE Pelée)		
†1772		Java	2,000
	Violent quake split Papandayang Mt.; entire town wiped out.		
1773	June 7	Santiago, Guatemala	58,000
	Quake demolished city. The few survivors moved inland 20 mi. to found new city.		
1778		Tauris, Persia	1,000s
	Quake downed 15,000 buildings.		
	July 3	Smyrna	100s
	Quake caused great damage.		
†1783	Feb. 5-Mar. 28	Calabria, Italy	40,000
	Quake destroyed 181 towns; shocks felt in area of 88,000 sq. mi.		
1784	July 23	Exinhian, Armenia	5,000
	Tremendous damage near Exinhian; many buried.		
1787		Philippines	100s
	Quake left whole island in ruins.		
1788	Oct. 12	Lucia, West Indies	900
	Quake destroyed city.		
1789	Sept. 30	Borgo di San Sepolero, Tuscany	1,000
	Quake caused heavy damage.		
1792	Feb. 10	Hizen, Japan	15,000
	Quake inundated many cities including Higo and Shimabara; 12,000 buildings destroyed after eruption of Unzendake.		
1793	Feb. 8	West Tsugaru	12
	Quake smashed 164 buildings.		
	†Apr. 1	Unsen	53,000
	Quake near Japanese volcano; floods of water drowned populace.		
1794	June	Torro del Greco, Italy	1,000s
	Quake swallowed city following eruption of Mt. Vesuvius. (SEE Vesuvius)		
1797		Calabria, Italy	50,000
	Quake demolished city.		
	†Feb. 4	Quito, Ecuador	40,000
	Quake staggered South America; cities of Sante Fe and Panama badly damaged.		
	Sept. 1	Cumana, Ecuador	1,000s
	Quake shook many cities including Quito and Binbamba.		
1800	Sept. 26	Constantinople	100s
	Quake destroyed Royal Palace and many buildings.		
1802	Dec. 9	Sado, Japan	19
	Quake destroyed 1,100 buildings; Sea of Kisagata was changed to land after *tsunami*.		
1804	July 10	Uzen, Ugo. Japan	75
	Quake created *tsunami* that turned Sea of Kisagata to plain island.		
1805	July 26	Naples & Calabria	26,000
	Quake destroyed many cities including Frosoleme.		
1810	Aug. 11	St. Michaels, Azores	100s
	Village of Las Casas sank and left a lake of boiling water.		
	Sept. 25	Ugo Kampuzane, Japan	59
	Quake destroyed 1,129 buildings.		
1811	Dec. 16-Feb. 7	New Madrid, Mo.	
	The "grand-daddy" of Middle West quakes. The tremors lasted 54 days, dropping the earth's surface 30 to 40 feet at some places.		
†1812	Mar. 26	Caracas, Venezuela	20,000
	Quake destroyed city.		
	†Dec.	San Juan Capistrano, Calif.	40
	Quake collapsed roof of church.		
1817	Apr.	Chang-Ruh, China	2,800
	Quake overthrew many provinces.		
1818	Mar.	Philipopolis, Turkey	1,000s
	Quake engulfed entire city.		
1819		Vostitza, Greece	1,000s
	Quake destroyed the ancient Aegium.		
	June 16	Cutch, India	1,543
	Quake destroyed 10,000 houses; shocks felt in area of 1,900,000 sq. mi.		
	Aug.-Sept.	Genoa, Italy	20,000
	Quake ruined many cities including Palermo.		
1822	May 7	Carthago, Costa Rica	100s
	Quake overwhelmed town.		
	Aug. 10	Aleppo, Asia Minor	20,000
	Quake destroyed town.		
	†Nov. 19	Chile	10,000
	Western coast permanently raised.		
1825	Apr. 5	Blida, Algiers	7,000
	Quake caused heavy damage.		
1827		Fort Kolitaran, India	1,000
	Violent quake near Lahore.		
1828	Feb. 2	Casamicciola, Island of Ischia	28
	Quake destroyed many buildings.		
	Dec. 28	Echigo Nagaoka, Japan	1,443
	Quake destroyed 750 homes.		
1829	Mar. 21	Mureia, Spain	6,000
	Quake caused great destruction.		
1830	May 26-27	Canton, China	6,000
	Quake destroyed large area.		
	Aug. 19	Yamashiro, Japan	151
	Quake shook town.		
1833	Dec. 7	Echigo, Uzen, Japan	42
	Quake destroyed 1,013 buildings.		
1834	Feb. 14	Borgotaro & Pontermoli, China	100s
	Quake delivered 40 shocks.		
†1835	Feb. 20	Concepcion, Chile	5,000
	Quake destroyed city; uplifted coastal areas including Santiago.		
	Apr. 29	Calabria	1,000
	Quake buried Naples and Corenza.		
	Oct. 12	Castigliore, Calabria	100
	Small quake in city.		
1837	Jan. 22	Jaffa	13,000
	Quake severely shook area.		
	†Aug. 2	St. Thomas	500
	Quake & cyclone brought horror to area.		
1839	Jan. 11	Port Royal, Martinique	700
	Quake destroyed half of island; rest damaged.		
1840	May 7	Cape Haytiem, St. Domingo	5,000
	Quake destroyed 2/3 of town.		
	July 14	Ternate	1,000s
	Island laid waste after quake.		
	July 27	Mt. Ararat, Armenia	100s
	Quake ruined 3,137 houses.		
	Oct. 30	Zante	100s
	Quake buried area.		
1841		Shinano, Japan	12,000
	Quake buried town.		
	†Aug. 27	Cartago, Costa Rica	4,000
	Quake collapsed 1,000s of homes & 100s of civic monuments.		
1842	May 7	Cape Haytiem, St. Domingo	10,000
	Quake destroyed town; large explosion from powder magazine followed.		
1843	Feb. 4	Pointe-à'-Pitre, Guadeloupe	100s
	Quake devastated Antigua, St. Thomas and St. Christopher.		
1844	May 8	Shinano and Echigo, Japan	12,000
	Quake destroyed 34,000 buildings.		

Major Earthquakes

Date		Place	Deaths
1847	Oct. 23	Attixico, Mexico	1,000s
	Quake destroyed city.		
		Zenkoji, Japan	34,000
	Quake demolished town.		
1851	Mar. 7	Rhodes & Macri	600
	Quake caused mountain to fall, crushing populace.		
	Aug. 14	Melfi, Italy	14,000
	Quake destroyed southern part of country.		
†1852	Aug. 20	Santiago, Cuba	100s
	Quake destroyed southern part of island. (SEE Etna)		
	Sept. 16-30	Manila, Philippines	1,000s
	Quake left city badly damaged.		
1853	Mar. 11	Odawara, Japan	79
	Quake destroyed 3,300 buildings.		
	May 4	Shiraz, Persia	10,000
	City destroyed.		
	July 15	Cumana, Venezuela	800
	City badly shaken; artillery company buried in quarters.		
	Aug. 18	Thebes, Greece	1,000s
	City destroyed; shocks felt throughout country.		
†1854	Apr. 16	St. Salvador	5,000
	One-fourth of island destroyed.		
	July 9	Japan	2,400
	Tsunami followed quake and destroyed 5,000 structures in Yamato, Iga, and Ise.		
	†Dec. 22	Japan	3,000
	Tsunami followed quake; 60,000 buildings destroyed.		
1855	Feb. 28	Broussa, Turkey	100s
	Quake nearly destroyed town.		
	Nov. 11	Edo, Japan	6,757
	Quake destroyed village and 50,000 buildings.		
	Dec. 12	Tokyo, Japan	10,000
	Quake partly destroyed city.		
1856	Mar. 2	Moluccas Islands	3,000
	Quake & volcanic eruption on Island of Great Tanger.		
	Oct. 12	Candia, Mediterranean	750
	Quake caused extensive damage on eastern shore.		
†1857	Mar. 21	Tokyo, Japan	107,000
	Massive earthquake started widespread fires that were aided by cyclonic winds of 60 m.p.h.		
	†Dec. 16	Calabria, Italy	10,000
	Quake caused great loss of life.		
1858	Feb. 21	Corinth	100s
	Entire area nearly inundated.		
†1859	Mar. 22	Quito, Ecuador	5,000
	City inundated by quake.		
	July 17	Erzeroum, Armenia	1,000s
	Quake buried city.		
1860	Mar. 20	Mendosa, S.A.	7,000
	Violent quake shattered city.		
1861	Mar. 20-23	South America	6,000
	Quake destroyed cities of San Juan and San Louis.		
1863	Apr. 22	Rhodes	300
	Quake destroyed 13 villages including herds of cattle.		
	†July 3	Manila, Philippines	1,000
	Quake caused immense damage.		
	Aug. 13-15	Peru & Ecuador	25,000
	Quakes devastated South America with shocks.		
1865	July 18	Macchia & Bendilla, Sicily	64
	Quake destroyed 200 houses.		
1867	Feb. 4	Argostoti, Cephalonia	50
	Village received slight tremor.		
	Mar. 9	Mitylene, Asia Minor	1,000
	Quake buried city.		
†1868	Aug. 13-15	Central America	25,000
	Quake caused tremendous loss of life and property. (SEE South America)		
	Oct. 21	California	40
	Quake struck north-central area.		
†1870	May 11-12	Oaxaca, Mexico	100
	Quake razed ½ of town.		
1872	Mar. 14	Iwami & Hamada, Japan	537
	Quake leveled 4,094 buildings.		
	Mar. 26-27	California	30
	Quake destroyed several small towns.		
	Apr. 3	Antioch, Syria	1,600
	Quake buried city.		
	Dec. 14-15	India	500
	Quake destroyed cities of Lehree, Eastern Catchi and Sind.		
1873	Mar. 19	San Salvador, Brazil	50
	Quake leveled city but populace had advance warnings.		
	June 29	Northern Italy	75
	Quake damaged much property.		
1874	July 22	Azagra, Spain	200
	Quake produced great landslip.		
	Sept. 3	Antigua, Guatemala	100s
	Quake caused damage in many cities.		
1875	May 3-5	Karsa Hissa, Asia Minor	1,000s
	Quake buried many cities.		
	May 12	Smyrna	1,000s
	Quake caused great loss of life.		
	†May 15	Colombia	16,000
	Quakes inundated city.		
	May 16-18	Colombo, Chile	14,000
	Many towns including San Jose de Cucota destroyed.		
1876	June 15	Japan	28,321
	Quake caused 100-ft. *tsunamis* which razed 300 mi. of the northeastern coast destroying 6,222 buildings.		
1877	May 10	South America & Sandwich Islands	1,000s
	Quake caused great destruction at Iguigua, Peru & Hilo.		
1878	May 14	Cua, Venezuela	600
	Quake destroyed city; shook Caracas.		
	†Oct.	San Salvador	1,000s
	Quake destroyed city along with towns of Santiago de Marie, Guadeloupe & Incuapa.		
1880	Sept. 13	Valparaiso, Chile	200
	City badly shaken; village of Illapel buried.		
1881	Mar. 15	Casmicciola, Italy	114
	Quake destroyed city; shook southern part of country.		
	†Apr. 3	Scio, Italy	5,000-7,000
	City buried by quake.		
1883	July 27	Java & Sumatra	1,000s
	Both islands devastated. (SEE Krakatoa)		
	July 28	Ischia, Italy	1,800
	Quake destroyed city. (SEE Krakatoa)		
	Aug. 26-28	Sundra Straits, Netherland Indies	36,000
	Quake destroyed 2/3 of island. (SEE Krakatoa)		
	†Oct. 16	Anatolia, Asia Minor (Turkey)	1,000
	Quake destroyed many towns; 20,000 left destitute.		
1884	May 19-20	Island of Kishm, Persian Gulf	200
	Quake destroyed 12 villages.		
	Dec. 25	Andulusia, Malaga	266
	Quake leveled most structures.		
†1885	June-July	Kashmir, India	3,100
	Quakes raped the land; destroyed 70,000 dwellings.		
	Aug. 2	Vernoe & Tashkend, Asia	54
	Shocks from quake damaged central regions.		
	Dec. 3-5	Msila, Algeria	30
	Slight quake in village.		
	Dec. 25-Jan. 2	Granada, Spain	1,000
	Quake destroyed Alhama and Periana.		

Date		Place	Deaths
1886	Aug. 27	**Ionian Islands**	300
		Terrible quakes at Morea, Malta and others.	
	†Aug. 31	**Charleston, S.C.**	100
		Heaviest recorded quake along East Coast.	
†1887	Feb. 24	**Riviera (France and Italy)**	2,000
		Quake hit Switzerland, France and Northern Italy.	
	May 5	**Owyhyhee, Hawaii**	167
		Quake shook island.	
	June 13	**Vernoe, Turkestan**	140
		Quake devastated cities including Almatensky.	
	Aug. 27	**California**	170
		Quake hit West Coast including Montezuma.	
	Dec. 4	**Bisignano, Calabria**	25
		Small quakes also struck Cosenza.	
1888		**Tukushima, Japan**	600
		Quake struck province 165 mi. north of Tokyo.	
	Mar. 7	**Yun Nan, China**	4,000
		Quake inundated city.	
1891	Jan. 15	**Gouraya & Villebourg, Algeria**	40
		Quake wrecked both cities.	
	Sept. 9	**San Salvador**	100s
		Quake caused great destruction in Central America.	
	†Oct. 28	**Japan**	7,000
		Quake smashed both Mino & Owari; 20,000 structures leveled with shocks felt in area of 243,000 sq. mi.	
1892		**Peru**	25,000
		Country devastated by quake.	
	July 30	**San Cristobal, Mexico**	100s
		Quake destroyed every structure in city.	
†1893	Feb. 8	**Zante**	100s
		Quake shook island off W. coast of Greece; 1000s homeless.	
	Nov. 19	**Kuchan & Samarcand, Persia**	12,000
		Severe quakes in both cities.	
1894	Nov. 17	**Calabria, Italy**	100
		Quake shook area.	
1895	May 24	**Paramthia, Epirus**	1,000s
		Quake left city in ruins.	
†1896	June 15	**Japan**	28,000
		Quake followed by *tsunamis* leveled Sanriku.	
1897	June 12	**Assam, India**	1,542
		India's worst quake to this date. All buildings within 3,000 sq. mi. destroyed; 8.7 on Richter Scale.	
1898		**Japan**	22,000
		Tsunami followed quake and raped country.	
	Jan. 5	**Moluccas, Ambonia**	50
		Mild shocks on island.	
1899	Sept. 20	**Aidin, Asia Minor**	1,600
		Quake destroyed city and 2 villages.	
	Oct. 12	**Ceram, Dutch East Indies**	100s
		Quake destroyed city.	
	Dec. 31	**Tiflis, Russia**	1,000
		Quake damaged province; destroyed 6 villages.	
1900	Oct. 30	**Guaronas, Caracas**	25
		Quake left city in shambles.	
1901	Nov. 8-12	**Erzerum, Armenia**	22
		Quake caused 50 shocks; many houses downed.	
1902	Feb. 13-18	**Schemacha, Transcausia**	2,000
		District destroyed; Czar contributed 150,000 rupies.	
	†Apr. 18	**Guatemala**	12,200
		Series of earthquakes destroyed city & 18 towns; 80,000 homeless.	
	May 8	**St. Pierre, Martinique**	40,000
		Island destroyed after eruption of Mt. Pelée. (SEE Pelée)	
	Dec. 16	**Andijan, Turkestan**	10,000
		Quake destroyed district of Ferghana; 15,000 houses leveled.	
1903	Apr. 29	**Van & Melazguird, Armenia**	860
		Quake devastated entire area; many cattle & sheep killed.	
†1905	Mar. 4	**India**	100s
		Series of quakes struck northern part of country; 1,000s injured.	
	†Apr. 4	**Kangra, India**	19,000
		City inundated; 8.7 on Richter Scale.	
	June 1	**Scutori, Albania**	100
		Quake leveled 500 houses; many injured.	
	†Sept. 8	**Italy**	5,000
		Seven-day series of quakes wiped out 25 villages.	
1906	Jan. 4	**Masaya, Nicaragua**	1,000s
		Quake followed by volcanic eruption.	
	Feb. 14	**Port of Boca Grande, Colombia**	100s
		Quake followed by tidal wave destroyed port.	
	Mar. 17	**Kagi, Formosa**	1,250
		Quake destroyed 5,556 houses; 2,329 injured.	
	†Apr. 18	**San Francisco, California**	700
		City destroyed; 28,188 houses destroyed; large fire afterward. 8.3 on Richter Scale.	
	†Aug. 16	**Valparaiso, Chile**	1,500
		Quake left 100,000 homeless.	
†1907	Jan. 14	**Kingston, Jamaica**	1,400
		Quake demolished city.	
	Jan. 22	**Simalu, Sumatra**	1,500
		Island inundated.	
	Oct. 21	**Katta-Kurgan & Samarkand, Asia**	14,000
		Tremendous quakes at both cities.	
	Oct. 23	**Calabria, Italy**	600
		Quake destroyed city and adjoining villages.	
1908	June 12	**Chang**	100s
		Houses with families swallowed by fissure opening in mountain.	
	†Dec. 28	**Messina, Sicily**	160,000
		Quake destroyed 98% of dwellings; 170,000 sq. mi. shaken. 7.5 on Strasbourg Scale.	
1909	Jan. 23	**Luristan, Persia**	5,500
		Quake destroyed province.	
	Apr. 23	**Lisbon, Portugal**	40
		Quake injured 100.	
	June 3	**Upper Padang, Sumatra**	230
		Quake injured many.	
	Oct. 22	**Belput, India**	25
		Railway station on the Quetta Line destroyed.	
1910	May 4	**Cartago, Costa Rica**	242
		City destroyed.	
1911	Jan. 5-12	**Kebery, Russian Turkestan**	300
		Quake destroyed town; shook Pispek area.	
	June 7	**Mexico City**	63
		Heavy damage; 75 people injured.	
	Oct. 15	**Catania, Sicily**	20
		Mild shock throughout city.	
1912	July 20	**Guadalajara, Mexico**	100s
		Quake almost destroyed city.	
	Aug. 11	**Dardanelles, Turkey**	3,000
		Quake destroyed many towns throughout region.	
1914	Mar. 16	**Hondo, Japan**	250
		Island badly shaken.	
	May 9	**Mt. Etna, Sicily**	182
		Village surrounding mountain destroyed. King and Pope sent aid.	
	Oct. 13	**Kronia, Turkey**	3,000
		Quake destroyed province.	
	Nov. 28	**Western Greece & Ionian Islands**	23
		Violent shocks felt across area.	
	Dec. 9	**Peru**	50
		Many towns badly damaged.	

Major Earthquakes

Date		Place	Deaths	Description
1915	Jan. 13	Avezzano, Italy	30,000	Quake destroyed 60 towns.
1916	July 6	Caltanissetta, Sicily	300	Quake buried 100 miners.
	Aug. 20	Italy	30	Quake injured 150; shocks felt in Berlin, Germany.
1917	Jan. 6	Formosa, China	300	Quake destroyed capital.
	Jan. 26	Bali, Malay Archipelago	550	Quake wrecked island.
	Dec. 29	Guatemala, Mexico	2,500	Quake destroyed city in 2 separate shocks.
1918	Oct. 11	Puerto Rico	150	Quake followed by sea wave wrecked island.
	Oct. 22	Guatemala, Mexico	150	Quake wrecked city second straight year.
1919	July 1	Tuscany, Italy	127	Quake destroyed city; thousands injured. King Emmanuel visited area.
1920	Jan. 4	San Joaquim, Mexico	100s	City wiped out; shocks felt at Georgetown University.
	Mar. 10	Tiflis, Caucasus	100s	Quake devastated region.
	Sept. 8	Pisa, Italy	100s	Quake razed 2 towns; Leaning Tower threatened.
	Dec. 6	Tepelin & Saseno, Albania	100s	Tidal wave followed quake.
	Dec. 11	Argentina	150	Severe shocks in several provinces.
	†Dec. 16	Kansu, China	180,000	Quake destroyed province; 8.6 on Richter Scale.
1922	Nov. 11	Atacama, Chile	600	Quake caused cities to disappear; U.S. President Harding sent aid.
1923	Mar. 24	China	3,000	Quake destroyed 70 sq. mi. of territory.
	Apr. 14	Korea	100s	Earth & tidal disturbance shook country.
	Apr. 21	Petropaulousk, Siberia	21	Tidal wave followed quake.
	May 5	Soula Sela, Asia Minor	100s	Quake destroyed town.
	May-June	Persia	6,000	Quake caused heavy loss of life in Northwest Mountains.
	July 4	Tibet, China	100s	Heavy loss of life and property at frontier.
	†Sept. 1-3	Tokyo & Yokohama, Japan	143,000	Both cities demolished; 600,000 homes destroyed. Measured 8.2 on Richter Scale.
	Sept. 10	Calcutta, India	50	Tremors shook city.
	Sept. 20	Persia	157	Quake destroyed 9 villages; 22 partially.
	Sept. 25	Persia	125	Another quake hit area.
1924	Jan. 4	Mt. Fujiyama, Japan	30	Shocks felt at base of mountain.
	Jan. 15	Japan	scores	Severe quake hit Tokyo & Yokohama.
	Mar. 4	Costa Rica	scores	Strongest shocks in 25 years.
	May 14	Armenia	50	Quake destroyed several cities.
	Aug. 9	Turkestan	41	Quake destroyed 3,100 houses.
	Sept. 16	Erzerum, Armenia	200	Great destruction throughout district.
	Sept. 20	Erzerum, Armenia	60	District hit again; 300 villages destroyed.
	Nov. 8	Algeria	22	Quake left 3,000 homeless.
	Nov. 13-14	Island of Java	664	Quake wrecked towns and villages.
	Dec. 18	Suriagao, Philippines	24	Serious quake on island.
1925	Jan. 12	Ardahan, Russian Armenia	140	Quake destroyed 4 regions; 2,000 homeless.
	Mar. 16	Talifu, China	6,500	Violent quake at Yunan Province.
	May 23	Japan	278	Quake devastated Toyo-oka and Kinosaki Springs; 1,000s homeless and 900 injured.
1926	Mar. 5	Peloponnesus, Greece	100s	City badly shaken.
	May 2	Pandjang Sumatra, East Indies	1,032	City destroyed, Soengeiboeloe and Solok badly damaged.
	May 24	Sapporo, Japan	1,000s	Quake preceded volcanic eruption.
	July 1	Fort Dekok, Sumatra	222	Quake destroyed village; heavy damage at Pandjang.
	Aug. 31	Horta Island Fayal (Azores)	200	Quake inundated town.
	Oct. 22	Armenia	400	Quake shook entire Republic; not a single structure left standing.
	Nov. 3	Armenia	1,500	Quake shook area for 15 days; 34 villages destroyed.
	Nov. 26	Managua, Nicaragua	scores	Quake destroyed 50% of the houses.
1927	Feb. 14-16	Bosnia, Yugoslavia	91	Quake devastated Herzegovnia, Dalmatia and Ljubliana. Crack in bed of Adriatic began disasters.
	Mar. 7	Tango (Japan)	3,000	Quake measured 7.9 on Richter Scale.
	Mar. 27	Central Japan	1,000s	Earthquake shook central & western parts; 83% of bldgs. affected.
	Apr. 14	Santiago, Chile	50	City badly shaken.
	May 14	Belgrade, Yugoslavia	100s	Many parts of country shaken.
	May 22	Kansu, China	100,000	Severe quake wrecked province.
	July 11	Palestine & Transjordania	268	Casualties in 20 towns; Nablus half-destroyed.
1928	Apr. 14	Balkan Peninsula & Aegean Island	56	Philippopolis & Bulgaria in ruins; 1,000s homeless.
	Apr. 15	Jaen, Peru	39	Quake shook southern part of country; many casualties.
	Apr. 16	Smyrna, Turkey	60	City devastated; shocks felt in Constantinople.
1929	Jan. 16	Suiyan, China	100s	Quake caused heavy damage in famine zone.
	Jan. 18	Cumana, Venezuela	50	City destroyed, American missionaries missing.
	May 3	Northern Khorassan, Persia	1,000s	Quake destroyed 1,000 villages; 1,000s homeless.
	May 20-27	Sivas, Turkey	117	Quake destroyed 74 villages; Northern Anatolia shaken.
	May 30	Villatuer, Argentina	35	Half of town destroyed; many injured at Villa Real and Las Malvinas.
	July 26	Ecuador	60	Tremors felt throughout country.

Date		Place	Deaths
	July 28	**Turnikeuy, Turkey**	**1,000**
	Quake destroyed city, Northern Anatolia shaken.		
1930	**May 6**	**India**	**3,600**
	Entire country devastated; Burma and Pegu heaviest hit.		
	July 23-25	**Irpino, Italy**	**1,500**
	Quake wiped out 25 communes.		
	Nov. 22	**Valona, Albania**	**30**
	Quake razed 900 houses.		
	Nov. 25	**Japan**	**285**
	Quake rips 600-mi. area from Osaka to Kuikui; 146 houses destroyed and 4,637 badly damaged.		
	Dec. 5	**Burma, India**	**36**
	Intense shocks throughout country.		
	Dec. 24	**Los Andes, Argentina**	**39**
	Quake left many homeless at Salta and La Poma.		
1931	**Jan. 2**	**Oaxaca, Mexico**	**106**
	Quake wrecked entire city.		
	Mar. 7	**Bulgarian Frontier, Yugoslavia**	**150**
	Quake destroyed city of Piraun. Wide damage left 500 injured and 1,000 houses leveled; 10,000 homeless people faced lack of supplies, storms and wolves.		
	Mar. 31	**Managua**	**1,000**
	Quake caused $15 million damage.		
	Apr. 29	**Gori, Russia**	**489**
	Quake wiped out 27 villages.		
	Sept. 2	**Hawkes Bay, New Zealand**	**230**
	This country's largest quake.		
1932	**Feb. 23**	**Santiago, Cuba**	**100**
	Two shocks wrecked city.		
	July 23	**Cuyutian, Mexico**	**34**
	Quake followed by tidal wave wrecked city; Manzanillo and Colima also damaged.		
	Sept. 29	**Chalcidice, Greece**	**500**
	Quake left 20,000 homeless; 1,000 hurt.		
	Dec. 25	**Kansu, China**	**70,000**
	District of Kaotai devastated.		
†1933	**Mar. 3**	**Sanriku, Japan**	**3,000**
	Northeastern coast hit by *tsunamis* after quake; 8,851 houses and 8,000 boats destroyed; 8.6 on Richter Scale.		
	†Mar. 10	**Long Beach, California**	**120**
	Quake caused $50 million damage.		
	Apr. 24	**Cos, Greece**	**200**
	Island wrecked; some damage in Sporades.		
	June 26	**Sumatra, Dutch East Indies**	**76**
	Island devastated.		
	Aug. 30	**Chengtu, China**	**100**
	Quake shook area.		
	Dec. 3	**Szechwan Province**	**400**
	Quake wrecked entire province.		
1934	**Jan. 16**	**Nepal, India**	**9,040**
	Severe quake thoughout country at Monghyr, Muzufferpur and Darbhanga.		
	Dec. 15	**Diarbekir, Turkey**	**20**
	Mild shocks at city.		
1935	**Apr. 21**	**Taihoku, Formosa**	**3,185**
	Quake was preceded by eruption of Asama Yama, a Japanese volcano silent for years.		
	May 18	**Kars, Turkey**	**500**
	Quake left 2,000 injured at district.		
	May 31	**Quetta, India**	**56,000**
	City devastated; 100 miles of surrounding area inundated.		
	July 17	**Formosa**	**39**
	Slight quake on island.		
	Oct. 13	**Tovildolinsky, U.S.S.R.**	**50**
	Quake injured 300.		
1936	**Jan. 10**	**Tuguerrew, Colombia**	**100s**
	Many villages wiped out in south.		
	July 13	**Taltal, Chile**	**50**
	Northern coast rocked; 100 houses leveled.		
1937	**July 26**	**Veracruz & Puebla States, Mexico**	**30**
	Quake left many injured.		
†1939	**Jan. 24**	**Chile**	**50,000**
	Quake razed 50,000 sq. mi.; 8.3 on Richter Scale.		
	Nov. 24	**Anatolia, Turkey**	**43**
	Quake caused heavy damage.		
	†Dec. 27	**Erzincan, Turkey**	**50,000**
	Quake destroyed 50,000 houses.		
1940	**Feb. 23**	**Soysalli, Turkey**	**120**
	Kayseri province wiped out.		
	May 25	**Lima, Peru**	**200-300**
	Worst quake in 50 years. Port of Callao had 5,000 injured.		
	July 31	**Central Analolia, Turkey**	**1,000**
	City of Peyik destroyed.		
	Nov. 9-10	**Ploesti, Rumania**	**400**
	Worst quake in country's history; 800 injured.		
1941	**Mar. 1**	**Larissa, Greece**	**25**
	Quake leveled 40% of houses near Thessaly.		
	Sept. 12	**Agri, Turkey**	**200**
	Forty villages in Van Province destroyed.		
	Dec. 17	**Formosa**	**319**
	Quake wrecked southern part of island. Communications cut for 2 days; 437 injured.		
1942	**May 13**	**Guayuquil, Ecuador**	**100s**
	Country's chief port wrecked.		
	Dec. 7	**Central Anatolia, Turkey**	**800**
	Quake destroyed many villages.		
1943	**June 21**	**Adapazari, Turkey**	**1,304**
	Quake destroyed 1,000 buildings; Hendek, Geyue and Arifiye also hit.		
	Sept. 10	**Tottori, Japan**	**1,400**
	Quake ruined city. Tokyo radio reported "damage was slight"; 7.4 on Richter Scale.		
1944	**Jan. 15**	**San Juan, Argentina**	**5,000**
	Quake destroyed 9 villages in the Andes.		
	Feb. 1	**Gerede, Turkey**	**1,458**
	Violent quake in Ankara area.		
1945	**Nov. 30**	**Pasni, India**	**400**
	Quake followed by a tidal wave.		
1946	**Feb. 13**	**Algeria**	**276**
	Series of quakes jolted country.		
	May 31	**Varto, Turkey**	**1,300**
	Quake destroyed 95% of city.		
	June 1	**Eastern Turkey**	**1,339**
	Country ripped by quake.		
	Aug. 4	**Dominican Republic**	**73**
	Quake leveled 4 towns in northern section.		
	Nov. 10-13	**Ancash, Peru**	**700**
	City in the Andes leveled; 7.4 on various scales.		
	†Dec. 21	**Honshu, Japan**	**2,000**
	Quake and *tsunami* affected 60,000 sq. mi.		
1947	**Feb. 13**	**Algeria**	**276**
	Quake shattered country.		
	June 1	**Eastern Turkey**	**1,339**
	Quake caused mass suffering.		
	Aug. 5-9	**Dominican Republic**	**73**
	Quake leveled 4 towns; number injured impossible to estimate.		
	Dec. 21	**Japan**	**1,061**
	Quake followed by 6 *tsunamis* spread over 60,000 sq. mi. leaving 100,000 homeless, 1,092 injured and 165 missing.		
1948	**Jan. 25-27**	**Panay Island, Philippines**	**27**
	Quakes lasted several days.		
	June 28	**Fukui, Japan**	**3,215**
	City destroyed; 7.3 on various scales.		

Date		Place	Deaths
	Oct. 4	**Kagi, Formosa**	**1,250**
	Quake left 2,329 injured and 5,556 houses leveled.		
	Oct. 5	**Askhabad, Iran**	**200**
	Series of quakes wrecked city leaving 600 children "orphaned" and 6,000 injured.		
1949	**Apr. 19**	**Chile**	**62**
	Central part of country shook.		
	†Aug. 5	**Ecuador**	**6,000**
	Quake razed 53 towns.		
	Aug. 18	**Erzerum, Turkey**	**256**
	Quake left 1,000 injured.		
1950	**Feb. 1**	**Bushire, Iran**	**20**
	Quake on the Persian Gulf.		
	May 21	**Cuzco, Peru**	**56**
	Quake destroyed 80% of city; 900-year-old capital of the former Inca Empire shaken, 137 injured.		
	July 8-11	**North Santander, Colombia**	**139**
	Quakes rocked area.		
	†Aug. 15	**Assam, India**	**1,000**
	Quake smashed 2,000 houses. Measured 8.7 on Richter Scale and 8.6 on Strasbourg Scale.		
1951	**Jan. 18-21**	**Papua Territory, New Guinea**	**3,000**
	Quake followed eruption of Mt. Lamington.		
	May 6	**Jacuapa, San Salvador**	**200**
	Quake wrecked city.		
	Aug. 13	**Turkey**	**44**
	Quake devastated northwestern part of country.		
	Oct. 22-23	**Hualien, Formosa**	**44**
	Quakes lasted 2 days.		
1952	**Jan. 3**	**Turkey**	**93**
	Entire country shook, many homeless.		
	Mar. 4	**Tokaichi, Japan**	**600**
	Quake measured 8.6 on Richter Scale, 8.3 on Strasbourg Scale.		
	Dec. 30	**Costa Rica**	**21**
	Quake struck near Irazu volcano.		
1953	**Feb. 22**	**Turud, Iran**	**531**
	Quake damaged 25 villages.		
	Mar. 18	**Canakkale & Balikesir, Turkey**	**1,200**
	Quake left 50,000 homeless.		
	Aug. 9-13	**Zante & Ithaea, Ionian Island**	**500**
	Extended quake left 92,700 homeless.		
	Sept. 10	**Cyprus**	**40**
	Quake left 100 seriously injured and 1,000s homeless.		
1954	**Feb. 5**	**Thessaly, Greece**	**31**
	City buried; 160 persons injured, 5,000 structures damaged, and 29,000 persons homeless.		
	Sept. 9-12	**Orleansville, Algeria**	**1,250**
	City destroyed. Measured 6.7 on Strasbourg Scale.		
1955	**Apr. 4**	**Philippines**	**432**
	Quake lasted 7 hours; 2,000 injured and 11,500 homeless.		
	Apr. 14	**Kiangtin, Sikiang, Red China**	**39**
	Quake left 113 injured.		
1956	**Mar. 16**	**Lebanon**	**145**
	Quake left 25,000 homeless.		
	June 10-17	**Kabul, Afghanistan**	**2,000**
	Country suffered for 8 days.		
	July 19	**Thera, Greece**	**43**
	Quake left 60% homeless on island. Measured 7.7 on Strasbourg Scale.		
	Nov. 11	**Fars Province, Iran**	**268**
	Series of quakes near Persian Gulf.		
1957	**May 26**	**Bolu, Turkey**	**66**
	Quake shook a large area in the north.		
	July 2	**Caspian Coast, Iran**	**200**
	Quake left 10,000 homeless.		
	†July 28	**Mexico City, Mexico**	**70**
	Quake shook city and areas near Acapulco.		
	Dec. 4	**Altai, Outer Mongolia**	**1,200**
	Quake measured 8.6 on Richter Scale.		
	Dec. 13-17	**Farsinaj, Iran**	**1,392**
	Western village leveled, 6,000 injured and 1,000s homeless.		
1958	**Jan. 15**	**Arequipa, Peru**	**128**
	Quake in the Andes.		
	Jan. 19	**Esmeralda, Ecuador**	**20**
	Slight quake.		
	Aug. 16-21	**Iran**	**191**
	Quake left 984 injured.		
1960	**Jan. 13**	**South America**	**2,199**
	Great quakes in Bolivia, Peru, and Chile; $622 million damage.		
	Feb. 21	**Melouza & Beni Illmane, Algiers**	**47**
	Three quakes shook villages.		
	†Feb. 29-Mar. 1	**Agadir, Morocco**	**12,000**
	Seventy % of city destroyed.		
	Apr. 24	**Lar (Persia)**	**1,000**
	Quake measured 5.75 on various scales.		
	†May 21-30	**Chile**	**5,700**
	Series of violent quakes followed by *tsunamis* and eruptions.		
	June 11	**Dehkuyeh, Iran**	**700**
	Quake destroyed village; 50 injured.		
	Sept. 1	**Colombia**	**40**
	Quakes left 300 injured.		
1961	**Dec. 20**	**Colombia**	**20**
	Mild quake.		
†1962	**Sept. 2**	**Iran**	**10,000**
	Worst quake in country's history.		
1963	**Feb. 21-22**	**Barce, Libya**	**300**
	Quake left 15,000 homeless.		
	Mar. 20	**Bali**	**1,100**
	Severe damage in the wake of Mt. Agung.		
	July 26	**Skopje, Yugoslavia**	**1,070**
	Quake left 80,000 homeless.		
	Sept. 2	**Gulmarg, Kashmir Valley**	**100**
	Quake shook 50 sq. mi.		
1964	**Jan. 18**	**Paiho & Tungshan, Taiwan**	**100**
	Severe damage to both cities.		
	†Mar. 27	**Alaska**	**118**
	One of the strongest quakes in history; $500 million damage.		
	June 16	**Niigata, Japan**	**27**
	Quake left 377 injured; 5 missing.		
	July 15	**Guerrao, Mexico**	**36**
	Pacific Coast struck; 65 injured.		
1965	**Feb. 18-24**	**Sanana Island, Indonesia**	**71**
	Quake destroyed 2,800 buildings and 14 bridges.		
	†Mar. 28	**Chile**	**470**
	Quake caused $200 million damage.		
	May 3	**San Salvador, El Salvador**	**100**
	Quake jolted capital city; 500 injured and 7,000 homeless; 7.5 on various scales.		
	Sept. 17-18	**Japan**	**50**
	Typhoon Trix and 7 quakes devastated country.		
1966	**Mar. 8**	**Hopei, China**	**unavailable**
	Extensive damage in Hingtai area; 8.6 on various scales.		
	Mar. 20-22	**Bwamba & Bundibugyo, Uganda**	**79**
	Both towns destroyed; 8.0 on various scales.		
	Apr. 26	**Tashkent, U.S.S.R.**	**10**
	Quake destroyed 20% of buildings; 300,000 homeless.		
	May 18	**Kivu Providence, Africa**	**90**
	Congo badly shaken.		
	June 29	**Bajhang, Nepal**	**150**
	Quake left 20,000 homeless.		

Date		Place	Deaths
	Aug. 19-23	**Turkey**	**2,529**
	Quake destroyed 100 towns leaving 100,000 homeless in 4 provinces.		
	Oct. 17	**Lima, Peru**	**92**
	City badly shaken.		
1967	**Feb. 9**	**Guacamayas, Colombia**	**100**
	Quake injured 420; measured 7.5 on various scales.		
	Feb. 20	**Malang, East Java**	**26**
	Quake shook village.		
	Mar. 11	**Madjene, Indonesia**	**37**
	South Celebes struck.		
	July 22	**Anatolia, Turkey**	**83**
	Quake left 110 injured.		
	July 26	**Erzincan & Tunceli, Turkey**	**112**
	Quake left 200 injured.		
	July 30-31	**Caracas, Venezuela**	**277**
	Quakes from Andes to the Caribbean.		
	Nov. 11	**Dedar, Yugoslavia**	**20**
	Border town struck; 80% of city destroyed leaving 204 injured; 6.25 on various scales.		
	Dec. 11	**India**	**200**
	Quake injured 1,000; 6.25 on various scales.		
1968	**Jan. 14-25**	**Sicily**	**235**
	Quake shook 600 sq. mi. in West Central area, 50,000 homeless; 9 on various scales.		
	May 16	**Honshu & Hokkaido, Japan**	**39**
	Islands badly shaken; 2,000 homes destroyed; 7.8 on various scales.		
	Aug. 2	**Luzon & Manila, Philippines**	**307**
	Quake caused hotel to collapse on 500 people; 7.8 on various scales.		
	Aug. 10-15	**Tuguan Island, Indonesia**	**100s**
	Island disappeared after second quake.		
	Aug. 31	**Khurasan, Iran**	**12,000**
	Quake devastated province. (SEE Qir Valley)		
1969	**Jan. 3-4**	**Khorassan, Iran**	**50**
	Quake left 2,000 homeless.		
	Mar. 28	**Alasehir, Turkey**	**53**
	Quake left 350 injured.		
	Mar. 29	**Addis, Ethiopia**	**23**
	Quake hit desert town leaving 350 injured.		
1970	**Mar. 28**	**Gediz, Turkey**	**1,100**
	City in west razed.		
	May 30	**Yungay, Peru**	**66,794**
	Resort city inundated; 600,000 homeless.		
	July 30	**Iran**	**100**
	Quake shook scores of villages; 200 injured; 6 on various scales.		
	Dec. 9	**Ecuador & Peru**	**82**
	Quake struck border.		
1971	**Feb. 6**	**Tuscania, Italy**	**scores**
	City destroyed, 4,000 homeless; 6 on various scales.		
	Feb. 9	**Los Angeles, California**	**65**
	Quake caused damage of $1 billion.		
	May 12	**Burdur, Turkey**	**57**
	Quake struck city.		
	May 23	**Bingol, Turkey**	**800**
	Country severely hit.		
	July 9	**Chile**	**90**
	Quake cracked North Central region; injured 250 and left 100,000 homeless.		
1972	**Mar. 20**	**Juanjil, Peru**	**30**
	Quake destroyed half of town.		
	†April 10	**Qir Valley, Iran**	**5,044**
	Quake shook a 250-mile radius leveling 58 villages.		
	Dec. 23	**Managua, Nicaragua**	**7,000**
	Worst tremors in country's history; 200,000 left homeless; 6.25 on various scales.		
†1973	**Sept. 29**	**Mexico**	**700**
	Quake ruined 300 mi. of the S.E. including scores of villages & towns.		
1974	**May 9**	**Japan**	**30**
	Quake injured 77.		
	Oct. 3	**Lima, Peru**	**73**
	Quake destroyed 60% of Canete, 120 mi. S. of Lima.		
	Dec. 28	**Pakistan**	**5,200**
	Quake ruined 9 towns.		
1975	**Feb. 4**	**China**	**unavailable**
	A major quake with a reading of 7.3 on Richter Scale hit near Ansham, Manchuria.		
	Sept. 6	**Lice, Turkey**	**2,312**
	Town leveled; 6.8 on Richter Scale.		

Major Fires and Explosions

(† indicates entries profiled in General Narrative. Fires involving one building, an institution, or organization are listed under the proper name, all others are listed under place name.)

Date		Place	Deaths
538 B.C.		**Babylon, Mesopotamia**	1,000s
	Fire destroyed greater part of city including hanging gardens following capture by Persians.		
390		**Rome, Italy**	100s
	Fire broke out after sacking by Gauls.		
146		**Carthage**	1,000s
	Fire destroyed entire city.		
86		**Athens**	100s
	City partially destroyed after sacking by Romans under Sulla.		
A.D. 59		**Lyons, France**	100s
	City burned to ground; Nero offered assistance.		
64		**Rome, Italy**	100s
	City burned for 8 days, 75% of area destroyed. Fire started in the Circus Maximus and was allowed to spread by Emperor Nero.		
500		**Alexandria, Egypt**	100s
	Fire consumed great library of classical antiquity.		
798		**London, England**	
	Fire destroyed most of city.		
982		**London, England**	
	City again nearly destroyed.		
1106		**Venice, Italy**	
	City nearly destroyed by fire.		
1118		**Nantes, France**	
	Most of city destroyed.		
1137		**York, England**	
	Fire completely destroyed city.		
1212		**London, England**	3,000
	Fire began at the London Bridge on the Southwark side and to the north and south. Most of the city was destroyed.		
1292		**Carlisle, England**	
	Fire completely destroyed city.		
1379		**Memel, U.S.S.R. (now Klaipeda, Lithuania, U.S.S.R.)**	
	Fire destroyed most of city. This same disaster occurred 5 times in 7 centuries.		
1405		**Berlin, Germany**	
	Great fire in city.		
1457		**Memel, U.S.S.R.**	
	Fire destroyed most of city.		
1491		**Dresden, Germany**	
	Fire destroyed city.		
1540		**Memel, U.S.S.R.**	
	Fire destroyed most of city.		
1544		**Leith, England**	
	Town destroyed by fire.		
1570		**Moscow, Russia**	200,000
	Fire devastated city, mass suffering.		
1577		**Venice, Italy**	
	Historic city again devastated by fire.		
1598		**Tiverton, England**	33
	Fire destroyed 400 houses.		
1612		**Cork, Ireland**	
	Most of city burned.		
1614		**Stratford-upon-Avon, England**	
	Historic cultural center destroyed by fire.		
1615		**Seville, Spain**	scores
	Fire destroyed Teatre Atarazanas.		
1624		**Oslo, Norway**	
	Fire destroyed most of city.		
1634		**Berne, Germany**	
	Fire devastated city.		
1645		**Boston, Massachusetts**	3
	Gunpowder explosion destroyed 1/3 of city.		
1666	Sept. 2-6	**London, England**	8
	The Great Fire destroyed 396 acres, 13,200 houses, and 400 streets. Edifices ruined included St. Paul's, the Royal Exchange, Guildhall and many public buildings. Insurance Institute for fire established 1 yr. later.		
1675		**Northampton, England**	
	Town nearly destroyed by fire.		
1676		**Jamestown, Virginia**	
	City burned to ground.		
1678		**Memel, U.S.S.R.**	
	Fire destroyed most of city.		
1680		**Berne, Germany**	
	City again struck by fire.		
1689		**Copenhagen, Denmark**	210
	Fire destroyed Castle of Amalienborg.		
1694		**Warwick, England**	
	Town ½ destroyed, contributions rebuilt damaged area.		
1700		**Edinburgh, Scotland**	
	City ruined by fire.		
1707		**Lisbon, Portugal**	
	City razed by fire.		
1715		**Wapping, England**	50
	Fire destroyed 150 houses.		
1728		**Copenhagen, Denmark**	
	City almost destroyed, 1,650 structures burned.		
1729		**Constantinople, Turkey**	7,000
	Fire destroyed 12,000 houses.		
1748	Mar. 25	**London, England**	
	Most destructive damage since the great fire of 1666, fire began in Change-Alley and destroyed 200 houses.		
1750	Jan.	**Constantinople, Turkey**	
	City razed, $15 million damage—1,000 houses destroyed.		
1751		**Stockholm, Sweden**	
	Fire destroyed 1,100 structures.		
1752		**Moscow, Russia**	
	Great fire, 18,000 structures destroyed.		
1756		**Constantinople, Turkey**	
	Great fire, 15,000 structures burned.		
1769		**St. Nazaire, Brescia**	3,000
	Explosion destroyed ¼ of city; powder stored in church ignited by lightning.		
1772		**Smyrna**	
	Fire destroyed 3,000 houses, 4,000 businesses, and $40 million damage.		
1778		**Saragosso, Spain**	77
	Fire destroyed Teatro Colissea; governor among victims.		
1781		**Paris, France**	20
	Fire destroyed Palais Royal.		
1782		**Constantinople, Turkey**	100
	Fire raged 3 days, destroyed 10,000 houses and 50 mosques.		
†1788	Mar. 21	**New Orleans, Louisiana**	scores
	Fire destroyed 856 buildings; $3 million damage.		
1790		**Karlskrona, Sweden**	
	Fire destroyed 1,300 structures.		
1795	June 21	**Copenhagen, Denmark**	
	Fire destroyed 1/3 of city.		
1811	Dec. 26	**Richmond, Virginia**	70
	Richmond Theater fire.		

Date		Place	Deaths
1812		**Moscow, Russia**	
	Russian incendiaries started fire after occupation by Napoleon's Army, 31,000 buildings destroyed—$150 million damage.		
1822		**Canton, China**	
	Fire destroyed 85% of city.		
1824	**Mar. 22**	**Cairo, Egypt**	**4,000**
	Fire devastated city, mass suffering.		
	Nov. 15-17	**Edinburgh, Scotland**	**10**
	Fire caused $4 million damage, reform regulations started immediately afterward.		
1825	**Nov. 7**	**New Brunswick, Canada**	**160**
	Forest fire destroyed 4 million acres, covered over 100 mi.		
1834	**Oct. 16**	**London, England**	
	Fire destroyed houses of Parliament, original warrant for the execution of Charles I lost.		
1835	**Dec. 16**	**New York, N.Y.**	
	Fire destroyed 654 buildings, $20 million loss—13 acres ruined.		
1836	**Dec 16**	**Washington, D.C.**	
	Fire destroyed General Post Office, over 10,000 valuable works of art ruined.		
	Dec. 30	**St. Petersburg, Russia**	**700**
	Lehman's theater fire.		
†1838	**Apr. 27-28**	**Charleston, S.C.**	**4**
	City gutted; damage in millions.		
1839	**Oct. 4**	**Philadelphia, Pa.**	
	Fire destroyed 52 buildings.		
†1842	**May 5**	**Hamburg, Germany**	**100**
	Fire destroyed 1,992 houses and $35 million damage, 20% of city ruined.		
1845	**Apr. 10**	**Pittsburg, Pa.**	**2**
	Fire destroyed 1,100 buildings, $10 million damage.		
	May	**Canton, China**	**1,670**
	Theater fire, heavy casualties.		
	May 28	**Quebec, Canada**	
	Fire destroyed 1,500 buildings.		
	June 20	**New York, N.Y.**	**6**
	Fire destroyed 1,300 buildings, $6 million damage.		
	June 28	**Quebec, Canada**	
	Fire destroyed 1,300 buildings.		
	Dec. 16	**New York City**	
	Fire destroyed same district as 10 yrs. earlier.		
1846	**June 12**	**St. John's, Newfoundland**	
	City nearly destroyed, 6,000 homeless—$15 million damage.		
	†June 12	**Quebec, Canada**	**45**
	St. Louis Theater fire.		
	July 13	**Nantucket, Mass.**	
	Fire destroyed 300 buildings.		
1847	**Mar. 6**	**Carlsrube, Baden, Germany**	**150**
	Fire at the Grand Ducal Theatre.		
†1848	**Aug. 16**	**Constantinople, Turkey**	**200**
	Fire destroyed 2,500 shops and $15 million damage.		
	Aug. 17	**Albany, N.Y.**	
	Fire destroyed 300 buildings, 25 steamboats—damage $3 million.		
1848	**Sept. 9**	**Brooklyn, N.Y.**	
	Fire destroyed 300 buildings.		
1849	**May 17**	**St. Louis, Mo.**	
	Fire destroyed 15 city blocks, 25 steamboats and $4 million damage.		
1850	**June 21**	**Cracow, Poland**	
	Fire destroyed many sections of city.		
	†July 9	**Philadelphia, Pennsylvania**	**39**
	Fire destroyed 400 bldgs. in slum districts; damage over $1 million.		
	Sept. 15	**San Francisco, Calif.**	
	Third and most destructive fire in 3 years, 1,500 buildings burned — $4 million damage.		
1851	**Mar. 12**	**Nevada, Calif.**	
	Fire destroyed 200 buildings, damage $1½ million.		
	†May 3	**San Francisco, Calif.**	**30**
	Fire destroyed 70% of city, 2,500 buildings and $3.5 million damage.		
	May 14	**Stockton, Calif.**	
	Fire caused $1½ million damage.		
	Aug. 24	**Concord, N.H.**	
	Fire destroyed downtown business district.		
	Dec. 24	**Washington, D.C.**	
	Fire at Congressional Library, 35,000 volumes and works of art destroyed.		
1852	**July 8**	**Montreal, Canada**	
	Fire destroyed 1,200 houses, damage $5 million.		
1853	**July 14**	**New York, N.Y.**	
	Fire destroyed Crystal Palace Museum, damage in the millions, city's worst conflagration since destruction of Harper & Brothers publishing house.		
1854	**Oct. 6**	**Gateshead, England**	**50**
	Fire swept city.		
1854	**July 30**	**Jersey City, N.J.**	
	Fire destroyed 30 houses and factories.		
	Aug. 25	**Milwaukee, Wisc.**	
	Fire destroyed most of city.		
	Aug. 25	**Troy, N.Y.**	
	Fire destroyed 100 houses and factories.		
	Oct. 8	**Memel, U.S.S.R.**	
	Fire destroyed most of city.		
1856	**Nov. 8**	**Syracuse, N.Y.**	
	Fire destroyed 100 bldgs.; damage over $1 million.		
†1857	**Mar. 21**	**Tokyo, Japan**	**107,000**
	Massive fires broke out after tremendous quake; winds of 60 m.p.h. spread the blaze.		
	June 7	**Leghorn, Italy**	**50-100**
	Fire at the Tentro degli Aquidotti.		
	Oct. 19	**Chicago, Ill.**	**14**
	Fire at large store on South Water St.; $800,000 damage.		
1858	**June 29**	**London, England**	
	London Docks exploded, $2 million damage.		
1863	**Jan. 17**	**Santiago, Chile**	**2,000**
	Fire at the Jesuit Church.		
1865		**Karlstadt, Sweden**	**10**
	Fire destroyed most of city.		
	†Feb. 8	**Philadelphia, Pa.**	**20**
	Fire destroyed 50 bldgs. in 3-sq.-blk. area; damage over $500,000.		
1866	**July 4**	**Portland, Me.**	
	Fire destroyed 200 acres, 1,000 buildings and $10 million damage.		
	Oct. 13	**Quebec, Canada**	
	Great fire, 2,500 buildings destroyed.		
†1869	**Oct. 1**	**Indianapolis, Indiana**	**27**
	Explosion at State Fair crushed women & children; 56 injured.		
†1870	**June 5**	**Constantinople, Turkey**	**900**
	Fire destroyed 3,000 structures in suburb of Pera, $25 million damage.		
†1871	**Oct. 8**	**Chicago, Ill.**	**250-300**
	The "great fire" left 90,000 homeless, 18,000 structures burned, and damage of $200 million.		
	†Oct. 8	**Peshtigo, Wisc.**	**1,500**
	Greatest forest fire in North America to this date, windstorm swept blaze over 4 million acres of timber forest.		

Major Fires and Explosions

Date		Place	Deaths	Description
1872	Nov. 9	**Boston, Mass.**	12	City's great conflagration destroyed 930 buildings; over $75 million damage.
1874	Feb. 14	**London, England**	2	Fire at Belgrave Square, $10 million damage.
1876	Apr. 12	**St. Hyacinth, Canada**		Fire destroyed great part of city, $15 million damage.
	†June 17	**Ayr, England**	29	Templeton & Sons Manufacturing Co. fire; victims mostly women employees.
	†Dec. 5	**Brooklyn, N.Y.**	295	Brooklyn Theater destroyed by fire.
†1881	Dec. 8	**Vienna, Austria**	850	Fire at Ring Theater.
1882	Jan. 31	**New York, N.Y.**	12	Fire at the New York World Newspaper Building.
	July 21	**Kingston, Jamaica**		Great fire, $6 million damage.
	†Dec. 13	**Kingston, Jamaica**	24	Terrible fire swept through business district; damage over $10 million.
1877	June 20	**St. John, N.B., Canada**	100	Great fire, $13 million damage.
1879	June 1	**Irkutsk, Russia**		Great fire, $5 million damage.
†1881	Mar. 23	**Nice, France**	70	Opera House fire from lamps lighting stage.
†1883	Jan. 10	**Milwaukee, Wisc.**	71	Fire at Newhall Hotel, victims were trapped on upper floors.
	Jan. 13	**Berditschoft, Russian Poland**	430	Fire destroyed Circus Ferroni.
1885	Jan. 3	**Adelaide, South Australia**	13	Fire destroyed Academy of Music Theatre, all victims firemen.
†1887	May 25	**Paris, France**	200	Fire at the Opera Comique Theatre.
	†Sept. 4	**Exeter, England**	200	Exeter Theater burnt down.
†1888	Mar. 21	**Oporto, Portugal**	200	Baquet Theater left demolished.
1889	June 6	**Seattle, Wash.**		Fire destroyed 64 acres, $15 million damage.
	Aug. 4	**Spokane, Wash.**	2	Fire destroyed entire business section, $10 million damage.
†1892	June 4	**Oil City, Pa.**	130	Fires & floods created a human hell.
†1894	Sept. 1	**Hinckley, Minn.**	600	Forest fire destroyed 200,000 acres.
1895	Dec. 12	**Baltimore, Md.**	24	Fire at the Front Street Playhouse.
†1897	May 4	**Paris, France**	150	Fire at Grand Bazar De Charité.
	Nov. 20	**Melbourne, Australia**		Flinders lane fire, damage in millions.
†1899	Mar. 17	**New York, N.Y.**	92	Windsor Hotel holocaust, damages in millions — 14 victims jumped to their death.
1900	Apr. 26	**Ottawa & Hull, Canada**		Fire caused great destruction in both cities, $15 million damage.
	†June 30	**Hoboken, N.J.**	326	Pier fire, $10 million damage.
1901	Jan. 14	**Denton, England**	14	Hat factory exploded near Manchester.
	May 3	**Jacksonville, Fla.**		Fire at city, $10 million damage.
	June 6	**Antwerp**		Fire at the Custom House, $10 million damage.
1902	Sept. 20	**Birmingham, Ala.**	115	Church caught fire, destroyed.
1903	Jan. 27	**London, England**	51	Colney Hatch Asylum caught fire, destroyed in 1 hr.
	Oct. 16	**Aberdeen, Wash.**	4	Fire called "city's black Friday," 140 buildings destroyed — millions in damage.
	†Dec. 30	**Chicago, Ill.**	602	Fire at Iroquois Theater, regulations were changed drastically as a result. Worst theater fire in America's history.
†1904	Feb. 7	**Baltimore, Md.**	1	Fire destroyed 75 city blocks, $85 million damage.
	Apr. 19	**Toronto, Canada**		Great fire, $13 million damage.
	June 15	**New York, N.Y.**	1,021	Excursion steamer caught fire and burned, victims aboard the *General Slocum* were women and children. (SEE *General Slocum*)
1905	Sept. 10	**Fairchance, Penn.**	19	Rand powder mills exploded.
	Nov. 19	**Glasgow, Scotland**	39	Lodging house fire, 32 injured, victims suffocated.
†1906	Apr. 18	**San Francisco, Calif.**	700	Fire followed Great Earthquake, 75% of city destroyed — 3,000 acres.
	Nov. 28	**Witten, England**	28	Roburite factory exploded, 200 injured.
1907	Jan. 9	**Pittsburgh, Pa.**	59	Steel works exploded, 7 injured — many missing.
	Feb. 26	**Montreal, Canada**	17	Fire at Hochelaga protestant school.
	May 2	**Canton, China**	20	Explosion of a gunpowder magazine, tremendous damage.
1908	Jan. 13	**Boyertown, Pa.**	170	Fire at Rhoades Opera House.
	†Mar. 4	**Collinwood, O.**	176	Lake View Elementary School holocaust, victims students.
	†Apr. 12	**Chelsea, Mass.**	12	City destroyed by fire, $6 million damage.
	Aug. 1-3	**Fernie, British Columbia**	100	Bush fire left 6,000 homeless, $10 million damage.
1909	Feb. 14	**Acapulco, Mexico**	300	Flores Theater fire, panic followed.
1910		**Idaho**	85	Forest fire destroyed 2 million acres of trees.
	Jan. 19	**Constantinople, Turkey**		Chiragan Palace destroyed with all archives of the Chamber of Deputies, damage of $7 million.
	Mar. 28	**Okorito, Hungary**	320	Great fire in village, 110 injured.
	Oct. 1	**Los Angeles, Calif.**	21	Explosion at the Los Angeles Times Building.
1911	Jan. 10	**Brussels, Belgium**		Fire destroyed Exposition, $10 million damage.
	Feb. 1	**Communipaw Terminal, N.J.**	30	Forty tons of dynamite exploded.
	†Mar. 25	**New York, N.Y.**	145	Triangle Shirtwaist Factory fire on the 8th, 9th & 10th floors of the Asch Bldg.; victims were immigrant women.
†1912	Mar. 18	**San Antonio, Texas**	26	Explosion of boiler of Southern Pacific train under repair.

Date		Place	Deaths	
†1913	July 21	**Jackson, Miss.**	35	Oakley Prison Farm fire caught Negro convicts lock in their cells.
	†July 22	**Binghamton, N.Y.**	50	Binghamton Clothing Company caught fire.
	Oct. 9	**Atlantic Ocean**	136	Fire destroyed the S.S. *Volturno* at sea. (SEE *Volturno*)
1914	Mar. 9	**St. Louis, Mo.**	37	Missouri Athletic Club fire.
	June 25-26	**Salem, Mass.**		Fire destroyed city, $12 million damage.
1915	Sept. 27	**Ardmore, Okla.**	44	Gasoline tank car explosion, two city blocks wrecked.
	Sept. 31	**Muemiswyl, Switzerland**	30	Dust explosion at comb factory, fire followed.
	Oct. 20	**Paris, France**	52	Munitions factory explosion.
	Nov. 31	**Wilmington, Del.**	31	DuPont Powder Co. exploded; company offered $1 million reward to find guilty party.
	Dec. 11	**Havre, Belgium**	110	Munitions works explosions, 1,000 injured.
1916	Feb. 6	**Skoda, Austria**	195	Arsenal exploded.
	Feb. 20	**Nish, Serbia**	43	Munitions magazine explosion, all victims Bulgarians.
	Mar. 4	**Fort Double Couronne, France**	30	Munitions storehouse explosion, many injured.
	Mar. 21	**Paris, Texas**		Fire destroyed 1,500 buildings, $14 million damage.
	Apr. 4	**Kent, England**	170	Powder factory exploded, many injured.
	July 14	**Tatoi, Greece**	32	Summer residence of King Constantine destroyed by fire, lasted 4 days.
	July 24	**Cleveland, Ohio**	26	Tunnel explosion, workmen buried.
	July 30	**N. Ontario, Canada**	184	Forest fire destroyed town of Matheson.
	Aug. 8	**Koenigsberg, Germany**	50	Ammunition shipment exploded.
	Nov. 16	**La Satannaya, Russia**	1,000	Ammunition explosion destroyed many buildings, injuries heavy.
	Dec. 6	**Kent, England**	26	Munitions plant explosion, all victims women.
	Dec. 31	**St. Ferdinand de Halifax, Canada**	45	Convent asylum destroyed by fire, all victims retarded girls.
1917	Jan. 19	**Silvertown, Essex, England**	300	Munitions factory explosion near London.
	Feb. 2	**Chicago, Ill.**	30	Two buildings demolished by gas explosion, many missing.
	Feb. 7	**Aix-la-Chapelle, Belgium**	26	Explosion on railway, victims laborers.
	Feb. 20	**Archangle, Russia**	1,500	Explosion while munitions steamer was unloaded, 3,000 injured.
	Apr. 10	**Chester, Pa.**	133	Eddystone Ammunition Corp. blew up after powder ignited; victims mostly women.
	June 23	**Bloeweg, Bohemia**	1,000	Munitions factory explosion, many injured.
	Aug. 6	**Henningsdorf, Germany**	300	Munitions factory explosion.
	Aug. 18	**Montreal, Canada**	25	Curtiss & Harvey Co. plant rocked by series of explosions.
	Aug. 26	**Petrograd, Russia**	100	Three factories exploded, many injured.
	Oct. 6	**Petrograd, Russia**	100	Theater used as temporary hospital destroyed by fire.
	†Dec. 6	**Halifax, Nova Scotia, Canada**	1,600	Ammunitions ship exploded, 1,000 buildings and 75 acres destroyed.
1918	Feb. 15	**Montreal, Canada**	55	Grey Nunnery fire, all victims children.
	Mar. 16	**Nova Scotia**	20	Lumber camp fire.
	†Apr. 13	**Norman, Oklahoma**	38	Oklahoma State Hospital for the Insane fire, few survived.
	May 18	**Oakdale, Pennsylvania**	210	Aetna Chemical Co. TNT explosion, many missing.
	July 2	**Midlands, England**	60	Shell-fishing factory exploded.
	Aug. 3	**Hamont Station, Belgium**	1,750	Ammunition trains exploded, victims German soldiers.
	Sept. 22	**Woellersdorf, Austria**	382	Munitions factory fire and explosion, victims were girls.
	Oct. 4	**Morgan, New Jersey**	64	Gillespie & Co. shell-loading plant destroyed by series of explosions of TNT.
	†Oct. 12	**Minnesota**	800	Forest fires caused $175 million damage.
1919	Jan. 7	**Pittsburgh, Pennsylvania**	20	Film Exchange building wrecked by explosion.
	Feb. 1	**Longwy, France**	64	Munitions train exploded.
	May 21	**Cedar Rapids, Iowa**	25	Douglas Starch Works exploded, 100 injured.
	June 11	**Constantinople, Turkey**		Yildez Kiosk Palace destroyed by fire, last vestige of the Ottoman Empire.
	June 20	**San Juan, Puerto Rico**	150	Mayaguez movie theater fire.
1920	Apr. 8	**Ponca City, Oklahoma**	32	Rooming house exploded.
	Apr. 25	**Hiroshima, Japan**	40	Forest fire destroyed 25,000 acres.
	Sept. 11	**Callao Bay, Peru**	30	Dynamite explosion on coast.
1921	Aug. 10	**Hiroshima, Japan**	100	Powder magazine exploded, origin unknown.
	Sept. 21	**Oppau, Germany**	565	Badische Anilin plant exploded after test of new gas, 4,000 injured; town destroyed.
	Oct. 26	**Savona, Italy**	100s	Forest fire caused explosion at Sant Elena Fortress, many injured.
	Dec. 6	**Saarlous, Rhenish Prussia**	100	Oil tank exploded at Nobel Dynamite works.
1922	Apr. 6	**Malaga, Spain**	60	Fire destroyed Customs House.
	May 18	**Rome, Italy**	20	Santo Spirito Hospital fire, all victims patients.
	May 26	**Blumau, Austria**	20	Powder explosion.
	Sept. 13	**Smyrna, Asia Minor**	100s	City destroyed, $110 million damage.
	Sept. 28	**La Spezia, Italy**	174	Falconara Fort exploded by lightning, 1,000 injured.
†1923	May 17	**Camden, S.C.**	76	Cleveland Rural Grade School fire, lamp overturned at graduation exercises.

Major Fires and Explosions

Date		Place	Deaths	Description
	†Sept. 1	Tokyo & Yokohama, Japan	143,000	Fire followed earthquake, 70% of cities destroyed; $140 million damage.
	†Sept. 17	Berkeley, Calif.	24	Fire destroyed 600 buildings, $10 million damage.
	Oct. 5	Ukraine, Russia	60	Kiev Synagogue fire, panic followed; 100 injured.
	Oct. 13	Warsaw, Poland	28	Fort blew up in city, 158 injured.
1924	Jan. 3	Pekin, Ill.	40	Corn Products Co. building exploded, 42 injured.
	Mar. 1	Nixon, N.J.	26	Ammonite Co. plant TNT explosion, many injured and missing.
	Mar. 24	Chow-t'sun, China	300	Fire 40 mi. E of Tsinan Shatung Province.
	May 28	Bucharest, Rumania	40	Explosion at Cotroceni Ammunition depot outside city, $3 million damage.
	Sept. 21	Smyrna	100	Fire at movie theater.
	†Dec. 24	Hobart, Okla.	36	Babb's Switch School fire, Christmas tree started blaze.
	Dec. 27	Otaru, Japan	120	Harbor explosion, dynamite cargo ignited.
1925	Feb. 1	Melbourne, Australia		Fire destroyed knitting mills, loss in millions.
	Mar. 1	Kharput, Turkey	160	Munitions plant explosion.
	May 25	Peking, China	300	Mukden Arsenal exploded, many injured.
	Nov. 22	Ahwaz, Persia	70	Soldiers victims of powder blast.
1926	Apr. 7	Mannheim, Germany	40	Powder factory explosion, 50 injured.
	†July 19	Lake Denmark, N.J.	30	Massive explosion at U.S. Naval Ammunition Dump started by lightning; damage over $85 million.
	Aug. 12	Csepel, Hungary	24	Manfried Weiss munitions works explosion, 300 injured.
	Sept. 5	Drumcollogher, Ireland	47	Movie theater fire.
	Nov. 27	East Garden, China	50	Canton Prison strike fire, complete destruction.
	Dec. 13	St. Auban, France	19	Explosion at chemical electrometallurgical works, 70 injured.
†1927	Jan. 9	Montreal, Canada	78	Laurier Palace Theater fire, victims all children.
	Aug. 1	Kiushiu Is., Japan	38	Deck explosion on mine-layer, 47 injured.
	Oct. 24	Tammerfors, Finland	21	Movie theater fire, many injured.
	Nov. 14	Pittsburgh, Pa.	28	Gas tank exploded in plant of Equitable Gas Co., 600 injured; 5,000 homeless.
1928	Feb. 27	Moriago, Italy	35	Movie theater fire.
	Mar. 6	Kodoes, Java	20	Fireworks factory explosion.
	June 19	Mexico City, Mexico	19	Boiler in bathhouse exploded.
	July 29	Lodz, Poland	40	Fuks & Hagria chemical factory explosion, 100 injured.
	†Sept. 22	Madrid, Spain	110	Fire at Novedades Theater, 350 injured.
	Sept. 26	Ft. Cabreriza, Morocco	38	Powder depot exploded.
	Nov. 8	Lynn, Mass.	23	Explosion & fire at Preble Box Toe Factory, many injured.
1929	Jan. 22	Tatavia, Turkey	70	Fire left 2,500 homeless, 400 houses destroyed.
	Mar. 4	Sofia, Bulgaria	28	Arsenal explosion, 12 injured.
	†Mar. 12	Igolkino, Russia	150	Movie theater fire, operator negligent.
	May 10	Xochilapa, Mexico	60	Forest fire destroyed town.
	†May 15	Cleveland, O.	121	Cleveland Clinic Hospital explosion, victims died from gas fumes.
	May 17	Iwie, Poland	100	Fire destroyed town, 4,000 homeless.
	May 29	Saghalien, Japan	41	Forest fire destroyed 1,046 houses.
	Sept. 5	Brescia, Italy	22	Powder factory explosion.
	Dec. 31	Paisley, Scotland	72	Glen Motion Picture Theater fire, victims all children.
1930	Mar. 10	Seoul, Korea	104	Moving picture theater fire.
	Mar. 20	Kirin, China	130	Movie house fire.
	Apr. 17	Cadiz, Philippines	20	Insular Lumber Co. fire, many injured.
	Apr. 18	Gaesti, Rumania	154	Church fire, Queen Marie & Regency council attend funeral.
	†Apr. 21	Columbus, O.	322	Fire at the Ohio State Penitentiary, most victims were in hospital or locked cells.
	Oct. 19	Wuchow, China	650	Tea house district fire.
	Dec. 3	Midas Geraes, Brazil	36	Freight car loaded with dynamite exploded and destroyed 3 buildings.
1931	Apr. 31	Nictheroy, Brazil	100	Munitions plant at naval laboratory exploded.
	May 5	Yuchu Fortress, China	100	Tremendous explosion, many injured.
	May 7	Yamanaka, Japan	20	Fire destroyed village; Emperor sent relief.
	†July 24	Pittsburgh, Pa.	48	Little Sisters of the Poor Home for-the-aged fire.
	Aug. 13	Macao, China	26	Ammunition depot explosion, 32 injured.
1932	Feb. 28	Shakok, China	160	Theater fire, 300 injured.
	May 19	Italian Somaliland	54	Fire destroyed S.S. *Georges Phillipar* at sea, $6 million damage. (SEE *Georges Phillipar*)
	July 10	Nanking, China	100	Ammunition storage depot explosion.
	July 13	Concepcion, Chile	20	Fire at Esmeralda Theater, victims all children.
	Dec. 21	Itoigawa, Japan	22	Fire destroyed 500 houses.
1933	Jan. 20	Morelia, Mexico	23	Dynamite explosion in city.
	Feb. 10	Neunkirchen, Germany	100	Gas tank exploded at the Neunkirchen Iron Works.
	Feb. 21	Shanghai, China	81	Rubber factory exploded, 120 injured.
1934	Mar. 14	Lalibertad, Salvador	250	Dynamite exploded in front of explosives warehouse.

Date		Place	Deaths
	Mar. 21	**Hakodate, Japan**	1,500
	Great fire, much property damage.		
	Mar. 24	**Lynchburg, Va.**	22
	Fire at the Federal Transient Relief Bureau.		
	May 14	**Hong Kong, China**	40
	Gas tank explosion, 100 injured.		
	Aug. 4	**Nakang, Japan**	25
	Dynamite explosions outside city, 8 injured.		
	Sept. 8	**New Jersey Coast**	133
	Luxury liner *Morro Castle* caught fire and burned on a voyage from Cuba to New York.		
1935	June 13	**Reinsdorf, Germany**	52
	Westphalian & Anhalt Explosive Works destroyed, 375 hurt.		
	July 28	**Taino, Italy**	33
	Bickford-Smith munitions factory exploded, 17 injured.		
	Oct. 23	**Shanghai, China**	190
	Explosion at Anti-Red ammunition store.		
	Oct. 30	**Lanchow, China**	2,000
	Great explosion at arsenal.		
1936	Jan. 31	**Scottsboro, Ala.**	20
	Motor truck filled with black convicts exploded, 2 injured.		
	Feb. 14	**Tientsin, China**	150
	Fire destroyed slum districts.		
	Feb. 17	**Valparaiso, Chile**	29
	Film explosion followed by fire.		
	Mar. 13	**Taipa Is., China**	23
	Fireworks factory exploded, victims women and children.		
	Mar. 17	**Tuliuchen, China**	221
	Fire at theater about to be destroyed.		
	Apr. 6	**Gainesville, Ga.**	57
	Hardware store and supply company fire.		
	June 15	**Tallinn, Estonia**	40
	Munitions factory explosion near city.		
	June 15	**Hyderabad, India**	20
	Movie theater destroyed by fire.		
1937	Feb. 13	**Antung, China**	685
	Movie theater fire, victims women and children.		
	†Mar. 18	**New London, Tex.**	294
	School exploded, natural gas cause.		
	July 5	**Hiroshima, Japan**	20
	Fire in sanitarium.		
	July 17	**Chunking, China**	110
	Powder factory exploded, 300 injured.		
	Dec. 20	**Tomita, Japan**	48
	School destroyed by fire, 20 injured.		
1938	Jan. 11	**Madrid, Spain**	100s
	Subway explosion, used to store ammunition.		
	Jan. 18	**St. Hyacinthe, Quebec**	47
	Sacred Heart College destroyed by fire, many injured.		
	Feb. 23	**Egypt (lower)**	23
	Four villages destroyed by fire.		
	May 16	**Atlanta, Ga.**	38
	Terminal hotel destroyed by fire.		
	Oct. 28	**Marseilles, France**	100
	Nouvelles Galleries & Hotel de Norilles destroyed by fire.		
	Nov. 6	**Oslo, Norway**	29
	O. Andersson's studio destroyed by fire.		
1939	Mar. 2	**Halifax, Nova Scotia**	20
	Queen Hotel destroyed by fire.		
	June 4	**Zacatepec, Mexico**	22
	Movie theater destroyed by fire.		
	Sept. 11	**Lemnos Is., Greece**	40
	Movie theater destroyed by fire.		
	Nov. 14	**Lagunillas, Venezuela**	47
	Oil town wrecked by fire.		
	Dec. 3	**Kowloon, China**	42
	Two tenement houses burned.		
	Dec. 14	**Brachto, Transylvania**	62
	Cellulose plant exploded, chlorine gas — 40 injured.		
1940	Jan. 29	**Toluca, Mexico**	25
	Bus burned, 36 injured.		
	†Apr. 23	**Natchez, Miss.**	198
	Rhythm Night Club burned, victims all black.		
	May 7	**Bogota, Colombia**	103
	Munic Palace destroyed by fire, 125 injured at Santander anniversary celebration.		
	Aug. 29	**Bologna, Italy**	38
	Munitions works exploded, many injured.		
	Sept. 22	**Sogamoso, Colombia**	20
	Fire in movie theater, victims children crushed in panic.		
1941	Jan. 10	**Polichka, Czechoslovakia**	80
	Munitions plant explosion.		
	June 9	**Ft. Smederovo, Yugoslavia**	1,500
	Ammunition dump explosion, 200 injured.		
	July 6	**Guadalajara, Mexico**	87
	Movie theater destroyed by fire.		
	Oct. 31	**Huddersfield, England**	41
	Clothing factory destroyed by fire.		
1942	July 21	**Limbourg Province, Belgium**	200
	Chemical factory exploded, village destroyed; 1,000 injured.		
	†Nov. 28	**Boston, Mass.**	491
	Cocoanut Grove Night Club destroyed by fire, 100s injured; actor Buck Jones victim.		
	Dec. 3	**Pernambuco, Brazil**	20
	Bus caught fire, 6 injured.		
	Dec. 13	**St. John's, Newfoundland**	100
	Fire at Knights of Columbus service man's dance; exits locked.		
1943	Feb. 24	**Cavan, Ireland**	35
	Orphanage fire, 13 injured.		
	†Sept. 7	**Houston, Tex.**	55
	Gulf Hotel fire, 32 injured.		
	Sept. 17	**Norfolk, Va.**	25
	Naval Air Station depth charge explosion, 350 injured.		
	Dec. 11	**Grenoble, France**	73
	Powder factory explosion, 1,000s homeless.		
†1944	Apr. 14	**Bombay, India**	1,376
	Steamship exploded, fire destroyed docks and residential area.		
	†July 6	**Hartford, Conn.**	168
	Ringling Bros. Circus tent fire, 250 hurt. Worst circus fire in history to this date.		
	†July 17	**Port Chicago, California**	321
	Vast explosion when ships loaded with TNT & cordite exploded at wharf in city.		
	†Oct. 20	**Cleveland, Ohio**	112
	East Ohio Gas Co. exploded, 50 blocks of fire; $15 million damage.		
	Nov. 2	**Ivy, France**	27
	Two trains, loaded with German ammunition, exploded.		
	Nov. 28	**RAF Bomb Depot, England**	175
	Burton-on-Trent, England, explosion, many injured and trapped.		
1945	Jan. 31	**Auburn, Me.**	17
	One woman and 16 children died in wooden house used as day nursery.		
	Feb. 26	**Paris, France**	20
	Munitions dump explosion, 30 hurt.		
	June 19	**Santiago, Chile**	383
	Braden copper mine fire, many injured.		
	July 7	**Saragossa, Spain**	30
	Powder warehouse explosion, 32 injured.		

Major Fires and Explosions

Date		Place	Deaths	
	Oct. 25	**Asniers-en-Bessin, France**	33	Ammunition dump explosion.
	Dec. 24	**Hartford, Conn.**	17	Niles St. hospital fire, 26 injured.
	Dec. 29	**Codroipo, Italy**	23	Ammunition dump explosion.
1946	Apr. 8	**Saigon, S. Vietnam**	20	Ammunition dump explosions, many injured.
	†June 5	**Chicago, Illinois**	61	LaSalle Hotel fire, 200 hurt.
	Aug. 18	**Vergarola, Yugoslavia**	43	Pile of mines from WW II exploded on beach, 57 injured.
	Oct. 23	**Menade, N. Celebes**	34	Japanese sea mines exploded, many injured.
	†Dec. 7	**Atlanta, Ga.**	119	Winecoff Hotel fire, 90 injured. Worst hotel disaster in America's history.
	†Dec. 12	**New York, N.Y.**	37	Ice plant fire destroyed tenement.
1947	Feb. 8	**W. Berlin, Germany**	86	Karlslust Dance Hall fire.
	Mar. 28	**Corregidor**	21	Japanese booby trap exploded.
	†Apr. 16-18	**Texas City, Texas**	552	French liner *Grandcamp* exploded, most of city destroyed with damage of $100 million.
	July 28	**Brest, France**	20	Norwegian nitrate ship *Ocean Liberty* exploded, 500 injured with $5 million damage.
	July 31	**Paris, France**	22	Caserne des Tourelles women's prison fire.
	Aug. 18	**Cadiz, Spain**	149	Naval torpedo & mine factory exploded, great damage.
	Aug. 30	**Rueil, France**	87	Select Theater fire, scores injured.
	Oct. 21	**Hoff, Germany**	28	Fire destroyed asylum.
	†Nov. 18	**Christchurch, N. Zealand**	41	Ballantyne's Department Store fire, many missing.
	Dec. 28	**Hankow, China**	400	Riverfront blaze wrecked harbor.
1948	Feb. 10	**St. John's, Newfoundland**	34	Old age home destroyed by fire.
	Apr. 7	**Shanghai, China**	20	Monastery fire, Buddhist monks victims.
	†July 28	**Ludwigshafen, Germany**	184	I.G. Farben chemical works exploded, 6,600 injured and $15 million damage.
	Sept. 22	**Hong Kong, China**	135	Chemical warehouse fire and explosion.
†1949	Apr. 5	**Effingham, Ill.**	77	St. Anthony's Hospital destroyed by fire, 20 victims were newborn babies.
	July 26	**Tarancon, Spain**	25	Army ammunition dump exploded.
	†Sept. 2	**Chungking, China**	1,700	Fire destroyed 10,000 structures on waterfront.
	Sept. 17	**Toronto, Canada**	120	Steamer *Noronic* caught fire and burned.
	Nov. 9	**Bootle, England**		Fire destroyed Gladstone dock, $5 million damage.
	Dec. 14	**Sioux City, Ia.**	21	Swift & Co. packing plant exploded, 100 injured.
†1950	Jan. 7	**Davenport, Ia.**	40	Mercy Hospital fire, all but 1 victim were mental patients.
	May 6-7	**Rimouski, Quebec**	10	Fire destroyed half of city, 2,000 homeless and $12 million damage.
	May 19	**South Amboy, N.J.**	31	Pennsylvania R.R. docks exploded, 202 injured.
	June 26	**Homs, Syria**	60	Fuel depot exploded, 93 persons injured.
1951	Jan. 30	**Hoquiam, Wash.**	20	Fire in elderly persons' rest home.
	June 15	**Montreal, Canada**	35	Hospice of Ste. Cunegonde fire, victims most female inmates.
	Dec. 22	**Tijuana, Mexico**	41	Fire at Christmas party for needy and orphaned children, 98 injured.
1952	Apr. 18	**Tottori, Japan**		Fire destroyed 5,300 homes, $8 million damage.
	Aug. 29	**Smyrna, Turkey**	21	Tobacco plant fire, 137 injured.
1953	Jan. 1	**Valparaiso, Chile**	48	Highway Dept. warehouse exploded, 350 injured.
	Feb. 14	**Fuchu, Japan**	23	Fireworks factory exploded.
	†Mar. 29	**Littlefield, Fla.**	33	Fire destroyed Littlefield Nursing Home, songwriter Arthur Fields was victim.
	Apr. 6	**Nantsechu, Formosa**	54	Ammunition disposal dump exploded, 250 injured.
	†Apr. 16	**Chicago, Ill.**	35	Haber Corp. electrical appliance firm flash fire.
	June 14	**Sao Paulo, Brazil**	70	Drygoods store fire spread to dance hall.
	June 27	**Beira, E. Africa**	40	Waterfront fire killed dockworkers.
	June 30	**Guatemala City**	21	Grocery store explosion set fire to houses.
	Aug. 18	**Bengazi, Libya**	50	Ammunition explosion.
	Sept. 12	**Wuensdorf, Germany**	20	Ammunition explosion.
	Oct. 16	**Boston, Mass.**	36	Explosion below deck of American aircraft carrier *Leyte*, 40 injured.
1954	Apr. 3	**Pusan, S. Korea**	40	Fire destroyed slum area called "Little Chicago," 3,700 homeless — 100 injured.
	May 7	**Braco Forte Is., Brazil**	20	Powder & oil installation exploded, victims were firemen.
	Nov. 4	**Sao Paulo, Brazil**	20	Fireworks factory explosion destroyed school next door, victims children and 2 teachers.
	Dec. 10	**Manila, Philippines**	26	Fireworks factory exploded.
1955	Feb. 12	**Chicago, Ill.**	29	Barton Hotel fire on "skid row."
	Feb. 17	**Yokohama, Japan**	97	Flash fire in Canadian-operated Roman Catholic old women's home; Mrs. Hisako Oyama, who gave Puccini themes for *Madame Butterfly,* was a victim.
	Apr. 3	**Sclessin, Belgium**	38	Movie theater caught fire, audience panicked.
	May 18	**Wielopolo, Poland**	58	Converted schoolroom turned theater caught fire.
	May 21	**Limbdi, India**	42	Cotton mill fire.
	†June 11	**Lemans, France**	82	Grand Prix racing car went out of control, caught fire and crashed into grandstand.
	Aug. 10	**Andover, O.**	22	Restaurant & several buildings caught fire & exploded from lightning.

Date		Place	Deaths
	Sept. 23	Gomex Palacio, Mexico	40
	Two dynamite trucks exploded after crash with train.		
	Dec. 7	Frankfort-on-the-Main, Germany	27
	Apartment building rocked by explosion.		
1956	Feb. 13	Gerze, Turkey	20
	Fire destroyed 85% of the business districts and 850 homes.		
	May 17	Takoradi, Africa	25
	Ammunition dump exploded, victims were Gold Coast soldiers.		
	†Aug. 7	Cali, Colombia	1,200
	Dynamite truck convoy exploded, 8 city blocks destroyed.		
	†Nov. 25	Cleveland National Forest	11
	Forest fire destroyed 40,000 acres.		
1957	Jan. 20	Taiwan, Formosa	36
	Artillery-range shell explosion, victims children.		
	Jan. 21	Kandy, Ceylon	20
	Wedding party fire, thatched cottage destroyed and bride killed.		
	Feb. 13	Kowloon, China	51
	Tenement block destroyed by fire.		
	†Feb. 17	Warrenton, Mo.	72
	Katie Jane Memorial Home flash fire.		
	Mar. 3	Sukkur, Pakistan	21
	Fireworks factory explosion.		
	June 23	Pusan, S. Korea	48
	Waterfront slum district explosion.		
	July 1	Naha, Okinawa	32
	Sunken ammunition ship exploded when approached by divers.		
1958	Mar. 19	New York, N.Y.	24
	Loft building fire killed employees of Monarch Underwear Co.		
	Apr. 18	Naho, Okinawa	40
	Sunken munitions ship exploded, victims were scrapping hull.		
	June 23	Rio de Janeiro, Brazil	110
	Fireworks explosion in the Santo Amarco marketplace.		
	July 20	Kokin-Breg, Yugoslavia	26
	Hydroelectric explosion at top-secret military area.		
	Nov. 8	Montreal, Canada	21
	Fire in tenement district.		
	†Dec. 1	Chicago, Ill.	93
	Our Lady of Angels parochial grade school fire, victims included 90 children and 3 nuns — cause unknown.		
	†Dec. 16	Bogota, Colombia	84
	Fire in department store at Christmas time.		
1959	Mar. 5	Little Rock, Ark.	21
	Arkansas Negro Boys Industrial Reformatory fire.		
	Mar. 17	Ilford, England	
	Main shopping center of London suburb destroyed by fire, damage was $42 million and was called London's "worst fire of the century."		
	Apr. 10	Lingayan Gulf, Philippines	38
	World War II bomb, taken from sunken ship, exploded in fishing village.		
	†June 23	Stalheim, Norway	34
	Stalheim Hotel fire, victims all American tourists — 35 injured.		
	June 28	Ogeechee River, Ga.	22
	Two tank cars exploded on bridge, victims were swimming and picnicking below.		
	July 8	Hadersley, Denmark	55
	Overloaded Danish excursion launch exploded.		
	Dec. 13	Dortmund, W. Germany	26
	Two apartment houses exploded and caught fire, gas leak.		
1960	Mar. 1	Pusan, Korea	63
	Fire in chemical plant.		
	†Mar. 4	Havana, Cuba	100
	La Coubre munitions ship exploded at Talia Tiedra dock, warehouses burned — 200 burned.		
	Mar. 23	Sasabi Mts., Japan	23
	Dam construction site dynamite explosion.		
	Mar. 28	Glasgow, Scotland	20
	Dockside warehouse fire and explosion, all victims were firemen. Greatest number ever killed in a single British fire.		
	June 11	Liverpool, England	22
	Local store caught fire.		
	†July 14	Guatemala City	225
	Guatemala City Insane Asylum fire; inmates numbered 1,500.		
	†Nov. 13	Amude, Syria	152
	Movie house caught fire, all victims children.		
	Dec. 19	Brooklyn, N.Y.	49
	American aircraft carrier *Constellation*, under construction, caught fire — damage $75 million. (SEE *Constellation*)		
1961	Jan. 7	San Francisco, Calif.	20
	Thomas Hotel caught fire.		
	May 3	Caracas, Venezuela	38
	Fireworks factory exploded, 50 injured.		
	May 15	Hong Kong, China	25
	Tenement district fire.		
	Dec. 13	Gdansk, Poland	22
	Shipyard fire, victims were at work on the hull of a ship when it burnt out.		
	†Dec. 17	Niteroi, Brazil	323
	Gran Circo Norte-Americano tent fire at suburb of Rio de Janeiro, Adilson Marcelino Aviles confessed to arson for revenge on circus owners.		
1962	Mar. 3	Aleppo, Syria	31
	Gasoline tank truck and a car collided and exploded.		
	Mar. 4	Emamzadeh-Hassan, Iran	19
	Basement fireworks store exploded.		
	Sept. 7	Parana, Brazil	250
	Brazil's richest coffee state caught fire after a 7-month drought, 500 injured — 300,000 homeless.		
	†Oct. 3	New York, N.Y.	23
	One-ton boiler exploded in business offices of the N.Y. Telephone Co., 94 injured.		
1963	May 4	Giourbel, Senegal	64
	Crowded movie theater flash fire, 18 people badly burned.		
	Aug. 13	Gauhati, India	32
	Indian government explosives dump exploded.		
	Oct. 31	Indianapolis, Ind.	68
	Indianapolis State Fair Grounds Coliseum gas explosion, 335 injured.		
	Nov. 18	Atlantic City, N.J.	26
	Fire destroyed Surfside Hotel, 21 injured.		
	†Nov. 23	Fitchville, O.	63
	Golden Age Nursing Home destroyed by fire.		
	Dec. 29	Jacksonville, Fla.	21
	Roosevelt Hotel fire, Donna Axum—the then Miss America—was rescued.		
1964	May 7	Manila, Philippines	28
	Office & apartment building wrecked by 2 explosions.		
	July 15	Tokyo, Japan	19
	Fire in 10 warehouses, all victims firemen.		
	†July 23	Bone, Algeria	85
	Ammunition ship *Star of Alexandria* blew up while being loaded at dock.		

Major Fires and Explosions

Year	Date	Place	Deaths	Description
	Aug. 25	Atlatlahuca, Mex.	45	Explosion at town fiesta.
	Dec. 18	Fountaintown, Ind.	20	Nursing home fire.
1965	Mar. 1	Lasalle, Canada	28	Apartment caught fire.
	Aug. 9	Searcy, Ark.	53	Explosion and fire at the Titan-2 missile silo, 2 injured.
	Oct. 30	Cartagena, Colombia	47	Fireworks explosions followed by fire in the public market, 100s injured.
1966	Mar. 11	Minakami, Japan	31	Two ski resort hotels caught fire.
	Apr. 23	Lapinlahti, Finland	29	Mental hospital destroyed by fire.
	Aug. 13	Melbourne, Australia	29	Salvation Army Home caught fire, worst fire disaster in human life in Australia's history.
	†Dec. 7	Erzurum, Turkey	68	Army barracks fire.
1967	Feb. 7	Montgomery, Ala.	25	Flash fire at Dale's Penthouse Restaurant atop 10-story apt. bldg.
	Feb. 7-9	Mt. Wellington, Tasmania	52	Forest fire destroyed 12 townships and charred the ground 40 mi. around. Worst forest fire in Tasmanian history.
	May 4	Mapanas-on-Samar Is., Philippines	21	Dynamite explosion wrecked fishing village.
	†May 22	Brussels, Belgium	322	Fire at L'Innovation Dept. Store.
	†July 26	Jay, Fla.	37	Fire swept through locked barracks of prison work camp.
1968	Feb. 26	Shrewsbury, England	22	Shelton Mental Hospital fire, 11 injured.
	May 11	Vijayawada, India	58	Wedding hall fire.
	Nov. 18	Glasgow, Scotland	20	Furniture factory warehouse fire, bars on windows prevented escape.
†1969	Dec. 2	Notre-Dame-du-Lac, Canada	38	Home for the aged caught fire, 30 injured.
1970	Jan. 9	Marietta, O.	27	Nursing home fire.
	Jan. 24	Semarang, C. Java	50	Oil pipe leak started fire, 41 injured.
	Mar. 20	Seattle, Wash.	19	Hotel fire, 16 injured.
	Apr. 9	Osaka, Japan	73	Underground subway construction explosion, 280 injured—27 buildings destroyed.
	May 22	United Arab Republic	41	Brush fires destroyed 660 homes, temperatures reached 118 degrees.
	Nov. 1	St. Laurent du Pont, France	144	Roadside dance hall fire, exits blocked.
	Dec. 20	Tucson, Ariz.	28	Pioneer International Hotel fire, 8 of its 11 stories burned—28 injured.
1971	Feb. 3	Brunswick, Ga.	25	Building which manufactured magnesium trip flares for use in Indochina exploded, 100 injured.
	Mar. 6	Burghoezli, Swit.	28	Psychiatric clinic fire.
	Apr. 20	Bangkok, Thailand	24	Fire at the Imperial Hotel, 9 victims were Americans.
	Oct. 28	Cairo, Egypt		Opera House built in 1869 to celebrate the opening of Suez Canal burned down, equipment was among the world's richest.
	†Dec. 25	Seoul, S. Korea	163	Taeyunkak Hotel fire lasted 8 hrs., propane gas used as cooking fuel was cause.
1972	Mar. 11	Minsk, Russia	100	Television and radio plant exploded, officials reprimanded for "criminal negligence."
	Mar. 30	Rio de Janeiro, Brazil	21	Fire in the country's largest oil refinery, 48 badly injured.
	†May 13	Osaka, Japan	118	Playtown Cabaret atop Sennichi Department Store caught fire, many victims leaped to their deaths.
	May 24	Jakarta, Indonesia	72	Five-hr. blaze at Tandjund Prior Harbor, $1 million damage.
	July 5	Sherbornne, England	31	Cold Harbor mental hospital fire.
	Sept. 1	Montreal, Canada	36	Blue Bird Cafe fire; 54 hospitalized.
	Sept. 24	Rhodes, Greece	31	Fire at fashionable restaurant, most victims Scandinavian tourists.
1973	Feb. 7	Paris, France	21	Elementary school fire, 4 adults and 17 children victims.
	Feb. 10	Staten Island, N.Y.	40	World's largest liquefied gas storage tank exploded, damage $31 million.
	Aug. 3	Isle of Man, England	51	Amusement park fire, victims all children.
	Sept. 1	Copenhagen, Denmark	35	Hafnia Hotel, country landmark, caught fire in its upper floors.
	Nov. 29	Kumamoto, Japan	101	Department store fire, 84 injured—no fire escapes.
	Dec. 13	Tachov, Czechoslovakia	80	Explosion demolished a dormitory.
†1974	Jan. 22	Heusden, Belgium	25	School of the Sacred Heart fire; victims children.
	†Feb. 1	Sao Paulo, Brazil	177	Joelma Building became a towering inferno when fire started on the 12th floor.
	June 2	Scunthorpe, England	29	Explosion rocked chemical plant.
	June 17	Lahore, Pakistan	40	Fire gutted entire bldg.
	Sept. 5	Nigeria	67	Fire swept river passenger boat in the South.
	Oct. 31	Allahabad, India	42	Explosion & fire on train started by negligence with fireworks.
	†Nov. 2	Seoul, Korea	78	Time Go-Go Club atop the Dawang Bldg. became a towering inferno.
1975	Jan. 22	Marikina, Philippines	51	One of the worst fires in the city; victims were women working in commercial building factory.
	Mar. 28	Rijeka, Yugoslavia	25	Fire in the maternity wing of Kucic Hospital caused mass deaths of incubated babies.
	Dec. 12	Mina, Saudi Arabia	138	Fire swept tent city; 100s injured.

Major Floods

(† indicates entries profiled in General Narrative)

Date	Place	Deaths
2400 B.C.	**World** The great deluge or flood, accompanied by worldwide earthquakes as reported in Genesis.	1,000s
1760	**Attica (Greece)** Deluge of Oxyges, often called the "Second Deluge."	1,000s
1504	**Deucalion (Greece)** Inundation destroyed Thessaly, often called the "Third Deluge."	1,000s
322	**Ephesus (Asia Minor)** Inundation destroyed city, rebuilt 2 decades later.	1,000s
241	**Rome, Italy** Tiber overflowed, all houses and buildings in lower part of city swept away.	100s
A.D. 7	**England** Inundation in valley of the Thames, cattle destroyed.	100s
9	**England** Humber overflowed, country inundated.	100s
14	**England** Severn overflowed, tremendous damage.	100s
15	**Rome, Italy** Tiber overflowed, great damage. Senate proposed to diminish its waters by diversion to the chief tributaries.	100s
29	**England** Trent overflowed, great damage.	100s
33	**Chester, England** Dee overflowed, town submerged.	100s
37	**England** Medway overflowed, most cattle drowned.	100s
48	**England** Thames overflowed, 4 counties submerged.	10,000
80	**England** Severn overflowed, most cattle drowned.	100s
86	**England** Medway overflowed.	100s
95	**England** Humber overflowed, 50 mi. of country submerged.	100s
115	**England** Severn overflowed, most cattle drowned.	100s
131	**Dorsetshire, England** Sea inundated 20 mi. inland.	100s
155	**Edinburgh, Scotland** City inundated, great damage.	100s
214	**England** Trent valley overflowed, stream extended 20 mi. from ordinary course.	100s
218	**Tweed, England** Great damage in and around city.	100s
245	**Lincolnshire, England** Inundation of sea submerged 1,000s of acres.	100s
250	**England** Ouse overflowed, most cattle drowned.	100s
268	**England** Humber overflowed, great property damage.	100s
317	**Kent, England** Isle of Thanet inundated, great property damage.	100s
323	**Ferne Is., England** Inundation submerged area and all inhabitants.	100s
330	**Lancashire, England** Sea irrupted, area inundated.	100s
352	**England** Severn valley inundated, great damage.	100s
353	**Cheshire, England** Thousand of acres inundated, great loss of livestock.	3,000
365	**Egypt** Inundation followed quake, great damage.	100s
368	**Sicily** Sea inundated, great damage.	100s
387	**Cheshire, England** Dee overflowed, great damage.	100s
393	**Egypt** Unusual inundation of Nile, great damage.	100s
419	**Hampshire, England** Sea overflowed, great damage.	100s
441	**Wales** Sea submerged great parts of North and South, most cattle drowned.	100s
469	**Constantinople** Four days of rain inundated city, great damage.	100s
479	**London, England** Thames overflowed for miles, great destruction.	100s
487	**England** Severn valley submerged, great damage.	100s
525	**Edessa (Mesopotamia)** City, known as "Antioch of the Fair Streams," inundated.	100s
529	**England** Humber overflowed, most cattle drowned.	100s
536	**Northumberland, England** Tweed overflowed, most cattle drowned.	100s
540	**France & Italy** Rain caused great inundations in both countries.	100s
552	**Greece** Flooding of sea, portions submerged.	100s
570	**Italy** Great inundation caused by rains.	100s
575	**England** Essex, Suffolk and Norfolk inundated from the sea.	100s
579	**France & Italy** Inundations accompanied by great rains.	100s
590	**Italy** Great inundations followed by plague.	100s
634	**Munster, Ireland** City submerged, great damage.	100s
649	**Cheshire & Lancashire, England** Inundations from the sea.	100s
669	**Kent, England** Medway overflowed, great damage.	100s
684	**Isle of Sikokf, Japan** Inundation submerged 500,000 acres, quake followed.	1,000s
685	**Ireland** Great inundation from sea.	100s
690	**Veneto & Liguria, Italy** Great inundations caused by incessant rain.	100s
758	**Glasgow, Scotland** Inundation drowned 400 families.	1,000
813	**England** Severn overflowed, 7,000 cattle drowned.	2,000
819	**France** Great inundation throughout country followed by rain.	100s
834	**Northumberland, England** Tweed overflowed over 30 mi., most cattle drowned.	100s
840	**Germany** Rhine overflowed from rains.	100s
935	**Southampton, England** Great inundation, area submerged.	100s
952	**Bagdad (Asiatic Turkey)** Euphrates overflowed, ½ of city submerged.	100s

Major Floods

Date		Place	Deaths
959		**Bagdad**	100s
		Euphrates overflowed, ¾ of city submerged.	
968		**Persian Gulf**	1,000s
		Inundations followed quakes, many cities submerged; new islands formed.	
973		**England**	100s
		Great overflow of Thames.	
1012		**England & Germany**	100s
		Danube and other rivers overflowed.	
1014		**England**	100s
		Great inundations along coast, many seaport towns ruined.	
1016		**Ireland**	100s
		Excessive rain caused great inundations, most cattle died.	
1020		**England**	100s
		Great inundations followed by plague.	
1040		**Germany**	100s
		Great inundations throughout country.	
1046		**England**	100s
		Severn valley inundated, most cattle drowned.	
1076		**Bagdad**	100s
		Tigris overflowed, city inundated.	
1086		**England**	100s
		Rain inundated country, plague followed.	
1088		**Bagdad**	100s
		Tigris overflowed, much damage.	
1090		**Constantinople**	100s
		Continuous inundations for months.	
1094		**Ireland**	100s
		Great inundations throughout country.	
1099		**England & Holland**	1,000s
		Rain and sea inundations on festival of St. Martin.	
1100		**Flanders**	100s
		Great inundation, town of Ostend submerged.	
1105		**England**	100s
		Great inundation followed by plague.	
1118		**England**	100s
		Constant inundations all year.	
1133		**France**	100s
		Rain caused great inundations.	
1134		**Flanders**	100s
		Great inundation from the sea.	
1152		**Germany**	100s
		Rhine overflowed from excessive rains.	
1157		**Italy**	100s
		Tiber overflowed, country inundated.	
1161		**Sicily**	12,000
		Inundations of the sea and many rivers.	
1162		**Holland**	100s
		Inundation from sea, most cattle drowned.	
1170		**Friesland & Utrecht, Holland**	1,000s
		Tremendous inundation, at Utrecht; people fished within the walls of town.	
1172		**Germany**	100s
		Rhine overflowed, great damage.	
		Ireland	100s
		Inundation devastated country.	
1173		**Zuyder-zee, Holland**	100s
		Whole area submerged, limits later extended from deluge.	
1188		**England**	100s
		Inundations from sea destroyed most cattle.	
1208		**France**	1,000s
		Inundations destroyed bridges & houses; "greatest ever seen in country."—Short.	
1211		**Perth, Scotland**	100s
		Tay & Anan overflowed, King narrowly escaped in boat—most of his court drowned.	
1212		**Sicily**	1,000s
		Inundation wiped out country.	
1219		**Nordland (Norway)**	36,000
		St. Lawrence Lake burst, all cattle drowned.	
1220		**Poland**	100s
		Constant rain inundated country.	
1228		**Friesland, Holland**	100,000
		Irruption of the sea devastated country.	
1230		**Italy & France**	100s
		Tiber overflowed, France submerged.	
1232		**Austria**	100s
		Danube overflowed, great damage.	
1240		**Lambeth, England**	100s
		Thames overflowed from heavy rain.	
1251		**Shannon, Ireland**	100s
		Great inundation throughout area.	
1260		**Germany**	100s
		Rhine overflowed, great damage.	
1266		**Scotland**	100s
		Tay & Forth overflowed, great damage.	
1277		**Friesland, Holland**	1,000s
		Great inundations formed the Dollert Sea.	
1278		**Italy**	100s
		Tiber overflowed, great damage.	
1286		**Holland**	1,000s
		Whole country on both sides of the Zuyder-zee submerged.	
1287		**Salandria**	15,000
		Fifteen islands submerged by the sea.	
		Winchelsea, England	100s
		Great inundation of sea, over 300 houses swept away.	
1291		**Damascus (Syria)**	100s
		Streams overflowed throughout country.	
1304		**Damascus**	100s
		Country inundated.	
1333	**Nov.**	**Florence**	100s
		Arno overflowed, great damage.	
1339	**Mar. 22**	**Tyne, England**	100s
		City inundated, great damage.	
†1421	**Apr. 17**	**Dort, Holland**	100,000
		One of the most destructive inundations in history, 72 villages submerged—20 never resurfaced.	
1446		**England & Holland**	1,000s
		Flood similar to 1421.	
1483		**England**	100s
		Severn overflowed for 10 days, settled waters later were called "The Great Waters."	
1515		**Germany**	1,000s
		"All Germany like a sea, and Cracovia submerged."—Short.	
1524		**Naples, Italy**	100s
		Tremendous inundation throughout city.	
1526	**Jan.-Mar.**	**England**	100s
		Three-month deluge destroyed cornfields, pastures and livestock.	
1529	**June 13**	**Switzerland**	100s
		Great inundation at Basle.	
†1530	**Nov. 1**	**Holland**	400,000
		Dikes failed, country inundated.	
1534		**Poland**	100s
		Extensive inundations throughout the country.	
1551	**Jan & Feb.**	**Mariapod, Austria**	100s
		Inundations lasted months.	
1553	**Jan. 19**	**Germany & Holland**	100s
		Rhine overflowed, great damage.	

Date		Place	Deaths	Description
1565		**Louvain, France**	100s	Inundation from sea, strong winds.
†1570	Nov. 1	**Holland**	50,000	Strong winds broke dikes, Friesland submerged with at least 20,000 victims—many other villages wiped out.
†1574	Oct. 1-2	**Leyden, Holland**	20,000	Flood ended Spanish siege of Leyden, washing away troops.
1606	Jan. 20	**England & Holland**	1,000s	Flood called the "Severn Estuary."
1607		**England**	100s	Serious inundations at Gloucestershire and Somersetshire, 257 houses wiped away at Coventry.
1617		**Catalonia (Spain)**	35,000	Inundation devastated country.
1619	July	**Thuringia (Germany)**	100s	Rain caused great inundation.
1623		**Austria & Hungary**	100s	Danube greatly overflowed.
1627		**Apulia (Naples)**	100s	Great inundations.
	Sept.	**Austria**	100s	Cloudburst overflowed Danube.
1629	June 20	**Mexico City, Mexico**	1,000s	Deluge from mountains, effects continued for years.
1630		**Scotland**	100s	Great inundation in the Clyde.
1633		**Cork, Ireland**	100s	Inundation wiped out public buildings and bridges.
1637	Sept. 1	**E. Friesland, Holland**	100s	Several inundations.
1642		**Kaifong, China**	300,000	City besieged by rebels and embankments destroyed, inundation followed.
1643		**Thuringia (Austria)**	100s	Great inundations.
1646		**Holland, Friesland, Zealand**	110,000	Series of great inundations.
1660	Nov. 11	**England**	100s	Thames valley inundated.
1705		**Limerick, Ireland**	100s	Fifty percent of the city drowned.
1717		**Zealand, Denmark**	1,300	Country devastated.
1723		**Madrid, Spain**	100s	Great inundation, many prominent people drowned.
1730		**Concepcion, Chile**	100s	Entire city inundated.
1762		**Burhanpoor, Dacca**	100s	Taptee overflowed, ¼ of city inundated.
		Lisbon, Portugal	100s	Great destruction of city.
1763		**Ireland**	250	Nore overflowed, 400,000 acres submerged.
1764	Jan.	**Dublin & Cork, Ireland**	100s	Great inundations at both cities & other parts of country.
1767		**Wales**	100s	Worst inundations in this area for centuries.
	Jan.	**England**	100s	Irruption of sea caused terrible inundations throughout country.
	Jan.	**Lochinabar, Scotland**	100s	Annan poured into village; houses, cattle and corn wiped out.
†1771	May 27	**Richmond, Va.**	150	All rivers in Virginia E. of Allegheny Mts. overflowed, James most serious inundation.
1775		**Rotterdam, Holland**	100s	Meuse overflowed, great damage.
1787	Sept.	**Navarre, France**	2,000	Great flow from mountains wiped out populace.
1787-88		**Punjab, India**	15,000	Inundations in Behar and other N.W. provinces, 100,000 cattle drowned.
1791		**Cuba**	3,000	Rain caused great inundation, 12,000 cattle drowned.
1800		**St. Domingo, West Indies**	1,400	City inundated.
		China	1,000s	Great damage throughout country.
1801		**Holland & Germany**	100s	Sea coasts wrecked.
1802	Apr. 14	**Lorca, Spain**	1,000	Reservoir burst, city under 20 leagues.
1811	Apr.	**Pesth, Hungary**	100s	Danube overflowed, 24 villages swept away.
1813		**Silesia & Poland**	10,000	Inundation wiped out French army under Macdonald & much populace in both countries.
	Sept. 14	**Widdin, Germany**	2,000	Danube overflowed, corps of Turkish men surprised and wiped out.
1816	Mar. 21	**Germany**	1,000s	Vistula overflowed, villages submerged.
†1824	Nov. 19	**St. Petersburg, Russia**	10,000	Neva overflowed, water submerged city 1 story deep.
1829	Apr. 9	**Danzig, Poland**	1,200	Vistula broke dikes, destroyed 10,000 cattle and 4,000 houses.
	Aug. 9	**Scotland**	100s	Spey & Findhorn overflowed to 50 ft., known as the "Moray Floods."
1830	Feb.	**Vienna**	100s	Inundations submerged dwellings of 50,000 people.
1832		**Coringa, Hindustan**	100s	Great and deadly inundation.
1833	Oct.	**Canton, China**	1,000	Inundations caused by rains swept away 10,000 houses.
1840	Oct. 31-Nov. 4	**France**	100s	Saone rose to its highest level in 238 years, Lyons, Avignon, & La Gaillotiere submerged.
1841	Jan. 6	**Middlesex, England**	100s	Brentford and surrounding districts inundated.
	July 18	**Schuylkill River, Pa.**	20	Floods capsized boats.
1845		**China**	1,000s	Yellow Sea overflowed, whole provinces submerged.
1846		**France**	100s	Central and West destroyed, 100 million francs damage.
1851-66		**China**	millions	The sunken Peking-Shanghai-Hankow triangle was responsible for the deaths of 40-50 million during 15-year period. (SEE China, 1954)
1852	Feb. 5	**Holmfirth**	90	Reservoir burst after heavy rain, valley inundated.
	June	**Gundagai, Australia**	89	Murrumbidgee overflowed, 1/3 of population wiped out.
1853	Nov. 2	**Cork, Ireland**	50	Lee overflowed, St. Patrick's bridge wiped out.
1864	Mar. 12	**Sheffield, England**	250	Bradfield Reservoir burst at the Dale Dike.
	Oct. 5	**India**	45,000	Ganges overflowed near its mouth by high winds.

Major Floods

Date		Place	Deaths	
1866	Nov. 16-17	**England (North)**	100s	Great damage in Yorkshire, Lancashire, & Leeds.
1872	Sept. 1	**Khandeish & Nassick, India**	100s	Area of Bombay Presidency inundated, most cattle destroyed.
1874	May 16	**Northampton, Mass.**	144	Reservoir burst, Mill River Valley submerged; $1 million damage.
	†April	**Mississippi River**	200-300	Floods inundated 10s of 1,000s of acres.
	July 24	**Eureka, Nev.**	30	Rain and waterspout submerged area.
	July 26	**Pittsburgh, Penn.**	220	Rainstorm overflowed rivers, Allegheny badly damaged.
1875		**Kirn, Germany**	37	Waterspout burst, great loss of property.
	June 22	**France (South)**	1,000	Towns of Toulouse, Verdun & many villages wiped away by overflow of Garonne, $150 million damage.
	August	**India (North-west)**	1,000s	Provinces inundated, great property damage.
1876		**Bengal, India**	200,000	Ganges & Brahmaputra overflowed from winds of hurricane.
		China (North)	1,000s	Great inundations in provinces.
	Dec. 3	**Adrianople, Turkey**	100s	Rain inundated city, 1,000 houses wiped out—great damage.
1877	June	**Szegedin, Hungary**	100s	Theiss overflowed, 6,500 houses submerged.
1879	Mar. 12	**Szegedin, Hungary**	77	Great inundation devastated area.
	Oct. 16-17	**Murcia, Spain**	1,000	Inundation submerged 2,000 houses, provinces of Andalusia wiped away.
1882	Jan. 21	**Ohio & Mississippi**	138	Great inundations in valleys, $15 million damage.
1883	Jan. 11	**Worms, Germany**	60	Great destruction near city.
	July 11	**Ontario, Canada**	30	Inundation in Thames Valley.
	Aug. 26-28	**Java & Sumatra**	36,000	Eruption of Krakatoa inundated both islands by sea waves.
1884	June 23	**Galicia, Germany**	21	Inundation destroyed railway bridge over the Vistula.
1886		**Galveston, Texas**	38	Storm started floods, city ruined.
†1887	Spring	**China**	1,500,000	Yellow River overflowed, 50,000 sq. mi. submerged—most villages wiped out.
1888	Mar. 26-27	**Germany**	100s	Elbe & Vistula overflowed, 200 villages submerged.
	May 8	**Canton, China**	3,000	Canton overflowed, 100s of villages submerged.
	June 17-20	**Mexico**	100s	Heavy rains caused inundations throughout country.
1889	Jan. 1	**Shantung, China**	1000s	Yellow overflowed, great damage.
	†May 31	**Johnstown, Pa.**	2,500	South Fork Dam burst, 30 acres submerged 40 ft.
†1890	Jan/Apr.	**Mississippi River**	100	Floods inundated 5,000 sq. mi.
1891	June 20	**Consuegra, Spain**	1,781	Flood left town submerged.
	July 21	**Foochoo, China**	100s	Yang-tse-Kiang overflowed, great destruction of property.
	July 26	**Posen, Poland**	100	Inundation destroyed life and property.
	Oct. 25	**Limoux, France**	20	Inundations collapsed many buildings.
1892	May 25	**St. Louis, Mo.**	250	Mississippi overflowed.
	†June 4	**Oil City, Pa.**	130	Floods & fire created a human hell.
	Oct. 13-15	**Yorkshire, England**	30	Towns of York, Leed and others inundated, great loss of livestock.
	Oct. 15	**Genoa, Italy**	35	Great destruction of property outside city, most bridges collapsed.
1893	Apr. 13	**St. Louis, Mo.**	250	Mississippi overflowed.
	August	**U.S. (South Atlantic Coast)**	2,000	Floods pushed by hurricane winds.
	Aug. 14	**Hungary**	48	Upper part of country submerged.
1894	Apr. 28	**Quebec, Canada**	24	Noir overflowed from landslide, livestock and property destroyed.
1895	Jan. 9	**Menduza, Argentina**	23	Great destruction at city.
1896	Mar. 2	**Mesopotamia**	100s	Tigris overflowed, great loss of life and property.
	Nov. 4	**Sao Miguel, Azores**	30	Great destruction on islands.
	Dec. 31	**Greece**	100s	Inundations submerged most northern villages.
1899	July 5	**Texas**	200	Brazos overflowed, most victims black.
	Oct. 7-8	**Salem, England**	40	Inundations wiped out villages.
1900	Aug. 15	**Japan**	200	Inundations throughout country.
	†Sept. 8	**Galveston, Tex.**	6,000	Inundations, hurricanes and strong winds, $100 million damage.
	Sept. 22	**Calcutta & Delhi, India**	50	Inundations left both towns in waste.
1901	July 15-24	**Han-kan, China**	100s	Yang-tze overflowed, tremendous property damage.
	Aug. 24	**Zargaza, Spain**	23	City inundated, much damage.
1902	July 5	**Tennessee**	25	Inundation in and around basin, damage $6 million.
	Sept. 15	**S. Bengal, India**	100s	Inundations wiped out 25 villages, 6,000 homeless.
†1903	May-June	**Kansas City, Mo.**	100s	Great destruction along Kansas and Saline rivers.
	†June 14	**Heppner, Ore.**	325	Willow Creek overflowed and wiped away 1/3 of town.
	July 6	**Oakford Park, Pa.**	50	Pacolet overflowed, $4 million damage.
1904	Feb. 12	**China**	100s	Dam burst on Hwange-ho, heavy damage.
	July 10-13	**Manila, Philippines**	200	Inundation caused by cloudburst submerged town of San Juan del Monbe, rain fell for 27 hrs.—27 in. high.
1905	Jan. 15	**Nesdal, Norway**	67	Inundation overflowed Loenvand, mass of rock wiped away houses and livestock—Boedal heavily damaged.

Date		Place	Deaths
1906		**Hong Kong, China**	**10,000**
	Great inundation at city.		
1907	**Jan. 11**	**Tanah, Sumatra**	**400**
	Wave inundated islands, Simalu submerged.		
	June 20	**Trikala, Thessaly**	**300**
	Town submerged, 1,000 wooden houses wiped out.		
	Sept. 24-27	**Malaga**	**100**
	Towns and communes submerged, much personal injury.		
1908	**Apr. 14**	**Han-kau, China**	**2,000**
	Inundation at the junction of the Han-kiang and Yangtze-kiang, 700 junks submerged.		
	May 21-24	**Texas**	**26**
	Brazos, Trinity, Angelina & Colorado overflowed, cities of Dallas & Fort Worth hit hard—6,000 people evacuated.		
	June 22	**China**	**100s**
	Fu & West overflowed, crops & property destroyed.		
	July 18	**Asia Minor**	**100s**
	Destructive inundations throughout area.		
†1909	**July 21**	**Texas (Coast)**	**41**
	Sluggish hurricane wrecked Bay City; $2 million damage across coast.		
	July 31	**Kirin, Manchuria**	**1,000**
	Province of Chergchun inundated, 7,000 houses submerged.		
1910		**Paris, France**	**35**
	Seine overflowed, $200 million damage.		
	June 15	**Switzerland**	**26**
	Great inundation, victims mostly children.		
	June 15-16	**Hungary**	**259**
	Inundation, caused by cloudburst, submerged large part of country.		
†1911	**Sept.**	**China**	**100,000**
	Yangtze overflowed, lake formed 80 mi. long and 35 mi. wide; another 100,000 people died of starvation weeks later.		
†1912	**Apr.**	**Mississippi River**	**250**
	Floods left 30,000 homeless; $10 million damage.		
1913	**†Mar. 25**	**Ohio (Ind. & Ill.)**	**500**
	Miami, Muskinghum, & Ohio overflowed, cities of Dayton, Middletown, Hamilton, Piqua & Zanesville ruined.		
	Aug. 10	**India**	**465**
	Country devastated, great damage.		
	†Dec. 2	**Texas**	**177**
	Brazos, Guadalupe, Colorado & Little overflowed, $9 million damage.		
†1914	**Jan.**	**Otay Valley, California**	**22**
	Floods caused $10 million in damages to crops and houses.		
	Sept. 6	**Kiao-chau, China**	**1,000s**
	West overflowed, 3 million homeless.		
	Oct. 23	**San Antonio, Texas**	**20**
	Flash floods swept away houses.		
1915	**June 12**	**Canton, China**	**100,000**
	City wiped out, Dwangtung & Dwangsi heavily damaged.		
	Aug. 3	**Erie, Penn.**	**78**
	Flash floods caused $6 million damage.		
	Aug. 16	**Texas**	**101**
	Tropical storm flooded cities of Galveston, Houston, Taylor, & Waco.		
	Sept.	**Erie, Pa.**	**30**
	Floods at Mill Creek caused by cloudburst.		
1916	**Jan. 14**	**Netherlands**	**10,000**
	North Sea overflowed from heavy gales.		
	†Jan. 27	**Otay Valley, Calif.**	**22**
	Lower Otay Dam and Reservoir failed, $10 million damage.		
	May 12	**South Africa**	**150**
	Flash floods caused great damage.		
	Aug. 9	**Cabin Creek, W. Va.**	**60**
	Cloudburst flooded narrow valley, damage in millions.		
	Sept. 20	**Bohemia**	**250**
	Flash floods left great property damage.		
1917	**Jan. 1**	**Clermont, Australia**	**100**
	Flash floods in Queensland.		
	Oct. 1	**Tientsin, China**	**100s**
	Floods inundated 15,000 sq. mi., millions homeless, $50 million damage.		
	Oct. 30	**Natal, S. Africa**	**100**
	Unusual rains caused great damage.		
1918	**Feb. 19**	**Zululand, Africa**	**100s**
	Umvolosi overflowed, many missing.		
1919		**Puerto Rico**	**116**
	Country inundated, $4 million damage.		
	Oct. 2	**Spain**	**100**
	Many southeastern cities inundated.		
1920	**May 30**	**England**	**20**
	Lud overflowed from cloudburst.		
	July 10	**Seoul, Korea**	**100**
	Han overflowed, great damage.		
	Sept. 13	**Luzon Is., Philippines**	**50**
	Great damage in provinces.		
1921	**Jan. 19**	**Pachuca, Mexico**	**50**
	Two dams burst, area flooded.		
	†June 2-3	**Pueblo, Colo.**	**120**
	Arkansas rose 20 ft., damage $25 million.		
	June 19	**Japan**	**130**
	Unusual rainy season produced flash floods.		
	Aug. 9	**Yamagata, Japan**	**24**
	Province inundated by flash floods.		
	Aug. 25	**Shantung, China**	**100s**
	Yellow overflowed, 100s of villages wiped out.		
	†Sept. 7-11	**San Antonio, Tex.**	**51**
	Nine major streams overflowed, $5 million damage.		
	Oct. 29	**Britannia, Brit. Columbia**	**26**
	Floods broke through creek, part of Port Coquitclaim destroyed.		
	Nov. 21	**Sicily**	**60**
	Floods wiped out villages.		
1922	**June 23**	**Rumania**	**20**
	Flash flood hit coastal area.		
1923	**June 9**	**Russia**	**400**
	Volga overflowed, great damage.		
	Dec. 1	**Dezzo, Italy**	**1,000**
	Rivers in the north overflowed, many dikes burst.		
1924	**Mar. 28-29**	**Belle Fourche, S.D.**	**26**
	Rain on 5-in. snowfall inundated area.		
	July 15	**China**	**1,000s**
	Chu-kiang overflowed, great damage at Canton, Chihli, & Ganon.		
	Aug. 6	**India**	**100**
	Floods in south left 50,000 homeless.		
	Aug. 7	**Taihoku, Formosa**	**700**
	Tamsui overflowed, city almost destroyed.		
1925	**July 15**	**Seoul, Korea**	**100s**
	Floods ruined city, famine followed.		
1926	**Jan. 1**	**Belgium**	**100s**
	Country inundated, restoration required throughout.		
	Jan. 8	**Nayarit, Mexico**	**100**
	Towns inundated throughout state.		
	May 26	**Kitsura, Japan**	**400**
	Flood burst dam, town destroyed.		

Major Floods

Date		Place	Deaths	
	June 25	**Leon, Mexico**	**100**	Santiago and Gomez overflowed, Coecillo dam burst and destroyed ½ of town.
	July 1	**Belgrade, Yugoslavia**	**100s**	Danube overflowed, city submerged, loss at $50 million.
	July 2	**Niigata, Japan**	**400**	Storms inundated area, damage at $5 million.
	Aug. 4	**Hupeh, China**	**3,000**	Yangtze overflowed, dikes burst in S.E. province.
	Sept. 25	**Moore Haven, Fla.**	**350**	Hurricane winds overflowed Lake Okeechobee.
†1927	Apr. 19	**Mississippi River**	**313**	Lower Mississippi overflowed from severe rainstorms, 18 million acres were inundated in 6 states.
	†May 29-30	**Morgan County, Kentucky**	**89**	Floods from Morgan County in the north to Harlan County in the south, $7 million damage—12,000 homeless.
	July 27	**Baroda, India**	**1,000**	Reservoir burst banks, great damage.
	Aug. 18	**Siberia**	**100**	Maritime provinces flooded, 40,000 homeless.
	Sept. 3	**Bukovina, Rumania**	**100s**	Entire areas inundated, damage 40 million lei.
	†Nov. 3-4	**New England**	**168**	Streams through Vermont to Connecticut flooded, $40 million damage.
	Nov. 27	**Oran, Algeria**	**100s**	Storms burst dam and started landslides.
†1928	Mar. 12-13	**San Francisquito Valley, Calif.**	**350**	St. Francis Dam failed, $15 million damage.
	June 29	**Kiushio, Japan**	**100s**	Floods ruined city.
	Aug. 4	**Shantung, China**	**2,000**	Tawen overflowed, great damage.
	Sept. 3	**Korea**	**400**	Flash floods throughout country.
	Sept. 10-16	**Florida (Southern)**	**2,000**	Lake Okeechobee overflowed from tropical hurricane, Belle Glade, Pahokee & South Bay inundated. (SEE Lake Okeechobee)
1929	Jan. 2	**Hondo, Japan**	**100s**	Coast flooded, 20 villages ruined.
	Feb. 18	**Thrace, Greece**	**100**	Vast area inundated, 7 rivers overflowed.
	Mar. 23	**Alabama-Tennessee**	**34**	Most rivers overflowed, $10 million damage.
	Apr. 5	**Tasmania**	**39**	Torrential rains burst dams & destroyed bridges.
	May 3	**Syria**	**50**	Euphrates overflowed, country submerged.
	May 21	**Iraq**	**100**	Tigris & Euphrates overflowed, country submerged.
	June 18	**Seville, Colombia**	**40**	Town destroyed, Quilcase overflowed from landslide.
	July 13	**Tabriz, Persia**	**375**	Cloudburst inundated several villages, 5,000 houses destroyed.
	July 15	**Rumania**	**24**	Bistritza, Moldava & Serth overflowed from heavy rains.
	July 22	**Anatolia, Turkey**	**500**	Black Sea region inundated, many missing.
	Aug. 23	**Yugoslavia**	**65**	Cloudburst in Balkan States left 2,000 homeless, great damage.
	Aug. 24	**Dera, India**	**300**	Indus Valley inundated, cholera epidemic followed.
1930	Mar. 4	**France (South)**	**221**	Tarn overflowed, 10,000 homeless, $50 million damage.
	May 19	**Bakau, Rumania**	**60**	Heavy rains left 1,000s homeless.
	July 14	**Korea**	**200**	Flash flood left 1,000s homeless.
	Oct. 23	**Tampico, Mexico**	**100s**	Torrential rains flooded area, the Alamo submerged.
	Nov. 18	**Manizales, Colombia**	**32**	Landslide dammed Aguacatal River outside city.
1931	July 10	**Kwantung Prov., China**	**500**	West overflowed, many missing.
	Aug.	**China**	**millions**	Hwang-ho River overflowed—called by some the worst flood disaster in history.
	Aug. 11	**Maluan, India**	**100**	Flash floods left 1,000s homeless.
	Aug. 15	**San Pedro Jicayan, China**	**200**	Panuco & Tamesi overflowed, 16 villages submerged.
	Aug. 18	**Hankow, China**	**100s**	Chiakow dike collapsed, 1,000s fled city.
	Aug.-Sept.	**China**	**140,000**	Yangtze River valley inundated from Shanghai to Hangkow, 2 million homeless, $50 million damage.
	Sept. 8	**N. Honan, China**	**700**	Yellow overflowed, 20,000 homeless.
	Dec. 19	**Tunis, Morocco**	**30**	Flash floods near city.
1932	Feb. 13	**Nelson Is., Alaska**	**38**	Floods wiped out 7 villages of area, many missing.
	Apr. 7	**Soroca, Rumania**	**80**	Flash floods caused peasants to attack villages for failure to render aid.
	June 27	**China**	**100s**	Yellow rose 2 ft., 1,000s homeless, cholera epidemic followed.
	Aug. 1	**China**	**500**	Chu Kiang (Canton River) overflowed by heavy rains, cholera & bubonic plague followed.
	Aug. 3	**Harbin, Manchuria**	**3,000**	Sungari overflowed, all crops ruined, 35,000 houses wiped out.
	Aug. 31	**China**	**1,100**	Tung overflowed, walls held back the Canton.
	Nov. 22	**Huila, Colombia**	**100**	Fortalecillas overflowed, floods & landslides followed.
1933	Mar. 4	**Mayaguez, Puerto Rico**	**50**	Rain overflowed Yaguez, 500 homes destroyed, many missing.
	Apr. 22	**Albania**	**26**	Flash floods on coast.
	June 26	**Tungjen, China**	**1,000s**	Mayen overflowed, valley inundated.
	July 4	**Rakuto Valley, Korea**	**55**	Flash floods at area.
	July 10	**Czechoslovakia**	**36**	Carpathian streams overflowed, many villages wiped out.
	Aug. 2	**China**	**1,000s**	Wei overflowed, millions of acres submerged.
	Aug. 16	**Jamaica**	**70**	Island inundated, $2 million damage.
	Sept. 1	**Shenchow, China**	**50,000**	Yellow overflowed, 500,000 homes destroyed, famine throughout area.
†1934	Jan. 1	**La Canada Valley, Calif.**	**40**	Western extension of the San Gabriel Range overflowed, $5 million damage—500 houses destroyed.
	Jan. 11	**Mendoza, Argentina**	**70**	Gush of water from Andes wiped out province.

Date		Place	Deaths	
	Apr. 4	Oklahoma (Western)	22	Torrential rains inundated state.
	May 14	Tiberias, Palestine	20	Cloudburst flooded village, many houses destroyed.
	July 14	Assam, Japan	100s	Flash flood west of city, many missing.
	July 17	Warsaw, Poland	100	Vistula overflowed, 60,000 peasant families homeless.
	Dec. 1	Australia	35	Terrible damage in Yarra, eastern Port Phillip streams, & central and south Gippsland.
1935	Mar. 16	Tientsin, China	100s	Yellow overflowed, 250,000 homeless.
	May 30-31	Colorado & Nebraska	110	Republican River Valley overflowed to 1½ miles, 275,000 acres submerged—21,000 cattle drowned.
	June 3	Mexico	400	Actopan overflowed, wide area submerged.
	June 19	Chimalpa, Mexico	21	Flash flood at city.
	July 4	Hankow, China	30,000	Yellow & Yangtze overflowed, 3 provinces wiped out, damage at $300 million—5 million homeless.
	Aug. 23	Japan (North)	52	Flash flood injured 75.
	Oct. 24	Bulgaria	40	Struma overflowed, great damage.
	†Oct. 25	Jeremie, Haiti	2,000	Widespread floods when the Grand Anse, Voldrogue, & Roseauc Rivers overflowed.
	Dec. 26	Antalya, Turkey	92	Southwestern district flooded, 1,000s homeless.
	Dec. 27	Skodar, Albania	40	Flash flood at city.
1936	Feb. 26	New England & Quebec	29	Floods caused damage in millions.
	Mar. 27	Ohio	107	Ohio River rose to its highest level since 1762, $270 million damage.
	July 1	Texas	26	Cloudburst flooded Guadalupe & San Antonio river basins, $2 million damage.
	Oct. 9	Brazil	30	Andagueda overflowed, large area engulfed.
	Nov. 19	Osaruzawa, Japan	100s	Reservoir dam burst, at least 300 dead with 100s missing.
	Dec. 7	Philippines	100	Cagayan overflowed, 80,000 homeless.
†1937	Jan.	Ohio	137	Great flood caused $418 million damage, worst inundation in 24 years.
	Apr. 11	Kogendo Prov., Korea	90	Floods at E. coast left many missing, large number of vessels ruined.
	Aug. 3	Rangoon, Burma	50	Floods left 3,000 homeless.
	Aug. 9	North Korea	300	Flash floods left 100s injured.
	Nov. 23	Jamaica	50	Cloudbursts flooded islands.
†1938	Feb. 27	San Bernardino, Calif.	87	Rain up to 30 in. flooded the San Bernardino & San Gabriel Mt. areas, damages of $79 million.
	June 11	Kweichow, China	2,000	Yangtze overflowed, 10 counties suffered.
	June 29	Tokyo, Japan	100s	Rains caused inundations which lasted weeks.
	July 3	Kentucky (Eastern)	78	Triplett & Frozen creeks overflowed in Rowan & Breathitt counties, $2 million damage.
	Aug. 10	Nonda, India	100	United Provinces inundated, great damage.
	Aug. 16	North Korea	100s	Rains caused worst floods in 16 yrs.
	Sept. 23	New York & New England	500	Most disastrous flood in America's history, $350 million damage. (SEE Long Island, N.Y.)
	Nov. 31	Celebes	113	Flash floods throughout country.
	Dec. 2	Urfa, Turkey	72	Whole region inundated.
1939	June 29	Bulgaria (North)	160	Storms caused inundations, great damage.
	†Sept.-Nov.	China	200,000	Floods devastated country, 10 million homeless—25 million faced starvation.
	Sept. 6	California (Southern)	45	Floods from storms caused $2 million damage.
1940	Aug. 15	Kaifeng, China	100s	Yellow overflowed, Honan Prov. ruined.
1941	Oct.	Kansas, Oklahoma, Missouri	47	Basins of Grand River Dam & Lake of the Ozarks overflowed.
	Dec. 14	Huaraz, Peru	3,000	Earth slide sparked inundations, residential area swept away.
1942	Feb. 1	Urubamba, Peru	100s	Rimac overflowed, 1,500 homeless.
	May 21	Honesdale, Pa.	33	Lackawaxen River overflowed.
	Sept. 28	E. Shensi Prov., China	3,000	Yellow overflowed, 40,000 homeless.
	Dec. 1	El Cobre, Venezuela	32	Flash flood at area.
1943	Apr./June	U.S. (Central States)	60	Floods caused over $172 million damage in several states; Michigan hardest hit.
	Aug. 4	Rajputana, India	10,000	Khari overflowed, many villages submerged.
	Aug. 5	West Virginia	21	Flash flood in central part of state, crops & livestock destroyed.
	Dec. 14	State of Sinaloa, Mexico	30	Area inundated, great damage.
1944	Apr. 9	Buenos Aires, Argentina	60	Naposta Grand overflowed from heavy rains, large area washed out.
	Sept. 10	Mexico	50	Rains inundated 7 towns, many missing.
1945	Jan. 29	Chavin, Peru	169	Mosna overflowed, broke dike above city.
	Mar. 28	Petropolis, Brazil	30	Flash flood at area.
	Oct. 19	Media Luna, Cuba	20	Vicana & Macaca overflowed, area ruined.
1946	May 12	Turkey	2,000	Floods wiped away several villages.
	June 29	Korea	45	Record rainfall inundated southern area, 1,000s homeless.
1947	Mar. 23	Warsaw, Poland	76	Vistula overflowed, 50,000 homeless.
	April	Warren, Pa.	29	Floods inundated city; wide area affected.
	June 13	Turkey	21	Rain & hail inundated 10 villages.

Date		Place	Deaths	
	June 15	Ciudad, Mexico	40	Cloudburst flooded area, many injured.
	July 6	Chengtu, China	1,000	Chinkiang overflowed, 100,000 homeless.
	Aug. 17	Colombo, Ceylon	20	Worst flood in country's history to this date left 1,000s homeless.
	Sept. 15	Tokyo, Japan	2,000	Floods throughout area left 400,000 homeless, many missing.
	Sept. 29	Lahore, India	1,000	Floods drowned Moslem refugees.
	Oct. 30	Egido, Venezuela	40	Montalban overflowed, village destroyed.
	Nov. 10	Turkey	100s	Seyhan overflowed, many villages engulfed.
1948	Feb. 21	Turkey (South)	100s	Dikes burst on Seyhan & Ceyhan rivers.
	May 28	Vanport City, Ore.	26	Columbia overflowed, worst flood disaster in 54 yrs. Damage $140 million in 3 states.
	May 30	Iyang Dist., China	330	Yangtze overflowed, 8,000 acres submerged.
	†May-June	Columbia River	51	British Columbia, Washington & Oregon inundated.
	June 6	Amasya, Turkey	92	Flash flood crippled area.
	June 20	Foochow, China	1,000	Worst flood since 1918, 300,000 homeless.
	July 25	Ordou, Turkey	22	Rains inundated area on Black Sea.
	July 26	Japan	30	Ida overflowed, victims schoolchildren.
	Aug. 4	La Buayra, Venezuela	26	Flash flood injured 30.
	†Aug. 7	Fukien Prov., China	1,000	Yellow overflowed, 3 million homeless.
	Sept. 17	Ichinoseki, Japan	850	Rains burst dikes on Iwai River.
	Dec. 16	Brazil	600	Minas Geraes & Rio de Janeiro areas flooded, 1,000s injured or homeless.
	Dec. 20	Isfahan, Iran	100	Area inundated, 20,000 homeless.
1949	Apr. 7	Telkief, Iraq	50	Cloudburst inundated area.
	May 20	Maecio, Brazil	100	Cloudburst inundated Alagoa State. Many injured.
	June 2	Sao Francisco, Brazil	70	Flash flood inundated area.
	June 20	Anatolia, Turkey	20	Floods in N. Central, Tokat inundated.
	June 25	Pachuca, Mexico	54	Flash flood crippled area.
	July 17	China	57,000	Yangtze overflowed, worst flood since 1931—20 million homeless.
	Oct. 14	Guatemala	600	Nation inundated by rains, 60,000 homeless—$25 million damage.
	Nov. 4	Caracas, Venezuela	50	Guaira overflowed, over 200 injured.
	Nov. 22	Cyprus	22	East coast smashed with water, worst since 1929.
	Nov. 24	Colombia	30	Rio Mayo overflowed, S.W. inundated.
1950	Mar. 17	Quito, Ecuador	20	Chanchan overflowed, area isolated.
	Apr. 4	Ceunca, Ecuador	50	Tomebamba overflowed, city submerged.
	†May/July	Nebraska	23	Floods inundated 60,000 acres.
	June 8	Meshed, Iran	36	City inundated, many missing.
	June 25	W. Virginia	26	Flash floods in N.C. area, damage great.
	July 7	Anhwei Prov., China	477	Summer floods left 1 million homeless and 5 million acres of crops damaged.
	†Aug.	China	489	Five million acres submerged, 10 million homeless.
	Sept. 20	N. Punjab, India	200	Bihar State inundated, 12,000 homes ruined, 1,100 sq.mi. submerged.
	Oct. 16	La India, Nicaragua	23	Tropical storm sparked flash flood.
1951	Jan. 1	Morocco, Africa	71	Rharb Plain inundated by rain, 300 homeless, many missing.
	Feb. 10	W. Java, Indonesia	25	Monsoon rains left 1,000s homeless.
	May 19	Formosa	300	Flash floods throughout island.
	June 15	Kashmir, India	25	Brahmaputra overflowed, 1,000s evacuated.
	†July	Kansas	50	Missouri & Kansas rivers overflowed, Pres. Truman declared disaster area, $1 billion damage.
	July 13	Honshu, Japan	144	Floods ruined Kyoto Prefecture, many missing.
	Aug. 19	Mukden, Manchuria	1,800	Liang overflowed, 1,000s missing.
	Aug. 23	Mexico	260	Cities of Tampico, Valles & Cardenas ruined when 6 rivers overflowed from hurricane rains.
	Sept. 15	Kotwara, India	50	Flood washed out Nayar River bridge.
	†Nov. 13	Po Valley, Italy	173	Po overflowed, many northern cities ruined, 160,000 homeless.
1952	July 3	Honshu, Japan	50	Floods left 70,000 homeless.
	Aug. 16	Bristol Channel, England	19	Lyn overflowed, many towns evacuated, damage $6 million.
	Aug. 31	Zamboanga Prov., Philippines	74	Two-day rain flooded area, $2 million damage.
†1953	Feb. 1	Holland	1,835	Storms overflowed North Sea, worst disaster in the Netherlands since 1421.
	Feb. 9	N. Sumatra, Indonesia	82	Floods left 32 missing, damage in millions.
	Mar. 11	Jaramijo, Ecuador	26	Bravo overflowed, 532 homeless.
	June 2	Venice, Italy	24	Deluge left St. Mark's Sq. 10 in. deep with water.
	June 22	Hyderabad, India	80	Sabari overflowed near city.
	June 27	Kyushu, Japan	684	Floods left 1 million homeless, 2,097 injured.
	July 17	Kyushu, Japan	638	Inundations off Honshu coast; 120,000 homeless, 100s missing, 5,700 injured.
	Aug. 2	San Rafael, Ecuador	20	Six rivers overflowed, great damage.
	Aug. 4	Vaz, Iran	265	Flash flood wiped out 4,000 houses.

Year	Date	Place	Deaths	Details
	Aug. 6	**Karachi, Pakistan**	**50**	Rains collapsed huts in villages, 500 injured.
	Aug. 15	**Kyoto, Japan**	**143**	Flash flood at Kizu River Valley broke Taisho Dam, 100s missing.
	Aug. 24	**Shwegyin, Burma**	**100s**	Town destroyed, 4,000 evacuated, many missing.
	Oct. 17	**Spain**	**50**	Floods in the North, $20 million damage.
	Oct. 19	**Calabria, Italy**	**62**	Northern areas submerged, damage in millions.
1954	Feb.	**Australia**	**26**	Cyclone caused northern rivers to overflow, damage in millions.
	Feb. 21	**Australia**	**23**	Northeast coast had worst floods in its history.
	†June 24-30	**Rio Grande**	**185**	Floods brought on by heavy rains caused $5 million damage.
	†Aug. 1	**China**	**40,000**	Yangtze overflowed at record 96.06 ft., 10 million evacuated.
	†Aug. 10	**Shigatse, Tibet**	**500-1,000**	Flood devastated 2nd largest city in Tibet.
	†Sept. 17	**Farahzad, Iran**	**2,000**	Flash flood wiped away pilgrims at Moslem shrine.
	Sept. 29	**British Honduras**	**29**	Floods resulted from hurricane Gilda.
	Sept. 31	**Kazvin, Iran**	**150**	District swamped, 1,000 homeless.
1955	Feb. 26	**Maitland, Australia**	**22**	Cyclone caused 7 rivers to overflow, 10,000 homes in 20 towns affected.
	Aug. 28	**Taipokow, China**	**21**	Flash flood near Hong Kong.
	Oct. 7-12	**India & Pakistan**	**1,700**	Worst floods in century, 100,000 homeless. Calcutta, Ganges & Bramaputra rivers inundated 10,000 sq.mi. Losses continued for over a month.
	Oct. 13	**Puerto Cortes, Costa Rica**	**30**	Heavy rains inundated area, wiped out village.
	Oct. 13	**Volos, Greece**	**23**	Flash flood injured 18.
	Oct. 15	**United States**	**42**	Northeast states flooded from extra-tropical cyclone, damage in 10s of millions.
	Oct. 18	**Mexico**	**100**	Torrential rain isolated 3 states, 3 rivers overflowed.
	Dec. 5	**Madras, India**	**120**	Heavy rains left 500,000 homeless.
	Dec. 18	**Lebanon (North)**	**140**	Country's worst flood this century, Tripoli cut in half, many missing.
	Dec. 28	**Algeciras, Colombia**	**40**	Flash flood swamped 80 homes.
1956	January	**Yuba City, California**	**74**	Worst flood disaster since 1906 earthquake, 50,000 homeless—$100 million damage.
	July 11	**Karachi, Pakistan**	**100s**	Monsoon floods wiped out 500,000 homes, crops ruined.
	July 22	**Isfahan, Iran**	**450**	Heavy floods caused $60 million damage, 1,000s homeless.
	July 26	**Afghanistan**	**51**	Heavy rains inundated Bamian Valley & Kandahar Prov.
	Aug. 24	**Adiejaman, Turkey**	**138**	Flash flood swamped province.
	Sept. 31	**India**	**100**	Flash flood on the Gandak River, wide area submerged.
	†Oct. 24	**Uttar Pradesh, India**	**50**	Jumna overflowed, capital threatened.
	Oct. 30	**Colombia**	**21**	Scattered floods throughout country.
	Dec. 26	**Passa Quatro, Brazil**	**36**	Flash flood left 100 injured.
	Dec. 27	**Minanao, Philippines**	**21**	Floods throughout area, Pres. Magsaysay declared state of calamity.
1957	May 16	**Juazeiro, Brazil**	**28**	Bahia State inundated, 5,000 homeless.
	July 16	**Philippines**	**230**	Agno overflowed, 4,000 homeless in Pangasinan Prov.
	July 21	**S. Shantung Prov., China**	**550**	Yi & Shu overflowed, 1,000s homeless.
	July 25	**Kyushu, Japan**	**513**	Torrential rains flooded N.W. area, 60,000 homes ruined—many persons missing.
	Aug. 18	**Kashmir, India**	**39**	Flash floods near Tibetan border.
	Sept. 16	**Tabriz, Iran**	**122**	Floods submerged area.
	Oct. 14	**Valencia, Spain**	**68**	Turia overflowed, damage in millions.
	Oct. 26	**India (Northeast)**	**400**	Dam burst, wiped out frontier village.
	Nov. 9	**Nellore, India**	**53**	Heavy rains wiped out 43 villages in Andhra State.
	Dec. 6	**Rio de Janeiro, Brazil**	**60**	Floods left 1,000s homeless, scores missing.
	Dec. 23	**Ceylon**	**225**	Floods left 200,000 homeless, coastal areas submerged.
1958	Apr. 2	**California**	**16**	Heavy rains inundated state, Pres. Eisenhower declared disaster area—$50 million damage.
	July 3	**Iowa**	**21**	Southwest part of state inundated, Pres. Eisenhower declared disaster area.
	July 7	**South Korea**	**40**	Heavy rains inundated area, 2,000 families homeless.
	July 12	**Kunrund, India**	**24**	City inundated by heavy rains.
	July 28	**Buenos Aires, Argentina**	**60**	City flooded, many missing.
	Sept. 15	**Mexico (Central)**	**26**	Floods caused 30,000 to evacuate near capital.
	Sept. 31	**France**	**27**	Flash floods on the Gardon & Vidourle rivers.
1959	Jan. 9	**Rivadelago, Spain**	**130**	Torrential rains burst dam, technicians stood trial.
	Jan. 21	**United States**	**23**	Flash floods inundated East & Midwest areas from Ohio to Kentucky—$100 million damage.
	Mar. 29	**Tananarive, Malgache**	**143**	Torrential rains inundated Port Berger & Manaru, 100,000 homeless.
	Apr. 12	**Latin America**	**124**	Argentina, Brazil, Uruguay property damage at $60 million.
	May 1	**Port-au-Prince, Haiti**	**40**	Heavy rains caused flash floods.
	May 19	**Union of So. Africa**	**60**	Cape Prov. & Natal inundated, $15 million damage.
	June 13	**Hong Kong, China**	**36**	Heavy rains inundated area.
	June 31	**Caserio Las Juntas, Colombia**	**185**	Village wiped out by flash flood.

Date		Place	Deaths
	July 14	**Kyushu Is., Japan**	41
	Heavy rains inundated 30,000 homes.		
	July 15	**Karachi, W. Pakistan**	98
	Torrential rains overflowed Chenabl, broke dikes, 150,000 homeless.		
	July 18	**Kashmir, India**	139
	Heavy rains inundated area.		
	Aug. 8	**Taiwan (Formosa)**	700
	Central & South inundated, many missing.		
	Sept. 18	**Surat, India**	500
	Dike burst on Tapti River, 15,000 homeless.		
	Sept. 28	**Rio Grande do Sul, Brazil**	100
	Pardo overflowed from flash floods.		
	Oct. 10	**W. Bengal, India**	70
	Damodar River Valley inundated, 500,000 dwellings destroyed.		
	†Dec. 3	**Frejus, France**	412
	Storm broke Malpasset Dam, 6-mi. area inundated.		
1960	Mar. 11	**Brazil (Central)**	100
	Worst flash floods in yrs. in coastal areas.		
	Aug. 25	**Orissa, India**	47
	State inundated, 1½ million homeless.		
	Sept. 18	**Italy (Alps)**	36
	Tiber overflowed from heavy rains, many injured.		
	Oct. 28	**Chinandega, Nicaragua**	325
	State inundated after record flash floods, 5,000 homeless.		
1961	June 27	**Japan**	265
	Coastal floods damaged $60 million in property, 1,300 hurt and many missing.		
	July 12	**Poona, India**	140
	Floods left 90,000 homeless.		
	July 12	**Namwon, S. Korea**	100
	Dam burst by flood waters, American helicopters saved many.		
	July 20	**Charleston, W. Va.**	21
	Heavy rains caused flash floods, Pres. Kennedy designated it disaster area.		
	Oct. 9	**Bihar, India**	1,000
	State inundated, many homeless.		
	Nov. 11	**East Africa**	200
	Heavy rains inundated Kenya & Somalia, 1 million homeless—300,000 near starvation.		
†1962	Feb. 16	**Germany (North Sea Coast)**	343
	Storm broke dikes in north, 30,000 evacuated from Hamburg—500,000 homeless.		
	Aug. 18	**Assam, India**	73
	Tista overflowed, 200,000 homeless.		
	Aug. 18	**Florencia, Colombia**	41
	City inundated, many missing.		
	Aug. 28	**Suchon, So. Korea**	242
	Flash floods left many homeless and missing.		
	†Sept. 26	**Barcelona, Spain**	445
	Flash floods caused $80 million damage, 1,000s injured.		
1963	Apr. 25	**Herat, Afghanistan**	107
	Flash flood at city.		
	July 16	**East Pakistan**	30
	Floods left 1,200,000 homeless.		
	July 21	**Kashmir, India**	100s
	Flash floods left many injured.		
	Sept. 20	**Uttar Pradesh, India**	237
	Heavy rains inundated area, 200,000 homeless.		
	Oct. 9	**Belluno, Italy**	2,000
	Heavy rains inundated Piave River Valley, damage in millions.		
	Nov. 19	**Haiti**	500
	Floods and landslides inundated Grand Riviare du Nord, all crops ruined.		
1964	Jan. 20	**Brazil**	100
	Jequitinhonha River Valley inundated, 100,000 homeless.		
	June 8	**Montana**	24
	Heavy snow-melt from mts. flooded N.W., Pres. Johnson proclaimed major disaster area.		
	†July 18-19	**Japan**	108
	Torrential rains flooded W. coast, many missing.		
	Aug. 26	**Punjab, India**	32
	One million homeless in Bihar State.		
	Oct. 5	**Macherla, India**	120
	Reservoir burst, monsoon flooded 7 states.		
	Dec. 6	**Philippines**	100s
	Southern area smashed, many missing.		
	Dec. 14	**South Vietnam**	500
	Two provinces demolished, 3,000 homeless.		
	Dec. 22	**California-Oregon-Idaho**	40
	Snow, rain & high winds devastated 3 states, damage at $1 billion.		
1965	Mar. 28	**El Cobre, Chile**	400
	Earthquake burst dam in La Calera, village flooded.		
	Apr. 13-May 8	**Mississippi River**	19
	Winter snow & ice melted and inundated 1,000 miles along river—40,000 homeless & $200 million damage.		
	Apr. 24	**Pernambuco, Brazil**	20
	Acarau overflowed, 10,000 homeless.		
	†June 16-26	**Colorado**	23
	South Platte & Arkansas overflowed from heavy rain and damaged 7 states from Colorado to Nebraska.		
	July 2	**Chile (Central)**	41
	Bio overflowed, 70,000 homeless in Valparaiso, Santiago & Concepcion.		
	July 3	**Laos**	50
	Song overflowed.		
	July 16	**South Korea**	94
	Central area floods left 190,000 homeless, 100s missing.		
	July 24	**Japan (West)**	28
	Heavy rains caused inundations and landslides.		
	Aug. 12	**India (Central)**	32
	Flash flood inundated area.		
	Aug. 20	**Morocco**	22
	Ourika Valley inundated.		
	Aug. 22	**Nayarit, Mexico**	24
	Rain near Texas borders inundated area.		
	Sept. 1	**Italy**	55
	Storms inundated central & northern areas.		
	Sept. 24	**Morocco**	37
	Kehmis N'Gua inundated.		
	Dec. 22	**Tipuani, Bolivia**	31
	Flash flood left 150 homeless.		
1966	Jan. 11	**Rio de Janeiro, Brazil**	300
	Record rain caused inundations & landslides, 5,000 homeless.		
	Mar. 11	**Jordan (South)**	70
	Flash floods left 3,000 homeless, many missing.		
	June 12	**Hong Kong, China**	55
	Two-week rain caused city's worst flood, 6,000 homeless.		
	July 14	**Ulan Bator, Mongolia**	100s
	Heavy rains inundated area, city paralyzed.		
	Sept. 7	**W. Bengal, India**	21
	Rain overflowed rivers, 100,000 homeless in Malda area.		
	Sept. 14	**Iran**	42
	Thirty villages flooded in N.W., many injured.		
	Oct. 15	**Algeria**	50
	Worst rain in 30 yrs., 1,000s homeless.		
	†Nov. 4-6	**Florence, Italy**	113
	Worst flood in 1,000 yrs. hit country, cities of Florence, Rome, Naples & Venice swamped. Art damage alone in millions. (SEE Florence)		

Date		Place	Deaths
	Nov. 6	**Panama**	**30**
	Pacora-Chepo area inundated, 400 homeless—many missing.		
	Nov. 6	**Austria**	**23**
	Rain caused flash floods.		
1967	**Jan. 23**	**Brazil**	**620**
	Heavy rains inundated states of Rio de Janeiro and Sao Paulo.		
	Feb. 19	**Rio de Janeiro, Brazil**	**119**
	Heavy rains collapsed 2 buildings, city inundated—4,000 homeless.		
	Mar. 16	**Karachi, Pakistan**	**27**
	Lyari overflowed, 100,000 homeless.		
	Mar. 19	**Caraguatatuba, Brazil**	**160**
	Rains inundated area N. of Sao Paulo.		
	June 9	**Manila, Philippines**	**26**
	Rain flooded area followed by landslides.		
	Aug. 2	**Nagpur, India**	**20**
	Floods outside city.		
	Aug. 19	**Sudan (East)**	**30**
	Heavy rains flooded area, 100s missing.		
	Aug. 31	**Niigata & Yamagata, Japan**	**53**
	Floods injured 36, many missing.		
	Sept. 5	**India (Central)**	**100s**
	Monsoon rains inundated area, 1 million homeless.		
	Sept. 10	**India**	**100s**
	Nanaksagar Dam burst.		
	Oct. 10	**Buenos Aires, Argentina**	**40**
	Heavy rains inundated city, 40,000 evacuated.		
	Oct. 19	**Taiwan**	**69**
	Typhoon inundated country, 20,000 stranded—many missing.		
	Nov. 26	**Lisbon, Portugal**	**457**
	Rainfall flooded area, Quintas worst hit, 1,000s homeless.		
	Nov. 31	**Java (Central)**	**112**
	Irrigation dam burst, official arrested for criminal negligence.		
1968	**July 13**	**East Pakistan**	**140**
	Flash floods left 1,000s homeless.		
	†Aug. 7-14	**Gujaret, India**	**1,000**
	Heavy rains inundated 3 N.E. states, great damage.		
	Oct. 1	**Taiwan**	**19**
	Heavy rains caused widespread floods.		
	†Oct. 1-4	**India**	**1,000**
	Three N.E. states inundated by floods and landslides.		
	Nov. 2	**Sikkim, India**	**260**
	Floods caused $2 million damage.		
	Nov. 3-6	**Biella & Valle, Italy**	**120**
	Torrential rains inundated N.W. part of country.		
1969	**Jan. 18-26**	**California (Southern)**	**91**
	Torrential rains left 9,000 homeless, $35 million damage.		
	Jan. 25	**Khuzestan Prov., Iran**	**20**
	Floods in south gutted 50 villages and left 30,000 homeless.		
	Mar. 16	**Mundau Valley, Brazil**	**230**
	Torrential rains inundated northeastern state of Alagoas.		
	Mar. 17	**Minnesota-Wisconsin**	**21**
	Spring floods swept 8 states, 25,000 homeless—$100 million damage.		
	Apr. 6	**Azerbaijan, Iran**	**20**
	Torrential rains inundated province.		
	July 4	**Cleveland, O.**	**41**
	Rainstorms caused inundations along Lake Erie at holiday time.		
	Aug. 20	**Virginia**	**67**
	Torrential rains from hurricane Camille struck west & central part of state, $132 million damage.		
	†Sept.-Oct.	**Tunisia**	**542**
	Rain fell for 38 days, 50,000 homes gutted.		
1970	**Jan. 5**	**Mendoza, Argentina**	**27**
	Rain collapsed Prado Dam, 600 mi. W. of Buenos Aires.		
	June 1	**Rumania & Yugoslavia**	**170**
	Worst inundations in East European history, 250,000 homeless—damage at $1 billion.		
	July 7	**South Korea**	**39**
	East and southern coasts inundated by 5 days of torrential rain, $5 million damage.		
	July 22	**Himalayas**	**543**
	Flash flood from raging rivers in the foothills wiped out 25 buses, 5 taxis and an army vehicle.		
	July 23	**Pernambuco, Brazil**	**47**
	Torrential rains inundated northeastern state, capital city of Recife 50% submerged.		
	Aug. 16	**Dacca, E. Pakistan**	**100**
	Rivers overflowed, great damage to crops & property.		
	Sept.	**India (Western)**	**600**
	Inundations which lasted 3 weeks wiped out the Gujarat states, 20,000 homeless.		
	Sept. 2	**Luzon Is., Philippines**	**40**
	Three days of heavy rain inundated island, state of national emergency declared.		
	Sept. 8	**Pyinmana, Burma**	**90**
	Flood waters drowned spectators of a bridge construction 250 mi. N. of Rangoon.		
	Sept. 9	**Maricopa, Ariz.**	**21**
	Central area inundated, $1 million damage.		
	Oct. 8	**Genoa, Italy**	**17**
	Refinery tank burst, large area inundated.		
	Oct. 12	**Puerto Rico**	**60**
	Week of floods left 10,000 homeless, $100 million damage.		
	Oct. 30-Nov. 1	**South Vietnam**	**306**
	Rain gutted 5 northern provinces; 204,000 homeless—80% of rice crop ruined.		
	Nov. 12	**Colombia**	**370**
	Worst rainy season in 40 yrs. left 50,000 homeless, $20 million damage.		
	Dec. 14	**Indonesia & Antara**	**90**
	Inundations & landslides in both countries.		
1971	**Jan. 5**	**Malaysia**	**50**
	Torrential rains inundated 8 of nation's 11 states, 114,000 people evacuated.		
	Jan. 29	**Mozambique**	**60**
	Northeastern section of the Portuguese E. African territory inundated, 20,000 homeless.		
	Jan. 31	**Quelimane, Mozambique**	**1,000**
	Zambezi overflowed, north coast submerged.		
	Feb. 26	**Rio de Janeiro, Brazil**	**130**
	Flash flood left 1,000s homeless, water up to 6 ft. deep.		
	Apr. 26-28	**Salvador, Brazil**	**140**
	Four days of rain inundated city, 10,000 homeless—$6 million damage.		
	Aug. 17	**Hong Kong, China**	**90**
	Inundation & storms left 2,500 homeless, damage in millions.		
	Aug. 30	**N. Vietnam**	**100,000s**
	Red and other streams rose to unprecedented levels, inundation was called worse than 1945 which took 1 million victims.		
1972	**Feb. 26**	**Logan County, W. Va.**	**107**
	Coal mine waste waters broke through a 200-ft. high makeshift dam, 14 towns heavily damaged.		
	Mar. 13-June	**Bangla Desh**	**427**
	Storms & floods lasted 3 months, 650 sq.mi. submerged—10,000 people in 17 villages marooned.		

Date	Place	Deaths	Description
Mar. 23	Piura, Peru	30	Chira & Piura overflowed, many cities & 40,000 people affected.
Mar. 31	Tunisia (Western)	150	Rain overflowed Mejerda, 26,000 homeless—15% of cereal crop ruined.
†May 3	Mexico City, Mexico	37	Floods ruined 500 structures; winds tore off 4,000 roof-tops.
May 25	Mississippi River		Inundations lasted record 77 days, $420 million damage.
†June 9	Rapid City, South Dakota	236	Floods caused over $100 million damage, destroyed 1,200 homes, and wrecked 5,000 autos.
†July	Japan	370	Floods & landslides caused $472 million damage.
July 9	Guadalajara, Mexico	30	Cloudburst inundated 3 towns on Lake Chapala.
†July 19	Manila, Philippines	289	Floods started by rainstorms left over 45,000 homeless.
†Aug. 7	Nepal	105	Floods followed monsoon rains.
Aug. 12-Sept. 4	Punjab, Sind.	3,000	Indus overflowed & submerged 20,000 sq.mi., 2 million acres of crops & 3,000 villages wiped out. Officials called it the worst natural disaster in the nation's history.
†Aug. 19	South Korea	463	Floods caused by massive rains engulfed country.
Nov. 14	South Vietnam	60	Thousands of acres submerged at Hoai Nhon, Sn Nhon, Qui Nhon & Binh Dinh.
Nov. 23	Luzon, Philippines	54	Typhoon & flooding left 800,000 homeless.
1973 May 3	Mexico City, Mexico	37	Thunderstorm caused flash flood, 100,000 homeless.
Aug. 26	India & Bangla Desh	253	Rain overflowed rivers in both countries.
†1974 Mar. 24	Tubarao, Brazil	200	Floods overwhelmed city, 100,000 fled, damage over $250 million.
May 1	Brazil	200	Floods & landslides swept country.
Aug. 10	Bangla Desh	3,000	Floods followed monsoon rains.
Aug. 11	Himalayan Mountains	300	Floods brought on by incessant rains.
Aug. 20	Luzon, Philippines	78	Floods caused by monsoon rains left millions homeless.
1975 Jan. 10	Thailand	131	Heavy rains caused floods; 10,000 homeless.

Major Marine Disasters

(† indicates entries profiled in General Narrative)

Date | **Place** | **Deaths**

1502 July — Spanish Fleet — 500
Fleet commanded by Admiral Antonio de Torres was devastated by hurricane off Mona Island, Hispaniola; the 30 caravels carried gold for Columbus.

1504 — Spanish Flotilla — 175
Fleet commanded by Captain Juan de la Cosa foundered in a storm in the Bahia de Uraba, S.A.

1525 Oct. — unidentified — 72
The Spanish vessel foundered in a hurricane off Havana on a voyage to Veracruz.

†1528 Sept. 22 — Narvaez Expedition — 380
Excursion of Spanish explorers devastated by hurricane near Apalache Bay on the Gulf of Florida.

1545 July 20 — *Mary Rose* — **73**
The British vessel foundered in a squall on a voyage from Portsmouth to Spithead.

1551 — unidentified — 140
The French pirate ship foundered on the coast of Iaquana, Hispaniola.

†1553 — New Spain Flota — 100s
The fleet of 20 ships was devastated by a hurricane 5 days out of Veracruz on a voyage to Havana; only 2 of the vessels reached land & those survivors were massacred by the Indians.

1554 — Villafane's Armada — 100s
General Angel de Villafane's immense armada entered the Bermuda Triangle & 3 of his large ships were never heard from again. (SEE Bermuda Triangle)

1555 Jan. 21 — *Santa Maria la Blanca* — **85**
The 220-ton Spanish galleon wrecked in the port of San Juan de Ulva.

1558 Feb. 6 — *Maestre Pedro de Mata* — **60**
The urca of large fleet foundered in a storm near Rio Alvarado.

1559 Aug. 20 — Spanish (expedition) — 600
The fleet was caught in a hurricane off Tampa, Fla. (SEE Tampa Bay, Florida)

†Sept. 19 — Bay of Santa Maria (disaster) — 100s
The 13-vessel fleet under the command of the Governor of Florida was smashed in ½ by a hurricane.

1577 — Manrique's Fleet — 100s
Huge treasure fleet commanded by Don Antonio Manrique sailed into the Bermuda Triangle & vanished. (SEE Bermuda Triangle)

†1586 Spring — *St. James* — **450**
The Portuguese ship foundered in heavy wind while she rounded the Cape of Good Hope.

†1588 Aug.-Oct. — Spanish Armada — 4,000-10,000
The 26,000-man fleet left La Corona, Spain, for England and was demolished while it crossed the English Channel.

1590 Nov. — Flota de Nueva Espana — 1,000
The 63-ship Spanish flota was devastated by a storm in the Gulf of Mexico: among those lost were the navy's *La Trinidad, La Piedad, Nuestra Senora de la Concepcion,* & the *Nuestra Senora del Socorro.*

†1591 Aug. 10 — Grand Fleet — 500
Hurricanes wiped out Spanish treasure fleet on its annual run from Havana to Spain.

1593 Dec. 17 — unidentified — 28
The French ship smashed into reef at Bermuda.

1599 — *San Augustin* — **100s**
The Manila galleon foundered off San Francisco on a voyage from the Philippines to Acapulco.

1600 Sept. 12 — Flota de Nueva Espana — 1,000
The Spanish flota smashed by a hurricane off the coast of Villa Rica; 2 weeks later the remaining ships encountered another storm on the voyage to Veracruz.

1610 — unidentified — 142
The British privateer foundered off the Isle of Pines on a voyage from Plymouth, England.

unidentified — 53
A ship of unknown origin foundered in strong winds off the coast of Zacatula.

1615 Aug. 30 — Flota de Nueva Espana — 100s
Spanish flota of 41 ships caught in storm off Islas Tranquila & Arena; all passengers & crew drowned.

1618 Oct. — *Almiranta* — **100s**
The Honduran ship foundered near the Fort Pierce Inlet.

1621 — unidentified — 30
The patache advise boat was sunk by a tidal wave close to the Dry Tortugas on a voyage from Veracruz to Spain.

1622 Sept. 6 — Spanish Convoys (disaster) — 1,000s
The Armada de Tierra Firme & the Tierra Firme Flota were devastated by a hurricane which wrecked at least a dozen vessels; this is considered the worst disaster to have occurred in the Florida Keys in 50 years to this date.

1623 — *Nuestra Senora de la Picdad* — **112**
The Portuguese navio wrecked at Isla Mujeres.

May — *Espiritu Santa el Mayer* — **250**
The 480-ton Spanish galleon was devastated by huge waves at the mouth of the Bahama Channel on a voyage from Havana.

†1628 Aug. — *Vasa* — **50**
The Swedish flagship sank on her maiden voyage before she even cleared Stockholm Harbor.

1629 June — *Batavia* — **40**
The Dutch merchant ship wrecked on the coral reef at Houtman's Abrolhos Islands near Australia. Out of 316 soldiers, sailors, company officials, women and children, 100 were murdered by stranded mutineers.

1631 — unidentified — 100s
The Dutch merchantman smashed into St. Martin Island in the Lesser Antilles; a Spanish ship attempted to pick up the survivors but she too foundered in an unexpected storm—only 8 survived.

Oct. 21 — Flota de Nueva Espana — 300
The Spanish flota of 19 ships was smashed by a hurricane 1 week out of Veracruz on a voyage to Havana & Spain.

1634 — *San Juan Agustin* — **40**
The Spanish galleon foundered in a storm off Havana between Rio de Puercos & Bahai Honda.

1637 Feb. 27 — *Caballon* — **150**
The Spanish slave nao wrecked on the rocks at Las Hormigas near Callao, S.A.

1641 Sept. 27 — Nueva Espana Flota — 100s
The convoy was devastated in a storm.

†1643 Nov. 1 — *Nuestra Senora De La Concepcion* — **324**
The flagship of the Spanish silver fleet foundered in a hurricane N. of Hispaniola.

1650 — unidentified — 100s
Twenty-eight vessels of different nationalities foundered in a hurricane off Basseterre in the Lesser Antilles.

Date		Place	Deaths
1650's		**Manila Galleons**	1,000s

These vessels would sail to California & Mexico from the Philippines but epidemics of smallpox would consistently claim 100s of lives; in 1657 2 such ships lost 650 persons to disease.

†1654 Aug. 15 *Sparrowhawk* **28**
The Dutch vessel broke to pieces in a typhoon off the Korean coast.

1656 *Nuestra Senora de la Maravillas* **644**
The 650-ton Spanish galleon collided with another galleon & sank on the Little Bahama Bank just N. of Memory Rock.

May *Verqulde Draeck* **186**
The Dutch ship foundered off Batavia reefs.

1660 Mar. 26 **Virginia Merchant** **179**
The British merchantman foundered off Bermuda on a voyage from Plymouth to Jamestown.

1664 **Abermenai Ferry** **79**
Ferryboat started by Edward I capsized on her run between Caernarvon to the southernmost tip of Newborough Warren; townspeople blamed the disaster on the "wrath of God" because the ferry was built from wood stolen from the dismantled Llanddwyn Church.

1666 Aug. 4 **unidentified** **100s**
Two huge British warships foundered in a hurricane in English Harbor, Antiqua. (SEE Guadeloupe)

1669 Jan. 12 *Oxford* **200**
The 240-ton British privateer frigate caught fire & exploded at the Isle of Ash, Hispaniola.

1678 May 3 **French Fleet** **1,200**
Eighteen warships & 2 privateers wrecked on a reef on Aves Island, S.A.

†1679 Sept. 18 *Griffin* **31**
The 40-ton ship, built by explorer Robert Cavalier, disappeared after she set sail from Green Bay, Wisc.

Aug. 3 **unidentified** **174**
The 350-ton Spanish galleon foundered in a storm at the mouth of the Plate River.

1680 Aug. 3 **unidentified** **100s**
Twenty French ships & 2 British foundered in a hurricane in Cul-de-Sac Bay, Martinique.

1681 **Tierra Firme Armada** **100s**
A large number of ships foundered on a voyage from Cartagena to Porto Bello; included were the galleons *Santa Teresa* & the *Nuestra Senora de la Soledad.*

1684 *San Juan de Dios* **100s**
The Spanish nao foundered on the Playa de Panque, Chile; on board was the new bishop of Concepcion.

1687 **Dutch Fleet** **700**
Nineteen merchantmen foundered in a storm off Cayenne, French Guiana.

1689 **N.S.** *de Concepcion y San Yosef* **100s**
The Spanish ship disappeared in the Bermuda Triangle. (SEE Bermuda Triangle)

1691 Sept. 1 *Harwich* **71**
The British warship wrecked on Mount Edgecumbe.

1693 Nov. 21 *Mordaunt* **scores**
The 46-gun British warship smashed into the Los Colorado Reefs, Cuba.

1695 Sept. **H.M.S.** *Winchester* **400**
The British warship, 60-gun vessel, foundered off Key Largo, Fla.; wreckage located in 1940.

Oct. **unidentified** **600**
A dozen French ships foundered off Martinique in a hurricane.

1698 **unidentified** **400**
The Portuguese carrack foundered on the coast off Georgetown, British Guiana.

†1700 Sept. 3 *Rising Sun* **97**
The Scottish frigate foundered off Charleston, S.C.

1703 Nov. 26 *Newcastle* **193**
The British vessel sank at Spithead during a great storm.

Nov. 26 *Reserve* **173**
The British vessel lost in the great storm at Yarmouth.

1704 *Castle del Rey* **132**
The 18-gun, 300-ton privateer smashed into the shoals off Sandy Hook on a voyage from Manhattan.

1707 Oct. 22 *Association* **86**
The British vessel foundered in a storm with other vessels off the Scilly Isles.

1709 Dec. 25 *Solebay* **43**
The 32-gun British vessel foundered near Boston neck.

1710 Aug. *Caesar* **26**
The Rhode Island sloop ran ashore on Dighy Cut in the Bay of Fundy.

1711 *Zuytdorp* **286**
Dutch (Zeeland) ship wrecked off Australia.

†Aug. 22 **English Armada** **2,000**
Eight English transports foundered in bad weather at Egg Island, Labrador.

Oct. 15 *Edgar* **82**
The 70-gun British vessel exploded at Spithead.

†1715 July 31 **Capitanas** **1,000**
The 11-ship Spanish flota was devastated by massive hurricane off the Florida coast.

1724 Sept. 12 *Almiranda* **120**
The Spanish nao along with the *La Tolosa* foundered at Cape Samana, Hispaniola.

1725 **Flota de Nueva Espana** **400**
The Capitana foundered in a fire in Campeche Sound in the Gulf of Mexico.

1726 June 9 *Zeewyk* **100**
The Dutch East Indiaman wrecked off Houtman's Abrolhos Islands.

1732 Jan. *Nuestra Senora de la Concepcion* **500**
The huge Spanish galleon foundered at the entrance of Veracruz.

1738 *Princess Augusta* **250**
The German immigrant ship wrecked off the northern tip of Sandy Point, Block Island; most victims of the voyage died of contaminated water during the journey.

1739 *Adriatick* **100s**
The British merchantman foundered off Cape Hatteras on a voyage from London to Virginia.

Jan. **unidentified** **290**
The German vessel foundered near Cape Henry on a voyage from Germany to the James River.

1741 July *Vease Pink* **scores**
The British troop transport smashed on a reef on the Morant Keys off Jamaica.

1742 Mar. 20 *St. Auguasies* **400**
The Spanish warship wrecked on Anegada on a voyage from San Sebastian, Spain, to Havana.

1744 Sept. 21 *Golchester* **50**
The 50-gun British vessel wrecked at Kentish Knock.

Oct. 5 *Victory* **110**
The 100-gun British vessel foundered near the isle of Alderney.

1746 **Portuguese Fleet** **100s**
Thirteen ships disappeared in a storm while they sailed past Barbado on a voyage from Pernumbuco, Brazil, to Lisbon.

1749 *Pearl* **81**
The British slave ship foundered at Barbuda in the Lesser Antilles.

Date		Place	Deaths
	Apr. 13	*Pembroke*	**330**
	The 60-gun British vessel foundered off Porto Novo.		
	Apr. 13	*Namur*	**50**
	The 74-gun British vessel foundered near Fort St. David, East Indies.		
1752	**July 26**	**The** *Prince*	**scores**
	The French East India Company's ship caught fire on a voyage to Pondicherry & foundered at the latitude of 8 degrees 30 minutes S. & longitude 5 degrees W.		
1755		*Hazard*	**80**
	The French slave ship wrecked at Barbuda on a voyage from Africa to Hispaniola.		
1757		*Duke of Cumberland*	**25**
	The British merchantman wrecked off Cape Henry on a voyage from the Canaries to Virginia.		
		Anamaboo	**100s**
	The slave ship of unknown origin foundered off St. Helena Sound on a voyage from Africa to Rhode Island.		
1758		**unidentified**	**200**
	The British privateer foundered in a hurricane at Sandy Point in the Lesser Antilles.		
	Apr. 13	*Prince George*	**400**
	The 80-gun British vessel caught fire and burned at lat. 48 N. on a voyage to Gibraltar.		
	Nov. 29	*Lichfield*	**130**
	The 50-gun British vessel foundered on the coast of Barbary.		
1759	**Sept. 25**	*Tilbury*	**57**
	The 60-gun British vessel foundered off Louisbourg.		
1760	**Feb. 14**	*Ramillies*	**73**
	The 90-gun British vessel wrecked on St. Nicholas Island, Plymouth.		
	June 22	*Racehorse*	**100s**
	The British slave ship wrecked on Frying Pan Shoals on a voyage from Africa to South Carolina.		
	Nov. 3	*Ann*	**18**
	The 14-gun Royal British Navy frigate, outward bound from Liverpool, was wrecked at Dinnas Dinelle when struck by a severe north-westerly wind.		
1761	**Jan. 1**	*Duc d'Aquitaine & Sunderland*	**124**
	The two British vessels foundered in a storm off Pondicherry.		
	Oct. 25	*Griffin*	**50**
	The British man-of-war foundered off Bermuda.		
1763		*Pitt Packet*	**100s**
	The British vessel foundered in Delaware Bay on a voyage from Belfast to Philadelphia.		
1767		*Good Intent*	**300**
	The British slave ship foundered off Cape Hatteras on a voyage from Africa.		
1770		*L'Orriflame*	**700**
	The 1,200-ton French galleon foundered in a storm on the coast off Valparaiso, S.A.		
1772	**Jan. 2**	*Intelligence*	**21**
	The British merchantman sank at the entrance of Cape Francois, Hispaniola.		
	Aug.	**Hispaniola**	**280**
	Twenty-eight French ships sank in a violent gale.		
1773	**Oct. 18**	*Dove*	**82**
	The British slave ship foundered off the coast of Florida on a voyage to St. Augustine.		
1775		*Repulse*	**32**
	The 32-gun British vessel foundered off Bermuda.		
1776		*Clara*	**120**
	The 30-gun frigate-of-war foundered off Banco Ingles, Montevideo.		
	Sept. 6	**French-Dutch Convoy**	**6,000**
	Hurricane sank 100 merchantmen at Point Bay, Martinique.		

Date		Place	Deaths
1777	**Nov. 11**	*Aurora*	**100s**
	The British troop-transport wrecked off Cape Hatteras.		
1779	**Aug. 28**	**Martinique**	**1,000s**
	Hurricane sank over 70 ships at same site of violent storm 3 yrs. earlier.		
1780	**Oct.**	**Dutch Convoy**	**100s**
	Hurricane sank 7 ships off Orange Town in the Lesser Antilles. (SEE Barbados, West Indies)		
	†Oct. 3-4	*Phoenix*	**200**
	The 44-gun British frigate wrecked on the shoals of Cabo de la Cruz, Cuba, during the "Savanna-la-Mar" hurricane.		
	Oct. 9	*Juno*	**300**
	The 40-gun French frigate wrecked on Dominica during a hurricane. (SEE Barbados, West Indies)		
	Oct. 10	**French-English Fleet**	**1,000s**
	Tremendous hurricane sank over 100 ships; included were the *Andromeda, Laurel, Deal Castle, & Endymion.* (SEE Barbados, W. Indies)		
	Nov. 3	*Hussar*	**62**
	The 28-gun British frigate ran aground at Pot Rock, in the East River, N.Y.		
1781		*Earl of Cornwallis*	**scores**
	American privateer foundered at Bassiterre in the Lesser Antilles.		
1782	**Aug. 4**	*Swan*	**130**
	The British sloop foundered off Waterford.		
	†Sept.	**Royal Navy Disaster**	**3,500**
	After the Battle of the Saints the Royal Navy captured 5 French warships but on their return voyage the Sept. "line storm" devastated the party; included in the wrecks were the *Ville de Paris* with 800 victims, also the *Centaur, Hector, Glorieux & Ramilies.* (SEE *Centaur*)		
†1783		*Erfprinz*	**303**
	The Dutch warship sank off Cape Cod.		
		Dragon	**60**
	The 60-cannon Spanish warship foundered on "Bajo Nuevo" in the Gulf of Campeche.		
		Cato	**54**
	The British vessel wrecked on the Malabar coast.		
	Mar. 13	*Count Belgioiso*	**147**
	The Indiaman vessel foundered off Dublin Bay.		
	Nov. 23	*Ontario*	**190**
	The British sloop wrecked a few miles off Oswego on Lake Ontario.		
1785		*La Boussole & L'Astrolabe*	**21**
	The merchant ships foundered off the coast of Alaska.		
		Faithful Stewart	**200**
	The Scottish immigrant ship foundered off Cape Henlopen on a voyage from Londonderry to Philadelphia.		
	Dec. 5	*Abermenai*	**55**
	The ferryboat sank on the Menai Strait.		
1786	**Jan. 6**	*Halsewell*	**386**
	The East Indiaman vessel wrecked on the Seacombe Isle off Purbeck.		
1787	**May 17**	*Sisters*	**500**
	The British slave ship foundered in heavy winds in the Mona Passage on a voyage from Africa to Havana.		
1790	**Dec. 8**	*Clermont*	**110**
	The British packet foundered on Salt Island during a voyage from Holyhead to Dublin.		
1791		*King George*	**280**
	British slave ship wrecked on Barbados.		
	Mar. 18	*Betty & Mary*	**46**
	The vessel out of Newry smashed on the Hoyle, Liverpool Bay.		
	Aug. 28	*Pandora*	**35**
	The British frigate, which carried some of the *Bounty* mutineers, wrecked on the Great Barrier Reef.		

Date		Place	Deaths
†1792	**Aug. 29**	*Royal George*	**900**
	Famous 108-gun British battleship capsized at Spithead while being repaired.		
1795	**Aug. 2**	**Immigrant Ship**	**100s**
	Unidentified vessel foundered off Cape Charles in a gale.		
1796	**May 13**	*Cormorant*	**95**
	The 18-gun British sloop-of-war exploded at Port-au-Prince.		
	Sept. 19	*Amphion*	**200**
	The British frigate exploded at the dock of Plymouth; her cargo of high explosives apparently was set off by a drunken sailor.		
1797	**Jan. 17**	*Droits de l'Homme*	**140**
	The 74-gun French ship sank 10 days out of Bantry Bay.		
	Nov. 16	*La Tribune*	**300**
	The British vessel foundered off Halifax.		
	Dec. 2	*Hunter*	**75**
	The 18-gun British warship ran aground on Hog Island.		
1798		*De Braak*	**35**
	The 16-gun British warship capsized off Lewes; the vessel's cargo was over 100 tons of treasure.		
		Resistance	**290**
	The British ship exploded in the Straits of Banca.		
1799	**Mar. 15**	*Guadalupe*	**147**
	The Spanish frigate foundered off Cape San Antonio, Cuba.		
	Oct. 11	*Lutine*	**47**
	The British ship wrecked off Vlieland near Holland.		
	Oct. 25	*Amaranthe*	**22**
	The British sloop-of-war foundered off the coast of Florida.		
	Oct. 25	*Nassau*	**100**
	The 64-gun British vessel foundered between Langstone and Chichester.		
	Nov. 5	*Sceptre*	**291**
	The 64-gun British vessel wrecked in Table Bay off the Cape of Good Hope.		
1800	**Jan. 14**	*Queen*	**369**
	The British transport wrecked on Trefusis Point.		
	†Mar. 17	*Queen Charlotte*	**700**
	The British frigate caught fire and burned off Leghorn.		
	Nov. 7	*Leocadia*	**140**
	The 34-gun Spanish frigate foundered near Punta Santa Elena, Ecuador.		
1801	**Mar. 16**	*Invincible*	**400**
	The 74-gun British ship wrecked at Harborough Sands, Yarmouth.		
1802		*General Oglethorp*	**23**
	The American ship foundered off Whale Key, Bahamas.		
	Feb. 10	*Margate*	**23**
	The British vessel foundered near Reculver.		
	Oct. 27	*Juno*	**425**
	The Spanish frigate, with a cargo valued at $300,000, sank to a depth of 180 ft. off Cape May, N.J.		
1803		*York*	**491**
	The British ship foundered in the North Sea.		
	Sept. 30	*Victory*	**27**
	The British vessel sank at Liverpool.		
	†Nov. 19	*Nautilus*	**27**
	The British sailingship wrecked on the rocks of Macao.		
	Nov. 29	*Fanny*	**46**
	The British vessel foundered in the Chinese Sea.		
1804		*Francizhena*	**scores**
	The Portuguese merchantman wrecked on Barbados on a voyage from Brazil to Lisbon.		
	Apr. 2	*Apollo*	**29**
	The West Indian frigate ran aground near Figuera, Portugal, while it shepherded a convoy.		
1805	**Feb. 5**	*Earl of Abergavenny*	**250**
	The East Indiaman vessel foundered on the Bill of Portland.		
	Oct. 23	*Aeneas*	**340**
	The British transport foundered off Newfoundland.		
	Dec. 21	*Aurora*	**300**
	The British transport wrecked on the Goodwin Sands.		
†1806	**Aug. 23**	*Rose in Bloom*	**21**
	The American coastal vessel foundered in a hurricane near Barnegat Inlet, N.J.		
	Sept. 21	*King George*	**106**
	The British packet foundered on the Hoyle bank on a voyage from Park-gate to Dublin.		
	Oct. 27	*Athenien*	**347**
	The 64-gun vessel foundered near Tunis.		
1807	**Jan. 22**	*Felix*	**74**
	The 12-gun British vessel wrecked near Santander.		
	Feb. 1	*Blenheim*	**590**
	The 74-gun British sailing vessel foundered in the Indian Ocean during a typhoon near the island of Rodriguez.		
	Feb. 1	*Java*	**280**
	The British sailing vessel lost with the *Blenheim* in the same typhoon.		
	Feb. 14	*Ajax*	**250**
	The 74-gun British vessel caught fire and burned off Tenedos.		
	Mar. 4	*Blanche*	**45**
	The British frigate wrecked on the French coast.		
	Nov. 11	*Firefly*	**scores**
	The 12-gun British warship sank off Curacao Island, S.A.		
	Dec. 29	*Anson*	**60**
	The 44-gun British vessel wrecked in Mount's Bay on the Lee Bar near Pothleven.		
1808		*Ardilla*	**34**
	The Spanish 18-gun vessel foundered off the Gulf of Mexico.		
1809		*Dominica*	**62**
	The 10-gun British war brig sank off Tortola, Virgin Islands.		
	Jan. 9	*Morne Fortune*	**41**
	The 12-gun British warship wrecked on Martinique.		
	Jan. 21	*Primrose*	**125**
	The British brig sank on the Manacles.		
	Aug. 13	*Frith*	**40**
	The passage boat sank in the Frith of Dornoch.		
†1810	**Dec. 22**	*Minotaur*	**570**
	The British frigate wrecked on a large sand reef outside the entrance of Texel, on the Haak Bank, Holland.		
1811	**Feb. 13**	*Pandora*	**30**
	The 38-gun sloop wrecked off Needles, Jutland.		
	Dec. 4	*Salanha*	**300**
	The frigate foundered on the Irish coast.		
	†Dec. 24	*St. George (& Defence)*	**2,000**
	The British ship *St. George* lost her anchor in a gale and was carried to Wingo Sound to be refitted and the ship *Defence* was sent to assist; both foundered in a gale at their meeting place.		
1813		*Subtle*	**50**
	The British warship sank off St. Barthelemy Is. in the Lesser Antilles.		
	Aug.	**unidentified**	**3,000**
	Forty-two ships foundered in a hurricane.		
1814	**Jan. 14**	*Queen*	**350**
	The British transport foundered on Trefusis Point, Falmouth.		
1815		*Sylph*	**115**
	The 18-gun English warship wrecked on Southampton Bar, Long Island.		

Date	Place	Deaths

Apr. 24 *San Pedro Alcantara* **50**
The 64-gun Spanish warship caught fire & exploded in the Caribbean off Coche Island.

†**1816** *Medusa* **155**
The French frigate sank off the coast of Africa.

Jan. 30 *Seahorse* **380**
The British transport foundered near Tramore Bay.

Jan. 31 *Lord Melville* **&** *Doadicea* **200**
The two British transports foundered in bad weather near Kinsdale.

Nov. 10 *Harpooner* **200**
The British transport foundered near Newfoundland.

1817 Oct. 23 *William and Mary* **60**
The British packet wrecked on the Willeys rocks in the Bristol Channel.

1819 *Frederick* **22**
The Australian sailing vessel wrecked in the Flinders Group, off the western head of Bathurst Bay, Qld.

†**July 27** *Firebrand* **75**
The schooner wrecked in the great hurricane on the Mississippi Gulf Coast. (SEE Mobile, Alabama)

Dec. 30 *Consulado* **120**
The Spanish brig foundered in a storm with the *Guia.*

1820 Mar. 18 *Ariel* **79**
The British vessel foundered in the Persian Gulf.

Dec. 5 *Tal-y-foel* **Ferry** **25**
The vessel sank due to too much sail on a windy day while sailing from Caernavon.

1821 Aug. 8 *Earl of Moira* **40**
The British vessel wrecked on the Burbo Bank near Liverpool.

†**Sept. 17** *Washington* **20**
The schooner foundered in a hurricane in the Bay St. Louis on the Mississippi Coast.

1822 Apr. 21 *Albion* **45**
The 470-ton English vessel was blown down by heavy winds 20 days out of New York on a voyage to Europe.

1823 *Nereide* **290**
The French merchantman foundered off the California coast on a voyage from the Far East to S.A.

Mar. 26 *Alert* **113**
The packet foundered between Dublin and Liverpool.

May 16 *Robert* **60**
The British vessel foundered on a voyage from Dublin to Liverpool.

1824 May 15 *Aetna* **24**
The Citizens' Line steamer blew up in New York harbor.

†**1825 Mar. 2** *Kent* **81**
The 1,530-ton East Indiaman vessel caught fire & sank.

Apr. 14 *Teche* **20**
The 295-ton steam side-wheel, built in 1820, exploded at Natchez, Miss.

Oct. 21 *Comet* **70**
The 94-ton passenger steamship, built in 1821, collided with the steamship *Ayr* off Kempoch Point and sank 165 yards from shore.

1828 Apr. 14 *Acorn* **115**
The sloop was lost off Halifax Station, Nova Scotia.

1829 June 4 *Fulton the First* **33**
The American steam frigate exploded in the Brooklyn Navy Yard.

1830 Feb. 24 *Helen Macgregor* **60**
The 400-ton Mississippi River paddle steamer, built in 1823, exploded at Memphis, Tenn.

Apr. 16 *Newry* **40**
The British passenger vessel foundered near Bardsby.

1831 Aug. 18 *Rothsay Castle* **127**
The 75-ton wooden paddle steamer, built in 1816, wrecked on a sand bank at the entrance to the Menai Strait.

Aug. 19 *Lady Sherbrooke* **263**
The immigrant ship, on a voyage from England to Quebec, foundered off Cape Ray, N.J.

1832 Apr. 9 *Brandywine* **155**
The 483-ton Mississippi River steamboat, built in 1829, caught fire and burned at Randolph, Tenn.

June 2 *Hornet* **20**
The steam side-wheel capsized on the Ohio River.

1833 Feb. 15 *Hibernia* **150**
The British vessel caught fire and burned at W. long. 22 degrees - S. lat. 4 degrees.

May 11 *Lady of the Lake* **215**
The sailing vessel wrecked on an iceberg on a voyage from England to Quebec.

May 14 *Loch Fyne* **36**
The 1,213-ton iron clipper ship, built in 1826, sailed from Australia for Lyttleton, N.Z., and disappeared.

June 7 *Peruvian* **50**
The 226-ton steam side-wheel, built in 1831, exploded at Natchez, Miss.

Aug. 31 *Amphitrite* **133**
The 208-ton chartered convict ship was run aground on the French coast near Boulogne, broke in two, and all but 3 drowned.

Oct. 9 *George Washington* **50**
The 605-ton steam side-wheel, built in 1833, stranded at Long Point, Ontario.

Oct. 11 *Lady Munro* **75**
The 250-ton bark wrecked on the Island of Amsterdam in the Indian Ocean.

Oct. 27 *New England* **20**
The vessel exploded on the Connecticut River.

Oct. 31 *Saint Martin* **31**
The 143-ton steam side-wheel, built in 1832, caught fire at Donaldsonville, La.

1834 Jan. 9 *Lady Munro* **70**
The British vessel foundered on a voyage from Calcutta to Sydney.

June 16 *Washington* **30**
The steamer caught fire and burned off Dunkirk, N.Y.

Oct. 24 *Boonslick* **30**
The steam side-wheel collided with the steamboat *Mississippi Belle* at St. Louis, Mo.

1835 Apr. 12 *George III* **134**
The convict ship wrecked on a rock at the entrance to the D'Entrecasteaux Channel, N.S.W.

May 14 *Neva* **218**
The 837-ton convict ship, built in 1825, wrecked on the rocks at the Bass Strait near King's Island.

July 17 *Enchantress* **50**
The immigrant ship wrecked on the cliffs of Bruny Island on the D'Entrecasteaux Channel, N.S.W.

1836 Mar. 13 *Ben Franklin* **20**
The vessel exploded at Mobile, Ala.

Oct. 11 *Clarendon* **37**
The 345-ton British sailing ship ran aground in a gale at Blackgang Chine, Isle of Wight.

Oct. 26 *Royal Tar* **32**
The British wooden paddle steamer, built in 1836, caught fire and burned in Eastport Harbour.

†**Nov. 21** *Bristol* **84**
The American bark wrecked off Far Rockaway, N.Y.

1837 Jan. 2 *Mexico* **116**
The bark wrecked at Hempstead Beach, N.Y.

May 8 *Ben Sherrod* **200**
The Mississippi River steamboat, built in 1836, caught fire at Black Hawk, La.

Aug. 15 *Dubuque* **27**
The vessel collapsed in the Mississippi River.

Date		Place	Deaths	Description
	Oct. 9	*Home*	**96**	The 537-ton steam side-wheel, built in 1837, foundered off Cape Hatteras, N.C.
	Oct. 31	*Monmouth*	**300**	The 135-ton steam side-wheel, built in 1836, collided with the *Tremont* at Profit Island, Mississippi River.
1838	**Jan. 26**	*Killarney*	**29**	The East Indiaman vessel caught fire and burned at sea.
	Apr. 21	*Oronoko*	**100**	The 367-ton steamboat, built in 1831, exploded at Princeton on the Mississippi River.
	Apr. 26	*Moselle*	**85**	The steam side-wheel blew up on the Ohio River at Cincinnati.
	June 14	*Pulaski*	**101**	The 687-ton steamboat, built in 1837, had a boiler explosion at the New River Inlet, N.C.
	June 16	*Washington*	**50**	The vessel caught on fire and burned on Lake Erie.
	Sept. 27	*Forfarshire*	**45**	The 270-ton Scottish coastal ship, built in 1834, was wrecked in a gale and broke in two on a voyage to Dundee, Scotland.
	Nov. 21	*Protector*	**170**	The East Indiaman vessel sank at Bengal.
	Nov. 25	*Gen. Brown*	**60**	The vessel exploded on the Mississippi River.
1839		*Dispatch*	**21**	The Australian ship caught fire and burned in the Tasman Sea on a voyage to London.
	Jan. 7	*Diligence*	**57**	The British revenue cutter hit stormy weather in the Irish Channel and ran aground on the coast of Ireland.
	Jan. 9	*Lockwoods*	**53**	The Liverpool-owned immigrant ship wrecked off Lensowe near the Cumberland coast.
	May 6	*George Collier*	**26**	The 402-ton steam side-wheel, built in 1835, exploded on the Mississippi River.
1840	**Jan. 13**	*Lexington*	**156**	The 488-ton wooden paddle steamer, built in 1835, caught fire at Eaton's Neck, N.Y.
	May 7	*Hinds*	**51**	The 130-ton steam side-wheel, built in 1836, foundered near Natchez, Miss.
	June 17	*Lord William Bentinck*	**85**	The British passenger ship foundered near Bombay.
	Aug. 9	**Brig** *Florence*	**60**	The ship foundered off Newfoundland.
	Nov.	*Persian*	**24**	The vessel exploded on the Mississippi River.
	Nov. 13	*Fairy*	**63**	The 233-ton sloop, built in 1826, ran aground and wrecked on the coast of Norfolk, Eng.
1841	**Jan. 4**	*Thames*	**62**	The 500-ton steamship foundered in a gale off the Brow of Ponds Reef, Scilly Isles.
	Feb. 13	*Lamplighter*	**19**	The 186-ton steam side-wheel, built in 1835, foundered at East Pass, Fla.
	Feb. 20	*Governor Fenner*	**123**	The 500-ton American sailing ship, built in 1831, collided with the paddle steamer *Nottingham* 15 mi. west of Holyhead, Eng.
	Feb. 22	*Creole*	**34**	The 192-ton steam side-wheel, built in 1839, caught fire at Torras, La.
	Mar. 12	*President*	**136**	The British-American steamer foundered in a storm on a trans-Atlantic run from New York to Liverpool.
	May 18	*Minstrel*	**148**	The 300-ton sailing vessel, built in 1830, ran aground and wrecked on the Red Island Reef.
	Aug. 6	*Caroline*	**37**	The 407-ton steam side-wheel, built in 1841, became snagged at Plum Point, Tenn.
	Aug. 9	*Erie*	**242**	The 497-ton steam side-wheel, built in 1837, burned near Silver Creek, N.Y.
1842	**July 9**	*Shamrock*	**68**	The vessel exploded on the St. Lawrence River.
	Aug. 27	*Waterloo*	**190**	The 414-ton convict ship, built in 1815, foundered in a gale at Simon's Bay, the Cape, S. Africa.
	Sept. 26	*Armada*	**41**	The British steamer sank off Metis.
	Oct. 13	*Eliza*	**30**	The 206-ton steam side-wheel, built in 1841, became snagged at Bird Island, Mo.
	Oct. 21	*Reindeer*	**21**	The steamer sank off Point Sauble, Lake Michigan.
	Nov. 12	*Reliance*	**115**	The 1,515-ton sailing ship, built in 1827, ran aground in a gale off Merlement, near Boulogne.
1843	**Jan. 7**	*Monk*	**19**	The British cargo ship, overloaded with 140 pigs, sprang a leak and struck the North Bank on a voyage from Porthdinllaen to Liverpool.
	Jan. 13	*Conqueror*	**77**	The 800-ton vessel, built in 1835, was wrecked in a gale off the French coast near Boulogne.
	Apr. 8	*Solway*	**35**	The 1,700-ton British steamship, built in 1841, wrecked on the Baldargo Reef, near the island of Sisargo.
	Oct.	*Clipper*	**50**	The 174-ton Ohio River steamboat, built in 1843, exploded on the lower Mississippi River.
1844	**Jan. 3**	*Shepherdess*	**70**	The Ohio River steamboat snagged on a submerged tree near St. Louis, Mo.
	Mar. 1	*Buckeye*	**80**	The 170-ton Mississippi River steamboat, built in 1837, was run down by the steamboat *DeSoto* at Atchafalaya, La.
	July 9	*Pegasus*	**52**	The British steam-packet foundered off the Fern Islands.
	Oct. 23	*Lucy Walker*	**60**	The steam side-wheel exploded at New Albany, Ind.
	Dec. 14	*Belle of Clarksville*	**36**	The 250-ton steam side-wheel, built in 1843, collided with another Mississippi River steamboat at Memphis, Tenn.
1845	**Jan. 8**	*Belle Zane*	**75**	The vessel sank in the Mississippi river.
	June 16	*Manchester*	**30**	The British steamer foundered off the Vogel Sands near Cuxhagen.
	July 26	*Terror*	**67**	The 326-ton ship, built in 1813, disappeared in heavy ice at lat. 74° 48 ′ N - long. 66° 13′ W.
	Sept. 30	*Charterhouse*	**66**	The 2,025-ton steamship foundered during a storm off Hainan Head.
	Oct. 27	*Plymouth*	**25**	The 150-ton steam side-wheel, built in 1844, collided with the *Lady Madison* near Shawneetown, Ill.

Date		Place	Deaths
1846	Feb. 15	*John Minturn*	28
	The ship ran aground at Squam Beach, N.J.		
	Aug. 4	*Cataraqui*	414
	The 400-ton immigrant ship, built in 1840, ran aground in a gale off the west coast of King's Island, Bass Strait.		
	†Sept. 6-7	*New York*	21
	The steamer foundered in a hurricane in the northwestern Gulf of Mexico.		
	Nov. 21	*Maria*	30
	The 692-ton steam side-wheel, built in 1844, collided with the *Sultan* at Natchez, Miss.		
	Nov. 27	*Atlantic*	42
	The 1,112-ton steam side-wheel stranded off Fishers Island, New York, and wrecked.		
1847	Jan. 16	*Sirius*	20
	The 703-ton paddle steamship, built in 1837, wrecked on the Smith's Rocks near Ballycotton.		
	Feb. 12	*Tweed*	72
	The 1,800-ton paddle-steamer, built in 1841, wrecked on the Alecranes on a voyage to Veracruz, Mex.		
	Mar. 17	*Sovereign*	44
	The 214-ton Australian paddle steamer, built in 1839, foundered on the south passage of Moreton Bay.		
	Apr. 29	*Exmouth*	251
	The 320-ton immigrant sailing ship, built in 1835, foundered on the rocks of the Runs of Islay.		
	May 19	*Carrick*	170
	The 275-ton brig, chartered as an immigrant ship, foundered in a gale on the St. Lawrence River.		
	June 4	*Edna*	20
	The 183-ton steam side-wheel, built in 1842, exploded at Colombia, La.		
	June 29	*Star Spangled Banner*	20
	The 275-ton steam side-wheel, built in 1845, snagged at Baton Rouge, La.		
	Nov. 19	*Talisman*	50
	The Mississippi River steamboat collided with another steamboat and sank.		
	Nov. 21	*Phoenix*	240
	The 302-ton steam screw, built in 1845, caught fire and burned at Sheboygan, Wisc.		
	Dec. 20	*Avenger*	265
	The 1,445-ton steam frigate, built in 1845, wrecked on the Sorelli Rocks off the Island of Galita.		
	Dec. 29	*A. N. Johns*	60
	The 199-ton steam side-wheel, built in 1847, exploded at Trinity, Ky.		
1848	Jan. 18	*Yalobusha*	35
	The 80-ton steam side-wheel, built in 1837, caught fire at Donaldsonville, La.		
	Feb. 29	*Omega*	115
	The 1,277-ton sailing vessel, built in 1840, foundered in the mid-Atlantic and the captain transferred passengers to other ships; the rescue ships all foundered while the *Omega* regained control and was saved.		
	Mar. 20	*Benares*	25
	The 400-ton paddle steamer, built in 1847, caught fire near Rajmahal on the Ganges River.		
	Mar. 24	*Commerce*	100
	The 300-ton immigrant ship, built in 1840, ran aground off the coast of Nova Scotia.		
	May 27	*Clarksville*	21
	The 484-ton steam side-wheel, built in 1845, caught fire and burned at Napoleon, Ark.		
	Aug. 9	*Edward Bates*	53
	The vessel exploded on the Mississippi River.		
	†Aug. 28	*Ocean Monarch*	178
	The 1,301-ton American sailing vessel, built in 1843, caught fire 6 mi. off Great Orme's Head, North Wales, and sank.		
	Sept. 16	*Concordia*	28
	The vessel exploded at Plaquemine, La.		
	Nov. 21	*Wyandotte*	30
	The 314-ton steam side-wheel, built in 1847, snagged near Vicksburg, Miss.		
1849	Mar. 1	*Floridian*	193
	The 500-ton American bark, built in 1840, foundered in a gale and wrecked on the Long Sand off Harwich.		
	Apr. 3	*Hannah*	60
	The 287-ton brig, built in 1826, struck an ice floe and foundered in 40 minutes while on a voyage from Newry to Quebec.		
	May 10	*Maria*	109
	The 300-ton sailing vessel, built in 1835, struck an iceberg 50 mi. from St. Paul's Island on a voyage to Quebec.		
	June 19	*Richard Dart*	36
	The brig wrecked on Prince Edward Island, South Indian Ocean.		
	June 27	*Charles Bartlett*	135
	The 400-ton American brig, built in 1840, collided with the *Europa* at 50° 49′, long. 29° 30′.		
	†Oct. 6	*St. John*	27
	The 400-ton immigrant ship, built in 1840, wrecked on Grampus Rocks outside Boston.		
	Nov. 9	*Hanover*	26
	The sailing ship wrecked on the rocks at the entrance to the Bath Harbor, Maine.		
	Nov. 11	*Caleb Grimshaw*	92
	The 800-ton immigrant ship, built in 1840, caught fire after it sailed from Liverpool to America.		
	Nov. 15	*Louisiana*	86
	The 376-ton steam side-wheel, built in 1848, exploded at New Orleans, La.		
1850		*Queen of the West*	32
	The 1,060-ton Canadian ship, built in 1849, was lost at sea.		
	Mar. 4	*Orline St. John*	41
	The 349-ton steam side-wheel, built in 1847, caught fire at Bridgeport, Ala.		
	Mar. 23	*Troy*	22
	The steamship exploded near Black Rock, New York.		
	Mar. 29	*Royal Adelaide*	400
	The 450-ton paddle steamship, built in 1842, foundered at Margate on a voyage to London.		
	Apr. 18	*Anthony Wayne*	50
	The steamer exploded near Vermillion, Lake Erie.		
	Apr. 23	*Belle of the West*	34
	The 249-ton Mississippi steamboat, built in 1841, exploded at Warsaw, Ky., on the Ohio River.		
	May	*Commerce*	40
	The American steamer collided off Grand River, Canada.		
	†June 17	*G. P. Grittith*	295
	The 587-ton steam side-wheel, built in 1848, caught fire at Mentor, Ohio.		
	June 19	*Orion*	60
	The 899-ton passenger ship, built in 1850, wrecked on the rocks of Portpatrick Harbor.		
	Oct. 23	*Neiri Shevket*	516
	The 90-gun Turkish line-of-battle ship exploded while lying off the arsenal at Constantinople; negligence in the transfer of ammunition was the cause.		
	Oct. 29	*Sagamore*	20
	The 66-ton steam side-wheel, built in 1850, exploded at San Francisco, Calif.		
	Oct. 30	*Donna Maria II*	200
	The Portuguese Navy frigate was blown to bits in the harbor of Macoa; reason of explosion is unknown.		

Date		Place	Deaths
	Nov. 20	*Edmund*	**96**

The 400-ton immigrant ship, built in 1840, had her masts wrecked by a gale and smashed into the Duggerna Rocks off the Bay of Kilkee.

Dec. 14 *Anglo-Norman* **100**
The vessel exploded at New Orleans, La.

Dec. 17 *South America* **30**
The vessel caught fire on the Mississippi River.

Dec. 17 *Knoxville* **19**
The vessel exploded on the Mississippi River.

1851 **Jan. 29** *John Adams* **123**
The Mississippi River steamboat wrecked on an obstacle 200 mi. from Memphis.

Feb. 10 *Autocrat* **30**
The Mississippi River steamboat was rammed by another steamboat.

Feb. 20 *St. Louis* **20**
The 210-ton steam side-wheel, built in 1847, exploded at St. Louis, Mo., when used as a ferryboat.

Mar. 2 *Oregon* **60**
The vessel exploded on the Mississippi River.

June 10 *Atiet Rohoman* **175**
The 500-ton Indian sailing ship, built in 1840, lost her rudder and foundered near Bombay.

July 25 *Randolph* **27**
The 500-ton Indian sailing vessel, built in 1840, wrecked on a voyage to Calcutta.

Sept. 29 *Brilliant* **100**
The vessel exploded on the Mississippi River.

Oct. 23 *Henry Clay* **28**
The 221-ton steam screw, built in 1849, foundered near Long Point, Ontario.

Nov. 27 *Archer* **34**
The 147-ton steam side-wheel, built in 1844, collided with the *Die Vernon* at Grafton, Ill.

Nov. 29 *Molly Grath* **20**
The 75-ton steam stern wheel, built in 1851, collided with the *Pontiac No. 2* near Owensboro, Ky.

Dec. 9 *Clermont* **20**
The 121-ton steam side-wheel, built in 1845, wrecked at White River, Ark.

†1852 **Jan. 4** *Amazon* **140**
The 3,000-ton wood paddle steamer, built in 1851, caught fire and exploded 110 mi. W.S.W. of the Scillies.

Jan. 25 *DeWitt Clinton* **36**
The 265-ton steam side-wheel, built in 1847, became snagged at Memphis, Tenn.

†Jan. 28 *General Warren* **42**
The 309-ton steam side-wheel, built in 1844, stranded at Astoria, Ore.

†Feb. 26 *Birkenhead* **455**
The 1,400-ton British paddle frigate, built in 1846, struck an uncharted rock off Danger Point, 50 mi. from Cape Town.

Apr. 2 *Redstone* **40**
The steamer exploded on the Ohio River.

Apr. 3 *Glencoe* **60**
The 428-ton steam side-wheel, built in 1846, exploded at St. Louis, Mo.

Apr. 9 *Saluda* **35**
The 233-ton steam side-wheel, built in 1846, exploded at Lexington, Mo.

Apr. 25 *Prairie State* **20**
The 314-ton steam side-wheel, built in 1849, exploded at Pekin, Ill.

Apr. 26 *Chickamauga* **20**
The 309-ton steam side-wheel, built in 1851, collided with the *W.B. Clifton* at French Island, Evansville, Ind.

May 9 *Favorite* **21**
The Australian schooner foundered in a gale off Cape Howe on a voyage to Sydney.

July 4 *St. James* **35**
The 347-ton steam side-wheel, built in 1850, exploded at Lake Pontchartrain, La.

July 28 *Henry Clay* **60**
The 386-ton steam side-wheel, built in 1851, burned at Hudson River, Yonkers, N.Y.

†Aug. 20 *Atlantic* **100s**
The 1,155-ton steam side-wheel, built in 1848, collided with the steamer *Ogdensburg* near Long Point, Ontario, Can.

Aug. 22 *Franklin No. 2* **32**
The vessel collapsed on the Mississippi River.

Sept. 3 *Reindeer* **31**
The 790-ton steam side-wheel, built in 1850, exploded at Bristol Landing, Saugerties, Hudson River, N.Y.

Sept. 7 *Fairfield* **20**
The 434-ton wooden sailing ship, built in 1833, ran aground in a gale 110 mi. S. of Port Natal.

Sept. 29 *Mobile* **71**
The 1,000-ton American sailing vessel, built in 1851, wrecked on Blackwater Bank on a voyage from Liverpool.

Oct. 8 *Successor* **64**
The 423-ton British bark, built in 1849, was destroyed by a monsoon.

Dec. 24 *Lily* **30**
The British vessel stranded on the Calf-of-Man and exploded.

1853 **Feb. 15** *Queen Victoria* **67**
The 248-ton paddle steamer, built in 1837, wrecked on the cliffs of Howth, N. of the Bailey light.

Feb. 16 *Independence* **140**
The vessel caught fire off the coast of California.

Mar. 23 *Farmer* **32**
The 158-ton steam side-wheel, built in 1849, exploded at Galveston, Texas.

Apr. 11 *Larriston* **31**
The 474-ton wooden steamship, built in 1852, collided with the American frigate *Plymouth* and a short time later wrecked on the rocks of Turnabout Island, 80 mi. from Foochow.

Apr. 30 *Ocean Wave* **28**
The American steamer caught fire and burned off Kingston, Lake Ontario.

May 4 *William and Mary* **170**
The 257-ton immigrant ship, built in 1849, wrecked on the rocks off the Bahamas.

May 15 *Monumental City* **33**
The 768-ton screw steamship foundered in the Mallacoota Inlet, near Gabo Island, Vic.

May 20 *Aurora* **26**
The 400-ton sailing ship, built in 1845, foundered 46 degrees N., long. 38 degrees W.

June 7 *Nessree* **350**
The 500-ton Indian sailing ship, built in 1840, ran aground near Habshee Jungeera, 35 mi. S. of Bombay.

†Sept. 29 *Annie Jane* **348**
The 1,294-ton immigrant ship, built in 1853, foundered off Bara Island in the Hebrides.

Oct. 19 *Dalhousie* **59**
The 754-ton wooden ship, built in 1848, foundered 15 mi. W.S.W. of Beachy Head.

Nov. 26 *Marshall* **48**
The 307-ton steamship, built in 1846, collided with the bark *Woodhouse* off Kilnea, 5 mi. from the Newsand Float near the mouth of the Humber River.

Date		Place	Deaths
	Dec. 24	*St. George*	**51**

The immigrant passenger ship, loaded with Irish, caught fire and burned in the mid-Atlantic.

1854 Jan. 3 *Staffordshire* **175**
The 1,817-ton sailing vessel, built in 1851, wrecked on the Blonde Rock, Cape Sable.

†Jan. 14 *San Francisco* **300**
The 3,000-ton paddle steamship, built in 1853, sank in Atlantic 45 days out on her maiden voyage.

†Jan. 20 *Tayleur* **349**
The 1,997-ton sailing vessel, built in 1853, foundered in the Irish Sea, off Lambay Island.

Jan. 28 *Georgia* **60**
The 326-ton steam side-wheel, built in 1851, exploded at Lake Pontchartrain, La.

Mar. *City of Glasgow* **450**
The 1,610-ton screw steamship, built in 1850, sailed from Liverpool and disappeared.

Mar. 5 *Caroline* **45**
The 103-ton steam side-wheel, built in 1853, caught fire and burned at White River, Ark.

Mar. 9 *John L. Avery* **75**
The 323-ton steam side-wheel, built in 1853, snagged at Fort Adams, Miss.

Mar. 20 *Monroe* **30**
The 183-ton steam side-wheel, built in 1848, capsized near Natchez, Miss.

Apr. 15 *Secretary* **50**
Vessel blew up at San Pablo, Calif.

Apr. 16 *Powhatan* **250**
The 900-ton American immigrant ship, built in 1839, grounded into a bar several miles off the coast of Barnegat, N.J.

Apr. 29 *Favourite* **201**
The 450-ton immigrant ship, built in 1845, collided with the American ship *Hesper* off Start Point, England.

May 3 *Winchester* **25**
The 600-ton sailing packet, built in 1845, sank in the mid-Atlantic; most of the 447 passengers were rescued.

May 10 *Lady Nugent* **409**
The 642-ton wooden ship, built in 1840, disappeared in the Bay of Bengal after she left Madras.

May 31 *Europa* **20**
The 841-ton sailing ship, built in 1851, caught fire and burned one day out of Plymouth, England.

Sept. 27 *Charlotte* **117**
The 535-ton hired transport, built in 1844, foundered in a storm outside Port Elizabeth.

†Sept. 27 *Arctic* **322**
The 2,850-ton wooden paddle steamship, built in 1849, collided with the small French steamship *Vesta* 65 mi. S.W. of Cape Race, Newfoundland.

Oct. 8 *E. K. Collins* **23**
The 942-ton steam side-wheel, built in 1854, caught fire at Amherstburg, Ontario.

Nov. 13 *New Era* **300**
The immigrant ship wrecked near the New Jersey coast.

Nov. 14 *Prince* **143**
The 2,710-ton steamship, built in 1854, wrecked in a storm outside the Black Sea with a cargo worth over $5 million.

Nov. 14 *Resolute* **41**
The 639-ton sailing ship, built in 1851, foundered in a gale off Balaclava.

Nov. 28 *Nile* **30**
The 700-ton steamship, built in 1849, wrecked near St. Ives.

Dec. 31 *George Canning* **96**
The 700-ton sailing vessel, built in 1845, foundered in a gale off the Elbe on a voyage to Hamburg.

1855 Jan. 9 *Guiding Star* **480**
The 2,013-ton clipper ship, built in 1853, disappeared with all immigrant passengers and crew in a huge ice field at 44° S., 28° W.

Jan. 20 *Janet Boyd* **28**
The 230-ton bark, built in 1839, wrecked on Margate Sands in bad weather.

Jan. 27 *Pearl* **80**
The 78-ton steam side-wheel, built in 1854, exploded at Yolo, Calif.

Feb. 25 *Morna* **21**
The 363-ton steamship, built in 1854, wrecked on the North Bishop's Rock, off St. David's Head.

May 3 *John* **200**
The British immigrant vessel wrecked on the Menacles Rocks near Falmouth.

June 30 *Lexington* **30**
The 312-ton steam side-wheel, built in 1850, exploded at Rome, Ind.

1856 Jan. 5 *Belle* **30**
The 66-ton steam side-wheel, built in 1853, exploded at Sacramento, Calif.

Jan. 23 *Pacific* **186**
The 2,860-ton wooden paddle steamer, built in 1849, sailed from Liverpool and disappeared.

Feb. 14 *John Minturn* **60**
The New Orleans packet wrecked off Squam Beach, N.J.

Feb. 29 *John Rutledge* **135**
The 1,600-ton American sailing ship, built in 1840, struck an iceberg off the Newfoundland Banks.

Feb. 21 *Great Duke* **29**
The 2,000-ton American sailing ship, built in 1845, wrecked on the rocks of St. Gowan's Head, near Milford Haven in a gale.

Mar. 15 *New Jersey* **51**
The 85-ton steam screw, built in 1836 and used as a ferryboat, burned at Philadelphia, Pa.

Mar. 30 *Cazador* **315**
The 350-ton Chilean paddle-steamship, built in 1850, wrecked on the Carranza Rocks, 18 mi. S.W. of Constitution, Chile.

May 30 *Pallas* **82**
The 316-ton bark, built in 1826, wrecked on St. Paul's Island on a voyage to Quebec.

June 3 *Josephine Willis* **69**
The 786-ton New Zealand packet ship, built in 1840, collided with the *Mangerton* 9 mi. S.S.W. of Folkestone and sank.

July 16 *Northern Indiana* **50**
The American steamer caught fire and burned on Lake Erie.

Aug. 10 *Nautilus* **20**
The 898-ton steam side-wheel, built in 1854, stranded at Last Island, Ga.

Sept. 5 *Ocean Home* **77**
The 646-ton American sailing vessel, built in 1840, collided with the American vessel *Cherubim* off Lizard Light after she sailed from Rotterdam.

Sept. 24 *Niagara* **60**
The vessel caught fire and burned on Lake Michigan.

Oct. 24 *Toledo* **40**
The 585-ton steam screw, built in 1854, foundered at Port Washington, Wisc.

Oct. 29 *Superior* **34**
The 567-ton steamer, built in 1845, became stranded at Grand Island, Mich.

Date	Place	Deaths

Nov. 2 *Lyonnais* **130**
The 1,070-ton iron screw steamship, built in 1846, collided with the barque *Adriatic* off Nantucket Island, Mass.

Nov. 4 *J. W. Brooks* **50**
The 312-ton steam screw, built in 1851, sank off Duck Light, Ontario.

1857 May 21 *Pacific* **24**
The 350-ton bark foundered off the coast of New Zealand.

May 31 *Louisiana* **55**
The 1,056-ton steam side-wheel, built in 1850, caught fire at Galveston, Texas.

June 26 *Montreal* **250**
The steamer caught fire & sank 12 mi. from Quebec.

Aug. *Champion* **32**
The 249-ton Australian passenger cargo steamship, built in 1854, collided with the steamship *Lady Bird* near Cape Otway.

Aug. 20 *Dunbar* **121**
The 1,321-ton Australian ship wrecked at South Head, Sydney, with a cargo worth $250,000.

Sept. 12 *Central America* **427**
The 1,200-ton United States mail steamship, built in 1852, sprang a leak and foundered in heavy sea at 31-25 N. - 77-10 W. The ship was insured for $1.25 million and carried $1.5 million in gold.

Sept. 23 *Leffort* **826**
The 84-gun Russian line-of-battle ship, with 70 women and children on board, foundered in a storm off the island of Hogland in the Gulf of Finland. The ports had been left open to provide fresh air for the passengers.

Oct. 24 *Catherine Adamson* **21**
The 768-ton clipper ship, built in 1855, wrecked off the Inner North Head, Sydney, Aus.

Nov. 2 *Maritana* **27**
The 991-ton sailing ship, built in 1857, wrecked on the Shag Rocks one mi. E. of Boston.

1858 Jan. 20 *Fanny Fern* **20**
The 190-ton steam stern wheel, built in 1853, exploded at Lawrenceburg, Ind.

Mar. 1 *Eliza Battle* **29**
The 315-ton steam side-wheel, built in 1858, caught fire at Kemps Ledge, Tombigbee River, Ala.

Apr. 22 *Ocean Spray* **23**
The 371-ton steam side-wheel, built in 1857, caught fire and burned at St. Louis, Mo.

Sept. 13 *Austria* **471**
The 2,383-ton Hamburg-Amerika liner, built in 1857, caught fire and foundered in the North Atlantic.

1859 Feb. 28 *Princess* **70**
The 715-ton steam side-wheel, built in 1855, exploded at Baton Rouge, La.

Apr. 24 *St. Nicholas* **60**
The 666-ton steam side-wheel, built in 1853, exploded at St. Francis Island, Helena, Ark.

Apr. 28 *Pomona* **386**
The 1,181-ton American immigrant ship, built in 1856, sank 7 mi. off Ballyconigar on the Irish coast.

Aug. 4 *Admella* **83**
The 395-ton Australian passenger steamship foundered off Cape Northumberland, South Australia.

†Oct. 25 *Royal Charter* **438**
The 2,719-ton British auxiliary ship, built in 1854, wrecked on the sands of Moelfre Bay.

Oct. 26 *Troy* **23**
The 340-ton steam screw, built in 1849, foundered at Point Dubuque on Lake Huron.

Nov. 21 *Indian* **27**
The 1,764-ton steamship, built in 1855, wrecked on rocks near Cape Race, N.S.

Dec. 25 *Blervie Castle* **57**
The Australian ship foundered in the English Channel.

1860 Jan. 6 *Northerner* **36**
The 1,012-ton steam side-wheel, built in 1847, stranded at Cape Mendocino, Calif.

Feb. 20 *Hungarian* **205**
The 2,190-ton steamship, built in 1859, foundered in the dark off Cape Sable, Nova Scotia.

Feb. 25 *Nimrod* **45**
The 583-ton paddle steamer, built in 1843, wrecked on the rocks off St. David's Head on a voyage to Cork, Ire.

June 24 *B. W. Lewis* **40**
The 472-ton steam side-wheel, built in 1858, exploded at Cairo, Ill.

†Sept. 8 *Lady Elgin* **287**
The 1,037-ton steam side-wheel, built in 1851, collided with the schooner *Augusta* off Winnetka, Ill.

Sept. 9 *Camilla* **121**
The 549-ton British sloop, built in 1847, disappeared in a typhoon off the coast of Japan.

Oct. 31 *H. R. W. Hill* **39**
The 602-ton steam side-wheel, built in 1852, exploded at Baton Rouge, La.

Nov. 3 *Baltic* **20**
The 399-ton steam side-wheel, built in 1856, exploded at Mobile, Ala.

Nov. 23 *Docotah* **24**
The 698-ton steam screw copper carrier, built in 1857, wrecked at Buffalo, N.Y.

1861 June 4 *Canadian* **35**
The 1,926-ton passenger ship, built in 1860, sank in the Straits of Belle Isle near Liverpool.

Oct. 30 *Keystone State* **33**
The 1,354-ton steam side-wheel, built in 1849, stranded at Saginaw Bay, Mich.

1862 Feb. 23 *Cambridge* **42**
The 242-ton steam stern wheel, built in 1856, became snagged at Grand Claise, Ark.

Feb. 27 *Prince* **74**
The 223-ton steam side-wheel, built in 1859, became snagged near Hickman, Ky.

April *Mars* **50**
The Waterford steamer wrecked on a rock near Milford Haven.

†July 27 *Golden Gate* **198**
The 2,057-ton steam side-wheel, built in 1851, caught fire north of Manzanillo, Mexico.

Aug. 13 *West Point* **76**
The 409-ton steam side-wheel, built in 1860, collided with the *George Peabody* at Ragged Point, Potomac River.

Oct. 10 *Bencoolen* **26**
The 1,415-ton wooden sailing ship, built in 1855, was wrecked in Boda Bay.

Dec. 20 *Lifeguard* **46**
The steamer sailed from Newcastle and disappeared off Flamborough Head.

†1863 Feb. 7 *Orpheus* **190**
The 1,706-ton British steam corvette, built in 1860, foundered while she approached the harbor of Manukau on the W. coast of New Zealand.

Mar. 28 *Sunbeam* **34**
The 398-ton steam side-wheel, built in 1861, foundered outside Eagle Harbor, Mich.

Date **Place** **Deaths**

Apr. 27 *Anglo-Saxon* **237**
The 1,700-ton trans-Atlantic passenger ship, built in 1856, crashed into rocks during heavy fog at Clam Cove, 4½ mi. N. of Cape Race, N.F.L.

Apr. 27 *Milton Willis* **26**
The 83-ton steam screw, built in 1859, exploded at San Pedro, Calif.

Aug. *Planet* **35**
The American steamer foundered in Lake Superior.

†**Aug. 3** *Ruth* **30**
The 702-ton steam side-wheel, built in 1862, caught fire and burned at Columbus, Ky.

Sept. *City of Madison* **156**
The 419-ton steam side-wheel ammunition carrier, built in 1860, exploded at Vicksburg, Miss.

Oct. *Water Witch* **20**
The 369-ton steam screw, built in 1862, foundered on Saginaw Bay, Mich.

1864 **Jan.** *All Serene* **23**
The Australian cargo ship capsized 50 mi. S. of Tonga.

Feb. 22 *Bohemian* **20**
The 2,190-ton liner, built in 1859, struck a rock and sank near Portland, Maine.

June 8 *Berkshire* **35**
The 649-ton steam side-wheel burned at Poughkeepsie, N.Y.

July 21 *B. M. Runyan* **100**
The 443-ton steam side-wheel, built in 1857, snagged at Gaines Landing, Miss.

Nov. 4 *Racehorse* **99**
The 695-ton British gunboat, built in 1860, wrecked on rocks off Chafee Cape at the southern entrance to the Gulf of Pechelli, China.

Nov. 24 *Stanley* **34**
The 552-ton steamship, built in 1858, wrecked in the Tyne on a voyage to Aberdeen.

Dec. 22 *North America* **197**
The 1,651-ton steam screw, built in 1864, foundered at 31-10-00 N. - 78-40-00 W.

Dec. 22 *Bombay* **92**
The 2,782-ton British line-of-battleship, built in 1827, caught fire and burned off Montevideo at the Flores Island.

1865 **Jan. 14** *Lelia* **50**
The 1,100-ton paddle steamer, built in 1864, sprang a leak off Great Orme's Head and was abandoned.

Jan. 27 *Eclipse* **27**
The 223-ton steam stern wheel, built in 1862, exploded at Johnsonville, Tenn.

Mar. 25 *General Lyon* **400**
The 1,076-ton steam screw, built in 1864, caught fire off Cape Hatteras, N.C.

Apr. *City of Dunedin* **40**
The 463-ton schooner-rigged paddle steamer, built in 1863, sailed from Wellington, New Zealand, and disappeared.

Apr. 23 *Fiery Star* **78**
The 1,361-ton full-rigged clipper ship, built in 1851, was severely damaged in a gale near the Hauraki Gulf which forced the captain to abandon ship. Only the handful that remained aboard lived.

†**Apr. 26-27** *Sultana* **1,547**
The 1,720-ton steam side-wheel, built in 1863, was hopelessly overloaded and exploded, then burned 8 mi. from Memphis, Tenn.

May 16 *Athens* **29**
The 739-ton mail steamship, built in 1856, foundered near Moville Point.

Date **Place** **Deaths**

May 29 *Governor Troop* **40**
The 154-ton steam side-wheel, built in 1859, burned near Augusta, Ga.

July 30 *Brother Jonathan* **171**
The 1,359-ton steam side-wheel, built in 1851, stranded off Seal Rocks near Crescent City, Calif. The vessel carried an Army payroll of $500,000.

Aug. 9 *Pewabic* **40**
The 738-ton steam screw, built in 1863, collided with the *Metour* near Thunder Bay, Mich.

Aug. 24 *Eagle Speed* **265**
The immigrant vessel foundered near Calcutta.

Oct. 15 *Atlanta* **48**
The 1,054-ton steam screw foundered at 36-03-00 N. - 72-30-00 W.

Oct. 20 *Niagara* **75**
The 797-ton steam side-wheel, built in 1864, collided with the *Post Boy* near Helena, Ark.

Oct. 23 *D. H. Mount* **24**
The 321-ton steam screw, built in 1863, foundered between Cape Hatteras, N.C., and Jacksonville, Fla.

Oct. 25 *Tennessee* **34**
The 1,148-ton steam side-wheel, built in 1854, foundered at sea off Savannah, Ga.

Dec. 26 *Constitution* **40**
The 944-ton steam screw, built in 1863, stranded at Cape Lookout, N.C.

†**1866** **Jan. 11** *London* **220**
The 1,752-ton British auxiliary steamship, built in 1864, encountered very heavy weather in the Bay of Biscay and sank a short time later.

Jan. 28 *Miami* **40**
The 175-ton steam stern wheel, built in 1863, exploded at Napoleon, Ark.

Jan. 30 *Missouri* **65**
The 856-ton steam side-wheel, built in 1864, blew up at Newburg, Ind.

Apr. 3 *Monarch of the Seas* **738**
The immigrant sailing ship left Liverpool and foundered in a gale. A letter was found in a bottle months later which described the disaster.

Apr. 16 *Jeddo* **150**
The 1,059-ton sailing ship, built in 1865, caught fire and burned in the Straits of Sunda.

Apr. 26 *Windsor* **28**
The 223-ton steam side-wheel, used as a ferryboat, disappeared near Detroit, Mich.

May 14 *General Grant* **73**
The 1,103-ton American sailing ship wrecked near Disappointment Island, one of the Auckland group. The survivors lived on the Island for 18 months before being rescued.

July 12 *Cowarra* **60**
The 439-ton Australian steamship, built in 1860, ran aground on Oyster Bank outside Newcastle, N.S.W.

†**Oct. 3** *Evening Star* **261**
The 2,014-ton steam side-wheel, built in 1863, foundered off Tybee Island, Ga,

Nov. 10 *Ceres* **38**
The steamship ran ashore at Carnshore Point, Wexford.

Dec. 6 *Deutschland* **57**
The 2,898-ton liner, built in 1866, ran into a snowstorm after she crossed the North Sea and wrecked on the Kentish Knock sands.

Dec. 27 *Fashion* **43**
The 1,194-ton steam side-wheel, built in 1865, caught fire at Baton Rouge, La.

Date | Place | Deaths

1867 Jan. 17 *John Raine* **59**
The 541-ton steam side-wheel, built in 1858, caught fire at Greenville, Miss.

Feb. 17 *David White* **35**
The 636-ton steam side-wheel, built in 1853, exploded at Columbia, Miss.

May 21 *Wisconsin* **23**
The 352-ton steam screw, built in 1852, caught fire and burned at Grenadine Island, Lake Ontario.

Oct. 9 *Home* **80**
The steamship was damaged by buoy on Gedney Channel, New York Harbor; finally foundered 6 mi. N. of Oglethorpe Light.

†Oct. 29 *Rhone (Wye* & others) **124**
The 2,738-ton British liner, built in 1865, wrecked on the rocks of Salt Island near the Virgin Islands, during the great hurricane of 1867.

Dec. 24 *Raleigh* **24**
The 868-ton steam side paddle, built in 1865, burned off Charleston, S.C.

1868 Mar. 18 *Magnolia* **80**
The 375-ton steam side-wheel, built in 1858, exploded at California, Ohio.

†Apr. 9 *Sea Bird* **68-103**
The 638-ton steam side-wheel, built in 1859, caught fire and burned near Evanston, Ill.

June *Istria* **23**
The bark sank near Diamond Shoals, N.C.

June 20 *Morning Star* **50**
The 1,075-ton steam side-wheel, built in 1862, collided with the bark *Courtland* west of Lorain, Ohio.

June 20 *Courtland* **31**
The steamer collided with the *Morning Star* west of Lorain, Ohio.

Sept. 7 *Hippocampus* **26**
The 152-ton steam screw, built in 1867, stranded at St. Joseph, Mich.

Nov. 25 *Hibernia* **78**
The 2,000-ton Scottish steamer, built in 1865, foundered at 43-20 N., long. 29 W. on a voyage to Glasgow. The victims all died in their lifeboats.

†Dec. 4 *America (& United States)* **72**
The 2 large steamboats collided & burned on the Ohio River.

1869 Jan. 11 *Augusta Dinsmore* **23**
The 850-ton steam screw, built in 1863, stranded at Cape Lookout, N.C.

Feb. 11 *Mittie Stephens* **37**
The 224-ton steam side-wheel, built in 1863, caught fire at Caddo Lake, La.

Feb. 14 *St. Vincent* **20**
The 834-ton sailing ship, built in 1863, wrecked on the Moko Moko Rocks, N. of Cape Turakirate in a gale.

Feb. 20 *Radetzky* **345**
The 1,826-ton Austrian steam frigate, built in 1861, exploded between the islands of Lissa and Lesina in the Adriatic.

Mar. 9 *Blue Jacket* **32**
The 1,790-ton Australian clipper ship, built in 1854, caught fire and was abandoned on a voyage to Liverpool.

Mar. 29 *Italian* **32**
The 1,860-ton steamship, built in 1861, wrecked off Cape Finisterre.

June 11 *Gulf City* **22**
The steamer disappeared off Lookout Shoals, N.C.

Sept. 12 *Carnatic* **27**
The 1,870-ton mail steamship, built in 1862, wrecked at the mouth of the Gulf of Suez.

Oct. 27 *Stonewall* **209**
The 879-ton steam side-wheel, built in 1866, caught fire and burned 40 mi. from Cairo, Ill.

†1870 Jan. 23 *Oneida* **120**
The 1,032-ton American frigate, built in 1861, collided with the British steamship *Bombay* outside Yokohama Harbor.

†Jan. 31 *City of Boston* **191**
The 2,278-ton liner, built in 1864, left New York for Liverpool and disappeared.

Mar. 18 *Normandy* **34**
The 550-ton British paddle steamship, built in 1863, collided with the steamship *Mary* off the Isle of Wight.

May 9 *Slaney* **41**
The 301-ton British gun vessel, built in 1857, sank in a typhoon off Drummond Island Reef, Paracels, China.

June 25 *Harlech Castle* **23**
The Australian ship sailed from Melbourne for Newcastle and disappeared.

Sept. 6 *Captain* **483**
The 4,272-ton twin-screw ironclad, built in 1870, was caught in rain squalls at the Bay of Biscay and capsized.

Oct. 9 *Mariposa* **36**
The 1,089-ton steam screw, built in 1864, foundered off the Florida coast.

Oct. 19 *Cambria* **169**
The 1,997-ton iron steamship, built in 1869, struck on the rocks off Donegal, Ireland.

Oct. 20 *Varuna* **72**
The American steamer, en route from New York to Galveston, sank off the Florida coast.

†Dec. 18 *Gorgone* **122**
The French steam-corvette disappeared in a hurricane near the port of Brest on a voyage to Cherbourg.

1871 Jan. 14 *T. L. McGill* **58**
The vessel caught fire on the Mississippi River.

Jan. 27 *Kensington* **150**
The vessel collided off Cape Hatteras, N.C.

July 30 *Westfield* **104**
The steam-screw ferryboat exploded in New York harbor.

Aug. 27 *Ocean Wave* **75**
The 272-ton steam side-wheel, built in 1854, exploded at Point Clear, Ala.

Oct. 15 *R. G. Coburn* **31**
The American steamer foundered on Saginaw Bay.

Dec. 20 *Delaware* **42**
The 3,243-ton British steamship, built in 1865, wrecked during a gale at Mincarlo, Scilly Isles.

1872 Apr. 14 *Rona* **60**
The 1,215-ton iron paddle steamship, built in 1862, collided with the *Ava* 20 mi. from Turnabout.

Aug. 24 *America* **65**
The 4,560-ton paddle steamship, built in 1869, caught fire in the harbor of Yokohama.

Aug. 30 *Metis* **30**
The 1,359-ton steam screw, built in 1865, collided with the schooner *Nettie Cushing* off Watch Hill, R.I.

Nov. 2 *Serica* **29**
The 708-ton China tea clipper, built in 1863, wrecked on the Paracel Islands.

Dec. 22 *Germany* **25**
The 3,244-ton steamship, built in 1868, wrecked at Pointe de Coubre, River Gironde.

†1873 Jan. 22 *Northfleet* **300**
The 951-ton sailing ship, built in 1853, was anchored off Dungeness when the Spanish steamship *Murillo* smashed into her and cut her down to the waterline.

Date		Place	Deaths
	Mar. 1	*Chacabuco*	**24**

The 999-ton iron sailing ship, built in 1869, collided with the steamship *Torch* 15 mi. from Orme's Head, North Wales.

Mar. 1 *Boyne* **20**
The British bark wrecked off Mohilo Bay, Cornwall.

†Apr. 1 *Atlantic* **560**
The 3,607-ton crack liner, built in 1871, wrecked upon the rocks off Meagher Island, near Halifax, N.S.

May 8 *Cadiz* **62**
The 945-ton passenger ship, built in 1858, wrecked on Wizard Rock, off Brest.

Aug. 23 *Geo. Wolfe* **30**
The vessel blew up on the Mississippi River.

Sept. 15 *Ironsides* **27**
The American steamer foundered on Lake Michigan.

Nov. 22 *Ville du Havre* **226**
The 3,950-ton French liner, built in 1866, collided in mid-Atlantic with the iron clipper *Loch Earn* and sank.

Dec. 14 *Ella* **32**
The London and Hamburg steamer sailed from London and foundered in a gale.

1874 Feb. 14 *Queen Elizabeth* **23**
The 2,630-ton British steamship, built in 1872, wrecked on a ridge of shingle in Gibraltar Bay.

Mar. 17 *Manchu* **55**
The 804-ton wood steamship, built in 1866, foundered on a voyage from Nagasaki to Shanghai.

May 23 *British Admiral* **80**
The 1,808-ton White Star liner, built in 1873, was wrecked on the rocks of King's Island, Bass Strait.

July 26 *Pat Roger* **50**
The steam screw ship caught fire and burned on the Ohio River.

Oct. 20 *Maju* **24**
The British iron ship foundered in a gale off the Hebrides.

Oct. 22 *Brooklyn* **20**
The 466-ton steam side-wheel, built in 1866, exploded on the Detroit River, Mich.

†Nov. 17 *Cospatrick* **468**
The 1,200-ton immigrant ship, built in 1856, caught fire and burned off Auckland, New Zealand.

Nov. 29 *La Plata* **68**
The 1,218-ton iron screw steamship, built in 1862, foundered after a gale on a voyage from Woolwich to Rio Grande do Sull.

Dec. 16 *Cortes* **25**
The British coal carrier foundered in the Bay of Biscay on a voyage to Aden.

1875 Feb. 24 *Gothenburg* **102**
The 501-ton Australian passenger ship wrecked on the Great Barrier Reef, near Flinders Passage.

Apr. 14 *Stuart Hahnemann* **37**
The 1,997-ton sailing ship, built in 1874, capsized in a squall on a voyage from Bombay to Liverpool.

May 7 *Schiller* **314**
The 3,421-ton German liner, built in 1873, wrecked on the Retarrier Ledges near Scilly Isles.

May 8 *Cadiz* **62**
The British steamer wrecked on Wizard Rock, Brest.

May 31 *Vicksburg* **47**
The 2,484-ton liner, built in 1872, foundered 120 mi. S.E. of Cape Race.

†June 30 *Strathmore* **49**
The 1,472-ton sailing ship, built in 1875, ran aground on the Twelve Apostle Rocks and the survivors were rescued 6 months later.

Sept. 10 *Equinox* **23**
The American steamer foundered on Lake Michigan.

Nov. 4 *Pacific* **237**
The 875-ton paddle steamer, built in 1854, collided with the sailing ship *Orpheus* 40 mi. S. of Cape Flattery.

Nov. 9 *City of Waco* **53**
The vessel burned at Galveston, Texas.

†Dec. 6 *Deutschland* **157**
North German Cloud passenger liner struck Kentish Knock shoals.

Dec. 29 *Dante* **22**
The 1,743-ton steamship, built in 1874, was rammed by a Norwegian bark in St. George's Channel.

1876 Feb. 17 *Strathclyde* **38**
The 1,255-ton steamship, built in 1871, collided with the German steamship *Franconia,* 2½ mi. from Dover.

July *Geltwoed* **27**
The 1,056-ton bark was found wrecked in Ricoli Bay on a voyage to Melbourne.

July 9 *St. Clair* **27**
The 236-ton steam screw, built in 1867, caught on fire and burned at 14-Mile Point, Mich.

Aug. 12 *Great Queensland* **569**
The 1,794-ton Australian wooden sailing ship, built in 1852, exploded at sea near Cape Finisterre. The disaster was the worst in the history of Australian immigration.

Sept. 11 *Dandenong* **40**
The 575-ton Australian steamship, built in 1865, foundered near Jervis Bay.

Dec. 25 *Ambassador* **23**
The 1,951-ton British steamer, built in 1872, collided with the American ship *George Manson.*

†Dec. 29 *Circassian* **28**
British ship torn in half during salvage operations.

1877 Jan. 5 *George Cromwell* **30**
The 802-ton side-wheel, built in 1862, stranded off Cape St. Mary, Newfoundland.

Jan. 20 *George Washington* **25**
The 804-ton steam side-wheel, built in 1862, stranded off French Mistaken Point, Newfoundland.

June 15 *Eten* **120**
The 1,853-ton steamship, built in 1871, wrecked on the rocks off Cape Ventanas.

Sept. 11 *Avalanche* **94**
The 1,210-ton Australian iron sailing ship, built in 1874, was rammed by the sailing ship *Forest* 15 mi. S. by W. of Portland, Vic.

†Nov. 24 *Huron* **100**
The 1,041-ton steam screw crashed off the Oregon Inlet.

Nov. 29 *Atacama* **104**
The 1,822-ton steamship, built in 1870, foundered 22 mi. S. of Caldera, Chile.

1878 Jan. 31 *Maetopolis* **100**
The vessel wrecked near the North Carolina coast.

†Mar. 24 *Eurydice* **398**
The 921-ton British frigate, built in 1843, foundered in icy weather 3 mi. E.N.E. off Bonchurch on the Isle of Wight.

May 31 *Grosser Kurfurst* **284**
The 6,663-ton German turret ironclad, built in 1875, collided with the *Konig Wilhelm* in clear weather near Folkestone.

June 1 *Loch Ard* **50**
The 1,693-ton sailing ship, built in 1873, ran aground at Curdies Inlet, 27 mi. from Cape Otway, Victoria.

July 23 *James Service* **24**
The 455-ton Australian bark, built in 1869, was wrecked S. of Fremantle, Western N.S.W.

†Sept. 3 *Princess Alice* **645**
The 251-ton river steamship, built in 1865, collided with the *Bywell Castle* near Woolwich, Eng.

Date		Place	Deaths
	Nov. 26	*Pomerania*	48
	The 3,382-ton liner, built in 1873, collided with the bark *Moel Eilian* off Dover, Eng.		
	Dec. 10	*Emily B. Sonder*	28
	The vessel sank off Cape Hatteras, N.C.		
	†Dec. 18	*Byzantin*	210
	The 906-ton French steamship, built in 1854, collided with the British steamship *Rinaldo* near Gallipoli.		
1879	Mar. 1	*Vingorla*	68
	The 578-ton British India steamship, built in 1875, sprang a leak and sank 90 mi. N. of Bombay.		
	Mar. 19	*Arrogante*	47
	The 1,000-ton French warship, built in 1864, foundered in heavy waves off the island of Hyeres, near Toulon.		
	May 24	*Ava*	70
	The 2,600-ton British India liner, built in 1873, was rammed by the sailing ship *Brenhilda,* 70 mi. from Sandheads at the mouth of the Hooghy.		
	Nov. 22	*Waubuno*	24
	The American steamer disappeared on the Georgian Bay.		
	†Dec. 2	*Borussia*	174
	The 2,075-ton Dominion liner, built in 1854, sprang a leak and sank in the Atlantic.		
†1880	Jan. 31	*Atlanta*	290
	The 923-ton British sailing frigate, built in 1844, disappeared after she sailed from Bermuda.		
	Feb.	*Vingola*	66
	The steamer sprang a leak and sank 70 mi. N. of Bombay.		
	June 11	*Narraganssett*	27
	The steamer collided with the *Stoningham* off Long Island Sound and sank.		
	June 28	*Seawanhaka*	24
	The steamer caught fire & burned in the East River, N.Y.		
	Sept. 4	*Vera Cruz*	71
	The American steamer foundered in a hurricane in the North Atlantic.		
	†Oct. 15	*Alpena*	101
	The 653-ton steamer foundered in Lake Michigan.		
	†Nov. 24	*Uncle Joseph*	250
	The 823-ton French steamship, built in 1870, collided with the Italian steamship *Ortiga* off La Spezia.		
1881	Feb. 7	*Bohemian*	35
	The 3,052-ton British steamship, built in 1870, was wrecked on a reef of rocks near Mizen Head, Cork, Ireland.		
	Apr. 26	*Doterel*	143
	The 1,124-ton British sloop, built in 1880, exploded from the gases of paint which ignited the ammunition racks while anchored at Ponta Arenas.		
	Apr. 29	*Tararua*	102
	The 828-ton New Zealand steamship, built in 1864, wrecked on the Waipapapa Reef near South Island.		
	May 24	*Victoria*	200
	The overloaded steamer capsized in the Thames River, Canada.		
	Aug. 30	*Teuton*	236
	The 2,313-ton steamship, built in 1869, wrecked 4 mi. off Quoin Point near Cape Agulhas.		
	Oct.	*Balclutha*	22
	The 262-ton Australian steamship, built in 1860, foundered off Gabo Island, N.S.W.		
	Oct. 4	*Koning der Nederlanden*	90
	The 3,063-ton Dutch steamship, built in 1872, broke her propeller at lat. 5°S.-long. 64°E. and sank.		
	Oct. 11	*Corsica*	21
	The 1,581-ton British cargo ship, built in 1863, foundered off Cape Rosa.		
	Oct. 21	*Clan Macduff*	32
	The 2,328-ton steamer, built in 1870, sprang a leak during bad weather 40 mi. S. of Roche Point, Ire.		
	Nov. 5	*Albion*	32
	The British steamer wrecked on the Atlantic coast of Colombia.		
1882	Feb.	*Kosmos*	21
	The British steamer foundered off Killa.		
	Feb. 4	*Bahama*	20
	The British steamer foundered between Puerto Rico and New York.		
	Feb. 28	*Livadia*	23
	The Shields steamer sank off Yarmouth.		
	Apr. 1	*Douro*	23
	The 2,846-ton liner, built in 1865, collided with the Spanish steamship *Yrurac Bat* 50 mi. W. of Cape Finisterre.		
	Apr. 1	*Yrurac Bat*	36
	The 2,197-ton Spanish steamship, built in 1871, collided with the British liner *Douro* 50 mi. W. of Cape Finisterre.		
	May 18	*Manitoulin*	30
	The American steamer caught fire and burned at Georgian Bay.		
	July 4	*Sciota*	57
	The vessel collided on the Ohio River.		
	July 7	*Adder*	65
	The 1,556-ton Dutch monitor-ram, built in 1871, foundered in a gale in the North Sea off Scheveningen.		
	Aug. 23	*Armenian*	23
	The 1,123-ton Liverpool steamship, built in 1871, foundered in the Baltic.		
	†Sept. 14	*Asia*	123
	The 350-ton steamer, built in 1872, wrecked near Lonely Island, Georgian Bay, Lake Huron.		
	Oct. 28	*Gulf of Panama*	22
	The 1,592-ton steamship, built in 1880, foundered off Texel on a voyage to Bremen.		
	Nov. 16	*Winton*	24
	The British cargo ship, built in 1880, sank 30 mi. N.W. of Ushant.		
	Dec. 15	*Langrigg Hall*	24
	The 1,394-ton iron bark, built in 1880, wrecked on South Rock on a voyage to Calcutta from Liverpool.		
†1883	Jan. 19	*Cimbria*	340
	The 3,037-ton Hamburg-American liner, built in 1867, collided in the dark with the *Sultan* off the Island of Borkum.		
	Feb. 1	*Kenmure Castle*	32
	The 1,951-ton iron brig-rigged steamship, built in 1873, foundered in a gale in the Bay of Biscay.		
	Mar.	*Wykeham*	22
	The British steamer sank near Lisbon.		
	Mar. 7	*Navarre*	45
	The 552-ton British steamship, built in 1866, foundered 200 mi. off Spurn Head on a voyage to Leith.		
	Mar. 17	*Dunstaffnage*	23
	The 1,945-ton sailing ship, built in 1881, foundered off Aberdeen.		
	Apr. 24	*British Commerce*	25
	The steamer sank after a collision with the *County of Aberdeen* off Selsey Bill.		
	May 3	*Grappler*	70
	The vessel caught fire at Vancouver Islands, British Columbia.		
	†July 3	*Daphne*	195
	The 460-ton coasting steamship, built in 1883, sank at her initial launch with the relatives of the victims as witnesses.		

Date		Place	Deaths
	July 3	*Ludwig*	75
	The 3,987-ton Belgian liner, built in 1861, sailed from Antwerp for Montreal and disappeared.		
	Nov. 8	*Iris*	35
	The British vessel sank off Cape Villano.		
	Nov. 14	*Manistree*	30
	The 561-ton steam screw, built in 1867, sank on Lake Superior.		
	Dec. 11	*Auk*	22
	The Liverpool steamer sank at South Henden.		
†1884	Jan. 18	*City of Columbus*	97
	The 1,999-ton steam screw, used as a passenger ship, sank off Devils Bridge Reef, Gay Head, Mass.		
	Jan. 25	*Simla*	20
	The ship collided with the *City of Lucknow* in the English Channel off the Isle of Wight.		
	Jan. 27	*Juno*	30
	The British iron ship became stranded in the Mersey during a gale.		
	†Apr. 3	*Daniel Steinmann*	124
	The 1,790-ton steamer, built in 1875, wrecked on the Madrock Shoal just before she entered Halifax Harbor, N.S.		
	Apr. 18	*State of Florida*	123
	The 3,138-ton steamship, built in 1875, collided with the *Poenema* 1,200 mi. from Ireland.		
	May 6	*Senorine*	62
	The French brig foundered off Great Bank, N.F.L.		
	May 11	*Syria*	59
	The 1,010-ton sailing ship, built in 1868, foundered in a gale in the Fiji Islands, near Suva.		
	July 21	*Gijon*	168
	The 1,843-ton Spanish steamship, built in 1872, collided with the British steamer *Laxham* near Cape Villano.		
	Sept. 22	*Wasp*	52
	The 465-ton British gunboat, built in 1881, wrecked off Tory Island near the coast of Ireland.		
	Nov. 27	*Durango*	20
	The British screw steamer was rammed by the Luke Bruce in the English Channel.		
1885	Sept.	*Merchantman*	70
	The British vessel wrecked on Sands Head.		
	Nov. 7	*Algoma*	54
	The 1,773-ton Canadian steamer, built in 1883, foundered on Lake Superior.		
†1886	Jan. 11	*London*	220
	The 1,752-ton British steamship & sailing vessel, built in 1864, sank in a storm 200 mi. S.W. of Lund's End, Eng.		
	Jan. 20	*Kapunda*	298
	The 1,095-ton ship collided with the bark *Ada Melmore* off the Brazilian coast.		
	Feb. 9	*W. R. Carter*	125
	The 563-ton steam side-wheel, built in 1864, exploded near Vicksburg, Miss.		
	Apr. 11	*Taiaroa*	45
	The 438-ton steamship, built in 1875, ran aground and wrecked at the mouth of the Clarence River.		
	May 30	*Ly-EE-Moon*	76
	The 745-ton Australian steamship foundered off Cape Green.		
	July	*Young Dick*	170
	The Queensland labor vessel foundered near Hinchinbrook.		
	Aug. 26	*Ferntower*	50
	The 943-ton steamship, built in 1867, foundered near Saigon.		
	Oct. 15	*Malleny*	20
	The 1,053-ton iron sailing ship, built in 1868, wrecked on the Tuskar Rock, Bristol Channel.		

Date		Place	Deaths
	Dec. 14	*Harvey Mills*	22
	The 2,186-ton wooden ship, built in 1876, foundered in a gale near Cape Flattery, Washington.		
	Dec. 23	*Ville de Victoria*	32
	The 2,548-ton French liner, built in 1883, collided with the British ironclad warship *Sultan* and sank.		
1887	Jan. 20	*Kapunda*	303
	The 1,095-ton sailing ship, built in 1875, collided with the bark *Ada Melmore* S. of Maceio, Brazil.		
	Mar. 17	*Tasmania*	34
	The 4,488-ton liner, built in 1884, wrecked on the Les Moines Rocks off Point Roccapina.		
	Apr. 28	*Benton*	150
	The Chinese steamer foundered after a collision.		
	May 1	*John Knox*	29
	The 2,069-ton steamship, built in 1883, stranded at the South-West Island channel off St. John's, Newfoundland.		
	June 17	*Champlain*	22
	The steamer caught fire on Lake Michigan.		
	July 10	*Mystery*	24
	The sloop capsized off Jamaica Bay, Long Island.		
	Sept. 2	*Falls of Bruar*	24
	The Glasgow steamer sank off Yarmouth.		
	Sept. 10	*Wasp*	73
	The 715-ton British gunboat, built in 1887, disappeared on a voyage from Sheerness to Shanghai.		
	Oct. 19	*Cheviot*	25
	The 1,226-ton Australian iron steamship, built in 1870, wrecked on the rocks at Back Beach, Portsea.		
	Oct. 29	*Vernon*	41
	The steamer foundered on Lake Michigan.		
	Nov. 15	*Wah Yeung*	400
	The British steamship caught fire and burned outside Hong Kong.		
	†Nov. 19	*W. A. Scholten*	134
	The 3,300-ton Dutch liner, built in 1874, collided with collier *Rosa Mary* 4 mi. E. of the Admiralty Pier, Dover.		
1888	Jan. 4	*Alfred D. Snow*	28
	The 1,987-ton American wood sailing ship, built in 1877, wrecked off Waterford, Ireland.		
	Aug. 14	*Geiser*	119
	The 1,818-ton liner, built in 1881, collided with the liner *Thingvalla* 30 mi. S. of Sable Island and capsized.		
	Sept. 13	*La France*	87
	The French steamer collided with the Italian ship *Sud America* near the Canary Islands.		
	Dec. 24	*Kate Adams*	23
	The vessel caught fire on the Mississippi River.		
1889	Feb. 3	*Nereid*	23
	The Newcastle steamer collided with the Scottish ship *Killochan* off Dungeness.		
	†Mar. 16	*Trenton* (& others)	147
	The *Trenton, Vandalia, Nipsic, Adler,* & *Eber* were overwhelmed in a hurricane in the harbor of Apia, Samoan Islands.		
1890	Feb. 17	*Duburg*	400
	The vessel sank in the China Sea.		
	Jan. 13	*Marlborough*	30
	The 1,191-ton full-rigged ship, built in 1876, disappeared on a voyage from New Zealand to London.		
	Jan. 27	*Loch Moidart*	30
	The 2,081-ton iron bark, built in 1881, ran aground at Callandzoog, near Dieppe.		
	†Mar. 1	*Quetta*	146
	The 2,254-ton British screw steamer, built in 1881, wrecked on the rocks near Somerset, Torres Straights.		

Date — Place — Deaths

Mar. 28 *Dunedin* **34**
The 1,320-ton iron ship-rigged, built in 1874, foundered in a storm near Cape Horn.

May 22 *Gulf of Aden* **73**
The 2,366-ton British steamship, built in 1887, foundered on a voyage to Valparaiso.

July 13 *Sea Wing* **97**
The steamer was lost in a storm on Lake Papin, Minn.

Aug. 28 *Portuense* **25**
The 1,470-ton steamship, built in 1875, foundered in a cyclone 250 mi. from Barbados.

†Sept. 19 *Ertogrul* **587**
The 2,344-ton Turkish frigate, built in 1863, foundered in a gale off the S. coast of Japan.

Oct. 29 *Viscava* **61**
The 2,458-ton Spanish steamship, built in 1872, collided with the American schooner *Cornelius Hargreaves* off the New Jersey coast.

Nov. 10 *Serpent* **173**
The 1,770-ton British light cruiser, built in 1888, wrecked on the Punta Buey Reef.

Dec. 1 *Thanemore* **48**
The 3,032-ton liner, built in 1867, caught fire and foundered near Flemish Gap.

Dec. 13 *Talookdar* **22**
The 2,120-ton sailing ship, built in 1885, collided with the German steamship *Libussa* and sank on a voyage to South America.

Dec. 25 *Shanghai* **200**
The 3,088-ton British paddle steamer, built in 1873, caught fire and burned 6 mi. from Mud Fort, River Yangtze.

1891 Mar. 9 *Marana* **22**
The 2,177-ton steamship, built in 1880, foundered in the great snowstorm of 1891 at the Cornish coast in the Falmouth area.

Mar. 10 *Bay of Panama* **24**
The 2,365-ton steel sailing ship, built in 1883, ran aground in a snowstorm at Nare Point near the mouth of the Helford River.

†Mar. 17 *Utopia* **576**
The 2,731-ton liner, built in 1874, collided with the battleship *Anson* in the Bay of Gibralter and sank in a short time.

Mar. 24 *Strathairly* **19**
The 1,919-ton British steamship, built in 1876, wrecked on the coast of Chicamicomico, N.C.

Mar. 31 *Roxburgh Castle* **21**
The 1,844-ton British cargo ship, built in 1880, collided with the sailing ship *British Peer* 140 mi. S.W. of the Scilly Isles.

Apr. 30 *St. Catharis* **90**
The British steamer foundered off the Caroline Islands.

May 30 *Taramung* **23**
The 1,281-ton Australian steamship, built in 1880, disappeared in a gale off Cape Gabo.

Aug. 28 *Gambier* **21**
The 1,030-ton Australian passenger ship sank after a collision in Port Phillip.

Sept. 12 *Taormina* **40**
The 1,594-ton Italian steamship, built in 1873, collided with the Greek steamship *Thessalia* and sank off Cape Sunion, Greece.

Nov. 2 *Enterprise* **70**
The Indian steamer foundered off Port Blair, Andaman Islands, in a cyclone.

Dec. 12 *Enterkin* **30**
The 1,698-ton sailing ship, built in 1889, ran aground in a heavy gale on the Galloper Sands.

1892 Jan. 10 *Namchow* **414**
The 1,712-ton Chinese steamship, built in 1870, broke her propeller and sank off Cupchi Point, China.

May 15 *Earl of Aberdeen* **21**
The 2,205-ton four-masted ship, built in 1886, wrecked on the Hat and Barrels reef off Penbrokeshire.

May 21 *Solimoes* **125**
The 3,700-ton Brazilian iron clad, built in 1875, ran aground and wrecked off Cape Polonio, Uruguay.

Aug. 9 *Ajax* **35**
The 882-ton German steamer, built in 1889, collided with the steamer *Rundeberg*.

Aug. 30 *Western Reserve* **26**
The steamer foundered on Lake Superior.

Oct. 10 *Bokhara* **125**
The 2,944-ton liner, built in 1873, was driven off course in rough weather and wrecked on the Pescadores.

†Oct. 27 *Roumania* **113**
The 3,387-ton steamship, built in 1880, wrecked near Peniche, Portugal, in bad weather.

Oct. 28 *W. H. Gilcher* **21**
The steamer foundered on Lake Huron.

Nov. 25 *Chishima* **75**
The 753-ton Japanese gunboat, built in 1890, collided with the *Ravenna* off Iyo in the Inland Sea of Japan.

Nov. 28 *Greystroke* **24**
The Hartepool steamship wrecked near Cuxhaven.

†1893 Feb. 8 *Trinacria* **34**
The 2,107-ton liner, built in 1871, wrecked on the rocks off Cape Vilano near Spain.

May 13 *Countess Evelyne* **24**
The 1,354-ton steamship, built in 1882, collided with the Irish steamship *City of Hamburg* near the coast of Cornwall.

†June 22 *Victoria* **358**
The 10,470-ton British battleship, built in 1887, collided with the 10,000-ton *Camperdown* and sank in 10 minutes on a voyage from Beyrout to Tripoli.

Sept. 4 *Spirit of the Dawn* **21**
The 716-ton iron bark, built in 1869, wrecked on a reef near Antipodes Island.

Sept. 19 *Roosalka* **178**
The 2,026-ton Russian monitor, built in 1867, foundered in the Gulf of Finland.

Sept. 30 *Evelyn* **20**
The 1,202-ton iron barque, built in 1863, disappeared after she passed Cook Strait in a gale.

Oct. 14 *Dean Richmond* **21**
The steamer foundered on Lake Erie.

Nov. 7 *Albany* **24**
The steamer collided on Lake Huron.

Nov. 18 *Hampshire* **24**
The London steamer sank off St. Ives, Cornwall.

Dec. 5 *Jason* **27**
The British vessel disappeared on a voyage from Calcutta to Boston.

1894 Jan. 28 *Port Yarrock* **25**
The 1,379-ton bark, built in 1886, wrecked at Brandon Bay, Tralee.

Mar. *Colintrave* **31**
The 1,747-ton Scottish ship sailed from Newcastle, N.S.W., for San Francisco and disappeared.

June 25 *Norge* **600**
The American steamer wrecked off the Rockall Reef in the North Atlantic.

July 8 *Vladimir* **100**
The Russian ship collided with the Italian ship *Columbia* off Tarhankut.

Date **Place** **Deaths**

Oct. 28 *Wairarapa* **78**
The 1,786-ton steamship, built in 1882, wrecked on the cliffs of Great Barrier Island.

Oct. 30 *Tormes* **21**
The 1,644-ton Spanish steamship, built in 1877, wrecked off the Crow Rock near Pembroke.

Nov. 14 *Culmore* **22**
The 1,720-ton British sailing ship, built in 1890, foundered near Spurn Head, Yorkshire.

Dec. 22 *Abydos* **19**
The 1,339-ton steamer, built in 1871, foundered off the Isle of Man.

Dec. 29 *Prescott* **22**
The 1,941-ton steamship, built in 1873, sailed from Sunderland to Marseilles and disappeared.

Dec. 30 *Osseo* **26**
The 1,463-ton bark, built in 1889, foundered off Holyhead.

1895 **Jan.** *Florence* **21**
The 809-ton Scottish vessel sailed for Panama and disappeared.

Jan. 21 *Chicora* **24**
The steamer foundered on Lake Michigan.

†Jan. 30 *Elbe* **335**
The 4,510-ton German liner was rammed by the British vessel *Crathie* off Lowestoft & foundered soon afterwards.

Feb. *Menai* **22**
The British ship sailed from Newcastle N.S.W. for Tocopilla, Chile, and disappeared.

Feb. *Cumbrae* **23**
The 1,360-ton Australian ship sailed from Newcastle, N.S.W., for Valparaiso and disappeared.

†Mar. 11 *Reina Regente* **402**
The 5,000-ton Spanish cruiser, built in 1887, foundered S.W. of Cape Carminal between Cape Tarifa and Cape Trafalgar.

Apr. 11 *Dundrennan* **25**
The 1,950-ton sailing ship, built in 1880, foundered off Struis Point.

May 20 *Dom Pedro* **161**
The 3,000-ton French ship, built in 1879, wrecked on the Fraguina Reef near Villagarcia.

May 22 *Gravina* **168**
The 618-ton Spanish passenger steamship, built in 1878, foundered in a cyclone off the Philippines.

May 27 *Colima* **173**
The 2,906-ton steamer, built in 1873, exploded 50 mi. S. of the Mexican port of Manzanillo.

July *Lady Lawrence* **25**
The 1,384-ton British ship sailed from Newcastle, N.S.W., for Valparaiso and disappeared.

July 21 *Maria P.* **148**
The 722-ton Italian steamship, built in 1886, collided with the Italian steamship *Ortiga* at the entrance to the Gulf of Spezia, off Isda del Tino.

Aug. 7 *Catterthun* **65**
The 2,179-ton Australian liner, built in 1881, wrecked on the rocks of Sugarloaf Point near Sydney.

Sept. 19 *Sanchez Barcaistegui* **28**
The 935-ton Spanish sloop-of-war, built in 1876, collided with the *Mortera* off Cape Mora.

Nov. 21 *Principia* **28**
The 2,749-ton British cargo ship, built in 1881, caught fire and wrecked near the Faroe Islands.

1896 **Feb. 13** *Pearl* **40**
The Australian wooden steamboat collided with the yacht *Lucinda* and sank on the Brisbane River. This disaster was Australia's worst river accident.

Date **Place** **Deaths**

Mar. 7 *Matadi* **25**
The 2,683-ton British cargo ship, built in 1889, exploded at Boma, West Africa.

Apr. 15 *Elbe* **334**
The 4,510-ton liner, built in 1881, collided with the steamship *Crathie* and sank in the North Sea 20 min. later.

Apr. 30 *On Wo* **255**
The 1,354-ton British steamship, built in 1870, collided with the steamship *Newchwang* near Woosung.

June 16 *Drummond Castle* **243**
The 3,706-ton British steamer, built in 1881, wrecked on the Pierres Vertes rocks at the S. entrance to the Fronveur Sound one day from London.

July 23 *Iltis* **68**
The 489-ton German gunboat, built in 1878, ran aground during a typhoon 9 mi. S.E. of Shan-tung promontory.

Sept. *Castlebank* **28**
The 1,542-ton Scottish ship sailed from Newcastle, N.S.W., for Tocapilla, Chile, and disappeared.

Nov. 26 *J. H. Jones* **26**
The steamer sank on Georgian Bay.

Dec. 7 *Salier* **281**
The 3,214-ton German steamship, built in 1875, ran aground on the Corona Reefs, Arosa Bay.

1897 **Feb. 3** *City of Agra* **41**
The 3,274-ton British steamship, built in 1879, was wrecked in a gale at Aron Bay, 6 mi. E. of Cape Villano.

Feb. 9 *Cyranus* **20**
The 1,653-ton Glasgow ship, built in 1880, wrecked on the rocks off Ile de Sein, Ushant.

Mar. 3 *Siracusa* **24**
The 1,726-ton German steamship, built in 1879, wrecked near Neguay, Cornwall.

Mar. 5 *Utrecht* **100**
The steamer sank near Ushant on a voyage from Rotterdam to Java.

Mar. 8 *Ville de St. Nazaire* **34**
The 2,640-ton French liner, built in 1870, sprang a leak 1 day out of New York and foundered in a hurricane off Cape Hatteras.

June 9-10 *Aden* **75**
The 3,925-ton schooner-rigged steamship, built in 1892, wrecked into rocks along the Red Sea.

Sept. 20 *Ika* **75**
The 110-ton Austrian pleasure steamship, built in 1885, collided with the British steamer *Tyria* near Fiume.

Oct. *Glenfinlas* **30**
The 2,148-ton British ship sailed for Manila from Newcastle, N.S.W., and disappeared.

1898 **Feb.** *Midas* **23**
The British sailing vessel disappeared off the coast of Japan.

Feb. 15 *Maine* **264**
The 6,682-ton American battleship, built in 1890, exploded while at anchor off Morro Castle, Havana.

Feb. 16 *Flachat* **78**
The 2,175-ton French liner, built in 1880, wrecked on the rocks of Anaga Point, Teneriffe.

Feb. 20 *Asia* **22**
The 1,398-ton sailing ship, built in 1883, foundered off Cape Cod.

Mar. 14 *Mohegan* **106**
The 6,889-ton liner, built in 1898, wrecked on the Maen Voces Rock in the Varsis Ledge near Falmouth.

Date		Place	Deaths
	Mar. 22	*Helen W. Almy*	**41**
	The 315-ton American wooden bark, built in 1859, capsized near Point Bonita on a voyage to the Klondyke.		
	Mar. 24	*Lydle*	**30**
	The French steamer foundered in the English Channel.		
	May 5	*Maitland*	**21**
	The 880-ton paddle steamship, built in 1870, wrecked on the rocks off Barrenjoey Lighthouse, near Broken Bay, N.S.W.		
	May 24	*Mecca*	**53**
	The 1,460-ton British steamship, built in 1873, sank in a collision on a voyage from Calcutta to Rangoon.		
	†July 4	*Bourgogne*	**571**
	The 7,395-ton French liner, built in 1885, collided with the British ship *Cromartyshire* 60 mi. S. of Sable Island 2 days out of New York.		
	Nov. 18	*Atlanta*	**28**
	The 1,753-ton iron sailing ship, built in 1885, foundered off Newport, Oregon.		
	†Nov. 26	*City of Portland*	**157**
	The 1,517-ton passenger steamer, built in 1890, foundered off Peaked Hill Bars, Provincetown, Mass.		
	Nov. 28	*Clan Drummond*	**37**
	The 2,908-ton steamship, built in 1882, sank in bad weather in the Bay of Biscay.		
	Dec. 16	*Ilios*	**20**
	The 2,020-ton steamship, built in 1882, collided with the steamship *Pierremont* near Soutar, South Shields.		
1899	**Jan. 14**	*Andelana*	**20**
	The 2,395-ton sailing ship, built in 1922, sank during the night while moored at Tacoma.		
	Mar. 5	**Cape Melville, Qld.**	**300**
	Cyclones sank 66 pearling luggers near the Cape.		
	†Mar. 30	*Stella*	**100**
	The 1,059-ton channel steamship, built in 1890, foundered on the Black Rock, 8 mi. from Alderney.		
	Apr. 11	*Hoche*	**24**
	The French fishing boat sank off Mizen Head.		
	Apr. 24	*Loch Sloy*	**31**
	The 1,280-ton Scottish bark, built in 1877, wrecked on Brothers Rock at the mouth of the Gulf of St. Vincent, N.S.W.		
	May 15	*Ohau*	**22**
	The 740-ton New Zealand steamship, built in 1884, foundered in a gale near Cape Campbell.		
	Aug. 14	*Resolute*	**54**
	The 460-ton steamship, built in 1883, collided with the steamship *Scindia* in the Hooghli, Calcutta.		
	Dec. 17	*Pierre Le Grand*	**45**
	The 3,610-ton French steamship, built in 1882, disappeared in the Adriatic.		
	Dec. 24	*Ariosto*	**21**
	The 2,920-ton steamship, built in 1887, foundered off the coast of North Carolina.		
1900	**Feb. 15**	*Pavillac*	**37**
	The Atlantic steamer disappeared on a voyage from New York to Havre.		
	Feb. 25	*Glenelg*	**31**
	The 210-ton Australian steamship, built in 1875, wrecked on the coast of Victoria.		
	Feb. 27	*Planet Mercury*	**40**
	The British steamer wrecked near Yarmouth, N.S.		
	Mar. 9	*Cuvier*	**26**
	The 2,299-ton British steamship, built in 1883, collided with the East Goodwin lightship.		
	May 8	*Sierra Nevada*	**22**
	The 1,523-ton British sailing ship, built in 1877, wrecked near Port Phillip, Australia.		
	May 13	*City of Paducah*	**23**
	The Mississippi River steamboat foundered near Grand Tower.		
	June 30	*Main, Bremen, Saale*	**300**
	German vessel exploded at Hoboken, N.J. (SEE Hoboken)		
	Sept. 10	*Gordon Castle*	**20**
	The 2,045-ton steamship, built in 1871, collided with the Hamburg steamer *Stormarn* in Cardigan Bay.		
	Sept. 18	*Charkieh*	**38**
	The 1,533-ton cargo ship, built in 1865, sank near the Doro Channel in the Aegean Sea.		
	Oct. 3	*Faidherbe*	**24**
	The 1,589-ton French steamship, built in 1882, collided in the fog with the French steamer *Mitidja.*		
	Nov. 10	*Monticello*	**36**
	The British steamer foundered off Nova Scotia.		
	Nov. 14	*City of Vienna*	**20**
	The 1,080-ton Irish cargo ship, built in 1885, collided in the Bristol Channel and sank.		
	Dec.	*Mobile*	**26**
	The British vessel disappeared in the Atlantic.		
	Dec. 16	*Gneisenau*	**38**
	The 2,856-ton German training corvette, built in 1879, wrecked on the rocks off Malagna Harbor, Spain.		
	Dec. 28	*Primrose Hill*	**33**
	The 2,520-ton four-masted bark, built in 1886, wrecked off the South Stack, Holy-head.		
1901	**Jan. 17**	*Kaisari*	**26**
	The 2,494-ton steamship, built in 1886, wrecked off Reunion Island.		
	Feb. 3	*Lucerne*	**24**
	The 1,944-ton steamship, built in 1878, ran aground at Trinity Bay, N.F.		
	†Feb. 22	*Rio De Janeiro*	**131**
	The 3,548-ton steamer, built in 1878, was struck below the water line in bad weather off Point Fort, near Mile Rock, San Francisco Bay, Calif. The vessel has never been found and was worth $1,000,000.		
	Mar. 19	*Rydalmere*	**25**
	The 1,270-ton bark, built in 1875, foundered in a gale off Cape de Gata on the Spanish Mediterranean coast.		
	Mar. 21	*Federal*	**30**
	The 2,403-ton steamship, built in 1890, disappeared off the Australian coast near Gabo Island.		
	Mar. 22	*Taher*	**20**
	The British steamer wrecked at Port Louis, Mauritius.		
	Apr. 1	*Aslam*	**180**
	The 2,541-ton Turkish transport, built in 1872, wrecked near Yembo.		
	Aug. 14	*Islander*	**70**
	The 1,495-ton Canadian steamer, built in 1888, struck an iceberg and sank in Steven's Passage, Alaska. Vessel carried $3,000,000 in gold.		
	Aug. 19	*City of Golconda*	**40**
	The Ohio River steamboat capsized on the Ohio.		
	Aug. 25	*Noranmore*	**39**
	The 5,640-ton Belgian steamship, built in 1898, capsized in a gale off Athina, Black Sea.		
	Sept. 16	*Hudson*	**24**
	The steamship foundered on Lake Superior.		
	Sept. 18	*Cobra*	**67**
	The 350-ton British destroyer, built in 1901, foundered near the Outer Dowsing Shoal.		

Date		Place	Deaths
	Dec. 2	*Condor*	**104**
	The British steamer disappeared off Esquimalt, British Columbia.		
	Dec. 24	*Polstjernan*	**22**
	The 1,656-ton Swedish steamship, built in 1881, wrecked in bad weather off Korso, S. of Gronskar.		
1902	**Jan. 2**	*Walla Walla*	**42**
	The 3,070-ton American steamship, built in 1881, collided with the French bark *MAX* 11 mi. N. of Mendocino.		
	Jan. 31	*Chanaral*	**21**
	The Dunkirk sailer sank off Ushant.		
	Mar. 4	*Tiber*	**21**
	The 1,736-ton steamship, built in 1870, foundered 80 mi. E. of Halifax.		
	May 6	*Camorta*	**739**
	The 2,119-ton British steamship, built in 1880, was lost in a typhoon near Rangoon.		
	July 15	*Luga*	**30**
	The steamer wrecked on the Luga, Russian coast.		
	July 21	*Primus*	**112**
	The pleasure steamer collided with the *Hausa* on the Lower Elbe and sank.		
	July 30	*Prins Alexander*	**40**
	The 1,009-ton Dutch steamship, built in 1872, collided with the steamship *Ban Hin Guan* off Malacca.		
	Aug. 17	*Highfields*	**23**
	The British bark collided with the German steamer *Kaiser* off Cardiff and sank.		
	Oct. 31	*Enero*	**22**
	The 2,047-ton Spanish steamship, built in 1898, collided with the steamship *Stregulus* near Dungeness.		
	Nov. 5	*Elingamite*	**30**
	The 1,675-ton Australian steamship wrecked at Three Kings Islands, N.Z.		
	Nov. 21	*Bannockburn*	**20**
	The steamer disappeared on Lake Superior.		
	Dec. 3	*Neptuno*	**29**
	The Spanish steamer sank in the Bay of Biscay.		
	Dec. 8	*Parthenon*	**28**
	The 1,308-ton Greek steamship, built in 1877, disappeared off the Black Sea coast of Turkey.		
1903	**Feb. 3**	*Van Stabel*	**27**
	The 2,349-ton French bark, built in 1901, foundered off Monarch Island, Hebrides.		
	Feb. 26	*Ottercaps*	**30**
	The British steamer foundered in a gale at Feuntenot near Audierne.		
	May 26	*Huddersfield*	**22**
	The steamer sank at Schelde on a voyage from Antwerp to Grimsby.		
	June 2	*Arequipa*	**63**
	The British steamer foundered at Valparaiso.		
	†June 7	*Liban*	**150**
	The 2,308-ton French steamship, built in 1882, collided with the steamship *Insulaire* and sank outside Marseilles.		
	Oct. 26	*Savoyard*	**36**
	The French sailer foundered near Brest.		
	Oct. 29	*Tokai Mary*	**48**
	The 1,121-ton Japanese steamship, built in 1868, collided with the Russian steamship *Progress.*		
	Dec. 8	*Pylaros & Assos*	**50**
	The Greek steamships collided in the port of Ithaca.		
1904	**Mar. 20**	*Lady Cairns*	**22**
	The 1,287-ton sailing ship, built in 1869, collided with the German bark *Mona* 25 mi. E. of the Kish lightship, Kingstown.		
	May 15	*Yoshino*	**329**
	The 4,160-ton Japanese light cruiser, built in 1892, collided with the armored cruiser *Kasuga* in the thick fog southward of the Liao-Tung peninsula.		
	†June 15	*General Slocum*	**1,021**
	The 1,284-ton Hudson River paddle-steamship, built in 1891, caught fire when she approached the Hell Gate channel in New York City.		
	June 20	*Delfin* **(No. 150)**	**20**
	Foundered in Neva River, this Russian 150-ton (submerged) submarine was penetrated through open hatches by wash from passing tug off Baltic port of Kronstadt.		
	†June 28	*Norge*	**651**
	The 3,318-ton Danish steamship, built in 1881, wreched on the rocks at Rockall on a voyage from Copenhagen.		
	July 10	*Nemesis*	**31**
	The 1,393-ton Australian steamship, built in 1880, disappeared on a voyage to Melbourne.		
	Aug. 13	*Inverkip*	**22**
	The Australian ship sank in a collision with the *Loch Carron* off the Fastnet, southern Ireland.		
	Nov. 5	*Brier Holme*	**20**
	The 921-ton iron barque dynamite carrier, built in 1876, blew up after she wrecked on a reef at Elliot Cove, S.W. of Tasmania.		
1905	**Mar. 15**	*Khyber*	**23**
	The 2,026-ton British sailing ship, built in 1880, foundered in a gale and ran aground at Porthgwarra, Cornwall.		
	Apr. 27	*Yuen Wo*	**30**
	The 2,522-ton British steamship caught fire and burned at Tungchow, Yangtze River.		
	June 3	*Afghanistan*	**23**
	The bark was sunk in a collision with the *Caesar* in the Straits of Dover.		
	June 25	*Georg Stage*	**22**
	The 206-ton Danish training ship, built in 1882, collided with the British steamship *Ancona* near Copenhagen.		
	July 21	*Bennington*	**65**
	The 1,710-ton United States gunboat, built in 1890, exploded in the harbor at San Diego, Calif.		
	Aug. 28	*Peconic*	**20**
	The 1,855-ton steam screw, built in 1881, foundered near Fernandina, Fla.		
	Sept.	*Loch Vennachar*	**26**
	The 1,485-ton iron clipper ship foundered off Kangaroo Island, N.S.W.		
	Sept. 2	*Iosco*	**19**
	The 2,051-ton steam screw, built in 1891, sank off Huron Island, Lake Superior.		
	Sept. 10	*Mikasa*	**599**
	The 15,200-ton Japanese battleship, built in 1902, caught fire and exploded at the naval base of Sasebo.		
	Nov. 17	*S-126*	**33**
	The 420-ton German torpedo boat, built in 1905, sank in a collision off the German coast.		
	Nov. 18	*Hilda*	**125**
	The 848-ton British steamship, built in 1882, wrecked on a reef called Pierres des Portes on a voyage to St. Malo.		
1906	**Jan. 21**	*Aquidaban*	**212**
	The 4,950-ton Brazilian ironclad, built in 1885, exploded off Jacarapagua near Rio de Janeiro.		
	Jan. 22	*Valencia*	**129**
	The American steamer lost off Vancouver Island.		
	Mar. 14	*British King*	**27**
	The 3,042-ton steamer, which carried a cargo of oil, foundered when a group of barrels broke through her side.		

Date **Place** **Deaths**

Apr. 19 *Comte de Smet de Naeyer* **34**
The 1,863-ton training ship, built in 1904, foundered off Ushant due to heavy weather.

May 29 *Lismore* **22**
The 1,676-ton sailing ship, built in 1885, wrecked at Santa Maria, Chile.

†**Aug. 4** *Sirio* **442**
The 2,401-ton Italian liner, built in 1883, wrecked on the rocks of the Hormigas Islands off the Spanish coast.

Sept. 18 **Hong Kong Harbor** **1,000**
A typhoon wrecked 12 ships.

Sept. 25 **Hinduian (boat)** **206**
The vessel, loaded with Hindus, capsized in the Indus.

Oct. 14 *Hankow* **100s**
The steamer caught fire and burned in Hong Kong Harbor.

Oct. 18 *St. Lucie* **21**
The 165-ton steam side-paddle, built in 1888, foundered at Elliotts Key, Fla.

Oct. 23 *Hermann* **23**
The German steamer sank after a collision near the East Goodwins.

Nov. 18 *Dix* **45**
The 130-ton steam screw, built in 1904, collided with the steamer *Jeanie* at Al-Ki Point, Wash.

Dec. 1 *D. M. Clemson* **24**
The 5,531-ton steam side-wheel, built in 1903, disappeared after she sailed from Lorain, Ohio.

1907 **Mar. 12** *Jena* **120**
The vessel exploded at Toulon, France. (SEE *Liberté*)

Jan. 13 *Pengwern* **25**
The Liverpool steamer ran aground at Cuxhaven and wrecked.

†**Feb. 12** *Larchmont* **332**
The 1,605-ton wooden paddle steamer collided with schooner *Harry Knowlton* near Block Island, R.I.

†**Feb. 21** *Berlin* **127**
The 1,775-ton steel steamer wrecked at the mouth of the Maas.

Feb. 21 *Imperatrix* **40**
The Austrian liner foundered in Cretan waters.

Feb. 22 *Marion* **24**
The 206-ton steam screw, built in 1905, burned at Wadmalaw Sound, S.C.

Apr. 3 *Arthur Sewall* **28**
The 3,209-ton ship sailed from Philadelphia, Pennsylvania, and disappeared.

June 27 *Violette* **22**
The Gravelines schooner sank off the coast of Ireland.

†**July 20** *Columbia* **100**
The 2,721-ton steam screw iron vessel, built in 1880, collided with the steamer *San Pedro* at Point Arena, Calif.

Oct. 11 *Cyprus* **22**
The 4,900-ton steam side-wheel, built in 1907, foundered near Deer Park, Wisc.

Nov. 26 *Kaptan* **110**
The Mahsousseh steamer foundered in the North Sea.

1908 **Mar. 23** *Matsu-Maru* **300**
The steamer sank after a collision at Hakodate, Japan.

Apr. 25 *Gladiator* **28**
The 5,750-ton British cruiser, built in 1896, collided with the S.S. *St. Paul* and ran aground near Black Rock.

Apr. 27 *Yarmouth* **20**
The 806-ton steamship, built in 1903, foundered on a voyage from Rotterdam to Harwich.

Apr. 30 *Matsushima* **200**
The training cruiser exploded off the Pescadores.

June 24 *Larache* **38**
The Spanish steamer wrecked on the rocks near Muros.

Date **Place** **Deaths**

Aug. 26 *Dunearn* **51**
The 3,142-ton British cargo ship, built in 1895, foundered in a typhoon near Goto Island.

Sept. 1 *Amazon* **20**
The British bark disappeared off the Welsh coast.

Sept. 20 *Star of Bengal* **112**
The 1,877-ton bark, built in 1873, stranded at Coronation Island, Alaska.

Sept. 30 *Stabul* **140**
The Turkish ferry steamer sank after a collision outside the harbor of Smyrna.

Nov. 7 *Taish* **150**
The steamship sank off the island of Etorofy.

Nov. 25 *Sardinia* **120**
The 2,474-ton steamship, built in 1888, caught fire 1 mi. out of Malta and wrecked on the rocks of Ricasoli.

Nov. 30 *D. M. Clemson* **24**
The steamer foundered on Lake Superior.

Dec. 2 *Soo City* **19**
The 670-ton steam screw, built in 1888, foundered off the Gulf of St. Lawrence.

1909 **Jan. 31** *Clan Ranald* **40**
The 3,596-ton turret deck steamship, built in 1900, foundered when she crossed the Gulf of St. Vincent, S.A.

Feb. 12 *Penquin* **74**
The 824-ton New Zealand ship, built in 1864, wrecked on Tom's Rock, 15 mi. from Wellington.

Mar. 5 *Maori* **34**
The 5,317-ton steamship, built in 1893, wrecked on the rocks near Duiker Point on a voyage to New Zealand.

May 9 *Adella Shores* **27**
The steamer disappeared on the Great Lakes of America.

†**July 28** *Waratah* **211**
The 9,339-ton steamship, built in 1908, sailed from Durban and disappeared in a gale near Cape Town.

Aug. 24 *Colombian* **80**
The Argentine steamer collided with the German steamer *Schesien* near the Montevideo harbor.

Oct. 25 *Hestia* **35**
The 3,790-ton steamship, built in 1890, wrecked on the rocks off Grand Mannan Island in the Bay of Fundy.

Nov. 14 *La Seyne* **101**
The 2,379-ton French mail steamship, built in 1870, collided with the British India liner *Onda* in the Rheo Straits on a voyage to Singapore.

Dec. 3 *Ellan Vannin* **35**
The 380-ton steamship, built in 1860, foundered near the mouth of the Mersey on a voyage to Liverpool.

Dec. 9 *Marquette and Bessemer No. 2* **36**
The 2,514-ton steam screw, built in 1905, foundered on Lake Erie.

1910 **Jan. 12** *Czarina* **30**
The 1,045-ton steam screw iron vessel, built in 1883, stranded at Coos Bay, Ore.

Feb. 10 *General Chanzy* **159**
The 2,257-ton liner, built in 1891, wrecked on the rocks off the N.W. coast of the island of Minorca.

Feb. 13 *Lima* **50**
The British liner wrecked off Huamblin Island.

Feb. 18 *F. S. Ciampa* **24**
The Italian steamer wrecked at Dunwotly Bay off the coast of Ireland.

Mar. 16 *Loodiana* **175**
The 3,269-ton British steamship, built in 1884, disappeared on a voyage to Colombo.

May 15 *Skerryvore* **22**
The 3,371-ton British cargo ship, built in 1892, collided with the German bark *J. C. Vinnen* off Hastins.

Date		Place	Deaths
	May 26	*Pluviose*	**27**
	The French submarine collided with a mail steamer near Calais.		
	Aug. 16	*Martos*	**30**
	The 1,427-ton Spanish steamship, built in 1883, collided with the German steamship *Elsa* 32 mi. W. of Tarifa.		
	Sept. 9	*Pere Marquette 18*	**27**
	The 2,090-ton steam screw steel vessel, built in 1902, foundered near Sheboygan, Wisc.		
	Oct. 11	*Arkadia*	**37**
	The 2,206-ton steam screw disappeared after she sailed from New Orleans, La.		
	Oct. 13	*Cranford*	**23**
	The 2,293-ton British steamship, built in 1888, foundered in a hurricane near Hartlepool.		
	Nov. 7	*Abhona*	**91**
	The 4,422-ton British India liner, built in 1910, foundered in stormy weather on way to Rangoon.		
1911	**Feb. 6**	*Glenbank*	**23**
	The 1,481-ton Norwegian sailing ship, built in 1893, foundered in a hurricane near Legendre Island, N.S.W.		
	Mar. 23	*Yongala*	**142**
	The 3,664-ton steamship, built in 1903, disappeared in a hurricane after she sailed from MacKay, Queenland.		
	May 23	*Taboga*	**60**
	The 649-ton passenger steamship, built in 1898, wrecked on a rock off Punta Mala, Panama.		
	Aug. 8	*Emir*	**86**
	The 1,291-ton French passenger steamship, built in 1882, collided with the S.S. *Silverton* after a departure from Gibraltar.		
	Aug. 9	*Fifeshire*	**24**
	The 5,812-ton liner, built in 1898, became stranded S. of Cape Guardafui near Aden.		
	Sept. 4	*Tucapel*	**31**
	The 2,967-ton Chilean steamship, built in 1900, foundered at Camana Beach, N. of Quiloa, near Mollendo.		
	Sept. 11	*Rosedale*	**26**
	The 164-ton Australian steamship foundered near Sydney.		
	†Sept. 25	*Liberté*	**235**
	The 14,865-ton French battleship, built in 1905, blew up in the harbor of Toulon; no reason was given as to the cause.		
	Nov. 23	*Romagna*	**60**
	The 678-ton Italian passenger ship, built in 1910, foundered in a gale off Rovigno.		
	Nov. 23	*Harusame*	**45**
	The 365-ton Japanese destroyer, built in 1902, foundered in a gale off Cape Shima.		
1912	**Jan. 4**	*Tathra*	**24**
	The 483-ton Australian steamship, built in 1907, foundered off Ambryn Island, New Hebrides.		
	Jan. 10	*Russ*	**172**
	The 1,078-ton Russian passenger ship, built in 1906, foundered in a gale outside the Danube.		
	Jan. 18	*Wistow Hall*	**54**
	The 3,314-ton steamer, built in 1890, wrecked on the Tempion Rock, North Haven.		
	Feb.	*Genoa*	**24**
	The 1,942-ton steamship, built in 1890, disappeared in a heavy gale in the North Sea.		
	Mar. 18	*Foxley*	**30**
	The 4,274-ton steamship, built in 1906, became stranded on St. John Narborough Island at the Straits of Magellan.		
	Mar. 21	*Koombana*	**125**
	The 3,668-ton Australian ship, built in 1908, foundered in a typhoon on a voyage to Broome, Western Aus.		
	†Apr. 14	*Titanic*	**1,517**
	The 45,000-ton British White Star liner struck an iceberg in the North Atlantic on her maiden voyage from Southampton to New York City.		
	June 8	*Vendemiaire*	**24**
	French 550-ton (submerged) sub cut in half by French battleship *St. Louis* during maneuvers off Cape de la Hague between Aurigny Island and Cape Hague.		
	Sept. 28	*Kichemaru*	**1,000**
	The Japanese steamer foundered off the coast of Japan.		
	†Oct. 27	*Princess Sophia*	**346**
	The Canadian steamer foundered in a violent snowstorm after she departed Skagwag for Vancouver.		
	Dec. 20	*Florence*	**22**
	The 2,492-ton British steamship, built in 1889, foundered in Marine's Cove, St. Mary's Bay, near Cape Race.		
1913	**Jan. 1**	*El Dorado*	**39**
	The 3,531-ton steam screw, built in 1884, sailed from Baltimore, Md., and disappeared.		
	Jan. 3	*Rosecrans*	**36**
	The 2,976-ton steam screw iron vessel, built in 1883, stranded at the Columbia River Bar, Ore.		
	Jan. 27	*Pangani*	**30**
	The 3,054-ton German bark, built in 1903, collided with the French steamship *Phryne* off Cap la Hague and sank in minutes.		
	†Mar. 1	*Calvados*	**200**
	The 353-ton British steamer sank in the Sea of Marmora.		
	Mar. 7	*Alum Chine*	**40**
	The 1,767-ton steamship, built in 1905, exploded at Baltimore, Md.		
	†Aug. 17	*State of California*	**40**
	The 2,266-ton steam screw iron vessel, built in 1879, foundered at Gambler Bay, Alaska.		
	†Oct. 9	*Volturno*	**136**
	The 3,600-ton steamship, built in 1906, caught fire in mid-Atlantic and sank.		
	Nov. 9	*Charles S. Price*	**28**
	The 6,322-ton steam screw, built in 1910, foundered on Lower Lake Huron.		
	Nov. 9	*Isaac M. Scott*	**28**
	The 6,372-ton steam side-wheel steel vessel, built in 1909, disappeared on Lake Huron.		
	Nov. 9	*Henry B. Smith*	**26**
	The 6,631-ton steam screw, built in 1906, was lost in a storm.		
	Nov. 9	*Argus*	**24**
	The 4,707-ton steam side-wheel, built in 1913, foundered on Lake Huron.		
	Nov. 9	*Hydrus*	**24**
	The 4,714-ton steam screw steel vessel, built in 1903, disappeared near Lexington, Mich.		
	Nov. 9	*John A. McGean*	**23**
	The 5,100-ton steam screw vessel, built in 1908, foundered on Lake Huron.		
	Nov. 9	*James Carruthers*	**22**
	The 7,862-ton Canadian steamship, built in 1913, sank during a storm on Lake Huron.		
	Nov. 15	*Bridgeport*	**26**
	The ship sank in the St. Lawrence; cause unknown.		
1914	**Jan. 14**	*Oklahoma*	**25**
	The 5,853-ton tanker, built in 1908, foundered and broke in two 50 mi. S. of Sandy Hook, N.J.		
	†Mar. 5	*Principe de Asturias*	**445**
	The 8,371-ton Spanish liner, built in 1914, wrecked on the rocks 3 mi. E. of Ponta Boi and sank 20 fathoms.		

Date		Place	Deaths
	Mar. 31	*Southern Cross*	**173**
	The 537-ton Newfoundland sealer, built in 1886, foundered in a blizzard near Cape Race.		
	Apr. 27	*Benjamin Noble*	**20**
	The steamer disappeared on Lake Superior.		
	†May 15	*Joseph F. Luckenbach*	**29**
	The vessel wrecked off coast of South Carolina.		
	†May 29	*Empress of Ireland*	**1,027**
	The 14,500-ton steamship, built in 1906, collided with the Norwegian steamer *Storstad* on the St. Lawrence River.		
	Sept. 18	*Fisgard II*	**21**
	The 6,010-ton British training ship, built in 1870, foundered off Portland Bill.		
	Sept. 18	*Francis H. Leggert*	**65**
	The 1,606-ton steamer, built in 1903, foundered off the Columbia River, Ore.		
	Oct. 30	*Rohilla*	**83**
	The 7,409-ton British hospital ship, built in 1906, wrecked on the rocks S. of Whitby in a gale.		
	Nov. 26	*Bulwark*	**788**
	The 15,000-ton British battleship, built in 1902, exploded at the harbor of Sheerness while being loaded with ammunition. No reason was ever given for the disaster.		
	Nov. 23	*Hanalei*	**23**
	The 666-ton steam screw, built in 1901, stranded at Bolinas Point, Calif.		
	Dec. 3	*Endeavor*	**24**
	The 331-ton Australian steamship, built in 1908, foundered on a voyage to Macquarie Island.		
	Dec. 7	*Vedra*	**34**
	The 4,057-ton tanker, built in 1893, stranded on Walney Island off Barrow and exploded.		
	Dec. 12	*Bogor*	**33**
	The 3,621-ton Dutch steamship, built in 1898, was wrecked on a reef off Leixoes.		
	Dec. 27	*Success*	**60**
	The 385-ton British destroyer, built in 1901, foundered off Fifeness.		
1915	**Jan. 13**	*Viknor*	**295**
	The 5,386-ton auxiliary cruiser, built in 1888, foundered off the Tory Island in bad weather.		
	Feb. 6	*Erne*	**70**
	The 550-ton British destroyer, built in 1903, wrecked on the coast of Aberdeenshire.		
	Mar. 25	*F-4 (SS-23)*	**21**
	American 400-ton (submerged) sub sank 1½ mi. off Honolulu, Hawaii, due to the corrosion of the lead lining of her battery tank which caused heavy water seepage and loss of control.		
	Apr. 3	*Prins Mauritz*	**49**
	The 2,121-ton Dutch steamship, built in 1900, lost in a hurricane 90 mi. N.E. of Cape Hatteras, N.C.		
	May 27	*Princess Irene*	**45**
	The 5,934-ton liner, built in 1914, exploded in Sheerness Harbor.		
	†July 24	*Eastland*	**852**
	The 1,961-ton excursion steamer, built in 1910, capsized in the Chicago River, Chicago, Illinois.		
	Aug. 13	*Marowinjne*	**87**
	The vessel lost off the Gulf of Mexico.		
	Aug. 16	*Sam Houston*	**56**
	The vessel wrecked at Galveston, Tex.		
	Aug. 16	*San Jacinto*	**50**
	The vessel wrecked off Galveston, Tex.		
	Nov. 2	*Santa Clara*	**21**
	The 1,588-ton steam screw, built in 1900, stranded at Coos Bay, Ore.		
	Nov. 3	*Orteantan*	**36**
	The 2,293-ton steam screw ship, built in 1880, sailed from New York City and disappeared.		
	Nov. 17	*Anglia*	**150**
	The 1,862-ton hospital ship, built in 1900, struck a mine near Folkstone Gate, England.		
	Dec. 30	*Natal*	**405**
	The 13,500-ton British armored cruiser, built in 1907, caught fire and exploded in Cromarty harbor.		
1916	**Mar. 16**	*Prins Willem II*	**53**
	The 1,621-ton Dutch steamship, built in 1890, disappeared in European waters on a voyage to Paramaibo.		
	May 8	*S. R. Kirby*	**20**
	The 2,338-ton steam side-wheel iron vessel, built in 1890, foundered near Eagle Harbor, Mich.		
	May 9	*Roanoke*	**45**
	The 2,354-ton steam screw, built in 1882, foundered at Port San Luis, Calif.		
	June 5	*Eneonore*	**30**
	The vessel capsized on the Mississippi River.		
	July 17	*C. W. Morse*	**25**
	The 509-ton steam screw sailed from New York and disappeared.		
	Aug. 2	*Leonardo Da Vinci*	**248**
	The 22,000-ton Italian battleship, built in 1911, caught fire in Taranto Harbor and had a series of explosions.		
	†Aug. 29	*Hsin Yu*	**1,000**
	The Chinese steamer collided with the *Hai-Yung* off the coast of China.		
	Oct. 20	*Imperatriza Maria*	**200**
	The 22,500-ton Russian battleship, built in 1914, caught fire and her ammunition exploded at Nikolaieff Dockyard in the Baltic Sea.		
	Oct. 20	*James B. Colgate*	**24**
	The 1,713-ton steam screw vessel, built in 1892, foundered on Lake Erie.		
	Oct. 20	*Merida*	**23**
	The 3,329-ton steam screw steel vessel, built in 1893, lost between Southeast Shoal and Long Point, Lake Erie.		
	Nov. 3	*Connemara*	**82**
	The 833-ton British steamer, built in 1897, collided into the S.S. *Retriever* near Carlingford Bar in heavy weather.		
	Dec. 8	*Bob*	**40**
	The 589-ton barge, built in 1916, foundered off the Gulf of Mexico.		
	Dec. 26	*Maryland*	**34**
	The 2,419-ton steam screw, built in 1890, foundered at 39-00-00 N. - 67-00-00 W.		
1917	**Jan. 14**	*Tsukuba*	**200**
	The 13,750-ton Japanese battleship, built in 1905, caught fire and exploded in Yokosuka Harbor.		
	Jan. 29	*K-13*	**34**
	The British sub flooded when engaged in initial tests at Gareloch. (SEE *Squalus)*		
	Feb. 21	*Mendi*	**627**
	The 4,230-ton British steamship, built in 1905, collided with the liner *Darro* off St. Catherine's Point and sank in 20 minutes.		
	†July 9	*Vanguard*	**804**
	The 19,250-ton British battleship, built in 1909, had an internal explosion due to the ignition of ammunition at Scapa Flow.		
	Dec. 6	*Tuscarora*	**30**
	The 2,386-ton steam screw, built in 1890, sailed from Montreal, Can., and disappeared.		
	Dec. 17	*F-1*	**19**
	The submarine sank at San Diego, Calif.		

Date		Place	Deaths
	Dec. 30	*Mont Blanc*	1,158

The 3,121-ton steamship, built in 1899, collided with the Norwegian steamship *Imo* off Halifax, Nova Scotia. The *Mont Blanc* carried a cargo of 5,000 tons of high explosive which destroyed 3,000 dwellings, injured 10,000 people, and caused $30,000,000 damage. (SEE Halifax)

1918 **Jan. 9** *Racoon* **91**
The 920-ton British destroyer, built in 1910, foundered in a snowstorm off the N. coast of Ireland.

Feb. 8 *Boxer* **70**
The 280-ton British destroyer, built in 1894, sank in a collision in the English Channel.

Feb. 24 *Florizel* **92**
The 3,081-ton British cargo ship, built in 1909, wrecked 7 mi. N. of Cape Race, N.F.L.

Feb. 26 *Cherokee* **23**
The tugboat sank in a storm off Delaware Capes.

Mar. 22 *Gaillardia* **90**
The 1,290-ton British Navy sloop, built in 1917, blew up while laying mines across the North Sea.

Mar. 23 *Arno* **79**
The 550-ton destroyer, built in 1914, foundered in a collision off the Dardanelles.

Apr. 4 *Bittern* **60**
The 360-ton British destroyer, built in 1897, collided with the S.S. *Kenilworth* near Portland Bill.

May 1 *City of Athens* **66**
The 3,648-ton steam screw collided with the French cruiser *La Glorie* off Atlantic City, N.J.

May 16 *Taher* **20**
The 2,004-ton Canadian steamship, built in 1908, foundered off Port Louis, Mauritias.

†July 5 *Columbia* **87**
The 222-ton steam side-wheel, built in 1897, foundered at Pekin, Ill.

†July 12 *Kawachi* **500**
The 24,420-ton Japanese battleship, built in 1910, blew up by an internal explosion at Tokoyama Bay.

Sept. 17 *San Gabriel* **20**
The 561-ton steam screw steel vessel, built in 1903, foundered near Cape Lucas, Mexico.

Oct. 5 *Lake City* **30**
The 2,485-ton steam screw, built in 1917, collided with the steam screw *James McGee* off Key West, Fla.

Oct. 6 *Ontranto* **425**
The 12,124-ton steamship collided with the transport *Kashimir* in the Irish Sea.

Oct. 25 *Princess Sophia* **398**
The 2,320-ton Canadian steamship, built in 1912, struck the Vanderbilt Reef, Lynn Canal near Alaska and sank in a violent gale after being wedged in a snowstorm 40 hours.

Nov. 24 *Cerisoler* **38**
The American mine sweeper disappeared on Lake Superior.

†1919 **Jan. 1** *Iolaire* **300**
The 362-ton British steam yacht, built in 1902, smashed on rocks near Stornoway, Scotland.

†Jan. 17 *Chaouia* **460**
The 4,334-ton French steamer wrecked off the Strait of Messina.

Sept. 9 *Valbanera* **488**
The Spanish passenger ship lost in hurricane off the Dry Tortugas near Florida. (SEE Florida Straits)

Sept. 9 *Corydon* **27**
The 2,351-ton steam screw, built in 1918, foundered off the Florida coast.

Sept. 19 *Monisla* **28**
The 1,697-ton steam screw, built in 1916, sailed from Mobile, Ala., and disappeared.

Oct. 28 *Muskegon* **29**
The 1,148-ton steam side-wheel iron vessel, built in 1881, smashed into a pier at Muskegon, Mich.

Nov. 9 *Polar Land* **51**
The 4,130-ton vessel vanished off Nova Scotia.

Nov. 12 *John Owen* **22**
The 2,128-ton steam screw, built in 1889, sank on Lake Superior near Caribou Island, Mich.

Nov. 19 *T. W. Allan* **26**
The 113-ton schooner, built in 1870, sailed from New Bedford, Mass., and disappeared.

Dec. 18 *Manxman* **40**
The 4,827-ton Canadian cargo ship, built in 1888, foundered after she left Nova Scotia.

Dec. 19 *J. A. Chanslor* **38**
The 4,938-ton steam screw steel vessel, built in 1910, stranded at Cape Blanco, Ore.

Dec. 29 *Anton Von Driel* **26**
Belgian ship sank off Newfoundland.

1920 **Jan. 9** *Treveal* **36**
The 5,200-ton steamship, built in 1918, wrecked on the Kimmeridge Ledge off Weymouth.

Jan. 11 *Afrique* **553**
The 5,404-ton French liner, built in 1907, wrecked on the Roche-Bonne Reefs, 50 mi. from LaRochelle. Worst French maritime disaster since the loss of *LaBourgogne* in 1898.

Jan. 26 *Mielero* **22**
The 5,596-ton steam screw steel vessel, built in 1917, foundered at 31-45-00 N. - 78-40-00 W.

Mar. 15 *Lux* **121**
The 2,621-ton French passenger ship, built in 1893, foundered off the Balearic Islands.

Apr. 18 *William O'Brian* **40**
The 5,211-ton steam screw sailed from New York City and disappeared.

Aug. 20 *Superior City* **29**
The 4,795-ton steam side-wheel steel vessel collided with the steamer *Willia L. King* near Whitefish Point, Lake Superior, and sank to a depth of 40′.

1921 **Jan. 2** *Santa Isabel* **278**
The 2,488-ton Spanish steamship, built in 1916, wrecked off the island of Salvora in the Bay of Arosa.

Jan. 20 *K-5* **57**
British 1,092-ton (submerged) sub disappeared in the Bay of Biscay, 120 mi. S.W. of the Scilly Islands while on a routine practice with 4 other "K" class subs.

Jan. 20 *Hewitt* **42**
The 5,398-ton steam screw, built in 1914, sailed from Sabine, Texas, and disappeared.

Mar. 3 *Hong Moh* **842**
The 3,954-ton British steamship, built in 1881, foundered in a storm on White Rocks, Lamock Island, off Swatlow.

Mar. 5 *Madimba* **43**
The 2,013-ton Belgian ship, built in 1919, collided with the Belgian steamer *Italier* on a voyage to Matiadi.

†Mar. 18 *Hong Koh* **1,000**
The overcroweded Chinese steamer struck a rocky reef near Swatlow Harbor; panic & riot capsized the vessel.

June 13 *Canostota* **49**
The 4,904-ton American steamship sailed from Sydney for Wellington, Australia, and disappeared.

June 26 *Fitzroy* **31**
The 623-ton Australian steamship, built in 1912, foundered in a gale near Cape Hawke, N.S.W.

Date	Place	Deaths
Aug. 6	*Alaska*	42
	The 3,709-ton steam side-wheel, built in 1899, struck Blunts Reef off the California coast.	
Oct. 20	*Santa Rita*	35
	The 5,237-ton steam screw steel vessel, built in 1902, sailed from New Orleans, La., and disappeared.	
1922 Mar. 23	*H-42*	26
	British 500-ton (submerged) sub sank off Europa Point, Gibraltar, after being rammed by British destroyer.	
May 20	*Egypt*	87
	The 7,941-ton liner, built in 1897, collided with the French steamship *Seine* near Ushant.	
Aug. 26	*Niitaka*	300
	The Japanese cruiser foundered in a storm off Kamchatka, U.S.S.R.	
Aug. 28	*Itata*	190
	The 1,971-ton Chilean steamship, built in 1873, wrecked in heavy weather at Coquimbo.	
1923 Feb. 14	*Lukkos*	25
	The 1,744-ton Dutch ship, built in 1921, sailed from Antwerp for Tangier and disappeared.	
Mar. 28	*Douglas Mawson*	20
	The 167-ton Australian steamship foundered in a cyclone in the Gulf of Carpentaria, Qld.	
Apr. 24	*Mossamedes*	237
	The 4,615-ton liner, built in 1895, ran aground on the coast of Angola.	
May 6	*Okara*	81
	The 5,291-ton British India cargo steamship, built in 1895, foundered at 19°N., long - 91°E.	
June 26	*Sumatra*	44
	The 584-ton steamship, built in 1889, foundered in a gale off Port Macquarie.	
Aug. 20	*Klupfel*	42
	The 3,959-ton German ship, built in 1922, foundered in a storm between Terschelling and Borkum which caused the crew and captain to take to lifeboats. All the men drowned.	
Aug. 21	*Ro-31* **(ex.-***No. 26)*	88
	Japanese 1,000-ton (submerged) sub flooded after premature opening of hatch and sank off Osaka, Japan; 5 survivors.	
†1924 Jan. 10	*L-24*	48
	British submarine sank off Portland Bill.	
Mar. 11	*Santiago*	25
	The 3,325-ton American steamship, built in 1906, foundered 60 mi. S.E. of Cape Hatteras.	
Mar. 19	*No. 43*	46
	Japanese submarine sank in a collision off Saesebo, Japan.	
June 6	*Yahiko Maru*	32
	The 2,653-ton Japanese steamship, built in 1888, foundered 10 mi. S.E. of Hainan Head.	
June 12	*Mississippi*	48
	Vessel exploded off San Pedro, Calif.	
Sept. 21	*Clifton*	27
	The 1,713-ton steam side-wheel, built in 1892, foundered at Lake Huron, Michigan.	
1925 Feb. 26	*Christina-Reuda*	21
	The steamer became stranded off La Rochelle, France, and wrecked.	
Apr. 19	*Raifuku Maru*	48
	The 5,867-ton Japanese steamship, built in 1918, foundered at lat. 41° 43′N. - long. 61° 39°W.	
May 8	*Norman*	22
	The vessel capsized on the Mississippi River.	
Aug. 18	*Mackinac*	47
	The vessel exploded at Narragansett Bay, R.I.	
Aug. 22	**Indian (ferry)**	100
	The boat capsized at Meghna, India.	
Aug. 26	*Sebastiano Veniero*	54
	Italian 925-ton (submerged) sub collided with the S.S. *Capena* underwater in the Mediterranean Sea halfway between Syracuse and Cape Passero, Sicily.	
Sept. 25	*S-51* **(SS-***162)*	33
	American 1,230-ton (submerged) sub collided with the passenger-cargo vessel *City of Rome* off Block Island, R.I.	
Oct. 7	*Margarita*	36
	The 4,443-ton Greek ship, built in 1901, disappeared in a gale on a voyage from East London to Dakar.	
Nov. 12	*M-1* **(ex- HMS** *K.18)*	69
	British 1,950-ton (submerged) sub collided with the Swedish steamer *Vidar* while running submerged in the English Channel off Start Point, England.	
1926 Jan. 26	*Laristan*	28
	The 4,293-ton steamship, built in 1916, foundered at 45° 12′N. - long. 43° 12′W.	
Mar. 17	*Fagernes*	21
	The 3,204-ton Italian steamship, built in 1916, collided in the dark 2 hours out of Swansea.	
Apr. 5	*Dorrigo*	22
	The 715-ton Australian steamship, built in 1913, foundered a few hours after she left Brisbane, 14 mi. S.E. of Double Island Point.	
Apr. 26	*Chichibu*	230
	The 1,540-ton, 3-masted iron steamer, built in 1873, stranded in a storm off Paramushiru, Kurile Island.	
Aug. 27	*Buryvestrick*	160
	The steamship crashed into the Cronstadt River Pier at Leningrad and all drowned.	
Sept. 8	*Haleakala*	35
	The 5,587-ton steam screw, built in 1919, foundered at 25-00-00 N. - 66-00-00 W.	
Oct. 16	**Chinese Troopcarrier**	1,200
	The Chinese troopship exploded on the Yangtze River.	
Oct. 22	*Valerian*	86
	The 1,250-ton British sloop, built in 1916, foundered in a hurricane off Gibbs Hill, Bermuda.	
Oct. 22	*Eastway*	22
	The 5,832-ton steamship, built in 1915, foundered on a voyage from Norfolk, Virginia, to Pernambuco.	
Dec. 20	*Linseed*	45
	The vessel capsized on the Hudson River, N.Y.	
1927 Jan. 8	*John Tracy*	26
	The 2,469-ton, 253′ steam screw foundered off Highland Light, Truro, Mass.	
Mar. 18	*Chongfu*	100
	The steamer wrecked off Luchow on the Yangtze River.	
May 31	*Negros*	108
	The steamer foundered in a typhoon off the Philippines.	
June 14	*Shahzada*	21
	The 2,246-ton steamship, built in 1904, sprang a leak and sank 50 mi. from the Sandheads on a voyage to Akyab.	
July 28	*Favorite*	26
	The excursion boat capsized in a squall on Lake Michigan.	
Aug. 19	*Leyden*	37
	The tugboat capsized in the Pasig River, Philippines.	
Aug. 24	*Warabi*	102
	The 770-ton Japanese destroyer, built in 1921, collided with the *Zinty* in the Bungo Channel and sank to 60 fathoms in minutes.	
Aug. 24	*Columbia*	23
	The 152-ton schooner, built in 1923, foundered off Sable Island, Nova Scotia.	
Sept. 20	*Gentoku Maru*	278
	The Japanese steamer capsized in Tsingtao Bay.	

Date		Place	Deaths
	†Oct. 25	*Principessa Mafalda*	314
	The 9,210-ton Italian liner, built in 1908, foundered 90 mi. from Abrolhos Island when her boilers burst.		
	Dec. 6	*Kamloops*	21
	The steamer disappeared on Lake Superior.		
	†Dec. 17	*S-4*	40
	The American submarine was rammed & sunk by the destroyer *Paulding* off Provincetown, Mass.		
1928	Feb. 5	*Trentinian*	43
	The post boat, which carried a cargo of gasoline, exploded on the Mekong River, Indo-China.		
	Feb. 20	*Hsin Ta-Ming*	300
	The Chinese steamship collided with the steamer *Atsuta Maru* and sank in the Yangzte River.		
	July 6	*Angamos*	283
	The 5,975-ton Chilean transport, built in 1890, wrecked on the rocks off Punta Morguillas, S. of Lebu.		
	July 18	*Cap Lay*	40
	The steamer wrecked on a rock in the Songtambo River near Indo-China.		
	Aug. 6	*F-14*	27
	Italian 318-ton (submerged) sub collided with the Italian destroyer *Giuseppe Missori* while surfacing 7 mi. W. of Brioni Is. off Pola in the Adriatic Sea.		
	Aug. 15	*Hsin Hsu-Tung*	500
	The Chinese steamer foundered on the Yangtze River.		
	†Oct. 4	*Ondine*	43
	The 787-ton French submarine disappeared off Vigo, Spain.		
	†Nov. 12	*Vestris*	110
	The 10,494-ton steamship, built in 1912, foundered one day out of New York in bad weather.		
	†Dec. 22	*Kobenhavn*	60
	The 3,901-ton Danish motorship, built in 1921, disappeared on a voyage from Buenos Aires to Melbourne; 7 years later the remains of her lifeboat filled with skeletons was found on the S.W. African coast buried in the sand.		
1929	Jan. 2	*Malakoff*	27
	The 4,597-ton French ship, built in 1903, wrecked off Port Mahon, Minorca Is.		
	Jan. 13	*Seiner*	21
	The 346-ton screw steamer, built in 1922, foundered at 41-05-00N. - 67-10-00W.		
	Jan. 16	*Hsin Wah*	401
	The 1,940-ton Chinese steamship, built in 1921, wrecked on the rocks off Wagan Island on a voyage to Hong Kong.		
	Jan. 20	*Teesbridge*	30
	The 3,898-ton steamship, built in 1905, foundered 300 mi. E. of Cape Race.		
	July 21	*Hsin Kong*	60
	The 2,146-ton Chinese ship, built in 1906, sank off Shantung Promontory.		
	Aug. 29	*San Juan*	71
	The 2,152-ton steam screw, built in 1882, collided with the steam screw *S. C. T. Dodd* at Pigeon Point, Calif.		
	Sept. 9	*Andaste*	25
	The 1,430-ton steam screw, built in 1892, foundered at Grand Haven, South Chicago, Ill.		
	Oct. 22	*Milwaukee*	52
	The 2,933-ton American car ferry, built in 1902, foundered between Milwaukee and Grand Haven, Wisc.		
	Dec. 7	*Radyr*	21
	The 2,357-ton steamship, built in 1918, foundered in Bideford Bay.		
	Dec. 21	*Lee Cheong*	200
	The Chinese steamer foundered in a gale off Fukien Point near Hong Kong.		
	Dec. 25	*Varna*	27
	The 1,820-ton Bulgarian steamship, built in 1902, sank in a collision in the Sea of Marmara.		
	Dec. 31	*Warnea*	27
	The steamer sank after a collision with an unnamed vessel in the Sea of Marmora.		
1930	Jan. 12	*St. Genny*	23
	The 425-ton British tug, built in 1918, foundered in a gale 30 mi. N.W. of Ushant.		
	Apr. 19	*Federico Gorolla*	20
	The 2,180-ton Italian steamship, built in 1889, suffered a boiler explosion between Zante and Cephalonia.		
	Apr. 27	*Condor*	100
	The 423-ton British river steamer, built in 1897, capsized near Nagorbari on the river Jamuna, Eastern Bengal.		
	May 23	*Asia*	100
	The steamship caught fire in the Jeddah Harbor.		
	June 4	*Georaga*	64
	The steamer sank off Teneriffe, Colombia, a tree smashed into her hull.		
	June 9	*Lithung*	100
	The steamer wrecked on the rocks in the Yangtze River.		
	June 10	*Pinthis*	50
	The 1,111-ton American tanker, built in 1919, collided with the American steamship *Fairfax* outside Fall River on a voyage to Boston.		
	Aug. 12	*Tongan*	77
	The 1,141-ton Chinese steamship, built in 1891, collided with the Chinese steamship *Lienhsung* off Shantung Promontory.		
	Sept. 16	*South Coast*	19
	The 301-ton steam screw, built in 1887, foundered off Oregon coast.		
	Nov. 23	*Luise Leonhardt*	30
	The 3,464-ton German ship, built in 1921, wrecked at the W. Point of Vogelsand by the Elbe lightship.		
	Dec. 19	*Oberon*	41
	The 3,008-ton Finnish steamship, built in 1925, collided with the Finnish steamship *Arcturus* 7 mi. S. of Laeso Trindel lightship and sank in minutes.		
	Dec. 30	*Torefjell*	24
	The steamer sank off the coast of Norway.		
1931	Feb. 10	*Kikusui Maru*	50
	The steamer sank in a collision with the *Porthos* near the coast of Kobe.		
	Feb. 16	**Chinese (steamer)**	100
	The vessel sank in the Pearl River.		
	Mar. 12	*Tachi*	300
	The steamer exploded and sank in the Yangtze River.		
	Mar. 16	*Viking*	20
	The sealer exploded off Horse Island at White Bay, N.F.L.		
	Mar. 19	*Chang Kiang*	250
	The French steamship sank in the China Sea off Amoy.		
	May 22	*Rabotchi No. 9*	35
	Russian 784-ton (submerged) sub disappeared after test dive in the Gulf of Finland, 100 mi. S.E. of Helsingfors, Baltic Sea.		
	June 14	*St. Philibert*	368
	The 189-ton French passenger steamer, built in 1923, foundered in a squall off the island of Noirmontier.		
	Aug. 8	*Kwong Sang*	38
	The 2,283-ton steamship, built in 1902, ran aground in a typhoon on the island of Foyan, N. of Foochow.		
	Oct. 21	*L-55* **(ex. HMS** *L-55)*	50
	Russian 1,150-ton (submerged) sub emerged in the path of the German steamer *Gratia* and sank in the Gulf of Finland 35 mi. W. of Leningrad, Russia.		

Date | **Place** | **Deaths**

Dec. 10 *Liro* **20**
The 1,333-ton Esthonian ship, built in 1876, foundered in bad weather on a voyage to Tallinn.

Jan. 26 *M-2* **60**
The British submarine lost off Portland Bill, England.

Feb. 5 *Eleanor Nickerson* **21**
The 143-ton oil screw, built in 1927, collided with Belgian steam screw *Jean Jabot*.

Feb. 15 *Taikai Maru* **38**
The 2,792-ton steamship, built in 1897, disappeared on a voyage from Vladivostok to Aomori.

†May 19 *Georges Philippar* **54**
The 17,359-ton liner, built in 1931, caught fire 5 mi. from Cape Guardafui in the Gulf of Aden.

May 27 *Iling* **44**
The steamship capsized in the Yangtze River.

July 8 *Promethee* **66**
French 2,060-ton (submerged) sub flooded from failure of hydraulic MBT vents and sank off Cherbourg, France.

†July 26 *Niobe* **69**
The German naval training vessel sank in the Baltic Sea off the island of Fehmarn; victims were trapped in their cabins.

Aug. 7 *Azana* **22**
The fishing boat capsized in a gale off Cangas de Morrazo.

Sept. 9 *Observation* **37**
The 122-ton steam screw, built in 1888, caught fire after an explosion on the East River, N.Y.

Sept. 29 *Nevada* **38**
The 5,645-ton American ship, built in 1920, ran aground on the eastern point of Amatignak Island, Aleutians.

Nov. 14 *Genchu Maru* **36**
The 3,208-ton Japanese steamer, built in 1918, ran aground in a typhoon on the E. coast of Edzu.

Dec. 6 *Sawarabi* **106**
The 820-ton Japanese destroyer, built in 1921, sank in a gale off Formosa.

Dec. 26 *Hsin Fuh-Tai* **35**
The 2,831-ton Chinese ship, built in 1894, ran aground off Northwest Horne.

1933 **Jan. 16** *Hsin Ningtain* **300**
The steamer foundered in bad weather in Hangchow Bay.

Mar. 6 *Antung* **70**
The 3,509-ton British ship, built in 1926, ran aground in the fog 3½ mi. S. of Mofo Point, Hainan Island.

Mar. 14 *Kinsen Maru* **25**
The Japanese tramp steamship sank 400 mi. E. of Bowen, Qld.

May 6 *Rouslan* **33**
The Russian salvage steamer sank off the South Cape.

July 10 *Toonan* **168**
The 1,482-ton Chinese steamship, built in 1881, collided with the Japanese *Choshun Maru* 13 mi. off the Southeast Promontory, Shantung.

July 26 **Russian (launch)** **70**
The vessel capsized in the Volga River, the captain was sentenced to death for the ship being overloaded.

Oct. 2 **Japanese (excursion boat)** **33**
The vessel capsized off Misumi.

Oct. 24 *Tronoh* **28**
The steamship foundered in a storm off Singapore, China.

Nov. 15 *Saxilby* **27**
The 3,630-ton steamship, built in 1914, disappeared in bad weather 400 mi. off the S. coast of Ireland.

Nov. 17 *Seiten Maru* **30**
The vessel sank off Loochoo Island, China.

1934 **Mar. 12** *Tomoduru* **97**
The 527-ton Japanese torpedo boat, built in 1933, sprang a leak off Sasebo and was towed back but the ship flooded and drowned the occupants.

Apr. 7 *Yuan Shun* **29**
The 1,759-ton Chinese steamship, built in 1903, sank 40 mi. outside Woosung.

†Sept. 8 *Morro Castle* **133**
The 11,520-ton electric screw steamer, built in 1930, caught fire 6 mi. off Asbury Park, N.J.

1935 **Jan. 25** *Mohawk* **45**
The 5,896-ton liner, built in 1926, collided with the Norwegian steamer *Talisman* off Mantoloking, N.J.

Feb. 2 *Gerd* **21**
The 2,323-ton Swedish ship, built in 1907, sank after she collided with the Finnish bark *Lingard* near Vinga.

Feb. 18 *Fulung* **100**
The steamer sank off Wuhuko, China.

Feb. 26 *Blairgowrie* **26**
The 3,259-ton British cargo steamer, built in 1924, disappeared in the Atlantic.

May 12 **Russian (ferryboat)** **28**
The vessel, which carried all schoolchildren, sank in the Psiol river, U.S.S.R.

May 29 *Marechal de Luxembourg* **40**
The schooner foundered off Newfoundland.

June 27 *San Lunon* **140**
The merchant ship capsized at Hoiping, China.

July 2 *Midori Maru* **104**
The steamer collided with the *Senzan Maru* and sank in the Inland Sea, Japan.

July 13 **Chinese (steamer)** **100**
The vessel capsized at Tinghai, Chekiang Province.

July 25 *B-3* **55**
Russian 1,138-ton (submerged) sub emerged and collided with the Russian battleship *Marat* in the Gulf of Finland, Baltic Sea.

Oct. 12 *Vardulia* **37**
The 5,735-ton steamship, built in 1917, disappeared in a gale 700 mi. W. of Malin Head.

Nov. 11 *Inebolu* **26**
The 1,080-ton ship, built in 1892, foundered outside Pelican Point at the entrance of Izmir harbor in bad weather.

Nov. 21 *Sheaf Brook* **21**
The steamer foundered in the mid-Atlantic.

1936 **Jan. 1** *Paringa* **31**
The steamship sank in the Bass Strait.

Jan. 12 *Iowa* **34**
The 5,724-ton steam screw steel vessel, built in 1920, foundered at Peacock Spit, near Cape Disappointment, Wash., in a hurricane.

Feb. 4 *Vargas-Gomez* **21**
The steamship capsized off Posadas, Buenos Aires.

Feb. 5 *Unman Maru* **45**
The freighter sank off Cape Shinomi, Japan.

May 13 *Ming Chiang* **40**
The 329-ton Chinese motorship, built in 1925, wrecked at Shuangyutzu near Wanhsien.

July 13 *Marie* **23**
The merchant ship sank in a typhoon off the Philippines.

Aug. 13 *Oranaise* **36**
The 1,806-ton French ship, built in 1915, capsized 40 mi. E. of Mostaganem.

Sept. 17 *Pourquoi Pas* **33**
The 443-ton steamer, engaged in Polar research, wrecked on the rocks in a strong wind off Western Iceland.

Date		Place	Deaths
	Sept. 19	*Long Island*	**42**

The 390-ton fishing steamer foundered off the Overalls Lightship near Delaware in a 70 m.p.h. wind.

Oct. 20 *Van Der Wijk* **34**
The 2,633-ton Dutch steamship, built in 1921, foundered in bad weather near Tandjong Pakis between Sourabaya and Samarang.

Nov. 8 *Isis* **39**
The 4,454-ton German motorship, built in 1922, sank in the Atlantic.

1937 **Jan. 28** *San Matteo* **40**
The 3,757-ton Italian steamship, built in 1904, wrecked on the Stolp Bank, 17 mi. N. of Stolpmunde in a gale.

Feb. 10 *Otaru Maru* **36**
The 1,464-ton Japanese ship, built in 1905, foundered in a blizzard 40 mi. S. of Yatsunobe, Awomori Prefecture.

Dec. 22 *Hisar* **24**
The 2,398-ton wooden Turkish ship, built in 1919, ran aground at Irva Deresi in the Black Sea.

1938 **Feb. 12** *Admiral Karpfanger* **60**
The Belgian trainingship was found wrecked on the shore at Windbound Bay, Navarin Island, near Cape Horn.

Mar. 8 *Anglo Australian* **38**
The 5,456-ton steamship, built in 1927, disappeared 60 mi. off Fayal.

June 1 **Egyptian (riverboat)** **30**
The vessel capsized at Maghagha, Egypt.

Aug. 5 **Portuguese (motorboat)** **29**
The small craft sank at Quarteira Beach, Portugal.

1939 **Jan. 16** *Cambay Star* **28**
The freighter sank off the Arabian Sea.

Jan. 22 *Bouker No. 65* **65**
The scow capsized in the East River, N.Y.

Feb. 2 *I-63* **75**
The Japanese submarine collided with another submarine and sank in the Bung Channel.

May 23 **Spanish (bark)** **59**
The fishing vessel capsized off Santander, Spain.

†May 23 *Squalus* **26**
The American submarine sank off Portssmith, New Hampshire.

†June 1 *Thetis* **99**
The British submarine sank in the Irish Sea.

†June 15 *Phenix* **71**
The French submarine sank off Indo-China.

July 24 *SC-424* **34**
Russian 587-ton (submerged) sub sank after a collision off Murmansk, Soviet Russia.

Aug. 24 *Itacare* **76**
The steamer sank off Ilheos, Bahia, Brazil.

Sept. 24 *Spray* **22**
The fishing boat capsized off Port Magu, Calif.

Oct. 16 *Hsin Ta Kou Maru* **300**
The Japanese launch capsized in the Yangtze Delta.

Dec. 12 *Indigirka* **750**
The 2,336-ton Russian steamer, built in 1886, wrecked on a reef in the Okhotsk Sea on the N. coast of Hokkaido Island.

Dec. 12 *Duchess* **129**
The 1,375-ton British destroyer, built in 1932, collided with the battleship *Barham* in the North Channel off the W. coast of Scotland.

Dec. 23 *Kizilirmak* **20**
The 2,794-ton Turkish ship foundered in bad weather 6 mi. W. of Sinop in the Black Sea.

Dec. 24 *Pepitaperz* **46**
The trawler sank off Villa Real de Santo Antonio, Portugal.

Date		Place	Deaths
1940	**Jan. 21**	*Orazio*	**106**

The 11,669-ton Italian liner, built in 1927, caught fire one day out of Genoa.

Feb. 25 **Spanish (sailboat)** **30**
The vessel sank off Vigo, Spain.

Mar. 9 *Marie Yette* **21**
The patrol boat collided with the tanker *Spramex* at Bordeaux, France.

Apr. 20 **Chinese (steamer)** **240**
The passenger vessel capsized in an attempt to avoid a collision with another vessel on the Chailing River, 121 mi. from Chunking.

June 28 *Paganini* **220**
The 2,427-ton Italian troopship, built in 1928, caught fire and sank 12 mi. off Durazzo.

June 28 *Fraser* **40**
The 1,375-ton Canadian destroyer, built in 1931, collided with the British cruiser *Calcutta* in the Gironde estuary.

Aug. 3 *Moraleda* **80**
The 785-ton Chilean passenger ferry, built in 1912, wrecked on Lynch Rock, Fairway Island.

Aug. 29 *I-67* **89**
The 1,638-ton Japanese submarine foundered in a heavy storm.

Aug. 31 *Albionic* **25**
The 2,468-ton steamship, built in 1924, sailed from Wabana, N.F.L., and disappeared.

Sept. 19 *Shelbrit I* **21**
The 1,025-ton British coastal tanker, built in 1928, caught fire and blew up in the Moray Firth.

Oct. 14 **Turkish (boat)** **23**
The sailing vessel capsized off Gorele.

Oct. 22 *Margaree* **140**
The 1,375-ton Canadian destroyer, built in 1932, collided with a merchant ship during the night in the North Atlantic.

Nov. 2 *Regulus* **35**
The 837-ton Philippine motorship, built in 1938, foundered in a typhoon off Cagayancillo Island.

Nov. 12 *William B. Davock* **22**
The 4,200-ton American steamship, built in 1907, foundered in a storm off Pentwater, Lake Mich.

Nov. 25 *Patria* **280**
The 11,885-ton French liner, built in 1914, exploded at Haifa.

Dec. 30 *City of Bedford* **48**
The 6,402-ton British steamship, built in 1924, collided with the *Bodnant* and sank at 60°03′N., 23°01′E.

1941 **Jan. 3** *Soemba* **34**
The 6,718-ton Dutch steamship, built in 1924, sank 300 mi. S.E. of Cape Race.

Feb. 15 **Belgian (raft)** **30**
A raft with 35 children capsized off Hasselt.

Mar. 24 *Cities Service Denver* **20**
The 9,316-ton steam screw, built in 1921, burned 130 mi. E. of Charleston, S.C.

Apr. 20 *Blenheim* **138**
The 1,807-ton Norwegian steamer, built in 1923, caught fire and exploded in the Porsangerfjord.

†June 16 *O-9* **33**
The 480-ton American submarine sank in a test dive off the coast of New Hampshire.

Oct. 2 *L-61* **70**
Japanese 2,100-ton (submerged) sub sank after collision with gunboat off Iki Island, Japan.

Dec. 7 *Sauternes* **25**
The 1,049-ton British steamship, built in 1922, sank in a gale off Svino, Faroe Islands.

Date		Place	Deaths
	Dec. 7	*Windflower*	**23**
	The 925-ton Canadian corvette, built in 1940, was sunk in a collision in the W. Atlantic.		
1942	**Jan. 1**	*Waziristan*	**47**
	The 5,135-ton British steamship, built in 1924, disappeared 300 mi. N.W. of Jan Mayen Island.		
	Jan. 8	*Lamoriciere*	**277**
	The 4,713-ton French liner, built in 1921, foundered in a storm off Minorca on a voyage to Algiers.		
	Jan. 15	*Wigry*	**25**
	The 1,859-ton Polish steamship, built in 1912, wrecked on the S.W. coast of Iceland.		
	Feb. 3	*Klondyke*	**26**
	The 1,563-ton barge, built in 1921, stranded at the junction of Elk and Susquehanna rivers, Turkey Point, Md.		
	Feb. 7	*S-26*	**32**
	The American submarine collided and sank off Panama.		
	Feb. 8	**Yangtze River (steamer)**	**200**
	The vessel capsized off Ichang, China.		
	Feb. 12	*White Crest*	**47**
	The 4,365-ton British steamship, built in 1928, was lost in a gale 900 mi. W. of Inishtrahull.		
	†Feb. 18	*Truxton* (& *Pollux*)	**189**
	The 1,193-ton American destroyer, built in 1920, wrecked in a gale off St. Lawrence, N.F.		
	Apr. 10	**Greek (boat)**	**209**
	The vessel, filled with women and children, sank in the Aegean Sea.		
	Apr. 11	*Fanefjeld*	**24**
	The 1,354-ton Norwegian ship, built in 1920, foundered off Isafjord.		
	May 11	**French (ferryboat)**	**30**
	The vessel exploded near Bordeaux, France.		
	July 18	*Atilay*	**38**
	The Turkish submarine sank off the Dardanelles.		
	Sept. 22	**American (motorboat)**	**25**
	The vessel sank on Lake Huron.		
	Oct. 2	*Curacao*	**338**
	The British cruiser was rammed by the *Queen Mary* off the English coast and sank.		
	Oct. 21	*Laos*	**58**
	The steamer sank in a typhoon off Indo-China.		
	Nov. 12	*Tensan Maru* & *Kobe Maru*	**46**
	The two steamers collided and sank in the East China Sea.		
	Dec. 31	*Maiden Creek*	**20**
	The 5,731-ton American steamship, built in 1919, foundered in the Atlantic on a voyage to New York.		
1943	**Jan. 1**	*Arthur Middleton*	**66**
	The 7,176-ton steamship, built in 1942, exploded outside Oran.		
	Jan. 11	*Ihsan*	**20**
	Motorboat sank in a squall off Istanbul, Turkey.		
	Jan. 24	*Ville de Tamatave*	**88**
	The 6,276-ton French liner, built in 1931, foundered in a gale.		
	Apr. 14	*Ulven*	**33**
	Swedish 850-ton (submerged) sub sank after mine collision off Marstrand, Sweden.		
	May 3	*Oneida*	**31**
	The 2,664-ton American ship, built in 1919, foundered 300 mi. E. of Sydney, N.S.W.		
	June 18	*Moncyr*	**56**
	The packet boat exploded and burned off Carralinho, Brazil.		
	Oct. 20	**U.S. Navy**	**88**
	Two blacked-out tankers collided in the night off Palm Beach, Fla.		
	Dec. 17	**U.S. Army**	**25**
	Small vessel, on maneuvers, capsized on Lake Pontchartrain, La.		
	Dec. 22	*Suffolk*	**37**
	The collier disappeared off Montauk Pt., N.Y.		
1944	**Jan. 3**	*Turner*	**138**
	The U.S. destroyer caught fire & exploded off Ambrose Lightship, N.Y.		
	Jan. 7	*St. Augustine*	**30**
	The Navy patrol vessel collided E. of Cape May, N.J., with a U.S. freighter.		
	Feb. 26	*William H. Welch*	**62**
	The 1,344-ton American steamship, built in 1943, ran aground at Black Bay, Loch Ewe.		
	Mar. 12	*J. Pinkney Henderson*	**69**
	The American Liberty ship collided with the *Senior* outside New York on the Atlantic.		
	Apr. 7	**U.S. Liberty Ship**	**62**
	The vessel wrecked in storm and broke in 3 in the mid-Atlantic.		
	Apr. 14	*Fort Stikine*	**336**
	The 7,142-ton British cargo ship, built in 1942, blew up in the crowded Bombay docks. (SEE Bombay, India)		
	May 31	**Liberty Ships**	**100s**
	Storm caught fleet off the Farallon Islands.		
	July 17	*Quinault Victory*	**270**
	The 7,608-ton American ship, built in 1944, exploded while being loaded with munitions at Port Chicago. (SEE Port Chicago)		
	†Sept. 14	*Warrington*	**344**
	The 1,840-ton American destroyer, built in 1937, foundered in a hurricane off the Bahamas in the company of 4 other small vessels. (SEE United States [East])		
	Oct. 19	*Juan Casiano*	**21**
	The 7.064-ton Mexican ship, built in 1919, sank in a storm 90 mi. off Savannah.		
	†Dec. 17	*Spence*	**341**
	The 2,050-ton American destroyer, built in 1942, foundered in a typhoon E. of Samar in the Philippines. (SEE Luzon Islands, Philippines)		
	†Dec. 17	*Monahan*	**250**
	The 1,395-ton American destroyer, built in 1935, foundered in a typhoon E. of Samar. (SEE Luzon Islands, Philippines)		
	†Dec. 17	*Hull*	**139**
	The 1,395-ton destroyer, built in 1934, foundered in a typhoon E. of Samar. (SEE Luzon Islands, Philippines)		
1945	**Feb. 5**	*Springhill*	**21**
	The American tanker exploded after a collision with the Panamanian tanker *Pan-Clio* in upper New York Bay.		
	Mar. 20	*Mapocho*	**78**
	The 2,652-ton Chilean steamship, built in 1882, caught fire and sank off Frente Caleta Buena.		
	Apr. 9	*John Harvey*	**360**
	The American Liberty ship exploded in the harbor at Bari, Italy; 1,730 persons were injured.		
	Apr. 9	*St. Mihiel*	**20**
	The American freighter collided with the tanker *Nashbulk* in the fog off the Massachusetts coast.		
	Apr. 11	*Panama*	**45**
	The 6,650-ton motorship, built in 1915, foundered in mid-Atlantic.		
	Apr. 23	*PE-56*	**49**
	The 430-ton American patrol boat exploded off Maine.		
	Aug. 6	*Ajudante*	**54**
	The Brazilian river steamer collided with a Colombian gunboat on the Amazon River.		

Date		Place	Deaths
	Sept. 29	*Empire Patrol*	**33**

The 3,334-ton British motorship, built in 1928, caught fire and burned 38 mi. off Port Said.

Nov. 8 — **Chinese (river steamer)** — **1,550**
The vessel, loaded with Chinese soldiers, sank off Hong Kong.

Dec. 14 — **Japanese (transport)** — **238**
The vessel foundered in a storm off Shikoku.

1946 **Feb. 9** — **Egyptian (river boat)** — **50**
The vessel capsized and sank near Tima.

Feb. 14 — *Yukon* — **32**
The 5,747-ton American steamship, built in 1889, ran aground and wrecked in Johnston Bay, Prince William Sound.

Mar. 24 — *Kinkazan Maru* — **170**
The Japanese ferryboat capsized off Honshu.

June 27 — *C-4* — **46**
Spanish 1,290-ton (submerged) sub was rammed while cruising submerged by the Spanish destroyer *Lepanto* 8 mi. off Soller, Balearic Islands, Spain.

July 31 — *Duque de Caxias* — **27**
The Brazilian transport caught fire off the Brazil coast; 1,600 passengers were rescued.

Aug. 2 — *Vitya* — **295**
The steamer, loaded with celebrants of Aga Khan's golden jubilee, sank in Lake Nyassa, Tanganyika, Africa.

Oct. 29 — *Ebisu Maru* — **497**
The 490-ton Japanese motorship, built in 1935, struck a wreck and broke in 3 places near Chinampo, Korea.

Dec. 5 — *U-2326* **(ex-German)** — **26**
French 256-ton (submerged) sub sank from unknown causes off Toulon, France.

Dec. 21 — *Enticer* — **21**
The British tug foundered off China.

1947 **Jan. 18** — *Chekiang* — **400**
The small Chinese steamer sank in the Yangtze River off Woosung after a collision.

†Jan. 19 — *Chimara* — **393**
The 1,800-ton Greek passenger liner struck a mine off the tip of the Attica peninsula on a voyage from Salonika.

Mar. 1 — *Navadoc* — **24**
The 2,250-ton Canadian freighter foundered 22 mi. E. of Portland, Me.

Apr. 16 — *Grandcamp* — **33**
The 7,176-ton steamship, built in 1942, caught fire and caused a tremendous explosion at Texas City, Tex. (SEE Texas City, Texas)

Apr. 18 — *Sir Harvey Adamson* — **269**
The 1,030-ton steamship, built in 1914, foundered in a gale on a voyage from Rangoon to Tajoy and Mergui.

Apr. 23 — *Samtampa* — **39**
The 7,219-ton British steamship, built in 1943, wrecked in bad weather at Sker Point, Porthcawl.

June 19 — *Chienkuo* — **100**
The steamer wrecked on the rocks in the North River, Kwangtung Province, China.

July 1 — *Panigaglia* — **68**
The steamer exploded when her cargo of munitions was being unloaded near Civitavecchia, Italy.

†Sept. 11 — *Reina del Pacifico* — **25**
The refitted World War II troopship used for passenger duty had a boiler explosion in the Irish Sea.

Sept. 7 — **Brazilian (ferries)** — **30**
The 2 vessels collided off Rio de Janeiro in Guanabara Bay.

Sept. 11 — *Island Queen* — **20**
The excursion steamer exploded at a dock in Pittsburgh, Pa.

Oct. 23 — *Mallard* — **62**
The 193-ton British tug, built in 1903, sank in a cyclone while at anchor at Motirchara in the Muscal Channel.

Nov. 14 — *Clarksdale Victory* — **49**
The 7,607-ton steamship, built in 1945, wrecked on Hippa Reef, 140 mi. S.W. of Ketchikan, Alaska.

Dec. 2 — *Castillo Coca* — **26**
The 1,739-ton Spanish steamship, built in 1919, wrecked on the rocks at Sogano Point off Ferrol.

Dec. 26 — *Kina* — **49**
The Danish motorship was wrecked off northern Samar.

1948 **Jan. 19** — *Cautin* — **150**
The Chilean steamship foundered in the Imperial River.

Jan. 31 — *Samkey* — **43**
The 7,219-ton ship, built in 1943, disappeared in the Bermuda Triangle.

Sept. 1 — *Euzkera* — **44**
The 350-ton Honduran yacht, built in 1894, capsized 150 mi. N. of Puerto Colombia; she was being used as a circus ship and 59 animals were also lost.

Nov. 14 — *Hopestar* — **40**
The 5,627-ton cargo steamship, built in 1936, foundered in storm weather in the Atlantic.

†Dec. 3 — *Kiangya* — **2,750**
The 3,731-ton Chinese passenger ship, built in 1939, was on a voyage from Shanghai to Ningpo when she hit a mine, exploded, and sank 15 mi. off the Woosung breakwater.

1949 **Jan. 27** — *Tai Ping* — **1,500**
The 2,493-ton Chinese steamship, built in 1921, collided with Chinese steamship *Kien Yuan* in fog in Bonham Strait, N. of Chusan Island.

May 31 — *Kearney* — **28**
A Liberty ship from the American carrier was overwhelmed by the sea off Norfolk, Va.

June 11 — *Kjoebenhavn* — **150**
The Danish vessel sank; she struck a mine in the Kattegat.

July 9 — *Corum* — **59**
The Turkish steamer exploded in Istanbul.

July 26 — **Indian (ferryboat)** — **140**
The vessel, filled with pilgrims, capsized in the Marabada River at Indore.

Aug. 23 — *China Victor* — **500**
The 3,283-ton Chinese steamship, built in 1919, was being unloaded at Kaohsiung, Formosa, when fire broke out and the ship blew up.

†Sept. 17 — *Noronic* — **118**
The 6,905-ton Canadian steamship, built in 1913, caught fire in the Toronto harbor and sank the next day.

Oct. 4 — *Fournier* — **77**
The Argentine minesweeper wrecked on a submerged rock and sank in the Magellan Straits.

Oct. 18 — *Maystone* — **20**
The British collier collided with the British carrier *Albion* during a gale off Britain's North Sea coast.

Nov. — **Chinese Army Vessel** — **6,000**
The Nanking News Service disclosed that an army evacuation ship had exploded in Manchuria and sunk earlier in the month.

†1950 **Jan. 12** — *Truculent* — **55**
The British submarine was rammed by the Swedish tanker *Divinia* , in the Thames estuary, England.

Feb. 28 — *Clam* — **27**
The 7,404-ton British motor tanker, built in 1927, wrecked at Reykjanes near Iceland.

Apr. 30 — *Hsinan* — **70**
The Chinese communist steamer collided with the *California Bear* off Dairen, Manchuria.

Date		Place	Deaths
	July 9	*Indian Enterprise*	73
	The 7,319-ton British cargo ship, built in 1946, exploded in the Red Sea.		
	Aug. 25	*Benevolence*	23
	The 11,800-ton American steamship, built in 1944, collided with the steamship *Mary Luckenbach* at San Francisco Bay.		
	Nov. 15	**Yugoslavian (ferry)**	94
	The vessel capsized on the Sava River near Orasje.		
	Dec. 1	*I. P. Suhr*	20
	The 1,999-ton Danish ship, built in 1927, foundered 5 mi. S. of Sandhammaren.		
	Dec. 10	*Tomi Maru*	26
	The 725-ton motorship, built in 1949, foundered off the N.W. coast of Kyushu.		
†1951	Apr. 16	*Affray*	75
	The British submarine disappeared in the English Channel off the Isle of Wight; she was located Sept. 12 in 258 feet of water in the Channel.		
	Apr. 20	*Esso Greensboro* & *Esso Suez*	39
	The 2 Standard Oil tankers collided in dense fog and caught fire in the Gulf of Mexico, 190 mi. S. of Morgan City, La.		
	May 31	**German (excursion boat)**	60
	The vessel, which carried mostly children, exploded on the Spree River.		
	Aug. 13	*Bess*	37
	The 1,116-ton Norwegian motorship, built in 1939, capsized on her way to Oslo.		
	Sept. 1	*Pelican*	46
	The fishing boat, used as a pleasure ship, capsized in rough seas off Montauk Point, N.Y.		
1952	Mar. 27	*Apnok*	21
	The South Korean freighter collided with the ammunition carrier *Mt. Baker.*		
	†Apr. 26	*Hobson*	175
	The American destroyer collided with the aircraft carrier *Wasp* and sank in the Atlantic.		
	Apr. 26	*St. Paul*	30
	The American cruiser had a powder blast in her gun turret; this was the worst disaster of the Korean War.		
	July 20	**unidentified**	50
	Sailboat capsized off Mindoro Island.		
	Sept. 9	**Yugoslavian (ferry)**	86
	The vessel turned over in a storm in the Danube River near Belgrade.		
	Sept. 23	*La Sibylle*	47
	French submarine never surfaced after dive off Toulon; reports stated ship must have burst.		
	Oct. 7	*Norman*	20
	The trawler ran aground off Greenland.		
	Oct. 23	*Brito*	21
	The Chilean Navy tug wrecked on the rocks and exploded off Puerto Quintero, Chile.		
	Dec. 15	**Paraguayan (launch)**	32
	The river vessel capsized off Paraguay.		
	Dec. 17	*Melanie Schulte*	35
	The 6,170-ton German motor cargo ship, built in 1952, disappeared on a voyage from Narvik to Mobile.		
1953	Jan. 2	**Philippinean (motorboat)**	80
	The craft sank off Cebu Island with 180 on board.		
	Jan. 8	**Colombian (steamer)**	20
	The small coastal vessel foundered off Colombia.		
	†Jan. 9	*Chang Tyong-Ho*	249
	The 146-ton South Korean passenger ship capsized in heavy seas off Pusan.		
	Jan. 17	**Indian (boat)**	32
	The vessel, loaded with Hindu pilgrims, wrecked off Calcutta.		
	†Jan. 31	*Princess Victoria*	121
	The 2,694-ton British motorship, built in 1947, foundered off the mouth of Loch Ryan.		
	Feb. 4	**Indonesian (ferry)**	58
	The vessel capsized and sank off Okinawa.		
	Feb. 21	**Philippinean (ferry)**	30
	The vessel was lost off Luzon.		
	Mar. 8	*Sollom*	54
	Minesweeper sank off Egypt.		
	†Apr. 4	*Dumlupinar*	81
	The 1,526-ton Turkish submarine collided, in the dark, with the 4,000-ton Swedish freighter *Naboland* and sank in the Dardanelles 3 mi. N. of Canakkale.		
	Apr. 29	**Colombian (ship)**	67
	The coastal vessel sank off the coast.		
	July 17	**Indian (ferryboat)**	60
	The vessel capsized in the Sutlej River near New Delhi.		
	Aug. 1	*Monique*	120
	The French liner disappeared in the South Pacific.		
	Sept. 2	**U.S. Army**	20
	The military craft sank in a training exercise at Ft. Bragg, N.C.		
	†Oct. 16	*Leyte*	36
	The American aircraft carrier caught fire and caused a blast at Charleston Naval Yd., Boston.		
	Nov. 16	*Vittoria Claudia*	20
	The 2,745-ton Italian steamship, built in 1905, collided with the French motorship *Perou* 2 mi. S.E. of Dungeness.		
1954	Jan. 10	*Nedjan*	21
	The Swedish freighter foundered in a Baltic storm.		
	Feb. 7	*Laforey*	20
	The 609-ton British trawler, built in 1949, wrecked on Sendiogane rocks, near Batalden, N.W. of Floro.		
	Mar. 6	*Guadelete*	33
	The Spanish Navy cutter foundered in a gale off Gibraltar.		
	†May 26	*Bennington*	107
	The 32,000-ton American aircraft carrier exploded and burned near Quonset Point, Rhode Island.		
	Aug. 15	*Sittang River*	40
	The ferryboat capsized in Burma.		
	†Sept. 26	*Toyo Maru*	794
	The 4,337-ton Japanese train ferry, built in 1947, capsized in a typhoon outside Hakodate. The captain was found guilty of negligence.		
	Oct. 7	*Mormackite*	36
	The 6,195-ton American ship, built in 1945, foundered in bad weather 110 mi. E.S.E. of Cape Henry, Va.		
	Nov. 30	*Tresillian*	24
	The 7,373-ton motorship, built in 1944, foundered 150 mi. N.W. of the Bishop Rock.		
	Dec. 7	*Southern Districts*	24
	The 3,337-ton freighter disappeared off the Gulf of Mexico and the wreckage was found 2 weeks later near Sand Key, Fla.		
	Dec. 8-9	**European Coast**	121
	Storms caused 16 ships to founder along the French, English and Irish coasts.		
1955	Jan. 26	*Lorella*	20
	The 559-ton British trawler, built in 1947, capsized in a hurricane N.E. of North Cape, Iceland.		
	Feb. 14	*Akebono Maru No. 6*	22
	The 342-ton Japanese trawler, built in 1947, collided with the South Korean frigate *No. 61* near Ukushima.		

Date		Place	Deaths
	May 11	*Shiun Maru*	**173**
	The Japanese ferryboat collided with the freighter *Udaka Maru* in the fog and foundered on a voyage from Honshu to Shikoku.		
	June 9	**Indian (ferry)**	**32**
	The vessel capsized in the Ganges River, 10 mi. from Allahabad, India.		
	June 9	*Johannishus*	**20**
	The Swedish tanker collided with the Panamanian freighter *Buccaneer* and burned in the English Channel.		
	July 13	*Geologist*	**20**
	The 6,155-ton British cargo ship, built in 1944, collided with the *Sunprincess* at 10° 49′N. - 61° 40′W.		
	July 14	**African (launch)**	**22**
	The vessel, which carried Mau Mau terrorists on their way to an island prison, capsized on Lake Victoria, off Nairobi, Kenya.		
	Nov. 4	*To An*	**23**
	The steamer foundered off the Formosa Strait.		
	Nov. 13	*Joyita*	**25**
	The empty launch was found off the Fiji Islands; all passengers were missing.		
	Nov. 26	*Cetus*	**21**
	The 738-ton Philippine motorship, built in 1943, capsized on the Cagayan River, Philippines.		
1956	**Jan. 12**	*Taishin-Ho*	**70**
	The coastal ship caught fire and burned when docked at Samchopo, S. Korea.		
	Jan. 18	*Salem Maritime*	**25**
	The American oil tanker caught fire and exploded while docked at Lake Charles, La.		
	Feb. 12	**Nile River (ferryboat)**	**22**
	The vessel capsized near Mansoura, Egypt.		
	Apr. 7	**Nigerian (motorboat)**	**28**
	The vessel sank near the harbor of Badagri.		
	May 13	**Indonesian (motorboat)**	**73**
	The overloaded vessel capsized off Tegal in the Java Sea.		
	†July 25	*Andrea Doria* (& *Stockholm*)	**52**
	The 29,083-ton luxury liner, built in 1953, was struck below her navigating bridge by the Swedish-American liner *Stockholm* off Nantucket Is., Mass.		
	†Sept. 15	*Pelagia*	**33**
	The 7,282-ton American freighter, launched in 1943, foundered in bad weather.		
	Oct. 20	*Lepus*	**25**
	The 2,294-ton Philippine ship, built in 1911, foundered in a typhoon.		
	Nov. 12	*Ave del Mar*	**28**
	The Spanish fishing boat wrecked on a reef and sank in Vigo Bay, Sp.		
	Nov. 17	**Formosan (ferryboat)**	**102**
	The vessel wrecked on a reef and sank on a voyage from Formosa to the Pescadores.		
1957	**Mar. 6**	**German (ferry)**	**28**
	The overloaded ferry capsized in the Elbe River, E. Germany.		
	Mar. 28	**Indonesian (ferry)**	**40**
	The overloaded ferry capsized in the Tjitarum River, 40 mi. E. of Jakarta.		
	Apr. 10	**India (boats)**	**150**
	Two vessels sank due to alarmed pilgrims who caused both to list in the Godvari River in Central India.		
	Apr. 12	**Japanese (wooden vessel)**	**96**
	The overloaded vessel wrecked on a reef and sank off the coast of Onomichi, Japan.		
	Apr. 14	**Korean (tugboat)**	**27**
	The vessel capsized in the Yellow Sea near Wolmi I., Korea.		
	May 17	**Yangtze (riverboat)**	**100**
	The vessel burned and sank at Wuhan, China.		
	June 2	**Indian (ferry)**	**20**
	The vessel capsized in the Damodar River, 80 mi. from Calcutta.		
	July 5	**Indian (boat)**	**20**
	The vessel capsized in the Godvari River, 50 mi. from Ahmadnagar.		
	†July 14	*Eshghabad*	**270**
	The Russian fishing vessel struck a reef between Salyan & Baku in the Caspian Sea.		
	Aug. 28	*Ciudad de Buenos Aires*	**94**
	The 3,754-ton Argentine ferry, built in 1914, collided with the steamship *Mormacsurf* at Km. 123, Martin Garcia Channel, River Plate.		
	Sept. 8	**Korean (ferryboat)**	**23**
	The vessel capsized off Wandi I., South Korea.		
	†Sept. 22	*Pamir*	**81**
	The 3,103-ton 4-masted steel bark, built in 1905, foundered in a hurricane 600 mi. W. of the Azores.		
	Oct. 7	**Indian (passenger boat)**	**50**
	The vessel capsized in the Jaibharali Tejpur River, Assam State, India.		
	Nov. 6	*Luapula*	**42**
	The riverboat capsized off Kabimba, Belgian Congo.		
	Dec. 22	*Narva*	**28**
	The 2,044-ton British cargo ship, built in 1943, foundered.		
1958	**Jan. 26**	*Nankai Maru*	**166**
	The 494-ton motor ferry, built in 1956, foundered in a storm in Kii Strait between Shikoku Island and Wakayama.		
	†Feb. 19	*Seistan*	**57**
	The 7,440-ton motorship, built in 1957, caught fire and exploded at Bahrein.		
	Feb. 19	*Bonitas*	**22**
	The 5,636-ton Italian steamship, built in 1929, sprang a leak and sank near Cape Lookout.		
	Mar. 1	*Uskudar*	**350**
	The 148-ton Turkish ferry, built in 1927, foundered in a gale in Izmit Bay outside Izmit.		
	Mar. 15	**unidentified**	**58**
	The ship sank off Bawean Is., East Java.		
	Mar. 22	*Dodecanessos*	**20**
	The Greek coastal vessel foundered in a hurricane near Rhodes.		
	July 21	**Indian (boat)**	**47**
	The boat capsized in a gale in Kerala State, India.		
	Sept. 27	*Arnel*	**23**
	The 1,026-ton Portuguese ship, built in 1955, wrecked off Santa Maria Island, Azores.		
	Nov. 18	*Carl D. Bradley*	**29**
	The 10,028-ton steamship, built in 1927, foundered off Gull Island, Lake Michigan.		
	Oct. 12	**Philippinean (ferry)**	**75**
	The overloaded motor launch sank with fiesta celebrants off Cebu Is., Philippines.		
	Oct. 17	**Soviet (trawler)**	**22**
	The fishing trawler wrecked in the Shetland Islands.		
	Oct. 20	*Guarani*	**37**
	The picket boat disappeared off Argentina.		
†1959	**Jan. 30**	*Hans Hedtoft*	**95**
	The 2,875-ton motorship, built in 1958, struck an iceberg 30 mi. S.E. of Cape Farewell and sank with all aboard.		
	Feb. 9	*Blue Wave* & *Julie*	**47**
	The two Newfoundland trawlers capsized in icy waters N.E. of N.F.L.		

Date		Place	Deaths
	Apr. 14	**Indian (boat)**	35

Small boat capsized when it crossed the Sarda River near the Indian-Nepalese border.

	May 8	*Dandarah*	150

The Nile River excursion boat foundered off Qalyub, 10 mi. N. of Cairo.

	Aug. 22	*Pilar II*	90

The Philippine inter-island vessel sank off Palawan Island in Typhoon Iris.

	†Oct. 27	*Sinola*	27

The 1,580-ton Mexican motorship, built in 1943, foundered in a storm off Manzillo. (SEE Minatitlan, Mex.)

1960	Feb. 24	**Pakistan (riverboat)**	20

The riverboat capsized off Chittagong.

	Mar. 4	*La Coubre*	75

The freighter exploded at the Havana dock while her cargo of ammunition was unloaded. (SEE Havana)

	Mar. 21	**Ethiopian (ship)**	50

The vessel foundered in the Red Sea; on board were Yemenites expelled from Ethiopia.

	Apr. 6	**Persian (vessel)**	57

The motor launch capsized in a storm at the Persian Gulf near Kuwait.

	May 12	**Indian (vessel)**	60

The overloaded Indian boat, which carried pilgrims, capsized in the Krishna River in Andhara State.

	June 13	**Polish (boat)**	21

The Polish excursion boat, which carried 18 teenagers, capsized in the Dunajec Mountain River.

	Oct. 25	*El Gamil*	22

The 1,356-ton Egyptian steamship, built in 1904, foundered in the Red Sea.

	Dec. 2	*Iri*	22

The British freighter disappeared in the Atlantic.

	Dec. 14	*World Harmony*	53

The Greek tanker collided with the Yugoslav tanker *Peter Zorankic* and caused a fire and explosion in the Turkish Strait, Bosporus.

	†Dec. 19	*Constellation*	50

The 80,000-ton U.S. aircraft carrier, world's largest at that time, caught fire in her Brooklyn Naval Yard berth.

1961	Jan. 7	**Iran (motor launch)**	88

The Iranian motor launch sank in the Persian Gulf en route from Iran to Kuwait.

	Jan. 11	*Price*	43

The 27-ton Moroccan yacht foundered in a storm in the Mediterranean off Alhucemas Bay.

	Apr. 2	**Indian (motor launch)**	30

The motor launch capsized in the Shatt-al-Arab River in Iran.

	†Apr. 8	*Dara*	236

The 5,030-ton British India liner, built in 1948, exploded on her return to the port of Dubai in the Persian Gulf.

	June 7	*Aung Teza*	67

The 999-ton Burmese ship, built in 1960, capsized 80 mi. S. of Moulmein.

	July 7	*Save*	259

The 2,037-ton Portuguese motorship, built in 1951, caught fire and exploded in the mouth of the River Linde.

	Sept. 3	*Vencendor*	54

The coaster sank off Buenaventura, Colombia.

	Sept. 29	*Starcarrier*	27

The 5,561-ton Norwegian motorship, built in 1948, caught fire and exploded in Diego Suarez harbor.

	Nov. 5	*Clan Keith*	68

The 7,129-ton steamship, built in 1942, was wrecked in a gale on the Ecueils des Sorelles Rocks, off Cap Bon, Tunisia.

Date		Place	Deaths
	Dec. 7	*Combined I*	28

The 1,722-ton Panamanian motorship, built in 1948, foundered during a storm off Ladd Reef, 650 mi. S.W. of Manila.

1962	Jan. 1	**Indian (riverboat)**	70

The Indian passenger boat foundered off the port of Mhapal on the Savitri River.

	Jan. 7	*Sabac*	28

The 2,811-ton Yugoslav steamship, built in 1922, collided with the British motorship *Dorrington Court* 6 mi. S.E. of Dover.

	Mar. 14	*Hedia*	20

The 2,434-ton Liberian steamship, built in 1915, foundered near Galatia Island after she reported in "all well."

	Oct. 21	*Sanct Svithun*	41

The 2,172-ton Norwegian motor vessel, built in 1950, wrecked outside the harbor of Rorvik in Northern Norway.

	Nov. 18	*Munakata Maru*	39

The 1,972-ton Japanese oil tanker collided with the 21,634-ton Norwegian *Tharald* at the port of Kawasaki in a Tokyo Bay channel.

1963	Jan. 4	*Djandji Radjan*	105

The Indonesian ferry caught fire and sank in Toba Lake in North Sumatra.

	Jan. 18	**South Korean (ferry)**	90

The 35-ton coastal vessel foundered in a storm in the Yellow Sea on a voyage to Mokpo.

	Feb. 4	*Marine Sulphur Queen*	39

The 524-ton tanker disappeared on a voyage from Beaumont, Tex., to Norfolk, Va.; 2 life jackets were later found.

	†Apr. 10	*Thresher*	129

The 4,300-ton American nuclear submarine, launched in 1960, sank in the Atlantic, E. of Boston.

	†May 4	**Maghagha Ferry**	221

Ferryboat, which contained Moslem pilgrims, capsized and sank in the upper Nile River at Maghagha.

	July 2	**Burmese (schooner)**	113

The vessel sank 1 mi. from the port of Moulmein.

	July 11	*Ciudad de Asuncion*	53

The 2,330-ton Argentine riverboat caught fire and sank in the River Plate Estuary, 50 mi. E. of Buenos Aires.

	July 20	*Tritonica*	33

The 12,863-ton British ore carrier collided with the *Roonagh Head* in the St. Lawrence River near the village of Petite-Riviere.

	Aug. 17	*Midori Maru*	55

The 300-ton ferryboat foundered in the East China Sea 18 mi. off Okinawa.

	Oct. 23	**South Korean (ferry)**	49

The vessel capsized in the Han River near Seoul; all aboard were children.

	†Dec. 22	*Lakonia*	128

The 20,314-ton Greek cruise liner, built in 1930, caught fire and burned 180 mi. N. of Madeira.

1964	Feb. 10	*Voyager*	79

The 2,800-ton Australian destroyer, built in 1958, collided with the aircraft carrier *Melbourne* S. of Sydney. This was Australia's greatest peacetime marine disaster to this date.

	Apr. 2	*Kadavulevu*	70

The schooner capsized and caught fire off Fiji, Japan.

	July 23	*Star of Alexander*	100

The United Arab Republic freighter exploded when her 2,000 tons of ammunition were being unloaded at the Algerian port of Bone. (SEE Bone, Algeria)

Date	Place	Deaths

Dec. 22 *San Patrick* **32**
The freighter disappeared in the Aleutian Islands; wreckage later sighted.

1965 May 23 *Malawi* **150**
The ferry capsized in crocodile-infested waters when guide cables broke at Shire River, Liwonde, Malawi.

June 6 *Luisa* **32**
The tanker exploded and sank at Bandar Mashur.

Aug. 5 *Apollo* **28**
Freighter collided with trawler near Esposende, Portugal.

†Nov. 13 *Yarmouth Castle* **89**
The Panamanian cruise ship caught fire and burned in the Caribbean, E. of Miami.

1966 Jan. 10 *Monte Palomares* **38**
The ferry sank in the North Atlantic.

Jan. 25 *Permina* **89**
The vessel sank at Belawan, Sumatra.

Jan. 31 **Indian (ships)** **80**
The passenger launch and steamer collided at the Chanpur Port in the Brahmaputra Region.

May 15 *Pioneer Cebu* **100**
The vessel sank in a typhoon off the Philippines.

May 24 *Kaitawa* **30**
The 2,500-ton British collier ran aground on the Pandora Banks and wrecked 10 mi. off the northern-most tip of New Zealand.

July 17 *Alva Cape* **32**
The tanker collided with the tanker *Texaco Massachusetts* and exploded at Kill Van Kull, N.Y.

Oct. 22 *Golden State* **26**
The 7,598-ton American freighter collided with the Philippine coastal steamer *Pioneer State* off the Philippine Islands.

Oct. 25 **Indian (riverboat)** **100**
The East Indian vessel sank on the Kosi River near Patna.

†Oct. 26 *Oriskany* **43**
The 42,000-ton United States aircraft carrier caught fire and exploded in the Gulf of Tonkin.

Nov. 3 *Progress* **26**
The ferry ran aground in a storm at Madras, India.

Nov. 31 *Daniel J. Morrell* **28**
The 603-ft. ferry broke up and sank on Lake Huron.

†Dec. 12 *Heraklion* **230**
The Greek ferry foundered in a storm when a 16-ton refrigerator trailer broke loose in the Sea of Crete.

1967 Jan. 14 *Hanil-Ho* **50**
The South Korean ferry collided with the *Chungnam-Ho* off South Korea.

Feb. 28 *Tukan* **57**
The Soviet fishery ship sprang a leak and sank off Hanstholm, Jutland.

May 5 **Sudanese (riverboat)** **60**
The vessel capsized in the Blue Nice River near Singa, East Central Sudan.

May 23 *Circle* **38**
The tanker exploded and burned 100 mi. S. of Toulon, France.

†July 29 *Forrestal* **134**
The 75,900-ton American aircraft carrier caught fire off Vietnam. This was the worst American Navy disaster since World War II.

Aug. 10 **Rumanian (lake steamer)** **153**
The vessel capsized in the middle of Lake Tel in a storm.

Sept. 21 *Fiete Schulze* **24**
The ferry sank in stormy seas off Spain.

Date	Place	Deaths

Sept. 25 **Indian (motorboat)** **150**
The vessel capsized and sank in the Ganges Delta near Faridpur.

1968 Jan. 10 *St. Romanus* **20**
The British fishing trawler foundered off the northern coast of Iceland.

Jan. 22 **Indian (vessel)** **40**
The vessel sank in the Ganges River 10 mi. N. of Benares.

†Jan. 26 *Dakar* **69**
The 1,800-ton Israeli submarine disappeared 100 mi. W. of Cyprus.

Jan. 26 *Kingston Peridot* **20**
The British fishing trawler foundered in stormy seas off the coast of Iceland.

†Jan. 27 *Minerve* **52**
The 190-ft. French submarine disappeared 25 mi. S.E. of Toulon.

Mar. 29 **Indian (boat)** **60**
The vessel capsized in a strong wind in the Gogra River near Chapra.

Apr. 10 *Wahine* **51**
The 8,944-ton New Zealand ferry, one of the world's largest, blew apart on Barrett's Reef in a 123 m.p.h. windstorm.

†May 21 *Scorpion* **99**
The 3,075-ton American nuclear submarine disappeared in the Atlantic, S.W. of the Azores. She was located in Nov. 1968 400 mi. S.W. of the Azores at 10,000 ft. below the surface.

May 31 **Indian (ferryboat)** **30**
The craft capsized in a gale on the Ganges River near Calcutta.

June 14 *World Glory* **20**
The tanker foundered in heavy seas and broke up off the coast of S. Africa.

Oct. 30 *Rio Esmeraldas* **40**
The motorship sank off Ecuador coast.

Dec. 22 *Federal Queen* **40**
The schooner capsized off Cannovan Island, Grenadines, W. Indies.

†1969 Jan. 14 *Enterprise* **27**
The 90,000-ton U.S. warship raged with fire after a loose bomb exploded on flight deck.

Mar. 13 *NR 4553* **24**
The 125-ft. Russian tanker collided with the tanker *Esso Honduras* off North Carolina.

Apr. 6 *Union Faith* **25**
The 10,750-ton Taiwan freighter collided with an oil barge on the Mississippi River under the Great New Orleans Bridge.

†June 2 *Frank E. Evans* **74**
The American destroyer collided with the Australian aircraft carrier *Melbourne* 650 mi. S.W. of Manila in the South China Sea.

June 21 *Zambesi River* **108**
A barge, which carried 150 Portuguese troops, capsized 190 mi. N. of Beira, Mozambique.

July 30 **Indian (launch)** **50**
The overloaded vessel capsized in the rain swollen Godavari River.

Aug. 15 **Egyptian (launch)** **24**
The vessel sank in the Nile River.

Aug. 18 *Lake Geneva* **24**
A French pleasure boat sank between Thonon-les-Bains and Evian-les-Bains; all aboard were teen-agers.

Date		Place	Deaths
	Aug. 25	*Noongah*	**20**
	The freighter capsized in a gale off Sydney, Australia.		
	Sept. 14	**East Pakistani (boat)**	**25**
	The river vessel capsized near Dacca.		
	Nov. 5	*Keo*	**36**
	The 639-ft. Liberian tanker broke in 2 in a storm 120 mi. S.E. of Nantucket, Mass.		
	Dec. 26	*Badger State*	**25**
	The 8,166-ton American ship foundered in heavy seas 600 mi. N.E. of Midway Is.		
1970	**Jan. 9**	**Ecuador (motorboat)**	**50**
	The vessel sank in the shark infested Guayaquil Gulf.		
	Feb. 1	*Akrotiri*	**21**
	The Greek ship caught fire in her engine room when anchored at the Rumanian port of Constanta.		
	Mar. 1	**Ceylonese (boat)**	**61**
	The vessel capsized at Jaffna.		
	†Mar. 4	*Eurydice*	**57**
	The French submarine exploded in the Mediterranean 35 mi. E. of Toulon, France.		
	July 5	**Indian (ferry)**	**150**
	The launch capsized in the Krushna River, 33 mi. from Masulipatamo on India's E. coast.		
	Aug. 1	*Christena*	**125**
	The Caribbean motor launch capsized and sank in the Caribbean off St. Kitts; the coast guard was not notified for 2½ hours.		
	Sept. 3	**Indian (boat)**	**68**
	The vessel capsized in the flooded Krishna River in Bijapur.		
	Nov. 5	**South Korean (ferry)**	**29**
	The vessel capsized off Chunchon.		
	Dec. 15	*Namyong-Ho*	**308**
	The 62-ton South Korean ferryboat sank when 150 crates of tangerines shifted to one side of the vessel 50 mi. off the southern coast of Korea.		
	Dec. 23	*Northern Dancer*	**24**
	The 9-ton passenger ship collided with the 900-ton *Aquadud* while anchored 80 mi. off the Java coast.		
1971	**Mar. 7**	*Niki*	**23**
	The freighter struck sunken wreckage in the English Channel off Folkestone.		
	Mar. 29	*Texaco Oklahoma*	**33**
	The American tanker, which carried 220,000 barrels of oil, broke in 2 110 mi. N.E. of Cape Hatteras.		
	May 22	*Meteor*	**32**
	The Norwegian cruise ship caught fire and exploded 75 mi. off Vancouver, B.C.		
	Aug. 28	*Heleanna*	**54**
	The 11,232-ton Greek ferryboat, which carried twice the number of passengers allowed, caught fire in the Adriatic.		
	Nov. 21	*Beethoven II*	**106**
	The passenger ship sank in heavy seas off the central Philippines.		
1972	**Jan 2**	*Qatari*	**40**
	The ship sank in a storm off island of Qais in the Persian Gulf.		
	Jan. 9	*Dona Anita*	**42**
	The 7,840-ton African freighter foundered in stormy weather W. of Vancouver Island, B.C.		
	Feb. 2	*V. A. Fogg*	**39**
	The 572-ft. American tanker disappeared after she sailed from Freeport, Tex., with a cargo of highly volatile benzine residue.		
	Mar. 6	*San Nicolas*	**28**
	The Liberian tanker disappeared on a voyage from Brazil to New Orleans; wreckage was later found in the Gulf of Mexico.		
	†May 11	*Royston Grange* **(&** *Tien Chee)*	**84**
	The British cargo ship collided with the Liberian oil tanker, *Tien Chee,* in the fog 7 mi. from Montevideo, Uruguay.		
	June 9	*Kaigata Maru*	**20**
	The Japanese fishing trawler caught fire and sank in the Atlantic.		
	June 28	*Tarsos*	**22**
	The Greek oil tanker was rocked by an explosion at the repair dock of Bombay.		
	†Aug. 21	*Texanita* **(&** *Oswego Guardian)*	**47**
	The Greek oil tanker collided with the Taiwan tanker *Oswego Guardian* in the fog 20 mi. S. of the Cape of Good Hope near So. Africa.		
	Nov. 15	*World Hero*	**44**
	The 150-ton Greek super tanker collided with a Greek troop carrier off Piraeus, Greece; the captain and 2 crew members were charged with manslaughter.		
1973	**Feb. 22**	*Bombay Maru*	**200**
	The freighter collided with a Japanese ferry which carried 280 passengers in Rangoon port.		
	Mar. 22	*Anita*	**30**
	The Norwegian freighter was lost in heavy fog off Cape May, N.J.		
	Mar. 22	*Norse Variant*	**30**
	The Norwegian freighter was lost in heavy fog off Cape May, N.J.; 1 survivor.		
	May 6	*Ghazi*	**250**
	The river launch collided with the launch *Dighipir Express* near Dacca and sank immediately.		
	May 10	*Swamasaore*	**300**
	The overloaded motor launch sank in Padma River and was located 2 days later 100 ft. down river.		
	May 18	*O Arbiru*	**23**
	The Portuguese freighter foundered in a storm near Indonesia.		
	June 26	*Saudi*	**50**
	The Indian cargo and passenger capsized in the shark-infested sea off Cape Guardafui in the northeast corner of Africa.		
	Oct. 28	*Ushuala*	**24**
	The Argentine transport collided with the freighter *Rio V* in the Rio de la Plata estuary, 90 mi. from Buenos Aires.		
	Dec. 19	*Oriental Monarch*	**31**
	The 15,000-ton Liberian freighter sprang a leak in her engine room & sank in stormy weather in the Pacific 500 mi. W. of Vancouver Is.		
	Dec. 24	*Jambeli*	**163**
	The overloaded Ecuadorean ferryboat capsized in the Pacific Ocean between Puerto Bolivar and Guayaquil.		
1974	**Feb. 22**	**unidentified**	**157**
	The Korean tug capsized in the harbor of Chungmu, 210 mi. S. of Seoul.		
	Feb. 26	**unidentified**	**43**
	The Mexican Navy tug sank in the Gulf of Mexico.		
	Apr. 21	**unidentified**	**100**
	The fishing schooner capsized in a storm 150 mi. S.E. of Rangoon.		
	May 1	**unidentified**	**250**
	The motor launch capsized off Bangla Desh.		

Date		Place	Deaths
	Sept. 26	**unidentified**	**200**
	The Soviet destroyer caught fire & sank in the Black Sea; this was the worst peacetime naval disaster since the *Thresher.*		
	Sept. 28	**unidentified**	**31**
	The Panamanian freighter foundered in a typhoon 400 mi. E. of Hong Kong.		
	Oct. 25	**unidentified**	**200**
	The crowded ferry capsized 90 mi. S.W. of Dacca, Bangla Desh.		
	Nov. 9	*Pacific Ares*	**33**
	The freighter transporting steel collided with tanker hauling liquified gas in Tokyo Bay.		
	Nov. 15	**unidentified**	**50**
	Small craft sank due to her weight of 25 extra people in the Egyptian Nile.		
1975	**Jan. 25**	**unidentified**	**100**
	Ferryboat and steamer collided in the Burizana River.		
	June 29	**unidentified**	**80**
	Passenger boat capsized in Ganges near Patna, India.		
	Aug. 3	*Red Star Numbers 240 & 245*	**400**
	The two Chinese excursion boats collided and sank in West River near Canton, China.		
	Aug. 24	**unidentified**	**29**
	Small flotilla of ferryboats sank in Joao Pessoa, Brazil; victims children.		
	Oct. 1	**unidentified**	**50**
	Steamer sank 800 miles inland on the Amazon River.		
	Oct. 24	**unidentified**	**150**
	Two-deck ferry capsized on run from Rangoon, Burma, to Kyonmanga.		
	Nov. 10	*Edmund Fitzgerald*	**29**
	The 729-ft. ore boat sank in a storm in Lake Superior; called the worst Great Lakes disaster in 17 years.		

Major Mine Disasters

(† indicates entries profiled in General Narrative)

Date	Place	Deaths
1705 Oct. 3	**Durham, England** Gateshead colliery explosion.	30
1708 Aug. 18	**Durham, England** Fatfield colliery explosion.	69
1710	**Durham, England** Bensham colliery explosion; because of vagueness of records this pit disaster could be confused with the one 2 yrs. earlier.	60
1737 Aug. 5	**Cumberland, England** Corpshill colliery explosion.	22
1743 Jan. 18	**Durham, England** North Burdick colliery explosion.	17
1766 Apr. 16	**Durham, England** South Biddick colliery explosion.	27
1767 Feb. 27	**Durham, England** Fatfield colliery explosion.	39
1794 June 9	**Durham, England** Picktree colliery explosion.	30
June 11	**Durham, England** Harraton colliery explosion.	28
1799 Oct. 11	**Lumley, England** Fence Houses colliery explosion.	39
1805 Oct. 21	**Northumberland, England** Hebburn colliery explosion.	35
Nov. 29	**Durham, England** Oxclose colliery explosion.	38
1812 May 25	**Durham, England** Felling (Brandlings' Main) colliery explosion.	92
1813 Sept. 28	**Fatfield, England** Hall Pit colliery explosion.	32
1815 May 3	**Northumberland, England** Heaton colliery explosion: mine flooded.	80
June 2	**Newbottle, England** Success colliery explosion.	57
1817 June 3	**Harraton, England** Row colliery explosion.	38
Dec. 18	**Rainton, England** Fence Houses colliery explosion.	27
1819 July 19	**Northumberland, England** Sheriff Hill colliery explosion.	35
1821 Oct. 23	**Wallsend, England** "A" Pit colliery explosion.	52
1823 Nov. 3	**Rainton, England** Plain colliery explosion.	59
1826 Jan. 17	**Durham, England** Jarrow colliery explosion.	34
May 30	**Townley Main, England** Stella colliery explosion.	38
1830 Aug. 3	**Durham, England** Jarrow colliery explosion.	42
1833 May 9	**Springwell, England** "B" Pit colliery explosion.	47
1835 June 18	**Northumberland, England** Wallsend colliery explosion.	102
1837 July 28	**Cumberland, England** Workington colliery explosion; mine flooded.	27
Dec. 6	**Northumberland, England** Springwell colliery explosion.	27
1838 Oct. 24	**Lowca, England** John Pit colliery explosion.	40
†1839 Mar. 18	**Richmond, Virginia** Black Heath mine exploded; all the internal works of the mine were blown to pieces—2 men escaped.	53
June 28	**South Shields, England** St. Hilda's colliery explosion.	52
1843 Feb. 14	**Pembrokeshire, Wales** Landshipping colliery inundation.	40
1844	**Richmond, Virginia** Black Heath mine again exploded.	11
Sept. 28	**Northumberland, England** Haswell colliery explosion.	95
1845 Aug. 2	**Glamorgan, Wales** Crombach colliery explosion.	28
Aug. 21	**Durham, England** Jarrow colliery explosion.	39
1846 Jan. 14	**Monmouthshire, Wales** Risca colliery explosion.	35
1847 Feb. 19	**Pottsville, Pennsylvania** Spencer mine exploded by carburetted hydrogen gas.	7
Mar. 5	**Barnsley, England** Oaks colliery explosion.	73
1848 Oct. 28	**Cumberland, England** Whinney Hill colliery explosion.	30
1849 Jan. 24	**Yorkshire, England** Darley Main colliery explosion.	75
June 5	**Durham, England** Hebburn colliery explosion.	33
1850	**Winterpock, Virginia** Cox's mine at Clover Hill exploded.	7
Nov. 12	**Durham, England** Houghton colliery explosion.	26
1851 Mar. 15	**Renfrewshire, Scotland** Nitshill colliery explosion.	61
Aug. 18	**Durham, England** Washington colliery explosion.	35
Dec. 20	**Rawmarsh, England** Warren Vale colliery explosion.	52
1852 May 10	**Glamorgan, Wales** Middle Dyffryn colliery explosion.	65
May 10	**Glamorgan, Wales** Gwendreath colliery inundated.	26
May 20	**Preston, England** Cappull colliery explosion.	36
1853 Mar. 24	**Wigan, England** Ince Hall (Arley Pits) explosion.	58
1854 Feb. 18	**Lancashire, England** Ince Hall colliery explosion.	89
May 15	**Richmond, Virginia** Chesterfield mine exploded.	9
1855 Mar. 19	**Coalfield, Virginia** The Midlothian coal mine exploded.	55
1856 July 15	**Glamorgan, Wales** Cymmer colliery explosion.	114
1857 Feb. 19	**Yorkshire, England** Lundhill colliery exploded.	189
July 31	**Ashton under Lyne, England** Heys colliery explosion.	40
1858 Feb. 2	**Ashton under Lyne, England** Bardsley mine exploded.	53
Dec. 11	**Leigh, England** Tyldesley colliery exploded.	25
1859 Apr. 13	**Winterpock, Virginia** Bright Hope mine at Clover Hill exploded.	9
1860 Mar. 3	**Burradon near Killingworth, England** Coal mine explosion.	74
Dec. 1	**Risca, Wales** Black Vein Pit colliery exploded.	142

Date		Place	Deaths
	Dec. 20	**Northumberland, England**	22
	Hetton Mine exploded.		
1861	June 11	**Derbyshire, England**	21
	Inundation in the Claycross mines.		
1862	Jan. 16	**Northumberland, England**	204
	New Hartley colliery explosion.		
	Feb. 19	**Merthyr, South Wales**	47
	Cethin mine gas explosion.		
	Dec. 8	**Yorkshire, England**	59
	St. Edmund's main colliery exploded.		
1863		**Winterpock, Virginia**	17
	Raccoon mine at Clover Hill exploded.		
	Mar. 6	**Northumberland, England**	26
	Coxlodge colliery explosion.		
	Oct. 17	**Port Talbot, South Wales**	34
	Morfa colliery exploded.		
1865	June 16	**Monmouthshire, South Wales**	26
	Tredegar colliery exploded.		
	Dec. 20	**Glamorgan, South Wales**	34
	Explosion at Cethin Cyfartha colliery.		
1866	Jan. 23	**Wigan, England**	30
	Explosion at Park Lane colliery due to firedamp.		
	Oct. 31	**Durham, England**	24
	Pelton Fell colliery exploded.		
	Dec. 12-13	**Barnsley, England**	361
	Oaks colliery, Hoyle Mill exploded; 28 searchers killed the following day by fresh explosion.		
	Dec. 13	**Staffordshire, England**	91
	Talk-of-the-Hill mine exploded.		
1867	Apr. 3	**Winterpock, Virginia**	69
	Bright Hope mine at Clover Hill again exploded.		
	Oct. 16	**St. Etienne, France**	24
	Fire damp explosion.		
	Nov. 8	**Pontypridd, Wales**	178
	Explosion at Ferndale colliery, in the Rhondda Valley, attributed to naked lights.		
1868	Aug. 6	**Jemmapes, Algeria**	47
	Fire damp explosion.		
	Nov. 28	**Wigan, England**	62
	Hindley-Green colliery exploded.		
	Dec. 26	**Lancashire, England**	26
	Haydock colliery exploded.		
1869	Apr. 1	**Wigan, England**	62
	High Brooks colliery explosion.		
	June 10	**Pontypridd, South Wales**	53
	Ferndale colliery exploded.		
	July 21	**Lancashire, England**	59
	Haydock Pit colliery exploded.		
	†Sept. 6	**Plymouth, Pennsylvania**	110
	Coal mine fire at Avondale colliery.		
	Nov. 15	**Wigan, England**	30
	Low Hall colliery exploded.		
1870	Feb. 14	**Taibach, South Wales**	30
	Morfa colliery explosion.		
1871	Jan. 10	**Chesterfield, England**	26
	Reinishaw Park colliery exploded.		
	Feb. 24	**Pontypridd, South Wales**	38
	Pentre colliery exploded.		
	Aug. 14	**Pittston, Pennsylvania**	17
	The Eagle Shaft mine fire; flames instantly rushed from the shaft to the height of 200 ft. above the surface.		
	Sept. 6	**Wigan, England**	70
	Ince Moss colliery exploded.		
	Sept. 27	**Grisons, Switzerland**	30
	Colliery explosion.		
	Oct. 25	**Durham, England**	30
	Colliery exploded.		
	Nov. 9	**St. Etienne, France**	50
	Seaham colliery exploded.		
1872	Mar. 28	**Atherton, England**	27
	Lovers' Lane colliery explosion.		
	Oct. 7	**Yorkshire, England**	34
	Morley colliery disaster caused by carelessness and poor discipline.		
	Nov. 8	**Montceax, France**	38
	Colliery exploded.		
	Nov. 8	**Mambourg, England**	21
	Coal pit exploded when machine broke.		
	Nov. 14	**Walsall, England**	22
	Pelsall-Hall disaster caused by influx of water from an old-working.		
1873	Feb. 18	**North Staffordshire, England**	20
	Explosion at Talke colliery.		
	May 13	**Nova Scotia**	75
	Explosion and fire at Drummond colliery.		
	June 10	**Shamokin, Pennsylvania**	10
	Henry Clay mine exploded by carburetted hydrogen gas.		
1874	Apr. 19	**Dunkinfield, England**	54
	Astley Pit explosion caused by gross ignorance.		
	Nov. 20	**Rotherham, England**	23
	Warren colliery explosion caused by naked lights.		
1875	Aug. 30	**Kidsgrove, England**	43
	Explosion at Bunker's Hill caused by a gunpowder fuze.		
	Dec. 4	**New Tredegar, England**	22
	Powell Duffryn pit exploded.		
	Dec. 6	**Barnsley, England**	140
	Swaithe Main colliery exploded.		
	Dec. 14	**Mons, Belgium**	110
	Explosion at a Frameries colliery near city.		
1876	Feb. 4	**St. Etienne, France**	30
	Jabin Pit colliery exploded.		
	May 20	**Coalfield, Virginia**	8
	Midlothian mine exploded.		
	July 24	**Nortonville, California**	6
	Black Diamond mine exploded.		
1877	Feb. 14	**Graissessac, France**	55
	Graissessac mine exploded by firedamp.		
	Mar. 8	**Swansea, England**	19
	Worchester New colliery exploded.		
	May 9	**Wadesville, Pennsylvania**	7
	Wadesville mine exploded by carburetted hydrogen gas.		
	Oct. 11	**Lancashire, England**	36
	Pemberton colliery exploded.		
	Oct. 22	**Lanarkshire, Scotland**	207
	Blantyre colliery exploded.		
1878	Mar. 9	**Kersley, England**	43
	Unity Brook colliery exploded.		
	June 7	**Haydock, England**	189
	Wood Pit colliery exploded.		
	Sept. 11	**Abercarn, Wales**	268
	Ebbw Vale colliery exploded leaving 119 survivors.		
	Nov. 21	**Sullivan, Indiana**	8
	Sullivan mine exploded.		
1879	Jan. 13	**Pontypridd, Wales**	63
	Dinas Middle Pit in the Rhondda Valley exploded.		
	May 6	**Audenried, Pennsylvania**	6
	Audenried mine exploded by carburetted hydrogen gas.		
	July 2	**Lanarkshire, Scotland**	28
	High Blantyre mine exploded.		
1880	Jan. 21	**Newcastle-under-Lyne, England**	62
	Leycett mine caved in.		
	Mar. 5	**Nanticoke, Pennsylvania**	6
	Nanticoke mine No. 2 exploded by carburetted hydrogen gas.		
	Apr. 1	**Anderlaus, France**	20
	Colliery explosion.		
	July 15	**Risca, Wales**	120
	Black Vien colliery exploded.		
	†Sept. 8	**Sunderland, England**	161
	Seaham colliery exploded.		

Year	Date	Place	Deaths	Description
	Dec. 10	Penygraig, South Wales	101	Great explosion at Navy Steam Coal Mine; few survivors.
1881	Feb. 7	Tunstall, England	25	Whitfield colliery near Shell exploded.
	Mar. 4	Almy, Wyoming	38	Almy mine exploded.
	Dec. 9	Cockerell, Belgium	66	Cockerell colliery exploded.
	Dec. 19	Wigan, England	48	Abram colliery exploded.
1882	Feb. 3	Coalfield, Virginia	32	Midlothian mine again exploded.
	Feb. 16	Trimdon Grange, England	68	Trimdon Grange colliery exploded.
	Apr. 18	Durham, England	37	Tudhoe colliery at Weardale exploded.
	May 2	Atherstone, England	32	Baddesley colliery explosion.
	May 24	Shenandoah, Pennsylvania	5	Kohinoor mine exploded by carburetted hydrogen gas.
	Nov. 7	Claycross, England	45	Park House pit exploded.
1883	Jan. 9	Coulterville, Illinois	10	Coulterville mine exploded.
	Feb. 16	Braidwood, Illinois	69	Coal mine flooded; all drowned.
	June 23	Australia	22	Creswick gold mine exploded.
	Nov. 7	Altham, England	68	Moorfield colliery near Aeerington exploded.
1884	Feb. 20	West Leisenring, Pennsylvania	19	West Leisenring mine exploded.
	†Feb. 24	Crested Butte, Colorado	59	Coal mine exploded at Crested Butte.
	†Mar. 13	Pocahontas, Virginia	112-150	Laurel mine explosion ignited by open lamp.
	Oct. 27	Uniontown, Pennsylvania	14	Youngstown mine exploded.
1885	Mar. 2	Durham, England	42	Usworth mine exploded.
	Mar. 6	Karwin, Poland	53	Count Larish's mines exploded.
	Mar. 17	Camphausen, Germany	140	Mine near Saarbruck exploded.
	June 4	Saarbrueken, Germany	17	Fire damp in a coal pit.
	June 18	Lancashire, England	178	Mine near Clifton Hall colliery exploded at 9:30 A.M.
	Oct. 21	Plymouth, Pennsylvania	6	Plymouth mine No. 2 exploded.
	Dec. 23	Pontypridd, South Wales	81	Two hundred entombed at Mardy colliery.
1886	Jan. 12	Almy, Wyoming	13	Almy mine No. 2 exploded.
	Jan. 21	Newburg, West Virginia	39	Newburg mine exploded.
	Mar. 8	Dunbar, Pennsylvania	6	Uniondale mine exploded.
	Aug. 30	Scranton, Pennsylvania	6	Fair Lawn mine exploded by carburetted hydrogen gas.
	Sept. 24	Schalke, Germany	45	Mine in Westphalia exploded.
	Oct. 2	Altofts, England	22	Pope and Pearson's colliery near Wakefield exploded.
	Nov. 26	Wilkes-Barre, Pennsylvania	12	Conyagham mine exploded by carburetted hydrogen gas.
	Dec. 2	Fence Houses, England	28	Elemore colliery exploded.
1887	Feb. 18	Pontypridd, Wales	39	National colliery exploded.
	Mar. 1	Belgium	69	Chateus Pit in the Beanbryn collieries exploded.
	Mar. 5	Mous, Belgium	130	La Boule Quaregnon colliery exploded.
	Mar. 23	Bulli, Australia	85	Accumulation of gas was ignited by shot firing and caused explosion. A bitter strike had just been settled and many inexperienced miners were on duty.
	Apr. 4	Savannah, Oklahoma	18	Old Savannah mine No. 2 exploded.
	May 4	Vancouver Island	170	Victoria colliery at Nanaimo caught fire; all entombed.
	May 28	Lanarkshire, Scotland	73	Udston colliery exploded.
	June 4	Dour, France	34	Escouffiax coal mine exploded.
	June 8	Geisenkirchener, Prussia	60	Hibernia colliery exploded.
1888	Feb. 16	Camphausen, Germany	40	Kreuzgraben coal mine exploded.
	Mar. 29	Rich Hill, Missouri	24	Keith and Perry mine No. 6 exploded due to gas accumulation and careless inspection.
	Apr. 19	Cumberland, England	30	St. Helen's colliery exploded.
	June 4	Vancouver Island	76	Wellington collieries exploded.
	Nov. 3	Clinton County, Pennsylvania	17	Kettle Creek mine exploded.
	Nov. 3	Aueyron, France	40	Colliery exploded near city.
	Nov. 4	Cransac, France	80	Fire damp at the Mines of Campagnae.
	Nov. 9	Frontenac, Kansas	40	Shaft No. 2 exploded due to ignition of gas that came in contact with other explosive properties.
	Nov. 13	Dour, Belgium	21	Mine explosion.
1889	Jan. 3	Esperanza, Spain	27	Esperanza colliery exploded from fire damp.
	Jan. 18	Cheshire, England	23	Hyde colliery exploded.
	Mar. 13	Wrexham, North Wales	20	Pendwn Pit colliery exploded.
	July 3	St. Etienne, France	184	Verpilleux mine explosion caused by fire damp.
	Sept. 5	Penicuik, England	63	Mauricewood colliery caught fire; 2 escaped.
	Oct. 16	Longton, England	64	Mossfields colliery exploded.
1890	Feb. 1	Plymouth, Pennsylvania	8	Nottingham mine exploded due to carburetted hydrogen gas.
	Feb. 6	Monmouthshire, Wales	176	Lianerch colliery near Abersychan exploded; 26,000 lbs. collected.
	Feb. 18	Nievre, France	44	Colliery at Decize exploded.
	Mar. 10	Port Talbot, South Wales	87	Morfa colliery exploded.

Date		Place	Deaths
	May 15	**Ashley, Pennsylvania**	**26**
	Jersey mine No. 8 exploded due to lit naked lamp in the presence of gas.		
	July 29	**St. Etienne, South France**	**109**
	Pelissier mine exploded.		
	Sept. 1	**Boryslaw, Austria-Hungary**	**80**
	Boiler exploded in mine; victims suffocated.		
	Sept. 12	**Stassfurt, Germany**	**20**
	Loederbury district's local mine exploded.		
	Sept. 15	**St. Wendel, Saarland**	**24**
	Maybach Pit colliery exploded.		
	Nov. 30	**Bohemia**	**87**
	Brux mine flooded.		
1891	**Jan. 5**	**Polish Ostrau**	**50**
	Count Wilezek's coal mines exploded.		
	Jan. 21	**Tchevotoneff, Russia**	**44**
	Tchevotoneff coal mine exploded.		
	Jan. 27	**Mount Pleasant, Pennsylvania**	**109**
	Coal mine exploded near Mammoth due to fire damp.		
	Feb. 22	**Nova Scotia**	**123**
	Springhill mines exploded.		
	May 22	**Pratt City, Alabama**	**11**
	Pratt No. 1 mine exploded from opened lamp near gas.		
	Sept. 20	**Forchies, Belgium**	**27**
	Monceau Fontaine mine exploded from fire damp.		
	Dec. 6	**St. Etienne, France**	**73**
	Mine explosion caused through fire damp.		
†1892	**Jan. 7**	**Krebs, Oklahoma**	**100**
	Mine No. 11 exploded due to early firing of shots.		
	Mar. 11	**Mons, Belgium**	**153**
	Anderlues colliery again exploded.		
	†May 10	**Roslyn, Washington**	**45**
	Roslyn mine exploded; naked lamps ignited gas.		
	Aug. 26	**Tondu, South Wales**	**112**
	North Park Slip colliery explosion.		
	Sept. 1	**Frameries, Belgium**	**25**
	Agrappe colliery exploded.		
1893	**Jan. 10**	**King, Colorado**	**27**
	Como mine exploded, caused by "a windy shot."		
	Feb. 17	**Mazarron, Spain**	**27**
	Impensada lead mine exploded; men suffocated.		
	Apr. 11	**Pontypridd, South Wales**	**63**
	Fire at the Great Western colliery in the Rhondda Valley.		
	July 4	**Dewsbury, England**	**139**
	Combs colliery exploded.		
	Aug. 20	**Dortmund, Germany**	**50**
	Fire damp caused mine explosion.		
1894	**June 23**	**Cilfynydd, South Wales**	**290**
	Explosion at Albion colliery, 3 miles from city.		
1895	**Jan. 14**	**No. Staffordshire, England**	**Scores**
	Diglake colliery flooded at Andley.		
	Feb. 4	**Zaborze**	**33**
	Fire damp explosion in the Queen Louise mine.		
	Feb. 27	**Cerillos, New Mexico**	**24**
	White Ash mine explosion caused by 2 men sent to take up track who ignited a body of standing gas which ignited coal dust.		
	†Mar. 20	**Red Canyon, Wyoming**	**62**
	Coal mine No. 5 explosion caused by a blown-out shot.		
	Apr. 18	**Lake Watcom, Washington**	**23**
	Blue Canyon mine exploded from a blast that ignited gas and dust.		
	June 10	**Upper Silesia**	**550**
	Antonien colliery caught fire; only 50 men survived.		
	July 25	**Bochum, Germany**	**33**
	Prinz von Preussen mine exploded.		
	Dec. 19	**Cumnock, North Carolina**	**39**
	Cumnock mine exploded from gas ignited by open lights.		
	Dec. 20	**Dayton, Tennessee**	**28**
	Nelson mine exploded from opened lights in "marked-out" rooms.		
1896	**Jan. 14**	**Mahrish-Ostrauv, Moravia**	**23**
	Hermengilde coal mine caught fire.		
	Jan. 27	**Ferndale, South Wales**	**57**
	Tylorstown colliery exploded.		
	†Feb. 18	**New Castle, Colorado**	**49**
	Vulcan mine explosion caused by an explosive placed on a lump of coal which blocked chute and covered a small quantity of dust and slack which set off gas.		
	Apr. 13	**Durham, England**	**20**
	Brancepeth colliery explosion.		
	Apr. 30	**Yorkshire, England**	**63**
	Micklefield colliery exploded. Relief fund started by Queen at £50—total 20,000 by Oct. 6.		
	June 28	**Pittston, Pennsylvania**	**58**
	Coal mine caved in.		
	Nov. 19	**Westphalia, Germany**	**25**
	Blumenthal colliery exploded.		
	Dec. 20	**Reschitza, Hungary**	**36**
	Reschitza colliery exploded.		
1898	**Mar. 17**	**Belmez, Spain**	**75**
	Sainte Isabelle mine exploded.		
	Apr. 19	**Leicestershire, England**	**35**
	A "gob" fire at Whitwick colliery.		
	July 16	**Morgenrot, Germany**	**24**
	Paulus colliery mine shaft rope broke; men fell 200 ft.		
1899	**Aug. 18**	**Pontyrhyl, Wales**	**21**
	Llest colliery exploded.		
	Dec. 9	**Carbonado, Washington**	**31**
	Carbon Hill mine No. 7 exploded due to ignition of a small quantity of gas by the forced rising of dust.		
†1900	**Mar. 6**	**Red Ash, West Virginia**	**46**
	Red Ash mine explosion caused by excess accumulation of dust.		
	†May 1	**Scofield, Utah**	**200**
	Winter Quarters No. 1 and 4 mines explosion caused by accidental explosion of black powder ignited by either a windy or a blown-out shot.		
	May 23	**Cumnock, North Carolina**	**23**
	Cumnock mine explosion believed caused by broken gauze in a safety lamp.		
1901	**Apr. 16**	**Johannesburg, South Africa**	**26**
	Geldenhuis Deep mine exploded.		
	May 24	**Senghenydd, Wales**	**81**
	Universal colliery exploded.		
	May 27	**Dayton, Ohio**	**20**
	Richland mine exploded by a blown-out shot at the head of a cross entry, followed by the explosion of a keg of powder.		
	Oct. 26	**Diamondville, Wyoming**	**22**
	Diamondville mine explosion occurred when gas was ignited while fighting a fire.		
1902	**Jan. 24**	**Oskaloosa, Iowa**	**20**
	Lost Creek mine No. 2 exploded by fire shot which ignited flammable gases.		
	May 19	**Coal Creek, Tennessee**	**184**
	Fraterville mine exploded by gas accumulated because of inadequate ventilation ignited by open lights.		
	May 23	**Ferme, British Columbia**	**150**
	Crow's Nest Pass colliery exploded.		

Date		Place	Deaths	
	†July 10	Johnstown, Pennsylvania	112	Rolling Mill mine exploded due to a worker who ignited gas by using his naked lamp for better light.
	July 31	New South Wales, Australia	95	Mt. Rembla coal mine exploded due to fire damp and coal dust. Australia's worst disaster; memorial service held annually.
†1903	June 30	Hanna, Wyoming	169	Hanna mine No. 1 exploded due to fire burning close to gas accumulated in the workings.
1904	Jan. 25	Cheswick, Pennsylvania	179	Harwick mine explosion entombed 179 men. Mr. S.N. Taylor, mining engineer, lost life during rescue.
†1905	Mar. 23	Virginia City, Alabama	112	Virginia City mine exploded due to windy shot in which too much dynamite was used.
	Mar. 10	Clydach Vale, Wales	33	Cambrian colliery explosion.
	†Mar. 18-19	Red Ash, Virginia	24	Rush Run and Red Ash mines exploded on 2 occasions; the second blast killed rescuers.
	†Apr. 3	Zeigler, Illinois	49	Zeigler mine exploded due to ignition of explosive gas.
	July 11	Wattstown, South Wales	119	Explosion in the National colliery.
	Dec. 2	Diamondville, Wyoming	18	Diamondville mine No. 1 dust explosion caused by a blown-out shot.
1906	Jan. 4	Coaldale, West Virginia	22	Coaldale mine explosion was the result of a keg of powder which exploded and inflamed the dust.
	Feb. 8	Parral, West Virginia	23	Parral mine explosion ignited by the opened light of a driver.
	Mar. 10	Courrieres, France	1,060	Explosion in the Courrieres coal mines, near Lens, in the Pas de Calais; worst in France's history.
	Mar. 22	Century, West Virginia	23	Century mine No. 1 explosion caused by a blown-out shot.
	Mar. 29	Nagasaki, Japan	250	Explosion in the Takashima coal mine.
	Oct. 3	Pocahontas, Virginia	36	Pocahontas mine explosion caused by a blown-out shot which ignited gas and dust.
	Oct. 14	Grange, England	25	Explosion at Wingate colliery; many injured.
1907	Jan. 23	Primero, Colorado	24	Primero mine explosion origin unknown.
	Jan. 28	Rhenish, Prussia	158	Reden colliery explosion.
	†Jan. 29	Stuart, West Virginia	84	Stuart mine explosion caused by an open light.
	Feb. 4	Thomas, West Virginia	25	Thomas mine No. 25 explosion caused by open lights.
	Sept. 8	Esperanza, Mexico	27	Explosions in the Esperanza mines caused by fire damp; many injured.
	Dec. 1	Fayette City, Pennsylvania	34	Naomi mine exploded due to fire damp augmented by coal dust.
	†Dec. 6	Monongah, West Virginia	362	Monongah mines No. 6 and 8 exploded by gas ignited by open lights or dust clouds ignited by electric arcs.
	†Dec. 16	Yolande, Alabama	57	Yolande mine No. 1 explosion started by gas ignited by an open lamp.
	†Dec. 19	Jacob's Creek, Pennsylvania	239	Darr mine explosion may have been caused by the projection of flames into a gaseous and dusty atmosphere or by an open light.
	Dec. 31	San Antonio, New Mexico	30	All entombed by explosion at the Cortage mines.
1908	Mar. 4	Staffordshire, England	26	Mine fire in the Hampstead colliery.
	Mar. 28	Hanna, Wyoming	59	Hanna mine No. 1 suffered from 2 explosions leaving 21 forever entombed.
	July 1	Jusovka, Russia	200	Great colliery explosion.
	Aug. 18	Wigan, England	75	Maypole colliery explosion.
	Nov. 11	Westphalia, Germany	360	Explosion of the Radbod mine.
	†Nov. 28	Marianna, Pennsylvania	154	Rachel and Agnes mine after a blown-out shot in the face of No. 3 Blanche entry.
	†Dec. 29	Switchbach, West Virginia	50	Lick Branch mine explosion was propagated by dust.
1909	Jan. 10	Zeigler, Illinois	26	Zeigler mine explosion started at south entry where a fire had previously raged.
	Jan. 12	Switchbach, West Virginia	67	Lick Branch mine explosion was caused by an overcharged shot which ignited the coal dust.
	Jan. 31	Primero, Colorado	149	Mine exploded while 150 men were working; one man rescued.
	Feb. 16	Durham, England	168	West Stanley colliery explosion.
	June 23	Wehrum, Pennsylvania	21	Lackawanna mine No. 4 disaster caused by a miner who planted 2 sticks of dynamite in a hole used the previous day and not cleaned of the coal dust.
	Oct. 29	Glamorgan, Wales	27	Darran mine explosion.
	†Nov. 13	Cherry, Illinois	259	Coal mine fire due to negligence.
†1910	Jan. 31	Primero, Colorado	75	Primero mine explosion; cause unknown.
	Feb. 1	Browder, Kentucky	34	Browder mine explosion was ignited by open lights and the explosion was spread by coal dust and kegs of black powder.
	Apr. 20	Mulga, Alabama	40	Mulga mine explosion propagated by dust.
	†May 5	Palos, Alabama	84	Palos mine No. 3 explosion ignited by an open flame on a body of gas.
	May 11	Whitehaven, England	136	Wellington colliery explosion.
	†Oct. 8	Starkville, Colorado	56	Starkville mine explosion caused by ignition of dust.
	Nov. 8	Delagua, Colorado	79	Victor American mine No. 3 explosion caused by fire in a crosscut.
	Dec. 21	Hulton, England	344	Number 3 Bank Pit colliery explosion.
1911	Jan. 20	Casimir, Russian Poland	40	Fire in colliery.
	Feb. 9	Trinidad, Colorado	17	Cokedale mine disaster was caused by a blown-out shot in a room, accentuated by the detonation of a sack of dynamite left near the face of the room, and propagated by coal dust.

Date		Place	Deaths
	Apr. 7	Throop, Pennsylvania	72
	Pancoast colliery caught fire; cause unknown.		
	†Apr. 8	Littleton, Alabama	128
	Banner mine explosion caused by propagation of gas.		
	Apr. 24	Elk Garden, West Virginia	23
	Ott mine No. 20 disaster started by a shot fired in the face of an air course had blown out, which ignited dust already stirred up by previous shots.		
	July 15	Sykesville, Pennsylvania	21
	Sykesville mine explosion originated at an entry face by ignition of gas and dust by the flame of a shot or by an open light.		
	Nov. 18	Vivian, West Virginia	18
	Bottom Creek mine explosion was ignited by the open lights of a survey party entering an abandoned room.		
	Dec. 9	Briceville, Tennessee	84
	Cross Mountain mine explosion caused by an open light.		
1912	Mar. 20	McCurtain, Oklahoma	73
	San Bois mine No. 2 explosion caused by the open lights of men waiting in the entry under direct charge of the foreman.		
	Mar. 26	Jed, West Virginia	83
	Jed mine explosion caused by miner's open light in a butt entry filled with gas.		
	July 9	Yorkshire, England	88
	Cadeby Main colliery blew up twice.		
	Aug. 13	Abernant, Alabama	18
	Abernant mine explosion was caused by the open light of a Negro laborer.		
1913	Apr. 23	Finleyville, Pennsylvania	98
	Cincinnati mine explosion started when a miner fired a shot that broke into a clay vein which liberated a gas blower.		
	May 17	Belle Valley, Ohio	15
	Noble mine explosion started when a new door was installed in the 8th entry which released gas upon naked lights.		
	Aug. 2	Tower City, Pennsylvania	20
	East Brookside mine explosion started by a cave-in which released gas with explosive force.		
	Aug. 5	Glasgow, Scotland	22
	Fire in mine.		
	Aug. 22	Bangalore, India	50
	Miners fell down shaft.		
	Oct. 14	Sengenhydd, Wales	439
	Explosion in the Universal colliery; 500 rescued.		
	†Oct. 22	Dawson, New Mexico	263
	Stag Canyon mine No. 2 disaster caused by overcharged shot.		
	Nov. 18	Acton, Alabama	24
	Acton mine No. 2 explosion originated from overcharged and blown-out shots of black powder.		
	Dec. 8	Rybnik, Poland	16
	All victims suffocated in Rybnik mine.		
	Dec. 16	New Castle, Colorado	37
	Vulcan mine explosion started by an open shot in a chute.		
1914	Jan. 20	Dortmund, Germany	22
	Fire damp caused explosion in mine.		
	Mar. 9	Ekaterinoslav, Russia	24
	Mine exploded.		
	†Apr. 28	Eccles, West Virginia	181
	Eccles mines No. 5 and 6 exploded due to open light near gas.		
	June 19	Lethbridge, Alberta	236
	Hill Crest Collieries, Ltd., mine No. 20 wrecked by explosion, many entombed.		
	July 28	Dortmund, Germany	15
	Fire raged through a pit.		
	Oct. 5	Mulga, Alabama	16
	Mulga mine explosion ignited by gas accumulation and an open light.		
	†Oct. 17	Royalton, Illinois	52
	North mine No. 1 explosion caused by a miner's open light.		
	Dec. 1	Hokkaido, Japan	437
	Mineral mine caught fire.		
1915	Feb. 6	Carlisle, West Virginia	21
	Carlisle mine explosion occurred when a door was left partly open all night which allowed gas to accumulate and a miner ignited it the following morning with an open light.		
	Feb. 9	South Wellington, British Columbia	21
	Victims drowned in colliery.		
	†Mar. 2	Layland, West Virginia	115
	Layland mine No. 3 disaster caused by poor ventilation and the absence of fire-bosses.		
	Apr. 13	Shimonoseki, Japan	236
	Coal mine explosion.		
	Aug. 31	Boswell, Pennsylvania	19
	Orenda mine explosion was ignited by a railroad car's sparks.		
	Nov. 9	Essen, Germany	9
	Kaiser Co. mine exploded.		
	Nov. 16	Ravensdale, Washington	31
	Northwestern mine exploded due to carelessness with smoking materials.		
	Nov. 30	Boomer, West Virginia	23
	Boomer mine No. 2 explosion ignited by gas from a pillar section exposed to open lights.		
1916	Feb. 11	Ernest, Pennsylvania	27
	Ernest mine No. 2 explosion ignited by open lights.		
	Nov. 14	Palos, Alabama	30
	Bessie mine explosion ignited by machinemen with open lights.		
	Dec. 13	Stone City, Kansas	20
	Fidelity mine No. 9 exploded when gas in a room face was ignited by an open light.		
†1917	Apr. 27	Hastings, Colorado	121
	Hastings mine disaster caused by a mine inspector who struck a match to relight his safety lamp.		
	†June 8	Butte, Montana	163
	Speculator metal mine exploded.		
	Aug. 4	Clay, Kentucky	62
	West Kentucky mine No. 7 explosion was ignited by an open light.		
	Nov. 29	Christopher, Illinois	17
	Old Ben mine No. 11 exploded when a pumpman ignited gas with an open light.		
1918	Jan. 12	Podmore Hall, England	155
	Minnie Pit colliery explosion.		
	Sept. 28	Royalton, Illinois	21
	North mine No. 1 exploded after a fire was thought to be under control but some flames escaped which ignited gas.		
1919	Apr. 29	Majestic, Alabama	22
	Majestic mine exploded after open lights ignited gas.		
	May 26	Moravia, Czechoslovakia	78
	Czechs attribute disaster to negligence.		
	June 5	Wilkes-Barre, Pennsylvania	92
	Coal powder explosion caused by powder kegs ignited in tunnel.		
	Sept. 18	Ovledo, Spain	19
	Mine fire; all men suffocated.		

Date		Place	Deaths
	Oct. 20	Cornwall, England	31
	Levant tin mine collapsed.		
1920	Mar. 11	Mexico City, Mexico	136
	El Bordo mine burned.		
	July 16	Sapporo, Japan	200
	Mine exploded.		
1921	Jan. 24	Oelsnitz	36
	Mine exploded at Saxony.		
	June 20	Berne, Switzerland	202
	Most Oenis mine exploded; many missing.		
	June 21	Westphalia, Germany	83
	Mine exploded in city.		
1922	Feb. 2	Gates, Pennsylvania	25
	Gates mine No. 2 explosion caused by the use of a nonpermissible single-shot blasting magneto.		
	Apr. 30	Transylvania, Rumania	100
	Great explosion in mine.		
	Sept. 5	Whitehaven, England	39
	Haig colliery explosion.		
	Nov. 6	Spangler, Pennsylvania	77
	Reilly mine No. 1 explosion caused by a miner's open light.		
	Nov. 22	Dolomite, Alabama	90
	Dolomite mine No. 3 explosion was ignited by an arc from a 3,300-volt armored cable.		
1923	Feb. 8	Dawson, New Mexico	120
	Stagg mine No. 1 explosion set off by trolley and feed wires which caused arcs to touch dust dislodged from timbers.		
	Feb. 9	Cumberland, British Columbia	33
	Mine exploded.		
	Feb. 10	Beuthen, Silesia	176
	More than 600 miners entombed; many unaccounted for to this day.		
	July 28	Yorkshire, England	27
	Maltby colliery explosion.		
	†Aug. 14	Kemmerer, Wyoming	99
	Frontier mine No. 1 explosion occurred when a fire boss attempted to relight his flame safety lamp with a match.		
	Sept. 23	Dombrova, Poland	110
	Reden coal mine exploded followed by fire.		
	Sept. 25	Falkirk, Scotland	40
	Redding mine flooded; 1 escaped.		
	Nov. 6	Beckley, West Virginia	27
	Glen Rogers mine explosion caused by an arc from an electric drill.		
1924	Jan. 25	Johnston City, Illinois	33
	McClintock mine exploded as a result of open lights used by trackmen.		
	Jan. 26	Shanktown, Pennsylvania	`36
	Lancashire mine No. 18 exploded when a "flameproof" mining machine ignited gas.		
	†Mar. 8	Castle Gate, Utah	173
	Castle Gate mine No. 2 explosion caused by a cap lamp being relit.		
	Mar. 28	Yukon, West Virginia	26
	Yukon mine No. 2 exploded when 3 miners set off gas with their open lights.		
	†Apr. 28	Benwood, West Virginia	119
	Benwood mine disaster caused by accidental ignition of gas.		
	Aug. 11	Fukushima Province, Japan	72
	Gas explosion in coal mine.		
	Sept. 16	Sublet, Wyoming	39
	Sublet mine No. 5 explosion caused by the ignition of gas by an arc from a locomotive trolley.		
1925	Feb. 11	Dortmund, Germany	121
	Mine exploded; 200 entombed, many missing.		
	†Feb. 20	Sullivan, Indiana	52
	City mine exploded from open lights; propagated by coal dust.		
	Mar. 17	Barrackville, West Virginia	33
	Barrackville mine No. 41 exploded after a door was left open which allowed gas to accumulate.		
	Mar. 26	Lorraine, France	50
	Mine elevator cable broke; mine boycotted after disaster.		
	Mar. 30	Northumberland, England	38
	Explosion at Montague colliery; all victims entombed.		
	May 27	Farmville, North Carolina	53
	Carolina mine explosion caused by overcharged shot of explosive.		
	Sept. 4	Pingyang, Korea	150
	Teihaku coal mine exploded.		
	Oct. 16	Faunsdorf, Austria	100s
	Cave in of an elevator shaft buried victims.		
	Dec. 10	Irondale, Alabama	53
	Overton mine No. 2 exploded due to carried carbide lights.		
†1926	Jan. 13	Wilburton, Oklahoma	92
	No. 21 mine exploded when gas was lit by an open light.		
	Jan. 14	Farmington, West Virginia	19
	Jamison mine No. 8 explosion caused by an open light.		
	Jan. 29	Helena, Alabama	27
	Mossboro mine No. 1 exploded when blown-out shots raised and ignited coal dust.		
	Feb. 3	Horning, Pennsylvania	20
	Horning mine No. 4 exploded from the sudden increase of gas.		
	Mar. 8	Eccles, West Virginia	19
	Eccles mine No. 5 explosion was ignited by an arc from the controller of a cutting machine as it was brought to the face.		
	Aug. 26	Clymer, Pennsylvania	44
	Clymer mine No. 1 exploded when gas had accumulated in places ventilated by a blower fan when a door was left open and lighted by an electric arc from a trolley wire.		
	Aug. 28	Burma, India	20
	Tiger Camp mine had landslide; many injured.		
	Oct. 4	Rockwood, Tennessee	27
	Rockwood mine exploded when gas came into contact with open lights.		
	Oct. 9	Dannhauser, Africa	118
	Durham Navigation colliery exploded; 154 entombed.		
	Dec. 9	Francisco, Indiana	37
	Francisco mine No. 2 exploded due to unreported accumulation of gas.		
1927	Mar. 1	Commonwealth, Wales	52
	Mine shaft explosion entombed victims; King and Queen sent messages of condolence.		
	Apr. 18	Hainault, Belgium	21
	Levan De Mons mine exploded.		
	Apr. 30	Everettville, West Virginia	97
	Federal mine No. 3 explosion was caused by gas and dust.		
1928	Jan. 9	West Frankfort, Illinois	21
	No. 18 mine explosion caused by lack of line curtains which led to the accumulation of gas.		
	Jan. 30	Sawaroso, Java	35
	Victims suffocated in coal mine fire.		
	Feb. 11	Ontario, Canada	39
	Hollinger Consolidated Gold mine caught fire.		

Date		Place	Deaths
	†May 19	**Mather, Pennsylvania**	**195**
	Mather mine No. 1 explosion started by an arc from a non-permissible storage battery locomotive.		
	June 30	**St. Entienne, France**	**51**
	Gas explosion followed by fire in mine.		
	Dec. 9	**Mirocchio Lake, Peru**	**26**
	Mirocchio mine exploded.		
1929	**Jan. 26**	**Liaoyang, Manchuria**	**103**
	Explosion in mine near city.		
	†Mar. 21	**Parnassus, Pennsylvania**	**46**
	Kinlock mine explosion was ignited by an electric arc from open electric equipment.		
	Mar. 31	**Brussels, Belgium**	**23**
	Mine exploded; many injured.		
	Sept. 14	**Belgrade, Yugoslavia**	**20**
	Mine exploded; many injured.		
	Sept. 19	**Saarbruecken, Germany**	**23**
	Coal mine explosion.		
	Dec. 17	**McAlester, Oklahoma**	**61**
	Old Town mine explosion originated from a lit cigarette.		
1930	**Feb. 6**	**Standardville, Utah**	**23**
	Standard mine explosion caused by open doors.		
	Feb. 22	**Northburg, Germany**	**31**
	Eschweiler mine exploded from fire damp.		
	July 10	**Neurode, Germany**	**99**
	Gas explosion at Wenceslaus mine.		
	Aug. 15	**Princeton, British Columbia**	**41**
	Blakeburn mine of Coalmont Coal Co. exploded and entombed 46.		
	Oct. 21	**Alsdorf, Germany**	**256**
	Great mine blast; cause remained mystery.		
	Oct. 25	**Saarbruecken, Germany**	**92**
	Maybach colliery exploded; 36 hurt.		
	Oct. 27	**McAlester, Oklahoma**	**30**
	Wheatley mine No. 4 exploded after explosive gas had accumulated in the face of a crosscut when a line curtain was removed while coal was loaded out.		
	Nov. 5	**Millfield, Ohio**	**82**
	No. 6 mine exploded from gas and dust.		
1931	**Jan. 28**	**Dugger, Indiana**	**28**
	Little Betty mine explosion caused by open lights.		
	Jan. 29	**Whitehaven, England**	**27**
	Explosion at Haig colliery 2 miles off coast under sea.		
	Feb. 12	**Manchuria, China**	**3,000**
	Fire in the Fushun coal mines; all deaths denied but confirmed by Chinese papers two days after disaster.		
	Nov. 20	**Yorkshire, England**	**45**
	Bentley colliery blast trapped many.		
1932	**Feb. 8**	**Charleroi, Belgium**	**20**
	Mine blast; 22 rescued.		
	Feb. 27	**Boissevain, Virginia**	**38**
	Boissevain mine explosion caused by ignition of dust from windy shots.		
	Aug. 6	**Hokkaido, Japan**	**57**
	Mine exploded.		
	Nov. 12	**Lancashire, England**	**27**
	Garwood Hall colliery explosion; some injured.		
	Dec. 9	**Yancy, Kentucky**	**23**
	Zero mine explosion caused by an open shot.		
	Dec. 24	**Moweagua, Ill.**	**54**
	Moweagua mine explosion was caused when a circuit breaker blew out after the starting whistle sounded.		
1933	**June 3**	**Sakito, Japan**	**46**
	Coal mine explosion left 30 injured.		
1934	**Aug. 6**	**Big Stone Gap, Virginia**	**17**
	Derby mine No. 3 explosion caused by the ignition of dust.		
	Sept. 22	**Wrexham, Wales**	**265**
	Gresford colliery suffered great blast; Crown sent sympathy.		
1935	**Jan. 21**	**Gilberton, Pennsylvania**	**13**
	Gilberton colliery disaster caused by flame safety lamps being used by untrained miners.		
	May 13	**Tsinan, Shantung, China**	**400**
	Stream flooded mine shaft; troops sent in to stop riot by relatives.		
	July 14	**Fukuoka, Japan**	**63**
	Mitsui mine explosion entombed victims.		
	July 25	**Calcutta, India**	**33**
	Mine explosion; 43 injured.		
	Oct. 26	**Kiushiu Island, Japan**	**83**
	Mine explosion near Fukuoka trapped 120.		
1936	**Jan. 31**	**Jharia, India**	**37**
	Loyabad colliery exploded; fire followed.		
	June 20	**Kukuoka, Japan**	**31**
	Gas explosion in mine.		
	Aug. 6	**Yorkshire, England**	**58**
	Woodmoor colliery explosion left many lost; 9 rescue squads sent in to search.		
	Aug. 31	**Bochum, Westphalia, Germany**	**20**
	Explosion left many injured.		
	Oct. 3	**LaBouverie, Belgium**	**19**
	Mine explosion; 30 injured.		
	Oct. 12	**Fukuoka Prefecture, Japan**	**19**
	Gas explosion in mine.		
1937	**Mar. 19**	**Johannesburg, South Africa**	**39**
	Gas blast in mine outside city.		
	July 2	**Staffordshire, England**	**30**
	Holditch colliery explosion.		
	July 15	**Sullivan, Indiana**	**20**
	Baker mine exploded as a result of ignition of gas by carbide lights.		
	Sept. 6	**Sofia, Bulgaria**	**40**
	Gas explosion in mine near city.		
	Oct. 15	**Woodward, Alabama**	**34**
	Mulga mine exploded when dust was ignited.		
	Nov. 11	**Tsumakoi, Japan**	**100s**
	Sulfur mine had 2 of 4 shafts flooded; 950 unaccounted for.		
1938	**Mar. 13**	**Singareni, India**	**147**
	Fire in the coal fields; many injured.		
	Apr. 22	**Hanger, Virginia**	**45**
	Keen Mountain mine exploded when fired adobe shots ignited dust.		
	May 10	**Markham, England**	**79**
	Gas explosion in mine; 40 injured.		
	Oct. 6	**Yubari, Hokkaido, Japan**	**151**
	Coal mine exploded.		
1939	**Jan. 22**	**Fukuoda, Japan**	**92**
	Onura mine blast left many missing.		
	June 23	**Johannesburg, South Africa**	**24**
	Elevator broke; 20 injured.		
	July 14	**Providence, Kentucky**	**28**
	Duvin mine exploded when coal dust was ignited by an explosive blast.		
	Oct. 2	**Palau, Mexico**	**69**
	Coal gas blast in mine.		
	Oct. 7	**St. Etienne, France**	**37**
	Mine exploded.		
	Oct. 28	**Fife, Scotland**	**35**
	Valleyfield colliery explosion.		
	Nov. 10	**Morioka, Japan**	**34**
	Fumes trapped over 200 in mine.		

Date		Place	Deaths
1940	**Jan. 10**	**Bartley, West Virginia**	**91**
	Pond Creek mine No. 1 exploded when an electric arc started an ignition.		
	Feb. 28	**Istria Province, Italy**	**60**
	Arsa coal mine explosion left 100 injured.		
	†Mar. 16	**Neffs, Ohio**	**72**
	Willow Grove mine No. 10 exploded as a result of an overcharged shot of pellet black.		
	Mar. 29	**Tsingtsing, China**	**204**
	Mine blast in West Hopeh Province left 159 injured.		
	Apr. 27	**Black Sea Coast, Turkey**	**37**
	Coal mine explosion off the coast.		
	May 26	**Kokura, Japan**	**40**
	Coal mine explosion buried victims.		
	†July 15	**Portage, Pennsylvania**	**63**
	Sonman East mine explosion was ignited by a collapsing roof.		
	Sept. 12	**Oita, Japan**	**50**
	Mitsubishi Mining Co. coal mine exploded.		
	Nov. 29	**Cadiz, Ohio**	**31**
	Nelms mine blew up when an arc from a non-permissible drill ignited gas and coal dust.		
	Dec. 15	**Northern Bucharest, Rumania**	**51**
	Mine blast trapped 200.		
1941	**July 29**	**Yorkshire, England**	**20**
	Grigglestone colliery exploded.		
	Oct. 27	**Daniel Boone, Kentucky**	**15**
	Daniel Boone mine explosion caused by smoking.		
	Nov. 3	**Nordegg, Alberta, Canada**	**27**
	Coal mine explosion; 4 bodies recovered.		
1942	**Jan. 1**	**Staffordshire, England**	**57**
	Sneyd colliery exploded.		
	Jan. 27	**Mount Harris, Colorado**	**34**
	Wadge mine exploded due to poor ventilation.		
	Apr. 26	**Honkeiko, Manchuria**	**1,549**
	Worst colliery explosion in history.		
	May 12	**Osage, West Virginia**	**56**
	Christopher mine No. 3 explosion was caused by an arc in the control box of a cutting machine.		
	July 9	**Pursglove, West Virginia**	**20**
	Pursglove mine No. 2 disaster caused by a fall of roof rock.		
†1943	**Feb. 27**	**Washoe, Montana**	**74**
	Smith mine explosion orginated by the ignition of an explosive mixture of gas by an open light in the face region of the mine.		
	†Aug. 28-29	**Sayreton, Alabama**	**28**
	Sayreton mine No. 2 explosion ignited by an arc from the controller of a combination trolley and cable-reel locomotive.		
1944	**Mar. 24-25**	**Lumberport, West Virginia**	**16**
	Katherine mine No. 4 exploded from a series of fires.		
	July 5	**Bellaire, Ohio**	**66**
	Powhatan coal mine caught fire and was sealed.		
1945	**May 9**	**Sunnyside, Utah**	**23**
	Sunnyside mine No. 1 exploded when coal dust was raised and ignited.		
	Sept. 13	**Vryheid, South Africa**	**52**
	Mine exploded; 14 injured.		
	Dec. 26	**Fourmile, Kentucky**	**25**
	Belva mine No. 1 explosion caused by a man smoking.		
1946	**May 8**	**Dampremy, Belgium**	**21**
	Mine blast outside city.		
1947	**Mar. 25**	**Centralia, Illinois**	**111**
	Centralia mine No. 5 explosion caused by an underburdened shot which ignited dust.		
	Aug. 15	**Whitehaven, Cumberland, England**	**104**
	William mine exploded; 2 police dogs used to search for missing bodies.		
	Aug. 22	**Durham, England**	**20**
	Morrison North mine exploded.		
1948	**Mar. 14**	**Trieste Territory, Yugoslavia**	**71**
	Racha coal mine exploded.		
	Apr. 17	**Aguas Caliente, Peru**	**41**
	Copper mine exploded.		
	Apr. 20	**Sallaumines, France**	**13**
	Coal mine explosion caused 130,000 French miners to strike for better safety regulations.		
1949	**Oct. 19**	**Oberschlema, Germany**	**100**
	Flood in mine.		
	Nov. 6	**Zwickau, Germany**	**70**
	Uranium mine exploded.		
	Nov. 17	**Goa, India**	**40**
	Landslide in manganese mine.		
	Nov. 29	**Johanngeorgenstadt. East Germany**	**—**
	Berlin Telegraf reported 2,300 miners killed in uranium mine blast; U.S.S.R. denied report and claimed only 1 death but on Dec. 5 the Leipzig fire brigade chief reported 3,700 dead.		
1950	**May 20**	**Gelsenkirchen, Germany**	**55**
	Belgian owned mine exploded from coal dust.		
	Sept. 26	**Derbyshire, England**	**80**
	Creswell colliery caught fire.		
1951	**Jan. 2**	**Tatabanya, Hungary**	**81**
	Mine explosion in the West.		
	May 29	**Durham, England**	**81**
	Easington coal mine explosion.		
	†Dec. 21	**West Frankfort, Illinois**	**119**
	New Orient mine No. 2 disaster caused by smoking.		
1952	**Jan. 13**	**Stellarton, Nova Scotia**	**19**
	MacGregor coal mine exploded.		
	Apr. 19	**Zwickau, East Germany**	**47**
	Coal mine exploded.		
	July 28	**Yeungsham, China**	**140**
	Wolfram mine blast.		
	Dec. 15	**Camarines, Philippines**	**49**
	Marsman gold mine flooded.		
1953	**Feb. 1**	**Oberschlema, East Germany**	**22**
	Uranium mine flooded.		
	Apr. 25	**Angangueo, Mexico**	**33**
	American Smelting and Refining silver and zinc mine caved in.		
	Oct. 24	**Seraing, Belgium**	**26**
	Gas explosion at the Charbonnages du Many coal mine.		
1954	**Mar. 25**	**Chorzow, Silesia, Poland**	**45**
	Coal mine explosion blamed on sabotage.		
	Aug. 31	**Kushiro, Japan**	**34**
	Taiheto coal mine exploded.		
	Nov. 13	**Farmington, West Virginia**	**15**
	Explosion of methane gas at the Jamison Coal & Coke mine.		
	Dec. 11	**Parasia, India**	**64**
	Mine flooded and caved in.		
1955	**Jan. 24**	**Zonguldak, Turkey**	**39**
	Underground coal mine explosion.		
	Feb. 6	**Bihar State, India**	**55**
	Coal mine explosion 100 mi. west of Calcutta.		
	Mar. 22	**Morgnano, Italy**	**24**
	Coal mine exploded.		
	Apr. 21	**Minas Gerais State, Argentina**	**30**
	A 40-ft. deep trench collapsed on victims who attempted to dig a gold mine at a place where a nugget had been found.		

Date		Place	Deaths
	July 16	**Niedershlema, East Germany**	**33**
	Uranium mine caught fire.		
	Aug. 3	**Gelsenkirchen, West Germany**	**40**
	Dust explosion killed Ruhr miners in the Dahlbusch coal mine.		
	Nov. 1	**Akahira, Hokkaido, Japan**	**60**
	Coal mine exploded outside city.		
1956	**Mar. 2**	**Motize, Mozambique**	**34**
	Coal mine exploded.		
	†Aug. 8	**Marcinelle, Belgium**	**270**
	Casier du Bois coal mine caught fire; worst mine disaster in Belgian history.		
	Aug. 27	**Upper Silesia, Poland**	**29**
	Mine fire; victims were gas poisoned.		
	Nov. 1	**Springhill, Nova Scotia**	**38**
	Cumberland Ry. & Coal Co.'s mine No. 4 exploded.		
†1957	**Feb. 4**	**Bishop, West Virginia**	**37**
	No. 34 mine explosion was caused by non-permissible conditions and poor ventilation.		
	Nov. 19	**Muirkirk, Scotland**	**17**
	Kames colliery exploded.		
	Nov. 25	**Yawata, Kyushu, Japan**	**18**
	Higashi Nakazaru colliery flooded after a dynamite charge.		
†1958	**Feb. 19**	**Asansol, India**	**181**
	Explosion in one mine caused 2 others to be flooded; entire crew trapped.		
	May 7	**Nagasaki, Japan**	**29**
	Coal mine flooded.		
	Aug. 28	**Zabreze, Poland**	**72**
	Coal mine fire caused by the "murderous negligence" of 2 mine workers.		
	Oct. 1	**Podvis, Yugoslavia**	**60**
	Coal mine fire started when a transformer exploded; worst mine disaster in Yugoslavia history.		
	†Oct. 23	**Springhill, Nova Scotia**	**74**
	Cumberland Rail & Coal Co.'s mine No. 2 exploded 4,000 ft. below ground level; some survivors were entombed 8 days.		
	Oct. 27	**McDowell County, West Virginia**	**22**
	Bishop mine No. 34 explosion caused by a blast that ignited a mixture of methane and air.		
1959	**Sept. 18**	**Lanarkshire, Scotland**	**47**
	Augengeich colliery caught fire when an electric exhaust fan burst into flames; worst mine disaster in Scottish history.		
	Nov. 25	**Szuesci, Hungary**	**31**
	Coal mine explosion.		
1960	**Jan. 21**	**Coalbrook, South Africa**	**417**
	Clydesdale colliery suffered a rock slide 515 ft. below the earth's surface; 440 miners were trapped.		
	Feb. 1	**Yubari, Hokkaido, Japan**	**32**
	Japanese coal mine exploded.		
	Feb. 22	**Zwickau, East Germany**	**49**
	Karl Marx coal mine exploded; many miners were trapped for days.		
	Mar. 8	**Logan, West Virginia**	**18**
	Island Creek Coal Co.'s Holden mine No. 22 caught fire.		
	May 22	**Ostrava, Czechoslovakia**	**54**
	Hlubina coal mine exploded.		
	June 28	**Abertillery, Wales**	**45**
	Six Bells colliery suffered an explosion and cave-in.		
	Sept. 20	**Kawasaki Machi, Japan**	**67**
	A Japanese coal mine exploded and was flooded.		
	Sept. 25	**Prague, Czechoslovakia**	**20**
	Mine fire outside city.		
1961	**Mar. 2**	**Terre Haute, Indiana**	**22**
	Viking Coal Corp.'s mine exploded.		
	Mar. 15	**Fukuoka, Japan**	**26**
	Yahata mine exploded.		
	July 8	**Dulna Suce, Czechoslovakia**	**108**
	Gas explosion in coal mine.		
†1962	**Feb. 7**	**Volklingen, Germany**	**298**
	Luisenthal mine exploded; cause believed gas leakage.		
	Feb. 27	**Banovici, Yugoslavia**	**54**
	Country's largest lignite mine suffered 2 explosions.		
	Mar. 9	**Heessen, Westphalia, West Germany**	**31**
	Fire damp explosion in coal mine.		
	Mar. 22	**Hapton Valley, England**	**16**
	Mine blast left many injured.		
	Nov. 5	**Ny-Aalesund, Norway**	**21**
	King's Bay mine exploded.		
	†Dec. 6	**Carmichaels, Pennsylvania**	**37**
	U.S. Steel Corp.'s Robena mine No. 3 suffered an explosion 650 ft. underground.		
	Dec. 12	**Carletonville, South Africa**	**34**
	Driefontein gold mine collapsed; mine was considered world's richest gold mine in output and potential.		
1963	**Aug. 28**	**Moab, Utah**	**18**
	A severe explosion at a potash mine located ½-mile underground.		
	Oct. 24	**Broistedt, West Germany**	**29**
	Lengede iron mine collapsed and flooded.		
	Nov. 9	**Umuta, Japan**	**452**
	Mitsui Miiki coal mine disaster caused by leakage of coal gas.		
	Dec. 4	**Tatabanya, Hungary**	**26**
	Coal mine explosion.		
1964	**Feb. 9**	**Keelung, Formosa**	**17**
	Shui Kang mine exploded.		
	June 14	**Karkar, Afghanistan**	**74**
	Coal mine exploded.		
1965	**Feb. 2**	**Lens, France**	**21**
	Coal mine exploded.		
	Feb. 22	**Hokkaido, Japan**	**35**
	Mine suffered blast and cave-in.		
	Feb. 24	**Rumania**	**41**
	Uricani mines exploded.		
	Mar. 19	**Amasya, Turkey**	**68**
	Government-owned lignite mine had a series of gas explosions followed by fire.		
	Apr. 8	**Nagasaki, Japan**	**30**
	Mine exploded which set off cave-in.		
	†May 17	**Tonypandy, Wales**	**31**
	Mine, scheduled to be closed, exploded.		
	†May 28	**Dharbad, India**	**375**
	East India coal mine exploded; worst disaster in country's history for collieries.		
	†June 1	**Fukuoka, Japan**	**236**
	Yamano Coal Co. mine exploded due to gas leakage.		
	†June 7	**Kakanj, Yugoslavia**	**128**
	Coal mine had a methane gas explosion; country's worst mine disaster in 20 years.		
†1966	**Oct. 21**	**Aberfan, Wales**	**144**
	Landslide collapsed colliery, victims mostly children.		
1967	**Jan. 19**	**Greymouth, New Zealand**	**19**
	Underground dust mine exploded.		
	July 25	**Johannesburg, South Africa**	**50**
	Anglo-American Corp.'s Western Deep Levels gold mine lost 50 workers when they were shoved down a shaft when they attempted to escape the cold; most of the workers suffocated or were crushed to death.		
	Sept. 5	**Antofagasta, Chile**	**21**
	Chuguicamata copper mine exploded.		

Major Mine Disasters

Date		Place	Deaths
1968	Mar. 6	**Belle Isle, Louisiana**	21
	Cargill, Inc. salt mine caught fire; first salt mine fire since 1920.		
	Nov. 20	**Mannington, West Virginia**	78
	Mountaineer Coal Co. mine No. 9 exploded; investigators entered the mine 4 days later and found no trace of the 78 trapped men.		
1969	Mar. 31	**Barrotean, Mexico**	180
	Altos Hornos de Mexico mine had a gas explosion followed by fires; worst mining disaster in Mexican history.		
	July 7	**Juifang, Taiwan**	30
	Worst coal mine disaster in Taiwan history.		
1970	Mar. 15	**Breza, Yugoslavia**	38
	Coal mine explosion.		
	Apr. 5	**Ostrava, Czechoslovakia**	26
	Coal mine explosion.		
	June 6	**Sharig, Pakistan**	30
	Explosion devastated government operated mine.		
	Sept. 7	**Sorrange, West Pakistan**	24
	Gas explosion started cave-in which blocked pit entrance.		
	Sept. 24	**Zambia**	89
	Mufulira copper mine caved in; worst mine disaster in Zambia's history.		
	Dec. 30	**Wooton, Kentucky**	38
	Underground explosion at the Finley Coal Co. mine; the mine had been ordered shut in June.		
1971	May 16	**Sinjabi, West Pakistan**	32
	Coal mine exploded.		
	June 16	**Hunedoara, Rumania**	51
	Mine disaster occurred 150 mi. northwest of Bucharest.		
	Dec. 1	**Keelung, Taiwan**	48
	Seven Star mine explosion.		
1972	May 2	**Kellogg, Idaho**	91
	Sunshine Silver mine erupted viciously into a blaze; Sunshine officials called the disaster a "1 in 50 million shot."		
	†June 6	**Wankie, Rhodesia**	427
	Wankie colliery was destroyed with 3 gas explosions; 464 men were trapped.		
	Oct. 21	**Teheran, Iran**	34
	Underground explosion in coal mine.		
	Nov. 2	**Hokkaido, Japan**	31
	Methane gas explosion in coal mine.		
1973	Feb. 8	**Johannesburg, South Africa**	23
	Underground fire in the West Drien fontein gold mine.		
	Mar. 19	**Bihar, India**	47
	Jitpore colliery had a series of explosions caused by methane gas.		
1975	Nov. 3	**Figols, Spain**	27
	Gas explosion in coal mine.		
	Dec. 27	**India**	100s
	Blast at the Chasnala colliery in the Dhanpad region, 160 miles northwest of Calcutta.		

Miscellaneous Disasters

(† indicates entries profiled in General Narrative)

Date		Place	Deaths	
1843	Jan. 13	**Donegal, Ireland**	27	Mass drowning of fishermen by violent gale off coast.
	Jan. 15	**England**	80	Fishermen drowned in snowstorm off the Morne coast, in the County Down.
1844	Feb. 23-24	**Scarborough, England**	21	Heavy gales of wind from S.S.W. caused mass drownings.
	Mar. 31	**Flanitz, Balearic Is.**	404	Wall collapsed during Palm Sunday procession, 199 seriously injured.
	May	**Flers in the Orne, England**	20	Panic in church caused by false alarm crushed victims, 50 injured.
	Nov. 2	**Oldham, England**	21	Large factory collapsed, many injured.
1845	Apr. 7	**U.S., East**	60	Mass drowning when floating theatre capsized on the Hudson River.
	†Apr. 10	**Yarmouth, England**	250	Suspension bridge collapsed from weight of spectators gathered to see a clown in a boat pulled by geese.
	May 1	**Lyons, France**	20	Panic on bridge crushed & trampled victims.
	May 7	**Vienna**	30	Mass drowning when boat capsized near city.
1846	Jan. 3	**Zivelle, Holland**	15	Mass drowning when boat capsized.
	Apr. 4	**Werden, Germany**	45	Mass drowning after ferryboat upset.
	Nov. 3	**France**	23	Aurach overflowed, victims drowned.
1852	Dec. 25	**Holmfirth, England**	70	Reservoir burst in village.
1856	Apr. 3	**Island of Rhodes**	4,000	Lightning ignited powder vault in the Church of St. John.
1857	July 7	**Leghorn, Italy**	150	Small fire started stampede in the Theatre degli Aquidotti, over 300 injured and fire was rapidly put out.
1861	Feb. 24	**Yorkshire, England**	40	Laborers on the Rosedale railway sought shelter during most severe ice storm & froze to death at the Esklitt Huts over the moors.
1864	July 21	**Philadelphia, Pa.**	Scores	Walls collapsed on lunatics at Blockley Almshouse.
1865	July 14	**Zermat, Switzerland**	4	Mountain climbing disaster during the conquest of the Matterhorn.
1866	Sept. 14	**Johnstown, Pa.**	Scores	Crowd of 3,000, who waited for presidential train, collapsed bridge; many seriously injured.
1867	Sept. 6	**Chittenden, Vt.**	Scores	Temporary seats which held 8,000 collapsed at county fair, many injured.
1869	July 4	**Richmond, Va.**	Scores	Bridge collapsed during political rally, among victims was Col. James R. Branch, a strong Senate candidate.
1870	Jan. 27	**Liverpool, England**	21	Stampede started by a drunkard in St. Joseph's Catholic Church.
1876	Apr. 7	**Aberdeen, Scotland**	32	Mass drowning when overloaded ferryboat capsized on the River Dee.
1877	May 23	**Rockford, Ill.**	11	Winnebago County Courthouse collapsed.
	June 5	**England**	12	Witcombe Bridge collapsed on victims.
1878	June 29	**Schwelm, Germany**	27	Tunnel collapsed near city.
	Oct. 12	**Liverpool, England**	37	Stampede in the Coloseum Theatre when 4,000 people rushed for one exit during panic.
1880	Feb. 9	**Constantinople, Turkey**	200	Barracks 3 stories high collapsed at festival near city, all victims soldiers.
	†Sept. 17	**Ebro River, Spain**	275	Battalion of Spanish infantry drowned when their pontoon raft collapsed.
1883	Feb. 20	**New York City**	15	Panic among children caused stampede at the Sisters of Notre Dame School.
	†June 15	**Sunderland, England**	200	Panic caused stampede at Victoria Hall, victims children attending Sunday School. (SEE Victoria Hall)
	July 25	**Baltimore, Md.**	65	Pier on North Point, Tivoli, collapsed; worst disaster in this city since explosion of steamer *Medora*.
1884	Nov. 1	**Glasgow, Scotland**	14	Panic in the Star Theatre.
1885	June 12	**Thiers, France**	30	Spectators buried by collapse of roof upon leaving murder trial, at least 100 injured.
1887	Jan. 18	**London, England**	17	Panic in the Spitalsfield's Theatre.
	July 1	**Austria**	200	Ferryboat capsized, mass drowning of pilgrims.
	†July 10	**Zug, Switzerland**	70	New $80,000 dam burst; damage in millions of francs.
1888	Apr. 4	**Zelya, Mexico**	18	Panic & stampede when bull ring tent burned.
	Aug. 11	**Valparaiso, Panama**	70	Mena Reservoir burst, damage over $8 million.
1889	Nov. 1	**Glasgow, Scotland**	50	Building fell on the Templeton's Carpet Factory.
1890	July 10	**Osaka, Japan**	59	Mass drowning at vessel launching.
1891	Nov. 4	**Montana**	17	Cage fell in the Anaconda Mine.
1892	June 15	**Covington, Ky.**	20	Licking River Bridge collapsed, all victims workmen.
1893	June 9	**Washington, D.C.**	22	Floor in Ford's Theatre Bldg. fell on government clerks.
	June 22	**Borisoglebsk, Russia**	130	Panic & stampede in the church of Romano.
1895	Aug. 8	**New York City**	14	Ireland Bldg. collapsed, many indictments followed.
†1896	May 26	**Victoria, B.C.**	54	Streetcar wreck during celebration of Queen Victoria's birthday.
	Nov. 29	**Baroda, India**	29	Panic & stampede during Viceroy's visit.
1898	Jan. 3	**London, Canada**	30	City Hall floor collapsed.
†1900	July 4	**Tacoma, Washington**	41	Streetcar went out of control.
1905	Mar. 18	**Santiago, Chile**	Scores	Lyric Theatre collapsed, many injured.

Date		Place	Deaths
	Apr. 7	**Madrid, Spain**	**100s**
	Water reservoir under construction collapsed on over 400 workmen, weak pillars were blamed.		
1913	**May 24**	**Long Beach, Calif.**	**35**
	Pier collapsed.		
	Aug. 7	**Germany**	**17**
	Boat capsized, all drowned.		
1917	**July 1**	**Niagara Falls, N.Y.**	**11**
	Car plunged into whirlpool rapids.		
	Aug. 8	**Greenland**	**90**
	Fishermen with 7 vessels lost in gale.		
	Aug. 12	**Cape Cod, Mass.**	**19**
	Fishermen drowned when dories capsized.		
	Aug. 19	**Dover, England**	**16**
	Streetcar accident left 40 injured.		
1918	**Feb. 28**	**China**	**730**
	Stands collapsed at races, victims women & children.		
	June 30	**Sioux City, Iowa**	**39**
	The Ruff building collapsed on victims.		
	Sept. 30	**Key West, Fla.**	**20**
	Sailors drowned when naval tender capsized.		
†1919	**Jan. 15**	**Boston, Mass.**	**21**
	Molasses flood.		
	June 15	**Tuscaloosa, Ala.**	**19**
	Mass drowning, gasoline launch capsized.		
1920	**Sept. 6**	**Globeville, Col.**	**10**
	Streetcar collision at city.		
1921	**Sept. 10**	**Chester, Pa.**	**21**
	Faulty iron plate collapsed bridge, many injured.		
1922	**Jan. 28**	**Washington, D.C.**	**107**
	Knickerbocker Theatre roof collapsed on audience, heavy accumulation of snow blamed.		
	June 11	**City Island, N.Y.**	**56**
	Mass drownings when gale swamped boats.		
	July 13	**Cairo, Egypt**	**14**
	Roof of mosque collapsed, 20 injured.		
	Nov. 19	**Gulf of California**	**60**
	Mass drowning when boat capsized at landing.		
1923	**Jan. 3**	**Kelso, Wash.**	**30**
	Mass drowning when bridge collapsed.		
	Jan. 24	**Berlin, Germany**	**15**
	Floor of the Tageblatt Bldg. collapsed.		
	Mar. 13	**China**	**22**
	Mass poisoning of rice, 5 cooks blamed.		
	Aug. 13	**Pyrenees Mt.**	**23**
	Motor coach loaded with tourists plunged down ravine near St. Sauveur.		
1924	**Apr. 2**	**Spain**	**20**
	Bridge collapsed over Guadalquivir River.		
	Oct. 19	**Athens, Greece**	**25**
	Stampede at theatre as result of false alarm, 18 injured.		
1925	**Mar. 7**	**Azov Sea**	**150**
	Russian fishermen lost when ice broke.		
	Apr. 1	**Germany**	**67**
	Pontoon bridge collapsed over Weser River, all victims soldiers.		
	May 23	**Breton, France**	**28**
	Mass drowning of fishermen in storm.		
	July 22	**Melbourne, Australia**	**15**
	Verandas of theatre collapsed, many injured.		
	Oct. 22	**Tanta, Egypt**	**54**
	Mass drowning when bridge parapet collapsed.		
1926	**Apr. 29**	**Russia**	**50**
	Mass drowning when temporary bridge collapsed.		
	Sept. 20	**Sundarbans, India**	**174**
	Mass drowning when native craft capsized in storm off coast of Bengal.		
1927	**Apr. 23**	**Japan**	**50**
	Mass drowning of fishermen when craft sank off Saghalien Is.		
	June 18	**Rosellon, Colombia**	**40**
	Textile plant collapsed on workers.		
	Aug. 9	**Shanghai, China**	**33**
	Open shelter collapsed, 150 injured.		
	Aug. 28	**Nanche, Mexico**	**20**
	Mass drowning of rebels.		
	Oct. 30	**Ireland**	**50**
	Mass drownings when gale struck fishing fleet.		
1928	**July 18**	**Germany**	**100**
	Mass drownings from heat wave on the Oder & Rhine rivers.		
	Sept. 9	**Monza, Italy**	**21**
	Autos went out of control at Grand Prix.		
	Oct. 9	**Prague, Czechoslovakia**	**36**
	Seven-story bldg. collapsed, 64 survivors buried over 30 hrs.		
	Oct. 18	**Vincennes, France**	**19**
	Apartment house collapsed, mass demonstrations followed.		
1929	**Sept. 20**	**Port Vallarta, Mexico**	**30**
	Mass drowning when storm smashed launch.		
1930	**Mar. 3**	**Warsaw, Poland**	**30**
	Mass drowning in Lake Narogzna.		
	Apr. 2	**Kyushu Is., Japan**	**81**
	Ferry capsized, many missing.		
	Apr. 21	**Cairo, Egypt**	**20**
	Boat capsized on Nile.		
	July 12	**Buenos Aires, Argentina**	**60**
	Trolley car plunged into Riacho River.		
	July 22	**Coblenz, Germany**	**40**
	Mass drowning during celebration of Rhineland liberation.		
	Aug. 16	**Belgrade, Yugoslavia**	**22**
	Boat capsized in River Drake.		
	Aug. 18	**Calcutta, India**	**32**
	Mass drowning when ferryboat upset.		
	Dec. 8	**Bombay, India**	**30**
	Poison lizard in soup fed to masses.		
1931	**Mar. 1**	**Valdivia, Chile**	**12**
	Band overturned their small launch on Lake Llanguihue.		
	Apr. 9	**Korea**	**125**
	Storm caused mass drownings of Japanese fishermen.		
	May 3	**Lindau, Germany**	**10**
	Squall capsized boat on Lake Constance.		
	June 3	**Libourne, France**	**15**
	Bridge collapsed near city when its cables were being tested.		
	Aug. 4	**Georgetown, S. Car.**	**22**
	Bus loaded with picnickers plunged into Sampit River.		
1932	**Apr. 21**	**Bastia, Corsica**	**15**
	Roof of Palace of Justice collapsed, many injured.		
	Aug. 30	**Aguas Buenas, Puerto Rico**	**22**
	Truck plunged 30 ft. into rocky stream bed, 30 injured.		
	Nov. 13	**Warsaw, Poland**	**18**
	Wall of brewery wakehouse collapsed, 13 injured.		
	Dec. 13	**Germany**	**11**
	Mass drowning of skaters in Moselle & Rhine rivers.		
1934	**Jan. 8**	**Kyoto, Japan**	**76**
	Crowd stampeded when they bade farewell to troops, liquor blamed.		
	Mar. 15	**Beirut, Lebanon**	**27**
	Three-story bldg. collapsed.		
	July 22	**Ossining, N.Y.**	**15**
	Bus fell from 35-ft. ramp & burst into flames, 18 injured.		
	Aug. 8	**Bialystoke, Poland**	**12**
	Bus plunged into river, 4 survivors.		

Date		Place	Deaths
1935	Mar. 8	**Batavia, Java**	80
	Mass poisoning from sweetmeats.		
	Mar. 11	**Lyungyu, China**	20
	Mass drowning when bus crashed through bridge.		
	Apr. 10	**Canton, China**	60
	Theatre collapsed, 200 injured.		
	June 29	**Casablanca, Morocco**	13
	Overturned bus burst into flames, 8 injured.		
	July 14	**Turnhout, Belgium**	11
	Bus plunged into canal.		
	Aug. 12	**Cairo, Egypt**	20
	Truck fell on yacht, many injured.		
	Dec. 22	**Hopewell, Va.**	14
	Atlantic Greyhound bus plunged through open drawbridge.		
1936	May 13	**Hamamatsu, Japan**	38
	Chemical poisoning in rice cakes left 1,722 ill.		
	May 26	**Czechoslovakia**	33
	Mass drowning of children when their wagon fell from ferryboat on the Thaya River.		
	June 8	**Bucharest, Rumania**	20
	Grandstand collapsed at the 6th anniversary celebration of King Carol's return to throne, 700 injured.		
	June 15	**China**	34
	Mass drowning of fishermen when gale shattered fleet.		
	July 7	**Chicago, Ill.**	26
	Mass drowning of people during heat wave.		
	July 26	**Freudenstadt, Germany**	20
	Motor lorry plunged over embankment, 40 injured.		
	Oct. 13	**Banha, Egypt**	22
	Bus fell into canal near city, all victims drowned.		
1938	Mar. 7	**Cartagena, Colombia**	10
	Truck overturned, many injured.		
	May 1	**Atlixo, Mexico**	10
	Truck crashed near city, 32 injured.		
	May 2	**Oporto, Portugal**	20
	Bus crashed near city.		
	June 20	**Fukuoka, Japan**	15
	Poisoned rice cakes left 11 sick.		
	June 21	**Brest-Litovsk, Poland**	30
	Mass drowning of peasants.		
	Sept. 11	**Oviedo, Spain**	10
	Bus crashed, 20 injured.		
	Dec. 27	**South Korea**	39
	Tunnel caved in on workers.		
1939	Jan. 2	**Istanbul, Turkey**	22
	Mass drowning in the Black Sea.		
	May 2	**Nantao, China**	18
	Roof collapsed, 44 injured.		
1940	Apr. 21	**Slayton, Minn.**	11
	Car crash left 2 injured.		
	Sept. 18	**Chiba, Japan**	20
	Streetcar-auto collision in prefecture, 100 injured.		
1941	Feb. 20	**Zlen, Czechoslovakia**	16
	Car plunged into river near city, victims all German cops.		
	Sept. 23	**Casablanca, Morocco**	10
	Bus accident left 56 injured.		
	Oct. 26	**Clanton, Ala.**	15
	Bus caught fire after it struck bridge rail, 8 injured.		
1942	Sept. 9	**Quetame, Colombia**	18
	Bus skidded into river, all victims drowned.		
	Oct. 3	**Lumberton, Ohio**	11
	Truck-bus collision near city.		
1943	Mar. 4	**London, England**	178
	Air-raid shelter jam suffocated victims.		
	Apr. 31	**Scotland**	15
	Plane crashed into bus in S.E. area of country.		
	June 6	**Nashville, Tenn.**	18
	Army truck plunged down embankment near city, 8 injured.		
	Oct. 26	**Merida, Mexico**	36
	Church staircase collapsed, many injured.		
	Dec. 14	**Campbell, N.Y.**	11
	Truck & bus collision near city, 8 injured.		
†1944	Mar. 2	**Salerno, Italy**	426
	Mass asphyxiation when train stalled in tunnel.		
	Oct. 22	**Marlborough, England**	10
	Bus & truck collided, 21 injured.		
1945	Dec. 29	**Puebla, Mexico**	36
	Two buses collided, 29 injured.		
1946	Jan. 3	**La Paz, Bolivia**	26
	Truck plunged into river near city.		
	June 25	**Joplin, Mo.**	12
	Bus hit cow then plunged down embankment, 28 injured.		
1947	Apr. 28	**Uruapan, Mexico**	36
	Truck ran off mt., fire followed.		
	May 12	**Zagazig, Egypt**	40
	Bus plunged into canal near city.		
	July 13	**Usti, Czechoslovakia**	26
	Streetcar collision.		
	Oct. 15	**Mazagan, Fr. Morocco**	15
	Bus-truck collision near city.		
1948	Dec. 18	**Delle, Utah**	13
	Two Burlington Trailways buses collided, 44 injured.		
1949	Feb. 20	**Paraia, Cape Verde**	100s
	Wall collapsed on people who waited for Government food handout.		
†1950	May 25	**Chicago, Ill.**	33
	Streetcar smashed into gasoline truck loaded with 8,000 gals. of gas.		
	Dec. 28	**Lima, Peru**	13
	Exhaust fumes from bus, driver held for negligence.		
†1951	Oct. 22	**Atlanta, Ga.**	39
	Bootleg whiskey poisoned 100s of blacks, many were blinded for life.		
	Dec. 4	**Chatham, England**	23
	Suburban bus rammed into formation of cadets. Worst road accident in British history to this date.		
1952	Jan. 5	**Salvador, Brazil**	15
	Bus-streetcar crash followed by fire, 20 injured.		
	Feb. 11	**Cuernavaca, Mexico**	17
	Truck crashed S. of city on Acapulco Highway.		
	Mar. 12	**Salvador, Brazil**	33
	Bus-truck collision near city, 40 injured.		
	May 26	**Chonomas, Mexico**	24
	Truck overturned near city, 26 injured.		
	July 18	**Ayacucho, Peru**	15
	Truck crashed near city, 39 injured.		
	Aug. 30	**Toprakkale, Turkey**	13
	Truck overturned, 36 injured.		
	Sept. 2	**Chiclayo, Peru**	21
	Truck plunged into gorge, 7 injured.		
1953	Mar. 20	**Washington, N.J.**	10
	Car crashed head-on with trailer-truck, 10 members of same family killed.		
	†Apr. 14	**Caracas, Venezuela**	53
	Stampede in church started by panic, many victims children.		
	July 6	**Trujillo, Peru**	21
	Bus-car crash near city, 18 injured.		
	July 31	**Morrisburg, Ontario**	20
	Bus rammed stalled truck & plunged into Williamsburg Canal, 19 saved of 39.		
	Sept. 20	**Baker, Calif.**	10
	Car & trailer-truck collided head on.		

Year	Date	Place	Deaths	Description
1954	**Jan. 30**	**Trois Rivieres, Quebec**	**15**	Bus-truck collision near city, 10 injured.
	Apr. 22	**Lima, Peru**	**33**	Truck plunged off bridge near city.
	Apr. 29	**San Luis Prov., Argentina**	**11**	Truck plunged into river, 6 injured.
	June 7	**N. Beach, Md.**	**10**	Two-car collision near city.
	July 31	**Whitesburg, Ky.**	**11**	Car crashed into cliffs and burst into flames on U.S. Hwy. 119, worst disaster which involved a single car to this date.
1955	**Jan. 17**	**Tucuman, Argentina**	**11**	Truck crashed near city, 22 injured.
	†**June 11**	**Grand Prix**	**83**	Racing disaster when two cars collided and smashed into spectators at Le Mans, France. (SEE Grand Prix)
	Aug. 6	**Kimpos Airbase, S. Korea**	**10**	U.S. Army truck plunged through bridge rail, 9 injured.
	Oct. 11	**Mazatlan, Mexico**	**11**	Truck overturned.
	Nov. 7	**Buta, E. Congo**	**13**	Truck plunged off bridge into ravine, 6 injured.
	Nov. 20	**Waterbury, Neb.**	**10**	Cars collided head-on near city.
	Dec. 31	**Niigata, Japan**	**124**	Wall collapsed at Shinto shrine rite, panic followed.
1956	**Feb. 4**	**Ciudad Campeche, Mexico**	**14**	Truck crashed into bus while attempting to avoid cyclist, 20 injured.
	Feb. 7	**Algiers**	**10**	Trucks collided near country, 16 injured.
	Mar. 23	**Rawalpindi, Pakistan**	**35**	Holiday crowd stampeded on bridge, 60 injured.
	Apr. 21	**Camala, Chile**	**38**	Labor truck plunged off bridge near city.
	June 6	**Madrid, Spain**	**17**	Dance floor collapsed on wedding guests, 30 injured.
	July 2	**La Paz, Bolivia**	**19**	Labor truck crashed on mt. rd. outside city, 14 injured.
	Aug. 20	**Medellin, Colombia**	**12**	Truck plunged into ravine near city, 23 injured.
	Sept. 22	**Abu Seri, Egypt**	**11**	Truck crashed into festival crowd, 50 injured.
	Oct. 5	**Virden, Canada**	**10**	Two cars collided on Trans-Canada Hwy.
	Oct. 22	**Karachi, Pakistan**	**48**	Two-hundred ton concrete girder collapsed on workmen at harbor project, 28 injured.
	Nov. 18	**Pusan, S. Korea**	**14**	Army truck plunged into ravine near city, 39 injured.
	Dec. 14	**Vitoria de Santo Antao, Brazil**	**10**	Two trucks crashed near city.
1957	**Jan. 14**	**Accra, Ghana**	**13**	Trucks collided near city.
	May 25	**Benson, Ill.**	**11**	Cars crashed outside city.
	June 6	**Fayetteville, N.C.**	**20**	Truck loaded with farm workers collided with tractor-trailer near city.
	June 13	**Ft. Campbell, Ky.**	**14**	Truck fell into creek, 9 injured.
	July 26	**Cairo, Egypt**	**64**	House caved-in at city.
	Nov. 2	**Cairo, Egypt**	**20**	Apt. bldg. collapsed at city.
	Dec. 22	**San Antonio, Chile**	**21**	Head-on collision of 2 buses, 31 injured.
	Dec. 23	**Medellin, Colombia**	**15**	Bus slid off cliff outside city, 10 injured.
	Dec. 24	**Durban, S. Africa**	**12**	Bus plunged into river outside city, 40 injured.
1958	**Apr. 31**	**Prestonburg, Ky.**	**28**	School bus plunged over 50-ft. cliff into Big Sandy River, worst disaster of this type to date.
	May 18	**Acros de Valdevez, Portugal**	**16**	Bus plunged down ravine outside city, 28 injured.
	June 17	**Soledad, Calif.**	**12**	Farm bus loaded with Mexican laborers caught fire, 19 injured.
1959	**June 2**	**Schuylkill Haven, Pa.**	**11**	Propane gas truck caught fire & exploded on hgwy. after collision.
	June 8	**Phoenix, Ariz.**	**16**	Bus overloaded with Mexican farm workers smashed into tree, 32 injured.
	July 27	**Japan**	**75**	Mass drownings at beaches from heat wave.
	Sept. 17	**Barletta, Italy**	**55**	New apt. bldg. collapsed.
	Oct. 8	**New Brunswick, N.J.**	**12**	Bus collided with empty tank truck, explosion followed.
1960	**Jan. 9**	**La Paz, Bolivia**	**37**	Truck slid off mt. road outside city.
	Jan. 26	**Seoul, S. Korea**	**31**	Stampede in train injured 38.
	Aug. 25	**Turvo River, Brazil**	**59**	Bus plunged off bridge into water.
	Oct. 17	**Quito, Ecuador**	**35**	Overloaded bus plunged in gully 40 mi. N. of city.
†1961	**Jan. 15**	**New York**	**28**	U.S. Air Force's Texas Tower No. 4 collapsed in an icy northeast storm 80 mi. S.E. of city.
	June 1	**Paris, France**	**20**	Ancient quarries & caves collapsed in suburb outside city.
	Aug. 2	**Lake Lucerne, Switzerland**	**16**	American tour bus plunged into water, 22 survivors.
1963	**Mar. 1**	**Tecunaman, Guatemala**	**64**	Crowded bus crashed outside city.
	May 18	**Pahokee, Fla.**	**27**	Bus loaded with migrant workers plunged into canal.
	June 10	**Escalante, Utah**	**12**	Truck loaded with Boy Scouts overturned, 35 injured.
	Aug. 30	**Yeotmal, India**	**128**	Mosque collapsed, 98 injured.
	Nov. 3	**New York City**	**11**	Car entered dead-end st. and plunged into Harlem River, 3 survivors sued city for negligence.
	Dec. 24	**Calca, Peru**	**15**	Bus plunged off mt. outside city, 25 injured.
†1964	**May 25**	**Lima National Stadium**	**218**	Stampede at soccer game; 1,000s panicked.
	July 11	**Bergerac, France**	**10**	Truck skidded into crowd that watched Tour de France bicycle race near city.
	Aug. 16	**Savoy Alps, France**	**17**	Bus plunged into ravine; 14 victims children.
	Aug. 19	**Cuernavaca, Mexico**	**14**	Truck plunged off road outside city.
	Aug. 31	**Belo Horizonte, Brazil**	**11**	Bus crashed near city.
	Nov. 6	**Piracicaba, Brazil**	**28**	New 13-story bldg. collapsed, 15 injured, damage over $700,000.
	Nov. 29	**Jalapa, Mexico**	**24**	Stadium stampede as 5,000 rushed toward exits.

Date		Place	Deaths	Description
	Dec. 20	**Vidago, Portugal**	**15**	Bus collided with truck outside city.
1965	**Jan. 31**	**Guadalajara, Mexico**	**19**	Panic at music festival, 26 injured.
	Apr. 15	**American Falls, Ida.**	**10**	Worst head-on collision in state's history.
	Aug. 28	**Vinton, La.**	**11**	Truck had head-on collision with Greyhound bus, 28 injured.
	Aug. 30	**Seoul, S. Korea**	**15**	Bus plunged off cliff, 12 injured.
	Dec. 18	**Havana, Cuba**	**20**	Floor & ceiling of Hotel Luz collapsed, many injured.
	Dec. 23	**Middleburg, S. Africa**	**37**	Truck went out of control, victims young workers.
	Dec. 24	**Medford, Ore.**	**13**	Bus skidded & overturned outside city, 26 injured.
1966	**Apr. 25**	**Walfergem-Asse, Belgium**	**11**	Bakery truck smashed into students on sidewalk, the group was studying hgwy. safety.
	May 1	**Karbala, Iraq**	**23**	Moslem pilgrims suffocated in crush of 100,000, many injured.
	June 17	**Moscow, Russia**	**64**	Bus accident, driver received 10 yrs. in prison for "lack of discipline."
	June 27	**Agra, India**	**40**	Bus caught fire outside city, 30 injured.
	June 28	**Sharoud, Iran**	**42**	Bus plunged into valley outside city, 20 injured.
	July 25	**Niederbrechen, Germany**	**33**	Bus plunged off hgwy., most victims were Belgian school children.
	Aug.	**Japan**	**100s**	Mass drowning caused by heat wave, 100s missing.
	Aug. 7	**Japan**	**75**	Mass drownings caused by rough ocean.
	Nov. 19	**Durban, S. Africa**	**40**	Bus plunged into river outside city.
	Dec. 18	**Qum, Iran**	**25**	Buses collided outside city.
	Dec. 19	**Belo Horizonte, Brazil**	**11**	Bus & truck collided outside city, 18 injured.
	Dec. 29	**Celaya, Mexico**	**24**	Buses collided outside city, 48 injured.
1967	**Jan. 5**	**Philippines**	**83**	Two buses loaded with pilgrims collided 30 mi. S. of Manila, this is the worst traffic accident to this date.
	Mar. 24	**San Antonio, Texas**	**10**	Car collided with station wagon which carried 15 members of 2 families.
	July 13	**Genoa, Italy**	**13**	Truck collided with 2 cars outside city, victims all soldiers.
	Aug. 13	**Madras, India**	**17**	Stampede of Hindu pilgrims.
	Aug. 26	**Lima, Peru**	**35**	Truck plunged down embankment, 28 injured.
	Oct. 13	**Izmir, Turkey**	**25**	Bus plunged into ravine outside city.
	Dec. 15	**Jhelum, Pakistan**	**42**	Head-on collision of 2 buses outside city.
	Dec. 25	**Tala River, Argentina**	**16**	Bus plunged into water near Tafi del Valle.
1968	**Jan. 26**	**Conquista, Brazil**	**13**	Bus skidded into lake outside city.
	Mar. 7	**Baker, Calif.**	**20**	Bus collided with car, 12 injured.
	Mar. 17	**Lagos, Nigeria**	**19**	Bus & truck collided outside city.
	Mar. 18	**Rampur, India**	**27**	Bus ran off road outside city.
	June 13	**Kisumu, Kenya**	**34**	Bus crashed outside city.
	June 23	**Buenos Aires**	**71**	Panic at soccer stadium started worst stampede in Argentine history, 130 injured.
	July 22	**Japan**	**72**	Millions crowded beaches to escape heat, mass drowning left 7 missing.
	Aug. 14	**Lima, Peru**	**12**	Bus ran off mt. hgwy. 250 mi. N. of city.
	Aug. 18	**Gifo, Japan**	**30**	Two sightseeing buses swept into river by landslide after typhoon.
	Sept. 21	**Turkey**	**14**	Bus plunged off mt. rd.
	Oct. 3	**Pracmuap Khiri Khan, Thailand**	**11**	Truck plunged into river outside city, many missing.
	Oct. 14	**India**	**21**	Bus crash in northern Kashmir.
	Dec. 6	**Bolivia**	**50**	Swollen rivers swept away 3 trucks 345 mi. S. of La Paz, all victims drowned.
1969	**Aug. 5**	**India**	**27**	Bus, loaded with pilgrims, plunged down Himalayan ravine.
	Sept. 22	**India**	**33**	Swalior-Bhopal bus plunged into Parbati River.
	Oct. 2	**Lima, Peru**	**21**	Bus collided with freight truck, 25 seriously burned.
	Oct. 5	**Madura, India**	**26**	Bus & jeep collided 90 mi. from city, 40 injured.
	Nov. 29	**Guadalajara, Mexico**	**20**	Catholic church collapsed during inaugural services, many injured.
1970	**Jan. 8**	**Montes Calaros, Brazil**	**23**	Bus-truck collision outside city.
	Feb. 21	**Kafanchan, Nigeria**	**52**	Passengers injured in train wreck killed in truck crash on way to hospital.
	Mar. 14	**Pachuca, Mexico**	**27**	Two buses collided head-on, 32 injured.
	Mar. 21	**Quito, Ecuador**	**56**	Overloaded bus plunged into Ambalo River S. of city, 61 injured.
	Oct. 9	**Chamba, India**	**42**	Bus fell off road down mountain.
	Dec. 18	**Rawalpindi, India**	**26**	Bus plunged off bridge into canal outside city, all victims drowned.
1971	**Jan. 3**	**Benue Plateau, Nigeria**	**26**	Truck crashed bridge, 34 injured.
	Feb. 4	**Belo Horizonte, Brazil**	**63**	Government exhibit hall under construction collapsed on 200 workers during lunch hour.
	Feb. 5	**Ibjar, Iran**	**30**	Bus fell down deep gorge near city.
	May 10	**Kapyong, S. Korea**	**77**	Overloaded bus plunged into reservoir outside city.
	May 24	**Panama Canal**	**38**	Commuter bus plunged through guard rail on bridge.
	†Sept.	**Al Basrah, Iraq**	**459**	Mass mercury poisoning kept secret for 2 yrs.

Date		Place	Deaths
†1972	Jan. 23	**New Delhi, India**	100
		Mass poisoning at wedding feast; liquor contained wood alcohol and varnish.	
	†June 25	**Caceres, Spain**	22
		Bus plunged down ravine.	
	†July 3	**Amritsar, India**	27
		Bus collided with truck.	
	†July 10	**Chandka Forest, India**	24
		Elephants went on rampage, 5 villages stampeded.	
	July 19	**Sao Domingos, Brazil**	30
		Bus fell off ferry ramp into Capim River.	
	July 28	**Burgas, Bulgaria**	40
		Bus plunged into river, 9 injured.	
	†Aug. 8	**Zarand, Iran**	39
		One of the worst traffic accidents in history when 2 buses collided on narrow highway.	
	†Aug. 27	**Quito, Ecuador**	19
		Bus fell down 150-ft. ravine in the North.	
	Aug. 28	**Behshahr, Iran**	39
		Two buses collided near city, 40 injured.	
	†Sept. 16	**Naga City, Philippines**	100
		Mass drowning when religious celebrants collapsed old wooden bridge.	
	Sept. 30	**Saraburi, Thailand**	20
		Truck collided with bus, 15 injured.	
	Oct. 11	**Medenine, Tunisia**	20
		Army truck crashed into 2nd vehicle, victims were Tunisian workers who had emigrated to Libya.	
	Dec. 12	**Slogoimo, Indonesia**	49
		Bus crashed & caught fire, 13 injured.	
1973	Mar. 13	**Baguedano, Chile**	45
		Two buses collided 40 mi. N.E. of Antofagasta, this country's worst traffic disaster.	
	May 2	**Salvador, Brazil**	39
		Bus disaster claimed 13 children among victims.	
	July 6	**Alwar, India**	78
		Bus disaster 100 mi. S.W. of Delhi.	
	July 21	**Iran**	48
		Bus plunged into river in the North, one-half the victims were children.	
†1974	Feb. 17	**Zamalek Stadium**	49
		Stampede at soccer game in Cairo. (SEE Zamalek Stadium)	
	June 29	**San Mateo Atenco, Mexico**	29
		Bus smashed into bridge.	
	July 25	**Mexico City**	24
		Multiple bus accidents left 71 injured.	
	July 28	**Belem, Brazil**	69
		Bus collided with truck 250 mi. S. of city.	
	Aug. 11	**Ankara-Istanbul**	21
		Bus collision left 41 injured.	
	Sept. 9	**Zambia**	26
		Bus crash victims included a member of Parliament.	
	Nov. 26	**Indian-Nepal Border**	142
		Suspension bridge collapsed.	
1975	Jan. 1	**Japan Alps**	23
		Bus which carried holiday skiers slid off road into lake.	
	Jan. 29	**Ecuador**	30
		Bus went over embankment between Quito & Lago Agrio.	
	Feb. 24	**Medellin, Colombia**	20
		Bus plunged down mt.	
	May 19	**New Delhi**	66
		Truck which carried wedding party struck by train.	
	May 27	**North Yorkshire, England**	32
		Bus plunged through wall of Dibble's Bridge; brake failure blamed.	
	July 5	**Iran**	21
		Head-on collision between bus and truck near port of Bandar-Abbas.	

Major Plagues, Epidemics, Famines, and Droughts

(† indicates entries profiled in General Narrative)

Date	Place	Deaths
3500 B.C.	**Egypt**	**1,000s**
	Earliest recorded famine.	
†1708	**Egypt**	**1,000s**
	Start of the 7 years' famine; entire Earth affected.	
1491	**Egypt**	**1,000s**
	Massive plagues described in Exodus.	
767	**The World**	**1,000s**
	Plague swept planet, recorded by Petavius.	
503-443	**India**	**1,000s**
	Great pestilence & famine extended during reign of the Emperor Jei-chund.	
453	**Rome**	**1,000s**
	Plague left city desolate.	
436	**Rome**	**1,000s**
	Famine caused great multitudes to throw themselves into the Tiber.	
430	**Athens, Greece**	**1,000s**
	Plague gripped the city, Thucydides described masses of bodies piled in the streets.	
187	**Greece, Egypt & Syria**	**1,000s**
	Plague claimed 2,000 victims daily as noted by Pliny.	
164	**Europe & Near East**	**1,000s**
	Smallpox spread from Rome through Europe, to Persia for 15 years.	
23	**Rome, Italy**	**1,000s**
	Tiber overflowed, which led to widespread starvation, Augustus Caesar initiated one of the first famine relief projects.	
A.D. 6	**Rome, Italy**	**1,000s**
	Famine at city.	
10-5	**Ireland**	**1,000s**
	Crop failure brought great famine.	
42	**Judea**	**1,000s**
	Famine desolated country.	
51	**Greece**	**1,000s**
	Famine throughout country.	
54	**England**	**1,000s**
	Most "grevious" famine.	
76	**Ireland**	**1,000s**
	Famine throughout country.	
79-88	**Italy**	**1,000s**
	Pestilence and famine almost annihilated the Roman world; 10,000 died in Rome in 1 day.	
104	**England & Scotland**	**1,000s**
	Famine in both countries.	
107	**England**	**1,000s**
	Famine caused by long rains.	
151	**Wales**	**1,000s**
	Most severe famine.	
160	**England**	**1,000s**
	Famine & great starvation.	
167	**Roman Empire**	**1,000s**
	First of a series of great plagues.	
169	**Roman Empire**	**1,000s**
	Second in series of great plagues.	
173	**England**	**1,000s**
	Famine after severe frost & snow.	
175	**Rome, Italy**	**1,000s**
	Famine throughout area.	
189	**Roman Empire**	**1,000s**
	Third plague to ravage civilization in 20 yrs.	
192	**Ireland**	**1,000s**
	Bad harvest started country's first emigration.	
228	**Italy**	**1,000s**
	Masses starved.	
238	**Scotland**	**1,000s**
	Second great famine in decade.	
250-65	**Roman Empire**	**1,000s**
	Bubonic Plague crippled nation, 5,000 victims died daily in Rome, many cities completely depopulated.	
259	**Wales**	**1,000s**
	Famine so terrible the populace ate the bark of trees and were "pined" to death.	
272	**England**	**1,000s**
	Famine so terrible that people ate the bark of trees.	
288	**Great Britain**	**1,000s**
	Famine throughout country.	
306	**Scotland**	**1,000s**
	Famine lasted 4 yrs., was described as "most grevious & fatal."	
307	**Cappadocia, Asia Minor**	**1,000s**
	Famine occupied area.	
310	**England**	**40,000**
	Famine occurred, yr. varied from 308 to 338.	
325	**England**	**1,000s**
	Severe, bitter famine.	
331	**Antioch**	**1,000s**
	City so starved that a bushel of wheat sold for 400 pieces of silver.	
336	**Syria**	**1,000s**
	Famine with plague.	
370	**Phrygia**	**1,000s**
	Famine desolated country.	
381	**Antioch**	**1,000s**
	Plague & famine during reign of Theodosius the Great.	
410	**Rome, Italy**	**1,000s**
	Famine followed by plague.	
430	**Great Britian**	**1,000s**
	Plague left just enough alive to bury the dead.	
434	**Italy**	**1,000s**
	Famine & plague throughout country.	
444	**Great Britain**	**1,000s**
	Epidemic of Bubonic Plague.	
446	**Constantinople**	**1,000s**
	Most severe famine.	
450	**Italy**	**1,000s**
	Famine described by Dufresnoy caused parents to eat their children.	
466	**Great Britain**	**1,000s**
	Famine with a "bad, fatal air" as described by Short.	
475	**Europe**	**1,000s**
	North end of continent visited by locusts, crops destroyed, famine followed.	
484	**Africa**	**1,000s**
	Drought brought great famine.	
515	**Great Britain**	**1,000s**
	Famine called "most afflictive."	
520	**Venice, Italy**	**1,000s**
	Famine forced Theodoric the Great to relieve city.	
523	**Scotland**	**1,000s**
	A most terrible famine.	
527	**Wales**	**1,000s**
	Famine in the North.	
531	**Wales**	**1,000s**
	Famine and a small plague in the South.	

Major Plagues, Epidemics, Famines, and Droughts

Date	Place	Deaths
535-539	**Ireland**	1,000s
	Loss & scarcity of food brought long famine.	
537	**Scotland & Wales**	1,000s
	"Dearth" in both countries.	
538	**Italy**	1,000s
	Country suffered great famine.	
542	**Roman Empire**	1,000s
	Bubonic plague caused immense mortality.	
547	**Italy**	1,000s
	Second famine in decade.	
558	**Europe, Asia & Africa**	Millions
	Bubonic Plague swept continents, 7,500 died daily in Constantinople.	
576	**Scotland**	1,000s
	A most fatal famine.	
590	**England**	1,000s
	Famine followed great flood.	
592 Jan.-Sept.	**England**	1,000s
	Long drought with locusts.	
600-4	**France**	1,000s
	Long period of starvation.	
605	**England**	1,000s
	Famine from heat & drought.	
625	**Great Britain**	1,000s
	"Grevious" famine throughout country.	
664	**Ireland**	1,000s
	Famine preceded 2nd appearance of Buidhe Chonnail.	
667	**Scotland**	1,000s
	"Most grevious" famine.	
669	**France**	1,000s
	Serious famine throughout country.	
	Ireland	1,000s
	Great scarcity of food for long duration.	
680	**Great Britain**	1,000s
	Famine followed 3 yrs. drought.	
683	**Syria & Libya**	1,000s
	Famine in both countries.	
695-700	**England & Ireland**	1,000s
	Famine caused widespread cannibalism.	
703-6	**Italy**	1,000s
	Famine of long duration.	
712	**Wales**	1,000s
	Famine throughout country.	
718	**Syria**	1,000s
	Famine brought mass starvation.	
746	**Wales**	1,000s
	"A great dearth."	
746-749	**Constantinople**	200,000
	Plague ruined city and spread to Calabria, Greece, & Sicily.	
748	**Scotland**	1,000s
	Famine throughout country.	
759	**Ireland**	1,000s
	Famine throughout kingdom for long duration.	
768	**Ireland**	1,000s
	Famine accompanied by earthquake.	
772	**Chichester, England**	34,000
	Epidemical disease throughout area.	
	Ireland	1,000s
	Drought caused famine.	
774	**Scotland**	1,000s
	Plague & great famine.	
780	**England, Wales & Scotland**	1,000s
	Famine left countries desolate.	
791	**Wales**	1,000s
	A most "grevious" famine.	
803	**Scotland**	1,000s
	A most terrible famine.	
822-823	**England & Scotland**	1,000s
	Short described a famine that starved 1,000s.	
824-825	**Ireland**	1,000s
	"A great dearth."	
836	**Wales**	1,000s
	Famine with the ground covered with dead bodies of men & beasts as described by Short.	
845	**Bulgaria**	1,000s
	Great famine throughout country.	
850	**Paris, France**	1,000s
	Famine crippled city.	
851	**Italy & Germany**	1,000s
	Famine in both countries.	
856-860	**Scotland**	1,000s
	Starvation for 4 years.	
863	**Scotland**	1,000s
	Plague accompanied famine.	
868	**Paris, France**	1,000s
	City again crippled by famine.	
872	**England**	1,000s
	Locusts destroyed crop, famine followed.	
873	**Paris, France**	1,000s
	Famine again crippled city.	
879	**The World**	1,000s
	Famine gripped all nations.	
883	**Italy**	1,000s
	A most terrible famine.	
887-888	**England**	1,000s
	Famine caused a most "grevious" 2 yrs.	
890	**Scotland**	1,000s
	"A great dearth."	
895-897	**Ireland**	1,000s
	Invasion of famine brought great dearth.	
896-899	**Paris, France**	1,000s
	City starved for long duration.	
898	**France**	1,000s
	Famine throughout country.	
900	**England**	1,000s
	Famine throughout country.	
917-918	**Kashmir, India**	1,000s
	Area became vast burial ground, Jhelum River overflowed with bodies.	
931	**Wales**	1,000s
	Famine throughout country.	
932	**France**	1,000s
	Famine throughout country.	
936	**Scotland**	1,000s
	Cannibalism brought on by "grevious" famine.	
945-946	**France**	1,000s
	Famine of long duration.	
946	**Italy**	1,000s
	A shocking & "grevious" famine.	
954-958	**England, Scotland & Wales**	40,000
	Famine of 4-yr. duration, plague desolated Scotland.	
962	**England**	1,000s
	Famine brought by frost, plague also ravaged London.	
963-964	**Ireland**	1,000s
	Intolerable famine forced parents to sell their children.	
968	**Fustat, Egypt**	600,000
	Low Nile brought great famine in the vicinity of city, a new city was founded a short distance away called Cairo today.	
	Europe	100s
	Famine throughout continent, Germany & Scotland suffered heaviest.	
969	**England**	1,000s
	Wind storms blew away grain crops, famine followed.	

975 **Paris, France** **1,000s**
Mass starvation.
976 **England** **1,000s**
Great famine noted by John of Brompton.
987 **Albania** **1,000s**
Great dearth throughout country.
987-1059 **France** **Millions**
Famine occurred on an average of 1 every 18 months, people feared the millennial was a signal of the end of the world.
989 **England** **1,000s**
"Grevious" famine caused by rains in winter, no plowing or sowing.
1004 **England** **1,000s**
A famine such as no man could remember.
1005 **England** **1,000s**
Great famine caused Sweyn the Dane to retire.
1008 **Wales** **1,000s**
Famine with plague.
1012 **England - Germany** **1,000s**
Famine of long duration.
1016 **Europe** **1,000s**
Famine crippled continent.
1022 **Hindustan** **1,000s**
Drought followed famine during reign of Musaood I, whole countries were entirely depopulated.
1025 **England** **1,000s**
Famine from rains & plague.
1025-1026 **Egypt** **1,000s**
Great famine during reign of Calipate of Zahir.
1042 **Byzantine Empire** **1,000s**
Famine ravaged nation.
1047 **Ireland** **1,000s**
Snow & frost produced great famine.
1047-1048 **Scotland** **1,000s**
Famine stilled country for 2 yrs.
1050 **England** **1,000s**
Barrenness of the land caused great famine & mortality.
1051 **Mexico** **1,000s**
Famine forced the Toltecs to migrate.
1052-1060 **Hindustan** **1,000s**
Seven yrs. of drought at Ghor burned the earth and brought mass death from famine & heat.
1058 **Poland** **1,000s**
Great famine throughout country.
†1064-1072 **Egypt** **40,000**
Nile failed to flood and brought great famine & cannibalism, areas from Fustat to Cairo were cut off from supplies by the horsemen of the Lewata Berbers.
1068 **England** **1,000s**
Severe winter brought famine & plague.
†1069 **England** **50,000**
Famine followed Norman invasion, also cannibalism.
1073 **England** **1,000s**
Famine caused mass mortality so severe that the living were too weak to care for the sick or bury the dead.
1078 **Constantinople** **1,000s**
Short described famine & plague brought on by "the multitudes of strangers."
1080 **Denmark** **1,000s**
Famine throughout country.
1086 **England** **1,000s**
Excessive rains brought on fever & famine.
1087 **Denmark** **1,000s**
Famine so terrible that King Olaf II was surnamed the "Hungry."
England **1,000s**
Famine followed by great pestilence.

1093 **England** **1,000s**
Stow recorded "a great famine & mortality."
1094-1095 **London, England** **1,000s**
Plague took many lives in city.
1095 **Ireland** **1,000s**
Plague throughout country.
1097 **Sept.-Dec.** **Palestine & Egypt** **100,000**
Plague & famine during the 1st crusade.
1099 **England** **1,000s**
Rains & floods brought famine, tempests, & bad air.
1106 **England** **1,000s**
Barren land brought famine & plague.
1111 **London, England** **1,000s**
Plague followed winter famine.
1116 **Ireland** **1,000s**
Great famine caused mass cannibalism.
1117 **England** **1,000s**
Year's incessant rain brought terrible famine.
1120 **Jerusalem** **1,000s**
Short described a famine "with plague of mice and locusts."
1121-1122 **England** **1,000s**
Long & cruel frost brought great famine.
1123-1124 **France & Germany** **1,000s**
Terrible weather brought famine & great plague.
1124 **England** **1,000s**
Famine spread due to great poverty, bodies lay unburied everywhere.
1126 **England** **1,000s**
Great scarcity of food brought on by incessant summer rains, a sextarius of wheat sold for 20s.
1130-1131 **Rome, Italy** **1,000s**
Great famine in city.
1135-1137 **England** **1,000s**
Drought then famine.
1141 **England** **1,000s**
Beginning of a decade of famine.
1151-1152 **Europe & Palestine** **1,000s**
Famine throughout both areas.
1153 **Ireland** **1,000s**
Famine in Munster spread all over country.
1157 **England** **1,000s**
Floods of autumn destroyed grain & fruit, pestilence followed.
Italy **1,000s**
Great snow & frost brought famine.
1172 **Ireland** **1,000s**
Plague hastened Henry II's departure.
1175 **England** **1,000s**
Pestilence then great dearth.
1176 **Wales** **1,000s**
Famine with great mortality.
1183 **England & Wales** **1,000s**
Great famine stilled both countries.
1193-1196 **England & France** **1,000s**
Incessant rains caused such famine that common people perished everywhere followed by a pestilence of acute fever.
†1199-1202 **Egypt** **100,000**
Most severe famine to plague country, Nile failed to rise.
1200 **Ireland** **1,000s**
Starvation for 1 yr. brought on by cold.
1200-1201 **Egypt** **1,000s**
Failure of the Nile to rise brought great famine & cannibalism.
1203 **England** **1,000s**
Long rains brought famine & great mortality.

Major Plagues, Epidemics, Famines, and Droughts

Date	Place	Deaths	
	Ireland	**1,000s**	Famine so severe that priests ate flesh meat during Lent.
1204	**Ireland**	**1,000s**	Immense plague swept country.
1209	**England**	**1,000s**	Rainy summer & severe winter produced famine.
1218	**Damietta, Egypt**	**67,000**	Pestilence left only 3,000 survivors in the city.
1224	**England**	**1,000s**	Dry winter with poor harvest brought on famine.
1227	**Ireland**	**1,000s**	Great famine throughout country.
1230	**Rome, Italy**	**1,000s**	Deluge of the Tiber produced famine.
1235	**England**	**1,000s**	Famine & plague, 20,000 deaths in London alone; people consumed horse flesh, bark of trees, grass, etc.
1239	**England**	**1,000s**	Great famine saw parents consume offspring.
1243	**Hungary**	**1,000s**	Tartar invasion left great famine.
1248	**Germany**	**1,000s**	Famine throughout country.
1252	**England**	**1,000s**	Lack of rain for months killed crops, huge loss of cattle.
1258	**England**	**1,000s**	Famine followed great "dearth," again 20,000 died in London.
1262	**Ireland**	**1,000s**	Plague & hunger produced great mortality.
1264	**Egypt**	**1,000s**	Severe famine was relieved by efforts of Bibars, founder of the Mameluke Empire.
1268	**Sicily**	**1,000s**	Terrible famine spread to Vienna.
1271	**Canterbury, England**	**1,000s**	District suffered from famine which followed violent inundation.
	Ireland	**1,000s**	Pestilence & famine throughout country.
1281	**Poland**	**1,000s**	Famine throughout country.
1291	**India**	**1,000s**	Lack of rain caused terrible famine in the provinces of Delhi.
1294	**England**	**1,000s**	Famine gripped country, widespread death among poor.
1295	**England**	**1,000s**	Terrible harvest caused mass mortality among poor.
	Ireland	**1,000s**	Great "dearth" which lasted more than yr.
1297	**Scotland**	**1,000s**	Great pestilence & famine.
1298	**England**	**1,000s**	Food so scarce that communion in the churches was halted.
1299	**Persia**	**1,000s**	Country ravaged by famine & pestilence.
1314	**Great Britain**	**1,000s**	Famine forced people to devour flesh of horses, dogs, cats & vermin.
	Ireland	**1,000s**	Famine caused great civil insurrection.
	Thuringia, Poland & Silesia	**1,000s**	Lengthy, awful famine.
1315-1317	**Europe**	**1,000s**	Disease & starvation claimed 10% of population of central & western part of continent.
1316	**England**	**1,000s**	Universal dearth with such mortality among the poor that the living could scarcely bury the dead.
	Ireland	**1,000s**	A dearth so terrible that captured Scots were eaten at siege of Carrickfergus.
1317	**Ireland**	**1,000s**	Great famine followed Bruce's invasion.
1321	**England**	**1,000s**	This famine is regarded by many as the last serious famine in this country.
1333-1337	**China**	**6,000,000**	Great famine may have been source of Europe's Black Death, 4 million victims died in the area of Kiang alone.
1340	**Italy**	**1,000s**	The Black Death terrified country.
1341	**Scotland & England**	**1,000s**	Great "dearth" in which people ate horses, dogs & cats to sustain life.
1342	**India**	**1,000s**	Famine in Delhi provinces starved almost all inhabitants.
1344-1345	**India**	**1,000s**	Famine extended entire whole of Hindustan.
1347	**Italy**	**1,000s**	Famine destroyed 2/3 of populace, absolute starvation followed by plague.
†1348-1666	**Europe**	**25,000,000**	The Bubonic Plague, forever known as the Black Death, wiped out 1/3 of the Continent to create the greatest disaster in history; 200 persons buried daily in London alone; over 1 million lost in Germany & total annihilation of Cyprus & Ireland. (SEE Black Death)
1350	**Barbary**	**1,000s**	Grain from England caused great dearth.
1350-1355	**France**	**1,000s**	Famine followed Black Death, a small cask of herring sold for 30 golden crowns.
1353	**England & France**	**1,000s**	Great famine reported by Rapin.
1358	**England**	**1,000s**	Great "dearth" known as the second pestilence.
1361	**Poland**	**1,000s**	Famine throughout country.
1361-1362	**France & England**	**1,000s**	Plague in Paris & London.
1367	**France & England**	**1,000s**	Dreadful plague again in Paris & London.
1369	**France & England**	**1,000s**	Third plague to have struck Paris & London in decade.
1370	**Ireland**	**1,000s**	Plague throughout country.
1374-1375	**Italy**	**1,000s**	Famine desolated country.
1382-1385	**Ireland**	**1,000s**	Pestilence known as the Fourth.
1386	**Smolensk, Russia**	**1,000s**	Plague left only 5 persons alive in town.
1407	**London, England**	**30,000**	Great pestilence famished city.
1410	**Ireland**	**1,000s**	Great famine throughout country.
1412-1413	**India**	**1,000s**	Great drought brought famine in the Ganges-Jumna delta.
1433	**Ireland**	**1,000s**	Great & severe famine.
1440	**Scotland**	**1,000s**	Famine throughout country.

Date	Place	Deaths
1442	**Sweden**	**1,000s**
	Famine terrified country.	
1447 Spring	**Ireland**	**1,000s**
	Famine followed poor crops.	
1454	**South America**	**1,000s**
	Yellow fever wiped out Mayan race.	
1466	**Ireland**	**1,000s**
	Plague brought about by famine.	
1470	**Dublin, Ireland**	**1,000s**
	Plague wasted city.	
1471	**Orissa, India**	**1,000s**
	A most severe famine.	
	Oxford, England	**1,000s**
	Terrible pestilence claimed more victims than the country's total war of the preceding 15 yrs.	
1485	**London, England**	**1,000s**
	Sweating sickness also called Sudor Anglicus noted by Delaune.	
1491	**Ireland**	**1,000s**
	Famine referred to as "The Dismal Year."	
1495	**India**	**1,000s**
	Great "dearth" in Hindustan.	
1497	**Ireland**	**1,000s**
	Intolerable famine brought mass mortality.	
1499-1500	**London, England**	**30,000**
	Fatal plague forced Henry VII & his court to flee to Calais.	
1502	**Hispaniola**	**1,000**
	Half of expedition led by Spanish explorer DeLares killed by yellow fever.	
1506	**London, England**	**1,000s**
	Sweating sickness induced mortality in 3 hrs.	
1507	**West Indies**	**1,000s**
	First outbreak of smallpox in Western Hemisphere following visit of Columbus.	
1508	**Hispaniola**	**46,000**
	Outbreak of yellow fever all but wiped out native population for next 6 yrs.	
1517	**England**	**1,000s**
	Sweating sickness wiped out ½ of the population in the capital towns & Oxford was depopulated.	
1520	**Mexico**	**3,000,000**
	Smallpox carried into the country by Spaniards.	
1521	**India**	**1,000s**
	Famine in the Sind area.	
	England	**100s**
	Famine greatly inflated the price of wheat, mortality followed.	
1522	**Ireland**	**1,000s**
	Great famine throughout country.	
	Limerick, Ireland	**1,000s**
	Visitation of plague.	
1527	**England**	**100s**
	Great scarcity of bread in London & throughout country.	
1528	**England**	**1,000s**
	Sweating sickness throughout country.	
	Venice, Italy	**1,000s**
	Famine in city.	
July	**Italy**	**21,000**
	Epidemic of typhus.	
1529	**Germany**	**1,000s**
	Sweating sickness throughout country in North.	
1530's	**Tuscany**	**100,000**
	Brutal outbreak of typhus.	
1540	**Sardinia**	**1,000s**
	Famine desolated island.	
1540-1543	**India**	**1,000s**
	Another famine of long duration in Sind.	
1544	**Budapest, Hungary**	**30,000**
	Typhus decimated the Imperial army at Hoachim of Brandenburg besieging the city.	
1545	**Cuba**	**250,000**
	Typhus epidemic scourged area.	
1551	**England**	**1,000s**
	Fifth visit by sweating sickness.	
1552	**Metz, Germany**	**30,000**
	Half of the Imperial army under Emperor Charles wiped out by typhus.	
1557	**Russia**	**1,000s**
	Severe famine worsened by rains & great cold, Volga hardest hit.	
1560	**Brazil**	**Millions**
	Smallpox epidemic throughout country.	
1563	**London, England**	**20,000**
	Pestilence & famine terrified city.	
1577	**Oxford, England**	**500**
	Judge, jury & spectators at the infamous Black Azzizes.	
1581	**Persia**	**1,000s**
	Country desolated by famine & plague.	
1586	**Hungary**	**1,000s**
	Famine throughout country.	
	Ireland	**1,000s**
	Wars of Desmond brought famine & cannibalism.	
1588-1589	**Ireland**	**1,000s**
	Another famine which forced cannibalism.	
1591	**Italy**	**1,000s**
	Famine throughout country.	
1594-1598	**India**	**1,000s**
	Famine followed by plague & cannibalism.	
1595-1596	**Italy & Germany**	**1,000s**
	Famine spread across wide area.	
1598	**Pegu**	**1,000s**
	A most "grevious" famine.	
1600	**Russia**	**500,000**
	Famine & plague throughout country, another 30,000 died in Livonia.	
1601-1603	**Ireland**	**1,000s**
	Famine & plague throughout country.	
1603-1604	**England**	**50,000**
	Plague claimed 30,578 victims in London alone.	
†1608	**Jamestown, Virginia**	**62**
	Starvation followed fire in 1st English settlement.	
1611	**Constantinople**	**200,000**
	Great attack of pestilence.	
1618	**Naples, Italy**	**8,000**
	Outbreak of diphtheria.	
1625	**England**	**40,000**
	Plague claimed 35,417 victims in London.	
1630	**Vince, Italy**	**500,000**
	Plague devastated city & spread northward to Tyrol.	
	Deccan, India	**100,000**
	Famine during reign of Shah Jahan (Taj Mahal) followed by floods, 30,000 died in Surat alone.	
1631	**Asia**	**1,000s**
	A famine caused by drought across continent.	
1632	**France**	**80,000**
	Plague took 60,000 lives in Lyons.	
1650-1652	**Russia**	**1,000s**
	Starvation brought on by high price of grain, people ate sawdust.	
1656	**Italy**	**400,000**
	Famine in Rome followed by dreadful plague which spread from Sardinia to Naples for 6 months; disease started from infected military transport.	

Major Plagues, Epidemics, Famines, and Droughts

Date	Place	Deaths
1661	**Punjab, India** Famine brought on by drought.	1,000s
1664	**London, England** Great plague kept fires lit to purify air for 3 days to stop infection; historians argue disease was not stopped until the great fire of Sept. 1666.	100,000
1669-1670	**India** Earliest famine of note in this country.	3,000,000
1672	**Naples, Italy** Bubonic plague in city.	400,000
	Lyons, France Bubonic plague scourged city.	60,000
1677	**Hyderabad, India** Excessive rain brought famine, every village virtually wiped out.	1,000s
1690	**Ireland** Disease & famine across country.	1,000s
1693	**France** Awful famine noted by Voltaire.	1,000s
1703	**India** Famine in the Thar & Parkar districts of Sind.	1,000s
1709	**France** Severe famine throughout country.	1,000s
1711	**Austria & Germany** Epidemic of bubonic plague.	500,000
1720	**Marseilles, France** Ship from Levant carried plague over wide area.	60,000
1721	**Boston, Mass.** Smallpox wiped out 1/10 of population.	1,000
1727-1729	**Ireland** Wheat & corn scarce, mortality high.	100s
1733	**India** Famine throughout northwestern provinces.	1,000s
1739	**France** A most severe famine.	1,000s
	India Famine throughout Delhi & surrounding areas.	1,000s
1739-1740	**Ireland** Frost destroyed potato crop, price of wheat soared.	1,000s
1740	**Messina** Plague starved island.	40,000
1741	**Cadiz, Spain** Epidemic of yellow fever.	10,000
1745-1752	**India** Horrible, extended famine in Nara districts of Sind, Thar, & Parkar.	Millions
1748	**England** Famine extended for months.	1,000s
1750	**London, England** Judges, sheriff, aldermen & spectators died of typhus after exposure to prisoners.	50
1760	**Syria** One of the worst plagues in history noted by Abbe Mariti.	100,000
1769	**France** Famine so dreadful as to cause 5% mortality rate.	1,000s
†1769-1770	**Hindustan, India** First great Indian famine of record, some estimates say 1/3 of province died.	3,000,000
1770	**Bohemia** Famine & pestilence throughout country.	168,000
	Poland & Russia Famine & pestilence caused mass suffering.	20,000
1773	**Bassora, Persia** Pestilence depopulated city & surrounding neighborhood.	80,000
1775	**Cape de Verde** Great famine at area.	16,000
1778	**British Navy** Typhus spread through all ships of the line.	4,801
1781-1783	**India** Famine in the Carnatic and the Madras settlement.	1,000s
1782-1784	**India** Intolerable famine in the province of Sind which included Thar & Parkar.	Millions
1783-1784	**India** Lack of rain caused famine from Zahore to Karumnasa.	1,000s
1787-1788	**India** Famine in Behar & northwest provinces of Punjab; rain & floods were eagerly awaited.	1,000s
†1788	**Jamaica** Famine caused by ruination of crops by hurricanes; victims black slaves.	15,000
1789	**Roven, France** Province suffered 'grevious' famine.	1,000s
†1790-1791	**India** Almost total failure of rain caused the infamous Poji Bara or Skull Famine, cannibalism was rampant in Bombay, Orissa & Madras.	1,000s
1791	**India** Black ants destroyed all vegetation in Kach, this area would be visited with such regularity by famines & plagues that it was described as a terribly God-forsaken place.	1,000s
1792	**Egypt** Plague throughout country.	800,000
1793	**Philadelphia, Pa.** Widespread epidemic of yellow fever.	1,000s
1798	**England** Smallpox reached height of epidemic which raged for years.	80,000
1799	**Africa** Plague took 247,000 lives in Fez & 3,000 daily in Barbary.	300,000
1800	**Spain** Epidemic of yellow fever.	80,000
1802	**Santo Domingo** Yellow fever crippled Napoleon's army.	29,000
1803	**Haiti** Yellow fever destroyed all but 3,000 of French punitive expedition.	22,000
1803-1804	**India** Great famine brought on by drought, locusts, war and mass migration.	1,000s
1804-1805	**Gibraltar & Spain** Pestilent disease ravaged for 2 yrs.	25,000
1804-1807	**India** Starvation of the poorer classes in the Bombay Presidency.	1,000s
1810	**China** First great famine of century in this country.	Millions
1811	**China** Second great famine.	Millions
1812	**Vilna, Russia** Napoleon's army in retreat from Moscow wracked by typhus.	25,000
1812-1813	**India** Country devastated by famine, locusts, plague of rats & masses of starved immigrants.	Millions
1813	**Poland** Famine brought on by supplies being intercepted.	5,000
1813-1814	**India** Famine in many parts of the Agra district.	1,000s
1815	**Indonesia** Famine followed eruption of Tomboro which spoiled land & crops. (SEE Tomboro)	70,000

Date	Place	Deaths
1816-1817	**Ireland**	**737,000**
	Severe famine swept country.	
1816-1819	**Ireland**	**20,000**
	Epidemic of typhus caused great mortality.	
1819	**Tours, France**	**1,000s**
	Diphtheria epidemic lasted for months.	
	India	**1,000s**
	Famine in the Allahabad and neighboring districts due to late harvest of crop.	
1820-1822	**India**	**1,000s**
	Famine caused considerable suffering in the Madras district.	
1820-1822	**India**	**1,000s**
	Famine in Upper Sind & nearby provinces caused crop failure.	
1822	**Ireland**	**1,000s**
	Great & dreadful famine caused civil unrest that forced execution or deportation of ringleaders.	
1824-1825	**India**	**1,000s**
	Lack of rain brought severe drought & famine in Delhi, Madras Presidency & the Carnatic & Western districts.	
1825-1826	**India**	**1,000s**
	Lack of rain brought famine in the northwest provinces & blight in Sangor & Nerbada.	
1826-1837	**Europe**	**Millions**
	Cholera epidemic killed 900,000 in 1831, continent scourged for years.	
1827-1828	**India**	**1,000s**
	Famine in Hindustan & drought across Jumna.	
1828	**Gibraltar**	**1,000s**
	Epidemic fever which resembled the plague.	
†1833	**India**	**200,000**
	Disaster called "Guntoor famine" wiped out district.	
1833-1835	**India**	**1,000s**
	Famine in the Madras Presidency, locusts destroyed all the crops.	
1837-1838	**India**	**800,000**
	Lack of rain caused absolute drought in the northwest.	
1838-1839	**India**	**1,000s**
	Great scarcity of food caused mass migration from Surat & the Bombay Presidency.	
1840-1862	**The World**	**Millions**
	Epidemic of cholera infected the earth for 2 decades.	
1846	**China**	**Millions**
	Third great famine to cripple country this century.	
†1846-1847	**Ireland**	**1,029,552**
	Great potato famine caused immigration to America.	
†1847 Apr. 21	**Donner Party**	**42**
	Frontier expedition stranded in snow at Truckee Pass, Calif., famine and cannibalism followed.	
1847-1848	**London, England**	**15,000**
	Influenza epidemic infected city.	
1849	**China**	**Millions**
	Famines in the first-half of this century took over 45 million lives.	
1851-1855	**England**	**250,000**
	Tuberculosis claimed 50,000 victims a year.	
1853-1854	**India**	**1,000s**
	Great food shortage in the Bellary district of the Madras Presidency.	
1854	**Messina**	**16,000**
	Cholera epidemic for a year.	
1860-1861	**India**	**1,000s**
	Lack of rain in the Delhi territory made the great Nujjufghur Jheel entirely dry for the first time in its history.	
1863	**England**	**30,000**
	Scarlet fever swept country.	
1863-1875	**The World**	**Millions**
	Cholera epidemic continued for a decade; over 300,000 victims died in 1866 in Eastern Europe.	
†1866	**India**	**1,500,000**
	Lack of rain caused awful famine in the lower provinces of Bengal, Orissa, Behar.	
Mar.	**Dublin, Ireland**	**100s**
	New incurable disease that caused purple blotches to emerge on skin.	
1868-1870	**India**	**1,000s**
	Poor crops for several years caused starvation in Rajputana & the northwest and central provinces, great number of cattle died.	
1870	**France**	**23,697**
	Smallpox struck both German & French armies; Germans, practicing vaccination, lost only 297.	
1871-1872	**Persia**	**1,000s**
	Severe famine throughout country.	
1874-1875	**Asia Minor**	**150,000**
	Famine ravaged area, deaths are up to July '74.	
†1876-1877	**India**	**6,000,000**
	One of the longest famines on records brought about by great crop failure, more than 36 million people affected. Cholera accounted for half the lives lost.	
1877	**Brazil**	**1,000s**
	Great drought in the northern provinces exposed 200,000 to famine.	
†1877-1878	**China**	**Millions**
	Famine in the North affected 70 million people, 9 million died in an area the size of France.	
1878	**U.S., Southern**	**14,000**
	Epidemic of yellow fever.	
	Morocco	**1,000s**
	Provinces of Soos, Haha, & Antuga suffered from extreme famine.	
1889-1890	**The World**	**Millions**
	Influenza epidemic affected 40% of the earth's population.	
1891	**Russia**	**1,000s**
	One of the most severe famines ever to visit country followed by 2 more in 20 yrs.	
1892-1894	**China**	**1,000,000**
	Drought brought great famine.	
1893-1894	**The World**	**Millions**
	Cholera epidemic spread everywhere.	
1896-1897	**India**	**5,000,000**
	Drought caused famine & widespread disease.	
†1898	**India**	**1,000,000**
	Great mortality; death toll recorded until 1901.	
Oct.-Nov.	**Turkestan**	**1,000s**
	Plague throughout area.	
1899-1900	**India**	**1,250,000**
	Drought caused millions to starve with millions more dead from disease which followed.	
1899-1901	**India**	**1,000,000**
	Famine of long duration.	
1900	**Cuba**	**Scores**
	Yellow fever broke out among troops during Spanish American War.	
1900-1901	**Sydney, Australia**	**136**
	Plague continued intermittently for year.	
1901	**Hong Kong, China**	**1,509**
	Plague claimed 100 victims weekly for months.	
Apr.-Oct.	**Egypt**	**83**
	Plague reported 173 cases.	
1902 Apr.-July	**Egypt**	**147**
	Plague again infected area.	

Major Plagues, Epidemics, Famines, and Droughts

Date	Place	Deaths	
1903	Panama Canal	20,000	Yellow fever epidemic peaked among canal workers.
Jan.-Aug.	India	600,000	Plague throughout wide area.
Mar.-Apr.	Punjab, India	130,000	Disastrous epidemic of plague.
Apr.-Aug.	Hong Kong, China	915	Plague infected city.
Aug.	Niuchwang, China	1,000s	Great mortality from plague.
1904	India	1,000,000	Plague in Bombay, Bengal, the N.W. provinces and the Punjab; death rate averaged 18,000 per week with record weeks of over 40,000.
1905	India	500,000	Plague in Bombay, N.W. Presidency, and the Punjab; weekly mortality rate reached 20,000 with drops to 5,000.
	Greece	6,000	Malaria affected 1 million residents.
1906	India	356,700	Plague throughout country.
	China	1,000s	Floods in Yangtze affected 10 million people who resided in an area the size of Kentucky.
	Russia	1,000s	Second great famine equal to 1891.
1907	India	1,316,000	Plague continued in country.
1908	India	148,700	Plague of long duration began to level off.
	Hong Kong, China	109	Plague with 133 cases reported.
1909 May	Tuantsiu, China	100s	Bubonic Plague throughout southern area claimed 50 victims daily.
1910-1911	Manchuria	60,000	Pneumonic Plague epidemic.
1910-1913	China & India	Millions	Bubonic Plague ravaged both countries for great duration.
1911	China	1,000s	Famine identical to the one of 1906.
	Russia	1,000s	This famine climaxed ones of 1891 & 1906, 30 million people were affected but no accurate statistics of dead.
1914-1924	Russia	20,000,000	Famine & influenza reduced population by staggering proportions.
1915 June-Aug.	Serbia	150,000	Typhus epidemic raged all summer.
1916	Armenia	1,000s	Famine & disease brought mass suffering, after one census 2,277 deaths had occurred in 50-day period.
1917-1921	Russia	3,000,000	Endless epidemic of typhus.
1917-1919	The World	25,000,000	Influenza claimed 13 million victims in India, over 500,000 in America, & millions in Africa & Europe.
1920-1921	China	500,000	Drought starved 20 million in North.
1921	India	500,000	Epidemic of cholera.
1921-1922	Russia	Millions	Drought affected over 20 million, Maxim Gorki desperately requested help from America which was granted.
1921-1923	India	Millions	Bubonic Plague took incredible toll.
1924	India	300,000	Another outbreak of cholera.
	Los Angeles, Calif.	33	Plague quickly stamped out.
1926-1930	India	500,000	Incredible devastation by smallpox.
1928-1929	China	3,000,000	Famine equal to 1877-78 but modern transportation spared some victims in Shensi, Honan, & Kansu; starvation continued until 1931.
1929 Sept.	Panama	20	Over 200 cases of smallpox reported, ships fumigated.
1930 Jan.	Tunis	56	Bubonic Plague claimed Arab victims, 600 segregated.
Jan.	Germany	40	Mysterious disease struck Mennonite refugees, 50 others ill.
Feb.	Ionacatepec, Mexico	600	Smallpox claimed victims in fortnight.
Feb.	Balut & Sarangani	200	Smallpox epidemic struck island group.
Aug.	Belgian Congo	40,000	Drought brought famine to Ruada Province, 1,000s emigrated to Uganda.
1931	United States	17,000	Diphtheria killed children across country.
1932-1934	U.S.S.R.	5,000,000	Famine created by collectiveness among peasants.
1933 Sept. 20	Manchuria	1,000	Plague struck 2 cities, mainly Bubonic but some Pneumonic.
Oct. 1	China	50,000	Mysterious disease struck south-central area.
1935	Uganda	2,000	Strange epidemic of Bubonic Plague.
1935-1936	Santa Rem, Brazil	700	Malarial jungle fever struck area with great intensity.
1936	West China	5,000,000	Drought & famine brought incredible horror.
Feb.	Calcutta	400	Smallpox epidemic.
†1939 Sept.-Nov.	China	200,000	Famine followed great flood.
1942 Feb.	Greece	1,000s	Famine gripped country, 2,000 men, women & children died each day of cholera, typhus, typhoid & dysentery.
1943	India	Millions	Famine during world war.
	Kwangtung, China	1,000,000	Famine & disease caused people to sell children for supplies.
1946	Hunan Prov., China	60,000	Famine caused by drought, help for needy enormous.
Nov.	Hong Kong, China	530	Smallpox claimed more than half of 820 cases reported.
1947	U.S.S.R.	1,000s	Famine caused by exporting of grain which left peasants starved, not reported until 1963.
Sept.-Dec.	Egypt	10,276	Outbreak of cholera.
1948 July-Aug.	Changchun, Manchuria	1,000s	Great rise in prices caused starvation to reach upwards of 500 deaths per week.
1950 Aug.	Bihar, India	50	Famine claimed victims throughout state.

Date		Place	Deaths
1954	**Jan.**	**Sudan**	**100s**
	Smallpox epidemic claimed 40 victims a day.		
	Feb.	**Saigon, S. Vietnam**	**50**
	Outbreak of smallpox.		
1956	**May-Dec.**	**Iraq**	**300**
	Smallpox epidemic had 2,500 cases in 7 months.		
1957	**Feb.-Apr. 1**	**Calcutta**	**946**
	Smallpox epidemic, 141 victims in 1 wk.		
1958	**Jan.-July**	**India**	**16,000**
	Epidemic of smallpox & cholera lasted 7 months.		
	April	**E. Pakistan**	**50,000**
	Outbreak of cholera & smallpox.		
	Sept.	**E. Indonesia**	**515**
	Smallpox & cholera struck area.		
1959	**Mar. 14**	**Port-au-Prince, Haiti**	**200**
	Food shortage caused by drought in Jean-Rabel area.		
1960	**Nov. 28**	**Fortaleza, Brazil**	**20**
	Defective rabies serum left 120 ill.		
1961	**Jan. 14-Feb. 4**	**Java**	**143**
	Smallpox epidemic in central area, over 2,500 cases.		
	Apr. 5	**Nyasaland**	**103**
	Smallpox epidemic throughout area.		
1963	**June 26**	**India**	**1,000s**
	Famine in W. Bengal & Assam, 200,000 in state of starvation.		
1964	**Jan.-Feb.**	**Java**	**1,000**
	Famine spread throughout central area, 500 died a month.		
	Apr. 15	**Nyasaland**	**21**
	Smallpox outbreak in area.		
1965	**June 11**	**Belgian Congo**	**500**
	Smallpox epidemic in region.		
1966	**June 11**	**Sumatra**	**400**
	Western area struck by smallpox epidemic.		
	Dec. 18	**Pakistan**	**107**
	Smallpox infected country.		
1967	**Jan.-Apr.**	**India**	**4,000**
	Smallpox reported in 15 of 17 states.		
	Mar.-May	**East Pakistan**	**1,500**
	Smallpox infected area.		
	Oct.	**Tjiamis, W. Java**	**70**
	District had 700 smallpox cases reported.		
1967-8	**Nov.-Feb.**	**Karachi, Pakistan**	**100s**
	Smallpox epidemic lasted 4 months, exact toll of dead unknown.		
1968	**July-Sept.**	**Nigeria**	**800,000**
	Famine caused incredible starvation, deaths could be in millions.		
1970		**Yemen**	**300**
	Famine in earlier part of year affected 1,500,000; rains which lasted 1 month brought relief.		
1971	**Sept.**	**Al Basrah, Iraq**	**459**
	Mercury poisoned cargoes of American barley & Mexican wheat, over 6,500 people reported to hospitals.		
1972		**Iraq**	**100s**
	Mercury poisoning caused mass suffering from brain damage, blindness & paralysis.		
	†May	**India**	**800**
	Drought roasted 14 states; 50 million people suffered; crop loss over $400 million.		
1973-1974		**Africa & India**	**200,000**
	Drought caused mass starvation, reliable population records do not exist.		
1974	**Jan. 1-June 31**	**India**	**30,000**
	Worst smallpox epidemic of century to strike country, over 103,000 cases reported since beginning of that year.		
1975	**Aug.**	**Honduras**	**100s**
	Drought destroyed 90% of bean & corn crops.		
	Sept.	**Patna, India**	**50**
	Cholera in capital of Bahir State.		
	Oct.	**Papua, New Guinea**	**500**
	Influenza epidemic swept area.		

Major Railway Wrecks

(† indicates entries profiled in General Narrative)

Date		Place	Deaths
†1833	Nov. 8	**Hightstown, N.J.**	2
	Camden & Amboy train derailed, broken axle.		
1836	Apr. 1	**Frankfort, Ky.**	3
	Lexington & Ohio train derailed, broken cable.		
	Oct. 2	**Fairview, Pa.**	2
	Pennsylvania train derailed, broken axle.		
1837	Aug. 11	**Suffolk, Va.**	3
	Portsmouth & Roanoke train had a head-on collision with a lumber train, disregard to schedule.		
1839	July 4	**Union Sq., N.Y.**	2
	Harlem train boiler exploded.		
1840	Dec. 18	**Springfield, Mass.**	4
	Western train smashed through brick wall, runaway train.		
†1842	May 8	**Versailles, France**	54-100
	Carriages caught fire, victims locked in.		
1844	Sept. 2	**Reading, Pa.**	4
	Reading train boiler exploded.		
1847	Oct. 27	**Athol, Mass.**	4
	Vermont & Massachusetts train fell into Miller River, bridge collapsed.		
	Nov. 6	**Brookline, Mass.**	6
	Boston & Worcester train derailed, loosened brake rod.		
1848	Nov. 3	**Salem, Mass.**	6
	Eastern train had America's first head-on collision which involved a special excursion train.		
1851	Sept. 4	**Stuyvesant, N.Y.**	3
	Hudson River train collided with a cow.		
1852	Sept. 15	**Almond, N.Y.**	5
	Erie train rear collision, failure to provide flag protection.		
	Oct. 7	**Weirs, N.H.**	6
	Boston, Concord & Montreal train rear collision, failure to protect a stalled train.		
1853	Jan. 6	**Andover, Mass.**	6
	Boston & Maine train derailed, broken axle.		
	Apr. 23	**Chicago**	21
	Michigan Central & Michigan Southern collided, failure to obey timetable.		
	†May 6	**South Norwalk, Conn.**	46
	New Haven train fell into Norwalk River, engineer went through open draw.		
	Aug. 2	**Bulls Island, N.J.**	11
	Belvider & Delaware train collided with a cow.		
	Oct. 5	**Straffan, Ireland**	16
	Ireland's first major railway disaster, rear collision of passenger train.		
†1854	July 4	**Riverwood, Md.**	34
	Baltimore train head-on collision, conductor disregarded orders.		
	Oct. 27	**Baptist Creek, Ont.**	47
	Great Western Canada train collided in dense fog, switchman disregarded orders.		
†1855	Aug. 29	**Columbus, N.J.**	21
	Camden & Amboy train collided with carriage, sole operator backed into train crossing at excessive speed.		
	†Nov. 1	**Gasconade, Mo.**	22
	The Pacific Railroad of Missouri train fell into river, bridge collapsed.		
†1856	July 17	**Camp Hill, Pa.**	66
	Reading train collided with the Aramington, conductor disregarded schedule.		
†1857	Mar. 17	**Hamilton, Ont.**	66
	The Great Western Canada train fell into Des Jardines Canal, bridge collapsed.		
1858	Aug. 23	**Round Oak, England**	14
	Oxford, Worcester & Wolverhampton Railway collision.		
1861	Aug. 25	**Clayton Tunnel, England**	23
	London & Brighton train collision.		
	Sept. 17	**Huron, Ind.**	28
	The Ohio & Mississippi train fell into river, bridge collapsed.		
†1864	June 29	**St. Hilaire, Canada**	90
	Grand Trunk train fell into Richelieu Canal, engineer went throught an open draw.		
	†July 15	**Shohola, Pa.**	148
	Erie train collided head-on with prisoner train, telegraph operator gave all-clear signal.		
	Sept. 1	**Barnesville, Ga.**	30
	Macon & Western train had head-on collision with military train, confusion in shipment of supplies.		
1865	Aug. 25	**Reynolds, Tenn.**	35
	Louisville & Nashville train crashed, trestle collapsed.		
1867	June 26	**Great Indian Peninsular**	100
	Train plunged into river between Bhosawal and Hhundwah.		
	Aug. 20	**Abergale, N. Wales**	33
	Irish mail and luggage train ignited barrels of oil and exploded.		
	†Dec. 18	**Angola, N.Y.**	42
	Lake Shore train derailed, forward axle of rear truck of the rear car was slightly bent.		
†1868	Apr. 15	**Carr's Point, N.Y.**	26
	Erie passenger train broke track & fell down 100-ft. gorge.		
1870	Feb. 26	**Oxford, Miss.**	19
	Mississippi Central train crashed, trestle collapsed.		
	May 12	**Eureka, Mo.**	19
	Missouri Pacific train head-on collision, switchman disregarded orders.		
†1871	Feb. 6	**Wappingers Creek, N.Y.**	21
	Hudson River train derailed, collided with oil cars.		
	Feb. 25	**St. Nizaire, France**	60
	Train exploded with cargo of gunpowder near city.		
	†Aug. 26	**Revere, Mass.**	30
	Eastern train rear collision, excessive speed.		
1872	June 22	**Belleville, Ont.**	25
	Grand Trunk train derailed, engine broke off the line.		
	†Dec. 24	**Prospect, Pa.**	25
	Buffalo, Corry & Pittsburgh train collapsed bridge, broken wheel and fire.		
1873	May 7	**Perth, England**	21
	Train derailed near city.		
1874	Sept. 10	**Norwich, England**	26
	Two-train collision, telegraph clerks tried for manslaughter.		
	Dec. 24	**Shipton, England**	34
	Great Western train fell over embankment, tire of wheel broke.		
1876	Jan. 8	**Odessa, Russia**	68
	Train derailed on embankment near city.		
	†Dec. 29	**Ashtabula, Ohio**	92
	Lake Shore train fell into river, bridge collapsed in snowstorm. Worst American rail disaster to this date.		
†1878	Oct. 8	**Wollaston Station, Mass.**	21
	Old Colony train derailed, misplaced switch.		
1879	Jan. 11	**Phillippopolis, Turkey**	200
	Military train collapsed bridge.		
	†Dec. 28	**Dundee, Scotland**	75
	Train and Tay Bridge blown into river.		

Date		Place	Deaths
†1880	Aug. 11	**Mays Landing, N.J.**	40
		West Jersey & Atlantic train rear collision, second section followed too close.	
	†Oct. 9	**Pittsburgh, Pa.**	32
		Pennsylvania train rear collision, disregarded signals.	
†1881	June 24	**Cuartla, Mexico**	216
		Morelos train collapsed bridge, fell into San Antonio River.	
1882	July 13	**Tcherny & Bastigeur, Russia**	178
		Moscow Kursk train derailed, 8 carriages overturned.	
	Sept. 3	**Hugstetten, Germany**	70
		Baden train derailed.	
1883	July 27	**Carlyon, N.Y.**	23
		Rome, Watertown & Oldensburg train collided with freight car, brakes improperly secured.	
†1884	Jan. 2	**Toronto, Ontario**	30
		Grand Trunk train head-on collision, disregarded orders.	
	July 16	**Penistone, England**	24
		Manchester, Sheffield & Lincolnshire train wrecked on Bullhouse Bridge, broken crank axle.	
†1886	Sept. 14	**Silver Creek, N.Y.**	20
		Nickel Plate Road train head-on collision, other train disabled.	
†1887	Feb. 5	**White River, Vt.**	32
		Vermont Central train derailed and caught fire, broken rail.	
	†Mar. 14	**Forest Hills, Mass.**	24
		Boston & Providence train crashed, Busey Bridge collapsed.	
	†Aug. 10	**Chatsworth, Ill.**	82
		Toledo, Peoria & Western train crashed, bridge burned.	
	Nov. 15	**Hexthorpe, England**	25
		Manchester & Sheffield train smashed into Midland train.	
1888	Mar. 17	**Blackshear, Ga.**	23
		Atlantic Coast Line train derailed, trestle collapsed.	
	†Oct. 10	**Mud Run, Pa.**	64
		Lehigh Valley train rear collision, disregarded signal.	
	Oct. 20	**Salandra & Grassam, Italy**	22
		Train buried by landslide between cities.	
	Oct. 29	**Borki Station, S. Russia**	21
		Imperial train derailed, weak tracks.	
†1889	June 12	**Armagh, Ireland**	75
		Two special trains of the Great Northern Railway had rear collision due to excessive speeds.	
†1890	Aug. 19	**Quincy, Mass.**	23
		Old Colony Road train derailed, jack left on track.	
	†Sept. 19	**Shoemakerville, Pa.**	23
		Coal and merchant trains collided head-on.	
	Nov. 14	**Topsin, Greece**	40
		Train derailed near Salonica.	
†1891	June 14	**Bale, Switzerland**	120
		Excursion train collapsed bridge.	
	†July 3	**Ravenna, Ohio**	25
		Erie train rear collision, disregarded time interval.	
	July 27	**St. Maude, France**	44
		Excursion train collision near Paris.	
	Sept. 24	**Burgos, Spain**	25
		Train collision near city.	
	Nov. 23	**Central Russia**	31
		Kosloff train derailed on bridge.	
	Dec. 8	**Lahore, India**	70
		North & Western train collision 75 mi. from city.	
1893	Oct. 19	**Battle Creek, Mich.**	26
		Grand Trunk train head-on collision, disregarded orders.	
1895	Feb. 28	**Mexico City, Mexico**	140
		Train derailed, fell down gorge near city.	
	Nov. 16	**Cleveland, Ohio**	17
		Cleveland trolley fell from Central Viaduct, open draw.	

Date		Place	Deaths
†1896	May 26	**Victoria, B.C.**	54
		Trolley fell into gorge, iron bridge collapsed.	
	†July 30	**Atlantic City, N.J.**	60
		Reading Pennsylvania train collision, failure to exercise due caution and give right of way.	
1899	Feb. 18	**Forrest, Belgium**	21
		Calais Express and local train collided near Brussels.	
	May 12	**Exeter, Pa.**	34
		Reading train rear collision, failure to observe 5-min. interval.	
	Aug. 6	**Bridgeport, Conn.**	29
		Bridgeport Traction Co. trolley derailed, Peck's Pond bridge lacked guard rails.	
	Aug. 24	**Mapocho River, Chile**	60
		Train derailed, fell into river.	
1900	June 23	**McDonough, Ga.**	35
		Southern train wrecked, washout.	
	July 4	**Tacoma, Wash.**	41
		Trolley derailed, brake failure.	
1901	Aug. 31	**Nyack, Mont.**	34
		Great Northern train rear collision, runaway freight.	
	†Nov. 27	**Seneca, Mich.**	20
		Wabash train head-on collision, misinterpretation of orders.	
1902	May 12	**Pittsburgh, Pa.**	23
		Pennsylvania train exploded.	
	Sept. 1	**Berry, Ala.**	21
		Southern train derailed and fell down embankment, cause unknown.	
	Sept. 11	**Mangapatnan, Madras**	62
		Mail train wrecked, bridge collapsed.	
	Sept. 27	**Douai, France**	20
		Express train derailed near city.	
	Dec. 20	**Byron, Cal.**	27
		Southern Pacific train rear collision, hot box in forward train.	
	†Dec. 26	**Wanstead, Ont.**	28
		Grand Trunk train head-on collision, engineer's error.	
1903	Jan. 28	**Wesfield, N.J.**	23
		Central New Jersey train rear collision, disregarded signals.	
	June 27	**San Arsenslo, Spain**	100
		Bilbao-Zarogoza train derailed into Najerilla River.	
	†July 7	**Rockfish, Va.**	23
		Southern train head-on collision, misinterpretation of orders.	
	†Aug. 7	**Durand, Mich.**	22
		Wallace circus train rear collision, engineer asleep.	
	Aug. 10	**Les Couronnes, France**	84
		Paris Underground train caught fire and exploded.	
	Nov. 14	**Kentwood, La.**	32
		Illinois Central train rear collision, rear protection failure.	
	†Dec. 23	**Laurel Run, Pa.**	64
		Baltimore and Ohio train derailed, timber fallen from earlier freight blocked track.	
†1904	Aug. 7	**Eden, Colo.**	96
		Missouri Pacific train wrecked, Steele's Hollow Bridge collapsed in flood.	
	†Sept. 24	**Hodges, Tenn.**	63
		Southern train head-on collision, orders disregarded.	
	Oct. 10	**Warrensburg, Mo.**	29
		Missouri Pacific train head-on collision, overlooked second section on "dead man's curve."	
†1905	May 11	**Harrisburg, Pa.**	22
		Pennsylvania train derailed then exploded.	
	June 17	**Patapsco, Md.**	26
		Western Maryland train head-on collision, disregarded orders.	

Date		Place	Deaths
	July 27	Hall, England	21
	Liverpool & Southport train collided with stationary train.		
	Oct. 27	Victoria, Miss.	23
	Frisco train derailed, broken rail.		
†1906	Mar. 16	Florence, Colo.	34
	Denver & Rio Grande train head-on collision, orders were not delivered.		
	June 30	Salisbury, England	28
	High speed derailment & collision.		
	Oct. 28	Atlantic City, N.J.	57
	Pennsylvania train derailed on the Thorofare drawbridge.		
	†Nov. 12	Woodville, Ind.	43
	Baltimore & Ohio train head-on collision, second section overlooked.		
	Dec. 28	Elliot Junction, England	21
	Newcastle & Berwick train wrecked in collision near Arbroath.		
	†Dec. 30	Washington, D.C.	43
	Baltimore & Ohio train rear collision, signals unobserved.		
†1907	Jan. 2	Volland, Kansas	32
	Rock Island train head-on collision, engineer's error.		
	Mar. 28	Colton, Calif.	22
	Southern Pacific derailed, misplaced switch.		
	†May 11	Surf, Calif.	33
	Southern Pacific train derailed.		
	†June 20	Salem, Mich.	30
	Pere Marquette train head-on collision, misinterpretation of orders.		
	Sept. 15	Canaan, N.H.	26
	Boston & Maine train head-on collision, misinterpretation of orders.		
	Sept. 19	Encavnacion, Mexico	63
	Train wreck at city.		
1908	Apr. 20	Melbourne, Australia	28
	Two trains collided at Braybrook Station outside city.		
	May 8	Moradabad, India	120
	Train wrecked, failure in the "tablet" system.		
	Sept. 25	Young's Point, Mont.	23
	Northern Pacific train head-on collision, violation of time schedule.		
1909	Jan. 15	Dotsero, Colo.	20
	Denver & Rio Grande train head-on collision, orders disregarded.		
	Nov. 28	Sapperton, B.C.	22
	Great Northern train wrecked, washout.		
1910	Mar. 1	Wellington, Washington	96
	Two trains buried by avalanche.		
	Mar. 21	Green Mountain, Ia.	55
	Rock Island train derailed, track in terrible condition.		
	Sept. 21	Kingsland, Ind.	34
	Fort Wayne & Wabash train head-on collision, disregard for time table rules.		
	†Oct. 4	Staunton, Ill.	36
	Illinois Traction train head-on collision, second section overlooked.		
†1911	Aug. 25	Manchester, N.Y.	28
	Lehigh Valley train derailed, broken rail.		
1912	July 4	Corning, N.Y.	39
	Lackawanna train rear collision, signals disregarded.		
	July 5	Ligonier, Pa.	
	Ligonier Valley train head-on collision, orders disobeyed.		
1913	Apr. 4	Congo, Africa	23
	Train derailed on bridge, fell into gorge.		
	Sept. 2	Wallingford, Conn.	21
	New Haven train rear collision, outmoded signals.		
	Dec. 6	Costesi, Rumania	100
	Train collision near city.		
†1914	Aug. 5	Tipton Ford, Mo.	47
	Kansas City Southern train head-on collision, complete disregard for orders.		
	Sept. 15	Lebanon, Mo.	27
	Frisco train wrecked, washout.		
†1915	Jan. 18	Guadalajara, Mexico	600
	Train derailed, fell into gorge.		
	†May 22	Gretna Green, Scotland	227
	Caledonian trains head-on collision.		
1916	Mar. 5	Nish, Serbia	40
	Berlin-Constantinople train wrecked near city.		
	Mar. 21	Sayula, Mexico	50
	Mexican Central train wrecked near city.		
	Mar. 29	Amherst, Ohio	26
	New York Central train rear collision, collided with another wreckage.		
	Aug. 12	Brookvale, Pa.	28
	Southern Cambria train collision, runaway train.		
	Nov. 7	Boston, Mass.	40
	Streetcar fell into Fort Point Channel, open draw.		
	Nov. 10	Chirimoya, Mexico	40
	Troop train telescoped near Celaya.		
	Nov. 12	Berlin, Germany	19
	Balkan Express train ran down victims, all women.		
	Nov. 19	Behesa & San Miquel, Mexico	150
	Inter-Oceanic train wrecked on way to Veracruz.		
1917	Jan. 28	Tshura, Rumania	500
	Train wrecked near city.		
	Feb. 27	Mount Union, Pa.	20
	Pennsylvania train rear collision, lack of proper protection.		
	Aug. 14	Petrograd & Moscow, Russia	60
	Train wrecked between cities.		
	Sept. 28	Kellyville, Okla.	23
	Frisco train head-on collision, complete disregard for orders.		
	†Dec. 12	Modane, France	543
	Troop train derailed, out of control from wide tracks.		
	Dec. 20	Shepherdsville, Ky.	46
	Louisville & Nashville train rear collision, complete disregard for signals.		
†1918	June 22	Ivanhoe, Ind.	53
	Michigan Central train rear collision, empty circus train; engineer asleep.		
	†July 9	Nashville, Tenn.	101
	Nashville, Chattanooga & St. Louis train head-on collision, misinterpretation of orders.		
	Sept. 24	Dresden, Germany	31
	Train wreck at station.		
	Oct. 15	Bucharest, Rumania	100
	Bucharest Express train derailed near city.		
	†Nov. 2	Brooklyn, N.Y.	97
	Brooklyn Rapid Transit train derailed, made curve at excessive speed at Malbone St. tunnel.		
1919	Jan. 12	South Byron, N.Y.	22
	New York Central train rear collision, complete disregard for signals.		
	Apr. 17	Lemans, France	21
	Troop train collision near city.		
	Oct. 5	Mexico City, Mexico	60
	Train derailed in city.		
	†Dec. 20	Onawa, Me.	23
	Canadian Pacific train head-on collision, misinterpretation of orders.		
1920	Oct. 9	Paris, France	40
	Paris-Mantes train smashed into freight near city.		
	Oct. 9	Venice, Italy	23
	Train collision near city.		
	Dec. 22	Petrograd, Russia	212
	Train wrecked near city.		

Date	Place	Deaths
1921 Feb. 6	**Felixdorf, Austria** Train wrecked near city.	25
†Feb. 27	**Porter, Ind.** New York Central & Michigan Central crossing collision, complete disregard for signals.	37
June 25	**Paris, France** Lille-Paris train wrecked near city.	23
Dec. 5	**Woodmont, Pa.** Reading train head-on collision, complete disregard for signals.	27
1922 Aug. 1	**Tarbes, France** Train wrecked with pilgrims on way to Lourdes.	40
†Aug. 5	**Sulphur Springs, Mo.** Missouri Pacific train rear collision, complete disregard for signals.	34
Oct. 22	**Larubanya, Rumania** Train wrecked near city.	30
Dec. 13	**Humble, Tex.** Southern Pacific train side collision, engine ran off main track.	22
1923 Feb. 8	**Duesseldorf, Germany** Troop train in collision near city.	28
May 7	**Havana, Cuba** Train collision near city.	50
May 31	**Kreiensen, Germany** Train wreck at city.	47
July 3	**Vintelanca, Rumania** Bucharest-Jassy mail train smashed into freight.	63
July 3	**Acheres, France** Le Havre-Paris train derailed.	40
Aug. 24	**Lida, Russia** Train wrecked near city.	50
†Sept. 27	**Cole Creek, Wyo.** Burlington train wrecked, Cole Creek bridge collapsed in storm.	31
1924 Mar. 15	**Bareilly, India** Train derailed by tornado.	50
1925 Jan. 13	**Herne, Germany** Express and local trains collided.	23
Apr. 9	**Las Dianas, Spain** Electric trains collided near city.	20
Apr. 10	**Barcelona, Spain** Electric train smashed into wall of tunnel.	24
May 30	**Moscow, Russia** Taskent Express collided with suburban train.	50
†June 16	**Hackettstown, N.J.** Lackawanna train derailed, washed over earth blocked crossing.	50
Oct. 27	**Victoria, Miss.** Frisco train derailed, broken rail.	21
Nov. 13	**Dunaburg, Russia** Warsaw-Riga Express wrecked by freight near city.	22
1926 Mar. 15	**Virilia River, Costa Rica** Train derailed on bridge.	248
Aug. 19	**Hanover, Germany** Express train derailed, loosened rails.	21
Sept. 5	**Waco, Colo.** Denver & Rio Grande train derailed, excessive speed.	30
Sept. 24	**Hiroshima, Japan** Train wrecked near city.	40
Dec. 11	**Tiehling, Manchuria** Southern Manchuria trains collided near city.	25
Dec. 23	**Rockmart, Ga.** Southern train head-on collision, misinterpretation of orders.	20
1927 Feb. 24	**Tampico, Mexico** Monterey train wrecked 45 mi. from city.	40
Aug. 26	**Chamonix, France** Train plunged over 40-ft. cliff.	29
1928 Jan. 28	**Mandalay & Rangoon, India** Train derailed, fell off bridge.	40
June 10	**Nuremburg, Germany** Munich-Frankfort train fell down embankment near city.	22
June 27	**Darlington, England** Train wrecked at city.	25
Sept. 11	**Bruenn, Czechoslovakia** Paris-Berlin-Vienna train wrecked.	21
Oct. 26	**Recea, Rumania** Train wrecked, victims later looted by bandits.	35
1929 Apr. 5	**Boboca, Rumania** Train wrecked.	20
Sept. 24	**Perm-Viatka, Russia** Trans-Siberian mail train wrecked.	45
1930 Apr. 6	**Oita, Japan** Train exploded near city.	20
May 31	**Leningrad, Russia** Train wrecked near city.	22
1932 Jan. 7	**Moscow, Russia** Train collision near city.	50
May 24	**Harbin, Manchoukuo** Freight train smashed into passenger train near city.	40
Sept. 14	**Tlemcen, Algeria** French Foreign Legion train derailed, fell 250 ft.	50
1933 Aug. 21	**Namchang, China** Train wrecked near city.	40
Oct. 26	**Evreux, France** Train derailed near city.	30
Dec. 23	**Lagny, France** Local train smashed into Nancy express.	150
1934 Mar. 20	**Sverdlovsk, Russia** Trains collided near city.	33
1935 Sept. 24	**Loyang, China** Troop train wrecked at Honan Province.	200
Dec. 24	**Gross Heringen, Germany** Berlin-Basel train smashed into local.	20
1936 Oct. 24	**Tenchatang, China** Train wrecked, military officer blamed.	28
1937 July 16	**Patna, India** Delhi-Calcutta train derailed near city.	160
Dec. 4	**Madrid, Spain** Two trains collided near city.	20
Dec. 10	**Castlecary, England** Rear collision in heavy snow.	35
1938 Apr. 4	**Plumtree, S. Rhodesia** Freight and passenger trains collided.	23
Apr. 5	**Yencheng, China** Train wrecked in city.	80
May 30	**Balaclava, Jamaica** Train wrecked near station.	37
†June 19	**Saugus, Mont.** Milwaukee train wrecked, Custer Creek Bridge washed out by flood.	47
Aug. 21	**Trichinopoly & Madura, India** Train derailed between cities.	20
Dec. 21	**Mexico City, Mexico** Train wrecked near city.	40
Dec. 25	**Bessarabia, Rumania** Trains collided near Kishinev.	80
1939 Feb. 11	**Barcelona, Spain** Train wrecked outside city.	35
Oct. 8	**Berlin, Germany** Trains collided.	20
Nov. 31	**Transylvania, Rumania** Train derailed and overturned.	22
Dec. 22	**Magdeburg, Germany** Trains collided near city.	132
Dec. 22	**Freidrichshafen, Germany** Train wrecked near city.	99

Major Railway Wrecks

Date		Place	Deaths
1940	Jan. 28	**Osaka, Japan**	200
	Trains collided at city, caught fire.		
	†Apr. 19	**Little Falls, N.Y.**	30
	New York Central train derailed, made curve at excessive speed.		
	May 4	**Vallon, France**	21
	Train wrecked near city.		
	†July 31	**Cuyahoga Falls, Ohio**	41
	Pennsylvania train head-on collision, complete disregard for orders.		
	Nov. 4	**Traunton, England**	27
	London-Penzance train derailed near city.		
	Dec. 3	**Velilla de Ebro, Spain**	41
	Trains collided.		
	Dec. 15	**Iguala Caztal, Mexico**	25
	Trains derailed.		
1941	Jan. 11	**Paris, France**	20
	Train collision at Austerlitz Station.		
	Oct. 2	**Himeji & Okayama, Japan**	40
	Train collision between cities.		
	Dec. 24	**Johannesburg, So. Africa**	35
	Train derailed outside of city.		
	Dec. 30	**Hazenbrouck, France**	49
	Train wreck near city.		
	Dec. 30	**Eccles, England**	23
	Two passenger trains collided.		
1942	May 17	**Karachi, India**	22
	Northwestern Railway train wreck.		
	Dec. 27	**Almonte, Ont.**	36
	Canadian Pacific train rear collision, direct violation of standard rules.		
1943	Aug. 29	**Wayland, N.Y.**	27
	Lackawanna train collision, main track thwarted at switch.		
	†Sept. 6	**Frankford Junction, Pa.**	79
	Pennsylvania train (Congressional Limited) derailed, burned-off journal.		
	Dec. 16	**Buie, N.C.**	72
	Atlantic Coast train derailed in double accident.		
†1944	Mar. 2	**Salerno, Italy**	426
	Train stalled in tunnel and victims suffocated.		
	Mar. 26	**Tucuruvi, Brazil**	31
	Suburban train derailed near city.		
	July 6	**High Cliff, Tenn.**	35
	Louisville & Nashville train derailed, wide guage on tracks.		
	†Aug. 4	**Stockton, Ga.**	47
	Atlantic Coast train derailed, broken rail.		
	Sept. 14	**Terre Haute, Ind.**	29
	Chicago & Eastern Illinois trains head-on collision, complete disregard for signals.		
	Nov. 7	**Aguadilla, Spain**	500
	Train collision and fire in Leon Province Tunnel.		
	†Dec. 31	**Ogden, Utah**	50
	Southern Pacific train rear collision, complete disregard for signals.		
1945	Feb. 1	**Cazadero, Mexico**	100
	Nation Railways special pilgrim train collided with freight train 100 mi. N. of Mexico City.		
	Aug. 9	**Michigan, N.D.**	34
	Great Northern train rear collision, lack of protection for rear.		
	Aug. 25	**Cochabamba, Bolivia**	35
	Train derailed near city.		
	Sept. 30	**Bourne End, England**	43
	Train derailed at crossover.		
1946	Jan. 1	**Lichfield, England**	20
	New Year's Day train collision.		
	Mar. 20	**Aracaju, Brazil**	185
	Train derailed near city.		
	†Apr. 25	**Naperville, Ill.**	45
	Burlington train rear collision, complete disregard for signals.		
	Nov. 12	**Revigny sur Ornain, France**	35
	Train wrecked 35 mi. E. of Paris.		
†1947	Feb. 18	**Gallitzin, Pa.**	24
	Pennsylvania train derailed, made curve at excessive speed.		
	May 18	**Comilla, Bengal**	36
	Train derailed outside city.		
	July 10	**Canton, China**	200
	Passenger train derailed, plunged into river.		
	†Sept. 1	**Dugald, Ont., Canada**	31
	Canadian National train head-on collision, complete disregard for orders.		
	Oct. 24	**South Croyton, England**	31
	Two electric trains collided in fog.		
	Oct. 26	**Goswick, England**	24
	Train derailed near city.		
1948	Apr. 17	**Winsford, England**	24
	Mail and passenger train collision.		
	Sept. 14	**Napan, Korea**	40
	Local crashed into American troop train 120 mi. S. of Seoul.		
1949	Feb. 12	**Mora la Nueva, Spain**	30
	Madrid-Barcelona train fell down 40-ft. embankment.		
	Feb. 19	**Port d'Atelier, France**	43
	Locomotive smashed into passenger train.		
	Apr. 28	**Orlando, So. Africa**	74
	Triple electric train collision 10 mi. from Johannesburg.		
	Oct. 11	**Buenos Aires, Argentina**	25
	Freight and suburban train collided.		
	Oct. 22	**Nowy Dwor, Poland**	200
	Danzig-Warsaw train derailed, made curve at excessive speed.		
	Nov. 15	**Waterval Bowen, Africa**	56
	Train plunged into river off 70-foot bridge.		
1950	Jan. 30	**Sirkind, India**	54
	Train collision on E. Punjab Ry.		
	Feb. 17	**Rockville Center, L.I.**	31
	Long Island train side collision, complete disregard for signals.		
	Apr. 6	**Rio de Janeiro, Brazil**	108
	Leopoldina train plunged into Indios River, bridge collapsed.		
	May 7	**Jasidih, India**	81
	Punjab mail train crashed near city.		
	May 25	**Chicago, Ill.**	33
	Streetcar collided with gasoline truck, explosion followed.		
	†Sept. 11	**West Lafayette, Ohio**	33
	Pennsylvania train rear collision, complete disregard for signals.		
	Nov. 21	**Canoe River, B.C.**	21
	Canadian National head-on collision, operator's mistake.		
	†Nov. 22	**Richmond Hill, L.I.**	79
	Long Island train rear collision, complete disregard for signals.		
	Dec. 21	**Podivin, Czechoslovakia**	21
	Train smashed into bus.		
†1951	Feb. 6	**Woodbridge, N.J.**	84
	Pennsylvania train derailed, excessive speed on temporary rail.		
	Apr. 4	**Sakuragicho, Japan**	104
	Inter-urban train caught fire, broken power line blamed.		

Date		Place	Deaths
	June 8	**Nova Iguacu, Brazil**	**54**
	Train smashed into stalled gasoline truck 20 mi. from Rio. Brazil's worst rail disaster to this date.		
	Aug. 24	**Metz, France**	**20**
	Two French trains collided outside city, confusion in operation of signals.		
	Oct. 6	**Montenegro, Colombia**	**26**
	Avalanche buried train.		
	Nov. 12	**Weber Canyon, Wyo.**	**20**
	City of San Francisco rammed City of Los Angeles in blizzard.		
	Dec. 17	**Carneiro, Brazil**	**53**
	Train jumped tracks outside city.		
1952	**Mar. 4**	**Pavuna River, Brazil**	**119**
	Train rammed 2 derailed cars of Central Rio de Janeiro train, broken rail blamed.		
	May 17	**Adana, Turkey**	**26**
	Train derailed in the south.		
	May 18	**Bikaner, India**	**45**
	Passenger and freight train collision, misinterpretation of orders.		
	July 9	**Pzepin, Poland**	**160**
	Train wrecked outside city.		
	†Oct. 8	**Harrold-Wealdstone, England**	**112**
	Perth-London train rammed local commuter train at Harrold-Wealdstone station.		
	Oct. 16	**Lagos, Nigeria**	**40**
	Lagos-Offa train collided with crane near city.		
	Oct. 20	**Frere, So. Africa**	**23**
	Johannesburg-Durban train derailed.		
	Dec. 31	**Budapest, Hungary**	**20**
	Train wrecked, railroad worker hanged for negligence.		
1953	**Jan. 3**	**Iwon, Korea**	**27**
	Freight train derailed and ran off bridge.		
	Feb. 15	**Comodoro, Rivadavia, Argentina**	**24**
	Excursion train derailed and fell down a 150-ft. embankment.		
	Feb. 15	**Benevento, Italy**	**22**
	Bari-Naples train derailed, ran through closed switch.		
	Feb. 21	**Mexico City, Mexico**	**60**
	Suburban trolley car wrecked.		
	†Mar. 27	**Conneaut, Ohio**	**21**
	Pennsylvania train derailed after collision, damaged track by unsecured lading when a 35-ft. pipe bent a rail.		
	Dec. 18	**Sydenham, Australia**	**46**
	Electric trains collided.		
	†Dec. 24	**Waiouri, New Zealand**	**155**
	Wellington-Auckland train derailed, volcanic eruption of Raupchu volcano damaged track.		
	Dec. 24	**Sakvice, Czechoslovakia**	**103**
	Prague-Brno-Bratislava train smashed rear of local train, crew negligence blamed.		
1954	**Jan. 20**	**Taurus Mts., Turkey**	**20**
	Freight fell down incline into passenger train, brakes blamed.		
	Jan. 21	**Sind Desert, Pakistan**	**100**
	Oil and mail express train collided and burned 75 mi. N. of Karachi.		
	Jan. 30	**Kafr el Zayat, Egypt**	**28**
	Cairo-Alexandria passenger train ran over crowd who waited to greet Egyptian Pres. Mohammed Naguib.		
	Jan. 31	**Seoul, Korea**	**46**
	Passenger train collided with truck.		
	Feb. 8	**Benares, India**	**22**
	Cars of a ballast train overturned on workers.		
	Feb. 12	**Diamantina, Brazil**	**30**
	Train and bus collided.		
	Feb. 26	**Mexico City, Mexico**	**23**
	Runaway car smashed into locomotive.		
	Mar. 31	**New Delhi, India**	**31**
	Train, which carried explosives, blew up.		
	July 3	**Chateaubourg, France**	**20**
	Freight train smashed into passenger train.		
	July 24	**Wurms, W. Germany**	**21**
	Passenger train smashed into bus at grade crossing.		
	Sept. 2	**Negros Islands, Philippines**	**82**
	Logging train derailed on bridge.		
	Sept. 24	**Hyderabad, India**	**137**
	Train fell through water-logged bridge 50 mi. E. of city.		
	Dec. 2	**Louvain, Belgium**	**21**
	Passenger train wrecked outside of city.		
1955	**Feb. 7**	**Union of South Africa**	**46**
	Two-train collision between Johannesburg and Durban.		
	Apr. 3	**Guadalajara, Mexico**	**300**
	Train derailed, fell into canyon.		
	May 12	**West Java**	**46**
	Passenger train derailed in mountains.		
	July 14	**Beni Mazar, Egypt**	**20**
	Freight train jumped track and ran over passenger platform.		
	July 17	**San Bernardo, Chile**	**49**
	Passenger train smashed into station.		
†1956	**Jan. 22**	**Los Angeles, Calif.**	**30**
	Sante Fe train derailed, made curve at excessive speed.		
	Feb. 14	**Santiago, Chile**	**21**
	Holiday and freight train collision.		
	Feb. 25	**Burnitz, E. Germany**	**32**
	Freight train smashed into Dresden-Leipzig Express.		
	†Sept. 2	**Mahbubnagar, India**	**85**
	Passenger train fell into flooded ravine, bridge collapsed from heavy rain.		
	†Sept. 5	**Robinson, N.M.**	**20**
	Sante Fe train head-on collision, switch left open.		
	Nov. 23	**Marudaiyar, India**	**143**
	Madras-Tuticorin train fell into flooded river, bridge collapsed.		
	Dec. 16	**Taguasco, Cuba**	**22**
	Havana Express head-on crash with passenger train.		
1957	**Mar. 15**	**Tampere, Finland**	**24**
	Two express trains collided in snowstorm.		
	Apr. 7	**Magno, Brazil**	**20**
	Two passenger trains collided outside Rio de Janeiro.		
	June 5	**Cortazar, Mexico**	**24**
	Passenger and freight train collided outside city.		
	July 19	**Bollene, France**	**24**
	Nice-Paris train derailed.		
	Aug. 4	**Villaverde, Spain**	**21**
	Spanish Army troop train rammed into locomotive.		
	†Sept. 1	**Kendal, Jamaica**	**175**
	Twelve-car excursion train broke apart and fell into ravine, brakes blamed.		
	Sept. 7	**Nozieres, France**	**23**
	Paris-Nimes Express train derailed.		
	Sept. 29	**Gambar, W. Pakistan**	**300**
	Express collided with standing oil train, passengers burned alive.		
	Sept. 29	**Ibadan, Nigeria**	**44**
	Lagos-to-Kano train fell over an embankment into flood waters.		
	Oct. 20	**Catalca, Turkey**	**89**
	Simplon Express collided into local train.		
	Nov. 16	**Chatonnay, France**	**28**
	Freight and farmer train collision, freight on wrong track.		
	Nov. 23	**Padali, India**	**50**
	Bombay-Calcutta mail train derailed and wrecked.		

Year	Date	Place	Deaths	Description
	Dec. 4	St. John's, England	92	Two commuter trains collided in dense fog outside London.
	Dec. 9	Codogno, Italy	20	Milan-Rome express train smashed into truck.
1958	Jan. 1	Ambala, India	32	Two passenger trains collided.
	Feb. 24	Pathankot, India	30	Ammunition train exploded.
	Mar. 7	Santa Cruz, Brazil	67	Commuter train pile-up, one ran into two others halted by storm signal.
	May 8	Paciencia, Brazil	128	Electric commuter trains collided, signal error. Brazilian Pres. ordered resignations of 3 top officials of the Cental de Brasil line.
	May 21	Bombay, India	30	Train derailed N.E. of city.
	June 22	Orizaba, Mexico	20	Mexico City-Veracruz train fell down mountain side.
	June 26	New Canada Junction, S. Africa	20	Train derailed outside Johannesburg.
	†Sept. 15	Bayonne, N.J.	48	New Jersey Central train wrecked, disregard for signals caused open draw.
	Dec. 14	Fortaleza, Brazil	20	Rescue train which carried drought victims wrecked over an embankment.
1959	May 28	East Priangan, W. Java	110	Passenger train fell into ravine, conductor blamed.
	June 5	Sao Paulo, Brazil	48	Commuter trains collided, rush hour confusion.
	June 20	Lauffren, Germany	43	Express train rammed bus, crossing signal mix-up.
1960	Feb. 7	Sewell, Chile	25	Copper mining train derailed, ran over 30-ft. embankment.
	May 15	Leipzig, E. Germany	59	Passenger trains collided, failure to understand signals at station.
	†Nov. 14	Pardubice, Czechoslovakia	110	Passenger trains collided, failure to understand signals.
1961	Jan. 9	Barcelona, Spain	25	Trains collided at junction, failure to observe signals.
	Mar. 24	Kotri, Pakistan	22	Train derailed at grade crossing, jumped tracks.
	July 9	Chiayi, Taiwan	49	Train smashed bus at crossing, disregard for signals.
	June 18	Vitry Le Francois, France	24	Strasbourg-Paris express train derailed, jumped tracks.
	Oct. 5	Hamburg, Germany	33	Commuter train collision, repair train in wrong place.
	Oct. 24	Calcutta, India	50	Express train wrecked, fell down embankment 150 mi. from city.
	Dec. 14	Greeley, Colo.	20	Union Pacific City of Denver train smashed school bus at crossing, bus driver indicted for manslaughter.
	Dec. 23	Catanzaro, Italy	69	Last car of train broke loose, fell into gorge.
1962	Jan. 8	Woerden, Netherlands	91	Express train collided commuter train, excessive speed in fog. This country's worst train disaster.
	Feb. 22	Cali, Colombia	40	Freight and passenger train head-on collision.
	May 3	Tokyo, Japan	163	Freight and commuter train collision, sideswiped each other. Second commuter train smashed into wreckage, 9 workers held on criminal negligence.
	May 31	Voghera, Italy	63	Freight train collision with standing passenger train, excessive speed.
	June 12	Buenos Aires, Argentina	33	Commuter train smashed into school bus at crossing.
	July 9	Garmsar, Turkey	49	Freight train collided with a crowded bus.
	July 21	Dumraon, India	69	New Delhi-Calcutta train collision with standing freight train, excessive speed.
	July 23	Velars-sur-Ouche, France	40	Paris-Marseilles train derailed, middle car fell 150 ft.
	July 23	Bucharest, Rumania	32	Passenger train derailed, made curve at excessive speed.
	July 28	Steelton, Pa.	19	Pennsylvania train derailed, track alignment error.
	Oct. 9	Warsaw, Poland	40	Chopin Express train derailed, heavy fog on flawed track.
	Nov. 5	Kumanovo, Yugoslavia	23	Train derailed outside city.
	Dec. 26	Lincoln, England	20	London-Edinburgh train rear collision, first train derailed.
1963	Jan. 4	Katihar, India	35	Mail train rear collision, passenger train was standing in junction.
	Apr. 11	Indonesia	37	Jakarta-Bandong train fell into 200-ft. ravine, brakes inadequate.
	Nov. 9	Yokohama, Japan	162	Passenger trains wrecked, both ran into derailed freight train.
	Dec. 24	Szolnok, Hungary	43	Passenger train wrecked, crashed into standing freight train.
1964	Jan. 14	Jajinci, Yugoslavia	66	Commuter and passenger train rear collision, latter train was stalled in station.
	Feb. 1	Altamirano, Argentina	70	Express and freight train collision, latter train stalled and both exploded.
	†July 26	Custoias, Portugal	94	Passenger train derailed, rear car fell off track. Worst rail disaster in this country's history.
	Nov. 1	Langhagen, E. Germany	39	Trains had head-on collision, engineer disregarded stop signals.
	Dec. 20	Tocotalpa, Mexico	41	Freight and passenger train collision, freight engineer was asleep and fled into jungle afterwards.
1965	Feb. 10	Barcelona, Spain	25	Madrid-Barcelona mail train burned, wooden coaches caught fire.
	Oct. 4	Kwa Mashu, Africa	81	South African train derailed, 3 cars fell off tracks.
	Dec. 9	Toungoo, Burma	76	Head-on train collision near city.
	Dec. 18	Villar de los Alamos, Spain	30	Paris-Lisbon and local train head-on collision.
1966	Feb. 16	Split, Yugoslavia	29	Coal train and passenger rear collision, brake failure.
	May 31	Bucharest, Rumania	38	Rumanian train collision, Railroad Minister Dumitrav Simulesco replaced for alleged rail-personnel deficiencies.
	June 13	Bombay, India	60	Suburban trains collided.

Date		Place	Deaths	
	Oct. 24	**Lakhiseri, India**	35	Express train ran down people who waited on track.
	Dec. 28	**Tervel, Spain**	28	Two-train head-on collision.
1967	**June 6**	**Langenweddingen, E. Germany**	82	Double-decker commuter train smashed into gas truck at crossing, most victims children. Railway gate operators sentenced to 5 yrs. for negligence.
	July 6	**Korat, Thailand**	43	Express train smashed into passenger bus at crossing.
	Nov. 5	**London, England**	49	Hastings-to-Hudson train derailed, fractured rail.
1968	**Mar. 15**	**Santa Maria de la Almeda, Spain**	26	Train and trolley car collision.
	Mar. 18	**Hubli, India**	52	Express and passenger train rear collision, latter train was stationary.
	Sept. 20	**Depot, Indonesia**	50	Head-on train collision near city.
	Dec. 22	**Budapest, Hungary**	43	Passenger and freight train head-on collision, excessive speed by pass.
1969	**Jan. 31**	**Chonan, S. Korea**	35	Passenger trains rear collision, engineer completely disregarded signal.
	Feb. 3	**Raihind, Pakistan**	29	Train smashed into bus at crossing.
	Feb. 17	**Johannesburg, So. Africa**	20	Passenger trains head-on collision.
	Mar. 21	**Perus & Caieiras, Brazil**	35	Electric and locomotive train head-on collision, power failure.
	Mar. 25	**La Louviere, Belgium**	25	Passenger trains head-on collision.
	May 2	**Sofia, Bulgaria**	25	Passenger train derailed, car fell off rails.
	July 29	**Mlada Boleslav, Czechoslovakia**	24	Passenger train collided with bus.
1970	**Jan. 11**	**Santa Marta, Colombia**	36	Train smashed into bus.
	Jan. 28	**Johannesburg, So. Africa**	30	Train smashed into school bus.
	Feb. 1	**Buenos Aires, Argentina**	139	Express and stalled commuter train collision, disregard for signal. Worst rail disaster in Argentina history.
	Feb. 16	**Lagalanga, Nigeria**	81	Four-coach train derailed and fell into ravine, survivors (52) killed in crash with truck on way to hospital.
	Aug. 10	**Plencia, Spain**	33	Passenger and empty freight train collision, erroneous signal for exit given one of the trains.
	Oct. 14	**Onyang, S. Korea**	44	Train smashed into school bus, railroad crossing unmanned.
	Dec. 11	**Brno, Czechoslovakia**	32	Budapest-Berlin train smashed into wagons, signalman error.
1971	**Feb. 9**	**Aitrang, W. Germany**	30	Trans-Europe Bavarian Express jumped the tracks, train going 48 m.p.h. over speed limit.
	Feb. 14	**Bosnia, Yugoslavia**	34	Passenger train caught fire in a tunnel.
	May 27	**Radevormwald, W. Germany**	45	Passenger and freight train head-on collision, freight engineer responsible.
	July 21	**Rheinweiler, Switzerland**	25	Switzerland Express jumped tracks, made curve at excessive speed.
†1972	**Mar. 30**	**Potgietesrus, South Africa**	38	Diesel locomotive plunged off railroad trestle into river bed.
	†June 4	**Jessore, Bangladesh**	76	Passenger train smashed into stopped train.
	†June 16	**Vierzy, France**	107	Railway collision inside Vierzy Tunnel.
	†July 21	**Lebrija, Spain**	76	Madrid-Cadiz Express and local train head-on collision, local ran through red signal at earlier station.
	Aug. 5	**Rawalpindi, Pakistan**	65	Train smashed into standing freight train.
	Oct. 9	**Saltillo, Mexico**	204	Passenger train derailed, made curve at excessive speed. Surviving crewmen were charged with negligent manslaughter.
	Oct. 29	**Southeast Germany**	21	Express trains collided in heavy fog, engineer overlooked stop signal.
	†Oct. 30	**Chicago, Ill.**	45	Illinois Central Gulf Railroad commuter trains collided, conductor failed to protect rear as his train backed up.
	Oct. 30	**West Central Turkey**	30	Passenger train head-on collision with track-repair train, signals disregarded.
	Nov. 6	**Fukui, Japan**	28	Express train fire in 9-mi. tunnel, deadly fumes spread through tunnel.
1973	**Jan. 30**	**Kecskemet, E. Hungary**	24	Passenger train collided with bus.
	Feb. 2	**Medjez-Sfa, Algeria**	35	Passenger train jumped the tracks.
	Mar. 16	**Central Cuba**	24	Train derailed over bridge, one car fell into river.
1974	**Mar. 28**	**Lourenco Marques, Mozambique**	32	Two trains collided near capital.
	†Aug. 30	**Zagreb, Yugoslavia**	150	Passenger train smashed into station at night.
	Nov. 6	**Cotonov, Dahomey**	80	Two passenger trains collided 43 miles west of city.
1975	**Jan. 18**	**Cairo, Egypt**	27	Locomotive derailed due to excess speed.
	Feb. 28	**London, England**	41	Worst subway crash in city's history.
	May 23	**Rabat, Morocco**	34	Train derailed 35 mi. northeast of city.
	June 8	**Munich, Germany**	35	Head-on collision on the Munich-Bad Tolz line 30 mi. south of city.
	Oct. 20	**Mexico City, Mexico**	27	Subway trains collided; 60 injured.

Major Storms

(† indicates entries profiled in General Narrative)

Date		Place	Deaths	Description
479 B.C.		Potidraea, Greece	1,000s	Seismic sea wave in the Gulf of Kassandra.
426		Central Greece	1,000s	Violent shock in the Gulf Maliakos & Euboea was followed by 3 *tsunamis* which overwhelmed Orobiae (Roviae), Atlanti (Talantonisi), & Opous.
375		Helike, Greece	100s	Seismic sea wave inundated city.
A.D. 365		Greece, Asia Minor, Crete	100s	Sea retired then roared back, great damage.
416		Sumatra	1,000s	Huge waves swept the coast.
670		England	Scores	Deadly frost descended on country.
684	Nov. 29	Shikoku, Japan	1,000s	Severe quake followed by *tsunami* sank 8 sq. mi.
740	Oct. 26	Turkey, Thrace, Constantinople	100s	Sea retired then spawned huge wave, widespread destruction.
850	Nov. 27	Japan Sea	100s	*Tsunami* smashed N. coast.
869	July 9	Japan	1,000	North coast shaken by quake, *tsunami* destroyed Oshu & Rikusen, 100 villages ruined.
881		Cordova, Spain	100s	Great sea wave on the coast.
887	Aug. 26	Settsu, Japan	100s	Seismic sea wave smashed coast & neighboring areas.
987-988		England	Scores	Great frost lasted 120 days.
1050		Cyclades Is. of Greece	Scores	Small *tsunami* struck Santorin accompanied by submarine volcanic eruption.
1059		England	100s	Cold followed by plague & famine.
1069		Syria, Ramla, Palestine & Egypt	100s	Sea retired then roared back, coast inundated.
1114-1115		England	100s	Most severe winter to date.
1134	Oct. 1	England & Netherlands	100s	Sea rose & inundated coasts, may not have been seismic.
1240	May 22	Kamakura, Japan	100s	Seismic wave struck province of Sagami.
1281	July 17	Kiushin Is., Japan	99,997	Typhoon wiped out Chinese fleet of 3,500 ships.
1293		Japan	30,000	Seismic sea wave devastated coast.
1344		Constantinople	100s	Waves inundated shore of city.
†1359		Chartres, France	1,000	Hailstorm & lightning devastated army of Edward III, 6,000 horses also killed.
1361	Aug. 3	Nankaido, Japan	1,000s	Sea retired & produced seismic wave which devastated coastal cities of Settsu, Awa, Yukiminato, & Osaka.
1389	Mar. 20	E. Sporadas (Chios)	Scores	Quake spawned wave which destroyed fortress of city & damaged majority of churches.
1402		Syria	1,000s	Sea retired & delivered disastrous seismic wave.
1481	Oct. 3	Cape Santa Cruz	Scores	Disastrous quake set off seismic wave at island.
1494	July 16	Cape Santa Cruz	Scores	Violent hurricane recorded by Columbus.
1498		Cape Verde Islands	Scores	Great heat then rain for 7 days as recorded by Columbus 480 mi. S.W. of area.
1498	Sept. 20	Japan	1,000s	Seismic sea wave followed quake on the coast of Kii, Ise, Mikawa & Sagami.
1500	July 10	Totomo, Japan	100s	Quake followed by *tsunami* wrecked city.
1502	July	Hispaniola	500	Hurricane sank 20 ships which carried gold for Columbus.
1508	Aug. 3	Santo Domingo	Scores	Gale destroyed all thatched houses & 20 sailing vessels.
1509	July 10	Hispaniola, W. Indies	100s	Hurricane destroyed Santo Domingo; this visitation was considered mark of divine pleasure.
	Sept. 14	Turkey	1,000s	Quake caused giant wave to overwhelm walls at Constantinople and Galata, damage widespread.
1510	Sept. 21	Settsu, Japan	100s	Giant wave along coast.
	Oct. 10	Totomi, Japan	100s	Tidal wave along coast.
1515	July	Puerto Rico	Many	Hurricane claimed large number of Indians as victims.
1526	Oct.	Espaniola	100s	Island suffered worst hurricane in years, rivers overflowed their banks.
1528	Oct. 2	Apalachee Bay, Fla.	390	Tropical storm struck fleet called the Narvaez Expedition.
1530		San Juan	Scores	Hurricane caused rivers to overflow, crops & herds were swept away, all undertakings suspended.
	Sept. 1	Venezuela	100s	Giant wave along coasts of Paria, Cumana, & Cubacoa—sea raised more than 20 ft. & fell again.
†1533	July 26-Aug. 31	Puerto Rico	2,000	A trio of hurricanes demolished Spanish settlement; victims black slaves.
1543		Venezuela	Scores	Tidal waves along coasts.
1546		Middle East	100s	Sea wave struck Palestine, Joppa, Sichem, Nablus & Rama.
1562	July 25	Japan	100s	Three tidal waves struck coasts of Yatsuchiro & Higo.
	Oct. 28	Santiago, Chile	1,000s	Seismic sea wave extended along 30 leagues of coast, widespread damage.
1570	Feb. 8	Concepcion, Chile	1,000s	Seismic sea wave raped city, widespread damage.
†1574	Oct. 1-2	Leyden, Holland	20,000	Dikes gave way during fierce storm drowning Spanish troops about to siege Leyden.
1575	Dec. 16	Chile	1,000s	Seismic sea wave struck from La Imperial to Castro, inner port of Valdivia wrecked, damage immense with 2 Spanish galleons demolished.
1586	Jan. 18	Honshu, Japan	1,000s	Great sea waves wrecked central area.
	July 9	Lima, Peru	100s	Sea rushed in 14 fathoms high along coast & inundated shore.

Date | **Place** | **Deaths**

Sept. **Japan** **1,000s**
Giant sea wave inundated country, many houses swept away.

1591 **July 26** **St. Michael's, Azores** **100s**
Turbulent water, giant waves.

Aug. 10 **Atlantic Ocean** **500**
Gale struck the Grand Fleet on its annual treasure run from Havana to Old Spain.

†1596 **Sept. 4** **Uryû-jima, Japan** **700**
Tsunami covered 3/4 of island off coast of Japan. Shortly after, the area submerged 30 fathoms.

1604 **Heraklion, Crete** **1,000s**
Seismic sea wave followed destructive quake, coast depressed.

Nov. 24 **Chile & Peru** **1,000s**
Seismic wave followed quake, Arica in Chile inundated.

1605 **Jan. 31** **Japan** **5,000**
Sea retired, giant waves struck Kiushiu, Shikoku, Kazusa, Awa & Satsuma.

1611 **Dec. 2** **Japan** **1,783**
Giant sea wave flooded Yamada, Sanriku & Hokaido, wave at Koyatori was 100 ft. high.

1612 **Nov. 8** **Heraklion, Crete** **100s**
Shock spawned seismic sea wave, great damage on N. coast of is.

1614 **Nov. 26** **Takata, Etigo, Japan** **100s**
Tsunami spawned by quake wrecked area.

1615 **Arica, Chile** **100s**
Tidal wave & quake wrecked city.

Jan. **England** **Scores**
Known as "The Cold Yeare," deep snow claimed much livestock.

1616 **Sept. 9** **Japan** **100s**
North coast struck by tidal wave.

1622 **May 5** **Sostis, Ionian Is.** **100s**
Cape was swept away by sea.

1626 **Italy** **100s**
Sea retired and returned to inundate Fortore & San Nicandro.

1629 **Feb. 27** **Cythera, Crete** **Scores**
Tsunami followed quake.

Aug. 1 **Banda Is., Dutch W. Indies** **Scores**
Wave of 50 ft. damaged area & many vessels.

1630 **Banda Neirra, Moluccas** **Scores**
Sea waves overflowed shore.

1633 **Mar. 1** **Isu, Japan** **100s**
Wave swept coast at Atami.

Nov. 5 **Zante, Ionian Is.** **100s**
Seismic sea wave swept area.

1635 **Aug. 15** **New England** **Scores**
Violent storm caused great damage.

†1638 **Oct. 21** **Widecombe-in-the-Moor, England** **50**
Tornado crushed church filled with congregation.

1640 **Japan** **700**
Tidal wave drowned victims.

Apr. 4 **Belgium, France & Holland** **Scores**
Disturbed waters inundated large area.

1642 **St. Kitts, W. Indies** **Scores**
Hurricane wrecked 23 vessels & destroyed all houses & cotton-tobacco crops.

1646 **Apr. 5** **Constantinople, Turkey** **Scores**
Violent rush of sea, ships thrown ashore.

†1650 **Lesser Antilles** **1,000s**
Hurricane wrecked Basseterre; 28 ships lost in storm.

Sept. 29 **Cyclades (Santorin)** **100s**
Submarine explosion disturbed Kaimeni, Sikinos & Patmos, waves over 90 ft.

1656 **Guadeloupe** **100s**
Hurricane destroyed most houses, all domestic animals, & every vessel in harbor with most of their crews.

1657 **Mar. 15** **Concepcion, Chile** **100s**
City inundated by 3 seismic waves.

1658 **Europe (North)** **Scores**
Members of the army of Charles X of Sweden died crossing the ice from Holstein to Denmark.

1661 **Jan. 8-9** **Formosa** **Scores**
Violent agitation of sea.

1662 **Oct. 30** **Hiuga & Osumi, Japan** **100s**
Great wave struck coast.

1664 **Guadeloupe & St. Kitts** **Scores**
Violent hurricane & quake destroyed potato crop.

†1666 **Aug. 4** **West Indies** **1,000s**
Hurricane struck Guadeloupe, Martinique & St. Christopher; fleet of 17 sailing vessels with 2,000 troops went down in the storm. (SEE Guadeloupe)

1667 **Ragusa & Dalmatia** **100s**
Series of 4 sea waves ravaged area.

1672 **Cyclades (Santorin)** **100s**
Shock spawned sea wave which swallowed up island of Kos (Stanchio).

Apr. **Eastern Sporades** **100s**
Shock spawned *tsunami,* great damage at Tenedos Is.

1673 **May 20** **Halmahera Island** **Scores**
Moderate sea wave struck area.

Aug. 12 **Ternate, Dutch W. Indies** **100s**
Island struck by powerful sea wave.

1674 **Feb. 17** **Amboina, Dutch W. Indies** **Scores**
Moderate group of 3 waves struck area, victims mostly at Hitu.

May 6 **Hitu, Dutch W. Indies** **Scores**
Moderate wave struck area.

Aug. 10 **Barbados** **200**
Hurricane leveled 300 houses & wrecked 8 ships.

1675 **Barbados** **Scores**
Island devastated by hurricane, all crops destroyed, aid was requested from the British but refused.

1677 **Lima, Peru** **100s**
Sea erupted with great violence along coast.

Apr. 13 **Miyako, Japan** **100s**
Three seismic waves struck city, also damage at Rikuchu, Tsugara, & Nambu.

Dec. 7 **Luzon, Philippines** **Scores**
Waves struck wide area.

1678 **U.S., Lake Ontario** **Scores**
Storm wrecked bark, first lake disaster in this area.

June 17 **Santa Fe, Peru** **100s**
City N. of Lima ravaged by sea waves.

1679 **Aug. 26** **U.S., Lake Huron** **100s**
Severe gale sank *Griffin* on the upper lakes.

†1680 **Aug. 3** **Martinique** **1,000s**
Hurricane shattered island, 22 ships in Cul-de-Sac Bay sank with large loss of life.

†Aug. 15 **Santo Domingo** **1,000s**
Hurricane swept area; 25 French warships sank in harbor with total loss of life.

1681 **Antigua** **100s**
Island was left desolate by violent hurricane.

1686 **Chile** **100s**
Quake spawned seismic wave, great destruction.

1689 **Nevis** **100s**
Hurricane swept away ½ of inhabitants.

1690 **Antigua** **100s**
Shock spawned wave, area left desolate.

1692 **Mar. 4** **New Haven, Conn.** **Scores**
Violent storm of wind & rain, another followed 1 week later.

June 7 **Jamaica** **3,000**
Quake spawned giant wave, town of Port Royal destroyed in 3 min.

Date		Place	Deaths
†1694	Sept. 27	**Barbados**	3,000
	Hurricane swept island; 26 British merchantmen sank in Carlisle Bay.		
†1695	Oct.	**Martinique**	100s
	Hurricane swept island, dozen French ships lost with over 600 drowned off western side.		
1697		**U.S., East**	Scores
	Hurricane struck several states.		
1699		**Charleston, S. Carolina**	Scores
	Violent storm swept through area.		
1703	July 1	**Genoa, Italy**	Scores
	Sea descended 6 ft. then rushed back.		
	†Nov. 27	**England**	1,000s
	The "Great Storm" of November wrecked over 100,000 houses & crippled the Royal Navy.		
	Dec. 30	**Japan**	5,233
	Greatest *tsunamis* ever, 4 waves smashed Sagami, Awa, Kazusa, Oshima & Musasi.		
†1705		**Havana, Cuba**	100s
	Hurricane swept area; 4 Spanish warships & crew lost in harbor.		
	Nov. 26	**Chile & Peru**	Scores
	Shock & waves struck Arica & Arequipa.		
1707	Oct. 28	**Japan**	4,900
	Twelve great seismic sea waves ruined coastal cities of Kyushu, Shikoku, Honshu & Izu.		
1708	Nov. 28	**Amboina, Dutch E. Indies**	Scores
	Great sea wave, moderate damage.		
1711	Sept. 5	**Amboina, Dutch E. Indies**	Scores
	Three moderate waves struck bay.		
†1713	Sept. 16-17	**N. Carolina**	70
	Third hurricane of note in this area, violent winds blew bldgs. down.		
1716		**Oshima Is., Japan**	Scores
	Sea wave struck coast.		
1717	Feb. 18	**New England**	Scores
	Great snowstorm throughout wide area.		
1719		**Sweden**	7,000
	Great snowstorm struck caravan on journey to Drontheim.		
†1722	Aug. 28	**Port Royal, Jamaica**	400
	Hurricane destroyed 26 merchant vessels and wasted town.		
	Dec. 27	**Villanova, Portugal**	Scores
	Seismic sea wave wasted all S. coast from Cape St. Vincent.		
†1723	Sept. 11	**New Orleans, La.**	24
	Destructive hurricane struck city.		
1724		**Lima, Peru**	Scores
	Eight-ft. wave sank 19 ships, Callao inundated.		
1728	Sept. 14	**Charleston, S. Carolina**	Scores
	Great storm at city.		
1730	July 8	**Concepcion, Chile**	100s
	Seismic wave wrecked city, Valparaiso inundated.		
1732	Feb. 25	**Acapulco, Mexico**	Scores
	Great movement of the tide, sea left Plaza 10 ft. deep.		
†1737		**Japan**	1,000s
	Tsunami destroyed town of Kamaishi.		
	Sept. 9	**West Indies**	Scores
	Hurricane did great damage at St. Louis, St. Domingo, St. Kitts, & Montserrat.		
	†Oct. 7	**Bay of Bengal, India**	300,000
	Cyclone created monstrous storm wave of 40 ft., 20,000 ships destroyed at mouth of Hooghly River.		
1744	Oct. 20	**Jamaica**	100s
	Hurricane ruined island, 104 vessels with 182 men drowned at sea alone.		
1746	Oct. 28	**Callao, Peru**	Scores
	City smashed by 2 waves, one had a height of 80 ft.		
1747	Oct. 24	**Leeward Islands**	100s
	Twin hurricanes wrecked area, 50 ships lost.		
1748	May 14	**Aeghion, Peloponnesus**	100s
	Shock followed by destructive *tsunami* ruined city.		
1751	Mar. 5	**Concepcion, Chile**	100s
	Fourth quake with disastrous *tsunamis* to level city, Juan Fernandez Is. also wrecked.		
	Mar. 12	**New England**	Scores
	Area swept by violent storm.		
	May 24	**Chile**	100s
	Quake followed by great *tsunami* struck Concepcion, Juan Fernandez, & Santiago.		
	Oct. 18	**Azua, Santo Domingo**	Scores
	City overwhelmed by huge sea wave.		
1752	Sept. 15	**Charleston, S.C.**	95
	Hurricane wrecked harbor & caused great damage to agriculture, another hurricane struck area earlier in month.		
1754	Aug. 18	**Amboina, Dutch E. Indies**	Scores
	Moderate sea wave off S.E. coast.		
	Aug. 20	**Acapulco, Mexico**	Scores
	Most violent wave in this area since 1732, sea rose 15 ft. above normal.		
	Sept.	**St. Domingo**	Scores
	Hurricane destroyed 1,700 hogs, drove 12 ships ashore & ruined the sugar & indigo plantations.		
	Oct. 24	**New England**	Scores
	Great storm accompanied by heavy waves.		
1755		**Santiago, Cuba**	Scores
	Sea wave nearly inundated city.		
	†Nov. 1	**Lisbon, Portugal**	31,000
	One of the worst quakes with seismic waves in history; waves 15 to 40 ft. along the Portuguese & Spanish coasts.		
1756		**St. Simon's Is., Ga.**	Score
	City flooded during storm.		
1757	July 9	**Azores**	Scores
	Great sea eruption at Gracia, the Pic & St. George Is.		
1758		**Florida**	100s
	Tropical cyclone struck N.W., 40 drowned at St. Mark's.		
1759	Sept.	**Gulf Stream**	100s
	Extreme gale sank Tortugas & other islands, great snow followed.		
1761	Mar. 31	**Lisbon, Portugal**	Scores
	Sea rose 8 ft. & retired in & out, a 6-ft. wave also struck Cornwall, England.		
1762	Dec. 9	**West Indies**	Scores
	Storm followed quake & destroyed the walls of Carthagena, the castle at Santa Maria was wrecked with many other structures.		
1763	Sept. 1	**Moluccas, Dutch E. Indies**	Scores
	Sudden rise of sea inundated land.		
1766		**Mayon, Philippines**	1,000s
	Typhoon & floods caused immense mud slides, great damage to property.		
	Mar. 8	**Hirosaki, Japan**	1,335
	Tidal wave destroyed 7,500 bldgs.		
	Aug. 13	**Martinique**	90
	Hurricane wrecked St. Pierre, 35 ships demolished.		
1767	Apr. 24	**Barbados & Martinique**	Scores
	Moderate wave at area.		
1768	Oct. 25	**Havana, Cuba**	1,000
	Brief hurricane destroyed 4,000 dwellings; included were 98 public bldgs.		
1769		**St. Nazaire, Brescia**	3,000
	Lightning set off powder stored in church, 1/6 of city destroyed.		

Date		Place	Deaths
	Aug. 29	**Satsuma, Japan**	**100s**
	Sea wave at city.		
1770	**June 2**	**West Indies**	**1,000s**
	Quake with huge wave left 500 victims buried in the ruins of Port-au-Prince with 1 bldg. left standing; La Croix de Bouguet was swallowed up.		
1771	**Apr. 24**	**Isigaki-zima, Japan**	**9,400**
	Sea wave swept area.		
†1772	**Sept. 1-3**	**Ocracoke Bar, N.C.**	**50**
	Hurricane drove 15 ships ashore at Edenton, N.C.		
1773	**May 6**	**Africa**	**Scores**
	Group of waves, some 30 ft. high, struck N. coast at Algiers & Tangeria.		
	Aug. 14	**Massachusetts**	**Scores**
	Very violent storm in the east.		
1775		**Haiti**	**100s**
	Three shocks spawned huge wave, great damage.		
	†Sept. 2	**Bar, N.C.**	**150**
	Hamlet wiped out by hurricane, great destruction to corn crop.		
	†Sept. 9	**Newfoundland, Canada**	**4,000**
	Hurricane ripped apart Irish & English fishing boats, houses on land collapsed.		
1779	**Aug. 28**	**Martinique**	**1,000s**
	Hurricane smashed area that was just recovered from storm 3 yrs. earlier; over 70 ships lost.		
1780	**Oct. 3-5**	**Savanna-la-Mar**	**1,000s**
	Hurricane caused sea to overflow ½ mi., every man, beast, or vegetable life was claimed as victim. (SEE *Phoenix*)		
	†Oct. 9	**St. Eustatius**	**5,000**
	Hurricane leveled Orange Town.		
†1780	**Oct. 10**	**Barbados, West Indies**	**20,000**
	Hurricane destroyed every house on Barbados & devastated Martinique, St. Lucia, & St. Eustatius; 40 ships which carried 4,000 soldiers were also lost.		
1781	**Aug. 1**	**Jamaica**	**Scores**
	Gale sank 2 loaded vessels, drove 97 on shore.		
1782		**Barbados**	**1,000s**
	Gale devastated region, 3,000 victims lost at sea alone.		
1783	**Feb. 5**	**Messina**	**36,000**
	Violent sea rose 20 ft. & retired immediately.		
1784	**July 30**	**Jamaica & Santo Domingo**	**Scores**
	Hurricane destroyed many bldgs. & wrecked or damaged all vessels.		
1785	**Aug. 27**	**Jamaica**	**Scores**
	Hurricane swept through area.		
1786	**Sept. 2**	**Barbados**	**Scores**
	Hurricane claimed victims in the ruins of their houses.		
1787	**Mar. 14**	**San Marcos, Mexico**	**Scores**
	Seismic sea waves struck along coasts of Oaxaca, Michoacan, & Tehuantepec, height was estimated at 36 ft.		
	Sept. 19	**South Carolina**	**23**
	Tropical cyclone caused great damage.		
	Sept. 23	**Belize, British Honduras**	**100**
	Hurricane with heavy rains caused sea to rise, great damage, 11 square-rigged vessels lost.		
1788	**July 27**	**Alaska**	**Scores**
	Tidal wave overflowed at Sannak, Unga & Shumigan Is., great no. of hogs drowned.		
	†Sept.	**Caravel, Martinique**	**100s**
	Hurricane swept natives into sea; 50 ships lost.		
†1789	**Dec.**	**Coringa, India**	**300,000**
	Cyclone caused 3 great waves which left city in ruins.		
1791	**June 21**	**Havana, Cuba**	**3,000**
	Rain produced great flood, 11,700 head of cattle perished.		
1792	**Feb. 10**	**Shimabara, Japan**	**15,000**
	Tsunami set off by quake devastated peninsula with series of slides & waves.		
	Apr. 1	**Shimbara, Japan**	**707**
	Explosive eruption of the sea.		
1793		**Buenos Aires**	**19**
	Lightning struck city 37 times during thunderstorm.		
	Feb. 8	**Adigasawa, Japan**	**100s**
	Quake followed by *tsunami* displaced coast.		
1794	**Sept. 1**	**Louisiana**	**Many**
	Lower coast swept by hurricane, most horses & cattle along Mississippi River lost.		
1797	**Feb. 10**	**Padang, Sumatra**	**100s**
	Powerful waves inundated town.		
1798	**Nov. 17-21**	**New England**	**100s**
	Snowstorm buried area, tunnels had to be cut through snow to rescue survivors from houses.		
1799		**Sumatra**	**Scores**
	Wave 50 ft. above water level struck coast.		
	June 29	**Miakoshiura, Japan**	**Scores**
	Sea wave also struck Kaga.		
1802	**Aug.**	**Amboina, Dutch E. Indies**	**Scores**
	Quake caused sea to rise very high.		
1804	**Apr. 4**	**Georgia**	**Many**
	Tornado swept from Jones Co. to Columbia Co., most destructive in state until 1875.		
	July 10	**Uzon, Japan**	**75**
	Wave struck city.		
	†Sept. 12	**United States (South)**	**500**
	Great tropical cyclone in Ga. & S.C.		
	Sept. 12	**Broughton Is., Ga.**	**75**
	West Indies hurricane swept American coast, victims black slaves.		
1805	**June 5**	**United States (Midwest)**	**Many**
	Violent tornado swept through Mo. to Jonesboro, Ill.		
1806	**Aug. 24**	**United States (East)**	**30**
	Hurricane sank vessel *Rose in Bloom* and ruined cotton crop, N.C. hardest hit.		
	†Sept. 9-11	**Dominica, Guadeloupe**	**131**
	Hurricane caused Roseau River to overflow, town inundated from all directions.		
1807	**June 26**	**Luxembourg**	**230**
	Lightning struck magazine fortress & ruined lower part of town.		
1809	**May 28**	**Cincinnati, O.**	**Many**
	Three tornadoes struck city minutes apart.		
†1811	**Sept. 10**	**Charleston, S.C.**	**500**
	Tornado destroyed large parts of city, one of the worst recorded twisters in American history.		
1812	**June 23**	**Marseilles, France**	**100s**
	Violent movement of sea.		
	†Aug. 19	**Louisiana**	**45**
	Hurricane wrecked 53 vessels & demolished all small craft, damage on land was similar.		
	Oct. 14	**Trinidad, Cuba**	**Scores**
	Hurricane wrecked 500 houses & damaged most vessels in the harbor of Casilda.		
1813	**Aug. 10**	**Martinique**	**3,000**
	Two hurricanes struck island, rebellion started among Negro slaves.		
	Aug. 27-28	**South Carolina**	**Scores**
	Tropical cyclone caused great tides, mass drownings, 1/3 of rice crop ruined.		
1815	**Apr. 10**	**Sumbawa, Dutch W. Indies**	**Scores**
	Violent wave 12 ft. high.		
	Sept. 1	**West Indies**	**Scores**
	Hurricane swept area, Leeward Is. hardest hit, 14 sailboats lost.		
	Oct. 18-19	**Jamaica**	**Scores**
	Hurricane swept E. ½ of island, most rivers flooded.		
	Nov.	**Bali, Dutch E. Indies**	**Scores**
	Great wave inundated land.		

Date		Place	Deaths	
1817	Aug. 23	**Peloponnesus (Achaia)**	100s	Severe shock caused *tsunami* to sweep downtown section.
	†Oct. 21	**Martinique**	200	Hurricane swept island; 7 British merchantmen sunk.
1818	Mar. 18	**Benguelen, Sumatra**	Scores	Sea retired & returned with great force.
1819	Apr. 11	**Copiapo, Chile**	Scores	Sea overflowed land 600 meters, damage at Caldera.
	June 11	**France**	9	Lightning struck the church of Chateau Neuf les Montiers, 82 injured.
	†July 27-28	**Mobile, Alabama**	200	Hurricane wrecked many vessels; included was the schooner *Firebrand* with 75 victims.
1820	Dec. 29	**Macassar, Celebes Is.**	Scores	Wall of water 60 to 80 ft. struck fort of Boelekomba, great damage at Nipa-Nipa & Serang-Serang.
1821	Jan. 6	**Zante Is., Greece**	100s	Shock set off severe seismic wave, many houses carried away.
	Sept. 15	**Petite Coquille Is., La.**	100s	Gale off La. coast demolished military quarters & an entire garrison.
1822	June	**Burisal & Backerunge, India**	50,000	Cyclone drowned victims at the mouth of the Ganges.
	Sept. 4	**North Inlet, S.C.**	37	Tornado forced tide to record height, 7 houses & 1 church destroyed.
	Sept. 27-28	**Carolinas**	300	Tropical cyclone caused mass drownings, North Island lost 120 blacks & 5 whites.
	Nov. 19	**South America**	Scores	Seismic sea wave felt from Copiapo to Valdivia.
1823	Nov. 30	**St. Pierre, Martinique**	Scores	Quake with high tide caused great damage in harbor.
†1824	Sept. 15	**St. Simon Island (Ga.)**	83	Hurricane lashed coast; victims slaves.
1825		**Mayon, Philippines**	1,500	Storm sparked great landslip, wide destruction.
	†July 26	**Puerto Rico**	374	Hurricane left 1,210 injured & leveled 7,000 houses, barometer at Guadeloupe fell 1.86 in.
1827		**Chernabura Is., Aleutian Is.**	Scores	Tidal wave accompanied by quake and eruption of a volcano on Unimak.
1828	Dec. 18	**Echigo, Japan**	Scores	Sea wave at Kiushu.
	Dec. 29	**Celebes Islands**	Scores	Sea retired & roared back several times at Boelekomba & Macassar.
†1831	Aug. 10-11	**Barbados, W. Indies**	1,500	One of the most destructive hurricanes in history, damage over $7.5 million.
1833	Jan. 29	**Bengkulen, Sumatra**	Scores	Great sea wave destroyed breakwater, ships torn from anchors.
	May	**Calcutta, India**	50,000	Region at mouth of Hooghly inundated by cyclone, 300 villages destroyed.
	Dec. 7	**Japan**	Scores	Sea retired & roared back at Echigo, Sado Is., & Uzen.
1834	Feb. 9	**Ishikari, Japan**	Scores	Three waves smashed coast.
	†Sept. 23	**Santo Domingo**	1,000s	Destructive hurricane destroyed most houses & crops on island.
1835		**Hanasaki, Japan**	Scores	Great wave struck coast.
	Feb. 20	**Santiago, Chile**	Scores	Quake with waves 50 ft. high struck from Copiapo to Chiloe & from Juan Fernandez to Mendoza.
	June 19	**New Brunswick, N.J.**	Many	Atlantic tornado flushed all water from bed of Raritan River.
	†Sept. 12-18	**Florida Keys**	100	First well-reported hurricane to strike area from Key West to Cape Canaveral.
†1837	Aug. 2	**St. Thomas**	500	Cyclone & quake brought horror to area.
	Oct. 9	**Carolinas**	90	Tropical cyclone, most victims marine casualties.
	Nov. 7	**Chile & Hawaii**	100s	Destructive wave at Concepcion & Hilo, Valvidia completely destroyed.
1838		**Calcutta**	215	Cyclone, only a few yards in diameter, destroyed 1,245 houses in 16-mi. area.
1839		**Coringa, India**	300,000	Cyclone caused 40-ft. wave which destroyed 20,000 vessels and most of the city.
	Dec. 15	**Gloucester, Mass.**	41	Gale wrecked 41 vessels in harbor.
†1840	May 7	**Natchez, Miss.**	317	Most destructive tornado in America to this date, damage over $1 million, over 109 badly injured.
†1841	July 21-22	**Hong Kong, China**	100s	Typhoon caused great destruction & suffering throughout area.
	†Sept.	**St. Jo, Florida**	4,000	Hurricane destroyed every structure & all inhabitants.
	†Oct. 3	**Truro, Mass.**	57	Known as "the October Gale," most deaths occurred around the coastal area.
	Nov. 26	**Banda Neira, Moluccas**	Scores	Violent wave 8 to 9 ft. high smashed S. coast.
1842	May 7	**Haiti**	Scores	Destructive tidal wave smashed N. coast.
	June 16	**Natchez, Miss.**	500	Second great tornado to strike city in 2 yrs.
	July 12	**North Carolina**	Scores	One of the worst hurricanes to have struck area to this date, some ships disappeared & great loss of livestock.
1843		**Japan**	Scores	Two giant waves struck E. coast of Kushuro, Nemuro & Yezo.
	Jan. 5-6	**Sumatra**	Scores	Great sea wave struck S.E. coast of Baros & Nias Is.
	Sept. 13	**Port Leon**	14	Storm & gales left city in ruins.
†1844	Aug. 4	**Matamoros, Mexico**	70	Violent hurricane leveled all but 3 structures.
1846	April	**Truckee Pass, Calif.**	42	Snow marooned pioneer emigrants forever known as the "Donner Party." (SEE Donner Party)
	Oct. 11	**Havana, Cuba**	100s	Hurricane wrecked or damaged most bldgs., many vessels sunk.
	†Oct. 11-12	**Key West, Fla.**	46	Hurricane with such force as to annihilate 92 of 104 vessels in harbor & unroof or destroy 594 houses.
1847	Oct. 31	**Kondul, Bay of Bengal**	Scores	Great wave inundated small island.
1849	June 17	**La Serena, Chile**	Scores	Shock set off seismic sea wave.
	†Oct. 6	**United States (East)**	145	Coastal hurricane swept from Long Is. to New Eng., brig *St. John* wrecked on rocks off Cohasset. (SEE *St. John*)

Date		Place	Deaths
1850	July 18	**United States (Southeast)**	20
	Tropical cyclone swept the Car.-Va. area, loss of life was on the Schuylkill River.		
1851	Aug. 22	**Cambridge, Mass.**	Scores
	Tornado with path 60 yds. wide swept to Medford, great damage.		
1852	Apr. 13	**New Harmony, Ind.**	16
	Tornado struck 200-mi. area, $400,000 damage.		
	Nov. 26	**Amboina, Dutch E. Indies**	Scores
	Giant wave 26 ft. high struck coast.		
1853		**India**	84
	Hailstorm killed 3,000 cattle. (SEE Moradabad, India)		
	July 15	**Cumana, Venezuela**	Scores
	Violent quake followed by tidal wave.		
1854	Jan. 20	**Ohio**	Many
	Tornado struck Knox Co., Brandon & Mt. Vernon; damage severe.		
	July 9	**Japan**	2,400
	Tidal wave smashed Yamato, Iga & Ise; 5,000 bldgs. leveled.		
	†Dec. 22	**Japan**	3,000
	Quake produced *tsunami,* great damage to vessels, houses & bridges.		
1856	April 3	**Island of Rhodes**	4,000
	Lightning struck powder vaults in the church of St. John.		
		Hokkaido, Japan	Scores
	Tidal wave struck coast at Iburi & Oshima.		
	†Aug. 13	**Last Island, La.**	137
	Hurricane swept away all houses, vessel *Star* was anchored at area with 400 passengers of whom 25% lost their lives.		
	Nov. 13	**Chios Island**	100s
	Great shock set off large *tsunami.*		
1857	Sept. 12	**Carolinas**	100s
	Hurricane swept coasts, many vessels sunk; included was the *Central America* with nearly 400 victims.		
1858	Nov. 13	**Celebes Islands**	Scores
	Tidal wave caused considerable damage.		
1859	Sept. 25	**Banda Neira, Dutch E. Indies**	Scores
	Wave of great force smashed S. coast.		
	Oct. 20	**Patjitan, Java**	Scores
	Strong wave smashed coast.		
	Oct. 25-26	**Wales**	100s
	Storm off coast wrecked vessel *Royal Charter* with 450 lives, disaster known as the "Royal Charter Storm."		
1860	Sept. 11	**United States (Middle Gulf Coast)**	40
	Hurricane & gale swept area, Lake Borgne hardest hit.		
1861	Feb. 16	**Anjer Banjis, Sumatra**	Scores
	Powerful tidal wave smashed area.		
	Mar. 9	**Padang, Sumatra**	100s
	High wave swept inland.		
	June 5	**Krawang & Pakis, Java**	Scores
	Wave of great force struck area.		
	Nov. 2-3	**Boston, Mass.**	22
	Storm struck area, vessel *Maritania* wrecked on rock 1 mi. E. of Boston Light.		
†1862	Feb. 24	**Gloucester, Mass.**	122
	Hurricane called "February Blow of '62."		
	July 27	**Canton, China**	40,000
	Typhoon demolished waterfront area, all buildings leveled.		
1863	June 3	**S. Luzon, Philippines**	100s
	Quake produced giant seismic wave.		
†1864	Oct. 5	**Calcutta, India**	50,000
	Cyclone caused sea wave 40 ft. high, city & 200 ships destroyed in moments.		
1867		**St. Thomas, W. Indies**	1,000s
	Tsunami caused by quake caused more damage than the storm 30 yrs. earlier.		
	Dec. 18	**Keelung, Formosa**	100s
	Wave swept harbor, great landslides followed.		
1868	Apr. 2	**Hawaiian Islands**	100s
	Waves of 50 ft. swept villages of Keauhou & Punaluu away.		
†1869	Oct. 5	**United States (Northeast)**	50
	Rainstorm deluged several states, Mass. hardest struck, schooner *Rio* lost in St. Andrews Bay with 17 victims.		
1870	Oct. 7-8	**Matanzas, Cuba**	800
	Hurricane struck old city E. of Havana.		
1871	Mar. 2	**Dutch E. Indies**	100s
	Waves swept Tagulandag Is. & an 84-ft. wave swept 600 ft. inland at Buhias.		
†1872	Apr. 15	**Zanzibar**	200
	Hurricane destroyed 150 ships.		
1873	May 22	**United States (Midwest)**	Many
	Tornado caused great damage from Keokuk, Ia., to Peoria, Ill.		
	Aug. 24-25	**Nova Scotia, Canada**	600
	Cyclone destroyed 1,223 vessels within a few days, deaths may have reached 600.(SEE Newfoundland, Canada)		
1874	July 25	**Pittsburgh, Pa.**	134
	Cloudbursts outside city drowned or crushed victims, damage $500,000.		
1875		**Mayon, Philippines**	1,000s
	Worst disaster since 1766, typhoon & floods caused mass mud slides.		
	Mar. 20	**Georgia**	Many
	Most destructive tornado in state to this date, path was 200 mi. long.		
	Sept. 15	**Indianola, Tex.**	176
	Hurricane from the northeast wiped out 3/4 of town, winds up to 100 m.p.h.		
†1876	Oct. 31	**Backergunge, India**	100,000
	Tropical hurricane & cyclone forced water to rise from 10 to 40 ft. at mouth of the Megna in ½ hr., all crops destroyed.		
1877	June 4	**Mt. Carmel, Ill.**	16
	Tornado caused $40,000 damage.		
	Sept. 21-Oct. 5	**Curacao**	100s
	Hurricane with giant waves knocked down all tall bldgs., damage $2 million.		
1878	Jan. 23	**Chile & Peru**	Scores
	Sea waves inundated coastal towns of Arequipa & Iquique.		
	Mar. 24	**Ventnor, Isle of Wight**	100s
	Storm was a narrow strip 400 mi. long & 3 mi. in breadth—thus began the term "line squalls." British frigate *Eurydice* sank with over 300 hands, only 2 survived.		
	Aug. 9	**Wallingford, Conn.**	34
	Tornado caused $200,000 damage.		
	Aug. 29	**Makuslin, Unalaska Is.**	100s
	Quake and tidal wave destroyed town.		
†1879	Feb. 21-22	**Gloucester, Massachusetts**	157
	Hurricane smashed coast, fishing fleet wiped out.		
	Apr. 16	**Walterboro, S.C.**	Many
	Tornado struck 3 states, damage over $100,000.		
	†May 30	**Irving, Kans.**	50
	Two tornadoes, minutes apart, ripped city & mass area, fear remained for weeks.		
	†Dec. 28	**Dundee, Scotland**	75
	Gale swept country and destroyed Tay Bridge which resulted in great rail disaster. (SEE Dundee, Scotland)		
†1880	Apr. 18	**Marshfield, Mo.**	101
	Series of 24 tornadoes leveled city & caused damage over $2 million from Ark. to Wisc.		
1881		**Haifung, China**	30,000
	Great storm drowned or starved victims.		

Date	Place	Deaths
July 15	**Odessa, Minn.**	16
	Tornado damaged 247 bldgs., damage over $1½ million.	
†Aug. 18	**Martinique**	700
	Hurricane caused over $10 million damage.	
Aug. 27	**Carolina Coasts**	700
	Cyclone caused damage of $1½ million, 335 dead at Savannah, Ga.	
Oct. 5	**Haifong, China**	1,000s
	Typhoon swept area.	
1882 June 5	**Bombay, India**	100,000
	Storm & tidal wave blasted area.	
†June 17	**Grinnell, Ia.**	160
	Most destructive tornado in state to this date, over $600,000 damage in wide area.	
1883 Apr. 21	**Rochester, Minn.**	31
	Tornado destroyed 1,351 bldgs. with over $200,000 damage.	
Apr. 22	**Beauregard, Miss.**	40
	Tornado destroyed every structure in town, over $450,000 damage.	
Aug. 27	**Sumatra & Java**	36,000
	Eruption of Krakatoa caused 100-ft. sea wave equal to a 12-story bldg.; it inundated 295 towns & villages & destroyed 5,000 ships. (SEE Krakatoa)	
Sept. 11	**Carolinas**	53
	Tropical cyclone caused mass damage, over 100 vessels wrecked in Bahamas.	
†1884 Feb. 9	**South Carolina (and Southern U.S.)**	800
	Series of 60 tornadoes destroyed over 10,000 structures in Ala., Ind., Ky., Miss., N. & S. Car. & Tenn.	
1885 June	**Mexico**	170
	Cloudburst wiped out 25% of town's populace.	
Aug. 21	**South Carolina**	21
	Tropical cyclone struck coastal sections, great destruction at Charleston, damage $1,690,000.	
Nov. 6	**Philippines**	10,000
	Cyclone swept islands, damage in millions.	
1886 Jan. 6-13	**United States (Mid-Southwest)**	80
	Great blizzard struck 5 states without warning; Ia. had 20 deaths, Kans. lost 80% of its cattle.	
Apr. 14	**Minnesota**	74
	Tornadoes destroyed entire business district of Sauk Rapids & devastated Cedar Cloud, damage over $400,000.	
May 14-15	**Anderson, Ind.**	43
	Tornado caused over $1 million damage, its path extended to Seneca Co., Ohio.	
†Aug. 19	**Indianola, Texas**	176
	Hurricane destroyed town, never rebuilt.	
Oct. 11	**Cameron Parish, La.**	50
	Tropical cyclone wrecked city.	
†Oct. 12	**Sabine, Tex.**	150
	Hurricane inundated 20 mi. inland, almost every structure in area was shaken from its foundation.	
1887	**India**	1,000s
	Cyclone caused tremendous inundation over the Ganges delta.	
Sept. 23	**Philippines**	100s
	Great sea wave along the Tiburon Peninsula, sea retired 20 ft. & roared back.	
1888 Feb. 19	**Mt. Vernon, Ill.**	16
	Tornado, with path 62 mi. long, caused over $400,000 damage.	
†Mar. 11-14	**United States (East)**	400
	Great blizzard, known for its effect on New York City where over 200 lives were lost; overall loss over $7 million.	
Mar. 12	**New Guinea**	Scores
	Seismic sea wave engulfed N. coast.	
†Apr. 30	**Moradabad, India**	250
	Moradabad district, 100 mi. from city, was pounded with hailstones the size of baseballs for 2 hrs.	
Aug. 21	**Wilmington, Del.**	12
	Tornado struck 4-Co. area, damage over $150,000.	
Aug. 31-Sept. 8	**Cuba**	1,000
	Hurricane caused giant waves to wipe whole towns, Turks Is., Great Inagua, & Mexico heavily damaged.	
1889 Mar. 16	**Samoa**	186
	Hurricane smashed the Apia harbor & destroyed U.S. vessels *Trenton* & *Vandalia* plus German vessels *Adler* & *Eber*. (SEE *Trenton*)	
Sept. 9-12	**United States (Atlantic Coast)**	40
	Tropical cyclone caused over $2½ million damage.	
†1890 Mar. 27	**Louisville, Ky.**	106
	Tornado destroyed over $3 million worth of property at city and close districts.	
Aug. 19	**Wilkes Barre, Pa.**	16
	Tornado destroyed most structures, damage over $500,000.	
1891 Feb. 8	**United States (Mid-Northwest)**	23
	Blizzard has been called the worst ever known, frozen winds of 30 to 80 m.p.h. struck Ia., Neb., & S. Dak.	
Aug. 18	**Martinique**	700
	Most severe W. Indian hurricane, over $10 million damage in 4 hrs.	
1892 Apr.	**Kansas**	40
	Tornadoes struck several towns.	
June 14	**Minnesota**	50
	Tornado swept across five counties.	
1893 July 6	**Pomeroy, Ia.**	89
	Tornado, with path 50 mi. long, caused over $200,000 damage.	
†Aug. 27	**Georgia (& South Carolina)**	1,000
	Hurricane spawned wave that submerged the islands between Charleston, S.C., & Savannah, Ga.—damage over $1 million.	
†Oct. 1	**Louisiana**	2,000
	Hurricane caused great damage to shipping and property loss in millions, La. hardest hit.	
Oct. 13	**Carolinas**	22
	Tropical cyclone left N.C. greatly damaged.	
1894 Sept. 21	**United States (Northeast)**	48
	Series of 4 tornadoes caused $350,000 damage in Ia. & Minn.	
Oct. 8	**Apalachicola, Fla.**	Many
	Tropical cyclone struck city.	
1896 May 15	**Sherman, Tex.**	78
	Tornado raped town, over $150,000 damage.	
†May 25	**Oakland Co., Mich.**	47
	Tornado caused over $400,000 damage, Detroit narrowly escaped its wrath.	
†May 27	**St. Louis, Mo.**	306
	Damage from tornado was over $12 million, 2,500 hurt.	
†June 15	**Japan**	28,000
	Tsunami over 100 ft. high destroyed 13,000 houses, with a wind velocity of 480 m.p.h.	
July 23-24	**Shantung, China**	100s
	Storm off coast wrecked many vessels, included was the legendary *Iltis*.	
Sept. 28-29	**Cedar Keys, Fla.**	114
	Tropical cyclone caused damage of $7 million.	
Sept. 29	**United States (South)**	30
	Tropical cyclone struck Ga. & S.C.	
Nov. 25-28	**United States (Northwest)**	29
	Blizzard caused great suffering & loss of livestock in Minn. & N. & S. Dak.	
1897 Sept. 21	**Philippines**	100s
	Greatest sea wave ever recorded to this date at islands.	

Date		Place	Deaths
1898	**Jan. 12**	**Ft. Smith, Ark.**	**51**
	Tornado with path 120 mi. long, caused over $450,000 damage.		
	Jan. 31-Feb. 1	**United States (East)**	**26**
	Worst American snowstorm since 1888, damage to property and shipping over $2 million.		
	May 18	**United States (Midwest)**	**40**
	More than $1 million in damages in Ill., Ia., & Wisc. in a storm sweeping eastward from Muscatine, Ia.		
	Aug. 2-3	**Florida**	**27**
	Tropical cyclone swept most of state.		
	Oct. 2	**United States (South)**	**100s**
	Tropical cyclone struck coastal area, 179 dead in Ga.		
	Nov. 26-27	**New England**	**455**
	Storm accompanied by heavy snowfall wrecked 142 vessels off coast; most notable was the *Portland.*		
1899	**Apr. 27**	**Kirksville, Mo.**	**34**
	Tornado caused over $250,000 damage.		
	June 12	**New Richmond, Wisc.**	**100**
	Tornado struck on Circus Day with town loaded with tourists, damage extensive.		
	†Aug. 8	**Puerto Rico**	**3,000**
	Hurricane swept length of area, coffee crop worth over $7 million destroyed.		
	Sept. 30	**Ceram**	**100s**
	Great wave on S. coast.		
†1900	**Sept. 8**	**Galveston, Texas**	**6,000**
	West Indian hurricane swept tidal wave through city, area inundated up to 16 ft., damage over $20 million.		
	Nov. 20	**United States (South)**	**73**
	Six tornadoes caused $500,000 damage in Ala., Ark., & Miss.		
1901	**Mar. 25**	**Birmingham, Ala.**	**25**
	Storm struck city.		
	Nov. 13	**Great Britain**	**210**
	Storm wrecked over 50 vessels off coast.		
1902	**May 18**	**Goliad, Tex.**	**114**
	Tornado injured 250, damage over $50,000.		
†1903	**Jan. 13**	**Society Islands**	**1,000**
	Tsunamis of 40 ft. ruined South Pacific group.		
	†June 1	**Gainesville, Ga.**	**203**
	Tornado & windstorm smashed cotton mill which employed 750, damage over $1 million.		
1905	**May 9**	**Marquette, Kan.**	**30**
	Tornado wrecked town.		
	May 10	**Snyder, Okla.**	**97**
	Tornado destroyed 100 houses, damage over $300,000.		
	July 5	**Montague, Texas**	**40**
	Tornado struck Co., great number injured, 20 buildings leveled.		
	July 7	**Salvador**	**33**
	Republic ripped apart by storm.		
	July 12-20	**New York City**	**91**
	Long heat-wave scorched metropolis.		
	Nov. 28	**Minnesota**	**40**
	Storm over Great Lakes caused $2 million damage.		
1906	**Mar. 2**	**Meridian, Miss.**	**24**
	Tornado wrecked city.		
	†Sept. 18	**Hong Kong, China**	**10,000**
	Tropical cyclone accompanied by *tsunami* struck city.		
	Sept. 27	**Pensacola, Fla.**	**32**
	Worst storm to strike area in 175 yrs., damage over $2 million, wind velocity was 83 m.p.h.		
	†Oct. 18	**Florida Keys**	**129**
	Hurricane struck N. Atlantic coast, most victims were laborers building the Florida East Coast Railroad who were quartered on houseboats.		
	Oct. 21	**Coatepeque, San Salvador**	**100s**
	Storm devastated area, Chulo volcano inundated villages.		
1908	**Apr. 24**	**Alabama**	**210**
	Two tornadoes struck state, 1 in the north & outside Montgomery.		
	June 5	**Kan. & Neb.**	**27**
	Tornadoes struck several towns in northern Kan. & southern Neb.		
	Dec. 28	**Reggio di Calabria**	**50,000**
	Tidal wave caused paradise to vanish.		
1909	**Mar. 8**	**Brinkley, Ark.**	**64**
	Tornado damaged 100s of structures, damage over $600,000.		
	Apr. 30	**United States (South & Midwest)**	**125**
	Series of cyclones devastated Ala., Ga., Ill., Miss., Mo., & Tenn.		
	May 30	**Zephyr, Tex.**	**30**
	Tornado leveled town.		
	†July 21	**Texas (coast)**	**41**
	Hurricane destroyed ½ of city, tide at Galveston rose 10 ft. above normal, damage over $2 million.		
	†Aug. 27	**Mexico**	**1,500**
	Hurricane smashed N.E. coast, property loss from floods enormous.		
	†Sept. 10-20	**Louisiana, Mississippi, & Alabama**	**350**
	Hurricanes lashed area for week, La. & Miss. had damage over $5 million.		
	Dec. 25-26	**United States (East)**	**28**
	Christmas snowstorm caused over $20 million damage, Boston and vicinity hardest hit.		
1911	**Apr. 13**	**United States (Southwest)**	**23**
	Tornado hit Kans. & Okla., 4 towns leveled.		
	June 15	**Trieste, Italy**	**100**
	Hurricane smashed area.		
	July 3-11	**United States (East)**	**380**
	Ten-day heat wave caused great suffering in N.Y. & Pa.		
	Sept. 22	**Vesuvian, Italy**	**50**
	Hurricane caused great property damage.		
	Oct. 9	**Ortiz, Mexico**	**27**
	Storm left many missing, great property damage.		
	Nov. 11	**United States (Midwest)**	**23**
	Cyclone damage in millions, Ill. & Wisc.		
†1912	**Sept. 16**	**Taito, Formosa**	**107**
	Typhoon left 293 injured, 91,400 houses demolished, & 115,700 shaken.		
	†Nov. 18	**Black River, Jamaica**	**100**
	Early morning hurricane, with winds of 120 m.p.h. & great tidal waves, left island in ruins.		
1913	**Mar. 13**	**United States (Midwest & South)**	**100s**
	Windstorms produced heavy damage in Vincennes, Ind., Peoria, Ill., and in Tenn. & La. towns.		
	Mar. 21	**United States (South)**	**140**
	Entire region below Mason-Dixon line struck by storms, train service & power stopped.		
	†Mar. 23	**Omaha, Neb.**	**115**
	Tornado ruined city, over $3.5 million damage; neighboring areas also severely struck.		
	Mar. 23	**Terre Haute, Ind.**	**21**
	Tornado destroyed 300 houses, damage over $1 million.		
	May 11	**Philippines**	**100s**
	One of the most serious typhoons in decades smashed the area.		
	Aug. 26	**Tokyo, Japan**	**100s**
	Wave, attached to *tsunami,* gutted 15,000 houses; damaged railroads & crops.		
	Sept. 6	**France - Spain**	**26**
	Storms & rain caused great destruction in both countries.		
	Nov. 7-11	**United States (East-Midwest)**	**230**
	Snowfall over 35 in. wrecked 8 ships on Lake Huron with cargo valued at $2 million.		

Date		Place	Deaths
	Dec. 11	**Freetown, Sierra Leone**	**250**
	Tornado claimed many natives, great damage.		
1914	**Jan. 11**	**Russia**	**150**
	Snowstorm isolated northwest area.		
	†Jan. 12	**Kagoshima, Japan**	**35**
	Tsunami struck waterfront, 112 injured.		
	June 24	**Lake Constance, Germany**	**35**
	Storm over area, victims fishermen.		
1915	**Feb. 12**	**Manua Is., Samoa**	**22**
	Hurricane, *tsunami* & quake shook area, 1,000s faced starvation.		
	May 6	**United States (South)**	**21**
	Cyclone storms caused property damage in La. & Miss.		
	July 7	**Cincinnati, Ohio**	**20**
	Tornado struck city, area isolated for hrs.		
	July 25	**Hang Chow Bay, China**	**100s**
	Typhoon struck coast, damage great.		
	†Aug. 16	**Galveston, Tex.**	**275**
	Hurricane ravaged coast, tide at city rose 12 ft. above normal, wind velocity was 120 m.p.h.; damage over $50 million. Greatest storm of century to this date.		
	Aug. 26	**Luzon, Philippines**	**180**
	Typhoon leveled town of Tobacco, 800 injured, damage over $1 million.		
	†Sept. 29	**New Orleans, Louisiana**	**275**
	Hurricane smashed Gulf Coast, 90% of bldgs. destroyed in wide area, damage over $13 million.		
	Nov. 10	**United States (Mid-Southwest)**	**50**
	Tornado, with swath 16 mi. wide, left damage in millions at Kans., Neb., & S. Dak.		
1916	**Apr. 20**	**United States (Midwest)**	**20**
	Tornado struck Kan. & Mo., large property damage.		
	June 5	**United States (Midwest & South)**	**100**
	Tornadoes plowed through Ark., Ill., Miss., & Mo., damage over $250,000.		
	July 10-29	**Chicago, Ill.**	**305**
	Heat wave scorched city.		
	July 11	**Vienna, Austria**	**31**
	Tornado struck city, scores injured.		
	July 20	**Columbo, Ceylon**	**200**
	Typhoon struck coast.		
	July 24	**Spain**	**50**
	Hurricane razed provinces of Saragossa, Soria, Valladolid, Leon, & Pontevedro.		
	Aug. 15	**Kingston, Jamaica**	**20**
	Hurricane caused great damage to fruit crop.		
	Aug. 30	**Dominica, Br. West Indies**	**50**
	Hurricane, with 70 m.p.h. winds, wrecked 200 bldgs. & damaged the lime crop.		
	Oct. 5	**Virgin Islands**	**40**
	Cyclone devastated Torotola, Anagada & St. John.		
	Dec. 1	**Pendicherry, India**	**1,000**
	Cyclone smashed French possession, great damage.		
1917	**Mar. 11**	**Newcastle, Ind.**	**24**
	Tornado swept wide area, Nat'l Guard called to protect city from looters, damage over $600,000.		
	†Mar. 23	**New Albany, Ind.**	**45**
	Tornado swept through N. side of city, 2,500 homeless, damage over $2 million.		
	†May 26-27	**Illinois (through Mississippi)**	**249**
	Tornado left 1,200 injured at Ala., Ky., Ill., & Ind.; Matoon, Ill., had 53 victims with damage over $1.2 million. (SEE Mattoon, Ill.)		
	May 31	**Mo. & Ill.**	**67**
	More than 200 injured in southeast Mo. & southern Ill. towns.		
	June 5-6	**United States (Midwest)**	**249**
	Tornado caused over $3 million damage in Kans., Ky., Mich., & Mo.		
	July 27-Aug. 3	**New York City**	**190**
	Heat wave broke 25-yr. record.		
	Sept. 19	**Amoy, China**	**600**
	Typhoon destroyed all craft in harbor.		
1918	**July 6**	**Guam**	**500**
	Typhoon left population destitute & all crops destroyed.		
	Aug. 21	**Tyler, Minn.**	**36**
	Tornado destroyed business section, damage over $1 million.		
	†Sept. 1	**Louisiana**	**34**
	Hurricane destroyed 25-mi. area, wind velocity of 100 m.p.h. caused over $5 million damage.		
	†Sept. 30	**Tokyo, Japan**	**1,619**
	Typhoon left 1,000s homeless, 2,000 boats destroyed, damage in the millions of yen.		
1919	**Mar. 16**	**United States (South)**	**35**
	Tornado caused $1 million damage from Delhi, La., to Sunflower Co., Miss.		
	Apr. 6-9	**United States (South)**	**100**
	Tornadoes swept Ark., Okla., & Tex., damage severe.		
	†June 22	**Fergus Falls, Minn.**	**59**
	Tornado leveled town, over $3 million damage, 228 houses demolished.		
	†Sept. 9-10	**Florida Straits**	**772**
	Worst hurricane to strike southern coast this century, damage over $2 million at Corpus Christi, Tex.; Spanish steamer *Valbanera* disappeared with 488 victims. (SEE Corpus Christi, Tex.)		
1920	**Jan. 20**	**Norway**	**37**
	Gale off coast, victims fishermen.		
	†Mar. 28	**Indiana, Ohio**	**71**
	Series of 11 tornadoes caused over $3 million damage in Ill., Ind., Mich., O., & Wisc.		
	†Mar. 28	**United States (South)**	**38**
	Three tornadoes caused $2 million damage in Ala. & Ga.		
	†Mar. 28	**Chicago, Ill.**	**28**
	Tornadoes which struck several states destroyed 113 bldgs., injured 325 persons & left damage over $3.5 million around area of city.		
	Apr. 20	**United States (South)**	**160**
	Series of 3 tornadoes smashed area from Oktibbeha Co., Miss., to Jackson Co., Ala.; over $2 million damage.		
	May 2	**Peggs, Okla.**	**71**
	Cyclone destroyed town, 30% of population killed.		
	May 30	**England**	**20**
	Cloudburst overflowed River Lud.		
	Oct. 1	**Japan**	**100s**
	Typhoon struck East coast.		
1921	**Feb. 10**	**Gardner, Ga.**	**32**
	Cyclone wiped out hamlet.		
	Apr. 15-16	**Texarkana, Ark.**	**97**
	Series of 30 tornadoes swept all the Southern states, damage over $2½ million.		
	Dec. 24	**United States (South)**	**44**
	Storm injured 100 in Ark., La., Miss., & Tenn.		
1922	**Jan. 27-29**	**United States (Atlantic Coast)**	**140**
	Great snowstorm from S. Car. to Mass., Knickerbocker Theater in D.C. collapsed with 98 victims.		
	Apr. 8	**United States (Southwest)**	**42**
	Twelve tornadoes caused over $1 million damage in Okla. & Tex.		
	Apr. 17	**United States (Midwest)**	**32**
	Tornado injured 500 in Ark., Ill., & Ind.		
	May 21	**Wisconsin**	**25**
	Tornado smashed 4 counties, great damage.		
	June 11	**New York**	**50**
	Violent storm swept state, many bathers drowned.		
	Aug. 2-3	**Swatlow, China**	**60,000**
	Great typhoon smashed area, 1,000s homeless, 300 fishermen drowned off Kurile Islands.		

Date		Place	Deaths
1923	Feb. 13-14	**United States (Mid-Northwest)**	28
	Blizzard with winds of 63 m.p.h. struck Mich., N. & S. Dak., & Wisc.		
	Mar. 11-12	**United States (Midwest)**	48
	Heavy, wet snow caused $4 million damage.		
	Mar. 18	**United States (Midwest)**	900
	Tornado ripped through Ill., Ind., & Mo., 2,500 injured & property damage in millions.		
	Apr. 4	**Pineville, La.**	14
	Tornado destroyed town.		
	Apr. 25	**Oklahoma**	100
	Several towns hit by twisters.		
	May 14	**Mitchel Co., Tex.**	21
	Tornado struck area; $50,000 damage.		
	July 10	**Rostov, Russia**	23
	Hailstorm struck Don dist., many cattle killed.		
	†Sept. 1	**Japan**	143,000
	Tsunami caused by earthquake damaged Tokyo & Yokohama, great fire followed. (SEE Tokyo, Japan)		
	Nov. 5	**Qaxaca, Mexico**	100
	Storms devastated area.		
1924	Jan. 27	**Saloniki, Greece**	159
	Exceptional cold prevailed throughout country.		
	Mar. 15	**Bareilly, India**	50
	Tornado struck train.		
	Mar. 27	**United States (Midwest & Southwest)**	24
	Tornadoes, storms swept through Kan., Okla., Mo., O.		
	Apr. 27	**Japan**	100
	Storm struck Sea of Japan, victims fishermen.		
	†Apr. 29-30	**South Carolina (and Southern U.S.)**	115
	Series of 22 tornadoes caused over $10 million damage in Ala., Ark., Ga., La., N. & S. Car., Okla., & Vir.		
	May 26-27	**United States (South)**	43
	Series of 11 tornadoes caused over $1 million damage in Miss. & N. Car.		
	†June 28	**Lorain, Ohio**	78
	Northern part of state hit by 4 tornadoes, 7,000 homeless, over $11 million damage.		
	Aug. 29	**Virgin Islands**	80
	Hurricane, with winds of 110 m.p.h., destroyed 100s of houses & damaged 1,000s of others.		
	Sept. 12	**Kobe, Japan**	20
	Typhoon hit area, wrecked docks.		
	Sept. 21	**Eau Clare, Wisc.**	60
	Cyclone smashed northern part of state, scores injured, over $600,000 damage.		
	Oct. 10	**Cagayan Valley, Philippines**	30
	Typhoon hit area, many missing.		
†1925	Mar. 18	**Illinois (& Midwest)**	689
	Vicious tornadoes swept Ill., Ind., & Mo. with damage over $16 million. (SEE Annapolis, Mo., & Murphysboro, Ill.)		
	Apr. 25	**Primorsk, Korea**	200
	Region hit by deep snow.		
	June 8	**Philadelphia, Pa.**	71
	Heat wave at city, scores prostrated.		
	June 28	**Luzon, Philippines**	100s
	Typhoon smashed central area, great damage.		
	July 17	**Hong Kong, China**	140
	Rain fell for 11 hrs., great property damage.		
	Oct. 23	**Persian Gulf**	1,000s
	Bahrein & Henjam pearl fleets struck by cyclone.		
	Dec. 23	**Japan**	100
	Northern coast hit by storm, 40 vessels capsized.		
1926	Apr. 1	**Madaripur, India**	50
	Tornado razed 7 villages at Bengal.		
	May 28	**Burma**	2,800
	Cyclone & *tsunami* devastated country.		
	July 5	**Germany**	31
	Storm caused great damage.		
	July 21	**Rugovo, Serbia**	100
	Cyclone devastated city.		
	July 26	**West Indies**	100s
	Hurricane struck Bahamas, Santo Domingo & Puerto Rico, 4,000 homeless, damage over $8 million.		
	Aug. 26	**Houma, La.**	25
	Hurricane from Gulf of Mexico swept state, $1 million damage.		
	Sept. 4	**Oshima, Japan**	100
	Typhoon devastated area, over $100 million damage, worst storm in recent years.		
	†Sept. 15-22	**Florida**	450
	Hurricane smashed state from Miami to Palm Beach, 1,000s injured, damage over $100 million.		
	Sept. 20	**Bengal, India**	174
	Storm sank native craft off coast.		
	Sept. 21	**San Andreas, Spain**	51
	Storm gutted several cities.		
	Sept. 22	**Encarnacion, Paraguay**	178
	Hurricane caused by dust clouds left 300 injured, heavy damage.		
	Sept. 30	**China**	2,000
	Typhoon smashed coast, lighthouse submerged.		
	†Oct. 20	**Cuba**	650
	Hurricane flattened 150 sq. mi. area of Matanzas & Havana Prov., more than 10,000 destitute, 325 bldgs. leveled in Havana in hr.		
	Oct. 22	**Bermuda**	100
	Hurricane caused great damage off coast, maximum winds of 120 m.p.h.		
	Nov. 6	**Batangas, Philippines**	100s
	Province smashed by typhoon, tidal wave & flood—100s missing.		
	Nov. 25-26	**United States (South)**	78
	Series of 14 tornadoes caused over $1 million damage in Ala., Ark., Mo., & Tenn.		
	Dec. 25	**France**	20
	Cold weather gripped country.		
1927	Jan. 18	**Russia**	100s
	Great cold claimed many victims.		
	Feb. 13	**Niigata, Japan**	91
	Prefecture dazzled by blizzard.		
	Feb. 17	**Pleasant Hill, La.**	40
	Tornado struck area, 100 injured.		
	Mar. 5	**Madagascar**	500
	Cyclone struck E. coast of island, port of Tamatave ruined.		
	Mar. 18	**Green Forest, Ark.**	40
	Tornadoes wrecked Saline & Carroll counties, heavy property damage.		
	Apr. 11	**Sequoyah, Okla.**	13
	Tornado injured 44, caused over $328,000 damage.		
	†Apr. 12	**Rock Springs, Texas**	74
	Tornado wrecked town, $1½ million damage.		
	Apr. 14	**Morocco-Spain**	23
	Hurricane struck coasts, 59 injured, damage over $10 million.		
	Apr. 19	**United States (Midwest)**	31
	Tornado caused over $2 million damage in Ill, Mo., Neb., & Okla.		
	†May 9	**Poplar Bluff, Mo.**	142
	Series of 36 tornadoes caused over $8 million damage in Ind., La., Mich., Mo., La., & Tex.; Poplar Bluff, Mo., hardest hit.		
	June 1	**Germany**	21
	Cyclone at Dutch border wrecked 3 villages, 50 injured.		
	Aug. 18	**United States**	28
	Storm battered Eastern Seaboard, 5 schooners lost with crew.		

Year	Date	Place	Deaths	Description
	Sept. 13	Kiushiu Is., Japan	719	Typhoon destroyed 1,850 houses, flooded 3,000 others, & left 2,500 acres submerged.
	Sept. 26	Kwangtuag, China	5,000	Typhoon & tidal wave smashed area.
	†Sept. 29	St. Louis, Mo.	85	Five-minute tornado wrecked city, damage over $25 million, 1,800 homes destroyed.
	Oct. 28	England	22	North struck by gales & rains.
	Oct. 30	Irish Coast	50	Gale wiped out fishing fleet.
	Nov. 4	N. Madras, India	100s	Cyclone devastated area, Nellore partly wrecked.
1928	Jan. 3	Baku, Azerbaijan	100	Violent storms menaced the trans-Caucasian region.
	Jan. 12	Djetisuisk, Turkestan	70	Blizzard devastated district.
	Jan. 28	Great Britain	20	Rain & windstorm struck from S. of England to Scotland, 300 injured.
	Feb. 4	Hokkaido Is., Japan	40	Violent snowstorm capsized fishing boats off coast.
	Feb. 12	Europe	50	Western part of continent swept by gales, Scandinavia hardest hit.
	July 4	New York City	23	Storm swept shore, 3 million fled area.
	Aug. 18	Haiti	100s	Tropical storm left 10,000 homeless, villages wrecked.
	Aug. 19	Djidjelli, Algeria	20	Hurricane & quake swept coast, city in ruins, 200 injured.
	†Sept. 10-16	West Indies & Florida	5,000	Hurricane swept vast area, 1,870 injured. (SEE Lake Okeechobee)
	†Sept. 13	Guadeloupe	900	Hurricane swept islands, communications cut, damage over $50 million.
	Sept. 13	India	60	Blizzard claimed pilgrims as victims.
	Nov. 13	Villa Maria, Argentina	41	Cyclone swept area.
	Nov. 16	England	41	Gales smashed E. coast, many bldgs. damaged.
	Nov. 24	Philippine Islands	50	Typhoon swept villages, great damage.
	Nov. 25	Netherlands	58	Country ravaged by gales, great destruction.
	Nov. 27	Philippines	200	Typhoon raped islands south of Manilla, 10,000 homeless on Leyte.
	Dec. 23	Cottabato, Philippines	500	Area swept by tidal wave, 20 ships lost.
1929	Jan. 2	Hondo, Japan	150	Gales & *tsunami* destroyed 100s of homes, many injured.
	Feb. 11-17	Belgium	50	Cold wave lasted week, whole continent suffered.
	Feb. 26	United States (South)	28	Storm swept many states.
	Apr. 10	Swifton, Ark.	53	Tornadoes struck wide area, 200 injured, $1 million damage.
	Apr. 25	Statesboro, Ga.	48	Tornadoes ripped south central area, 100s injured, damage over $2 million.
	May 27	Leyte, Philippines	119	Typhoon inundated 6 villages, damage over $500,000.
	July 5	Austria	20	Hurricane swept country, crops damaged.
	Sept. 3	Philippines	250	Typhoon struck Luzon & Manila areas, 1,000s homeless.
	Sept. 20	Philippines	26	Typhoon struck Catanduanes & Rapurapu, 7,000 homes destroyed.
	Sept. 27	Nassau, Bahamas	20	Storms struck area.
1930	Jan. 9	China	100s	Snow & dust storm ravaged area for 2 days from Mongolian deserts to Yangtze Valley.
	Jan. 10	China	15,000	Worst cold in 60 yrs. at inner Mongolia & Suiyuan dist. of No. Shansi, both famine areas.
	Apr. 20	Leyte, Philippines	100s	Typhoon swept 14 towns, 1,000s homeless.
	May 1	Homer, Neb.	24	Tornado swept 4 states, many persons injured.
	May 3	Aniway Bay, Japan	100s	Typhoon struck area, over $3 million damage.
	May 6	Frost, Texas	69	Tornado leveled town, 100 injured; damage over $2 million.
	June 13	Macedonia, Greece	22	Hail storm with stones as large as tennis balls.
	July 9	United States (Midwest)	106	Heat wave in 5 states, broke 29-yr. record.
	July 18	Korea & Japan	258	Torrential rains & typhoon leveled 5,400 houses, damage over $50 million.
	July 25	Piave Valley, Italy	22	Hurricane injured 100, 200 homes damaged.
	July 28	Adrianople, Turkey	22	Worst tornado in 100 yrs. broke every window in city, 80% of homes destroyed & Sultan Selim's mosque.
	†Sept. 3	Santo Domingo, D.R.	4,000	Hurricane left 5,000 injured, damage over $40 million, all corpses cremated.
	Sept. 21	France	250	Equinoctial gale swept seaside resorts off Breton coast.
	Nov. 7	Pulo-Condor Island	50	Area smashed by typhoon, victims natives.
	Nov. 14	Loochow Is., Japan	100s	Typhoon, with winds over 160 m.p.h., caught 100s of fishermen by surprise.
	Nov. 19	Bethany, Okla.	23	Tornado wrecked ½ of town, 124 injured.
	Nov. 21	United States (Northwest)	23	Blizzard lasted 5 days in 7 states.
1931	Jan. 5	Leyte Prov., Philippines	100	Typhoon devastated area.
	Jan. 12	China	100s	North suffered extreme cold.
	Jan. 12	Japan	30	Blizzard derailed train, tore roofs off 1,000 houses.
	June 27	United States	1,016	Heat wave struck 12 states, temperatures over 100°.
	Aug. 25	China	100s	Central area struck by worst typhoon since 1925.
	†Sept. 10	Belize, Brit. Honduras	1,500	Hurricane & tidal wave caused damage over $7.5 million.
	Sept. 12	Formosa	26	*Tsunami* struck south followed by torrential rains.
	Sept. 16	Veracruz	50	Hurricane wrecked 20 boats in harbor, great damage in Lower Cal.
	Oct. 13	Tokyo, Japan	31	Wind & rain struck central area, 6,000 homes flooded.

Date		Place	Deaths
1932	Feb. 8	**Reunion Island**	45
	Cyclone smashed area.		
	†Mar. 21-22	**United States (South)**	268
	Tornadoes struck Ala., Tenn., S.C., Ky., & Va.; 3,000 injured, 8,500 homeless. (SEE Alabama)		
	Apr. 30	**Jolo, Philippines**	99
	Tsunami destroyed 2/3 of town.		
	May 5	**Annam, Fr. Indo-China**	500
	Typhoon smashed area farms & R.R.'s destroyed.		
	May 5	**Mymensingh, India**	70
	Tornado swept area, victims buried in ruins.		
	June 2	**Ismail, Rumania**	80
	Hurricane wrecked city, great damage.		
	June 22	**Honan, China**	200
	Hailstorm struck western section of area.		
	Aug. 14	**Galveston, Texas**	39
	Hurricane smashed southern part of state, 100s injured.		
	Sept. 12	**Loyang, China**	100s
	Rain & wind storms swept area.		
	†Sept. 26	**Puerto Rico**	225
	Hurricane swept island, 3,000 injured, damage over $30 million.		
	†Nov. 9	**Santa Cruz del Sur, Cuba**	2,500
	Storm wave, with winds of 210 m.p.h., resulted in one of the island's most disastrous hurricanes.		
	Nov. 9	**Cayman Is., Br. W. Indies**	80
	Hurricane left 300 injured, over $1 million damage.		
†1933	Mar. 3	**Sanriku, Japan**	3,000
	Tsunami caused by underwater quake brought 30-ft. wave over city.		
	Mar. 14	**Tennessee**	34
	Tornado swept state, 200 injured, Nashville had damage over $2 million.		
	Mar. 30-31	**United States (South)**	89
	Series of 29 tornadoes caused damage over $1½ million in Ala., La., Miss., & Tex.		
	May 1	**Webster Parish, La.**	23
	Tornado caused over $1 million damage.		
	May 9	**Kentucky**	34
	Tornado traveled from Monroe to Russell Co., damage over $200,000.		
	June	**Trinidad**	13
	Hurricane left 1,000 homeless & damage over $3 million, towns in Venezuela also suffered great damage.		
	Aug. 23	**United States (East Coast)**	62
	New York City battered by hurricane, damage in millions.		
	Sept. 1	**Cuba**	406
	Hurricane swept coast, 100,000 homeless, sugar crop wiped out.		
	Sept. 4	**Texas**	22
	Coast battered by hurricane, 2,000 homeless.		
	Sept. 16	**North Carolina**	21
	Hurricane smashed coast, $1 million damage.		
	†Sept. 24	**Tampico, Mexico**	100s
	Second hurricane in 10 days left city in waste, damage over $5 million.		
	Nov. 3	**Philippines**	20
	Typhoon struck coast.		
	Dec. 13	**Europe**	37
	Snow covered continent, birds fell to ground in Prussia.		
	Dec. 26-31	**United States (East)**	68
	Heavy snow in New York City & Penn.		
1934	Jan. 28	**Korea**	41
	Blizzard swept coast.		
	Feb. 25	**North Carolina**	20
	Tornado isolated cities, 3 other states hit.		
	Mar. 15	**Queensland, Australia**	64
	Storms swept area.		
	†June 8	**El Salvador**	2,000
	Hurricane left 3,000 homeless, Western Honduras also severely damaged.		
	July 17	**Moraxitza Val., Yugoslavia**	30
	Severe storms caused great damage at area.		
	July 22	**St. Louis, Mo.**	415
	Three-week heat-wave.		
	†Sept. 21	**Osaka, Japan**	4,000
	West swept by typhoon, great reconstruction needed.		
	Oct. 15	**Manila, Philippines**	69
	Typhoon with torrential rain devastated area.		
	Nov. 2	**Annam, Fr. Indo-China**	250
	Typhoon smashed coast.		
	Nov. 14	**Mauban, Philippines**	300
	Most violent typhoon in yrs. ruined town.		
1935	Feb. 4	**Nablus, Palestine**	24
	Rainstorms deluged area.		
	Apr. 6	**Luzon, Philippines**	70
	Island devastated by typhoon, Samar Province razed.		
	Apr. 7	**United States (South)**	26
	Freak tornado left 150 injured in La. & Miss.		
	Aug. 5	**Fukien Prov., China**	100s
	Typhoon smashed South, riots followed.		
	†Aug. 25	**Newfoundland, Canada**	Scores
	Hurricane demolished dozens of villages & fishing fleets.		
	†Sept. 2	**Florida Keys**	400
	Hurricane wrecked southern coast, great loss of life at Vet. Camp. No. 1, damage over $40 million.		
	Sept. 27	**Japan**	254
	Rainstorms left many missing.		
	†Oct. 25	**Jeremie, Haiti**	2,000
	Hurricane ruined area, great damage.		
	†Oct. 25	**Honduras**	150
	Weakened hurricane managed to destroy most banana plantations. (SEE Jeremie, Haiti)		
	Dec. 26	**Luzon, Philippines**	39
	Province smashed by typhoon, a 7,000-ton freighter was hurled into rocks.		
	Dec. 27-29	**United States (South)**	212
	Worst ice storm in 3 decades caused $2 million damage in Ark., Ga., & Tenn., transportation halted.		
1936	Feb. 11	**Bulgaria**	100
	Blizzard with temp. 49° below zero.		
	Feb. 23-24	**United States (West)**	26
	Snow with blizzard conditions in Nev. & Cal., 32 in. fell in 24 hrs., over 700 cars stalled.		
	†Apr. 2	**United States (South)**	23
	Series of 12 tornadoes caused over $3 million damage in Ala., Ga., & N. & S. Car.; Cordelle, Ga., had 23 victims & 289 bldgs. destroyed. (SEE Cordelle, Ga.)		
	†Apr. 2-6	**United States (South)**	421
	Series of 22 tornadoes caused over $22 million damage in Ala., Ark., Ga., Tenn., & S. Car.; Tupelo, Miss., had 195 victims. (SEE Gainsville, Ga.)		
	May 1	**Burma**	36
	Cyclones struck Kyaukpyo & Akyab districts, 200,000 homeless.		
	July 6	**Canada**	500
	Two-week heat wave forced 1,000s to invade city beaches.		
	Aug. 16	**Hong Kong, China**	100
	Worst typhoon since 1922 buried workmen at region.		
	Aug. 28	**Korea**	1,104
	Typhoon injured 1,028, many missing.		
	Oct. 2	**Japan**	70
	Typhoon struck ships off coast, Hokkaido Is. damaged.		
	Oct. 11	**Manila, Philippines**	546
	Typhoon isolated area, 100s missing.		

Date		Place	Deaths	
	Oct. 30	**India**	**162**	Tornado left 15,000 homeless, tobacco depot collapsed on victims.
1937	**Jan. 27**	**Europe**	**57**	Blizzards & gales struck west to Balkans.
	Aug. 5	**North Korea**	**130**	Typhoon left 18 injured.
	Sept. 1	**Hong Kong, China**	**100**	Typhoon struck area, wind velocity set record.
	Nov. 11	**Philippines**	**30**	Typhoon struck wide area, 3,000 homeless at Manila, 30,000 at Bulacan Province.
	Nov. 18	**Philippines**	**247**	Typhoon wrecked most coconut groves, damage over $4 million.
1938	**Sept. 1**	**Tokyo, Japan**	**99**	Countryside N. of city smashed by typhoon.
	†Sept. 17-21	**Long Island, N.Y.**	**600**	Hurricane smashed Eastern Seaboard, damage over $400 million.
	†Sept. 29	**Charleston, S.C.**	**32**	Group of 5 tornadoes injured 150, destroyed 100 bldgs., damage over $2 million.
	Oct. 7	**Philippines**	**22**	Central area struck by typhoon, all victims drowned.
	Nov. 24-25	**United States (East)**	**37**	Snowfall broke records in N.Y., Penn., & Vir.
1939	**Jan. 2**	**Istanbul, Turkey**	**22**	Cold wave struck city.
	Apr. 16-17	**United States (South)**	**41**	Series of 24 tornadoes caused $500,000 damage in Ala., Ark., La., Miss., & Tex.
	Sept. 28	**Southern California**	**57**	Hurricane storms ripped coast, worst Sept. storm in weather bureau history to this date.
	Dec. 4	**Masbate Is., Philippines**	**23**	Typhoon swept several provinces.
1940	**Jan. 21-24**	**Shanghai, China**	**650**	Southern Provs. struck by cold wave.
	Jan. 23-24	**United States (South & East Coast)**	**26**	Snowstorm swept almost to Mississippi Coast, damage in millions.
	Jan. 31	**Japan**	**78**	North central area struck by blizzards.
	July 10	**Seoul, Korea**	**52**	Typhoon left 1,000s homeless, 100 injured & 96 bridges destroyed.
	July 24	**Chile**	**100s**	Torrential rains inundated cities of Antofagasta, Tocopilla, Iquique, Taltal, Calama for 48 hrs.
	Sept. 7	**Bonin Is., Japan**	**100s**	Typhoon left 1,000s homeless at area 500 mi. S.E. of Hondo, Japan.
	Sept. 28	**Formosa**	**50**	Southern area struck by typhoon, 5,000 homes leveled, crops destroyed.
	Oct. 14	**Bombay, India**	**28**	Cyclone caused extensive damage, many small craft ruined.
	Nov. 11-12	**United States (Mid-Northwest)**	**157**	Armistice Day blizzard struck 6 states from Mich. to S. Dak., damage over $10 million, great loss of life on Lake Michigan.
	Dec. 26	**Cuba-Mexico**	**21**	Winds of gale force & torrential rains caused great damage.
	Dec. 29	**Santa Madalena Domar, Madiera**	**20**	Gale and rainstorm leveled village, victims swept out to sea.
1941	**Jan. 31**	**Shanghai, China**	**200**	Severe cold took the lives of beggars & indigents, victims mostly children.
	Feb. 16	**Spain & Portugal**	**140**	Storm lashed both countries, crops ruined, damage over $10 million.
	Mar. 15-16	**United States (Northwest)**	**151**	Blizzard & gales swept states from Minn. to S. Dak., deaths caused by exposure & carbon monoxide in stalled cars.
	†May 21	**Cape Girardeau, Mo.**	**23**	Tornado wrecked 233 homes & caused $4 million damage in 5 minutes.
	May 25	**Barisal, India**	**5,000**	Storm leveled villages in the Ganges Delta, great property damage.
	July 21	**Tokyo, Japan**	**35**	Typhoon lashed wide area in wake of 7-day rain, 26,000 homes flooded at Shizuoka.
	Sept. 29	**Tegucigalpa, Honduras**	**100s**	Hurricane lashed across the Caribbean, northern coast devastated, 1,000s homeless.
	Sept. 29	**Cuba**	**21**	Hurricane struck coast, victims fishermen.
	Oct. 1	**Japan**	**100s**	Typhoon swept island of Kyushu & S. Hondo, many fishermen lost off port of Kurosaki.
1942	**Feb. 5-6**	**United States (South)**	**23**	Series of 16 tornadoes caused over $2 million damage in Ala., Ark., Ga., Miss., Tenn., & S. Car.
	Feb. 15	**Shanghai, China**	**100s**	Cold wave struck area.
	†Mar. 16	**Baldwyn, Miss.**	**65**	Two tornadoes caused $1 million damage in 25 min.
	Apr. 29-30	**United States (Southwest)**	**21**	Series of 9 tornadoes caused $200,000 damage in Col., Kans., Mo., Neb., Okla., & S. Dak.
	†June 12	**Oklahoma City, Okla.**	**35**	Violent tornado struck at night, damage over $300,000, 100 houses destroyed.
	July 15	**Formosa**	**205**	*Tsunami* smashed coast.
	†Oct. 16	**Bengal, India**	**40,000**	Province ruined by cyclone, winds reached 150 m.p.h.
	Nov. 14	**Calcutta, India**	**670**	Cyclone with torrential rains swept coastal area 200 mi. from city.
	Nov. 28	**Kyushu, Japan**	**63**	*Tsunami* left 30,000 people isolated, 560 homes destroyed & 240 submerged.
1943	**Oct. 9**	**Mexico**	**52**	Hurricane struck 150-mi. stretch along Pacific coast, 102 injured.
1944	**Apr. 16**	**United States (South)**	**38**	Tornado injured more than 500, great damage at Ga. & S. Car.
	†June 23	**Shinnston, W. Va. (& Pennsylvania)**	**151**	Series of tornadoes caused over $2 million damage.
	†Sept. 8-16	**New England**	**389**	Hurricane caused $50 million damage in several states with winds up to 140 m.p.h.
	†Sept. 14	**United States (East)**	**100s**	Hurricanes struck New England states for days.
	†Oct. 13-21	**Cuba (& U.S. East Coast)**	**300**	Hurricane struck coasts, $20 million citrus crop ruined.
	†Dec. 17-18	**Luzon Islands, Philippines**	**790**	Admiral Halsey's Third Fleet was caught in storm while refueling 500 mi. E. of Luzon, 3 vessels were lost and a dozen severely damaged.

Year	Date	Place	Deaths	Description
1945	Feb. 12	United States (South)	41	Series of 7 tornadoes caused over $2 million damage in Ala. & Miss.
	†Apr. 12	Oklahoma (Arkansas & Missouri)	112	Tornado swept through Ark. & died out in Mo., damage over $3 million.
	Nov. 30	New England	34	Two-day storm caused great property damage.
	Dec. 24-25	Carolinas	30	Worst ice-storm in 2 decades.
1946	Jan. 4-6	United States (South)	80	Series of 12 tornadoes caused over $5 million damage in Ark., Miss., & Tex.
	†Apr. 1	Hilo City, Hawaii	179	Vicious tidal wave wrapped railroad tracks around trees, caused over $10 million damage & hospitalized 100s.
	Oct. 8	Flores, Azores	27	Hurricane struck Santa Cruz harbor, 57 fishing boats sunk.
	Oct. 22	Italy	22	Torrential rains struck northern area.
	Oct. 27	Sardinia, Italy	40	Storm left 20 injured.
	Nov. 2-6	United States (Southeast)	27	Heavy snow, planes grounded for 3 days.
	Nov. 13	Visayas, Philippines	400	Typhoon left 1,000s homeless, many missing, downtown business section of Cebu City submerged.
	†Dec. 21	Honshu, Japan	2,000	*Tsunami* & quake affected 60,000 sq. mi.
1947	Jan. 30	United States (Midwest & South)	20	Tornado swept 5 states, great damage at Ala. & Mo.
	Jan. 30-Feb. 8	Berlin, Germany	258	Cold wave lasted 10 days, exposure & starvation worst in 150 yrs.
	†Apr. 9	Texas (Oklahoma & Kansas)	169	Series of 8 tornadoes caused over $15 million damage in Kans., Okla., & Tx.; Woodward, Okla., demolished. (SEE Woodward)
	June 1	Pine Bluff, Ark.	37	Tornado left 500 homeless, 100s injured, damage over $1 million.
	Sept. 4-21	Florida & Gulf Coasts	51	Hurricane battered area, damage over $100 million.
	Oct. 7	Hong Kong, China	2,000	Typhoon struck fishing fleet off coast.
	Dec. 2	Portugal	165	Hurricane sank fishing fleet off N. coast.
	Dec. 26-27	United States (East)	55	Snow up to 30 in. in N.Y., N.J., & N. Eng.
1947-1948		United States (Midwest)	39	Worst ice storm to hit Mo. in 2 decades, Ia. & Okla. also heavily damaged.
1948	Jan. 24-31	United States (South)	38	Ice storm caused $20 million damage in Ark., Miss., & S. Car.
	Jan. 25	Shanghai, China	150	Cold wave, all victims children.
	Jan. 31	Reunion Island	300	Hurricane left 1,000s homeless.
	Mar. 19	Alton, Ill.	42	Tornado swept from Mo. to Shelby, Ill., damage over $3 million.
	Mar. 26	Indiana	20	Tornado swept state, damage over $3 million.
	June 17	China	190	Typhoon in the area of Tungting Lake.
	July 4	Shanghai, China	34	Windstorm left over 100 injured.
	Aug. 24-30	New York	33	Week of heat caused beaches to overcrowd, 50-yr. record of 98.9 degrees beaten.
	Sept. 6	Turin, Italy	80	Storms caused heavy damage throughout area.
	Sept. 17	Ichinoseki, Japan	500	Typhoon struck huge area, great injury & damage.
	Oct. 2	Hainan Is., China	30	Typhoon caused $5 million damage.
	Nov. 17-20	United States (Southwest)	29	The "November" blizzard caused $6 million damage in Col., Kans., & Neb.
	Nov. 22	Bombay, India	35	Cyclonic storm stopped power & transportation systems, most victims seamen.
	Dec. 19-20	United States (Northwest)	24	Area blanketed by 19½-in. snowfall, 3rd highest on record.
	Dec. 27	Shanghai, China	43	Cold wave struck city, deaths from exposure.
1948-9	Dec. 31-Jan. 1	United States (South)	23	Series of 6 tornadoes caused over $2 million damage in Ark., La., Miss., & Tenn.
1949	Jan. 1	Teheran, Iran	60	Snowfall left 73,000 homeless.
	Jan. 1-14	United States (West)	121	Severe blizzard in the Great Basin, Middle Rockies & N.W. Great Plains.
	Jan. 3	Arkansas	57	Tornado struck state from Columbia to Lincoln Co., damage over $1 million.
	Jan. 3	Europe (Western)	39	Cold wave & high gales caused highway & maritime accidents.
	Jan. 22-28	United States (Mid-Southwest)	28	Ice storm struck Okla., Tex., & Wisc.
	Mar. 1	Ruhr, Germany	30	Gales devastated area.
	Mar. 24-26	United States (Mid-South West)	57	Series of 42 tornadoes caused over $12 million damage in Ill., Ind., Ia., Kans., Ky., Mo., Neb., & Okla.; Cape Girardeau, Mo., had 23 victims.
	June 20	Kyushu, Japan	100s	Typhoon struck city, many missing; government charged with willful neglect.
	July 23	Shanghai-Okinawa	67	Typhoon storms injured 100s & damaged 40,000 structures.
	Aug. 7	China	1,000	Typhoon struck Pootung-Nanhwei area.
	Oct. 4	Naples, Italy	32	Storm struck area, many missing.
	Oct. 17	Guatemala	300	Two-day storm raised havoc throughout area.
	Oct. 27	India	1,000	Cyclone wrecked S.E. coast, 50,000 homeless.
	Nov. 2	Cebu, Philippines	26	Typhoon struck central area, 20,000 homeless.
	Dec. 8	Korea	1,000s	East coast wrecked by typhoon.
1950	Jan. 12-14	United States (West)	75	Great snowfall with winds over 72 m.p.h. at Tatoosh Is., Ore.
	Jan. 29	Himalayan Mts., Asia	500	Snow & cold caught many Chinese refugees.
	Feb. 13	Arkansas-Louisiana	31	Tornadoes hit 4 states, 200 injured, many homes smashed.
	Aug. 27	Chile	27	Tropical storm ripped western provs., $2 million damage.

Date	Place	Deaths
Sept. 3	**Japan**	**100s**
	Typhoons devastated huge area, Kobe-Osaka-Kyoto worst hit, 100,000 homeless.	
Sept. 20	**E. Punjab, India**	**70**
	Gales & rains left 200,000 homeless, 25,000 homes leveled.	
Oct. 16	**La India, Nicaragua**	**23**
	Storm swept through city.	
Nov. 20	**New York City**	**44**
	Rainstorm with winds up to 62 m.p.h. wrecked wide area, 407,000 bldgs. lost power, disaster later classified as gale.	
Nov. 23-28	**United States (East)**	**88**
	Heavy snowfall, extremely low temp., damage over $20 million in the Carolinas & Ohio.	
Nov. 25-28	**United States (Northeast)**	**295**
	Gales at near hurricane force struck 22 states, Conn., Mass., Vt., hardest hit, damage over $50 million.	
Nov. 27	**Mexico City, Mexico**	**27**
	Cold wave.	
1951 **Jan. 4**	**Comoro Is., Madagascar**	**500**
	Two-day tornado razed Hombo, many missing.	
Jan. 28-Feb. 4	**United States (Central)**	**200**
	Ice storm caused $60 million damage in N. Eng., Tenn., & Tex.	
Feb. 8	**Europe (West)**	**22**
	Freak storm struck from Bay of Biscay to Great Britain, many stranded.	
Mar. 10-14	**Iowa**	**23**
	Great snowfall throughout state.	
May 14	**Faridpur, Pakistan**	**100**
	Tornado struck E. Bengal area, many missing and hurt.	
Aug. 1-18	**Texas**	**42**
	Weeks of heat roasted state.	
†**Aug. 17**	**Jamaica**	**154**
	Hurricane left 1,000s homeless. (SEE Charlie)	
Aug. 21	**Tampico, Mexico**	**38**
	Gulf hurricane with winds of 158 m.p.h. wrecked wide area, martial law declared.	
Oct. 14	**Kyushu, Japan**	**448**
	Series of typhoons left 100s missing, southern area wrecked, damages of $28 million.	
Oct. 21	**Calabria, Italy**	**109**
	Week of storms wrecked province, 1,000s homeless.	
Nov. 2-5	**United States**	**136**
	Great frost in 25 states.	
Nov. 9	**Italy (North)**	**41**
	Storms ripped area, great havoc followed.	
Nov. 22	**Philippines**	**60**
	Typhoon smashed central areas, many missing.	
Dec. 9	**Cebu, Philippines**	**724**
	Typhoon devastated central area, 60,000 homeless, some missing.	
Dec. 25	**Epi Is., New Hebrides**	**100**
	Hurricane ripped apart area.	
Dec. 27-30	**Europe**	**63**
	Hurricane struck continent from Bay of Biscay to Great Britain, some missing.	
1952 **Jan. 13**	**California**	**26**
	Worst blizzard in ½ century, 196 passengers stranded on stalled train 3 days.	
Jan. 22-23	**United States (Northwest)**	**21**
	Blizzard struck N. & S. Dak. & Minn.	
Jan. 29	**Fiji Islands**	**30**
	Hurricane swept across area.	
Feb. 4-13	**Europe (West)**	**90**
	Nine-day snowstorm devastated area.	
Feb. 18-19	**New England**	**47**
	Snow totaled 31 in.	
Mar. 20-23	**United States (Mid-Northwest)**	**27**
	Great snowfall covered 8 states; included were Neb., Minn., & Wy.	
†**Mar. 21-22**	**United States (South)**	**208**
	Series of 31 tornadoes caused worst damage since 1932, over $15 million in Ala., Ark., Ky., Miss., Mo., & Tenn. (SEE Dierks, Ark.)	
June 16	**United States (East)**	**160**
	Heat wave sent temperatures over 100° in 17 states for 5 days.	
June 22	**Kyushu, Japan**	**23**
	Typhoon destroyed or flooded 2,500 homes.	
July 12	**Japan**	**83**
	Rainstorms devastated west.	
Aug. 12	**Mexicali, Mexico**	**30**
	Area suffered from 5-day heat wave.	
Sept. 21	**Tebessna, Africa**	**25**
	Sudden cloudburst at area.	
Sept. 23	**Petatlan, Mexico**	**113**
	Hurricane ripped through Guerrero State.	
Oct. 22	**Philippines**	**500**
	Typhoon devastated central areas, many missing, $50 million damage.	
Nov. 14	**Formosa**	**67**
	Typhonic winds of 115 m.p.h. ripped S.W., 500 injured, over 1,000 homes destroyed.	
Nov. 30	**Madras State, India**	**350**
	Cyclonic storm damaged 200,000 homes, many missing.	
Nov. 31	**Albertsville, S. Africa**	**35**
	Tornado flattened area, over 500 injured.	
†**Dec.**	**London, England**	**12,000**
	Fog affected city for weeks, expense estimated at $22 million.	
1953 **Jan. 8-11**	**United States (East)**	**49**
	Ice storm caused damage in millions in Md., N.Y., & Penn.	
Feb. 18-21	**United States (Northwest)**	**24**
	Snowdrifts to 16 ft. in Col., Ia., & Minn.	
†**Mar. 13**	**Texas (& Oklahoma)**	**20**
	Series of 17 tornadoes caused over $2 million damage in Ark., Miss., Okla., Tenn., & Tex.	
Mar. 18	**Pakistan**	**21**
	Tornado injured over 100.	
†**May 11**	**Waco, Texas**	**114**
	Tornado wrecked city & surrounding area, 1st twister ever recorded in area, damage over $42 million.	
June 6	**Japan (West)**	**29**
	Typhoon injured 40, $20 million damage.	
†**June 8**	**Flint, Mich.**	**116**
	Series of 8 tornadoes struck Mich. & Ohio, rated 10th worst in country's history, damage over $19 million.	
†**June 9**	**Worcester, Mass.**	**90**
	Worst New Eng. tornado in 75 yrs., $52 million in property damage, 3,000 homeless.	
June 11	**Deccan, India**	**100s**
	Record heat-wave scorched plateau.	
June 26	**Honshu, Japan**	**134**
	Heaviest rainfall in 61 yrs., 101.1 in., left 100s missing.	
July 8	**Punjab, Pakistan**	**111**
	Temperature rose to 111.02.	
July 9	**Andes Mts., Chile**	**25**
	Sudden storm caught tourists by surprise.	
Aug. 22	**Chile**	**33**
	Rain & windstorms caused heavy damage.	
†**Sept. 25**	**Vietnam (& Japan)**	**1,300**
	Typhoon struck central coast, Hue hardest hit, 1,000s homeless.	
Sept. 25	**Osaka, Japan**	**276**
	Typhoon smashed south, 993 injured, 19,000 homes destroyed—100s missing.	

Date		Place	Deaths	
	Dec. 3	Vicksburg, Miss.	30	Tornadoes struck 3 states, 1,000s homeless, $25 million damage.
1954	Jan. 3-10	Europe (Central)	80	Baltic storm caused severe blizzards.
	Jan. 14	United States (Northeast)	76	Snowstorm & cold waves throughout area.
	Feb. 2	Europe	100	Week-long cold wave struck continent.
	Feb. 28-Mar. 5	Ohio	24	Heavy snow & zero temp. throughout area.
	Mar. 29-30	United States (Central)	22	Cold wave in 26 states.
	June 23	Japan	26	Monsoon struck S.W. area, 25 injured.
	Aug. 17	Kyushu, Japan	30	Typhoon destroyed 500 homes, flooded 4,000 others.
	†Aug. 26-31	United States (Northeast)	60	Hurricane Carol ripped through 10 states, $461 million damage, 1,000s homeless. (SEE Carol)
	Sept. 10-13	New England	22	Hurricane Edna swept 5 states, damage in millions.
	Sept. 12	Kyushu, Japan	80	Typhoon with 100 m.p.h. winds left 66 injured, 15,000 homes damaged.
	†Sept. 26	Hakodate, Japan	1,600	Typhoon smashed wide area, ferry sank with 40 Americans aboard, many victims missing. (SEE *Toyo Maru*)
	†Oct. 12-16	Haiti	100	Hurricane Hazel struck southern peninsula, 100,000 homeless, many missing.(SEE Hazel)
	†Oct. 15	United States (South)	255	Hurricane Hazel struck 5 states & Washington, D.C., 1,000s homeless, $50 million damage. (SEE Hazel)
	†Oct. 16	Toronto, Canada	56	Hurricane Hazel wrecked city, damage over $24 million. (SEE Hazel)
	Nov. 26-30	England	58	South & Midlands lashed by gales, storm described as worst in 30 yrs.
	Dec. 28-30	United States (Southeast)	57	Snow & sleet storms in Kans., Okla., & Tex.
1955	Jan. 1-7	Europe (West)	39	Blizzards & cold waves throughout area.
	Jan. 6	Leyte, Philippines	23	Storm left 2,000 homeless.
	Feb. 1	Tunica, Miss.	30	Two tornadoes ripped apart city & nearby states, 100 bldgs. demolished.
	Feb. 18-20	United States (Northwest)	23	Severe blizzards with winds to 65 m.p.h. in N. & S. Dak., Neb., & Wy.
	Mar. 20-25	United States (West)	47	Heavy snow with high winds & blizzards in Col., Id., Mont., 200 injured.
	†May 25	Udall, Kans.	111	Monster tornado wrecked city & swept through 4 other states; Pres. Eisenhower declared disaster area.
	May 26	Santa Catarina, Brazil	22	State torn apart by tornado.
	June 4	India	23	North scorched by heat wave.
	July 9	Mexico	20	Rainy season caused severe damage.
	July 17	South Korea	21	Heavy rains caused $1 million damage.
	†Aug. 4-18	United States (Atlantic Coast)	310	Hurricanes Connie & Diane caused over $1.5 billion damage in 10 states, from Vir. to N.E., from their origin 700 mi. E. of the Fr. West Indies. (SEE Connie)
	Aug. 28	Formosa	40	Typhoon smashed S.E. part of country.
	Aug. 31-Sept. 8	California	107	Ten-day heat wave set record for sustained high temperatures.
	†Sept. 19	Tampico, Mexico	200	Hurricane Hilda struck the central & northern Gulf Coast with gale-like winds, floods & great destruction followed. (SEE Hilda)
	†Sept. 22-28	Caribbean	500	Hurricane Janet was the 10th and most violent of the season, areas of great damage included the Windward Islands, Grenada and the Yucatan Peninsula of Mexico. (SEE Janet)
	Oct. 1	Kyushu, Japan	50	*Tsunami* caused $30 million damage, 1,100 bldgs. ruined by fire, many persons missing.
	†Oct. 7-12	India (& Pakistan)	1,700	Monsoons caused tremendous flooding; 3,500 sq. mi. of cropland swamped; 10,000 villages wiped out.
	Oct. 14-17	United States (East)	44	Tropical cyclone struck 8 states on the Atlantic Coast; Conn. was hardest hit.
	Dec. 4	Madras, India	30	Three-day rainstorm left 1,000s homeless, damage at $1 million.
1956	Jan. 8-10	United States (East)	40	Severe ice storm in Me., N. Eng., & Penn., damage over $2 million.
	†Feb. 1-29	Europe	907	Snow & bitter cold sieged continent from England to Siberia, crop loss $2 billion.
	Feb. 1-8	United States (Southwest)	23	Snow continued for 92 straight hrs., in N. Mex., & Tex., damage in millions.
	Mar. 16-17	United States (East)	162	One of the most crippling wind & snowstorms in a generation in N. Eng., N.Y., & Penn.
	Apr. 2-3	United States (Mid-Southwest)	45	Tornadoes & windstorms struck 13 states from Mich. to Tex., $15 million damage.
	Apr. 7	Portuguese E. Africa	107	Cyclone wrecked districts of Nampula & Niassa and wiped out town of Memba.
	Apr. 15	Birmingham, Ala.	22	Tornado wrecked rural community near city, 200 injured, 1,100 homeless.
	July 6	Philippines (Central)	39	Tropical storm struck islands, victims mostly fishermen.
	†Aug. 2	Hangchow, China	1,960	Typhoon injured 1,200 & destroyed 38,000 homes. (SEE Wanda)
	Aug. 7	China	2,161	Typhoon swept over provinces of Chekiang, Honan & Hopeh, extensive damage in all areas. (SEE Wanda)
	Aug. 17-18	Japan & Okinawa	30	Typhoon struck coast of both countries.
	Sept. 8-10	Philippines-Japan	42	Typhoon Emma smashed 4 countries with 140 m.p.h. winds, damage in millions.
	Sept. 17	Nemours, Algeria	21	Cyclone swept through West.
	†Sept. 22	Grenada	230	Atlantic hurricane destroyed over 40,000 homes & devastated resort town.
	Sept. 26-27	Okinawa & Japan	23	Typhoon Harriet struck coasts, many victims died in earthslide.
	Oct. 30-31	Honshu, Japan	82	Heavy rainstorms struck central & eastern part of area.

Major Storms

Date		Place	Deaths	
	Nov. 12	S. Vietnam	56	Hurricane swept western sections.
	Dec. 2-8	Java	30	Eastern area deluged by typhoons & floods.
	Dec. 8-9	Jakarta	45	Typhoon & landslides destroyed 7,500 homes in the Indonesian Archipelago.
	Dec. 12-16	United States (East)	29	Ice storm in N. Eng., N.J., & N.Y.
1957	Jan. 23-31	United States (Southwest)	23	Severe ice storm in Kans., Okla., & Tenn.
	Mar. 22-25	United States (Southwest)	40	Blizzards caused $6 million damage in Kans., N. Mex., & Okla.
	Apr. 2-6	United States (Southwest)	45	Tornadoes & snowstorms struck large area.
	Apr. 19-27	Texas	11	Tornadoes & rainstorms forced evacuations of 1,000s from southern & central sections of state.
	May 11	East Pakistan	50	Tornadoes capsized 4 river boats.
	May 16	Silverton, Tex.	21	Tornado swept through town.
	May 20	Kansas City, Mo.	39	Tornado struck suburb of city.
	May 25-27	Hong Kong, China	23	Torrential rains & floods swept city.
	†June 27	United States (South)	534	Hurricane Audrey leveled Cameron, La., & devastated surrounding coastal regions of Texas, damage over $40 million. (SEE Audrey)
	June 27	Japan & Formosa	86	Typhoon Virginia struck both countries and disappeared in the China Sea.
	July 2-8	Europe	340	Week-long heat wave affected 4 countries, Italy suffered most casualties (145).
	July 13-28	Helsinki, Finland	25	Lightning, caused by 2 wks. of storms, terrified city.
	July 25-28	Kyushu Is., Japan	513	Torrential rains caused worst flood in 4 yrs., 500 injured & 100s missing.
	Sept. 26	Okinawa	53	Typhoon Faye, with winds of 146 m.p.h., wrecked shipping & military installations & left many victims missing.
	Oct. 18	Suleimaniyah, Iraq	27	Hailstorm struck city.
	Dec. 27	Bahrein Island	20	Sudden storm struck Persian Gulf & wrecked $1½ million off-shore Shell drilling rig.
1958	Jan. 26-27	Japan	271	Storms off east & southern coasts wrecked 7 ships.
	Feb. 7-11	New York State	21	Blizzards lasted 4 days; Syracuse had snow of 37 in.
	†Feb. 15-16	United States (Northeast)	500	Snowfall paralyzed transportation, damage $520 million in Del., N.J., & N. Car.
	Mar. 19-22	United States (East)	63	Snowstorm caused $20 million damage in N.Y., Penn., & Vir.
	May 27	India	26	Heat wave in states of W. Bengal, Behar, & Orissa.
	June 3	India	100	Heat wave in provinces of Bihar, Jodhpur, & Andhra.
	June 4	Colfax, Wisc.	30	Tornadoes struck 90-mi. area in N.W., $10 million damage; 350 injured.
	June 16	Caxaca State, Mexico	200	Pacific storm wrecked 21 fishing vessels off coast.
	June 28	Saudi Arabia	35	Heat wave struck 600,000 Moslems on Mecca pilgrimage.
	July 17	Taiwan	21	Typhoon Winnie struck E. coast.
	Sept. 18	Japan	24	Typhoon struck wide area, some persons missing.
	†Sept. 27-28	Japan	615	Typhoon Ida accompanied by great storm left 10,000 homeless, rainfall in Tokyo was 16 in. (SEE Ida)
	Nov. 15-19	United States (Northwest)	34	Blizzards & gales struck the Rocky Mt. states.
	Dec. 20-21	Rio de Janeiro, Brazil	46	Heavy rains throughout district.
	Dec. 26-27	Japan	60	Coastal storms surprised fishermen.
1959	Feb. 10	St. Louis, Mo.	22	Tornado struck residential area, 5,000 homeless; $12 million damage.
	Feb. 28	Bahrein	500	Windstorm from Persian Gulf swept state.
	Mar. 7	United States (Midwest)	46	Heavy snow caused multiple accidents.
	Mar. 11-13	United States (East)	93	Snowfall of 20 in. with blizzard in N. Eng., & N.Y.
	Mar. 26-29	Malagache Republic	100	Torrential rains & storms made 100,000 homeless—another 400,000 evacuated from capital city, Tananarive.
	Apr. 24	Madagascar	305	Cyclones & floods left 83,200 homeless.
	July 4	Pakistan	139	Monsoon rains flooded the Jhelum, Chenab & Ravi rivers.
	July 11	Korea	57	Heavy rains in southern areas.
	Aug. 14	Japan (Central)	137	Typhoon Georgia swept through area.
	Aug. 20	Fukien, China	720	Typhoon Iris struck province, 100s missing.
	Sept. 17-19	South Korea & Japan	699	Typhoon Sarah smashed both coasts, $50 million damage.
	†Sept. 26-27	Honshu, Japan	5,000	Typhoon Vera, worst in country's history, struck central area with 160 m.p.h. winds & left 1 million homeless. (SEE Vera)
	Oct. 16	Okinawa	28	Typhoon Charlotte swept coastal areas.
	Oct. 27	Manzanillo, Mexico	1,452	Hurricane struck Pacific port of Colimba state, torrential rains & huge mud slides followed.
	Dec. 6-10	England & W. Europe	132	Storms struck both coasts, most fatalities were at sea.
1960	Feb. 12-15	United States (Central)	43	Snowfall in 12 states from La. to N. Eng.
	Feb. 18-20	United States (East)	26	Snowfall in 6 states from Md. to N. Eng., damage in millions.
	Mar. 1	Mauritius Island	42	Indian Ocean typhoon left 68,000 homeless.
	Mar. 2-5	United States (Central)	81	Snowfall in 10 states from Ill. to N. Eng.
	May 5-6	Oklahoma	30	Tornadoes & storms injured over 200 in S.E. section of state.
	†May 22	Philippines	113	Typhoon Lucille caused by Chilean earthquakes. (SEE Lucille)
	†May 23	Hilo City, Hawaii	61	*Tsunami* with wave 2 stories high struck inland city.

Date	Place	Deaths
June 1-21	**India**	395
	Heat wave throughout North.	
June 9	**Hong Kong, China**	30
	Typhoon Mary struck city with 135 m.p.h. winds, 18,000 homeless.	
June 19	**West Pakistan**	30
	Heat wave throughout area.	
June 27	**Luzon, Philippines**	104
	Typhoon Olive struck northern coast, 60,000 homeless, $30 million damage.	
July 31	**Taiwan**	104
	Typhoon Shirley smashed island, 50,000 homeless.	
Aug. 26	**South Korea**	24
	Typhoon Carmen ripped up coast.	
Aug. 31	**Japan**	41
	Typhoon Della struck off southern coast.	
†Sept. 4-12	**Puerto Rico**	106
	Hurricane Donna caused floods & high tides, 600 injured.	
†Sept. 4-12	**Florida-New England**	22
	Hurricane Donna struck the Atlantic coast, 1,000s evacuated. It has been called "most destructive" in U.S. Weather Bureau history. (SEE Donna)	
Oct. 7	**Philippines**	51
	Typhoon Kit struck the islands.	
†Oct. 10	**East Pakistan-India**	4,000
	Cyclone & tidal wave devastated offshore islands of Ramgati & Hatia and along coast of Bay of Bengal.	
Oct. 13	**Philippines**	41
	Typhoon Lola struck islands.	
†Oct. 31	**East Pakistan**	10,000
	Cyclone & tidal wave again smashed Bay of Bengal coastal area, both disasters destroyed 900,000 homes & killed over 150,000 cattle.	
Nov. 3	**Nicaragua**	325
	Storms & floods routed area.	
Dec. 10-12	**United States (East)**	108
	Heavy snowfall with high winds in N.Y., Penn., & Vir.	
Dec. 13	**New England**	29
	Blizzard paralyzed transportation.	
1961 Jan. 19-20	**United States (East)**	37
	Snowstorm in 8 states from N. Car. to N.Y.	
Mar. 19	**Colla, East Pakistan**	266
	Tornadoes devastated area.	
Sept. 11-14	**Texas Coast**	39
	Hurricane Carla, called the fiercest in 61 yrs., smashed 4 states but most residents had moved inland.	
Sept. 17	**Japan (Central)**	185
	Typhoon Nancy struck area, 137,000 homeless.	
†Oct. 31	**Belize, Br. Honduras**	314
	Hurricane Hattie wrecked the capital city, 40% of bldgs. destroyed; 30% badly damaged. (SEE Hattie)	
1962 May 24	**Mexico**	50
	Heat wave scorched country.	
July 8	**Kyushu, Japan**	50
	Typhoon smashed coast.	
Aug. 5	**Yilan, Taiwan**	87
	Typhoon struck area, 1,400 injured, 1,000 houses destroyed.	
Aug. 9	**Philippines**	23
	Typhoon struck area, many missing.	
Sept. 1	**Hong Kong, China**	128
	Typhoon left 27,000 homeless, many injured.	
Oct. 28	**Thailand (South)**	769
	Typhoon smashed N. coast, $19 million damage.	
†Dec. 3-7	**London, England**	136
	Worst fog in 10 yrs. blanketed city & the Midlands.	
Dec. 29-31	**United States (Northeast)**	21
	Gale & zero temp. throughout area.	
†1963 May 28-29	**Chittagong, East Pakistan**	22,000
	Storm devastated area, twice the impact as 1960 disaster, 1 million mud homes destroyed.	
June 21	**South Korea**	186
	Storms struck provinces, 175 injured.	
Sept. 11	**China**	92
	Typhoon Gloria caused $11 million damage, Communist gov't ordered repair work completed in 2 months.	
†Sept. 30-Oct. 9	**Cuba-Haiti**	5,000
	Hurricane Flora left over 275,000 homeless, destroyed 90% of Cuba's coffee crop & the island's economy. (SEE Flora)	
Oct. 8	**East Pakistan**	79
	Typhoon caused great damage, 1 million homeless.	
1964 Apr. 12	**Jessore, Pakistan**	400
	Cyclonic storm smashed villages, 100s injured & missing.	
†June 13-14	**Hyderabad, Pakistan**	332
	Rain & windstorms leveled 100s of homes.	
†June 30	**Philippines**	43
	Storm struck Manila & N. Luzon, worst since 1882, $30 million damage. (SEE Winnie)	
July 3-16	**India**	22
	Monsoon rains lasted 13 days at Uttar, Pradesh & Punjab states.	
July 24	**Italy**	21
	Worst heat wave in 30 yrs.	
July 30	**Brazil**	21
	Heat wave along coast.	
Aug. 7-14	**South Korea**	69
	Rainstorm lasted 7 days.	
†Aug. 22-27	**Haiti**	138
	Hurricane Cleo smashed coast, Guadeloupe & Miami badly hit, damage over $200 million. (SEE Cleo)	
Sept. 5	**Hong Kong, China**	700
	Storms & typhoon delayed Olympic Games, China released official figures 2 weeks later.	
Sept. 12	**Seoul, S. Korea**	100s
	Rainstorm lasted 3 hrs., many missing.	
Sept. 24	**Kyushu Is., Japan**	30
	Storm left 1,000s homeless.	
Oct. 3	**Larose, La.**	21
	Storms started by Hurricane Hilda left 160 injured.	
Oct. 13	**Java, Indonesia**	34
	Heavy rains at city.	
Nov. 19	**Philippines (Central)**	100s
	Storms smashed area, 100,000 homeless.	
Dec. 23	**Ceylon-India**	1,800
	Cyclone caused tidal wave to sweep area, many missing.	
†1965 Apr. 11	**Indiana (& Midwest)**	271
	Tornadoes struck 4 states, worst disaster in Indiana history, damage in millions.	
†May 11-12	**Ganges Delta, East Pakistan**	12,000
	Cyclone wiped out 5 million homes.	
June 1-2	**East Pakistan**	12,047
	Cyclone with tidal wave left millions homeless, 1,000s in coastal areas starved.	
June 16	**Assam, India**	144
	Heat wave with temp. up to 107.2°.	
June 18	**South Taiwan**	31
	Typhoon Dinah left 89 injured, much property damage.	
July 18	**China (South)**	200
	Storm surprised fishermen off coast.	
July 19	**Chile**	96
	Worst rainstorm in 10 yrs. left 70,000 homeless in 22 provs.	
Aug. 5	**Okinawa, Japan**	26
	Storms left 100s homeless.	
Sept. 9	**New Orleans, La.**	62
	Hurricane Betsy left city a major disaster area, damage throughout state $85 million.	

Year	Date	Place	Deaths	Description
	Sept. 10	Japan	114	Typhoon struck coast, $5 million damage.
	†Dec. 15	East Pakistan	1,000s	Cyclone smashed Chittagong; Box's Bazaar area, 80% of all structures on Kutubdia Is. destroyed.
	Dec. 27	Sao Paulo, Brazil	135	Heat wave, all victims children.
1966	Jan. 29-31	United States (East)	201	Snowfall to 3 ft., winds over 60 m.p.h. from N.Y. to Vir.
	Jan. 30	Samoa	90	Typhoon caused great damage.
	Mar. 2-5	United States (Northwest)	26	Snowfall cont'd 4 days in N. & S. Dak., Minn., & Neb., over 100,000 head of cattle lost.
	Mar. 3	Mississippi	52	Tornado swept central area, Jackson, Tuscaloosa, & Aliceville hit, damage $12 million.
	Mar. 28-29	Rio de Janeiro, Brazil	73	Rainstorms over weekend deluged N.E. area.
	June 4-11	Bihar, India	300	Heat wave lasted 8 days.
	June 6	San Rafael, Honduras	73	Rainfall of 30 in. at area.
	June 8	Topeka, Kan.	20	Tornado caused $100 million damage; 4,000 homeless. Pres. Johnson declared major disaster area.
	June 28	Honshu, Japan	32	Typhoon struck area.
	July 1-13	New York City	100s	Heat wave set record (103°) for this century at city, death rate 650 above normal for period.
	July 11-17	St. Louis, Mo.	146	Heat wave lasted week, temp. over 100° every day.
	July 15-26	Seoul, S. Korea	67	Heavy rains drove 30,000 from homes.
	Aug. 1-8	Japan	354	Heat wave caused mass drownings, many missing.
	†Sept. 24-30	Caribbean	3,600	Hurricane Inez smashed the Dominican Republic, Cuba, & Guadeloupe; Haiti was called "the valley of death." (SEE Inez)
	Sept. 24	Japan	174	Typhoons Ida & Helen, with winds up to 202 m.p.h., leveled 17,000 houses; damage over $10 million.
	Oct. 2	Chittagong, Pakistan	35	Cyclone smashed area, extensive damage.
1967	Jan. 7	United States (Midwest)	23	Snowstorm hit Great Lakes from Ill. to Wisc.
	Jan. 9	Mexico City, Mex.	20	Snowstorm swept Gulf Coast to Mexico.
	Apr. 21	Chicago, Ill.	52	Tornadoes struck 8 states, Ill. Nat'l Guard activated, damage over $20 million.
	May 2	Munshiganj, India	80	Cyclone devastated wide area, 100s injured.
	May 10	Guadalajara, Mexico	70	Heat wave throughout area, most victims children.
	June 2	India	37	Heat wave at Bihar & W. Bengal states.
	July 9	Kobe, S. Korea	347	Typhoon Billie wrecked area, many missing.
	July 24	Karachi, India	26	Monsoon caused floods, 100,000 homeless.
	Sept. 20	Texas	49	Hurricane Beulah spawned record 60 tornadoes, 328 coastal towns destroyed, damage over $1 billion.
	Oct. 11	Bay of Bengal, India	51	Storm left 100s missing.
	Oct. 19	Taiwan & N. Philippines	73	Typhoon Carla struck both coasts.
	Oct. 28	Japan	30	Typhoon Dinah swept coast.
	Nov. 4	Philippines	24	Typhoon Emma caused damage of $5 million.
	Nov. 19	S. California	22	Heavy rains left property damage in millions.
1968	Jan. 15	Glasgow, Scotland	20	Storm, with winds of 125 m.p.h., damaged 70,000 tenements.
	May 6	Ark., Iowa, Ill.	72	Ten-state area hit by 45 tornadoes, damage over $40 million.
	May 29	Durango, Mexico	70	Heat wave at area, all victims children.
	July 12	Mexicali, Mexico	40	Heat wave at city.
	July 22	Japan	72	Heat wave caused great drownings.
	July 28	Japan	22	Typhoon struck S. coast.
	Nov. 1	Orissa, India	35	Cyclone ripped coastal dists.
1969	Jan. 3	Rio de Janeiro, Brazil	25	Heat wave at city.
	Jan. 23	Mississippi	29	Tornado struck 40-mi. area of hill country, great damage.
	Feb. 9-10	United States (Northeast)	64	Blizzard covered area.
	Apr. 14	East Pakistan	165	Storm left 1,200 injured.
	May 22	Bay of Bengal, India	100s	Cyclone & rainstorms wrecked coastal dists.
	July 4	Ohio	41	Thunderstorms called largest weather disaster in state's history, 14 counties affected.
	Aug. 2	South Korea	85	Monsoon rains left 12,000 homeless.
	Aug. 17	United States (South)	258	Hurricane Camille devastated La. & Miss., 1,000s homeless, damage over $1 billion; costliest storm to this date.
	Sept. 15	Pusan, S. Korea	250	Worst rainstorms in 60 yrs. hit S. coast for 3 days, scores missing.
	Sept. 27	Taiwan	47	Typhoon Elsie injured 66, damaged 200 houses.
	Oct. 4	Taipei, Taiwan	75	Typhoon Flossie flooded ½ of city, 31,000 homeless.
	Oct. 8	Tunisia	500	Ten days of rainstorms destroyed 50,000 homes.
	Nov. 10	Rio de Janeiro, Brazil	35	Heat wave at city, 440 treated for dehydration.
1970	Apr. 18	Texas	25	Tornadoes swept through 200-mi. area of Panhandle, 11 towns hit, damage in millions.
	May 11	Lubbock, Tex.	23	Tornadoes, with winds of 200 m.p.h., left $102 million in damages.
	June 17	Puerto Rico	50	Heavy rains inundated area, 1,600 families homeless.
	Aug. 3	Cuba-Fla.-Texas	31	Hurricane Cecilia smashed Gulf Coast, damage over $400 million.
	Aug. 22	Japan	20	Typhoon Anita struck off coast.

Date | Place | Deaths

Sept. 8 — Pyinmana, Burma — 90
Torrential rains flooded area.

Sept. 11 — Quezon Prov., Philippines — 144
Typhoon destroyed 90% of homes in 3 towns, damage over $2 million.

Sept. 11 — Venice, Italy — 30
Whirlwind, at speeds of 125 m.p.h., left 100s injured.

Sept. 18 — South Korea — 28
Torrential rains injured 35, left 7,000 homeless.

†Oct. 14-15 — Philippines — 1,500
Two typhoons struck country in 10 days, 500,000 homeless in 24 provs., 90,000 houses destroyed.

†Oct. 23 — Dacca, E. Pakistan — 100
Cyclone struck 9 dists., 3 engulfed by tidal waves.

†Nov. 12 — Ganges Delta, East Pakistan — 300,000-500,000
Cyclone & tidal wave struck Hatia, Sandwip, Kutubdia and many other islands, over 100,000 people missing. This has been called worst disaster of century.

Nov. 19 — Manila, Philippines — 30
Storm spawned typhoon, 25% of city damaged. Strongest storm to hit city since 1882.

Dec. 31 — Rhone Valley, France — 21
Record snowfall at area.

†1971

Feb. 21 — Mississippi (Louisiana & Tennessee) — 110
Tornadoes swept 3 states, over $8 million damage.

Feb. 27 — Rio de Janeiro, Brazil — 130
Heavy rains throughout state.

July 18 — Seoul, S. Korea — 70
Torrential rains left 3,600 homeless at area.

Aug. 6 — Japan & S. Korea — 78
Typhoon smashed coast, Kyushi Is. worst hit.

†Aug. 17 — Hong Kong, China — 130
Typhoon with winds over 120 m.p.h., caused over $2 million damage. (SEE Rose)

Sept. 7 — Japan — 38
Storm, known as Virginia, struck central Pacific coast.

Sept. 8 — Japan — 53
Typhoon smashed coast, many injured.

Oct. 23 — South Vietnam — 89
Typhoon Hester, with winds over 135 m.p.h., struck 3 provs. & destroyed town of Namhoa.

Oct. 29 — Cuttack Dist., India — 10,000
Cyclone & tidal wave devastated Orissa State, 100,000s homeless.

Oct. 30 — United States (West) — 24
Massive snowstorm left 3-ft. drifts in Utah & Wyo.

Nov. 25 — W. Java, Indonesia — 90
Tropical storm off coast, victims fishermen.

1972

Jan. 3 — Argentina — 100
Ten-day heat wave with temperatures over 100°.

Feb. 10 — Iran — 1,000s
Week-long snow dumped 26-ft. drifts across country, 1,000s missing.

Mar. 12 — Peru — 28
Rain fell for month, 150,000 homeless.

†Apr. 2 — Nasirabad, N. Bangladesh — 200
Tornado left 25,000 homeless.

May 2 — Mexico City, Mexico — 36
Thunderstorm injured 70, left 100,000 homeless.

May 8 — India — 676
Month-long heat wave, with highs at 120°, scorched N. part of country.

†June — India — 800
Monsoon rains came later than anytime this century; heat wave scorched 14 Indian states with damage over $40 million to sugar cane & jute crop.

†June 21-26 — United States (East) — 118
Hurricane Agnes swept 7 Atlantic Coast states, 200,000 homeless, damage over $100 million.

June 24-25 — Philippines — 100
Typhoon Ora caused $5 million damage & left 26,000 families homeless at Luzon, E. Visayas, & Bicol regions.

Sept. 16-17 — Japan — 50
Typhoon Helen destroyed 400 houses and sank 75 ships off coast.

Oct. 22 — Rajdhan Pass, India — 75
Windstorm buried mountain porters 43 mi. N. of Srinagar, Kashmir.

Dec. 2 — Japan — 24
Storm struck islands from Hokkaido to Kyushu.

1973

Jan. 10 — San Justo, Argentina — 50
Tornado, with 100 m.p.h. winds, leveled all bldgs. & left 300 injured.

Jan. 17 — Iberian Peninsula — 22
West coast struck by worst storm in 25 yrs., winds of 80 m.p.h.

Apr. 4-7 — Colorado — 30
Blizzard killed 10,000 cattle, populace stranded.

Apr. 13 — Faridpur, Bangladesh — 240
Province struck by 90 m.p.h. winds, 4,000 injured, 10,000 homeless.

Apr. 14 — Manikgang, Bangladesh — 1,000s
Tornadoes destroyed 13 villages, 12 others damaged.

May 21 — Peshavar, Pakistan — 20
Windstorm injured 100.

May 27 — United States (South) — 48
Tornadoes made both states major disaster areas, damage over $100 million in Ark. & Ala.

July 7 — Guadalajara, Mexico — 30
Cloudburst injured 27, over 1,200 homeless.

Sept. 24 — Japan — 60
Northern area had 12-in. deluge, storm caused mass destruction.

†1974

Jan. 16 — English Channel — 35
Worst storm in 20 yrs. ravaged both coasts of England & the Continent.

Mar. 25 — Bangladesh — 300
Storm swept southern coast.

†Apr. 3 — Xenia, Ohio — 34
Tornado wiped out town; 11 states affected with damage well over $500 million.

June 8-10 — United States (Midwest) — 30
Tornadoes & flash floods hit Ark., Kans., & Okla.

July 11 — Japan & S. Korea — 108
Typhoon Gilda caused $334 million damage.

Sept. 19-20 — Honduras — 5,000
Hurricane Fifi devastated country.

Nov. 1 — Philippines — 52
Typhoon caused $5 million crop loss.

Dec. 25 — Darwin, Australia — 50
Cyclone "Tracy" destroyed 90% of city.

1975

Jan. 14 — United States (Midwest) — 50
Blizzards with 50 m.p.h. winds swept the central plain.

Jan. 27 — Philippines — 30
Tropical storm caused tidal waves & landslides along the South China Sea.

May. 11 — Burma — 187
Cyclone smashed the Irrawaddy delta region.

Aug. 24 — Japan — 22
Typhoon Rita washed out 22,000 homes & 40 bridges.

Oct. 24 — Mazatlan, Mexico — 29
Hurricane Olivia hit city.

Nov. 30 — Puerto Rico — 61
Hurricane Eloise swept islands.

Major Volcanic Eruptions

(† indicates entries profiled in General Narrative)

Date	Place	Deaths
1400 B.C.	**Santorini** Volcano near Crete wiped out the Minoab civilization and initiated the legend of Atlantis.	1,000s
†1226	**Etna** First known eruption of Europe's largest volcano 10,870 ft., located on the eastern shore of Sicily.	100s
†1170	**Etna** Second eruption of historic volcano.	100s
†1149	**Etna** Giant volcano's 3rd eruption, attributed to the expulsion of the demigod Hercules from Sicily.	100s
†525	**Etna** Eruption noted by Pythagoras.	100s
†477	**Etna** Greek historian Thucydides made mention of a great explosion which destroyed Catania.	1,000s
†396	**Etna** Explosion destroyed Naxos & rerouted the army of Carthaginian general Himileo.	100s
†140	**Etna** Minor eruption of giant crater.	40
†126	**Etna** Molten lava poured into Ionian Sea, contaminated fish caused mass deaths.	100s
†122	**Etna** Ash destroyed Catania, disaster brought about 1st relief fund for victims.	1,000s
†A.D. 79 Aug. 24	**Vesuvius** City of Pompeii completely buried, rediscovered in 1595 with victims clutching bags of coins, 100s of casts were made of the bodies.	16,000
†203	**Vesuvius** The 3,842-ft. volcano overwhelmed several villages.	Scores
†472	**Vesuvius** Ash from volcano covered all of Europe.	100s
†1036	**Vesuvius** Great paths of lava rushed to the sea.	Scores
†1049	**Vesuvius** Identical eruption to 1036.	Scores
†1169	**Etna** Volcano's first disastrous eruption for centuries, Catania was destroyed with 50 other cities.	15,000
†1198	**Vesuvius** Eruption so great it activated the neighboring crater of Solfatara Lake.	Scores
†1302	**Vesuvius** Ischia, dormant for over 1,400 years, activated by eruption.	Scores
†1329	**Etna** Eruption of great volcano.	100s
†1362	**Oeraefa Jokull** Great Icelandic volcano swept away 40 farms with melted ice and snow.	200
†1522	**Masaya** Several Nicaraguan towns demolished by volcanic eruption.	100s
†1536	**Etna** Another eruption in Sicily.	1,000s
†1538 Sept. 29	**Vesuvius** New crater ("Monte Nuovo") formed, killed dozens of Neapolitan spectators.	Scores
1549	**Aqua** Guatemalan volcano (Volcan de Aqua, Volcano of Water) unleashed lake on Spanish capital on Lower Sloyes.	1,000s
†1591	**Taal** First recorded outbreak of Philippine volcano located 40 mi. S. of Manila on Luzon.	1,000s
†1616	**Mayon** Philippine volcano erupted for 1st time; scores of villages destroyed.	1,000s
1623	**Irazu** The 11,326-foot Costa Rican volcano wiped out half a dozen villages.	100s
†1631 Dec. 12	**Vesuvius** Italian volcano poured 7 streams of lava out of 1 crater, several villages were destroyed.	18,000
1638	**Peak** The 10,466-ft. volcano on Timor blew itself up, replaced by lake.	100s
1650	**Asamayama** Volcano obliterated villages in Shinano.	100s
†1669 March	**Etna** Lava flow destroyed Catania, 14 other villages.	20,000
†1693 Sept.	**Etna** Volcanic eruption devastated Catania.	18,000
1698	**Cotopaxi** The 19,550-ft. volcano consumed Tacunga, Ecuador.	100s
†1707	**Vesuvius** Flash eruption; Naples hardest hit.	100s
1711	**Abo** Volcano on Sanguir Island buried dozens of villages under rocks & ashes.	1,000s
1717	**Fuego** Volcano in Guatemala devastated Ciudad Vieja.	100s
†1718	**Soufriere** First eruption of volcano located on the north end of St. Vincent Island, entire area buried by ash.	100s
1741	**Cotopaxi** The 19,550-foot Ecuadorian volcano sent down block of ice, lava & scoria, water rushing at 56 feet per second; 600 houses were demolished.	1,000
1744	**Cotopaxi** Tremendous eruption of highest active volcano on earth in Ecuador was heard 636 miles away.	100s
1749 Aug. 11	**Taal** Philippines volcano destroyed several villages.	100s
†1754 May 13	**Taal** Philippines volcano wiped out towns of Taal, Tanauan, Sala, Lipa & Balayan.	100s
†1755	**Etna** Eruption blasted 5,000-mi. area in company with the Lisbon, Portugal, earthquake.	36,000
†1759 Sept. 28	**Jorullo** Mexican volcano rained rocks over Aguasarco area.	100s
1764	**Momotombo** Nicaraguan volcano 4,125 feet high destroyed several villages. (Author Victor Hugo named this volcano "The Bald and Nude Colossus.") Erupted for an estimated 5,000 years.	100s
†1766 Oct. 23-30	**Mayon** The 2,421-meter Philippine volcano's 2nd great eruption, mass destruction was aided by tornadoes (baguios), floods & landslips.	2,000

Date	Place	Deaths	Description
†1772	**Papandayan**	3,000	The 8,750-ft. Java volcano destroyed 40 villages & most cattle & coffee plantations; the eruption reduced its size to 5,000 ft.
†1779-80 Dec.-Jan.	**Sakurajima**	300	The 3,506-ft. Japanese volcano consumed villages of Furusato, Arimura, Waki & Kurokami.
†1779 Aug. 8	**Vesuvius**	Scores	Volcano destroyed several villages, threw lava, scoria & stones 10,000 feet.
†1783	**Asamayama**	5,000	The 8,131-ft. mt. poured tons of rock on 48 Japanese villages.
†June 11-Aug. 3	**Skaptar Jokul**	9,000	Volcanic eruption caused a national disaster in Iceland; 1/5 of its population, 4/5 of the sheep & 1/2 of the cattle (11,460) were destroyed.
†June	**Laki**	10,000	The greatest flow of lava from any volcano in recorded history; after 6 months, over 123,500 acres of Iceland was covered by lava.
†1785	**Soufriere**	Scores	Volcanic eruption killed many Indians.
1789	**Kilauea**	100	Hawaiian volcano threw off lethal gases, killing farmers.
1790	**Kilauea**	100s	Hawaiian volcano destroyed a division of the Hawaiian Army with an explosive eruption.
1792 Feb. 10	**Unzen dake**	15,000	Eruption destroyed cities of Higo & Shimabora.
†1793	**Miyi-Yama**	53,000	Volcano on the island of Java erupted & destroyed area.
†Apr. 1	**Unsen**	53,000	Volcanic eruption with series of quakes left lava stream 425 mi. in length.
†1794 June	**Vesuvius**	100s	Volcano overwhelmed city of Torre del Greco.
	Tunquraohua	40,000	Volcano overwhelmed Ecuadorian city of Riobemba; accompanied by earthquake.
	Tuxtla	Scores	Mexican volcano, 5,000 ft. high, 80 miles southwest of Veracruz wiped out several villages.
1800	**Mt. Guntur**	100s	Volcano on Java filled valley with lava, over-ran fleeing farmers, destroyed 6 villages.
†1812 Apr. 27-30	**Soufriere**	1,000s	West Indies volcano eruption followed great quake at Caracas by 35 days.
†1814 Feb. 1	**Mayon**	2,200	The 8,077-ft. Philippine volcano sent torrrent of fire, lava & hot stones into villages.
†1815 Apr. 5	**Tomboro**	11,974	Eruption sent ash 40 mi. E. to Bima, 300 mi. to Java, & 217 mi. to Celebes; only 26 people survived; 37,000 on neighboring islands starved to death as an indirect result.
†1822 Oct.	**Galung Gung**	1,000	Huge, inactive volcano razed 40 mi. of Java in 5 hrs.
†Oct.	**Galung Gung**	3,000	Second eruption in 4 days destroyed 114 villages.
†1825	**Mayon**	1,500	Philippine volcano erupted causing great landslips of mud & rock.
†1835 Jan. 20-23	**Coseg̈üina**	300	Western Nicaraguan volcano erupted for 3 days, rocks & intense heat claimed victims at its base.
1843	**Guntur**	1,000s	Javanese volcano cast out 30 million tons of ashes.
†	**Etna**	36	Crater, 7,000 ft. above village of Bronte, burst apart, & left 20 injured.
1844	**San Miguel**	100s	Volcano destroyed several El Salvador villages.
†1853	**Mayon**	53	Philippine volcano's lava boiled natives.
†June 24	**Niuafou**	70	Volcanic island between Samoa & the Fiji Islands destroyed village of Angaha.
1856 March	**Abo**	3,000	Many villages destroyed in volcanic explosion.
1867	**Gunung-Salak**	100s	Javanese volcano threw down such a quantity of cinders and lava that dozens of streams were dammed, cesspools and marshes which bred for 22 years epidemics which killed more than 1 million natives.
1868 Apr. 2	**Mauna Loa**	77	The 13,675-foot Hawaiian volcano gave off 122 shocks, destroying 100 houses.
†1872 Apr. 24	**Vesuvius**	Scores	Sightseers from Naples engulfed by lava flow.
June	**Mirapi**	4,000	Volcano on Java destroyed several towns in Kadu Province.
†1877 June 26	**Cotopaxi**	1,000	Volcano poured rocks & lava into nearby Ecuadorian villages.
†1883 Aug. 27	**Krakatoa**	36,000-50,000	Island in the Sundry Straits erupted with such force as to cause a shock felt around the world; this is the most famous volcanic disaster.
1886 June 10	**Tarawera**	Scores	New Zealand volcano split in two; 8-mile-long fissure opened 20 new craters; ashes covered 4,000 sq. miles.
†1888 July 9	**Mayon**	24	Towns of Libog & Legaspi partially destroyed by volcanic eruption.
†July 15	**Bandaisan**	461	Ancient Japanese volcano poured tons of rocks into a 10-sq.-mi. area in northern Hunshu.
1892 June	**Abu**	2,000	Volcanic eruption on Sanquir near Java.
†1897 June 23	**Mayon**	400	Philippine volcano caused mass destruction similar to 1814.
†1902 Apr. 13	**Tacona**	1,000	City of Retalbulen, Guatemala, buried under lava, stones and ashes.
†May 6-13	**Soufriere**	3,000	Pelée neighbor on St. Vincent's Island sent 7 separate streams of lava on its hypnotized victims.
†May 8	**Pelée**	30,000-36,000	Martinique volcano devoured St. Pierre with lava blast only to strike again several months later.
†Aug. 30	**Pelée**	2,000	Second eruption in 4 months, St. Pierre again devastated.
†Oct. 24	**Santa Maria**	6,000	Volcano 12,361 feet high in Western Guatemala wiped out a score of villages.
1905 Apr. 4	**Vesuvius**	105	Villagers of San Giuseppe sought protection in church but the weight of eruptive ash collapsed the roof.
1909	**Kelut**	5,500	Eruption menaced Indonesia.
†1911 Jan. 28	**Taal**	98	Philippine volcano caught U.S. engineer party at Bayuyungan.

Date		Place	Deaths	
	†Jan. 30	**Taal**	1,335	Philippine volcano smothered 13 villages, most located on Volcano Is.
†1914		**Mayon**	100s	Volcanic eruption ruined town of Cagsauga.
	Jan. 12	**Sakurajima**	35	Violent eruption of Japanese volcano, 3,506 feet high, destroyed 17 villages, damaged Kagoshima City, injured 112.
	Sept.	**Whakari**	Scores	Eruption of White Island volcano near New Zealand killed every employee of sulfur works, only pet cat survived.
†1917	June 6	**Boqueron**	450	Volcano in El Salvador erupted and showered San Salvador with burning sand.
†1919		**Keluit**	5,500	Java volcano flooded neighboring valleys, victims drowned instantly.
1926	Apr. 17	**Mauna Loa**	Scores	Hawaiian town of Hoopuloa engulfed by lava flow 40 feet high.
†1928	July 1	**Mayon**	200	Several villages destroyed.
	†Aug. 4-5	**Rokatinda**	226	Eruption in the Netherlands East Indies spawned landslides & floodwaves, 4 villages covered with ash.
	†Nov. 7	**Etna**	Scores	Rivers of lava destroyed town of Mascati & village of Nunziata.
†1929		**Vesuvius**	100s	Lava streams poured over a dozen villages.
	Nov. 4	**Santa Maria**	100s	Guatemalan volcano destroyed crops, casualties uncertain, 100s missing.
	Nov. 30	**El Nimo Jesus**	38	Victims all Guatemalan Preb. missionaries.
†1931	Dec. 13-28	**Merapi**	1,300	The Javanese volcano poured lava 4 mi. long, 200 yrds. wide & 80 ft. high.
1935	May 4	**Ararat**	100s	Volcanic eruption followed great quake, 1,600 homes were leveled and great damage throughout Turkey.
1937	May 29	**Volcanic Island**	500	Submarine crater burst, town of Rabaul, New Guinea, destroyed.
	Sept. 7	**Batana**	100s	Violent eruption 250 mi. S.E. of Rabaul, N.G., smoke rose 15,000 ft. in the heavily populated native territory.
1940	July 12	**Miyake**	Scores	First eruption in 65 yrs. forced 1,000s to evacuate area 200 mi. S. of Tokyo.
1941	Apr. 15	**Colima**	100s	Volcanic eruption accompanied quake and set forest fires throughout Mexican state 300 mi. E. of Mexico City.
†1944	Mar. 18-25	**Vesuvius**	100	Lava flow ruined crops & vineyards at Salerno-Torre Annaunziata region.
	June 10	**Paricutin**	3,500	The 9,213-ft. volcano buried Mexican towns of San Juan de Parangaricutiro & Paricutine with lava.
1947	Jan. 12	**Cerro Negro**	Scores	Nicaraguan volcano destroyed 280 sq. mi., Leon City greatly damaged.
1948	Oct. 18	**Villarica**	40	Four Chilean villages destroyed, death toll inaccurate due to scores missing.
1949	May 27	**Purace**	17	Students of Popayan Univ., Colombia, victims.
1950	Sept. 15	**Hibok Hibok**	84	Camiguin Islands forced to evacuate 3 villages.
1951	Jan. 21	**Lamington**	6,000	New Guinean volcano destroyed population on its northern shores.
	Dec. 2-8	**Hibok Hibok**	248	Philippines suffered 2 eruptions in 6 days, 20,000 homeless, typhoon hampered rescue work.
1958	June 24	**Aso**	Scores	Great damage around base of Japanese volcano, many injured.
1960	May 21-30	**Chile**	5,700	Volcanic eruptions, violent quakes & a *tsunamis* rocked country for days.
1961	Mar. 22-June 3	**Ebulobo**	Scores	Volcano active for 9 wks., 40,000 vacate homes at Marapi area.
†1963	Mar. 20	**Agung**	1,200	The 10,308-ft. mt. poured lava over Sebudi, Sebih, & Sorgah in Bali; 200,000 left homeless.
1964	Mar. 2	**Villarrica**	Scores	Chilean volcano's eruption caused 30,000 to flee.
†1965	Sept. 28	**Taal**	200	Worst eruption since 1911, state of calamity declared, village of Alas-As demolished.
1966	Aug. 22	**Awa**	28	Sangi Island ruined, 60 children missing, 2,000 injured.
	Aug. 27	**Kelut**	82	East Javanese village destroyed, 52 injured, many missing.
1968	July 30	**Arenal**	78	Costa Rican volcano erupted after 50 yrs., damage over $44 million with nation's economy retarded for decades predicted.

Notable Wartime Sinkings

Date | **Place** | **Deaths**

1849 **April 5** *Christian VIII* **700**
The Danish Navy wooden line of battleships, armed with 86 guns, blew up after a fierce bombardment by the Germans at Eckernfolde.

1862 **March 8** *Congress* **257**
The 1,869-ton United States Navy frigate, built in 1841, was sunk by the *Merrimac* during the American Civil War while lying at anchor off Newport News; also rammed and sunk was the American sloop-of-war *Cumberland.*

1877 **May 11** *Lutfi Djelil* **200**
The 2,700-ton Turkish Navy ironclad, built in 1870, was sunk by Russian artillery outside the fortress of Matchin on the Danube.

1894 **July 20** *Kow Shing* **1,450**
The 2,124-ton Chinese steamship, built in 1883, was torpedoed and sunk by the British in the Asian Strait.

1898 **Feb. 15** *Maine* **260**
The 6,682-ton United States Navy battleship, built in 1890, was at anchor off Morro Castle, Havana, Cuba, when a mine allegedly exploded under the ship; this disaster started the Spanish-American War of 1898.

July 3 *Viscaya* **200**
The 6,889-ton Spanish Navy armored cruiser, built in 1891, was sunk by American battleships off Asseradores, 15 mi. from Santiago.

1904 **Feb. 10** *Yenisei* **410**
The 3,000-ton Russian Navy minelayer, built in 1900, struck a mine and sunk at the entrance to Ta-lien Bay.

Apr. 13 *Petropavlovsk* **600**
The 11,354-ton Russian Navy battleship built in 1894, struck a mine and sank at the entrance to the harbor of Batoum.

May 15 *Hatsuse* **540**
The 15,240-ton Japanese battleship built in 1899, was sunk by Russian artillery off Port Arthur; 2/3 of the 740 men of the crew perished.

Dec. 12 *Takasago* **363**
The 4,160-ton Japanese cruiser, built in 1897, struck a mine between Port Arthur and Chefoo on the Yellow Sea; 162 survived.

1905 **May 27** *Ossliabya* **347**
The 12,674-ton Russian Navy battleship, built in 1901, was sunk by Japanese artillery at the battle of Tsu Shima.

May 27 *Navarin* **500**
The 10,206-ton Russian battleship, built in 1895, was sunk by Japanese torpedoes on a voyage to Vladivostok.

May 27 *Borodino* **830**
The 13,516-ton Russian Navy battleship, built in 1904, was blown up by Japanese artillery in the Straits of Tsu-Shima between Japan & Korea; only one survivor was picked up.

May 27 *Imperator Alexander II* **836**
The 13,516-ton Russian Navy battleship, built in 1904, was sunk during the battle of Tsu-Shima; 4 survived.

May 28 *Dimitri Donskoi* **200**
The 5,893-ton Russian Navy armored cruiser, built in 1885, was sunk after a long battle with 2 Jap cruisers off the island of Matsushima.

Aug. 23 *Takachiho* **243**
The 3,700-ton Japanese light cruiser, built in 1885, struck a mine on the Japanese coast and sunk; 10 survived.

Date | **Place** | **Deaths**

1914 **Aug. 28** *Koln* **507**
The 4,350-ton German light cruiser, built in 1909, was blown to bits by the British at the battle of the Heligoland Bight.

Sept. 22 *Hogue* **1,400**
The 12,000-ton British Navy armored cruiser was sunk along with the *Aboukir* & the *Cressy* by the German submarine *U-9* off Ymuiden; 60 officers & 777 men survived.

Oct. 11 *Pallada* **500**
The 7,775-ton Russian Navy cruiser built in 1906, was torpedoed by a German submarine in the Baltic.

Nov. 1 *Monmouth* **678**
The 9,800-ton British Navy armored cruiser, built in 1901, was sunk in a battle with the Germans off Coronel, Chile.

Nov. 1 *Good Hope* **900**
The 14,100-ton British Navy armored cruiser, built in 1901, was blown up in battle off Coronel, Chile.

Nov. 4 *Yorck* **300**
The 9,050-ton German armored cruiser, built in 1906, was struck in a minefield and sunk near Jade Bay.

Nov. 14 *Karlsruhe* **261**
The 4,320-ton German Navy light cruiser, built in 1912, was blown up 350 mi. E. of Trinidad.

Dec. 8 *Leipzig* **268**
The 3,250-ton German Navy light cruiser, built in 1906, was lost in the battle of the Falkland Islands.

Dec. 8 *Gneisenau* **650**
The 11,600-ton German Navy armored cruiser, built in 1906, was sunk after a lone battle off the Falkland Islands.

1915 **Jan. 1** *Formidable* **547**
The 15,000-ton British Navy battleship, built in 1901, was torpedoed and sank during training exercises off Portland Bill.

Jan. 24 *Blucher* **870**
The 15,500-ton German Navy armored cruiser, built in 1908, was sunk by British artillery in a battle at Dogger Bank.

Mar. 18 *Irresistible* **200**
The 15,000-ton British Navy battleship, built in 1902, was sunk in battle off the Dardanelles.

Mar. 18 *Bouvet* **610**
The 12,205-ton French Navy battleship, built in 1898, suffered an internal explosion & capsized in the Dardanelles Narrows while in battle with the guns of Fort Messudieh.

Apr. 27 *Leon Gambetta* **578**
The 12,416-ton French Naval armored cruiser, built in 1903, was sunk by an Austrian sub off the coast of Italy.

May 7 *Lusitania* **1,198**
The 30,396-ton British liner, built in 1907, was topedoed by a German submarine 10 mi. S. of the Old Head of Kinsale on a voyage to England; this sinking influenced the United States to enter W.W. I.

May 13 *Goliath* **570**
The 12,950-ton British Navy battleship, built in 1900, was attacked and sunk by the Turkish destroyer, *Mouavenet-Millieh,* in Morto Bay.

Aug. 13 *Royal Edward* **1,386**
The 11,117-ton Canadian liner, built in 1906, was sunk by a German submarine 6 mi. W. of Kandeliusa Island.

Date		Place	Deaths
	Oct. 15	*Hawke*	**500**

The 7,350-ton British Navy protected cruiser, built in 1893, was sunk by German submarines while on her Northern Patrol duty near Cromarty; 4 officers & 66 men survived.

Oct. 23 *Prinz Adalbert* **550**
The 9,050-ton German armored cruiser, bult in 1901, was sunk by English submarines near Libau.

Nov. 4 *Le Calvados* **740**
The 1,658-ton French transport, built in 1890, was torpedoed & sunk by the German submarine *U-38* off Oran.

Nov. 7 *Undine* **260**
The 2,715-ton German Navy light cruiser, built in 1902, was sunk by British submarines in the Baltic; few survived.

Dec. 8 *Scharnorst* **765**
The 11,600-ton German Navy armored cruiser, built in 1906, was sunk in a fierce battle with the British off the Falkland Islands.

Dec. 18 *Persia* **334**
The 7,974-ton liner, built in 1900, was torpedoed 71 mi. S.E. by S. of Cape Martello, Crete.

1916 **Jan. 20** *Breslau* **218**
The 4,550-ton German Navy light cruiser, built in 1911, struck a minefield and sank sank off Kusu Bay, Dardanelles.

Feb. 8 *Admiral Charner* **374**
The 4,750-ton French Navy cruiser, built in 1893, was torpedoed 15 mi. off the Syrian coast; of the 14 survivors only 1 lived.

Feb. 26 *La Provence* **1,200**
The 13,753-ton French liner, built in 1906, was sunk by German torpedoes while on transport service in the Central Mediterranean.

May 31 *Frauenlob* **320**
The 2,715-ton German Navy light cruiser, built in 1902, was sunk after exchanging fire with British cruisers off Jutland.

May 31 *Pommera* **840**
The 12,997-ton German battleship, built in 1905, was sunk by 8 torpedoes at the Battle of Jutland.

May 31 *Indefatigable* **1,010**
The 18,750-ton British Navy battle cruiser, built in 1909, was sunk in the Battle of Jutland; only 2 survivors were picked up.

May 31 *Queen Mary* **1,266**
The 28,000-ton British Navy battle cruiser, built in 1913, was sunk in the Battle of Jutland; only 9 soldiers survived.

May 31 **Battle of Jutland** **9,823**
This was the greatest of all sea conflicts with the British having lost 3 battle cruisers, 3 cruisers, & 7 destroyers with a death toll of 328 officers and 5,769 men; the Germans lost 1 battleship, 1 battle cruiser, 2 destroyers & 4 light cruisers with a death toll of 160 officers & 2,385 men.

June 1 *Wiesbaden* **570**
The 4,900-ton German Navy light cruiser, built in 1913, was sunk by British artillery at the Battle of Jutland; 1 survived.

June 5 *Hampshire* **640**
The 10,850-ton British Navy armored cruiser, built in 1905, struck a minefield and sank in 15 minutes between Marwick Head & the Brough of Birsay.

Nov. 25 *Suffren* **648**
The 12,750-ton French battleship, built in 1899, was torpedoed & sunk by the German submarine *U-52* 90 mi. W. of the Burlings.

1917 **Mar. 19** *Danton* **296**
The 18,400-ton French Navy battleship, built in 1911, was sunk by German torpedoes off the S.W. coast of Sardinia.

Apr. 15 *Arcadian* **277**
The 8,939-ton transport liner, built in 1899, was sunk by a torpedo in the Aegean, 26 mi. N.E. of Milo.

May 4 *Transylvania* **413**
The 14,348-ton British liner, built in 1914, was sunk by torpedoes a few miles S. of Cape Vado, Gulf of Genoa.

Dec. 30 *Aragon* **610**
The 9,588-ton British liner used as an auxiliary transport, built in 1905, was attacked and sunk by submarines while anchored outside the port of Alexandria.

1918 **Jan. 21** *Louvain* **224**
The 1,830-ton British steamship, built in 1897, was torpedoed by a German submarine on a voyage from Malta.

June 27 *Llandovery Castle* **234**
The 11,423-ton French troop carrier, built in 1914, was torpedoed by a German submarine 114 mi. W. of Fastnet; the vessel at the time was serving as a medical carrier & her Red Cross insignia was prominently displayed & illuminated.

July 14-15 *Djemnah* **442**
The 3,716-ton French liner, built in 1875, was torpedoed while carrying troops through the Mediterranean at night.

Oct. 10 *Leinster* **480**
The 2,646-ton Irish steamship, built in 1897, was torpedoed by the Germans on voyage from Kingstown to Holyhead.

1938 **Mar. 16** *Baleares* **300**
The 10,000-ton Spanish Nationalist Navy heavy cruiser, built in 1931, was torpedoed during fierce battle 70 mi. off Cape Palos.

June 23 *Kiang Hsin* **1,000**
The 3,373-ton Chinese steamship, built in 1905, was bombed & sunk by Japanese aircraft in the area of Yochow, Yangtze River.

1939 **Sept. 1** *Athenia* **138**
The 13,581-ton British liner, built in 1923, was torpedoed a few hours after war was declared between England & Germany; the liner was attacked by a German submarine 250 mi. W. of Inishtrahull, Donegal, Ireland.

Sept. 17 *Courageous* **515**
The 22,500-ton British Navy aircraft carrier, built in 1916, was sunk by German torpedoes outside Devonport.

Oct. 14 *Royal Oak* **810**
The 29,150-ton British dreadnought battleship, built in 1914, was struck in the bow by a German torpedo while lying at anchor at the harbor at Scapa.

Nov. 3 *Rawalpindi* **265**
The 16,697-ton converted British liner, built in 1925, was sunk by German artillery S.E. of Iceland.

1940 **Apr. 9** *Eidsvold* **185**
The 4,166-ton Norwegian Navy coast deference ship, built in 1900, was sunk by German destroyers outside the port of Narvik.

Apr. 9 *Blucher* **1,000**
The 10,00-ton German Navy heavy cruiser, built in 1937, was torpedoed and blown-up off the island of Oscarsborg.

Date	Place	Deaths

Apr. 10 *Pionier* **1,000**
The 3,285-ton German motorship, built in 1933, struck a mine and sank in the Kattegat.

May 29 *Waverley* **350**
The 537-ton British minesweeper, built in 1899 as a paddle steamship, was sunk during the Dunkirk Evacuation.

May 29 *Wakeful* **600**
The 1,100-ton British Navy destroyer, built in 1915, was sunk at the Dunkirk Evacuation.

June 1 *Scotia* **210**
The 3,454-ton British steamship, built in 1921, was sunk by German aircraft at the Dunkirk Evacuation.

June 1 *Skipjack* **300**
The 815-ton British Navy fleet minesweeper, built in 1934, was attacked & sunk by 40 German aircraft during the evacuation of Dunkirk.

June 8 *Glorious* **1,200**
The 22,500-ton British Navy aircraft carrier, built in 1917, was sunk by German battleships off Narvik along with British destroyer escorts *Acastra* & *Ardent.*

June 13 *Scotstown* **350**
The 17,046-ton British Navy steamship, built in 1925, was sunk by a German submarine 200 mi. W. of Inishtrahull.

July 2 *Arandora Star* **751**
The 15,501-ton British Blue Star liner, built in 1927, was torpedoed 75 mi. W. of Bloody Foreland, Ireland; victims were German and Italian internees being transported to Canada.

July 3 *Bretagne* **960**
The 22,189-ton French Navy dreadnought battleship, built in 1913, was attacked by aircraft of the Fleet Air Arm and capsized at the naval harbor of Oran, Mers-el-Kebir.

1941 **Mar. 25** *Britannia* **249**
The 8,799-ton British liner, built in 1926, was sunk by the German raider Thor 720 mi. W. of Freetown; the victims were passengers and crew.

Mar. 28 *Fiume* **500**
The 10,000-ton Italian Navy heavy cruiser, built in 1931, was sunk at the Battle of Cape Matapan.

Mar. 29 *Zara* **500**
The 10,000-ton Italian Navy heavy cruiser, built in 1930, was sunk by British battleships off Cape Matapan.

Apr. 26 *Diamond* **500**
The 1,375-ton British Navy destroyer along with the destroyer *Wryneck* was sunk in the Gulf of Nauplia during the evacuation of British troops from Greece.

Apr. 26 *Wryneck* **900**
The 900-ton British Navy destroyer, built in 1918, was sunk along with the *Diamond* in the Gulf of Nauplia; 50 survived.

May 7 *Pinguin* **400**
The 7,766-ton German Navy commerce raider, built in 1936, was sunk in battle with the *Cornwall* in the vicinity of the Socotra Island.

May 22 *Fiji* **241**
The 8,000-ton British Navy cruiser, built in 1939, was sunk by the Luftwaffe off the island of Antikithera.

May 22 *Gloucester* **804**
The 9,600-ton British Navy cruiser, built in 1937, was sunk by a heavy bomb while on rescue operations off the island of Antikithera.

May 23 *Hood* **1,338**
The 43,100-ton British Navy battle cruiser, built in 1919, was sunk by the *Bismarck* in the Denmark Strait between Iceland & Greenland; only a few survived.

Date	Place	Deaths

May 27 *Scharnhorst* **1,425**
The 26,000-ton German Navy dreadnought battleship, built in 1936, was pursued & sunk by the British 60 mi. N.E. of North Cape.

May 27 *Bismarck* **1,900**
The 35,000-ton German Navy dreadnought battleship, built in 1939, was torpedoed and destroyed after an extensive search 550 mi. W. of Land's End.

June 12 *Ardena* **700**
The 1,092-ton Greek steamship, built in 1915, struck a mine & sank off Argostoli.

June 17 *Lancastria* **3,900**
The 16,243-ton British troop ship was sunk by German aircraft off St. Nazaire.

Aug. 19 *Sibir* **400**
The 3,767-ton Russian motorship fitted as a hospital ship, built in 1929, was attacked by German aircraft in the Gulf of Finland, 1,100 survived.

Sept. 18 *Neptunia* **5,000**
The 19,475-ton Italian liner was converted into a transport along with her sister ship the *Oceania* in 1941; both vessels were sunk by the same submarine off Tripoli, Libya.

Nov. 19 *Sydney* **645**
The 6,830-ton Australian cruiser, built in 1934, was sunk by the German raider *Kormoran* in the Indian Ocean 300 mi. from Carnarvon, W. Australia.

Dec. 7 **Pearl Harbor** **3,303**
The attack at Hickham Field by 51 Japanese aircraft resulted in the sinking of 1 battleship, the *Arizona;* 1 battleship capsized, the *Oklahoma;* 6 battleships badly damaged; 3 cruisers badly damaged; 3 destroyers bombed and sunk; 3 odd-ships badly damaged. The Japanese loss in ships was 3 midget submarines. Loss in personnel was 2,343 officers & men killed; 960 missing and believed drowned; 1,272 wounded.

Dec. 9 *Prince of Wales* **762**
The 35,000-ton British Navy dreadnought battleship, built in 1939, was demolished along with the *Repulse* by Japanese aircraft off the N.W. coast of Malaya.

Dec. 14 *Galatea* **470**
The 5,220-ton British Navy light cruiser, built in 1934, was sunk by a German submarine off Alexandria.

Dec. 17 *Corregidor* **500**
The 1,881-ton Philippine steamship, built in 1911, struck a mine & sank near Manila Bay.

Dec. 19 *Neptune* **766**
The 7,175-ton British Navy cruiser, built in 1935, struck a minefield and sank off Tripoli.

1942 **Jan. 19** *Lady Hawkins* **250**
The 7,988-ton Canadian liner, built in 1928, was torpedoed & sunk between Cape Hatteras & Bermuda.

Feb. 13 *Giang Bee* **223**
The 1,646-ton British steamship, built in 1908, was torpedoed & sunk 1 day out of Singapore in the Banka Strait; most passengers were women & children.

Feb. 28 *Perth* **359**
The 6,980-ton Australian Navy cruiser, built in 1934, was sunk in battle with the Japanese in the Sunda Strait.

Mar. 26 *Jaguar* **194**
The 1,690-ton British destroyer, built in 1938, was torpedoed & sunk by a German submarine off the coast of Libya.

Mar. 28 *Galilea* **768**
The 8,040-ton Italian liner, built in 1918, was sunk by a British submarine 10 mi. from Antipaxo.

Date		Place	Deaths
	Apr. 9	*Hermes*	**802**

The 10,850-ton British Navy aircraft carrier, built in 1919, was attacked and sunk by 70 dive bombers 80 mi. S. along the coast of Ceylon.

Aug. 15 *Baependy* **300**
The 4,801-ton Brazilian liner converted to a transport, built in 1899, was torpedoed between Rio de Janeiro & Manaus; as a result of the sinking, war was declared against the Axis Powers 7 days later.

Sept. 12 *Laconia* **2,276**
The 19,695-ton British liner, built in 1922, was sunk by German torpedoes 500 mi. S. of Cape Palmas, Liberia.

Sept. 14 *Sikh* **275**
The 1,870-ton British Navy destroyer, built in 1937, was sunk during a raid on the Libyan port of Tobruk.

Oct. 30 *President Doumer* **260**
The 11,898-ton French liner, built in 1933, was sunk by a German submarine somewhere N. by E. of Madeira.

Nov. 8 *Hartland* **200**
The 1,975-ton British Navy cutter, built in 1929, was sunk during participation in the attack on Oran, Algeria.

Nov. 11 *Hecla* **279**
The 11,000-ton British Navy depot ship, built in 1940, was sunk by a German submarine W. of the Straits of Gibralter.

Nov. 23 *Tilawa* **280**
The 10,006-ton British liner, built in 1924, was sunk by a torpedo on a voyage from Bombay to Mombasa.

1943 **Jan. 6** *Benalbanach* **397**
The 7,153-ton liner converted to an auxiliary transport, built in 1940, was sunk by German aircraft E. of Algiers on a voyage to North Africa.

Feb. 7 *Henry R. Mallory* **270**
The 6,063-ton American passenger liner, built in 1916, was sunk by a wolf pack on a voyage from the United States to Iceland.

Mar. 13 *Empress of Canada* **352**
The 21,517-ton liner, built in 1922, was torpedoed by an Italian submarine 400 mi. S. of Cape Palmas.

Apr. 20 *Sidi-Bel-Abbes* **611**
The 4,392-ton French steamship, built in 1929, was sunk by a German submarine 10 mi. N. of the Habibas Islands, near Oran; 520 survived.

June 17 *Yoma* **484**
The 8,131-ton British liner, built in 1928, was sunk by a German submarine off Bunghazi.

Aug. 27 *Egret* **194**
The 1,200-ton British Navy sloop, built in 1938, was sunk by a German glider bomb off the coast of N.W. Spain.

Sept. 23 *Itchen* **228**
The 1,445-ton British Navy frigate, built in 1941, was sunk by German submarines S. of Iceland; on board were 80 survivors from the earlier sunk *St. Croix.*

Oct. 16 *Kari* **1,200**
The 1,925-ton Norwegian steamship was captured and used by the Germans as a troop transport when she was torpedoed and sunk by a British submarine 260 mi. W.N.W. of Ushant.

Nov. 24 *Liscombe Bay* **800**
The 6,730-ton American aircraft carrier, built in 1943, was sunk by a Japanese submarine while she approached the Makin Islands.

Nov. 26 *Rohna* **1,050**
The 8,602-ton British liner, built in 1926, was attacked & sunk by 30 German bonbers while on convoy duty to India from Oran.

Dec. 26 *Scharnhorst* **1,425**
The 26,000-ton German Navy dreadnought battleship, built in 1936, was sunk by British destroyers 60 mi. N.E. of North Cape; 36 survived.

1944 **Feb. 12** *Khedive Ismail* **1,271**
The 7,513-ton British Ministry of War Transport, built in 1922, was torpedoed & sunk in the vicinity of the Maldive Islands.

Feb. 18 *Penelope* **415**
The 5,270-ton British Navy cruiser, built in 1935, was sunk by German torpedoes off Anzio, Italy.

Feb. 25 *Mahratta* **220**
The 1,920-ton British Navy destroyer, built in 1941, was torpedoed & sunk by a German submarine in the Barentz Sea while on convoy duty on a voyage to North Russia.

Mar. 16 *El Madina* **380**
The 3,962-ton Indian steamship, built in 1937, was sunk by a Jap. submarine while transporting troops from Calcutta to Chittagong.

Aug. 21 *Kite* **217**
The 1,250-ton British Navy sloop, built in 1941, was attacked & sunk while on convoy to Russia.

Nov. 12 *Tirpitz* **1,000**
The 42,500-ton German battleship, built in 1940, was sunk after a 3-year effort by the British Naval command off the coast of Norway; the Royal Air Force used 12,000 lb. bombs to sink the vessel.

Dec. 24 *Leopoldville* **808**
The 11,509-ton Belgian liner, built in 1929, struck a torpedo or mine while ferrying troops from Southhampton to Cherbourg.

1945 **Jan. 29** *Serpens* **200**
The 7,176-ton American steamship, built in 1943, was sunk by the Japanese near Tulgi, Solomon Islands.

Jan. 30 *Wilhelm Gustloff* **7,700**
The 25,484-ton German holiday cruiser, built in 1937, was torpedoed by a Russian submarine outside the port of Danzig; on board were 8,700 passengers of which 1,000 survived.

Feb. 10 *Steuben* **3,000**
The 14,660-ton German troop liner, built in 1923, was sunk by a Russian submarine between Stolpe Bank & the Pomeranian coast.

June 16 *Twiggs* **200**
The 2,050-ton American destroyer, built in 1943, was attacked & sunk by Japanese aircraft off Okinawa.

July 4 *Bahia* **333**
The 3,150-ton Brazilian Navy light cruiser, built in 1909, was torpedoed off the N.E. coast of Brazil.

Nov. 8 *Hai Chu* **1,800**
The 1,078-ton Chinese steamship, built in 1923, struck a mine and sank near Boca Tigris, at the mouth of the Canton River.

World's War Dead

Year	War	Number Killed
1479 B.C.	Egyptian Invasion of Asia	5,000
1305-1288	Egyptian-Hittite Wars	10,000
724-721	Samarian Invasion of Israel	10,000
612	Fall of Assyria	10,000
609	Egyptian Conquest of Judah	5,000
605	Babylonian-Egyptian War	5,000
586	Egyptian Conquest of Babylon	5,000
583-573	Babylonian-Phoenician War	20,000
546	Persian Conquest of Lydia	10,000
539	Persian Conquest of Babylon	10,000
499-401	Persian-Greek Wars	40,000
480-474	Wars of Sicily	20,000
458-447	First Peloponnesian War	15,000
429-405	Great Peloponnesian War	100,000
409-341	Carthaginian Invasion of Sicily	100,000
395-362	Greek City-States' Wars	20,000
390-334	Gallic Invasion of Rome	10,000
338-332	Macedonian Conquests	200,000
321-305	Second Roman-Samite War	5,000
301-146	Wars of the Hellenistic Monarchies	100,000
298-295	Third Roman-Samite War	50,000
283-275	Wars during Rise of Rome	35,000
264-241	First Punic War	50,000
225-222	Conquest of Gisalpine Gaul	5,000
219-202	Second Punic War	200,000
197	Second Macedonian War	10,000
168	Third Macedonian War	20,000
149-146	Third Punic War	50,000
146	Roman Conquest of Greece	11,000
135-132	First Servile War	5,000
103-99	Second Servile War	5,000
86-66	First Mithridatic War	5,000
83-82	Marius-Sulla Civil War	8,000
73-71	Third Servile War	15,000
73-66	Third Mithridatic War	10,000
58-52	Gallic Wars	150,000
53-45	Wars of the First Triumvirate	75,000
43-31	Wars of the Second Triumvirate	75,000
A.D. 11-16	Germanic Wars of the Roman Empire	40,000
43-84	Roman Conquest of Britain	100,000
58-62	Parthian Wars of the Roman Empire	10,000
66-70	Jewish Wars of the Roman Empire	1,000,000
132-135	Jewish Wars of the Roman Empire	50,000
194-197	Civil Wars of the Roman Empire	25,000
226	Wars of Sassanian Persia	4,000
251-269	Gothic Invasions of the Roman Empire	150,000
312-394	Civil Wars of the Roman Empire	150,000
328-348	Persian Wars of the Roman Empire	50,000
355-366	Germanic Invasion of the Roman Empire	10,000
359	Roman-Persian Wars	30,000
376-378	Gothic Invasion of the Roman Empire	25,000
402-476	Wars of the Western Roman Empire	200,000

Year	War	Number Killed
451-452	Wars of the Western Roman Empire	30,000
500-633	Teutonic Conquest of Britain	15,000
502-531	Byzantine-Persian Wars	75,000
532	Nika Revolt	12,000
533-559	Wars of the Byzantine Empire	35,000
578	Byzantine-Persian Wars	1,000
615-627	Byzantine-Persian Wars	75,000
624-630	Mohammed's Conquest of Arabia	2,000
633-636	Moslem Conquest of Syria	17,000
637-641	Moslem Conquest of Persia	25,000
641-642	Moslem Conquest of Egypt	5,000
642-655	Teutonic Conquest of Britain	3,000
643	Moslem Conquest of Africa	10,000
656-661	Moslem Civil Wars	3,000
673-678	Moslem-Byzantine Wars	30,000
698	Moslem Conquest of North Africa	10,000
711-718	Moslem Conquest of Spain	10,000
711-1492	Spanish-Moslem Wars	300,000
717-718	Moslem-Byzantine Wars	40,000
718-732	Moslem Invasion of France	30,000
773-796	Conquests of Charlemagne	20,000
837-1016	Danish Invasions of Britain	25,000
881-886	Northern Invasions of France	4,000
891-955	Wars of the German States	7,000
939	Spanish-Moslem Wars	5,000
1000-1227	Wars of Scandinavia	25,000
1014	Invasion of Ireland	6,000
1054	Rise of Scotland	10,000
1066-1071	Norman Conquest of England	10,000
1071-1116	Byzantine-Turkish Wars	15,000
1081-1085	Norman-Byzantine Wars	5,000
1093-1292	English-Scottish Wars	5,000
1097-1102	First Crusade	100,000
1100-1106	Norman Civil War	2,000
1107-1108	Byzantine-Norman War	5,000
1119-1144	Crusader-Turkish Wars	5,000
1139-1184	Portuguese-Moslem Wars	12,000
1147-1148	Second Crusade	5,000
1153-1187	Crusader-Turkish Wars	5,000
1154-1237	German Invasions of Italy	15,000
1189-1191	Third Crusade	5,000
1194-1214	English-French Wars	6,000
1204-1208	Fourth Crusade	5,000
1214-1260	Mongol Wars, Era of Genghis Khan	300,000
1215-1217	Barons' War of England I	4,000
1218	Civil Wars of Bulgaria	3,000
1230	Bulgarian-Greek Wars	2,000
1230-1243	Wars of the Seljuk Turks	25,000
1242	English-French Wars	500
1244	Sixth Crusade	7,000
1250	Seventh Crusade	10,000
1254	Byzantine-Bulgarian Wars	3,000
1260	Bohemian-Hungarian Wars	2,000
1263	Norse Invasion of Scotland	2,000
1264-1267	Barons' Wars of England II	5,000
1268	Crusader-Turkish Wars	5,000
1270	Eighth Crusade	10,000
1274-1281	Mongol Wars, Invasion of Japan	50,000
1278	German-Bohemian Wars	1,000
1282	English Conquest of Wales	5,000

World's War Dead

Year	War	Number Killed
1289-1291	Crusader-Turkish Wars	25,000
1296-1305	English-Scottish Wars	10,000
1302-1385	Flemish Wars	15,000
1306-1328	English-Scottish Wars	10,000
1313-1325	Holy Roman Empire Civil War	5,000
1315-1386	Swiss-Austrian Wars	10,000
1318	English-Irish Wars	1,000
1322	Barons' Revolt in England	500
1331-1333	Japanese Civil Wars	10,000
1332	Scottish Civil War	2,000
1337-1453	Hundred Years' War	50,000
1339-1394	Austrian-Swiss Wars	5,000
1346-1422	English-Scottish Wars	12,000
1358	Jacquerie Uprising in France	4,000
1362	Danish-German War	2,000
1379	War of Chioggia	4,000
1389	Turkish Conquest of Serbia	15,000
1391-1402	Mongol Wars, Tamerlane's Conquests	100,000
1420-1434	Hussite Wars	30,000
1422-1478	Swiss Milanese Wars	15,000
1430	Turkish-Venetian Wars	1,500
1444	Swiss-French Wars	3,000
1448	Turkish-Hungarian Wars	20,000
1453	Conquest by Turks	9,000
1455-1485	Wars of the Roses	10,000
1465-1477	Swiss-Burgundian War	20,000
1470-1499	Turkish-Venetian Wars	5,000
1471	Danish-Swedish Wars	1,000
1494-1499	French Invasions of Italy	5,000
1499	Swiss-Swabian War	5,000
1502-1514	French-Spanish Wars in Italy	10,000
1503	French-Spanish Wars	5,000
1507-1525	French Wars in Italy	50,000
1509-1510	Spanish Conquest from Moors	10,000
1510	Portuguese Conquest of Goa	2,500
1511-1514	English-French Wars	10,000
1513-1543	English-Scottish Wars	50,000
1514	Turkish Invasion of Persia	5,000
1517	Turkish Invasion of Egypt	2,000
1521-1566	Turkish Wars (Reign of Suleiman)	200,000
1522	Capture of Rhodes by Turks	50,000
1524-1527	Spanish Invasion of Rome	10,000
1525	German Peasants' Revolt	1,000
1529-1530	Siege of Vienna by Turks	10,000
1542-1543	English-Scottish Wars	5,000
1544-1558	English-French Wars	5,000
1547-1555	German Reformation Wars	10,000
1557-1559	Spanish-French Wars	25,000
1562-1628	French Religious Wars	20,000
1563-1582	Polish-Russian Wars	8,000
1565	Siege of Malta by Turks	9,000
1565-1568	Spanish-French War in Florida	1,000
1566-1568	Turkish Invasion of Europe	8,000
1567-1648	Netherlands War of Independence	75,000
1570-1571	Conquest of Cyprus by Turks	8,000
1571	Defeat of the Turkish Fleet by Austria	35,000
1587-1591	English-Spanish Wars	10,000
1592-1598	Swedish-Polish Wars	5,000
1593-1603	Turkish-Austrian Wars	12,000
1600	War of the Unification of Japan	30,000
1618-1630	Swedish-Polish Wars	5,000

Year	War		Number Killed
1618-1648	The Thirty Years War		198,000
	France	80,000	
	Austria	118,000	
1621	Polish-Turkish Wars		5,000
1632	French Civil Wars		1,000
1635-1659	Spanish War		200,000
1637-1774	Indian Wars - Colonial Era		2,000
1642-1651	English Civil War		30,000
1646-1669	Venetian-Turkish Wars		15,000
1648-1649	Second English Civil War		3,000
1651	Polish-Cossack War		10,000
1652-1653	First English-Dutch War		2,000
1656-1658	Spanish-French Wars		4,000
1661-1662	Chinese-Pirate Wars		3,000
1663-1664	Austrian-Turkish Wars		17,000
1665-1667	Second English-Dutch War		8,000
1666-1685	Scottish Covenanter's Revolt		5,000
1672-1678	War with Holland and her Allies		220,000
	France	120,000	
	Holland	100,000	
1683-1699	The Great Turkish War		120,000
1688-1697	War of the Grand Alliance		360,000
	France	160,000	
	England-Holland	200,000	
1689-1692	Jacobite Insurrections, Resistance to the Glorious Revolution		7,000
1697-1716	Austrian-Turkish Wars		20,000
1700-1721	Great Northern War		45,000
1701-1711	Hungarian Insurrection		7,000
1701-1714	War of the Spanish Succession		1,000,000
	Austria	100,000	
	Holland & England	250,000	
	Piedmont	50,000	
	France, Bavaria & Spain	600,000	
1715	Jacobite Insurrections, "The Fifteen"		3,000
1716-1718	War of 1716-18		40,000
1737-1739	War of 1737-39		20,000
1718-1719	The Quadruple Alliance Against Spain		20,000
1733-1735	War of the Polish Succession		64,000
	Austria	14,000	
	France	50,000	
1740-1748	The War of the Austrian Succession		168,100
	Austria	28,100	
	France	140,000	
1745-1746	Jacobite Insurrections, "The Forty-five"		2,500
1754-1763	French and Indian War		7,000
1756-1763	The Seven Years' War		325,000
	Austria	150,000	
	France	175,000	
1761	Afghan-Maratha Wars		13,000
1769-1774	Turkish-Russian Wars		10,000
1775-1783	American Revolutionary War		10,435
	United States	4,435	
	England	6,000	
1778-1779	War of the Bavarian Succession		20,000
1782	Indian Wars-American Revolution		100
1788-1790	The War of Joseph II Against Turkey		10,000

Year	War		Number Killed
1789-1790	Insurrection In the Austrian Netherlands		2,664
	Austria	364	
	Belgian Patriots	2,300	
1790-1794	Indian Wars-Old Northwest		1,300
1792-1801	The French Revolutionary Wars		no figure
1792-1797	War of the First Coalition		194,700
	Austria	94,700	
	France	100,000	
1793-1796	French Civil War		120,000
1793-1802	France & England Naval War		13,200
	France	10,000	
	England	3,200	
1798-1801	French Expedition into Egypt		65,000
	France	15,000	
	Mamelukes, Arabs, Turks, English	50,000	
1798-1799	French War with Naples		1,600
	Naples	1,500	
	France	100	
1799-1801	War of the Second Coalition		154,520
	Austria, Russia, Turkey, Portugal, & the Kingdom of Naples	79,520	
	France	75,000	
1802-1803	Santo Domingan Expedition of French		30,000
1803-1804	Maratha-British War II		5,000
1805-1815	The Napoleonic Wars		
1805	War of the Third Coalition		75,000
	Austria	20,000	
	Russia	25,000	
	France	30,000	
1809	Austria against France and the Rhine Confederation		181,200
	Austria	71,200	
	France	90,000	
	Allied Troops	20,000	
1811-1819	Colombian War of Independence		1,000
1812	Russian Campaign of Napoleon		540,000
	France	340,000	
	Russia	200,000	
1812-1815	War of 1812		7,500
1813-1814	Indian Wars - Creek		2,000
1813-1814	The Wars of Liberation (Operations of 1813)		545,000
	Russia	100,000	
	Prussia	70,000	
	Austria	45,000	
	England	25,000	
	Spain	20,000	
	Portugal	7,000	
	Bavaria	5,000	
	Sweden	3,000	
	France	220,000	
	Rhine Confederation Troops	18,000	
	Poland	13,000	
	Italy	12,000	
	Naples	3,000	
	Croatia	1,000	
	Denmark	1,000	
	Other Allied Troops	2,000	
1813-1814	The Wars of Liberation (Operations of 1814)		211,000
	Russia	45,000	
	Austria	25,000	
	Prussia	25,000	
	Wurttemberg & Bavaria	5,000	
	England & Portugal	15,000	
	Saxony	1,000	
	France	90,000	
	Italy	5,000	
1815	War of the Hundred Days		16,200
	Austria	1,500	
	France	14,700	
1815	The War with Naples, June		2,160
	Austria	460	
	Naples	1,700	
1817-1818	British-Maharattan War		2,500
1817-1818	Chilean War of Independence		2,000
1821	Venezuelan War of Independence		500
1821-1827	Greek War		18,000
1822	Ecuadorian War of Independence		500
1823	French-Spanish War		1,000
	France	400	
	Spain	600	
1823-1826	First Anglo-Burmese War		17,000
1824	Peruvian War of Independence		3,000
1824-1826	British-Ashanti War		1,500
1825	British-Bhartapur War		500
1825-1830	Javanese War		18,000
1826-1828	Russo-Persian War		6,000
1827	Navarino Bay War		3,180
	England	80	
	France	40	
	Russia	60	
	Turkey	3,000	
1828-1829	Russo-Turkish War		130,000
	Russia	50,000	
	Turkey	80,000	
1831	First Polish War		6,500
1831-1832	First Syrian War		12,500
1832	Indian Wars - Black Hawk		300
1832-1840	Egyptian Revolt Against Turkey		4,000
1835-1836	Texan War		1,800
1838-1840	Boer-Zula War		3,000
1838-1842	First British-Afshan War		20,000
1839-1840	Second Syrian War		10,000
1839-1842	Russian-Khivan War		5,000
1840-1847	French-Algerian War		3,000
1841	Peruvian-Bolivian War		1,000
1842	Opium War		500
1845-1846	First British-Sikh War		4,000
1846-1848	Mexican-American War		19,000
	United States	13,000	
	Mexico	6,000	
1848	Orange Free State War		100
1848-1849	Austro-Sardinian War		9,000
	Austria-Hungary	5,600	
	Italy-Sardinia	3,400	

World's War Dead

Year	War		Number Killed
1848-1849	Hungarian War		59,500
	Austria-Hungary	45,000	
	Russia	14,500	
1848-1849	Second British-Sikh War		2,500
1849	First Schleswig-Holstein War		6,000
	Germany-Prussia	2,500	
	Denmark	3,500	
1849	Roman Republic War		2,500
	France	500	
	Austria-Hungary	250	
	Two Sicilies	250	
	Papal States	1,500	
1851-1852	La Plata War		1,500
	Brazil	600	
	Argentina	900	
1853-1856	Crimean War		265,000
	England	22,000	
	France	95,000	
	Italy-Sardinia	3,000	
	Turkey	45,000	
	Russia	100,000	
1855-1864	Indian Wars - Sioux		500
1856-1857	Anglo-Persian War		2,000
	England	500	
	Iran	1,500	
1857-1859	Sepoy War		4,000
1858-1859	First Turco-Montenegran War		6,500
1858-1859	Second Turco-Montenegran War		3,500
1859-1860	Spanish-Moroccan War		10,000
	Spain	4,000	
	Morocco	6,000	
1859	Italian Unification War		22,500
	France	7,500	
	Italy-Sardinia	2,500	
	Austria-Hungary	12,500	
1860	Italo-Roman War		1,000
	Italy-Sardinia	300	
	Papal States	700	
1860-1861	Italo-Sicilian War		1,000
	Italy-Sardinia	600	
	Two Sicilies	400	
1861-1865	American Civil War		647,528
	Union Forces	359,528	
	Confederates	258,000	
	Confederate deaths in Union prisons		30,000
1862-1867	Franco-Mexican War		20,000
	Mexico	12,000	
	France	8,000	
1863	Ecuadorian-Colombian War		1,000
	Colombia	300	
	Ecuador	700	
1863-1864	Second Polish War		6,500
1864	Second Schleswig-Holstein War		4,500
	Germany-Prussia	1,000	
	Austria-Hungary	500	
	Denmark	3,000	
1864-1868	Indian Wars - Cheyenne & Arapahoe		1,000
1864-1870	La Plata War		110,000
	Brazil	100,000	
	Argentina	10,000	
1865-1866	Spanish-Chilean War		1,000
	Peru	600	
	Chile	100	
	Spain	300	
1866	Seven Weeks War		36,000
	Germany-Prussia	10,000	
	Italy-Sardinia	4,000	
	Hanover	500	
	Bavaria	500	
	Baden	100	
	Saxony	500	
	Wuerttemberg	100	
	Hesse Electorate	100	
	Hesse Grand Duchy	100	
	Meckleburg-Schwerin	100	
	Austria-Hungary	20,000	
1868-1878	Ten Years' War		100,000
1870-1871	Franco-Prussian War		185,000
	Bavaria	5,500	
	Germany-Prussia	37,500	
	Baden	1,000	
	Wuerttemberg	1,000	
	France	140,000	
1872	Indian Wars - Apache		800
1873-1878	Dutch-Achinese War		7,500
1875-1877	Balkan War		10,000
1877	Indian Wars - Nez Perce		700
1877-1878	Russo-Turkish War		285,000
	Russia	120,000	
	Turkey	165,000	
1878	Bosnian War		4,000
1878-1880	Second British-Afghan War		4,000
1879	British-Zulu War		4,000
1879-1881	Russian-Turkmen War		1,000
1879-1883	Pacific War		14,000
	Chile	3,000	
	Peru	10,000	
	Bolivia	1,000	
1882-1884	Franco-Indochinese War		8,000
1882-1885	Mahdist War		20,000
1884-1885	Sino-French War		12,000
	France	2,000	
	China	10,000	
1885	Central American War		1,000
	Salvador	200	
	Guatemala	800	
1885	Serbo-Bulgarian War		3,000
1890	Indian Wars - Ghost		200
1894-1895	Franco-Madagascar War		7,000
1894-1895	Sino-Japanese War		15,000
	Japan	5,000	
	China	10,000	
1895-1896	Cuban War		50,000
1895-1896	Italo-Ethiopian War		10,000
1896-1898	First Philippine War		2,000
1897	Greco-Turkish War		2,000
	Turkey	1,400	
	Greece	600	
1898-1902	Spanish-American War		16,000
	United States	5,000	
	Spain	11,000	
1899-1902	Boer War		22,000
1899-1902	Second Philippine War		5,000
1900	Boxer Rebellion		1,000
1904-1905	Russo-Japanese War		130,000
	Japan	85,000	
	Russia	45,000	
1906	Central American War		1,000
	Guatemala	400	
	Honduras	300	
	Salvador	300	

Year	War		Number Killed
1907	Central American War		1,000
	Nicaragua	400	
	Honduras	300	
	Salvador	300	
1909-1910	Spanish-Moroccan War		10,000
	Spain	2,000	
	Morocco	8,000	
1911-1912	Italo-Turkish War		20,000
	Italy-Sardinia	6,000	
	Turkey	14,000	
1912-1913	First Balkan War		80,000
	Yugoslavia-Serbia	15,000	
	Greece	5,000	
	Bulgaria	30,000	
	Turkey	30,000	
1913	Second Balkan War		60,000
	Yugoslavia-Serbia	18,500	
	Greece	2,000	
	Rumania	1,500	
	Turkey	20,000	
	Bulgaria	18,000	
1914-1918	World War I		8,545,800
	United States	116,000	
	England	908,000	
	Belgium	87,500	
	France	1,350,000	
	Portugal	7,000	
	Italy-Sardinia	650,000	
	Yugoslavia-Serbia	48,000	
	Greece	5,000	
	Rumania	335,000	
	Russia	1,700,000	
	Japan	300	
	Germany-Prussia	1,800,000	
	Austria-Hungary	1,200,000	
	Bulgaria	14,000	
	Turkey	325,000	
1916	U.S. Expedition Against Villa		420
	Villa	400	
	United States	20	
1917-1921	Russian Nationalities War		50,000
1919	Hungarian-Allies War		10,000
	Czechoslovakia	2,000	
	Rumania	3,000	
	Hungary	5,000	
1919-1922	Greco-Turkish War		50,000
	Turkey	20,000	
	Greece	30,000	
1921-1926	Riffian War		30,000
	France	5,000	
	Spain	25,000	
1925-1927	Druze War		5,000
1931-1933	Manchurian War		60,000
	Japan	10,000	
	China	50,000	
1932-1935	Chaco War		130,000
	Paraguay	50,000	
	Bolivia	80,000	
1935-1936	Italo-Ethiopian War		20,000
	Italy-Sardinia	4,000	
	Ethiopia	16,000	
1936-1939	Spanish Civil War		611,000
	Nationalists	110,000	
	Executed	86,000	
	Republicans	175,000	
	Executed	40,000	
	Civilians	200,000	
1937-1941	Sino-Japanese War		1,000,000
	Japan	250,000	
	China	750,000	
1939	Russo-Japanese War		19,000
	Russia	1,000	
	Mongolia	3,000	
	Japan	15,000	
1939-1940	Russo-Finnish War		90,000
	Russia	50,000	
	Finland	40,000	
1939-1945	World War II		15,843,000
	(Some statistics of overall deaths of combatants and non-combatants have been placed as high as 55 million.)		
	United States	406,000	
	Canada	39,300	
	Brazil	1,000	
	England	270,000	
	Holland	6,200	
	Belgium	9,600	
	France	210,000	
	Poland	320,000	
	Italy-Sardinia	17,500	
	Yugoslavia-Serbia	75,000	
	Greece	77,000	
	Bulgaria	10,000	
	Rumania	10,000	
	Russia	7,500,000	
	Norway	2,000	
	Ethiopia	5,000	
	South Africa	8,700	
	China	1,350,000	
	Mongolia	3,000	
	Australia	29,400	
	New Zealand	17,300	
	Germany-Prussia	3,500,000	
	Hungary	75,000	
	Italy-Sardinia	60,000	
	Bulgaria	9,000	
	Rumania	290,000	
	Finland	42,000	
	Japan	1,500,000	
1945-1946	Indonesian War		1,400
	England	1,000	
	Holland	400	
1945-1954	Indochinese War		100,000
1947	Nationalist Chinese-Formosan War		100
1947-1948	Madagascan War	2,000	
1947-1949	First Kashmir War		1,500
1948-1949	Palestine War		8,000
	Israel	3,000	
	Iraq	500	
	U.A.R.	2,000	
	Syria	1,000	
	Lebanon	500	
	Jordan	1,000	
1950-1953	Korean War		1,893,100
	United States	55,000	
	Canada	310	
	Colombia	140	
	England	670	
	Holland	110	
	Belgium	100	
	France	290	
	Greece	170	
	Ethiopia	120	
	Turkey	720	
	Korea South	415,000	
	Thailand	110	
	Philippines	90	
	Australia	270	
	China	900,000	
	Korea North	520,000	

World's War Dead

Year	War		Number Killed
1952-1955	British-Kenyan War		800
1954-1962	Algerian War		15,000
1956	Russo-Hungarian War		30,000
	Russia	5,000	
	Hungary	25,000	
1956	Sinai War		3,230
	England	20	
	France	10	
	Israel	200	
	U.A.R.	3,000	
1956-1959	Tibetan War		40,000
1961-1973	Vietnam War		546,000
	United States	46,000	
	Chinese, North & South Vietnamese	500,000	
1962	Sino-Indian War		1,000
	China	500	
	India	500	
1965	Second Kashmir War		7,000
	Pakistan	4,000	
	India	3,000	
1967	Six Days' War		21,000
	Israel	900	
	United Arab Republic	11,500	
	Syria	2,500	
	Jordan	6,100	
1969	Football War		2,000
	Honduras	1,200	
	Salvador	800	

GRAND TOTAL. . . 42,790,637

Bibliography

Thousands of books, pamphlets, periodicals, reports, papers and newspaper clippings, as well as interviews and extensive correspondence with survivors and experts in the fields of disasters were used in researching this work. What follows are only the basic reference sources employed in the writing, compiling, and preparation of this narrative encyclopedia.

General

Books

Adams, Frank D. *The Birth and Development of the Geological Sciences.* New York: Dover, 1954.

Aeschylus. *Persae.*

Allen, Frederick Lewis. *Only Yesterday.* New York: Harper, 1931.

———. *Since Yesterday.* New York: Harper, 1940.

Allen, John Stuart. *Atoms, Rocks and Galaxies.* New York: Harper, 1942.

Allen, Shirley W. *Conserving Natural Resources.* New York: McGraw-Hill, 1959.

Allen, Troy. *Disaster.* Chatsworth, California: Barclay House, 1974.

Ames, Gerald, and Wyler, Rose. *The Earth's Story.* New York: Creative Educational Society and the American Museum of Natural History, 1957.

Andrews, Charles M. *The American Nation.* New York: Harper, 1904.

———. *The Colonial Period of American History: The Settlements.* New Haven: Yale University Press, 1939.

Aubert de la Rue, Edgar. *The Tropics.* New York: Knopf, 1957

Bahme, Charles W. *Handbook of Disaster Control.* Los Angeles: Bahme, 1952.

Ball, Robert S. *The Earth's Beginning.* New York: Appleton, 1902.

Banner, Hubert S. *Great Disasters of the World.* London: Hurst & Brackett, 1931.

Barcus, Frank. *Freshwater Fury.* Detroit: Wayne State University Press, 1960.

Beltrami, Giacomo Constantine. *A Pilgrimage in Europe and America.* London: Hunt & Clarke, 1828.

Bertin, Leon, et. al. *Larousse Encyclopedia of the Earth.* New York: Prometheus, 1961.

Bicknell, Ernest P. *Pioneering with the Red Cross.* New York: Macmillan, 1935.

Billings, Marland P. *Structural Geology.* New York: Prentice-Hall, 1954.

Bixby, William. *Havoc: The Story of Natural Disasters.* New York: Longmans, Green, 1961.

Blainey, Geoffrey. *The Tyranny of Distance.* Melbourne, Australia: Sun Books, 1966.

Blair, T.A. *Weather Elements.* New York: Prentice-Hall, 1953.

Blumenstock, David I. *The Ocean of Air.* New Brunswick, N.J.: Rutgers University Press, 1959.

Boardman, Mabel T. *Under the Red Cross Flag at Home and Abroad.* Philadelphia: Lippincott, 1915.

Bodant, Gaston. *Losses of Life in Modern Wars.* London: Oxford University, 1916.

Boder, David P. *I Did Not Interview the Dead.* Urbana: University of Illinois Press, 1949.

Botkin, B.A. *Sidewalks of America.* Indianapolis: Bobbs-Merrill, 1954.

Botley, C.M. *The Air and Its Mysteries.* London: Bell, 1938.

Brooks, C.E.P. *Climate Through the Ages.* New York: McGraw-Hill, 1949.

———. *Climate in Everyday Life.* New York: Philosophical Library, 1951.

Brown, John P. *Old Frontiers.* Kingsport, Tenn.: Southern Publishers, 1938.

Buckingham, Clyde E. *Red Cross Disaster Relief: Its Origin and Development.* Washington: Public Affairs Press, 1956.

Butler, Pierce. *The Unhurried Years.* Baton Rouge: Louisiana State University Press, 1948.

Byers, Horace R. *General Meteorology.* New York: McGraw-Hill, 1959.

The Center for Research Libraries Catalogue (5 vols.). London: Mansell Information Publishing, 1969.

Challinor, J. *A Dictionary of Geology.* Cardiff: University of Wales, 1962.

Clark, Charles Manning Hope. *A History of Australia.* Melbourne, Australia: Oxford University Press, 1962.

Clayton, H.H. *World Weather.* New York: Macmillan, 1923.

Cleland, Herdman F. *Geology, Physical and Historical.* New York: American Book Co., 1929.

Collier's Encyclopedia (24 vols.). New York: Crowell-Collier, 1969.

Commons, John R., and others. *History of Labor in the United States.* New York: Macmillan, 1921.

Congdon, Don. *The Thirties.* New York: Simon & Schuster, 1962.

Conrad, Joseph. *The Mirror of the Sea.* London: Dent, 1933.

Corbett, Edmund V. *Great True Stories of Tragedy & Disaster.* New York: Archer House, 1963.

Daly, Reginald A. *Our Mobile Earth.* New York: Scribners, 1926.

Day, A. Grove. *Hawaii and Its People.* New York: Duell, Sloan and Pearce, 1960.

Deacon, J. Byron. *Disasters and the American Red Cross in Disaster Relief.* New York: Russell Sage Foundation, 1918.

Devens, R.M. *American Progress, or The Great Events of the Greatest Century.* Chicago: Hugh Heron, 1882.

Dewey, Edmund R. *The 177-Year Cycle in War, 600 B.C.-A.D. 1957.* Pittsburgh: Foundation for the Study of Cycles, 1964.

Douglas, Marjory Stoneman. *The Everglades: River of Grass.* New York: Rinehart, 1947.

Downey, Fairfax. *Disaster Fighters.* New York: Putnam, 1938.

Duff, D.V. *Palestine Picture.* London: Hodder & Stoughton, 1936.

Dulles, Eleanor L. *Depression and Reconstruction.* Philadelphia: University of Pennsylvania Press, 1937.

Dulles, Foster Rhea. *The American Red Cross: A History.* New York: Harper, 1950.

Dumas, Samuel, and Knud Otto Vedel-Petersen. *Losses of Life Caused by War.* London: Oxford University, 1923.

Dunbar, Carl O. *Historical Geology.* New York: Wiley, 1949.

Edey, Maitland A. (ed.), and others. *Time Capsule/1927.* New York: Time-Life Books, 1968.

Eggenberger, David. *A Dictionary of Battles.* New York: Crowell, 1967.

Encyclopedia Americana (30 vols.). International Edition. New York: Americana, 1971.

Encyclopedia International (20 vols.). New York: Grolier, 1971.

Encyclopedia of Australia. London: Frederick Wayne, 1968.

Encyclopedia of the Philippines (20 vols.). Manila: Exequiel Floro, 1949.

Facts on File. New York: Person's Index, Facts on File (1941 to present).

Faulkner, Georgene. *Red Cross Stories for Children.* Chicago: Daughaday, 1917.

Fenneman, Nevin M. *Physiography of Western United States.* New York: McGraw-Hill, 1931.

———. *Physiography of Eastern United States.* New York: McGraw-Hill, 1938.

Flint, Richard F. *Glacial Geology and the Pleistocene Epoch.* New York: Wiley, 1947.

Flint, Timothy. *A Condensed Geography and History of the Western States, or the Mississippi Valley* (2 vols.). Cincinnati: E.H. Flint, 1828.

Fodor, Eugene (ed.). *Hawaii, 1966.* New York: McKay, 1966.

Fort, Charles. *Book of the Damned.* New York: Holt, 1941.

Fuller, J.F.C. *The Conduct of War, 1789-1961.* London: Eyre and Spottiswoode, 1961.

Gamow, George A. *A Planet Called Earth.* New York: Viking, 1963.

Garbell, M.A. *Tropical and Equatorial Meteorology.* New York: Pitman, 1947.

Gardner, Martin. *Fads and Fallacies in the Name of Science.* New York: Dover, 1957.

Garrison, Webb. *Disasters That Made History.* New York: Abingdon, 1973.

Gayarre, Charles. *History of Louisiana* (4 vols.). New York: Harper (vol. 1-2), Wiley (vol. 3), Redfield (vol. 4), 1854-1866.

Gilbert, Grove K. *An Introduction to Physical Geography.* New York: Appleton, 1904.

Godby, A.H. *Great Disasters and Horrors in the World's History.* St. Louis: Royal, 1890.

Gregory, Winifred. *American Newspapers, 1821-1936.* New York: Wilson, 1937.

Griffen, Bulkley S. (ed.). *Offbeat History, A Compendium of Lively Americana.* New York: World, 1967.

Hall, James. *Sketches of History, Life and Manners in the West* (2 vols.). Philadelphia: H. Hall, 1835.

Halliburton, Richard. *Complete Book of Marvels.* Indianapolis: Bobbs-Merrill, 1941.

Harbottle, Thomas Benfield. *Dictionary of Battles from the Earliest Date to the Present Time.* London: S. Sonneschien, 1904.

Hart, Adolphus M. *History of the Valley of the Mississippi.* New York: Newman and Ivison, 1853.

Hawks, Ellison. *The Book of Natural Wonders.* New York: Tudor, 1937.

Hayden's Dictionary of Dates & Universal Information (25th ed.). New York: Putnam, 1911.

Haydon, Brownlee. *The Great Statistics of Wars Hoax.* Santa Monica, Calif.: Rand Corp., 1962.

Heller, Robert C. (ed.). *Geology and Earth Sciences Sourcebook.* New York: Holt, Rinehart & Winston, 1965.

Heninger, S.K., Jr. *A Handbook of Renaissance Meteorology.* Durham, N.C.: Duke University Press, 1960.

Herodotus. *The History.*

Hoehling, A.A. *Disaster.* New York: Hawthorn, 1973.

Holmes, A. *Principles of Physical Geology.* London: Nelson, 1965.

Horan, James D. *The Desperate Years.* New York: Crown, 1962.
Houghton, Henry G. (ed.). *Atmospheric Explorations.* New York: Wiley, 1958.
Huberty, Martin R., and Flock, Warren L. (eds.). *Natural Resources.* New York: McGraw-Hill, 1959.
Humphreys, W.J. *Weather Proverbs and Paradoxes.* Baltimore: Williams and Wilkins, 1934.
———. *Ways of the Weather.* Lancaster, Pa.: J. Cattel, 1943.
Huntington, Ellsworth. *Civilization and Climate.* New Haven: Yale University Press, 1915.
Hurd, Charles. *The Compact History of the Red Cross.* New York: Hawthorn, 1959.
Huschke, Ralph E. *Glossary of Meteorology.* Boston: American Meteorology Society, 1959.
Inwards, Richard. *Weather Lore.* London: Rider, 1950.
Johnson, Robert Underwood, and Buel, Clarence. *Battles and Leaders of the Civil War* (4 vols.). New York: Century, 1887-88.
Kartman, B., and Brown, L. *Disaster!* New York: Pellegrini and Cudahy, 1948.
Kearney, Paul. *Disaster on Your Doorstep.* New York: Harper, 1953.
Keller, Helen Rex. *A Dictionary of Dates.* New York: Macmillan, 1934.
Keesing's Contemporary Archives. London: Keesing's Publications (1931 to present).
Kimble, George H.T. *Our American Weather.* New York: McGraw-Hill, 1955.
King, Edward, *The Southern States of North America.* London: Blackie & Son, 1875.
Klingbergs, Frank L. *Historical Study of War Casualties.* Washington, D.C.: United States Secretary of War Office, 1945.
Koeppe, Clarence E., and De Long, George C. *Weather and Climate.* New York: McGraw-Hill, 1958.
Krick, Irving P., and Fleming, Roscoe. *Sun, Sea and Sky.* Philadelphia: Lippincott, 1954.
Lahee, Frederick H. *Field Geology.* New York: McGraw-Hill, 1941.
Lane, Frank W. *The Elements Rage.* Philadelphia: Chilton, 1965.
Langmuir, Irving. *The Collected Works of Irving Langmuir* (12 vols.) New York: Pergamon, 1962.
Leach, Maria (ed.). *Dictionary of Folklore, Mythology and Legend.* New York: Funk and Wagnalls, 1949.
Leet, L. Don. *Disasters and Disaster Relief* (vol. 309). Philadelphia: American Academy of Political and Social Science, 1957.
———. *Causes of Catastrophe.* New York: McGraw-Hill, 1948.
Leet, L. Don, and Judson, Sheldon. *Physical Geology.* Englewood Cliffs: Prentice-Hall, Inc., 1950.
Leighton, Isabel (ed.). *The Aspirin Age.* New York: Simon & Schuster, 1949.
The Lincoln Library of Social Studies (3 vols.). Columbus: Frontier Press, 1970.
Longstreth, Morris. *Understanding the Weather.* New York: Macmillan, 1953.
Longwell, Chester R. *Physical Geology.* New York: Wiley, 1948.
Malone, Thomas Francis (ed.). *Compendium of Meteorology.* Boston: American Meteorological Society, 1951.
Mannes, Alfred. *Insurance: Facts and Problems.* New York: Harper, 1938.
Marquard, L. *The Story of South Africa.* London: Faber and Faber, 1955.
Masselman, George. *The Cradle of Colonialism.* New Haven: Yale University Press, 1963.
Mather, Kirtley F. *The Earth Beneath Us.* New York: Random House, 1964.
Mather, Kirtley F., and Mason, Shirley L. *A Source Book in Geology.* New York: McGraw-Hill, 1939.
Merrill, George P. *The First One Hundred Years of American Geology.* New Haven: Yale University Press, 1924.
Miller, Denning. *Wind, Storm and Rain.* New York: Coward-McCann, 1952.
Mitchell, R.J., and Leys, M.D.R. *A History of London Life.* New York: Longmans, Green, 1958.
Monnett, V.E., and Brown, H.E. *The Principles of Physical Geology.* Boston: Ginn, 1921.
Moore, Ruth. *The Earth We Live On.* New York: Knopf, 1963.
Morison, Samuel Eliot. *The Oxford History of the United States.* London: Oxford, 1928.
Morse, Joseph Laffan (ed.). *The Unicorn Book of 1954.* New York: Unicorn Books, 1955.
Namowitz, Samuel N. *Earth Science: The World We Live In.* Princeton: Van Nostrand, 1953.
Nieder, Charles. *Man Against Nature.* New York: Harper, 1954.
Nelson, Bruce. *Land of the Decotahs.* Minneapolis: University of Minnesota Press, 1946.
Nelson's Encyclopedia (30 vols.). Chicago: Columbia Educational Books, 1940.
Nesbitt, Paul H. *The Survival Book.* Princeton: D. Van Nostrand, 1959.
The New Encyclopedia Britannica (30 vols.). Chicago: Encyclopedia Britannica, 1973.
Newton, Douglas. *Disaster, Disaster, Disaster.* New York: Franklin Watts, 1961.
Norman, Eric. *Weird Unsolved Mysteries.* New York: Award Books, 1969.
Norman, John Roxborough. *A History of Fishes.* New York: Hill & Wang, 1963.
Parry, J.H. *Europe and a Wider World.* London: Hutchinson's University Library, 1949.
———. *The Age of Reconnaissance.* London: Weidenfeld and Nicolson, 1963.
Pearl, Richard M. *1001 Questions Answered About Earth Science.* New York: Dodd, Mead, 1962.
Polo, Marco. *The Travels of Marco Polo.* Modern Library.
Powell, John Walker. *An Introduction to the Natural History of Disaster.* Baltimore: University of Maryland, 1954.
Putnam, William C. *Geology.* New York: Oxford University Press, 1964.
Reclus, Elise. *The Ocean, Atmosphere and Life.* New York: Harper, 1873.
Rice, C.M. *Dictionary of Geological Terms.* Ann Arbor: Edward Bros., 1941.
Richardson, Lewis F. *Statistics of Deadly Quarrels.* Pittsburgh: Boxwood, 1960.
Riddick, Floyd M. *The United States Congress Organization and Procedure.* Washington: National Capitol Publishers, 1949.
Robinson, Donald. *The Face of Disaster.* Garden City, N.Y.: Doubleday, 1959.
Rogers, Agnes, with Allen, Frederick Lewis. *I Remember Distinctly, A Family Album of the American People.* New York: Harper, 1947.
Sann, Paul. *The Lawless Decade.* New York: Crown, 1960.
Shand, S.J. *Earth Lore.* New York: Dutton, 1938.
Shannon, David (ed.). *The Great Depression 1929-1941.* New York: Macmillan, 1948.
Shapley, Harlow. (ed.). *Climatic Change.* Cambridge: Harvard University Press, 1953.
Shaw, H. *Applied Geophysics.* London: Her Majesty's Stationery Office, 1936.
Shaw, William Napier. *The Drama of the Weather.* Cambridge: Cambridge University Press, 1940.
Sheldon, A.E. *Nebraska Old and New.* New York: University Publishing, 1937.
Singer, J. David, and Small, Melvin. *The Wages of War 1816-1965: A Statistical Handbook.* New York: John Wiley & Sons, Inc., 1972.
Spectorsky, A.C. (ed.). *The Book of the Mountains.* New York: Appleton-Century-Crofts, 1955.
———. *The Book of the Sky.* New York: Appleton-Century-Crofts, 1956.
———. *The Book of the Earth.* New York: Appleton-Century-Crofts, 1957.
Spencer, Edgar Winston. *Basic Concepts of Physical Geology.* New York: Crowell, 1962.
Sorokin, Pitirim A. *Man and Society in Calamity.* New York: Dutton, 1943.
Stamp, L.D. (ed.). *A Glossary of Geographical Terms.* London: Longmans, 1961.
Standard American Encyclopedia (15 vols.). Chicago: Consolidated, 1939.
Stimpson, George. *A Book About A Thousand Things.* New York: Harper, 1946.
Stokes, J. Lort. *Discoveries in Australia.* London: T. and W. Boone, 1846.
Strahler, Arthur N. *The Earth Sciences.* New York: Harper & Row, 1963.
Street, A.G. *Farmer's Glory.* London: Faber, 1937.
Sutton, Ann, and Sutton, Myron. *Nature on the Rampage.* New York: Lippincott, 1962.
Talman, Charles F. *The Realm of the Air.* Indianapolis: Bobbs-Merrill, 1931.
Tannehill, Ivan R. *Weather Around the World.* Princeton: Princeton University Press, 1943.
Taylor, Bayard. *A Visit to India, China and Japan.* New York: Putnam, 1855.
Thucydides. *History of the Peloponnesian War.*
The Times-World Index Gazetteer. London: Times, 1965.
Trevelyan, George Macaulay. *England Under Queen Anne.* New York: Longmans, 1930.
Tufty, Barbara. *1001 Questions Answered About Natural Land Disasters.* New York: Dodd, Mead, 1969
Twain, Mark. *Roughing It* (vols. I and II). New York: Harper, 1899.
Vlekke, B.H.M. *Nusantara: A History of the East Indian Archipelago.* Cambridge: Harvard University Press, 1943.
Wallace, Lew. *An Autobiography.* New York: Harper, 1906.
The War of the Rebellion: A Compilation of the Official Records of the Union and Confederate Armies, 4 series, 128 vols. Washington: Government Printing Office, 1880-1910.
Ward, Christopher. *The War of the Revolution.* New York: Macmillan, 1952.
Webster's New Geographical Dictionary. Springfield, Mass.: Merriam, 1972.
Wenstrom, William H. *Weather and the Ocean of Air.* Boston: Houghton-Mifflin, 1942.
Wheeler, Raymond H. *War, 599 B.C.-1950 A.D.: Indexes of International and Civil War Battles of the World.* Pittsburgh: Foundation for the Study of Cycles, 1951.
Wise, Henry Augustus. *Los Gringos: Or An Inside View of Mexico and California, with Wanderings in Peru, Chile and Polynesia.* London: Richard Bentley, 1849.
Woodbury, Angus M. *Principles of General Ecology.* New York: Blakiston, 1954.
Wright, Quincy. *A Study of War.* Chicago: University of Chicago, 1942.
Year (1947-1954). New York: Simon & Schuster.
Zumberge, James H. *Elements of Geology.* New York: John Wiley, 1963.
Zweig, Stefan. *The World of Yesterday.* New York: Viking, 1943.

Periodicals, Bulletins, Pamphlets, Papers, Reports

Annual Report For Short-Lived Phenomena. Smithsonian Institution, Washington, May, 1971.
Conference on Field Studies of Reactions to Disasters. National Opinion Research Center, University of Chicago, 1953.
Federal Disaster Insurance. U.S. Senate Report, Washington, 1956.
Fritz, Charles E., and Mathewson, J.H. *Convergence Behavior in Disasters.* Committee on Disaster Studies, Washington, 1957.

———. "The Human Being in Disaster." *Annals of the American Academy of Political and Social Science,* January, 1957.
Hertell, Joseph A. "Medical Preparedness for Disaster." *Journal of the American Medical Association,* March 8, 1958.
Hinsley, Joseph W. "Hospital Operational Preparedness." *Journal of the American Medical Association,* March 8, 1958.
Glass, Albert J. "Management of Mass Psychiatric Casualties." *Military Medicine,* April, 1956.
Logan, Leonard, Killian, Lewis M., and Marrs, Wyatt. *A Study of the Effect of Catastrophe on Social Disorganization.* Operations Research Office, Washington, 1952.
Perry, Stewart E., and others. *The Child and His Family in Disaster.* National Research Council, Washington, 1956.
The Problems of Panic. Committee on Disaster Studies, Washington, 1955.
Raker, John W., Wallace, Anthony F.C., Rayner, Jeanette F., and Eckert, Anthony W. *Emergency Medical Care in Disasters.* Committee on Disaster Studies, Washington, 1956.
Report of Relief Activities. American National Red Cross, Washington, 1928.
Titmuss, Richard M. *Problems of Social Policy.* His Majesty's Stationery Office, 1950.

Air Crashes

Books

Aircraft Year Book. Boston: Small, Maynard, 1921.
Allen, C.B. *The Wonder Book of the Air.* Chicago: Winston, 1936.
Allward, Maurice. *Safety in the Air.* New York: Abelard-Schuman, 1967.
The American Heritage History of Flight. New York: Simon & Schuster, 1962.
Baldwin, Munson. *With Brass and Gas.* Boston: Beacon, 1967.
Barlay, Stephen. *The Search for Air Safety, An International Documentary Report on the Investigation of Commercial Aviation Accidents.* New York: Morrow, 1970.
Barker, Ralph. *Great Mysteries of the Air.* New York: Macmillan, 1967.
Becker, Beril. *Dreams and Realities of the Conquests of the Skies.* New York: Atheneum, 1967.
Berget, Alphonse. *The Conquest of the Air.* New York: Putnam, 1911.
Berrimen, A.E. *Aviation.* New York: George H. Doran, 1913.
Bonney, Walter T. *The Heritage of Kitty Hawk.* New York: Norton, 1962.
Brennan, Dennis. *Adventures in Courage: The Skymasters.* Chicago: Rilley & Lee, 1968.
Briand, Paul L. *Daughter of the Sky.* New York: Duell, Sloan and Pearce, 1960.
Canby, Courtlandt. *A History of Flight.* New York: Hawthorn, 1963.
Charke, Basil. *The History of Airships.* London: Herbert Jenkins, 1961.
Curtiss, Glenn H., and Post, Augustus. *The Curtiss Aviation Book.* New York: Frederick A. Stokes, 1912.
Dallison, Ken. *When Zeppelins Flew.* New York: Time-Life Books, 1969.
Dene, S. *Trail-blazing in the Skies.* Akron: Goodyear Tire & Rubber, 1943.
Dudley, E. *Monsters of the Purple Twilight.* London: George C. Harrap, 1960.
Duke, Neville, and Lanchbery, Edward (eds.). *The Saga of Flight.* New York: John Day, 1961.
Eckener, H. *My Zeppelins* (trans. by D. Robinson). London: Putnam, 1958.
FAA Statistical Handbook of Aviation. Washington: Federal Aviation Agency, 1970-75.
Farmen, Richard, and Farmen, Henry. *The Aviator's Companion.* London: Mills and Boon, 1910.
Fechet, James E. *Flying.* Baltimore: Williams & Wilkins, 1933.
Ferris, Richard. *How It Flies.* New York: Nelson, 1910.
Fokker, Anthony H.G. *Flying Dutchman.* New York: Holt, 1931.
Fortune Airline Study. Chicago: Time, 1962.
Foulois, Maj.-General Benjamin D., with Glines, Col. C.V. *Memoirs, From the Wright Brothers to the Astronauts.* New York: McGraw-Hill, 1968.
Gamble, C.F. Snowden. *The Story of a North Sea Air Station.* London: Neville Spearman, 1967.
Gibbs-Smith, Charles H. *The Wright Brothers.* London: Science Museum, 1963.
———. *Air Rescue!* New York: Ace, 1961.
Glines, Carroll V. *The Compact History of the United States Air Force.* New York: Hawthorn, 1963.
———. *The Modern United States Air Force.* Princeton: Van Nostrand, 1963.
———. *Lighter-Than-Air Flight.* New York: Watts, 1965.
———, with Mosley, W.F. *The DC-3.* Philadelphia: Lippincott, 1966.
———. *Helicopter Rescues.* New York: Four Winds, 1966.
Godson, John. *Unsafe at Any Height.* New York: Simon & Schuster, 1970.
Goldstrom, John. *A Narrative History of Aviation.* New York: Macmillan, 1930.
Gorham, Maurice. *Sound and Fury.* London: Percival Marshall, 1948.
Grahame-White, Claude, and Harper, Harry. *The Aeroplane: Past, Present, and Future.* Philadelphia: Lippincott, 1911.
———. *Heroes of the Air.* New York: Hodder and Stoughton, 1912.
Halacy, D.S., Jr. *America's Major Air Disasters.* Derby, Conn.: Monarch, 1961.
Harper, Harry. *Man's Conquest of the Air.* London: J. Gifford, 1942.
———. *Winged World, The Coming of the Air Age.* London: J. Gifford, 1946.
Heinmuller, John P.N. *Man's Right to Fly.* New York: Aero Print, 1945.
Hoehling, A.A. *Who Destroyed the Hindenberg?* New York: Little, Brown, 1962.
Hood, J.F. *The Story of Airships.* London: Arthur Barker, 1968.
Jackson, Robert. *Airships.* Garden City, N.Y.: Doubleday, 1973.
Jane, Fred T. *All the World's Aircraft.* London: Sampson, Low, Marston, 1913.
Kelly, Fred C. *The Wright Brothers.* New York: Harcourt, Brace, 1943.
Kirschner, Edwin J. *The Zeppelin in the Atomic Age.* Urbana: University of Illinois Press, 1957.
Knight, Clayton. *Plane Crash.* London: Elek, 1958.
Langsdorff, Werner Von. *LZ-129 Hindenberg.* Frankfurt, 1936.
Launay, A. *Historic Air Disasters.* Shepperton, England: Ian Allen, 1967.
Lehmann, Capt. Ernst A. *Zeppelin.* London: Longmans, Green, 1937.
Lipsner, Captain Benjamin B. *From Jennies to Jets.* Chicago: Follett, 1951.
Loening, Grover Cleveland. *Monoplanes and Biplanes.* New York: Munn, 1911.
———. *Our Wings Grow Faster.* New York: Doubleday, Doran, 1935.
Lowell, Capt. V.W. *Airline Safety Is a Myth.* London: Bartholomew House, 1967.
Magoun, F. Alexander, and Hodgins, Eric. *A History of Aircraft.* New York: McGraw-Hill, 1931.
———. *Sky High, the Story of Aviation.* Boston: Little, Brown, 1935.
Mason, J.K. *Aviation Accident, Pathology.* London: Butterworth, 1962.
McMahon, John R. *The Wright Brothers: Fathers of Flight.* Boston: Little, Brown, 1930.
Meager, G. *My Airship Flights, 1915-1930.* London: William Kimber, 1970.
Middleton, E.C. *The Great War in the Air* (4 vols.). London: Waverley, 1920.
Miller, Francis Trevelyan. *The World in the Air* (2 vols.). New York: Putnam, 1930.
Mitchell, Brig. Gen. William. *Memoirs of World War I.* New York: Random House, 1960.
Mooney, Michael. *The Hindenberg.* New York: Dodd, Mead, 1972.
Neilsen, Thor. *The Zeppelin Story.* London: Alan Wingate, 1955.
Olley, Captain Gordon P. *A Million Miles in the Air.* London: Hodder and Stoughton, 1934.
Palmer, Henry R., Jr. *This Was Air Travel.* Seattle, Wash.: Superior, 1960.
Rintelen, Franz von. *The Dark Invader.* New York: Macmillan, 1933.
Robinson, Douglas H. *The LZ-129, Hindenberg* (Famous Aircraft Series). New York: Arco, 1964.
———. *The Zeppelin in Combat.* London: Foulis, 1966.
Rolfe, Douglas, and Dawydoff, Alexis. *Airplanes of the World.* New York: Simon & Schuster, 1962.
Rolt, L.T.C. *The Aeronauts: A History of Ballooning, 1783-1903.* London: Longmans, Green, 1966.
Rosendahl, Charles E. *Up Ship.* New York: Dodd, Mead, 1931.
———. *What About the Airship?* New York: Scribners, 1938.
Santos-Dumont, Alberto. *My Airships.* New York: Century, 1904.
Saunders, H.A. *Per Ardua: The Rise of British Air Power, 1911-1939.* London: Oxford University Press, 1944.
Scott, Col. Robert L. *Runway to the Sun.* New York: Scribners, 1945.
Serling, R.J. *The Probable Cause.* New York: Doubleday, 1962.
Shamburger, Page. *Tracks Across the Sky, The Story of the Pioneers of the U.S. Air Mail.* Philadelphia: Lippincott, 1964.
Shirer, William L. *Berlin Diary.* New York: Knopf, 1941.
Sikorsky, Igor I. *The Story of the Winged-S.* New York: Dodd, Mead, 1938.
Simmonds, Ralph. *All About Airships.* New York: George H. Doran, 1911.
Smith, C.H. Gibbs. *A History of Flying.* London: Batsford, 1953.
Smith, Dean C. *By the Seat of My Pants.* Boston: Atlantic Monthly, 1961.
Smith, Henry Ladd. *Airways: The History of Commercial Aviation in the U.S.* New York: Knopf, 1942.
Smith, R.K. *The Airships Akron and Macon.* Annapolis: U.S. Naval Institute, 1950.
Stewart, O. *Danger in the Air.* London: Routledge & Kegan Paul, 1958.
Sutton, Sir Graham. *Mastery of the Air.* New York: Basic Books, 1965.
Titler, Dale M. *Wings of Mystery.* New York: Dodd, Mead, 1966.
Toland, John. *Ships in the Sky.* New York: Holt, 1957.
Tyler, Poyntz. *Airways of America.* New York: Wilson, 1958.
Vaeth, J. Gordon. *Graf Zeppelin.* New York: Harper, 1958.
Villard, Henry Serrano. *Contact! The Story of the Early Birds.* New York: Crowell, 1968.
Vivian, E.C., and Marsh, W.L. *History of Aeronautics.* London: W. Collins Sons, 1921.
Whitehouse, Arch. *The Early Birds.* Garden City, N.Y.: Doubleday, 1965.

Whitnah, D.R. *Safer Skyways. Federal Control of Aviation, 1926-1966.* Ames: Iowa State University Press, 1966.

Williams, Archibald. *Conquering the Air. The Romance of the Development and Use of Aircraft.* New York: T. Nelson, 1926.

Winter, Lumen, and Degner, Glenn. *Minute Epics of Flight.* New York: Grosset & Dunlap, 1933.

Wykeham, P.G. *Santos-Dumont: A Study in Obsession.* London: Putnam, 1962.

Periodicals

Adelt, Leonhard. "The Last Trip of the *Hindenberg.*" *Reader's Digest,* November, 1937.

"Aftermath." *New Yorker,* August 11, 1945.

"Aftermath." *New Yorker,* July 27, 1946.

"After the Game." *Time,* March 20, 1950.

"Air Crash . . . What Caused It? . . . Who's to Blame? . . . The Skilled Men with Answers—If There Are Any." *Newsweek,* May 25, 1959.

Bailey, Ronald. "Those Who Cared Enough to Take Separate Planes." *Life,* July 15, 1962.

"Bolt from the Fog." *Newsweek,* August 6, 1945.

Blank, Joseph. "Atlanta: Aftermath of a Tragedy." *Redbook,* June, 1963.

"Bolivia 927! Turn Left." *Time,* November 14, 1949.

Brean, Herbert. "Agony and Enigma In a Dark River." *Life,* February 16, 1959.

"CAT's Claws." *Time,* April 11, 1960.

"The Cherry Orchard." *Time,* June 15, 1962.

"Civil Defense." *Nation,* December 31, 1960.

Collins, Paul. "When the Air Mail Began." *Liberty,* April 20, 1929.

"CPA Comet Took Off Nose High." *Aviation Week,* April 6, 1953.

"Crash Delays CPA Comet Plans." *Aviation Week,* March 9, 1953.

"Crash in Lake Michigan." *Newsweek,* July 3, 1950.

"Crowded Sky." *Time,* July 28, 1967.

"Death Comes at Ermenonville." *Time,* March 18, 1974.

'Death in a DC-6." *Newsweek,* Oct. 31, 1947.

"Death in the Air." *Time,* December 26, 1960.

"Death in the Skies." *Time,* September, 1969.

"Detective Story." *Newsweek.* February 4, 1952.

"Diving With Both Wings on Fire." *Life,* March 18, 1966.

"The Downfall of a Dirigible." *Literary Digest,* November 17, 1921.

Driggs, LaTourette Laurence. "The Fall of the Airship." *Outlook,* September 7, 1921.

"The Daughter of the Stars!" *Outlook,* September 16, 1925.

"E Between Nine & Ten." *Time,* December 29, 1952.

"Electra in the Wind." *Time,* May 16, 1960.

"End of a Pilgrimage." *Time,* November 27, 1950.

"Excessive Speed of TWA DC-9 Cited in Airport Midair Crash." *Aviation Week,* June 12, 1967.

"A Falling Leaf." *Newsweek,* March 14, 1966.

"The Fatal Starlings." *Time,* October 24, 1960.

"Fire in the Sky." *Time,* May 16, 1960.

"Flight into Death." *Newsweek,* August 25, 1958.

"GI Tragedy." *Newsweek,* November 20, 1961.

Gordon, Arthur. "He Found Out Why the Comets Blew Up." *Saturday Evening Post,* February 19, 1955.

"The Great DC-10 Mystery." *Time,* April 8, 1974.

"The Greatest Aerial Disaster." *Literary Digest,* September 3, 1921.

Howard, W.H.L. "Steps in the Evolution of Mail Carrying." *Flying,* June, 1918.

"The Hills of Hebron." *Time,* December 1, 1967.

"The Human Side of the Shenandoah Disasters." *Literary Digest,* September 26, 1925.

"I Could Hear Screams. . ." *Newsweek,* December 26, 1960.

"In a Thunderstorm." *Newsweek,* July 2, 1962.

"Interruption." *New Yorker,* September 1, 1945.

"In the Clouds." *Time,* August 6, 1945.

"It Was Beautiful: Stevie's Memory of a Fairy Book." *Life,* December 26, 1960.

Jones, F.H. "'Aircraft Accident Investigation—The Analysis of the Wreckage." *Canadian Aeronautics and Space Journal,* December, 1962.

"Like a Wounded Eagle." *Newsweek,* December 29, 1952.

"Locked Controls." *Time,* January 5, 1953.

Marquess of Donegall. "On Board the Dirigible Hindenberg." *Fact Digest,* October, 1936.

Mather, Margaret. "I Was on the Hindenberg." *Harper's Magazine,* November, 1937.

McGill, Ralph. "Those Who Cared for the Important Things." *Life,* July, 1962.

Moore, Taylor Samuel. "The Lesson of the Shenandoah." *Independent,* October 24, 1925.

Newton, E. "The Investigation of Aircraft Accidents." *Journal of the Royal Aeronautical Society,* March, 1964.

". . . A Nightmare of the Air Age." *Life,* December 26, 1960.

"No Survivors." *Time,* November 24, 1952.

"Off the Screen." *Newsweek,* February 14, 1966.

"Only Three Minutes." *Newsweek,* June 29, 1953.

"A Question of Safety." *Newsweek.* December 26, 1960.

Reals, W.J. and Danielson, R.E. "Flight Fatalities Studied, Autopsy Investigation of Aircraft Accidents." *Journal of the Kansas Medical Society,* August, 1963.

Ruppenthal, Karl M., "Crash of a System . . ." *Nation,* December 31, 1960.

"Sad Reminders of an Aerial Tragedy." *Life,* April 10, 1960.

Scott, David H. "Scott's Corner." *Flying Magazine,* October, 1967.

"The Shenandoah Verdict." *Literary Digest,* January 16, 1926.

"Skyscraper Crash." *Life,* September 6, 1945.

"Violent End of Quest for Beauty." *Life,* July 15, 1962.

"What Crumpled Up the ZR-2?" *Literary Digest,* September 24, 1921.

"What Did Matter." *Time,* November 17, 1961.

"The Worst Ever." *Time,* August 9, 1971.

"The Worst Single Day." *Time,* March 11, 1966.

Bulletins, Pamphlets, Papers, Reports, Studies

A Brief History of Air Transportation of Mail. Post Office Dept., Washington, D.C.

A Study of U.S. Air Carrier Accidents Involving Fire, 1955-1964. CAB Bureau of Safety, Washington, 1965.

Pilots' Weather Handbook. Civil Aeronautics Administration, Washington, 1955.

U.S. Air Mail Service. Post Office Department, Washington, D.C., 1921.

Avalanches & Landslides

Books

Albright, John Grover. *Physical Meteorology.* New York: Prentice-Hall, 1939.

Atwater, Montgomery M. *The Avalanche Hunters.* Philadelphia: Macrae Smith, 1968.

Bentley, Wilson A., and Humphreys, W.J. *Snow Crystals.* New York: McGraw-Hill, 1931.

Bowen, Ezra. *Book of American Skiing.* Philadelphia: Lippincott, 1963.

Bragg, William Henry. *Concerning the Nature of Things.* London: Bell, 1925.

Browne, Belmore. *Conquest of Mount McKinley.* New York: Putnam, 1913.

Brown, T. Graham, and De Beer, Gavin. *The First Ascent of Mont Blanc.* London: Oxford University Press, 1957.

Clark, R. *The Early Alpine Guides.* London: Hutchinson, 1949.

———. *Great Moments of Rescue.* London: Hutchinson, 1951.

Coolidge, William Augustus Breroort. *The Alps in Nature and History.* New York: Dutton, 1908.

———. *Alpine Studies.* London: Longmans, Green, 1912.

Conway, William Martin. *The Alps from End to End.* Westminster, England: A. Constable, 1895.

De Beer, G. *Early Travellers in the Alps.* London: Sidgwick & Jackson, 1930.

———. *Alps and Men.* London: E. Arnold, 1932.

———. *Travellers in Switzerland.* London: Oxford University Press, 1949.

Dole, C. Minot. *Adventure in Skiing.* New York: Franklin Watts, 1965.

Eckel, Edwin B. (ed.). *Landslides and Engineering Practice.* Washington: National Research Council, 1958.

Forbes, J.D. *Travels Through the Alps of Savoy.* Edinburgh. n.p., 1843.

Fraser, Colin. *The Avalanche Enigma.* New York: Rand McNally, 1966.

Frutinger, Hans. *Snow Avalanches Along Colorado Mountain Highways.* Fort Collins, Col.: Rocky Mountain Forest and Range Experiment Station, 1964.

Gallegher, Dale. *The Snowy Torrents.* Alta, Utah: U.S. Forest Service, 1967.

Gos, C. *Alpine Tragedy* (trans. by Malcolm Barnes). New York: Scribners, 1948.

Greely, A.W. *American Weather.* New York: Dodd, Mead, 1888.

Humphreys, W.J. *Weather Rambles.* Baltimore: Williams and Wilkins, 1937.

Kugy, J. *Son of the Mountains.* New York: Thomas Nelson, 1938.

Lunn, Sir Arnold Henry Moore. *The Alps.* London: Williams and Norgate, 1914.

———. *A History of Skiing.* London: H. Milford, 1927.

Mathews, C.E. *The Annals of Mont Blanc.* London, 1898.

McConnell, B.G. *Great Landslide at Frank, Alta.* Ottawa, Canada: Canadian Dept. of the Interior, 1904.

Nakaya, Ukichiro. *Snow Crystals.* Cambridge: Harvard University Press, 1954.

Quervain, M.R. *Avalanche Classification.* Toronto: International Association of Scientific Hydrology, 1957.

Seligman, Gerald. *Snow Structure and Ski Fields.* New York: Macmillan, 1936.

Sennett, Alfred Richard. *Across the Great St. Bernard.* London: Bemrose and Sons, 1904.

Sharpe, C.F. *Landslides and Related Phenomena.* New York: Columbia University Press, 1938.

Shackleton, Ernest. *South.* London: William Heinemann, 1919.

Smith, Albert. *The Story of Mont Blanc.* London: D. Bogua, 1853.

Talman, Charles F. *The Realm of the Air.* Indianapolis: Bobbs-Merrill, 1931.

Thomas, Lowell. *Book of the High Mountains.* New York: Julian Messner, 1964.

Tyler, J.E. *The Alpine Passes, 960-1250 A.D.* London: B. Blackwell, 1930.

Wechsberg, Joseph. *Avalanche!* New York: Knopf, 1958.

Periodicals

Atwater, Montgomery M. 'Snow Avalanches.' *Scientific American,* January, 1954.

———, and others. "Avalanche Research." *Appalachia Magazine,* December, 1954, June, 1955.

"Avalanche." *Newsweek,* January 22, 1962.

"Avalanche, the 'White Death' Strikes the Alps." *Life,* June 29, 1951.

Bentley, Wilson A. "Work on Snow Crystals." *National Geographic,* Vol. 15, 1904.

———. "The Magic Beauty of Snow and Dew." *National Geographic,* Vol. 43, 1923.
"Carpet of Death." *Time,* January 19, 1962.
Cecil Alter, J. "Why the Snow Slides from the Mountain Slopes." *Monthly Weather Review,* Vol. 40, 1912.
Church, J.E. "Snow Perils and Avalanches." *Scientific Monthly,* Vol. 56, 1943.
Close, Upton. "Where the Mountains Walked." *National Geographic,* May, 1922.
Colton, F.B. "Weather Fights and Works for Man." *National Geographic,* Vol. 84, 1943.
Conway, W. Martin. "Mountain-Falls." *Contemporary Review,* December, 1894.
Grob, W. "Some Thoughts About Avalanches." *Sierra Club Magazine,* Vol. 35, 1950.
Hicks, Jim. "We Welsh Are All the Same—We Dig Our Roots Deep." *Life,* November 14, 1966.
Ludlum, David M. "Extremes of Snowfall in the United States." *Weatherwise,* Vol. 15, 1962.
McDowell, Bart. "Avalanche!" *National Geographic,* Vol. 121, 1962.
"Mud Bath." *Newsweek,* February 10, 1969.
"The Murderous Mountain." *Time,* October 28, 1966.
Needham, Joseph. "The Earliest Snow Crystals." *Weather,* Vol. 16, 1961.
"Never One Like This." *Newsweek,* October 31, 1966.
Putnam, W.L. "Snow Conditions." *Appalachia Magazine,* 1-5(28-29), 1950-53.
Riddell, J. "Six Minutes Too Soon." *British Ski Year Book,* 1952.
Roch, A. "On the Study of Avalanches." *Sierra Club Magazine,* Vol. 36, 1951.
Seligman, Gerald. "Comments on Avalanche Research." *Journal of Glaciology,* April, 1953.
Smythe, F.S. "Some Physical Characteristics of Snow Avalanches." *Alpine Journal,* Vol. 41, 1929.
"Sudden Snows." *Time,* January 29, 1951.
Vokes, H.E. "Landslide." *Natural History,* Vol. 49, 1942.
"Where Men Met Mud." *National Geographic,* October, 1969.
Worden, William L. "The Deadly Mountain that Walks." *Saturday Evening Post,* January 1, 1955.

Bulletins, Pamphlets, Papers & Reports

Atwater, Montgomery M., and Kozial, F.C. "The Alta Avalanche Studies." U.S. Forest Service, 1950.
Bucher, E., and others. *Snow and Its Metamorphism.* U.S. Army Corps of Engineers, 1954.
Eckel, Edwin B. (ed.). *Landslides and Engineering Practice.* National Research Council, Washington, 1958.
Hennes, Robert G. *Analysis and Control of Landslides.* University of Washington Bulletin, 1936.
Snow Avalanches. U.S. Dept. of Agriculture, Washington, 1961.
Snow Survey Safety Guide. U.S. Soil Conservation Service, Washington, 1958.
Some Extremes of Snowfall. U.S. Weather Bureau, Washington, 1955.
Turtle Mountain, Frank, Alberta. Commission Report, Canadian Dept. of Mines, Ottawa, 1912.
Voellmy, A., *On the Destructive Force of Avalanches.* Alta, Utah, U.S. Forest Service, 1964.

Droughts, Famines, Floods, Plagues

Books

Adams, William Forbes. *Ireland and Irish Emigration to the New World from 1815 to the Famine.* New Haven: Yale University Press, 1932.
Alley, Rewi. *Man Against Flood.* Peking: New World Press, 1956.
Baghcladi, Abdul Latif al-, *The Eastern Key* (trans. by Ivey E. Videan and Sayid Zand). London: Allen & Unwin, 1965.
Bancroft, Herbert Howe. *History of California* (vol. V.). San Francisco: The History Company, 1886.
Bardach, John. *Downstream: A Natural History of the River.* New York: Harper and Row, 1964.
Barrows, H.K. *Floods, Their Hydrology and Control.* New York: McGraw-Hill, 1948.
Bartel, Roland (ed.). *London in Plague and Fire.* Boston: Heath, 1957.
The Battle of the Floods: Holland in February, 1953. Amsterdam: Netherlands Booksellers and Publishers, 1953.
Baumhoff, Richard G. *The Damned Missouri Valley: One Sixth of Our Nation.* New York: Knopf, 1951.
Beale, Rev. David J. *Through the Johnstown Flood.* Philadelphia: Hubbard, 1890.
Beckett, J.C. *A Short History of Modern Ireland.* New York: Harper and Row, 1952.
Bhatia, B.M. *Famines in India.* New Delhi, India: Asia Publishing House, 1963.
Bogart, Dean B. *Floods of August-October, 1955, New England to North Carolina.* Washington: U.S. Government Printing Office, 1960.
Breasted, James A. *History of Egypt.* New York: Scribners, 1909.
Brooks, C.E.P., and Glasspoole, J. *British Floods and Droughts.* London: Benn, 1928.
Browne, W.G. *Travels in Africa, Egypt and Syria, 1792-1798.* London: Cadell & Davies, 1806.
Bryant, Edwin. *What I Saw in California.* Philadelphia: Appleton, 1848.
Burkhardt, Jacob. *The Age of Constantine.* Garden City, N.Y.: Doubleday, 1956.
Burnett, Peter Hardemann. *Recollections and Opinions of an Old Pioneer.* New York: Appleton, 1880.
Carleton, William. *The Black Prophet.* New York: D.J. Sadlier, 1874.
Carlyle, Thomas. *Reminiscences of My Irish Journey in 1849.* New York: Lovell, Coryell, 1885.
Chambers, J.S. *The Conquest of Cholera.* New York: Macmillan, 1938.
Cleary, James Mansfield. *Proud Are We Irish.* Chicago: Quadrangle, 1966.
Cleland, Robert Glass. *Pathfinders* ('A Tragedy on the Trail'). Los Angeles: Powell, 1929.
Connell, K.H. *The Population of Ireland, 1750-1845.* Oxford, England: Clarendon Press, 1950.
Costigan, Giovanni. *A History of Modern Ireland.* New York: Pegasus, 1969.
Coulton, G.G. *The Black Death.* London: E.Benn, 1929.
Cronise, Titus Fey. *The Natural Wealth of California.* San Francisco: H.H. Bancroft, 1868.
The Dance of Death. Washington: Rare Books Division of the Library of Congress, 1945.
Dodwell, Henry. *The Founder of Modern Egypt.* Cambridge: Cambridge University Press, 1931.
Drioton, Etienne, and Vandier, Jacques, *L'Egypte.* Paris: Presses Univeritaires de France, 1952.
Dunbar, Edward E. *The Romance of the Age.* New York: Appleton, 1867.
Eckart, Allan. *A Time of Terror.* Boston: Little, Brown, 1965.
Edwards, R. Dudley, and Williams, Desmond (eds.). *The Great Famine.* New York: New York University Press, 1957.
Eldredge, Zoeth Skinner. *The Beginnings of San Francisco* (2 vols.). San Francisco: Z.S. Eldridge, 1912.
———. *History of California* (5 vols.). New York: Century History Company, 1915.
Erman, Adolf (trans. by A.M. Blackman). *Literature of the Ancient Egyptians* (re-issued as *The Ancient Egyptians, A Sourcebook of Their Writings* with added material by William Kelly Simpson). New York: Harper, 1966.
Freeman, Thomas Walter. *Pre-Famine Ireland: A Study in Historical Geography.* Manchester, England: Manchester University Press, 1957.
Gasquet, F.A. *The Great Pestilence.* London: S. Marshall, Hamilton, Kent, 1893.
Gibbs, Sir H.A.R. *Studies in the Civilization of Islam.* London: Routledge & Keegan Paul, 1962.
Glanville, S.R.K. *The Legacy of Egypt.* New York: Oxford University Press, 1942.
Greenwood, Major. *Epidemics and Crowd Diseases.* New York: Macmillan, 1935.
Grunebaum, Gustave E. von. *Medieval Islam.* Chicago: University of Chicago Press, 1946.
Haggard, Howard W. *The Lame, the Halt, and the Blind.* New York: Harper, 1932.
Harland, Jacob Wright. *California '36 to '48.* San Francisco: Bancroft Library, 1888.
Hayes, William C. *The Scepter of Egypt* (2 vols.). Boston: Harvard University Press, 1959, 1960.
Hazen, Allen. *Flood Flows.* New York: Wiley, 1930.
Hecht, Ben. *A Child of the Century.* New York: Simon & Schuster, 1954.
Hecker, J.F.C. *The Epidemics of the Middle Ages.* London: Trubner, 1859.
Herbert, Thomas, and Miller, Martin. *America's Greatest Flood and Tornado Calamity.* Chicago: Thomas H. Morrison, 1913.
Herodotus. *Histories.*
Hersey, John. *Here to Stay.* New York: Knopf, 1963.
Hirst, L.F. *The Conquest of Plague.* Oxford, England: Clarendon Press, 1953.
Hittel, Theodore H. *History of California.* San Francisco: N.J. Stone & Co., 1885.
Hitti, Philip. *History of the Arabs.* London: Macmillan, 1937.
Hoover, Herbert. *The Memoirs of Herbert Hoover, 1920-1933, The Cabinet and the Presidency.* New York: Macmillan, 1952.
Houghton, Eliza P. Donner. *The Expedition of the Donner Party and Its Tragic Fate.* Chicago: A.C. McClurg, 1911.
Hoyt, William G., and Langbein, William B. *Floods.* Princeton: Princeton University Press, 1955.
Hurst, H.E. *The Nile.* London: Constable, 1952.
Ibn Khaldun. *The Mugaddimah, An Introduction to History* (3 vols.). (trans. by Franz Rosenthal.). New York: Pantheon, Bollingen, 1958.
Insects: The Yearbook of Agriculture, 1952. Washington: Government Printing Office, 1952.
Jacks, G.V., and Whyte, R.O. *Vanishing Lands.* New York: Doubleday, Doran, 1939.
James, George Wharton. *Heroes of California.* Boston: Little, Brown, 1910.
Kaster, Joseph (ed.). *Wings of the Falcon, Life and Thought of Ancient Egypt.* New York: Holt, Rinehart and Winston, 1968.
Kellog, C.E. *The Soils That Support Us.* New York: Macmillan, 1941.
Kelly, Charles. *Salt Desert Trails.* Salt Lake City: Western Printing Co., 1930.
Kenyon, Frederic. *The Bible and Archaeology.* New York: Harper, 1940.
Krutch, Joseph Wood. *The Desert Year.* New York: William Sloan, 1952.
Lane, Edward William. *Modern Egyptians.* London: Ward Lock, 1890.
Lane-Poole, Stanley. *The Story of Cairo.* London: J.M. Dent, 1902.
Lefebvre, Gustave, *Romans et Contes Egyptians de L'Epogue Pharaonique.* Paris: Adrien-Maisonneuve, 1949.
Leo Africanus (al-Hasan ibn Muhammad al-Wazzan al-Fasi). *History and Description of Africa.* London: Haklyt Society, 1896.
Leopold, A. Starker. *The Desert.* New York: Time, 1962.
Leopold, Luna B., and Davis, Kenneth S. *Water.* New York: Time, 1966.

Loveday, Alexander. *History and Economics of Famines in India.* London: G. Bell, 1914.
Ludwig, Emil. *The Nile.* Garden City, N.Y.: Garden City, 1947.
Macardle, Dorothy. *The Irish Republic.* New York: Farrar, Straus and Giroux, 1965.
MacDonough, Oliver. *A Pattern of Government Growth: 1800-1860: The Passenger Acts and Their Enforcement.* London: MacGibbon and Kee, 1961.
Major, Ralph H. *Disease and Destiny.* New York: Appleton-Century, 1936.
Marshall, Logan. *The True Story of Our National Calamity of Flood, Fire and Tornado.* Chicago: L.T. Myers, 1913.
Marston, R.B. *War, Famine and Our Food Supply.* London: S. Low, Morston, 1897.
McClellan, Rollander Guy. *The Golden State.* Philadelphia: W. Flint, 1872.
McDowell, Robert B. *Social Life in Ireland, 1800-45.* Dublin: C.O. Lochlainn, 1950.
McGlashen, C.F. *History of the Donner Party.* Stanford: Stanford University Press, 1940.
Meinzer, Oscar E. *Hydrology.* New York: McGraw-Hill, 1947.
Milne, Lorcus J., and Milne, Margery. *The Balance of Nature.* New York: Knopf, 1960.
Mitchel, John. *The Last Conquest of Ireland.* Glasgow: Cameron, Ferguson, 1890.
———. *Jail Journal.* Dublin: M.H. Gill, 1914.
Moorehead, Alan. *The White Nile.* New York: Harper, 1960.
———. *The Blue Nile.* New York: Harper, 1962.
Montet, Pierre. *Everyday Life in Egypt.* London: Edward Arnold, 1958.
Murray, Margaret A. *The Splendor That Was Egypt.* New York: Philosophical Library, 1949.
Nash, Vaughan. *The Great Famine.* London: Longmans, Green, 1900.
Nohl, Johannes. *The Black Death, A Chronicle of the Plague* (trans. by C.H. Clarke). New York: Ballantine, 1960.
Norton, Henry Kittredge. *The Story of California from the Earliest Days to the Present.* Chicago: A.C. McClurg, 1913.
O'Brien, George. *Economic History of Ireland From the Union to the Famine.* New York: Longmans, Green, 1921.
O'Brien, William P. *The Great Famine in Ireland.* London: Downey, 1896.
O'Conner, Sir James. *History of Ireland, 1801-1924.* New York: George H. Doran, 1926.
O'Connor, Richard. *Johnstown, the Day the Dam Broke.* Philadelphia: Lippincott, 1957.
O'Faolain, Sean. *The Irish.* New York: Devin-Adair, 1949.
O'Hegarty, Patrick Sarsfield. *History of Ireland Under the Union, 1801-1922.* London: Methuen, 1952.
Owen, Robert Dale. *Footfalls on the Boundary of Another World.* Philadelphia: Lippincott, 1877.
Pomfret, John Edwin. *The Struggle for Land in Ireland, 1800-1923.* Princeton: Princeton University Press, 1930.
Powell, John Wesley. *Exploration of the Colorado River of the West.* Washington: Smithsonian Institute, 1875.
Quigley, Hugh. *The Irish Race in California.* San Francisco: A. Roman, 1878.
Rawlinson, H.G. *A Concise History of the Indian People.* London: Oxford University Press, 1965.
Rensch, H.E., Rensch, E.G., and Hoover, Mildred Brooke. *Historic Spots in California.* Stanford: Stanford University Press, 1933.
Russell, Lady Dorothea. *Medieval Cairo and the Monasteries of the Wadi Natrum.* London: Weidenfeld & Nicholson, 1962.
Russell, Thomas H. *Flood and Cyclone Disasters.* Chicago: Thomas H. Morrison, 1913.
Salaman, Redcliffe N. *The History and Social Influence of the Potato.* Cambridge: Cambridge University Press, 1949.
Smith, Goldwin. *Irish History and Irish Character.* London: J.H. & J. Parker, 1862.
Smith, William Stevenson. *Ancient Egypt.* Boston: Boston Museum of Fine Arts, 1960.
Soule, Frank. *The Annals of San Francisco.* New York: Appleton, 1855.
Stewart, Desmond. *Young Egypt.* London: Wingate, 1958.
———. *Cairo, 5500 Years.* New York: Crowell, 1968.
Stewart, George. *Ordeal by Hunger.* New York: Henry Holt, 1936.
Studies in Holland Flood Disaster, 1953. Amsterdam: Institute for Social Research, 1953.
Tannehill, Ivan R. *Drought, Its Causes and Effects.* Princeton: Princeton University Press, 1947.
Taylor, Bayard. *Eldorado* (2 vols.) New York: Putnam, 1850.
Thackeray, William Makepeace. *Irish Sketch Book.* Philadelphia: Lippincott, 1872.
Thomas, Lowell. *Hungry Waters, The Story of the Great Flood.* Philadelphia: John C. Winston, 1937.
Thornton, Jesse Quinn. *Oregon and California in 1848.* New York: Harper, 1849.
Triplett, Frank. *Conquering the Wilderness.* New York: N.D. Thompson, 1886.
Walford, Cornelius. *Famines of the World: Past and Present.* London: Edward Stanford, 1879.
Webb, Walter Prescott. *The Great Plains.* Boston: Ginn, 1931.
Wilson, John A. *The Culture of Ancient Egypt.* New York: Phoenix, 1956.
Woodham-Smith, Cecil. *The Great Hunger: Ireland 1845-49.* New York: Harper and Row, 1962.
Ziegler, Philip. *The Black Death.* New York: John Day, 1969.
Zinsser, Hans. *Rats, Lice and History.* Boston: Little, Brown, 1934.

PERIODICALS

"Act of God." *Time,* August 16, 1954.
"After the Deluge." *Newsweek,* January 9, 1956.
"Again the Black Horsemen." *Time,* August 22, 1949.
Allyn, H.M., "The Black Death, Its Social and Economic Results." *Annals of Medical History,* Vol. 7, 1925.
"The Angriest Deluge." *Newsweek,* October 29, 1956.
Anonymous. "Report of Famines in Orissa and Bihar." *Calcutta Review,* Vol. 16, 1868.
"At a Tragic Stroke." *Newsweek,* September 19, 1955.
Barton, Clara, "Philanthropy at Johnstown." *North American Review,* Vol. 149, 1889.
Bean, J.J.M.W., "Plague, Population and Economic Decline in the Later Middle Ages." *Economic History Review,* Vol. 15, 1963.
"The Big Flood." *Time,* December 19, 1969.
Bigler, H.W. "Diary of H.W. Bigler." *Overland Monthly,* September-October, 1887.
Bleasdale, A. "The Measurement of Rainfall." *Weather,* Vol. 14, 1959.
Bordue, Erich. "Some Hydrological Aspects of the Flood of August, 1955." *Geographical Review,* Vol. 47, 1957.
Brooks, Charles F., and Thiessen, Alfred H. "The Meteorology of Great Floods in the Eastern United States." *Geographical Review,* April, 1937.
"California A-Flood." *American Forests,* February, 1956.
Clemens, George R. "Cut-offs Lower Flood Crests." *Engineering News Record,* November 17, 1938.
Cook, H.L. "Flood Abatement by Headwater Measures." *Civil Engineering,* March, 1945.
Cunningham, H.S. "Indian Famines." *East India Association,* Vol. 28, 1897.
Danvers, L. "Historical and Recent Famines in India." *Society of Arts,* Vol. 34, 1886.
"Death from the Hills." *Newsweek,* June 19, 1972.
"Death in Lamaland." *Time,* August 23, 1954.
Degroot, Henry. "The Donner Party." *Overland Monthly,* July, 1870.
Digges, E.W. "Determination of Flood Control Benefits." *Civil Engineering,* August, 1941.
Elliot, C.A. "Recent Famines in India and Report of the Second Famine Commission." *Asiatic Quarterly,* Vol. 8, 1899.
"The Flood." *Newsweek,* December 22, 1969.
"Flood and Fire." *Volunteer Fireman,* March, 1937.
"The Floods Came." *Time,* October 3, 1955.
"Flood Fire Fighting." *Fire Protection,* February, 1937.
Fries, Fred W. "Valley of Death." *American Heritage,* March, 1953.
Furrel, J.W. "Indian Famines and the Duty of Government." *Calcutta Review,* Vol. 66, 1874.
"Fury of the Arno in the Beloved City of Dante." *Life,* November 18, 1966.
Graves, Ralph A. "Fearful Famines of the Past." *National Geographic,* Vol. 32, No. 2.
"The Greatest Famine of the Century." *Missionary Review of the World,* May, 1900.
Grosvenor, Gilbert M., and Neave, Charles. "Helping Holland Rebuild Her Land." *National Geographic,* Vol. 106, 1954.
Harrington, E.R. "Sitting Ducks Along the Rio Grande." *Engineering News-Record,* March 6, 1952.
Henry, Alfred J. "The Distribution of Maximum Floods." *Monthly Weather Review,* Vol. 47, 1919.
———, and others. "Ice in Rivers." *Monthly Weather Review,* Vol. 46, 1918.
Horn, S.J. "The Flood of 1937 in the Ohio Valley." *Civil Engineering,* May, 1937.
Horton, R.E. "The Melting of Snow." *Monthly Weather Review,* Vol. 43, 1915.
"Hunger Makes All Men Brothers." *Life,* August 23, 1954.
Jarvis, C.S. "Flood Stage Records of the River Nile." *Transactions of the American Society of Civil Engineers,* Vol. 101, 1936.
Kennedy, M.E. "Radio for Flood Emergencies." *Engineering News-Record,* February 26, 1942.
Klein, H.C. "Flood Plain Zoning and Evacuation." *Quarterly of the National Fire Protection Association,* April, 1939.
Langbein, W.B. "Flood Insurance." *Journal of Land Economics,* November, 1953.
"Lessons Learned from Recent California Floods." *American City,* May, 1956.
MacKaye, Benton. "Democracy in Flood Control." *Survey-Graphic,* September, 1940.
Maycock, A.L. "A Note on the Black Death." *Nineteenth Century,* Vol. 47, 1925.
McMaster, John Bach. "The Johnstown Flood." *Pennsylvania Magazine of History and Biography,* Vol. 57, 1933.
Murphy, Virginia Reed. "Across the Plains in the Donner Party (1846)." *Contemporary Review,* October, 1890.
North, Arthur W. "The Cut-Off." *Sunset Magazine,* December, 1915.
"No Time for Gaiety." *Newsweek,* March 27, 1967.
"Ohio City Shrugs Off a Flood." *Life,* February 11, 1952.
Peterson, Elmer T. "Big Dam Foolishness." *Country Gentleman,* May, 1952.
"Rapid Recovery." *Newsweek,* June 26, 1972.
"Remarkable Story of the Sufferings and Experiences of the Historical Donner Party." *Grizzly Bear,* January, 1908.
Renouard, Y. "La Peste Noir." *Revue de Paris,* March, 1950.

Richardson, H.W. "Rehabilitation of the Ohio Valley." *Engineering News-Record,* March 11, 1937.

Robbins, H. "A Comparison of the Effects of the Black Death on the Economic Organization of France and England." *Journal of Political Economy,* Vol. 36, 1928.

"A Royal Fury." *Time,* November 18, 1966.

Russell, J.S. "Effects of Pestilence and Plague." *Comparative Studies in Society and History,* Vol. 7, 1966.

"The Sandbags Were Men." *Newsweek,* August 16, 1954.

Segoe, L. "Flood Control and the Cities." *American City,* March, 1937.

Shuler, E.W. "A Rise Down the Canyon." *Scientific Monthly,* August, 1930.

Simpich, Frederick. "Men Against the Rivers." *National Geographic,* Vol. 71, 1937.

Singh, Khushwant. "Waiting for the Monsoon." *New York Times Magazine,* August 26, 1973.

Stiles, William W. "How a Community Met a Disaster, Yuba City Flood, December, 1955." *Annals of the American Academy of Political and Social Science,* Vol. 309, 1957.

Stokes, Frank. "The Last Man Out." *Touring Topics,* February, 1929.

Sturges, Samuel Davis, Jr. "Floods." *Annals of the American Academy of Political and Social Science,* Vol. 309, 1957.

Thompson, J.W. "The Aftermath of the Black Death and the Aftermath of the Great War." *American Journal of Sociology,* Vol. 26, 1920-21.

Todd, Oliver J. "Taming 'Flood Dragons' Along China's Hwang Ho." *National Geographic,* Vol. 81, 1942.

Velen, Victor, and Velen, Elizabeth. "Florence: After the Flood." *Saturday Review,* December 24, 1966.

"Visitor to California." *Time,* January 9, 1956.

Waggoner, W.W. "The Donner Party and Relief Hill." *California Historical Society Quarterly,* December, 1931.

"The Wanton Waters." *Newsweek,* January 2, 1956.

Wedell, P.M. "Location of the Donner Family Camp." *California Historical Society Quarterly,* March, 1945.

Wolman, Abel. "Problems in Developing A National Flood Policy." *Transactions of the American Society of Civil Engineers,* Vol. 103, 1938.

Bulletins, Pamphlets, Papers, Reports

Clifford, Roy A. *The Rio Grande Flood.* Committee on Disaster Studies, Washington, 1956.

Edwards, W.F. *Donner Lake.* Truckee, Calif., 1883.

Emergency Flood Conditions. California Director of Public Works, 1940.

Final Report of the Special Committee on Floods and Flood Prevention. American Society of Civil Engineers, 1917.

Flood Damage and Flood Control Activities in Asia and the Far East. Bureau of Flood Control, United Nations, 1950.

The Flood Problem in Fire Prevention and Protection. National Board of Fire Underwriters, New York, 1939.

Jarvis, Clarence S. *Floods in the United States.* U.S. Geological Survey, Washington, 1936.

The Kansas City Flood and Fire of 1951. University of Oklahoma Research Institute, 1952.

Manual for Flood Recovery Program. Connecticut Flood Recovery Committee, Hartford, 1956.

The Ohio-Mississippi Valley Flood Disaster of 1937. American Red Cross, Washington, D.C., 1937.

Report on Flood Recovery Program to General Assembly. Connecticut Flood Recovery Program, Hartford, January, 1957.

Report on Floods and Flood Damage. Insurance Executives Association, New York, 1952.

Troxell, H.C., and Peterson, J. *Flood in La Canada Valley.* California, U.S. Geological Survey, 1937.

Water Resources Activities in the United States: Floods and Flood Control. U.S. Senate Report, Washington, 1960.

Earthquakes and Volcanoes

Books

Aitken, Frank, and Hilton, Edward. *A History of the Earthquake and Fire.* San Francisco: E. Hilton, 1906.

Andrews, Allen. *Earthquake.* London: Angus & Robertson, 1963.

Anonymous. *The Agadir, Morocco, Earthquake, February 29, 1960.* New York: American Iron and Steel Institute, 1962.

Anonymous. *The Riddle of the Earth.* New York: Brentano's, 1925.

Atherton, Gertrude (ed. by Erskine Caldwell). *Golden Gate Country.* New York: Duell, Sloane & Pearce, 1945.

Ball, Robert S. *The Earth's Beginnings.* New York: Appleton, 1902.

Baretti, Guiseppe Marco Antonio. *Journey from London to Genoa.* London: T. Davies, 1770.

Barns, Thomas A. *Across the Great Craterland to the Congo.* London: E. Benn, 1923.

Barrymore, John. *Confessions of an Actor.* London: Robert Holden, 1926.

Bean, Walton. *Bess Ruef's San Francisco.* London: Cambridge University Press, 1952.

Berg, Glen V., and Stratta, James L. *Anchorage and the Alaska Earthquake of March 27, 1964.* New York: American Iron and Steel Institute, 1964.

Bergamini, David, *Japan's Imperial Conspiracy.* New York: Morrow, 1971.

Berry, James. *The Earthquake of 1906.* San Francisco, 1907.

Bonney, Thomas G. *Volcanoes, Their Structure and Significance.* New York: Putnam, 1899.

Bowden, Arthur T. *Man's Physical Universe.* New York: Macmillan, 1943.

Bronson, William. *The Earth Shook, the Sky Burned.* New York: Doubleday, 1959.

Brown, Mrs. Hugh. *Lady in Boomtown.* Palo Alto, Calif.: American West, 1968.

Bullard, Fred M. *Volcanoes: In History, In Theory, In Eruption.* Austin: University of Texas Press, 1963.

Bullen, K.E. *Introduction to Theoretical Seismology.* Cambridge: Cambridge University Press, 1953.

Bureau of Social Affairs. *The Great Earthquake of 1923 in Japan.* Tokyo: Home Office, 1926.

Busch, Noel Fairchild. *Two Minutes to Noon.* New York: Simon & Schuster, 1963.

Byerly, G. *Seismology.* New York: Prentice-Hall, 1942.

Carnota, John Smith Athelstane. *The Marquis of Pombal.* London: Longmans, Green, Reader and Dyer, 1871.

Carrington, R.C. *Pompeii.* Oxford, England: Clarendon Press, 1936.

Caruso, Dorothy. *Enrico Caruso. His Life and Death.* London: J. Werner Laurie, 1946.

Chapin, Henry, and Smith, F.G.W. *The Ocean River.* Philadelphia: Saunders, 1953.

Chauncy, Charles. *Earthquakes in Spain and Portugal as Well as in New England.* Boston: Edes & Gill, 1756.

Cheke, Marcus. *Dictator of Portugal.* London: Sidgwick & Jackson, 1938.

Cleland, Robert Glass. *A History of California.* New York: Macmillan, 1923.

Coleman, Satis N. *Volcanoes New and Old.* New York: John Day, 1946.

Correspondence Relating to the Volcanic Eruptions in St. Vincent and Martinique in May, 1902. London: Parliament, 1902.

Cotton, C.A. *Volcanoes as Landscape Forms.* Christchurch, New Zealand: Whitcombe and Tombs, 1944.

———. *The Earth Beneath.* Christchurch, New Zealand: Whitcombe and Tombs, 1945.

Cressy, George B. *Asia's Land and Peoples.* New York: McGraw-Hill, 1944.

Cromie, William J. *Exploring the Secrets of the Sea.* Englewood Cliffs: Prentice-Hall, 1962.

Daly, Reginald Alworth. *Our Mobile Earth.* New York: Scribners, 1926.

Dana, J.D. *Characteristics of Volcanoes.* New York: Dodd, Mead, 1890.

Darwin, Charles. *Geological Observations.* New York: Appleton, 1896.

———. *Journal of Researches.* New York: Appleton, 1896.

Davison, Charles. *A Manual of Seismology.* Cambridge: Cambridge University Press, 1921.

———. *A History of British Earthquakes.* Cambridge: Cambridge University Press, 1924.

———. *The Founders of Seismology.* Cambridge: Cambridge University Press, 1927.

———. *The Japanese Earthquake of 1923.* London: Thomas Murby, 1936.

———. *Great Earthquakes.* London: Thomas Murby, 1936.

Day, Arthur L. *Some Causes of Volcanic Activity.* Washington: Franklin Institute, 1924.

Dickelmann, William. *San Francisco Earthquake and Fire, April 18, 1906.* San Francisco: N.p., 1906.

Dutton, C.E. *Earthquakes.* London: John Murray, 1906.

Eiby, G.A. *About Earthquakes.* New York: Harper, 1957.

Engle, Eloise. *Earthquake!* New York: John Day, 1966.

English, G.L., and Jensen, D.E. *Getting Acquainted with Minerals.* New York: McGraw-Hill, 1958.

Erskine, Wilson. *Katmai.* New York: Abelard-Schuman, 1962.

Fenton, Carroll Lane. *Our Amazing Earth.* New York: Doubleday, Doran, 1938.

———. *Earth's Adventures.* New York: John Day, 1942.

Fenton, C.L., and Fenton, M.A. *The Rock Book.* New York: Doubleday, Doran, 1940.

———. *Mountains.* New York: Doubleday, Doran, 1942.

Frazer, J.G. *Pausanias' Description of Greece.* London: Macmillan, 1897.

Freeman, John R. *Earthquake Damage and Earthquake Insurance.* New York: McGraw-Hill, 1932.

Froude, James Anthony. *Oceana, or England and Her Colonies.* New York: Scribners, 1886.

Fuller, Myron L. *The New Madrid Earthquake.* Washington: U.S. Geological Survey, 1912.

Funston, Frederick. *Memories of Two Wars.* London: Constable, 1912.

Furneaux, Rupert. *Krakatoa.* Englewood Cliffs: Prentice-Hall, 1964.

Garesche, William A. *Complete Story of the Martinique and St. Vincent Horrors.* New York: L.G. Stahl, 1902.

Geike, Archibald. *Ancient Volcanoes of Great Britain* (2 vols.). London: Macmillan, 1897.

Genthe, Arnold. *As I Remember.* New York: Reynal & Hitchock, 1936.

———, and Irwin, Will. *Pictures of Old Chinatown.* New York: Moffat, Yard, 1909.

Gentry, Curt. *The Last Days of the Late, Great State of California.* New York: Putnam, 1969.

Gillis, Mabel R. *California: A Guide to the Golden State.* New York: Hastings House, 1939.

Glassock, C.B. *The Big Bonanza.* Indianapolis: Bobbs-Merrill, 1931.

Greely, Adolphus W. *Earthquake in California, April 18, 1906.* Washington: U.S. Government Printing Office, 1906.

Gregory, John Walter. *Earthquakes and Volcanoes.* London: Benn, 1929.

Gutenberg, B., and Richter, C.F. *On Seismic Waves.* Leipzig: Gerlands Beitrage zur Geophysik, 1934-36.

———. *Seismicity of the Earth and Associated Phenomena.* Princeton: Princeton University Press, 1949.

———. *The Internal Constitution of the Earth.* New York: Dover, 1951.

Hale, George W. *Earthquakes: Their Origin and Phenomena.* Deadwood, S.D.: n.p., 1902.

Hall, Maxwell. *Notes on Hurricanes, Earthquakes.* Kingston, Jamaica: Jamaica Meteorological Service, 1916.

———. *Earthquakes in Jamaica from 1688 to 1919.* Jamaica: Jamaica Meteorological Service, 1922.

Heck, Nicholas Hunter. *Earthquakes.* Princeton: Princeton University Press, 1936.

Heilprin, Angelo. *Mont Pelee and the Tragedy of Martinique.* Philadelphia: Lippincott, 1903.

———. *The Tower of Pelee.* Philadelphia: Lippincott, 1904.

Heintze, Carl. *The Circle of Fire, The Great Chain of Volcanoes and Earth Faults.* New York: Meredith, 1968.

Henry, Neil (pseudonym for Marshall Everett). *Complete Story of the San Francisco Earthquake.* Chicago: Bible House, 1906.

Herbert, Don, and Bardossi, Fulvio. *Kilauea: Case History of a Volcano.* New York: Harper & Row, 1968.

Hewitt, R. *From Earthquake, Fire and Flood.* New York: Scribners, 1957.

Hill, M.N. (ed.). *The Sea.* New York: Interscience, 1962.

Himmelwright, A.L.A. *The San Francisco Earthquake and Fire, 1906.* New York: Roebling Construction Company, 1906.

Hittel, John S. *A History of the City of San Francisco.* San Francisco: H.L. Bancroft, 1878.

Hittel, Theodore H. *History of California.* San Francisco: N.J. Stone, 1898.

Hobbs, William H. *Earthquakes, An Introduction to Seismic Geology.* New York: Appleton, 1907.

Hodgson, E.A. *Bibliography of Seismology.* Ottawa: Dominion Observatory, 1929.

Hodgson, John H. *Earthquakes and Earth Structure.* Englewood Cliffs: Prentice-Hall, 1964.

Hoffman, Frederick L. *Earthquake Hazards and Insurance.* New York: Spectator, 1928.

Holmes, Arthur. *Principles of Physical Geology.* London: Nelson, 1965.

Houston, Edwin J. *Wonder Book of Volcanoes and Earthquakes.* New York: Frederick A. Stokes, 1907.

Hulley, Clarence C. *Alaska, Past and Present.* Portland, Oregon: Binfords & Mort, 1970.

Hutton, F.W. *Tarawera Volcanic District.* Wellington, New Zealand: Government Printer, 1887.

Iacopi, Robert. *Earthquake Country.* Menlo Park, Calif.: Lane, 1964.

Imamura, Akitune. *Theoretical and Applied Seismology.* Tokyo: Maruzen, 1937.

Irving, Robert. *Volcanoes and Earthquakes.* New York: Knopf, 1962.

Jackson, Robert. *Thirty Seconds at Quetta: The Story of an Earthquake.* London: Evans, 1960.

Jaggar, T.A. *Volcanoes Declare War.* Honolulu, Hawaii: Paradise of the Pacific, 1945.

James, Marquis, and James, Bessie R. *Biography of a Bank.* New York: Harper, 1954.

Jeffreys, Harold. *Earthquakes and Mountains.* London: Methuen, 1950.

———. *The Earth.* Cambridge: Cambridge University Press, 1952.

Johnson, Gaylord. *Story of Earthquakes and Volcanoes.* New York: Julian Messner, 1938.

Johnson, George R. *Peru from the Air.* New York: American Geographical Society, 1930.

Jones, Horace L. *The Geography of Strabo.* New York: Putnam, 1927.

Jordan, David Starr (ed.). *The California Earthquake of 1906.* San Francisco: A. M. Robertson, 1906.

Judd, J.W. *Volcanoes.* London: Kegan Paul, 1893.

Keeler, Charles A. *San Francisco Through Earthquake and Fire.* San Francisco: P. Elder, 1906.

Keene, Sir Benjamin. *Private Correspondence.* Cambridge, England: The University Press, 1933.

Kendrick, Thomas D. *The Lisbon Earthquake.* London: Methuen, 1955.

Kennan, George. *The Tragedy of Pelee.* New York: Outlook, 1902.

Kennedy, John Castillo. *The Great Earthquake and Fire, San Francisco, 1906.* New York: Morrow, 1963.

Key, Pierre V.R. *Enrico Caruso: A Biography.* Boston: Little, Brown, 1922.

Kingdon-Ward, Jean. *My Hill So Strong.* London: Cape, 1952.

Knott, C.F. *The Physics of Earthquake Phenomena.* London: Clarendon, 1908.

Kraus, George. *High Road to Promontory.* Palo Alto, California: American West, 1969.

Lacroix, A. *La Montagne Pelee.* Paris: Mason, 1904.

Lafler, Henry A. *How the Army Worked to Save San Francisco.* San Francisco: Calkins Newspaper Syndicate, 1906.

Langley, Henry G. *The San Francisco Director.* San Francisco: Published by author, 1906.

Lawson, Andrew. *The California Earthquake of April 18, 1906* (2 vols.). Washington, D.C.: Carnegie Institute, 1969.

Leet, Lewis Don. *Practical Seismology and Seismic Prospecting.* New York: Appleton-Century, 1938.

———. *Earth Waves.* Boston: Harvard University Press, 1950.

———, and Leet, Florence. *Earthquakes: Discoveries in Seismology.* New York: Dell, 1964.

Ley, Willy. *Days of Creation.* New York: Viking, 1941.

Linthicum, Richard. *Complete Story of the San Francisco Horror.* Chicago: Trumbull White, 1906.

Livingstone, Alexander P. *Complete Story of San Francisco's Terrible Calamity.* San Francisco: Continental, 1907.

Longwell, Knopf, and Flint. *Outlines of Physical Geology.* New York: Wiley, 1941.

Lucretius. *On the Nature of the Universe.*

Lyell, Charles. *Principles of Geology* (2 vols.). London: John Murray, 1875.

Lynch, Joseph. *Our Trembling Earth.* New York: Dodd, Mead, 1940.

Macaulay, Rose. *They Went to Portugal.* London: J. Cape, 1946.

Macelwane, J.B. *When the Earth Quakes.* Milwaukee: Bruce, 1947.

Mackay, Margaret. *Angry Island: The Story of Tristan da Cunha, 1506-1603.* Chicago: Rand McNally, 1964.

Mallet, Robert. *Great Neopolitan Earthquake of 1857.* London: Chapman and Hall, 1862.

Marcus, Rebecca B. *The First Book of Volcanoes and Earthquakes.* New York: Franklin Watts, 1963.

Mather, Cotton. *Earthquakes in England.* Boston: T. Fleet, 1727.

Mather, Increase. *A Discourse Concerning Earthquakes in New England.* Boston: Printed by Timothy Green for Benjamin Eliot, 1706.

Matuzawa, Takeo. *Study of Earthquakes.* Tokyo: Uno Shoten, 1964.

Menard, Henry W. *Marine Geology of the Pacific.* New York: McGraw-Hill, 1964.

Milne, John. *Earthquakes and Other Movements.* Philadelphia: P. Blakiston's, 1939.

Milne, Lorus J., and Milne, Margery. *The Mountains.* New York: Time, 1962.

Morris, Charles. *The Volcano's Deadly Work.* New York: W.E. Scull, 1902.

Mowbray, Jay Henry. *Italy's Great Horror of Earthquake and Tidal Wave.* New York: G.W. Berton, 1909.

Niddrie, David. *When the Earth Shook.* New York: Devin-Adair, 1962.

Noe-Nygaard, Arne. *Sub-Glacial Volcanic Activity in Ancient and Recent Times* (trans. by W.E. Calvert). Copenhagen: Hagerups Forlag, 1940.

Noyes, Isaac P. *The Problem of the Tides and the Problem of the Earthquakes.* Washington: Published by the author, 1906.

Ollier, Cliff. *Volcanoes.* Cambridge, Mass.: MIT Press, 1969.

Padang, Maur Neumann van. *Catalogue of the Active Volcanoes of Indonesia.* Naples, Italy: International Volcanological Association, 1951.

Paul, William, and Warschauer, Douglas M. *Solids under Pressure.* New York: McGraw-Hill, 1963.

Perret. Frank A. *The Vesuvius Eruption of 1906, Study of a Volcanic Cycle.* Washington, D.C.: Carnegie Institution, 1924.

———. *The Eruption of Mt. Pelee.* Washington, D.C.: Carnegie Institution, 1935.

Pliny the Younger. *Letters.*

Poole, Lynn, and Poole, Gray. *Volcanoes in Action: Science and Legend.* New York: McGraw-Hill, 1962.

Pough, Frederick H. *All About Volcanoes and Earthquakes.* New York: Random House, 1953.

Prescott, William H. *History of the Conquest of Mexico.* New York: Modern Library, n.d.

Richter, Charles F. *Elementary Seismology.* San Francisco: W.H. Freeman, 1958.

Rink, Paul. *A.P. Giannini.* Encyclopedia Britannica, 1963.

Rittman, Alfred. *Volcanoes and Their Activity.* New York: Wiley, 1962.

Roberts, Elliott. *Volcanoes and Earthquakes.* New York: Pyramid, 1967.

Rodriguez, Mary Louis Bine. *The Earthquake of 1906.* San Francisco: n.p., 1951.

Rusk, C.E. *Tales of a Western Mountaineer.* Boston: Houghton-Mifflin, 1924.

Russell, Israel C. *Volcanoes of North America.* New York: Macmillan, 1897.

Sapper, K. *Vulkankunde.* Stuttgart, Germany: Engelhorn, 1927.

Scheidegger, A.E. *Principles of Geodynamics.* Berlin: Springer Verlag, 1958.

Searight, Frank T. *The Doomed City.* Chicago: Laird & Lee, 1906.

Searle, E.J. *City of Volcanoes.* Auckland, New Zealand: Paul, 1964.

Shand, Samuel James. *Eruptive Rocks.* New York: Wiley, 1947.

Shephard, Francis P. *Submarine Geology.* New York: Harper, 1963.

———. *The Earth Beneath the Sea.* Baltimore: Johns Hopkins Press, 1967.

Soley, John C. *Sources of Volcanic Energy.* New York: Putnam, 1924.

Squier, E.G. *The Volcanoes of Central America and the Geographical and Topographical Features of Nicaragua, as Connected with the Proposed Inter-Oceanic Canal.* New York: Published by the author, 1850.

Steinbrugge, Karl V. *Earthquake Hazard in the San Francisco Bay Area.* Berkeley: Institute of Governmental Studies, University of California, 1968.

Stetson, James B. *San Francisco During the Eventful Days of 1906*. San Francisco: Murdock, 1906.
Sutherland, Monica. *The San Francisco Disaster*. London: Barrie & Rockliffe, 1959.
Swanberg, W.A. *Citizen Hearst*. New York: Scribners, 1961.
Tazieff, Haroum. *The Orion Book of Volcanoes*. New York: Orion, 1961.
———. *Volcanoes*. London: Prentice-Hall, 1962.
———. *When the Earth Trembles*. New York: Harcourt, Brace & World, 1964.
Thomas, Gordon, and Witts, Max Morgan. *The San Francisco Earthquake*. New York: Stein and Day, 1971.
Thorarinsson, Sigurdur, *Hekla on Fire*. Munich: Hanns Reich, 1956.
———. *Surtsey: The New Island in the North Atlantic*. New York: Viking, 1967.
Todd, Frank Morton. *Eradicating Plague from San Francisco*. San Francisco: C.H.C., 1909.
Tsuboi, C., and others. *Prediction of Earthquakes*. Tokyo: University of Tokyo, 1962.
Tyler, Sidney. *San Francisco's Great Disaster*. Philadelphia: P.W. Zeigler, 1906.
Tyrell, George W. *Volcanoes*. New York: Holt, 1931.
Verbeek, R.O.M. *Krakatoa*. Batavia: n.p., 1886.
Voltaire. *Poems-The Lisbon Earthquake*. Paris, London: E.R. DuMont, 1901.
Walker, G.W. *Modern Seismology*. London: Longmans, Green, 1913.
Weatherred, Edith Tozier. *San Francisco on the Night of April 18, 1906*. San Francisco: Bachrach, 1906.
White, Trumbull, and Linthicum, Richard. *Complete Story of the San Francisco Horror*. Chicago: Hubert D. Russell, 1906.
Wilcoxson, Kent. *Chains of Fire: The Story of Volcanoes*. Philadelphia: Chilton, 1966.
———. *Volcanoes*. London: Cassell, 1967.
Williams, Howel. *Crater Lake: The Story of Its Origin*. Berkeley: University of California Press, 1941.
Wilson, James Russel. *San Francisco's Horror of Earthquake and Fire*. Philadelphia: National, 1906.
Wright, Frank Lloyd. *An Autobiography*. New York: Longmans, 1932.
Wurtzburg, Charles Edward. *Raffles of the Eastern Isles*. Toronto: Musson, 1954.
Ybarra, T.R. *Caruso*. London: Crescent, 1954.
Young, John P. *San Francisco: A History* (Vol. II). Chicago: J.J. Clarke, 1928.
Yun, Leong Gor. *Chinatown Inside Out*. New York: Barrows Mussey, 1936.

Periodicals

"The Agony of Agadir, a City Shaken to Death." *Life*, March 14, 1960.
Alter, D. "Possible Connection Between Sunspots and Earthquakes." *Science*, May 14, 1920.
"Among the Craters of the Moon." *National Geographic*, March, 1924.
"Asking for Calm." *Time*, July 4, 1960.
"Back to the Scene of Ordeal." *Life*, July 11, 1960.
Billings, L.G. "Personal Experiences With Earthquakes." *National Geographic*, January, 1915.
Bird, Roland T. "Recording Earthquakes." *Natural History*, Vol. 52, 1943.
Blanchard, D.C. "Volcanic Electricity." *Oceanus*, November, 1966.
Boesen, Victor Hugo. "America's Greatest Earthquake." *Coronet*, September, 1941.
Boone, Andrew R. "Scientists Unite on Greatest War on Earthquakes." *Popular Science*, May, 1933.
Bowie, W. "Causes and Predictions of Earthquakes." *Science*, April 10, 1925.
Boxer, C.R. "Pombal's Dictatorship and the Great Lisbon Earthquake." *History Today*, November, 1955.
Branner, John C. "Structural Engineering and Earthquakes." *Engineering Record*, December 25, 1915.
Byerly, P. "Earthquake Mechanisms." *Science*, Vol. 131.
"Causes of Earthquakes." *Science*, July 10, 1925.
"The Causes of the Kingston Earthquake." *Outlook*, January 26, 1907.
Chase, Thomas. "An Account of the Lisbon Earthquake." *Gentleman's Magazine*, Vol. 83, 1813.
"Chile's Land of Fire and Water." *National Geographic*, July, 1941.
"Chile's Quake." *Newsweek*, February 6, 1939.
Cloud, Wallace. "The Next Big Quake . . . Where Will It Hit?" *Popular Science*, June, 1964.
Coleton, F. Burrows. "Our Home-town Planet Earth." *National Geographic*, Vol. 101, 1952.
"Counting the Dead." *Time*, April 24, 1972.
Crosby, Irving B. "The Earthquake Risk in Boston." *Journal of the Boston Society of Civil Engineers*, 1923.
Davison, Charles. "The Kingston Earthquake." *Nature*, January 24, 1907.
"The Dead City." *Time*, March 14, 1960.
"The Deadly Earth." *Newsweek*, May 30, 1960.
"Death in the Andes." *Time*, August 15, 1949.
Dewell, Henry D. "Earthquake Expectancy in California." *Engineering News Record*, January 21, 1926.
Digby, C.H. "How Japan is Facing the Calamity." *Asiatic Review*, October 1923.
"Disaster in the Andes." *Newsweek*, August 15, 1949.
"Disaster Strikes Ecuador." *Life*, August 22, 1949.
Eaton, Jerry P., and Murata, K.T. "How Volcanoes Grow." *Science*, October 7, 1960.
"Earthquake Dangers in the United States." *Scientific American*, September 25, 1915.
"Earthquake in Chile." *Bulletin of the Pan American Union*, March, 1939.
"The Earthquake in Europe." *Harper's Weekly*, March 5, 1887.
"The Earthquake on the Riviera." *Frank Leslie's Illustrated Newspaper*, March 5, 1887.
"The Earth Shook." *Newsweek*, August 28, 1950.
"Earthquakes." *Natural History*, Vol. 23, 1923.
"Effects of the Earthquake in Chile." *Missionary Review of the World*, April, 1939.
Fay, George T. "The Big Breakup." *FAA Horizons*, May, 1964.
"From Sea to Clouds in Ecuador." *National Geographic*, December, 1941.
"Fury of the Quake—200,000 Megatons." *Life*, April 10, 1964.
"Geography of Japan." *National Geographic*, July, 1921.
"God Speaks, Assam Shakes." *Life*, October 2, 1950.
"The Gods Speak." *Newsweek*, March 29, 1963.
Graves, William P.E. "Horror Strikes on Good Friday." *National Geographic*, July, 1964.
Gruening, Ernest, and Parks, Winfield. "Lonely Wonders of Katmzi, Alaska." *National Geographic*, June, 1963.
Hedworth, W.A. "Exploiting the Volcano." *Chamber's Journal*, May, 1936.
Heilprin, Angelo. "The Shattered Obelisk of Mount Pelee." *National Geographic*, Vol. 17, 1906.
"Hills That Walked." *National Geographic*, May, 1922.
Hovey, Edmund Otis. "The Eruption of La Sonfriere, St. Vincent, in May, 1902." *National Geographic*, Vol. 13, 1902.
Jagger, T.A. "Sakurajima, Japan's Greatest Volcanic Eruption." *National Geographic*, April, 1924.
"Japanese Gratitude." *Outlook*, December 5, 1923.
"The Kangra Earthquake of April 4, 1905." *Nature*, March 1, 1906.
Kingdon-Ward, F. "Notes on the Assam Earthquake." *Nature*, Vol. 167, 1951.
———. "Caught in the Assam-Tibet Earthquake." *National Geographic*, Vol. 101, 1952.
"The Kingston Earthquake." *Nature*, January 24, 1907.
Kithil, Karl L. "Prospecting by the Earth Wave Travel Method." *Engineering and Mining Journal*, December 11, 1926.
Koster, A.L. "City of the Dead." *Natural History*, Vol. 65, 1956.
Lear, John. "Our Trembling Earth." *Saturday Review*, May 2, 1964.
———. "Surtsey-Child of an Expanding Earth?" *Saturday Review*, July 3, 1965.
Lewis, Howard L. "Life Comes to a New Land." *Nature and Science*, December 6, 1965.
Lindner, Richard Clarence. "The Greatest Catastrophe in History." *Frank Leslie's Illustrated Newspaper*, January 14, 1909.
Maiuri, Armando, Bianchi, Peter V., and Battaglia, Lee E. "Last Moments of the Pompeians." *National Geographic*, November, 1961.
Martin, G.C. "The Katmai Eruption." *National Geographic*, February, 1913.
Martin, Sue, as told to Burgess, Alan. "The Night the World Fell Down." *Reader's Digest*, August, 1963.
Mathews, Samuel W. "The Night the Mountains Moved." *National Geographic*, Vol. 117, 1960.
Matthews, L.H. "The Fayal Earthquake." *Stone & Webster Journal*, October, 1926.
Miller, Maynard M. "What Causes Earthquakes." *National Geographic*, July, 1964.
"The Mystery of Earthquakes." *U.S. News and World Report*, April 13, 1964.
"Nicaragua, a Land of Lakes and Volcanoes." *National Geographic*, August, 1944.
"The Night the Earth Went Wild." *Time*, September 14, 1962.
Oldham, R.D. "The Character and Cause of Earthquakes." *Nature*, March 31, 1923.
———. "The Depth and Twofold Character of Earthquake Origin." *Journal of Geology*, July-August, 1926.
Ol Oliver, Jack. "Long Earthquake Waves." *Scientific American*, Vol. 200, 1959.
"On the Shore of a Ruined City." *Outlook*, October 3, 1923.
Paige, S. "Earthquakes." *Science Monthly*, January, 1925.
Parsons, Willard Hall. "Volcanoes in the Making." *Science Digest*, July, 1940.
Perret, Frank. "What to Expect of a Volcano." *Natural History*, Vol. 39, 1937.
Pratt, W.E. "Eruption of Taal Volcano." *Science Journal*, April, 1911.
Press, Frank. "Volcanoes, Ice and Destructive Waves." *Engineering and Science*, November, 1956.
"Quaking Death in Ecuador." *Reader's Digest*, November, 1949.
"Radioactivity and Earthquakes." *Science*, July 31, 1925.
Raffles, Sir Stamford. "Eruption of Tomboro." *Asiatic Journal* (p. 342), 1816.
Reeds, Chester A. "The Japanese Earthquake Explained." *Natural History*, Vol. 23, 1923.
———. "Volcanoes in Action." *Natural History*, Vol. 28, 1928.
"The Relation of Seismic Disturbances in the Philippines to the Geologic Structure." *Philippine Journal of Science*, August, 1913.
Richards, Adrian F., and Walker, Lewis Wayne. "Operation Cremation: A Personal Account of the Dramatic First Landing on a New Volcano." *Natural History*, Vol. 63, 1954.

"The Riviera Earthquake." *Harper's Weekly,* March 12, 1887.
Rockwood, Charles G. "Notice of Recent American Earthquakes." *American Journal of Science,* March, 1881.
Russell, I.C. "The Recent Volcanic Eruptions in the West Indies." *National Geographic,* Vol. 13, 1902.
———. "Volcanic Eruptions on Martinique and St. Vincent." *National Geographic,* Vol. 13, 1902.
Sanders, Donald. "Volcanic Islands." *Science World,* March 24, 1965.
Schmidt, Ruth A.M. "Geology in a Hurry." *Geotimes,* October, 1964.
Shamblin, A. Kent. "Task Force on the Move." *Journal of Insurance Information,* July-August, 1964.
Simpich, Frederick, Jr. "Fountain of Fire in Hawaii." *National Geographic,* March, 1960.
Smith, Myles W. "In the Wake of the Quake." *Journal of Insurance Information,* July-August, 1964.
Stocking, Hobart E. "The Greatest Explosion of All Time." *Natural History,* Vol. 51, 1943.
"Stricken Japan." *Outlook,* September 19, 1923.
Sullivan, Walter. "Why Volcanoes Explode." *New York Times Magazine,* March 13, 1966.
Takashashi, Taro, and Bassett, William A. "The Composition of the Earth's Interior." *Scientific American,* Vol. 212, 1965.
"The 10,000-Mile Disaster." *Time,* June 6, 1960.
Thomas, Mrs. Lowell, Jr. "An Alaskan Family's Ordeal." *National Geographic,* July, 1964.
Thomas, Mitchell. "The Routine . . . Is Only the Beginning." *Journal of Insurance Information,* July-August, 1964.
"Tide of Trees & Tigers." *Time,* September 4, 1962.
Tillotson, Ernest. "Earthquakes." *Geographic Magazine* (London), October, 1940.
———. "The Great Assam Earthquake of August 15, 1950." *Nature,* Vol. 167, 1951.
Torndorf, Francis A. "Guesswork of Science." *Scientific American,* August, 1926.
———. "A Symposium on Earthquakes." *Journal of the Washington Academy of Sciences,* May 4, 1926.
"Undersea Earthquake." *Senior Scholastic,* April 22, 1946.
"Wake in the Quake." *Newsweek,* August 22, 1949.
Wellington, George. "Earthquake!" *Chamber's Journal,* February, 1933.
Wexler, Harry. "Volcanoes and World Climate." *Scientific American,* April, 1952.
Winchester, James H. "When the Earthquake Struck Chile." *Reader's Digest,* December, 1960.
"The World Screamed." *Newsweek,* September 17, 1962.
"Worst Shake." *Time,* February 6, 1939.
Zoeller, Lawrence. "The Big Shake." *National Guardsman,* May, 1964.

Bulletins, Pamphlets, Reports, Studies

The Alaskan Earthquake. Office of Civil Defense Office, Secretary of the Army, 1964.
Alaska's Good Friday Earthquake. A Preliminary Geologic Evaluation. U.S. Department of the Interior, 1964.
"Americans Can Be Proud." *Congressional Record,* September 30, 1964.
American Institute of Architects and Engineers Joint Council Report of the Restoration and Development of Alaska. Federal Reconstruction and Development Planning Commission of Alaska, 1964.
Annual Reports of Advisory Committee in Seismology. Carnegie Institute, Washington, D.C., 1921-26.
Bulletin of the Seismological Society of America, Stanford University of California. (Vols. 1-17, ending with June, 1927).
Bulletin of the Seismological Society of America. Vol. 12, No. 4, December, 1922.
The California Earthquake of April 18, 1906. Carnegie Institution, Washington, D.C., 1908-1910.
Can Science Diminish Earthquake Danger? Bulletin of the Pan American Union, February, 1923.
Catalogue of the Active Volcanoes of the World. Naples, Italy, International Volcanological Association, 1951.
Day, Arthur L. *Some Causes of Volcanic Activity.* Smithsonian Institute (Publication No. 2845), Washington, D.C., 1926.
"The Earthquake in Alaska." *Congressional Record,* March 30, 1964.
Earthquake Studies. Commonwealth Club of California, San Francisco, September, 1925.
Hobbs, W.H. *The Cause of Earthquakes, Especially Those of Eastern United States.* Smithsonian Institute (Publication No. 2889), Washington, D.C., 1927.
Impact of Earthquake of March 27, 1964, Upon the Economy of Alaska. Office of Emergency Planning. Executive Office of the President, 1964.
Judd, J.W. *Eruption of Krakatoa.* Report to the Krakatoa Commission, Royal Society, London, 1888.
Milne, J. *Catalogue of Destructive Earthquakes.* London: British Association, 1911.
Operation Helping Hand, the Armed Forces React to Earthquake Disaster. Headquarters, Alaskan Command, U.S. Army, 1964.
Preliminary Report, Prince William Sound, Alaskan Earthquakes, March-April, 1964. Seismology Division, Coast & Geodatic Survey, 1964.
"Rebuilding of the Alaska Railroad." *Congressional Record,* September 23, 1964.
Reid, Harry Fielding, *The Lisbon Earthquake of November 1, 1755.* Bulletin IV, No. 2, June, 1914, Seismological Society of America.
Response to Disaster. Federal Reconstruction and Development Planning Commission for Alaska, 1964.
Scrase, F.J. *The Reflected Waves from Deep-focus Earthquakes.* London: Royal Society Proceedings, 1931.
Turner, H.H. *On the Four-Year Period in Earthquakes.* Royal Astronomical Society, December, 1925.
Volcanoes in the United States. U.S. Geological Survey, Government Printing Office, Washington, D.C., 1965.
Vulcanology. Bulletin No. 77, National Research Council. Stokes, W.L., and Varnes, D.J., *Glossary of Selected Geological Terms.* Colorado Scientific Society Proceedings, Vol. 16, 1955, Denver, Colo.
Walford, A.R. *The British Community in Lisbon, circa 1775.* Historical Association, 10th Annual Report, 1946-50.

Fires, Explosions & Mine Disasters

Books

Aitken, Frank W., and Hilton, Edward. *A History of the Earthquake and Fire in San Francisco.* San Francisco: Edward Hilton, 1906.
Andrews, Ralph W. *Historic Fires of the West, 1865-1915.* New York: Bonanza, 1966.
Angle, Paul M. *The Great Chicago Fire.* Chicago: Chicago Historical Society, 1946.
Asbury, Herbert. *Gem of the Prairie.* New York: Knopf, 1940.
———. *Ye Old Fire Laddies.* New York: Knopf, 1930.
Beebe, Lucius. *Boston and the Boston Legend.* New York: Appleton-Century, 1936.
Blatchford, E.W. *Memories of the Chicago Fire.* Chicago: Privately printed by Mr. & Mrs. Paul Blatchford, 1921.
Bradna, Fred. *The Big Top.* New York: Simon & Schuster, 1952.
Brayley, Arthur Wellington. *A Complete History of the Boston Fire Department, Including the Fire Alarm Service and the Protective Department from 1630 to 1888.* Boston: J.P. Dole, 1889.
Bronson, William. *The Earth Shook, the Sky Burned.* New York: Doubleday, 1959.
Coffin, Charles Carleton. *Story of the Great Fire: Boston Nov. 9-10, 1872, by Carleton, an Eye Witness.* Boston: Shepard and Gill, 1872.
Colbert, Elias, and Chamberlain, R. *Chicago and the Great Conflagration.* New York: n.p., 1871.
Colonial Laws of Massachusetts, Reprinted from Edition of 1672 with Supplements Through 1686. Published by Order of the City Council of Boston, 1887.
Conwell, Col. Russell H. *History of the Great Fire in Boston, Nov. 9 and 10, 1872.* Boston: B.B. Russell, 1873.
Court, Alfred. *My Life with the Big Cats.* New York: Simon & Schuster, 1955.
Critchell, R.S. *Recollections of a Fire Insurance Man.* Chicago: n.p., 1909.
Cromie, Robert. *The Great Chicago Fire.* New York: McGraw-Hill, 1959.
Dana, D.D. *The Fireman.* Boston: E.O. Libby, 1858.
Davis, Kenneth P. *Forest Fire; Control and Use.* New York: McGraw-Hill, 1959.
Dineen, Michal P. (ed.). *Great Fires of America.* Waukesha, Wisc.: Country Beautiful, 1973.
Dougherty, Thomas F., and Kearney, Paul W. *Fire.* New York: Putnam, 1931.
Duckham, Helen, and Duckham, Baron. *Great Pit Disasters.* Newton Abbot, England: David & Charles, 1973.
Ennis, John. *The Great Bombay Explosion.* New York: Duell, Sloan and Pearce, 1959.
Farr, Finis. *Chicago.* New Rochelle, N.Y.: Arlington House, 1973.
Goodspeed, Rev. E.J. *History of the Great Fires in Chicago and the West.* Chicago: n.p., n.d.
Graham, Jory. *Chicago.* Chicago: Rand McNally, 1968.
Greeley, W.B. *Forests and Men.* New York: Doubleday, 1951.
Guthrie, John D. *Great Forest Fires of America.* Washington: U.S. Dept. of Agriculture, 1970.
Harlow, Alvin T. *The Ringlings.* New York: Julian Messner, 1951.
Haywood, Charles F. *General Alarm.* New York: Dodd, Mead, 1967.
Hill, Charles T. *Fighting a Fire.* New York: Century, 1916.
Himmelwright, A.L.A. *San Francisco Earthquake and Fire.* New York: Roebling Construction Co., 1906.
Hirsch, Phil (ed.). *Fires.* New York: Pyramid, 1971.
Holzman, Robert S. *The Romance of Firefighting.* New York: Harper, 1956.
Hoyt, Edwin P. *The Guggenheims and the American Dream.* New York: Funk & Wagnalls, 1967.
Humphrey, H.B. *Historical Summary of Coal Mine Explosions in the United States, 1810-1958.* Washington, D.C.: U.S. Government Printing Office, 1960.
Jones, Arthur B. *Salem Fire.* Boston: Gorham Press, 1914.
Kenlon, Chief John. *Fires and Fire-Fighters: A History of Modern Firefighting with a Review of Its Development from Earliest Times.* New York: George H. Doran, 1913.
Kennedy, John C. *Great Earthquake and Fire.* New York: Morrow, 1963.
Kernan, J. Frank. *Reminiscences of the Old Fire Laddies and Volunteer Fire Departments of New York and Brooklyn.* New York: M. Crane, 1885.
Kirkland, Mayor Joseph. *Story of Chicago.* Chicago: Dibble, 1892.

——. *History of Chicago.* Chicago: Munsell, 1895.
Kogan, Herman, and Cromie, Robert. *The Great Fire, Chicago, 1871.* New York: Putnam, 1971.
Letters Written by a Gentleman in Boston to His Friend in Paris Describing the Great Fire. with Introductory Chapter and Notes by Harold Murdock. Boston: Houghton, 1909.
Lewis, Lloyd, and Smith, Henry Justin. *Chicago, the History of Its Reputation.* New York: Harcourt, Brace, 1929.
Lucas, Rex A. *Men in Crisis.* New York: Basic Books, 1969.
Marshall, Logan. *The True Story of Our National Calamity of Flood, Fire and Tornado.* Chicago: L.T. Myers, 1913.
Massachusetts Charitable Fire Society. *An Old Boston Institution; A Brief History, Organized 1872.* Boston: Little, 1893.
Masters, Robert V. *Going to Blazes.* New York: Sterling Publishing, 1950.
McCarthy, Chief John J. *The Science of Fighting Fire.* New York: W.W. Norton, 1943.
McCurdy, D.B. *Chicago's Awful Theater Horror.* Chicago: Memorial, 1904.
McIlvaine, Mabel. *Reminiscences of Chicago During the Great Fire.* Chicago: Lakeside Press, n.d.
Milford, Nancy. *Zelda.* New York: Harper & Row, 1970.
Miller, D., and others. *Fighting Fire: Great Fires of History.* Hartford: Dustin-Gilman, 1873.
Morris, John V. *Fires and Firefighters.* Boston: Little, Brown, 1954.
Murray, Marion. *Circus.* New York: Appleton-Century-Crofts, 1956.
Plowden, Gene. *Those Amazing Ringlings and Their Circus.* Caldwell, Idaho: Caxton, 1967.
Pratt, Walter Merriam. *The Burning of Chelsea.* Boston: Sampson, 1908.
Sachs, Edwin O. *The Fire at the Iroquois Theater, Chicago, 30th December, 1903.* London: British Fire Prevention Committee, 1904.
Searight, Frank T. *Doomed City.* Chicago: Laird & Lee, 1906.
Sewell, Alfred L. *The Great Calamity: Scenes, Incidents and Lessons of the Great Chicago Fire.* Chicago: Alfred L. Sewell, 1871.
Sheahan, James W., and Upton, George W. *The Great Conflagration: Chicago.* Chicago: n.p., 1871.
Sheldon, George W. *Story of the Volunteer Fire Department of the City of New York.* New York: Harper, 1882.
Stein, Leon. *The Triangle Fire.* New York: Lippincott, 1962.
Turnbull, Andrew. *Scott Fitzgerald.* New York: Scribners, 1962.
Wheaton, Elizabeth. *Texas City Remembers.* San Antonio, Texas: Naylor, 1947.
Williams, Harold A. *Baltimore Afire, Being an Account of One of America's Great Conflagrations.* Baltimore: Remington, 1954.

Periodicals

"The Acquittal, The Triangle Case." *Outlook,* January 6, 1912.
"Acting a Mine Disaster for Instruction." *Harper's Weekly,* January 23, 1909.
"Agony of the Oriskany." *Time,* November 4, 1966.
"An Anti-U.S. Motive in a Fire-Disaster." *U.S. News & World Report,* June 5, 1967.
Applegren, George. "Who Milked Mrs. O'Leary's Cow?" *Weekly Underwriter,* October 11, 1941.
"Assignment to Die." *Newsweek,* August 20, 1956.
"Atlanta: The Inferno." *Newsweek,* December 16, 1946.
"The Baltimore Fire." *Outlook,* February 13, 1904.
"The Baltimore Fire." *Review of Reviews,* February 20, 1904.
"Baltimore's Great Fire." *Harper's Weekly,* February 13, 1904.
"Blasts Have Chain Effect." *Life,* April 28, 1947.
"The Boston Fire." *Harper's Weekly,* November 30, 1872.
"The Brooklyn Calamity." *Harper's Weekly,* December 23, 1876.
Bruno, Frank J. "In the Path of the Flames." *Survey,* October 26, 1918.
"The Burning of the North German Lloyd Steamships and Docks, Hoboken, N.J." *Scientific American,* February 20, 1904.
Carstens, C.C. "From the Ashes of Halifax." *Survey,* December 29, 1917.
"Chicago Hotel Fire Kills 60 People." *Life,* June 17, 1946.
"Chiu Ming." *Time,* August 9, 1948.
"The Coal-Mine Horror in Virginia." *Frank Leslie's Illustrated Newspaper,* March 22, 1884.
"Coals Cost in Human Life." *Literary Digest,* February 24, 1923.
Collins, Charles. "The Night Chicago Wept." *Chicago Tribune Magazine,* October 8, 1956.
"The Collinwood Disaster." *Outlook,* March 14, 1908.
Deacon, J. Bryon. "When the City Burns." *Survey,* December 15, 1917.
"Death Before Dawn." *Time,* January 16, 1950.
"Death in the Gulf." *Newsweek,* November 7, 1966.
"Death in the Mine." *Literary Digest,* June 9, 1928.
"Death in the Rue Neuve." *Time,* June 2, 1967.
"Deep in Frosty Run." *Newsweek,* December 17, 1962.
"Disaster: Fire in Two Cities." *Newsweek,* June 17, 1946.
"Disaster Report." *New Republic,* June 9, 1947.
"Disaster Strikes." *Scholastic,* May 5, 1947.
"Disaster: Texas City Diary." *Newsweek,* April 28, 1947.
"Don't Jump." *Time,* June 17, 1946.
Ennis, John. "Disaster in Bombay Harbor." *Reader's Digest,* April, 1958.
"A Fearful Calamity." *Frank Leslie's Illustrated Newspaper,* December 23, 1876.
"Fire at the Nice Opera House." *Frank Leslie's Illustrated Newspaper,* April 30, 1881.
"Fire in the Big Top." *Newsweek,* January 1, 1962.
"The Fire Tragedy in Brussels." *Life,* June 2, 1967.
Foster, Reginald L. "The Story of the Great Hoboken Fire." *Munsey's Magazine,* September, 1900.
Foy, Eddie, and Harlow, Alvin F. "Disaster in Chicago." *American Mercury,* February, 1957.
Fryer, William J. "Lessons of the Baltimore Disaster." *Review of Reviews,* March 4, 1904.
Gadsby, Franklin. "The Hull-Ottawa Fire." *Canadian Magazine,* July, 1900.
"The Great Baltimore Fire." *Scientific American,* February 20, 1904.
"The Halifax Disaster Brings the Hazard of War Close to American Citizens." *Current Opinion,* January, 1918.
"Hands at a Gate of Grief." *Life,* September 17, 1956.
"Hell Below." *Newsweek,* February 19, 1962.
"The Home of New York Pays in Full." *News From Home,* Spring, 1946.
"The Horrors of War in Peace-Time." *Literary Digest,* July 31, 1926.
"Italians in Belgian Mines." *Economist,* August 18, 1956.
"Just Plain Hell." *Newsweek,* January 16, 1950.
Kenlon, Chief John. "What Was the Cause of the *Morro Castle* Disaster?" *Fire Engineering,* July, 1936.
Kenworthy, E.W. "U.S. Sabotage or Cuban Carelessness?" *New York Times Magazine,* March 13, 1960.
"The Late Disaster at Milwaukee." *Frank Leslie's Illustrated Newspaper,* January 20, 1883.
MacKaye, Milton. "Death on the Waterfront." *Saturday Evening Post,* October 26, 1957.
"The Men in the Mine." *Newsweek,* December 31, 1951.
"The Mine Catastrophe in West Virginia." *Harper's Weekly,* December 21, 1907.
"The Mine Explosion at Hanna." *Independent,* July 9, 1903.
"The Milwaukee Fire." *Harper's Weekly,* January 20, 1883.
"Montsanto, Dealing with a Disaster." *Nation's Business,* January, 1971.
"The *Morro Castle* Disaster." *Factory Mutual Record,* September, 1934.
"The *Morro Castle* Fire." *National Fire Prevention Quarterly,* October, 1934.
"*Morro Castle* of Ward Line Destroyed by Rapid Fire at Sea." *Fire Engineering,* October, 1934.
Moser, Don. "Fire in Alpha 107 Mike!" *Life,* November 25, 1966.
"Most Terrible Disaster on Record in America." *Frank Leslie's Illustrated Newspaper,* December 19, 1907.
"New Jersey's Sample of War." *Literary Digest,* July 24, 1926.
"Ohio's Prison Horror." *Literary Digest,* May 3, 1930.
Piver, Jack. "Insurance and the San Francisco Fire of 1906." *Pacific Insurance Magazine,* February-March, 1944.
"Pluperfect Hell." *Time,* April 28, 1947.
Ranck, Samuel H. "While a Great City Burns." *Independent,* February 18, 1904.
"Red Sky at Morning." *Time,* December 16, 1946.
"The Relief of Halifax." *Survey,* December 15, 1917.
Rogers, Joseph M. "The Baltimore Fire." *Review of Reviews,* March 4, 1904.
"The Shape of Things." *Nation,* January 5, 1952.
"So, It Is the Factory Again." *Time,* August 9, 1948.
"Strange Cargo." *Time,* July 31, 1944.
"A Subterranean Disaster." *Independent,* June 2, 1928.
Sullivan, Mrs. Alexander. "The Hoboken Catastrophe." *Catholic World,* August, 1900.
"Texas City Blows Up." *Life,* April 28, 1947.
"The Texas School Explosion." *School and Society,* April 3, 1937.
"Two Disastrous Fires in New York Harbor." *Harper's Weekly,* February 13, 1904.
"The Waterfront Fire in New York Harbor." *Independent,* February 25, 1904.
"Why?" *New Republic,* April 28, 1947.
"The Winecoff Hotel Fire and Its Lessons." *American City,* January, 1947.
"Worst Hotel Fire in U.S. History." *Life,* December 16, 1946.

Bulletins, Pamphlets, Papers, Reports

Air Attack on Forest Fires. U.S. Forest Service, Washington, 1960.
Best's Special Report Upon the San Francisco Losses and Settlements. New York: Alfred M. Best Co., 1907.
Chandler and Company's Full Account of the Great Fire in Boston, 1872.
Chicago Fire, 1871, Special Report. The Underwriters Salvage Corps., Cincinnati, Ohio, n.d.
Ellis, R.L., *Quality Protection or Bargain Prices.* New York: Fireman's Fund, 1937.
Fire Defense. National Fire Protection Association, 1942.
Full Account of the Great Fire in Chicago. G.F. Nixon, Chicago, 1871.
Guenzel, Louis, *The Iroquois Theater Fire In Chicago.* Chicago: L. Guenzel, 1945.
Hearings, Texas City Disaster, U.S. House of Representatives, Judiciary Committee. Washington, D.C.: Government Printing Office, 1954.

Killian, Lewis M., with Quick, Randolph, and Stockwell, Frank, *A Study of Responses to the Houston, Texas Explosion.* Committee on Disaster Studies, Washington, 1956.
Lange, A.P., *Tested in the Crucible of Actual Performance: The San Francisco Conflagration, April 18-21, 1906.* Berkeley: A.P. Lange, 1938.
The Laurier Palace Theatre Fire. Boston: National Fire Protection Association, 1927.
Pamphlets Relating to Conflagrations in the U.S., 1904-1916. National Fire Protection Association, Chicago.
Records Relating to the Early History of Boston Containing Miscellaneous Papers. Boston: Municipal Printing Office, 1900.
Report of Fire at Iroquois Theater. Chicago Underwriters Association, Chicago, 1904.
Report of the Chicago Relief and Aid Society of Disbursements of Contributions for the Sufferers by the Chicago Fire. Cambridge, Mass.: Riverside, 1874.
Report of the Commissioners Appointed to Investigate the Cause and Management of the Great Fire in Boston. Boston: Rockwell & Churchill, 1873.
Report of the Hotel LaSalle Fire. Cook County Inspection Bureau, Chicago, 1946.
Report of the Special Committee of the Board of Trustees of the Chamber of Commerce of San Francisco. 1906.
The San Francisco Conflagration of April, 1906. Special Report to the National Board of Fire Underwriters, New York, May, 1906.
Texas City, Texas Disaster. National Board of Fire Underwriters. New York: 1947.
Texas City, Explosion, Galveston, 1947. U.S. Coast Guard, Board of Investigation.
Wohl, Richard R. "The Chicago Fire." Unpublished article, Chicago Fire Insurance Library, 1957.

Marine Disasters

Books

Adams, Robert. *The Narrative of Robert Adams.* Boston: Wells and Lilly, 1817.
Adamson, Hans Christian. *Keepers of the Lights.* Philadelphia: Chilton, 1955.
Albion, Robert. *Maritime and Naval History.* Mystic, Conn.: Marine Historical Association, 1955.
Allison, J.E. *The Mersey Estuary.* Liverpool, England: University Press, 1949.
Ambler, Charles Henry. *A History of Transportation in the Ohio Valley.* Glendale, Calif.: Arthur H. Clark, 1932.
Anderson, Romola, and Anderson, R.C. *The Sailing Ship: Six Thousand Years of History.* London: Harrap, 1926.
Anonymous. *American Adventures by Land and Sea Being Remarkable Instances of Enterprise and Fortitude Among Americans. Shipwrecks, Adventures at Home and Abroad, etc.* New York: Harper, 1847.
Anonymous. *An Authentic Account of the Destruction of the Ocean Monarch, etc.* Liverpool, England: William McCall, 1848.
Anonymous. *An Authentic Narrative of the Loss of the Earl of Abergavenny East Indiaman.* London: Minerva Press, 1805.
Anonymous. *A History of Shipwrecks and Disasters from the Most Authentic Sources.* London: Whittaker, Treacher, 1833.
Anonymous. *A Home on the Deep, or The Mariner's Trials on the Dark Blue Sea.* Boston: Higgins, Bradley & Dayton, 1857.
Anonymous. *Horrible Shipwrecks and Dreadful Loss of Lives (the Heln McGregor.)* London: Catnach, Circa 1832.
Anonymous. *The Loss of the Kent, East Indiaman.* London: Society for Promoting Christian Knowledge, 1837.
Anonymous. *The Mariner's Chronicle: Containing Narratives of the Most Remarkable Disasters at Sea, Such as Shipwrecks, Storms, Fires and Famines.* New Haven: Durrie and Peck, 1834.
Anonymous. *The Mariner's Chronicle of Shipwrecks, Fires, Famines, and Other Disasters at Sea.* Philadelphia: J. Harding, 1849.
Anonymous. *The Mariner's Library, or Voyager's Companion, Containing Narratives of the Most Popular Voyages, etc., With Accounts of Remarkable Shipwrecks.* Boston: C. Gaylord, 1840.
Anonymous. *Narrative of Calamitous and Interesting Shipwrecks.* Philadelphia: Mathew Carey, 1810.
Anonymous. *A Narrative of the Loss of the Royal George, etc.* London: S. Horsey, 1841.
Anonymous. *Perils of the Ocean, or Disasters of the Sea.* New York: Murphy Publishers, n.d.
Anonymous. *Remarkable Shipwrecks, or A Collection of Interesting Accounts of Naval Disasters.* Hartford: Andrus and Starr, 1813.
Anonymous. *Shipwrecks and Disasters at Sea.* London: n.p., 1851.
Anonymous (By An Old Salt). *The Terrors of the Sea, As Portrayed in Accounts of Fire and Wreck, and Narratives of Poor Wretches Forced to Abandon Their Floating Homes Without Food or Water, Thus Compelling Them to Resort to Cannibalism with Its Attendant Horrors.* New York: Hurst, n.d.
Appleman, Burns, Gugeler and Stevens. *Okinawa, the Last Battle, U.S. Army in World War II (the War in the Pacific).* Washington, D.C.: Historical Division, Department of the Army, 1948.
Applin, Arthur. *Admiral Jellicoe.* London: Pearson, 1915.
Archer, Lt. *Circumstantial Account of the Wreck of His Majesty's Ship Phoenix.* London: T. Tegg, 1809.
Ashton, Philip. *Romance of Sea-Faring Life.* London: n.p., 1841.
Astley, Thomas. *A Collection of Voyages and Travels* (4 vols.). London: Published by author, 1745-47.
Aston, Major Gen. Sir George. *Memories of a Marine.* London: J.Murray, 1919.
Bacon, Sir Reginald H. *A Naval Scrapbook, 1877-1900.* London: Hutchinson, 1925.
———. *The Life of John Rushworth Earl Jellicoe.* London: Cassell, 1936.
Baker, William A. *Colonial Vessels.* Barre, Mass.: Barre, 1962.
———. *Sloops & Shallops.* Barre, Mass.: Barre, 1966.
Baldwin, Leland D. *Keelboat Age on Western Waters.* Pittsburgh: Universtiy of Pittsburgh Press, 1941.
Baldwyn, Hanson W. *Sea Fights and Shipwrecks.* Garden City, N.Y.: Doubleday, 1958.
Banbury, David. *Shipbuilders of the Thames and Medway.* London: David and Charles, 1971.
Banta, R.E. *The Ohio.* New York: Rinehart, 1949.
Barnaby, K.C. *Some Ships Disasters and Their Causes.* New York: A.S. Barnes, 1970.
Barrington, George W. *Remarkable Voyages and Shipwrecks.* London: Simpkin, Marshall, Hamilton, Kent, 1883.
Bartlett, C.J. *Great Britain and Sea Power, 1815-1853.* London: Clarendon Press, 1963.
Bassett, Fletcher S. *Legends and Superstitions of the Sea and of Sailors in All Lands and at All Times.* New York: Belford, Clark, 1885.
Beesley, Lawrence. *The Loss of the S.S. Titanic.* Boston: Houghton-Mifflin, 1912.
Berman, Bruce D. *Encyclopedia of American Shipwrecks.* Boston: The Mariners Press, 1972.
Boardman, S.L. (ed.). *The Naturalist of the Saint Croix: A Memoir of George A. Boardman.* Bangor, Me.: Privately printed, 1903.
Bowan, Dana Thomas. *Memories of the Lakes.* Daytona Beach, Fla.: D.T. Bowen, 1946.
———. *Shipwrecks of the Lakes.* Daytona Beach, Fla.: D.T. Bowen, 1952.
Boyd, Thomas. *Poor John Fitch, Inventor of the Steamboat.* New York: Putnam, 1935.
Boyer, Dwight. *True Tales of the Great Lakes.* New York: Dodd, Mead, 1971.
Boxer, Charles R. *The Portuguese Seaborne Empire.* New York: Knopf, 1969.
Bradlee, Frances. *Blockade Running During the Civil War.* Salem, Mass.: Essex Institute, 1925.
Branch, Edgar Marquess. *The Literary Apprenticeship of Mark Twain.* Urbana: University of Illinois Press, 1950.
Buchanan, Lamont. *Ships of Steam.* New York: McGraw-Hill, 1957.
Buckley, John, and Cummins, John. *A Voyage to the South-Seas in the Year 1740-1.* London: J. Robinson, 1743.
Bulkley, Mary Adams. *The Wreck of the S.S. Ville de Havre.* London: n.p., 1873.
Burgess, Robert F. *Sinkings, Salvages, and Shipwrecks.* New York: American Heritage, 1970.
Burr, Aaron. *Memoirs.* New York: Harper, 1858.
Burton, Hal. *The Morro Castle, Tragedy at Sea.* New York: Viking, 1973.
Capper, Col. James, *On the Winds and Monsoons.* London: J. Derbrett, 1801.
Carter, Hodding, *Lower Mississippi.* New York: Farrar & Rinehart, 1942.
Casson, Lionel. *The Ancient Mariners.* London: Gollancz, 1959.
Chatterton, E. Keble. *The Epic of Durkirk.* London: Hurst & Blackett, 1940.
Chittenden, Hiram Martin. *History of Early Steam Navigation on the Missouri River* (2 vols.). New York: Harper, 1903.
———. *History of the American Fur Trade of the Far West* (2 vols.). Stanford, California: Academic Reprints, 1954.
Churchill, A., and Churchill, J. *A Collection of Voyages and Travels* (8 vols.). London: T. Osborne, 1745.
Churchill, Winston. *The Gathering Storm.* New York: Houghton-Mifflin, 1948.
Cipolla, Carlo M. *Guns & Sails In The Early Phase of European Expansion.* London: Collins, 1965.
Clemens, Samuel L.*Life on the Mississippi.* Boston: J.R. Osgood, 1883.
Clarke, James Stanier. *Naufragia: or Historical Memoirs of Shipwrecks and the Providential Deliverance of Vessels* (2 vols.). London: I. Gold, J. Mawman, 1805-06.
Clowes, Sir William Laird. *The Royal Navy: A History* (7 vols.). London: Sampson Low, Marston, 1897-1903.
———. *Sailing Ships: Their History and Development.* London: Her Majesty's Stationery Office, 1932.
Coleman, Terry. *Going to America.* New York: Pantheon, 1972.
Cowburn, Philip. *The Warship in History.* New York: Macmillan, 1965.
Cox, E.G., *A Reference Guide to the Literature of Travel.* Seattle: University of Washington, 1935.
Cravens, W.F., and Cate, J.L. (eds.). *The Army Air Force in World War II* (volume V). *The Pacific, Matterhorn to Nagasaki.* Chicago: University of Chicago Press, 1953.
Cry, G.W., Haggard, W.H., and White, S.H. *North Atlantic Tropical Cyclones, 1886-1958.* Washington: U.S. Government Printing Office, 1959.
Cumings, Samuel. *The Western Pilot.* Cincinnati: Morgan, Lodge & Fisher, 1825.

Curtis, John. *The Shipwreck of the Stirling Castle.* London: George Virtue, 1838.

Dalyell, Sir J.G. *Shipwrecks and Disasters at Sea.* Edinburgh: A. Constable, 1812.

David, Evan J. *Great Moments of Adventure.* London: Duffield, 1930.

Deiss, Joseph Jay. *The Roman Years of Margaret Fuller.* New York: Crowell, 1969.

Dickinson, Captain Thomas. *A Narrative of the Operations for the Recovery of the Public Stores and Treasure Sunk in the H.M.S. Thetis, etc.* London: Longman, Rees, Orme, Brown, Green, and Longman, 1836.

Divine, Arthur D. *The Wake of the Raiders.* London: J. Murray, 1940.

Donovan, Frank. *River Boats of America.* New York: Crowell, 1966.

Dorsey, Florence. *Master of the Mississippi.* Boston: Houghton-Mifflin, 1941.

Drake-Brockman, H., *Voyage to Disaster.* Sydney, Australia: Angus & Robertson, 1963.

Duckworth, C.L.D., and Langmuir, G.E. *Railway and Other Steamers.* Glasgow: Shipping Histories, 1948.

Duffy, James. *Shipwreck and Empire.* Cambridge, Mass.: Harvard Universtiy Press, 1955.

Dugan, James. *The Great Iron Ship.* New York: Harper, 1953.

Duncan, Archibald. *The Mariner's Chronicle.* London: James Cundee, 1804.

Dundas, Sir Charles. *An Admiral's Yarns: Stray Memories of 50 Years.* London: H. Jenkins, 1922.

Edwards, Hugh. *God and Little Fishes.* London: Davies, 1963.

———. *Islands and Angry Ghosts.* New York: Morrow, 1966.

———. *The Wreck of the Half-Moon Reef.* New York: Scribners, 1970.

Ellet, Charles. *The Mississippi and Ohio Rivers.* Philadelphia: Lippincott, Grambo, 1853.

Elliot, James W. *Transport to Disaster.* New York: Holt, Rinehart & Winston, 1962.

Ellms, Charles (ed.). *Shipwrecks and Disasters at Sea; or Historical Narratives of the Most Noted Calamities and Providential Deliverances from Fire and Famine on the Ocean.* New York: I.J. Rouse, 1836.

Eskew, Garnett. *The Pageant of the Packets.* New York: Henry Holt, 1929.

Everett, Marshall. *Wreck and Sinking of the Titanic. The Ocean's Greatest Disaster.* New York: L.H. Walker, 1912.

Fairburn, William Armstrong. *Merchant Sail.* Center Lovell, Maine: Fairburn Marine Educational Foundation, 1945-1955.

Fincham, John. *A History of Naval Architecture.* London: 1851.

Fiske, John. *The Mississippi Valley in the Civil War.* Boston: Houghton, Mifflin, 1900.

Fitzgerald, Admiral C.C. Penrose. *The Life of Admiral Sir George Tryon.* Edinburgh: W. Blackwood, 1897.

Fletcher, R.A. *Steamships, the Story of Their Development to the Present Day.* Philadelphia: Lippincott, 1910.

———. *The Mercantile Marine.* London: Sir I. Pittman, 1912.

———. *In the Days of the Tall Ships.* New York: Brentano's, 1928.

Flexner, James Thomas. *Steamboats Come True: American Inventors in Action.* New York: Viking, 1944.

Fowler, Gene. *Timber Line.* New York: Covici, Friede, 1933.

Franzen, Anders. *Wasa.* Stockholm: Nanstedt and Bonnier, 1964.

Franks, H. George. *Holland Afloat.* London: Netherland, 1942.

Gardener, Arthur H. *Wrecks Around Nantucket.* Nantucket, Mass.: Gardner, 1877.

Gayarre, Charles. *History of Louisiana.* New Orleans: F.F. Hansell, 1903.

Gibbs, James A., Jr. *Shipwrecks of the Pacific Coast.* Portland, Oregon: Binfords & Mort, 1957.

Goodenough, Sir William. *A Rough Record.* London: Hutchinson, 1943.

Goodhart, Philip. *Fifty Ships That Saved the World.* London: Heinemann, 1965.

Gould, R.T. *Enigmas.* London: G. Bles, 1946.

Gosnell, H. Allen. *Guns on the Western Waters.* Baton Rouge: Louisiana State University Press, 1949.

Gracie, Archibald. *The Truth About the Titanic.* New York: Mitchell Kennerly, 1913.

Graham, Philip. *Showboats: the History of an American Institution.* Austin: University of Texas Press, 1951.

Hall, James. *The West: Its Commerce and Navigation.* Cincinnati: H.W. Derby, 1848.

Halsey, Admiral William F., with Bryan, J. *Admiral Halsey's Story.* New York: Whittlesey House, 1947.

Haring, Clarence H. *Trade and Navigation Between Spain and the Indies in the Time of the Hapsburgs.* Cambridge: Harvard University Press, 1918.

Harris, John. *Navigantium* (2 vols.). London: T. Bennet, 1705.

Hartsough, Mildred. *From Canoe to Steel Barge on the Upper Mississippi.* Minneapolis: University of Minnesota Press, 1934.

Havighurst, Walter. *Voices on the River: The Story of the Mississippi Waterways.* New York: Macmillan, 1964.

Heckman, William L. *Steamboating, Sixty-five Years on Missouri's Rivers.* Kansas City: Burton, 1950.

Heeres, J.E. *The Part Borne by the Dutch in the Discovery of Australia.* Amsterdam: F. Muller, 1899.

Hill, Forest G. *Roads, Rails and Waterways.* Norman: University of Oklahoma Press, 1957.

Hocking, Charles. *Dictionary of Disasters at Sea During the Age of Steam, Including Sailing Ships and Ships of War Lost in Action.* London: Lloyd's Register of Shipping, 1969.

Hoehling, A.A. *They Sailed Into Oblivion.* New York: Thomas Yoseloff, 1959.

———. *Great Ship Disasters.* New York: Cowles, 1971.

Hough, Richard. *Admirals in Collision.* New York: Viking, 1959.

Hovgaard, William. *The Modern History of Warships.* London: E. & F.N. Spon, 1920.

Howe, Henry. *Life and Death on the Ocean.* Cincinnati: Henry Howe, 1856.

Howland, S.A. *Steamboat Disasters and Railroad Accidents in the United States.* Worchester, Mass.: Dorr, 1846.

Hughes, Henry. *Immortal Sails.* Prescott, Ont.: T. Stephenson, 1969.

Hughes, Richard W.A. *In Hazard: A Sea Story.* New York: Harper, 1938.

Hurlbert, Archer Butler. *Waterways of Westward Expansion. The Ohio River and Its Tributaries.* Cleveland: A.H. Clark, 1903.

Inglefield, Sir Frederick Samuel. *Shipping Casualties.* London: His Majesty's Stationery Office, 1915.

Inglefield, Captain John Nicholson. *Narrative Concerning the Loss of His Majesty's Ship the Centaur.* London: J. Murray, 1783.

James, Isaac. *Providence Displayed.* Bristol, England: Printed by Riggs and Cottle for the author, 1800.

Janeway, James. *A Token for Mariners.* London: H.N. Publishers, 1708.

Jefferis, Roger, and McDonald, Kendall. *The Wreck Hunters.* London: George Harrap, 1966.

Jones, Ivor Wynne. *Shipwrecks of North Wales.* Newton Abbot, England: David & Charles, 1973.

Jones, Virgil Carrington. *The Civil War at Sea.* New York: Holt, Rinehart and Winston, 1960.

Karig, Captain Walter, and others. *Battle Report,* Volume V, *Victory in the Pacific.* New York: Rinehart, 1949.

Keeler, Ralph. *Vagabond Adventures.* Boston: Fields, Osgood, 1870.

Kellogg, Louise Phelps (ed.). *Early Narratives of the Northwest, 1634-1699.* New York: Scribners, 1917.

Kemp, P.K. *H.M. Submarines.* London: Bergert Jenkins, 1952.

Kerr, Admiral Mark. *The Navy in My Time.* London: Rich & Cowan, 1933.

Kerr, Robert. *General History and Collection of Voyages and Travels* (18 vols.). Edinburgh: W. Blackwood, 1811-1824.

Kingston, W.H.G. *Shipwrecks and Disasters at Sea.* London: Routledge, 1873.

Kirschten, Ernest, *Catfish and Crystal.* New York: Doubleday, 1960.

Knox, Dudley W. *A History of the United States Navy.* New York: Putnam, 1936.

Knox, J. *A New Collection of Voyages, Discoveries and Travels* (7 vols.). London: J. Knox, 1767.

LaCroix, Robert de (trans. by Cleugh James). *Mysteries of the Sea.* New York: John Day, 1956.

Landstrom, Bjorn. *The Ship.* London: Allen and Unwin, 1961.

Larn, Richard, and Carter, Clive. *Cornish Shipwrecks.* London: David and Charles, 1969-71.

Latrobe, Charles Joseph. *The Rambler in North America.* New York: Harper, 1835.

Lenton, H.T., and Colledge, J.J. *Warships of World War II.* London: I. Allan, 1964.

Lewis, M.A. *The Navy of Britain.* London: George Allen & Unwin, 1948.

———. *The History of the British Navy.* Harmondsworth, England: Penguin, 1957.

———. *The Spanish Armada.* London: Batsford, 1960.

Lighttoller, Charles. *Titanic and Other Ships.* New York: Ivor Nicholson and Watson, 1935.

Lipscombe, F.W. *The British Submarine.* London: A. & C. Black, 1954.

Lloyd, Christopher. *A Short History of the Royal Navy.* London: Methuen, 1942.

———. *The British Seaman, 1200-1860.* London: Collins, 1968.

Lloyd, James T. *Steamboat Directory and Disasters on the Western Waters.* Cincinnati: J.T. Lloyd, 1856.

Lloyd's Register of Shipping, Merchant Ships Totally Lost. London: Lloyd's, 1890.

Lockhart, J.G. *Perils of the Sea.* New York: Frederick Stokes, 1925.

Lonsdale, Adrian L., and Kaplan, H.R. *A Guide to Sunken Ships in American Waters.* Arlington, Va.: Compass Publications, 1964.

Lord, Walter. *A Night to Remember.* New York: Holt, 1955.

Lubbock, Basil. *The Last of the Windjammers.* Boston: C.E. Lauriat, 1927.

Lytle, William M. *Merchant Steam Vessels of the United States, 1807-1868.* Mystic, Conn.: Steamship Historical Society of America, 1952.

Mace, Ellis C. *River Steamboats and Steamboat Men.* Cynthia, Ky.: Hobson, 1944.

Macintyre, Donald. *The Thunder of the Guns: A Century of Battleships.* London: Frederick Muller, 1959.

———. *Admiral Rodney.* London: Peter Davies, 1962.

Maclay, E.S. *The History of the United States Navy, 1775-1894* (Vol. II). London: Bliss, Sands and Foster, 1894.

Macy, Obed. *The History of Nantucket.* Boston: Hilliard, Fray, 1835.

Maginnis, A.J. *The Atlantic Ferry.* New York: Macmillan, 1892.

Magoun, F. Alexander. *The Frigate Constitution and Other Historic Ships.* Salem, Mass.: Marine Research Society, 1928.

Mahan, A.T. *The Influence of Sea Power on History.* Boston: Little, Brown, 1890.

———. *The Influence of Sea Power Upon the French Revolution and Europe.* Boston: Little, Brown, 1892.

Major, R.H. *Early Voyages to Terra Australia.* London: Hakluyt Society, 1859.

Marcus, G.J. *A Naval History of England, the Formative Centuries* (Vol. I). London: Longman's, 1961.

Marder, Arthur J. *British Naval Policy, 1880-1905.* London: Putnam, 1941.

The Marine Observer's Handbook. London: Her Majesty's Stationery Office, 1963.

Markham, M.E., and Markham, F.A. *The Life of Sir Albert Hastings.* Markham, Cambridge, England: University Press, 1927.

Marx, Robert F. *Shipwrecks of the Western Hemisphere, 1492-1825.* New York: World, 1971.

Mattingly, Garrett. *The Defeat of the Spanish Armada.* London: Pelican, 1959.

McDermott, J.F. *The Lost Panoramas of the Mississippi.* Chicago: University of Chicago Press, 1958.

McDonald, Kendall. *The Wreck Detectives.* London: George G. Harap, 1972.

Merrick, George Byron. *Old Times on the Upper Mississippi.* Cleveland: A.H. Clark, 1909.

Methley, Noel T. *The Lifeboat and Its Story.* London: Sidgwick & Jackson, 1912.

Minnigerode, Meade. *Certain Rich Men.* New York: Putnam, 1927.

Moore, John Hamilton. *A New and Complete Collection of Voyages and Travels.* (2 vols.). London: A. Hogg, 1785.

Moorhouse, E. Hallam. *Letters of the English Seaman, 1587-1808.* London: Chapman & Hall, 1910.

Mordal, Jacques (trans. by Len Ortzen). *Twenty-five Centuries of Sea Warfare.* New York: Clarkson N. Potter, 1965.

Morison, John H. *History of American Steam Navigation.* New York: Frederick Ungar, 1958.

Morison, Samuel Eliot. *Maritime History of Massachusetts.* Boston: Houghton Mifflin, 1921.

———. *Admiral of the Ocean Sea.* Boston: Little, Brown, 1942.

———. *History of the United States Naval Operations in World War II.* Boston: Little, Brown, 1948.

Moscow, Alvin. *Collision Course, the Andrea Dorea and the Stockholm.* New York: Putnam, 1959.

Mowfat, Farley. *The Serpent's Coil.* Boston: Little, Brown, 1961.

Murray, Marischal. *Ships and South Africa.* London: Oxford University Press, 1933.

Neider, Charles (ed.). *Great Shipwrecks and Castaways, Authentic Accounts of Adventures at Sea.* New York: Harper, n.d.

Ogg, Frederick Austin. *The Opening of the Mississippi.* New York: Macmillan, 1904.

Ohrelius, Bengt. *Vasa, the King's Ship.* London: Cassell, 1962.

Olmstead, Frederick Law. *A Journey in the Seaboard Slave States.* New York: Dix and Edwards, 1856.

Oppenheim, M. *The Administration of the Royal Navy, 1509-1660.* London: Bodley Head, 1896.

Paddock, Judah. *A Narrative of the Shipwreck of the Ship Oswego.* New York: Collins, 1818.

Padfield, Peter. *The Titanic and the Californian.* New York: John Day, 1965.

Paine, Ralph D. *Lost Ships and Lonely Seas.* New York: Century, 1922.

Pares, Richard. *War and Trade in the West Indies.* Oxford, England: The Clarendon Press, 1936.

Parker, W.J. Lewis. *The Great Coal Schooners of New England, 1870-1909.* Mystic, Conn.: Marine Historical Association, 1948.

Parry, J.H. *The Age of Reconnaissance.* London: Weidenfeld and Nicholson, 1963.

———. *The Spanish Seaborne Empire.* New York: Knopf, 1966.

Pawlowski, Gareth L. *Flat-Tops and Fledglings.* New York: A.S. Barnes, 1971.

Pears, R. *British Battleships, 1892-1957.* London: Putnam, 1957.

Penn, C.D. *The Navy under the Early Stuarts.* Portsmouth, England: Gieve's, 1920.

Petersen, William J. *Steamboating on the Upper Mississippi.* Iowa City: Iowa State Historical Society, 1937.

Peterson, Mendel. *History Under the Sea.* Washington, D.C.: Smithsonian Institute, 1965.

Pope, John A. *A Tour Through the Southern and Western Territories of the United States of America.* New York: C.L. Woodward, 1888.

Potter, Israel. *Life and Remarkable Adventures of Israel R. Potter.* Providence, R.I.: Henry Trumbull, 1824.

Pratt, Fletcher. *Civil War on Western Waters.* New York: Henry Holt, 1956.

Purchas, Samuel. *Purchas His Pilgrimes, Containing a History of the World, in Sea Voyages and Land Travels, by Englishmen and Others.* London: H. Featherstone, 1626.

Putnam, George R. *Lighthouses and Lightships of the United States.* Boston: Houghton Mifflin, 1923.

Rattray, Jeanette Edwards. *The Perils of the Port of New York.* New York: Dodd, Mead, 1973.

Riley, James. *Sufferings in Africa.* New York: Riley, 1817.

Roskill, S.W. *The Defensive* (Vol. I), *The War at Sea (History of the Second World War).* United Kingdom Military Series. London: Her Majesty's Stationery Office, 1954.

Rosskam, Edwin. *Towboat River.* New York: Duell, Sloan & Pearce, 1948.

Samuel, Ray, and Huber, Leonard V., and Ogden, Warren C. *Tales of the Mississippi.* New York: Hastings House, 1955.

Samuels, S. *From the Forecastle to the Cabin.* New York: Harper, 1887.

Savigny, J.B. Henry, and Correard, Alexander. *The Loss of the Medusa.* London: H. Colburn, 1818.

Saxon, Lyle. *Father Mississippi.* New York: Century, 1927.

Schoolcraft, Henry Rowe. *Navigation of an Expedition through the Upper Mississippi to Itasca Lake.* New York: Harper, 1834.

Shaw, Frank H. *Full Fathom Five, A Book of Famous Shipwrecks.* New York: Macmillan, 1930.

Small, Isaac M. *Shipwrecks on Cape Cod.* Chatham, Mass.: Chatham, 1967.

Smith, S.E. (ed.). *The United States Navy in World War II.* New York: Morrow, 1966.

Snow, Edward Rowe. *Great Storms and Famous Shipwrecks of the New England Coast.* Boston: Yankee, 1943.

———. *Mysteries and Adventures Along the Atlantic Coast.* New York: Dodd, Mead, 1948.

———. *Great Gales and Dire Disasters.* New York: Dodd, Mead, 1952.

———. *The Vengeful Sea.* New York: Dodd, Mead, 1956.

———. *True Tales and Curious Legends.* New York: Dodd, Mead, 1969.

Soren, John. *Case of John Soren.* London: Cox and Bayliss, 1813.

Spratt, H.P. *The Birth of the Steamboat.* London: Charles Griffin, 1958.

Sprout, Harold, and Sprout, Margaret. *The Rise of American Naval Power.* Princeton: Princeton University Press, 1946.

Stick, David. *Graveyard of the Atlantic.* Chapel Hill: University of North Carolina Press, 1952.

———. *The Outer Banks of North Carolina.* Chapel Hill: University of North Carolina Press, 1958.

Thomas, R. *Remarkable Shipwrecks, Fires, Famines, Calamities, Providential Deliverances and Lamentable Disasters on the Sea.* New York: Ezra Strong, 1836.

Thoreau, Henry David. *Cape Cod.* New York: Crowell, 1961.

Throckmorton, Peter. *The Lost Ships.* London: Cape, 1965.

Tweedie, Sir Hugh. *The Story of a Naval Life.* London: Rich & Cowan, 1939.

Uren, Malcolm John Leggoe. *Sailormen's Ghosts.* Melbourne, Australia: Robertson & Mullens, 1940.

Uring, Nathaniel. *A History of the Voyages and Travels of Nathaniel Uring.* London: Cassell, 1928.

Villiers, Alan John. *Monsoon Seas, the Story of the Indian Ocean.* New York: McGraw-Hill, 1952.

———. *Posted Missing, the Story of Ships Lost Without Trace in Recent Years.* New York: Scribners, 1956.

———. *Wild Ocean, the Story of the North Atlantic and the Men Who Sailed It.* New York: McGraw-Hill, 1957.

———. *Men, Ships, and the Sea.* Washington: National Geographic Society, 1962.

Whiteside, Thomas. *Alone Through the Dark Sea.* New York: George Braziller, 1964.

Wiel, Althea. *The Navy of Venice.* London: John Murray, 1910.

Williams, Archibald. *A Book of the Sea.* New York: Sully and Kleinteich, 1916.

———. *All About Our Wonderful Ships.* London: Cassell, 1924.

Winocour, Jack (ed.). *The Story of the Titanic.* New York: Dover, 1960.

Wood, Walter. *Survivors' Tales of Famous Shipwrecks.* London: Geoffrey Bless, 1932.

Periodicals

Anonymous. "Shipwreck by Lightning, Destruction of Merchant Ships." *Nautical Magazine,* November, 1852.

"Another Disaster for the Navy—But a Tale of Heroism." *U.S. News & World Report,* June 16, 1969.

"Automatic Sprinklers for Ship Fires." *Factory Mutual Record,* October, 1949.

Baldwin, Hanson W. "When the Fleet Met the Great Typhoon." *New York Times Magazine,* December 16, 1951.

Bassler, Lt. R.E. "Tryon and the *Victoria.*" *United States Naval Institute Proceedings,* September, 1934.

"Blazing Example." *Newsweek,* November 29, 1965.

Boxer, C.R. "The Dutch East Indiamen: Their Sailors, Their Navigators, and Life On Board." *Mariner's Mirror,* Vol. 49, No. 2, 1963.

Bride, Harold. "Thrilling Tale by *Titanic*'s Surviving Wireless Man." *New York Times Magazine,* April 28, 1912.

"Captain Williams, of the *Oneida.*" *Harper's Weekly,* March 26, 1870.

Childs, Marquis. "River Town." *Harper's Magazine,* November, 1932.

"*Dakar* and *Minerve.*" *Newsweek,* February 12, 1968.
"A Deadly Battery." *Newsweek,* October 4, 1954.
"Depth 75 Fathoms." *Time,* June 30, 1941.
"Disaster by Moonlight." *Time,* June 13, 1969.
"The Disaster on Long Island Sound, in Which 142 Persons Lost Their Lives, the Captain's Boat Being the First to Leave the Sinking Ship." *Harper's Weekly,* March 2, 1907.
Dixon, Harold. "Three Men on a Raft." *Life,* April 6, 1942.
"The End of the *Evans.*" *Newsweek,* June 16, 1969.
"Ensign Copp, of the *Oneida.*" *Harper's Weekly,* April 2, 1870.
"$59 to Tragedy." *Time,* November 26, 1965.
"Finding the *Scorpion.*" *Newsweek,* November 18, 1968.
Fishman, Joseph F., and Perlman, V. "Murder Without Malice." *American Mercury,* vol. 56, 1920.
Foreman, Grant. "River Navigation in the Early Southwest." *Mississippi Valley Historical Review,* 15, no. 1.
Friedman, Paul, and Linn, Louis. "Some Psychiatric Notes on the *Andrea Doria* Disaster." *American Journal of Psychiatry,* November, 1957.
"Fun Ship to Nassau." *Newsweek,* November 22, 1965.
"The *General Slocum* Disaster." *Harper's Weekly,* June 25, 1904.
Gerber, Rudolph J. "Old Woman River." *Missouri Historical Review,* July, 1962.
"Hell Below Decks." *Newsweek,* June 7, 1954.
Huber, Leonard V. "Heyday of the Floating Palace." *American Heritage,* October, 1957.
"The Ill Fated *City of Columbus.*" *Frank Leslie's Illustrated Newspaper,* January 26, 1884.
Lacasse, Victoire. "The *Bourgogne* Disaster." *Harper's Weekly,* vol. 17, 1898.
Lewis, Henry Harrison. "Life Saving at Sea." *Munsey's Magazine,* September, 1900.
"The *Liberte* Disaster." *Outlook,* October 7, 1911.
"Loss of Her Majesty's Ship *Birkenhead.*" *Notes and Queries* (London), Jan.-June, 1921.
"The Loss of the *Cimbria.*" *Frank Leslie's Newspaper,* February 3, 1883.
"The Loss of the *Empress of Ireland.*" *Literary Digest,* June 13, 1914.
"The Loss of the *Morning Star.*" *Harper's Weekly,* March 19, 1870.
Martin, Pete. "Tragic Voyage." *Saturday Evening Post,* June 10, 17, 1944.
Maxwell, Patrick. "Perils and Captivity." *Miscellany,* 11, 1827.
McAdam, E.L., Jr. "Wordsworth's Shipwreck." *PMLA,* June, 1962.
McDonald, W.J. "The Missouri River and Its Victims." *Missouri Historical Review,* 21, nos. 2, 3, 4.
Murphy, Mark. "Eighty-Three Days." *New Yorker,* August 21, 28, September 4, 1943.
"Mystery at 400 Fathoms." *Time,* November 19, 1965.
"Mystery at Sea: Fate of a U.S. Atomic Sub." *U.S. News & World Report,* June 10, 1968.
"Mystery of the *Scorpion:* What Could Have Sunk It." *U.S. News & World Report,* June 17, 1968.
Nevin, David. "Outward Bound From Miami on a Shabby Ocean Liner." *Life,* November 26, 1965.
Nichols, George Ward. "Down the Mississippi." *Harper's New Monthly Magazine,* November, 1870.
"The *Noronic* Pyre." *NFPA Quarterly,* December, 1950.
"November's Fatal Gale." *Frank Leslie's Illustrated Newspaper,* December 8, 1877.
"One Hundred and Fifty Lives Lost in a Steamboat Disaster." *Frank Leslie's Illustrated Newspaper,* February 28, 1907.
"Overdue." *Newsweek,* June 10, 1968.
"Overhaul." *Newsweek,* November 22, 1965.
"Presumed Lost." *Newsweek,* June 17, 1968.
"Quiet Hour." *Newsweek,* June 10, 1968.
"Riddle of the *Hobson.*" *Time,* August 25, 1952.
"Seventy-three Fathoms Down." *Time,* June 30, 1941.
"Silence from the *Seamounts.*" *Time,* June 7, 1968.
Somers, Chester L. "Submarine Disasters in Peacetime, 1900-1971." *Proceedings of the U.S. Naval Institute,* May, 1972.
"A Terrible Wreck." *Harper's Weekly,* April 12, 1884.
"Too Many of Us." *Time,* December 13, 1948.
Townsend, R.C. "John Wordsworth and His Brother's Poetic Development." *PMLA,* March, 1966.
"Tragedy for a Leading Lady." *Time,* October 26, 1953.
"Tragic Glow of Disaster." *Life,* January 6, 1961.
"Truth about Safety at Sea—Lesson of One Disaster." *U.S. News & World Report,* November 29, 1965.
"Twin Disaster." *Time,* February 9, 1968.
"The Unlucky French Navy Suffers Its Eighth Disaster This Year Through the Explosion on the *Jena.*" *Frank Leslie's Illustrated Weekly,* April 4, 1907.
Walters, R.C. "The Story of the Wreck of the *Annie Jane.*" *Ragged School Union Magazine* (London), April, 1854.
"*Wasp* Splits the *Hobson,*" *Life,* May 12, 1952.
Williams, G. "Commodore Anson and the Acapulco Galleon." *History Today,* August, 1967.
Woolf, Alexander. "The Loss of the *Rio de Janeiro.*" *Overland Monthly,* April, 1901.

Bulletins, Papers, Pamphlets, Reports

"An Account of the Loss of the Grosvenor Indiamen." *Report by Alexander Dalrymple to the East India Company,* 1783.
Anonymous. *The Loss of the Earl of Abergavenny, East Indiaman* (Pamphlet). London: John Stockdale, 1805.
The Battle of the River Plate. His Majesty's Stationery Office, London, 1940.
Bibliography, U.S. Coast Guard, Washington, D.C., 1945.
"Disaster at Apia, Samoa." *Annual Report of the Secretary of the Navy, 1889.* U.S. Navy Department.
"Dreadful Hurricane in the West Indies." *Westminster Magazine,* Pamphlet No. 2, 1781.
A History of Navigation on the Tennessee River System. House Document No. 254, Washington, 1937.
Index of Marine Disasters from Fishers Island, Conn., to Cape Cod, Mass. Army Corps of Engineers, Newport, R.I., 1904.
Merchant Vessels of the United States, 1906-1968. U.S. Bureau of Navigation, Washington, D.C., 1968.
Notice to Mariners. U.S. Coast Guard, Washington, D.C., 1960.
Principal Marine Disasters, 1831-1932. U.S. Coast Guard, Washington, D.C., 1932.
Sessional Papers. House of Commons, 1852 (Vol. 30).
U.S. Revenue Cutter Service Annual Reports. Washington, D.C., 1912-13.
U.S. Steamboat Inspection Service Annual Reports. Washington, D.C., 1871-1934.
Wreck Information List. U.S. Hydrographic Office, Washington, D.C., 1945.

Railway Wrecks

Books

Adams, Charles Francis. *Notes on Railroad Accidents.* New York: Putnam, 1879.
Adams, John Quincy. *Memoirs: Comprising Portions of His Diary from 1795 to 1849,* Vol. 9 (ed. by Charles Francis Adams). Philadelphia: Lippincott, 1876.
The American Railway. New York: Scribners, 1897.
Alexander, E.P. *Iron Horses: American Locomotives 1829-1900.* New York: Bonanza, 1941.
Bebout, J.E., and Grele, R.J. *Where Cities Meet: The Urbanization of New Jersey.* Princeton: D. Van Nostrand, 1964.
Beebe, Lucius. *Mixed Train Daily, a Book of Short-Line Railroads.* Berkeley: Howell-North, 1961.
Black, Robert C. *Railroads of the Confederacy.* Chapel Hill: University of North Carolina Press, 1952.
Buford, Carey Clive. *The Chatsworth Wreck.* Fairbury, Ill.: Blade, 1949.
Conant, Michael. *Railroad Mergers and Abandonments.* Berkeley: University of California Press, 1964.
Conference of Mass Transportation (3 vols.—1966-68). Cleveland: Brotherhood of Railroad Trainmen.
Dixon, Frank H. *Railroads and Government.* New York: Scribners, 1922.
Dunbar, Seymour. *A History of Travel in America.* Indianapolis: Bobbs-Merrill, 1946.
Fagan, J.O. *Confessions of a Railroad Signalman.* New York: Houghton Mifflin, 1908.
Fiser, Webb S. *Mastery of the Metropolis.* Englewood Cliffs: Prentice-Hall, 1962.
Fishlow, Albert. *American Railroads and the Transformation of the Ante-Bellum Economy.* Cambridge: Harvard University Press, 1965.
Fleming, Howard. *Narrow Gauge Railroads of America.* Oakland, Calif.: Grahame Hardy, 1949.
Fogel, Robert. *The Union Pacific Railroad: A Case in Premature Enterprise.* Baltimore: Johns Hopkins Press, 1960.
———. *Railroads and American Economic Growth.* Baltimore: Johns Hopkins Press, 1964.
Futterman, Robert A. *The Future of Our Cities.* Garden City, N.Y.: Doubleday, 1961.
Gooden, Orville Thrasher. *Missouri and North Arkansas Railroad Strike, Studies in History, Economics and Public Law.* New York: Columbia University Press, 1926.
Goodrich, Carter. *Government Promotion of American Canals and Railroads, 1800-1890.* New York: Columbia University Press, 1960.
Gottmann, Joan. *Megalopolis,* Cambridge: M.I.T. Presss, 1961.
Grayland, Eugene C. *There Was Danger on the Line.* Auckland, New Zealand: Belvedere, 1954.
Greer, Scott. *The Emerging City.* New York: Free Press, 1962.
Griswold, Wesley S. *Train Wreck!* Brattleboro, Vermont: Stephen Greene, 1969.
Hall, Peter. *The World Cities.* New York: McGraw-Hill, 1966.
Hamilton, James A.B. *British Railway Accidents of the Twentieth Century.* London: Unwin, 1967.
Hill, Forest G. *Road, Rails and Waterways.* Norman: University of Oklahoma Press, 1957.
Holbrook, Stewart H. *The Story of American Railroads.* New York: Crown, 1947.
Howland, S.A. *Steamboat Disasters and Railroad Accidents in the United States.* Worcester, Mass.: Dorr, 1846.
Hull, Clifton E. *Shortline Railroads of Arkansas.* Norman: University of Oklahoma Press, 1969.
Hungerford, Edward. *Men and Iron: A History of New York Central.* New York: Crowell, 1938.
Johnson, Arthur M. *Boston Capitalists and Western Railroads.* Cambridge: Harvard University Press, 1967.

Keir, Malcolm. *The March of Commerce, Pageant of America* (Vol. 4). New Haven: Yale University Press, 1927.

Kimmel, T., and Kaiser, W. *Focus: The Changing City*. New York: Friendship Press, 1963.

Lane, Wheaton J. *From Indian Trails to Iron Horse, Travel and Transportation in New Jersey, 1620-1860*. Princeton: Princeton University Press, 1939.

Larimer, J. McCormick. *The Railroad Wrecker*. Muskogee, Okla.: Muskogee Press, 1909.

Lyon, Peter. *To Hell in a Day Coach*. Philadelphia: Lippincott, 1968.

MacGill, Caroline E., and others. *History of Transportation in the United States Before 1860*. Cambridge, Mass.: Peter Smith, 1948.

McCready, Albert L. *Railroads in the Days of Steam*. New York: American Heritage, 1960.

Mencken, August. *The Railroad Passenger Car: An Illustrated History of the First Hundred Years with Accounts by Contemporary Passengers*. Baltimore: Johns Hopkins Press, 1957.

Meredith, Matthew. *First Anniversary of the Mud Run Disaster*. Pittsburgh, Pa.: Oliver, 1889.

Nock, Oswald. *Historic Railway Disasters*. London: Allan, 1966.

Osborn, F., and Whittick, A. *The New Towns*. New York: McGraw-Hill, 1963.

Peet, Stephen D. *The Ashtabula Disaster*. Chicago: Goodman, 1877.

Reck, Franklin M. *The Romance of American Transportation*. New York: Crowell, 1962.

Reed, Robert C. *Train Wrecks*. Seattle: Superior, 1968.

Robertson, Archie. *Slow Train to Yesterday*. New York: Somerset, 1945.

Rodwin, Lloyd. *The Future Metropolis*. New York: George Braziller, 1961.

Rolt, Lionel T. *Red for Danger*. London: Bodley Head Press, 1955.

Ruppenthal, Karl M. *Transportation Frontiers*. Stanford: Stanford University Press, 1962.

Salisbury, Stephen. *The State, the Investor, and the Railroad*. Cambridge: Harvard University Press, 1967.

Seyfried, Vincent F. *The Long Island Railroad*. New York: n.p., 1961.

Shaw, Robert B. *Down Brakes: A History of Railroad Accidents, Safety Precautions and Operating Practices in the United States of America*. London: Macmillan, 1961.

Sites, James N. *Quest for Crisis*. New York: Simmons-Boardman, 1963.

Smith, Mildred H. *Early History of the Long Island Railroad*. Uniondale, N.Y.: Salisbury, 1958.

Starr, John W. *Lincoln and the Railroads*. New York: Dodd, Mead, 1927.

Stover, John F. *The Railroads of the South, 1865-1900*. Chapel Hill: University of North Carolina Press, 1955.

———. *American Railroad*. Chicago: University of Chicago Press, 1961.

Taylor, George Rogers. *The Transportation Revolution 1815-1860*. Vol. IV of *The Economic History of the United States*. New York: Rinehart, 1951.

———, and Nev, Irene D. *The American Railroad Network, 1861-1890*. Cambridge: Harvard University Press, 1956.

Transit Fact Book. New York: American Transportation Association, 1968.

Trips in the Life of a Locomotive Engineer. New York: Bradburn, 1863.

Throm, Edward L. *Popular Mechanics' Picture History of American Transportation*. New York: Simon & Schuster, 1952.

Vernon, Raymond. *Metropolis, 1985*. Garden City, N.Y.: Doubleday, 1963.

Weaver, Robert C. *The Urban Complex*. Garden City, N.Y.: Doubleday, 1964.

Williams, Archibald. *Brunel and the Romance of the Great Western Railway*. London: n.p., 1925.

———. *The Marvels of the Railway*. London: Seeley Service, 1924.

Wingo, Lowden (ed.). *Cities and Space*. Baltimore: Johns Hopkins Press, 1963.

Winther, Oscar. *The Transportation Frontier: Trans-Mississippi West 1865-1890:* New York: Holt, Rinehart and Winston, 1964.

With, Emile. *Railroad Accidents*. Boston: Little, Brown, 1856.

Yearbook of American Railroad Facts, 1965-1970. New York: Association of American Railroads.

Periodicals

"A Calamitous Week." *Time*, July 3, 1972.

"Farewell and Return." *Life*, September 18, 1950.

"The Forest Hills Disaster." *Harper's Weekly*, February 26, 1887.

"How It Was Done." *Time*, September 13, 1943.

"The Illinois Railroad Accident." *Harper's Magazine*, August 20, 1887.

"The Illinois Railway Disaster." *Frank Leslie's Illustrated Newspaper*, August 20, 1887.

"One Hundred and Forty-Seven Dead, Nobody Guilty." *Literary Digest*, January 6, 1912.

"Train Wreckage Where 83 Died." *Life*, February 19, 1951.

"The Trestle at Woodbridge." *Time*, February 19, 1951.

"Troop-Train Tragedy." *Newsweek*, September 18, 1950.

"Welcome & Sympathy." *Time*, January 4, 1954.

"The White River Disaster." *Harper's Weekly*, February 19, 1887.

Storms

Books

Albright, John Grover. *Physical Meteorology*. New York: Prentice-Hall, 1939.

Algue, Jose. *Cyclones of the Far East*. Manila: Bureau of Public Printing, 1904.

Andrews, Charles M. *The American Nation, Colonial Self-Government*. New York: Harpers, 1904.

Anonymous. *Awful Calamities; or the Shipwrecks of December, 1839, Being a Full Account of the Dreadful Hurricanes of December 15, 21, 27, on the Coast of Massachusetts, in which More Than 90 Vessels Were Lost, Also the Dreadful Disasters at Gloucester*. Boston: Barnes, 1840.

Arago, Francois. *Meteorological Essays*. London: Longmans, 1855.

Aubert de la Rue, Edgar. *Man and the Winds*. London: Hutchinson, 1955.

Barbour, Thomas. *A Naturalist in Cuba*. Boston: Little, Brown, 1945.

Battan, Louis J. *The Nature of Violent Storms*. New York: Doubleday, 1959.

Bigelow, Frank H. *Storms, Storm Tracks and Weather Forecasting*. Washington: Government Printing Office, 1897.

Bilham, E.G. *The Climate of the British Isles*. London: Macmillan, 1938.

Bishop, Morris. *The Odyssey of Cabeza de Vaca*. New York: Century, 1933.

Blair, Thomas Arthur. *Weather Elements*. New York: Prentice-Hall, 1942.

Blodget, Lorin. "List of Hurricanes on the Coast of the South Atlantic States, and on the North Coast of the Gulf of Mexico." *Climatology of the United States and the Temperate Latitudes of the North American Continent*. Philadelphia: Lippincott, 1857.

Blunt, Edmund M. *The American Coast Pilot*. New York: B.W. Blunt, 1867.

Bowie, E.H., and Weightman, R.H. *Types of Storms of the United States and Their Average Movement*. Washington: Government Printing Office, 1914.

Bradley, John H. *Autobiography of Earth*. New York: Coward-McCann, 1935.

Brooks, C.E.P. *Climate Through the Ages*. New York: McGraw-Hill, 1949.

———. *The English Climate*. London: English Universities Press, 1954.

Brooks, Charles F. *Why the Weather?* New York: Harcourt, Brace, 1935.

Brooks, Edward M. *Tornadoes and Related Phenomena*. Boston, Mass.: American Meteorological Society, 1951.

Burns, Sir Alan. *History of the British West Indies*. London: Allen and Unwin, 1954.

Cain, Ernest E. *Cyclone!* London: Stockwell, 1932.

Capper, James. *Observations on the Winds and Moonsoons, etc.* London: J. Debrett, n.d.

Carr, Archie. *High Jungles and Low*. Gainesville: University of Florida Press, 1953.

———. *The Windward Road*. New York: Knopf, 1956.

Carson, Rachel. *The Sea Around Us*. New York: Oxford University Press, 1951.

———. *Under the Sea Wind*. New York: Oxford University Press, 1952.

Catesby, Mark. *Natural History of Carolina, Florida and the Bahama Islands*. London: C. Marsh, 1754.

Caughey, John Walton. *Bernardo de Galuez in Louisiana*. Berkeley: University of California Press, 1934.

Chalmers, Lionel. *An Account of the Weather and Diseases of South Carolina*. London: Dilly, 1776.

Chapman, Frank M. *Camps and Cruises of an Ornithologist*. New York: Appleton, 1908.

Clarke, Mary Helm. *Major and Minor Keys of the Florida Reef*. Coral Gables, Fla.: Riviera, 1949.

Cline, Isaac Munroe. *Tropical Cyclones*. New York: Macmillan, 1926.

———. *Storms, Floods and Sunshine*. New Orleans: Pelican, 1945.

Cline, Dr. Joseph L. *When the Heavens Frowned*. Dallas: M. Van Nort, 1946.

Clowes, Ernest S. *The Hurricane of 1938 on Eastern Long Island*. Bridgehampton, N.Y.: Hampton Press, 1938.

Coast and Geodetic Survey, U.S. Department of Commerce. *Tsunami! The Story of the Seismic Sea-Wave Warning System*. Washington: Government Printing Office, 1965.

Conrad, Joseph. *Typhoon*. Garden City, N.Y.: Hanover House, 1953.

Corle, Edwin. *Desert Country*. New York: Duell, Sloan and Pearce, 1941.

Cornish, Vaughan. *Ocean Waves and Kindred Geophysical Phenomena*. London: Cambridge University Press, 1934.

Coronas, J. *The Climate and the Weather of the Philippines*. Manila: Bureau of Printing, 1920.

Crane, Verner W. *Benjamin Franklin and a Rising People*. Boston: Little, Brown, 1954.

Crouse, N.M. *The French Struggle for the West Indies*. New York: Columbia University Press, 1940.

Dampier, William. *A New Voyage Round the World* (2 vols.). London: Argonaut Press, 1927.

Davis, Albert B., Jr. *Galveston's Bulwark Against the Sea: History of the Galveston Sea Wall*. Galveston, Tex.: U.S. Corps of Engineers, 1961.

Davis, W.M. *Whirlwinds, Cyclones and Tornadoes*. New York: Lee and Shepard, 1884.

Defoe, Daniel. *The Storm or A Collection of the Most Remarkable Casualties and Disasters Which Happened in the Late Dreadful Tempest Both by Sea and by Land*. London: G. Sawbridge, 1704.

Dingle, Aylward Edward. *A Modern Sinbad: An Autobiography.* London: Harrap, 1933.
Dobreck, William. *The Law of Storms in the Eastern Seas.* Hong Kong: Noronha, 1904.
Douglas, Marjory Stoneman, *Hurricane.* New York: Rinehart, 1958.
Dove, Heinrich Wilhelm (trans. by Robert H. Scott). *The Law of Storms.* London: Longman, Green, Longman, Roberts & Green, 1862.
Dunn, Gordon E., and Miller, Banner I. *Atlantic Hurricanes.* Baton Rouge: Louisiana State University Press, 1960.
Edwards, Bryan. *The History Civil and Commercial of the British West Indies.* London: G. & W.B. Whittaker, 1819.
Eliot, J. *Cyclones of the Bay of Bengal.* Calcutta: Superintendent of the Government Printing Office, 1888.
Espinosa, Fr. Antonio Vazquez de. *Compendium and Description of the West Indies* (trans. by Charles Upson Clark). Washington, D.C.: Smithsonian Institute, n.d.
Espy, J. The *Philosophy of Storms.* Boston: Little, Brown, 1841.
Esquemeling, John. *The Buccaneers of America.* New York: Dutton, 1924.
Ferrel, William. *A Popular Treatise on the Winds.* New York: John Wiley, 1904.
Fleming, J.A. *Waves and Ripples.* New York: Macmillan, 1923.
Flora, Snowden D. *Tornadoes of the United States.* Norman: University of Oklahoma Press, 1953.
———. *Hailstorms of the United States.* Norman: University of Oklahoma Press, 1956.
Form, William H., Nosow, Sigmund, with Stone, Gregory P., and Westie, Charles M. *Community in Disaster.* New York: Harper, 1958.
Foster, Edgar E. *Rainfall and Runoff.* New York: Macmillan, 1948.
Fowler, John. *A General Account of the Calamities Occasioned by the Late Tremendous Hurricanes and Earthquakes in the West-India Islands, etc.* London: J. Stockdale, 1781.
Franklin, Benjamin. *The Papers of Benjamin Franklin* (ed. by L.W. Larabee). New Haven: Yale University Press, 1961.
———. *The Works of Benjamin Franklin* (ed. by John Bigelow). New York: Putnam, 1904.
Free, E.E., and Hoke, Travis. *Weather.* New York: McBride, 1928.
Froc, R.F. Louis. *Typhoon Highways in the Far East.* Shanghai, Zikawei: Catholic Mission Press, 1896.
———. *Atlas of the Tracks of 620 Typhoons, 1893-1918.* Shanghai: Catholic Mission Press, 1915.
Froude, James Anthony. *The English in the West Indies.* New York: Scribners, 1888.
Gage, Thomas. *A New Survey of the West Indies.* New York: McBride, 1929.
Gibson, Count D. *Sea Islands of Georgia.* Athens: University of Georgia Press, 1948.
Glueck, Nelson. *Rivers in the Desert.* New York: Farrar, Straus and Cudahy, 1959.
Greely, A.W. *American Weather.* New York: Dodd, Mead, 1888.
Hall, Maxwell. *Notes of Hurricanes, Earthquakes.* Kingston, Jamaica: Meteorological Service, 1916.
Halpine, Charles Greham. *A Pilot's Meteorology.* New York: Van Nostrand, 1941.
Hanna, A.J., and Hanna, K.A. *Lake Okeechobee.* New York: Bobbs-Merrill, 1948.
———. *Florida's Golden Sands.* New York: Bobbs-Merrill, 1950.
Hanna, Kathryn A. *Florida, Land of Change.* Chapel Hill: University of North Carolina Press, 1948.
Harding, Capt. Edwin T., and Kotsch, Capt. William J. *Heavy Weather Guide* (Parts I & II, Hurricanes, Typhoons). Annapolis: United States Naval Institute, 1965.
Hazen, Henry Allen. *The Tornado.* New York: Hodges, 1890.
Hearn, Lafcadio, *Chita: A Memory of Last Island.* New York: Harper, 1905.
Helm, Thomas. *Hurricane: Weather at Its Worst.* New York: Dodd, Mead, 1967.
Heninger, S.K., Jr. *A Handbook of Renaissance Meteorology.* Durham, N.C.: Duke University Press, 1960.
Herbert, Thomas, and Miller, J. Martin. *America's Greatest Flood and Tornado Calamity.* Chicago: Thomas H. Morrison, 1913.
Horgan, Paul. *Great River.* New York: Rinehart, 1957.
Jennings, Gary. *The Killer Storms, Hurricanes, Typhoons, and Tornadoes.* New York: Lippincott, 1970.
Johnston, Alexander Keith. "Chronological Table of the Principal Hurricanes which Have Occurred in the West Indies within 150 Years." *The Physical Atlas of Nautical Phenomena.* Philadelphia: Lippincott, 1850.
Johnston, Alua. *The Legendary Mizners.* New York: Farrar, Straus, 1953.
Kendrew, W.G. *Climatology.* Oxford: Clarendon Press, 1961.
Knebel, Fletcher, and Bailey, Charles. *No High Ground.* New York: Harper, 1960.
Kolobkov, N. *Our Atmospheric Ocean.* Moscow: Foreign Languages Publishing House, 1962.
Lane, Frank W. *The Elements Rage.* New York: Chilton, 1965.
Laughton, L.G.C., and Heddon, V. *Great Storms.* New York: W.F. Payson, 1931.
Lawrence, Alexander A. *Storm Over Savannah.* Athens: University of Georgia Press, 1951.
Lester, Paul. *The Great Galveston Disaster.* N.p., 1900.
London, Jack. *The Cruise of the Snark.* New York: Macmillan, 1911.
Lowery, Woodbury. *The Spanish Settlements in the United States.* New York: Putnam, 1911.
Ludlum, David. *Early American Hurricanes, 1492-1870.* Boston: American Meteorological Society, 1963.
Madariga, Salvador de. *The Rise of the Spanish-American Empire.* New York: Macmillan, 1947.
———. *The Fall of the Spanish-American Empire.* New York: Macmillan, 1948.
Marshall, Logan. *The True Story of Our National Calamity of Flood, Fire and Tornado.* Chicago: L.T. Myers, 1913.
Martin, Robert J. *Tornadoes in the United States, 1916-1937.* Washington: U.S. Weather Bureau, 1940.
Martin, Sidney Walter. *Florida During Territorial Days.* Athens: University of Georgia Press, 1944.
Mather, Increase. *Remarkable Providences.* Boston: Joseph Browning, 1684.
Maury, Matthew F. *Gales, Typhoons and Tornadoes.* Washington: Government Printing Office, 1851.
———. *Physical Geography of the Sea and Its Meteorology.* New York: Harper, 1855.
Means, Philip Ainsworth. *The Spanish Main.* New York: Scribners, 1935.
Memoirs of the Imperial Marine Observatory. Kobe, Japan: Imperial Marine Observatory, 1922.
Milham, W.I.*Meteorology.* New York: Macmillan, 1912.
Milligen-Johnson, George. *A Short Description of the Province of South Carolina, With an Account of the Air, Weather and Diseases of Charleston.* London: John Hinton, 1770.
Mineral Information Service. *The Biggest Splash in History: Giant Wave in Lituga Bay.* San Francisco: Division of Mines and Geology, State of California, 1964.
Minikin, Robert C. *Winds, Waves, and Maritime Structures.* London: Charles Griffin, 1950.
Morales-Carrion, Arturo. *Puerto Rico and the Non-Hispanic Caribbean.* Puerto Rico: University of Puerto Rico Press, 1952.
Moore, Harry Estill. *Tornadoes Over Texas.* Austin: University of Texas Press, 1958.
Moore, Willis L. *The New Air World.* Boston: Little, Brown, 1922.
Murchie, Guy. *Song of the Sky.* Boston: Little, Brown, 1954.
Nansen, F. *The First Crossing of Greenland.* London: Heinemann, 1890.
Normand, C.W.B. *Storm Tracks in the Bay of Bengal.* Calcutta: India Meteorological Dept., 1925.
Norton, Grady. *Florida Hurricanes.* Washington: U.S. Government Printing Office, 1936.
Ober, Frederick A. *Camps of the Caribbees.* Boston: Lee & Shepard, 1880.
———. *Our West Indian Neighbors.* New York: James Pott, 1912.
Ormerod, Leonard. *The Curving Shore.* New York: Harper, 1957.
Ousley, Clarence. *Galveston in 1900.* Atlanta: Wm. P. Chase, 1900.
Pares, Richard. *A West Indian Fortune.* London: Longmans, Green, 1950.
Parton, James. *The Life and Times of Benjamin Franklin.* Boston: Houghton-Mifflin, 1882.
Perley, Sidney. *Historic Storms of New England.* Salem, Mass.: Salem Press, 1891.
Piddington, Henry. *Conversations About Hurricanes: For The Use of Plain Sailors.* London: Smith, Elder, 1852.
———. *The Sailor's Hornbook for the Law of Storms.* London: Norgate, 1876.
Piston, Donald S. *Meteorology.* Philadelphia: Blakiston, 1941.
Pratt, Fletcher. *The Heroic Years.* New York: Smith and Haas, 1934.
Proudman, J. *Dynamical Oceanography.* New York: John Wiley, 1953.
Putnam, Palmer C. *Power from the Wind.* New York: D. Van Nostrand, 1948.
Ragatz, Lowell J. *The Fall of the Planter Class in the British Caribbean, 1763-1833.* New York: Century, 1928.
Rainsford, Marcus. *An Historical Account of the Black Empire of Hayti.* London: J. Cundee, 1805.
Ramsay, David. *The Natural History of South Carolina.* Newberry, S.C.: E.J. Duffie, 1858.
Redfield, W.C. *Hurricanes of the Atlantic.* New Haven, Conn.: B.L. Hamlen, 1846.
Reese, Joe Hugh. *Florida's Great Hurricane.* Miami, Fla.: L.E. Fesler, 1926.
Reid, Lt. Col. William. *An Attempt to Develop the Law of Storms, etc.* London: J. Weale, 1841.
Riehl, Herbert. *Tropical Meteorology.* New York: McGraw-Hill, 1954.
Reiter, Eimar R. *Jet-Stream Meteorology.* Chicago: University of Chicago Press, 1963.
Richards, Paul W. *The Tropical Rain Forest.* London: Cambridge University Press, 1952.
Rich, Shebnah. *Truro, Cape Cod.* Boston: D. Lothrop, 1884.
Rosenberger, F.C. (ed.). *Jefferson Reader.* New York: E.P. Dutton, 1953.
Russell, Charles Edward. *From Sandy Hook to 62°.* New York: Century, 1920.
Russell, Rolo. *On Hail.* London: Stanford, 1893.
Russell, Thomas H. *Flood and Cyclone Disasters.* Chicago: Thomas H. Morrison, 1913.
Schonland, B.F.J. *The Flight of the Thunderbolts.* Oxford, England: Clarendon Press, 1950.

Sears, Paul B. *This is Our World.* Norman: University of Oklahoma Press, 1937.
Semmes, Raphael. *Memoirs of Service Afloat.* Baltimore: Kelly, Piet, 1869.
Sewell, William G. *The Ordeal of Free Labor in the West Indies.* New York: Harper, 1863.
Shaw, William Napier. *The Air and Its Ways.* Cambridge: Cambridge University Press, 1923.
Simpson, Charles Torry. *Florida Wild Life.* New York: Macmillan, 1932.
Stewart, George R. *Storm.* New York: Random House, 1941.
Stick, David. *Graveyard of the Atlantic.* Chapel Hill, N.C.: University of North Carolina Press, 1952.
———. *The Outer Banks of North Carolina.* Chapel Hill: University of North Carolina Press, 1958.
Sverdrup, H.V., Johnson, M.W., and Fleming, R.H. *The Oceans.* New York: Prentice-Hall, 1946.
Tannehill, Ivan Ray. *Hurricanes.* Princeton: Princeton University Press, 1952.
———. *The Hurricane Hunters.* New York: Dodd, Mead, 1956.
Taylor, George F. *Aeronautical Meteorology.* New York: Pitman, 1941.
Taylor, Thomas Griffith. *Australian Meteorology.* Oxford: Clarendon Press, 1920.
Terry, T.P. *Terry's Guide to Cuba.* New York: Houghton-Mifflin, 1929.
Thomas, Percy H. *Electric Power from the Wind.* Washington, D.C.: Federal Power Commission, 1945.
Thompson, J. Eric. *Rise and Fall of the Mayan Civilization.* Norman: University of Oklahoma Press, 1955.
Thoreau, Henry David. *Cape Cod.* New York: Crowell, 1961.
Van Doren, Carl. *Benjamin Franklin.* New York: Viking, 1938.
Van Doren, Mark (ed.). *The Travels of William Bartram.* New York: Facsimile Library, 1940.
Viemeister, Peter E. *The Lightning Book.* Garden City, N.Y.: Doubleday, 1961.
Visher, S.S. *Tropical Cyclones of the Pacific.* Honolulu: Museum Publishers, 1925.
Waldo, Frank. *Modern Meteorology.* London: W. Scott, 1893.
Warden, David. *A Statistical, Political, and Historical Account of the United States of North America.* Philadelphia: T. Wardle, 1819.
Weems, John Edward. *A Weekend in September.* New York: Holt, 1957.
Williams, John Lee. *The Territory of Florida.* New York: A.T. Goodrich, 1837.
Williamson, J.A. *The Ocean in English History.* London: Oxford, 1941.
———. *Hawkins of Plymouth.* London: Black, 1949.
Willison, George F. *Behold Virginia.* New York: Harcourt, Brace, 1951.
Winthrop, John. *Winthrop's Journal* (2 vols.). New York: Scribner, 1908.
Wood, Eliott Colpoys. *A Guide to the Parish Church at Widecombe-in-the-Moor.* Exeter, England: Townsend, 1962.
Wright, Louis B. *The Atlantic Frontier.* New York: Alfred A. Knopf, 1947.

Periodicals

Abbe, Cleveland. "Wind and Waves." *Monthly Weather Review,* vol. 33, 1905.
Adolphe, Edward. "Tornado Coming." *Town Journal,* April, 1956.
Ainlay, George. "1944—Year of the Great Hurricane!" *Science Digest,* May 15, 1944.
Alexander, W.H. "Hurricanes, Especially Those of Puerto Rico and St. Kitts." *Monthly Weather Review,* vol. 33, 1905.
"Along Tornado Alley." *Newsweek,* April 26, 1965.
Arnold, Rudy. "After a Hurricane." *Popular Science,* vol. 134, 1939.
"Atlantic Hurricane." *Science News Letter,* September 23, 1944.
"Audrey's Day of Horror." *Time,* July 8, 1957.
Baden, Ira J., as told to Parham, Robert H. "My 45 Seconds Inside the Tornado." *Saturday Evening Post,* July 11, 1953.
"Bad Friday." *Time,* April 3, 1964.
Ballou, S.M. "The Eye of the Storm." *American Meteorological Journal,* 1902.
"The Balm After the Storm." *Christianity Today,* April 26, 1974.
Bathurst, G.B. "The Earliest Recorded Tornado." *Weather,* vol. 19, 1964.
"Battering Ram." *Newsweek,* October 17, 1955.
Beach, Stewart. "Awakening in the Isle of Dreams." *Independent,* September 29, 1928.
Bello, Francis. "Hurricane." *Fortune,* August, 1956.
Benton, George S. "More Hurricanes in Your Future." *Johns Hopkins Magazine,* October, 1955.
"Beshi...Beshi." *Newsweek,* December 9, 1970.
"The Big Sweep." *Time,* March 31, 1952.
"Big Twister." *Time,* June 6, 1955.
Blank, Joseph P. "Day of the 100 Tornadoes." *Reader's Digest,* October, 1974.
"A Blizzard in New York." *Harper's Weekly,* March 24, 1888.
"A Blizzard There Was." *U.S. News & World Report,* February 28, 1958.
Bodsworth, Fred. "Why We're Getting More Disastrous Hurricanes." *Maclean's Magazine* (Canada), September 15, 1956.
Bonacina, L.C.W. "The Widecombe Calamity of 1638." *Weather,* vol. 1, 1946.
———, and Simmonds, J. "Tornadoes Across England." *Weather,* vol. 5, 1950.
Boughner, C.C. "Hurricane Hazel." *Weather,* vol. 10, 1955.
Bowie, E.H. "Formation and Movement of West Indian Hurricanes." *Monthly Weather Review,* vol. 50, 1922.
"Broods of Tornadoes." *Newsweek,* November 13, 1920.
Brooks, Charles F. "Some Excessive Rainfalls." *Monthly Weather Review,* vol. 47, 1919.
———. "Hurricanes in New England." *Geographical Review,* vol. 29, 1939.
Brooks, John. "Five-Ten on a Sticky June Day." *New Yorker,* May 28, 1955.
Brown, Andrew H. "Men Against the Hurricane." *National Geographic,* vol. 98, 1950.
"Bustle of a Town Rebuilding in the Wake of a Tornado." *U.S. News & World Report,* August 15, 1974.
Byers, H.R. "On the Meteorological History of the Hurricane of November, 1935." *Monthly Weather Review,* vol. 63, 1935.
Calvert, E.B. "The Hurricane Warning Service and Its Reorganization." *Monthly Weather Review,* vol. 63, 1935.
"Capricious Carol." *Time,* September 13, 1954.
"A Capricious, Costly Storm." *Life,* October 25, 1954.
"Caribbean Typhoon." *Outlook,* September 17, 1930.
"Carol the Killer." *Newsweek,* September 13, 1954.
Carpenter, S.C. "Domestic Occurrences: Particular Account of the Storm Which Happened on the Coast of South Carolina, in September, 1804." *Monthly Register Magazine and Review of the United States,* January, 1805.
———. "Domestic Occurrences: Retrospective Account of the Tremendous Storm in October, 1804." *Monthly Register Magazine and Review of the United States,* February, 1805.
"Catastrophe." *Time,* July 3, 1944.
Chapel, L.T. "Winds and Storms on the Isthmus of Panama." *Monthly Weather Review,* vol. 55, 1927.
"A City in the Hands of the Receiver." *Outlook,* September 1, 1915.
Cline, Isaac M. "Tide and Coastal Currents Developed by Tropical Cyclones." *Monthly Weather Review,* vol. 61, 1933.
Colton, F. Barrows. "The Geography of a Hurricane." *National Geographic,* vol. 75, 1938.
"The Deadliest Tornado in America's History." *Literary Digest,* April 4, 1925.
"Death and Heroism in Lorain, Ohio." *Literary Digest,* July 26, 1924.
"Delirious Moment." *New Yorker,* September 23, 1944.
"The Destruction of Port Royal." *Gentleman's Magazine,* October, 1750.
"Devastation in the Delta." *Time,* March 8, 1971.
"Diseases That Follow Hurricanes." *Literary Digest,* October 18, 1930.
"Donna's Mad Fling." *Newsweek,* September 19, 1960.
Dunlop, J.G. "Spanish Depradations." *South Carolina Historical and General Magazine,* vol. 30, 1929.
Dunn, Gordon E. "Aerology in the Hurricane Warning Service." *Monthly Weather Review,* vol. 68, 1940.
———. "The Tropical Cyclone Problem in East Pakistan." *Monthly Weather Review,* vol. 90, 1962.
Dyke, R.A. "Excessive Rainfall of July 22-25, in Louisiana and Extreme Eastern Texas." *Monthly Weather Review,* vol. 61, 1933.
"Early and Deadly: Hurricane." *Life,* July 8, 1957.
"Earthquake in Turkey." *Life,* January 29, 1940.
"The Earth Shook, Seas Heaved, Winds Blew." *Newsweek,* June 6, 1960.
Emeny, Stuart. "Tidal Wave Kills 10,000 People." *News Chronicle,* November 14, 1942.
Espy, J.P. "Essays on Meteorology: Northeast Storms, Volcanoes, and Columnar Clouds." *Journal of the Franklin Institute,* October 18, 1836.
Evans, E.A., and McEachron, K.B. "The Thunderstorm." *General Electric Review,* 1936.
Fassig, Oliver L. "Discussion of Tropical Cyclone." *Monthly Weather Review,* vol. 57, 1929.
Fay, John. "The Galveston Tragedy." *Cosmopolitan,* November, 1900.
Faye, Stanley. "The Great Stroke of Pierre Lafitte." *Louisiana Historical Quarterly,* July, 1940.
"A Few Glimpses of What the Twister Did in St. Louis." *Literary Digest,* October 15, 1927.
Finnell, H.H. "The Dust Storms of 1954." *Scientific American,* 1954.
"First the Wind, Then the Waters..." *Newsweek,* April 26, 1965.
Frazier, R.D. "Early Records of Tropical Hurricanes on the Texas Coast in the Vicinity of Galveston." *Monthly Weather Review,* vol. 49, 1921.
"The Funnels of Fury." *Newsweek,* April 15, 1974.
"Galveston—What It was, and What It Will Be." *Harper's Weekly,* October 6, 1900.
Goulding, Samuel D. "Neither Storm, Nor Strife..." *Commonwealth,* May 26, 1939.
"Government Aid for Disaster Victims." *U.S. News & World Report,* August 21, 1972.
Graham, Howard E. "A Fire-Whirlwind of Tornadic Violence." *Weatherwise,* May, 1952.
Grau, Shirley Ann. "Storm." *New Yorker,* September 24, 1955.
Gray, R.W. "Florida Hurricanes." *Monthly Weather Review,* vol. 61, 1933.
"The Great Whirlwind." *Time,* September 25, 1944.
"Hail at Its Worst." *Literary Digest,* July 16, 1932.

Hall, Ferguson, and Brewer, Robert D. "A Sequence of Tornado Damage Patterns." *Monthly Weather Review*, vol. 87, 1959.

Hall, W.S. "All Over the Map." *Publisher's Weekly*, November 18, 1944.

Harold, Martin H. "What Makes A Typhoon Tick?" *Saturday Evening Post*, February 7, 1948.

Harvey, J.B. "An Historic Storm." *Weather*, June, 1951.

Havemann, Ernest. "The Night the Tornado Struck." *Saturday Evening Post*, August 13, 1955.

Havrwite, Bernhard. "The Height of Tropical Cyclones and the Eye of the Storm." *Monthly Weather Review*, February, 1935.

Haydon, Everette. "West Indian Hurricanes and the March Blizzard of 1888." *American Meteorological Journal*, 1889.

"Hazel's Fling." *Time*, October 25, 1954.

"Hell on Good Friday." *Newsweek*, April 6, 1964.

Hemingway, Ernest. "Who Murdered the Vets?" *New Masses*, September 17, 1935.

Henry, A.J. "The Frequency of Tropical Cyclones That Closely Approach or Enter Continental United States." *Monthly Weather Review*, vol. 57, 1929.

"Heroism and Suffering in the Typhoon at Hong Kong." *Harper's Weekly*, November 10, 1906.

Hersey, John. "Over the Mad River." *New Yorker*, September 17, 1955.

Holt, Hamilton. "Florida After the Storm." *Review of Reviews*, November, 1926.

"The Hong Kong Typhoon." *Outlook*, September 29, 1906.

"How a Twister Struck Haiti." *Literary Digest*, October 13, 1928.

"Human Flotsam of the Florida Hurricane." *Literary Digest*, October 9, 1926.

Hurd, W.E. "The North Atlantic Hurricane of October 13-29, 1926." *Pilot Chart of the North Atlantic Ocean*, October, 1926.

"Hurricane Audrey's Terrible Aftermath." *Life*, July 15, 1957.

"Hurricane-Wrecked Santo Domingo." *Literary Digest*, September 20, 1930.

"The Hurricane's Tragic Toll." *Literary Digest*, October 6, 1928.

"In the Wake of Disaster." *Newsweek*, July 8, 1957.

"Into a Hurricane's Eye." *Newsweek*, September 25, 1944.

"Invisible Monster." *Newsweek*, October 3, 1938.

"It Can Happen Almost Anywhere." *American City*, July, 1953.

Jagger, T.A. "The Great Tidal Wave of 1946." *Natural History*, June, 1946.

Justice, Alonzo A. "Seeing the Inside of a Tornado." *Monthly Weather Review*, vol. 58, 1930.

Kenney, Nathaniel T. "Our Changing Atlantic Coastline." *National Geographic*, vol. 122, 1962.

Kimball, H.H. "What Is a Storm Wave?" *Monthly Weather Review*, vol. 29, 1901.

Lemons, Hoyt. "Some Meteorological Aspects of Nebraska Tornadoes." *Monthly Weather Review*, vol. 66, 1938.

"Like the End of the World." *Newsweek*, November 30, 1970.

"Looking Into the Heart of a Tornado." *Reader's Digest*, June, 1942.

"A Lot of It." *Newsweek*, February 24, 1958.

Ludlam, F.H. "The Hailstorm." *Weather*, vol. 16, 1961.

Mackaye, Milton. "We're Cracking the Secrets of Weather." *Saturday Evening Post*, September 11, 1954.

Malin, James C. "Dust Storms, 1850-1900." *Kansas Historical Quarterly*, May-November, 1946.

Malkin, W., and Galway, J.G. "Tornadoes Associated with Hurricanes." *Monthly Weather Review*, vol. 81, 1953.

"Man vs. Nature: Still a Losing Fight." *U.S. News & World Report*, April 26, 1965.

Martin, Harold H. "What Makes a Typhoon Tick?" *Saturday Evening Post*, February 7, 1948.

McDonald, W.F. "Low Barometer Readings in West Indian Disturbances of 1932, and 1933." *Monthly Weather Review*, vol. 61, 1933.

———. "Lowest Barometer Reading in the Florida Keys Storm of September 2, 1935." *Monthly Weather Review*, vol. 63, 1935.

Miller, C.E. "Tornadoes, American Phenomena." *Nature Magazine*, May, 1945.

Miller, Eric. "American Pioneers in Meteorology." *Monthly Weather Review*, vol. 61, 1933.

Mitchill, Elisha. "On the Proximate Causes of Certain Wind and Storms." *American Journal of Science*, April 19, 1831.

Mitchill, Samuel Latham. "Some Particulars of a Terrible Hurricane." *Medical Repository*, August, 1804.

"Mobilization by Radio." *Literary Digest*, November 5, 1927.

"Mobilization for Relief." *Commonwealth*, October 7, 1938.

Moraes, Dom. "East Pakistan: The Wave." *New York Times Magazine*, January 10, 1971.

Moret, J.C. "Storms on the Sea Coast of the Mississippi." *De Bow's Review*, September, 1868.

Morgan, James A. "The Devil's Handkerchief Is Up." *Illustrated World*, May, 1921.

Moore, Willis L. "I Am Thinking of Hurricanes." *American Mercury*, September, 1927.

Munk, Walter H. "The Circulation of the Oceans." *Scientific American*, September, 1955.

Namias, Jerome. "The Jet Stream." *Scientific American*, October, 1952.

———. "Long Range Weather Forecasting." *Scientific American*, August, 1955.

"Nineteen Forty Four Hurricane." *Life*, October 2, 1944.

"The North Sea Breaks Bounds." *Economist*, February 24, 1962.

Oliver, F.W. "Dust Storms in Egypt." *Geographical Journal*, vol. 106, 1945.

"Ominous Sight of Tornado Over the Plains of Kansas." *Life*, June 20, 1955.

"One Big Snow Stops Wheels of U.S." *U.S. News & World Report*, February 28, 1958.

"On the Track of the Tornado Tragedy." *Literary Digest*, April 2, 1932.

"Our Hurricane Reporter." *Survey*, October, 1944.

"Out of the Doldrums." *Time*, September 25, 1944.

"The Pakistani Tragedy." *Newsweek*, November 30, 1970.

"Path of Destruction." *Newsweek*, June 22, 1953.

Paulhus, J.L.H. "Indian Ocean and Taiwan Rainfalls Set New Records." *Monthly Weather Review*, vol. 93, 1965.

"Picking Up the Pieces." *Newsweek*, April 13, 1964.

Pope, L.G. "The Wind's Whirligig of Death." *Popular Science Monthly*, May, 1928.

Redfield, William C. "Remarks on the Prevailing Storms on the Atlantic Coast, of the North American States." *American Journal of Science*, July, 1831.

———. "Note on the Hurricane of August, 1831." *American Journal of Science and Arts*, October, 1831.

———. "Observations on the Hurricanes and Storms of the West Indies and the Coast of the United States." *American Journal of Science and Arts*, January, 1834.

———. "On the Gales and Hurricanes of the Western Atlantic." *London Nautical Magazine*, April, 1836.

———. "On the Courses of Hurricanes with Notices of the Typhoons of the China Sea and Other Storms." *London Nautical Magazine*, January, 1839.

Reeds, Chester A. "Storms and Storm Tracks." *Natural History*, vol. 28, 1928.

Rossman, Fritz O. "Differences in the Physical Behavior of Tornadoes and Waterspouts." *Weather*, vol. 13, 1958.

Roth, Richard. "Hailstones and Hailstorms." *Weatherwise*, vol. 5, 1952.

"Round-Up on Hurricane Is Now Complete." *Science News Letter*, November 11, 1944.

"The St. Louis Tornado." *Literary Digest*, October 15, 1927.

"The September Gale." *Saturday Review*, December 3, 1938.

"The Shape of a Tornado." *Literary Digest*, September 20, 1924.

Shepherd, William G. "Beating the Hurricane." *Colliers*, November 17, 1928.

Shove, D. Justin. "Hail in History." *Weather*, vol. 6, 1951.

Simpson, R.H. "Hurricanes." *Scientific American*, vol. 190, 1954.

"Sixteen Miles Under." *Time*, January 8, 1940.

"Spinning Doom." *Time*, May 25, 1953.

Springer, Gertrude. "Our Hurricane Reporter." *Survey-Graphic*, October, 1944.

Stearns, W.D. "Storms of the Gulf of Mexico and Their Prediction." *American Meteorological Journal*, 1894.

Stewart, John A., and Gehman, Richard. "What's Wrong With the Weather?" *Collier's*, January 6, 1956.

Stewart, John Q. "New England Hurricane." *Harper's*, December, 1938.

Stuart, Ben C. "Early Texas Coast Storms." *Monthly Weather Review*, September, 1919.

Stocking, Hobart E. "Nine Day Wonders." *Natural History*, vol. 52, 1943.

Stoddart, D.R. "Catastrophic Storm Effects on the British Honduras Reefs and Cays." *Nature*, vol. 196, 1962.

"Storm Line." *Time*, June 22, 1953.

"Storm Line." *Time*, June 22, 1968.

Sumner, H.C. "The North Atlantic Hurricane of September 8-16, 1944." *Monthly Weather Review*, vol. 72, 1944.

Sutton, Graham. "The Energy of the Atmosphere." *Science*, November, 1965.

Talman, Charles F. "Ice from the Thunderclouds." *Natural History*, vol. 38, 1936.

Tannehill, Ivan Ray. "Some Inundations Attending Tropical Cyclones." *Monthly Weather Review*, vol. 55, 1927.

———. "Sea Swells in Relation to Movement and Intensity of Tropical Storms." *Monthly Weather Review*, vol. 64, 1936.

"The Terrible Twins." *Time*, May 28, 1965.

"Terrible Twisters." *Newsweek*, March 31, 1952.

"Terror in Turkey." *Newsweek*, January 8, 1940.

"Terrors of a Tropical Gale." *Independent*, October 9, 1926.

"That Truant, the Tornado." *Literary Digest*, April 18, 1925.

"Then It Hit." *Newsweek*, June 6, 1955.

"Tidal Wave." *Newsweek*, December 30, 1946.

Tindall, George B. "The Bubble in the Sun." *American Heritage*, August, 1965.

Tingley, F.G. "The Genesis of a Tropical Cyclone." *Monthly Weather Review*, vol. 59, 1931.

"Tornadoes in the South & Midwest." *Literary Digest*, April 17, 1920.

"Tornadoes Ravage Middle West." *Frank Leslie's Illustrated Newspaper*, June 14, 1917.

"Tornado's Wake." *McCalls*, April, 1956.

Toynbee, H. "On the Great Hurricanes, the Tracks of American Storms and the Ordinary Winds of the North Atlantic Ocean in August, 1873." *Nautical Magazine* (London), December, 1877.

"Tragic Autumn." *Newsweek*, October 25, 1954.

True, A.F. "The Structure of Tropical Cyclones." Proceedings of the U.S. Naval Institute, Annapolis, March, 1937.

"Tsunamis the Terrible." *Time*, April 15, 1946.

"Twirling Death." *Newsweek,* May 25, 1953.

"Twister Terror: Nature Runs Wild." *Time,* April 15, 1974.

"Two-Hundred-Mile-an-Hour Death." *Literary Digest,* April 18, 1936.

"Two Windy Girls on the Warpath." *Life,* September 26, 1960.

"Up the Valley." *Time,* April 23, 1965.

Vosburgh, Frederick G. "Men Birds Soar on Boiling Air." *National Geographic,* vol. 74, 1938.

"The Wake of Agnes." *Newsweek,* August 21, 1972.

Ward, D.C. Robert. "Tornadoes." *Outlook,* April 1, 1925.

"Weather—Gone and Coming." *Newsweek,* October 25, 1945.

"The West Indian Hurricane Toll." *Literary Digest,* September 29, 1928.

Wexler, Harry. "The Circulation of the Atmosphere." *Scientific American,* September, 1955.

"When Donna Got Lost." *Newsweek,* September 26, 1960.

Wherry, John A., and Peterson, Lloyd E. "Liaison on the Home Front." *Journal of Insurance Information,* July-August, 1964.

Wilson, June. "The Worst Storm in English History." *Country Life,* vol. 118, 1955.

"Wind, Water & Death." *Newsweek,* September 14, 1935.

"Wind, Water & Woe." *Time,* September 16, 1935.

"Winter's Greatest Storm." *Frank Leslie's Illustrated Newspaper,* March 24, 1888.

Woodward, Frances. "Wind and Fury." *Atlantic Monthly,* December, 1938.

"Worst Weather Ever." *Newsweek,* August 29, 1955.

Bulletins, Pamphlets, Papers, Reports

Alexander, William H. *West Indian Hurricanes.* U.S. Weather Bureau, Washington, 1902.

Bigelow, Henry B., and Edmondson, W.T. *Wind Waves at Sea, Breakers, and Surf.* U.S. Navy, Washington, 1947.

Brooks, Charles F. *The New England Hurricane of September, 1944.* Blue Hill Observatory Reprint No. 5, 1945.

Climate and Man. U.S. Dept. of Agriculture Yearbook, Washington, 1941.

Community Tornado Safety. U.S. Weather Bureau, Washington, 1960.

Dunn, Gordon., Namias, Jerome, and Seimpson, R.H. *Survey of the Hurricane Problem.* U.S. Weather Bureau, Washington, 1955.

Fassig, Oliver L. *Hurricanes of the West Indies.* U.S. Weather Bureau, Washington, 1913.

Garriott, Edward B. *West Indian Hurricane.* U.S. Weather Bureau, Washington, 1900.

Gregg, W.R., Tannehill, I.R., and others. "Testimony Regarding the Hurricane of September 2, 1935." *Hearings before the Committee on World War Veterans' Legislation,* Washington, 1936.

Heck, N.H. *List of Seismic Sea Waves.* Bulletin of the Seismological Society of America, October, 1947.

Howard, Richard A. *Sun, Sand and Survival.* U.S. Air Force, 1953.

Hurricane Rains and Floods of August, 1955, Carolinas to New England. U.S. Weather Bureau, Washington, 1956.

The Hurricane Warning Service. U.S. Weather Bureau, 1933.

Lapham, I.A. *List of the Great Storms, Hurricanes and Tornadoes of the United States.* Washington, Franklin Institute, 1872.

Lineham, Urban J. *Tornado Deaths in the United States.* U.S. Weather Bureau, Washington, 1957.

Losses Caused by Hail, 1909-1918. U.S. Dept. of Agriculture, Washington, 1922.

Mitchell, C.L. *West Indian Hurricanes and Other Tropical Cyclones of the North Atlantic Ocean.* U.S. Weather Bureau, Washington, 1924.

———. *Hurricanes of the South Atlantic and Gulf States, 1879-1928.* U.S. Weather Bureau, Washington, 1928.

National Hurricane Research Project. U.S. Weather Bureau, Washington, 1956.

Price, W. Armstrong. *Hurricanes Affecting the Coast of Texas from Galveston to Rio Grande.* Corps of Engineers, Washington, 1956.

Psychological First Aid in Community Disasters. Psychiatric Association Committee on Civil Defense, Washington, 1954.

Showalter, A.K., and Fulks, J.R. *Preliminary Report on Tornadoes.* U.S. Weather Bureau, Washington, 1943.

Thomas, Percy H. *Electric Power from the Wind.* Federal Power Commission, Washington, 1949.

———. *Aerodynamics of the Wind Turbine.* Federal Power Commission, Washington, 1949.

Tornado Occurrences in the United States. U.S. Weather Bureau, Washington, 1952.

Wallace, Anthony F.C. *Tornado in Worcester.* National Research Council, Washington, 1956.

Water. U.S. Dept. of Agriculture Yearbook, Washington, 1955.

The World's Heaviest Rains. U.S. Weather Bureau, Washington, 1955.

Newspapers

(The following newspapers were used extensively in research, some, like the *London Times,* the *Spectator,* and the *New York Times,* from their inception. Dates of use, unfortunately, are too numerous to cite here.)

Anchorage Daily News, Anchorage Times, Apalachicola Commercial Advertiser, Arkansas Gazette, Arizona Republic, Atlanta Constitution, Atlanta Journal, Atlantic City Press, Austin American-Statesman, Baltimore Patriot, Baltimore Sun, Bangor Times, Baton Rouge Advocate, Baton Rouge Gazette, Boston Evening Post, Boston Evening Traveller, Boston Globe, Boston Herald Traveler, Bridgetown Press, California Star, Charleston Courier, Charleston Mercury, Charleston Southern Patriot, Charlotte (N.C.) *Observer, Chicago Commercial Advertiser, Chicago Daily News, Chicago Herald Examiner, Chicago Inter-Ocean, Chicago Sun, Chicago Sun-Times, Chicago Times, Chicago Today* (also *Chicago Evening American* and *Chicago's American), Chicago Tribune, Christian Science Monitor, Cincinnati Enquirer, Cleveland Plain Dealer, Columbia Missouri Statesman, Columbus Evening Dispatch, Congressional Record, Connecticut Courant, Dallas Times-Herald, Denver Daily News, Denver Post, Denver Rocky Mountain News, Denver Times, Detroit Free Press,* the *Eastern Underwriter, East Hampton* (N.Y.) *Star, Edmonton* (Can.) *Journal, Fairbanks Daily News-Miner, Florida Herald, Galveston Citizen, Galveston News, Galveston Post, Georgia* (Savannah) *Republican, Grand Rapids Press, Harrisberg News, Hartford Courant, Hartford Times, Houston Chronicle, Houston Post, Houston Telegraph and Texas Register, Illinois Journal, Indianapolis News, Indianapolis Star, Indianola* (Tex.) *Bulletin, Jacksonville News, Jacksonville Times-Union, Jamaica Dispatch, Jewish Daily Forward, Kansas City Daily, Kansas City Star, Kansas City Times, Key West Inquirer, Kobe* (Japan) *Chronicle, Kodiak Bear, Kodiak Mirror, London Daily Graphic, London Daily News, London Evening Post, London Gazette, London Globe, London Morning Post, London Standard, London Times, Long Beach Press-Telegram, Los Angeles Examiner* (also *Los Angeles Herald-Examiner), Los Angeles Times, Louisiana Gazette, Manchester Guardian, Maryland Gazette, Meriden* (Conn.). *Record, Miami Daily News, Miami Herald, Milwaukee Journal, Milwaukee Sentinel, Minneapolis Tribune, Missouri State Journal, Mobile Mercury, Mobile Press, Mobile Register, Mobile Tribune, Montreal Gazette, Montreal Star, Nantucket Inquirer, Natchez Courier, Natchez Free Trader, National Observer, National Underwriter, Newark Daily Advertiser, Newark Evening News, New Bedford* (Mass.) *Standard Times, New Haven Register, New Jersey Mirror, New Orleans Bee, New Orleans Bulletin, New Orleans Daily Crescent, New Orleans Delta, New Orleans Picayune* (also *New Orleans Times-Picayune), New Orleans Times-Democrat, New York American, New York Call, New York Daily Graphic, New York Daily News, New York Evening-Journal, New York Express, New York Herald, New York Mercury, New York Post, New York Press, New York Spectator, New York Sun, New York Times, New York Tribune, New York World, New York World-Telegram, Norfolk Beacon, Norristown* (Pa.) *Herald, North Carolina Gazette, Omaha World, Orange County Register,* the *Oregonian, Orleans Gazette, Pacific Rural Press, Paris Herald, Pensacola Gazette, Pennsylvania Gazette, Pennsylvania Journal, Peshtigo Times, Philadelphia Daily News, Philadelphia Inquirer, Phoenix Arizona Republic, Pittsburgh Press, Portland Journal, Portland* (Me.) *Press Herald, Providence Journal, Richmond Times-Dispatch, Sacramento Bee, Sacramento Union, St. Joseph Times, St. Louis Evening Chronicle, St. Louis Globe-Democrat, St. Louis Post-Dispatch, St. Louis Times, Salem* (Mass.) *Register, San Antonio Light, Santa Barbara Press, San Francisco Bulletin, San Francisco Call, San Francisco Call-Bulletin, San Francisco Chronicle, San Francisco Examiner, San Jose Pioneer, South Carolina Gazette, Spectator, Springfield* (Mass.) *Union, Tallahassee Floridian, Tallahassee Sentinel, Toronto Star, Toronto Telegram, Trenton* (New Jersey) *State Gazette, Tucson Daily Reporter, Tucson Star, Vineyard* (Martha's Vineyard, Mass.) *Gazette, Virginia Gazette, Wall Street Journal, Washington Evening Star, Washington Post, Washington Square Daily News, Whitehall Evening Post, Wilmington Courier, Wilmington Recorder, Wilmington Star News, Winsted* (Conn.) *Evening Citizen, Yankton Press & Dakotan, Yarmouth* (Mass.) *Register.*

Miscellaneous Publications

Aerial Age, Aeronautics, Aeronautical Digest (later *Aereo Digest), Aircraft Journal, Airlanes, Airline Pilot, Air Power Historian, Air Service Journal, Airway Age, American Airmen, American Federalist, American Journal of Science, Aviation, Chronicles of the Sea, Commonweal, Fire Journal, Flying, Gentlemen's Magazine, Geographical Journal, Geographical Review, Japan Magazine, Justice, Kansas Historical Quarterly, Life and Labor, Living Age, London Magazine, Monthly Weather Review, National Geographic Magazine, Natural History, Naval Chronicle, New Wonderful Museum and Extraordinary Magazine, Popular Aviation, Popular Mechanics, Saturday Review, Science, Science Newsletter, Scientific American, Scots Magazine, Today's Health, Weatherwise.*

INDEX

A

B

C

D

E

F

G

H

I

M

N

O

P

Q

R

S

U

V

W

Y

Z